D1175607

Newsday

LONG ISLAND

THE CELEBRATED SERIES

OUR STORY

Written and Edited by the Staff of Newsday.

THIS VOLUME CONTAINS pages of the daily "Long Island: Our Story" series that appeared in Newsday from Sept. 28, 1997, through June 30, 1998. Portions of some of the series' 10 special sections also appear. Some pages have been adjusted for presentation in this book, which incorporates corrections published in Newsday.

ISBN 1-885134-14-2

Printed in Canada

To subscribe to Newsday, call 1-516-843-2000.

LONG ISLAND OUR STORY

Contents

Introduction

We hope this book will bring you and your family many hours of enjoyment over the years to come.

"Long Island: Our Story" became a labor of love for the Newsday staffers who were involved in its writing and editing for more than two years. Their journey through time was shared by more readers than any other newspaper series we know of.

Throughout the nine months of publication, the one question we heard repeatedly from readers was, "Will there be a book?"

Certainly, that question has been answered. What you hold in your hands is a book that you will return to from time to time to relive a Long Island moment or to answer a question about how our island developed through the centuries. It is a celebration of where we live, where we came from and who we are.

The essence of "Long Island: Our Story" is captured in this book. Some material from our special sections and added features could not be adapted for this volume.

We thank all of the people, libraries, historical societies and other organizations that helped guide us through our history.

Long Island is truly a wonderful place that helped shape the country's destiny in several key ways. So much happened here that is in danger of being forgotten or devalued. "Long Island: Our Story" set out to correct that. We hope it has.

Enjoy the book. Enjoy our Long Island.

Raymond A. Jansen,
Newsday Publisher

Newsday
THE LONG ISLAND NEWSPAPER

http://www.newsday.com MONDAY, SEPT. 29, 1997 50¢

The Birth of Long Island

CHAPTER 1

From a glacier as tall as a skyscraper to a fish-shaped island awaiting its first inhabitants

Newsday Photo / Jeff Schamberry

Colliding continents and towering glaciers forged our beaches and plains, valleys and hills

The Birth of Long Island

BY DAN FAGIN
STAFF WRITER

A half-billion years ago, it was a chain of volcano islands adrift in a tropical sea. Over untold millennia, it took new forms, like a lump of clay forever being reshaped.

Three hundred million years ago, the place that would become Long Island was a dinosaur swampland at the edge of a towering mountain range cast up by the slow-motion collision of continents. And just 20,000 years ago, it was a wasteland of woolly mammoths and iceberg lakes in the menacing shadow of a retreating glacier as tall as a skyscraper and as wide as a continent.

But not until 11,000 years ago — an eyeblink in the 4.6-billion-year life of Planet Earth — did the rising sea finally encircle a fish-shaped pile of sand pushed together by the newly departed ice sheet.

In geological terms, Long Island was born yesterday.

The oversize sandbar where we live is only the latest, temporary incarnation of a corner of the world that has been continuously reshaped by colliding continents, crumbling mountains, shifting sea level, pounding waves and titanic glaciers. And though Long Island is brand new by the time scale of history, the way we live upon it is profoundly influenced by the remarkable series of transformations that occurred here over hundreds of millions of years.

Skyscrapers are harder to build here because the bedrock, pressure-cooked in a series of ancient continental collisions, is buried too deeply to support them. Our underground water supply is abundant, but fragile, because it rests in porous sand from the eroded Appalachian Mountains. The hills and finger bays of the North Shore, and the rich plains to the south, were shaped by the great Canadian glaciers that came here at least twice. And thousands of waterfront homes teeter on the edge of disaster because of the erosion and rising sea level that have continued to make Long Island shimmy and shrink ever since the last ice sheet began retreating 22,000 years ago.

Despite these powerful legacies, a surprising amount of basic information about Long Island's past is either unknown or controversial. There are gaps in the time line when scientists have no idea what happened, and periods for which there are competing theories but no consensus among the experts.

The problem is that researchers — mostly geologists, since rocks and fossils are just about the only clues to Long Island's early history — have remarkably little to go on as they try to piece together a credible chronology. Plant and animal fossils usually aren't well preserved here because the climate is too wet, and many potential digging sites have been paved over. Worse still, the last glacier to visit the region changed the landscape so drastically that much of the earlier geological record is either buried or bewilderingly scrambled.

"It's like trying to put together a jigsaw puzzle with 70 or 80 percent of the pieces missing," said Ralph Lewis, an expert on the history of Long Island Sound and an associate state geologist at the Connecticut Geological and Natural History Survey. "Every time you get a new piece, you have to do more detective work. You have to modify the picture."

But there are a few places on Long Island — such as the rocky cliffs of Montauk or sandpits of Port Washington — where the landscape reveals buried secrets that geologists have struggled to decipher for more than a century.

On a muggy morning last summer, two men who have been exploring the Port Washington site for more than 25 years pondered its mysteries from a rocky perch overlooking the main pit.

For geologists Les Sirkin and Herb Mills, natural history is an almost mystical pursuit, and the abandoned sand pit just west of Hempstead Harbor is a temple. The mining stopped here decades ago, but lasted long enough to scrape away millions of tons of sand deposited by the last glacier, exposing sediments that have been in place for as long as 90 million years. The cliffs that the mining machines cut along the sides of the pit also have a story to tell: the jagged bands of white, gray and black on the cliff faces offer hints about the chaotic events that, layer by layer, built Long Island.

The sand pit is a portal to a time when Long Island did not exist as a distinct entity, but was instead an undifferentiated portion of a broad coastal plain that moved with North America as the continent drifted north from the tropics.

The bottom layer of that plain is bedrock from a series of continental collisions that began 450 million years ago. The slab was covered by a thick wedge of sandy sediment deposited over hundreds of millions of years by streams that ran to the coast from the eroding Appalachians. But what finally created Long Island was a glacier. Like a bulldozer pushing together a sand pile, the ice scraped along the top edge of the sandy wedge to form the Island's fish shape.

When he was younger, Sirkin, a research professor of earth sciences at Adelphi University, spent long days chipping at rocks while hanging suspended on ropes slung over the cliffs at the sand pits. Mills, too, has spent much of his life studying the jumbled cliff layers, trying to identify the choreography of ice, ocean and rock that created those markings over millions of years.

"In the sand pits, you can really start to see how all the pieces fit together," said Mills, who is curator of geology for the Nassau County museum system.

Understanding the evolution of Long Island requires a grasp of two key concepts, that the Earth's climate, and its land masses, are forever changing.

At various times, scientists believe, the world's average temperature has ranged from as low as 59 degrees to as high as 77 degrees, probably because of variations in the Earth's tilt and orbit,

Please see GLACIERS on Page 4

LI HISTORY.COM

Internet explorers can experience the virtual evolution of Long Island, with a bird's-eye view of the forces that shaped land and sea. Look for installments and enhancements to Long Island: Our Story at Newsday's special site, http://www.lihistory.com.

LEGACY

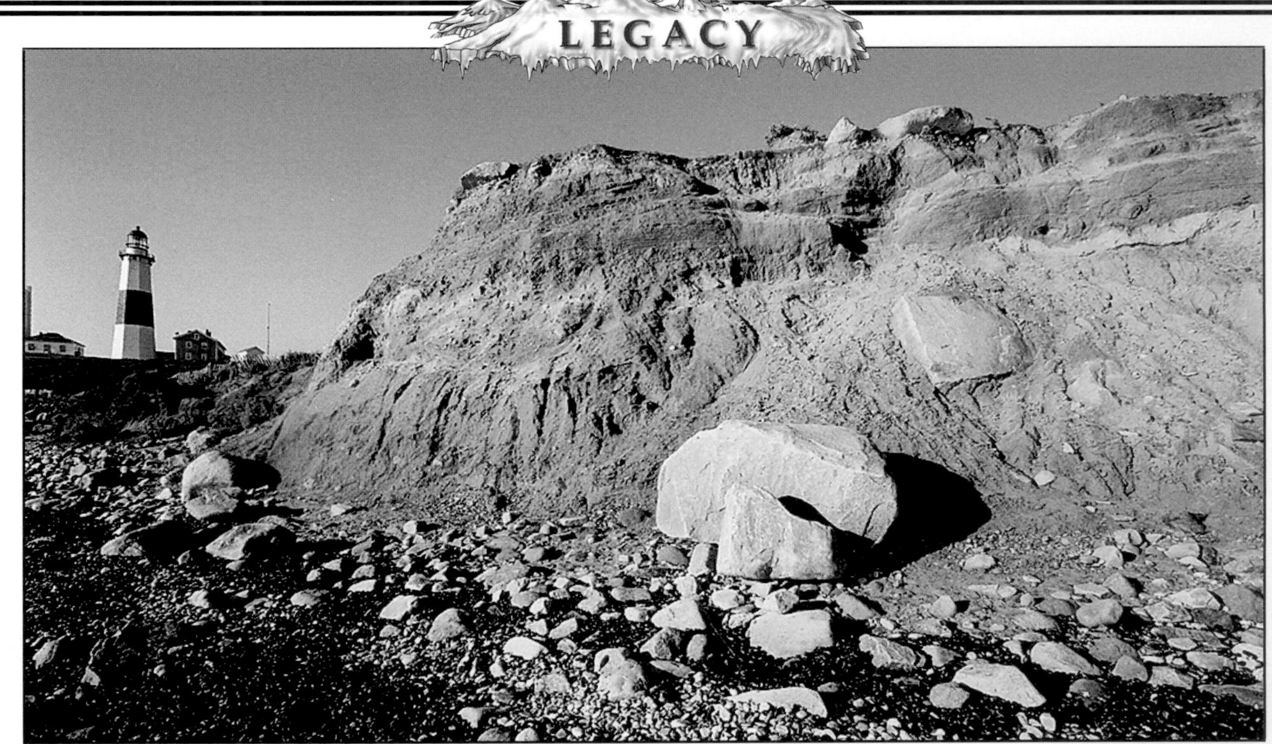

Newsday Photo / Bill Davis

SIGNS OF THE ICE AGE

Layered cliffs and large boulders, like the ones above at Montauk Point, are two of the most visible legacies of the glacier that left Long Island about 20,000 years ago. The dark striations on the cliff mark layers of clay deposited during the last Ice Age when the region was dotted with lakes filled with melting icewater. The thicker bands of white and gray on the cliffs show deposits from at least two glaciers. The boulders are not native to Long Island, but were broken off of New England bedrock and carried here by the bulldozing ice sheet.

In the Beginning

Long Island took more than 450 million years to form. Using a representative cross-section of earth, here is how geologists believe Long Island developed.

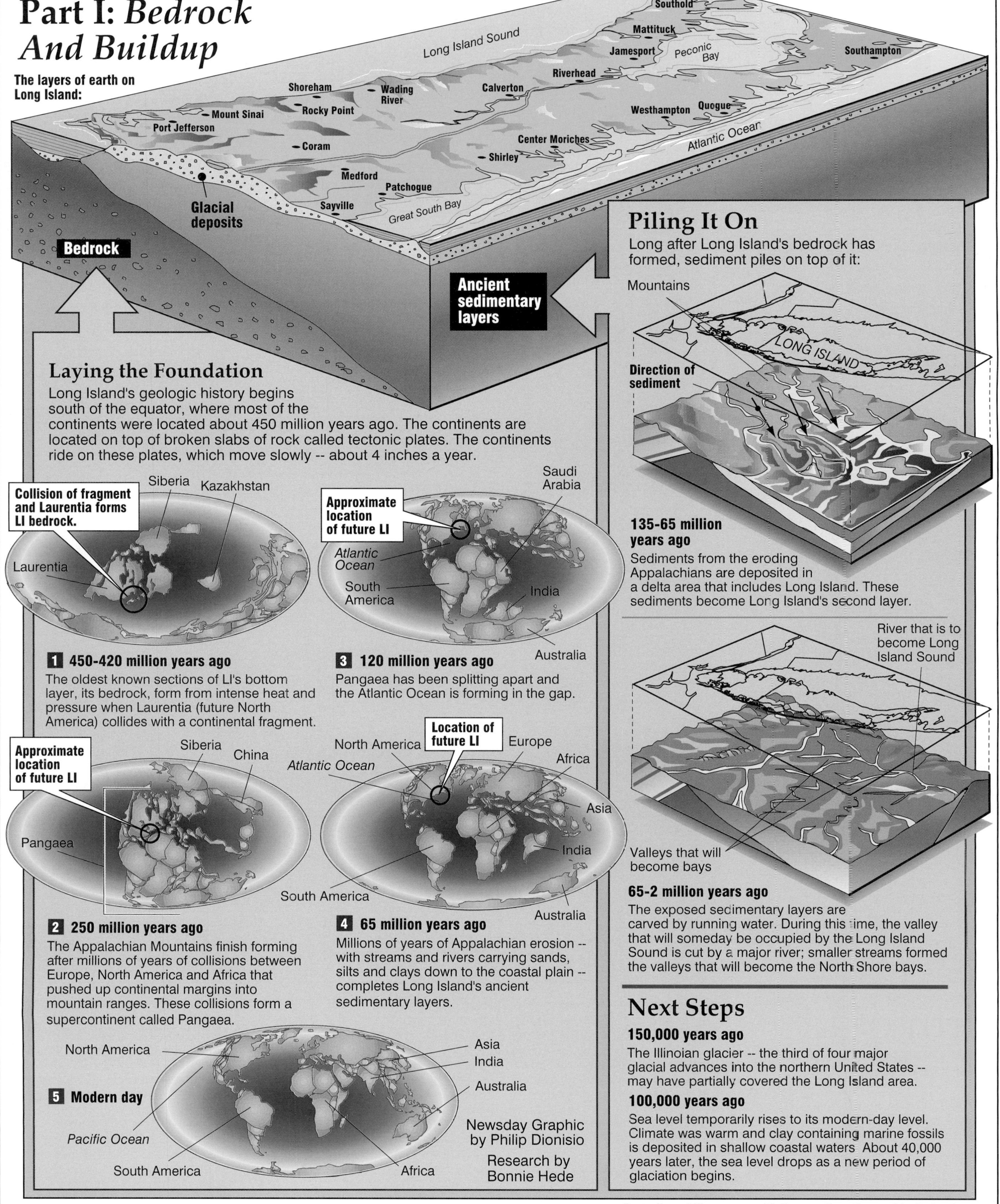

Part I: Bedrock And Buildup
The layers of earth on Long Island:
Long Island Sound
Southold
Mattituck
Jamesport
Peconic Bay
Southampton
Riverhead
Shoreham
Wading River
Calverton
Rocky Point
Mount Sinai
Port Jefferson
Westhampton
Quogue
Coram
Center Moriches
Atlantic Ocean
Shirley
Medford
Patchogue
Sayville
Great South Bay
Glacial deposits
Bedrock
Ancient sedimentary layers
Laying the Foundation
Long Island's geologic history begins south of the equator, where most of the continents were located about 450 million years ago. The continents are located on top of broken slabs of rock called tectonic plates. The continents ride on these plates, which move slowly -- about 4 inches a year.
Collision of fragment and Laurentia forms LI bedrock.
Siberia
Kazakhstan
Laurentia
1 450-420 million years ago
The oldest known sections of LI's bottom layer, its bedrock, form from intense heat and pressure when Laurentia (future North America) collides with a continental fragment.
Approximate location of future LI
Saudi Arabia
Atlantic Ocean
South America
India
Australia
3 120 million years ago
Pangaea has been splitting apart and the Atlantic Ocean is forming in the gap.
Approximate location of future LI
Siberia
China
Pangaea
2 250 million years ago
The Appalachian Mountains finish forming after millions of years of collisions between Europe, North America and Africa that pushed up continental margins into mountain ranges. These collisions form a supercontinent called Pangaea.
Location of future LI
North America
Europe
Atlantic Ocean
Africa
Asia
India
South America
Australia
4 65 million years ago
Millions of years of Appalachian erosion -- with streams and rivers carrying sands, silts and clays down to the coastal plain -- completes Long Island's ancient sedimentary layers.
North America
Asia
India
Australia
5 Modern day
Pacific Ocean
South America
Africa
Newsday Graphic by Philip Dionisio
Research by Bonnie Hede
Piling It On
Long after Long Island's bedrock has formed, sediment piles on top of it:
Mountains
LONG ISLAND
Direction of sediment
135-65 million years ago
Sediments from the eroding Appalachians are deposited in a delta area that includes Long Island. These sediments become Long Island's second layer.
River that is to become Long Island Sound
Valleys that will become bays
65-2 million years ago
The exposed sedimentary layers are carved by running water. During this time, the valley that will someday be occupied by the Long Island Sound is cut by a major river; smaller streams formed the valleys that will become the North Shore bays.
Next Steps
150,000 years ago
The Illinoian glacier -- the third of four major glacial advances into the northern United States -- may have partially covered the Long Island area.
100,000 years ago
Sea level temporarily rises to its modern-day level. Climate was warm and clay containing marine fossils is deposited in shallow coastal waters. About 40,000 years later, the sea level drops as a new period of glaciation begins.

Parts II and III appear with the continuations of today's story.

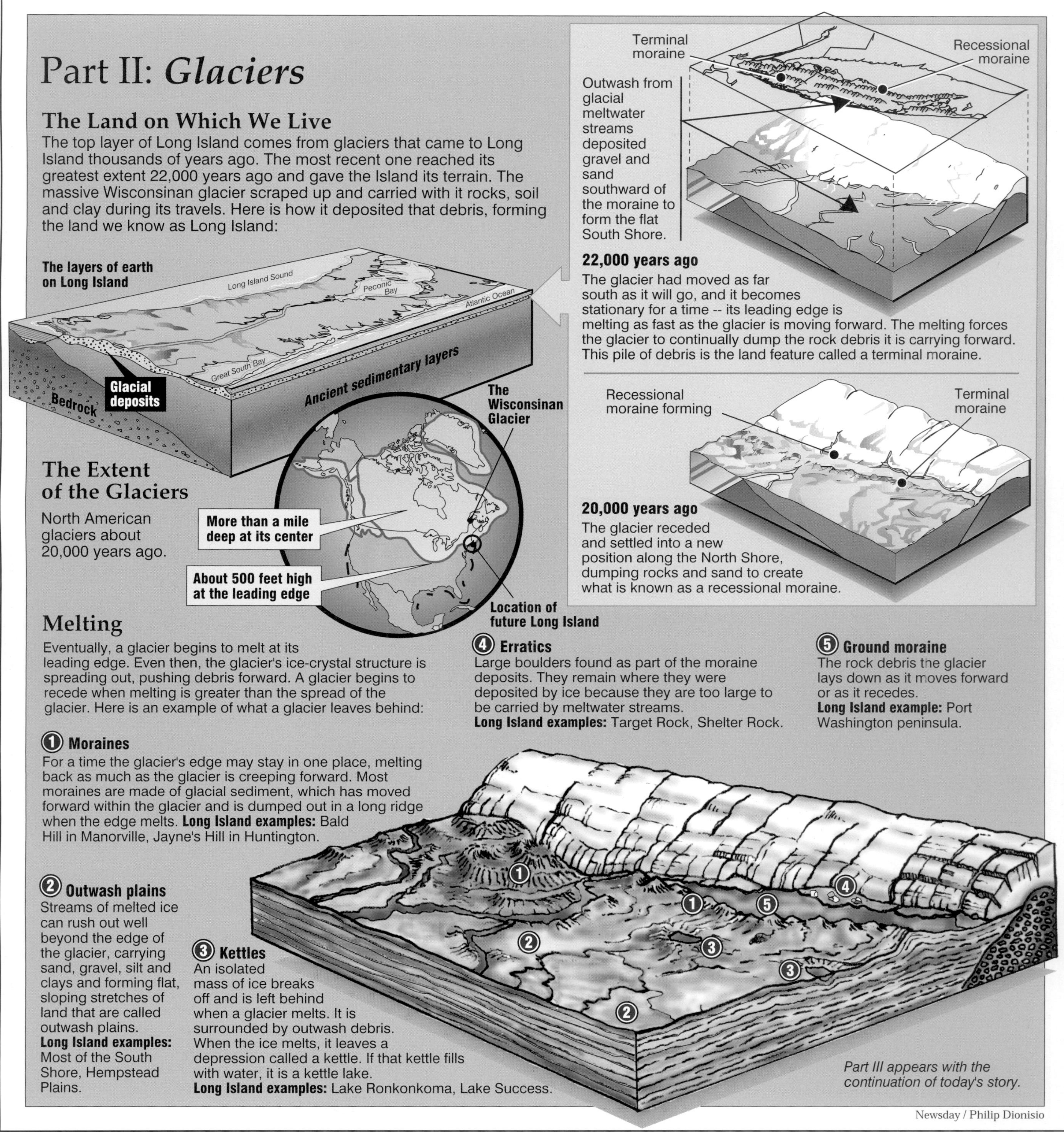

Part II: Glaciers
The Land on Which We Live
The top layer of Long Island comes from glaciers that came to Long Island thousands of years ago. The most recent one reached its greatest extent 22,000 years ago and gave the Island its terrain. The massive Wisconsinan glacier scraped up and carried with it rocks, soil and clay during its travels. Here is how it deposited that debris, forming the land we know as Long Island:
The layers of earth on Long Island
Long Island Sound
Peconic Bay
Atlantic Ocean
Great South Bay
Glacial deposits
Bedrock
Ancient sedimentary layers
Terminal moraine
Recessional moraine
Outwash from glacial meltwater streams deposited gravel and sand southward of the moraine to form the flat South Shore.
22,000 years ago
The glacier had moved as far south as it will go, and it becomes stationary for a time -- its leading edge is melting as fast as the glacier is moving forward. The melting forces the glacier to continually dump the rock debris it is carrying forward. This pile of debris is the land feature called a terminal moraine.
Recessional moraine forming
Terminal moraine
20,000 years ago
The glacier receded and settled into a new position along the North Shore, dumping rocks and sand to create what is known as a recessional moraine.
The Extent of the Glaciers
North American glaciers about 20,000 years ago.
The Wisconsinan Glacier
More than a mile deep at its center
About 500 feet high at the leading edge
Location of future Long Island
Melting
Eventually, a glacier begins to melt at its leading edge. Even then, the glacier's ice-crystal structure is spreading out, pushing debris forward. A glacier begins to recede when melting is greater than the spread of the glacier. Here is an example of what a glacier leaves behind:
1 Moraines
For a time the glacier's edge may stay in one place, melting back as much as the glacier is creeping forward. Most moraines are made of glacial sediment, which has moved forward within the glacier and is dumped out in a long ridge when the edge melts. Long Island examples: Bald Hill in Manorville, Jayne's Hill in Huntington.
2 Outwash plains
Streams of melted ice can rush out well beyond the edge of the glacier, carrying sand, gravel, silt and clays and forming flat, sloping stretches of land that are called outwash plains. Long Island examples: Most of the South Shore, Hempstead Plains.
3 Kettles
An isolated mass of ice breaks off and is left behind when a glacier melts. It is surrounded by outwash debris. When the ice melts, it leaves a depression called a kettle. If that kettle fills with water, it is a kettle lake. Long Island examples: Lake Ronkonkoma, Lake Success.
4 Erratics
Large boulders found as part of the moraine deposits. They remain where they were deposited by ice because they are too large to be carried by meltwater streams. Long Island examples: Target Rock, Shelter Rock.
5 Ground moraine
The rock debris the glacier lays down as it moves forward or as it recedes. Long Island example: Port Washington peninsula.
1
2
3
4
5
Part III appears with the continuation of today's story.

Newsday / Philip Dionisio

Birth of LI

GLACIERS from Page 2

in sunspot activity, and in the relative positions of the other planets. That 18-degree difference may not seem like much, but it has been enough to launch ice ages in which so much ocean water was trapped in glaciers that sea level dropped by hundreds of feet.

The Earth's surface keeps changing because it consists of seven large plates of solid rock, and two dozen smaller ones, that slide in different directions very slowly — usually a few inches per year. Earthquakes in California, volcanoes in Japan, and the growing Himalayan Mountains are all responses to colliding plates. Conversely, huge trenches such as the ones in Africa's Great Rift Valley appear where plates are pulling apart.

It was an ancient continental collision that formed the oldest, and hardest, rocks buried beneath Long Island.

For hundreds of millions of years, North America was located in the tropics, on or below the equator. The continent was rotated on its side so that the present-day East Coast faced south. Offshore, an arc of volcanic islands that resembled modern-day Japan slowly approached that coastline near the place where Long Island would take shape.

That island chain collided with North America about 450 million years ago, and the volcanic rocks were pushed deep into the Earth's crust, where intense heat and pressure hardened them. That super-hard bedrock eventually moved closer to the surface, and today probably lies beneath much of Long Island. It can be seen in the walls of a New York City water tunnel being dug 700 feet beneath Queens.

An entire continent, Africa, loomed off the North American coast when the next key event began, roughly 300 million years ago. The two continents slowly ground into each other for the next 100 million years, buckling at their edges and pushing up a vast mountain range, the Appalachians, that was taller than the present-day Rockies.

Dinosaurs were dominating life on

A Long Wait for Stonybrookadactyl

BY DAN FAGIN
STAFF WRITER

The weather was right: hot and sticky. So was the terrain: swampy. The right plants — subtropical ferns — grew here, too.

But Jurassic Parkway won't be in theaters anytime soon because so far, there's only indirect evidence that dinosaurs lived on the place that would become Long Island.

Dinosaur bones and footprints have been unearthed nearby in New Jersey, Connecticut and the upstate Hudson River Valley. But not here. The most glamorous fossils recovered on and near Long Island have instead been teeth from mammoths and mastodons — Ice Age elephants that lived tens of millions of years after dinosaurs disappeared from the region.

Dinosaur fossils are hard to find anywhere, and even tougher to unearth on Long Island. Except for a few exposed cliffs on the North Shore, in places like Garvies Point in Glen Cove and Roanoke Point north of Riverhead, almost all of the local rock that dinosaurs would have walked upon has since been buried beneath hundreds of feet of sand and gravel deposited by later glaciers.

Another problem is that Long Island's soil is saturated with water and rich in oxygen, which means bones tend to break down quickly before they can mineralize and become stone fossils.

"Surely there were dinosaurs around. It's just that conditions weren't right for preservation of bones," said Herbert Mills, curator of geology for Nassau County's division of museums.

But Mills and other local geologists haven't given up hope. On a recent trip to the Port Washington sand pits, where decades of sand mining removed newer glacial deposits and exposed the 90-million-year-old rock below, Mills noted that dinosaurs did not become extinct until 25 million years after the newly exposed rock was formed.

"You could very well be standing on a dinosaur bone," Mills told a visitor.

The Long Island region was often underwater when dinosaurs roamed the Earth. But at times when sea level was low enough, they probably thrived here because the climate was warmer, and swampier, than today, scientists believe. The eastern edge of North America was much closer to the equator, and included lots of marshy deltas from rivers that swept down from the newly formed Appalachian Mountains, which 200 million years ago were as tall as the Rockies are today.

Dinosaurs disappeared worldwide 65 million years ago when the climate cooled abruptly, perhaps because a giant asteroid or comet crashed into Mexico's Yucatan Peninsula and threw enormous amounts of dust into the atmosphere. On Long Island, studies of fossilized pollen show that the local vegetation suddenly switched from subtropical ferns to temperate flowering plants such as magnolia, willow and sassafras.

The richest fossil finds in the region have been in New Jersey, including the first dinosaur ever discovered in the United States: a duck-billed Hadrosaurus unearthed in 1858 and named for Haddonfield, where it was discovered. Bones from another species, Dryptosaurus, that resembled a smaller version of Tyrannosaurus rex also have been found at several sites around New Jersey.

"I think we had as many different kinds of dinosaurs as any place on Earth," said David Parris, curator of natural history at the New Jersey State Museum in Trenton. "If they're found in New Jersey, there's no reason why, theoretically, you couldn't expect to find them in New York, including Long Island."

So far, though, the only large-animal fossils found on or near Long Island have been much newer: the teeth, and occasionally tusks, of mastodons and woolly mammoths.

The two furry elephant-like beasts lived on Long Island for several hundred thousand years before disappearing about 11,000 years ago, casualties of warmer temperatures and hunting pressure from nomadic Indians who were beginning to enter the region. Mastodons were longer but had lower shoulders than mammoths, which resembled modern elephants except for their furry coats. On land, the fossil finds have been meager locally. Five teeth and a few bone fragments from a young mastodon were discovered by workers dredging a pond in Jamaica, Queens, in 1858 — the same year Hadrosaurus was found in New Jersey. The only other reported finding, a mastodon jawbone recovered on a Southold beach in 1823, was later discovered to have been brought to Long Island from Kentucky by a collector.

But the waters off Long Island's South Shore have been a treasure trove of mammoth and mastodon teeth and tusks, most of them caught in fishing nets. Dozens of teeth have been found over the years, and some are now on display in the Hall of Extinct Mammals on the fourth floor of the American Museum of Natural History.

Shifting sea level explains why so many fossils have been found offshore. During parts of the Ice Age, so much ocean water was locked up in glaciers that sea level was about 350 feet lower than today and the South Shore of Long Island was 80 miles farther south, revealing a broad coastal plain, an ideal habitat for the ancient elephants.

But mastodons don't fire the imagination like dinosaurs, and local geologists are eagerly awaiting the day when someone, somewhere on Long Island, stumbles on a buried dinosaur bone — Greatneckasaurus, perhaps, or Hicksvillatops.

"I believe such a find is possible," said Steve Englebright of the Museum of Long Island Natural Sciences in Stony Brook. "It could happen here."

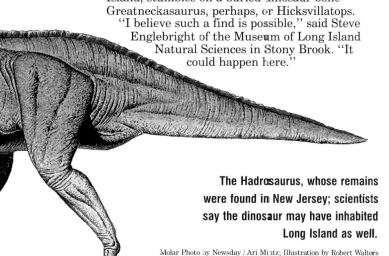

Where Beasts Roamed

Children clambering over a plastic mastodon statue in Baisley Pond Park in Queens have no way of knowing that they are playing at the only place where on Long Island where bones of the now-extinct Ice Age elephant have ever been found.

No sign marks the place where in 1858, workmen excavating part of the pond uncovered five molar teeth and a few fragments of an ivory tusk belonging to a young mastodon, buried beneath four feet of muck. The only reminder of the historic find is the new mastodon statue in the park's Sutphin Boulevard playground, which was renovated last summer.

Where those mastodon bones are today is mystery. Several local geologists say one tooth was part of Adelphi University's fossil collection, but faculty members now say they have no record of the tooth. All other mastodon and mammoth bones found in the Long Island region have been dredged up by fishermen trawling off the South Shore, in areas exposed during the last Ice Age, when sea level was more than 300 feet lower than today.

— **Dan Fagin**

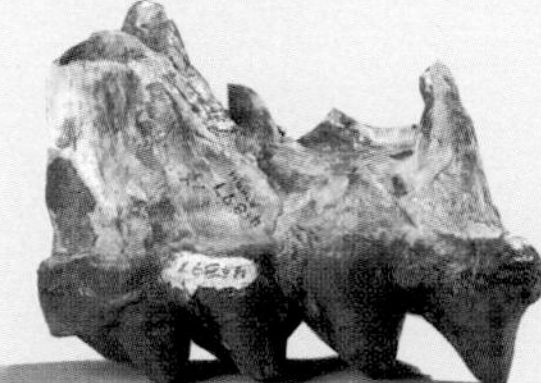

A mastodon molar found 40 miles off L.I. in 1950 is at the American Museum of Natural History.

The Hadrosaurus, whose remains were found in New Jersey; scientists say the dinosaur may have inhabited Long Island as well.

Molar Photo by Newsday / Ari Mintz; Illustration by Robert Walters

Earth by the time Africa and North America began drifting apart about 200 million years ago. The great reptiles probably thrived on the edge of the widening Atlantic Ocean, where majestic rivers swept down from the Appalachians into swampy deltas flecked with islands thick with ferns.

One of those rivers carved the valley that would become Long Island Sound, and they all carried away huge volumes of sediment from the eroding Appalachians. That sand piled up on the eastern flank of the mountain range and gradually formed a thick wedge on top of the older bedrock. That wedge still survives on Long Island, where the porous sand performs the vital job of storing most of our underground water supply.

The Long Island area was probably underwater much of the time that the dinosaurs lived, since the worldwide climate was so warm that relatively little ocean water was locked up in ice caps. But geologists know the area was exposed at least part of the time, because rocks found in Port Washington and elsewhere contain fossilized leaves from land plants similar to today's tulip and magnolia trees, leading Mills and other researchers to surmise that dinosaurs probably roamed here.

The Bahamas-like weather in which the dinosaurs thrived ended suddenly 65 million years ago. According to the current leading theory, a giant comet or asteroid hit the Earth, raising enormous dust clouds that blocked the sun. The dinosaurs died off quickly, and the cooling trend gradually picked up speed as North America continued to drift north and west toward its current position.

When it was in the tropics, North America had avoided several ice ages that struck other parts of the world. But this time, it would feel the full force of the big chill. Ice caps, developing first in Antarctica, eventually formed in Canada as well and began expanding south from Hudson Bay about 2.4 million years ago.

The Canadian ice sheet probably expanded and receded across the entire northern half of North America at least 16 times, lowering and raising sea level by hundreds of feet with each advance

Please see **GLACIERS** on Next Page

Birth of LI

GLACIERS from Preceding Page

and retreat. Just 22,000 years ago, when the last major glaciation was at its zenith, sea level was more than 300 feet lower than it is now, and the Atlantic shoreline was 80 miles south of present-day Fire Island.

Exactly how many times glaciers reached Long Island is uncertain. Most experts say there's no evidence the Island was glaciated more than twice, although some geologists think it happened five times or more. The first ice sheet was here either about 150,000 or 60,000 years ago, and the second 22,000 years ago, according to the majority view, based in part on Sirkin's research.

Monumental in size and power, the ice sheets changed everything in the region, and effectively built Long Island.

Before the glaciers arrived, Long Island was an indistinct part of a broad and flat plain that was often underwater. By the time the last ice sheet left, Long Island had an elevated central spine and distinctive north and south forks, all high enough to avoid the encroaching sea and survive as an exposed island.

Perhaps as much as 1,000 feet tall at its intimidating front edge, the last glacier, which is the one geologists know the most about, may have been even thicker farther north — thick enough to cover the tallest mountains in the Northeast, including 6,288-foot-tall Mt. Washington in New Hampshire.

The ice was so heavy that it distorted the Earth's crust, and probably also caused ice-free areas just beyond the glacier's southern edge to bulge up slightly. Thousands of years after that ice had retreated, land that had been squashed beneath the thickest parts of the glacier was still gradually rebounding. Newfoundland, for example, has bounced back more than 600 feet.

Like a snowplow clearing off a cement driveway, the glacier's leading edge scraped away the sandy deposits of the coastal plain wedge and exposed the bedrock below, which is why so many outcroppings of bedrock are visible today in New England but not Long Island.

Spreading south by perhaps one foot per day — a "glacial pace" that is remarkably fast by the timescale of geology — the expanding ice sheet not only bulldozed the sandy debris, it also sheared and carried off boulders as it scraped across bedrock. Some smaller rocks were moved more than 250 miles, which is why Mills has found cobbles in the Port Washington sand pits that came from Whiteface and Gore mountains in the upstate Adirondacks.

Fleeing the advancing ice sheet, an array of exotic cold-weather animals, many now extinct, moved into the Long Island area, including woolly mammoths, mastodons, ground sloths, saber-toothed tigers, elk-moose, caribou, musk oxen and wolves. Today, the teeth and bones of some of those Ice Age beasts are occasionally snared in fishermen's nets off the South Shore.

Scooping up massive amounts of rock and sand as it moved through Connecticut, the glacier then widened and deepened the ancient river valley that would later become Long Island Sound, and also broadened the narrow stream beds that would become the finger harbors of Long Island's North Shore.

The wide valley played another key role: It slowed the advancing ice sheet just before the world's climate grew warm enough to stop the glaciation.

By the time the glacier covered the northern half of Long Island, about 22,000 years ago, its edge was melting as fast as new ice was pushing down from Canada. More than 1,000 miles from where it began in Hudson Bay, the glacier finally stopped. Soon, the melting began to outstrip the production of new ice, and the ice sheet, like a Popsicle on a sidewalk, began to shrink.

In its wake, the retreating glacier left behind a Long Island landscape that it had dramatically transformed. A hilly ridge, or moraine, now marked the line where the ice sheet stopped. Made of bulldozed rock mixed with sand and gravel dumped by streams running down from the melting glacier, that moraine is still visible as Long Island's elevated central spine, which extends from Brooklyn to Amagansett before curving offshore. The offshore portion of that moraine has since been destroyed by ocean erosion but may once have constituted a third East End fork below the present-day Montauk peninsula.

The south-flowing icewater streams, including the Connetquot and Carmans Rivers, fed short-lived glacial lakes where icebergs floated. The swollen rivers also shaped fertile flatlands south of the moraine — most notably the Hempstead Plain, where the soil was rich with wind-blown silt that was also a gift of the glacier, since the fine powder came from rocks ground down by the ice sheet.

As it receded slowly, the glacier did more sculpting. Additional hilly moraines formed along the North Shore and North Fork, marking places where the ice sheet paused. Chunks of ice that broke free from the glacier and did not immediately melt formed deep depressions in the soil that later filled in with groundwater. The region's two biggest lakes, Ronkonkoma and Success, and many others, were formed in these "kettleholes." The glacier also left behind thousands of boulders that the ice sheet had sheared off the bedrock farther north and carried to Long Island.

By about 19,500 years ago, the glacier was off Long Island and slowly receding north. In the shadow of the retreating ice, a huge glacial lake that may have stretched from Queens to Martha's Vineyard filled the valley that would become Long Island Sound. That lake drained about 16,000 years ago, and the coastal plain was once again exposed. As the weather warmed, tundra vegetation gradually gave way to pine trees, and eventually chestnuts and oaks.

Still, Long Island was not yet an island. That process began roughly 15,000 years ago when the rising sea began entering the valley, probably near Fisher's Island. A few thousand years later, the ocean probably broke through at the valley's western edge.

Meanwhile, a new species was arriving in the area: Homo sapiens. Starting about 12,000 years ago, nomadic hunters, whose ancestors had trekked across the Bering Strait to Alaska 100 generations earlier, entered the region. Skillful hunters, these paleo-Indians probably quickly killed off the mammoths, mastodons and other large Ice Age animals.

Long Island finally earned its name about 11,000 years ago, or perhaps slightly later, when the rising ocean waters on the eastern and western edges of the ancient river valley finally

Part III: *The Finishing Touches*

Water was the final ingredient in forming Long Island as we know it. Dashed lines indicate current boundaries.

Glacial deposits
Long Island Sound
Atlantic Ocean
Water
Bedrock
Ancient sedimentary layers

17,500 years ago
The Wisconsinan glacier has receded from Long Island. Sea levels are still low, but gradually rising as the glacier melts. Lakes have been left in land depressions by the melting ice.

Current shoreline of Connecticut
LONG ISLAND
Future Long Island Sound
Ancestral Raritan River to the ocean
Lakes formed from melting ice

15,000-10,000 years ago
The Long Island Sound is being filled in with water from the ocean. Sea level continues to rise as the glacial ice melts back to Canada.

CONNECTICUT
NEW YORK
NEW JERSEY
LONG ISLAND
Long Island Sound
Ancestral Hudson River
Ancestral Raritan
Atlantic Ocean

8,000 years ago
Long Island as we know it begins to emerge, but it has yet to be carved into its modern form by waves and currents.

CONNECTICUT
NEW YORK
NEW JERSEY
LONG ISLAND
Atlantic Ocean

SOURCE: Herbert Mills, Nassau County Division of Museums; Henry Bokuniewicz, State University of New York at Stony Brook; PALEOMAP Project, University of Texas at Arlington; "Eastern Long Island Geology with Field Trips"; United States Geological Survey; "The Geological History of Long Island", Educational Leaflet No. 15 of the Nassau County Museum; "Roadside Geology of New York"; National Geographic World Atlas; "Icebergs and Glaciers"; "The Geological History of New York State"; "Planet Earth: Glacier"; "Physical Geology".

Newsday / Philip Dionisio

Throwing Stones in Academia

BY DAN FAGIN
STAFF WRITER

No, it's not an all-out war between two of the leading authorities on the natural history of Long Island. Let's just say relations are icy.

Les Sirkin and John Sanders tell two very different stories about the great glaciers that shaped Long Island, and neither geologist is shy about calling the other's ideas foolish — though the cutting remarks are never delivered directly, since the two rarely speak to each other.

The nicest thing that Sirkin, a 64-year-old research professor of earth sciences at Adelphi University, has to say about Sanders is: "John may be a great gadfly, but I don't think he's making an enormous impact on glacial geology."

Sanders, meanwhile, complains that Sirkin won't even consider evidence that his ideas might be wrong. "You can't dig with him and you can't ask questions. Now what does that tell you?" said the 71-year-old Sanders, a retired geology professor at Barnard College who is now affiliated with Hofstra University.

Their dispute is a personal one, but it also shows just how much of Long Island's history must still be written in pencil.

The biggest and oldest local controversy is over when, and how many times, ice sheets descended from Canada to form hills, lakes, cliffs, and every other familiar feature of Long Island.

That century-old argument would be easy to solve if rocks could be dated in the same way as fossils. But the standard technique of figuring out a fossil's age by measuring the decay of radioactive elements such as uranium and carbon-14 only works on bones, plants, or anything else that was once alive.

Instead, geologists study cliffs and other places where layers of rock are visible, and search those layers for buried shells, charcoal and other organic material that can be dated. They also ponder indirect evidence: fossilized pollen that shows whether the climate was cold enough for glaciers, and grooves cut into bedrock that reveal which direction the ice sheets moved.

Sirkin believes only two glaciers ever reached Long Island. He gives two possible dates for the first glacier, either 150,000 or 60,000 years ago, and thinks it covered at least the North Shore and probably additional areas before retreating into Canada.

The second glacier was here just 22,000 years ago, he says, and stopped halfway down Long Island, depositing a ridge of bulldozed rock — a moraine — stretching from Queens to Amagansett and continuing eastward toward Martha's Vineyard. As it retreated, the same glacier formed a second series of moraines near the North Shore, including the elevated spine of the North Fork, according to Sirkin.

Sanders gives a very different version. He believes that glaciers reached present-day Nassau and Suffolk Counties at least four times, that the two moraines were formed by different ice sheets, and that the last time ice was in either county was about 100,000 years ago. The 22,000-year-old glacier cited by Sirkin never made it south of Connecticut or east of Queens, according to Sanders.

A clear majority of geologists in the region agrees more with Sirkin than Sanders, who acknowledges that his own ideas conflict with what he calls the "prevailing dogma," which is also the version cited in Newsday's articles about Long Island history.

But Sanders isn't quitting. He and a Hofstra colleague, Charles Merguerian, continue to organize field trips, for amateurs and professionals alike, that are aimed at refuting Sirkin's ideas and boosting their own.

Sirkin, meanwhile, has also been busy trying to reach a wider audience, through a series of newly published books he has written about local geology.

Sanders bought one copy. But, so far, Sirkin hasn't signed up for a field trip.

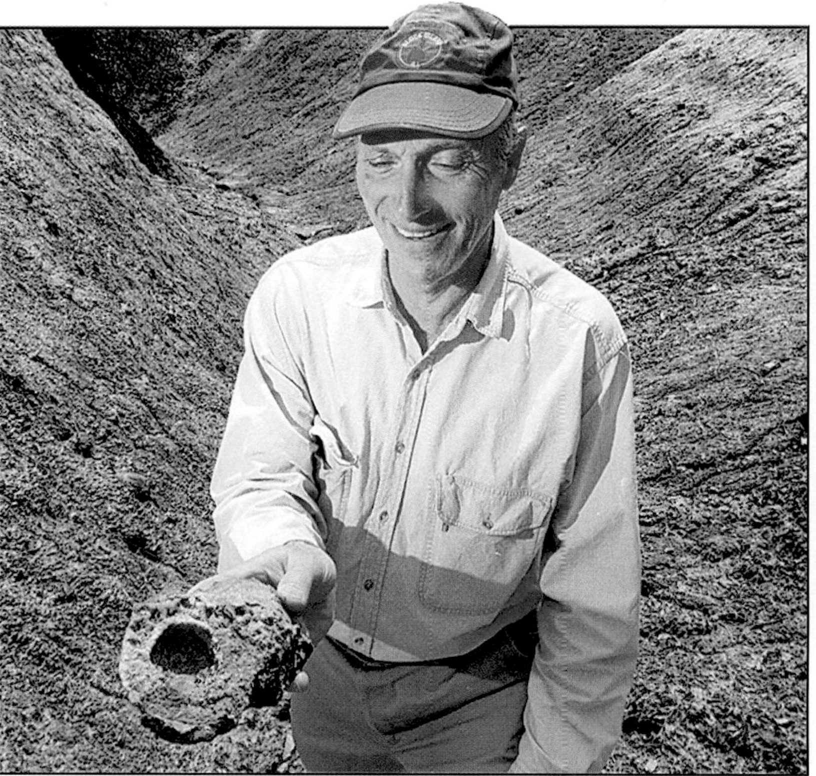

Newsday Photo / Bill Davis

Adelphi's Les Sirkin examines a concretion — a solid mass harder than surrounding rock — he found in a clay bed at the Port Washington sand pit. Below, John Sanders of Hofstra shows a line in a Montauk cliff that he says indicates a shift in the land.

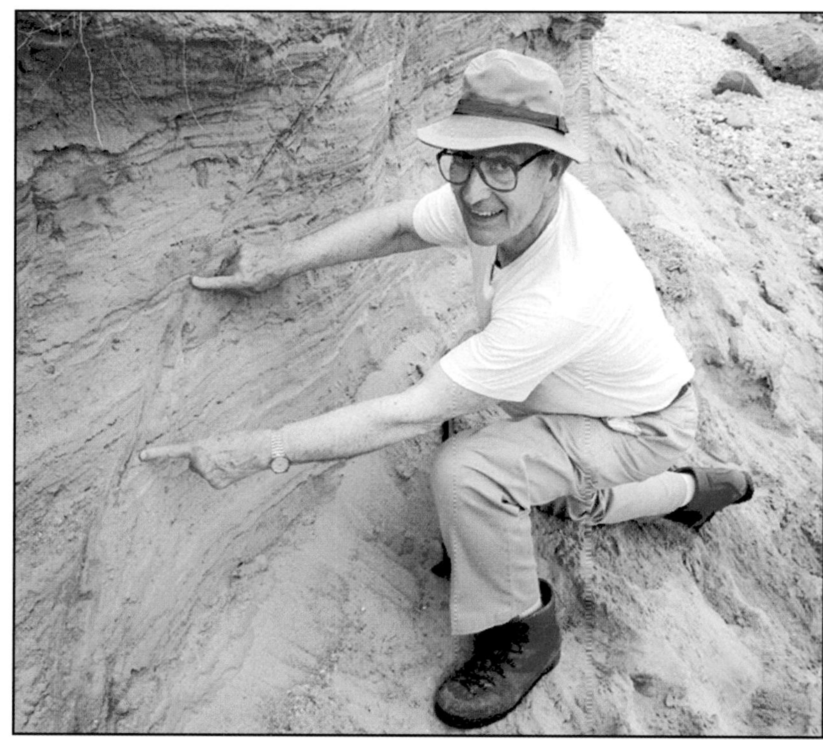

Newsday / Jessica Brandi Lifland

joined to form Long Island Sound.

But Long Island's evolution didn't end, and continues today, because storm erosion and the rising sea are still reshaping the Island.

The one-foot-per-century rise in sea level, and the pounding storm waves, are gradually shrinking the Island by pushing back the North Shore cliffs and cutting into the South Shore beaches. They also are gradually propelling the barrier islands inland. Fire Island, for example, is moving toward the South Shore at a rate of about 1.7 feet per year.

What happens next is uncertain; the only sure thing is that Long Island will keep changing. Many scientists suggest that emissions of carbon dioxide and other pollutants from burning oil and coal will speed the worldwide warming trend and escalate the sea-level rise, spelling disaster for shoreline communities in the coming century.

That's not the only possible scenario, however. There have been more than a half-dozen major ice ages in Earth's history, and each has apparently lasted anywhere from 20 million to 50 million years. But the last one began just 2 million years ago, and has consisted of 100,000-year cold periods — when much of North America was covered by ice — alternating with much shorter intervals of warm climate, usually lasting only about 10,000 years.The current period of warming has lasted more than 20,000 years.

"We may be running out of time," said John Sanders, a retired geology professor at Barnard College. "And the switchover, when it comes, is going to be very dramatic."

In other words, the glaciers may not be finished with Long Island just yet.

Newsday reporters, researchers, photographers, designers and editors have been working on "Long Island: Our Story" for as long as two years. In addition to the writers and others whose bylines and credits will appear in the daily installments, several people had key roles in the preparation of Chapter 1: Harvey Aronson, editor; Georgina Martorella, research; Jeff Schamberry, photo editing; Kathryn Sweeney, photo research; Robert Eisner, design; Larry Striegel, news editing; Tim Drachlis, graphic editing; and Mona Crawford, Internet site production.

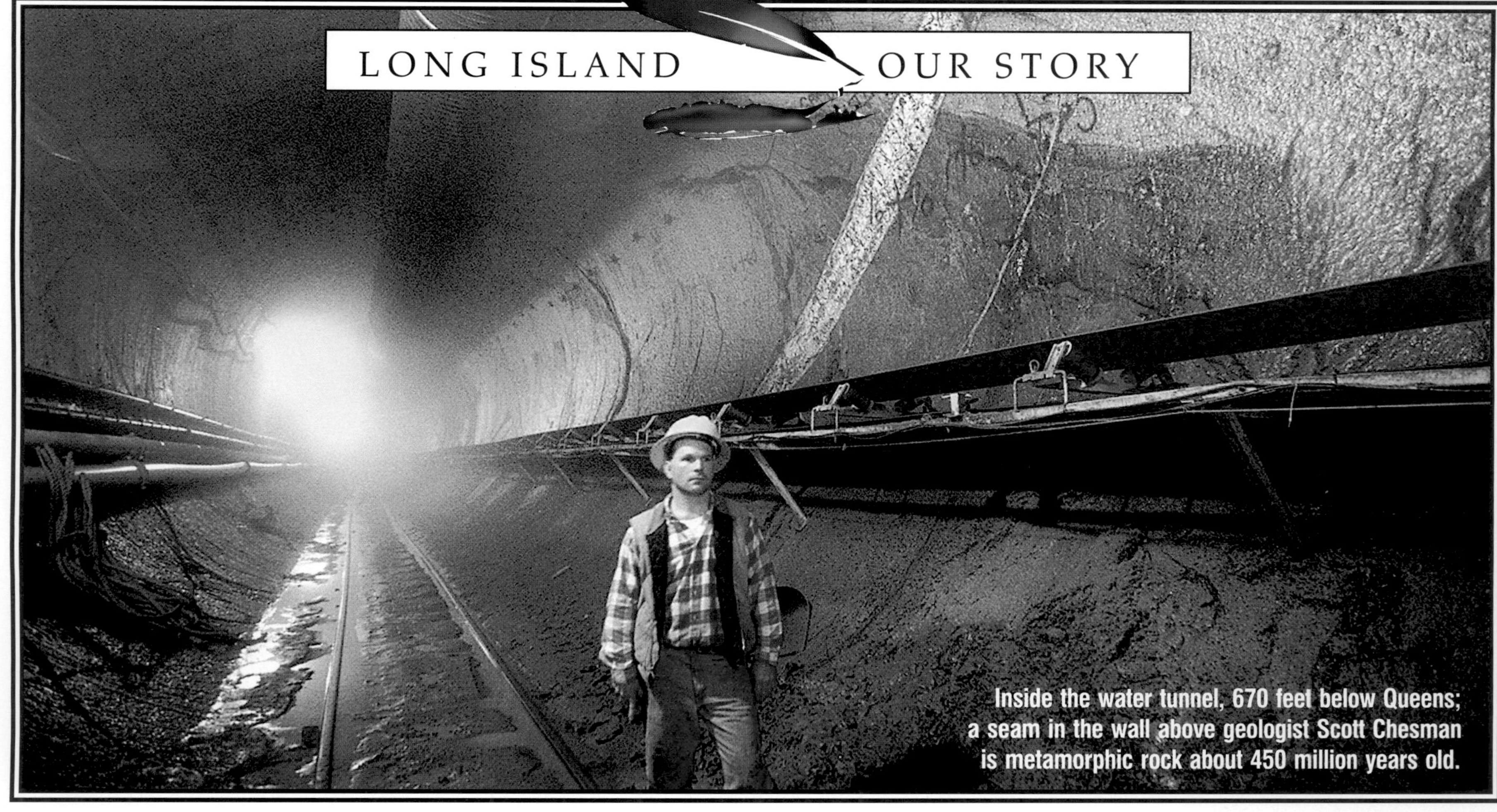

Inside the water tunnel, 670 feet below Queens; a seam in the wall above geologist Scott Chesman is metamorphic rock about 450 million years old.

Newsday Photo / Bill Davis

A new water tunnel offers rock-hard and ages-old clues about the formation of Long Island

In the Belly Of the Earth

BY DAN FAGIN
STAFF WRITER

Forged by the fiery collision of a now-vanished continent and a string of volcano islands, the oldest pieces of Long Island are a mystery whose secrets lie buried beneath hundreds of feet of sand and soil.

But there are clues, and some of the most intriguing are being revealed, inch by laborious inch, as a locomotive-sized machine drills a water tunnel through some of the hardest rock on Earth, 670 feet below Queens.

Much of the bedrock exposed by the drilling is 450 million years old. And while the primary purpose of the project is to bring more water to New York City, the incidental geology is fascinating in its own right. The long-hidden rock is the sturdy pedestal upon which eroding mountains and bulldozing glaciers later sculpted Long Island's familiar features, and it is the only real evidence of the Island's earliest history.

As revealed by the tunnel excavations, the ancient rock is anything but colorless. Even in the dim light of the construction lamps, the tunnel's sloping walls are a striking tableau of rippling stripes as delicate as spiderwebs and slashing faults as jarring as lightning bolts. Granite slabs speckled with garnet lie beside sheared-off chunks of blackish-green ocean crust and hardened lava from long-dead volcanoes.

"It's really extraordinary. It's the closest thing to a religious experience you can get in geology," said Charles Merguerian, a professor of structural geology at Hofstra University.

The epiphanies are few for bedrock experts on Long Island because here, unlike many other parts of the world, the only visible bedrock is a few small outcroppings at the northwestern edge of Queens in Long Island City. From there, the bedrock's upper boundary slopes steadily downward to the east and south. By the time that slope reaches central Suffolk County, the bedrock is more than 1,500 feet below the surface.

> **LI HISTORY.COM**
>
> See history in geology, with images of Long Island's Cretaceous sediments and fossils of plant and sea life. On the Internet, see http://www.lihistory.com.

No one knows whether the bedrock in Queens is similar to the unmapped rock beneath Nassau and Suffolk counties. "It's very possible that there may be a totally exotic piece of real estate down there under eastern Long Island that we don't even know about, possibly an old piece of Africa," Merguerian said, explaining that local bedrock could have originated in a different continent and been joined to North America after an ancient continental collision. "We have absolutely no clue."

Much of the sparse evidence that does exist has come from New York City's effort to build a third water tunnel to bring drinking water down from upstate reservoirs. The Queens leg of the tunnel is the latest in a series of digs that began in 1970 and will continue until the tunnel is finished in 2015.

On an afternoon when a driving rain had curbed activity at the surface, a crew of tunnel workers — or sandhogs, as they call themselves — was making steady progress near the bottom of an entry shaft in Maspeth that is more than twice as deep as the Statue of Liberty is tall. Monitoring the crew's progress in guiding the 640-ton boring machine was Scott Chesman, a former sandhog who is a geologist at the city Department of Environmental Protection.

His prime mission is to see how the ever-changing composition of the rock affects the progress of the $13 million machine. But Chesman is also mapping, analyzing and even videotaping the types of rock the machine encounters in hopes of shedding new light on the origin of Long Island's basement. He has only one chance to get it right, since the tunnel's exposed walls will later be covered with concrete. And the task is tricky because newer rock — a mere 360 million years old — has filled in crevices and faults in the older bedrock.

"It's rock psychology, you can see all the trauma that the rock's been through," said Chesman, pointing at an intricate pattern of older granite and younger volcanic rock.

The tunnel walls in Queens are streaked with major fault lines, and many of those cracks are packed so tight with groundwater that when struck by the drilling machine they gush water at a torrential rate — as much as 1,300 gallons a minute — that requires a fast grouting job by the sandhogs.

The many faults along the tunnel walls are powerful evidence that our region is in an earthquake zone. Large quakes were recorded in the New York City area in 1737 and 1884, and others are sure to follow, according to Merguerian. In fact, he said, the long gap between earthquakes means that the next one, when it comes, may be a big one.

Another key discovery in the tunnels has bolstered the leading theory about how at least some of Long Island's bedrock was formed.

A half-billion years ago, geologists believe, the continent that would later become North America was rotated in a different direction. The land that would become the east coast of the United States was facing south, just below the equator, near an offshore arc of islands.

When that island chain smashed into the coast about 450 million years ago, the oceanic rocks were pushed 10 miles deep into the Earth. There, temperatures as high as 1,300 degrees transformed the rock to its super-hard form.

Later cataclysms brought the bedrock to its present position near the surface, and added new wrinkles. For instance, additional local bedrock was formed 360 million years ago when a collision on the other side of the volcano arc created what would become New England, and still more was formed about 280 million years ago in the great collision with what became Africa that pushed up the Appalachian Mountains and formed the super-continent of Pangaea. North America and Africa have been drifting apart ever since Pangaea began breaking up about 200 million years ago.

Merguerian and other experts believe it is the first of those collisions that created most of Long Island's bedrock, and the tunnel excavations support that theory by revealing new evidence of a massive fault zone — called Cameron's Line — that stretches from central Massachusetts to Brooklyn and is thought to mark the impact zone of that first ancient collision 450 million years ago.

"You can actually see the characteristics of Cameron's Line in the subsurface geology," Merguerian said, referring to the fault lines. "It's right there on the tunnel walls."

Many secrets of the bedrock are still untold. But a skyscraper's length below the streets of Maspeth, inside the tunnel whose walls are covered with swirls and swoops of pressure-cooked rock, it is at least possible to begin to imagine the awesome power of the continental collisions that formed the solid foundation upon which Long Island was built.

Preserving deep reserves of water is LI's chief environmental issue

Ancient, Clean, Controversial

BY DAN FAGIN
STAFF WRITER

The oldest stuff at Jones Beach State Park isn't the 1950s rock and roll at the oldies shows, the vintage 1929 bathhouses, or even the Jones name, which comes from a British privateer who established a whaling outpost on the beach 300 years ago.

It's the drinking water, which probably predates even the 11th Century Venetian bell tower that was the model for Jones Beach's water tower.

The water in the park's brick-and-stone tower originated as rain that fell somewhere near the current site of the Long Island Expressway about 1,000 years ago and then trickled downward and toward the South Shore through layers of sand, gravel and clay. The water's journey finally ended when it was captured 1,100 feet below Jones Beach by wells that pumped it all the way up to the tower for use in faucets and showers.

As the millennium-long odyssey of Jones Beach's water supply shows, Long Island's aquifer system is not only the region's most vital natural resource and its chief environmental concern, it is also our strongest link with the ancient past.

Events that occurred tens of millions of years ago built the interconnected layers of water-bearing sand and gravel that extend as deep as 2,000 feet and make up the aquifer system. The water in those buried reservoirs consists entirely of rain that seeps through the Island's sandy soil and slowly moves down and sideways for hundreds or even thousands of years until it either drifts off the Island or is pumped back up to the surface again by water wells.

It is a bountiful supply that holds roughly 70 trillion gallons — enough to flood the entire surface of Long Island with more than 300 feet of water — and can withstand long droughts that dry up surface-water reservoirs like the ones that supply New York City. But it is also a fragile system that has been measurably altered by the suburbanization of Long Island, and by the more than 1,000 wells that collectively pump about 390 million gallons of water out of the aquifers every day.

Sewers and intense pumping have lowered the water table by a few feet in Nassau and western Suffolk, diminishing or even eliminating many shallow streams and lakes and causing underground salt water to seep inland deep below the shorelines.

Portions of the shallow and mid-range aquifer system are now so tainted by fertilizers, pesticides, industrial chemicals, gasoline and cesspools that water companies must either treat the water after they pump it up or abandon their shallow wells. Some of that contaminated groundwater also seeps into bays and harbors, contributing to pollution problems offshore.

The aquifer system's ability to renew itself with clean rainwater, meanwhile, has been diminished by the profusion of driveways, roads and parking lots. Drops that once fell directly on soil are now increasingly landing on concrete, where they pick up contaminants before trickling down into the aquifer system. Some of those contaminants can remain in groundwater for hundreds of years as droplets slowly seep downward.

The effects are so far-reaching that the concern over preserving the quality of Long Island's groundwater has become the single most important factor limiting the region's growth.

"The only true limit is water," said veteran planner Lee Koppelman, director of the Center for Regional Policy Studies at the State University at Stony Brook. "It is the limiting, controlling factor because we don't have any external sources of water — unless we're all going to buy Perrier. If we have environmental interests that we care about protecting, we have to limit our use of the aquifers and protect the recharge areas."

Long Island depends on groundwater because of events that began 100 million years ago, when the Appalachians were still a towering mountain range and the future Long Island was part of a bedrock plain sloping southeast from the Appalachian foothills to the eastern edge of North America.

Over tens of millions of years, streams carried sediments from the eroding mountains and deposited them on the bedrock in a series of distinct layers that eventually resembled a lopsided lasagna. At the northwestern edge of Queens, where the bedrock is at the surface, these sandy sediments are only a few feet deep. But in southeastern Suffolk County the layers of sand, gravel and clay occupy more than 2,000 feet between the surface and the bedrock.

The deepest and oldest layer, just above the bedrock, is a wedge of water-bearing sand and gravel known as the Lloyd aquifer. On top of the Lloyd is a thinner layer of clay called the Raritan. The next layer of sand, gravel and silt is the Magothy aquifer, deposited about 60 million years ago and the region's most important source of drinking water. Another clay barrier called Gardiner's Clay is on top of the Magothy, but only near the South Shore. And the uppermost layer is the narrow and polluted Upper Glacial Aquifer, composed of sand and rocky rubble that was bulldozed into the area by at least two ice sheets, the last one just 22,000 years ago.

The layer-cake composition means groundwater moves in predictable patterns, slowing and changing course when it reaches clay and speeding up in sand and gravel. Near the North Shore, groundwater tends to move more quickly toward Long Island Sound, and near the South Shore it moves toward the ocean. But in the middle of Long Island, rainwater moves slowly into the deepest aquifers that are becoming increasingly important sources of drinking water as shallower aquifers are contaminated.

That's why planners worry the most about protecting Long Island's central spine, including the Suffolk pine barrens. The recharge zone for the Magothy aquifer is only five miles wide, centered roughly on the Long Island Expressway. And only the middle half-mile of that zone recharges the deeper, cleaner Lloyd aquifer.

That's an immediate concern for the dozens of Long Island communities relying on rainwater that has been in the aquifer system anywhere from 10 to 50 years.

But even in places like Jones Beach, where the water is 1,000 years old, the quality of the water supply will eventually be determined by the way we treat our environment today. That is the unavoidable legacy of Long Island's aquifer system.

LI's Aquifers

The water Long Islanders drink is stored beneath the ground primarily in three layers.

Glacial aquifer
Water table
Runoff
Long Island Sound
Lakes
Evaporation while falling
Evaporation
Evaporation
Great South Bay
Fire Island
Atlantic Ocean
500 feet
Bedrock
1,000 feet
500 feet
1,000 feet
1,500 feet
Magothy aquifer
Raritan confining unit
Lloyd aquifer

Only water that lands in deep-flow recharge zone will reach the Lloyd aquifer

Ground water travel time in years

1. Glacial layer contains the newest water to the groundwater system.
2. The Magothy layer is the largest of the aquifer formations and holds the most water, much of which is hundreds of years old.
3. The Lloyd layer is largely untapped and contains the oldest water, some of which has been held in aquifers for more than 5,000 years.

0 MILES 10

Newsday / Philip Dionisio

SOURCE: Suffolk County Water Authority

Newsday Photo / Bill Davis

THE LOWLY SUMP

Sumps don't get much respect. Fenced-in eyesores, they take up precious space in suburbia. But the more than 3,000 basins on Long Island have at least two big jobs: controlling floods and recharging underground aquifers. Sewers in roads and parking lots collect rainwater and send it to nearby sumps, so that storm water need not be piped to bays and harbors. As more land is paved, sumps are places where rain can still penetrate the soil and reach aquifers. The basins range in size from 10,000 square feet to more than 20 acres. The problem is, by the time storm water reaches sumps it has been tainted by fertilizer, gasoline and other pollutants, which then enter aquifers. That's why planners concerned about protecting the water supply say sumps are no substitute for preserving open space.

The Sound is framed by Connecticut and Long Island in a photo taken in March from the Space Shuttle.

NASA Photo; Newsday Map

Once a river, then a valley, a lake, and recently the body of water we know today

The Evolution of LI Sound

BY DAN FAGIN
STAFF WRITER

It has been an ancient river, a fertile valley, a vast ice field, and a milky, iceberg-laden lake almost 200 miles long. What it hasn't been, until recently, is the saltwater estuary that makes Long Island a long island.

Long Island Sound is only about 11,000 years old — born yesterday, by the standards of geology. But it runs deep into the distant past. In fact, experts say, were it not for a river that formed tens of millions of years earlier when dinosaurs were still roaming the area, the Sound probably wouldn't exist today and Long Island would be part of Connecticut.

The signs of the Sound's varied history are everywhere, if you know where to look. Under its muddy bottom are beach ridges that radiate from the waterway's center like bathtub rings and mark its gradual expansion as sea level has risen. Embedded in its shoreline cliffs are dark-colored ribbons of clay from a now-vanished freshwater lake. Buried deep in its sediments are the shells of animals that thrived when the Sound was a valley laced with streams, and deeper still are the shadowy vestiges of the ancient river channels that first carved the valley in the time of the dinosaurs.

Geologist Ralph Lewis has been studying those signs for 16 years. Using submarines, sonar, drilling machines and even remote-controlled vehicles to explore the Long Island Sound's depths, Lewis and other experts have compiled a detailed chronology of the waterway's relatively recent birth, and its ancient antecedents.

"What's fascinating about Long Island Sound is that so much of the story happened in the last 12,000 years, when humans were here," said Lewis, an associate state geologist at the Connecticut Geological and Natural History Survey. "The first people who came to this area saw a completely different world than we see today. They watched Long Island Sound evolve."

The story actually begins tens of millions of years before the first Indians arrived, when the valley that would one day become Long Island Sound was carved by a river, or perhaps two rivers, that drained a broad, sandy coastal plain. Smaller tributary streams extended to the south onto present-day Long Island, and carved similar valleys that today are still recognizable as the harbor inlets of the north shore, from Little Neck Harbor in Queens all the way out to the gently curved bays of the North Fork.

But as with almost every other natural feature in the region, it took a series of huge ice floes descending from Canada — the glaciers — to transform that ancient valley into the shape we would recognize as Long Island Sound.

At least twice over the past 150,000 years, ice sheets with imposing front walls that may have been 1,000 feet tall plowed across that river valley.

As they moved, the glaciers widened and deepened the valley, scooping up a massive amount of rock and sand and carrying it south onto Long Island. Some of the scooped-up material ended up as a long ridge, called a terminal moraine, that marks the line where each glacier finally stopped and began receding north again as it melted. The glaciers, however, did not retreat steadily. Instead, they stuttered, creating new ridges called recessional moraines wherever they paused. Today, the locations of two of those moraines are marked by the elevated spines of the north and south forks of Long Island.

Each time a glacier retreated north, it left behind an extraordinary calling card: a large but temporary lake formed by the melting ice. On their north sides, these glacial lakes were bounded by the towering ice wall of the receding ice sheet, and on the south by the bouldery ridges of the moraines.

The last glacier, which probably arrived on Long Island about 23,000 years ago, is the one that researchers know the most about. As it slowly receded into New England about 2,000 years later, the glacier left in its growing wake a huge lake, or perhaps series of lakes, extending from Queens to Martha's Vineyard. Scientists call the Long Island Sound portion of that lake Glacial Lake Connecticut.

"You may have been able to canoe all the way from New York City to Buzzard's Bay [Massachusetts] in this one big freshwater lake," Lewis said.

Lake Connecticut was unlike anything Long Islanders would know today. It was deeper and colder than today's Sound and probably had no fish. Icebergs likely floated on its waters, and even its color was different: dim and milky because it contained so much "rock flour" — the powdery residue of rocks ground down by the glacier. Mastodons and giant sloths probably roamed the barren tundra of the lake's southern shoreline, while the towering, gray ice wall loomed on the opposite shore. As the ice continued to recede, short-lived glacial lakes later formed near Albany and Hartford, among other places.

About 3,000 years after it was born, Lewis said, Lake Connecticut drained through an eroded gap in the moraine ridge near Fisher's Island. For a short time, starting about 16,000 years ago, the ancient but newly broadened valley was once again exposed. But not for long, because about 1,000 years later, rising ocean waters came in through the same eroded gap — this time in the opposite direction. Eventually, the ocean broke through on the valley's western edge, too, and the Sound began to take shape.

But the Indian hunters who began arriving in the area soon afterward saw a waterway that looked very different than it does today. Long Island Sound at first was slender and small, and its shorelines were bare. Sea level was rising so quickly that there wasn't time for marshes — which can take decades to fully develop — to appear along its edges. Indeed, it wasn't until about 4,000 years ago, when the rate of sea level rise slowed, that the wetlands we know today began to appear along its coasts.

Since then, the Sound's waters have risen another 20 feet, enough to reclaim huge chunks of land that had not been submerged since the days of Lake Connecticut. But even today, Long Island Sound isn't finished growing. Erosion and rising sea level continue to cut into its shore cliffs and beaches, slowly expanding the boundaries of this young and ever-changing waterway.

LI HISTORY.COM

A glacier glossary on the Internet reveals the role glaciers played in shaping Long Island and Long Island Sound. You can also test your knowledge of Long Island Sound and learn about its legends and lore. See http://www.lihistory.com.

A tiny portion is all that remains of the once vast Hempstead Plains

The Prairie That Was

BY GEORGE DEWAN
STAFF WRITER

Toward the end of every August, the purple-pink, bell-shaped flowers of the sandplain gerardia burst into bloom in a small section of a 19-acre protected site in the southeast corner of Nassau Community College in Garden City. That the fragile, endangered member of the snapdragon family survives at all in this place is because its home is one of the last remnants of the great Hempstead Plains.

The first known prairie in America and one of its first major tourist attractions, the flat and treeless, grassy Hempstead Plains was formed thousands of years ago by the outwash of the glacier that sculpted Long Island. Visitors made long trips to see this natural wonder, and they were not disappointed: In May the birdfoot violets created a magnificent blue-violet mantle across the plain; later in the season, the prolific tall grasses appeared as a gray-green lake, shimmering gently in the wind.

Today, only about 80 acres of the original 60,000-acre Hempstead Plains have survived the intrusion of man. Like a wistful reminder of a Long Island that once was, these remnants sit in isolation amid the concrete and steel effusions of 20th Century suburbia. The land there is a dramatic reminder that on Long Island, geography has been our destiny.

Indians may have hunted and camped on the plain. Colonial white settlers used it as common pasturage for their sheep and cattle, and later, as sodbusters, they put the land to the plow. Horse-racing tracks were built. The military made good use of the plains, from pre-revolutionary militia encampments to 20th Century army bases. Its flat vistas were ideal for the airfields that were laid out in what became the Cradle of Aviation. Garden City arose on the plain, as did Levittown and Plainview and Plainedge. Massive shopping centers sprouted.

Where once there were footpaths, the plains are now criss-crossed by superhighways. The grasshopper sparrows and the upland sandpipers have not been seen in recent years, and the heath hen is certified extinct. The bushy rock rose and the hand-maid moth are fighting for survival. The center of the Hempstead Plains is now the heart of Nassau County, which has adopted the birdfoot violet as the official county flower, and given the remaining 80 acres protected status.

Before the expansion westward, where pioneers discovered the Great Plains beyond the Mississippi River, the Hempstead Plains was the only prairie Americans knew. Running from eastern Queens almost to the Suffolk County border, it was a true prairie, flat and almost treeless, covered by tall, coarse grasses like broom sedge, Indian Grass, Little and Big Blue Stem and a profusion of wildflowers.

For some time, experts have debated why the Hempstead Plains retained its unique prairie characteristics, but there is no consensus. One explanation is that its upper layer of soil, although rich and loamy, is very thin, and the underlying sand and gravel subsoil allows water to percolate quickly downward, leaching away many soil nutrients. Also, the sod formed by prairie grasses has deep and dense roots, almost impenetrable to other plants. And, frequent burnings by Indians and later the colonists encouraged the growth of prairie grasses but inhibited everything else.

One of the first travelers to take note the Hempstead Plains' unique quality was Daniel Denton, who wrote in 1670:

"Towards the middle of Long-Island lyeth a plain sixteen miles long and four broad, upon which plain grows very fine grass, that makes exceeding good hay, and is very good pasture for sheep or other cattel; where you shall find neither stick nor stone to hinder the horse heels, or endanger them in their races . . ."

In the earliest colonial days, the plain was not parceled out to individuals, but retained as common property, pasture land for everyone's cattle and sheep. When the Town of North Hempstead was separated from Hempstead in 1784, the town began to assign the plains land to individual farmers. But Hempstead Town retained the plains as common land for another century.

Little by little, acre by acre, the Hempstead Plains was put to other uses. First it was plowed over for the planting of crops. But at the turn of the 20th Century it became apparent that the flat Hempstead Plains was a natural terrain for the taking off and landing of the new flying machines. Aviation, which began as a pastime, became a major industry on Long Island.

Newsday Photos / Bill Davis

Nature Conservancy biologist Marilyn Jordan, left, at a preserved section of the Hempstead Plains; above, the sandplain gerardia, an endangered plant.

Today there are 19 acres at Nassau Community College, a plot managed by the Nature Conservancy. Directly to the south, across Charles Lindbergh Boulevard, there are another 60 acres, the Hempstead Plains Preserve, supervised by the Nassau County Department of Recreation and Parks. The tracts can be seen by arrangement with the agencies.

The county biologist most concerned with maintaining the preserve is Carole Neidich-Ryder. But, she says, if left untouched, the last 80 acres of the Hempstead Plains will disappear as a prairie.

What, she is asked, would the 80 remaining acres of the Hempstead Plains look like in 10 or 20 years if they were left completely alone? "It would look like the intersection of the Grand Central and the Cross Island Parkways," she replies.

Many nonnative species of plants are competing with native prairie grasses and flowers such as the rare sandplain gerardia, often crowding them out. The 60 acres south of Lindbergh Boulevard, for example, seem well on their way to that fate, as blackberry and dewberry brambles, black cherry, autumn olive, mugwort, bush clover and other nonnative plants and bushes are taking over.

Which leads to the intriguing conclusion that to keep the last of the Long Island prairie in its natural state, something unnatural will have to be done to it. It is going to have to be gardened.

"That's what environmental restoration is about," Neidich-Ryder says. "It's about the fact that we've changed our natural habitat in so many different places that to get it back to where it was, it's gardening. It's gardening on a grand scale. Yeah, there's no mistake about that."

So the Hempstead Plains has become a sort of living museum, but one that needs constant attention lest it become something else. "The Hempstead Plains is so small, and the environmental stress on it is so great, that if the humans don't help it along by cutting or burning, or taking off some of the plants that we don't need, it will be lost from the face of the Earth," she says. "You won't have it any more."

The Hempstead Plains

The Hempstead Plains is outwash of a glacier's retreat from Long Island.

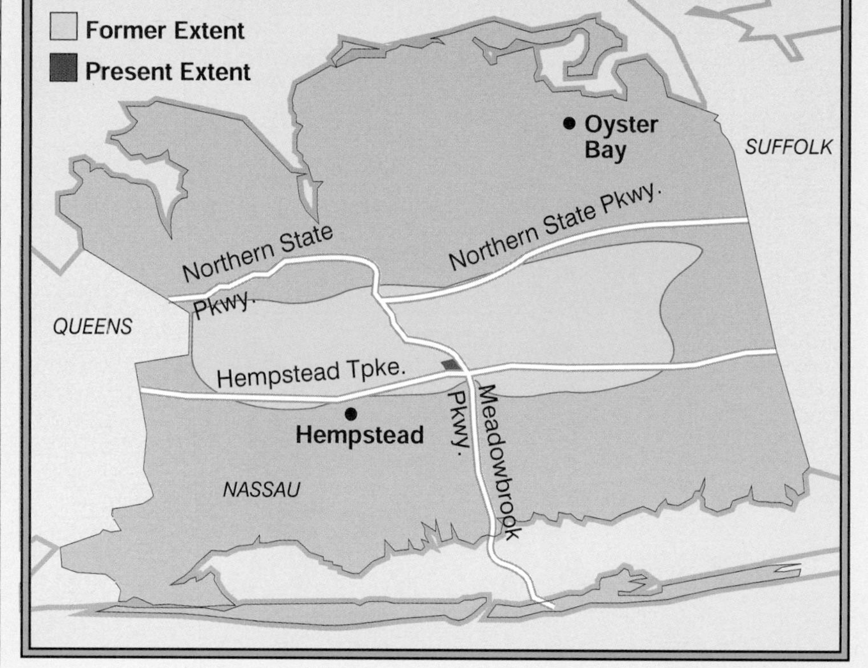

Newsday / Linda McKenney

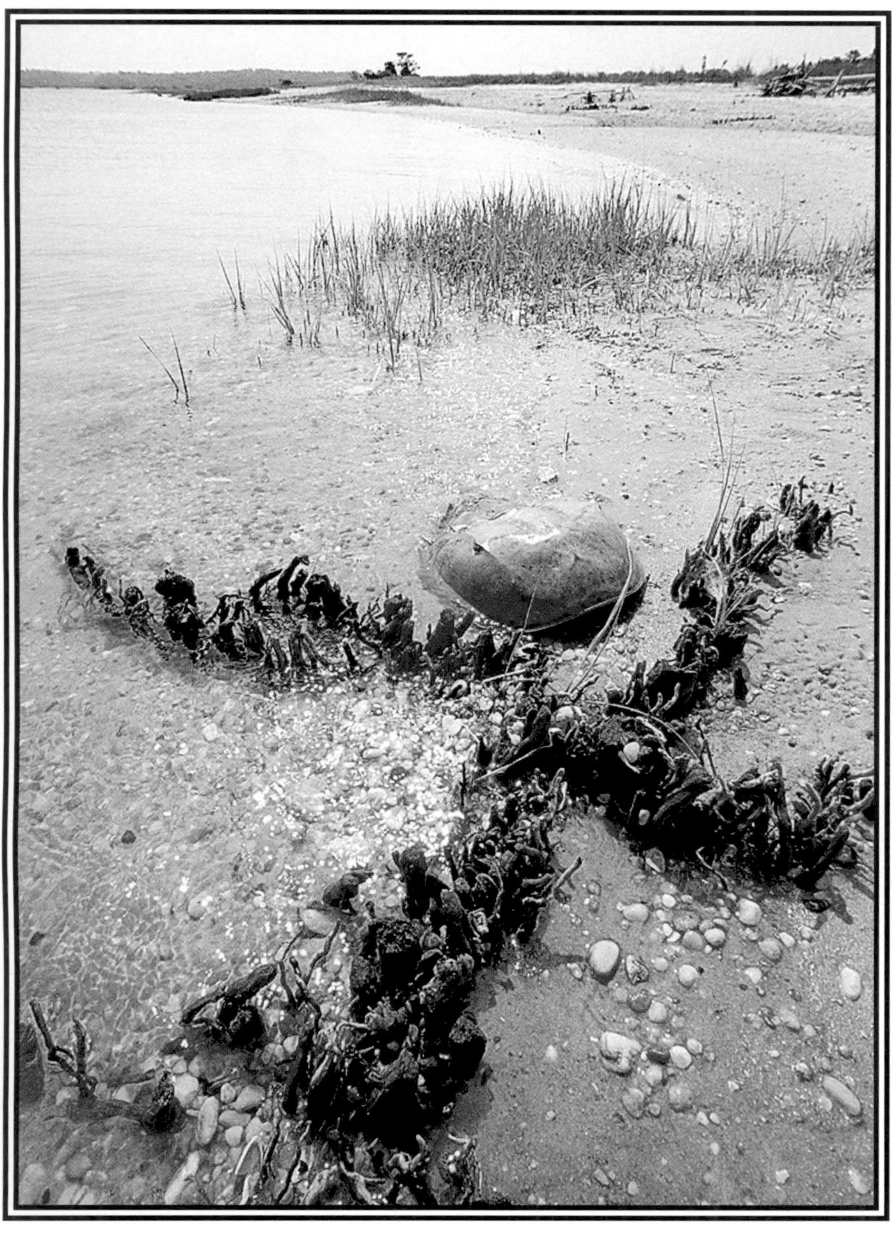

Newsday Photo / Bill Davis

Roots are all that remain of an ancient Atlantic white cedar tree that rose at the edge of Flanders Bay in Suffolk County. The rising sea wipes out the trees, creating the "ghost forests" of roots.

Ancient tree roots render haunting prophecy of shoreline erosion yet to come

Ghost Forests Send a Message

BY DAN FAGIN

STAFF WRITER

The ghost forest lies at the end of a rutted road through a piney woodland, beyond a stand of cedar and tupelo trees, across a grassy wetland and over a weathered dune to the edge of a gently arcing beach on the southern shore of Flanders Bay.

Coated with barnacles and diminished to their stumpy roots by erosion, the Atlantic white cedars on the beach at Hubbard County Park aren't much to look at. But the trees have been dead for thousands of years, and the story the ghost forest tells is about an island that is one of the most physically dynamic places on the planet.

Long Island is geological history in the making. While much of the world changes only along the multimillion-year time scale of sliding continental plates, Long Island undulates before our eyes, thanks to the tremendous forces of wind, tide and shifting sea level that pound away at an island made mostly of soft sand, not hard rock. Bluffs and beaches can give way at breathtaking speed, while barrier islands roll toward the mainland quickly enough for their movements to be tracked from year to year. And the foot-per-century worldwide rise in sea level is not only shrinking the Island at its edges, but also gradually pushing up the underground water table and flooding formerly dry land far from the coast.

"This is a dynamic place. You can stand on a cliff during a nor'easter and watch it eroding at your feet," said Les Sirkin, a research professor of Earth sciences at Adelphi University.

Nature isn't the only force changing Long Island, of course. Humans have had a powerful impact, especially during the last 50 years as the population of Nassau and Suffolk Counties has more than tripled to 2.6 million. Sea walls, jetties and dredging have altered the pattern of erosion. Drinking-water wells and sewer systems have slowed the natural rise in the water table, and development has drained many of the wetlands that would be expanding as the water table rises.

Although human activity has obscured many of the signs of Long Island's dynamism, they are still visible to the trained eye. And they denote the Island's continuing natural evolution as surely as a budding crocus signifies the passage from winter to spring.

Faded stripes on oceanfront cliffs mark oscillations in sea level, and so do

Long Island Forms

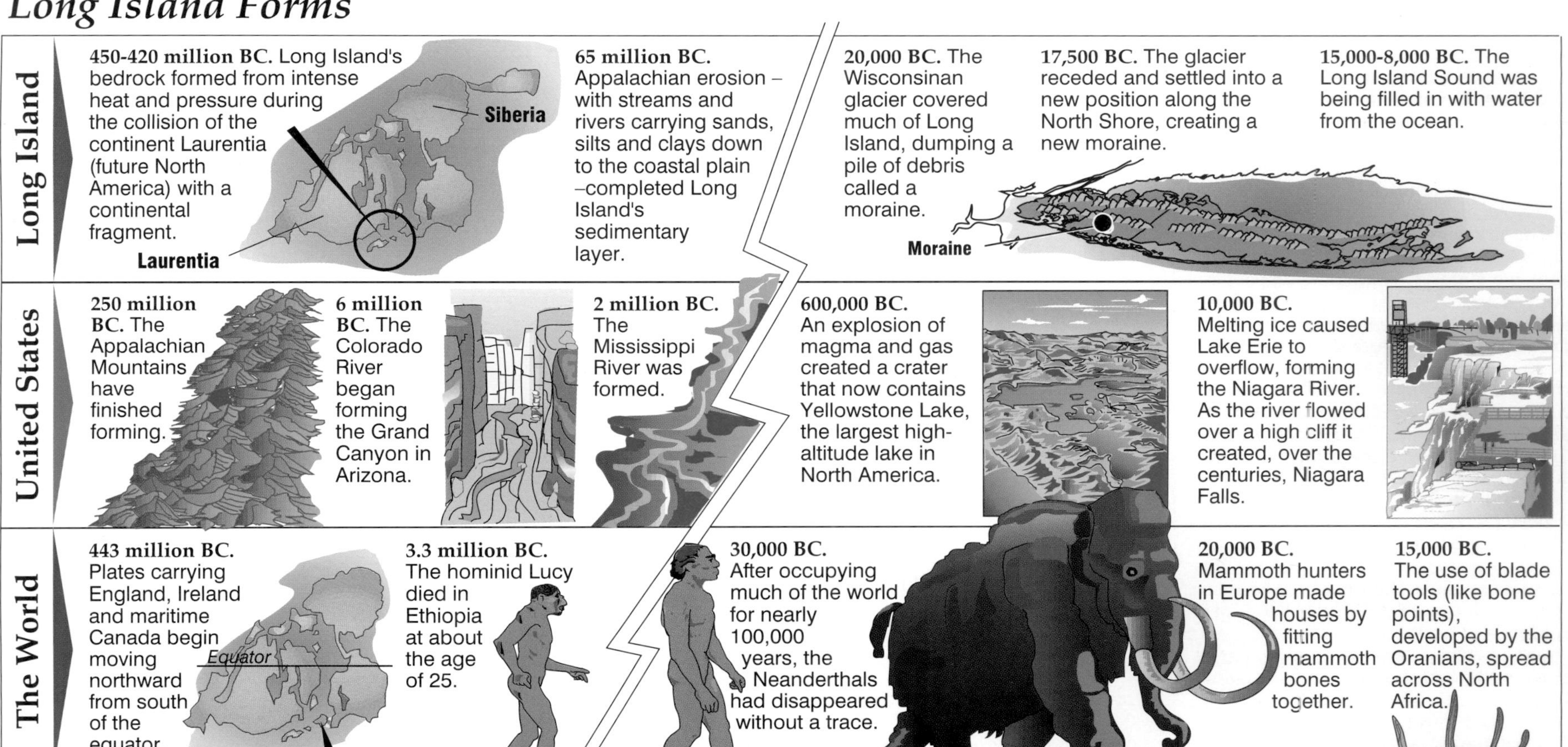

Long Island
450-420 million BC. Long Island's bedrock formed from intense heat and pressure during the collision of the continent Laurentia (future North America) with a continental fragment.
Siberia
Laurentia
65 million BC. Appalachian erosion – with streams and rivers carrying sands, silts and clays down to the coastal plain –completed Long Island's sedimentary layer.
20,000 BC. The Wisconsinan glacier covered much of Long Island, dumping a pile of debris called a moraine.
Moraine
17,500 BC. The glacier receded and settled into a new position along the North Shore, creating a new moraine.
15,000-8,000 BC. The Long Island Sound was being filled in with water from the ocean.
United States
250 million BC. The Appalachian Mountains have finished forming.
6 million BC. The Colorado River began forming the Grand Canyon in Arizona.
2 million BC. The Mississippi River was formed.
600,000 BC. An explosion of magma and gas created a crater that now contains Yellowstone Lake, the largest high-altitude lake in North America.
10,000 BC. Melting ice caused Lake Erie to overflow, forming the Niagara River. As the river flowed over a high cliff it created, over the centuries, Niagara Falls.
The World
443 million BC. Plates carrying England, Ireland and maritime Canada begin moving northward from south of the equator.
Equator
ENGLAND
3.3 million BC. The hominid Lucy died in Ethiopia at about the age of 25.
30,000 BC. After occupying much of the world for nearly 100,000 years, the Neanderthals had disappeared without a trace.
20,000 BC. Mammoth hunters in Europe made houses by fitting mammoth bones together.
15,000 BC. The use of blade tools (like bone points), developed by the Oranians, spread across North Africa.
B.C.
450 million years
250 million years
2 million years
600,000 years
32,000 years
22,000 years
17,000 years
15,000 years
12,000 years

Newsday / Philip Dionisio

LI HISTORY.COM

Learn how geologists and other scientists study Long Island using specialized maps. On the Internet, you'll see a tectonic map, a geologic map and a physiographic map and find out what information they supply to researchers. See http://www.lihistory.com.

the subtle stair-step beaches that lie above and below the water line. Shoreline landmarks like the Montauk Lighthouse and Ocean Parkway serve as fixed reference points to measure the long-term impact of erosion. And far from the coast, expanding swamps and shifting forest boundaries all point to a shrinking island.

Nowhere is Long Island's ever-changing topography more dramatically evident than in the ghost forests.

The term was coined by geologist Steve Englebright, a member of the state Assembly and curator of the Museum of Long Island Natural Sciences in Stony Brook who identified the ancient trees on several East End beaches, including Hubbard County Park, Montauk Point State Park and Mashomack Preserve on Shelter Island.

On a warm morning, Englebright tripped along the shoreline at Hubbard with the enthusiasm of a schoolboy on the first day of summer, waving his arms in sweeping gestures that took in the entire tableau of beach, dune, marsh, grassland and, finally, distant tree line — all of it undisturbed by humans.

"What you are seeing is the natural evolution of Long Island," he said. Toeing a desiccated tree root on the narrow beach while pointing to a line of cedars 100 yards inland, he said, "What used to live here now lives way back there."

Englebright explained that the Atlantic white cedar, rare in New York, tends to grow only on the boundary between grassland and forest. So the stubby cedar roots on the shore, he said, must be the remnants of ancient trees that were alive when the sea level was much lower, and when the beach was a few hundred feet farther out.

The twin forces of shoreline erosion and rising sea level not only changed the location of the beach, they set off an ecological chain reaction that pushed everything else back, too: the dune, the swamp, the grassland, and the line of cedars marking the beginning of the pine forest. "The pine barrens have been pushed back over the centuries, and this is the proof," Englebright said.

Tests on the ancient trees support his idea. Radiocarbon tests show that cedar roots on the beach at Montauk are 6,500 years old, and that similar stumps at Mashomack are 4,200 years old. The ghost forest at Hubbard County Park has not been tested, but Englebright believes that the cedar roots at the shoreline here are at least 3,000 years old.

The cedars aren't the only clue to the big changes at Hubbard.

Crouching at the shoreline and digging eight inches into the sand, Englebright pulled up a handful of peat. The dark-colored material consists of decomposed plants, and doesn't occur naturally under bare beaches. Instead, it forms at the bottom of densely vegetated wetlands like the swamp located 20 yards away from the shoreline at Hubbard. The peat under the beach, he said, must have been deposited centuries ago when sea level

Please see **CHANGES** on Next Page

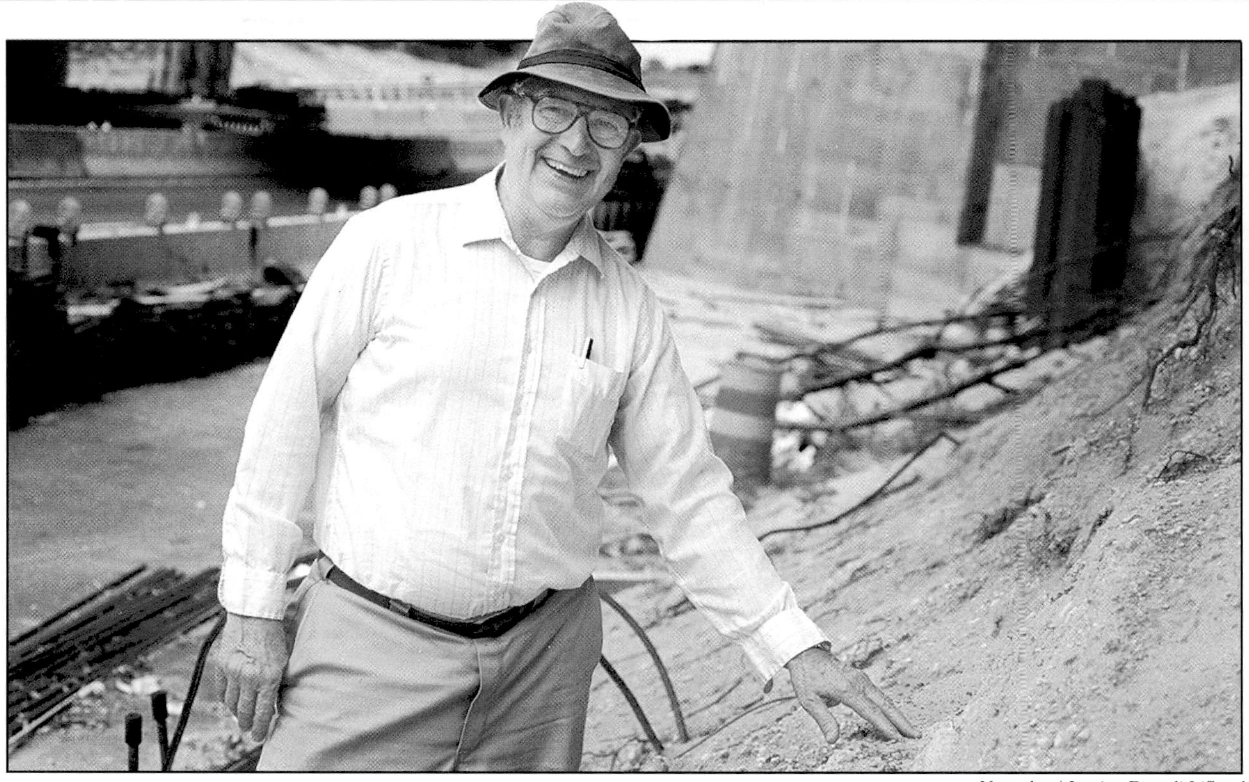

Newsday / Jessica Brandi Lifland

Retired professor John Sanders checks a newly exposed piece of ground at a construction site on the Northern State Parkway in Westbury. He hopes charcoal he found there in July can shed light on how many times glaciers reached Long Island.

They Do Geology on the Run

BY DAN FAGIN
STAFF WRITER

Just another day on the Northern State Parkway: bumper-to-bumper traffic, orange cones, and an Ice Age geologist in a floppy hat digging for ancient charcoal.

John Sanders smiled as he dug on a sweltering July morning, unlike the irritated drivers who had to slow down as they passed the Westbury road-widening project. A few weeks earlier, a construction crew had bulldozed the edge of a small hillside, exposing rocks buried for tens of thousands of years. Now the retired Barnard College geology professor was happily chipping at the newly created cliff with a metal tool.

"This is a really nice exposure," he said, admiring arched bands on the cliff face that he said suggested the passage of an ancient south-flowing stream fed by a melting glacier. His discourse on glacial history was difficult to hear over the passing traffic, but Sanders kept talking — and digging — anyway.

The small band of geologists who labor to reconstruct Long Island's distant past is accustomed to working in less-than-ideal conditions, and to taking advantage of whatever opportunities come along.

Chronically short of research funds, they piggyback onto other projects, including road work, sand mining, well-digging, water-tunneling and even toxic cleanups. After big storms, they race to the shoreline to see rocks and cliffs uncovered by the pounding surf.

They even wish for a nasty nor'easter now and then. "It's very opportunistic. You hope there's a nice big storm so you can get out there and see all the nice smooth [rock] surfaces," said Gilbert Hanson, a professor of geosciences at the State University at Stony Brook.

Lack of money isn't the only obstacle. So much of Long Island is already paved over that there aren't many good places left for fossil-hunting. Geologically rich sites such as the Flower Hill Bog in Manhasset have been destroyed by development, and many fossil cliffs around Long Island have been wrecked by seawalls and other erosion controls. The cliffs near the Montauk Lighthouse, a rich source of information for local geologists for more than a century, have been partially covered in recent years as the U.S. Army Corps of Engineers has tried to stave off erosion of Montauk Point.

What little geological research does take place on Long Island is almost conducted for public health or business reasons, not natural history. "There's not much geology for geology's sake," said Glen Richard, another Stony Brook geologist.

Much of what is known about Long Island's ancient history has been discovered almost as an afterthought. Charles Merguerian, a professor of structural geology at Hofstra University, has shed new light on the formation of Long Island's bedrock by studying the walls of the new water tunnel that New York City is digging 700 feet below Brooklyn and Queens. A chronology of Long Island glaciers developed by Les Sirkin, a research professor of earth sciences at Adelphi University, is based in part on his many years of research in the abandoned sand mines of Port Washington — a site that will soon be drastically altered by a planned 18-hole golf course and senior citizens housing complex.

Non-scientists have also done their part. Amateurs, mostly fishermen, have found all of the woolly mammoth and mastodon teeth discovered on or near Long Island. In 1967, for example, George Stires was fishing for ocean skimmer clams 70 miles south of the Rockaways when he netted a six-inch black object.

"It was pretty, so I took it home and washed it off, and after a while I called the Smithsonian," said Stires, of Bricktown, N.J. The object turned out to be the tooth of a mastodon, an Ice Age elephant species now extinct. It now resides in the Smithsonian Institution, where Stires has proudly visited it with his children.

The next important discoveries could come as a side benefit to the massive groundwater cleanup effort that is just getting underway in and around Brookhaven National Laboratory, Hanson said. Wells being dug in the area to test for chemical contamination also may be used to study long-buried sediments, just as they have at toxic-waste sites around Long Island.

Or maybe the next big revelation will come near Exit 33 on the Northern State. Sanders hopes that charcoal buried in the roadside cliff could shed some light on the controversial question of when, and how many times, the glaciers reached Long Island.

Unlike rocks, charcoal samples are relatively easy to test and date, and Sanders has already recovered one piece of charcoal he hopes to test soon.

He won't be able to get additional samples from the site, however. The little cliff on the side of the parkway, like so many other potential treasure troves for Long Island's natural historians, is due to be covered in concrete any day now.

Long Island — Not Really an Island?

BY DAN FAGIN
STAFF WRITER

Sure, it's long, but it's no island. The U.S. Supreme Court says so.

In a 12-year-old ruling that still prompts eye-rolling from scientists who study Long Island's geography, the high court declared that for purposes of international law Long Island is merely "an extension of the mainland" that is "integrally related" to Manhattan and the Bronx. The decision was unanimous, although many Long Islanders doubtless would have dissented if given the chance.

"Of course, Long Island is an island. But what I think is important as a scientist doesn't mean a hill of beans to the lawyers," said R. Lawrence Swanson. A trained oceanographer who runs the Waste Management Institute at the State University at Stony Brook, Swanson was an independent expert witness in the case.

For the last 11,000 years or so, ever since the rising sea filled in Long Island Sound, Long Island has inarguably met the geographic definition of an island: a piece of land surrounded by water at low tide. But the legal definition, naturally, is much more abstruse, and it took a long and costly court fight to determine that Long Island didn't meet it.

The issue wound up in court because the federal government and the states of New York and Rhode Island couldn't agree on who controls Long Island Sound and Block Island Sound. The states wanted to retain the power to regulate fishing, and to require state-licensed pilots to be on board ships passing through the waterway.

The is-the-Island-an-island controversy quickly became the key issue in the case. If Long Island was merely an extension of the mainland, as the two states argued, then under international law Long Island Sound and Block Island Sound would be inland bays controlled by the states instead of open waters under federal control.

Supreme Court Justice Harry Blackmun settled the issue — for the lawyers, at least — in a 1985 majority opinion that sided with the states and included a flawed geology lesson.

"Long Island and the adjacent shore [of Manhattan] also share a common geological history, formed by deposits of sediment and rocks brought from the mainland by ice sheets that retreated approximately 25,000 years ago," Blackmun wrote.

Not really, according to Swanson and several other experts. Glaciers did cover both places, but Manhattan and Long Island are different geologically.

Much of Manhattan consists of exposed bedrock hundreds of millions of years old, while Long Island is mostly loose sand and didn't even exist as a distinct entity until it was built up by bulldozing ice sheets over the last 150,000 years.

Blackmun also opined that before humans widened it, the East River was too narrow, shallow, and navigationally dangerous to be a significant barrier between Long Island and the boroughs of Manhattan and The Bronx.

Wrong again, according to Swanson. "It's just very clear from a geophysical and geological point of view that Long Island is an island separated by the mainland by a series of very complex tidal straits," he said.

Even off-Island experts agree the Island is an island.

"I never understood that Supreme Court decision," said Ralph Lewis, an associate state geologist at the Connecticut Geological and Natural History Survey and an expert on the history of Long Island Sound. "We didn't build those channels. It's a natural island."

LI HISTORY.COM

For the full text of the Supreme Court ruling, see http://www.lihistory.com.

Shoreline Erosion Yet to Come

CHANGES from Preceding Page

was lower and the site was a swamp.

Then Englebright walked to the inland edge of the dune and pointed out that it, too, is on the move. A wedge of overwashed sand now extends off the back edge of the dune and into the marshy grass that marks the edge of the swamp.

The swamp isn't standing still, either. Even as it loses ground to the dune on one edge, the freshwater wetland appears to be expanding on its opposite edge into the open grassland that leads to the forest. The swamp's expansion may be yet another consequence of sea level rise, Englebright said. Wetlands across Long Island have gradually expanded over the centuries because the freshwater aquifers beneath the Island float like a bubble on top of a curved bed of salt water. As sea level rises, the salt water compresses the bubble from all sides, forcing up the water table and flooding formerly dry areas.

What it all means is that gradually, the bay is wearing away the dune, the dune is creeping back into the swamp, the swamp is flooding the grassland, the grassland is expanding into the line of cedars, and the cedars are pushing back the pine barrens.

Throughout Long Island, similar chain reactions are underway — almost all of them set off by sea-level rise and shoreline erosion.

One of the most remarkable is occurring off the South Shore: the lurching march of Fire Island and other so-called "barrier islands" — a misleading term for a chain of sandbars neither stable nor strong.

Their movement toward the mainland is sporadic. But over the long run, the barrier islands are moving north by an average of 1.7 feet per year, except in places like Jones Beach and Long Beach that are moving more slowly because they have been hardened by man-made erosion controls, according to an analysis by Stephen Leatherman of the University of Maryland, an authority on barrier islands.

Erosion is propelling the islands inland. Prevailing northeast winds drive massive amounts of sand — up to 600,000 cubic yards per year in some areas of Fire Island — westward across the ocean beaches of the barrier islands, scouring their southern edge like sandpaper on soft wood. Sea-level rise also contributes to the erosion, as the breaking waves creep higher up on the sandbar. Calm winters and unique local conditions sometimes mask the overall trend, but on average, the barrier islands are losing roughly one or two feet of oceanfront each year.

The islands move, according to the prevailing theory, because continuing erosion makes them thin, and therefore vulnerable to washovers and breaches during heavy storms. When the ocean does break through, huge quantities of sediment are transferred from the front to the back side of the barrier islands, causing them to "roll" toward the mainland. Seawalls, inlet dredging, and sand replenishment projects can slow the natural migration of the barrier islands but cannot stop it over the long run.

All around mainland Long Island — a larger but similarly unstable sandbar — the same natural processes are reshaping the shoreline and the interior.

That is starkly evident at the mouth of the Nissequogue River in Smithtown. The offshore islands and salt marshes that 100 years ago protected the river's fragile freshwater wetlands have virtually disappeared because of storm erosion and rising sea level, said Henry Bokuniewicz, a professor of oceanography at the State University at Stony Brook.

The islands, which appear on old maps, are now visible only as darker patches on the blue water, indicating their presence below the water. Those islands once helped protect the river from the pounding waves of Long Island Sound. Now that they are gone, the once-broad salt marshes that guard the mouth of the river have withered to narrow spits. The destruction of the newly exposed salt marshes has allowed the Sound to invade the Nissequogue and push back the freshwater wetlands located farther up the river — although there isn't much space available for their retreat because of encroaching development.

The shift underway at the Nissequogue is a cautionary tale for Long Islanders who live on sand spits such as Bayville and Asharoken, and for the many more who live on Great South Bay, Huntington Bay, and the many other harbors and bays protected by those fragile barrier beaches.

Pointing at the wave-battered sand spits at the Nissequogue's mouth, Bokuniewicz said: "That is exactly what would be happening to Bayville right now" if the sandbar where that Nassau village sits had not been hardened by docks, driveways and all the other fixtures of dense development.

The key question for Long Islanders, of course, is what happens next? How long, and at what cost, will Bayville and many other vulnerable areas be able to avoid the fate of the Nissequogue sand spits?

There's no doubt in the minds of the scientists who study Long Island that the natural dynamism of this oversized sandbar will ultimately defeat the best efforts of humans to hold it in place.

Trying to stave off the effects of erosion and sea level rise "is like gambling — if you go on long enough you're going to lose," said Bokuniewicz.

A century from now, he said, Holland-style dikes may line large portions of the Long Island shoreline, with windmills to pump out the water-saturated land behind the walls. And Englebright predicts that the rising water table will eventually flood the back yards of thousands of homes in central Long Island.

When that time comes, the ghost forests of Hubbard County Park won't be the most vivid illustration of Long Island's dynamism any more.

That distinction instead will go to the ghost docks, ghost seawalls and ghost houses of coastal Long Island.

LEGACY

Newsday Photo / Ken Spencer

KETTLEHOLE LAKES

Lake Ronkonkoma is the largest of dozens of so-called "kettlehole lakes" that were formed on Long Island by the last glacier, which left the region about 20,000 years ago. Geologists believe the lakes were formed from large chunks of ice left behind by the receding ice sheet. When those pieces of ice finally melted, they left depressions in the sandy soil that were deep enough to be filled in by the slowly rising water table. Lake Success in Nassau County is another kettlehole.

If sea level keeps rising, many LI shore and inland communities can expect wet changes

More Floods in the Future?

BY DAN FAGIN
STAFF WRITER

On a moonlit night almost 20 years ago, a geologist snuck onto private land deep in the Calverton woods, canoed to the middle of a large pond and began lowering a long rope he had carefully knotted at three-foot intervals. He never got to the second knot.

When Steve Englebright's rope touched the bottom of Swan Pond after just four feet, instead of the 50 feet he was expecting, his secret midnight trip with two other environmental activists to study the pond suddenly became a mystery as well as a mission.

The mission was accomplished soon afterward when Suffolk County bought the property to block a planned golf course expansion. And the mystery is being unravelled two decades later as Englebright, now a state assemblyman, and other naturalists discover just how profoundly Long Island is being reshaped by a relentless but often overlooked force: the rising sea.

The Calverton Ponds Preserve, above, and geologist Steve Englebright, who theorizes that such places were once dry pine barrens that became bogs when the water table rose.

Newsday Photos / Bill Davis

Sea level around the world has risen about 350 feet since the climax of the last Ice Age 22,000 years ago, as gradually increasing global temperatures have melted polar ice and swelled the oceans. Few places on Earth have been changed as dramatically by the rising tide as Long Island.

Twenty thousand years ago, Long Island wasn't an island at all, but an elevated area of a broad coastal plain that extended as far south as Atlantic City. Since then, the rising sea has moved the southern shoreline 80 miles north, and flooded the valley we know as Long Island Sound.

If sea level continues to rise more than an inch per decade, and especially if that rate doubles or triples because of pollution-induced global warming, as many experts predict, Long Island will become a very different place over the next century.

The sea may split the narrow South Fork into at least three sections, and shoreline residents from Montauk to Long Beach will face a grim choice of either abandoning their property or building barriers to hold back the rising sea, as in Holland.

"In the long term, you can envision dikes around places like Oakdale and Bay Shore. All that would be missing are the tulips," said Henry Bokuniewicz, a professor of oceanography at the State University at Stony Brook and an expert on sea-level changes.

Windmills may be there, too, he said, because the shrinking coastline is only the most obvious of the many ways in which rising sea level is transforming Long Island. As in Holland, the rising ocean waters also are pushing up the underground water table, flooding formerly dry areas. That's why the Dutch use windmills: to pump out water-saturated land.

Some scientists think the water table may be rising even faster than sea level. Here's why: Long Island's freshwater aquifers are like a bubble floating on a curved bed of salt water. When sea level rises, the salt water compresses the bubble from below and from all sides, forcing the fresh water upward even faster than the rising sea.

Of course, none of these changes is happening overnight, and there are other complicating factors. Heavy rains raise the water table, and heavy pumping by water wells lowers it. The land isn't stable, either. Various parts of Long Island are still slowly rising or falling, in a residual effect of the last glacier. That ice sheet was so heavy that it temporarily distorted the Earth's crust, which is still gradually returning to its former shape 1000 generations after the glacier receded north.

Nor has the 20,000-year trend of warmer weather and higher seas been a steady rise. Almost all of the increase came during the first 14,000 years. Since then, the up-and-down oscillations have been small, although the experts do agree that the current trend is upward — abetted, most likely, by ever-increasing emissions of carbon dioxide and other so-called "greenhouse gases." These gases, byproducts of burning coal and oil, trap heat in the atmosphere like the window panes of a greenhouse.

It's possible, experts say, that the warming trend will end soon, and sea level will begin falling again. Rhodes Fairbridge, a retired professor of geology at Columbia University, has become famous among his peers for suggesting that temperature and sea level rise and fall in complex but predictable cycles. The cycles, he said, may follow shifts in the orbits of the nearby planets, since planetary alignment affects sunspot activity and the amount of solar radiation reaching Earth, two factors known to influence climate.

Markings on cliffs near his Amagansett home, Fairbridge said, show that sea level was actually about 10 feet higher 5,000 years ago than it is today, and has gone through several ups and downs since then, including a decline during the so-called "Little Ice Age" of 300 to 400 years ago and a subsequent rebound that is still continuing.

Until the next shift, the rising tide will continue to reshape the Island. The ocean will drown existing beaches and create new ones farther inland, while dry areas will become flooded marshes.

That's exactly what has happened at Swan Pond, the place Englebright discovered was only four feet deep when he made his secret expedition there 20 years ago.

Scientists have known for a long time that many of Long Island's lakes and ponds, including Lake Ronkonkoma and Lake Success, were so-called "kettlehole lakes" formed by large chunks of ice left behind by the last glacier. When those chunks melted, they left deep depressions that groundwater filled.

But Swan Pond and many nearby ponds in Calverton, Englebright discovered, were shaped like frying pans, not kettles.

Several years later, he began to figure out why. Digging 24 feet down into a Shelter Island swamp, Englebright uncovered dry sandy soil at the bottom that looked exactly like the sand now found in the pine barrens of Brookhaven and Southampton. Over hundreds or even thousands of years, he decided, the gradually rising water table must have transformed a dry area into a bog.

Englebright believes something similar happened at Swan Pond. Like the kettleholes, the pond was a product of the last Ice Age, but was formed by a thin layer of melting permafrost, not a big chunk of glacial ice. The shallow depression was exposed for thousands of years until the rising water table finally claimed it.

If the tide keeps rising, he said, many more formerly dry areas will eventually flood, including the back yards of suburban homes in communities farther inland, such as Middle Island and Yaphank. "Those neighborhoods are the next Calverton ponds," Englebright said, "whether they like it or not."

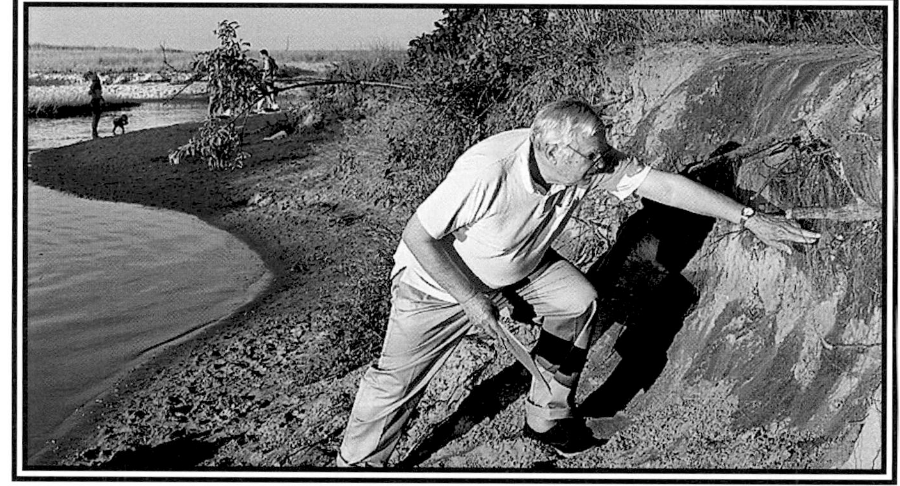

Pointing to markings on a cliff along Fresh Pond Creek in Amagansett, geologist Rhodes Fairbridge believes that perhaps 5,000 years ago, the sea was some 10 feet higher than today.

Despite humanity's efforts, erosion poses a relentless threat

Washed to the Sea

BY DAN FAGIN
STAFF WRITER

On a summer afternoon, the sun-dappled view of azure sky and turquoise sea stretches uninterrupted to an impossibly distant horizon.

But the view south from Montauk Point is a portal to the past for the scientists who study Long Island's natural history. They see something that isn't there anymore: a great ridge of sand and rock that constitutes what may have been the vanished third fork of the East End.

Local geologists have conflicting ideas about when and how a glacier built that ridge, but there's no argument about what obliterated it. Ocean erosion has been an inescapable fact of life on Long Island ever since the slowly rising sea began pounding away at that now-vanished ridge, probably about 12,000 years ago.

The relentless surf has not only chewed up cliffs and thinned beaches, it has also drastically reshaped Long Island over the centuries. And while Long Islanders remain focused on fighting the short-term effects of erosion, sometimes in costly and controversial ways, the Island's history teaches the humbling lesson that over the long run the sea will not be denied.

The missing ridge south of Montauk is perhaps the most dramatic example of erosion's power on Long Island. It is probably part of the terminal moraine, the line that marks the place where, 22,000 years ago, a glacier finally stopped expanding southward. As the great ice sheet retreated, it left a ridge of bulldozed rubble in its wake. Most of that moraine is still visible today as the elevated central spine of Long Island that roughly parallels the Long Island Expressway. But farther east, geologists believe, the moraine dipped south and left the present-day Island at Amagansett before curving northeast and continuing on to Martha's Vineyard.

As it receded back toward Canada, the glacier paused several times and deposited several recessional moraines that were so tall and wide that they became the Montauk peninsula and the north fork. Whether there were three forks on the East End is uncertian, since no one knows if water was ever in between the Montauk peninsula and the now-vanished moraine farther south. But what is certain is that a bouldery ridge on the ocean floor is all that remains of the missing moraine.

"That's an enormous amount of land. The fact that the entire terminal moraine is gone is a very impressive thing," said Les Sirkin, a research professor of earth science at Adelphi University. "In 12,000 years, several miles of terminal moraine have been totally eroded away."

No section of Long Island's 1,180-mile coastline is immune from erosion's effects, but the Montauk peninsula has been hit hardest because it is unprotected by barrier islands and lies squarely on the historic pathways of nor'easters and hurricanes. Over thousands of years, the area has been narrowed so severely that Long Island's axis has shifted like a weathervane from east-west to northeast-southwest. Massive amounts of sand have been taken from the vanished moraine and from the cliffs at Montauk and pushed west, blown by the prevailing northeast winds.

On a placid summer day at Jones Beach or Fire Island, it's hard to envision so much sand moving so quickly from east to west. But, in fact, at various spots along the South Shore, anywhere from 100,000 to 600,000 cubic yards of sand are pushed westward every year, according to studies by New York State. Storms blowing in from the west can briefly reverse the flow, but the dominant trend is for the sand to move from Montauk toward the Rockaways.

On the north shore, Long Island Sound has steadily licked at the base of these cliffs at Caumsett State Park on Lloyd Neck, causing higher ground to give way and tumble downward.

Newsday Photo / Bill Davis

The North Shore isn't as volatile. Calmer seas and the shore's many harbors all serve to keep more sand in place, so the sand transport rate anywhere along the shoreline is never greater than 100,000 cubic yards per year.

But the natural drift of sand along its North and South Shores can't be the only reason Long Island is slowly wasting away. It can't explain why the calmer North Shore is losing an average of one or two feet of shoreline every year, and so are parts of the South Shore that should be benefiting from the river of sand flowing west from Montauk.

What is happening, experts say, is that Long Island's coasts are also being hammered by a double whammy of rising sea level and inept erosion-control efforts by humans.

The ocean is slowly rising by about one foot per century, part of a 20,000-year trend that began when the glacier melted as it retreated toward Canada. What Long Islanders perceive as a vanishing beachfront is actually, in part, a gradually rising water line. The trend has worsened erosion by slowly raising the platform for the devastating storms that periodically strike the Island. During the very worst storms, waves can crest as much as eight feet higher than normal — enough to wash away more than 100 feet of beach in a few hours.

But even the nastiest winter storms cannot equal the havoc humans have wreaked through misguided erosion control efforts. On the South Shore, especially, the east-to-west flow of sand has been badly disrupted by the 69 major groins and jetties built to protect favored stretches of beach and keep six inlets navigable for boats. The most infamous example is in Westhampton, where the construction during the 1960s of 11 rocky groins projecting into the ocean has led to devastating erosion along Dune Road, just west of the sand-grabbing groins.

"We've made a lot of mistakes in the past," said Jay Tanski of the New York Sea Grant Institute at the State University at Stony Brook. "The interruption of the natural sand flow has caused very severe problems and the most spectacular erosion that we see."

Even the U.S. Army Corps of Engineers, which built many of those groins and jetties, now favors "soft" erosion-control methods such as building up protective dunes and pumping sand across inlets to avoid interrupting the natural sand flow. "I certainly don't like structures," said Joseph Vietri, deputy planning director of the corps' New York office. "It's true that most of the structures that have been built over the years to control erosion would never be built today."

But even those "softer" solutions won't be able to hold off coastal erosion indefinitely, Vietri acknowledged. Beach renourishment projects may be economically justifiable if they can hold the beach in place for 30 or even 50 years, he said. But over the longer term, if the sea continues to rise and current erosion patterns continue, controlling erosion will become so expensive that the only feasible option will be a strategic retreat.

"It's questionable whether there will ever be enough money to keep the shoreline from retreating over the long term," Vietri said. "If you look beyond 50 years, it becomes very hard to justify any of these projects."

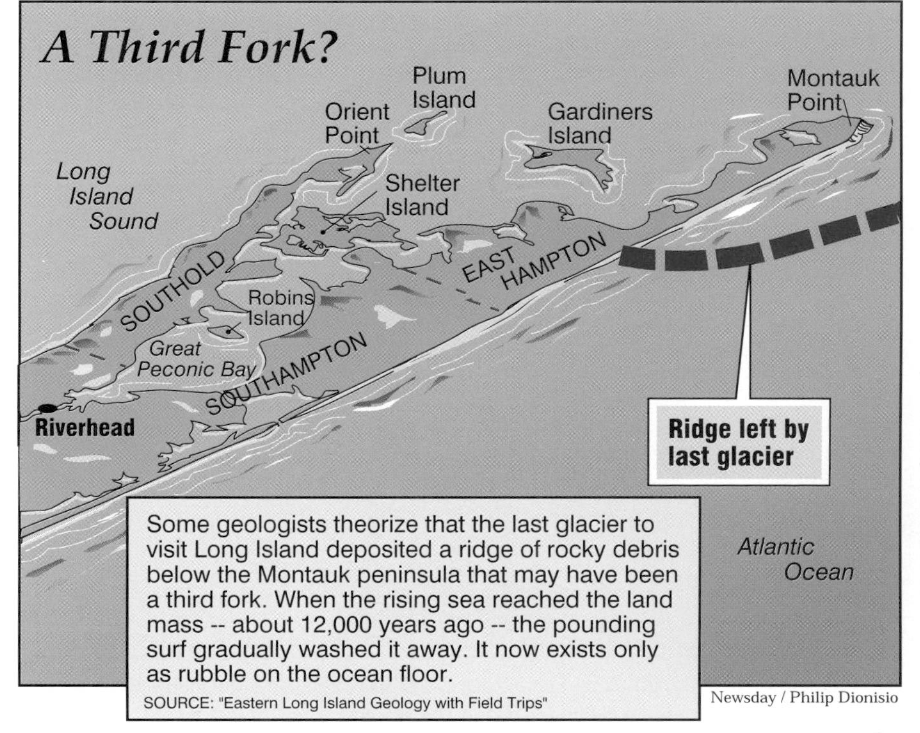
A Third Fork?
Plum Island
Orient Point
Gardiners Island
Montauk Point
Long Island Sound
Shelter Island
SOUTHOLD
EAST HAMPTON
Robins Island
Great Peconic Bay
SOUTHAMPTON
Riverhead
Ridge left by last glacier
Atlantic Ocean
Some geologists theorize that the last glacier to visit Long Island deposited a ridge of rocky debris below the Montauk peninsula that may have been a third fork. When the rising sea reached the land mass -- about 12,000 years ago -- the pounding surf gradually washed it away. It now exists only as rubble on the ocean floor.
SOURCE: "Eastern Long Island Geology with Field Trips"

Newsday / Philip Dionisio

Not totally pristine, the pine barrens is the closest thing we have to a natural museum

In Search of Prehistory

BY DAN FAGIN
STAFF WRITER

Up on Bald Hill in the Manorville-Riverhead hills, where Long Island's last wilderness climbs the bouldery ridge laid down by an ice sheet a thousand generations ago, the pine barrens forest seems exquisitely undisturbed, even primeval.

But very little about the pine barrens is exactly what it seems. For while the 100,000-acre collection of dry plains, stunted forests, grassy marshes and flower-ringed ponds is the closest thing we have to a living museum of natural history, it is an imperfect representation of prehistoric Long Island — if indeed that were possible.

The scrubby pine forests of south-central Suffolk County were only one of several kinds of forests that once blanketed Long Island. Researchers now believe that centuries of farming, lumbering and fire-setting — by American Indians and European settlers alike — actually expanded the pine barrens by removing other types of forests that were more economically useful.

"Long Island was settled so early, and so much of it was cut and burned and plowed for so long, that there's not many vestiges left," said Marilyn Jordan, a stewardship ecologist at the Nature Conservancy of Long Island. "You can't turn back the clock and go back in time."

Scientists have very little to go on as they try to reconstruct the history of the pine barrens, and even less for the denser forests of oak, chestnut, hickory, tulip, birch and other hardwoods that probably once dominated much of Long Island.

What little they do know comes from studying the early maps and reports of colonists and from analyzing fossilized pollen from trees and plants.

Nature never stands still, of course, which makes the researchers' task even more difficult. Pine forests have probably existed in North America for tens of millions of years, but any local trace of them was wiped out by the massive glaciers that scoured the Long Island landscape at least twice within the past 150,000 years. When the last ice sheet retreated north about 20,000 years ago, it left behind a frozen landscape in which practically nothing could grow.

Pollen specialists such as Les Sirkin, a research professor of earth sciences at Adelphi University, have reconstructed what happened next by studying microscopic pollen buried deep in bottom sediment of local lakes and peat-filled bogs.

In the oldest sediment, deposited just after the glacier left, Sirkin has found pollen from cold-weather herbs and grasses, not trees. As the weather warmed, spruce and fir forests became dominant, followed by pine and then oak and other hardwoods as temperatures leveled off about 6,000 years ago.

But while hardwoods grow well on the northern half of Long Island, conditions are different to the south, especially in Suffolk County.

There, rivers of melting ice from the departing glacier dumped a thick layer of sand and gravel that is low in nutrients and doesn't hold water well. Fires spread fast and far on the dry soil, and there aren't many creeks or wetlands. Taller, stronger hardwood trees generally won't grow, and neither do many crops, so the European colonists mostly avoided the hardscrabble pinelands they considered "barren."

It's a good thing they did, because the land they shunned sits above Long Island's last large reservoir of clean drinking water, as is a treasure trove of species found in few other places.

Through centuries of natural selection, or survival of the fittest, plants and animals in the pine barrens have adapted ingeniously to the harsh conditions. Local plants such as the bladderwort and the thread-leafed sundew eat insects to get the nitrogen and phosphorus that isn't available in the poor soil. Adapting to the tinderbox conditions, the globally rare twisted dwarf pines of Westhampton developed cones that open to disperse seeds only in the intense heat of a fire. Swamps of rare Atlantic white cedars thrive here, and so does Hessel's Hairstreak, an endangered butterfly that lives only in those cedar swamps.

The plants and animals adapted so well, in fact, that pine barrens species moved in to fill the void when the hardwood forests were destroyed by lumbering, and when the richer soils were exhausted by intense plowing. That has led a few botanists to suggest that the pine barrens is merely a scavenger ecosystem that owes its existence to human intervention.

Most researchers, though, believe that at least some parts of the pine barrens are indeed prehistoric, particularly areas near Moriches and Westhampton where soil conditions are worst. Traces of ancient charcoal, as well as pine pollen, suggest that pines and forest fires have been here for "at least four or five thousand years," said Ray Welch, a professor of biology at Suffolk Community College.

A pristine window into Long Island's past? Not quite. But the pine barrens, Welch said, "are as similar to what you would have found primevally on Long Island than anything else you can see now."

In other words, they're the best we've got left.

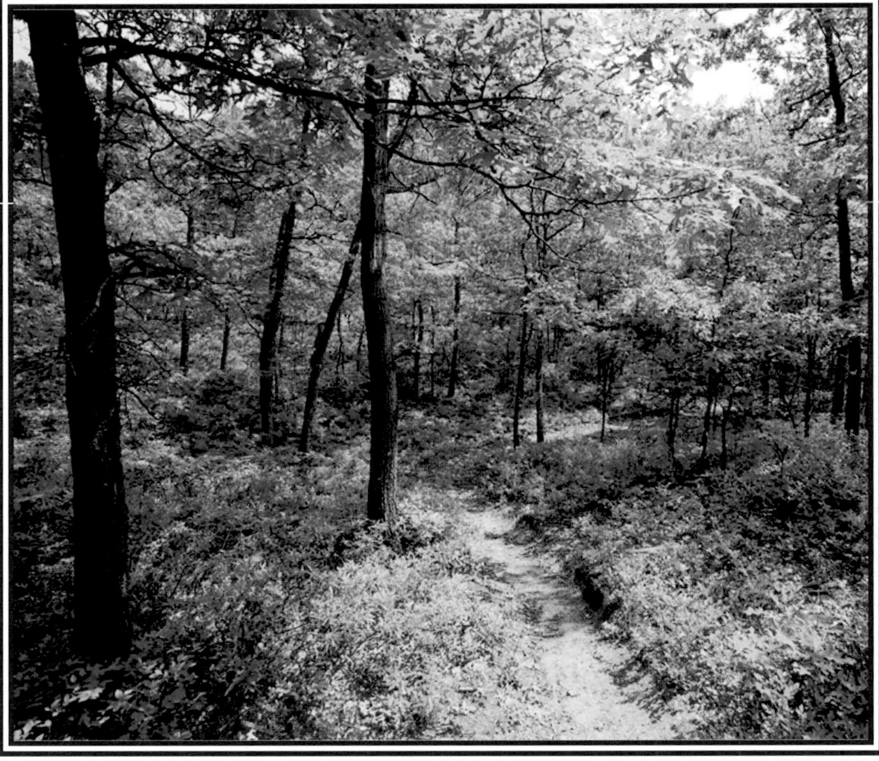

Newsday Photo / Bill Davis

The scrubby pine forests of Suffolk County were avoided by settlers as poor agricultural land. Above, the undeveloped Manorville Hills west of Riverhead

The Pine Barrens

BROOKHAVEN
Long Island Sound
RIVERHEAD
Riverhead
Long Island Expwy.
Sunrise Hwy.
William Floyd Pkwy.
SOUTHAMPTON
0 MILES 10

Newsday / Linda McKenney

HIKING, CAMPING, EXPLORING

There are hundreds of places to hike in the pine barrens. But here are four destinations ideal for first-time visitors:

1. Quogue Wildlife Refuge is great for bird-watching and viewing a progression of habitats, from tidal wetlands to upland forests. Hiking trails are marked, guides are available and there is a nature and wildlife rehabilitation center.

2. South Haven County Park, near Shirley, combines traditional park facilities (camping, fishing and sports fields) with a magnificently undisturbed stretch of the Carmans River. Canoers can continue under Sunrise Highway into the adjacent Wertheim National Wildlife Refuge. Hiking trails are marked.

3. Rocky Point Natural Resources Management Area is a large, mostly undisturbed forest. Visitors must first get an access permit (available by mail or in person from the state Department of Environmental Conservation's Stony Brook office) before hiking its many trails, including a 13-mile mountain bike loop. To witness the forest's recovery from the 1995 fire, park at Lot 18 on Whiskey Road and walk north to the fire site. The Paumanok Path, which runs all the way to Shinnecock, begins on the property.

4. Sears-Bellows County Park in Flanders is excellent for seeing ponds and hills deposited by the last glacier. Trails go up into the glacial moraine and past several coastal ponds, including one where swimming is allowed in season. There are campsites, a riding stable, and even the Big Duck, a 20-foot-tall East End landmark for more than 60 years.

— Dan Fagin

Environmentalists and developers battle over whether to build or preserve

Open Conflict Over Open Land

BY DAN FAGIN
STAFF WRITER

The War of the Woods is the handiwork of history.

Events that occurred in the distant past shape the ongoing struggle between preservationists and developers over the future of the vast pine barrens forest of east-central Suffolk County.

The 100,000-acre woodland of pitch pine and scrub oak exists because of a glacier that covered the northern half of Long Island 22,000 years ago, and the water-bearing sand deep beneath the forest's needle-covered floor is even older. Long Island's unique geology explains why the pine barrens were bypassed as the rest of the region rapidly developed, and it is also the reason that the fate of the region's last wilderness will help to forge the destiny of all Long Island.

Since 1995, an uneasy truce has prevailed in the pine barrens. That was the year that developers and environmental activists, after tortuous negotiations, reached a sweeping agreement that virtually forbids building in the 52,500-acre core zone and sets strict controls in the surrounding 47,500 acres.

But the war isn't over. Many of the land purchases and trades needed to implement the deal haven't occurred yet, and the two sides are still fighting over a mega-mall being built in Yaphank and other projects similarly proposed for the fringes of the pine barrens.

"It's a battle, day in and day out," said Richard Amper, executive director of the Long Island Pine Barrens Society, an environmental group that has spearheaded efforts to preserve the forest.

"These's still quite a lot of activity and pressure," agreed Bob Wieboldt of the Long Island Builders' Institute, which frequently spars with environmentalists over plans to build on the fringes of the forest.

The controversy won't go away because of two conflicting but inescapable truths about physical Long Island: the pine barrens is the only huge area left available for building, yet it also contains many of the region's rarest plants and animals and its largest undergound reservoir of uncontaminated drinking water. "The very same geology that created the rare flora and fauna also created the purest water supply," said Amper.

The pine barrens exist for the same reason the rest of Long Island exists: The glacier ran out of gas here. By about 22,000 years ago, the Earth's gradually warming climate was finally temperate enough for the ice sheet to melt as quickly as it was expanding. The glacier that had steadily advanced 1,000 miles south from Canada's Hudson Bay until it covered the entire northern half of North America finally stopped, and then began receding north again.

FAST FORWARD

How Today's Events Are Shaped by the Past

On Long Island, the leading edge of the ice sheet was resting on the central spine of Long Island when it stopped and reversed direction. In its wake, the glacier left behind an elevated ridge of sand and rock that roughly follows the path of the present-day Long Island Expressway.

Ice-water streams fed by the melting glacier ran south from that ridge and carried huge volumes of sediment to the flatlands of the present-day South Shore. Most of that sediment originated in Connecticut and was carried south by the ice sheet, so the soils on the South Shore took the characteristics of whichever rock types were hundreds of miles to the north. In western Long Island and the East End, the South Shore soils were fertile because of the rich granite that lay due north in Connecticut. But east-central Suffolk is below central Connecticut, where the dominant rock is sandstone. So the glacial streams covered a broad swath of South Shore from Yaphank to Westhampton with sand that was devoid of nutrients and too porous to hold rainwater.

In that harsh and dry environment where wildfires were common, plants and animals survived only through ingenious adaptations, such as the globally rare dwarf pine trees whose cones disperse their seeds in the intense heat of fires. A unique ecosystem arose in what became the pine barrens.

Because the trees were scrubby and the soil was poor, the pine barrens were mostly ignored by American Indians and later by Europeans. Instead, settlers farmed more fertile areas and cut down the sturdy hardwood forests of the North Shore, establishing a development pattern that largely excluded east-central Long Island.

By the 1980s, though, the eastward march of suburbia was cutting heavily into the Suffolk pinelands that probably once covered as much as 250,000 acres. What finally slowed that march was a combination of factors: economic recession, public backlash against traffic and other consequences of growth, and a growing appreciation of the environmental importance of protecting the pine barrens.

For the Long Island Pine Barrens Society and other groups that led the drive to protect the forest, preserving open space and the rare plants and animals who lived there was always a key motivator. But as they sought support from the broader public, preservationists emphasized the pine barrens' role in the aquifer system from which all residents of Nassau and Suffolk Counties get their drinking water.

"The main motivation was always the open space and habitat. That was a pretty hard argument to sell, but everybody gets pretty concerned about drinking water so that's what was emphasized," said Lee Koppelman, longtime executive director of the Long Island Regional Planning Board.

Very few Long Islanders get their drinking water directly from the pine barrens, and most probably never will because piping water over long distances is very expensive. Yet Long Island's unique geology assigns the pine barrens an important role in limiting contamination of the island-wide aquifer system. This is because water that falls on the pine barrens eventually migrates to other parts of the Island that do supply large amounts of drinking water.

Most of the rain that falls on the Island moves north to Long Island Sound or south to the ocean before it can reach and replenish the deepest aquifers. Only in a narrow five-mile-wide band that roughly parallels the Long Island Expressway does falling rain eventually reach the deep aquifers, and the pine barrens is the cleanest area in that so-called deep-flow recharge zone. Rain that falls in the pine barrens moves quickly through the sand and enters the aquifer system without picking up contaminants, eventually reaching deep water wells.

That's important because since the 1970s hundreds of shallow backyard wells have been abandoned due to contamination from fertilizer, pesticides and other pollutants. Many water companies now must treat groundwater before pumping it to customers, or extend tainted wells into the deeper, cleaner aquifers that have become crucial sources of drinking water.

"Because of our geology on Long Island, the only way to guarantee clean drinking water is to have the land above it undeveloped," said John Cryan, who co-founded the pine barrens society in 1978. "Over time, people on Long Island have come to understand that."

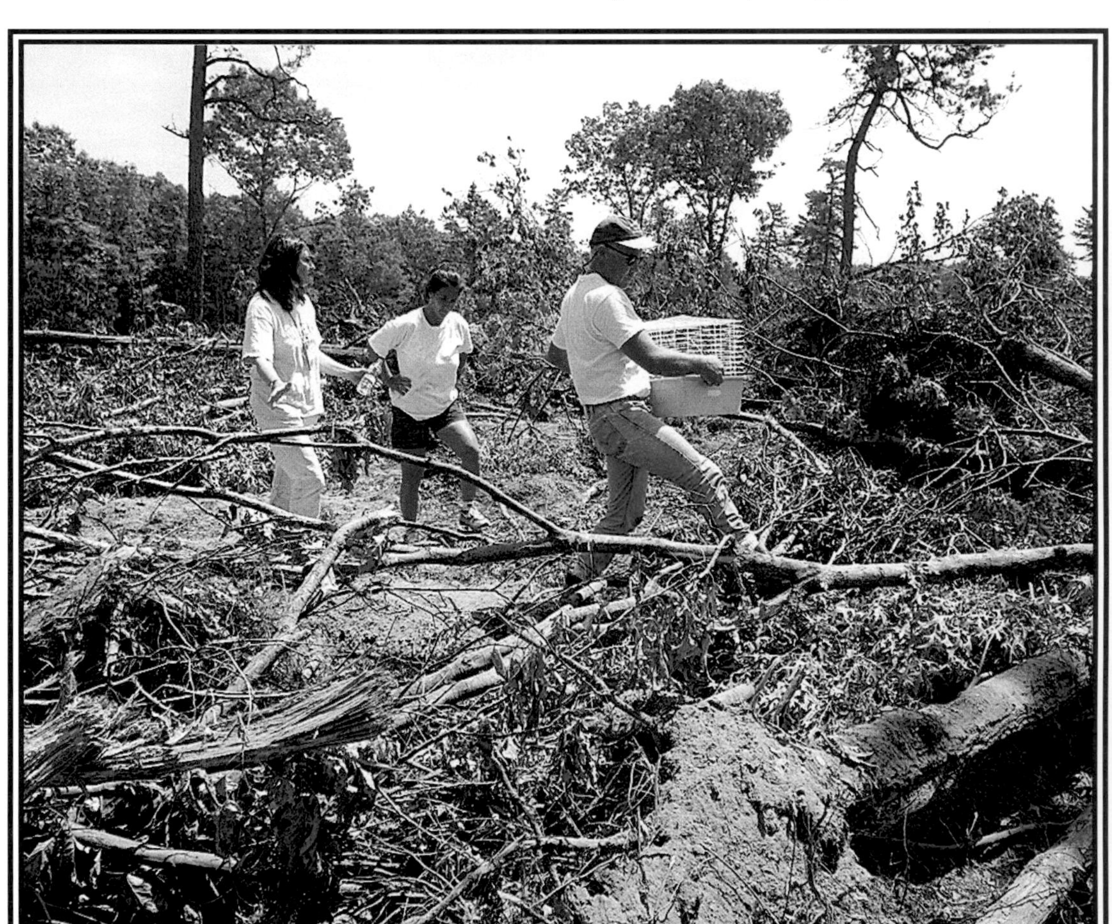

Photo by Maxine Hicks

A developer set aside a day at the construction site of a Yaphank mall last summer to allow environmentalists to look for box turtles. In addition, work was suspended for nearly a month to allow fledgling birds to mature.

Before people arrived, a pristine land of wildlife and sweet vegetation

When the Island Was New

BY IRENE VIRAG
STAFF WRITER

The dinosaurs had long vanished into legend and the great glacier had slipped back to its beginnings. Time and tide and the legacy of the ice blanket had forged the land into a fish-shaped island that stretched eastward into the ocean.

Long Island was beginning its transformation into Eden.

The sparse shrubs and grasses of the treeless tundra that followed the glacier had been replaced by forests of hemlocks and spruce. They in turn had given way to vast pine barrens and then to woods heavy with oak and chestnut and hickory trees and to swamplands filled with Atlantic white cedars and red maples and tupelos.

Life abounded in the streams and woodlands and along the shores of the new island. Horseshoe crabs mated in the surf and buck moths clung to each other in the pine barrens and dragonflies danced in the marshes.

Creatures of the Pleistocene Era had wandered across the land bridge that once traversed the oceans of the far north, and their kind still roamed the island. Saber-toothed tigers and huge dire wolves hunted mastodons and woolly mammoths. Elk and caribou and bears and musk oxen and ground sloths lived in the pristine wilderness, and as millennia passed, they gave way to smaller mammals — to deer and wolves and beavers and bobcats.

When the first people followed the mastodons and mammoths across the land bridge of the arctic regions, the place a poet would call Paumanok teemed with flora and fauna. There are no written records of that time about 12,000 years ago when Paleo-Indians came to the fish-shaped island, but geological evidence and educated guesses enable experts to sketch a picture of the way it probably was.

Tundra vegetation such as reindeer moss, cotton grass, low bush blueberries, cranberries and huckleberries still grow in the pine barrens. Fossilized pollen holds evidence of the tiga. Mammoth and mastodon teeth and tusks have been found in South Shore waters near the continental shelf that was dry land when humans arrived. Bison bones were discovered in the Hempstead Plains.

Atlantic white cedars at the edge of Flanders Bay in Suffolk County; the tree once flourished on Long Island but is rare today.

Newsday Photo / Bill Davis

LI HISTORY.COM

Prehistory meets the modern age in an interactive crossword puzzle devoted to Long Island geology. All the clues and answers come from stories in Chapter 1, which is available on the Internet at http://www.lihistory.com.

The pine barrens themselves are a relic. So are the 80 acres that are left of the 60,000-acre Hempstead Plains, once famous as the only prairie east of the Mississippi. Island Trees was just that — an island of trees in a sea of grass. Jamaica Bay is the descendant of a 24,000-acre wetland dominated by Atlantic white cedars, now a rare species in New York State.

Stroll the boardwalk at Jones Beach on a hot summer day when blankets and bodies litter the sand, or drive along the Long Island Expressway at rush hour and imagine what it must have been like when the first human stood upon the shore and gazed at the swelling sea or ran through the fragrant pine forests. Perhaps a line from a Joni Mitchell song comes to mind — "they paved paradise and put up a parking lot."

The paradise that was Long Island kept evolving. The same basic climate and vegetation that we know today took hold about 8,000 years ago when deciduous plants rooted in the silty soil. Oak trees shaded out the pines. *Spartina alterniflora*, a grass still found along north shore waterways, flourished in the salt marshes. Big game was becoming scarce and Indians started to settle near the bays and salt marshes plentiful with shellfish and the fresh-water streams laden with trout.

It was all still here when the first Europeans arrived. In 1670, Daniel Denton, a minister s son, wrote of his travels across Long Island. He catalogued mulberries, persimmons, "plums of all sorts," "grapes great and small" and "strawberries of which is such abundance in June, that the Fields and Woods are died red." Denton rhapsodized about "an innumerable multitude of delightful Flowers not only pleasing the eye, but smell, that you may behold Nature contending with Art, and striving to equal, if not excel many Gardens in England."

It was clear the land enchanted him — thickets of elder and sumac and "groves gleaming in spring with the white bloom of the dogwood, glowing in fall, with liquid amber and pepperidge, with sassafras, and the yellow light of the smooth shafted tulip tree."

Game abounded, although the settlers would hunt wolves and bobcats to extinction on the Island — even posting bounties for them. Denton saw deer, bear, polecats, and otters. And he told of wild turkeys, heath hens, quail, partridges, and "green silken frogs" whose singing rivaled that of the birds.

It was, he wrote, a place "where besides the sweetness of the Air, the Countrey itself sends forth such a fragrant smell that it may be perceived at Sea before they can make the Land; where no evil fog or vapour doth no sooner appear but a North-west or Westerly winde doth immediately dissolve it, and drive it away: What shall I say more? . . . that if there be any terrestrial Canaan, 'tis surely here, where the Land floweth with milk and honey."

It was a time before progress when a world was still new. Before paradise was lost.

A LONG-LIVED BLUEBLOOD

For an intimate glimpse of the past, check the shore during the high tides of the full and new moons in May and June. That's when horseshoe crabs do what comes naturally, the way they've been doing it for millions of years.

The male grabs the female with his front claws and rides piggy-back to shore on the high tide. The female lays thousands of bluish-green eggs in the sand, and the male fertilizes them. By mid-June, the crabs are on their way back to the continental shelf to bury themselves for the winter.

As species go, *limulus plyphemus* is prehistoric. Fossils show it existed 400 million years ago — long before the dinosaurs showed up, not to mention Long Island, the glacier and Homo sapiens.

Horseshoe crabs are true blue bloods and not just because of their lineage. Their copper-based blood is blue, not red like ours, which is iron-based. And they're not even crabs. They just molt like crabs. Their closest relatives are terrestrial arachnids like spiders and ticks.

Most horseshoe crab young are eaten by fish after the tide pulls them out to sea. But each female produces about 300,000 progeny a year. About 9 million horseshoe crabs are believed to be thriving along the East Coast of North America from the Bay of Fundy on down and west to the Yucatan Peninsula. So the species should be around for ages to come.

— **Irene Virag**

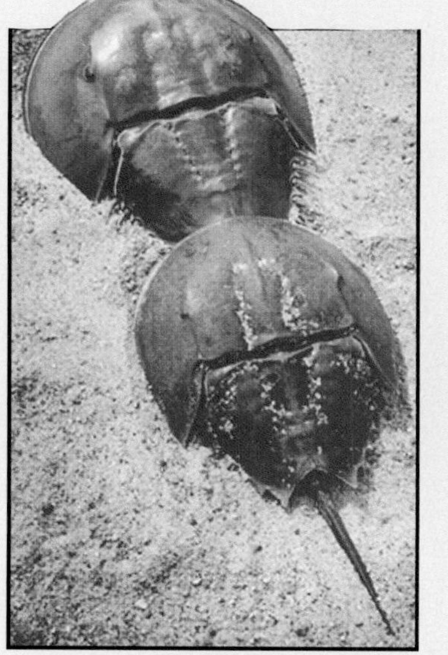

TIME MACHINE

PICTURING THE PAST AND PRESENT

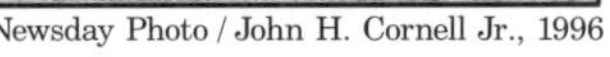
Newsday Photo / John H. Cornell Jr., 1996

Worn Away By the Tides

THEN & NOW

In the 1790s, hoping to insulate the planned Montauk Lighthouse from the crashing waves of the Atlantic, federal surveyors decided to build it on top of Turtle Hill, 297 feet from the tip of Montauk Point — about the length of a football field. Over time, however, the ocean — and heavy-footed climbers — steadily wore away the surrounding cliffs. The lighthouse is now just 70 feet from the water.

The photographs show the bluffs in the early 1900s compared with today. (In front of the lighthouse is a concrete sighting tower built during World War II.)

The U.S. Army Corps of Engineers has slowed the erosion in recent years by placing huge boulders at the base of the cliffs. In addition, a 1970s idea called "reed-trench terracing" has worked well. It involved a series of terraces covered with dead reed grass to prevent sand loss, and then a layer of soil and vegetation for stability. It was the idea of Giorgina Reid, a private citizen from Jackson Heights, Queens.

CHAPTER 2

The First Long Islanders

From the Paleo-Indians who arrived circa 10,000 BC to the European explorers who named Lange Eyland

Newsday / Bob Newman

Some 550 generations across 12 millennia occupied the Island before Europeans arrived

The First Long Islanders

BY STEVE WICK
STAFF WRITER

They arrived thousands of years ago when the ice was finally gone, a trickle of big-game hunters who sought out shelter near fresh water streams and lakes. They had been walking for centuries, generation after generation, traveling imponderable distances, continent to continent. When they arrived in the land that divided into two forks at its easternmost end like the tail of a great fish, they were as far east as they could go.

Surrounded by salt water, these new arrivals discovered that the bays were filled with food — shellfish of all varieties in unlimited quantities, and fish so numerous that when they migrated into shallow creeks they seemed to push out all the water.

In thick forests of pine and oak, they built shelters from tree branches and grasses, cultivated crops with stone tools, carved out canoes from tree trunks and used them to hunt whales and to journey great distances across open ocean. And for as long as 12,500 years — more than 550 generations of people, one following the other in an unbroken chain — they lived all to themselves on the long island by the ocean.

If Long Island's first residents had a name for themselves, it is lost in the mists of history. When Europeans arrived along the northeast coastline in the early 16th Century, floating ashore in their own great boats, they called the people they met Indians. What that first momentous encounter was like for the Indians can, for the most part, only be guessed at. But wispy clues are buried like precious gems in historical documents.

"Many years ago, when men with a white skin had never yet been seen in this land, some Indians were out fishing in the mouth of the Cohotatea [Hudson] River . . . spied at a great distance something remarkably large floating on the water," an Indian told a Moravian missionary in 1801. "Some believed it to be an uncommonly large fish or animal, while others thought it was a very big house floating on the sea."

If history is a chronology of events, there is little hard evidence of the earliest inhabitants of Long Island — a people called the Paleo-Indians. There is more about the Indians who were here when Europeans arrived — they are called the Woodland Period Indians — but nearly all of it was written by Dutch and English settlers. What constitutes the Indians' own writings can be seen in the mysterious symbols and squiggly lines they made on the deeds the Europeans used to claim land as their own. History you can hold in your hand has been found in the ground Long Islanders live, play and walk on — stone utensils the Indians used in virtually every aspect of their lives.

So much seems lost to the centuries. Their language, part of the Algonquian language group, is extinct, with only a few words saved for posterity. In one celebrated case, words were recorded by a man soon to be president — Thomas Jefferson — who traveled to Long Island on horseback to conduct research. But most of his notes were stolen. The Indians' social mores, how they raised their children, how they farmed, how groups living near each other on Long Island were related, how far they traveled, who their allies and their enemies were — all these remain shrouded in mystery.

Today, artists can only guess what they looked like. A drawing by Shinnecock artist David Bunn Martine shows a tall, lean, leather-clad man, decorated in a colorful belt made from shells, with bird feathers and porcupine quills adorning his hair. The earliest photographs, made in the 19th Century, show an entirely different people — formally dressed, stern, sometimes sad-eyed men and women staring into the camera like strangers in their own land.

One famous photo taken in 1867, shows Stephen (Talkhouse) Pharaoh — a Montaukett who was born and died on Montauk Point — sitting in a chair, his legs crossed, the long, graceful fingers of his left hand draped across his thighs, his right hand clutching a stout walking stick the way he once held a whaler's harpoon, his long black hair draped across his broad shoulders. If a people's history can be seen in a single photograph, it is perhaps found in this one.

"He is my great-great-uncle," said Robert Cooper, who sits in a home in a section of East Hampton called Freetown, where Indians and freed black slaves once lived. Old black-and-white photographs decorate his walls, monuments to his ancestors. "He is a stern-faced gentleman, isn't he? You know, he

LI HISTORY.COM

Past installments and enhancements to "Long Island: Our Story" are available on the Internet at Newsday's special site, http://www.lihistory.com.

A New World

The Paleo-Indians are believed to have followed the ice-free corridors between glaciers to reach North America about 14,000 years ago.

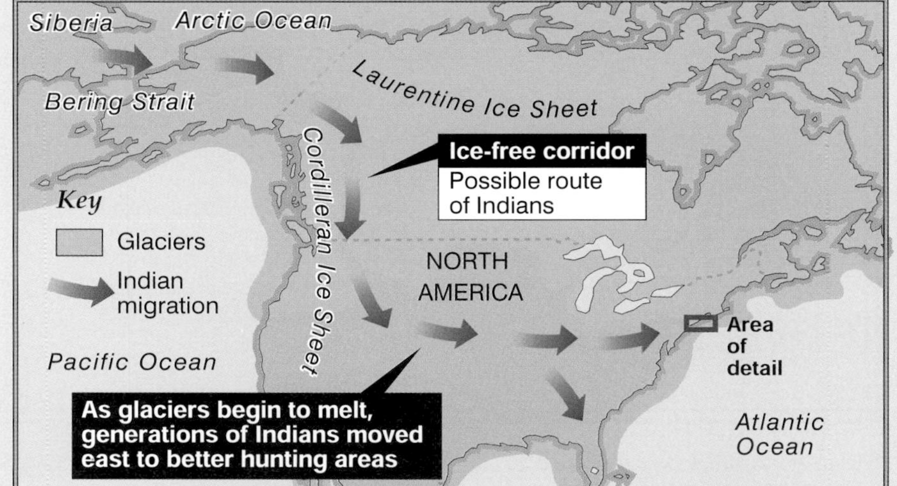

Where They Settled

People moved east onto Long Island about 12,500 to 8,000 years ago, after the last glacier moved north toward New England. At the time, Long Island was a tundra with little vegetation. Below is where the first inhabitants are believed to have lived during that period, as indicated by the discovery of fluted spear points.

Fluted spear points

Spear points found among the bones of prehistoric animals.

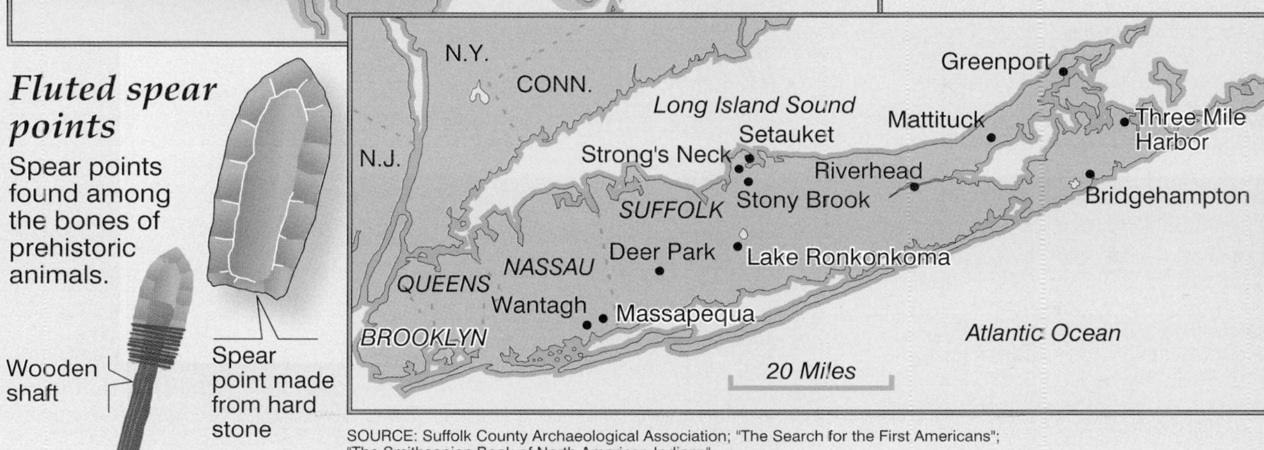

SOURCE: Suffolk County Archaeological Association; "The Search for the First Americans"; "The Smithsonian Book of North American Indians"

Newsday / Steve Madden

would walk from East Hampton to New York City in a single day. He was a Civil War veteran, and proud of it. He was born at a place on Montauk Point that used to be called Indian Fields. I believe he was of the last generation to live there before they were removed.

"He is buried there, too. Most days, even now, there is a flag on his grave. People sometimes leave little coins on his grave, little keepsake items. I believe that before he died in 1879, he could say he had been true to his heritage as much as he could. In a way, I guess, he was the last great Montaukett."

Stephen Pharaoh's story connects like the beads of a necklace, all the way back to an enigmatic Indian named Wyandanch, who also lived on Montauk Point. Wyandanch sold off thousands of acres of Long Island to the English after their arrival on the East End in the 1640s — actions that would reduce his people to guests on their former land.

For the most part, an examination of the record of Indian history on Long Island shows that Wyandanch's story, along with the stories of so many other Indians, remains untold.

"I think their history has been ignored," said John Strong, a professor at the Southampton Campus of Long Island University and the region's leading expert on Indians. "I don't think there's any question of that. There is a new way of looking at the Algonquian people that is essentially from the wigwam out, rather than from the outside in, as it always had been done. It is looking at what they saw, what they experienced. In a real sense, it's an effort to right a wrong in the telling of our history."

THE WAY THEY WERE

A special graphic appears on Pages 26-27

As taught for years in Long Island schools, the region's Indians lived in tribal groups that had names like Corchaug and Canarsie, Unkechaug and Setauket. They greeted the Europeans when they came and sold their land to the new arrivals. After that, they "disappeared" or "died off," vanishing from the landscape as if they had never really been here.

The "new" Indian history of which Strong is a leading proponent tells a far different story.

* * *

Experts divide the periods before Europeans arrived in the New World into four groups: Paleo-Indian Period, 12,500 to 8,000 BP (before present); Archaic Period, 8,000 to 3,000 BP; Woodland Period, 3,000 to 1,000 BP, and Late Woodland, 1,000 BP to the calendar year 1600.

It has been long accepted that the Paleo-Indians, whose origins are believed to be in Asia, walked across a land bridge between modern-day Siberia and Alaska when huge glaciers had absorbed enough ocean water to drop sea levels by up to 500 feet. This epic crossing took place more than 13,000 years ago. Once on the North American continent, the Paleo-Indians followed their prey — large, hairy, elephant-like beasts — wherever it took them, across vast and frozen distances.

Over the generations, small bands of hunters moved from Alaska down a north-south corridor between enormous walls of ice. The southern end of the corridor was in modern-day Montana. The Paleo-Indians carried spears tipped with what archeologists call Clovis points — intricately carved pieces of stone with characteristic fluting down the center. Named after a town in New Mexico where a similar point was found, they date to hunters who used them to kill big game. Fourteen such points have been found on Long Island.

"The Clovis points on Long Island are certainly suggestive of Paleo-Indians being there eleven thousand years ago," said James Adovisio, an archeologist who helped excavate a site in southwest Pennsylvania that suggests humans were there approximately 16,000 years ago. To arrive then, Adovisio said in an interview, would mean humans walked across the Bering Strait more than 30,000 years ago.

"Using these older numbers," said Adovisio, "then people were at Long Island well before the eleven-thousand date." He said the archeological community is involved in an intense debate about these numbers; to date, he said, no one has even named the people who might have preceded the Paleo-Indians to the East Coast. He said physical proof of an earlier occupation on Long Island may never be found, in part because the landmass shrank as huge glaciers melted and sea levels rose. The best archeological sites, he said, are now under water.

Whether their occupation was 11,000 years ago or 5,000 years earlier, it can only be imagined today how a people with such deep roots reacted when Europeans arrived on the scene in the early 16th Century. For their part, the first encounters gave the Europeans an opportunity to gather specimens they had never seen before and take them home — including Indians.

A little-known aspect of early exploration of the North American coastline — one certainly not discussed in social studies textbooks — is the kidnaping of Indians from coastal communities back to Europe, where they were sold into slavery. Kidnapings appear to have begun as early as 1500, when Portugese explorers went ashore somewhere on the north Atlantic coast, grabbed 57 Indians and took them back to Portugal, where they were sold on the auction block. Two years later, English sailors landed at Newfoundland and kidnaped three Indian men as proof they had made landfall. In July, 1525, a Spanish expedition abducted 58 men and women near what is now Newport, R.I., and brought them back to Spain.

"There are numerous examples of kidnapings up and down the coastline," said James Axtell, a historian at the College of William and Mary in Virginia. "A number of European countries were doing it." Records in England show North American Indians were used as sideshow acts, in some cases giving canoe demonstrations in the Thames River. There are accounts, Axtel said, of kidnaped Indians making it back to their homelands after being taken to Europe. Squanto, the celebrated Massachusetts Indian of

CLOVIS POINTS

Fourteen Clovis points — the stone spear tips used by Paleo-Indians — are known to have been found on Long Island, proof that Indians lived here more than 10,000 years ago. Experts say dozens of other points have probably been found and are sitting in garages, barns, cigar boxes, or private collections.

All 14 points were found in Suffolk, Nassau and Queens Counties, alongside creeks or, in the case of three found near Mt. Sinai, along the Long Island Sound waterfront. One was reported stolen from a private collection sometime in the 1960s.

Most of the 14 are in private collections and not available to the public. You can see the others at these locations:

Two intricately carved points are on display in the Southold Indian Museum. Garvies Point Museum and Preserve in Glen Cove has two points; the Sachem Public Library has two, and the Smithsonian Institution's Museum of the American Indian in Manhattan has four.

— Steve Wick

Newsday Photo / Bill Davis

A Paleolithic point found in Cutchogue, now at the Indian Museum in Southold.

Please see **FIRST** on Next Page

Paleo-Indians

FIRST from Preceding Page

American Thanksgiving stories, was taken from the Cape Cod area and, before 1620, was back home in time to greet the Pilgrims.

In spite of these incidents, Indians continued to greet Europeans when they arrived on their coastlines. A year before the Newport kidnapings, a group of Indians happily greeted Italian explorer Giovanni da Verrazano when, in the spring of 1524, he dropped anchor in the flooded valley of New York Harbor — the wooded landscape of Long Island to the east, a narrow, pointed island to his north. Everywhere, thick stands of forest ran to salt water.

" . . . Pursuing our voyage . . . we reached a new country, which had never before been seen by anyone, either in ancient or modern times . . ." Verrazano wrote on July 8, 1524, to Francis I, the king of France and sponsor of his expedition. He went on:

Many people who were seen coming to the seaside fled at our approach, but occasionally stopping, they looked back at us with astonishment, and some were at length induced, by various friendly signs, to come to us.

These showed the greatest delight in beholding us, wondering at our dress, countenances and complexion. They then showed us by signs where we could more conveniently secure our boat, and offered us some of their provisions . . .

They go entirely naked, except that about the loins they wear skins of small animals like martens fastened by a girdle of plaited grass, to which they tie, all round the body, the tails of other animals hanging down to the knees; all other parts of the body are naked. Some wear garments similar to birds' feathers.

The complexion of these people is black, not much different from that of the Ethiopians; their hair is black and thick, and not very long. It is worn tied back upon the head in the form of a little tail. In person they are of good proportions, of middle stature, a little above our own, broad across the breast, strong in the arms, and well formed in the legs and other parts of the body; the only exception to their good looks is that they have broad faces, but not all, however, as we saw many that had sharp ones, with large black eyes and a fixed expression. They are . . . acute in mind, active and swift of foot, as far as we could judge by observation. In these last two particulars they resemble the people of the east . . .

TO OUR READERS

Which is preferred, "Indian" or "Native American"? After interviewing scores of descendants, scholars, leaders and others for this series, Newsday chose to continue using Indian because it is widely accepted and used among descendants in the United States.

Literal objections have been raised against both terms. Indian originated with Christopher Columbus' mistaken belief that his ships had reached Asia. Native American has been criticized as reflecting neither the character of the early population nor the wishes of most of their descendants today.

On Long Island, opinion is divided. David Bunn Martine, a Shinnecock artist, says he is comfortable with the term Indian but calls himself, and his neighbors on the Shinnecock Reservation in Southampton, Shinnecocks. Robert Cooper, a descendant of the Montaukett chief Wyandanch, says he is comfortable with the term Native American, but, like Martine, uses Montaukett when talking about his own people.

"Long Island: Our Story" will also refer to "Algonquians." This word originated in French Canada and describes people who spoke similar languages, ranging from Labrador to the Carolinas and as far west as the Great Plains.

— **The Editors**

Except for a few spare references in some historical documents, the Indians' reaction to meeting Europeans is not known. One of them — written nearly two centuries after the fact — concerns the arrival in 1609 in New York Harbor of Henry Hudson, an Englishman working for the Dutch.

Many years ago, when men with a white skin had never yet been seen in this land, some Indians were out fishing at a place where the sea widens . . . espied at a great distance something remarkably large floating on the water . . . some believed it to be an uncommonly large fish or animal, while others (thought it was) a very big house floating on the sea.

Strong, in his book "The Algonquian Peoples of Long Island From Earliest Times to 1700," writes that this account was given in 1801 to a Moravian missionary named John Heckewelder. "As the floating house drew near," Strong writes, "word came back that it was a house of bright colors and crowded with people. The leader, who they thought at first must be a manito (spirit), was dressed in red pants and a red coat covered with glittering gold lace."

The man in the fancy red suit was Hudson, who was working for a Dutch conglomerate called the East India Co. He sailed his Half Moon into New York Harbor in early September, 1609. In an extraordinary account of the voyage, Hudson's mate, Robert Juet, wrote in his journal of their arrival that "this day the people of the country came aboard of us, seeming very glad of our coming, and brought green tobacco, and gave us of it for knives and beads. They go in deer skins loose, well dressed. They have yellow copper. They desire clothes and are very civil. They have great store of maize or Indian wheat, whereof they make good bread. The country is full of great and tall oaks."

After daylight on the morning of Sept. 5, Hudson sent a crew onto land to his east — Long Island. They encountered great numbers of men, women and children, Juet wrote, and saw huge trees and ate dried berries. They met Indians they invited aboard the Half Moon who had red copper tobacco pipes, and copper ornaments around their necks. "At night they went on land again," Juet wrote, "so we rode very quiet, but durst not trust them."

On Sunday, Sept. 6, Hudson sent a five-man crew ashore to explore. On their way back to the Half Moon, "they were set upon by two canoes, the one having twelve, the other fourteen men. The night came on, and it began to rain, so that their match went out; and they had one man slain in the fight, which was an Englishman named John Colman, with an arrow shot into his throat, and two more hurt. It grew so dark that they could not find the ship that night . . ."

The following morning, Juet wrote, Colman was carried to a point of land near present-day Coney Island. On a spot of cleared land not known today or marked with granite — the wide neck of land was named Colman's Point by Hudson's crew — he was laid to rest.

"I believe it's safe to say that Colman is the first European killed on Long Island and perhaps New York," said Charles Gehring, director of the New Netherlands Project at the New York State Library in Albany. "The Half Moon was made up of Englishmen and

Indians Appear

Long Island

10,500-8000 BC: Paleo Indians are thought to have moved onto Long Island after last glacier melted.

7000 BC: Large Ice Age animals disappeared.

6000 BC: Beginning of Archaic, or hunting and gathering, period.

3000 BC: Fish and shellfish added to the diet of Archaic people on Long Island.

2500 BC: Camp site was built at Wading River by Archaic period Indians. (The site later became the oldest Indian site found on Long Island.)

1000 BC: Beginning of Woodland period, or agricultural stage. Indians began using clay pottery on LI.

United States

11,000 BC. Asian big-game hunters rapidly settled in North America.

6000 BC. A climactic change brought forest to eastern North America while making the central and western parts of the continent more arid.

1500 BC. People in Minnesota and Wisconsin began learning the techniques of metallurgy.

200 BC. In Ohio, the Adena culture was being replaced by the Hopewell culture, trading people who smoked tobacco and used copper.

The World

8000 BC. A permanent village was established at Jericho. By 7500 the number of inhabitants was about 200.

4500 BC. Sailing boats seen along the Euphrates River for the first time.

2950 BC. Menes, the first king of Egypt, united Upper and Lower Egypt.

1200 BC. The Israelite tribes, who had left Egypt, arrived in Canaan.

30 AD. Jesus of Nazareth crucified by Roman authorities.

11,000 BC | 10,000 | 9000 | 8000 | 7000 | 6000 | 5000 | 4000 | 3000 | 2000 | 1000 | 0 | 100 AD | 200 | 300

SOURCE: "The Algonquian Peoples of Long Island From Earliest Times to 1700"; Suffolk County Archaeological Association; "American Facts and Dates"; "Chronicle of the World"

Dutchmen. Colman was an Englishman who had the misfortune to go ashore and get killed."

After burying Colman, Hudson headed the Half Moon farther up into the harbor. On Sept. 14, he moved into the river that would later bear his name, all the while encountering Indians in "great canoes . . . full of men." Several Indians were kidnaped and held on board to assure safe passage. They caught "great stores of very good fish," Juet wrote, and at several places on the river fought with small groups of Indians. In one case, a mate on the Half Moon cut off an Indian's hand with a sword. At one point, Hudson ordered a cannon fired at Indians on land, killing several.

After his bloody trip up and down the river, Hudson returned to Europe touting the wonders of New York. Two years later, he was followed by another Dutchman, a lawyer-turned-explorer named Adrian Block, on a ship called the Tiger. He returned to the Netherlands with a rich store of furs and two kidnaped Indians he called Valentine and Orson.

But it was Block's third trip to New York, in November, 1613, that made history.

On a November night, the Tiger, laden with beaver pelts destined for markets in the Netherlands, rode at anchor on the Hudson River side of the southern, pointed tip of Manhattan, near where the World Trade Center towers stand today. To Block's horror, the ship caught fire, which raged out of control. As he stood on the shore with his crew, Block watched the Tiger burn to the waterline.

Block and his crew then did the incredible — over a long, cold winter they built another ship. Cutting trees on the island, using tools retrieved from the burned wreckage, they built a 42-foot ship they christened the *Onrust*, the Restless. Eventually, Block made it home to the Netherlands.

In 1616, Block drew a map of the land the Dutch called *Lange Eylandt*. Block's Long Island looked like a series of islands pushed together, ending on the North Fork in a series of dots. On the south side, near where the South Fork juts out on his map, he wrote an Algonquian word, *Nahicans*, one of the first descriptions of Long Island Indians.

For the Indians of Long Island, the journey from their discovery by outsiders to their displacement from their land was relatively short. By 1636, the Dutch began making the first land purchases on Long Island, near the present-day Brooklyn Borough Hall. Large sections of Brooklyn were purchased for trade items such as cloth, kettles, axes, hatchets, knives and awls.

Nowhere in the Algonquian view of their world was there a provision for selling land. Nor did the Europeans believe the Indians "owned" land. What the Indians thought they were doing when they etched their unique marks on these deeds is not known today.

"At most," Strong said, "they thought they were sharing the land with the new people. They didn't believe these deeds were as final as they were."

Historical records show that the Dutch relationship with the Indians in western Long Island and near their principal settlement on Manhattan was murderous. One of the largest massacres occurred in present-day Massapequa, at a site where the Indians had built a log fort for their protection. There, in 1644, an English mercenary named John Underhill, hired out to the Dutch, killed more than 120 Indian men, women and children.

Years after the slaughter, an Oyster Bay resident wrote:

> *After the battle of Ft. Neck, the weather being very cold and the wind northwest, Capt. Underhill and his men collected the bodies of the Indians and threw them in a heap on the brow of a hill and then sat down on the leeward side of the heap to eat their breakfast. When this part of the county came to be settled, the highway across the neck passed directly over the spot where, it was said, the heap of Indians lay, and the earth in that spot was remarkably different from the ground about it, being strongly tinged with a reddish cast, which the old said was occasioned by the blood of the Indians.*

Only 54 years after Block wrote "Nahicans" on his map, Indian life on Long Island had undergone fundamental change. In numerous accounts, observers of the day wrote that Indian villages were being decimated by diseases. Reservations were set up where Indian communities were supposed to live and plant crops. All across Long Island, evidence that a people had once lived for 500 generations had faded.

In 1670, just 30 years after the English arrived to settle towns on the East End, a Hempstead minister's son, Daniel Denton, published an account he called "A Brief Description of New York." He wrote of the wonders of Long Island, a place he said was "capable of entertaining so great a number of inhabitants, where they may with God's blessings, and their own industry, live as happily as any people in the world . . ."

He continued:

> *To say something of the Indians, there is now but few upon the Island, and those few no ways hurtful but rather serviceable to the English, and it is to be admired, how strangely they have decreast by the Hand of God, since the English first settling of these parts; for since my time, where there were six towns, they are reduced to two small Villages, and it hath been generally observed that where the English come to settle, a Divine Hand makes way for them, by removing or cutting off the Indians either by Wars one with the other, or by some raging mortal Disease.*

FAST FORWARD

MONTAUKETTS SEEK RECOGNITION

In 1995, the descendants of the Montaukett Indians living on the South Fork did something they had never done before: They asked the federal government to formally recognize them.

The paperwork — called a notice of intent to seek recognition — was filed by Robert Pharaoh of Sag Harbor, a descendant of a long line of Montauketts going back to colonial times.

"We are in the process of assembling a tribal roll, along with geneological charts to show how we connect to the Montaukett people of the past," said Robert Cooper, a Montaukett who lives in East Hampton. Cooper can trace his ancestry back to the 17th Century, when English colonists arrived on the South Fork.

There are two tribes on Long Island that maintain reservations that date to the 18th Century and which have been recognized by New York State since Colonial times — the Shinnecocks in Southampton and the Poosepatucks in Mastic. No Indian group on Long Island has received federal recognition, nor has any sought it in the past. The Montauketts have not sought state recognition. Federal recognition is a rigorous process that requires a tribe having to prove its members today are bonafide descendants of the original tribe. To accomplish this, the modern-day group must show that the tribe, among other things, held meetings, kept tribal membership rolls and has tried to keep itself together as a group.

"We want to save our history and, if we can, construct a museum to our people on Montauk Point — our old land," Cooper said.

— Steve Wick

0-1000 AD: Smoking rituals, using round pipes, introduced around this time; more decorative pottery styles emerged.

500 AD. The Anasazi culture developed in Utah, Arizona and New Mexico. For protective reasons, the Anasazi contructed their villages on cliffs.

610 Mohammed began preaching in Mecca.

1000 AD: Late Woodland period began.

1000. Leif Ericson settled in Vinland, thought to be somewhere along the New England coast.

1066. William the Conqueror defeated Harold at the Battle of Hastings and became king of England.

1215. King John signed the Magna Carta.

1300. Pottery style called Windsor emerged on Long Island and in southern New England. (On the South Fork, pots have been found with small faces molded or carved on them.)

1300. Drought forced Pueblo Indians in Southwest to abandon cliff dwellings.

Oct. 12, 1492. Christopher Columbus stepped ashore on the West Indian island of San Salvador.

April 2, 1513. Juan Ponce de Leon discovered Florida and claimed it for Spain.

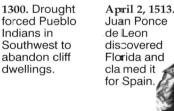

Oct. 31, 1517. Martin Luther posted his list of theses on the door of a Wittenberg church.

1524. Giovanni da Verrazano, sailing for France, dropped anchor in New York Harbor and was greeted by Indians in dugout canoes.

400 500 600 700 800 900 1000 1100 1200 1300 1400 1500 1600

Newsday / Steve Madden

The Way They Were

Archeologists divide the periods of Indian life on Long Island into four major stages: Paleo, Archaic, Woodland and Late Woodland. Here is what their lives may have been like:

Paleo

12,500 to 8,000 years ago

Environment: Tundra, with little vegetation.

Food: Hunted large animals, gathered food.

Shelter: Shelters were constructed against overhanging rocks or out of branches covered with animal skins, archeologists believe.

Community life: Paleo-Indians may have lived in communities of 40 to 50 people, composed of extended families and renewed by marriage to members of neighboring groups. The dog was probably domesticated during this period. The size of the community may have been determined by the number of young men needed to create an effective hunting team.

Tools: Spear points, made of hard, colored stone with long grooves chipped out of each side, were used to kill animals. In the Hudson Valley, archeologists' finds from this period include knives, scrapers and borers for working with hides, bone and wood.

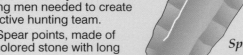

Spear point

Archaic

8,000 to 3,000 years ago

Environment: Warmer climate and more vegetation, including evergreen trees.

Food: New forests became home to new kinds of animals: deer, bear, wolves. People could gather berries, nuts and wild plants. Fish and shellfish were added to the diet.

Shelter: Probably lived in round or oval-domed wigwams, a framework of young trees covered with bark, reed mats or skins. It is not known whether people settled in one place or were nomadic in search of food.

Stone drills were used to pierce wood, bark and soft stone, probably twirled between palms.

Tools: Many new tools were invented for woodworking and food processing. Rattles and bowls were made from turtle shells. Thin quartz blades were mounted on handles for use as knives. A spear-thrower, weighted with a bannerstone for longer throws, was invented. Dugout canoe was introduced during this stage.

Clothing: Skins of beaver, deer and raccoon were used for clothing, blankets and wigwam coverings. Beads and pendants of shell and stone were hung around the neck.

Community Life: Social structure appears to have been based on a kinship system that probably linked families to a wide network of relations across Long Island, eastern New Jersey and southern New England. The familial network was reinforced with regular communal feasts and religious ceremonies. People usually married outside their own group, and evidence indicates a couple may have been able to choose the village of either spouse. Canoes were used to carry trade goods to neighboring communities.

Using a Spear-Thrower

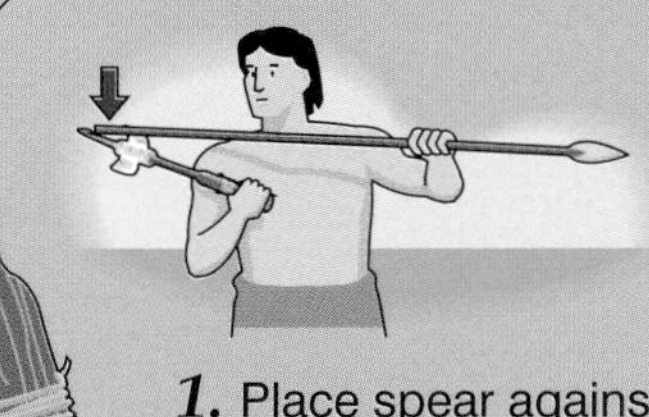

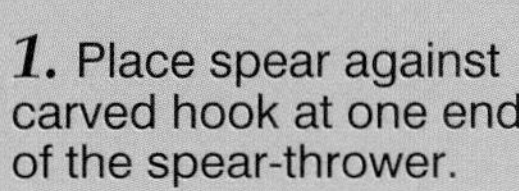

1. Place spear against carved hook at one end of the spear-thrower.

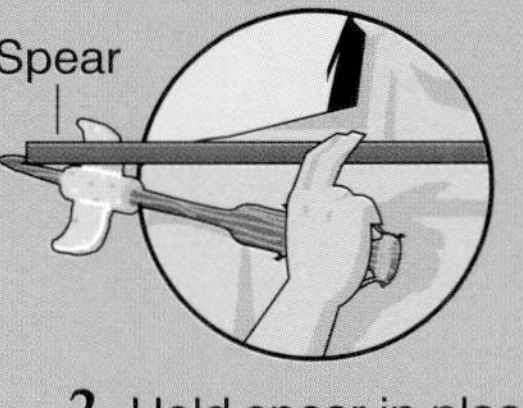

2. Hold spear in place with one or two fingers of hand holding the grip.

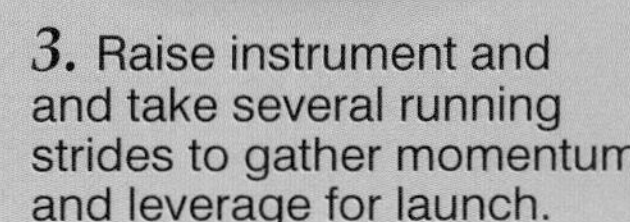

3. Raise instrument and and take several running strides to gather momentum and leverage for launch.

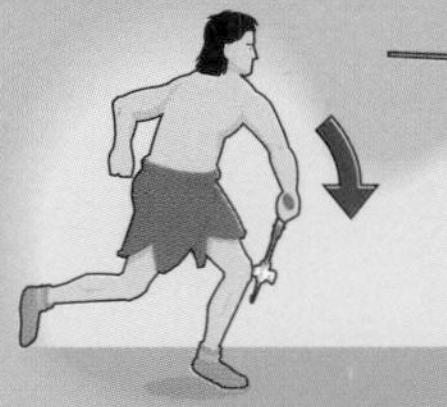

4. Thrust forward and downward with a snap as spear is released.

Woodland *(3,000 to 1,000 years ago)* *and Late Woodland* *(1,000 years ago to 1600 AD)*

3,000 to 400 years ago

Contact with Europeans

Environment: Similar to current day

Clothing: Natives greased themselves in animal fat to ward off cold in winter, mosquitos in summer and to make their hair and skin more attractive. Women wore their hair in braids before marriage, long after. Both sexes painted their faces every day, some were tattooed.

Community Life: More permanent, year-round communities were formed, ranging in size from 20 to 500 people. The smaller communities may have been campsites that served as hunting or fishing stations, with one or two structures. In the larger communities, wigwams and longhouses could have been spread out over a large area, but probably had a shared community gathering place, a burial place, planting grounds, sweat houses and other structures.

Recreation/Ceremonies: Archeologists have found stone balls and disks for games and stone puzzles. Ceremonies and feasts were held often: A full-moon festival celebrated the coming of spring; another in August celebrated the harvest. Powwows were held as a communal ceremony for the group, or for a sick person.

Tools: Clay pottery changed cooking methods; small amounts of sand or crushed shells were added to the clay to make the walls stronger; design tools were used to decorate the pots. Hunting was made easier with the bow and arrow; arrowheads became smaller and more triangular. Hoes were developed for agricultural use. Among the boned tools: awls, eyed needles, antler tines for flaking stone, turtle shell dishes, and beaver incisors used for woodworking.

Food: Women processed food by pounding, drying, cooking and smoking so it would not spoil. Cultivated plants – corn, pole beans, squash, pumpkins and melons – were brought to Long Island from Mexico late in the Woodland period. Ritual weeding took place in June. Evidence of abundant fishing includes stone netsinkers, bone fishhooks and antler harpoons.

The Mythical Thirteen Tribes of Long Island

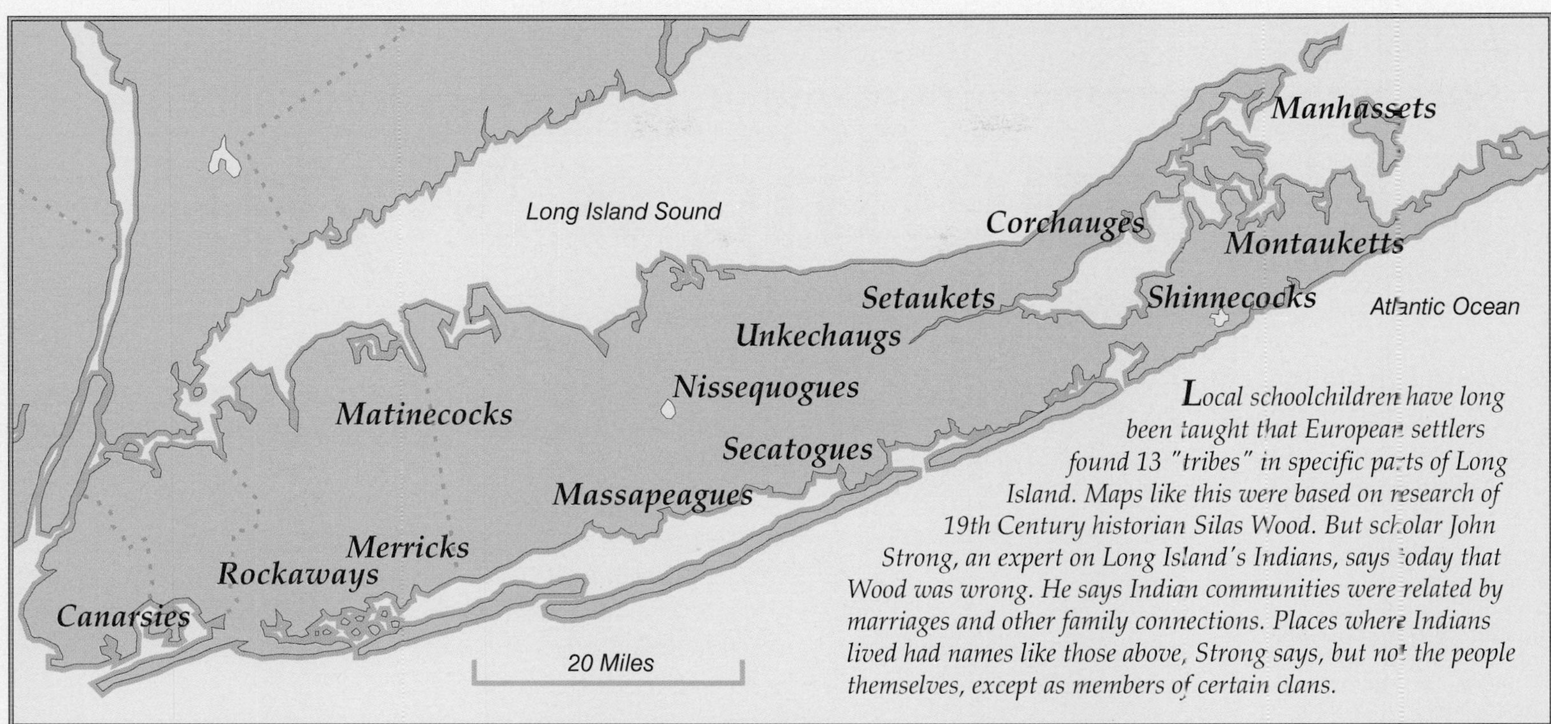

Local schoolchildren have long been taught that European settlers found 13 "tribes" in specific parts of Long Island. Maps like this were based on research of 19th Century historian Silas Wood. But scholar John Strong, an expert on Long Island's Indians, says today that Wood was wrong. He says Indian communities were related by marriages and other family connections. Places where Indians lived had names like those above, Strong says, but not the people themselves, except as members of certain clans.

Nutrients in the Indian Diet

Carbohydrates	Proteins/fats	Vitamins	Minerals
Ground nut	Black walnut, butternut	Lambs' quarters (A,B,E)	Oysters, shrimp, clams (calcium, iodine)
Pond lily	Hickory	Pokeweed (A,B,D)	Green leaf plants (calcium)
Jerusalem Artichoke (root)	White oak acorn	Berries, beach plum, grape, cranberry strawberry (vitamin C)	Hickory nuts (phosphorous)
Arrowhead	Game, animals, fish, fowl	Animal and fish liver (A,D)	Game animals, fish, fowl (copper, phosphorous)

Types of Shelter

Moderately large permanent or semi-permanent villages were established. People lived in oval or circular wigwams or in longhouses.

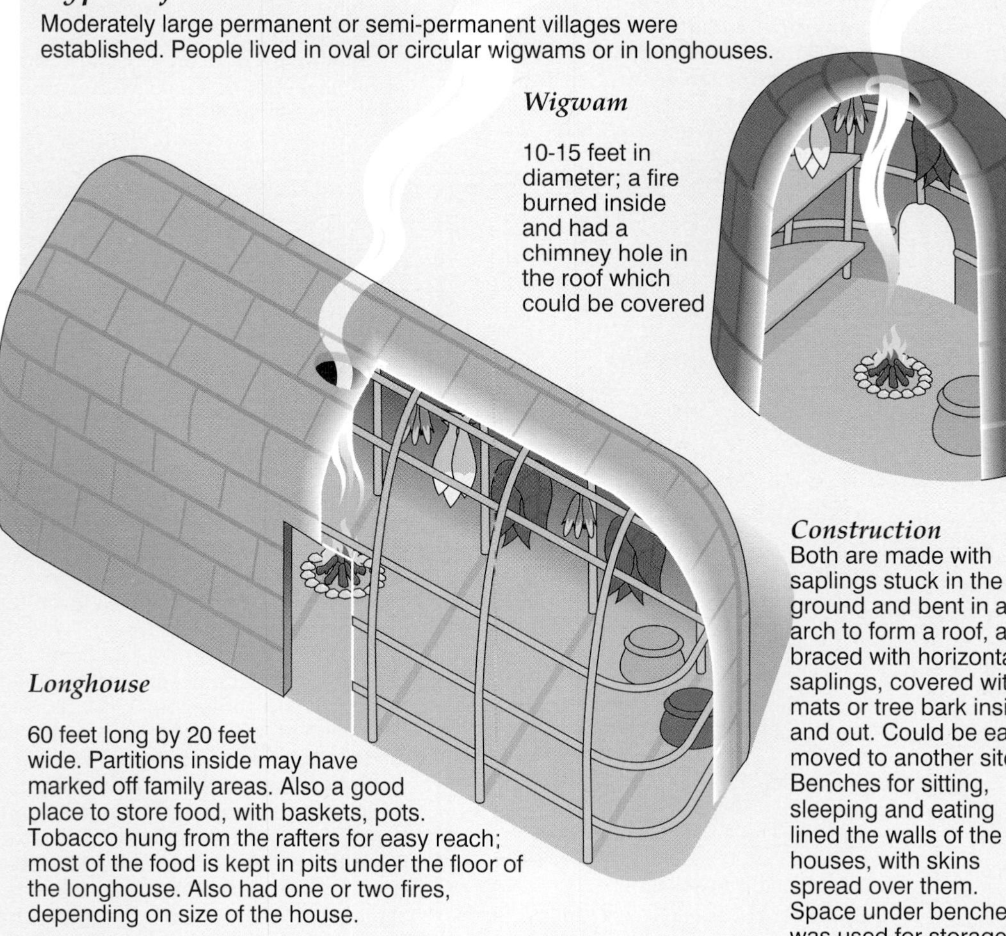

Wigwam

10-15 feet in diameter; a fire burned inside and had a chimney hole in the roof which could be covered

Construction

Both are made with saplings stuck in the ground and bent in an arch to form a roof, and braced with horizontal saplings, covered with mats or tree bark inside and out. Could be easily moved to another site. Benches for sitting, sleeping and eating lined the walls of the houses, with skins spread over them. Space under benches was used for storage.

Longhouse

60 feet long by 20 feet wide. Partitions inside may have marked off family areas. Also a good place to store food, with baskets, pots. Tobacco hung from the rafters for easy reach; most of the food is kept in pits under the floor of the longhouse. Also had one or two fires, depending on size of the house.

Cooking the Food

One technique used by Woodland indians to cook food involved the use of clay molds

1. Encase body in clay coat two fingers thick.

2. Place clay baking dishes in embers and cover with hot coals. Process cooks flesh in its own juices, preserving flavor and vitamins.

3. Mold can be broken open along outer edges, making a convenient serving dish. Scales and skin stick to the clay.

SOURCE: "The Algonquian Peoples of Long Island From Earliest Times to 1700": Suffolk County Archaeological Association; Nassau County Museum of Natural History

Newsday/ Steve Madden

Europeans apparently mistook Indian place names for tribal labels

Untangling a Myth

BY STEVE WICK
STAFF WRITER

When school children learn Indian history, they read in textbooks that there were 13 tribes on Long Island at the time Europeans arrived to claim the land.

These 13 tribes had formal names, such as Matinecock, and lived in well-defined geographical areas and nowhere else. The Matinecock, for example, lived along the North Shore of Nassau County and as far east as modern-day Huntington.

This is what school children on Long Island have been told for decades. But it's wrong.

"The 13 tribes has been a staple in generations of textbooks, on maps, and in newspaper articles," said John Strong, an expert on Long Island Indian history who teaches at Southampton College. "There were no such tribes. It's a myth. It's a good example of how what we are told about Indian history is largely provided by outsiders, who in this case got it wrong."

The myth goes back to the early 19th Century, when an amateur historian from Huntington named Silas Wood drew up a list of 13 Indian "tribes" he said existed on Long Island at the time of contact with Europeans. The list made him famous.

"Wood's list, with a few minor alterations made by local historians from time to time, has, unfortunately, become the standard reference for Native Americans of Long Island and has been repeated by historians and classroom teachers to the present day," Strong writes in "The Algonquian Peoples of Long Island From Earliest Times to 1700."

Strong says Indians on Long Island were connected by kinship systems. This means, he said, that communities were related by marriages and other family connections. The *place* the Indians lived in had a name, Strong says, but not the people themselves, except as members of certain clans, or social groups.

Wood's findings, which were based on a reading of land deeds made between Europeans and Indians, were included in an 1824 book called "A Sketch of the First Settlement of the Several Towns on Long Island." He listed 13 tribes — the Canarse, the Rockaway, the Merikoke, the Marsapeague, the Secatague, and the Patchague on the South Shore; the Matinecoc, the Nissaquague, the Satauket and the Corchaug, on the North Shore; the Shinnecoc, Manhanset and the Montauk on the South Fork and Shelter Island.

In addition to drawing up tribal names, Wood delineated specific territories for each group. For example, he wrote, "The Rockaway tribe claimed the territory around Rockaway, and more or less of the lands in Newtown and Jamaica. The Merikoke and the Marsapeague tribes extended from Rockaway through Queens county into Suffolk, on the south side of the island."

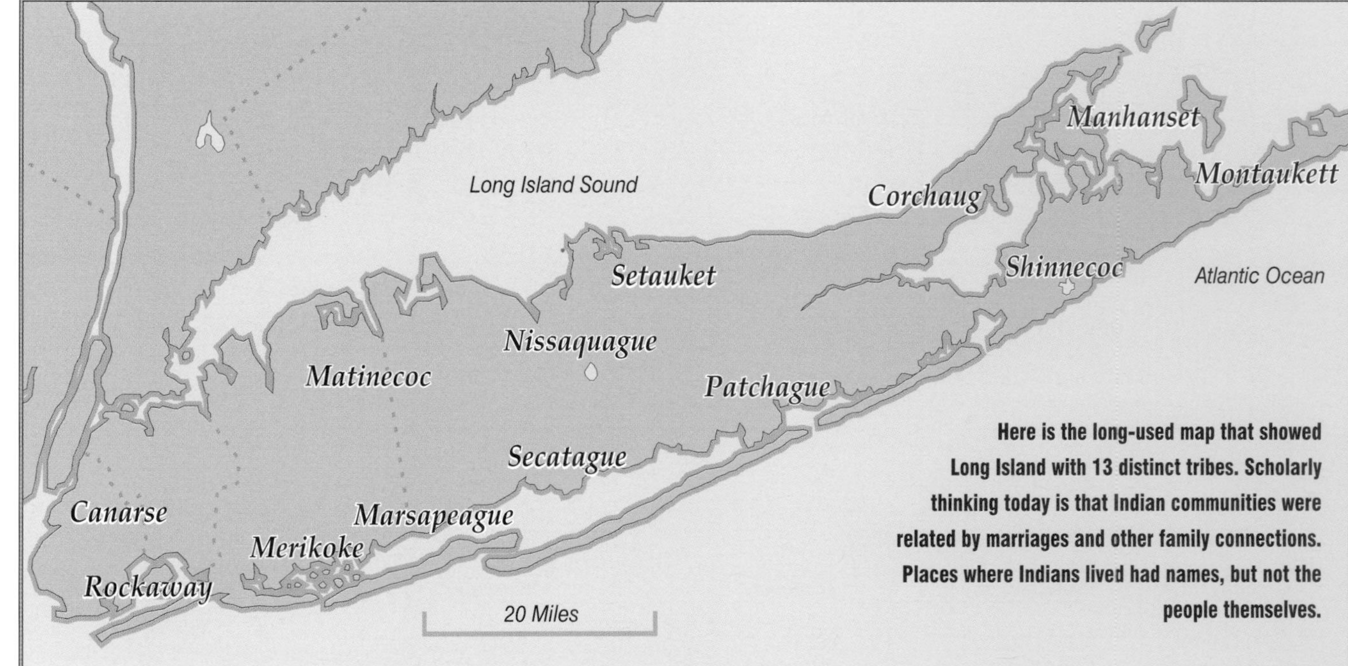

Here is the long-used map that showed Long Island with 13 distinct tribes. Scholarly thinking today is that Indian communities were related by marriages and other family connections. Places where Indians lived had names, but not the people themselves.

Newsday / Steve Madden

All this is a myth that has endured, Strong writes in his book, which was published this year. "The primary documents make it quite clear that there were no tribal systems on Long Island before the sporadic series of raids known as Governor Kieft's War, 1640 to 1645, which resulted in the deaths of more than one thousand Native Americans and a few dozen whites." At that time, Willem Kieft was the governor of the tiny Dutch colony that straddled the southern tip of Manhattan Island and the western shore of Long Island.

Upon arriving on Long Island, Europeans used to the social order of their home countries — villages populated by people who owned the land they farmed and lived on — looked for the same thing in their new land. But no such order existed here. The Algonquian-speaking people of Long Island did not, for example, understand the concept of ownership, and thus selling land was a foreign concept to them.

Looking for order and defined boundaries, the Dutch seem to have viewed the Indians they encountered at the west end of Long Island and along the Hudson River as being members of individual nations. The word "nations" and "tribes" are used interchangably in the Dutch records. There are also numerous Indian names cited by the Dutch as designating the people living in communities in and around New Netherlands. Today, these names — such as the Wappenas, Hogelanders, Wicquasgecks, Reckewacke, Mereckewacks, Tappanders, Massapeins, and the Zinkeeuw — are historical mysteries without answers.

The most current thinking on these odd-sounding names is that they may have referred to a specific location, not a group or an Indian community. Since the Algonquian language once spoken by Indians on Long Island is extinct — except for small vocabularies made in the 18th Century and a small colony of the last speakers of an Algonquian dialect in Canada — these words today can not be translated.

"Most experts today say these words were place names," said Walter Smith, a longtime member of the Southold Indian Museum and a lifelong amateur archeologist who lives in Orient. "In other words, the Indians were referring to the place they lived, not what they called themselves. They probably knew themselves as nothing more sophisticated than 'the People.' The Dutch, and later the English who did the same thing, evidently thought they were tribal names."

Wood's work was accepted as dogma as soon as he published his book. Fifteen years later in 1839, Benjamin Thompson, a historian and writer who lived in Setauket, published "A History of Long Island," which he dedicated to Wood. Thompson wrote that the Indians were divided into tribes which exercised "independent authority over separate portions of territory," and he listed the same 13 tribes. The leaders of these tribes, Thompson wrote, made fair and equitable transactions with Europeans for the land they had occupied for thousands of years.

After Thompson, another popular Long Island historian, Peter Ross, published, in 1902, a multi-volume history in which he listed the same 13 tribes. Ross, though, broke ranks with Thompson and others by arguing that Long Island's Indians were cheated out of their lands and pushed to the brink of extinction.

SILAS WOOD

The man who created the tribal myth was born on his family's farm in West Hills, in Huntington, in 1769, when Long Island was part of a British colony. A hilly, wooded place in the southern part of the town, West Hills was where Walt Whitman was born in 1819. A portrait of Silas Wood shows a dark-haired man with a narrow, unhappy face. He was a child during the Revolution, when British troops occupied portions of Long Island.

He attended Princeton College, and, in 1795, was elected to the New York State Assembly from Huntington. After leaving the Legislature, he practiced law in Huntington. It was while as an attorney, and later district attorney of Suffolk County, that he began to research his book.

He died in 1847, and is buried in Huntington. A 1970 article in a Long Island historical journal described Wood as Long Island's "first great historian."

Huntington Historical Society

Silas Wood, an amateur historian, drew up the list of 13 Long Island "tribes" he said existed when Europeans arrived.

Indian communities grew corn, beans, squash and tobacco in Long Island soil

Masters of Agriculture

BY STEVE WICK
STAFF WRITER

When Long Island was all theirs, Indians lived in small communal villages made up of grass-covered shelters that looked like large beehives. Their villages sat on necks of woodland and alongside tidal creeks that overflowed with food — food so plentiful it could be scooped out by the basketful.

Their thatched huts, called wigwams, were open at the top to let out smoke and were placed in no particular order. Fields where corn, beans, tobacco and squash were grown were laid out between huts. Some villages were very small, perhaps accommodating fewer than a dozen people, while others were large and spread out along shorelines.

"In my mind's eye," said Ralph Solecki, an archeologist who grew up near a creek in Cutchogue that was the site of a large Indian settlement, "I see a village that overlooks salt water, with fields around it where the corn is high, with thick woods on the north side as a wind barrier, and nearby a freshwater pond or spring. They would have everything they needed — food, water, wood — within easy reach. Long Island was an ideal place in so many respects."

These villages were scattered along Long Island's shorelines. A map made in 1639 by a Dutchman named Johannes Vingboons shows four longhouses — longer wigwams that held several families — on a jagged neck of land in present-day Brooklyn.

The Indians' villages were agricultural marvels. Over thousands of years, corn had moved from the Southwest and Mexico to the East Coast — passed along from Indian group to Indian group. It was planted in long, irregular rows. Between the rows, crops such as beans and squash were planted. Tobacco, another crop that had made its way from Mexico to the East Coast, also was planted and used in smoking rituals.

Newsday Photos / Bill Davis

Clay pots possibly used for cooking by Indians on Long Island, and at right, stone hoes used for planting, with a modern-day hoe for comparison, are on display at the Southold Indian Museum. Below, ax heads and a knife, characteristic of those used by late prehistoric Indians, at the Garvies Point Museum & Preserve in Glen Cove

Corn and beans were the stuff of myth. Some coastal Indians believed a crow that had flown from thousands of miles away brought them their corn and bean seeds. Other coastal natives, such as the Montauketts of the South Fork, passed on stories from generation to generation that it was a god who lived in the west who brought them the seeds.

Because of where the Indians lived on Long Island, their lives were tied to salt water. Their lush gardens were a complement to their harvesting of the creeks, where they could obtain prodigious amounts of oysters and clams, as well as migrating fish that appeared regularly in great numbers. Europeans who arrived in the mid-17th Century wrote that the Indians netted small fish such as bunker and alewives and carried them to their planting fields, burying a fish around each seed to fertilize the soil.

The Indians of Long Island were as tied to the seasons as any modern farmer. When a cluster of stars that astronomers call the Pleiades moved across the winter sky and disappeared beneath the western horizon in early May, they broke up the rich brown soil with stone-tipped tools and hoes made of clam shells and began to plant their corn.

Intriguing finds on Long Island, including a site near Mount Sinai Harbor, suggest the Indians tracked the movement of stars in the winter sky. A crude lunar calendar was found at the Mount Sinai site. When the stars suggested spring had arrived, Indian women dug up the fields for planting.

"They make heaps like molehills, each about two and a half feet from the others, which they sow or plant in April with Maize, in each heap five or six grains," wrote Isaack de Rasieres, a Dutchman who visited an Indian community in western Long Island in the early 1600s.

When the English arrived on the East End in the early 1640s, they discovered another feature of Indian agricultural practices — deep holes covered with woven mats that were used to store food during winter. The English called them "Indian barnes" and they disliked them because their livestock frequently fell through the mat roofs.

The old fields and villages of the Indians are long gone and memories have faded. But there are treasures of the past. One of them is a photograph taken in 1900 that shows a Shinnecock man named John Henry Thompson, dressed for the photographer in a three-piece suit. He is standing alongside a "barne," he has just made. It is covered with grass and sticks.

LI HISTORY.COM
Images of more artifacts and an explanation of their uses in everyday Indian life are available on the Internet at http://www.lihistory.com.

LEGACY

THE WIGWAM

The Long Island Indians lived in stick-built wigwams covered with bark and grass. The wigwams were tight and dry and could be erected quickly.

"Their houses are for the most part built after one plan . . ." wrote a Dutchman in a document called "Description of New Netherland," which is in the New York State archives in Albany. "They set various hickory poles in the ground according to the plan of the size of the building. The tops are bent together above in the form of a gallery, and throughout the length of these bent poles, laths are fastened. The walls and roofs are then covered with the bark of elm, ash, and chestnut trees; the bark is lapped over each other as a protection against a change of weather, and the smooth side is turned inward. The houses lodge fifteen families together, more or less, according to the dimensions."

One of the best descriptions of a longhouse — a longer and considerably larger version of a wigwam — was written by Dutch minister Jasper Danckaerts in the early 1600s. He wrote that 20 people lived in a longhouse that was 60 feet long and 15 feet wide. It was constructed of saplings bent over to form an arch that was covered with grass mats and layers of bark. — Steve Wick

A wigwam depicted in a painting by Dorothy Raynor at the Southold Indian Museum

Gods Of The Indians

Old Dutch writings relate some of what original Long Islanders believed of life and the afterlife

By Steve Wick
STAFF WRITER

Long Island Indians believed in an abundance of gods, in a devil who was responsible for evil, and in an afterlife in which their souls went west to live either in peace or in torment.

"There were the gods of the four corners of the earth," wrote Samson Occum, a Mohegan Indian from Connecticut who had converted to Christianity and — in the early 1760s — traveled to East Hampton to preach among the Montauketts. "And there was a god over their corn, another over their beans, another over their pumpkins, and squashes. There was one god over their wigwams, another of their fire, another over the sea, another of the wind, one of the day, and another of the night . . .

"But they had a notion of one great and good God, that was over the rest of the gods, which they called *Cauhluntoowut* . . .," he wrote in a letter to a friend in Connecticut, adding, "These were common notions with all the Long Island Indians."

These "common notions" had been reported more than a century before Occum wrote the letter, a copy of which is included in a massive collection called "The History & Archaeology of the Montauk," which chronicles the lives, legends and tribulations of the people Occum sought to convert.

Although Occum is regarded as a reliable observer, he had turned away from Indian beliefs when he converted to Christianity. The Indian view of their beliefs is for the most part lost to history. There is no written record in their own words of what they believed in. Like so much of Long Island Indian history, we view it from a secondary point of view — that of outsiders.

"As a child, I heard older relatives talk about things such as where they lived, or foods they ate, but religious practices were almost never discussed," said Robert Cooper, a Montaukett Indian who lives in East Hampton. "I know they believed in spirits, and believed in harmony with the Earth. They saw themselves as being one with the Earth, which was their mother. That's what I've taken from the old beliefs."

The earliest accounts of the Indians' religious beliefs were written by the Dutch soon after their arrival in the early 17th Century. These accounts show both the rich diversity of beliefs among different Indian communities and their common threads. For example, the Indians encountered by the Dutch appear to have shared a belief in life after death, in certain creation myths, and in a multitude of gods as well as a devil who was to blame when someone died.

"Respecting Religion, we as yet cannot learn that they have any knowledge of God, but there is something similar in repute among them," an unidentified Dutchman is quoted as stating in documents filed in the New York State Library. "They say that mention was made by their forefathers for many thousand moons, of good and evil spirits, to whose honor, it is supposed, they burn fires or sacrifices . . . The ministry of their spiritual affairs is attended to by one they call *Kitzinacka*, which, I think, is a Priest."

The same document states that the Indians believed a person's soul "goes up westward on leaving the body. There 'tis met with great rejoicing by the others who died previously; there they wear black Otter or Bear skins, which among them are signs of gladness . . . Death is the offspring of the Devil, who is evil."

The Indians did have an elaborate belief system, as well as creation myths, according to another document called "A Description of New Netherland":

> *They pay great reverence to the devil, because they fear great trouble from him when hunting and fishing; wherefore the first fruits of the chase is burnt in his honor, so that they may not receive injury. If they experience pain in any part, they say — A devil lurks in there. They fully acknowledge that a God dwells beyond the stars, who, however, gives himself no concern about the doings of Devils on earth: because he is constantly occupied with a beautiful Goddess, whose origin is unknown. She once came down from heaven into the water . . . and would have sunk, unless land had suddenly bubbled up under her feet. The land waxed bigger, so that erelong a whole globe was perceptible, which quickly produced all sorts of vegetables and trees. Meanwhile, the goddess brought forth a deer, bear and wolf, and again cohabited with these animals: She thus became pregnant, and lay in of divers sorts of creatures at one birth. From this arises the variety not only of animals, but also of men, which in color are either black, white, or sallow.*

The Dutch appear to have been particularly struck by how the Indians prepared their dead.

"The next of kin closes the eyes of the deceased," a document in "A Description of New Netherland" states, continuing:

> *After being waked there a few days, they are thus interred. The body hath a stone under the head . . . They place beside it a pot, kettle, a platter, spoon, money, and provisions, to be made use of in the other world . . . The men make no noise over the dead, but the women carry on uncommonly; they strike their breasts, tear their faces, call the name of the deceased day and night. The mothers make the loudest lamentations on the death of their sons. They cut off their hair, which they burn on the grave in the presence of all the relatives.*

As for what happened after death, Occum wrote in his letter:

> *Their souls go to the westward a great way off, where the righteous, or those that behaved themselves well in this world, will exercise themselves in pleasurable singing and dancing forever . . . They suppose the wicked go to the same place or country with the righteous; but they are to be exercised in some hard servile labor . . . such as . . . making a canoe with a round stone.*

Boston Public Library

Samson Occum, a Mohegan from Connecticut who preached Christianity on Long Island

LEGACY

PAUL CUFFEE'S GRAVE

The Rev. Paul Cuffee's grave sits all by itself in Hampton Bays, sandwiched between the railroad tracks and a busy highway. The stone marker is weather-beaten and broken in two.

To bring a measure of distinction to the site, Cuffee's descendants erected a small white fence around it. "He was someone who mattered, yet you would not know it the way his grave sits by the tracks," said Janine Tinsley-Roe of Bellport, a descendant. "But once upon a time, that was all Indian land."

Cuffee, a Shinnecock Indian, was born in Brookhaven Town. He became a celebrated minister, like his grandfather Peter John, who preached to the Indians of Long Island. Cuffee, who in his youth was an indentured servant to a Wading River farmer, became an enthusiastic convert in his early 20s.

He preached among Indian communities at Poospatuck, a small reservation near present-day Mastic Beach; at a part of Hampton Bays called Canoe Place, and, toward the end of his career, at Montauk. It is said he was a vigorous preacher whose services were attended by huge crowds.

When he died, a missionary society erected the stone (at right) that now — even though it is broken — marks his solitary grave. It reads, in part:

> In testifying the Gospel
> of the Grace of God
> He finished his course
> with Joy on
> 7th of March 1812
> Aged 55 years and
> Three Days

— **Steve Wick**

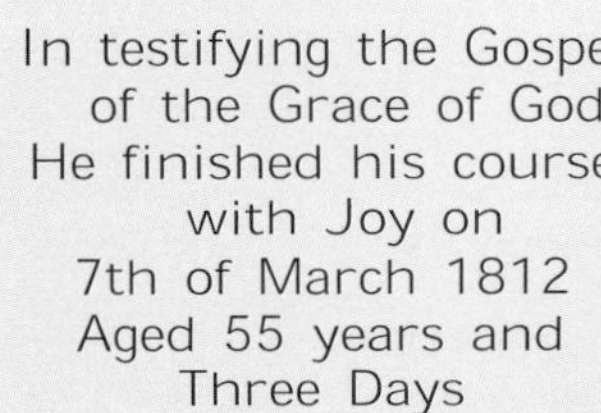

Newsday Photos / Bill Davis

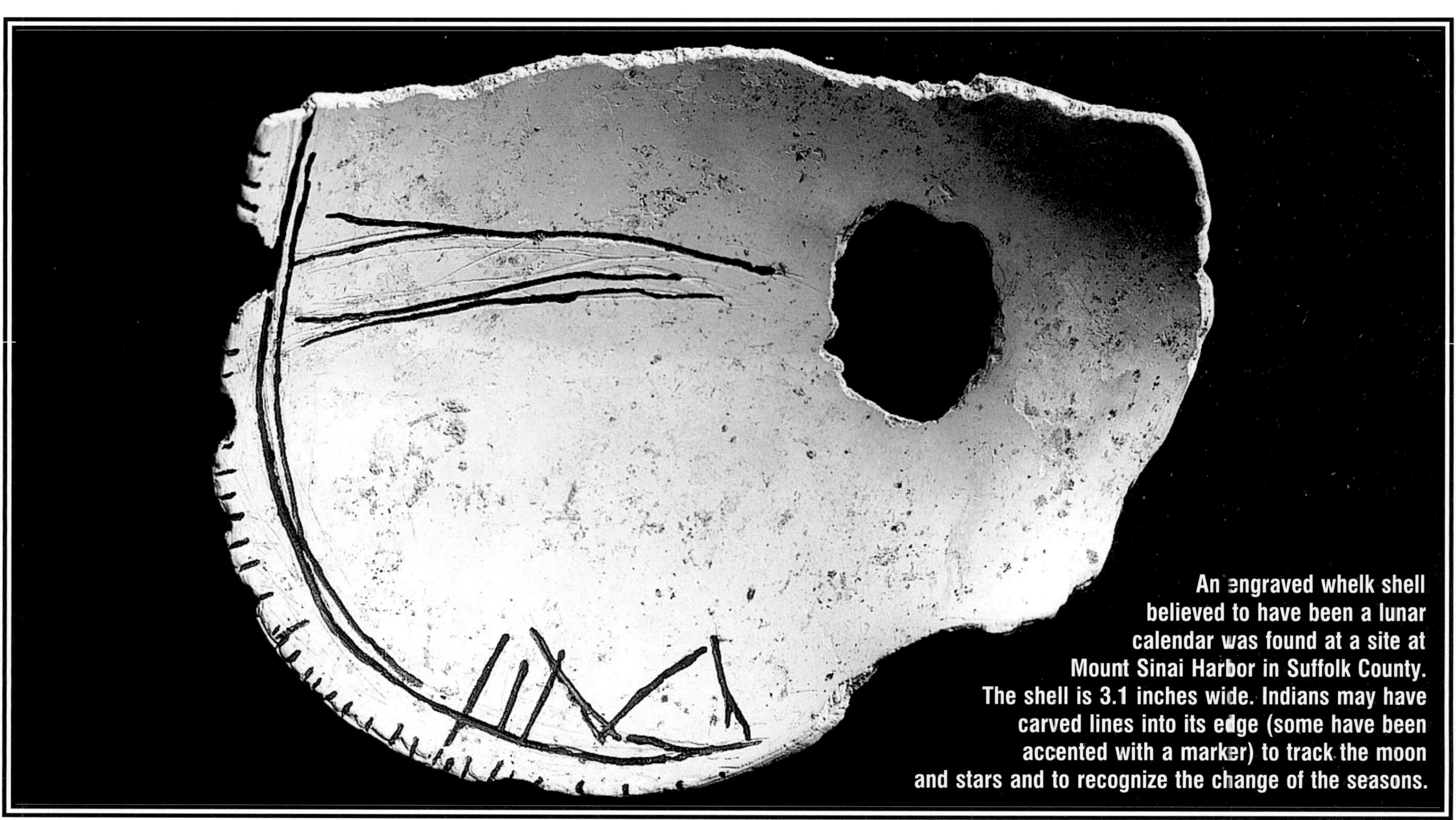

An engraved whelk shell believed to have been a lunar calendar was found at a site at Mount Sinai Harbor in Suffolk County. The shell is 3.1 inches wide. Indians may have carved lines into its edge (some have been accented with a marker) to track the moon and stars and to recognize the change of the seasons.

Buffalo Museum of Science

From birth to death, the Indians of Long Island marked the passing stages of life

A Time to Live, A Time to Die

BY STEVE WICK
STAFF WRITER

The Algonquian Indians of Long Island buried their dead with fanfare, exchanged gifts at weddings, partied at harvest time and held naming ceremonies for their children.

Although very little has been recorded by the Indians themselves about their social customs, there are accounts by observers that fill in the historical holes. When Samson Occum, a Mohegan from Connecticut, came to East Hampton to preach Christianity to the Montauketts in the 1760s, he found that old customs died hard. In one case, he described how children were not named until they had survived infancy.

"He [Occum] reported that several families often gathered together to hold a naming ceremony, which included dancing, feasting, and exchanges of gifts," historian John Strong writes in his book, "The Algonquian Peoples of Long Island." "There were two different ways of announcing the names. Some families had each recipient of a gift stand and shout the name of the child three times; others called upon a few elders to speak the name.

"This name was only the first of several the child would have during his or her lifetime. It was a common practice to take on a new name in response to a dream or an unusual personal experience or accomplishment."

Rites of passage were common among the Algonquians. Young people reaching their teenage years were singled out for special treatment — sort of like a boy today having a bar mitzvah or confirmation. Boys were sent into the woods alone to hunt and endure hardships. Girls experiencing their first menstruation were sequestered in a special wigwam for several days and their hair was cut off.

Marriage appears to have been a particularly big deal among the Indians — even though they didn't have catering halls for overpriced receptions. The father of a male child seeking to marry him off to a girl in his village presented animal gifts to the prospective bride's parents. If the parents agreed, they accepted the gifts.

"If there was an agreement," Strong, a professor at the Southampton Campus of Long Island University, writes, "a great wedding feast was prepared by both sets of parents and their families for all of the friends and relatives."

When adults married, it was much simpler. Basically, the partying was scaled back to include just the two families. But sometimes all ceremony was skipped and the man and woman chose to live together. In this case, the woman would come to the man's wigwam, and they would share a meal. Marriage was not always forever. According to Occum, divorce was commonplace.

Indian gravesites found on Long Island show that funeral rites were commonplace. In a few cases, personal belongings were included in the grave. In others, dogs were killed and placed in the grave. Strong writes of an archeologist digging near Sag Harbor who found the skeleton of a puppy in a shallow grave. In the late 1920s, a construction crew building a house near Lake Montauk found a wooden coffin that contained the remains of an adult female and a small dog. Copper pots, glass beads, and pipes were also in the grave. Strong believes that the dogs were included in graves to help guide the dead to the next life.

There were many rituals built around curing illnesses. A village herbalist had the task of administering herbal remedies and mixing plants. There were remedies for every illness. In addition, sweat lodges, which had important ritual signficance themselves, were also used to help cure the sick.

Lodges were constructed of sticks and covered with grass and clay. The clay covering turned the lodge into a virtual oven. The lodges were heated with hot stones piled in the center. As with modern-day steambaths, water was sprinkled on the hot rocks to produce steam. Often, herbs were consumed beforehand to increase sweating.

There were many rituals centered on stargazing. Western Long Island Indians "were careful observers of the heavens because they believed that the stars were living beings," Strong writes. The positions of stars relative to the seasons provided critically important information for harvests. These western Long Island Indians seem to have been particularly interested in phases of the moon, too. Tribal stargazers passed word to the community as to when to hunt, fish and plant.

A mystery to historians today are the engravings found on stone tablets at several locations on Long Island. It is unclear what role, if any, carvings made in the shape of idols and engravings such as these played in Algonquian social life.

Occum said the Montauketts used idols as a means of communicating with the spirit world. Western Long Island Indians kept small wooden dolls, called *nanitis,* according to historical records, which were considered sacred.

Engraved tablets found by archeologists at several Long Island sites seem to have served other purposes. Most beg more questions than they answer. One, found near Glen Cove, is carved with lines and other markings on both sides. A tablet in the collection of the East Hampton Library's Long Island collection is made of slate, with notches around the edge and with a cross-hatch pattern on one side and a rectangle inside a circle on the reverse side.

Strong, who has done the most work trying to uncover the meanings of these objects, says they are a mystery.

"We don't really know much about them, or how they fit into the Algonquian social order," he said. "There's even a dispute about some of the engraved tablets and carvings over whether they were made by the Algonquians at all. Some of what the Indians did on Long Island, and what they believed in, is beyond our understanding today."

Prized shells of local waters provided jewelry and currency used far beyond Long Island

An American Mint, Even Before Coins

BY STEVE WICK
STAFF WRITER

In the beginning, Long Island was *Sewanhacky.*

This Algonquian word — which roughly translates to "Place of Shells" — is found in Dutch records of land purchases in western Long Island.

"It is believed to come from the Delaware *sewan,* purple shell, and *hacky,* place," said Charles Gehring, the director of the New York State New Netherlands Project, in Albany, an effort under way to translate Dutch documents from the 17th Century. "The Algonquian words for shells are, apparently, the first name for Long Island."

Algonquian was a huge language group — spoken by hundreds of thousands of Indians on the East Coast — that was splintered by numerous dialects. For instance, Indians on the western end of Long Island spoke a Delaware-based dialect, while Indians on the eastern end spoke a Mohegan-Pequot dialect. Yet the words for shells that were used for Long Island appear to cross these different dialects.

According to Gehring, the name *Sewanhacky* first appears in deeds written in June, 1636, for land on the western end of Long Island. One deed from that month reads that it was "situate on the island called by them *Sewanhacky,* also *Sewanhacking.*" It is spelled differently in other Dutch deeds from that time, including *Suanhacky, Seawanhacky* and *Sewanhaka.*

Eleven years earlier, in 1625, a crude Dutch map of Long Island was emblazoned with the word *Matouwax.* By the late 1630s, when the English appeared on the East End, the Algonquian word *Pommanocc* appears in land records.

In the early 1900s, a scholar named William Tooker translated *Matouwax* from a southern New England Algonquian dialect as meaning "land of the periwinkle," or "country of the ear shell." Tooker translated *Pommanocc,* also from a southern New England dialect, as meaning "land of tribute."

For the Algonquian people of Long Island, shells in all their forms were used for jewelry, as trade goods and as a primitive form of money. The phrase "land of tribute" refers to the payments in shells made by Long Island Indians to dominant tribes along the southern New England coastline, such as the Pequots and the Narragansetts.

It is clear in historical records that Long Island's waters were an early American mint, producing the best shells found in the region.

"The documents show that the waters around Long Island teemed with shells," Gehring said. He pointed out that *wampum* — another Algonquian word for the shells — was traded from Indian group to Indian group as far west as the Great Plains. "These shells were highly valued."

There were two classes of wampum, white and purple. White wampum was made from the center column of the periwinkle, or conch shell. The purple wampum was made from the purple sections of large clam shells. The darker wampum was valued considerably higher than white wampum.

The shell pieces were ground, polished and cut into small cylinders. Each cylinder was then drilled with a stone tool and strung together in the form of a necklace. These shell pieces were also woven into belts, elaborate capes, earrings and headpieces. Scholars say the wampum was so highly prized that a gift of it from one tribe to another could prevent a war. Historians say a gift of wampum from a murderer to his victim's family could end animosity between the parties.

In addition to jewelry and as a form of tribute, wampum also was used as a payment for services for a shaman, or a medicine man, as part of a marriage proposal, and was often used in burial services. Wampum has been found in gravesites throughout New England and on Long Island. It also conferred status on a sachem, or leader.

Wampum stringing beads were carved from clamshells, at top, and sea whelks, above. These are on display at the Garvies Point Museum, Glen Cove.

Newsday Photos / Bill Davis

But it was when Europeans arrived, first the Dutch and then the English, that wampum took on new meaning. Soon after their arrival in New York waters, the Dutch realized the value of wampum to the Indians and began to set up elaborate trade networks. For instance, the Dutch began to trade wampum with the coastal Pequot Indians in Connecticut for furs obtained in upstate New York. The Pequots obtained their wampum in eastern Long Island bays, around modern-day Gardiners Island and Shelter Island.

By the mid-1630s, wampum was legal tender throughout New England and Long Island. When the English arrived later on eastern Long Island, one of the trade items they used to coax the Indians to sell their land was small metal tools that made the drilling of wampum pieces easier and quicker. These drills were called "muxes," a word that appears on many Long Island land deeds. Once metal drills were introduced to Long Island Indians, wampum began to be manufactured in great amounts.

Today, hundreds of years after it was made by Indian hands, wampum remains an item of great beauty.

"The shells are really beautiful stuff," said Walter Smith, a longtime member of the Southold Indian Museum, which has a large wampum collection. As he spoke, he showed off a prize piece — a necklace complete with shells carved in the shape of goose heads.

"Wampum was of enormous value to the Algonquian people, and became cash money to Europeans," Smith said. "Many people grew rich trading Long Island shells — the same shells we see today on all our beaches."

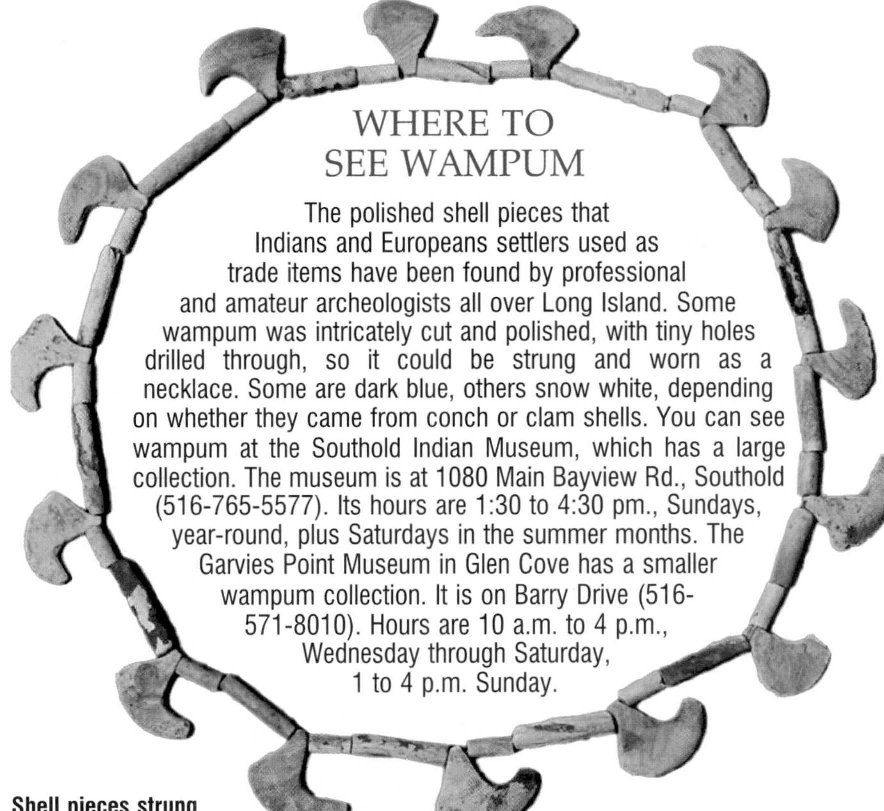

WHERE TO SEE WAMPUM

The polished shell pieces that Indians and Europeans settlers used as trade items have been found by professional and amateur archeologists all over Long Island. Some wampum was intricately cut and polished, with tiny holes drilled through, so it could be strung and worn as a necklace. Some are dark blue, others snow white, depending on whether they came from conch or clam shells. You can see wampum at the Southold Indian Museum, which has a large collection. The museum is at 1080 Main Bayview Rd., Southold (516-765-5577). Its hours are 1:30 to 4:30 pm., Sundays, year-round, plus Saturdays in the summer months. The Garvies Point Museum in Glen Cove has a smaller wampum collection. It is on Barry Drive (516-571-8010). Hours are 10 a.m. to 4 p.m., Wednesday through Saturday, 1 to 4 p.m. Sunday.

Shell pieces strung into a wampum necklace, on display at the Southold Indian Museum

Illustration by Teresa Shaw

Newsday Photos / Bill Davis

Above, the remains of Fort Corchaug sit near the tree line along a salt creek in Cutchogue. At left, a sketch by New Suffolk artist Teresa Shaw depicts the fort as a palisaded quadrangle with nearby wigwams and dugout canoes.

Archeologists hope a buried fort will reveal new secrets of Indian civilization

The Promise of Corchaug

BY STEVE WICK
STAFF WRITER

Deep in the woods alongside a salt creek on the North Fork, history is buried under a carpet of top soil and decayed leaves.

The history alongside a creek in Cutchogue is unlike anything that exists in the Northeast. It is more than 350 years old, and is mostly untrampled. There were others like it at one time on other creeks and woodsy hills nearby, but they are all gone now.

What once sat in these verdant woods was a log fort built by the Indians who lived on the North Fork at the time of contact with English colonists who arrived in the late 1630s. When they poked into the woods alongside the creek, the English found a fort made of logs, roughly rectangular in shape, and enclosing an area of less than three acres. All around it were the corn and bean fields that fed the Indians.

Today, 3½ centuries later, the secrets of Fort Corchaug, as the site is called, are hidden away underground.

"It is the rarest of rare," said Ralph Solecki, a Texas-based archeologist who grew up a quarter-mile from the site in a house in Cutchogue. "There is nothing else like it anywhere in the region because the other 17th-Century Indian forts have been lost. It is a wonder."

As a child, Solecki began finding arrowheads in farm fields around his house. As a teenager, he read an article that said a log fort had been built by the Indians in the late 1630s alongside a Cutchogue creek, was later abandoned and lost to time. In the summer of 1935, Solecki went looking on a nearby creek, but found nothing promising. Then an amateur archeologist told him to look on the west side of Downs Creek.

"The site was right where he said it was," Solecki said. "The farm it had once sat on was then owned by the Downs family. They'd had it since the early 1800s, and when I talked to the family they said stories about the fort had been passed down through the generations. It's clear now that the site was abandoned after the English came to the area. The logs would have fallen down and rotted away. Luckily, the family had cattle on the site, which had probably never been plowed. It was a miracle it had not been destroyed by farming practices."

Standing by the creek that day, Solecki could make out a low, rounded berm that protruded from the ground and ran perpendicular to the creek. The berm, he thought, probably anchored one wall of the fort. Just south of the fort was the remains of an ancient well, which he knew held potential as an archeological site. But it was the flat land where the fort once sat that intrigued him.

In the stillness alongside the creek, Solecki could vividly imagine the distant past — the four walls of the fort built as a refuge for the Indians, the salt creek on one side, farm fields on the other side. "It seemed incredible to me on that day, and it still holds true today, that this site was untrampled."

Solecki came back in the late 1940s to write his master's thesis on the site. What he found then, he said, convinced him that the fort was built with the help of Europeans as a defense against attack from Indians from New England, who traveled to eastern Long Island to collect shells. During a summer of digging, Solecki found Dutch trade goods on the site, which, he said, suggested that the fort may have been connected to a vast trading system that channeled wampum from the Peconic Bay to the Dutch in New Amsterdam. Near the ancient Indian well, Solecki found arrowheads more than 1,000 years old.

Today, the site and 105 acres around it — an area called Fort Neck in old Southold Town records — will be preserved under an accord signed last July. According to a plan submitted in June, the Peconic Land Trust, a nonprofit conservation group, bought the site from William Baxter of Stamford, Conn., for $1.2 million. A Georgia businessman, Russell McCall, agreed to buy back part of the tract from the Land Trust for $800,000. Plans for the fort site include an interpretive center, and a study center for archeologists and students.

When the site is acquired, archeologists have said they would like to begin serious work. They have excavated little more than 10 percent of the 105-acre tract. There may be a burial ground and the site of an ancient village in the woods and fields alongside Downs Creek. But just as it is, the historical importance of the fort is clear.

"There weren't that many forts along the eastern seaboard that can be documented as having been built by Native Americans in the Seventeenth Century," said Lorraine Williams, curator of archeology at the New Jersey State Museum in Trenton. She excavated part of the site in the 1960s.

Work at the site could fill in missing chapters in Long Island's extraordinary Indian history.

"To me, it's not a matter of arrowheads," said Elizabeth Hale, a member of the Shinnecock community in Southampton. "It's a matter of a social system that survived for thousands of years before people came and discovered us."

History professor John Strong, an expert on Indians of Long Island, at the Corchaug site; he is among those interested in what will be found when archeologists dig at the 105-acre tract.

A dying language once heard on Long Island is spoken by a few on a Canadian reserve

Keepers of a Lost Culture

BY STEVE WICK
STAFF WRITER

At left, Beulah Timothy — with a picture of her late father, Kennedy Snake — is one of perhaps 10 people fluent in the Munsee Delaware language at the Delaware Nation Reserve in Moraviantown, Ontario. The language was once spoken widely by Indians in the lower Hudson River area and western Long Island, and Timothy is a descendant of those peoples. Above is her former schoolhouse, now a woodshop, on the reserve. Below is a sign posted on the edge of the reserve.

Newsday Photos / Bill Davis

MORAVIANTOWN, Ontario

Beulah Timothy is a ghost of history. So is her brother, Richard Snake, and their childhood friend, Alma Burgoon.

Their home is the Delaware Nation Reserve, 3,000 acres of rich farmland 150 miles southwest of Toronto. Small, well-kept homes surrounded by cornfields dot the reserve, which is crisscrossed by gravel roads and bordered by a slow-moving muddy river called the Thames.

Their ancestors came here 200 years ago in the company of missionaries. It was the end of a long journey. The Delaware had been on the run for generations after fleeing the region of the lower Hudson River and western Long Island in the early 1640s to escape certain extinction in a war waged by Dutch settlers.

Nearly 500 people live at Moraviantown, as the reserve is known. They are ghosts of a long lost homeland that has forgotten them as much as they have forgotten it. Their history in New York and on Long Island has been all but obliterated by the passage of 3½ centuries and untold amounts of concrete and asphalt. Hidden away in Canada, the Delaware are a people forgotten by the land they were forced to flee.

But the lives of Richard Snake, Beulah Timothy and Alma Burgoon represent even greater anomalies within their world — they are the last speakers of a language called Munsee Delaware.

It was the language of New York, centuries before there was a New York, and Long Island, when no one but the Algonquian Indians knew it was an island. Munsee Delaware was the language that explorer Henry Hudson heard in 1607 as he sailed up the river that now bears his name; the language heard by another explorer, Adrian Block, who with his men spent the winter of 1613-14 on Manhattan Island building a ship they christened the Restless. It was the language heard by the Dutch as they expanded their settlements onto the western end of Long Island, pushing aside the Delaware and turning them into refugees. And it was a language spoken for hundreds of generations on Long Island.

That the descendants of those refugees still live as a community — that *anyone* anywhere can still speak the language — seems incredible.

"There're just a few speakers left," Timothy says in a soft voice. She is seated in the kitchen of her home, near the center of the reserve. Her brother sits across from her, smiling and laughing at her stories. Nearby, Burgoon looks through a hymn book translated into Delaware in the 1840s at the urging of the Moravian missionaries who brought a small band of Delaware to Canada in 1792.

Timothy ticks off the names of her neighbors who are fluent in Munsee Delaware. Eight to 10, she says. Maybe not that many, she's not really sure.

"All the elders spoke it when I was growing up. That's all we heard. Back then, when the young people went to school, they were sent home to learn English. All we spoke was Indian."

Multiple twists of fate brought the Delaware to rural Canada. Drive across their reserve, covered in corn by the middle of August, hear Delaware being spoken, hear children laugh at the playground by the Delaware First Nation office, and a visitor comes away thinking they must have fallen through a hole in the fabric of American history and landed safely in another world. The residents of the Delaware Reserve have been known to a small group of linguists and anthropologists who have studied them and listened to their language, but otherwise the world knows little about them.

These last speakers, nearly all of them elderly, are the rarest of the rare. Nearly every Algonquian language spoken on the East Coast before the arrival of Europeans is considered extinct, and many of them do not even have vocabularies or small word lists that can be held up as windows to lost worlds.

"Eastern Algonquian is for the most part extinct," said Ives Goddard, a linguist at the Smithsonian Institution who visited the Delaware Reserve in the early 1960s when there were more than 40 fluent speakers. "There are a few Algonquian speakers left in Maine, a very small community, but otherwise all the languages once heard from Maine to Florida are extinct."

Well, not quite extinct — Beulah Timothy, Richard Snake, Alma Burgoon and a few others are still speaking Munsee Delaware. But time is against their language. Snake, who is 59, is the youngest. Timothy is 81 and Burgoon is 69. Herb Snake, Richard's and Beulah's brother, who was fluent, died as summer began, and a name was removed from the list the aging speakers keep in their heads. Some of the remaining speakers on the reserve are infirm. Others will not see outsiders. The secrets of the language remain only with this small group, and there is no program on the reserve — or anywhere else in Canada or the United States — to teach the language.

"It's a miracle you can hear it at all," says Philip Snake, the tribal chief. "Our people are a miracle. We shouldn't be here, should we? That what's all those professors and anthropologists have been telling us for years. We've only been in Canada 200 years — a wink of the eye, really. We were down there for thousands of years. How many people even know we're still around?"

There is a fading sign alongside the gravel road that leads to the reserve that reads: "The creator put us in a special place for a reason." It was a long road that brought the Delaware to this special place.

Dutch explorers first encountered the Indians of the lower Hudson River in the fall of 1607, when the Half Moon piloted by Henry Hudson arrived on the scene. Soon afterwards, one of Hudson's men, John Coleman, was killed by Indians encountered on the western end of Long Island. Hudson later killed a number of Indians he met on his way back down the river after having proceeded almost to where Albany is today.

But it was not these events, or the later settlement of Manhattan Island and western Long Island by the Dutch, that turned the Indians into refugees. It was a war that erupted in the early 1640s and resulted in more than 1,000 Indian deaths across the region, including a massacre at a village in present-day Nassau County.

The Indian villages on Long Island were divided into bands, which the Dutch mistakenly called tribes. Linguistically, Long Island was divided in half — Munsee Delaware was spoken by Indian groups in the western half of the Island. They included the Canarsee, who lived in what is now Brooklyn; the Rockaway, a group on the South Shore; the Matinecock, who extended across the North Shore of Nassau and into Suffolk, and the Massapequa, a group in modern-day Nassau. The Indians on the eastern half of Long Island spoke dialects of Mohegan Pequot, another Algonquian language altogether.

In 1643, warfare between Dutch settlers and Indians spilled across the region. Some of the Indians in western Long Island may have fled east. Hundreds of others looked west for safety.

"The war spawned the mass movement of people west, past the Dutch settlements," said Goddard. "Groups moved to Staten Island, then into New Jersey, then past the Delaware River into eastern Pennsylvania."

By the early 1700s, the Delaware were living in different bands along the Susquehanna River, picking up and moving west when the frontier inched nearer to them. By the mid-1700s, they were in western Pennsylvania. And by the 1780s they were spread across eastern Ohio.

All the while, said Goddard, they were living in tight-knit communities away from whites, maintaining their Indian culture. "As they moved west, some groups went in different directions and were absorbed into other tribes," Goddard said. "In other words, they disappeared. But a large number stayed together. They were quite successful adjusting to the frontier and maintaining their way of life."

One band, the Turtle Clan, prospered in Ohio. After the Revolution, Goddard said, George Washington and Thomas Jefferson — who was fascinated with the Delaware language, as he would later be with eastern Long Island Indian languages — proposed turning what is now nearly all of Ohio into a protected Indian reservation. Their proposal was never enacted, however, which had fateful consequences for the Delaware.

Many of the Delaware settlements in eastern Ohio were under the protective tutelage of Moravian missionaries. The Moravians were Czechoslovakian Prot-

Please see **DELAWARE** on Next Page

Newsday Photo / Bill Davis

A prayer book has words in English on the left and Munsee Delaware on the right.

THE MUNSEE DELAWARE LANGUAGE

In the late 1970s, Canadian linguist John O'Meara traveled to the Delaware First Nation Reserve, in Ontario, to record the last speakers of Munsee Delaware. Among them was an elderly woman named Ethel Peters. Peters told O'Meara a witchcraft story she called "When My Uncle Was Bewitched." What follows is the first paragraph of that story, in Munsee Delaware and then in English.

Nii numoxoomus waak noohum kxanuwak nxah amiimunzal. Nii nguk wunaxoo-kihkayiin, nal ha wa nzhiis, nal waak ktakan oxkweesus. Aapwu-noohum-wiinamalsuw, lum'tiisiinee.

My grandfather and my grandmother had three children. My mother was the oldest, then there was my uncle, then another girl. My grandmother got sick early on, she had rheumatism.

A full version and a recording of "When My Uncle Was Bewitched" are available on the Internet at http://www.lihistory.com. In addition, you can hear 10 conversational phrases spoken in Munsee Delaware by Dianne Snake of the First Nation Reserve.

To hear conversational phrases and a recording of Ethel Peters reading "When My Uncle Was Bewitched" on the telephone, call 516-843-5454 or 718-896-6969 and enter category 8253 (touchtone required).

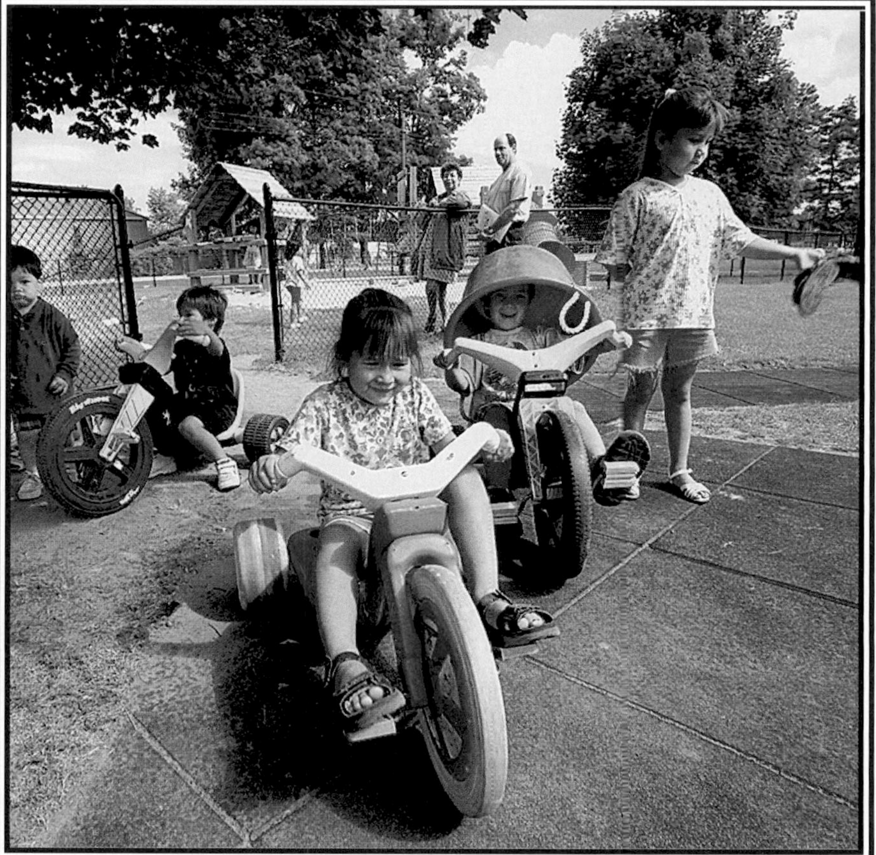

Newsday Photos / Bill Davis

Jolene Whiteye, at left, with a photo of her late grandfather, Joseph Whiteye, who spoke Munsee Delaware. Jolene is beginning studies in treaty law at the University of British Columbia this fall. Above, children play at the Moraviantown reserve. Today's generations are taught English; there is no program in which children or adults can learn Munsee Delaware.

The Keepers Of a Lost Culture

DELAWARE from Preceding Page

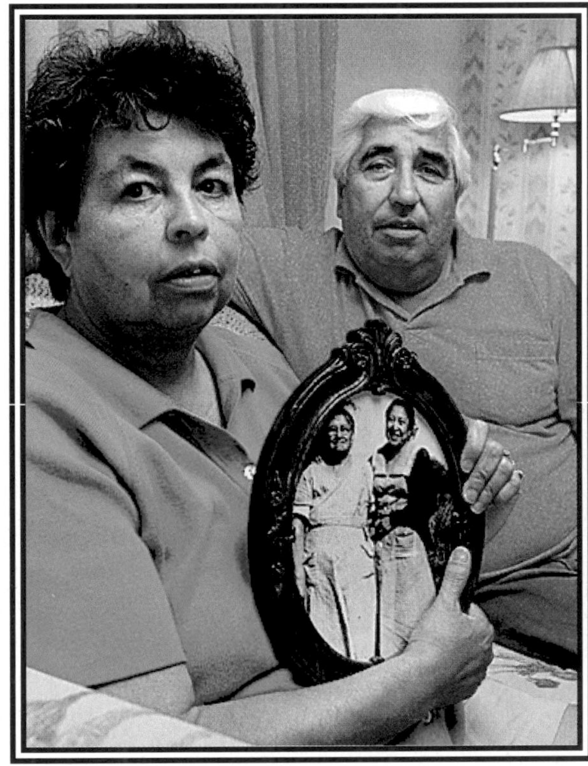

Newsday Photo / Bill Davis

Tribal chief Philip Snake and his wife, Dianne. "How many people even know we're still around?" the chief asks.

estants who saw their life's work in the conversion of the Delaware. But their protection could only go so far, and in 1782, near the mission town of Gnadenhutten, Ohio, 90 Christianized Delaware were massacred by white settlers.

It was this act that pushed the Turtle Clan to flee north into Michigan and, by 1792, into Ontario, to the banks of the Thames River, where their descendants live today and still consider themselves Christians.

"From what I understand, this journey began because there were a lot of land sales down there," said Darryl Stonefish, the Delaware Nation's researcher. "There were disputes over sales in the New York City area; there were massacres by the Dutch. There were a lot of small sales on Long Island, too. Sometimes, the native people didn't understand what a land sale really was."

Today, the Delaware have no real connection to their old homeland. Small groups have visited New York City. Richard Snake has visited Westchester County to look at an Indian burial ground. And Philip Snake said he regularly receives mail from federal officials in New York informing him, as a possible claimaint, about government land sales.

"They seem to think we have an interest in land down there," he said. "Our lives are right here. We have immediate needs here — like saving our language."

The Delaware do, however, have emotional links to Ohio. Numerous tribal members have traveled to Ohio to visit the massacre site. Many have seen a play about the massacre that is produced almost every summer in a town near the site. They know the histories of the Moravian missionaries who brought them to Canada.

When Canadian linguist John O'Meara arrived at Moraviantown in 1979, he found more than 20 fluent speakers — half the number Goddard found in the early 1960s. O'Meara made dozens of recordings of the speakers, and today, he wonders if soon his tapes will be all that there is of Munsee Delaware.

"I cannot see it surviving much past the turn of the century," he said.

Recently, O'Meara published a large dictionary of the language, based on the tapes he made at Moraviantown and other research. The dictionary is available through the University of Toronto Press.

* * *

The Delaware seem to laugh a lot.

Seated at Timothy's kitchen table, Dianne Snake — chief Philip Snake's wife, and a partial Delaware speaker — tells a joke in Delaware and everyone but a visitor cracks up. One joke is followed by another, all in Delaware. Did Hudson go back to England and Holland after his epic voyage and report that the Indians were always laughing?

When they finish laughing, Burgoon and Dianne Snake talk about the speakers who have died in recent years, including a woman named Ethel Peters, who told on tape, in Delaware, a witchcraft story. Everyone remembers her.

"Oh, I love that story," Burgoon says. Then she and Dianne Snake sing part of a Moravian hymn translated into Delaware. A quiet, graceful woman, Burgoon speaks of a bus trip she took to the massacre site in Ohio, where she planted a tree in remembrance of the 90 who were killed.

"Is there even a marker at that site?" Richard Snake asks. "It seems not that long ago when we found out we used to be in Ohio. Going down there, it was like going back home again." Speaking of the language, he says, "Someone was saying a long time ago, if you can't speak the language you're not Indian."

They all nod in sad agreement.

Suddenly, they're laughing again. What now?

"We've given you a name," Dianne Snake tells the visitor. She says it, a long gutteral word with a lot of "k" sounds. She spells it out on a pad of paper — *kehktaweewsiit.*

Asked what it means, she laughs again. "The nosy one," she says.

After speaking of his childhood at Moraviantown, Richard Snake says he wants to learn more about his ancestors' history — where they lived, how they lived, what happened to them. But the links back to Long Island are thin.

If he were to speak to schoolchildren learning Long Island history, what would he tell them?

"That we're still here," he says, smiling.

Turtle Clan's Trek to Moraviantown

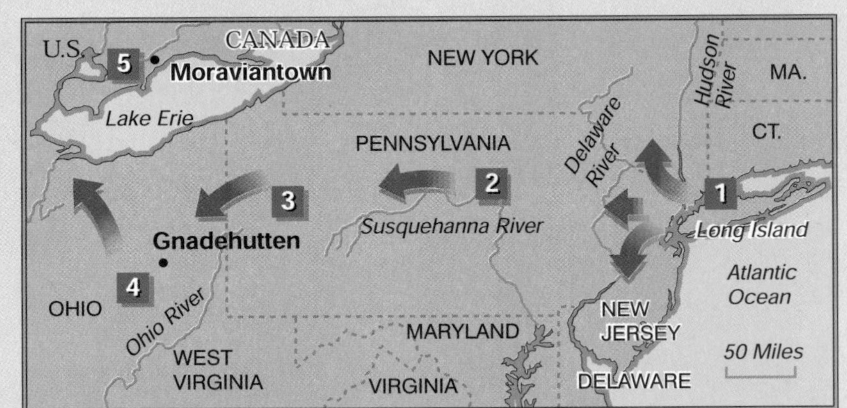

1. With Dutch and Indians at war in 1643, some Indians in the East, including western Long Island, fled to Staten Island, New Jersey and eastern Pennsylvania.

2. Indians lived along the Susquehanna River in the early 1700s.

3. By the mid 1700s, many of the Indians were living in western Pennsylvania.

4. Indians were spread across eastern Ohio by the 1780s. In 1782, 90 Delaware were massacred by white settlers in Gnadehutten, Ohio.

5. After the massacre, the Turtle Clan fled north to Michigan and by 1792, into Ontario, where its ancestors live today.

Newsday / Steve Madden

A robbery foils his work to save some of the Island's Algonquian language

Jefferson's Lost Legacy

BY STEVE WICK
STAFF WRITER

On June 13, 1791, two future presidents rode across Suffolk County on horseback.

Thomas Jefferson, who 15 years earlier wrote the Declaration of Independence, and who nine years later would be elected the third president of the United States, was one of the riders. On this day, he was secretary of state under President George Washington.

His saddle mates included his Virginia neighbor, James Madison, the Father of the Constitution, as he would one day be called, who in 1808 would be elected the fourth president. The two men were the best of friends. Jefferson called Madison "Jemmy."

On this day, a third man of distinction rode with them. He was William Floyd, the owner of a large estate near Mastic. With Jefferson, Floyd shared a unique honor — he, too, had scratched his name with a quill pen on the Declaration of Independence.

It was not necessarily presidential politics that brought them to a patch of woods near Floyd's estate. Jefferson had traveled to Suffolk County to meet a group of Unkechaug Indians in hopes of finding someone who knew their ancient language. The vocabulary compiled by Jefferson that day would be one of only two ever made of the Algonquian language of the Long Island Indians — and most of it would be lost to history when a trunk containing his notes was stolen off a boat while it was being shipped back to Monticello, his Virginia estate, at the end of his presidency.

The 271 words that survived are a gift to Long Island, historians say.

"Among Jefferson's many interests was Indian languages," said Kathleen Bragdon, a linguist at the College of William and Mary, Jefferson's alma mater. "It may be his least known, but he wanted to collect Algonquian vocabularies from the last speakers."

Jefferson found what he was looking for on an anemic stretch of farmland and woods by a salt creek near present day Mastic, where a group of Unkechaugs eked out a meager existence as farmers and fishermen. They lived in shacks along the woodsy fringe of well-tended farms and estates owned by Floyd's neighbors.

Among the group, Jefferson wrote that he found "but three persons of this tribe now who can speak its language. They are old women." From two of them, Bragdon said, Jefferson compiled a glossary of words, which were similar to vocabularies of Connecticut Indians who spoke an Algonquian language called Quiripi.

A month before they arrived on Long Island, Jefferson wrote to a family member that he and Madison would soon leave on a trip to Lake George, in upstate New York. From there, he wrote, they would cross into Vermont, travel by boat down the Connecticut River to New Haven, and then journey overland to New York and Philadelphia. But in a letter to Madison written the next day, Jefferson proposed a change in the itinerary. When they reached New Haven, he said, they should cross over to Long Island.

The two giants of the young American republic spent the night of June 12 at a Southold inn owned by a Christiana Peck. The next morning, they stopped at another inn, in Riverhead, and from there they rode south and west along well-traveled cart paths to Floyd's estate and the Indian village where Jefferson met the three women.

"Primarily, I think this trip to New York was more about politics than Indian languages," said Bernard Sheehan, a history professor at the University of Indiana. "After all, both these men would soon run for president. But Jefferson wanted to write down Indian languages because he was interested in their origins. He thought these languages proved that the American continent was older than Asia. He later changed his mind about this."

Thomas Jefferson, above in a portrait by Charles Wilson Peale done in 1791, the year he traveled to Long Island with James Madison. The journey is remembered on a plaque, left, at the public library in Southold.

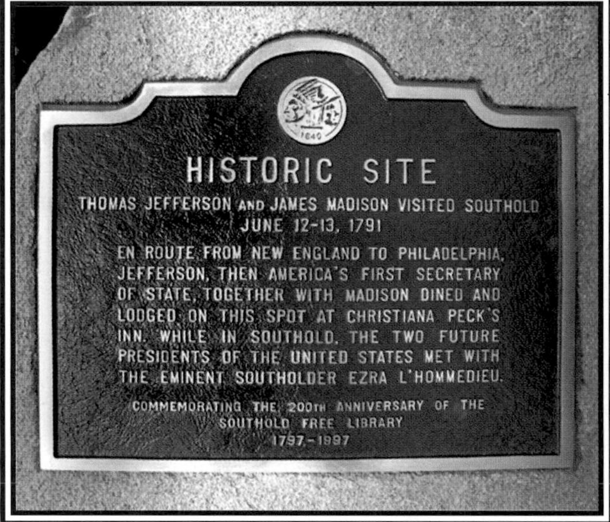

1640
HISTORIC SITE
THOMAS JEFFERSON AND JAMES MADISON VISITED SOUTHOLD
JUNE 12-13, 1791
EN ROUTE FROM NEW ENGLAND TO PHILADELPHIA, JEFFERSON, THEN AMERICA'S FIRST SECRETARY OF STATE, TOGETHER WITH MADISON DINED AND LODGED ON THIS SPOT AT CHRISTIANA PECK'S INN. WHILE IN SOUTHOLD, THE TWO FUTURE PRESIDENTS OF THE UNITED STATES MET WITH THE EMINENT SOUTHOLDER EZRA L'HOMMEDIEU.
COMMEMORATING THE 200TH ANNIVERSARY OF THE SOUTHOLD FREE LIBRARY
1797-1997

Top, Independence National Historical Park; Bottom, Newsday Photo / Bill Davis

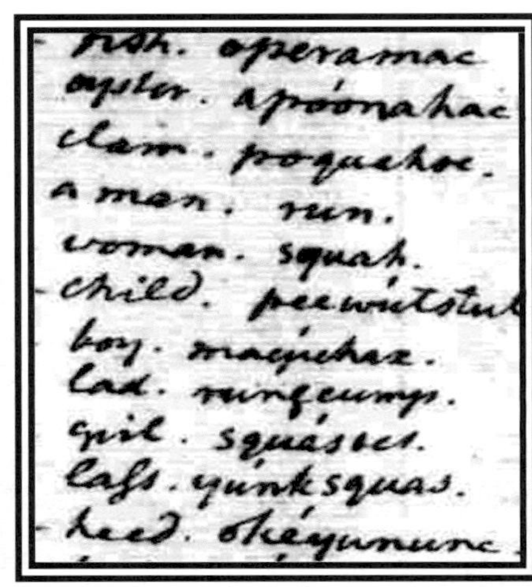
fish. operamac
oyster. apoonahac
clam. poquahoc.
a man. run.
woman. squah.
child. peewitstut
boy. maquchaz.
lad. runfeumps.
girl. squasses.
lass. yunksquas.
head. okeyununc

American Philosophical Society

A detail from Jefferson's hand-written glossary of language taken at the Unkechaug settlement in Suffolk County in 1791. Translations here include the words clam, man, woman, child and boy.

But much of Jefferson's research would be lost. When his presidency ended in 1809, he packed his belongings — including 50 Indian vocabularies he had collected over the past 30 years — into a trunk that was shipped to Virginia on a boat. On the last leg of its journey up the James River, the trunk was stolen and the contents tossed into the river.

In a letter, Jefferson described the loss:

An irreparable misfortune has deprived me of the Indian vocabularies which I had collected. They were packed in a trunk of stationary, and sent round by water with about thirty other packages of my effects, from Washington, and while ascending James River this package, on account of its weight and presumed precious contents, was singled out and stolen.

The thief, being disappointed on opening it, threw into the river all its contents, of which he thought he could make no use. Among these were the whole of the vocabularies. Some leaves floated ashore and were found in the mud but these were very few, and so defaced by the mud and water that no general use can ever be made of them.

The pages found in the mud were restored and ended up in the American Philosophical Society library, in Philadelphia. Copies of the Unkechaug vocabularies were made in the 1920s by Long Island historian Morton Pennypacker, who donated them to the East Hampton Library.

As for Jefferson, he said in a letter a few months after the loss of the Indian vocabularies that he was pleased that the culprit had been caught and put on trial. While the fate of the thief is not known, Jefferson, in that same letter, said he would no doubt be hanged.

LEGACY

INDIAN PLACE NAMES

Using his own methods, William Wallace Tooker drew up a list of common place names on Long Island and "translated" them into what he said was Algonquian. Here are some of them:

Agawom — The Indian name for Southampton.

Canarsie — A community in Brooklyn, among the first European settlements on Long Island. The name was also applied as a tribal name to the Indians who lived in the area. The name first appears in a 1647 land deed.

Copiag — A tract of land in Babylon. Tooker said some deeds use the name **Coppiage.**

Hauppauge — Tooker says this was not an Indian word, but it derived from one — **Wingan-hauppauge** — which was the name of a swampy area in Islip now called Hauppauge.

Mannatto — A hill in Oyster Bay rich in Indian lore. Tooker says the hill was also known as Manitou Hill and was said to be haunted by a great spirit.

Massapeague — Indians the English called **Massapeags** lived here. Tooker said there were two Indian forts in the southern part of Oyster Bay now known as Massapequa at the time of settlement. Any evidence of the forts today has been obliterated.

Mastic — A broad neck of land in southern Brookhaven Town. Tooker said this word was first applied to the neck bounded today by the Forge River. He said the word was spelled Mastuck in a 1692 deed, and Mastic in a second deed the following year.

Matinnecock — Tooker said this word applied to several locations in Oyster Bay. The English named the Indians who lived in this part of Long Island the **Matinnecocks.** Tooker said these Indians, after contact with Europeans, moved east and lived along the modern-day Nissequogue River in Smithtown.

Matsepe — The name of an Indian village in Oyster Bay. Some historical accounts say more than 120 Indians were killed here by Dutch troops in the late 1640s.

Montauk — Tooker said this word is a derivative of another Algonquian word, **Meuntacut,** which a 17th Century Indian deed indicates is the "high land" at Montauk Point. Other deeds spell it **Meantaucutt, Meantaquit, Meantucket, Meantauk** and **Mantack.**

Munnawtawkit — The Algonquin name for Fisher's Island, which Tooker said was a planting field used by the Pequots, who lived on the Connecticut coast.

Ronkonkoma — This word first appears in a deed from 1664, reading, "Bounds which they had formerly made into **Raconkumake,** a fresh pond about the midl of Long Island." Variations in other deeds include **Raconkamuck, Raconckamich,** and **Ronconhama.** Tooker translated the word to mean "boundary fishing place."

Sagamore Hill — This is, of course, the name Theodore Roosevelt bestowed on his house in Oyster Bay. Tooker said the name derives from a local Indian named **Mohannis,** who was a chief or sagamore. Local tradition is that the hill atop which the house was built was called Mohannis Cove or Mohannis Hill.

Newsday Photos / Jessica Brandi Lifland

A few of the Long Island place names derived from Indian language

Wickapogue — The Algonquian name for a farming district near Mecox Bay in Southampton Town. A 1668 deed said **Weequapaug** was owned by and Englishman referred to as "Goodman Halsey."

Wyandanch — In the 19th Century, Tooker wrote, this community was called West Deer Park. It was changed to **Wyandance** in 1889 and was named after the Montaukett Indian Wyandanch, who sold off huge sections of Long Island to the English — including areas far to the west of his home turf on the South Fork. Tooker — in what modern-day historians might construe as an insult — called Wyandanch "always the friend of the white settler."

Yaphank — The name of a creek in a deed dating to 1664; now the name of the hamlet in Brookhaven Town.

William Wallace Tooker's quest to recover lost words

Indian Names Were His Fame

BY STEVE WICK
STAFF WRITER

Early in this century, a Sag Harbor pharmacist tried to give Long Island back its Indian identity.

Using old deeds, land records, dusty historical documents and any Indian vocabularies he could get his hands on, even from groups far to the north of Long Island, William Wallace Tooker drew up a list of what he said were Indian place names for towns, villages and other sites all across Long Island.

The list was enormous — there were more than 500 place names and other "Indian" words on it. For many of the words, Tooker may have played fast with what few facts were available on long-extinct Algonquian languages and all but invented them. Still, scholars say, he got some of them right.

His list covers hundreds of towns and communities, such as *Setauket,* which Tooker said translated from Algonquian as "land at the mouth of the river," to obscure words like *Seapoose,* which he defined as an inlet that opened up into the ocean.

In many ways, Tooker was hooked on Indian history from childhood.

When he first began working as a pharmacist in the late 1860s, Tooker lined up his collection of Indian artifacts — he started collecting when he was 5 years old — in the store window. By the early 1880s, when he was in his mid-20s, Tooker began his career as the region's first ethnohistorian and writer on Long Island's Indian past. He later sold his artifact collection to a Brooklyn museum, and his writing is today a part of the local history collection at the John Jermain Library in Sag Harbor.

Jermain Memorial Library Photo
William Wallace Tooker

Calling himself an "Algonkinist," Tooker wrote that he had discovered Indian names for hundreds of hills, meadows, creeks and necks all across Long Island, and even drew up a list of Algonquian words he said were suitable for naming such things as hotels and country homes. While he never spelled out exactly how he did it, he did say he used various land records written at the time of European arrivals on Long Island, plus vocabularies made by Europeans of the Algonquian dialects along the Northeast coastline.

A 1955 article in the Long Island Forum said Tooker was so adept at translating Algonquian words that he could do it on cue — this even though very few vocabularies were ever recorded. Scholars say now that Tooker was, for the most part, making educated guesses loosely based on words drawn from other vocabularies. He published his list in 1911 in the form of a thick book called "Indian Place Names on Long Island." Prior to the publication of the book, hailed as the first attempt to translate Indian words found in historical records, Tooker published most of his work in weekly newspapers and anthropology journals.

"Tooker was one of those men of the late Nineteenth Century who saw themselves as amateur archeologists and anthropologists digging into the area's Algonquian past," said John Strong, who teaches at Southampton College. "Not a great deal has been written of the man himself, but it can be said that he dedicated his life to Long Island Indian history and his legacy is still with us."

Today, Tooker's Indian place names are controversial among scholars. But most of them say his landmark work still serves an important purpose in trying to unlock the long-buried Indian history of a suburban island.

"When Tooker did his work, the language he was attempting to translate was unknown and unknowable," said Ives Goddard, an Algonquian language expert at the Smithsonian Institution. "He looked at maps, old deeds, all kinds of colonial records, and then came up with his place names. Today, we would say those words he pulled out of records were incomprehensible and without real meaning.

"There was no science to what he did; it's mostly fanciful," Goddard added. "Some words you could say he's probably close, but with most of them he is certainly wrong. Unless you have a complete vocabulary, defining place names is just guesswork."

In other words, *Setauket* probably does not mean "land at the mouth of the river," and *Ronkonkoma,* No. 349 on Tooker's list, probably does not mean "the boundary fishing place."

Strong agreed: "His work was seen at the time as very original. And in a real sense it is useful today, but it can't be seen as definitive."

In a "remarks" section of his book, Tooker wrote that the Algonquian words collected by Thomas Jefferson in 1791 and John Gardiner in 1798, "and the names which I here present, are all that remain of the language as once spoken from Staten Island to Montauk Point."

Tooker came up with 486 place names — towns, villages, hills, sections of woods, rivers and necks of land across Long Island — and 99 "Indian" words he listed in an appendix. Of those words, Tooker wrote that they were "suitable for country homes, hotels, clubs, motorboats, etc."

But his main contribution to Long Island history is his place names. Historians across the Island have used his list for generations.

"I have read Tooker for years," Goddard said. "I keep his book right on the shelf by my desk. I take a generous view of my predecessors. He should not be beat up today for not figuring it out. After all, there were no native speakers he could have gone to to decipher the place names. His book can still contribute to our knowledge of Indian history on Long Island. And I'm sure he is right in some areas, and some of his cultural information is most valuable today.

"Tooker did the spade work, and that's good for us today."

LI HISTORY.COM

For an extensive list of local Indian place names compiled by William Tooker, see http://www.lihistory.com on the Internet.

Corn porridge called samp was a staple for both Indians and colonists

Dinner, and a Snack, Too

BY MICHELE INGRASSIA
STAFF WRITER

'Samp is a funny thing," a South Shore woman wrote to the Long Island Forum in 1946, referring to the once-ubiquitous porridge made from corn. "By it, one can prove whether one is a native Long Islander or not. For the native there's nothing quite like it in the world. For the others it is an awful mess, only fit for the pigs to eat!"

By today's sweet, fragile, don't-pick-it-'til-the-pot-boils standards, Long Island's coarse early corn *was* fit only for the pigs. Nevertheless, as far back as the Indians, it offered real nourishment. And by the time Dutch and English settlers arrived, it had become perhaps the single most important, and versatile, staple — to be boiled with meat; ground into flour for bread, and, most of all, simmered in a thick stew known as samp.

"Iroquois women could prepare up to forty different corn dishes," writes historian John A. Strong in his new book, "The Algonquin Peoples of Long Island From Earliest Times to 1700," "and a woman from a western tribe was able to recite, from memory, more than one hundred fifty detailed recipes."

One of the so-called "three sister" plants — sibling to beans and squash — corn first appeared in the Island's food supply about 1,000 years ago. But contrary to conventional wisdom, it was for centuries just a "luxury crop," says Strong. The reason may be that Indians lived in small, shifting encampments that effectively precluded them from cultivating corn — indeed, prehistoric kernels have been documented at only three sites on or near the Island: Bowmans Brook on Staten Island, Pleasant Hill near Shoreham, and Sebonac, near the Shinnecock Reservation.

Besides, early Indians managed just fine on what they hunted and gathered. "The food supply here was so plentiful, with shellfish, venison and wild plants like sunflowers and Jerusalem artichokes, that when corn was introduced there was no rush to it," says Strong, a Southampton College history professor.

Gradually, however, the Indians domesticated corn, which had found its way north from Mexico centuries before. Its value was evident not just in the Indians' gardens, but in their vocabulary, which contained at least seven different words for the crop. Among them: *wewauchum,* generic for corn; *seaump*, or pounded corn, and *yeokeheag*, for roast pounded corn.

By the time Europeans landed, there were six varieties — white, blue, red, yellow, orange and multicolor. "It is the common food of all," Dutch settler Adriaen van der Donck observed. "Young and old eat it; and they are so well accustomed to it, and fond of it, that when they visit our people, or each other, they consider themselves neglected unless they are treated with *sappaen,*" or samp.

Newsday Photos / Bill Davis

Indian corn, above, with a rock for pounding and a larger rock for a mortar, at the Southold Indian Museum; at left is a wooden mortar found in the 1930s in a marsh in the area of Fort Massapeag, in Massapequa. The wooden mortar is at the Garvies Point Museum in Glen Cove.

Plentiful, portable and nonperishable, corn quickly became critical to the settlers, who added European touches — salted beef, shellfish, herbs — to the Indians' fare. "If it were not for corn, the settlers could not have gone across the nation building a country," says Long Island food historian Alice Ross. Ironically, she says, it was wheat that the Dutch and English had expected to sustain them. But they soon realized that the wheat seeds they brought from the Connecticut River Valley would take years to cultivate.

Of course, before the hard corn could be eaten it had to be processed. And in the days before windmills, the Indians crafted a "samp pounder," an oversized mortar and pestle, to do the work. The mortar was fashioned from a three-foot tree stump that was seared and scraped until a 12- to 15-inch cavity was hollowed out. The spring pole to maneuver the pestle came from a nearby sapling, bent and poised over the mortar. The pestle itself was a long, heavy stick, rounded at the end and fastened to the spring pole.

To soften the corn, kernels were soaked overnight in water and lye — or hot ashes — then rinsed, dried and brought to the pounder. Particularly among the settlers, autumn Saturdays on Long Island were samp days, when villagers would cart their kernels to a central mortar, the thump, thump, thumping lasting into the early candlelight.

"There were a great many myths to go with the pounders," says Ross. "One holds that, if sailors were coming into Long Island at night or in the fog and didn't want their ship destroyed on the rocks, they would listen for the sound of corn being pounded."

Though the settlers took many recipes from the Indians, none was more important than the recipe for samp porridge, a heavy, stick-to-the-ribs corn, bean and meat stew. On its own, it was an everyday breakfast, lunch or dinner — even a snack in a pre-Doritos world. With salted beef, it was a Sabbath supper.

Most often, though, samp was a movable feast: Started on Saturday, it would simmer on the hearth all week, altered day by day with a bit of meat here, a drop of shellfish there. No one got bored. "By the end of the week, a popcorn-flavored crust had formed around the pot," Ross says. "Each family member would try to lift out the whole shell without breaking it, and whoever did got a special privilege."

Though corn myths have faded, and you won't find samp on any four-star menu, corn remains quintessential Long Island fare — albeit again more luxury than staple. Annually, says Bill Sanok of the Cornell Cooperative Extension in Riverhead, the Island grows about 18 million ears of sweet corn, each one meant to be picked and eaten before the summer sun goes down.

Developed about a century ago, that delicate corn has nothing in common with the coarse, flinty food that sustained centuries of Indians and settlers. True, a hard-kerneled crop remains, but the yield is barely 3 million ears per year. What becomes of it? "It's used," Sanok says, "for feeding animals."

LEGACY

Indian corn on the stalk last month at Krupski's Farm in Peconic

Indians and colonial settlers had hundreds of corn dishes, but before the late 1800s, no one wrote down recipes. This samp porridge, from food historian Alice Ross, is a version of the Eastern Woodlands Indians' nausamp.

Samp Porridge

1 pound beans (any type available)
1 pound yellow or white samp (hulled corn, hominy)
Preserved meat, such as corned beef or salt pork
Peeled and cut root vegetables to taste, such as potato, carrots, onion, parsley
Salt and pepper to taste

1. Soak beans in water overnight.
2. In the morning, put samp into a large kettle with enough water to cover by three inches. Bring to a boil, then simmer for several hours, until tender; add water and stir from time to time.
3. In another pot, cook soaked beans in water for 45 minutes, or until skins slip easily.
4. One hour before serving, add prepared vegetables to samp and continue cooking until tender. Add beans. Correct flavor. Serve. Note: This dish improves with age, and is better after two to three days.

Verrazano, discovering Long Island's southern and western shores, calls the land 'Flora'

A Visitor From Europe

BY STEVE WICK
STAFF WRITER

Early in the 16th Century, European explorers began to sail west across the mysterious vastness of the Atlantic Ocean, drawn by stories of virgin lands overflowing with riches, and schools of fish so thick they could thwart a ship's passage.

One of the many men who ventured west from Europe at that time was an Italian explorer named Giovanni da Verrazano, who was in the service of the French king, Francis I. Unlike other explorers who sailed into northern waters off what is today the coast of Canada, or Spanish explorers who traveled far to the south, Verrazano hit the mainland almost dead center, at the wide hip of sandy beach at present-day Cape Hatteras, N.C. From there, he began to slowly move north, marveling at everything he saw.

It was April, 1524, and Verrazano's boat, the Dauphine, was all alone in what to Europeans was a sparkling new world. He had left France in the company of three other ships, but storms claimed two and the third had turned around. On the 17th of that month, three decades after Columbus' monumental journey into Carribean waters, Verrazano piloted the Dauphine through a narrow cut between two land masses he did not know were islands and entered a wide, deep bay sheltered by thickly forested lands. On that day, he wrote in his journal:

We found a very pleasant place, situated amongst certain little steep hills; from amidst the hills there ran down into the sea a great stream of water, which within the mouth was very deep, and from the sea to the mouth of same, with the tide, which we found to rise 8 foot, any great vessel laden may pass up.

Verrazano was in what would more than a century later be called New York Harbor — the first European to sail there, and the first European to see the wooded western end of Long Island on the harbor's eastern shore. The "great stream of water" at the top of the harbor would later be named for the explorer who sailed far up it — Henry Hudson. Before he left, Verrazano came up with his own names, which were later inked onto his brother's map — the huge landmass to his east was christened "Flora," and the fingers of land that were split by the freshwater river he called "Angouleme," the family name of Francis I. Long Island and Manhattan Island now had European names.

That month, that year, in that place, Verrazano was a stranger in a land seen fresh by Europeans, but populated by hundreds of thousands of Indians who had lived along this coastline for thousands of years. He was a discoverer of an occupied land, but for his countrymen across the ocean, his discovery of new lands on their behalf was momentous. And it remains momentous today.

Pierpont Morgan Library

Verrazano in a type of poster made after his death. It describes him as a "grand captain," "commander of the sea for the Christian King Francis I" and "discoverer of the new France."

Brown University, John Carter Brown Library

A close-up detail from a 1556 map based on Verrazano's voyage shows Long Island only as a peninsula. It was labeled "Flora."

"What makes Verrazano unique is that he wrote about what he saw, and his brother, who was a mapmaker, drew maps of what they saw," said Charles Gehring, the director of the New Netherlands Project, in Albany.

His letter to Francis I, written in July when he was safely back in France, is the earliest description known to exist of the American coastline. The letter was written in an almost breathless tone — Verrazano had seen the promised land, and he wanted his king to know it.

On the 24th of February we encountered as violent a hurricane as any ship ever weathered . . . Pursuing our voyage towards the West, a little northwardly . . . we reached a new country, which had never before been seen by any one, either in ancient or modern times . . . Many people who were seen coming to the sea-side fled at our approach, but occasionally stopping, they looked back upon us in astonishment . . . They showed the greatest delight on beholding us, wondering at our dress, countenances, and complexion.

Describing his trip north along the coastline as he sailed toward New York Harbor, Verrazano spoke of an "outstretched country" with "beautiful fields and broad plains, covered with immense forests of trees, more or less dense, various in colors and delightful and charming in appearance." The land was so filled with forests of plants and flowers that its rich perfume wafted out to sea at "great distance" — the sweet fragrance of the American continent greeted Verrazano and

LI HISTORY.COM

Brown University, John Carter Brown Library

A LETTER TO THE KING

The full letter Giovanni da Verrazano wrote to King Francis I of France about his voyage to America can be found at http://www.lihistory.com. The Web site also carries all installments to "Long Island: Our Story."

At left, a detail from the 1556 map based on Verrazano's 1524 journey

Three Voyages — and a Tragic End

BY STEVE WICK
STAFF WRITER

Giovanni Da Verrazano was born in Florence, Italy, in 1470. He moved to France to work as a ship's navigator, and soon earned a reputation as a state-sponsored pirate who raided Spanish and Portuguese ships on the high seas. But it was his sailing along the American coast in 1524 that earned him the reputation that survives today.

There is a bust of Verrazano in Battery Park, in New York City, as well as a mural in the New York Custom House. Of course, there's also a bridge named after him — it spans the narrows he passed through when he entered New York Harbor between Brooklyn and Staten Island.

On his trip in 1524, he attached the first non-Indian names to large sections of the coastline, from modern-day Georgia to Canada. Some names were based on what he saw, while others were in honor of the French king, Francis I.

He named a section of the Georgia coastline "Field of Cedars." South of what today is called Cape Fear, N.C., he called the area he saw "Forest of Laurels." He named the area north of that "Annunciata."

The Hudson River region he called "Angouleme," which was both a family name of the French king and a principality. The bay itself he called "Bay of St. Marguerite." In his letter to Francis I, he said he picked the name of the king's sister "who vanishes the other matrons for modesty and talent."

At the end of his account to Francis I, Verrazano explained the purpose of his journey. 'My intention was in this navigation to reach Cathay and the extreme east of Asia, not expecting to find such an obstacle of new land as I found . . .'

A brave explorer no doubt, it seems Verrazano was also a skillful sycophant.

He named modern-day Block Island "Louisa Island," after the king's mother. The coastline and islands near modern-day Rhode Island he called "Refugio," or refuge. As he passed modern-day Cape Cod, he called the land "Armellini," and the finger of land at the end of Cape Cod he dubbed "Cape Pallavicino."

Verrazano evidently did not like the Indians he encountered on the Maine coast. He called this place "Land of Bad People." In the letter to Francis I, he said the Indians there were "full of uncouthness and vices, so barbarous that we were never able . . . to have any intercourse with them. They dress with the skins of bear, lynx, sea-wolves and other animals . . . They had no regard for courtesy . . . and they shot at us with their bows, sending forth the greatest cries, then fled into the woods."

At the end of his extraordinary account to his king, Verrazano explained what the purpose of his journey was. "My intention was in this navigation to reach Cathay and the extreme east of Asia, not expecting to find such an obstacle of new land as I found; and if for some reason I expected to find it, I thought it to be not without some strait to penetrate to the Eastern Ocean.

"And this has been the opinion of all the ancients, believing certainly our Western Ocean to be one with the Eastern Ocean of India without interposition of land."

Verrazano's second voyage, in 1527, was to Brazil. His third voyage, the following year, was to bring him back to the American coastline in the hope that he could find an opening to that "Eastern Ocean of India."

It didn't work out that way.

Instead of striking the American coast, the wind blew him to the West Indies. He stopped at one of the islands — some historians say it was Guadeloupe — where he went ashore to make contact. He was grabbed by a group of Indians, who killed him and then ate him.

— Steve Wick

tickled his imagination long before he actually saw it. He gushed over the plant life, and the abundance of animals and birds.

And he wrote about the people on the shore somewhere south of New York, where an incredible thing happened.

A young sailor was attempting to swim ashore through the surf to carry them some knick-knacks . . . When he came near three or four of them he tossed the things to them, and turned about to get back to the boat, but he was thrown over by the waves, and so dashed by them that he lay as it were dead upon the beach. When these people saw him in this situation, they ran and took him up by the head, legs and arms, and carried him to a distance from the surf; the young man, finding himself borne off in this way, uttered very loud shrieks in fear and dismay, while they answered as they could in their language . . . Afterwards they laid him down at the foot of a little hill, when they took off his shirt and trowsers, and examined him, expressing the greatest astonishment at the whiteness of his skin. Our sailors in the boat, seeing a great fire made up, and their companion placed very near it . . . imagined that the natives were about to roast him for food.

But as soon as he had recovered his strength . . . they hugged him with great affection and accompanied him to the shore; then leaving him . . . they withdrew to a little hill, from which they watched him until he was safe in the boat.

Verrazano's Travels

Giovanni da Verrazano was the first known European to sail into New York Harbor. Here is a look at this travels.

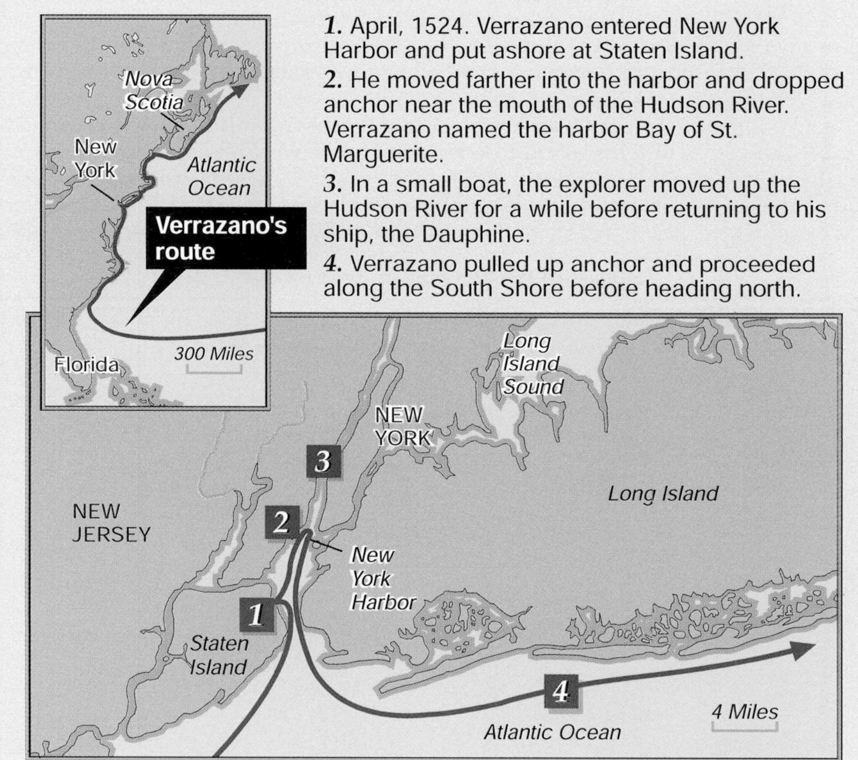
1. April, 1524. Verrazano entered New York Harbor and put ashore at Staten Island.
2. He moved farther into the harbor and dropped anchor near the mouth of the Hudson River. Verrazano named the harbor Bay of St. Marguerite.
3. In a small boat, the explorer moved up the Hudson River for a while before returning to his ship, the Dauphine.
4. Verrazano pulled up anchor and proceeded along the South Shore before heading north.
Nova Scotia
New York
Atlantic Ocean
Verrazano's route
Florida
300 Miles
Long Island Sound
NEW YORK
NEW JERSEY
Long Island
New York Harbor
Staten Island
Atlantic Ocean
4 Miles

Newsday/ Steve Madden

Proceeding north again, Verrazano wrote that they went ashore and kidnaped an Indian boy to take back to France, and tried to grab a young girl — "who was very beautiful and very tall" — but she screamed and they left her behind.

In April, the Dauphine entered New York Harbor, first passing through the deep, narrow cut between modern-day Staten Island and Long Island. After briefly putting ashore on the Staten Island side, Verrazano slipped farther into the harbor, which he named the Bay of St. Marguerite, after the French king's elder sister. He dropped anchor south of where the Hudson River flooded into the bay.

In a smaller boat, Verrazano ventured up the river "and found the country on its banks well peopled . . . dressed out with the feathers of birds of various colours." Farther up the river, they encountered a group of Indians in dugout canoes. After returning to the Dauphine, they pulled up anchor and proceeded along the south shore of Long Island, the first leg on the trip back to France, which they reached in early July.

But now, Long Island was on the map.

Ten months later, in May, 1525, the second European known to have sailed into — or, perhaps, only near — New York waters arrived on the scene. He was Estevan Gomez, who had left Portugal the previous August, a month after Verrazano had returned to France. Because his journal was lost, it is not known today just what Gomez saw or where, exactly, he visited.

It would be more than 80 years before a new wave of explorers arrived to explore New York Harbor, the rivers around it, and Long Island. They were the Dutch, and they were here to look for profits in this newfound land.

One of them would be the first to set foot on the Long Island landmass, and a second Dutchman would be the first to discover that it was an island.

By Steve Wick
STAFF WRITER

Newsday Photo / Bill Davis

At a class on the Poospatuck Reservation in Mastic, Margo Thunder Bird, left, teaches "the rabbit dance," an Indian sweetheart dance in which women choose their partners. "I always knew I would do something to help people know our history," Thunder Bird says.

Three who work to preserve and reveal the ways of Indian ancestors

Keeping Cultures Alive

Robert Cooper has spent years assembling the scattered pieces of his people's history. He has become an archaeologist of memories — collecting genealogies, family letters, burial records, photographs, anything that will help him understand the rich past of the Montaukett people.

In his own way, David Bunn Martine tries to do the same thing. An artist, Martine has painted portraits of his Shinnecock ancestors as a way of bringing them back to life. He also hosts a cable television show on the East End that features Indian topics, and he is working to improve the Shinnecock museum in Southampton.

On the Poospatuck Reservation in Mastic, Margo Thunder Bird uses what is left of a vocabulary collected in 1791 by Thomas Jefferson to return a small piece of an extinct Algonquian dialect to its original use. "Growing up, I always knew I would do something to help people know our history," Thunder Bird said. "And my mother always said the key to our identity was our language . . . I told her before she died I would do what I could to help bring it back."

The only intact Long Island-based Algonquian language is spoken on the Moraviantown Delaware Nation Reserve in Ontario. Neither Thunder Bird nor anyone on the Shinnecock Reservation knew of the existence of the Munsee Delaware speakers there. "I didn't know that language could be heard anywhere," said Martine. " We need to find out more about that."

Cooper, Martine and Thunder Bird are three voices for Indian history, a history that began on Long Island thousands of years before the first European ever set foot here. Theirs is a history that, for the most part, has been lost to time or hidden away in the privacy of family lives. What the Indians lost after Europeans arrived in the early 17th Century to build villages and towns, these three are trying to reclaim — even if it represents only a tiny slice of the lives their ancestors once lived.

Nearly every aspect of Algonquian culture that once existed on Long Island is gone. Much of that culture was pushed aside by Europeans within a generation or two of their arrival. It lives in the far distant past, too deep to be unearthed. Even in 1791, when Jefferson came to Long Island to hear Indian languages, he was hard pressed to find any fluent speakers.

Today, Long Island Indians try to understand the culture that was once here even as they have had to borrow from other Indian groups. The annual fall powwow held on the Shinnecock reservation in Southampton features a wide array of Indian customs, some found out West, and feels more pan-Indian than Long Island Indian.

"We have to dig deep to keep our culture alive," said Martine.

Martine and Thunder Bird live on reservations — Martine in Southampton, Thunder Bird in Mastic. Together, these reservations account for only a sliver of the land their ancestors lived on. But they are wellsprings for creativity, history and hope. They are Indian land, all that's left of it.

Cooper, who lives in the Freetown section of East Hampton — a wooded area east of the village where Montaukett Indians have lived since they were removed from Montauk Point in the 1880s by a real-estate speculator — uses his home as a family history center. He studies documents and digs deep for cultural tidbits that might help him understand where he comes from. He does all this, he said, in the hope that the Montauketts might get back the one thing they want the most — a piece of Montauk Point, their ancestral homeland.

Growing up in Freetown, Cooper listened to stories of relatives and other Indians who lived near his house. "I knew my elders; I heard their stories," he said. "I wanted to know what they knew. I didn't want it to die with them."

As a young man, Cooper began to assemble the pieces of a historical jigsaw puzzle — yellowed land records and house deeds, cemetery records and black-and-white photographs of long-dead Montauketts. When the puzzle began to come together, a picture emerged of a people who lived quietly, away from the public eye, all but forgotten by the society around them.

"They came alive for me when I put the photographs up on my wall in the living room," he said.

For David Martine, the desire to know more about his people also began in childhood.

"I have always been interested in our history," said Martine. "When I was younger, there was a limited number of places to go for our history, so we had to look ourselves and listen to oral histories. There were older Shinnecocks who knew a lot and listened when they were young. So it was there to be passed down. I always thought that it was important the history grow."

When he was young, Martine's grandmother was his personal historian. She knew Shinnecock history up close, and told her young grandson that her grandfather David Bunn had been one of 10 Shinnecocks — and one of three Bunns — to drown on a stranded ship called the Circassian, which foundered off Bridgehampton in the winter of 1876. It was a momentous event in Shinnecock history, changing forever the quiet Southampton reservation, where nearly every household was affected by the tragedy.

"My grandmother had the first Indian trading post on Long Island," Martine said. "She was always talking about our history. She preserved it; she passed it along. My goal at the Shinnecock museum on the reservation is to put our culture on display and to begin a language program to teach our young."

That is exactly what Thunder Bird has been doing on the Poospatuck Reservation.

"My parents taught us our history," she said. "They stressed it was our family's responsibility to understand and know our history. I listened to them, but I always wanted to learn more. It was my mother's wish that we begin a language project. Her belief was that our language was not 'lost,' as so many people said it was, but rather buried. She knew that our language was the true connection to our past."

Today, Thunder Bird teaches language classes on the reservation for children, using a word list collected by Jefferson in 1791. She is the only such language teacher on Long Island.

"That list was made right here — it's our language completely," she said. "It's our starting point and gives us a vocabulary we can use as a foundation. It's all very gratifying to hear a small child use those words."

LEGACY

Newsday Photo / Bill Davis

A TRIBUTE TO THEIR COMMUNITY

The Pharaoh Museum at Montauk County Park once exhibited relics of the Montaukett Indians, including a 5,000-year-old stone point and photos of people who lived on the site in the mid-19th Century, when it was Indian land. Currently closed, the museum is the only publicly operated one in Suffolk County dedicated to Indian history. A group called Friends of the Pharaoh Museum wants a larger facility at the park. Suffolk County officials say they hope to remodel the museum in 1998. Call 516-852-7878 for park information.

Hudson, embodying Europe itself, sets foot in a new land

Half Moon Arriving

BY STEVE WICK
STAFF WRITER

A group of Indians was fishing in the harbor when the Half Moon drifted ghostlike over the horizon. They thought the ship was a floating house, and the man on the deck — who wore a bright, red jacket — an evil spirit.

This man was no spirit — he was Europe itself waiting to break out of its confines and move west across the Atlantic Ocean in search of new lands. His name was Henry Hudson, an Englishman working for Dutch businessmen who sought a passage to the Orient. As he piloted his Half Moon through the narrows and into a deep harbor, Hudson hoped that this route would take him there.

It was Sept. 3, 1609. As the Half Moon lay at anchor, a flag with a crescent moon at the peak of its mast, Hudson could see an island between two rivers to his north. To his east was a vast, wooded land of mystery no European had yet explored. Giovanni da Verrazano had seen it 84 years before when he sailed into this same harbor, and named the land *Flora*. Now Hudson wanted to be the first to set foot on it.

Within a few years, the Dutch would give this place a different name — *Lange Eylandt*.

On the morning of Sept. 4, Hudson lowered a rowboat and set out to sound the harbor. He knew what every sailor in unexplored waters knew — to strike bottom could spell disaster. What they found was encouraging — the water in the harbor was deep all around.

Hudson's crew was divided between Englishmen and Dutchmen. Hudson himself was English-born, and already a well-known explorer. In 1607, he had sailed from England in search of a passage to Asia near the North Pole.

Word of Hudson's northern adventures reached the Dutch, who were setting up merchant companies to seek business in new lands and were eager to find their own paths to the Far East.

AP Illustration

Henry Hudson, the English explorer

They hoped such a passage existed somewhere near the center of the still unnamed American continent.

"Hudson stood before them full of enthusiasm, and expressed his ardent conviction that Asia might be reached by the Northeast," a historian wrote. Hudson was given command of the Half Moon.

After first heading toward northern waters, Hudson turned south, proceeding as far as the coast of Virginia, where the English, in 1607, had landed and set up the tiny colony at Jamestown. Then he turned north, as if homing in on the very narrows that Verrazano passed through.

On Sept. 3, Hudson's mate, an Englishman named Robert Juet, wrote in his journal:

The morning misty until ten o'clock, then it cleared, and the wind came to the south-south-east, so we weighed and stood to the northward. The land is very pleasant . . . At three o'clock in the afternoon, we came to three great rivers. So we stood along the northernmost, thinking to have gone into it, but we found it to have a very shoal bar before it, for we had but ten foot water. Then we cast about to the southward, and found two fathoms, three fathoms, and three and a quarter, till we came to the southern side of them, then we had five and six fathoms, and anchored. So we sent in our boat to sound, and they found no less water than four, five, six, and seven fathoms . . .

On Sept. 4, the Half Moon crept into the harbor, sounding every few minutes to make sure the water was deep enough. After dropping anchor, the small rowboat was lowered. Juet wrote:

Then our boat went on land with our net to fish, and caught ten great mullets, of a foot and a half long a piece, and a ray as great as four men could haul into the ship. So we trimmed our boat and road still all day. At night the wind blew hard at the north-west, and our anchor came home, and we drove on shore, but took no hurt, thanked be God, for the ground is soft sand and ooze. This day the people of the country came aboard of us, seeming very glad of our coming, and brought green tobacco, and gave us of it for knives and beads . . .

Juet seemed to have a hard time describing the marvels around him. On Sept. 5, he wrote in his journal:

In the morning as soon as the day was light, the wind ceased and the flood came. So we heaved off our ship again into five fathoms of water, and sent our boat to sound the bay, and we found there was three fathoms hard by the southern shore. Our men went on land there, and saw great store of men, women and children, who gave them tobacco at their coming on land. So they went up into the woods, and saw great store of very goodly oaks, and some currants. For one of them came aboard and brought some dried, and gave me some, which were sweet and good. This day many of the people came aboard, some in mantles of feathers, and some in skins of divers sorts of good furs. Some women also came to us with hemp. They had red copper tobacco pipes, and other things of copper they did wear about their necks. At night they went on land again, so we rode very quiet, but durst not trust them.

LI HISTORY.COM

The full text of the journal of Hudson crewman Robert Juet is available on the Internet at http://www.lihistory.com.

Corbis-Bettmann

Hudson is forced off his ship by his crew after a hard winter in 1611.

Explorer's Cold End

After the epic voyage up the river that now bears his name, Henry Hudson returned to the Netherlands and was soon being outfitted for another voyage, this time far to the north.

He set out in the spring of 1610, in the ship Discovery. By early summer, the Discovery was in icy waters in the far north of modern-day Canada, near the bay that today bears Hudson's name. There, he became trapped in the ice and was forced to spend the winter without provisions. The following spring, the Discovery's crew mutinied, and set Hudson and his son, John, adrift in a small boat. They were never seen again. — **Steve Wick**

A Hudson Crewman Is Killed

As the morning of Sept. 6, 1609, dawned, Henry Hudson ordered a group of men, including an Englishman named John Coleman, to go ashore. Coleman, whose name is sometimes spelled "Colman" in historical records, stepped into the small boat and began to paddle toward the shoreline on the far side of the narrows. This was *Lange Eylandt* — Long Island.

Later that day, after dark, Hudson's mate, Robert Juet, wrote, the men got into a fight with a group of Indians. "And they had one slain in the fight," he wrote, "which was an Englishman, named John Colman, with an arrow shot into his throat . . ."

It was the following morning before the men found their way back to the Half Moon. Later that day, Hudson took a party ashore to a point of land he named Coleman's Point, and buried the seaman. Coleman is the first European known to have been killed by an Indian in New York, and was the first European buried on Long Island.

— **Steve Wick**

An illustration imagines Henry Hudson's encounter with Indians in 1609 after his Half Moon arrived at the mouth of the river later named for the explorer.

Collection of the New-York Historical Society

By Steve Wick
STAFF WRITER

Dutch trader Adrian Block reaches America, and then sees his ship destroyed by fire

Stranded In A Strange Land

Few visitors to New York had more problems than Adrian Block.

Four years after Henry Hudson explored the big river that now bears his name, a Dutch ship called the Tiger left Holland en route for the same waters. Block, an enterprising Dutchman who had made two earlier visits to these waters, was the captain.

From a business point of view, the area was a gold mine waiting to be dug. Unlike Hudson — who sailed into New York waters hoping to get somewhere else — Block sailed here on purpose. An attorney in the Netherlands, Block was an inveterate explorer with an eye for profitable enterprises. The market for furs in Europe was enormous, and his earlier visits had convinced him that he could fill up his ship with furs and transport them back to the Netherlands for sale as coats and hats. Fortunes were waiting to be made.

Block's third voyage west began in the summer of 1613. Instead of approaching the harbor from the south, the way Hudson did, Block sailed down the coast and approached from the north, meeting coastal Algonquian Indians along the way and collecting some of their highly prized sea shells.

Two months after he left the Netherlands, he passed through the narrows that guard the entrance to what is now New York Harbor. Just where he went from there is not known, but within a few weeks he was anchored almost where the river emptied into the harbor, nearly at the southern tip of modern-day Manhattan Island, his ship filled to the gunwales with beaver and otter pelts.

While Block and his crew were camped on the island — close to where the World Trade Center now sits — disaster struck. While they stood helpless on the shore, the Tiger caught fire and burned to the waterline.

"I think we can all imagine what it must have been like to watch their ship burn," said Charles Gehring, director of the New Netherlands Project in Albany. "They were thousands of miles from home — with no way to get home."

The story of what happened to Block after the Tiger was destroyed by fire is one of the great sea stories of all time. Over a long, hard winter, Block and his crew did the incredible — they built a new ship.

"What they did was fantastic," Gehring said. "Just fantastic."

Block's men cut down trees, hewed the trees into planks, and with whatever tools they could salvage from the Tiger, they built a 44-foot-long sailing vessel. They christened it the Restless, a name that may well have reflected their moods during the long winter, and slid it into the river to begin a long voyage back to the Netherlands. A voyage in which they discovered that the land mass east of where the Tiger had burned was an island — a place known today as Long Island.

It is likely that the ship was built with few, if any, nails they were able to retrieve from the wreckage of the Tiger. The mast was hewed from a single tall tree. What they used for a sail is not known, nor just how long it took to construct the ship.

"Another incredible thing is that Block kept a journal," Gehring said. "We know this because a Dutch historian named Johannes DeLaet said he read it. This is our only clue, but that journal has never been found. We can only hope that one day it is found. But it is clear that Block had people on board who were carpenters and blacksmiths and others who could get the job done. But we don't know what he was thinking when the ship burned, how he felt, or just how they did the work. We just know they did it."

Block's journey is significant not only because of the construction of the Restless. It is likely, Gehring said, that Block found the keys to the Dutch's new kingdom — that upstate New York Indians such as the Mohawks would trade furs for wampum.

"I think it's Block who takes the wampum up the river, sees that the Mohawks were traveling hundreds of miles to the coastline to get wampum of their own, and strikes up a deal to trade shells for furs. He sees this and is the first to start it."

In the spring of 1614, after a long winter making the ship and living in huts, Block prepared the Restless for the long, uncertain trip home.

A 1937 Reginald Marsh painting of Adrian Block in the rotunda of the old U.S. Custom House at Bowling Green in Manhattan.

Newsday Photo / Bill Davis

Block's Ship Tells Tales Centuries After the Fire

In 1916, a laborer with a pick ax working on a new subway line in Lower Manhattan struck something. When he looked closer, he found a number of charred wooden beams.

The laborer, working beneath Greenwich and Dey Streets, had found the remains of Adrian Block's ship, the Tiger, which had burned to the water line 303 years earlier as it lay at anchor in the Hudson River loaded with a rich cargo of furs.

A foreman named James Kelly was called to the scene, and with mules he tried to pull the beams and a section of the ship's keel out of the ground. When that failed, he ordered a six-foot section of what turned out to be the ship's prow cut off. The workers also found a Dutch ax, trade beads, clay pipes, a chain and some cannon balls.

Today, the section of the Tiger is part of a display at the Museum of the City of New York. It is the only physical proof ever discovered of Block's incredible story — that the Tiger burned in the fall of 1613, leaving him and his crew stranded until they built a new ship.

Tests on the beams showed they were 420 years old. An iron bolt found on the site was forged in the year 1600, tests showed. When the World Trade Center was built in the 1960s, an attempt was made to recover the rest of the Tiger. Archeologist Ralph Solecki, a Cutchogue native who then taught at Columbia University, could not find it. He did find six bronze guns.

Museum of the City of New York

Timbers of Adrian Block's burned ship, the Tiger, were found in 1916 during a subway excavation. They now hang in the Museum of the City of New York.

In 1613, the waterline in that part of Manhattan Island was considerably farther inland. In the late 1700s, huge sections of lower Manhattan on the Hudson River were filled in, thus covering over the remains of the Tiger. Historians speculate that after the ship was burned to the waterline, Block's crew beached the charred hull in a small cove on the west side of what is now Greenwich Street.

— **Steve Wick**

Explorer Adrian Block realizes Long Island is an *island* and claims it for his home country

Property of the Netherlands

BY STEVE WICK
STAFF WRITER

As he launched his new ship, Adrian Block let the tide carry the Restless into New York Harbor. If he said something to his crew as they departed, it is not recorded in history. He could not wish away the realities of geography — their homes in the Netherlands were 3,600 miles away across the ocean.

Now a strong spring wind grabbed the sails and blew the ship into the narrow inlet on the east side of what is now Manhattan. This was the place the Dutch called *Hellegat,* today's East River, and Block had no idea what was on the other side, or for that matter whether he could safely pass through. It's very name — Hell Gate — indicated what the Dutch thought of it.

The tide roared through this narrow inlet like a cascading waterfall, making a fearsome racket, according to the mid-17th Century diary of an Englishman named Daniel Denton. No European had ever been through it.

"Block definitely had a problem," said Charles Gehring, the director of the New Netherlands Project in Albany. "At that point, all he was thinking of was how to get home. To the crew's joy, they made it through and discovered what they thought was an inland sea."

Thus began Block's voyage of discovery.

He was the first European to sail into Long Island Sound. Proceeding east, he entered a large freshwater river he called the "Fresh River" — today's Connecticut River — and then rounded the North Fork of Long Island and dropped anchor on the bay side of the South Fork. What is today Montauk Point, Block named *Hoeck van de Visschers,* or Point of the Fishers, evidently a reference to the Indian fishermen he encountered there. Once he saw the open ocean behind this point, Block knew what no other European knew — that the long, stout peninsula jutting out from the harbor was an island. He had now been completely around it, and he claimed it all for the Netherlands.

It is believed that Block's men made a landing on Montauk Point. Just where never has been ascertained, nor has the length of their stay. The one document that could give answers — Block's own journal — never has been found. But they were there, somewhere, perhaps waiting for a Dutch ship to pass by on the ocean side. Evidently one never came, because the Restless soon left and began to sail toward Cape Cod. Passing the high, rocky island east of Montauk Point — the same island Giovanni da Verrazano had seen and mapped — Block named it *Adrian Blocks eylandt,* or Block Island.

Off the New England coast, an unusual coincidence happened — the Restless crossed paths with another Dutch ship, the Fortune, captained by Block's friend Hendrick Christiaenzen. Block got on the Fortune and continued across the ocean to the Netherlands. History does not tell us what happened to the Restless.

Gehring believes it may have stayed briefly in New York waters before being sailed home. "I believe it got to the Netherlands, but no record has ever been found of what happened to it," he said. "It's a tantalizing mystery."

After Block returned to the Netherlands, his discoveries were recorded on a map, known as the "Adriaen Block Chart." The original of the chart is in the Dutch National Archives. Copies are available at the Melville Library at the State University at Stony Brook.

According to David Allen, the map librarian at Stony Brook, Block's chart depicts with remarkable accuracy the general outline of Long Island. Block's Long Island features two narrow forks at its eastern end, and bays on its North Shore. The only name on the map is *Nahican,* evidently an Algonquian place name. It cannot be translated today. The name does not appear on any other maps of Long Island. A 1635 Dutch map, which Allen said was based on Block's work, features the word *Matouwacs* across the south shore of Long Island. The meaning of that word is not known, either.

"Block was an instant celebrity in the Netherlands," Gehring said. "You know he's significant because he gets to have an island named after him. It's 'Adrian Block's Island,' his whole name. And it was a very important island. It's right there at the end of Long Island, right where you'd want to be, the perfect place to trade in both directions, north and south."

After his return, Block appeared before government officials, who after hearing his story declared the area he had surveyed *Nieuw Nederlandt,* New Netherland. A charter was issued to merchants to begin trading, and a settlement was envisioned on the island where Block had built the Restless. A new age in a new world had begun.

Block's Travels

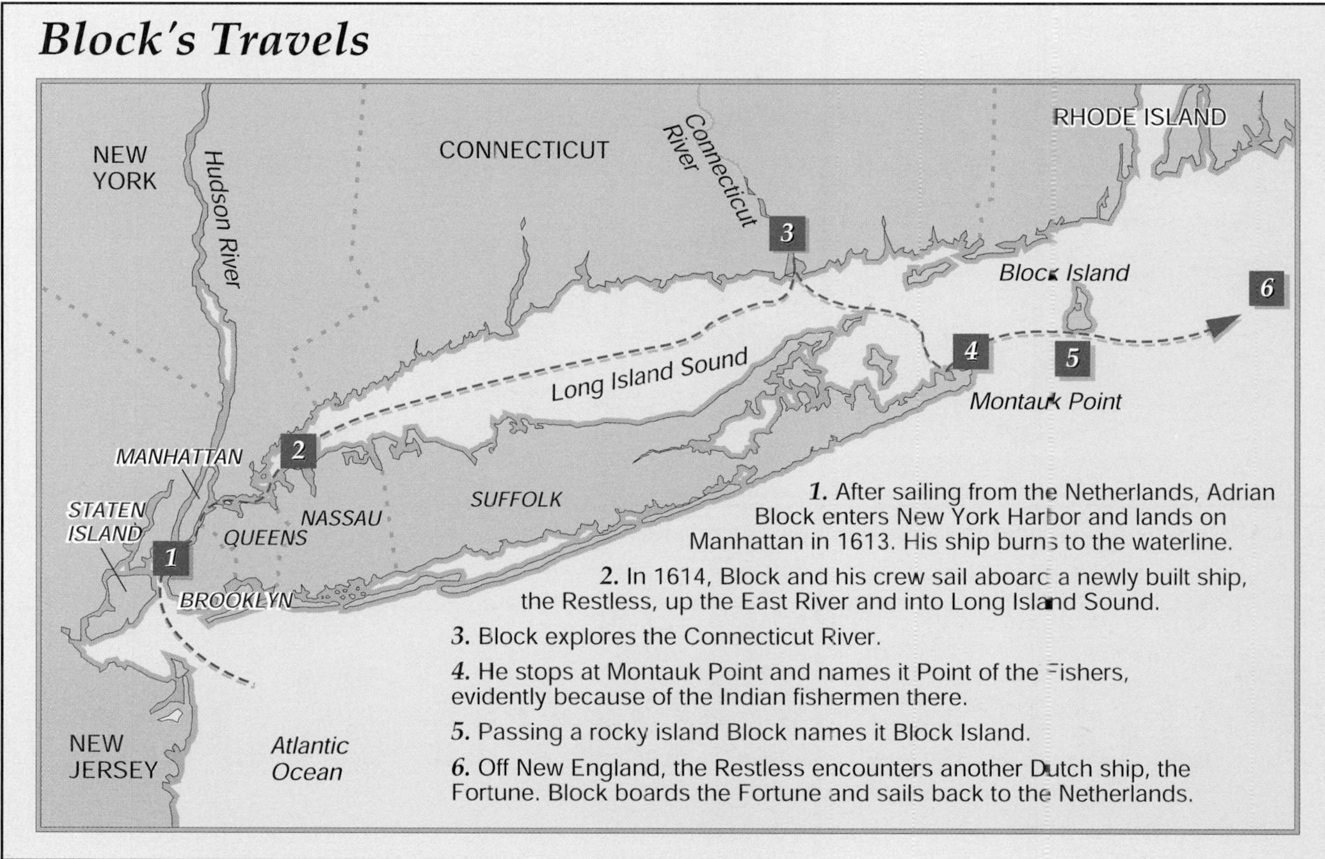
NEW YORK
CONNECTICUT
Connecticut River
RHODE ISLAND
Hudson River
Block Island
Long Island Sound
Montauk Point
MANHATTAN
STATEN ISLAND
QUEENS
NASSAU
SUFFOLK
BROOKLYN
NEW JERSEY
Atlantic Ocean
1. After sailing from the Netherlands, Adrian Block enters New York Harbor and lands on Manhattan in 1613. His ship burns to the waterline.
2. In 1614, Block and his crew sail aboard a newly built ship, the Restless, up the East River and into Long Island Sound.
3. Block explores the Connecticut River.
4. He stops at Montauk Point and names it Point of the Fishers, evidently because of the Indian fishermen there.
5. Passing a rocky island Block names it Block Island.
6. Off New England, the Restless encounters another Dutch ship, the Fortune. Block boards the Fortune and sails back to the Netherlands.

Newsday / Steve Madden

Having lost their ship to fire in 1613, Adrian Block and his crew build a new 44-foot ship from trees on Manhattan Island for the voyage back to the Netherlands. On the way they became the first Europeans to sail into Long Island Sound. Farther on, Block saw a rocky island east of Montauk Point and named it for himself — Block Island.

From "Old Times in the Colonies," 1880

SPECIAL: 17TH-CENTURY MAPS

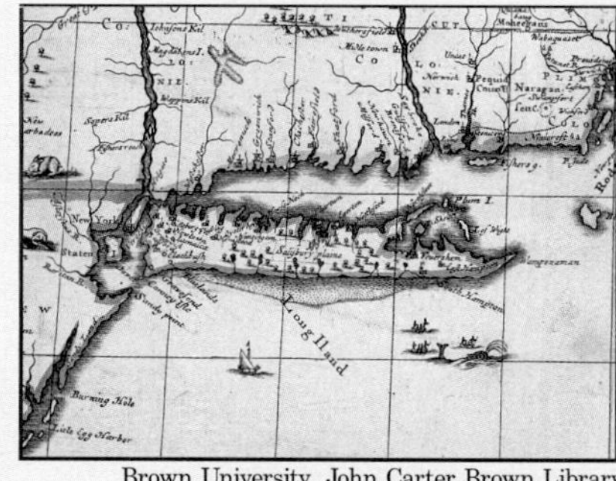

Brown University, John Carter Brown Library

Maps from the 17th Century show how European explorers came to understand the geography of Long Island, including the 1690 map at left.

See Following Pages.

•

Online: Click on http://www.lihistory.com to be linked to more maps, as well as all installments and enhancements to "Long Island: Our Story."

In an undated illustration, Dutchmen trade with native inhabitants in New York.

Collection of the New-York Historical Society

The Dutch add New Netherlands to their growing world empire

Putting Down Roots

BY STEVE WICK
STAFF WRITER

What Dutch business interests heard when Adrian Block returned to the Netherlands and told his story about spending the winter on Manhattan Island electrified them. Block had seen the future — a country filled with furs and ready to be conquered, settled and exploited.

Which is exactly what the Dutch now intended to do. At the beginning of the 17th Century, the Dutch were a major colonial power, promoting business interests in Asia and South America. To these businessmen, this new land would fit nicely into a growing world empire.

In 1614, the year of Block's return, Dutch merchants formed the New Netherland Co. Its goal was to sponsor voyages to the area between 40 and 45 degrees north latitude — the middle of present-day New Jersey to the coast of Maine. This huge region — with Long Island sitting dead center, a long, wooded finger of promise — now had a formal, European name.

"No Christian people had ever been there before," wrote a Dutch observer named Adriaen van der Donck in the mid-17th Century.

Soon, the Dutch were building a log fort on an island at the northernmost part of the Hudson River that was navigable for their ships, near present-day Albany. At about the same time, merchants in the Netherlands formed a second business entity, the West India Co., for the purposes of exploiting their new fur-rich land.

"During this time, there was wild competition between Dutch merchants to exploit this new area," said Paul Otto, an expert on the Dutch history of New York at Dordt College in Iowa. "The New Netherland Company was an effort to manage the competition, and when its charter ran out, the West India Company was set up. At that time, the Dutch were at war with Spain, although a truce was in effect.

"But the West India Company was different — it was an instrument of war designed to go against Spain's interests in the New World. It was empowered to create colonies, settle people, attack Spanish vessels, conduct trade and make treaties with the Indians. New Netherlands fell under the broad monopoly of this company."

By 1624, traders were establishing the fort near Albany. English colonists were in Virginia and Plymouth, and England was claiming the northeastern Atlantic Coast. To bolster their own claims, the Dutch moved to set up settlements. They sent groups of Walloons — French-speaking refugees from Belgium — to New Netherlands. One group went to what is now Governors Island. By 1626, these groups were consolidated on Manhattan Island.

That year, a Dutch official, Peter Minuit, purchased Manhattan for 60 guilders' worth of trade goods. In the mid-19th Century, a historian put the value of these goods at $24, but historians today say the figure is wrong.

"That amount represented about three or four months' salary for the average Dutch soldier who was part of the group," Otto said. "No deed for Manhattan Island has ever been found. You can't really see this in terms of dollars. There's no way to come up with an amount. On top of this, the Indians didn't even think they had sold anything; they didn't think they had to leave."

Soon, the southern tip of Manhattan Island, called New Amsterdam by the Dutch, was a construction site. Trees were cut down and small houses were erected, the streets nothing more than dirt cart paths. Windmills for making flour were built at the tops of creeks; sailing vessels lined new docksides. It was a tiny community walled off to the north by a thick forest laced with Indian trails. And to the east, across the ribbon of salt water that is today's East River, lay Long Island.

A 17th Century Dutch document called "Description and First Settlement of New Netherland" details the beginnings of New Amsterdam.

The Colony was planted at this time, on the Manhates where a Fort was staked out by Master Kryn Federycke, an engineer. It will be of large dimensions. The ship which has returned home this month brings samples of all the different sorts of produce there. The cargo consists of 7246 Beavers, 675 Otter skins, 48 Minx, 36 Wild cat, and various other sorts; several pieces of oak timber, and hickory.

The counting house there is kept in a stone building, thatched with reed; the other houses are of the bark of trees . . . There are thirty ordinary houses on the east side of the river which runs nearly north and south . . . Francois Molemaecker is busy building a horse mill, over which shall be constructed a spacious room sufficient to accommodate a large congregation, and then a tower is to be erected where the bells brought from Porto Rico will be hung . . .

The document says that, as the fort was being built, "two hundred and seventy souls, including Men, Women and Children," lived in the houses "in no fear, as the Natives live peaceably with them." Natives, no doubt, who remembered Block's winter on almost this same spot.

To the north of the tiny Dutch settlement, the English colony at Plymouth was beginning to grow. Neither liked the presence of the other, and it was only a matter of time before trouble began.

ORIGINAL SOURCE

ADRIAEN VAN DER DONCK

Adriaen van der Donck was an attorney from the Netherlands who traveled to New Amsterdam in 1641 and several years later published a book called "A Description of the New Netherlands." It was the first book published by a resident of what is now New York State.

Along with descriptions of the region, van der Donck tried to show that this land was Dutch-owned by right of discovery.

That this country was first found or discovered by the Netherlanders is evident and clear from the fact that the Indians or natives of the land, many of whom are still living, and with whom I have conversed, declare freely that before the arrival of the Lowland ship, the Half-Moon, in the year 1609, they did not know that there were any other people in the world than those who were like themselves, much less any people who differed so much in appearance from them as we did . . . There are persons who believe that the Spaniards have been here many years ago, when they found the climate too cold to their liking, and again left the country.

He also defined the borders of the New Netherlands — on the north was New England, the south Virginia. West, he wrote, was "undefined and unknown."

Many of our Netherlanders have been far into the country, more than seventy or eighty miles from the river and seashore. We also frequently trade with the Indians, who come more than ten or twenty days' journey from the interior, and who have been farther off to catch beavers, and they know of no limits to the country.

— Steve Wick

New-York Historical Society

Adriaen van der Donck

Some of the story of New York's first European settlers exists in thousands of old documents

The Dutch Paper Chase

By Steve Wick
STAFF WRITER

Charles Gehring was translating Dutch documents from the 17th Century when he found an account that he couldn't forget. It concerned a trip some Dutch businessmen made from Albany to western New York in the later part of the century.

"They were traveling to an Indian village near present-day Buffalo to explore trading opportunities," Gehring said. "They were hundreds of miles from any settlements. They wrote that when they came into the village, they encountered a white man named Charles Smith. They were stunned. He had been kidnaped years before in Virginia.

"He begged the Dutch to take him with them when they left. There's no record of what happened, but I don't get the sense they were able to leave with him. I don't know what ever became of Charles Smith."

The tale of the mysterious Charles Smith is one of thousands of stories Gehring has uncovered in the two decades he has been director of an ambitious effort called the New Netherlands Project. Gehring began it in the mid-1970s when he was hired to translate documents dating from the brief period between the arrival of Dutch explorers in New York waters, in the early 1600s, and ending when the Dutch were kicked out by the English in 1664.

"It is a fascinating period," Gehring said. "I've always thought the Dutch history of New York has been given short shrift by historians and scholars. It's as if they weren't here."

When he began the project, Gehring found that there were approximately 12,000 pages of Dutch records dating to the period when the region was called New Netherlands and the tiny community at the southern tip of Manhattan Island was New Amsterdam. These documents had first been stored in Manhattan and then, during the American Revolution when fires were common, had been taken by British officials to two prison ships anchored in the harbor, the Dutchess of Gordon and the Warwick, for safekeeping. After the war, New York officials brought them back to Manhattan and later to Albany, where Gehring has his office.

During the 19th and early 20th Centuries, scholars slogged through a small portion of the Dutch records, translating important government documents but leaving untouched thousands of pages related to social history and the everyday lives of the Dutch. Today, Gehring estimated, there are approximately 6,000 pages of flesh-and-blood history, written in 17th Century Dutch and waiting for his sharp eye and knowledge of the language.

The director of the New Netherlands Project, Charles Gehring, pores over 17th-Century Dutch documents, some singed in a fire. At right, the signature of New Amsterdam's Peter Stuyvesant

Photos by Dave Oxford

LI HISTORY.COM

Play an interactive crossword puzzle devoted to Indian life and early European settlers. All clues and answers come from stories in Chapter 2, which is available on the Internet at http://www.lihistory.com.

A linguist and teacher before he began the New Netherlands Project, Gehring can read and write in 17th Century Dutch, which he said is far different from modern Dutch. He likened it to comparing English today with Shakespearean English. But understanding the language is not enough — he has to decipher the handwriting, too.

"It took quite a while to get used to the handwriting. In the beginning, I'd look at a page and think, What are those letters? Now I can do it. It took a lot of time. In looking at the new documents, I also realized that some of the old translations were just incomplete. With what we've learned in recent years, we have a greater knowledge and can go back to these earlier translations and do a better job."

From what he has learned, a tremendous amount of material that relates to the Dutch occupation of New York is missing. For the most part, Gehring said, the state's records begin in 1642, 16 years after the Dutch purchased Manhattan Island from the Indians for 60 guilders worth of trade goods. Nothing before that year has been found. When the English arrived in force in 1664, the Dutch left, only to return in 1673 for another brief occupancy. But in between, Gehring said, official records continued to be written in Dutch.

Taken together, the documents already translated provide a wealth of material about how the Dutch lived, how they interacted with the Indians, and how their communities were set up. "It fascinated me that what they did here was the very model of a community in the Netherlands," Gehring said. "They transplanted what they knew exactly — from their church, to the poor house, the way streets were laid out, what the architecture was like. They brought all their institutions with them."

A fire that broke out in 1911 in the State Library in Albany nearly destroyed New York's past. More than 2 million documents — books, thousands of records pertaining to Indian transactions, English records before the Revolution — were lost. Some Dutch records were destroyed, and nearly all suffered burns and smoke damage.

Gehring receives no state funding for his effort. He raises his approximately $120,000 annual budget from private sources. It covers his work and the work of his assistant, Janny Venema, both of whom travel to the Netherlands to lose themselves in the Dutch Archives. Gehring said there is much to be done, and he wants to do it.

"I can't retire, and I don't want to," said the 58-year-old scholar. "I love what I do. I've learned so much that is now available to the pubic. You know, the Dutch came here from a small, crowded country. Their opportunities in this new country were limitless. They could look west and see nothing but immense space. Their ambitions soared here."

Hoping, in the Future, More Past Is Found

After more than 20 years translating Dutch documents and searching for lost ones, in New York and in the Netherlands, Charles Gehring yearns for what he has not found.

Here are some items he crosses his fingers will be turned up some day:

- Ships' logs belonging to Henry Hudson and Adrian Block. "There are references to them, but the actual logs have never been found," Gehring said. "I can only imagine the wonders in those logs."
- Records of the Dutch West India Co., presumed to have been discarded in the 1670s when the company was reorganized. Explorers such as Hudson and Block worked for the company.
- Correspondence from Dutch residents of New Netherlands to friends and relatives back home. "We know there was a stream of letters and other correspondence, but haven't found any," Gehring said.
- Copies of a newspaper called the New Netherland Marcurius, or Mercury. "There are just two references to the existence of the Mercury, otherwise we know nothing about it," Gehring said. "For all we know, they are in someone's attic, someone's trunk, a small museum somewhere that doesn't know what they are. They're a treasure waiting to be found." **— Steve Wick**

Early Maps Of Long Island

Maps made in the 17th Century help show how Europe came to understand Long Island. Italian explorer Giovanni da Verrazano entered New York Harbor in 1524, but it was not until 1609 that Englishman Henry Hudson sailed farther inland and found the river that would bear his name. In 1613-14, Dutch mariner Adrian Block sailed around Long Island and returned home with information that helped chart the East Coast. Here are four maps made from 1635 to 1690; two are Dutch and two English.

1635

Dutch cartographer William Janszoon Blaeu based this 1635 map — a close-up detail is seen at right — on charts drawn after the 1613-14 journey of Adrian Block. The map is notable for its illustrations, such as the Indian canoes in the ocean. Blaeu also depicted Long Island as a series of islands, not a large landmass. The Algonquian word "Matouwacs" is not easily translated today, but a 19th Century linguist believed it meant "Island of the Periwinkle." The map is unusual to today's eye because it is oriented with west at the top.

State University at Stony Brook Library, Special Collections Department

Long Island Studies Institute

1656

This is also a Dutch map; the cartographer was Nicholaes Visscher. The detail seen at left prominently features the Dutch words Lange Eylandt, for Long Island, over the Algonquian word Matouwacs. The map reflects the growth of Dutch and English settlements on Long Island, including "S. Holt" on the North Fork, for Southold, and "Garner's Eylant," for the island owned by Englishman Lion Gardiner. It also shows the island as a land mass and not a series of islands divided by channels, as on the Blaeu map. The map is the first to feature the evidence of the Hempstead Plains, according to cartography scholar David Allen, author of "Long Island Maps and Their Makers: Five Centuries of Cartographic History" (Amereon Ltd.). The plains are designated here by the words "Gebroken Landt," for broken land.

1675

This British map at right dates to 1675 and is believed to be the first map of colonial Long Island based on an actual survey; the cartographer, Robert Ryder, also was a professional surveyor. The map includes colors and shadings never seen before on a map of Long Island, and shows the barrier beaches along the South Shore.

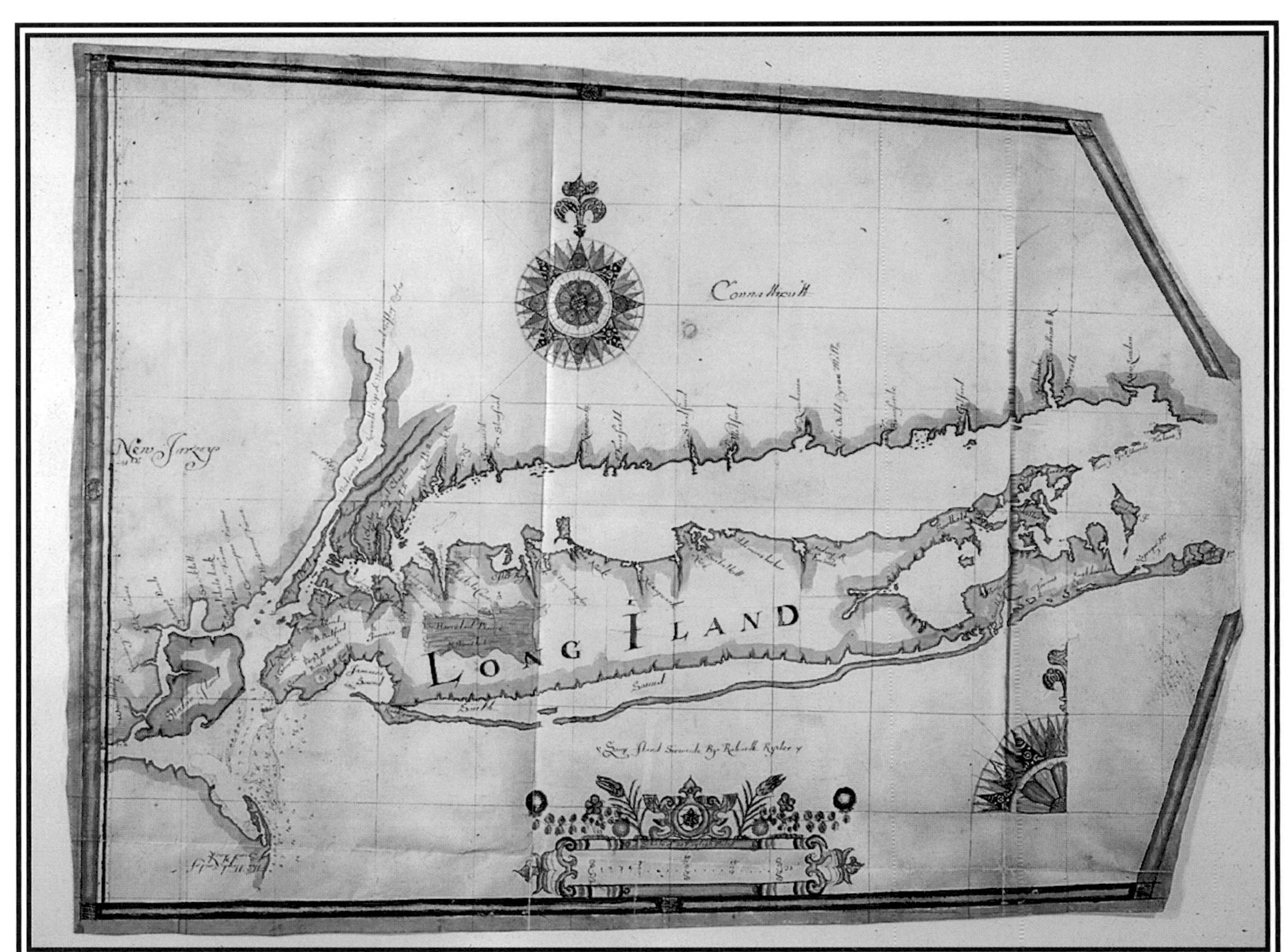

Brown University, John Carter Brown Library

1690

The map below is labeled "A Map of ye English Empire in the Continent of America," by Robert Morden. It dates to 1690. The detail here shows Indians whaling off the South Fork. It shows a wide, broad plain labeled the "Salisbury plaine," as well as community names, including Huntington, "Hemsteed," and Flushing. On the East End, Gardiner's Island is labled "I. of Wight," which was the name given to the island by Lion Gardiner after he bought it in 1639.

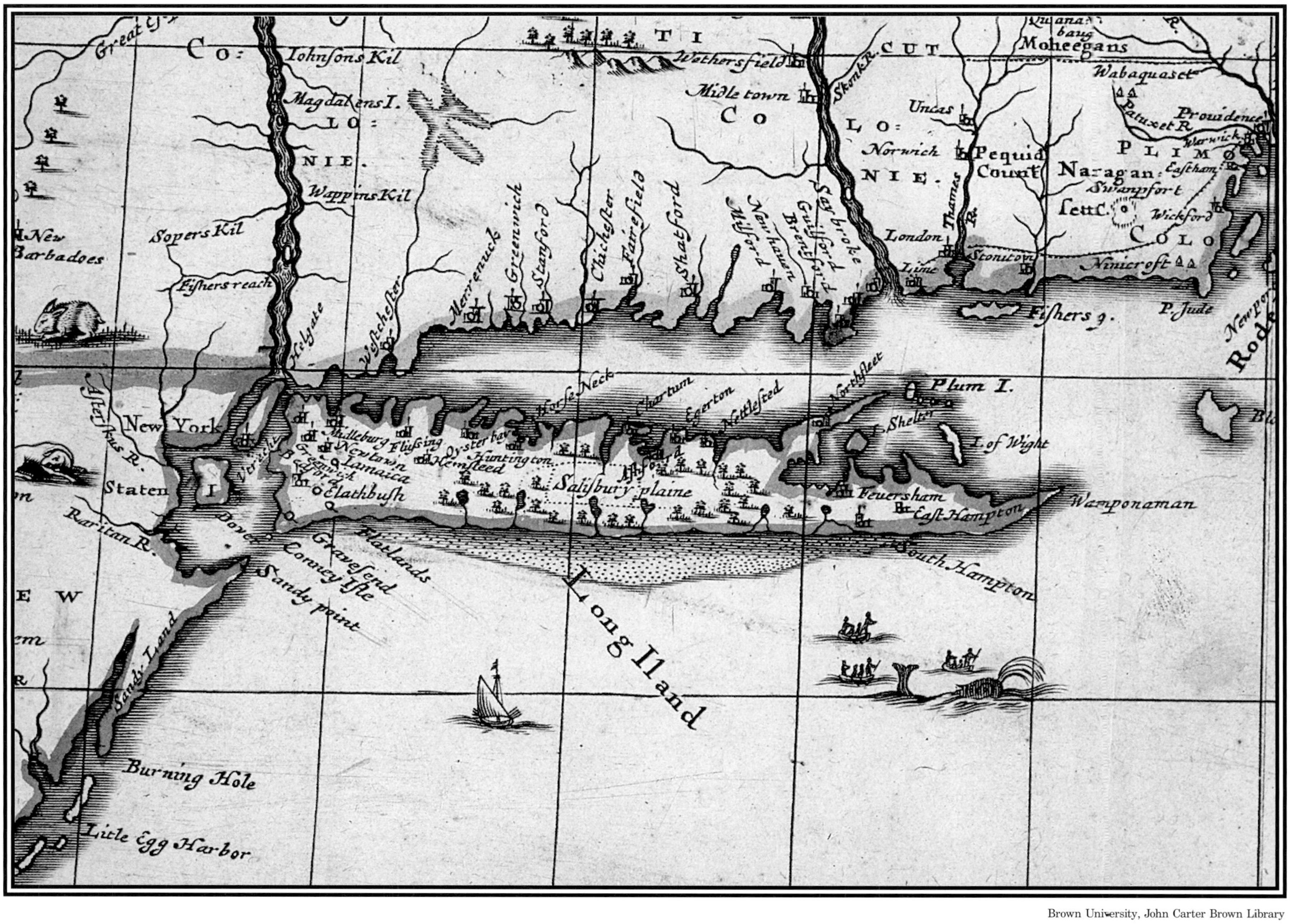

Brown University, John Carter Brown Library

Greater Patchogue Historical Society

TIME MACHINE

PICTURING THE PAST AND PRESENT

Newsday Photo / Bill Davis

Doing Business In Patchogue

For 104 years, Swezey's department store, shown above in 1910, has stood as a mercantile monument in Patchogue.

The department store, on the northwest corner of Main Street and Ocean Avenue, originally was called Swezey & Newins. Arthur M. Swezey and Fred Newins offered dry goods, carpets, furniture, crockery and glassware. The prominent clock tower was lost in a 1946 fire that also destroyed much of the building.

The small building adjacent to Swezey's on Main Street was Al Seitz' Tonsorial Parlors and Bath Room. The building next to it was Pape's, a candy and ice cream parlor.

The large structure on the far left, the Syndicate Building, contained a number of enterprises, including the post office, The Argus weekly newspaper and the Union Savings Bank. The bank opened for business in 1897 in the Swezey building, but outgrew the space and moved to the Syndicate Building in 1902, according to village historian Anne Swezey. She is married to Robert Swezey, whose father, John R. Swezey, was mayor of Patchogue from 1948-52 and a distant relative of Arthur.

CHAPTER 3

The Colonists

From the struggle between the Dutch and English for control of a new land to the eve of revolution

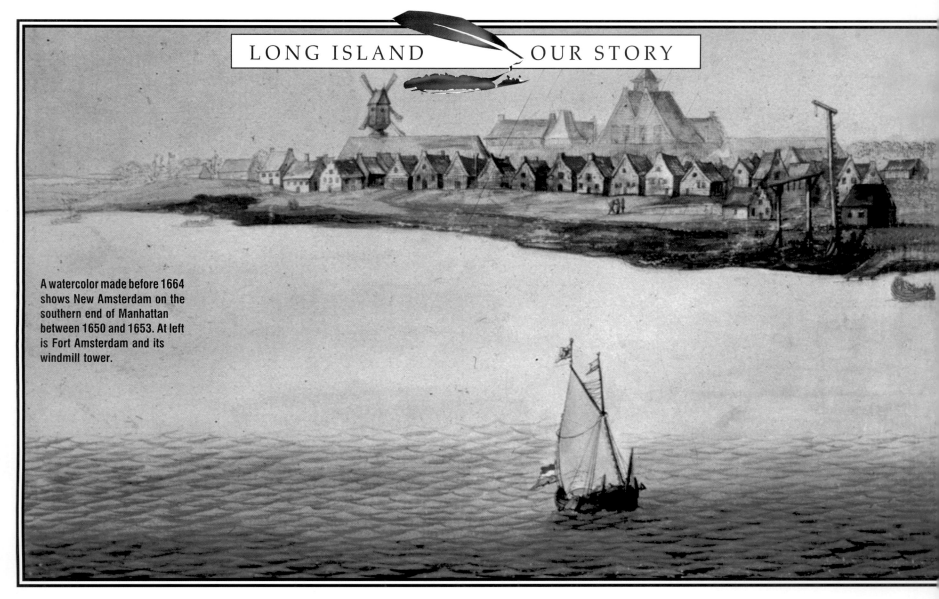

A watercolor made before 1664 shows New Amsterdam on the southern end of Manhattan between 1650 and 1653. At left is Fort Amsterdam and its windmill tower.

BY STEVE WICK
STAFF WRITER

A showdown develops as Dutch and English immigrants

The Colonial

As the 17th Century dawned in Europe, two powerful countries pushed west across the ocean on a search for new lands to exploit and settle. Their collision in the New World would decide the future of Long Island.

The two powers were the Netherlands and England. The Netherlands was enjoying a Golden Age — one of the smallest countries in Europe had become a wealthy superpower. Across the English Channel, England was on the verge of social upheaval that would propel thousands of its citizens out of the country on a search for a new England.

For the Netherlands, the New World represented a business opportunity; for the English, land for new settlements. They both laid claim to Long Island, where the Dutch took hold of the western end and, later, the English settled on the eastern end. In Europe, the English channel separated the two countries; on Long Island, it was 100 miles of wilderness occupied for thousands of years by bands of Indians.

Before their struggle was resolved, slavery would be introduced to the region; hundreds of Indians would be killed in a brutal episode called the Kieft War; an English engineer named Lion Gardiner would meet a Montaukett Indian named Wyandanch, and their friendship would leave a deep imprint on the history of Long Island; new towns would be settled, churches and schools built; a woman from East Hampton would be put on trial as a witch, and the Indians who had greeted the Europeans would be removed from their land and reduced to paupers.

The story begins on Manhattan Island.

By the mid-1620s, after nearly a decade of trading with the Indians along the great river discovered by Henry Hudson, the Dutch decided to establish a permanent presence at the southern end of what is today Manhattan Island. In its first few years, the tiny settlement was little more than a collection of log huts connected by dirt cart paths; a large warehouse in which furs and other trade items were stored; a church, and a handful of other structures. North of the settlement were open fields where sheep and cows grazed, and beyond that were dense woods and rocky outcroppings that extended all the way to the northern tip of the island.

Needing land to raise food and other crops, such as tobacco, the Dutch soon leapfrogged to western Long Island, a land of infinite promise and far better suited for homesites. Soon, small villages cropped up — New Ultrecht, Breuckelen, both named after towns in the Netherlands, and Gravesend. Ferries plied the river between the settlement at New Amsterdam, on Manhattan Island, and the farming villages on *Lange Eylandt*.

"In the beginning," said Paul Otto, a history professor at Dordt College in Iowa, "the Dutch were looking for trade opportunities and not permanent colonies. They were expanding their economy outward into areas such as sugar, tobacco and the slave trade, which was their real bread and butter. But the growth of the English colonies upset the balance, and endangered their claim to the new lands. They set up their colony at New Amsterdam so they could say they occupied the land and therefore it was theirs."

By the mid-1630s, English settlers had begun to push south along the southern New England coastline. As with immigrants leaving England and sailing to Massachusetts, the motivation for this move was in large part religious. Squabbles among religious leaders in Massachusetts led to conservative groups splitting off to look for new colonies where

LI HISTORY.COM

Play an interactive crossword puzzle devoted to the colonial period. All clues and answers were taken from stories in Chapter 3, which will be available on the Internet, as the series unfolds, at http://www.lihistory.com.

Newsday Photo / Bill Davis

THE RAPELJE FAMILY

Dutch documents say Sarah deRapelje, born in Brooklyn in 1625, was the first child of European settlers born in what would become New York State. Her parents, Joris Jansen DeRapelje and the former Catalyntje Trico, had come from Holland a few years earlier.

Today a Long Island family — including Anna B. Rapelje, 95, and her son, Peter W. Rapelje, 64, of Glen Cove, both at left — traces 12 generations back to Sarah's parents, with members in Glen Cove and Bayville. "We have four generations of Rapeljes still living on Long Island," Peter says.

Museum of the City of New York

settle on opposite ends of Long Island

Collision

church rules could be strictly enforced.

This push south into wilderness controlled by Indian groups such as the Pequots brought the Dutch and the English to within 50 miles of each other — the English in Connecticut, the Dutch in rural outposts on western Long Island and in what is now Westchester County.

But the English desire to settle the stretch of coastline that today runs from the mouth of the Connecticut River east to New London would spark a cataclysmic war and the nearly total slaughter of the Pequots, who occupied the land and had trading arrangements with the Dutch. It was this war that allowed for the nearly peaceful settlement of eastern Long Island by English colonists.

In the spring of 1637, soldiers led by two mercenaries, John Mason and John Underhill, attacked a Pequot fort near what is now Mystic. Hundreds were killed by the English, including women and children; many were burned alive when the fort was set ablaze. More than 1,000 Pequots were killed by English soldiers and their Indian allies in subsequent months. (Descendants of the few survivors were settled on a reservation that today is the site of Foxwoods, the world's most profitable casino.)

Documents show that one of the Indian leaders who hunted down Pequots and cut off their heads to present to the English was Wyandanch, a Montaukett who lived in the area of today's East Hampton. He did so at the behest of an Englishman named Lion Gardiner, and the two men would become fast friends until death. In the aftermath of the war, Gardiner purchased the island that today bears his family's name off the coast of East Hampton — he was the first Englishman to settle on eastern Long Island; his daughter, Elizabeth, was the first English child born in what is now New York State.

By 1640, small groups of English colonists followed in Gardiner's wake, sailing from Connecticut to both the North and South Forks of Long Island. They established tiny communities they called Southold — named for a village in England called Southwold — and Southampton. Each of the Long Island towns claims to have been first; there is no way today to prove it one way or the other.

History on Long Island is in large part an unbroken chain. In Southold, the first families included families such as Reeve, Wells, Terry, Tuthill and Booth, all of whom have descendants there today. The same is true in Southampton, where the earliest names — Howell, Halsey, Cooper and Sayre — also have descendants today.

By that same year, 1640, the Dutch had hundreds of settlers spread across western Long Island in small, remote farming villages. They also had English settlers in their area, and one was Deborah Moody, who was one of the first to settle in Gravesend, Breuckelen. A fighter for religious freedom, Moody was perhaps the most remarkable Long Island woman of the 17th Century. One of the earliest Dutch settlers on Long Island was Joris deRapelje, who in the mid-1620s lived near the present-day Brook-

Please see **DUTCH** on Next Page

A TALE OF TWO GOVERNORS

Peter Stuyvesant, *New Netherlands director-general, 1646-64*

He was nothing if not colorful: He limped around New Amsterdam on one good leg; his right leg had been amputated during a battle against the Spanish on the island of St. Martin, and when he arrived at New Amsterdam (Manhattan) in 1647 to serve as the governor of the Dutch territory, he was wearing a wooden leg embroidered with silver bands. He put his mark on colonial history when, in 1650, he negotiated the Hartford Treaty, which ceded the Connecticut River Valley to the English and divided Long Island in two. This division allowed the English to claim the bulk of the Long Island landmass, from Oyster Bay east; the Dutch took what is today Brooklyn and Queens. Stuyvesant was the last Dutch governor.

The Granger Collection

Stuyvesant, center, in a J.I.G. Ferris painting of the 1664 surrender of New Amsterdam.

Richard Nicolls, *New York governor, 1664-68*

His entrance onto the New World stage was grand. In March, 1664, England's King Charles II gave to his brother, James, the duke of York, all of the Atlantic coastline from Maine to Delaware. Long Island lay at the heart of this huge land grant. To seize it from the Dutch, a flotilla of warships commanded by Richard Nicolls, who was aboard his flagship, the Guinea, dropped anchor off Gravesend, Brooklyn. He threatened to destroy the Dutch fort on Manhattan Island, so the Dutch surrendered. Nicolls became the first English governor of New Amsterdam and renamed it New York to honor the duke of York. He is well regarded by historians. He is best known for a code called the Duke's Laws, designed primarily for Long Island, which were the first English laws passed in the colony of New York. He did not like criticism of the laws from Long Islanders, and he quit in 1667 and was replaced by Francis Lovelace. **— Steve Wick**

Colonial Collision

DUTCH from Preceding Page

lyn Navy Yard. Joris' daughter, Sarah, born in a Dutch village near Albany, was the first white child born in what was to become New York State. A descendant, Peter Rapelje, lives today in Glen Cove — another example of the unbroken chain.

From a European point of view, Long Island was now multi-national — Dutch at one end, English at the other.

"The Dutch saw where they were as New Netherlands, an extension of the old country," said Charles Gehring, director of the New Netherlands Project in Albany. "Their villages were Dutch, the language was Dutch, as were the customs and laws. New Amsterdam looked like a village in Holland. Even when non-Dutch settlers came into their area, they were part of the Dutch system."

At the opposite end of Long Island, the tiny communities of the North and South Forks were carbon copies of small, rural villages in England. Here, though, the church controlled all government affairs, and to be an official of any kind, a person had to be a member in good standing of the church. The church set the laws and the punishment for lawbreakers, and basically ran the day-to-day life of the town's residents. Nonchurch members — such as Quakers, whose practices were heretical to the Puritans — were punished, often severely.

Along with being outwardly pious, these early settlers also were superstitious. According to one early account, "If a rooster crowed on your doorstep, company was coming. If you dropped a fork, it was a man; a knife, a woman; a spoon, a child. A door hinge creaking was a sign of death. If the bottom of your feet itched, you were going to walk on strange ground. If your left ear burned, you would hear bad news; if your right, good news. If you spilled salt, put some in the fire so as to avoid a quarrel. Always take salt and a new broom into a house before moving in. Never cut a baby's nails until a year old or you will make a thief of it."

Superstitions were not always so benign. In the 1650s, an East Hampton woman, Goodwife Garlick, was tried for witchcraft after a woman neighbor — the daughter of Lion Gardiner — died unexpectedly. Her trial — at which she was acquitted — was the first of its kind on Long Island, and presaged a wave of witchcraft trials in New England.

The dramas played out by the English have no Dutch counterpart. The Dutch were spread thin across a wide area, raising tobacco, corn and livestock on land originally cleared by the Indians and trading for such items as beaver and otter pelts. In sharp contrast to the English settlements, New Amsterdam, the log hamlet at the southern tip of Manhattan Island, was home to an abundance of religions and nationalities. New Amsterdam, and all of New Netherlands, from Long Island to the small settlement near what is now Albany, was a commercial venture, not a religious one.

The colony's commercial underpinnings can be seen in a momentous action that occurred in 1626 — a ship holding 11 African slaves sailed into New Amsterdam. Dutch records attach names to some of the 11 — Paul d'Angelo, Simon Congo, Anthony Portugese and John Francisco. But it would be the English who would expand slavery across the region, with slaves doing farm work in every town on Long Island.

While relations between Indians and English would remain quiet in the aftermath of the Pequot War, this was not the case in the Dutch-held areas. In 1640, the year Southold and Southampton were established, a war broke out across Manhattan and western Long Island that would result in more than 1,000 Indian deaths, including a massacre of more than 100 Indians in what is today Massapequa. It was called the Kieft War, after the Dutch governor of the province, Willem Kieft, who would be recalled in disgrace to the Netherlands. He was lost at sea on his return trip.

Museum of the City of New York

The seal of New Netherlands, used on official Dutch documents after 1630, shows a beaver against a shield enclosed by wampum.

Importantly, it is not just modern-day historians looking back at the Kieft War who describe it as brutal — it was described that way by a Dutchman of the day, in a document dated in 1649. The author of the document, who does not name himself, was apparently an eyewitness to events and, more than likely, a government official disgusted by Kieft's behavior. He writes the document in a question-and-answer format to officials in the Netherlands with the hope of getting Kieft replaced. In the document, he rips into Kieft as a greedy and brutal tyrant who had "for a long time secretly intended to begin a war with the savages of New Netherland, because they had refused, on reasonable grounds, to give him a certain contribution . . ."

The author additionally states: "Further, they (the Indians) had allowed us to remain peaceably in their country . . . we were under obligations to them, and not they to us." In a reference to Dutch explorer Adrian Block — who, in 1614, spent the winter on Manhattan Island building a ship from scratch after his burned to the waterline — the author says, "that when our nation, having lost a ship there had built a new one, they had supplied them with victuals and all other necessaries, and had taken care of them for two winters till the ship was finished; consequently, we were under obligations to them, not they to us."

The author writes of Indians being beheaded by the Dutch, or burned alive. "Young children, some of them snatched from their mothers, were cut in pieces before the eyes of their parents, and the pieces were thrown into the fire or into the water; other babes were bound on planks and then cut through, stabbed and miserably massacred, so that it would break a heart of stone . . ."

With brute force, the Dutch could push the Indians off their land, but they could not keep the English away. For two decades after the Kieft War, the two nations lived in peace side by side on Long Island. In 1647, a new Dutch governor, Peter Stuyvesant, arrived on the scene at a time of increasing hostility between the two sides, with an English official in Massachusetts, William Bradford, predicting war.

There are few characters in colonial history quite like Stuyvesant. His tenure as a leader was long, 17 years, and he cut a fascinating figure — he had a peg leg embroidered with silver bands. He lost his right leg when it was crushed by a cannonball in a battle in the Caribbean. One surviving portrait of him, painted in 1660, shows a man with a broad, wide face.

When he arrived on the scene, Stuyvesant could see that English settlers were spilling into Dutch areas, so in 1650 he negotiated a treaty in Hartford that drew a line that began near present-day Greenwich, Conn.,, and crossed Long Island, beginning just west of what is now

Colonizing a New World

Long Island

1609. Members of Henry Hudson's crew from the Half Moon landed on Coney Island.

1624. First Dutch settlements established on Manhattan and Nutte (Governor's) Island.

1626. Peter Minuit of the Dutch West India Company purchased Manhattan Island from the natives for trade goods worth 60 guilders.

1639. Lion and Mary Gardiner move from Connecticut to Isle of Wight (Gardiners Island), land they bought from the Montauketts.

United States

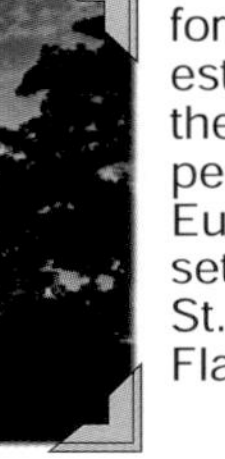

1565. Spanish forces established the first permanent European settlement at St. Augustine, Fla.

1587. Virginia Dare became the first English child born in North America at the Roanoke colony, which disappeared soon thereafter.

1607. More than 100 colonists founded the first permanent English settlement in Jamestown.

1620. Pilgrims arrived at Plymouth, Mass., after a 63-day voyage.

The World

1534. King Henry VIII became head of the English church, severing all religious ties to the Pope.

1543. Nicolaus Copernicus proposed that the Earth is not the center of the universe.

1558. Elizabeth I became queen of England.

1588. An English fleet defeated the Spanish Armada.

1603. King James I became ruler of England, uniting Scotland and England.

1520 1530 1540 1550 1560 1570 1580 1590 1600 1610 1620 1630 1640

Oyster Bay. West of this line was Dutch, east of it was English. But forces in Europe were to quickly undo the Treaty of Hartford.

"Beginning in the early 1650s, the Dutch and English began fighting in Europe over trade and naval supremacy," said Otto, the history professor at Dordt College. "The situation spilled over into the New World, where by the mid-1660s the English were moving to kick the Dutch out of New Netherlands. Locally, there was a desire for more territory and the English were pushing up against the Dutch borders."

The issue of who owned Long Island and the surrounding territory was settled — on paper, at least — when in March, 1664, Charles II gave his brother, James, the duke of York, a grant that covered the area from Maine south to the "De la Ware Bay." James organized a fleet of warships under the command of Richard Nicolls — who would become the first English governor of what is today New York State, and whose legacy can be seen in street names, such as Nicolls Road — and in late August he anchored off the shoreline of Gravesend and threatened to attack Fort Amsterdam. By early September, the Dutch agreed to leave, and James sent word of his victory to Massachusetts, signing his letter "ffrom New Yorke upon the Island of the Manhatoes."

Eighteen months later, the Dutch returned to retake Fort Amsterdam. They did not keep it for long, and in 1674, they gave it up permanently. Nicolls served as English governor from 1664-68, and under his leadership enacted the Duke's Laws, a code designed primarily for residents of Long Island. These were the first English laws in colonial New York, covering a number of political issues, and were deeply resented across Long Island because, among other things, the laws imposed taxes without popular consent.

Long Island was now a part of England.

HISTORICAL MARKERS: A BORDER DISPUTE

As the Huntington Town historian, Rufus Langhans liked to promote local history. So it was not surprising when he put up three historical signs in the town saying they marked the "international boundary" that divided Dutch and English Long Island.

Langhans, who died in 1994 at age 72 after serving 25 years as town historian, contributed greatly to understanding Long Island's past. He was right about the boundary, which was drawn in 1650 under the terms of the Treaty of Hartford, which created a formal border between the parts of the Island claimed by the two countries. But he got the location wrong — the line was not in Huntington.

The boundary was sought by the Dutch governor, Peter Stuyvesant, who realized that the English had spilled into areas controlled by the Dutch in the Connecticut River Valley and in Long Island. The line, according to the treaty, ran south from the "western edge of Oyster Bay," basically cutting modern-day Nassau County in two. So the actual "international boundary" was approximately 10 miles west of Langhans's markers.

The three Huntington markers were placed at these locations:

- On the southwest corner of Woodbury and Harbor Roads,
- Manetto Hill Road, 200 feet east of County Line Road,
- And Round Swamp Road and Old Country Road.

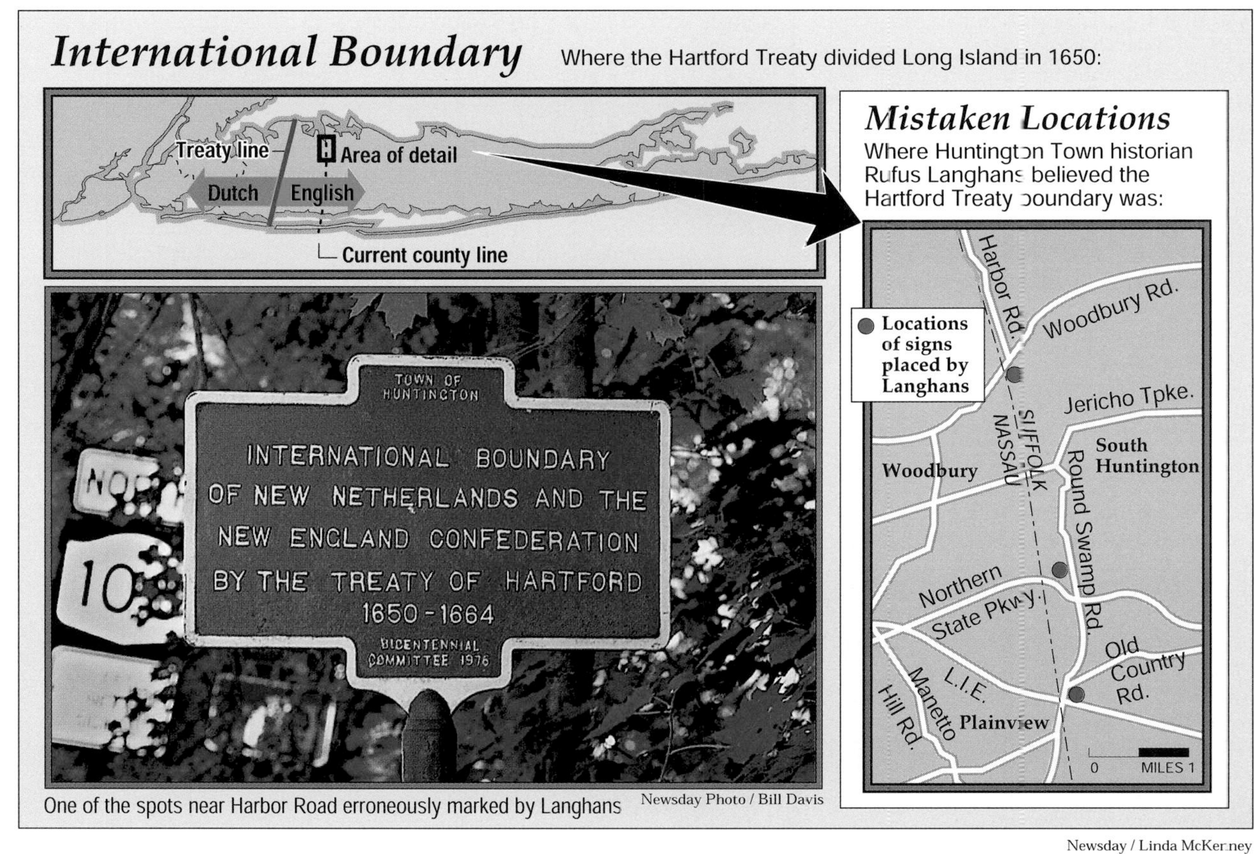

One of the spots near Harbor Road erroneously marked by Langhans Newsday Photo / Bill Davis

Newsday / Linda McKenney

1650. Treaty of Hartford was signed, dividing Long Island between Dutch (west) and English (east). Border was west of the present-day Nassau-Suffolk boundary.

1664. Dutch leader Peter Stuyvesant surrendered New Netherlands to the English; colony was renamed New York.

1692. New York Assembly renamed Long Island the "Island of Nassau," after William of Nassau of the Netherlands, husband of England's Queen Mary.

1766. Sons of Liberty in Oyster Bay protested the British stamp tax.

1689. First public school in North America was founded in Philadelphia.

1692. Salem witch-hunt began when some children claimed that three old women had bewitched them.

1754. The French and Indian War began with troops led by George Washington encountering French troops. The war ended in 1763.

March 22, 1765. The Stamp Act was passed. The act required the purchase of revenue stamps to be affixed to newspapers, pamphlets, almanacs, legal documents, playing cards and dice.

March 5, 1770. Seven colonists were killed in Boston by British troops. The incident became known as the Boston Massacre.

1649. England's King Charles I was beheaded and the country's monarchy is abolished. The monarchy was restored 11 years later.

1682. France's King Louis XIV moved the royal court to Versailles.

1725. Vitus Bering, a Danish sailor exploring the oceans for Peter the Great of Russia, discovered the straits separating North America and Asia.

1772. The monarchs of Austria, Prussia and Russia seized one-third of Poland's territory and began rule over half of its population.

SOURCE: "To Know the Place: Exploring Long Island History," edited by Joann P. Krieg and Natalie Naylor; "Long Island Before the Revolution"; Long Island Forum; "Chronicle of the World"; "The Encyclopedia of American Facts and Dates."

1650 1660 1670 1680 1690 1700 1710 1720 1730 1740 1750 1760 1770 1780

Newsday / Linda McKenney

The Dutch in Manhattan find lots of land for farming on the long island across the harbor

Breuckelen Becomes Home

BY STEVE WICK
STAFF WRITER

By the mid-1630s, the Dutch were ready to expand their base from the southern tip of Manhattan Island — a collection of clapboard houses, a church, a tavern, a large storehouse, orchards and cow pastures — to the unchartered wilds of Long Island.

Across the wide harbor east of New Amsterdam, as the Dutch called their tiny community, was a huge expanse of woods, open fields, salt marshes and bays filled with shells to make wampum, the coin of the new realm that could be used to buy furs from the Indians of the north. And more fertile open land for plantations than existed in all the countries of Europe combined.

Early in the summer of 1636, a decade after buying Manhattan Island, a group of Dutchmen began to make the first purchases of land on the place the Indians called Sewanhackey, the land of shells — Long Island. Within a few weeks, a total of 15,000 acres had been bought along the eastern shore of what is today Jamaica Bay. The Dutch called their new village *New Amersfoort.* It is today called Flatlands.

Later that same month, the Dutch took a giant step toward expanding their Long Island holdings when two Dutchmen and a Frenchman bought two tracts totalling 1,265 acres. One of the tracts was in a place the Dutch, trying to understand the mysteries of the Algonquian language, called Gowanus; the second was nearby.

"The reason the Dutch crossed over from Manhattan to Long Island was because they needed good pasture land," said Charles Gehring, the director of the New Netherlands Project, in Albany. "They needed land for their cattle, and Long Island had the space and Manhattan didn't. Long Island was cleared and flat, and Manhattan was rocky and hilly. Long Island represented the future."

In a flurry of real-estate activity over the next two years, the Dutch acquired much of the eastern half of present-day Brooklyn. They purchased the land from the Indians for what amounted to throwaway trinkets and everyday household items — duffel bags, knives, axes, awls, kettles and other cooking appliances. And they did not stop there. The increased demands for homesteads for new immigrants from the Netherlands pushed authorities to seek even more land, and as the decade of the 1630s ended, the Dutch had bought most of the land in present-day Queens County.

By the spring of 1639, as Dutch farmers began to plant their crops in western Long Island, there were only three other Europeans living to their east — an Englishman named Lion Gardiner, who had just moved onto the island that now bears his name, his Dutch-born wife, and their daughter, Elizabeth. As small as it was, their grand island-manor north of East Hampton was the first English colony on Long Island. Far to the west, separated by a wilderness of forests and streams, the Dutch were not bothered by the Gardiner family. They could sit contentedly on Manhattan Island, and on western Long Island, and think everything around them would soon be theirs.

In 1640, as other Englishmen and their families began to move in small groups to the eastern end of Long Island, the Dutch continued to buy up the west end. Large purchases in the southern part of Brooklyn by homesteaders secured Gravesend for the Dutch. They now had the land that overlooked the narrows at the mouth of the harbor.

By the spring of that year, large tobacco plantations were thriving near Gravesend and along the wooded fringes of the East River. Also that spring, in an act as final as an execution, a Delaware-speaking Algonquian the Dutch called Penhawitz signed away rights to a huge expanse near the center of Brooklyn — and thereafter became a refugee on his own land.

There were political reasons for the Dutch's aggressive land purchases, which displaced hundreds of Indians.

"In addition to finding pasture land, the Dutch needed to push settlements into Long Island as a counterbalance to the growing English presence on the East End," Gehring said. "The Dutch could not allow the English to take it all, so they knew they had to claim as much of the west end of the island as they could. But the Dutch also knew they couldn't stop the English from setting up villages on the East End, so the island essentially became both Dutch and English at the same time."

Six years later, as the Dutch population of western Long Island continued to grow, the director-general of the New Netherlands province, Willem Kieft, incorporated the area as Breuckelen, after the city of the same name in the old country.

Brooklyn was born.

Additional settlements followed, including a village called New Utrecht, which was just north of the entrance to New York Harbor. Dutch documents from the period say the first land owner in New Utrecht was a man named Cornelius Van Werckhoven, who divided the community into 50-acre lots. One of the first residents to live there, according to the documents, was a man named Jacob Swart, who was a carpenter. Swart built the first houses in New Utrecht.

"It's hard to imagine it today, but where these settlements were was very remote, a long way from other Dutch communities," Gehring said. "They were used to very close-together communities back in the Netherlands, back-to-back farmland. Here, it was just the opposite. Of course, this made the settlements very vulnerable during times of unrest with the Indians."

Unrest and bloodshed were to come.

Nassau County Museum Collection, Long Island Studies Institute

A detail from a 1666 map entitled "A plotte off ye situation of ye towns and places on ye west end of Long Island to Hempstead bounds." The map shows some early Dutch communities in Brooklyn, including Gravesend, Coney Island and Flatlands. A note in the upper left says the map was hand-copied "from original in State Library" in 1883.

LEGACY

POTATOES, DUCKS, CLAMS — AND TOBACCO

Before potatoes, there was tobacco.

When Dutch settlers arrived on western Long Island in the mid-1650s, they found the Indians had cleared huge areas for their own farming. One of their crops was tobacco, which years earlier the English had learned to grow in Virginia.

Early Dutch records for New York show that Long Island tobacco was highly prized. One account, written in 1654, says that tobacco was packed in "hogsheads," or barrels, and shipped to Europe for sale.

This account states:

. . . The planters must be informed that much depends on their cultivating and curing of the tobacco, for it is considered much stronger and pleasanter when it is pruned in time, during its growth; and if after drying it has a good yellow color, it has been found to be valued much higher here, bringing one half as much more than the Virginia tobacco . . . if well taken to heart, it may make the commonwealth and its inhabitants flourishing and wealthy.

Could it make Long Islanders wealthy today? Difficult to say. While being overwhelmingly a southern crop, tobacco is grown today in Pennsylvania and Connecticut. And as recently as 40 years ago, some farmers on the East End grew tobacco for personal use.

"My father and grandfather grew tobacco," said Joe Gergela, of the Long Island Farm Bureau. Both of their farms were in Riverhead. "But it would not be economical today because Long Island growers would be so small and they couldn't compete with the huge tobacco farms in the South. But it'll grow here, no question about that."

— **Steve Wick**

Baltimore Sun Photo / Jed Kirschbaum

Influences of the Netherlands live on centuries later in roads, buildings and names

Dutch Settlers Left Their Mark

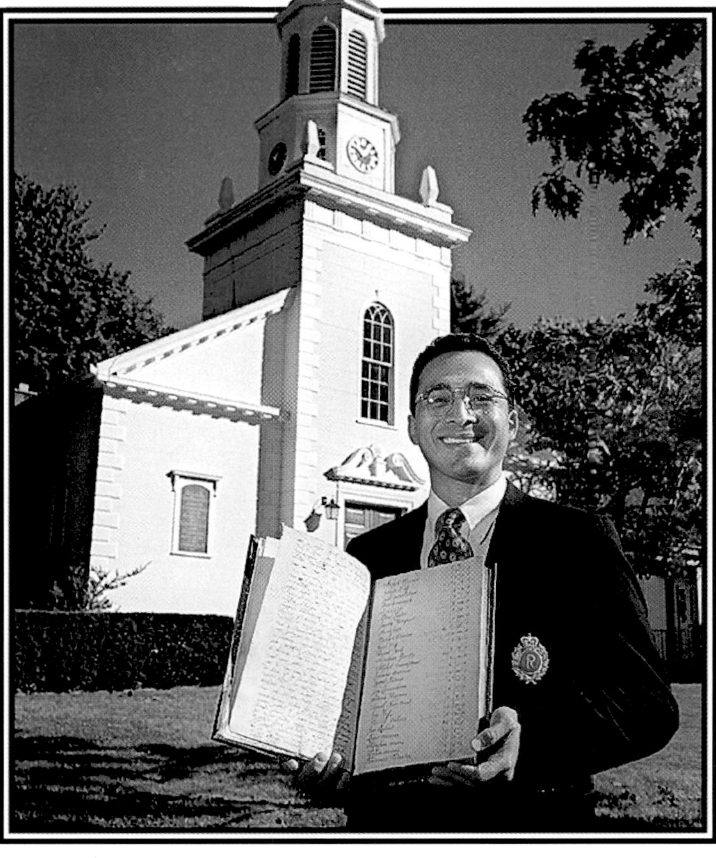

Pastor Allan B. Ramirez at the Brookville Reformed Church with Dutch-language church records from 1732-1788. The original church was built in 1734. The current building, the third on the site, went up in 1924-25.

Newsday Photo / Bill Davis

BY STEVE WICK
STAFF WRITER

In late September, the members of the Brookville Reformed Church gathered to celebrate the church's anniversary and to dig deep into the congregation's past.

Inside a safe were the original records of the church, founded in 1732, and written in a language once heard all over western Long Island — Dutch. "We have had the records in the church since it was founded," said the Rev. Allan Ramirez, the church's pastor.

The records tell the story of a small group of Dutch families that settled in a place that no longer exists on any map — Wolver Hollow. *Wolver*, in Dutch, means wolves. The group included families who had come from the Netherlands to establish farms in Oyster Bay, and in 1732 about dozen met in the farmhouse of Jurian Haff to form a church they called the "Protestant-Dutch Congregation of Oyster Bay in Queens County."

Two years later, the group had raised enough money to build a church, which stands today on Brookville Road. The church is both a monument to the people who founded it as well as a legacy to the Dutch, who governed their colony at New Netherlands for only a half-century before being evicted by the English for the last time in 1674.

Despite their short tenure, the Dutch left a deep imprint on the region they called New Netherlands — western Long Island, Manhattan Island and the Hudson River Valley north to Albany. They settled five towns on Long Island — Brooklyn, New Ultrecht, Flatlands, Flatbush and Bushwick, which had a total population of less than 1,000 when the English seized New Netherlands and renamed it New York.

The Dutch legacy has lingered for generations — in old houses, like the Wyckoff House in Brooklyn and the Jan Schenck house on display at the Brooklyn Museum; in street names; in churches and cemeteries; in a trove of documents written in Dutch, and in the language itself, spoken well into the 19th Century in parts of Brooklyn, along the Hudson River, and even in Oyster Bay.

"Our records show that Dutch was spoken well into the 1800s and the church records were written in Dutch until nearly the time of the Civil War," Ramirez said. "I don't think most people would think that Dutch was spoken in Oyster Bay that late."

Street and place names serve as reminders of Dutch history. In the Bronx, a golf course and park are named after a prominent 17th Century Dutch family — Van Cortlandt. In Brooklyn, Coney Island comes from the Dutch word *Conijn*, or Rabbit Island. Just north of Coney Island is a street named New Utrecht Avenue. In Williamsburg, a street is named Wallabout Avenue, which was the name the Dutch gave the water between Long Island and Manhattan Island. In Queens, there's Vanderveer Street and the Van Wyck Expressway, named after prominent 17th Century Dutch families.

One place name on Long Island has its roots in the Dutch language — Robins Island in Southold, which translates to Seal Island. And another, Fire Island, may have Dutch roots. The number four in Dutch is *vier*, which is pronounced fear but is often confused with the word fire, which in Dutch is *vuur*.

An excellent example of Dutch architecture is the Pieter Claesen Wyckoff House Museum, on Clarendon Road and Ralph Avenue, in Brooklyn.

Peter Claesen was 12 years old when he arrived in New Netherlands in April, 1637. He worked as a servant on a farm near Albany before moving to a plantation on Long Island where he raised tobacco. The house that Claesen — who later changed his name to Peter Claesen Wyckoff — is operated as a historic home by the New York City Department of Parks and Recreation.

A Dutch-era home is on display at the Brooklyn Museum. It is the Jan Schenck house, built around 1675, a year after the English took over. Schenck, who was born in the Netherlands, built the house in the area the Dutch called Flatlands, along the western edge of Jamaica Bay.

It is clear that, even when the English ruled, that Dutch influences stayed.

"A number of historians believed that the English very quickly changed everything, removing all the Dutch influences," said Eric Nooter, a Dutch-born historian who teaches in New York. "But that is wrong. The Dutch language could be heard on Long Island until the time of the Revolution. Meetings were conducted in Dutch; some church services were in Dutch, and many of the residents were bilingual, speaking English and Dutch."

The bound volumes that contain the history of the Brookville Reformed Church, as it is called today, show that Dutch was the official language until well into the 19th Century. "The volumes include financial records, births, deaths, all matter of church business," said Ramirez. He said a church member in the early 20th Century translated the records into English; recently, the original records were put on microfiche for safekeeping.

In Albany, Charles Gehring is custodian of a trove of Dutch documents that date to the New Netherlands period. Gehring oversees the New Netherlands Project, which seeks to preserve and translate these records while looking for undiscovered documents in New York and the Netherlands.

"The Dutch legacy lingered in many ways for a lot longer than most people have assumed," he said.

LEGACY

ARCHITECTURAL TREASURES

The **Wyckoff House Museum** at Clarendon Road and Ralph Avenue in Brooklyn, at right, is a legacy from Dutch occupation of New York. It is open weekdays by appointment; $2 for adults, senior citizens and children $1. Group tours can be arranged. Call 718-629-5400.

•

The flared eaves of a Dutch house also are seen in the **Minne Schenck house**, lower right. Built around 1723-30 in Manhasset, it now can be seen at the Old Bethpage Village Restoration. The village is open Wednesday-Sunday, late May through December; closed January-February and some holidays. Fee: $5; $3 ages 5-12 and over 60 (some events more); 516-572-8400.

THE DUTCH TRADITION AT HOFSTRA UNIVERSITY

There may be nothing on Long Island more Dutch than Hofstra University.

According to the university's archives, the school's seal is the coat of arms of the royal house of the Netherlands; the school flag is based on a flag planted in New Netherlands by Dutch settlers; the school's athletic teams are the Flying Dutchmen and Flying Dutchwomen; a dormitory complex is named the Netherlands, and the school's commencement ceremonies traditionally begin with greetings in Dutch.

In 1985, in honor of Hofstra's 50th anniversary, the Dutch government named a white hybrid tulip the Hofstra University tulip. It is the first tulip named for an American university.

The university is named after William S. Hofstra, who traced his roots to the Dutch province of Friesland. Hofstra was president of the Nassau Lumber Co. in Hicksville and Hempstead and was well-known for his charitable endeavors. He built an estate-style house in Hempstead in 1904, which he called The Netherlands. After his death in 1932, his widow stipulated in her will that the estate be used for a public purpose. Hofstra College was started in 1935.

— Steve Wick

Newsday Photos / Audrey C. Tiernan (Wyckoff), and Bill Davis

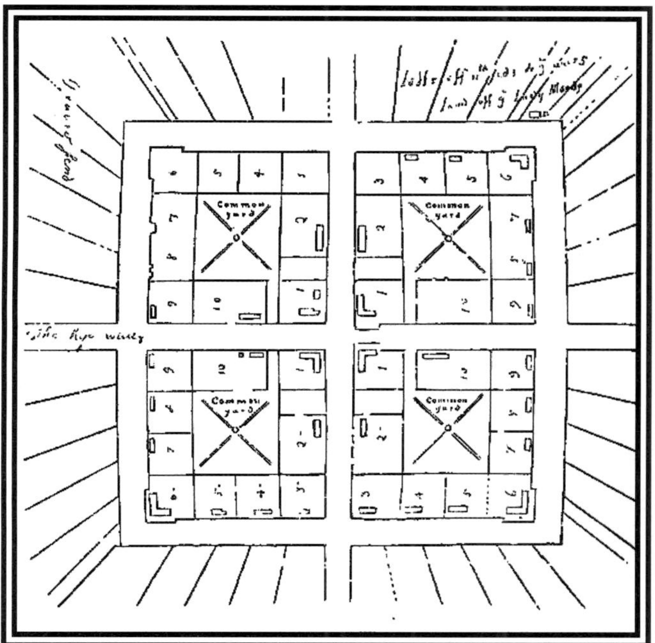

Newsday Photo / Ken Sawchuck

Both a 1645 plot map and a current aerial photo show the four-square-block area of Gravesend, Brooklyn, established by Lady Deborah Moody.

Religious dissenter Lady Deborah Moody set a precedent when she founded Gravesend

A 'Dangerous' 1600s Woman

BY GEORGE DEWAN
STAFF WRITER

Nobody knows where Lady Deborah Moody is buried, but an appropriate epitaph would have been what one official wrote about her in 1644: "Shee is a dangerous woeman."

Dangerous to the religious establishment she certainly was. This widowed, middle-aged English immigrant also was a most remarkable Long Island woman of the 17th Century. Moody was the founder of Gravesend, the only permanent settlement in early colonial America planned and directed by a woman.

"It was in a man's age that Lady Moody played a part which entitles her to a place among the leaders of that day," State Historian Alexander Flick told a meeting of the Long Island Historical Society in 1939.

The town patent granted to her by the Dutch in 1645 was unusual in that it gave Moody and her colleagues absolute freedom of conscience. Although the Dutch West India Co. had ordered that no church other than the Dutch Reformed was allowed in the entire colony of New Netherlands — making it unlawful to worship publicly in any other religion — Gravesenders would not be prosecuted for worshiping in any faith in their own homes.

For Moody, who was in her late 50s at the time, this was the moment that she had crossed the seas to achieve. But her success had been full of sacrifice and her journey long.

Moody was christened Deborah Dunch in London in 1586. She came from a wealthy family with both political and religious connections, but also one that believed strongly in civil liberties and religious non-conformity. She married Henry Moody, a well-connected landholder who was later given a knighthood, and thus she became Dame Deborah, or Lady Deborah. Her husband died in 1629, when she was about 33.

These were days of great religious turmoil in England, and Moody was attracted to Anabaptism, a Protestant sect that rejected infant baptism in the belief that baptism should be administered only to adult believers. Unable to live in the oppressive religious climate in England, she sailed for the Massachusetts Bay Colony in 1639.

Moody found the Puritan New England community just as oppressive, for her Anabaptist views were, to them, a "damnable heresy." In July, 1643, the governor, John Winthrop, wrote in his journal:

The lady Moodye, a wise and anciently religious woman, being taken with the error of denying baptism to infants, was dealt withal by many of the elders and others, and admonished by the Church of Salem (whereof she was a member), but persisting still, and to avoid further trouble, etc., she removed to the Dutch against the advice of her friends. Many others, infected with anabaptism, removed thither also. She was after excommunicated.

Somewhat surprisingly, given the equal rigidity of the Dutch Reformed Church in New Amsterdam, the director general, William Kieft, allowed Moody to settle on choice unoccupied land in what is now southern Brooklyn. There is disagreement on the origin of the town's name: some think that Kieft named it for his birthplace in Holland, Gravenzande, but others feel it comes from the English town of the same name at the mouth of the Thames River.

No sooner had the settlers moved into newly built quarters in Gravesend than they were attacked by Indians from up the Hudson River. Although the Indians were repelled, the group, which included at least 40 men, moved temporarily to Amersfoort (now Flatlands). At that point Moody considered returning to New England. Which led John Endecott, Winthrop's deputy, to write to his superior:

I shall desire that she may not have advice to returne to this jurisdiction, unless she will acknowledge her ewill [evil] in opposing the churches, and leave her opinions behinde her, ffor shee is a dangerous woeman.

Moody returned to Gravesend in 1645, and on Dec. 19, a patent was granted by Kieft that is memorable for the freedoms it allowed. In addition to allowing freedom of conscience, the patent also granted the right to create a self-governing town. With Moody supervising, a unique town plan was laid out.

"Gravesend was the only permanent settlement in America's early colonization period to have been initiated, planned, and directed by a woman," wrote Thomas J. Campanella in the fall, 1993, Landscape Journal. "In its elegant and logical simplicity, the plan of Gravesend was almost without precedent in the English New World."

The inhabited part of the town consisted of four squares of a little more than four acres each, with two main roadways bisecting north-south and east-west (today's McDonald Avenue and Gravesend Neck Road). Each of the four sections had 10 house lots surrounding a one-acre commons. Outside of the village itself were the individual, triangular pieces of 100-acre farms, called boweries, radiating out from the center like spokes from a wheel.

In 1652 war broke out across the Atlantic Ocean between the English and the Dutch. The result was increased tension in New Netherlands between the Dutch rulers and the English towns in western Long Island. That was aggravated in 1657, when the first Quakers came to New Netherlands, a move that infuriated the new director general, Peter Stuyvesant. In one of her last acts of dissension, Moody invited them to Gravesend, and the first Quaker meeting in the colonies was held in her house that year.

Seven years later, the entire Dutch colony would come under English rule, but Lady Moody would not live to see it. She died about 1659, at age 73. It was a quiet ending for the life of a woman whom the historian Flick called "The Grand Dame of Gravesend."

ANNE HUTCHINSON

There was another, better-known English-born religious dissenter in Massachusetts Bay Colony, one whose life paralled that of Deborah Moody. Her name was Anne Hutchinson.

In the summer of 1643, just about the time that Moody arrived in New Amsterdam, the widowed Hutchinson, 52, and all but one of her six children were murdered by Indians at a new colony at Pelham Bay. A 10-year-old daughter, Susanna, was captured and later ransomed from the Indians by the Dutch.

Although Bay Colony Gov. John Winthrop seemed to like Moody, he appeared to despise Hutchinson, whom he once called the "American Jesabel," from the biblical heretic Jezebel. Hutchinson was banished from the colony in 1638 for her antinomianism, the belief that the individual could experience God's grace directly, without a need for a church or a religion.

One reason we remember her today is that the Hutchinson River Parkway in Westchester County is named for Anne Hutchinson. — George DeWan

Violence escalates as a Dutch craftsman is murdered and Indians are massacred

Blood Flows, War Threatens

BY STEVE WICK
STAFF WRITER

By the winter of 1643, relations between the Dutch and their Indian neighbors had gone bad. Suddenly, there were killings on both sides and calls for war.

Several months earlier, the Dutch living on Manhattan Island went into panic when reports reached them that an elderly wheelwright, who lived on a farm north of their settlement in modern-day Westchester County, had been murdered by an Indian. Dutch records said the Indian "pretending a desire to buy something and whilst the old man was taking from the chest the cloth the Indian wanted, took up an ax and cut his head off . . ."

Soon, reports filtered up and down the Hudson River of attacks on Dutch settlements by Indians, and rumors of war spread quickly to the remote farming settlements on Long Island.

Willem Kieft, the Dutch official in charge at New Amsterdam, demanded that the Indians living near where the murder took place hand over the killer. They refused. Kieft was told the Indian who killed the old man "had only avenged the death of his Uncle, who had been slain over one and twenty years by the Dutch," according to the records.

Meeting with an official council called the Twelve Men, Kieft decided on war if the murderer was not soon in Dutch custody. Specifically, Kieft decided that an attack on the Indian villages should come when the men were off hunting.

"Thereupon, spies looked up the Indians who lay in their Village suspecting nothing, and eighty men were detailed under the command of Ensign Hendrick Van Dyck and sent thither," Dutch records say. But the guide leading the troops got lost in the darkness and could not find the village, and the men turned back.

Several weeks later, large groups of Indians from the north began to move south toward New Amsterdam, most likely to attack traditional Indian enemies in the south and to collect wampum. From the Dutch point of view, the Indians' purpose was to foment war against both the Dutch and the English along the southern New England coastline and the East End of Long Island. Kieft also claimed the Indians wanted to poison him. As with so much of Indian history in New York, it is not known today what motivated them. Their point of view does not exist in New York's recorded history.

The movement south of the northern Indians caused Indian groups near Manhattan Island to seek the protection of the Dutch. But Kieft was not in a charitable frame of mind. These may have been refugees, but they also were Indians. The Twelve Men met and presented Kieft with a plan to attack the refugee Indians across the Hudson River in modern-day New Jersey. The "design" — as the attack plan was called — was executed the same night as the meeting, Feb. 25, 1643, with Dutch soldiers attacking an encampment less than a mile from New Amsterdam. Eighty Indians were killed and 30 taken prisoner.

Of the attack by the Dutch, a book titled "A History of the City of Brooklyn," published in 1867, said the Indians were "remorselessly butchered . . . The story of that night is one of the saddest and foulest upon the pages of New Netherland's history." A Dutch account published in the mid-17th Century said ". . . young children were cut in pieces before the eyes of their parents, and the pieces were thrown into the fire or into the water; other babes were bound on planks and then cut through, stabbed and miserably massacred, so that it would break a heart of stone . . ."

This slaughter by the Dutch seems to have inspired other attacks. The Dutch living at the western end of Long Island asked for permission to attack their Indian neighbors. Kieft refused, fearing they might be "hard to conquer," according to the records.

But attacks on Long Island did occur, and panicked Dutch farmers on Long Island fled west, toward the protective shelter of New Amsterdam. To quell unrest, the Dutch invited a group of Long Island Indians to travel to New Amsterdam to conduct a peace treaty. The Indians paddled to New Amsterdam in their great dugout canoes and agreed to end hostilities.

It was not to last more than a few months.

Stock Montage Inc.

English religious dissenter Anne Hutchinson and five of her children, who had been living at the Pelham Bay area of the present-day Bronx, were killed by Indians during Indian-Dutch fighting in 1643. The above drawing was published in an 1880 book entitled "A Popular History of the USA."

A Martyred Missionary's Eyewitness Account

BY STEVE WICK
STAFF WRITER

The Rev. Isaac Jogues, a Jesuit priest from France, was murdered by Indians in 1646. He was the first Catholic missionary to work in what is now New York State, and he was the first to be martyred.

Before he was killed, Jogues wrote a brief account of his capture by upstate Indians, his release to Dutch authorities in New Amsterdam, where between August, 1642, and November, 1643, he witnessed the atrocities of the Dutch-Indian wars.

In 1642, six years after his arrival in Canada, he was captured by Mohawks somewhere in northern New York. A year later, he escaped and fled to Albany, where Dutch authorities put him on a boat and sent him downriver to New Amsterdam. There, he was put on a boat to France.

His keen eye during the 10 months he lived at New Amsterdam before sailing home to France provide readers today with an extraordinary look at a troubled time and place. He begins by describing the layout of the Dutch fort at New Amsterdam, saying there were 400 people living on the island "of different sects and nations," who spoke "eighteen different languages." They were Calvinists, Catholics, English Puritans, Lutherans and Anabaptists.

Of the bloodshed that spilled across the Lower Hudson River Valley and into western Long Island, Jogues wrote:

Some nations near the sea having murdered some Hollanders of the most distant settlement, the Hollanders killed 150 Indians, men, woman and children . . . And in the beginning of winter the grass being low and some snow on the ground they pursued them with six hundred men, keeping two hundred always on the move and constantly relieving each other, so that the Indians, pent up in a large island and finding it impossible to escape, on account of women and children, were cut to pieces to the number of sixteen hundred, woman and children included. This obliged the rest of the Indians to make peace, which still continues. This occurred in 1643 and 1644.

In 1646, Jogues was back in Montreal. In the fall of that year, he was working as a missionary in Mohawk country, near Lake George, where he had earlier lived as a captive. There, according to one account, the Indians blamed Jogues for the failure of their crops, and they killed him with an ax. Jogues' life and death are still remembered today in many Catholic schools. He was canonized in 1930.

LI HISTORY.COM

Museum of the City of New York

The Rev. Isaac Jogues

A description of New Amsterdam written by the Rev. Isaac Jogues two years before his death in 1646 is available on the Internet at http://www.lihistory.com.

Englishman John Underhill led the slaughter of Indians in defense of European settlers

A Man Hated and Hailed

BY STEVE WICK
STAFF WRITER

For a few months after the Dutch summoned Indian leaders from Long Island to their fort at New Amsterdam, there was peace across the region. But by the fall of 1643, the killing had begun anew.

As panicky settlers across western Long Island fled to the fort at New Amsterdam, Gov. Willem Kieft and his advisers reached out for help from the English community in Connecticut. While offering no troops, the English allowed for the raising of a small army of English mercenaries.

Enter John Underhill, a man with a reputation.

In Long Island history, there is no one like Underhill. He sailed from England to the Plymouth Colony in Massachussets in the early 1630s. By written accounts, he was no Puritan. He did not like being told how to live his life by church leaders.

Newsday Photo / Bill Davis

A plaque placed at the Underhill monument in Mill Neck shows Capt. John Underhill reading to Indians. His book says "Love One Another."

But he was useful when it came to fighting. When the English made war against the Pequots in Connecticut in 1637, Underhill helped lead the murderous assault against the Indians' log fort near present-day Mystic. By his own account, he and his men killed more than 1,000 Pequots — men, women and children — and put the torch to their fort and wigwams. As a people, the Pequots all but disappeared from the landscape after Underhill was through with them.

As the Dutch huddled behind pallisaded walls on Manhattan Island through the winter of 1643-44, Indian attacks along the fringes of their settlement picked up. In response, Dutch troops attacked Indian villages on Staten Island and in Westchester County.

Soon, Underhill, leading the army of mercenaries, arrived at New Amsterdam. Long Island historians of the 19th Century often wrote flattering lines about him, calling him a heroic Indian fighter who "saved" Europeans from extinction. But there is a markedly different view supported by the evidence.

"Underhill changed the history of Long Island, and southern New England," said John Strong, a professor at the Southampton Campus of Long Island University. "Before Underhill, the Indians on Long Island could think they could share the land with Europeans. After the Pequot War, and after other slaughters he participated in, that changed."

Underhill's claim to a bloody piece of Long Island history began in April, 1644. Dutch records of the day say that "seven savages" were arrested at Hempstead, an English village within the Dutch sphere of influence, on charges of killing pigs "though it was afterwards discovered that some Englishmen had done it themselves."

Hearing of the arrests, the Dutch governor in New Amsterdam, Kieft, sent Underhill and 15 or 16 soldiers, who promptly killed three of the seven Indians. "They then took the other four with them in the sailing boat, two of whom were towed along by a string around their necks till they were drowned, while the two unfortunate survivors were detained as prisoners at fort Amsterdam," according to a Dutch account written at the time. The report went on:

When they had kept them a long time . . . the director (Kieft) became tired of giving them food any longer and they were delivered to the soldiers to do as they pleased with.

The prisoners were immediately dragged out of the guard house and soon dispatched with knives of from 18 to 20 inches, which director Kieft had made for his soldiers for such purposes . . . that these knives were much handier for bowelling them. The first of these savages having received a frightful wound . . . dropped down dead. The soldiers then cut strips from the other's body . . . Kieft . . . stood laughing heartily at the fun.

The bloodbath on Long Island escalated when Underhill and his troops attacked a peaceful community of Indians, apparently at a site in modern-day Massapequa. When the shooting stopped, Underhill's troops had killed 120 Indians — the first and last Indian "battle" on Long Island.

Although this incident is well-documented in colonial records, the exact location of the massacre has been debated among historians for years. Some said the massacre occurred in present-day Queens; Strong and others, including famed archeologist Ralph Solecki, say the evidence strongly suggests it occurred at a site in Massapequa called Fort Neck. Confirmation would appear to have come in 1935, Strong has written, when the bones of 24 people were dug up during an excavation at the site.

In the late 19th Century, an Oyster Bay historian named Samuel Jones wrote this account:

After the battle of Ft. Neck, the weather being very cold and the wind northwest, Capt. Underhill and his men collected the bodies of the Indians and threw them in a heap on the brow of the hill, and then sat down on the leeward side of the heap to eat their breakfast. When this part of the county came to be settled, the highway across the neck passed directly over the spot where, it was said, the heap of Indians lay, and the earth in that spot was remarkably different from the ground about it, being strongly tinged with a reddish cast, which the old people said was occasioned by the blood of the Indians.

A historical marker noting the site of the slaughter stood on the corner of Merrick Road and Cedar Shore Road. It was evidently stolen in the early 1990s and never replaced.

Next, Underhill turned his attention to an Indian village in Westchester County. There, as he had in Mystic, he attacked Indians assembled in a fort, shot them and torched their wigwams. More than 180 Indians were killed.

Later, Underhill bought an estate in Oyster Bay called Killingworth, where he died in 1672. A marker on Factory Pond Road and Locust Valley-Bayville Road, in Lattingtown, notes the location of Killingworth. The marker describes Underhill as a "distinquished military officer, statesman and pioneer."

A huge obelisk to Underhill's memory was erected in 1907 by the Underhill Society of America, a genealogical group, on Factory Pond Road, in Mill Neck. It features four plaques on its base showing Underhill reading to a group of Indians who are kneeling worshipfully at his feet. On the cover of the book are the words, "Love One Another."

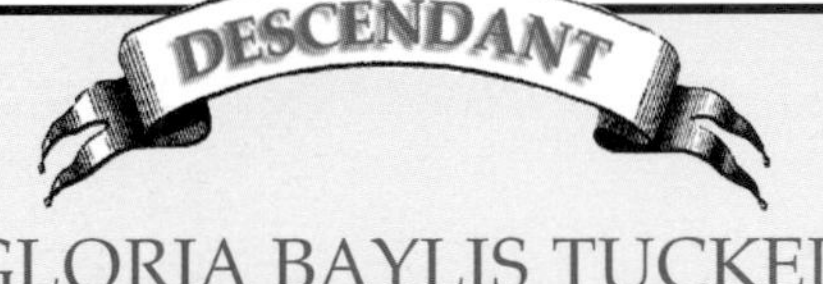

GLORIA BAYLIS TUCKER

Newsday Photo / K. Wiles Stabile

Gloria Baylis Tucker of the Underhill Society in front of the Underhill monument in Mill Neck.

Gloria Baylis Tucker may not have Underhill in her name, but her connection to Long Island's famed Indian fighter is secure.

It goes beyond being a 10th-generation direct descendant of Capt. John Underhill. She also lives on Underhill Place in Oyster Bay on property once owned by Underhill. She's president of the Underhill Burying Ground, the Mill Neck site where Captain John and hundreds of other Underhills are interred.

"I am a direct descendant by his second wife, Elizabeth Feake," says Tucker, who is "closing in on 80." Tucker's mother's mother was an Underhill.

Tucker joins close to 500 other descendants as a member of the Oyster Bay-based Underhill Society, which documents the family's history.

Tucker says the Underhills have seen the reputation of their ancestor shift over the years. Sometimes he's been hailed as the savior of the white settlers; other times he's been denounced as a barbarian. "I think he was a good man," Tucker says, citing the fact he had been named a captain in Massachusetts and in Connecticut as evidence of his military skills.

"It was unfortunate," she says of the Indians killed, "but he wasn't the only one . . . He was just doing a job." **— Bill Bleyer**

The tale of Smithtown's borders may be apocryphal, but it makes for a good story

The Legend Of the Bull

BY MOLLY MCCARTHY
STAFF WRITER

Sure, Paul Bunyan was a big guy. And Johnny Appleseed had a green thumb. But they've got nothing on Richard (Bull) Smith, the legendary founder of Smithtown.

After years of embellishing, Smith's tale has fermented into the tallest of them all. "I think it's a perfectly wonderful legend. I don't think there's another town in the United States that could match it, and we should keep it," said Louise Hall, the director of the Smithtown Historical Society. Here's how the legend shapes up today, more than 300 years later.

As the story goes, the Indians made a pact with Smith, an English settler who knew a good real-estate deal when he saw one: He could keep whatever land he circled in a day's time riding atop his trusty bull named "Whisper."

A clever man, Smith waited for the longest day of the year, circa 1665, to undertake the trek. He even trotted out one of Whisper's favorite cows the night before to trace the route. Her fetching scent would surely quicken Whisper's pace and get Smith to the end of the 55-mile border in time. He would start at the east end of what is now Smithtown, go south to Raconcamuck, now known as Ronkonkoma, then west to Hauppauge and north along what is today Veterans Highway and on to Town Line Road, which marks the town's western border, and finally north to the edge of Long Island Sound.

At noon, he — and the bull — rested. Smith munched on bread and cheese in a hollow, inspiring the name Bread and Cheese Hollow Road. Naturally, Smith got 'round, and Smithtown was his.

That's the legend. Now here's what historians say really happened. Before Smith ever thought of founding a town in his name, he came to Southampton.

Actually, Smith first got off the boat, the John of London, from England at the Massachusetts Bay Colony in 1635. Because land there was already scarce and the Puritans extremely severe, he soon made his way to Long Island.

The first mention of Smith, then spelled Smythe, in the Southampton town records was in 1643. Soon after his arrival, Smith befriended Lion Gardiner, the first lord of the manor of Gardiners Island, and quickly rose into the fledgling settlement's highest social circles.

Along the way, Smith must have tweaked a nose or two. In 1656, he was banished from Southampton for insulting the wrong people. The order is reprinted in Noel Gish's book, "Smithtown, New York: 1660-1929." It reads:

It is ordered by the general court that Richard Smythe for his Irreverent carriage towards the magistrates contrary to the order was adjudged to be banished out of the towne and he is to have a weeks liberty to prepare himself to depart, and if at any time he be found after this limited week within the towne or the bounds thereof he shall forfeit twenty shillings.

In Robert Gaston's 1939 mural, Richard Smith rides his bull around a giant area to set borders for Smithtown. "You hear it so often, you begin to believe it," Supervisor Pat Vecchio says of the tale.

Smithtown didn't come into play yet. Smith's next stop was Setauket, where in 1657 he set up house with his wife, Sarah, and their nine children.

Other forces were at work. The great Indian sachem Wyandanch gave Lion Gardiner a gift of land for rescuing his daughter, the Heather Flower, from a hostile tribe. Gardiner signed over the land that would become Smithtown to Smith in 1663. Smith either bought it or won it in a card game, depending on who's telling the story.

But the true tale doesn't end there. It took Smith a dozen more years of court battles to ensure that Smithtown was really his. When the English court didn't give him what he wanted, he tried the Dutch. And when the Dutch lost New York, he went back to the English. It went on and on. Finally, the last bits of Smithtown were declared his in the Andros Patent of 1677. Sounds like Smith was more of a bull than Whisper was.

"If you think about the fact that he got to two colonial governors with his boundary dispute, I think he was a very educated and determined man. He was absolutely determined to secure this land," said Hall. "I wouldn't call him pushy, that's too modern a word."

Though it's likely Smith's demeanor may have had something to do with inspiring the "Bull" myth, historians have come up with several theories. One is that Smith had a pet bull he liked to walk around town. Others point to Smith's coat of arms: A bull rising out of a shield decorated with six fleur-de-lis symbols.

Then there's Gish's theory, an interesting take on papal bulls. Apparently, papal bulls, decrees issued to settle matters of church and state, were very popular during the 17th Century. Papal bulls were sometimes used to resolve boundary disputes between dioceses or parishes. Gish argues that Smith could have issued his own "Smith Bull" to solve, once and for all, his boundary disputes with the Dutch, the English and the neighboring town of Huntington.

Of course, many people, especially Smithtown residents, dismiss these theories in favor of the fanciful fiction. It may be full of bull, but it's Smithtown's bull.

"When I first heard it, I thought it was somewhat farfetched, but it was a lovely story," said Smithtown Supervisor Pat Vecchio. "As the years go by, it seems less farfetched to me. You hear it so often, you begin to believe it."

Asked almost weekly about the legend, Hall has developed her own strategy for handling the ultimate question of authenticity. "I show them the map done for the town's bicentennial. We talk about whether there were Indian trails along the route and how the bull could have covered that much territory if it was covered in underbrush. Then I let them decide."

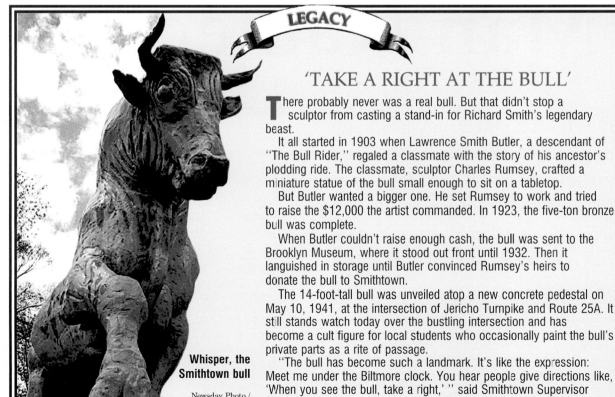

LEGACY

'TAKE A RIGHT AT THE BULL'

Whisper, the Smithtown bull

Newsday Photo / Bill Davis

There probably never was a real bull. But that didn't stop a sculptor from casting a stand-in for Richard Smith's legendary beast.

It all started in 1903 when Lawrence Smith Butler, a descendant of "The Bull Rider," regaled a classmate with the story of his ancestor's plodding ride. The classmate, sculptor Charles Rumsey, crafted a miniature statue of the bull small enough to sit on a tabletop.

But Butler wanted a bigger one. He set Rumsey to work and tried to raise the $12,000 the artist commanded. In 1923, the five-ton bronze bull was complete.

When Butler couldn't raise enough cash, the bull was sent to the Brooklyn Museum, where it stood out front until 1932. Then it languished in storage until Butler convinced Rumsey's heirs to donate the bull to Smithtown.

The 14-foot-tall bull was unveiled atop a new concrete pedestal on May 10, 1941, at the intersection of Jericho Turnpike and Route 25A. It still stands watch today over the bustling intersection and has become a cult figure for local students who occasionally paint the bull's private parts as a rite of passage.

"The bull has become such a landmark. It's like the expression: Meet me under the Biltmore clock. You hear people give directions like, 'When you see the bull, take a right,' " said Smithtown Supervisor Pat Vecchio.

— Molly McCarthy

Newsday Photo / Bill Davis

Englishman Lion Gardiner, center, fights Pequots at Old Saybrook, Conn., in 1637. The painting by C.S. Reinhart, done in 1877, is on display at the Gardiner family home on Gardiners Island.

A English builder fights Indians at a Connecticut fort, then turns his eyes to Long Island

A Man Named Lion

BY STEVE WICK
STAFF WRITER

'In the year 1635, I, Lion Gardiner, Engineer and Master of works of Fortification . . .''

So begins the account written by an Englishman named Lion Gardiner of his extraordinary life. His story opens in the Netherlands, where he served in the English army, moves to the Connecticut frontier, where he witnessed a bloody war of extermination against the Pequot Indians, and ends in East Hampton, where his family and his legend still live.

Born in England in 1599, Gardiner was an adventurer at an early age. His exact birthplace is not known, nor who his parents were. A laudatory description of Gardiner, published in 1885, gushed, ''He was . . . of fine military presence, well proportioned although slightly under the average height, with quiet face, eyes keen, intelligent and deep-set, and the manners and bearing of a gentleman.''

His recorded history begins in his early 30s, when he served in the English army in the Netherlands. There, in a protracted war between Protestants and Catholics, Gardiner earned a reputation as a ''master of works of fortifications'' — a fort builder.

His fame spread across the ocean, and in 1635 he was summoned by the backers of a fledgling English colony in what would become Connecticut. The tiny colony was in a precarious position — Dutch traders from New Amsterdam had begun to make inroads into the area, trading from their boats with the local Indians and constructing permanent outposts. By doing so, the Dutch hoped to keep the English from expanding south from the Massachusetts Bay Colony.

But the Dutch were the least of the colony's problems. Of even more immediate concern were the Pequots, a group with a fearsome reputation who lived along the same stretch of coastline where the English hoped to build settlements. Records of the day show the English feared and despised the Pequots, as did other Indian groups such as the Mohegans, who lived in the same territory.

Gardiner was 36 years old the year he and his Dutch-born wife, Mary, sailed to Massachusetts aboard the Bachelor, arriving in November after a stormy 3½-month voyage. The couple spent the winter in Massachusetts, and by April, 1636, they were living with a small group of colonists near the mouth of the Connecticut River. They were well south of the English settlements in an area largely untracked by white men.

Gardiner supervised the construction of a fort near the mouth of the Connecticut River, and commanded it while farms and homesites were carved out of the surrounding wilderness. As the fort was being built, two momentous events happened in his life — his wife gave birth to their son, David, the first white child born in what is now the state of Connecticut, and a war broke out with the Pequots that would forever change the fort-builder's life.

The event that historians call the Pequot War began with small-scale confrontations between Indians and Englishmen in the area of the fort and up and down the coastline. Distrust built, there were deaths on both sides, and officials of the Massachusetts Bay Colony decided to wage war on the Pequots.

FAST FORWARD

The Pequots' Comeback Pays Off Big

In 1637, the Pequots were massacred, their name officially erased from the maps of Connecticut. Today, they operate the most profitable casino in the world.

In 1992, the tiny Mashantucket Pequot Tribe opened Foxwoods Resort Casino on their reservation in Ledyard, Conn. It is today the western hemisphere's largest casino, with customers exceeding 50,000 a day. The casino's slot machines alone generate $50 million a month in revenues.

Once considered a scourge by their English enemies, the Pequots today are eastern Connecticut's largest employer and taxpayer. Historians say only a few Pequots survived the Pequot War, which was a bloodbath carried out at an Indian-built log fort near present-day Mystic by English soldiers. Survivors were hunted down throughout the countryside and eastern Long Island and killed; others were sent to live with other Indian groups.

By 1856, the original reservation of more than 2,000 acres had dwindled to 214 acres, with tribal members dispersed throughout the country. By the mid-19th Century, only two Pequot women remained on the reservation.

Their comeback began in the 1970s when tribal chairman Richard Hayward — the grandson of one of the two women who were the reservation's only residents — hired attorneys to help the Pequots regain some of their original reservation. Efforts to improve the local economy led to the casino's opening in 1992, which brought back many Pequot descendants. The tribe now has more than 500 members.

— Steve Wick

Photos by Evan Eile

Above, one of the many sculptures of American Indians at the Foxwoods Resort in Ledyard, Conn. At right, Bernadette Augustus of the Bronx plays roulette at the casino.

While it is clear in his own account — written as a letter to officials in Connecticut — that Gardiner distrusted and loathed the Pequots, he opposed an all-out war against them because he feared for his family as well as for the handful of others who were with him in the fort.

"It is all very well for you to make war who are safe in Massachusetts bay, but for myself and these few with me who have scarce holes to put our heads in, you will leave at the stake to be roasted," he wrote in his account. "I have but twenty-four in all, men, women and children, and not food for them for two months, unless we save our corn field which is two miles from home, and cannot possibly be reached if we are in war."

Gardiner's protests fell on deaf ears. When a group of soldiers — led by John Underhill and another Englishman, John Mason — reached the fort, Gardiner said, "You come hither to raise these wasps about my ears, and then you will take wing and flee away."

As the soldiers prepared for an attack on a nearby Pequot fort, Gardiner tried to keep his family and the others inside his own ramparts alive. Forays outside the walls to get food were dangerous events; some of his men were caught by Pequots and tortured — some were burned alive at a stake, their skin peeled off, according to Gardiner's account. One group of men, out on a hay-cutting mission, was set upon by Pequots who "rose out of the long grass . . . and took the brother of Mr. Mitchell, who is minister of Cambridge, and roasted him alive."

LI HISTORY.COM

Lion Gardiner left a legacy in the form of a journal that details his dealings with the Indians. For Gardiner's account, see http://www.lihistory.com on the Internet.

Gardiner himself narrowly escaped death when he went outside the fort's walls with 10 armed men and three dogs. A half mile away, they met up with a small band of Pequots — some of whom were wearing the clothes of murdered English settlers — and a fight ensued. Almost immediately, two men were killed. As the group fled toward the safety of the fort, another man was shot through the thighs with an arrow, another man was hit in the back, and as Gardiner pulled back toward the fort, he was struck in the thigh. The group, he wrote, had to fight "with our naked swords or else they (would have) taken us all alive . . ." In another incident a day or two later, "I was shot with many arrows . . . but my buff coat preserved me, only one hurt me."

After these incidents, Underhill and Mason assembled an army of more than 80 men to stay with Gardiner. To beef up the numbers, the English recruited nearby Mohegans — enemies of the Pequots. This army then attacked the Pequot fort near Mystic, slaughtering men, women and children and setting the building on fire. To historians today, the attack was a massacre unlike anything that had occurred in New England up to that point. To Englishmen at the time, it was a blessing. Gardiner wrote:

. . . and the Lord God blessed their design and way, so that they returned with victory to the glory of God and honour of our nation, having slain three hundred, burnt their fort, and taken many prisoners.

Underhill's account, published in London in 1639, boasted that more than 1,000 Pequots were killed, three times Gardiner's estimate. Historians say that English soldiers conducted mop-up operations for months after the attack on the fort, hunting down Pequots hiding in the woods, and killing hundreds more. In a few months in 1637, most members of the tribe were killed.

"It was a war of extinction," said Kevin McBride, an archeologist at the University of Connecticut.

The Pequots would agree. Today, the descendants of the survivors operate Foxwoods Resort Casino on a site not far from the massacre. They believe their history was distorted. "The Pequots never wrote down their histories at the time of contact with Europeans," said Shannan McNair, a spokeswoman for Mashantucket Pequot Tribal Nation. "So it's hard to know what was true and was said about the Pequots to justify the massacre."

After the massacre, Gardiner's life changed forever when an Indian from Long Island paddled his canoe over to Connecticut from Montauk. Spelling the Indian's name "Waiandance," Gardiner wrote in his account:

Three days after the fight came Waiandance, next brother to the old Sachem of Long Island . . . He came to know if we were angry with all Indians. I answered No, but only with such as had killed Englishmen. He asked whether they that lived upon Long Island might come to trade with us.

Gardiner said he would only trade with the Long Island Indians "if you will kill all the Pequots that come to you, and send me their heads . . . so he went away and did as I had said, and sent me five heads . . ."

And thus began the friendship of the English settler named Lion Gardiner and an Indian chief named Wyandanch. Two years later, his tour of duty in Connecticut over, Gardiner capitalized on his friendship with Wyandanch's people, whom the English called the Montaukett Indians, and bought some real estate on Long Island.

Lion Gardiner finds a 3,000-acre island for his home and forges a friendship with Wyandanch

The Settler and the Sachem

BY STEVE WICK
STAFF WRITER

The Pequot War behind him, Lion Gardiner took the first step into his new life and into Long Island history.

For reasons not known today, Gardiner decided that he would not return to England once he had completed building a fort at the mouth of the Connecticut River. As spring awoke in 1639, he began searching for a home for his wife and their baby son, David.

"I have always understood that Lion began his search by visiting islands," said his 20th-Century descendant, Robert David Lion Gardiner. Paddling away from the Connecticut coastline, Lion Gardiner visited the islands of eastern Long Island — Fishers Island, Plum Island, and then Shelter Island. But none suited his needs.

"He needed fresh water and these islands did not have streams," Robert Gardiner said.

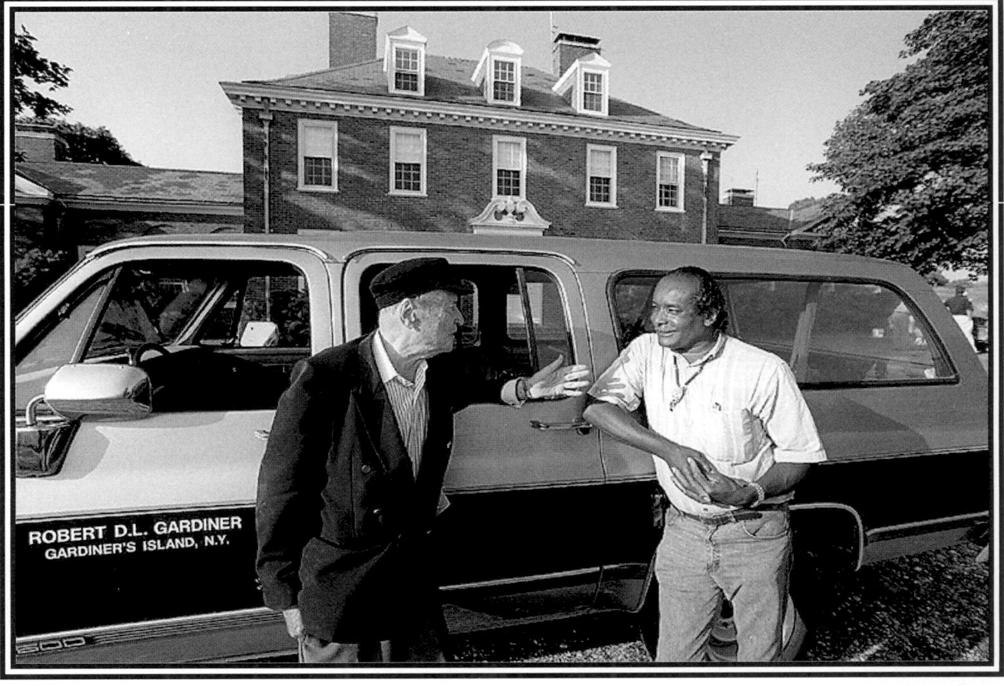

Newsday Photo / Bill Davis

Robert David Lion Gardiner, left, and David Cooper, descendants of the 17th-Century figures Lion Gardiner and Montaukett leader Wyandanch, respectively, on a visit to Gardiners Island last summer.

There was another island, called by the Montaukett Indians *Manchonat*, or the Island of Death, most likely because many Indians had died there during an epidemic. It was the easternmost island in the archipelago enclosed by the North and South Forks of Long Island. When Lion Gardiner paddled around that island, he was struck by its shape.

"He thought it resembled the Isle of Wight, in England," Gardiner said. "When he walked over it, he found it had magnificent forests, saltwater ponds and freshwater streams that he could dam and use for his livestock."

Gardiner had found his new home. Early in May, 1639 — four years after he and his wife, Mary, had sailed from Europe — Gardiner sat down with the Algonquian Indians who lived near the island and bought all 3,000 acres. From Gardiner's point of view, anyway, it was a real-estate purchase. In exchange for a place as magnificent and untrampled as any great estate in his native England, Gardiner gave the Indians a quantity of cloth, a gun, gunpowder and "a large black dog." To the Indians, who had no understanding within their culture of selling land, it may have been little more than an agreement to share the beautiful island with the Englishman.

The deed for the island contains Gardiner's signature and has the mark of the "sachem of Pomanocc," a man identified as Yovawan. Pomanocc is an Algonquian word that is untranslatable today; a linguist earlier in this century believed it meant "Island of Tribute." In buying the island for his small family, Gardiner had created the first English settlement on eastern Long Island. Soon after settling on the island, his daughter, Elizabeth, was born — the first English child born in what is now New York State. Gardiner's purchase was later ratified when he received a grant from King Charles I of England.

Historians say Gardiner's acquisition of the island — which he called the Isle of Wight before giving it his own name — could not have taken place without the consent of Wyandanch, the Montaukett Indian Gardiner met in the aftermath of the Pequot War. Wyandanch, whose people had been under the thumb of the Pequots, befriended Gardiner after their destruction — the enemy of his enemy was indeed his friend.

"Wyandanch's role in the transaction is not recorded, but he undoubtedly was the one who brought the two parties together," writes scholar John Strong in "The Algonquian Peoples of Long Island From Earliest Times to 1700."

Wyandanch had made the deal possible. Gardiner would later return the favor in dramatic fashion.

In the spring of 1653, a party of Niantic Indians attacked Wyandanch's village on Montauk Point, killing more than 30 in a place known for years after as "massacre valley." Prisoners were taken, one of whom was Wyandanch's daughter. To get her back, Gardiner traveled to Rhode Island and paid a handsome ransom.

Just what the circumstances of the daughter's kidnaping were are not known today. David Gardiner, Lion's descendant, wrote in 1840 that she was grabbed on her wedding day and her intended husband was killed. Indian history scholar John Strong has written that there is nothing in the records that supports that account.

The bond between the Indian and the Englishman seemed genuine. Based on appearances, it was a true friendship, one that was depicted — apparently by Wyandanch — in a number of deeds for large tracts of land the Montaukett sold to Gardiner. On these deeds, Wyandanch drew stick figures of two men, one an Indian, the other an Englishman.

One of the deeds was for a huge tract of land in modern-day Smithtown, whichWyandanch conveyed to Gardiner in the aftermath of his daughter's return to Montauk. On that deed, the stick figures are holding hands. Near the end of his life, Gardiner would be the largest landowner in Long Island history — nearly 100,000 acres.

No European ever got so much from any Indian as Lion Gardiner got from Wyandanch.

Last summer, on a day rich in history, descendants of both men met. Robert David Lion Gardiner and Robert Cooper, a descendant of Wyandanch who lives in East Hampton, traveled together to Gardiner's Island. There, they talked about the friendship between their ancestors.

"They were blood brothers," Gardiner said.

"I believe that, too," Cooper said. Both men were sitting on a bench overlooking a saltwater pond on the island.

"When Wyandanch died, Lion wrote a letter to a friend in Connecticut and said his heart was broken, his best friend was dead," Gardiner said.

When Gardiner got up from the bench, he said to Cooper, "Why don't you walk with me?"

"I'll walk with you anywhere," Cooper said, smiling.

Newsday Photo / Bill Davis

Gardiner, at home in East Hampton, with portraits of his ancestors

ROBERT DAVID LION GARDINER

On his island, Robert David Lion Gardiner is the lord of the manor — the 16th since his ancestor acquired Gardiners Island from the Indians and established the first English colony on Long Island.

"We are the oldest intact estate of its kind in America," Gardiner said. He is 86 years old, lives in Palm Beach, Fla., in the winter and in East Hampton in the summer months. He shares the use of the island and its elegant manor with his niece, Alexandra Goelet, her husband, Robert, and their two children. Gardiner also owns a mansion on Main Street in East Hampton Village that was once used by President John Tyler, who married a Gardiner woman named Julia.

Surely, no living person knows more about Gardiner family history than the current lord of the manor. He can talk about it until listeners jokingly beg him to stop. He has collected treasures since childhood. They include the original deed showing Lion Gardiner's purchase of Gardiners Island from the Indians, a cannonball unearthed at Fort Saybrook, which Lion built near the mouth of the Connecticut River, and priceless paintings from his family's past.

— **Steve Wick**

Did the chief give away too much, or did he have no choice in protecting his people?

Wyandanch, Ever an Enigma

BY STEVE WICK
STAFF WRITER

There are few clues and much conjecture about Wyandanch, the Montaukett chief who befriended Lion Gardiner and changed the course of Long Island history.

"I have always seen him as a strong man, a powerful man," said Robert Cooper. Born and raised in the Freetown section of East Hampton, Cooper traces his ancestry all the way back to Wyandanch. "I think he might have looked like Stephen Talkhouse Pharaoh."

A photograph of Pharaoh, himself a descendant of Wyandanch, that was taken in 1867 shows a tall, lean man with long, graceful fingers and shoulder-length black hair parted above his left eye.

The name Wyandanch, in different spellings, appears in only a handful of official records and personal letters. It is clear he was an influential man, a deal maker, and a man who put himself at the forefront of his people. The name is first mentioned in Lion Gardiner's account of the 1637 Pequot War, which he wrote in 1660.

In it, Gardiner writes, "Waiandance, next brother to the old Sachem of Long Island," traveled to Connecticut to meet him and to discuss trade possibilities between his people and the English. If the Indians could trade with the English, Wyandanch told Gardiner, he would make tribute payments to him, as he had done with the Pequots. Tribute payments were a form of protection money. The Montauketts, and presumably other Long Island Indian groups, paid the powerful Pequots to leave them alone; now Wyandanch proposed the same relationship with Gardiner.

In the long view of history, what are we to make of Wyandanch? Did he seek an alliance with the English to protect his people or was he used by Gardiner and others to sell off his people's ancestral lands?

"Wyandanch has to be seen in the context of the times," said Long Island Indian scholar John Strong. With hundreds of Pequots killed in a matter of days, the English were now seen by Indian groups of the area as the new power on the scene, one that could dominate them the way the Pequots had.

"My fix on Wyandanch is that he was astute enough to recognize what the English represented in the aftermath of the Pequot War," Strong said. This would explain why Wyandanch approached Gardiner just days after the English assault on the Pequot fort.

"He was probably both a realist and an opportunist. He knew he had to make accommodations to protect the Montauketts. The English gave him a lot of trade goods and status that increased his power, which was their intention. But we can't know today what was in his head."

SPECIAL POSTER

A copy and transcript of the 1659 Wyandanch-Gardiner deed

Next Page

History shows that, once Gardiner and Wyandanch met, their friendship lasted until Wyandanch's death. Gardiner said Wyandanch was "a true friend to the English" who warned them of threats made by northern Indians. He also tells of a time in the late 1640s when Wyandanch helped authorities in Southampton arrest two Indians for the murder of a white woman.

It is hard to know for certain today, Strong said, whether Gardiner was taking advantage of Wyandanch in hopes he would get favors later in terms of land deals.

"My first thought on that was that Wyandanch was a puppet used by Gardiner," Strong said. "But I think that assessment is too simplistic and does not take into consideration what it meant to be a Native American on Long Island at that time."

In 1660 — a year after conveying 10 square miles of what is today Smithtown and Setauket to Gardiner — Wyandanch was dead. In his account of the Pequot War, written that same year, Gardiner makes this comment about Wyandanch: ". . . for in the time of a great mortality among them he died, but it was by poison; also two-thirds of the Indians upon Long Island died . . ." Historians say this is a reference to a smallpox epidemic that year that killed thousands of Indians.

Strong said he suspects Wyandanch may have been poisoned by other Indian groups angered at him for selling their land to the English without their consent. Although there are records showing Wyandanch selling the English land in the western part of Long Island, far from his home territory, there is no hard evidence of his being murdered in retaliation.

Who had the motive to kill him? Perhaps the Corchaugs, on the North Fork, Strong speculates. Seeking to resolve questions about land ownership of large tracts, including Plum Island, Southold officials met in early 1659 with Wyandanch, hoping, it would seem, that he would sign on the dotted line and certify their ownership.

"Wyandanch asserted that the Corchaugs were not now, nor had they ever been, the owners of either the North Fork or Plum Island," Strong writes. The Montauketts owned these lands. A short time later, Wyandanch sold Plum Island to a Connecticut man for such items as a barrel of biscuits and some fish hooks.

The last document signed by Wyandanch involved a transaction with Lion Gardiner. In a letter, Gardiner said he was heartbroken at his friend's death. After his death, no Long Island Indian emerged as a deal maker for the English, nor do sachems — chiefs of their bands — appear in the record books. None was needed, since so much of the land was now in English hands.

Courtesy of David Bunn Martine

An illustration by Shinnecock artist David Bunn Martine shows how a 1600s Algonquian like Wyandanch might have dressed. Based on extensive research, Martine depicts a colonial garment with a wampum shoulder bandolier, leather armbands decorated with porcupine quill, a ceremonial club with shell inlay, and a squirrel-skin tobacco pouch decorated with deer hair.

ROBERT COOPER

Newsday Photo / Bill Davis

Cooper at the grave of an ancestor, Stephen Talkhouse Pharaoh, in a Montauk field

Robert Cooper can only imagine what his ancestor, Wyandanch, was like. But he likes what he imagines.

"He was a great figure," he said.

Cooper grew up in East Hampton, in a part of the town called Freetown, where freed slaves and Indians were settled and where a long line of his ancestors lived. For years he worked for the East Hampton Town Police Department and served on the Town Board. One of his actions on the board was to restrict any future development on Gardiners Island.

Cooper, 55, has spent years tracing his family's history, poring over family records and genealogies — records that take him through the Pharaoh family to Wyandanch.

Cooper has also worked to improve the tiny Pharaoh Museum at Montauk County Park, and hopes one day that the Montauketts will own a piece of their former homeland. "I want us to learn our history because without it we have nothing," he said.

— Steve Wick

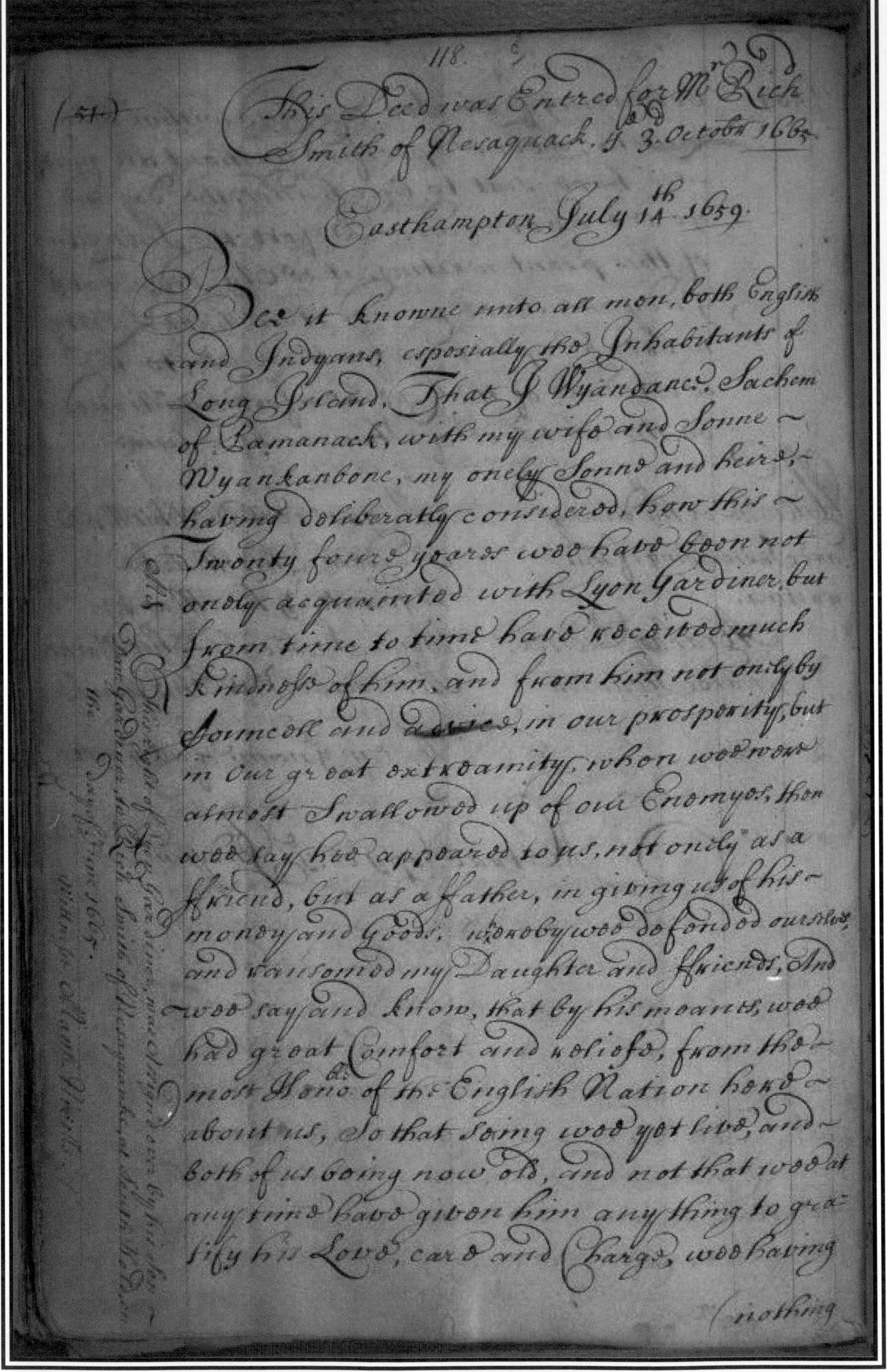

(21) 118.

This Deed was Entred for Mr Rich Smith of Nesaquack ye 3 October 1665

Easthampton July 14th 1659.

Bee it knowne unto all men, both English and Indyans, espesially the Inhabitants of Long Island, That I Wyandance, Sachem of Pamanack, with my wife and Sonne Wyankanbone, my onely Sonne and heire, having deliberatly considered, how this Twenty foure yeares wee have been not onely acquainted with Lyon Gardiner, but from time to time have received much kindnesse of him, and from him not onely by councell and advice, in our prosperity, but in our great extreamity, when wee were almost Swallowed up of our Enemyes, then wee say hee appeared to us, not onely as a ffriend, but as a ffather, in giving us of his money and Goods, whereby wee defended ourselves, and ransomed my Daughter and ffriends, And wee say and know, that by his meanes, wee had great Comfort and reliefe, from the most Honoble of the English Nation here about us, So that seeing wee yet live, and both of us being now old, and not that wee at any time have given him any thing to gratify his Love, care and Charge, wee having (nothing

(22) 119

nothing left that is worth his acceptance, but a Small Tract of Land, wch wee desire him to accept of for himselfe, his heires, Executors and Assignes for ever; Now that it may bee knowne how, and where this Land lyeth on Long Island, Wee say it lyeth betweene Huntington and Seataucut, the westerne Bounds being Cowharbour, Easterly Aca=taamunk, and Southerly crosse ye Island to the end of ye great hollow or valley or more then halfe through the Island, Southerly, and that this is our free Act and Deed, doth appeare by our hand Markes under written, Signed, Sealed and delivered in the presence of

Richard Smith
Thomas Chatfield.
Thomas Talmage.

Wyandance his Mark.
Wyankanbone his Mark.
The Sachems wife Suwahen Marke

Book of Deeds, New York State Archives, Albany

Wyandanch's Gift

After Englishman Lion Gardiner rescued the kidnaped daughter of Wyandanch in 1653, the grateful Montaukett chief gave the settler land between Huntington and Setauket. The deed seen here is a duplicate of the 1659 document that sealed the exchange. It was copied by hand, in 1665 for public record. The deed's text appears below (spellings are updated for ease of reading). Wyandanch, his son and wife used marks to sign the deed. Richard Smith, founder of Smithtown, was a witness. Notes in the margin reveal the subsequent transfer of the land from David Gardiner, Lion's heir, to Smith in 1665.

East Hampton, July 14th, 1659.

Be it known unto all men both English and Indians, especially the inhabitants of Long Island, that I, Wyandanch, sachem of Paumanack, with my wife and son Wyankanbone, my only son and heir, having deliberately considered how this twenty-four years we have been not only acquainted with Lion Gardiner, but from time to time have received much kindness of him, and from him not only by counsel and advice in our prosperity, but in our great extremity, when we were almost swallowed up of our enemies — then, we say, he appeared to us, not only as a friend, but as a father, in giving us his money and goods, whereby we defended ourselves, and ransomed my daughter and friends. And we say and know that by his means, we had great comfort and relief from the most honorable of the English Nation here about us. So that, seeing we yet live, and both of us being now old, and not that we at any time have given him anything to gratify his love, care and charge, we having nothing left that is worth his acceptance but a small tract of land, we desire him to accept for himself, his heirs, executors and assigns forever. Now that it may be known how and where this land lyeth on Long Island, we say it lyeth between Huntington and Setauket, the western bound being Cow Harbor [now Northport], easterly Acataamunk, and southerly, across the Island to the end of the great hollow or valley, or more than halfway through the island southerly; and that this is our free act and deed, doth appear by our hand marks under written. Signed, sealed and delivered in the presence of

[Signed] Richard Smith, Thomas Chatfield, Thomas Talmage, [and] Wyandanch, Wyankanbone, the Sachem's Wife [with their marks]

Questions of ownership and land use hang over the paradise between the forks

Gardiners Island: What Next?

BY STEVE WICK
STAFF WRITER

For 358 years it has been their island. The family's ownership has survived Indian wars, pillaging pirates, the Revolution, the Civil War and two World Wars. It has survived the income tax, the inheritance tax, the Depression and bitter feuds.

And the island is not cheap to maintain — nearly $2 million a year in upkeep and property taxes. Costs go up every year, too.

Today, Gardiners Island is the oldest family-owned estate of its kind in America, dating to the reign of Charles I of England.The 3,000-acre island holds a vast wealth of history. It has the largest stand of white oak in the Northeast, as well as rare birds, Indian artifacts, and one of the oldest wood-frame structures in New York State.

Its fields and forests, its manor house and barns, the carpenter's shed built in 1639, a stone wall built by slaves — all hold the collective memory of Long Island history.

Since the spring of 1639 it has been in the Gardiner family — but will the Gardiners have it much longer?

Robert David Lion Gardiner, the current lord of the manor, as each generation of Gardiners who have looked after the island have called themselves, is pessimistic. He is 86 years old, and has no children. On top of the issue of having no heirs, there's the thorny tax question.

"If you know anything about inheritance taxes in this country, how high they are, you will very quickly realize that it is all but impossible to keep this island in my family," Gardiner said as he toured the island last summer. Gardiner is worth millions of dollars, but said his own wealth, after taxes, will not be enough to keep the island going after his death.

"It's a miracle it has been in our family this long," Gardiner said.

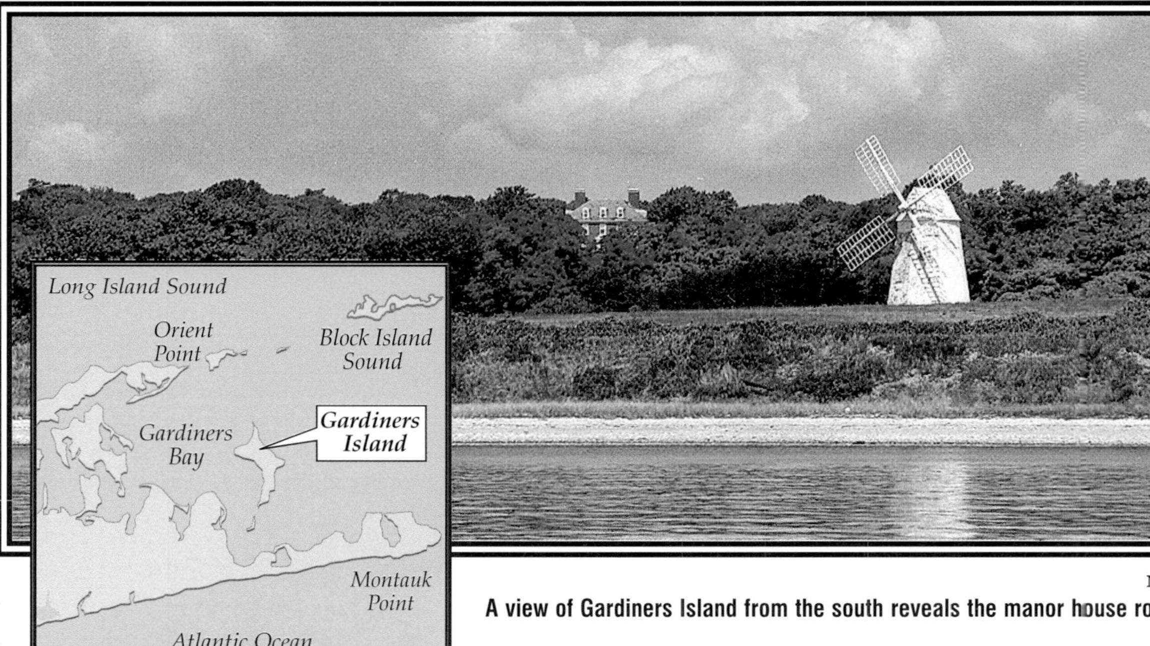

Newsday Photo / Bill Davis

A view of Gardiners Island from the south reveals the manor house roof and an old windmill.

Then there's the family situation. Gardiner shares the use of the island with his niece, Alexandra Goelet, to whom he does not speak. They have sued each other and warred for years over their sharing of the island and the question of its future. Gardiner has accused his niece of harboring a secret desire to cover the island with houses; for her part, Goelet has said in the past she has no such plan. She would not be interviewed for this story.

In the 1980s, Gardiner refused to pay his share of the taxes and upkeep, so the Goelets now carry that burden. But a court decision allowed Gardiner to continue using the island.

According to the legal agreements that tie the Gardiner family to their island, if Gardiner were to die today the ownership of the island would pass to his niece. Gardiner has said he does not want that to happen, and last summer, while touring the island and showing off its history and natural beauty, he said he was working on a plan to keep the island away from her.

"I am working on a plan to create the Robert David Lion Foundation which would own the island and make it available for small study groups," Gardiner said while sipping French champagne under the shade of a huge tree in front of the island's manor house. He is clearly an aristocrat in a country that doesn't have any.

Jack Raymond, a spokesman for the Goelets, said Gardiner does not have the legal right to convey the island. "He can't unilaterally do anything with the island," Raymond said.

Beyond the issue of the trust, Gardiner said he would not oppose government ownership of the island, or ownership by a private group such as The Nature Conservancy. In the past, federal, state and local governments have said acquisition of the island would be beyond reach. In 1989, the island was said to be worth more than $125 million. The Nature Conservancy has described the Peconic Bay system, and its islands, as one of the "last great places on Earth."

FAST FORWARD

Yesterday's Events Making News Today

So determined to keep the island out of his niece's hands, Gardiner has even gone hunting for a suitable heir. In 1989, he found a 48-year-old Mississippi businessman named George Green and made plans to legally adopt him as his "son." What made this Green different from a lot of other Greens was his middle name — Gardiner. The plan, however, fell through.

The family has nearly lost the island in the past.

In the mid-1660s, David Gardiner — the first Lion Gardiner's son — nearly lost the island through his own financial mismanagement. His mother, Mary, had to sell holdings in Connecticut and Smithtown to bail out the family and keep the island.

Centuries later, in 1937, the island was put up for sale by its owner. A few weeks before an auction of the island was to be held, another Gardiner — Sarah Diodati Gardiner — stepped in and bought the island. Upon her death in 1953, it passed to her nephew, Robert David Lion Gardiner, and his sister, Alexandra Creel. When Creel died, her rights passed to her daughter, Alexandra Goelet, and a son, who subsequently died.

Asked how the island managed to stay in the family, Robert David Lion Gardiner said last summer: "We have always married into wealth. We've covered all our bets. We were on both sides of the Revolution, and both sides of the Civil War. The Gardiner family always came out on top."

LION GARDINER'S GRAVE

Lion Gardiner died in East Hampton in 1663, two years after writing his memoirs. In 1888, a descendant, Sarah Gardiner, exhumed his grave in the South End Cemetery and made an important discovery — he had red hair.

"Sarah was my grandmother," said Robert David Lion Gardiner, the 16th lord of the manor. "She was concerned that Lion's sandstone grave marker was becoming badly eroded. She hired the architect who had designed St. Patrick's Cathedral in Manhattan to design a Gothic granite tombstone. But she wanted to make sure Lion's remains were really there, so when the workers were putting the tombstone in place she asked them to dig deeper.

"Lion was buried in his red British army officer's uniform, which was still visible even then. He was wearing a steel corset, a steel helmet, with a beautiful sword hitched to his belt. And she discovered he had a gray beard streaked with red. Some of the hairs were clipped off and distributed to members of the family inside a Tiffany crystal and diamond case."

Lion Gardiner's tombstone sits near the center of the cemetery. Historians say there is no tombstone like it anywhere in America. Designed by James Renwick — who in addition to designing St. Patrick's Cathedral also designed the Smithsonian Institution's original building in Washington, D.C. — the tombstone is carved in granite in the shape of a cathedral. Under the roof of the cathedral is a recumbent knight in steel hat and corset — the very image of Lion Gardiner, the engineer and warrior of the Pequot War. Gardiner's is one of only a few marked graves on Long Island of people born in the 16th Century — he was born in 1599.

Newsday Photo / Bill Davis

The Lion Gardiner sarcophagus at Old Cemetery, East Hampton

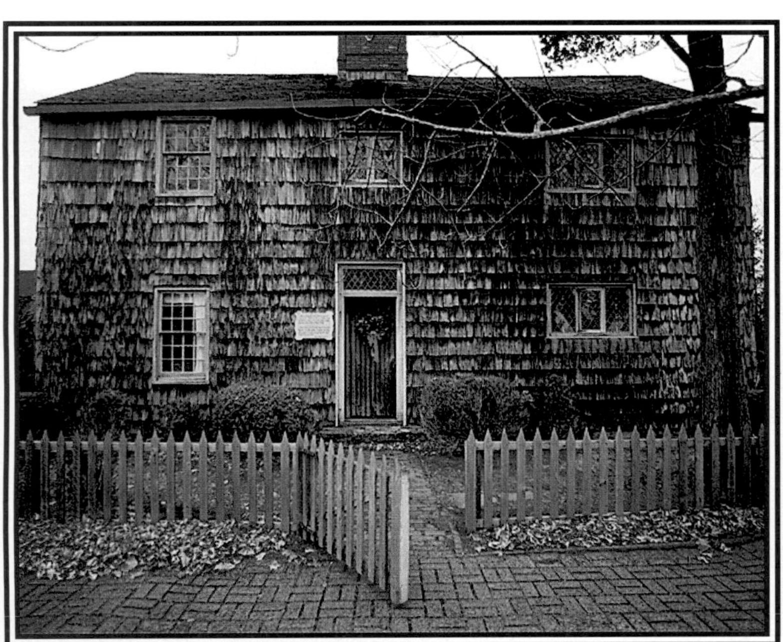

Newsday Photo / Bill Davis

THE OLD HALSEY HOUSE
In Southampton: one of the oldest English-type frame houses in the state

Newsday Photo / Bill Davis

THE OLD HOUSE
In Cutchogue: also one of the earliest English-style homes

Still standing, these homes help us imagine life as it was three centuries ago

Proud Old Houses

We see our history in our houses. Many homes of the colonial Long Islanders still exist. With an architecture influenced by the Dutch on the west end and by the English on the East End, these old structures have a story to tell. Here is a sampling of some of Long Island's earliest houses to be visited and enjoyed.

— **George DeWan**

OLD HALSEY HOUSE,

South Main Street, **Southampton.** Built by Thomas Halsey on this site in 1648, it is one of the oldest English-type frame houses in the state. Contains 17th- and 18th-Century furnishings, a Dominy clock and a rare 16th-Century "Breeches" Bible. (Check out Genesis 3:7. Most Bibles state Adam and Eve used fig leaves to make "aprons" to cover themselves; this one, a Geneva Bible, states "breeches.") Hours: 11 a.m.-5 p.m., Tuesday-Sunday, June 12-Sept. 15. Fees: $2; 50 cents children ages 6-12. Call 516-283-2494.

THE OLD HOUSE,

Case's Lane, at the Village Green, **Cutchogue**. Built in Southold by John Budd in 1649 and moved to Cutchogue between 1660 and 1662. Also one of the oldest English-type frame houses in the state. Has 17th- and 18th-Century furnishings. Hours: 1-4 p.m., Saturday-Monday, July-August; weekends, June and September. Fees: $1.50; 50 cents ages 12-16. Call 516-734-7113.

PIETER CLAESEN WYCKOFF HOUSE,

Clarendon Road and Ralph Avenue, **East Flatbush**, Brooklyn. Built about 1652 and thought to be the oldest frame house in New York City. Colonial furnishings, with documents dating from 1670 to 1866. Open: Monday-Friday, by appointment. Fee: $2 adults; senior citizens and children, $1. Call 718-629-5400.

VAN NOSTRAND-STARKINS HOUSE,

221 Main St., **Roslyn**. Built by William Van Nostrand in 1680 and acquired by the blacksmith Joseph Starkins in 1740, this is the oldest surviving building in Nassau County; has 18th-Century furnishings and archaeology exhibits related to the house. Hours: 1-4 p.m., Tuesday, Wednesday, Saturday, Sunday, June-October. Fee: $1. Call 516-625-4060.

VANDER ENDE-ONDERDONK HOUSE,

18-20 Flushing Ave., **Ridgewood**, Queens. The oldest fieldstone Dutch house left in New York City, it was built about 1709 by Paulus Van der Ende and purchased by Adrian Onderdonk in 1821. Serving as headquarters for the Greater Ridgewood Historical Society, the house is furnished in colonial style, except for one room, the Victorian Room. Open: Saturday, noon-4 p.m.; other days by appointment. Fee: $2 adults; age 12 and under, free. Call 718-456-1776.

Newsday Photo / Audrey C. Tiernan

PIETER CLAESEN WYCKOFF HOUSE
In East Flatbush: a legacy from the Dutch occupation of New York

Newsday Photo / Bill Davis

VAN NOSTRAND-STARKINS HOUSE
In Roslyn: the oldest surviving building in Nassau

Newsday Photo / Bill Davis

VANDER ENDE-ONDERDONK HOUSE
In Ridgewood: exhibits colonial artifacts found on site

A settlement is born in Hempstead, and its founders become wealthy

The Dutch Welcome the English

BY MOLLY McCARTHY
STAFF WRITER

The Dutch had a problem.

Nearly 20 years after they arrived on Manhattan Island, the settlement of New Netherlands in 1644 didn't extend eastward very much beyond where Brooklyn is today. The Dutch couldn't find enough immigrants to inhabit the vast Long Island territory they claimed.

So, the Dutch made a deal with the English. "The Dutch wanted settlers, and they were not afraid of the religion of the English," said Myron Luke, 92, the former Hempstead town historian. "They would have looked askance at the religious practices of other settlers such as the Quakers, but they welcomed the English."

Although they had driven out a group of Englishmen who built a house at Great Neck in 1640, the Dutch decided to give the English a try. That momentous decision led in 1644 to the founding of Hempstead, the first European settlement in present-day Nassau County.

In 1643, a small English settlement in Stamford, Conn., sent Robert Fordham and John Carman to Long Island to negotiate a land deal with the Indians. They hoped Long Island would provide a safe haven from Connecticut's increasingly belligerent Indian tribes.

"They must have looked across the Sound and saw the beautiful greenery of Long Island, and that was enough. It drew them like a touchstone," Luke said.

Fordham and Carman probably liked what they saw. They returned to Stamford with a deed signed by the Indians, granting them hundreds of thousands of acres, including half of a huge meadow known as the Hempstead Plains and all the land south to the ocean. After obtaining a patent from the Dutch, the Hempstead founders extended those claims to the necks of the north shore.

They built a fort and meetinghouse on the southern edge of the Hempstead Plains in the heart of today's Hempstead Village. Some historians believe the meetinghouse was located just east of where St. George's Episcopal Church stands today at 319 Front St. The 60,000-acre Hempstead Plains was used as common pastureland for the settlers' cattle and sheep.

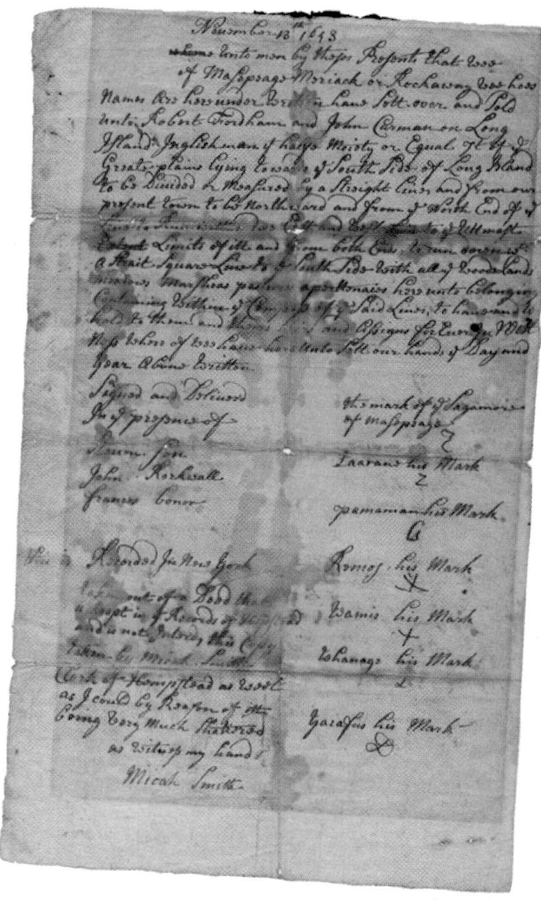

November 18th 1643
Know all men by these Presents that wee
of Massapeage Moriack or Rockaway wee whose
Names are hereunder written have sett over and Sold
unto Robert Fordham and John Carman on Long
Island Englishman ye halfe Moiety or Equal part of ye
Greate plains lying towards ye South side of Long Island
to be Divided & Measured by a Straight line and from our
present town to be Northward and from ye North End of ye
[illegible] East and West [illegible] ye Uttmost
Extent Limits of ille and from both ends to run downe with
a Strait Square line to ye South side with all ye woodlands
meadows marshes pastures appurtenances hereunto belonging
Containing within ye Compass of ye Said Lines, to have and to
hold to them and their [illegible] and Assignes for Ever In Witness whereof wee have hereunto sett our hands ye Day and
Year Above Written

Signed and Delivered
In ye presence of
[illegible]
John Rockwall
Francis Conor

the mark of ye Sagamore of Massapeage
Taarans his Mark
Apamaman his Mark
Romos his Mark
Wamis his Mark
Chanago his Mark
Yaracfus his Mark

Recorded In New York
taken out of a Deed that
is kept in ye Records of Hempstead
and is not Intered, this Copy
taken by Micah Smith
Clerk of Hempstead as well
as I could by Reason of its
being very much shattered
as witness my hand
Micah Smith

Nassau County Museum, Long Island Studies Institute

A town clerk's copy of the deed for the 1643 purchase of Hempstead from the Indians; signature marks — some are only an X — appear in a vertical row down the right side.

Even though Fordham and Carman didn't record their first glimpse of Long Island, Daniel Denton, the son of the minister who crossed the Sound with Hempstead's first settlers, did several years later in his 1670 treatise, "A Brief Description of New York." Denton described a virtual Eden, rich with fish, game and other bounty:

The Island is most of it of a very good soyle, and very natural for all sorts of English Grain; which they sowe and have very good increase of, besides all other Fruits and Herbs common in England, as also Tobacco, Hemp, Flax, Pumpkins, Melons, &c.

. . Yea, in May you shall see Woods and Fields so curiously bedecke with Roses, and an innumerable multitude of delightful Flowers not only pleasing to the eye, but smell, that you may behold Nature contending with Art, and striving to equal, if not excel many Gardens in England.

The Dutch agreed to grant the English a patent for Hempstead on several conditions. The English would have to attract at least 100 families to Hempstead by 1649, and answer ultimately to Dutch laws and customs.

The directors of the Dutch West India Co. wrote to Peter Stuyvesant, New Netherlands' director-general: "We have not found any very great objections to allow them [the English] for the present to come in reasonable numbers, but the appointment of Magistrates must absolutely be left to our directors."

Despite these restrictions, Hempstead settlers had a considerable amount of freedom. In the New England tradition, they held annual town meetings where local laws were enacted. And, unlike other Dutch towns, they tried their own criminal cases and appointed their own sheriff.

What historians know about the early days in Hempstead has been pieced together or inferred from later records. The earliest town record, consisting of original documents from its first decade, is often referred to as the "mouse-eaten book" and has been missing for some years.

Those records may have shed light on the naming of the town, a fact that remains in dispute even today. Some argue that Hempstead derived from Hemel-Hempstead, a small town north of London from which the English settlers may have hailed. Others are equally sure that the Dutch named Hempstead, spelled Haamstede, for a place on the island of Schouwen off the Netherlands coast.

The tale of Thomas Rushmore, as retold by his descendent Robert P. Rushmore of Garden City in "Thomas Rushmore: A Long Island Pioneer," published in 1994, illustrates the situation of one Englishman who came to Dutch Long Island:

Still a young man, Thomas Rushmore was a servant or apprentice to a lawyer in Hartford, Conn. After a few minor brushes with the law, he left New England for Hempstead, arriving about a dozen years after its birth.

Rushmore was after land and status, and it didn't take him long to acquire both. He bought a home lot for 10 pounds and, a year later, was elected as one of five Hempstead townsmen. He later served as town clerk and assistant to the town attorney.

Upon his death in 1683, Rushmore owned more than 300 acres across the town, including choice holdings in woodlands south of the Hempstead Plains, along the north shore in Great Neck and Manhasset and in what is today Westbury and Herricks. Among dozens of miscellaneous items listed in the appraisal of Rushmore's estate are two feather beds, four brass kettles, nine pewter platters, a silver dram cup, two washing tubs, a colt, a mare, an old linen wheel, a saw mill, a grist mill and two rights of commonage in the Town of Hempstead.

Like many of its English founders, Rushmore came to Hempstead and soon became a rich man.

From "History of the City of New York," 1877-1896

An illustration of the Newmarket racecourse in Hempstead

AMERICA'S FIRST RACECOURSE

"Towards the middle of Long-Island lyeth a plain sixteen miles long and four broad . . . and once a year the best horses in the Island are brought hither to try their swiftness."

— Daniel Denton, 1670

The first measured race course in America was set up on the great Hempstead Plains in the spring of 1665, less than a year after the English captured New Netherlands from the Dutch and began to put an English spin on life on western Long Island. On the order of the new English governor, Richard Nicholls — who thus became the father of racing in America — a course called Newmarket was laid out in what is today's Garden City. The oldest American racing trophy in existence, a silver porringer that is now owned by Yale University, was awarded on this course in 1668.

— George DeWan

New York has the most slaves in the North, almost half of them on Long Island

The Rise of Slavery

BY GEORGE DE WAN
STAFF WRITER

Long Island had the largest slave population of any rural or urban area in the North for most of the colonial era.

For almost two centuries, New York was a slave colony and Long Island was a slave island. Beginning with the introduction of 11 black slaves into New Netherlands in 1626, the number of slaves in New York grew to almost 20,000 on the eve of the Revolutionary War a century and a half later.

"Throughout the slave era in the north, New Yorkers held more enslaved Africans than the residents in the combined New England colonies or those in New Jersey or Pennsylvania," writes Richard S. Moss in his 1993 book, "Slavery on Long Island."

In 1698 there were 2,130 blacks in New York, almost all of them slaves, more than in any colony north of Maryland. Almost half of them were on Long Island. And one out of five Suffolk County residents was black, virtually all of them slaves.

Slavery in the New York colony was unlike that on the plantations of the Deep South, where close to a half-million slaves lived in servitude by the time of the Revolution, and would continue to be enslaved until the Civil War. New York State would not ban slavery within its borders until 1827, though two minor exceptions continued until 1841.

On Long Island, slaves were widely scattered about the thinly populated countryside, and although a wealthy 18th Century landowner like William Floyd in Mastic might have a dozen or so slaves, one, two or three was more common. So the daily family life of a Long Island slave was markedly different from his or her counterpart in the South, where large groups of blacks in separate slave quarters could at least share their religion, culture and social life, often with their own family members.

Long Island slavery may have been different, but it was slavery, nonetheless. Black men, and occasionally American Indians, were owned by white men, just as they owned cattle, sheep and farm implements.

Their daily life was regulated, both by the needs of their owners and by laws of the colony. The first major slave law came in 1702, titled "An Act for Regulating Slaves." No person could trade with a slave without permission of the slave's master or mistress. Owners could punish their slaves at their own discretion, though they were not allowed to take a slave's life or sever a body part. Slaves could not carry guns. Except when working for their owners, slaves could not congregate in groups larger than three, with whipping the penalty, up to 40 lashes. Towns could appoint a public whipper, who would be paid up to three shillings for each slave whipped.

Slaves worked in the fields alongside their owners, and many of them worked their way into more skilled jobs as craftsmen, such as shoemakers, blacksmiths and woodworkers. Female slaves also did outside work, but more often were used as household servants.

But because an owner usually had few slaves, married slaves were often forced to live apart, seeing each other only occasionally. They received little education. Many slaves converted to Christianity, and one of their few rewards was being allowed to go to church on Sunday.

The Granger Collection / Howard Pyle

An illustration of a 1600s slave auction in Manhattan; unlike at plantations in the South, slaves on Long Island lived just a few to a house, often away from friends and relatives.

Slavery got started in New Netherlands and in the South because there was an acute labor shortage in America. Even imported white indentured servants, who contracted to serve for a certain period of time, often seven years, were hard to obtain. The alternative for the farmer or the large householder was to purchase slaves.

In 1626, seven years after slaves had been introduced at Jamestown, Va., a ship carrying 11 male slaves sailed into the harbor at New Amsterdam. Only four of the names of the first slaves in New York are known for certain: Paul d'Angola, Simon Congo, Anthony Portugese and John Francisco, the names indicating that they were probably taken from Spanish or Portuguese slave ships captured at sea by privateers. They were immediately put to work by the Dutch West India Co. building roads, cutting timber, clearing land and helping construct a major fort at the southern tip of Manhattan.

For the next 38 years, until the British took over New Netherlands and renamed it New York, the Dutch slowly increased the numbers of slaves in the colony, including settlements on western Long Island in Kings and Queens Counties. Some slaves were imported directly from Africa, but the Dutch officials preferred to buy slaves who had been "seasoned" by a few years of living in the West Indies. By then they had gotten used to working as slaves, had picked up some of the new language, and in many cases had contracted and survived a bout with the killer disease smallpox, thus becoming immunized.

Nothing illustrates the difference between Dutch and English attitudes toward slavery better than an incident that occurred in New Amsterdam in 1644. Eleven male slaves, presumably the same 11 who first arrived in 1626, petitioned Director-General Willem Kieft to be freed along with their wives. They cited their long service to the Dutch West India Co. and their obligations to their families. Their request was granted, though it was on a "half-freedom" plan. That meant that they were given land grants for farming — out on the swampy edge of town that is now known as Greenwich Village — but required to give back annually part of their produce, and work for the company for wages whenever their services were required. And freedom was not given to their children.

Long Island beckoned some of the freed slaves. "Some of the early freed Negroes moved to Long Island and other neighboring areas where they joined whites in the founding of new towns," writes Vivienne L. Kruger in her 1985 doctoral dissertation. ". . . Francisco the Negro [John Francisco], one of the eleven slaves manumitted [freed] in 1644, became one of the twenty-three original patentees of Boswyck [Bushwick] in 1660."

Nothing comparable to this manumission of slaves by the Dutch occurred later under English rule. Manumission became rare until the later part of the 18th Century, and when it did occur, it was the act of an individual owner.

When Barnabus Wines of Southold

LI HISTORY.COM

THE STORY OF VENTURE SMITH

The story of one man's capture in Africa, his journey into slavery in America and eventually his freedom in Connecticut and Long Island, is detailed beginning on Page 72. Extended excerpts of his narrative, published in 1798, are available on the Internet at http://www.lihistory.com.

A Panicked Response To The 'Great Negro Plot'

Thirteen black men burned to death at the stake. Seventeen black men hanged. Two white men and two white women also hanged. All thirty-four were executed in New York City between May 11 and August 29, 1741, as part of the episode early New Yorkers called the "Great Negro Plot," or the "New York Conspiracy."

— **Thomas J. Davis, "A Rumor of Revolt"**

BY GEORGE DEWAN
STAFF WRITER

In the spring and summer of 1741, New York City's white residents panicked over what they saw as an imminent slave insurrection by its growing black population, augmented by "country slaves" from western Long Island.

The beginning was low-keyed, without any great portent of things to come. In late February of 1741 there was a middle-of-the-night burglary at the Broad Street shop of merchant Robert Hogg. Taken were a pair of silver candlesticks, some linen and a sack of silver coins. Arrested the next day and charged with the crime was a black slave named Caesar.

At the time, one out of every five residents of the city was a black slave. There were restrictive laws controlling slave activities on the books, but they were loosely enforced. New Yorkers still remembered a slave insurrection in 1712 involving arson and the murder of nine whites that resulted in the execution of 19 black slaves.

Caesar had been arrested at John Hughson's tavern on upper Broadway, where the slave's mistress, a white prostitute named Peggy Kerry, hung out. Hughson and his wife, Sarah, both white, came under immediate suspicion as receivers of the stolen goods. Investigators got lucky when they questioned a 16-year-old, white, indentured servant of the Hughsons named Mary Burton, who claimed to know something about the robbery, but said, "I'll be murdered or poisoned by the Hughsons and the negroes for what I should tell you."

Mary was held in protective custody and her tongue was loosened with promises of getting her released from her indenture. She accused the Hughsons of receiving stolen property from the slaves, and when the goods were found, the Hughsons were in trouble.

A new element was thrust into the escalating tensions when, on March 18, the first of a series of suspicious fires broke out in the city. The city council raised the possibility of a conspiracy of arsonists, and suspicions grew that black slaves were responsible. Four fires were set on April 6. As cries of "The Negroes are rising!" filled the air, mobs of angry white citizens roamed the streets to round up black slaves. Nearly a hundred were hauled off to jail.

Then, out of the blue, came a connection to the February burglary. It was provided to the grand jury by none other than Mary Burton.

The Granger Collection

A 19th Century engraving depicts the execution of a slave in 1741 following rumors of a consipiracy in New York City. Below, an illustration shows Africans packed into the cargo hold of a ship. The space shown is only 3 feet, 3 inches high.

New York Public Library / Schomburg Center for Research in Black Culture

Now she accused the Hughsons, Kerry, Caesar and other slaves of plotting to burn the city and massacre the whites. "In their common conversations they used to say that when all this was done, Caesar should be governor, and Hughson, my master, king," Mary told the jury.

With her damning testimony, many New Yorkers thought that 1712 was about to repeat itself.

Caesar and another slave named Prince were found guilty of burglary, and on May 11 they were both hanged. Two more slaves, Cuffee and Quack, were hanged on May 30, but not before they had accused dozens of others of being in on a conspiracy. Mary Burton spun wilder and wilder stories, making more accusations. Though her testimony was riddled with inconsistencies, no one seemed to care. Writing it all down, the prosecuting officials cast their net wider and wider.

Scores of alleged conspirators were hauled in and interrogated. Hughson, his wife and Kerry were tried on June 4 and found guilty of conspiracy. They were hanged eight days later.

One of the alleged conspirators was a slave from Brooklyn named Doctor Harry, who was accused of bringing poison to Hughson's tavern for blacks to use on themselves if convicted. He denied ever being at Hughson's, but was burned at the stake on July 18.

Other Long Island slaves were later implicated by testimony of a city slave named Jack, who said he once proposed burning a white man's shed. "In firing the shed, that'll fire the whole town," Jack said. "And then the Negroes in town, with the Negroes that'll come from Long Island, will murder the white people."

The arrests and trials and executions continued through the summer, until, on the last day of August, the paroxysm of fear, anger and suspicion virtually ended with the hanging of a white schoolteacher, John Ury. He was officially found guilty of conspiracy, but he was really tried because he was thought to be a Catholic priest, which he wasn't. Catholics were often discriminated against in the strongly Protestant city. What got Ury in trouble was his ability to read Latin.

Mary Burton got her reward from the city on Sept. 2, 1742. It totaled 100 pounds sterling, enough to pay off her indenture and set herself free, with 81 pounds left over.

Most historians agree that there was no grand slave conspiracy. But there were real racial problems in New York City in 1741, and they exploded in the conspiracy trials, which some have compared to the Salem witch trials of 1692.

"New York's officials indulged themselves and the public in acting out their fears," Davis, a history professor at Arizona State University, wrote recently in his book. "They simply deceived themselves by systematizing real disorders into a single scheme where all the enemies of the English world suddenly surfaced."

died in 1762, he not only freed two of his slaves, Peter and Pegg, but also gave them a generous legacy, according to Kruger. To Peter he gave "his chest and wearing apparel, and £10 [10 pounds sterling], also my gun and small iron pot, hoe, one scythe, one sickle." To Pegg he gave "all her wearing apparel, and her beding, three pairs of sheets, two chests, one pot, one trammel [an adjustable pothook for a fireplace crane], one pewter tongs, four old chairs, two basins, a linnen wheel, one cow and calf, one box." He also gave the two of them a half-acre of land.

The first slaves in Suffolk County were brought to Shelter Island from Barbados in 1654 by Nathaniel Sylvester to work on his large estate. Little by little, others on Long Island turned to slavery to solve their labor problems. There was a slave market in New York City, but a Long Island farmer more likely would find a slave for sale from another slaveholder in Suffolk or Queens Counties.

It was not always easy, however, to find a slave for sale, even for someone as well off as William Smith of the Manor of St. George, in Mastic. In an April 14, 1746, letter to his father-in-law, Henry Lloyd, Smith wrote:

> *I have taken a great deal of pains to buy a good slave but cannot get one. If you . . . could recommend any one to me I should take it as a great favor and will come and buy him as soon as I hear of any one to be sold.*

A slave might have been a farmer's most valuable possession. Moss says that by the middle of the 18th Century, the average cost of an adult male slave was about 38 pounds sterling. This would translate roughly to $5,000 in today's currency.

"Account books and other records indicate that owners generally sought to protect their valuable investment in slave property and therefore provided medical care similar to that available to the owners' families," writes Grania Bolton Marcus in her 1988 book, "Discovering the African-American Experience in Suffolk County, 1620-1860." "Some slave owners ordered clothing and shoes for their slaves from the same tailors, dressmakers and shoemakers who made their own clothing."

The rare Long Island farmer with a dozen or so slaves probably housed them in slave cabins separate from the main house. But slave owners with only one or two slaves might have them living in an attic, a cellar or some other out-of-the-way section of their own homes. The farmer might have employed indentured workers as well as casual labor, and when it came time to work the crops, all of them might be found in the fields, working side by side.

"Slavery in New York was quite different from the plantation slavery we often imagine," writes Marcus. "Few New Yorkers owned vast numbers of slaves: only seven people in the entire colony held 10 or more slaves, according to a

Please see **SLAVERY** on **Next Page**

One Slave's 36-Year Venture tc

BY JOYE BROWN
STAFF WRITER

For 13 years, the enslaved African worked Fishers Island.

As a boy, he spent hours combing, cleaning and untangling thick, coarse wool to feed the spinners' wheel or pounding bushels of corn to feed the chickens. As a man, he got into a dispute with his owner's son that left him bound, dragged and hanging by his wrists from a gallows.

Yet, when the suggestion came sometime later to steal his way to freedom, the slave called Venture balked. "I cast a deaf ear," he would recall in a narrative that appears to be the only published first-person account of slave life in colonial Long Island.

The suggestion was made by an indentured white servant named Heddy, who would not be put off.

After he had persuaded and much enchanted me with the prospect of gaining my freedom by such a method, I at length agreed to accompany him.

The decision made, Venture joined Heddy and two others to steal supplies and their master's boat. But the dangerous attempt — which took them to Montauk Point — failed.

"I informed my master that Heddy was the ringleader of our revolt and that he had used us ill," Venture said in "A Narrative of the Life and Adventures of Venture, A Native of Africa, But Resident Above Sixty Years in the United States of America," published in 1798. When he was in his 60s, Venture is believed to have related his story to a Connecticut schoolteacher, Elisha Niles.

Heddy was placed into custody. Venture was put back to work. And a few months later, he was forcibly separated from his wife and children and sold to a man in Connecticut.

Still, his hope for freedom did not die. Over the next 20 years, Venture would work to earn his freedom — cutting and cording acres of wood, signing on for whaling crews, catching eels and lobsters and growing watermelons. And he would also earn the freedom, one by one, of his wife and three of his four children. Along the way, he would accumulate and be cheated of wealth, become one of the first free black property owners in Suffolk County and become himself a slaveowner. While stories abound of his great strength and dedication to work in Connecticut, where he died at 77, little has been written of his time on Long Island.

The story of Venture is the stuff of legend. He was West African born, son of a tribal king, stood well over 6 feet tall and was estimated to weigh 300 pounds. It was not uncommon for him to canoe some 45 miles round-trip between Connecticut and Long Island to visit his family or to collect clams in Suffolk waters and cut wood. During the Revolutionary War, he was said to have made a good living ferrying Patriots fleeing British-occupied Long Island.

VENTURE SMITH'S LIFETIME JOURNEY

- **ABOUT 1729:*** Venture Smith is born in **Guinea**, son of the head of the Dukandarra tribe. (This is not modern Guinea. In colonial times, Guinea referred to a crescent of countries that ran roughly from Senegal to Nigeria.)
- **ABOUT 1736:** Smith is sold to slave-ship steward Robertson Mumford in the slave port of **Anamaboo, Ghana**. He was 7 years old. The ship's first stop is **Barbados**, where all of the enslaved Africans, except Smith and three others, are sold to planters. At **Narragansett, R.I.**, the ship's home port, Smith works for a time for his master's sister.
- **ABOUT 1737:** Smith goes to live with his owner at Fishers Island and works there for 14 years.
- **1765:** Smith buys his freedom after having worked for two masters in **Stonington, Conn.** He is 36.
- **ABOUT 1769:** Having earned enough money by working on Long Island, Smith buys the freedom of his two sons, and four years later buys the freedom of his wife.
- **ABOUT 1775:** Smith sells land he had bought in **Suffolk County** and moves to Connecticut. He settles down in **East Haddam, Conn.**, and acquires property.
- **1805:** Smith dies at age 77. His gravestone reads, "Sacred to the Memory of Venture Smith, African. Though the son of a King, he was kidnapped and sold as a slave, but by his industry he acquired money to purchase his freedom . . ."

* Dates are approximate because Smith in the narrative sets his birth year at "about 1729."

This African who would become American was born somewhere near the Gulf of Guinea in about 1729, son of Sangm Furro, head of the Dukandarra tribe. Sangm Furro had named his eldest son Broteer. When Broteer was 6, he watched enemy tribesmen kill his father. The narrative states:

I saw him while he was thus tortured to death . . . The shocking scene is to this day fresh in my memory and I have often been overcome while thinking of it . . . He was a man of remarkable strength and resolution, affable, kind and gentle, ruling with equity and moderation.

When Broteer was 6½, he was forced by his father's killers to march 400 miles through West Africa. Then he and his captors were captured and marched to the coastal slave-trading port of Anamaboo, Ghana. For a time, Broteer lived in a castle, where he was rested and fatted for market.

There came a day when the 7-year-old child climbed into a canoe crowded with Africans and was rowed to a massive boat resting in the harbor.

I was bought on board by one Robertson Mumford, a steward of said vessel, for four gallons of rum and a piece of calico, and called Venture on account of his having purchased me with his own private venture.

Thus I came by my name.

The boy now called Venture was among 260 Africans who would share a voyage to enslavement, suffering an outbreak of smallpox along the way. When the ship reached Barbados, not more than 200 of them were alive. All except Venture and three others were sold to planters there.

The ship then sailed for Rhode Island, where Venture worked a few months for Mumford's sister. Finally, at age 8, he was taken to Mumford's property on Fishers Island.

The first of the time of living at my master's house, I was pretty much employed in the house . . . My behavior had as yet been submissive and obedient. I then began to have hard tasks imposed upon me. Some of these were to pound four bushels [32 pounds] of corn every night in a barrel for poultry or be rigorously punished . . . These tasks I had to perform when only about nine years old.

Mumford's son, James, began to give Venture additional tasks. Venture became less submissive and on one occasion said no. James did not take the refusal lightly.

He then broke out into a great rage, snatched a pitchfork and went to lay me over the head therewith, but I as soon got another and defended myself with it, or likewise he would have murdered me . . . He immediately called some people who were within hearing working for him and ordered them to take his hair rope and come and bind me with it . . . He took me to a

Photo by Christopher Hatch

The graves of Meg and Venture Smith in East Haddam, Conn.

Slavery on LI

SLAVERY from **Preceding Page**

mid-18th Century census. It was much more common for an owner to have but one or two slaves working for him, indeed often working with him. In the town of Huntington, Long Island, for example, a total of 53 masters owned 81 slaves."

While the Dutch took an almost casual approach to the treatment and control of the slaves that were imported into the colony after 1626, everything changed after the British took over in 1664. The British, who controlled what was now New York, not only stepped up the importation of slaves into America, they passed a series of slave codes regulating slavery that made it harsher, repressive and more brutal.

How slaves lived under British rule was essentially how the slave codes said they could live. The rules covered marriage, slaves congregating, court protection, family life, ownership of property, bearing of arms and many other aspects of daily life.

Under the 1702 law, a slave who assaulted or struck any free Christian man or woman was subject to prison for up to 14 days, as well as "reasonable" corporal punishment. No slave could give evidence in any court, except against other slaves who were plotting to run away, kill their master or mistress, burn their houses and barns or destroy their corn or their cattle.

A 1706 law allowed "Negro, Indian and Mulatto slaves" to be baptized as Christians, pointing out that this would not, contrary to widespread opinion at the time, automatically free them from slavery. The law also stated that any child born of a slave woman would carry the slave status of the mother, apparently a reference to a child whose father was either a free black or a white slave owner.

The brutal murder of an entire family in Newtown (now Elmhurst) in January, 1708, led to a capital punishment statute against slaves later that year. A farmer named William Hallett, his pregnant wife and their five children were ax-murdered in their sleep by their two slaves, an Indian man named Sam and an unidentified black woman, apparently in the belief that they would fall heir to the property. They were arrested and found guilty at trial. They were executed in front of a large public gathering on Feb. 2, nine days after the murder, the woman burned at the stake, the man hanged. Two other black men were hanged as accessories.

In response, the Colonial Assembly on Oct. 20, 1708, passed "An Act For

Freedom

gallows made for the purpose of hanging cattle on and suspended me from it . . . I was released and went to work after hanging on the gallows about an hour.

When Venture was 22, he wed Meg, another of Mumford's slaves. Shortly thereafter, he cast his lot with Heddy and two of his friends and prepared for their ill-fated run toward freedom.

We privately collected, out of our master's store, six great old cheeses, two firkins of butter and one batch of new bread. We stole our master's boat, embarked and then directed our course towards the Mississippi River. We mutually confederated not to betray or desert one another on pain of death. We first steered our course for Montauk Point, the east end of Long Island.

When the group went ashore at Montauk for fresh water, Heddy stole the supplies and set off alone for East Hampton.

I then thought it might afford some chance for my freedom, or at least a palliation for my running away, to return Heddy immediately to his master, and inform him that I was induced to go away by Heddy's address.

Venture caught Heddy in Southampton. The entire group sailed back to bondage on Fishers Island.

Soon after, Venture was sold to Thomas Stanton of Stonington, Conn., who heaped so much abuse upon him that Venture complained to a local magistrate. The magistrate chastized Stanton. But he also ordered Venture to return to his owner, who had him handcuffed, chained and put up for sale.

Ultimately, he was bought by Oliver Smith, another Stonington resident. And he decided to try another path to freedom.

I asked my master one time if he would consent to have me purchase my freedom. He replied that he would. I was then very happy . . .

Venture had to slowly, almost painfully, stockpile an enormous sum to buy his freedom. He would hire himself out under an agreement to give Smith a portion of his earnings. Sometimes Smith gave permission for him to work for others; sometimes permission was denied. The task would take five years.

I hired myself out at Fishers Island, earning twenty pounds — thirteen pounds, six shillings of which my master drew for the privilege and the remainder I paid for my freedom.

Month after month, year after year, Venture sought outside work — with the bulk of the money going to his owner.

In October following, I went and wrought six months at Long Island. In that six months time, I cut and corded 400 cords of wood, besides threshing out 75 bushels of grain and received of my wages only 20 pounds.

Finally, Smith agreed to free him. The man who had been sold to slavery for rum and cloth paid an unusually high price — 71 pounds, two shillings, about $9,400 in today's money — for his own release.

He was 36 years old.

And he was angry:

I had already been sold three different times, made considerable money with seemingly nothing to derive it from, had been cheated out of a large sum of money, lost much by misfortunes, and paid an enormous sum for my freedom.

Still, Venture took his owner's last name as his own. He left Connecticut for Long Island and set to work again — this time to buy his family's freedom.

For the first four years of my residence . . . I spent my time working for various people . . . In the space of six months, I cut and corded upwards of 400 cords of wood . . . In the aforementioned four years, what wood I cut at Long Island amounted to several thousand cords, and the money which I earned amounted to 207 pounds, 10 shillings.

This money, I laid up carefully . . . All fine clothes I despised in comparison with my interest . . . expensive gatherings of my mates I commonly shunned and all kinds of luxuries I was perfectly a stranger to.

When he was 40, Venture worked on Ram Island, today part of Shelter Island. And by then he earned enough money to buy the freedom of his sons, Solomon and Cuff. At the time, he also bought his first slave "for no other reason than to oblige him." The man ran away.

With his sons (one of whom would die of scurvy at the age of 17), Venture looked to other ways of raising money — growing watermelons, fishing for eels and lobsters, joining on as crew for a whaling expedition headed by his old owner, Smith. At one point, Venture chartered a sloop so he could commute from Long Island to Rhode Island to sell wood.

He also began to buy land somewhere in Suffolk.

My temporal affairs were in a pretty prosperous condition. This and my industry was what alone saved me from being expelled from that part of the Island in which I resided, as an act was passed by the selectmen of the place, that all Negroes residing there should be expelled.

When Venture was 44, he was well pleased to buy his wife, Meg. He would describe her as "the wife of my youth, whom I married for love and bought with my money." Unknown to her owner, Meg was pregnant. Venture rejoiced that he would not have to buy another child. He also bought two more slaves. The first decided to "return to his own master." The second, "I parted with shortly after."

When he was 46, he purchased his eldest child, Hannah, from the Mumfords.

One year later, he sold his property on Long Island and moved to East Haddam, Conn. There, he continued to work and amassed a large amount of property and generated a wealth of tall tales that have been passed down from generation to generation.

It is said that he was so big that he passed through doors sideways, so strong that he never raised his ax higher than eye level because he wanted to chop wood, "not chop air." He was too big to ride on the back of a horse, so he rode in a two-wheeled cart behind. And when his horse did not behave, Venture would lift the animal's forelegs and "jounce" it a few times.

When he died in 1805, Venture Smith was one of the wealthiest men in East Haddam, with some 100 acres of land, three homes, boats and a fishery.

But there was always something he valued more.

My freedom is a privilege which nothing else can equal.

A CLOSER LOOK AT A SLAVE'S STORY

In his life's story, some of Venture Smith's Africa geography is wrong; and he makes no specific mention of where he owned land on Long Island or cut so many cords of wood.

But he's correct about essentials such as the Mumford family living on Fishers Island and in describing the slave port in Ghana and a slave ship in the harbor.

Why the discrepancies? Why the gaps?

There are answers, historians say, and the problems do not take away from the narrative's significance as one of the rare slave accounts of life in colonial Connecticut and Long Island.

Smith's recollections came when he was old and ill. He says he was born in Guinea. In the 1800s, Guinea referred to a crescent of countries in West Africa, roughly from Senegal to Nigeria, said Donald R. Wright, a history professor at the State University College at Cortland. Smith's narrative says he was marched in a straight line to reach the slave port in Ghana. That's impossible, Wright said, because of the curving coast.

Still, Smith correctly describes Anamaboo, a port town that exists today in Ghana. And he's correct in saying that a ship commanded by a Capt. Collingwood of Rhode Island was in the harbor at the time. Collingwood sailed from Rhode Island to West Africa in 1738, said Richard Coughtry, a historian at the University of Nevada-Las Vegas.

Connecticut history brims with documents and other remnants of Venture Smith. Many of his descendants live there. And in and around East Haddam, there are other reminders: a church Smith helped raise, his toolbox — and his gravestone, which in September was added to Connecticut's historic freedom trail. **— Joye Brown**

Book Cover From Schomburg Center for Research in Black Culture

---

Preventing the Conspiracy of Slaves." The law said that any slave who killed or conspired to kill anyone who was not black or a slave would be subject to execution. The owner of the executed slave would be reimbursed by the colony up to 25 pounds sterling.

As the years went by and the numbers of slaves increased, new laws were passed, piling on more restrictions. Import duties were placed on all slaves brought into the colony. The selling of oysters in New York by slaves was banned. The selling of rum and other strong liquors to slaves was prohibited. A 1712 law said that even freed slaves could not own property, reversing the Dutch law. And a slave could not own a gun, or even use a gun except with the permission of his master.

Local laws on Long Island also curtailed slave movements. In 1732, the Town of Brookhaven forbade slaves to be out at night except on an "extraordinary occasion." In 1734, one report in Hempstead said that 10 slave men had been imprisoned for being "unseasonably in a frolick." And in 1757, Smithtown passed a law "that no negro be found without a pass from his master, not to exceed one mile . . ."

Slaves were chattel, pieces of property that could be bought, sold, rented out and moved around at the will of the owner. They could be bequeathed to heirs. And even taxed. A 1702 law laying out sources of income for the colonial government listed import duties on black slaves along with mackerel, salt, barrel staves and cocoa nuts. The children of slaves automatically belonged to their owners.

The work of the slaves was varied. "Agriculture commanded the largest number of African-Americans as well as whites, but slaves occupied every rung of skilled and unskilled labor," writes Marcus. "They cut stone, made barrels, blacksmithed, manned fishing boats and whaling ships. African-American women were involved in the same complex domestic economy as white women, as well as in agricultural work and domestic service."

As the colonial period came to an end, on the eve of the Revolutionary War, slavery remained a potent force on Long Island. In the 1771 census, Kings County had 3,623 people, and almost one-third of them were black, most of them slaves. Queens, which included present-day Nassau County, had 10,980 residents, one-fifth of whom were black. Suffolk County by then had the largest population on Long Island, 13,128, and 11 percent were black.

At that time there were only faint stirrings of distaste for the slavery system on Long Island It would take a revolution, the formation of a new state government and the rising of abolitionist sentiment before New York State, the largest slave state in the North, would give up its peculiar institution.

Records offer clues to how slaves, human property, served the wealthy Lloyd family

Slave Life on Lloyd Neck

BY JOYE BROWN
STAFF WRITER

A spoon. A sock. A room.

A fireplace. A spinning wheel.

A kitchen, clams, red and white clay.

And a busy, isolated place, almost an island.

Each of them pieces, small parts of a portrait that can never be complete. To this day, the slaves of Lloyd Neck have no voice.

None wrote of their lives, of the day-to-day between birth and death. None, including the poet Jupiter Hammon, the most famous and pampered slave of the manor, wrote of their dreams, their thoughts, their joys or their fears.

There was Opium, also known as Obium, brought from Boston and passed from father to son. He made an unsuccessful attempt to flee. There was Hester, who would balk at being sold to slavery in the South. She was sold to a new owner in the North instead. There was Aurelia, brazen enough to refuse an order to return to her master's home. She was hired out to someone else.

And there were countless others, who were bought, sold, who lived and died and worked 3,000 acres of idyllic beauty joined by a tendril of land to the larger community of Huntington.

This much is known through the ledgers, letters, last wills and testaments of the Lloyd family; the lives of slaves as seen through the eyes of their masters. In often-bloodless prose, the masters of the manor provide a fascinating glimpse into colonial Long Island. It's a rare picture of slave life, even if it is incomplete and falls together like a crazy quilt with no batting.

* * *

Bill for Sale of Negress

Know all Men by these present that I Joseph Conkling . . . for and in consideration of Twenty five pounds Current money . . . sell and Convey unto Joseph & John Lloyd and to their heirs one Certain Negro Girl Named Phoebe of about Six Years of Age During the Term of her Natural Life . . .

— Sixth Day of December A.D. 1773

* * *

In 1685, James Lloyd of Boston bought the peninsula that now bears his name. He won a royal land grant that made it the Lordship and Manor of Queens Village. All this, and James, the first lord of the manor, never left Boston to even visit his little piece of England. At his death, his son, Henry, took over the land and built the first manor house. His four sons, Henry, John, Joseph and James, inherited the estate in 1763. Joseph would go on to build a second manor house in 1767.

Throughout the generations, the Lloyds worked the land and hired tenants and indentured servants. As that proved too few hands, they, like their neighbors across Long Island, bought slaves. And as necessity arose, they traded them, much as a modern boy might trade baseball cards.

* * *

From John Lloyd to Henry Lloyd:

If it is not asking more than becomes me . . . I Desire that I should be next purchaser of one of your Negro men. *October 16, 1746*

* * *

The spoon is made of dark wood, roughly carved, topped with the head of an African. The sock is made of flax, fed through a spinning wheel and left, now, oddly soft to the touch. It is monogrammed and the darning is as intricate as the original construction.

Each was representative of the work of Lloyd Neck slaves.

By all accounts, work was the center of a slave's life, especially at Lloyd Neck, where the earth bore more bounty than men could easily work alone. There were thousands of peach, plum and apple trees. There were fields of wheat, corn and other grains. There were clams and oysters to be pulled from the thick, night-black mud of waters that surrounded the manor on three sides. There was clay, red and white, to be dug and sold or shaped for the kiln. There were bass to be caught, deer to be hunted, livestock to be tended. And there were acres of oak and other timbers to be felled, corded and carted away for sale.

Inside, the work continued, with fires stubborn to start and greedy to be fed, food to be prepared, produce to be canned.

Twinned with work was commerce. The Lloyds were able traders and all things on the manor were geared toward contributing to its financial success. Sometimes, however, even a slave could force an exception.

* * *

From Henry Lloyd II to John Lloyd II:

I am much better pleas'd with Hesters being sold as she was with 10 pounds loss than she should be sent to Carolina against her will, though by what I can learn of the treatment Negroes meet with at the plantation she was design'd for is Such as that Some of those I have Sent prefer their Scituation to that they have left. *September 13, 1773*

* * *

At Lloyd Neck, some slaves probably lived in a room within the masters' house. Of course, the room more than likely had no fireplace and few, if any, windows — a sharp contrast to the bright, warm bedrooms in the front of the manor. And the slave's room might also have a spinning or flax wheel or a good supply of candles, so slaves could work well into the night.

For clothing, hand-me-downs appeared to be the order of the day. In colonial times, most clothing was made from wool and flax beaten down and spun to thread, most probably, by black hands. The newer cloth went to the backs and the beds of the masters.

Education was another matter. Hammon was taught to read and write and may have joined the Lloyd children at the manor schoolhouse. There is no sign that the same could be said of other slaves.

The Lloyds appeared to take some responsibility for the spiritual well being of slaves. Some believe they may have allowed slaves to accompany them as they worshipped, sitting in the family pew of a church in Huntington Village, or, more likely, their pew at an Anglican Church across the Sound in Stamford, Conn.

And as for physical well being, when Lloyd slaves fell ill, the family called in its own doctors.

* * *

From Dr. George Muirson to Henry Lloyd:

Jupiter is afflicted with Pains in his Leggs, Knees and Thighs, ascending to his Bowels, which in my esteem is a Gouty Rumatick Disorder to releave which and Prevent the Impending Danger (As You Observe) of It's Getting Up to his stomach . . . Give one of the Purges, In the morning fasting, and att night one of the boluses, the next day take away about 12 or 14 ounces of blood . . .

May 19, 1730

* * *

Slave marriages and deaths did not make the letters. There are no records of such mundane matters.

And there is no evidence of where slaves were buried. Markers, if there were any, have long since rotted away.

LEGACY

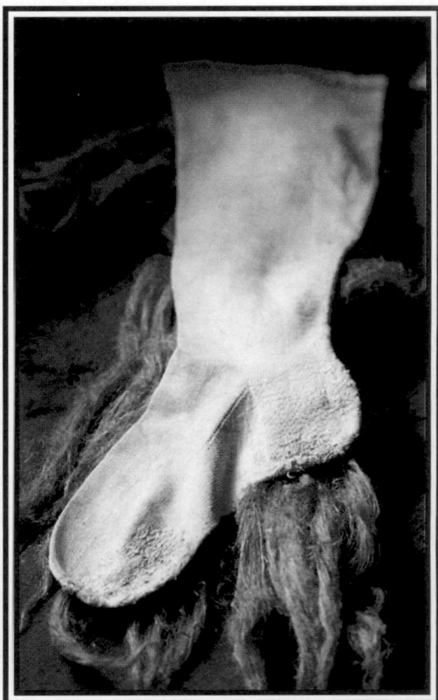

Newsday Photos / Bill Davis

AT JOSEPH LLOYD MANOR

"Slave Quarters," says the small sign at the entrance to the room above at the Joseph Lloyd Manor House (at left) on Lloyd Neck. If they lived in the main house, slaves often had a cramped back room with no source of heat. A spinning wheel in the room might allow them to work well past sunset. Above right is a linen sock made from flax. Jupiter Hammon, the first published black poet, lived at the manor house as a slave.

The Joseph Lloyd Manor House is open on weekends from late May through Columbus Day. Built in 1767, it overlooks Lloyd Harbor. Among its exhibits are a formal garden, 18th-Century furniture and decorative arts.

LI HISTORY.COM

More excerpts from the Lloyd family collection are available on the Internet at http://www.lihistory.com

LONG ISLAND OUR STORY

Tom Gall starts a farm in Oyster Bay and even buys a slave for himself

A Freed Slave on His Own

BY GEORGE DEWAN
STAFF WRITER

When Alice Crabb's will was probated in Oyster Bay in October, 1685, it contained a striking sentence about her slave, known as Black Tom: "I give to my negro man one calf one iron skellet one mare and his freedom and liberty."

Black Tom, later known as Tom Gall, is believed to be the first slave to be freed on Long Island.

To tell a single slave's story is made difficult by the scarcity of written records. Slaves usually had only a single name, and that was given to them by their masters, a name that was sometimes plain, sometimes fanciful: For every Jack or Sarah there was a Bacchus or a Pleasant Queen Anne. Being mostly illiterate, slaves rarely left personal accounts, and white owners had few occasions to write about them, except in ledgers indicating how much they paid for them or sold them for.

After Black Tom, there would not be many more slaves freed for another century. Manumission did not begin in earnest until the colonial period was over. But slaves strove for freedom in other ways. Some bought their freedom with wages earned over many years. Others ran away. Some gained sanctuary with upstate Indian tribes such as the Iroquois; others fled to the anonymity of New York City or shipped out as seamen on a vessel in a harbor.

The story of Black Tom can be pieced together from Oyster Bay Town documents that record land sales, slave sales, excerpts from wills and surveyors' notes.

One example:

This is to satisfy all whom it may concern, that I, Richard Crabb, have received from Lewis Morris one Negro boy called Owah of about the age of 12 or 13 years to be employed in such services and labor as my occasions shall require.

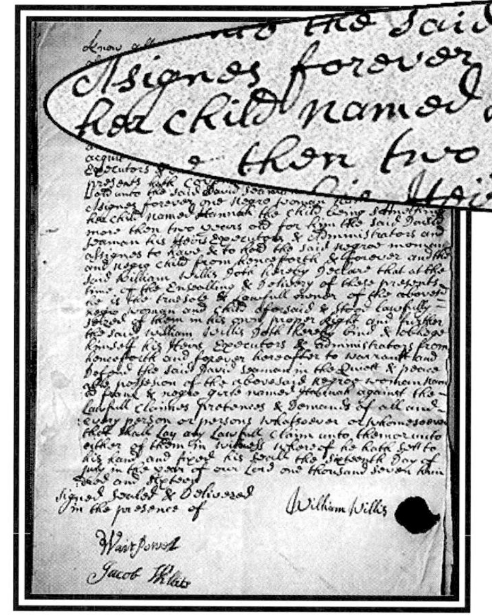

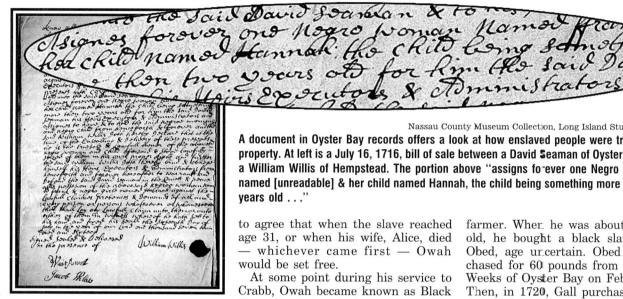

Nassau County Museum Collection, Long Island Studies Institute

A document in Oyster Bay records offers a look at how enslaved people were treated as property. At left is a July 16, 1716, bill of sale between a David Seaman of Oyster Bay and a William Willis of Hempstead. The portion above "assigns forever one Negro woman named [unreadable] & her child named Hannah, the child being something more than two years old . . ."

This was written by Alice Crabb's husband on Nov. 26, 1673. Owah was Black Tom's name at the time, and he apparently was a gift to Alice Crabb. The document does not say what Crabb paid for the young slave.

There were conditions put on the sale by Morris, who was the son of wealthy New Yorker Richard Morris. Crabb had to provide Owah with "sufficient diet and lodging, with good warm clothing." Also, and this was unusual for the time, Crabb had to agree that when the slave reached age 31, or when his wife, Alice, died — whichever came first — Owah would be set free.

At some point during his service to Crabb, Owah became known as Black Tom. He does not show up again in the records until he was freed at age 24 or 25 in 1685. To confirm her mother's intentions in her will, Crabb's daughter, Mary Andrews, swore to a statement on Oct. 26 that "Tom the Negro which was formerly my mother's servant . . . [is] therefore no longer in bondage, but to be a free man from the day of the date hereof to the day of his death . . ."

The newly freed Black Tom took the name Tom Gall, and he married a free black woman named Mary. He began farming, though it appears only as a squatter on a two-acre piece of property that was not his. In 1697, the town granted "unto Negro Tom and his children" the two-acre plot, plus another plot of four acres. He raised cattle or sheep, since in 1700 the town gave "Black Tom the Negro" his own earmark for "all his creatures." He also cultivated his own orchard.

Gall must have prospered as a farmer. When he was about 57 years old, he bought a black slave named Obed, age uncertain. Obed was purchased for 60 pounds from Nathaniel Weeks of Oyster Bay on Feb. 7, 1717. Then, in 1720, Gall purchased an additional eight acres of land from George Balden, or Baldwin, for 85 pounds. Two years later he sold the same parcel of land for 85 pounds to a Thomas Rodgers.

There are no records to indicate how Obed was used by Gall as a slave. But Tom and Mary Gall's daughter, whose name is not known, fell in love with Obed and they married. Four years after the Galls bought Obed, by then their son-in-law, they freed him from slavery.

Tom Gall's story fades away, rather than ends. At about age 67, he is mentioned in a 1727 land sale involving others. After that, nothing. How Gall and his wife died, where they died, where they are buried, these things are not known. His life begins and ends in the pages of the Oyster Bay Town Records. But this sketchy account of the life of Tom Gall is more than we know about the lives of most of the slaves who lived on Long Island.

REMINDERS OF LONG ISLAND SLAVERY

In Huntington, you can walk across the same floorboards and see the kitchen or the office where slaves worked at the **Joseph Lloyd Manor** house in Lloyd Neck.

There, the Society for the Preservation of Long Island Antiquities also runs programs for school groups that tell the story of Lloyd Neck slaves. "We are the only historic house on Long Island that acknowledges slaves and tries to shed light on their lives," said Kathleen Kane, a society member.

The house, located at Lloyd Lane and Lloyd Harbor Road, Lloyd Harbor, is open Sundays, from Memorial Day through Columbus Day.

These are some of the places Long Islanders can go to find out more about slavery.

In Setauket, there is the gallery at **Caroline Church**, which dates back to 1744 and may have been added to keep slaves segregated from other worshipers. In Mastic Beach, crosses were added next to the **William Floyd family cemetery** to mark the burial place of slaves Charles, Caeser, Harry, Sam, Pompey and Lon.

And at the **African American Museum** in Hempstead, school groups can learn more about slavery as part of the museum's program on African-Americans on Long Island. "It's very important that everyone know," said museum director Willie Houston.

Here are some other places you can visit:

St. John's Episcopal Churchyard (1765), Montauk Highway, Oakdale. Revolutionary War soldiers, American Indians and slaves (gravestones marked with "M" for male, "F" for female).

Youngs Memorial Cemetery (1658), Cove Road, Oyster Bay. Has graves of the Youngs' ancestors and their slaves.

St. David AME Zion Church, Eastville Avenue, Sag Harbor. Originally built by Lewis Cuffee and Eastville neighbors in 1840; believed to have been an Underground Railroad station for runaway slaves.

Valley Road Historic District, Community Drive, Manhasset. Remains of Success, a community of free blacks, former slaves and Matinecock Indians established 1829. Includes Lakeville AME Zion Church (1833), cemetery and two residences.

Tuthill Slave Cemetery (1830s), King Street and Narrow River Road, Orient. Dr. Seth Tuthill (1784-1850); his wife, Maria (died 1840), and many slaves with unmarked stones. Marker notes the Tuthills' wish to "be buried with their former servants." — **Joye Brown**

Newsday Photos / Bill Davis

Graves of slaves at the Floyd cemetery in Mastic; at left, the upper gallery at Caroline Church in Setauket is believed to have been added to seat slaves.

In the face of Dutch tyranny, 31 Queens residents defend Quaker rights to worship

Flushing Stands Up for Tolerance

BY GEORGE DEWAN
STAFF WRITER

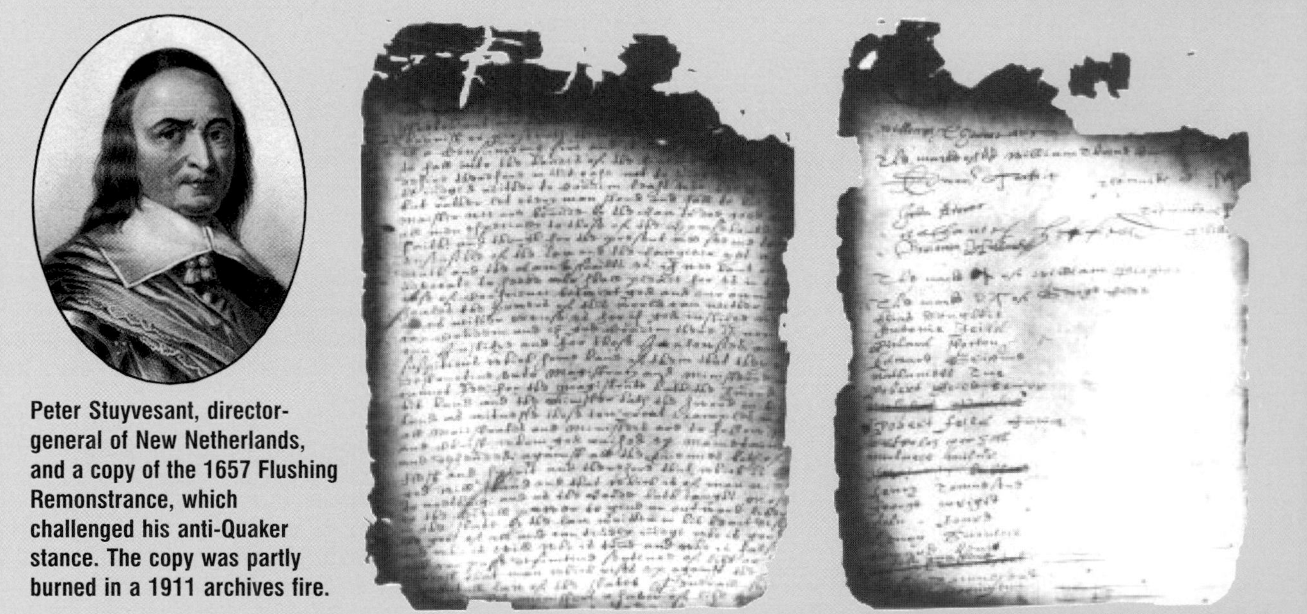

Peter Stuyvesant, director-general of New Netherlands, and a copy of the 1657 Flushing Remonstrance, which challenged his anti-Quaker stance. The copy was partly burned in a 1911 archives fire.

Stuyvesant, From "History of Long Island," 1902; Above, New York State Archives, Albany

To publicly proclaim the new Quaker religion on western Long Island was to risk arrest and banishment. To let a Quaker spend the night in your home could lead to a heavy fine.

The early years of Quakerism on Long Island were a struggle against religious intolerance. It would take a generation of civil disobedience for Quakers to worship without fear of reprisal.

One of the first, faltering steps toward religious freedom in America was taken in Queens when 29 residents of Flushing and two from Jamaica signed a protest to the Dutch governor that anticipated the First Amendment to the U.S. Constitution 137 years later. These were not Quakers; they included the town clerk, the sheriff and two local magistrates.

There was only one official religion in New Amsterdam, and that was the strict Calvinism of the mother country's Dutch Reformed Church. One of its chief practitioners was the director-general, Peter Stuyvesant, who despised Quakers, once calling them an "abominable and heretical sect."

Out of this oppressive setting came the remarkable 1657 document known as the Flushing Remonstrance. In it, the residents courageously and bluntly challenged Stuyvesant and his anti-Quaker laws.

"You have been pleased to send up unto us a certain prohibition or command that we should not receive or entertain any of these people called Quakers because they are supposed to be by some, seducers of the people," began the remonstrance, a form of grievance, signed Dec. 27, 1657, in the kitchen of the home of one of the signers, Michael Milner. "For our part, we cannot condemn them in this case, neither can we stretch out our hands against them, to punish, banish or persecute them . . ."

This attitude was consistent with the terms of the charter given to the town in 1645 by Stuyvesant's predecessor, Willem Kieft. The remonstrance ended with this memorable sentence:

Therefore, if any of these said persons come in love unto us, we cannot in conscience lay violent hands upon them, but give them free ingresse and regresse unto our town, and houses, as God shall persuade our consciences.

The Flushing charter was the most liberal given to any settlement in the colonies up to that point. It guaranteed the residents the right "to have and enjoy the liberty of conscience, according to the manner and custom of Holland, without molestation or disturbance . . ." Holland was noted at that time for its tolerance of religions of all kinds, although the Calvinism of the Dutch Reformed Church was the official religion at home and in New Netherlands.

Stuyvesant was furious. The grievance had been written by the Flushing town clerk, Edward Hart, and delivered by the sheriff, Tobias Feake, both of whom were immediately arrested and jailed, along with two town magistrates who had signed, William Noble and Edward Farrington. They were all later released, but Stuyvesant, laying most of the blame on the sheriff, had him fired.

> **LI HISTORY.COM**
> For the full text of the Flushing Remonstrance, a precurser to the freedom of religion clause in the U.S. Constitution, see http://www.lihistory.com on the Internet.

A handful of Quakers were causing problems for Stuyvesant out of proportion to their numbers. Begun as the Religious Society of Friends in England by George Fox about 1648, the Quakers — the origin of the name is not certain, but it apparently was first used in derision to refer to women who trembled and quaked in religious ecstasy — believe that God can be apprehended individually, without ministers, creeds or churches. This, of course, was heresy to both the Calvinists in New Netherlands and the Puritans in New England.

The first Quakers came to New England in 1656, where they were to be treated even more severely than Stuyvesant was to deal with them in New Netherlands. The first Quaker on Long Island was Richard Smith — the same "Bull" Smith who later founded Smithtown — who was banished from Southampton in October, 1656, for his "unreverend carriage" toward the magistrates.

In early August, 1657, a small vessel called the Woodhouse sailed into the harbor at New Amsterdam with 11 Quakers aboard. The two Dutch Reformed ministers, Johannes Megapolensis and Samuel Drissius, immediately reported to their superiors in Amsterdam.

"When the master of the ship came on shore and appeared before the Director-General, he rendered him no respect, but stood still with his hat firm on his head, as if a goat," the churchmen wrote on Aug. 14. They noted that the ship sailed the next morning with most, but not all, the Quakers aboard:

We suppose they went to Rhode Island; for that is the receptacle of all sorts of riff-raff people, and is nothing else than the sewer of New England . . . they left behind two strong young women. As soon as the ship had fairly departed, these began to quake and go into a frenzy, and cry out loudly in the middle of the street, that men should repent, for the day of judgement was at hand.

The women, Mary Weatherhead and Dorothy Waugh, were put in a filthy jail for eight days, then deported to Rhode Island.

Another of the Quaker ministers, Robert Hodgson, took off for Gravesend on Long Island, where he conducted the first Quaker meeting in the colonies, at the home of Dame Deborah Moody. Hodgson went on to Hempstead, where he was quickly arrested and charged with holding Quaker meetings. He was tied to the back of a cart and made to walk to New Amsterdam, where he was convicted as a heretic, fined 600 guilders, given two years at hard labor and whipped. He refused to pay the fine or work, and, through the intervention of Stuyvesant's sister, was soon released and banished.

"Director-General Stuyvesant was determined to repulse Quaker missionary efforts in New Netherland because he believed that the Friends posed a threat to the social order," wrote Mildred Murphy DeRiggi, a historian for Nassau County Museum Services, in her unpublished 1994 doctoral dissertation, "Quakerism on Long Island: The First Fifty Years, 1657-1797."

For a while, Stuyvesant was successful in repressing what he saw as the new Quaker menace to society. But not for long. Five years later, another Flushing resident, John Bowne, would confront the director-general in an incident that resonated all the way to Amsterdam.

LEGACY

Newsday Photo / Bill Davis

THE JERICHO MEETINGHOUSE

The Jericho Meetinghouse, on Old Jericho Turnpike in Jericho, is one of seven Quaker meetinghouses on Long Island. Built in 1788, it is best known as the place of worship of Elias Hicks, a farmer and an outspoken defender of civil and religious liberties. Hicks and his wife, Jemima, are buried on the grounds. Sunday meetings at Jericho are at 11 a.m. and are open to the public. The oldest Quaker meetinghouse, built in 1694, is in Flushing. Others are in Saint James, Manhasset, Locust Valley, Westbury and Bethpage.

John Bowne stands up to powerful Peter Stuyvesant in a blow for religious freedom

One Man's Quiet Resistance

BY GEORGE DEWAN
STAFF WRITER

Late in the afternoon of Sept. 1, 1662, John Bowne heard a pounding on the front door of his Flushing home. Both his pregnant wife, Hannah, and his 1½-year-old daughter, Marie, were very sick. With the infant in his arms, Bowne opened the door. He was faced by Director-General Peter Stuyvesant's sheriff, Resolve Waldron, backed by a company of soldiers armed with guns and swords. They were there to arrest him.

Thus began a long nightmare for the 34-year-old English-born farmer and businessman. His crime: allowing Quakers to worship in his house.

The governor, as Stuyvesant was often called, was about to ratchet up his campaign against the Religious Society of Friends. Bowne's wife had converted to Quakerism, and by 1662, he himself may have converted. And the Bowne house in Flushing, built the previous year, had become a center for Quaker meetings. Stuyvesant, erupting in anger, ordered Bowne arrested.

What followed was an extraordinary example of passive resistance and civil disobedience. We have Bowne's own version of what happened, written in a journal he kept from 1650 to 1694.

Soon after being jailed in New Amsterdam, Bowne asked to see Stuyvesant. He was turned down because Bowne refused to take off his hat in the governor's presence — a sign of deference to a superior that Quakers did not recognize. He was wearing the hat a day later, when he was taken to court.

"The Governor bade me put off my hat; but before I could make answer, he bade the schout [sheriff] take it off," Bowne wrote in his journal. Waldron tossed the hat on the floor by the door. Bowne continued:

Then he asked me about meetings, and after some words said I had broken their law. So he called for it and read it to me, wherein he termed the servants of the Lord to be heretics, deceivers, and seducers, and such like, and then asked me if I would deny that I had kept meetings . . .

I answered I shall neither deny nor affirm. Will you put us to prove it, said he. I said: Nay, I shall not put you to proving, but if you have anything against me you may act. Here I am in your hands ready to suffer what you shall be suffered to inflict upon me.

At the end of his short interview with the governor, Bowne walked to the door, picked up his hat, put it on and was escorted back to jail.

The Council of New Netherlands sentenced Bowne to a hefty fine of 25 Flemish pounds. It was to be paid in Indian wampum, which was still legal tender, primarily because of the scarcity of the various Dutch, Spanish, English and Portuguese money that was then in circulation. But Bowne still refused to pay. "So I was presently carried or guarded away to the dungeon and there put . . . and allowed nothing but coarse bread and water."

On Oct. 6 Bowne was moved to another jail, where his treatment became quite curious. His wife was allowed to visit him from time to time, as were some friends. His cell door was often left unlocked for hours. This was possibly in the hope that he would flee the province, since by this time Stuyvesant seemed to just want to get rid of him. Just before Christmas, Bowne was even allowed to visit his home in Flushing for three days, unescorted. To the astonisment of the sheriff, he returned to the jail to be locked up even before the scheduled time.

After three months of refusing to pay the fine, Bowne was told that he would be banished on the next ship to Holland. Stuyvesant invited Bowne to his home and offered him one last chance: Agree to leave the Dutch colony within three months and he would be set free. Bowne declined. Stuyvesant agreed to write a letter to directors of the Dutch West India Co. in Amsterdam, explaining why he had banished Bowne.

Bowne wrote in his journal:

So after I had spoken something as to my innocency towards them and how clear I was from desiring any hurt unto them or any revenge upon them for anything they had done against me, the Governor answered I thank you for it, and called me Goodman Bowne.

On Dec. 31, Bowne was shipped to Amsterdam. He presented his case to the directors in writing, but did not get to see them in person until May 25. Bowne told the directors that liberty of conscience had been promised to the people of Flushing in its 1645 patent, signed by Stuyvesant's predecessor, Gov. Willem Kieft. They seemed surprised to hear it. Bowne gave them a copy of the document, then left the room. When he returned, he was addressed by a Lord Perkins, who seemed to be in charge.

"Then he standing up set a bold face on a bad cause and told me they had read it and considered of it and did find it very good and liked it well." The directors were noncommittal about what they would do next, but they did tell Bowne that he could go home to Flushing.

What Bowne did not know at the time was that the directors, having received Stuyvesant's account of his treatment of Bowne, had already sent Stuyvesent a strongly critical response. They pointed out to Stuyvesant that they themselves would just as soon not have Quakers in the colony, but they sorely needed immigration and as large a population as possible to make New Netherlands a going concern.

The letter abruptly ended the persecution of the Quakers in New Netherlands. It read, in part:

You may therefore shut your eyes, at least not force peoples' consciences, but allow every one to have his own belief, as long as he behaves quietly and legally, gives no offence to his neighbors and does not oppose the government.

After a long journey homeward, by way of England and Barbados, Bowne arrived at his Flushing home on March 31, 1664, almost 19 months after he had been arrested. There is a story told that Bowne and Stuyvesant soon met on the street in Flushing, and that the following exchange took place:

Stuyvesant: "I am glad to see you safe home again."

Bowne: "I hope thou wilt never harm any more Friends."

Stuyvesant never got the chance. Five months later, the British invaded New Amsterdam, and he and his council surrendered quietly. New Netherlands was quickly renamed New York, and New Amsterdam became New York City. Within a few years, a Charter of Liberties and Privileges was passed, guaranteeing religious freedom to all citizens in the new British colony.

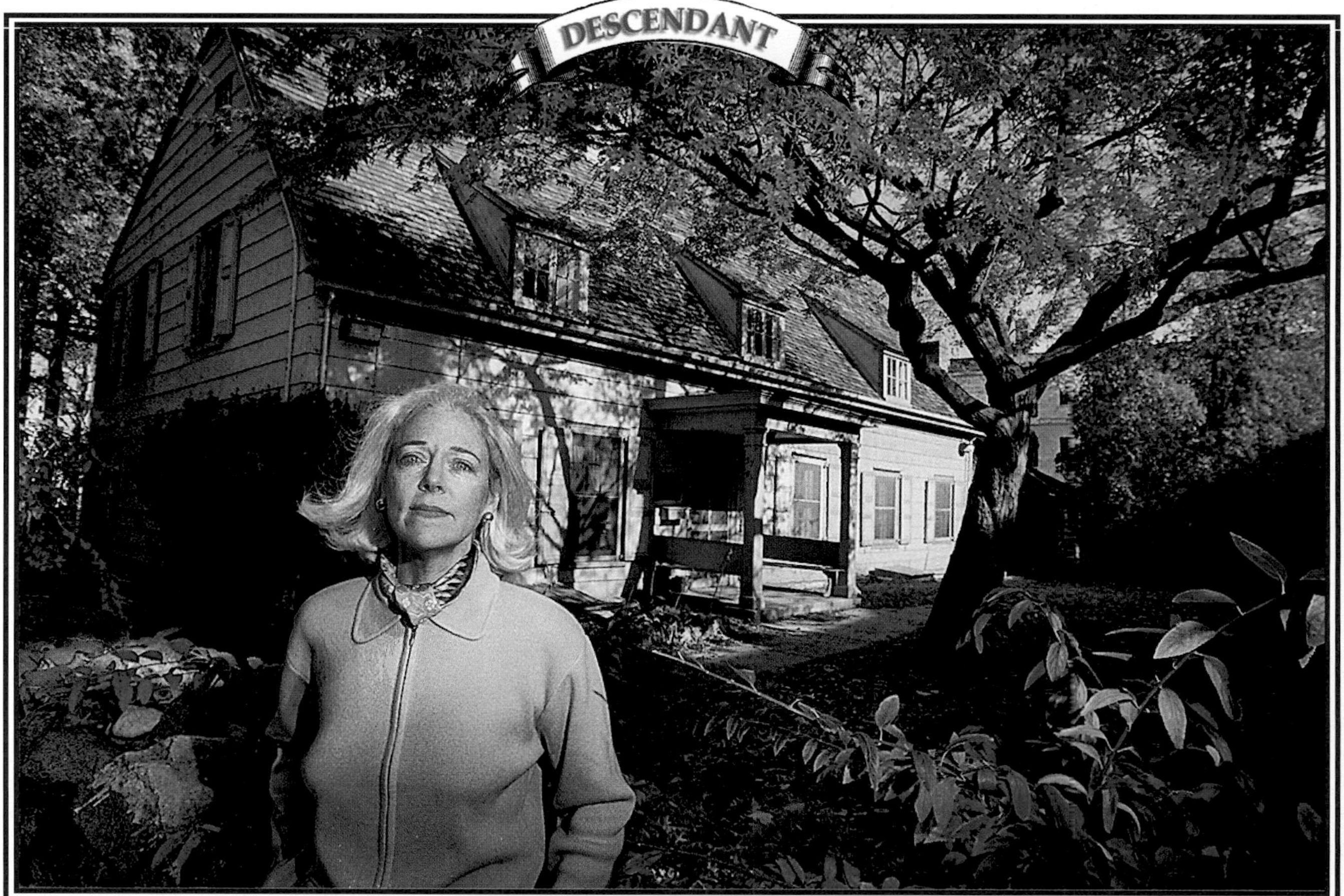

Newsday Photo / Bill Davis

PENELOPE BOWNE PERRYMAN

Penelope Bowne Perryman of East Islip proudly traces her ancestry 10 generations back to the noted Flushing dissenter, John Bowne. She regularly visits the Bowne House, where she is pictured above. "He's a very, very remarkable and inspiring man," Perryman said recently. "More people need to know what he did."

To find out what John Bowne did, visit his home at 37-01 Bowne St. in Flushing, Queens, which was built in 1661. Open to the public for guided tours by the Bowne House Historical Society on Saturday, Sunday and Tuesday, 2:30 p.m. to 4:30 p.m. Admission is $4 for adults, $3 seniors, $2 students. Call 718-359-0528.

A hanging inspires three Oyster Bay siblings to fight for the Quakers of New England

The Sisterhood of Friends

BY GEORGE DEWAN
STAFF WRITER

Mary Dyer, a middle-aged mother of six, was hanged as a Quaker from a sturdy branch of a great elm tree on Boston Common in 1660. A Puritan in the gathered crowd looked at the lifeless body and jested: "She hangs there as a flag for others to take example."

Three remarkable young Quaker sisters from Oyster Bay took example from Mary Dyer's death, but not in the way the scornful Puritan intended. Over a period of 17 years, from 1660 to 1677, Mary Wright, then Hannah Wright, then Lydia Wright, were so moved by the persecution of Quakers in New England that they went to Boston, each on her own, to testify in the courts of Puritan authority. For their efforts, they were jailed, pilloried and run out of town.

"Assertively and independently, each questioned the authority of ministers and magistrates, taking a course of action not considered appropriate for women in a paternalistic society," Mildred DeRiggi, a historian with the Nassau County Department of Museum Services, said at a 1996 history conference.

The oldest sister, Mary, who was 18 at the time of Dyer's death, traveled by herself to Boston a few months later. She went to demonstrate against the hanging of Mary Dyer, who after she had been banished, returned to Boston to continue preaching. Mary Wright, along with several Quakers from Salem, Mass., were all immediately jailed.

The next sister to challenge the authorities was Hannah, four years younger than Mary and a teenager also when she went to Boston. Although King Charles II by this time had halted the hanging of Quakers — four had been executed — a new Massachusetts law was in effect. It called for Quakers to be stripped naked to the waist, tied to the back of a cart and whipped through town after town until they were out of the colony.

The Granger Collection

AP Photo

A 19th Century engraving shows Puritans in the 1670s whipping Quakers in Boston, where a statue recalls martyr Mary Dyer.

Hannah's story is summarized in "The History of the Rise, Increase and Progress of the Christian People Called Quakers," a 19th Century book by William Sewel:

"Once, a girl . . . called Hannah Wright, whose sister had been banished for religion, was stirred with such zeal, that coming from Long Island, some hundreds of miles from Boston, into that bloody town, she appeared in the court there, and warned the magistrates to spill no more innocent blood. This saying so struck them at first, that they all sat silent; till Rawson the secretary said, "What, shall we be baffled by such a one as this? Come, let us drink a dram."

The youngest of the sisters, Lydia, was 22 in the summer of 1677 when she and other Quakers accompanied Margaret Brewster of Barbados when she entered a Puritan Church in Boston dressed as a penitent. "Brewster was barefoot, with her hair loose and with ashes on her head, her face blackened, and sackcloth covering her garments," DeRiggi said.

All of the Quakers were arrested. In August, they appeared in court for trial, and Lydia Wright's testimony before the magistrates — reproduced in a 1753 book by Joseph Besse, "A Collection of the Sufferings of the People Called Quakers" — shows she had remarkable poise for a young woman.

Gov. John Leverett: "Are you one of the women that came in with this woman into Mr. Thatcher's meeting-house to disturb him at his worship?"

Lydia Wright: "I was; but I disturbed none, for I came in peaceably, and spake not a word to man, woman or child."

Governor: "What came you for then?"

Wright: "Have you not made a law that we should come to your meeting? For we were peaceably met together at our own meeting house, and some of your constables came in and haled some of our Friends out, and said, 'This is not a place to worship God in.' Then we asked him 'Where we should worship God?' Then they said 'We must come to your public worship.' And upon the first-day following I had something upon my heart to come to your public worship, when we came in peaceably, and spake not a word, yet we were haled to prison, and there have been kept near a month."

S. Broadstreet: "Did you come there to hear the word of God?"

Wright: "If the word of God was there, I was ready to hear it." . . .

Juggins (a magistrate): "You are led by the spirit of the devil, to ramble up and down the country like whores and rogues a cater-wauling."

Wright: "Such words do not become those who call themselves Christians, for they that sit to judge for God in matters of conscience ought to be sober and serious, for sobriety becomes the people of God, for these are a weighty and ponderous people."

Governor: "Do you own [acknowledge] this woman?

Wright: "I own her and have unity with her, and I do believe so have all the servants of the Lord, for I know the power and presence of the Lord was with us."

Juggins: "You are mistaken: You do not know the power of God. You are led by the Spirit and Light within you, which is of the Devil. There is but one God, and you do not worship that God which we worship."

Wright: "I believe thou speakest truth, for if you worshipped that God which we worship, you would not persecute his people, for we worship the God of Abraham, Isaac and Jacob, and the same God that Daniel worshipped."

So they cried, "Take her away."

Margaret Brewster was stripped to the waist, given 20 lashes, tied to the back of a cart and drawn through town. Lydia Wright and the rest of the women were also tied to the cart, but not whipped. Thus banished, Lydia returned to Oyster Bay.

The Wright sisters were the daughters of Peter and Alice Wright, who were among the first settlers of Oyster Bay. The middle sister, Hannah, died at age 29 when her boat capsized while she was on a Quaker mission in Maryland. Both Mary and Lydia married, and in 1685 they moved with their families to New Jersey.

Newsday Photo / Bill Davis

The 1884 monument to Nathaniel Sylvester "and the last four Friends to be executed on the Boston Common."

SHELTERING ISLAND

During the period in which the Quakers were persecuted, Shelter Island was the only place outside of Rhode Island where a Quaker could go and worship without fear. Many who had been banished from the Massachusetts Bay Colony, including Mary Dyer, spent some time there, and it became a place of asylum for dispossessed Friends. This was all because of the strong Quaker beliefs of the Island's owner, Nathaniel Sylvester, and his wife, Grissell.

It is only a myth that the island was so-named as the place where shelter was given to persecuted Quakers. In fact, the name came earlier, and is derived from an Indian word meaning "island sheltered by islands."

In 1884, a monument to Sylvester was erected in the woods on his old property, and it includes a tribute to four Quakers hanged by the Puritans: Mary Dyer, Marmaduke Stevenson, William Robinson and William Leddra. Open-air Quaker meetings are held there from May through October. Open to the public, it is on a dirt road off Route 114, about 1.2 miles from the North Ferry, or 3.3 miles from the South Ferry. — George DeWan

A Southampton tax official passes himself off as owner of nearly one-third of Long Island

John Scott, Scoundrel

By Molly McCarthy
STAFF WRITER

Long Island — like the rest of the New World — was a land of opportunity. And one of the most flamboyant of those pioneering opportunists was John Scott.

Though Scott lived less than 10 years here, his escapades proved so legendary that he is almost always immortalized in history books as "Capt. John Scott of Long Island." By the age of 30, Scott claimed to own nearly a third of the Island and persuaded fellow English settlers to call him their president.

Historians have other names for him — rogue, rascal, adventurer and swindler. Today, he'd be called a con artist.

Born in England in 1634, Scott was sent to the Massachusetts Bay Colony as a boy during the fallout of his mother country's civil war. After an apprenticeship with a Quaker family, he went to sea and acquired the respectable title of captain. In 1654, Scott arrived in Southampton, where he tried just about any occupation that would earn him the capital to buy land. He was a blacksmith, whaler, fur trader and sea merchant. Soon, he was making real estate deals with the famous sachem, Wyandanch, whom he referred to in a land deed as "an ancient and great friend."

In 1658, Scott — by now a town tax commissioner of Southampton — set up house on land he purchased along the southern shore of Peconic Bay, where North Sea is today. After a flurry of negotiations with the Indians and settlers, the would-be land tycoon claimed to own parts of what now encompasses the Town of Brookhaven in addition to holdings in Hempstead, Quogue, Southampton, East Hampton and Huntington.

But his new property wealth was in jeopardy. If the Dutch who had settled the western end of Long Island won their claim to the rest, his holdings would be lost. He also had to worry about whether Connecticut or another colony would claim it. Connecticut Gov. John Winthrop had long insisted that his colony's charter included Long Island.

So, in 1660, the English settlers sent Capt. John Scott to the court of Charles II to make a case for an independent colony. Little did they know that Scott would be making a case for himself.

In England, Scott secured the right introductions, bought elegant clothes and donned a light-colored curling wig in the fashion of the day. A contemporary described Scott's appearance:

A proper well-sett man in a great light coulered Periwigg, rough-visaged, haveing large haire on his eyebrows, hollow eyde, a little squintain or a cast with his Eye, full faced about ye cheekes, with a Black hatt & in a streight boddyed coate cloath colour with silver lace behind.

To assure an audience with the king, Scott claimed to be a Scott of Scot's Hall in Kent. Though many historians later doubted his claim, Dorothea Scott, the heiress to Scot's Hall, was so charmed by the man that she vouched for his lineage and later gave him 2,000 pounds for what she believed to be 20,000 acres along the southern shore of Long Island.

Dorothea never saw the money again, not to mention the land, which was never Scott's to sell.

In his plea to Charles II, Scott asked for no less than to be appointed governor of Long Island. And, even though the king was said to approve of the idea, the request was denied by the king's Council of Foreign Plantations. Nevertheless, the rumor had already spread across the sea that Scott had been named governor.

Upon his return, Scott met with Connecticut officials and agreed to head an expedition to push the Dutch off Long Island and annex it to Connecticut. Then he huddled with representatives of the English towns on Long Island and persuaded them to elect him president until the "Duke of York, or His Majesty could establish a government among them."

With these conflicting loyalties to Connecticut and Long Island, Scott assembled some men and rode into New Netherlands to confront the Dutch. "This country you inhabit is unjustly occupied by your leaders," he shouted to Dutch settlers. "It belongs to the king of England and not to the Dutch. If you acknowledge his Brittanic majesty's sovereignty you will be permitted to remain in your homes. Otherwise you will be forced to leave."

In requesting a meeting with the Dutch governor, Peter Stuyvesant, Scott signed his missive, "President John Scott." Stuyvesant, who had heard rumors that Scott had been appointed governor of a new English colony, eventually agreed to the meeting.

Back in Connecticut, Winthrop got word of Scott's actions, and immediately called for his arrest. Among the charges were forgery, sedition, treason and "profanation of God's Holy Day."

A band of Winthrop's men sailed to Scott's newly established estate in Setauket, which the captain had named "Scot's Hall" after the great English manor. They took him to jail in Hartford. Scott's arrest did draw protests from many settlers, who still believed he had their best interests at heart.

After three months in prison, Scott escaped, returning to his estate.

He did not stay long. In February, 1665, after the duke of York established his government in New York, Scott was asked to produce a deed verifying his claim to "20 miles square in the heart of Long Island" — probably much of Brookhaven.

He didn't come up with the document. Instead, he skipped Long Island and headed for Barbados. His estate was sold, and his family left destitute.

Capt. John Scott of Long Island never returned.

A Never-Ending Battle for Primacy

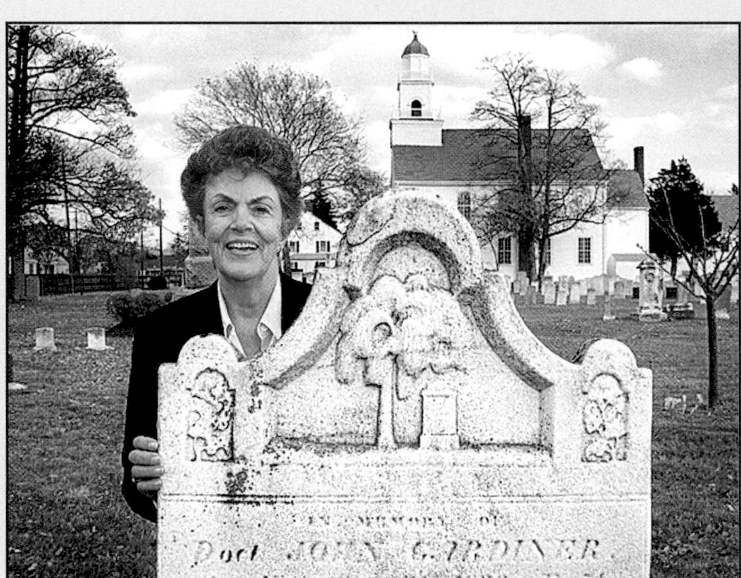

Newsday Photos / Bill Davis

Antonia Booth, Southold town historian, at the grave of John Gardiner, at the Old Burying Ground of the First Presbyterian Church, which traces its beginnings from 1640. Below, Robert Keene, Southampton historian, whose town got its start in the same year

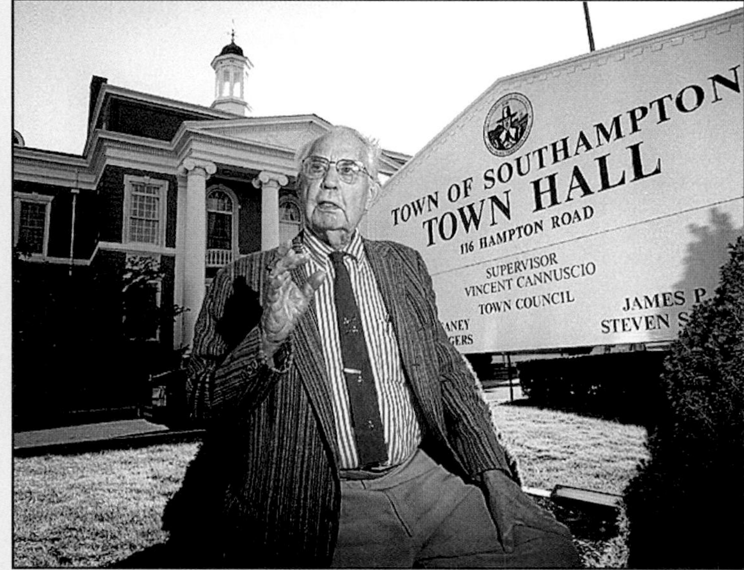

No. 2 Won't Do For Southold And Southampton

Which came first, Southold or Southampton? Both towns were started in 1640, and each claims to be the first English town on Long Island.

"This question has been argued since the 19th century," said Antonia Booth, the Southold town historian, who believes her town was first. "It's pretty obvious they came to the North Fork first. It was closer to Connecticut and easier to reach. Why sail around the North Fork to go to the South Fork?"

"Of course we were first," said Robert Keene, the Southampton town historian. "Our settlers came in early June; Southold was settled in the fall. But I don't think it's black and white — it can't really be nailed down. But we were first."

Documents in either town don't answer the question, which is why people have been arguing over it for more than a century. Southold documents suggest a church group arrived in the fall. But one theory says that the group would not have arrived at that time of year without an earlier group coming over to plant crops and build houses. This point is butressed by a Southold document that shows that a standing house was sold in August, months before the church group arrived.

Southampton documents suggest the first settlers arrived at a place called Conscience Point in early June, time enough to get crops in the ground and houses up before winter set in. But beyond a few pieces of paper in both towns, the question of which town came first can't be definitively answered.

In 1939, the then-Southold town historian, Wayland Jefferson, said he found a document called the Osmon Deposition that proved Southold was first. His discovery came as both towns were about to celebrate their 300th anniversaries. But it proved nothing — historians now say the document, which Jefferson never showed to anyone, was a fake.

After a century of often acrimonious debate on the subject, both town historians say it's time to talk about history that is knowable.

"What differences does it really make now?" Keene said. — **Steve Wick**

A Long Island farmer's wife is accused of witchcraft three decades before the trials in Salem

Witchhunt in East Hampton

BY GEORGE DEWAN
STAFF WRITER

One Friday in early February, 1657, 16-year-old Elizabeth Gardiner Howell lay feverish and delirious in her bed in the small, isolated village of East Hampton. Elizabeth's infant daughter had just been taken from her breast after feeding, and she crooned a psalm at the departing child. Suddenly, the teenage mother stiffened and shrieked:

"A witch! A witch! Now you are come to torture me because I spoke two or three words against you!"

Elizabeth's father, Lion Gardiner, the leading citizen of the community, was summoned from his home across the street.

"What did you see?" asked Gardiner.

"A black thing at the bed's feet," cried Elizabeth, violently flailing her arms to strike at what she saw.

By Sunday evening, Elizabeth Howell was dead. So began a chain of events that led to one of the first witchcraft trials in the American colonies, more than three decades before Salem, Mass., would be forever marked by the sign of the witch.

The accused was Goody Garlick, a woman in her 50s who lived just down the street. Her actual name was Elizabeth, the wife of Joshua Garlick, a farmer who had once worked for Gardiner on his nearby island — first called the Isle of Wight but later renamed Gardiners Island. Goody was a shortened form of Goodwife: Goodman and Goodwife were not names, but terms of address for a married person who was not of high rank — similar to Mr. or Mrs. — but also not lower class.

The death of young Elizabeth Howell got the little rural community of 33 families buzzing. Goody Simons told the local magistrates that as Elizabeth lay dying she told her that Goody Garlick was responsible. This led the justices, John Mulford, John Hand and Thomas Baker, to hold three weeks of hearings, where depositions were taken from 13 witnesses. All the direct quotations used in this account are copied verbatim from these depositions, which are in the Town of East Hampton archives.

On Saturday, Lion Gardiner's wife, Mary, who was ill herself, left her bed to visit her daughter. Elizabeth, who was the first English child to be born in New York State, put out her hand to her mother and began crying. "Oh, mother, mother," she said. "I am bewitched."

"I asked her who she saw," said Mary Gardiner. "And she said, 'Goody Garlick in the further corner and a black thing at the hither corner, both at the feet of the bed.' "

Goodwife Simons testified that Elizabeth had once gotten terribly upset with Joshua Garlick for being sharp-tongued with her when she went to his farm to look for her husband, Arthur, who was there threshing. On the second night of her sickness, Elizabeth told Goody Simons, who was staying with her, to go and get Goody Garlick.

"I could tear her in pieces," Elizabeth told Goody Simons. "She is a double-tongued woman! Did you not see her last night stand by the bed side ready to pull me in pieces? And she pricked me with pins."

A number of residents told the justices stories about Goody Garlick that hurt her case. Goody Edwards said that once Goody Garlick had requested that Edwards' daughter, who had recently given birth, provide her with some breast milk, which she did. The child immediately got sick. Edwards later told this story to Goody Davis, the wife of Foulk Davis. Goody Davis told Edwards that Goody Garlick had once made the same request of her own daughter, whose child quickly died.

Here is more of the testimony:

Thomas Tallmage said that he had once been at the house of Goody Davis:

[She was] speaking unto me about some accidents that had fallen out among them at the Island [Wight] as concerning the death of her child in what manner it was taken away and of an ox that had his leg broke and having reference in her speech concerning Goody Garlick as if she were a witch.

Richard Stratton said that, years earlier, he heard Goody Davis say that her own child died strangely at the Island. "She thought it was bewitched and she said she did not know of any one on the Island that could do it unless it were Goody Garlick."

Goody Birdsall heard Davis say that she had dressed her child in clean linen at the Island. "Goody Garlick came in and said how pretty the child doth look. And so soon as she had spoken Goody Garlick said the child is not well for it groaneth and Goody Davis said her heart did rise and Goody Davis said when she took the child from Goody Garlick she said she saw death in the face of it. And her child sickened presently upon it and lay five days and five nights and never opened the eyes nor cried till it died."

One person who did not testify, for whatever reason, was Goody Davis, who at one time lived on the Isle of Wight, as did the Garlicks. And as the testimony went on, it became increasingly apparent that it was this same Goody Davis who seemed to be Goody Garlick's chief accuser. Through the testimony of others, Davis accused Goody Garlick of having caused a catalog of unexplained happenings on the Island: a child that was "taken away in a strange manner," a man that was dead, a fat and lusty sow and her piglets that died during the birth, an ox with a broken leg.

By the end of the hearing, the focus seemed to have shifted to Goody Davis. Jeremiah Vaile, who lived next door to the Garlicks but who had once worked for Gardiner on the island, said that Gardiner was once asked if he thought that Davis' child had been bewitched. Gardiner, who didn't testify but whose word counted for something in the town, replied testily that "Goody Davis had taken an Indian child to nurse and for lucre of a little wampum had merely starved her own child."

In his 1996 book, "Imagining the Past," historian Timothy H. Breen took a close look at East Hampton history. He concluded that the Goody Garlick case was one of many instances of the East Hamptonites trying to establish a pecking order in their new little town.

"The investigation into witchcraft

The Granger Collection

Accusations fly in an illustration of the 1692 trial of two suspected witches in Salem, Mass., in an 1892 illustration by artist Howard Pyle.

SETAUKET, SCENE OF MORE CHARGES

Not long after Christmas, 1664, George Wood, a Setauket landowner and innkeeper, sickened and died. A while after that, his infant son followed him to the grave. These two deaths resulted in the only other witchcraft trial of Long Islanders.

Ralph and Mary Hall were indicted on charges of witchcraft and sorcery in connection with the death of the Woods. They were tried in the Court of Assizes in New York in October, 1665, the only witchcraft trial ever held in the State of New York. The Halls pleaded not guilty, and no public testimony was taken. The jury had some questions about Mary Hall, but none about Ralph Hall.

"We find that there are some suspicions by the evidence, of what the woman is charged with, but nothing considerable of value to take away her life," the jury said. "But in reference to the man we find nothing considerable to charge him with."

The couple returned to Setauket. Three weeks later they sold their property and moved north of New York City to what is now City Island.

— George DeWan

1650s East Hampton: A Litigious Society

The early inhabitants of East Hampton were a quarrelsome bunch, especially in the 1650s, when the town was just getting formed and the residents were jostling among themselves for status. But instead of getting into public fistfights or dueling matches at dawn, they accused each other of slander and defamation and took their cases to the town justices.

This was the atmosphere in which Goody Garlick was charged with witchcraft.

The issues were usually minor, but the outcomes major. One man accused a woman of slandering his wife by calling her a liar when she claimed her new petticoat had come all the way from England. A man accused another of overcharging him in a business transaction. A man claimed another man was going about town accusing his 17-year-old servant of being a masturbator.

But few claims were as odd and seemingly trivial as the pumpkin porridge case. In January, 1658, John Wooley, a servant of the Gardiners, filed a defamation suit against Mrs. John Hand, who happened to be the wife of one of the three judges, called townsmen. Out of the trial testimony comes this story:

Elizabeth Gardiner, wife of Lion Gardiner, had made pumpkin porridge, set it down and left the room. When she returned she was angered to learn that the porridge had been eaten. The culprits turned out to be two members of her own family, who she proceeded to berate angrily. But Wooley, it was claimed, stood nearby and made mocking noises, including "bow wou," apparently an imitation of a dog barking. Mrs. Hand, who wasn't even there, spread the story around town.

The trial went quickly. Wooley's witnesses agreed that he wasn't there when Elizabeth Gardiner reprimanded the culprits. Mrs. Hand's witnesses provided little support in her defense. The jury found in favor of Wooley, and fined Mrs. Hand 10 shillings plus court costs.

Then came the charges of witchcraft against Goody Garlick. "Early in February 1658 the inhabitants of East Hampton harvested a decade of ill will," writes historian Timothy Breen. ". . . The appropriate context for this particular trial is not the long story of New England witchcraft, but rather the short, local history of slander and defamation. For in this society, nothing could have been more damaging to a person's reputation than a charge of witchcraft." — **George DeWan**

Participants in the Investigation

The 1657 case of Goody Garlick offers a look at the small-town nature of early East Hampton. The community was founded by English settlers in 1648 and named Maidstone. For several years it was associated officially with the colony of Connecticut. The community at first had 34 home lots of eight to 12 acres each. (Home lots here are not drawn to scale.) This map shows the proximity of participants in the investigation that led three local justices to indict her for witchcraft. She was later tried and acquitted in Hartford.

1. *Jeremiah Vaile:* Lived next door to the Garlicks, and said that leading citizen Lion Gardiner was once asked if he thought that Goody Davis' late child had been bewitched. He said Gardiner lashed out at Davis for nursing an Indian child for pay while neglecting her own.

2. *Goody Brooks:* Heard Lion Gardiner's wife say that her daughter, Elizabeth Gardiner Howell, "was bewitched."

3. *Richard Stratton:* Heard Goody Davis say that her child died strangely at Gardiners Island, and she thought the child was bewitched. Davis said "she did not know of anyone on the Island that could do it unless it were Goody Garlick."

4. *Elizabeth Gardiner Howell:* Daughter of Lion Gardiner. Delirious and suffering a fever, she said she had seen a vision of Goody Garlick "in the further corner and a black thing at the hither corner." She died the next day.

5. *Thomas Tallmage:* He recalled a visit to the home of Goody Davis when there was a "reference in her speech concerning Goody Garlick as if she were a witch" but he could not confirm that "she did positively say that she was a witch."

6. *John Hand:* One of three justices in the case. His wife, Alice, testified of hearing Goody Davis say Goody Garlick brought misery wherever she lived, and would probably do so on moving from Gardiners Island to East Hampton.

7. *Goody Davis:* Wife of Foulk Davis, an early associate of Lion Gardiner. She is the most prolific source of stories linking Goody Garlick with witchcraft and was sued for defamation by the Garlicks. She did not give a deposition.

8. *Goody Simons:* A supposed victim of Garlick, she had suffered "fits" when Garlick's black cat had slipped into her house, according to case testimony.

9. *Ann Edwards:* Another accuser in the case.

10. *Goody Bishop:* Testified she heard the fitful Goody Simons once declare "that she would not have Goody Garlick nor Goody Edwards come near her."

11. *Lion Gardiner:* Father of Elizabeth Gardiner Howell, he had employed Goody Garlick's husband, Joshua, as a farmer on Gardiners Island. He was originally skeptical of charges against Elizabeth Garlick, but his wife and son-in-law were more inclined to believe the witchcraft charges.

12. *Goody Birdsall:* Testified to a story she heard from Goody Davis. Davis had said a visiting Garlick once admired Davis' child, but observed that the child was not well. Davis took the child from Garlick and the child became ill and died five days later.

13. *Samuel Parsons:* A friend of Arthur Howell, Elizabeth's husband. He had been visiting the Howells the night Elizabeth became ill.

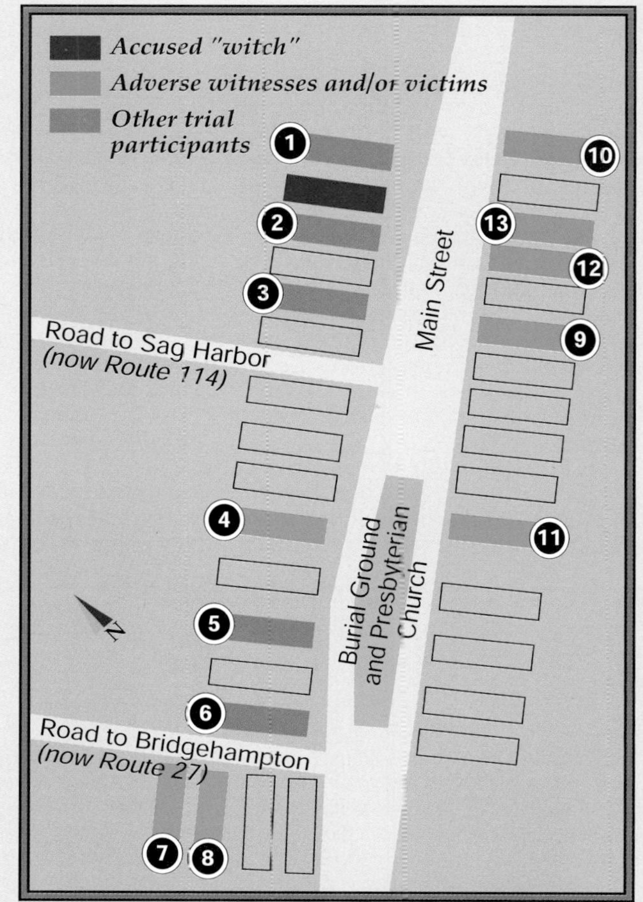

SOURCE: "Entertaining Satan: Witchcraft and the Culture of early New England," by John Putnam Demos; "Imagining the Past," by T.H. Breen.

Newsday / Linda McKenney

had uncovered no witch; rather, it had exposed once again a pattern of slander and defamation," Breen writes. "Discontented people in East Hampton who had come to this isolated extension of New England culture looking for a fresh start and some possible bettering of their lives had in their ambition turned on each other. As the witnesses poignantly revealed, no one in East Hampton seems to have experienced more disappointment than did Mrs. Foulk Davis."

Unable to make a decision, the three judges sent the case to Hartford, Conn., for a trial on charges of witchcraft. But for Joshua Garlick, the testimony was convincing enough. On behalf of his wife, he immediately entered an action of defamation against Goody Davis. There is no evidence that the defamation suit was ever tried.

The Hartford trial was held on May 5, in the Particular Court of Connecticut, with a panel of magistrates headed by the governor, John Winthrop. But it was anticlimactic. There may have been testimony, but the official record mentions none, although the East Hampton depositions were available.

The indictment shows how strongly the idea of a woman possessed by the devil, a witch, was embedded in the Puritan belief system:

Thou art indicted by the name of Elizabeth Garlick the wife of Joshua Garlick of East Hampton, that not having the fear of God before thine eyes thou has entertained familiarity with Satan the great enemy of God & mankind & by his help since the year 1650 hath done works above the course of nature to the loss of lives of several persons (with several other sorceries) & in particular the wife of Arthur Howell of East Hampton, for which both according to the laws of God & the established law of this commonwealth thou deservest to die.

The jury found Elizabeth Garlick not guilty, and she and her husband went home to East Hampton. They seemed to have lived peaceably, well into their 90s. Their chief nemesis, Goody Davis, appears to have died soon after the Hartford trial.

LI HISTORY.COM

For official reports of testimony in the Goody Garlick case and transcripts from other New York State witchcraft cases, see http://www.lihistory.com on the Internet.

Facing a British military threat, the Dutch surrender their hold on New Netherlands

England Expands Its Empire

BY STEVE WICK
STAFF WRITER

In August, 1664, an English soldier named Richard Nicolls sailed his warship into the deep water off the western Long Island shoreline, dropped anchor, and ordered the Dutch to leave their small community on Manhattan island.

It took only a few days for the Dutch to comply.

"It was a humiliating few days for the Dutch," said Charles Gehring, director of the New Netherlands Project in Albany. "Nicolls threatened to turn his ship's cannons on them, so they packed up and left."

Word spread across Long Island that the Dutch government, led by Peter Stuyvesant, the man with the wooden leg embroidered with silver bands, had surrendered and boarded a boat for the Netherlands. The Island's residents — from the Dutch farmers on the western end to the small, English villages on the East End — waited anxiously to see what changes would be wrought by Nicolls, who was installed as the new governor.

They did not have to wait long. Among Nicolls' first tasks was to redraw the map. What is today Staten Island, Long Island and Westchester — the heart of New Netherlands — was renamed Yorkshire. He then divided Yorkshire into three "ridings," or administrative districts. East Riding included all of the present-day Suffolk County; North Riding included Weschester County and nearly all of modern-day Queens County; West Riding took in Staten Island, what is now Kings County and a section of Queens County.

A sheriff was appointed for all of Yorkshire, and each riding had a deputy sheriff. A court system made up of justices of the peace, who would meet three times a year, was instituted. The foundation for English law was now in place across the region. In what would be his most significant contribution to New York history, Nicolls then compiled "the Duke's Laws," which contained the civil and criminal codes that covered all of Yorkshire. He named them for James, the duke of York, who was the brother of England's King Charles II. These laws also regulated Indian affairs, church activities and required all governments to keep public records.

"Municipal Goverment of the City of New York," 1906

An illustration portrays the fall of New Amsterdam as a flag is lowered and Peter Stuyvesant surrenders.

The English towns on Long Island, which had for more than two decades almost entirely governed themselves, were now under the umbrella of laws written in far-off New York — they were now a *part* of something much larger. They had a governor to answer to, and judges, and a set of laws where none before existed.

Hoping to sell the Duke's Laws to his new subjects, Nicolls held a political convention — a first for Long Island. He picked the tiny hamlet of Hempstead — the English village that had been under Dutch control — and summoned representatives from every English town on Long Island. In March, 1665, six months after the Dutch surrender, Dutch-speaking farmers from the west end and English-speaking villagers from the East End arrived in Hempstead to discuss the new laws that would govern their lives.

The Duke's Laws were based on codes that existed in New England. But there were modifications that troubled Long Islanders. The biggest gripe was that Nicolls made no provision for town meetings, an elected assembly or for public schools. Bowing to the Dutch, who had permitted religious dissidents such as Quakers, he allowed for religious tolerance, which was unheard-of in the church-dominated governments on the East End.

"Nicolls tried hard to find a middle ground between two very different people — the Dutch and the English," said Paul Otto, a history professor at Dordt College, in Iowa. "He is seen as doing a pretty good job, even though there was a great deal of complaining from both sides."

LI HISTORY.COM

The Duke's Laws covered all aspects of colonial life, including marriage, property, trade with Indians and even churchgoing. A sampling of these laws can be found on the Internet at http://www.lihistory.com.

The governor evidently wearied of the complaining, and he was replaced just three years after vanquishing the Dutch. His replacement was Francis Lovelace, who assumed power in April, 1667. Nicolls stayed on another year before sailing for England, where five years later he was killed in a sea battle. (His Long Island legacy can be found in street names such as Nicolls Road.)

But the Dutch flag would fly over Manhattan Island again.

In 1672, another war erupted between the Dutch and English on the high seas. The following year, a Dutch fleet plundered English shipping along the East Coast, then sailed into New York Harbor to reclaim their former colony. The Dutch commander, Cornelius Evertsen, sent a message ashore that he was here to take what "was theyr owne . . ." Soon, 600 Dutch soldiers landed on the west side of Manhattan, and the English promptly surrendered.

On July 30, 1673, the Dutch flag once again flew over the city. Once again, the maps were redrawn. New York was now New Netherlands.

But this was not to last. Fifteen months later, in October, 1674, the Dutch signed a treaty relinquishing their American claim for good, in exchange for other property concessions internationally. New York was back on the map. And so were the Duke's Laws.

THE DUKE'S LAWS

The Duke's Laws covered nearly every facet of life on Long Island and were published in alphabetical order — from how arrests were to be carried out, how juries were to be picked, to the amount of the bounty paid for dead wolves.

Although specifically directed at English and Dutch colonists, the laws also covered what Indians could and could not do. For example, Indians were required to fence in their corn fields and were specifically barred from practicing their own religion. "No Indian whatsoever shall at any time be suffered to powaw or performe outward worship to the Devil in any Towne within this Government," one section of the laws said.

There are detailed instructions of how churches were to be managed. For instance, a church was to be built in each community, capable of holding 200 people; ministers would have to present their credentials to the government to prove they were not "ignorant pretenders to the Ministery." The minister would be required to preach "constantly every Sunday and shall also pray for the King, Queene, Duke of York and the Royall Family."

Under the laws, a person, "either Christian or Indean," who kills a wolf would receive a payment by bringing the head to a constable. The payment would be "to the value of an Indean coat."

The laws set out rules by which a person could be arrested. For instance, a person could not be arrested on the sabbath. Jurors were to be paid "three shillings six pence per diem."

The laws also required marks, or brands, for horses in each town. Letters were designated in geographic order, east to west: A for East Hampton, B for Southampton, C for Southold, D for Seatalcott (Setauket), E for Huntington, F for Oyster Bay, G for Hempstead, H for Jamaica and I for Flushing. The letters are still in the seals of Huntington and Brookhaven, which uses Setauket's D.

A painting in the old Nassau County Courthouse in Mineola depicts the issuance of the Duke's Laws in 1664. At left, the Huntington seal, which even today has an "E," the town mark under the Duke's Laws.

Newsday Photos / Bill Davis

The Portuguese princess for whom Queens is named was an outsider in England

The Trials of Catherine

BY CARYN EVE MURRAY
STAFF WRITER

From the day she ascended the throne of England, circumstance conspired against the happiness of Catherine of Braganza, the Portuguese-born monarch for whom the borough of Queens is named.

Though she married into the English court of King Charles II in 1662, she always remained, in most ways, an outsider: She was Portuguese; her subjects were English. She was a devout Catholic ruling a nation of Anglicans. Her dress was conservative at a time when the trend was flamboyance and flair.

She struggled with the strange and baffling English language and customs of her new, adoptive homeland. And she grappled with political enemies and an unfaithful husband.

Even now, the Queen sits at the center of a controversy. A group of historians, artists, elected officials and Queens residents is opposing a move to build a statute honoring the queen. They object because Catherine and her husband profited from the enslavement of Africans.

Charles in 1664 chose to name the land for his queen after the property, the former Dutch colony of New Amsterdam, came under British control. He named the adjacent land Kings County — as a nod of recognition to himself. At the same time, he renamed the central island New York, honoring his brother, the duke of York.

(It was not the first or last time that Queens, Nassau or Suffolk would be named for English royalty. In 1693, the name of Long Island was legally changed to the island of Nassau by the state governor's council, in honor of the sitting English king, William III of the Netherlands, who descended from the German House of Nassau. The name was never terribly popular, and though the law was never repealed, it faded into disuse. The name would later reappear when Nassau County was formed on Jan. 1, 1899.)

Queen Catherine rarely found popular and public acceptance.

It was an unexpected twist for a life begun in the opulence, wealth and splendor of the Portuguese inner circle, where Catherine was born to the duke and duchess of Braganza on Nov. 25, 1638 — St. Catherine's Day.

Her infancy, in the somewhat remote town of Vila Vicosa, coincided with her homeland's own infancy at independence.

Portugal's throne, which had been controlled by Spain from 1580 to 1640, was becoming awash in nationalism, flexing its own political power: Catherine's father ascended to the throne to become John IV of Portugal, and he reigned until his death in 1656.

Friends of Queen Catherine

Catherine of Braganza wed England's Charles II in 1662

The fact that Catherine was a very eligible 18 years of age, with an enviable dowry at the time of her father's death, was no small matter. Portuguese advisers quickly turned matchmaker, certain that a union between Catherine and a bachelor ruler from a leading European power could secure Portugal's political future.

After a brief flirtation with the notion of wedding her to Louis XIV of France, advisers set their hearts and sights on the rakish Charles II, thus bolstering the strategic alliance with Britain.

Though marriage-minded, Charles also was very much mistress-minded. And infidelity was not to be the only trouble spot in Catherine's marriage.

In a nation of Anglicans, sparks flew often, as well as openly and brutally, between followers of the Anglican and Catholic churches.

Catherine didn't just have the wrong religion, she also lacked fashion sense and fluency: She spoke no English, and her conservative, stylized Iberian peninsula style dress clashed with the free-spirited British attire of the time.

For all this, she was criticized and reviled openly as a curious outsider — gaining detractors both inside and outside the court, particularly among the king's many mistresses, who conspired to have her ousted, even killed.

But she was not without some formidable assets: Her political position as the daughter of Portuguese royalty served her well, as did her steadfastness, her good nature — and her sizable dowry.

That dowry included a record cash payment of 500,000 pounds, for starters, and free trade with a number of Portuguese possessions, all of which gave Britain new economic strength as a trading power.

Though her dowry proved sound, her loyal and forgiving nature was tested many times over, as Charles' mistresses repeatedly bore him children — 14 in all — while Catherine miscarried twice and produced no heirs.

Playing upon the public's antipathy toward Catholics, the king's advisers, including the duke of Buckingham, hatched a number of plots against Catherine, proposing to Parliament that the queen be beheaded at the Tower of London — or, alternately, banished to America, where she might fade into obscurity and die.

Fully aware of all his wife had put up with over the years, and not unappreciative of her character and good nature, Charles defended her publicly in Parliament, and stood by her, declaring himself a loyal husband true to his wife.

Ultimately, that indeed came to pass. Manuel Andrade e Sousa, president and founder of the Friends of Queen Catherine, has studied Catherine's life, and he notes that the diarists of the time recorded a major shift in Charles' affections as the king grew older:

"The new mistress of the king is Catherine of Braganza," one wrote. On his deathbed in 1685, Charles begged Catherine for her forgiveness, which, of course, she gave.

After he died, his brother, James, became king. And Catherine began a quest to return home. It would take nine years and succeed only when her brother, then Portugal's king, helped her secure safe passage and the necessary funds. When she finally made it to Portugal, after a 30-year absence, she was greeted with cheers and fireworks.

On New Year's Eve, in 1705, Catherine died at the age of 68. An ocean away, the New World was taking shape.

FAST FORWARD

CONTROVERSY OVER A STATUE

Queen Catherine of Braganza, who never set foot in the borough named for her, is about to be put on a pedestal.

But not if the ad hoc Committee Against Queen Catherine has anything to say about it.

A 35-foot-tall statue of Catherine has been commissioned by the Friends of Queen Catherine, a nonprofit, international collective founded in 1988 to promote Catherine's connection to the borough of Queens.

Manhattan sculptor Audrey Flack, who won a 1992 competition to create the statue, has been working for five years on the design at the Tallis foundry in upstate Beacon. It is scheduled to be unveiled late next year as part of New York City's centennial celebration.

Over the past few months, however, a group of African-American educators, clergy, activists and elected officials has launched a national campaign to stop the statute. They say that Catherine and her husband, King Charles II, supported the enslavement of African people. Even if the two did not own slaves, the critics contend, they supported the system that allowed slavery to flourish in the colonies.

"We should be beyond enshrining the wrong history," said Jeffrey Kroessler, who teaches history at Long Island University in Brooklyn.

The $2.4-million monument, which includes the $1-million statue, is being paid for entirely by private fund-raising in the United States, Portugal and elsewhere in Europe. Meanwhile, a smaller, 10-foot-high bronze statue, which is already complete, will be installed next May on Lisbon's Tagus River waterfront in time for that city's World's Fair, Expo '98.

— Caryn Eve Murray and Merle English

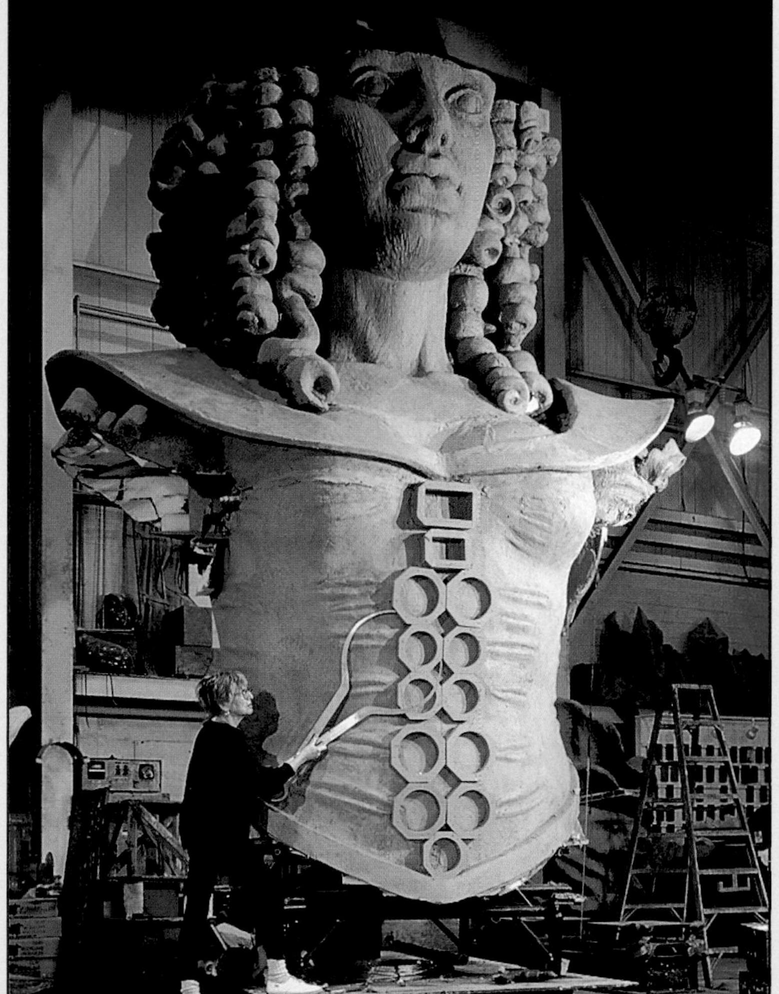

Friends of Queen Catherine

Part of the 35-foot bronze statue that would stand on the Queens side of the East River.

Modest trails put Long Island on the path to a network of thoroughfares

Historic Highways and Byways

BY SYLVIA ADCOCK
STAFF WRITER

The path leads through dense woods, overgrown with thickets and brambles, not far from the rush of traffic on Route 25A. Thick-trunked trees form a canopy overhead, with only splashes of sunlight allowed to break through.

Stony Brook neighbors know it as the old stagecoach trail, and indeed it was. Here, cutting through the northwest corner of the state university campus, is the original path of North Country Road, laid out in the early 1700s on an Indian trail as one of three main roads that crossed Long Island. The main roadway, today known as Route 25A, was moved north in the 1800s when the railroad came through. So modern touches like asphalt never marred this abandoned path that still holds the footprints of history.

Newsday Photo / Bill Davis

The old stagecoach trail, the original path of North Country Road, runs through property at the State University at Stony Brook. Note a relatively new addition: a fire hydrant on the left.

The story of roads on Long Island begins with Indian footpaths that were only two or three feet wide, often following animal trails that led to water. The first settlers followed the footpaths and some became roads.

At first, the roads were merely paths, often called cartways, cleared to connect the villages with surrounding farms. Old town records are full of accounts of new paths being laid out, sometimes cutting through a farmer's land.

In some cases, the landowners took pains to make sure that the traffic wouldn't disturb them. East Hampton Town records show that in 1668, Stephen Hand allowed the town to put a cart path through his land, but he specified that it could not be used to drive cattle, only for horses or ox "in the yoake." Today, Stephen Hands Path, long paved, still can be found on the map stretching north from Montauk Highway in the community of Hardscrabble.

Most of these early roads were local and did nothing to help travelers get from one end of the Island to the other. That changed in 1703 when the General Assembly of New York appointed highway commissioners in Kings, Queens and Suffolk Counties to lay out, clear and preserve public highways "to be and continue forever." These roads were to be four rods wide — about 18 feet — and their surface was only the dirt packed down by travelers. It was not until the next century that roads began to be improved with planks and with drainage ditches on either side.

These first true through-routes were often referred to as the "king's highway." The network began at the tiny Brooklyn ferry settlement where boats crossed the East River to Manhattan; part of the road later became Fulton Avenue. It stretched to Flatbush and branched off to the thriving village of Jamaica. Eventually the road went on to Hempstead.

The 1703 law declared that road repairs would be the responsibility of those people whose lands the roads traversed. The highway commissioners could decide if fences had to be destroyed, or they could allow "swinging gates" that would permit travelers to pass through.

Even then, there was squabbling between travelers and landowners. Travelers complained that the road was too narrow, while landowners complained that it was taking too much of their property. In 1721, court complaints were made against a group of Brooklyn landowners for encroaching on the roadway. Jan Rapalje and Hand Bergen, two of those accused, replied that they were no worse than their neighbors. "If all our neighbours are willing to make ye road according to law," they wrote, they were willing to do the same, "being they are not willing to suffer more than their neighbours."

Rapalje and Bergen appealed to the General Assembly, and soon another law was passed that helped compensate the landowners. If a majority of people in a town "should adjudge that part of the road near to the ferry was too narrow or inconvenient," they could ask the sheriff to summon a jury of 12. The jury could appraise the land that would be used to widen the road, and the amount would be levied and paid to the owners.

The through-routes spread from Brooklyn, and by 1733 three well-traveled roads had been established across the Island. They were known as North Country Road, Middle Country Road and South Country Road. Today, the name South Country Road remains on parts of Montauk Highway, as does Middle Country Road on parts of Jericho Turnpike. North Country Road followed much of the path of Route 25A.

The roads became more important when the first mail route was established. Before 1764, East End residents got their mail delivered by boat from Connecticut and others had to travel to New York to get their mail. But the postal route, a 239-mile circuit, changed that. A Scottsman named Dunbar delivered mail every two weeks, traveling to the East End along the North Shore and returning on the South Shore.

FAST FORWARD

WILL ROUTE 25A KEEP ITS CURVES?

Hundreds of years have passed since the first roadways were cleared on Long Island.

And we're still fighting over them.

Today, the focus is on the increased development that widened roads bring. Neighborhood activists have learned that a new or widened road can bring more cars, more noise and more development.

Which in turn bring more cars and more noise.

"Roads will absolutely define the community that they go through," said Jean Thatcher, president of Concerned Citizens for 25A, a North Shore group.

In recent years, Route 25A has been the focus of battles between neighborhood activists and the state Department of Transportation, which plans to rebuild part of that road in Cold Spring Harbor.

"They'd like to have all the little curves straightened out," said Barbara van Lieu, a St. James historian who wants to protect Route 25A. "You'd just lose the whole ambience of the area."

The state says the changes are needed for safety reasons.

Construction in the Cold Spring Harbor area is to begin in early 1998, but residents continue to battle to stop the changes. Stay tuned.

— **Sylvia Adcock**

But there were no road signs, and it was easy to get lost. Traveling by water across Long Island Sound was still preferred. In fact, the first map of the Island to show roadways did not appear until 1750. It shows a few lines stretching from the ferry at Brooklyn to Jamaica and Hempstead, where the road branches — one road continuing along the middle of the Island and another heading north to Smithtown.

The English mapmaker didn't name the roads, and he drew the lines faintly, almost as if he wasn't sure they'd stay.

In Stony Brook, the path once used by Indians and stagecoaches is now used by joggers and cyclists. In a sense, it has returned to its roots, worn down by the tread of those who may not realize history is under their feet.

Early Roads In 1780, mapmaker Bernard Romans showed these roads of Long Island. Many of the routes appeared on maps made in the 1750s. The Island's geography is shown as Romans drew it.

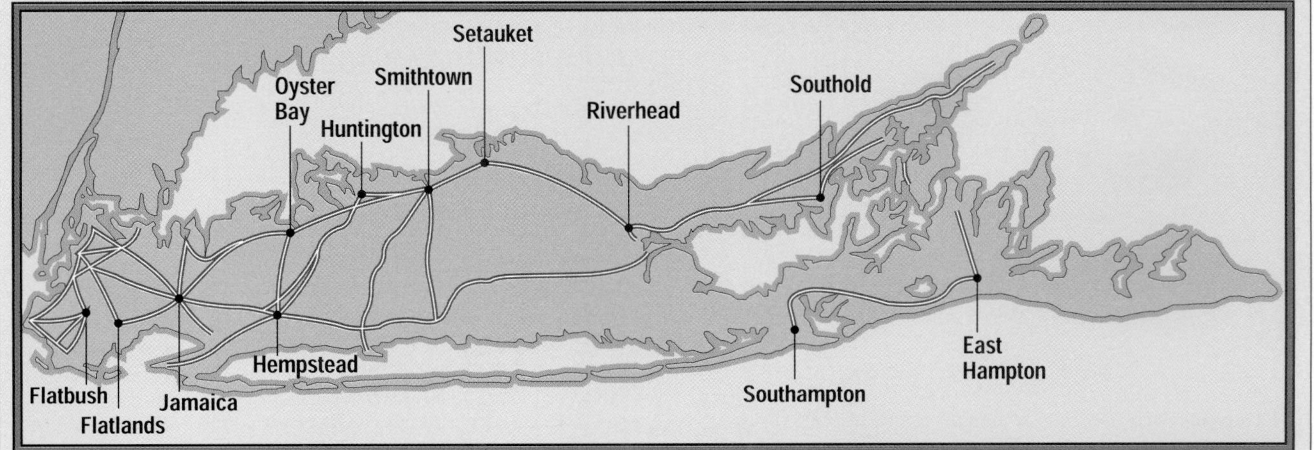

Newsday / Linda McKenney

He goes to sea with royal approval to attack England's enemies, and returns accused of piracy

The Legend of Capt. Kidd

By Steve Wick
STAFF WRITER

He was a respected member of his church in Manhattan and passed the collection plate on Sundays. He was an accomplished sailor and a businessman whom the king of England said was "well beloved." He was hired by powerful political figures to stop marauding vessels from preying on commercial ships. He buried a fortune in stolen treasure on Long Island.

His given name was William but he is better known by his title — Capt. Kidd. He is one of the most famous pirates in history.

Born in Scotland in 1645, Kidd went to sea as a young man, working on a merchant vessel between New York and London. He also served as a privateer — a commander of an armed private ship with official permission to prey on French and Spanish shipping in the Caribbean. By the mid-1690s, Kidd and his family were living in an elegant home on Pearl Street in Manhattan.

"The 17th Century was a tumultuous time," said Mildred DeRiggi of the Long Island Studies Institute at Hofstra University. "There was a gray area between being privateers attacking enemy shipping with government sanction as part of the war effort versus those plundering and smuggling purely for profit."

At that time, New York profited handsomely from the pirate trade. Goods were smuggled into the colony and many powerful public figures shared the booty. Pirates also used the harbors around Long Island to refit their ships and sell their loot — slaves, sugar, textiles, jewels and spices seized on the high seas.

Harpers Magazine

Newsday Photo / Bill Davis

A magazine illustration, at left, shows Capt. William Kidd's men burying treasure on Gardiners Island. Above, a swatch of fabric said to be part of Kidd's bounty. Below, a marker on Gardiners Island says, "Capt. Kidd's treasure was buried in this hollow and recovered, 1699."

Newsday Photo / John H. Cornell Jr.

In 1695, Kidd traveled to London in search of a royal commission as a privateer. There, he met up with a New York friend, Robert Livingston. A political figure and entrepreneur, Livingston was himself engaged in illegal trade with the French, England's mortal enemy.

Livingston introduced Kidd to the earl of Bellomont, who as a member of Parliament had manuevered to get himself named governor of the Massachusetts Bay Colony. Later, he would be named governor of New York. Bellomont and Livingston threw their support behind Kidd's plan to be a privateer, with the booty divided among the principals.

To give the plan the seal of approval, Bellomont persuaded King William to grant a royal commission. Some historians believe that the king was also to receive a share of whatever loot Kidd collected from pirates he captured — in other words, his majesty was now a partner in Kidd's venture.

Kidd set sail on a ship named the Adventure Galley. He returned to New York, where he loaned equipment from his ship to help in the building of Trinity Church in Lower Manhattan, which opened in 1698 under a royal grant. To this day, Kidd's name is engraved on pew No. 16: "Captain William Kidd, Commander Adventure Galley."

The truth of Kidd's venture is lost in the fog of history. What is known is that he sailed for the Indian Ocean to seek treasure. In May, 1698, the Adventure Galley with its 150-man crew dropped anchor off Madagascar. But 90 of his men deserted. Kidd abandoned the ship, which needed repair, and seized a rich Moorish vessel, the Quedah Merchant. By spring 1699, he was in the West Indies.

Meanwhile, back in England, sentiment had changed. Unbeknownst to Kidd, he had been declared a pirate by the British government. Bellomont, ensconced in Boston as governor of the Massachusetts Bay Colony, became a new man — turning against pirates and Kidd in particular. In May, 1699, Bellomont wrote that the inhabitants of Long Island were "a lawless and unruly people" protecting pirates who had "settled among them."

When Kidd learned that he had been declared a pirate, he transferred some of his loot to a sloop, the St. Anthony, and leaving the Quedah Merchant behind, set sail for New England to clear his name. He seems to have gone directly to Oyster Bay, where he contacted an attorney, James Emmot, whom he asked to approach Bellomont.

LI HISTORY.COM

Read the court account from a seaman who sailed with Captain Kidd and was accused of piracy. The testimony, dated May 28, 1700, is available on the Internet at http://www.lihistory.com.

That July, Bellomont wrote:

Captain Kidd in a sloop richly laden, came to Rhode Island, and sent one Emot to Boston to treat about his admission and security. He said Kidd had left the great Moorish ship he took in India, called the Quedah Merchant, in a creek on the coast of Hispaniola, with goods to the value of 30,000 pounds.

Kidd was no fool. He sent jewels to Bellomont's wife, and he buried a large amount of his treasure on Gardiners Island, a half-mile inland from its western coastline. He did this with the permission of the island's owner, Jonathan Gardiner, the grandson of Lion Gardiner. Kidd marked the burial spot with a cairn, a large pile of rocks. The vine-covered cairn still stands on the island, near a granite marker erected in the 19th Century. Kidd also gave Gardiner an expensive silk fabric — a piece hangs on a wall of the island's manor house.

With his bargaining chips in place, Kidd traveled to Boston. His best bet was the Quedah Merchant back in the Caribbean. He also carried proof that the ships he seized were French. But on July 6 he was arrested on piracy charges. Bellomont, his partner at the beginning, was now his enemy.

After arresting Kidd, the governor sent a messenger to Gardiners Island to seize the buried loot — estimated at the time to be worth 20,000 pounds (more than $1 million in today's value). All the treasure is believed to have been removed. Gardiner — who some historians have suggested was in league with Kidd — gave a statement to Bellomont in which he said that on the day he buried the treasure, Kidd convinced him to "take three negroes, two boys and a girl, ashore, to keep till he, the said Kidd, should call for them . . ."

Kidd gave Gardiner gifts of cloth and "four pieces of Arabian Gold." Gardiner said Kidd also buried "a chest and a box of Gold, a bundle of quilts, and four bales of goods." Two members of Kidd's crew, "who went by the names of Cook and Parrot," gave Gardiner "two bags of Silver . . . which weighed thirty pounds . . . a small bundle of gold, gold dust of about a pound weight . . . a sash and a pair of worsted stockings."

In February, 1700, Kidd arrived in London for trial. He was first charged with murdering one of his crewmen, William Moore. Two crewmen who had deserted testified against him. He was convicted and sentenced to hang.

To put another nail in Kidd's coffin, officials then tried him for piracy. He testified that the ships he seized in the Indian Ocean were French ships, but he was not allowed to introduce evidence to prove it. He was convicted again.

On May 23, 1701, Kidd stood on the gallows. When the floor fell out from under him, the rope broke and he survived. He was carried back up and hanged again. This time it worked.

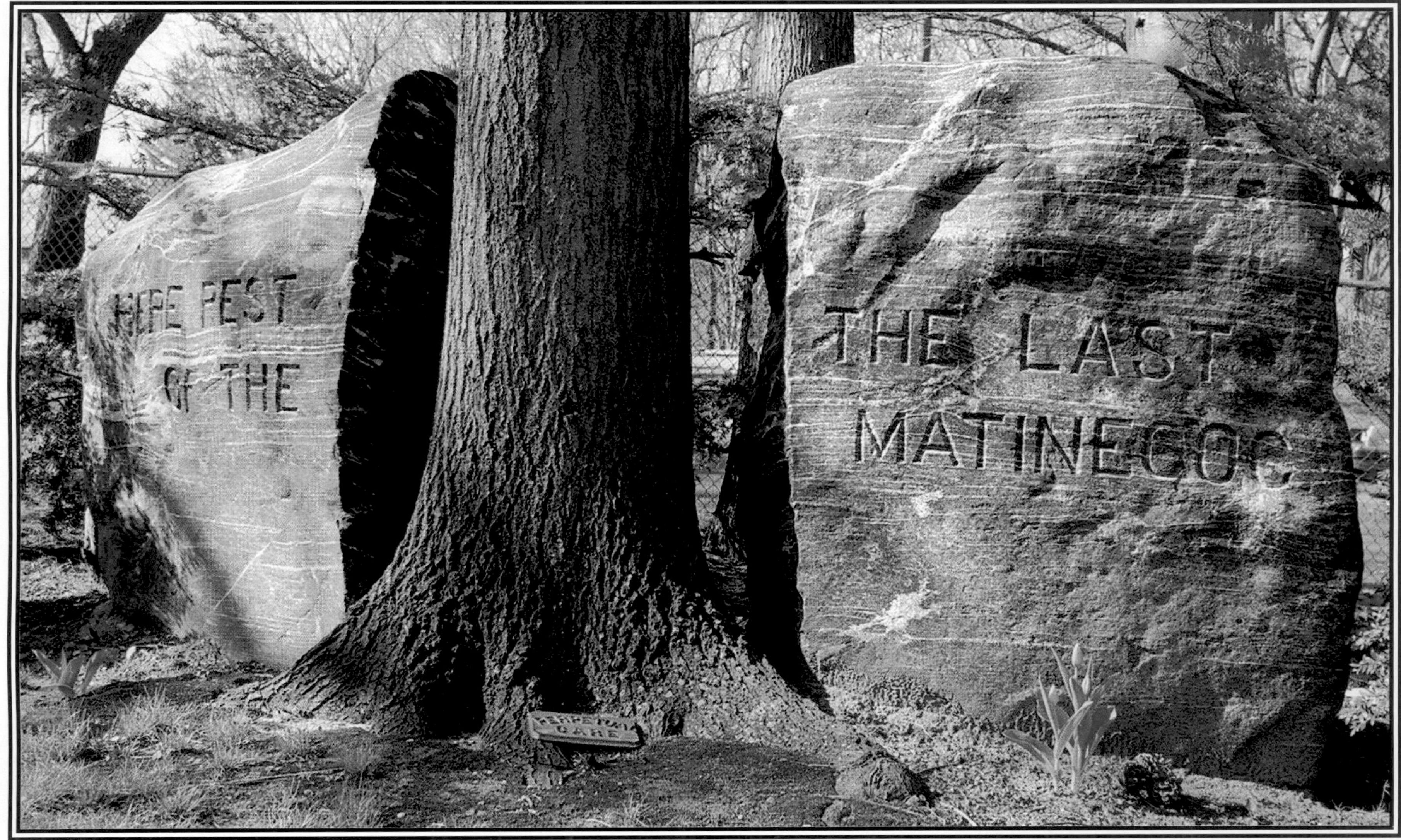

Newsday Photo / Bill Davis

By 1700, disease kills thousands of Long Island Indians, and survivors hold on to little land

A Devastated People

BY STEVE WICK
STAFF WRITER

The Montaukett Indians had lived on the windswept plain for thousands of years. But by the mid-18th Century they had reached a critical milestone in their history. They were, one of them wrote, in danger of becoming "Vagabonds on the Face of the Earth."

Every aspect of the Montauketts' lives had changed irrevocably in the more than 120 years since the English had arrived on the South Fork. Their language, their customs, how they viewed their world, how they worshiped their gods — all of it was gone. And their reservation on Montauk Point had been shrinking for decades as more of their land was bought up by their East Hampton neighbors in questionable land deals.

Hoping to regain some of the land, a Montaukett named Silas Charles dictated a letter to Cadwallader Colden, the lieutenant governor of New York, in 1764 and scratched his mark — an X — at the bottom. He began:

That your Petitioner and those Indians concerned with him, constitute a Tribe commonly distinguished by the name of the Montawk Indians, and . . . at present constitute about thirty families . . . That this tribe continued to live in the Neighborhood; living principally by Planting, Fishing and Fowling, gradually wasting away, and those who remain, now occupy a Tract upon Montawk Point . . .

That they are exposed to, and suffer great Inconveniences from the Contempt shewn to the Indian Tribes by their English Neighbors at East-Hampton, who deny them necessary Fuel, and continually encroach upon their occupations, by fencing more and more of the Indian's Lands, under Pretence of Sales made by their Ancestors.

That your petitioner and his Associates are in Danger of being crowded out of all their ancient Inheritance, and of being rendered Vagabonds upon the Face of the Earth . . .

Charles wanted a secure place for his people to live:

. . . that your honor would be pleased to grant and confirm to said Indians all the Lands on Montawk Point that may appear to be unsold by their Ancestors.

New York history does not record Colden's response, nor what, if any, efforts were made by the colony to help the Montauketts, who would continue to live at Montauk until they were permanently displaced in the 1880s by a real estate promoter.

But the letter reflects how poorly one of the communities of Long Island's first inhabitants was living 12 years before the beginning of the American Revolution. The fate of the Algonquians of Long Island had been sealed by the end of the 1600s — their communities decimated by disease, loss of land and poverty. By 1764, Long Island had changed dramatically since the first years of English and Dutch settlement. At the west end, prosperous farms straddled the girth of Brooklyn, and at the East End, the village of Sag Harbor was a busy port, home to a U.S. Customs House and wealthy inhabitants.

The eastern half of Long Island, which the British had first called the East Riding of Yorkshire, was now Suffolk County, named for a county in England. There, approximately 13,000 people lived. In the western half, home to Queens and Kings Counties, approximately 14,000 people lived. Across the region, towns were small, insular and set apart; there were no newspapers or colleges.

Indians were part of the landscape, either as individuals or in small groups, but often were not counted in town censuses. If counted at all, many were counted as slaves, along with blacks; others were indentured servants, working on sailing vessels, on farms, and living in small communities at the wooded fringes of towns and villages. When Thomas Jefferson came to Suffolk County in 1791, he found the remnants of the Unkechaugs living in a swampy tract near present-day Mastic. There were Shinnecocks in the western part of Southampton Town; and at Montauk, according to Charles, 30 families lived in small huts and cottages on land

AT LEFT: "HERE REST THE LAST OF THE MATINECOC," says a split stone at the Zion Episcopal Church cemetery in Douglaston. The remains of a large number of Matinecocks are buried there. The rock was unveiled during a ceremony in 1936. Despite the inscription, there are Matinecock descendants today on Long Island.

set aside by the town as a Montaukett reservation.

The Indians of Long Island were in trouble long before Charles wrote his letter.

In the mid-1630s, an English official in Connecticut said smallpox had killed great numbers of Indians — entire villages almost at once — and that the Indians living along the Connecticut River Valley were dying like "rotten sheep." Smallpox had long since ravaged Europe and many settlers to the new world were immune. Later that decade, the Dutch began buying land on western Long Island and the English began buying on the East End. Soon, there were accounts of mass Indian deaths on Long Island.

A Dutch account published in the 1650s indicates that a smallpox epidemic in the 1630s killed 90 percent of the Indian population in the New Netherlands region. In a brief account of his life, written in 1660, Lion Gardiner said a great plague roared through Long Island that year, killing two-thirds of the Algonquian population. There are no accounts that year of mass burials of Indians, but the number of dead surely ran into the thousands.

On April 2, 1661, an Indian leader in Flatlands, now part of Brooklyn, told an official of the Dutch government that, before Europeans arrived, his people were "a great and mighty people," who were now reduced to "a mere handful." In one Long Island town, this "mere handful" was subjected to punishment if they traveled into white areas.

According to scholar John Strong's "The Algonquian Peoples of Long Island From Earliest Times to 1700," officials in East Hampton at this same time ordered Indians not to come into white areas for fear they would bring diseases with them. Indians who violated the ban were fined or whipped.

Farther west on Long Island, Indian life was equally bleak. Daniel Denton, the son of the first minister in Hempstead, wrote an account, published in 1670, entitled "A Brief Description of New York: Formerly Called New-Netherlands." He wrote of the Indians, whose number had fallen only 30 years after the arrival of Europeans. Their deaths, he wrote, were the work of God:

To say something of the Indians, there is now but few upon the Island, and those few no ways hurtful but rather serviceable to the English, and it is to be admired, how strangely they have decreast by the Hand of God, since the English first settling of those parts; for since my time, where there were six towns, they are reduced to two small Villages, and it hath been generally observed, that where the English come to settle, a Divine Hand makes way for them, by removing or cutting off the Indians either by Wars one with the other, or by some raging mortal Disease.

"The Algonquian people on Long Island were overwhelmed in the first years after Europeans arrived," Strong said in an interview. "Their communities were devastated."

Refugees Went West and North

When the Kieft War erupted in 1643 across the lower Hudson River Valley, Manhattan island and western Long Island, hundreds of Indians fled west into New Jersey to escape the bloodshed.

These Indians escaped the rampages of Dutch soldiers and English mercenaries such as John Underhill, but they also escaped smallpox and other epidemics that ravaged Indian communities on the East Coast.

Most of the refugees — who spoke an Algonquian language called Munsee Delaware — settled in Pennsylvania, then Ohio, where a massacre occurred in the 1790s that pushed them into modern-day Canada. In Ontario, on a reservation called Moraviantown, modern-day descendants of the very Indians who greeted Henry Hudson in 1607, and who helped Adrian Block build a ship during the winter of 1613-14 on Manhattan island, live today.

And a tiny handful of them, perhaps no more than 10, still speak Munsee Delaware. They are the only fluent speakers in the world of any Algonquian language once spoken on Long Island.

But, in interviews, these Indians say they don't regard themselves as museum pieces — just survivors.

"We feel fortunate that we've been able to live the way we have," said Philip Snake, the chief of the Delaware Nation at Moraviantown. "Leaving New York was the best thing we did."

— Steve Wick

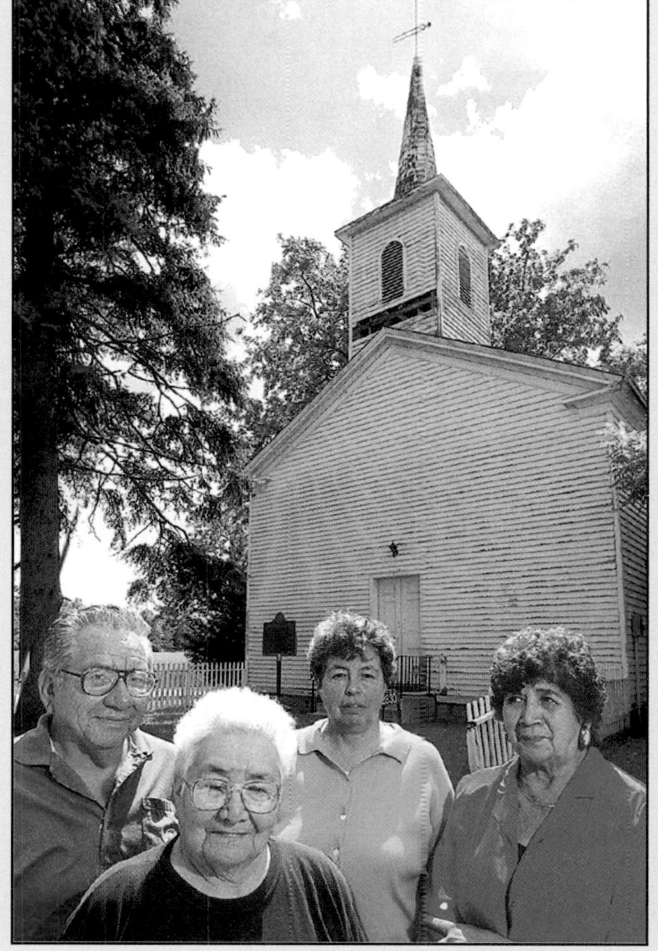

Newsday Photo / Bill Davis

Richard Snake, Beulah Timothy, Dianne Snake and Alma Burgoon, from left, are among residents of Ontario's Delaware Nation Reserve who still speak an Algonquian language once heard on Long Island.

Within a generation of Denton's observations, the remaining pockets of Indians on Long Island had been granted reservations. In nearly all of these cases, records show, the reservations were for the permanent use of the Indians. Historians who have examined these land deeds say questions of fraud permeate the deals. In addition, they say rum was given away when deeds were signed even though in most Long Island towns the sale of alcohol to Indians was illegal.

In June, 1687, New York Gov. Thomas Dongan gave the Matinecocks two reservations, one on each side of Hempstead Bay. The reservation on the west side was for 150 acres; on the east side, 200 acres. According to Dongan's grant, the Indians were to "have and to hold" these reservations forever. On top of this, the Indians themselves did not have the power to sell the land.

"I believe Dongan wrote that in because he was concerned about fraud and abuse," Strong said.

But "forever" didn't last long.

There are no records in Hempstead, or anywhere else, of the Matinecocks actually living on these reservations. Six years after the reservations were created by Dongan, the reserve on the east side of the bay was given as a gift by an Indian named Suscaneman to an Englishman, James Townsend — this in violation of Dongan's grant.

Historian Robert Grumet, who works for the U.S. Park Service in Philadelphia, said this deed is covered with "the scent of chicanery" because later actions by the Indians showed they believed this reservation was still theirs. There also are documents, Strong writes in his book, that show the same Indian who gave the reservation to Townsend giving another man, Moses Mudge, permission to build a house on the tract.

"The transaction from Suscaneman to Townsend is very suspicious," Strong said in the interview.

By 1711, Townsend had passed the land on to two sons-in-law, Thomas Jones and Abraham Underhill. "By that time, the remaining Matinecocks had been dispersed to small enclaves near English towns and were unable to protest," Strong writes. "It is possible that the tract is now part of Hempstead Harbor Beach County Park."

The situation was no better on the East End of Long Island.

By 1700, East Hampton had purchased all the remaining Montaukett lands. The town then granted the Indians residence rights on Montauk "forever." Here, as in Hempstead, "forever" was a relative term. By the mid-1880s, all the Montauketts had been permanently displaced from Montauk Point.

In Southampton in the early 1700s, town officials granted a "thousand year" lease to the Shinnecocks for a large tract of land east of what is now the Shinnecock Canal. Today, a huge piece of this land is occupied by two world-class golf courses. The thousand years ended in 1859, when the town sought to develop the hills on the north side of this tract and pressed the Indians to trade this land for an 800-acre tract on Shinnecock Neck, where their reservation is today. A group of Shinnecocks later testified before a congressional committee that the signatures on this trade agreement had been forged.

Also in 1700, an Englishman named William Smith set aside a 175-acre reservation for the Unkechaugs alongside a creek near modern-day Mastic. Again, the word "forever" was used in describing the Indians' use of the reservation. But by 1730, 100 acres had been taken back by the Smith family; later land transactions involving other parties reduced the reserve to approximately 50 acres.

There are people today on Long Island who trace their lineage to the Matinecocks, who were given the two reservations on Hempstead Bay. But their history on Long Island seems summed up on a carving on a rock in a church cemetery in Queens. The remains of a large number of Indians were unearthed in 1929 when a Queens road was widened. The remains were reburied in the Zion Episcopal Church in Douglaston.

At a ceremony in 1936 — attended by two Mattinecock descendants — a large rock was unveiled which had these words inscribed on them: "HERE REST THE LAST OF THE MATINECOC."

Newsday Photo / Bill Davis

As a sign of tribute, visitors sometimes place stones and coins on a marker at the Indian Field Cemetery in Montauk.

Christian missionaries set out to convert Algonquians in the 1600s and 1700s

Preaching To the Indians

BY STEVE WICK
STAFF WRITER

From their first encounter with the Indians of Long Island, Europeans sought to convert them to Christianity.

Although there does not appear to have been a well-organized crusade to convert the Indians of Long Island, there are accounts of individual missionaries working among them. In a few cases, the missionaires were Indians themselves.

The most famous of the Indian preachers was Samson Occum, a Mohegan from Connecticut who lived with the Montauketts and was ordained in East Hampton.

Besides being a Christian preacher, Occum appears to have been a crusader for the Indian way of life. After working in Montauk, and traveling throughout southern New England, he helped organize an effort to take Indians from Long Island to a religious colony upstate called Brotherton, northeast of Syracuse. There, Occum believed, their land would not be taken over by whites — which is what he saw happening on Long Island.

In retrospect, some historians have said that attempts to convert the Indians were part of a larger effort to assimilate them and their land holdings into white society.

From the beginning, European settlers were upset by the Indians' religious practices. In 1670, Daniel Denton, the son of a Hempstead minister, described the Indians' faith as "diabolical" in a journal he kept of his travels about Long Island. He described an Indian religious ceremony at which a "priest or pawaw" collected valuables from Indians that he put "upon the top of their low flat-roofed houses." Then, Denton wrote, the priest demanded "their God come and receive it . . . After they have wearied themselves, the priest by his Conjuration brings in a devil amongst them, in the shape sometimes of a fowl, sometimes of a beast, and sometimes of a man . . ."

Michael Smith, a Shinnecock who is an ordained minister at the Presbyterian Church on the tribe's Southampton Reservation, said some of those who sought to convert the Indians did it because they viewed it as the first step in eliminating them. "First get the land, then convert them, then eliminate them as a people," Smith said. "That was part of the attitude at the time."

But Smith said it would be simplistic to view all missionaries as working to harm Indians. He said Occum wanted to help them.

"There were missionaries who viewed the Indians' beliefs in taking care of each other and protecting the land as being something that could be incorporated into Christian teachings," Smith said. "And there were others who were brutal in what they did. Occum respected Indians enough, and viewed their culture as being in danger, to want to take them to a safer place."

That safer place was Brotherton, home to a mix of Indians from throughout New England and Long Island. Occum also traveled to England — where he was treated as a celebrity — to raise money for an Indian college that later became Dartmouth.

Occum left a deep imprint on Long Island. He arrived at Montauk in 1749, when he was 27. A few years later, he set up an Indian school to teach children reading and writing. He also nursed them, helped them settle their problems, hunted, fished and raised corn, and preached the gospel. While living at Montauk, he met and married a Montaukett named Mary Fowler, who was a descendant of Wyandanch.

In the early 1770s, a number of missionaries began looking for ways for Indians to live by themselves without pressure from white neighbors. By this time, the Montauketts were living impoverished lives, in grass huts and shacks, on Montauk Point. They had lost nearly everything that had been theirs.

Boston Public Library

Newsday Photo / Ken Spencer

Preacher Samson Occum, a Mohegan, moved to Montauk in 1749 to work among the Indians. He set up a school.

At left, the Presbyterian Church at the Shinnecock Reservation in Southampton. Pastor Michael Smith says some early missionaries harmed the Indians, and some helped.

A deed was secured to a tract of land upstate that was to be called Brotherton. It was meant to be an Indian colony run by Christian Indians; one of the residency rules, Gaynell Stone explains in her book, "The History and Archaeology of the Montauk," was that "no Indian with Negro or mulatto blood could possess any land."

In March, 1774, the first group arrived. Included were a number of Montaukett families. The colony was small until after the Revolution, when Occum led more families to Brotherton. Near the time of Occum's death in 1792, land problems cropped up in Brotherton, too, and in the early 1800s, many of the Indians there moved west to Wisconsin.

In her book, Stone points out a tragic footnote to the Brotherton story. Some Montauketts did not want to make the move west to Wisconsin, but were barred by East Hampton authorities from moving back to Montauk. A few years' absence had, somehow, canceled their rights to land that had been theirs for thousands of years.

History does not provide a simple answer as to who was better off — the Montauketts who stayed in East Hampton or those who fled upstate and later went to Wisconsin. Descendants of those who found refuge in Wisconsin live there today. By the 1880s, Montauketts who stayed in East Hampton were removed from Montauk Point. And, by the turn of the century, their tribe would be declared extinct by a Suffolk County judge.

ALMOST IN THE IVY LEAGUE

Dartmouth College on Long Island?

Samson Occum felt strongly enough about educating Indians that he traveled to England in the mid-1700s to raise money to establish a college. And he and his supporters first thought the college should be built in a farm field in Southold.

That site — called "Corchaug Pond" in the oldest records of the town — sat just west of what is today the hamlet of Southold, and south of Route 25. It was set aside as an Indian reservation in 1685; later, records show, local officials talked of relocating the Montauketts to the site.

In 1767, a minister named Nathaniel Walker, a friend of Occum's, wrote to a supporter about creating an Indian school on the site. The letter reads:

Mr. Occum tells me that there is a large tract of land on Long Island on ye North Side not far west of Southold . . . which he thinks may be procured for a small sum which is handy for fish oysters clams, so that much of the youth's living might be obtained therefrom . . . Will it not be worth while to look after that land . . .? You know the good temper of Long Island folks.

The college envisioned by Occum was not built in Southold for reasons that have never been made clear. It was built in New Hampshire and was named Dartmouth College. Today, students remember Occum by smoking clay pipes at graduation time and ice-skating during the winter on Occum Pond, which is, of course, next to Occum Ridge. **— Steve Wick**

European settlers adapt Old World recipes to American produce, grain, meat and fish

Colonial Cooks Stir a Rich Mix

BY ALICE ROSS

They carried their Englishness over the Atlantic and dreamed of re-creating the best of England in the New World. They brought the things they knew — their religion, their language, a technology that included essential iron and brass cooking equipment, and, of course, their beloved recipes.

Although today it is hard to imagine, the English settlers of 17th- and 18th-Century Long Island enjoyed a sumptuous and wholesome table, characterized by the roasts, pies and puddings that set their table apart from other cuisines of the day. Those with means found a rich base of ingredients: world-class beef, game and seafood, fine kitchen garden and dairy products, various orchard fruits and berries, substantial wheat breads, ciders and ales, and the exotic seasonings of Far Eastern colonies.

Emigrants make do with what is at hand. Wheat, for example, was not easy to grow, so good sense dictated substitutions of native corn, attractive for its easy agriculture, nutrition and pleasing flavor. Settlers cast Indian staples of corn, beans, pumpkins and squash into their own forms. Indian cornbreads (dumplings, ash-baked cakes or pan-baked flatbreads) were transformed with European products — yeast (and ultimately chemical leavenings), milk, eggs, fats and grains — to resemble Old World breads. In the same ways, local pumpkin, squash and even clams made their way into traditional puddings and pie fillings. Beans replaced English pease (dried field peas) in soups, porridges and baked dishes. And quahogs (American hard-shell clams) replaced fish in the fish-milk stews of coastal England and France to become New England chowder.

The Dutch on Long Island did much the same. They, too, grew New World foods alongside those from home, stored cranberries and pumpkins in root cellars chock-a-block with European cabbages, carrots, turnips, parsnips and onions, and dished them up together in Old World ways. Thus the American *citron*, a species of watermelon characterized by a great deal of rind particularly suited to candying, replaced expensive imported candied citron in Dutch "oley koeks," fried cakes or doughnuts. And cornmeal mushes often replaced more traditional buckwheat gruels.

This true melting pot, a combination of the best foods of two continents, spawned the colonial Long Island diet. Sometimes the wealth of flavors was enhanced by a shifting balance between luxuries and staples.

Newsday Photo / Bill Davis

Indian pudding, which includes nutmeg, raisins, stone-ground cornmeal and molasses, in the Smithtown studio of food historian Alice Ross.

For example, to the envy of less fortunate relatives at home, our ordinary farming folk enjoyed a great abundance of domesticated animals, wild game and fish; what with fresh butcherings and the preserved meats of smokehouses and brine kegs, they got to eat meat three times a day, and feasted on oysters at will. And when all else failed, there were salt cod and clams.

One English visitor noted that meats were eaten in larger quantities than vegetables. It would seem that assorted systems for holding hearth spits, long-legged spiders (frying pans), tin reflecting ovens, ceramic or iron stew pots and forged grid irons (broilers) were never idle.

Wood was another blessing. Colonial Long Island forests provided seemingly endless supplies of cordwood, enabling each family to fuel both its hearth and private bake oven. This was a distinct departure from Europe's commercial bakeries and trade-system control of grains and fuels. Indeed, most European women did not own a brick oven and had limited baking skills. However, once in the colonies, and with frontiers outpacing urban bakeries, American women tapped their own developing wheat and rye fields and wood lots. Easy access to inexpensive molasses from the Caribbean sugar mills encouraged the trend toward increased sweetening. Early Long Island recipe collections and diaries frequently included such baked goods as bread or "soft" and "hard molasses cakes" (cake and cookies), reflecting women's new cooking responsibilities and their growing international reputation as a nation of bakers.

Food historian Alice Ross' recent doctoral dissertation was about women, work and cookery in Suffolk County before 1920.

A Crookneck Or Winter Squash Pudding

This recipe was adapted from America's first cookbook, Amelia Simmons' "American Cookery," published in Hartford in 1796. It is likely that this extremely popular cookbook was known on Long Island, where commercial, religious and social ties to Connecticut were strong. It clearly reflects the new world culinary adaptations of southern New England, with which eastern Long Island was identified.

This early recipe is almost clear enough to follow in its original version, but its adaptation follows. It may be used as a pudding, a pie filling or a side dish with poultry or pork.

Core, boil and skin a good squash, and bruize [mash] it well; take 6 large apples, pared, cored and stewed tender, mix; add 6 or 7 spoonfuls of dry bread or biscuit, rendered fine as meal, half pint milk or cream, 2 spoons of rose-water, 2 do. [ditto] wine, 5 or 6 eggs beaten and strained, nutmeg, salt and sugar to your taste, one spoon flour, beat all smartly together, bake.

FOR THE MODERN COOK

2 medium winter squash, such as butternut or acorn, 3 to 3½ pounds
3 apples, peeled, cored and stewed, or ½ cup prepared applesauce
3 tablespoons unflavored bread crumbs
½ cup milk or cream
2 large eggs, beaten
2 tablespoons sugar, or to taste
2 tablespoons sweet wine, optional
1 teaspoon nutmeg
1 teaspoon salt, or to taste

1. Cut squash in half and remove seeds. Bake at 350 degrees for 40 minutes, or boil until tender. Cool and peel.
2. Place squash in large saucepan. Mash over moderate heat. Add stewed apples or applesauce, bread crumbs, milk or cream, beaten eggs and sugar and continue mashing, over heat, until thickened. Add wine, nutmeg and salt.
Or: Place combined ingredients in dish and bake at 375 degrees for 30 minutes, or until set. Serve hot. Makes 4 to 6 servings.

Newsday Photo / Bill Davis

Winter squash pudding

Indian Pudding

Indian pudding, a colonial English-American staple, was still going strong in 1848 when E. Leslie published "Directions for Cookery," from which this recipe is adapted. It makes a fine warm or cold dessert

2 cups milk
1 cup stone-ground cornmeal
2 tablespoons butter, melted
¾ cup unsulphured molasses, warmed
4 tablespoons sugar
3 eggs, well beaten
1 teaspoon cinnamon, or to taste
½ teaspoon nutmeg, or to taste
grated peel of ½ small lemon
½ cup raisins
sweetened whipped cream or sweet wine for topping

1. Preheat oven to 375 degrees. Heat milk with cornmeal. Whisk from time to time until thick. Heat molasses and butter, and whisk in sugar.
2. Gradually beat hot cornmeal mixture into beaten egg. Add cinnamon, nutmeg, lemon peel and raisins. Place in 8-inch-diameter glass baking dish or ceramic mixing bowl. Bake for 1¼ hours, or until top is rounded and set. Serve hot with toppings of whipped cream or sweet wine, if desired. Makes 4 to 6 servings.

Deep Hollow Ranch Photo

Jack, Frank and Phineas Dickinson and father Frank Sr. in '47; right, Frank Dickinson today.

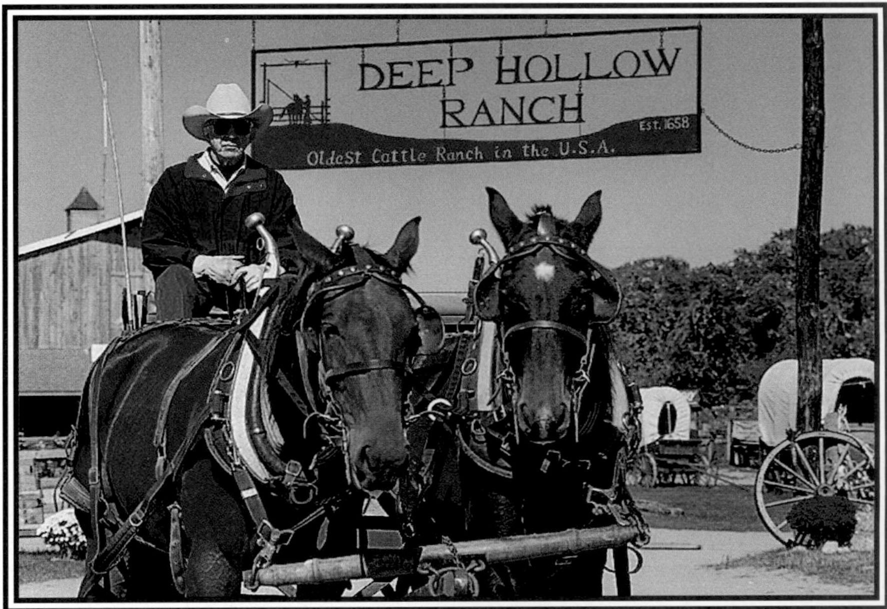

Newsday Photo / Bill Davis

Cattle, the area's colonial currency, continued to roam into the 20th Century

Ride 'Em, Island Cowboy

BY RIDGELY OCHS
STAFF WRITER

It was called "going on" in Montauk and Shank remembers it well. "All the local fellows used to help with the cattle drives," he said.

Starting at about 4 a.m. on a chilly spring day, Shank, just a teenager in the late '30s, and other hands would meet at his grandparents' farm in East Hampton, saddle up their horses and start driving about a hundred head of cattle — mostly cows, their calves and a few bulls belonging to farmers from all over the area — down Montauk Highway.

"Going through Amagansett, they'd roam into peoples' yards. You had to have a wagon with a team of horses for tired calves. They'd just lie down after a while," said Shank, whose real name is Frank Dickinson.

Twelve to 14 hours later, cattle and cowboys would arrive dusty and tired at Indian Field near Deep Hollow Ranch, three miles east of Montauk village. There the cattle, for $6 a head, would graze from May 1 to Nov. 1, when they "went off" Montauk — this time by trucks back to their farms or off to market.

These cattle drives only lasted three or four years in the late 1930s, Shank said, but they were part of a 300-year history of cattle, horses and sheep on Long Island. Indeed, there are those who say that Long Island is the birthplace of the American cowboy and that Montauk is the site of the oldest cattle ranching area in the country.

These claims are debatable. The Spanish introduced cattle and horses in the 1500s on this continent and other English colonies — notably Virginia — had large numbers of cattle by the beginning of the next century. But it is clear that cattle — and, yes, "cowboys," men who herded them — were an important part of the early history of the island.

In 1643 John Carman and Robert Fordham bought from the Indians 60,000 acres of blue-green grass known as Hempstead Plains, now the site of Garden City and other communities. Here cattle, sheep and hogs were pastured and then driven into New York City for sale.

Cattle, more than any other livestock, played a critical role in those days. "The cow was to the Hempstead planter what tobacco was to the Virginian," said Bernice Schultz in her 1940 history of "The Pastoral Period of Western Long Island." Instead of hard currency, cattle were used in exchange for goods; the Indians were paid for their land in cattle, and the governor would accept cattle as payment for land patents.

By the Revolution, there were 7,000 head of cattle and as many sheep in Hempstead and Oyster Bay, according to Schultz. In fact, one of the first large-scale cattle drives ever recorded in this country took place on the Hempstead Plains. On Aug. 22, 1776, as the Battle of Long Island was taking place, orders were given for the cattle to be driven eastward across the plains to keep them from falling into British hands. The colonists lost not only the battle, but also thousands of head of cattle.

Cattle — and pasture lands for them — were no less important in eastern Long Island.

On Aug. 6, 1660, the East Hampton town fathers bought a tract of land east of the town from the Montauk chief Wyandanch. By 1687, they had bought more land, obtaining all of what was called the "lands of Montauk," about 11,000 acres beginning at Napeague and extending to Montauk Point.

Although perhaps not the waist-high leaves of grass of the Hempstead Plains, these fields, bending down to the shimmering sea, were nonetheless rich pastures for grazing animals. Although now the vista is broken by low trees and scrub, "when I was a young boy," Shank said. ". . . It was nothing but rolling hills and grass."

The land was owned in common by citizens who would each pay to have cattle or sheep driven out to the Montauk pastures, where they would stay from spring to late fall and then be driven back to their farms for the winter. This common ownership system continued until 1879, a "phenomenon unequalled in the annals of American history," said William B. Jackson in an unpublished history written in 1942 on the common pasture system.

Three men were chosen each year to stay out with the cattle, sheep and horses and three houses were built several miles apart — First House in 1744, Second House in 1746 and Third House in 1797 — to accommodate these men and their families. First House has burned down, but Second House is now in the middle of the hamlet of Montauk and Third House in Indian Field — the quarters of Teddy Roosevelt when the Rough Riders were quarantined in Montauk in 1898 — is now part of Montauk County Park.

Ear marks, not brands, were used to identify the cows. Shank, whose family first came to East Hampton from Southold in the 1600s, said his family's ear marks were a "hollow crop in the right ear and a slit in the left." You can still see original lists of the ear marks in the East Hampton Public Library.

In 1879 East Hampton sold the "lands of Montauk" to a wealthy Brooklynite, Arthur Benson, for the grand sum of $151,000. Benson used it mostly for hunting and fishing, but some of the lands continued to be leased for grazing. Except for a 10-year period from 1926-36 and during World War II, cattle have grazed on what remains of the original pasture lands since then.

Shank's son-in-law, Rusty Leaver, bought about 20 acres across from Indian Field, south of Montauk Highway, in the late 1970s to raise horses and cattle. He and his wife, Diane, run Deep Hollow Ranch — now part of Montauk County Park — as concessionaires, using the 3,000 or so acres of county land for trail rides, maintaining the family's tie to the land. In the last few years, the ranch, which started as a dude ranch in 1937, has become well known for hosting the Back to the Ranch concerts.

And, yep, it still has cattle. Big ones. Longhorns.

Newsday Photo / Bill Davis

The second house built in Montauk is now a museum.

MONTAUK HOUSES

Second House. This 1746 farmhouse, the second house built in Montauk, was used by early herders; five rooms were later decorated by Victoria magazine. Montauk Highway, Montauk. Hours: 10 a.m to 4 p.m., Saturday and Sunday in June; same hours Thursday through Tuesday, July through September. Fee: $2, $1 under 12.

•

Third House. Built in 1749, it was used by herders. The house was rebuilt in the early 1800s and became a restaurant in the 1950s. Theodore Roosevelt and his Rough Riders recuperated there after the Spanish-American War. In Montauk County Park, Montauk. Open daily 8 a.m. to 4 p.m., May 26 through September, then weekends to Oct. 31; other times by appointment.

— Tom Morris

America's first commercial nursery was visited by President George Washington

The Blooming Of Flushing

BY GEORGE DEWAN
STAFF WRITER

At the western end of Flushing there is a dreary commercial patch that includes an auto parts store, an asphalt plant, a glass signs shop and a lumberyard, all bathed in the exhaust fumes of a constant flow of trucks and cars. Here and there alongside the cracked concrete sidewalks grow the ubiquitous ailanthus and the irrepressible chicory, its lavender flowers the only bright spot in a dismal panorama, a hint, perhaps, of a more fragrant past.

Here, more than 250 years ago, the air was filled with the more pleasing smells of apple, plum, peach, nectarine, cherry, apricot and pear. This unlikely garden spot was the site of the first commercial nursery in America, eight acres planted by Robert Prince in 1737, expanded eventually to 113 acres and continued by the Prince family until just after the Civil War.

Prince's Nursery gathered trees and plants from around the world for resale, and became renowned through the American colony for its exotic wares. George Washington, six months after he became the new nation's first president in the spring of 1789, made a trip by barge to visit the nursery. The British who occupied Long Island during the Revolutionary War had considered it so special that they put an armed guard around the nursery to protect it from predators. When Meriwether Lewis and William Clark explored the Northwest during the Jefferson Administration, many of the botanical treasures they found were sent back to the Prince Nursery.

In a 1771 broadside, the nursery advertised 33 different kinds of plum trees, 42 pear trees, 24 apple trees and 12 varieties of nectarines. On March 14, 1774, Prince's son, William, advertised in the New York Mercury:

William Prince at his nursery, Flushing Landing, offers for sale one hundred and ten Carolina magnolia flower trees raised from the seed — the most beautiful trees that grow in America — 4s [shillings] per tree, four feet high, fifty large Catalpa trees, 2s per tree, nine feet high to the under part of top and thick as ones leg; thirty or forty almond trees that begin to bear, 1s and 6d [pence] each; gooseberry bushes, 6d; Lisbon and Madeira grapevines; English and American strawberry plants; one thousand five hundred white and one thousand black mulberry trees; also Barcelona filbert trees, 1s.

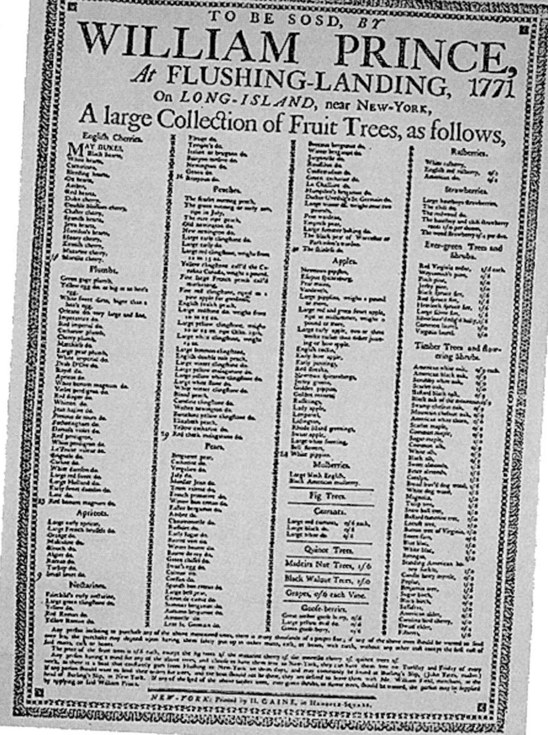
TO BE SOSD, BY
WILLIAM PRINCE,
At FLUSHING-LANDING, 1771
On LONG-ISLAND, near NEW-YORK,
A large Collection of Fruit Trees, as follows,

Queens Historical Society

A 1771 advertising notice from the Prince Nursery in Flushing

When Robert Prince opened his nursery, Flushing was a small, rural community and the business was built adjacent to Flushing Creek, allowing for shipping of plants and trees via Flushing Bay. First limited to the propagation and sale of fruit trees, the business later expanded to shade and ornamental trees, thus becoming a major force in the landscaping of Long Island.

The Revolutionary War led to the 7-year occupation of Long Island by the British in 1776, the Prince Nursery was cut off from most of the outside world, and business declined. It got so bad that at one point the nursery offered for sale 30,000 grafted cherry trees, proposing they be used as barrel hoops.

By 1789 the nursery had regained its business and its reputation. Washington, at heart a Virginia planter even though he had recently been sworn in as president, decided to pay a visit to the nursery. At the time, the seat of government was in New York City, and Washington lived in a house at the corner of Cherry and Pearl Streets. In his diary for Oct. 10, he notes:

"I set off from New York, about nine oclock in my barge, to visit Mr. Princes fruit gardens and shrubberies at Flushing." He was accompanied by Vice President John Adams and others. Washington was not overly impressed, perhaps because the nursery had not yet fully recovered from the war; or perhaps because his Virginia standards were so high. "These gardens, except in the number of young fruit trees, did not answer my expectations. The shrubs were trifling and the flowers not numerous."

Of course, it was October, not quite flower time on Long Island. And Washington's account books show that he later bought fruit from Prince's trees.

In 1793, William Prince Jr., Robert's grandson, established a new Prince nursery north of Broadway, now Northern Boulevard. The two nurseries would later be combined. Prince called it the Linnaean Gardens, after the Swedish naturalist Carolus Linnaeus, who at mid-century had devised the system of plant classification called binomial nomenclature, still in use today. For example, the American white oak is known as *Quercus alba*, consisting of a Latin genus name followed by a descriptive name.

William Jr. introduced in 1798 some of the first Lombardy poplars seen in America, advertising 10,000 of them for sale, from 10 to 17 feet in height. This tall, graceful and column-like tree that conjures up images of formal French allées became quickly popular on Long Island, in spaces where long avenues of trees could be planted. But a century later, interest in them waned.

There were failures as well. William Jr. decided in the spring of 1827 to raise silkworms, so he imported the first of a special variety of white mulberry trees, on whose leaves the silkworms feed. In a recent exhibit on the nursery at the Queens Historical Society, a small plaque read: "William Robert Prince — Imported mulberry trees to establish a cocoonery for silk worms — almost bankrupted the family business." Prince also was unsuccessful at growing wine grapes, in great part due to his inability to control a deadly fungus.

Beginning with the Prince family enterprise, Flushing became a community of nurseries as others sprang up to compete. Best-known was the Parsons Nursery, begun by the Quaker Samuel Parsons in 1838, and for a time the only grower of rhododendrons and hardy azaleas. It was located at the site of the present Flushing High School. Parsons introduced the pink-flowering dogwood, and in 1847 Parsons brought back from Belgium an oddity in a four-inch pot called the weeping European beech. This old tree, with several of its descendants surrounding it, still lives next to the Queens Historical Society at 143-35 37th Ave. There also were the Bloodgood Nursery and the Garretson Seed Farm.

As population pressure became more intense, Queens farmland was given up to the building of homes and businesses. So, too, did the nurseries die out in western Queens.

Queens Historical Society

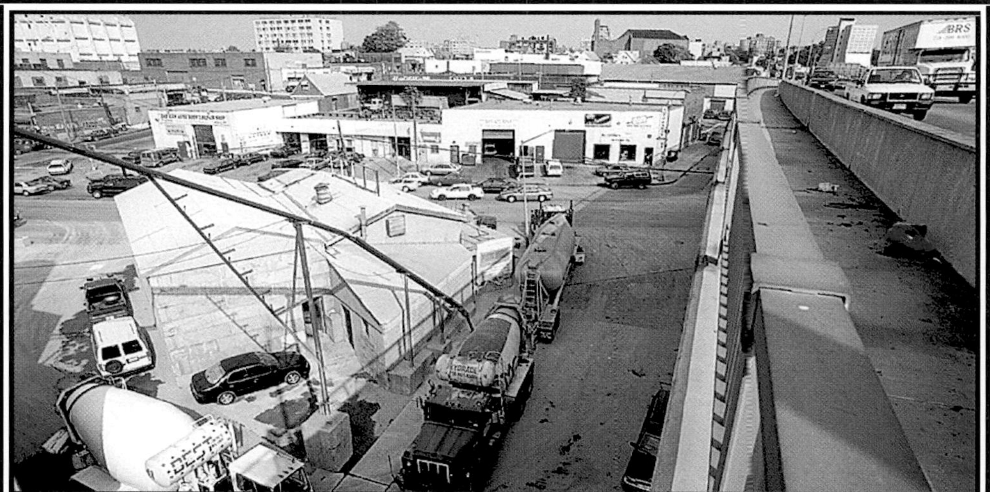

Newsday Photo / Bill Davis

A photo taken from Northern Boulevard looking toward Collins Place shows the former site of The Linnaean Gardens, run by William Prince Jr. At left, an 1876 map shows Collins Place two blocks from Flushing Creek and rows of trees still at the site. The Prince family ran nurseries until just after the Civil War.

The statesman and inventor came to Long Island, but did he set mile markers himself?

Measuring Franklin's Impact

BY MOLLY McCARTHY
STAFF WRITER

Ben Franklin was a man of great invention. And he prided himself in making things easier. Bifocals were hatched out of his near-sightedness. The lightning rod out of his fascination for electricity. A primitive odometer out of his need to measure early postal routes.

So it's possible that the author of "Poor Richard's Almanack" was the man responsible for a set of 30 stone mile markers laid in the mid-1700s along the King's Highway on the road from Riverhead to Orient. Of 30 milestones, 21 still line the roadway, known today as Route 25.

In a 1991 pamphlet, "Benjamin Franklin's North Fork Milestones," the late Robert P. Long, a local history buff from Southold, argued that Franklin, appointed postmaster general in 1753, personally set out the milestones in 1755 as he surveyed dozens of new postal routes. Long described Franklin in "high hat, ruffled shirt, [and] double-breasted cutaway coat," sitting in a carriage equipped with the crude odometer of his own invention.

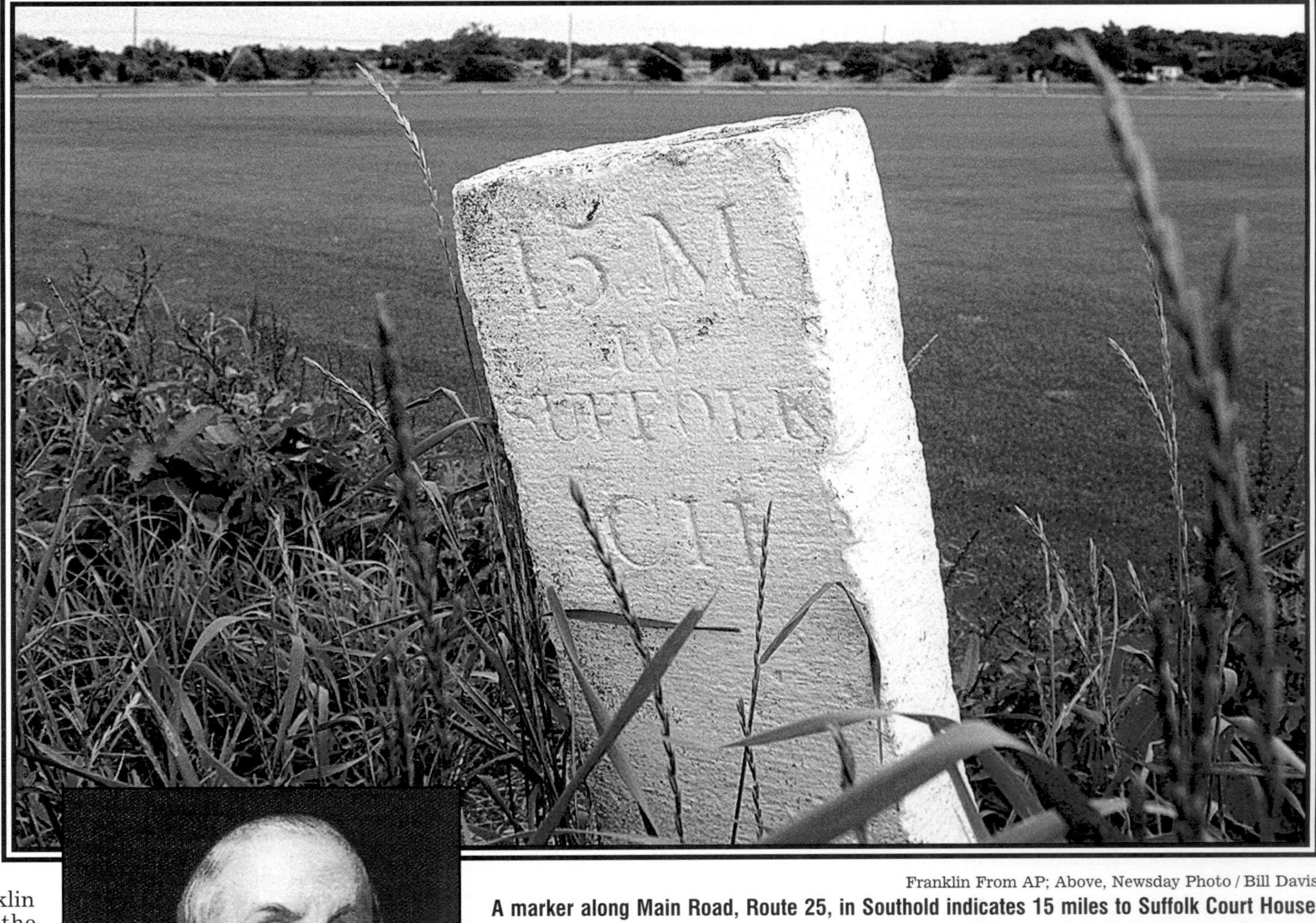

Franklin From AP; Above, Newsday Photo / Bill Davis

A marker along Main Road, Route 25, in Southold indicates 15 miles to Suffolk Court House, as Riverhead was known in the 1750s. Although one historian wrote that Ben Franklin was involved in their placement, others have not found evidence.

A small bell rang as the carriage reached each new mile, and Franklin instructed the laborers to drive the marker into the ground, according to Long's account. The markers, resembling worn tombstones, were etched with the distance to the Suffolk Court House, as Riverhead was called in those days. The scheme enabled local postmasters to calculate postal rates.

It's easy to imagine the great inventor coming up with such a plan. But in spite of Long's assertions, there's little proof that Franklin himself oversaw the installation of the milestones.

"I don't think there's anything that says Ben Franklin's tail was fastened to a seat in a wagon that took this route and laid these stones," said Ralph Williams, who preserved milestone 28, which sits in front of his Orient home. "It's all a bit inferential."

There are various sightings of Franklin in pre-revolutionary Long Island. And some of them are confusing. Augustus Griffin, a prominent Southold resident and prolific diarist, wrote in his journal in 1857 that Franklin visited Southold in 1755 on his way to visit his mother in Boston. The only problem here is that Franklin's mother died in 1752.

The journal entry does mention Franklin's odd new invention, but says nothing about mile markers. The carriage "was so contrived, with clock work or machinery of peculiar make, that a bell would be struck at the termination of every twenty rods," Griffin wrote.

Franklin spent the night at the inn of Samuel Griffin, Augustus' grandfather, who took him across the Sound the next morning to New London. So, on that particular trip, Franklin did not even make it to the end of the North Fork.

Long Island was a common route to New England from New York City and Philadelphia, so it is not surprising that Franklin, like other prominent gentlemen of his day, would have been spotted at local inns and taverns. In fact, a letter, dated Oct. 25, 1750, from Franklin to a colleague named Jared Eliot, mentions an earlier trip Franklin took through Long Island. Franklin asked Eliot to find out about a type of fence he saw during his travels. Franklin wrote:

I request you to procure for me a particular account of the manner of making a new kind of fence we saw at Southold, on Long Island, which consists of a bank and hedge. I would know every particular relating to this matter, as the best thickness, height, and slope of the bank; the manner of erecting it, the best time for the work, the best way of planting the hedge, the price of the work to laborers per rod or perch, and whatever may be of use for our information here, who begin in many places to be at a loss for wood to make fences.

Franklin's 32 volumes of collected writings make no mention of the mile markers or of a 1755 visit to Southold. Franklin spent much of that year in Philadelphia, traveling in January and February through southern New England, New York and New Jersey.

However, Franklin did take several months in 1763 to inspect post offices throughout New York and New England, so he could have simply laid the markers later than was originally thought.

Southold Town Historian Antonia Booth subscribes to the theory that Franklin himself left the unassuming stone legacies, citing the Eliot letter and Griffin journal as proof.

Others, while enchanted by the tale, believe Franklin probably had better things to do.

"Ben Franklin was a very efficient man, and I can't really see the efficiency of doing it himself," said Williams. "I can't imagine he had the time. I prefer to think of him worrying about matters of state."

LEGACY

CARRYING THE MAIL, ILLEGALLY

The first known mailman on Long Island loved his job so much he did it illegally.

His last name was Dunbar; his given name remains unknown. We learn about him from an enthusiastic 19th-Century amateur historian, Gabriel Furman. "A respectable old Scotchman, named Dunbar, was in the habit of riding a voluntary post between the city of New York along the south road to Babylon, and from thence a few miles to the east, and then across the island to Brookhaven," Furman wrote in his 1874 book, "Antiquities of Long Island." "He thus brought the inhabitants of the central portion of this island their letters and newspapers about once a week or once a fortnight, depending upon the state of the weather."

This was probably about 1778, when the British occupied the Island, and they didn't like free-lance mailmen. "Mr. Dunbar's business being an illegal one subjected him to severe penalties, and was only winked at by reason of its absolute necessity," Furman wrote.

— George DeWan

The hardships of a Long Island mother compel her to write, 'Dear Lord, deliver me'

Diary Of A Colonial Housewife

BY GEORGE DEWAN
STAFF WRITER

On a midsummer day in 1769, soon after her 55th birthday, Mary Cooper sat down wearily at a table in her Oyster Bay farmhouse, opened her diary, and with quill pen in hand began pouring out her anguish:

July the 13, 1769. Thirsday. This day is forty years sinc I left my father's house and come here, and here have I seene littel els but harde labour and sorrow, crosses of every kind. I think in every respect the state of my affairs is more then forty times worse then when I came here first, except that I am near the desierered haven. A fine clear cool day. I am un well.

In one of the few diaries written by a woman in the American colonies, Mary Cooper opened a window on 18th-Century colonial Long Island life. Another diary, written about the same time by Ebenezer Miller of Miller Place, adds to the picture we get of how people lived in the middle of the 18th Century.

Although Cooper and her husband, Joseph, were better off than the average farmers of the day — the family owned most of Cove Neck, and at times kept four slaves — the picture she presents of the constant hard work, family tragedies, church on the Sabbath and occasional entertainment was repeated on farms large and small across the Island.

Cooper married at 14, became a mother at 20 and had six children, all of whom caused her sorrow. Two died in infancy, two in childhood and the remaining two died before their parents.

On her dead children's birthdays, and those of her dead father and sister, she remembers and grieves:

Tuesday, September 8, 1772. This day is 18 years since my dear son Caleb was born. O alas, how is my expectation cut off.

Much of what was used on the farm was produced on the farm, and from sunup to sundown and after, there was work to be done. Cooper writes of cleaning house, cooking meals, drying apples, making sweetmeats and sausage, salting beef, washing and ironing clothes, baking mince pies, taking care of honeybees, making wine, drying cherries, processing flax, making soap, sewing, picking blackberries, making candles, and boiling souse, or pickled meat.

Cooper is constantly writing of her exhaustion and weariness:

Friday, July 7, 1769. Hot as yesterday. I am dirty and distressed, almost weared to death. Dear Lord, deliver me.

Despite the signs that the Coopers were fairly well off for their times, Cooper often writes of having creditors bothering her. Added to that were the constant demands being put on her to feed and house relatives:

Wednesday, August 23, 1769. A fine clear morning with a cold north wind. My hearte is burnt with anger and discontent, want of every nessesary thing in life and in constant feare of gapeing credtors consums my strenth and wasts my days. The horror of these things with the continuel cross of my family, like to so many horse leeches, prays upon my vitals, and if the Lord does not prevent will bring me to the house appointed for all liveing.

But there were amusements and social life as well. She and her friends had sewing and quilting bees, where the women would all work

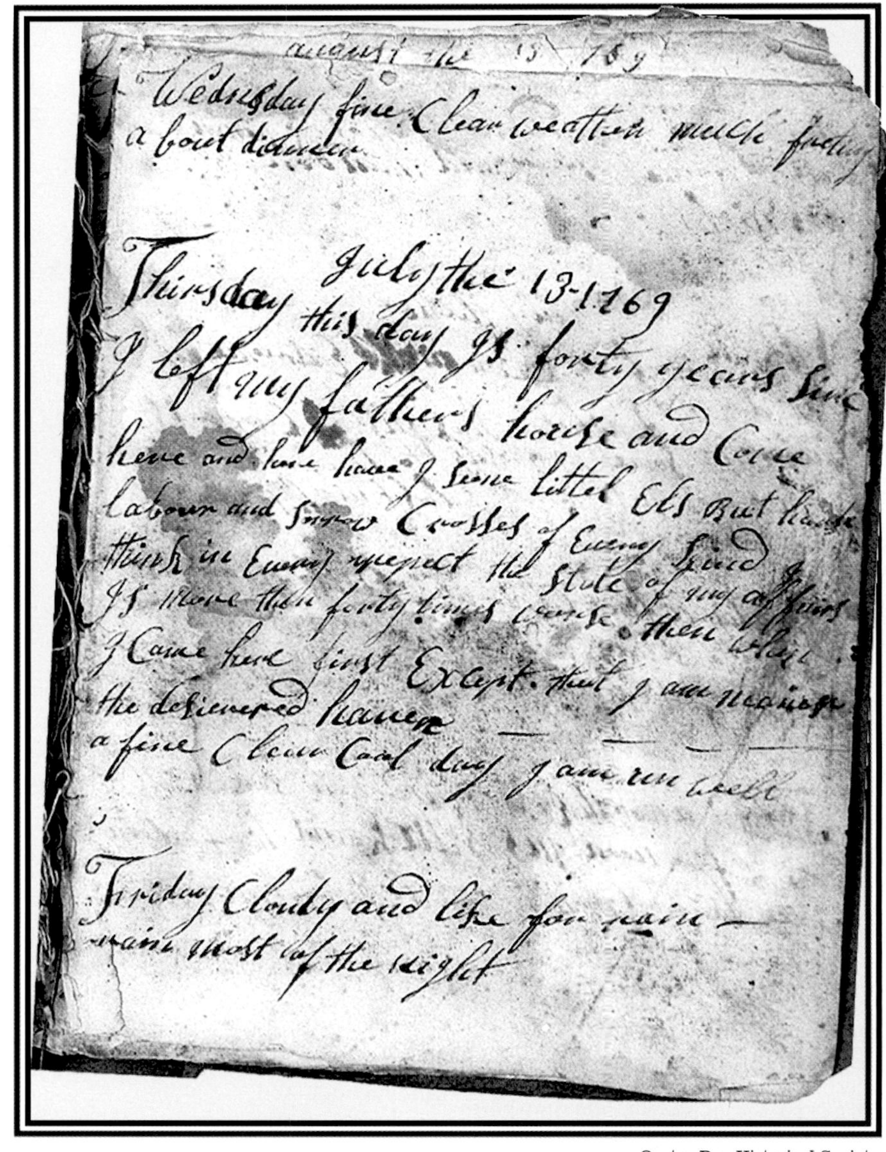

Thirsday July the 13-1769
this day is forty years sinc
I left my fathers house and Come
here and here have I seene littel Els But harde
labour and sorrow Crosses of Every kind I
think in Every respect the state of my affairs
is more then forty times worse then when I
Came here first Except that I am neare
the desiered haven
a fine Clear Cool day I am un well

Friday Cloudy and like for raine
raine most of the night

Oyster Bay Historical Society

A page from the diary of Cove Neck housewife Mary Cooper, open to Thursday, July 13, 1769.

Newsday

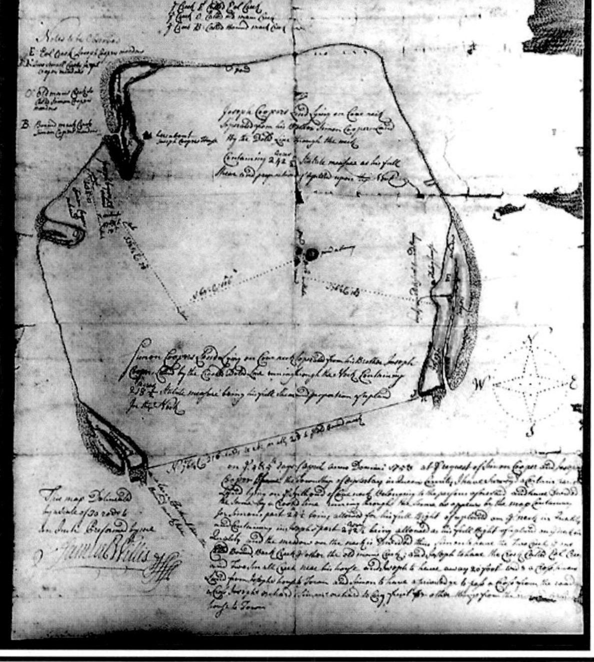

The New-York Historical Society

A hand-drawn survey map from April, 1753, at right, shows the properties of Joseph and Simon Cooper on Cove Neck. The outline of Cove Neck matches the peninsula as seen on the present-day map above.

Oyster Bay Historical Society

A drawing by contemporary artist John Collins shows the 1700s home of Mary Cooper. The house still stands but has been remodeled.

and gossip together. She records a barbecued-turtle feast, dancing, and, occasionally, seeing horse racing, which had been inaugurated a century earlier on the Hempstead Plains. On Aug. 29, 1769, she, with others, sailed across Long Island Sound to Connecticut in two hours — "very greatly against my will," she writes. "The tumulting waves look frightful."

Cooper was a member of the New Light Baptist Church, and may have occasionally gone to hear preaching by Jupiter Hammon, the black slave from nearby Lloyd Harbor who was America's first black poet. "I went to the New Light meetin to here a Black man preach," she writes on Aug. 27, 1769, and she has three references to hearing "Hammon" preach, although it cannot be confirmed that this is the same person.

Religion is Mary Cooper's solace:

1773. June the 29. Tuesday. South west wind, cloude, some thunder and a fine shower of rain this after noon and a bright rain bow appeared some thing longer then uesal which raised my thoughts to the bright relms of day. I longed to se that head once crowned with thorne, that dear parson treated with scorn and cruelty for sinful me. The dasling luster of his face I faint. I can find no word to express my ideas, my greatest vews seeme to be of my Jesus seated on a throne of glory in the bright relms of etarnel day. The pleasing luster of his eyes out shine the wonders of the skys. In raptures and sweet delight I fell a sleep. O, that my last moments may be like these.

Out in Suffolk County, Ebenezer Miller kept a diary of his farming activities between 1762 and 1768. Farming was the dominant way of life on colonial Long Island, and the rhythms of the seasons and the crops ordered the lives of its men, women and children. Miller's diary is most often a record of the commonplace rather than the unusual. Year after year, Miller recorded the endless cycle of farm life, activities that were repeated on farms from Queens to the East End.

In the spring he mended fences and plowed his fields to plant flax, oats and corn. By midsummer he was getting in his first crop of hay, harvesting rye and wheat, and a little later, pulling his flax, which would be spun to make linen. In September he made the first cider of the year, some of which would be drunk fresh, the rest barreled and which, when fermented, would be a potent brew. Later in September he gathered corn. As the weather got colder he gathered wood to supply him for the winter and gathered dung to fertilize the fields. In the winter it was time to prepare the flax for spinning, to thresh the oats and wheat, and to slaughter sheep, hogs and cattle for food. Wood was chopped and piled in the woodshed.

January, 1764:

Tuesday the 24 was a Very bad Snow Storm a great Snow fell to Day before this storm had been a fine Spell of Wether Very warm for Saturday february ye 10 Day we finished thrashing We have 32 bushels of wheat in the house

As with Cooper, Sundays were for church, and Miller notes the names of the preachers, including the Rev. Benjamin Tallmadge of Setauket. And then occasionally, something unusual does happen:

LI HISTORY.COM

Two months of entries from Mary Cooper's diary offer a glimpse of life on Long Island in 1769. See http://www.lihistory.com on the Internet.

1767. Joseph Robinson drowned June 11th. June ye 24 Noble [probably a slave] was hurt by a fall his Scull brok and 7 or 8 bitts of the Skull bone Taken out.

No mention is made of who did the surgery, but since trained surgeons were rare, it could have been the local blacksmith or some other local craftsman adept with his hands.

Major changes in the lives of country folk took place as the 17th Century gave way to the 18th, as a backbreaking, primitive way of life gave way to improvements both inside and outside the home.

"Work in the kitchens of the seventeenth century was hard and unrelenting," wrote John H. Braunlein in "Colonial Long Island Folklife," prepared for a 1976 exhibit at the Museums at Stony Brook. "When prosperity came, as it did to many eighteenth-century communities, few women found their positions improved. Early Long Island kitchens often lacked suitable fireplace utensils; without spits, hooks, or andirons, housewives made do with piles of stones, green wood, and sharply pointed sticks. These medieval conditions became largely obsolete during the 1700s, however, as metal kitchen implements became available."

In the fields, too, the later colonial period saw many changes introduced. By Mary Cooper's time, the old wooden plows had given way in many places to plows where the mouldboard, which pushed the earth aside, was covered with iron. The use of fertilizer, virtually unknown in the 17th Century, did not come into heavy use until the late 18th Century, so Cooper's and Miller's farms were probably heavily depleted of nutrients, with resulting low crop yields.

By 1700, hogs, sheep and cattle were plentiful, and became a widespread source of food. By the late colonial period these animals, plus horses, were being raised not just for food, but as a commercial venture, and were frequently exported to the West Indies in exchange for rum, sugar and molasses.

So there were changes, and life was getting better in late colonial Long Island. But there remained challenges for people like Mary Cooper. There was sickness and always family problems. She even had problems with her husband, whom she called Dade, in a marriage that does not sound terribly happy:

February the 2, Saturday, 1771. I am unwell and much aflected for fear of the small pox. I had envited some of my friends to come here to see Ester [her daughter] and dade would not let me have a turkey to rost for supper and I am so aflected and ashamed about it that I feele as if I should never get over it. I got to bed feared and distressed at 1 or 2 o'clok in the morning.

A FORK FOR YOUR TEA, SIR?

When Sarah Miller was a girl living in Montauk in the early 1700s, a new food called tea was introduced to the East End. The problem was, few people knew how to eat it.

"Mrs. Miller remembers well when they first began to drink tea on the East End of L. Island," John Lyon Gardiner, proprietor of Gardiners Island, wrote in his journal in 1793. Then 78, Miller was the mother of Gardiner's overseer, and she told him the story. He wrote in his journal:

She tells a number of curious stories about their awkward manner of trying it. One family boil'd it in a pot and eat it like samp porridge, another spread the leaves on his bread & butter, and brag'd at his having eat half a pound at a meal to his neighbor who was informing him how long a time a pound of tea lasted him.

She remembers the first teakettle that was in E. Hampton, it came ashore at Montauk in a [wrecked] ship (Capn Bell). The farmers come down their on business with their bottle, they could not find out the use of the tea kettle, which was then brought up to Old Governor Hedges, some said that it was for one thing & some another, while one more knowing than his neighbors affirmed it was the Ships which they all assented.

— George DeWan

Reaping the 'considerable' harvest of the New World's wealth on land and sea

The Well-Kept Colonies

BY GEORGE DEWAN
STAFF WRITER

In the year 1750, the prosperous Oyster Bay merchant Samuel Townsend sent out his sloop Solomon under Capt. John Jones on a voyage to the Virgin Islands. The single-masted ship was loaded with cargo: 76 barrels of flour, 26 barrels of pork, five quarter-barrels of butter, four casks of hams, beef and tongues, 4,250 barrel hoops, seven geese and 20 bushels of corn.

Townsend valued the cargo at 262 pounds sterling. It's value in current dollars: $35,000.

By the middle of the 18th Century, Long Island was no longer a rural backwater. It had progressed well beyond the early colonial subsistance level, where individual farmers lived in isolation and produced only what they themselves used. What Townsend was selling to the Virgin Islanders was the excess product of a bustling Long Island economy.

The ship would not come back empty, for the West Indies had products that Long Islanders and other New Yorkers wanted to buy, including rum, molasses, sugar and indigo. Other Townsend ships sailed to New York to buy British imports, like glassware, cutlery and expensive fabrics of all kinds, for resale in his general store in Oyster Bay.

At the retail level, Townsend catered to the needs of country folk who traveled miles for what he had to offer. Just a few days' entries from his General Store Data Book for 1750-1751 — now owned by the New-York Historical Society — lists the following for sale: salt, linen, onions, molasses, rum, brooms, combs, turnips, pepper, cotton handkerchiefs, nails, worsted caps, flax seed, calico, silk, ribbons, knives, buttons, garters, snuff boxes, and oznabrig, a coarse cotton fabric.

Ports on Long Island's North Shore were important points of entry for goods coming into the New York colony — both legally and illegally — as early as 1699, according to an entry in the journal of the Provincial Assembly: "A third part of the goods imported into the colony of New York were run into the four ports on Long Island, viz.: Setauket, Oysterbay, Musketo Cove [Glen Cove] and Southold." In the next 50 years, Sag Harbor and other ports would also become important.

Agriculture still dominated the Long Island economy in the late colonial period, and that included the raising of beef cattle, sheep and hogs. But as communities began to grow, they increasingly needed craftsmen to produce items that once might have been made at home. Millers, carpenters, weavers, tailors, brick makers, coopers and blacksmiths were in demand. But smaller communities could not support full-time specialists, so these early craftsmen often had to do more than one thing.

"Thus a farrier not only shod horses but worked as a blacksmith as well," wrote John H. Braunlein a few years ago in "Colonial Long Island Folklife." "A cabinetmaker might advertise himself as a carpenter, a joiner, and a wheelwright . . . A potter also might make shoes; a blacksmith might also be a capable mason."

The New-York Historical Society

An oil painting by G. Moore shows shipbuilding in New Netherlands in the 1600s. In the next century, under English rule, Long Island's economy grew as ships took agricultural bounty abroad and returned with technology and trade goods.

Then there was John Stuard, who in July, 1691, applied to the Town of Hempstead for 18 to 20 acres of tillable land near Plain Edge for his growing family. He offered his skills in return: "I am willing to settle among you, to follow the trade of a cooper, as also to practice the art of surgery."

In 1759 the Universal Gazeteer was published in Dublin, Ireland, and this is how it described Long Island: "The island principally produces British and Indian corn, beef, pork, fish, etc., which they send to the sugar colonies, from where they receive in return, sugar, rum, cotton and indigo; they also have a whale fishery, sending the oil and bone to England, in exchange for cloths and furniture. Their other fisheries here are very considerable."

Very considerable, indeed. Long Island's surrounding waters were as fertile as its land. Clams, oysters and scallops were abundant, as were a variety of fish, and much of this harvest was shipped to New York at a nice profit.

For some on the South Shore, there were profits also in whales that were driven ashore. An item in the Feb. 4, 1754, New York Mercury read: "Last week a small whale, twenty feet long, was towed up to New York by a sand boat from Rockaway, where it was found floating near the shore by some clammers." By this time, however, whales were disappearing, having been driven farther out to sea, and the whaling industry would not revive for another century, when commercial boats from Long Island would put out to sea in quest of huge profits.

Farmers were becoming entrepreneurs. "Progressive farmers, during the winter, built for themselves serviceable, sea-going boats such as sloops or two-masted schooners," Islip historian N.R. Howell wrote in 1949. "When their crops did not need attention they could take a load of wood to the city and bring back a load of horse manure for their farms. As the size of New York City increased, the farmers transported many cargoes of hay and grain for the horses of city folks."

With the waterways, especially Long Island Sound, being used as colonial highways, a shipbuilding industry developed, especially on the North Shore, with its better harbors and its forests. This meant a healthy economic stimulus to places like Southold, Setauket and Oyster Bay.

Payment for goods and services presented a great problem on colonial Long Island, as elsewhere. The British Parliament did not allow the export of English coins, and it refused to allow a separate mint to be established in America. As a result, the colonies relied heavily on silver and gold coins from Spain, or sometimes Portugal. But until individual colonies began emitting paper money during the late colonial period, much trading was done by barter.

"The services of surgeons, weavers, hatters, sailors, merchants, masons and other tradesmen were occasionally paid for in cash," Braunlein wrote. "More often, however, their labors were repaid in goods, for the economy of colonial Long Island was one of barter. Corn was exchanged for shoes, chairs were offered for rum, and weaving bought flour and butter."

All in all, Long Islanders in the late colonial period were doing well. Experts on the colonial economy such as Edwin J. Perkins have concluded that the general standard of living in the 13 colonies was the highest in the world by the 1770s, on the eve of the Revolutionary War.

In fact, Perkins says, when war came, colonial soldiers were normally two inches taller than recruits entering the service of the British Royal Marines. This, he says, is probably because they ate more meat.

In the town that will become Glen Cove, grain and lumber are grist for the mills

The Daily Grind

BY BILL BLEYER
STAFF WRITER

'Ship's biscuit'' — a slow-to-spoil wheat concoction with the consistency of concrete — was a staple of the 18th-Century sailor's diet. And sailors embarking from New York in the mid-1700s often tested their teeth on biscuit baked on Long Island.

Specifically, biscuit baked in a thriving, one-industry town called Musketa Cove. That industry was milling grain.

Like many other Long Island waterfront communities that could trap the tides or harness streams, Musketa Cove — which would become Glen Cove in the next century — symbolized commercial development in colonial Long Island. The magic word was gristmills. These served as economic generators for waterfront communities, providing business opportunities that rippled through the entire region.

Musketa Cove's gristmills were literally big business. One mill was so large that it contained 26 pairs of grinding stones. And another mill operated by the Walton family was big enough to spin off its own bakery to manufacture ship's biscuits on an export scale.

Mills were the reason the community was founded. In the 1660s, a building boom was under way in Manhattan and lumber was in short supply. A young Rhode Islander named Joseph Carpenter glimpsed a solution. He noticed that northwestern Oyster Bay not only had plenty of trees but a creek that could accommodate vessels. So he purchased 2,000 acres along Hempstead Harbor from the Matinecock Indians on May 24, 1668.

Carpenter and his partners, brothers Robert, Daniel and Nathaniel Coles and Nicholas Simkins, all of Oyster Bay, established the Musketa Cove Plantation. They retained the name the Matinecocks had given the area: Musketa (also spelled ''musquito''), which had nothing to do with bugs but translated roughly as ''the place of rushes.''

''The Five Proprietors of Musketa Cove Plantation,'' as they called themselves, dammed a small stream that ran through a valley roughly parallel to today's Glen Street. Carpenter built a sawmill for the partners and a gristmill for himself by the dam located near the foot of Mill Hill northeast of where the fire department is today. He agreed to grind the grain of the other proprietors ''tolle free for ever.'' Everybody else paid the miller with a one-twelfth portion of the final product.

By 1679, the sawmill was producing nine types of boards and lumber as well as wainscott, ''feather-edged'' boards for paneling, and custom-cut walnut for cabinets. The mills made the community such an important economic center that workers migrated out from the city, sleeping in mills or staying with friends. Mention of the sawmill ceases in the 1690s, probably because all easily accessible trees had been harvested.

But the grain-milling business was still going strong, so much so that just after the turn of the century, a family of wealthy New York City merchants decided to invest in waterfront land and purchase several of the mills. The acquisitions by three brothers — Jacob, Abraham and Isaac Walton — included a second gristmill near what is now Pulaski Street. They also set up the bakehouse to turn out ship's biscuit. Besides making a profit for themselves, the Waltons generated income for independent craftsmen. For example, the records of a local blacksmith named Mudge show that he did many jobs for them, fabricating and fixing equipment for their mills and ships.

The earliest mills were built on two ponds — Upper and Lower Mill Pond. Upper Mill Pond, which ran from what is now Pulaski Street to St. Patrick's Church, and part of Lower Mill Pond were eventually filled in. What's left is known today as Pratt Pond.

By the 1740s, the Waltons had competition. A second milling center developed when the Woolsey family set up shop in the Dosoris area of town near Long Island Sound. Benjamin Woolsey II and his brother Melancthon built tidal mills powered by saltwater that flowed in at high tide and ran out through the mill. John Butler and his family took over the mills or built their own in the 1750s. A painting of one of Butler's mills shows 26 pairs of grinding stones. ''This was clearly a major export operation,'' Glen Cove city historian Dan Russell said. The mills were ultimately taken over by Butler's son-in-law, Nathaniel Coles. One survived until it burned down in 1867.

The mills provided local farmers with a convenient market for their grains. ''The local mills before the Revolutionary War were turning out a fairly diverse range of flours,'' Russell said. ''It's not just wheat, it's not just corn, it's rye and even a minimal production of pea flour. It must have tasted awful. There was barley, and a lot of that probably went into making booze.''

Newsday Photo / Bill Davis

Office of the Mayor, City of Glen Cove

Pratt Pond, above, is what remains of Upper Mill Pond and Lower Mill Pond, where the earliest mills in Musketa Cove (now Glen Cove) were built. The large and profitable Musketa Cove sawmill, which is represented in the drawing at left, was the reason for the founding of the community. Ultimately, its gristmills became more important.

It Was A Smugglers' Cove, Too

The early entrepreneurs of Musketa Cove took advantage of their proximity to the water for more than milling — smuggling became the community's second industry. Lord Bellomont, the colonial governor in 1699, called Musketa Cove one of the four biggest smuggling ports on Long Island.

Smuggling then rarely involved gold or jewels. It meant trading with the occasional ship that carried goods to Musketa Cove rather than New York, where customs duties were collected. Because of the distance from the city, the illegal trading could go on in broad daylight. ''It was booze — rum, particularly, because we were already producing whiskey locally — chocolate, spices, silk,'' said Dan Russell, Glen Cove's city historian.

In 1693, a French privateer was spotted by British authorities at anchor off the town, probably to put goods ashore for illegal resale in New York City. A British frigate sailed from New York to capture the French bark and its crew but managed only to snag the captain. The British also arrested Nathaniel Coles for plotting to defraud crown and colony of customs duties. Officials released him several weeks later. When the Waltons arrived, they maintained local traditions — trading in contraband, primarily to supply their hotels and taverns in the city and their large fleet of transatlantic ships.

In 1728, wigmaker Josiah Milliken published an unusual official declaration denying that he had tipped off customs agents to the Waltons' basement full of smuggled wines and brandies. Aware of the Waltons' clout, he feared the rumor might ''turn to his Hurt and Damage.''

— **Bill Bleyer**

Colonists build mills to grind grain, saw wood and pump water

Harnessing Water and Wind

LEGACY

WINDMILLS AND GRISTMILLS

Long Island had hundreds of mills in the 17th and 18th Centuries. Here is a selection of mills that survive; a few are still in working order. Call ahead for schedule and fee information.

BRIDGEHAMPTON
Beebe Windmill, at Ocean Road and Hildreth Avenue; built 1820, moved 1915. Summer tours and children's activities. Call 516-537-1088.

EAST HAMPTON
Hayground Windmill, Windmill Lane, East Hampton; built 1801, moved 1950. Not open to the public.
Old Hook Windmill, North Main Street; built in 1806 by Nathaniel Dominy. Open in July and August. Call 516-324-0713.
Pantigo Windmill, on property of John Howard Payne historic site, 14 James Lane. Open by appointment; call 516-324-0713.

EAST ROCKAWAY
East Rockaway Grist Mill Museum, Woods and Atlantic Avenues, East Rockaway; burned by an arsonist in 1990, the 300-year-old mill is nearly restored. Open in summer, and by appointment. Call 516-887-6320.

GARDINERS ISLAND
Gardiners Island Windmill, built 1795 and rebuilt 1815. Not open to the public.

GREAT RIVER
Southside Sportsmens Club District (Connetquot River State Park), Sunrise Highway, has a mid-18th-Century windmill. Site has occasional tours (next is March 29). Call 516-581-1072 to register.

LITTLE NECK
Alley Pond Environmental Center, 228-06 Northern Blvd., has a working windmill for pumping water. Call 718-229-4000.

LLOYD HARBOR
Van Wyck-Lefferts Tide Mill, built at Huntington Harbor in the 1790s. The Nature Conservancy, which owns the mill, offers free boat tours to the site May through October. Call 516-367-3225.

ROSLYN
Roslyn Grist Mill, Old Northern Blvd., built 1715-41. It was converted to a teahouse in 1916 and is now the focus of restoration efforts.

ROSLYN HARBOR
Cedarmere, Bryant Avenue; home of 19th-Century American poet William Cullen Bryant, has a Gothic Revival mill from 1862. Cedarmere is open May through early November. Call 516-571-8130.

SADDLE ROCK
Saddle Rock Grist Mill, Grist Mill Lane; a restored tidal gristmill built around 1700. Open Sundays, May through October. Call 516-571-7900.

SHELTER ISLAND
Shelter Island Windmill, North of Manwaring Road; built in 1810 by Nathaniel Dominy in Southold, moved to Shelter Island in 1839 (used briefly during World War I). Moved to current location in 1926.

SMITHTOWN
New Mill and **Mill House**, New Mill Road at Stump Pond at Blydenburgh County Park; Mill House was built around 1801, New Mill around 1827. Open by appointment. Call 516-854-4949.
Wyandanch Club Historic District, Route 25, at Caleb Smith State Park, has remains of a 1795 gristmill. Park closed Mondays, April through September; closed Monday and Tuesday, October through March. Call 516-265-1054.

SOUTHAMPTON
National Golf Links, Sebonac Inlet Road; windmill dates to the early 1900s. It was once used to pump water.
Southampton Campus of Long Island University has a windmill built 1712-1714. It originally stood in the middle of Southampton Village and was moved to its present site in 1890. Now used for offices and a guesthouse.

STONY BROOK
Stony Brook Grist Mill, Harbor Road off Main Street; Long Island's most completely equipped working mill, dating to 1751. It features demonstrations. Open April through November. Call 516-751-2244.

WAINSCOTT
Wainscott Windmill, Main Street; built in 1813 and moved several times. Not open to the public.

WATER MILL
Corwith Windmill, Village Green, Montauk Highway; built in 1800 in Sag Harbor and moved in 1813; operated until 1887. Call 516-726-5984 for tour information.
Water Mill Museum, Old Mill Road; Long Island's first water-powered gristmill (1644), has been restored and displays early tools and colonial crafts. Open late May through September. Call 516-726-4625.

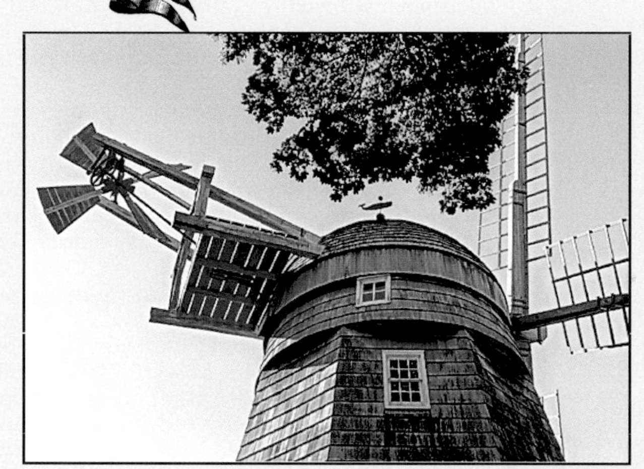

Newsday Photo / Bill Davis

A tail rotor on Bridgehampton's Beebe Windmill, above, would turn the top according to wind direction. Water Mill's Corwith Windmill, below, would be turned by rotating the long tail pole by hand.

Newsday Photo / George Argeroplos

Newsday Photo / Bill Davis

The Stony Brook Grist Mill is fueled by water diverted from a pond. Below, corn falls into a hopper, then is ground by a millstone.

Newsday Photo / Bill Davis; Dutch Mill, Right, "History of the City of New York"

BY GEORGE DEWAN
STAFF WRITER

The man who could harness the power of water and wind was a major figure in a colonial village. The miller and his gristmill were equaled in importance only by the blacksmith and his forge.

Before steam engines made them obsolete, there were hundreds of gristmills on Long Island. Whether they were water mills or windmills, they were built by craftsmen primarily for the milling of grain, but also for the sawing of wood and the pumping of water.

Few sights evoke the past more than a briskly revolving waterwheel next to a dammed-up stream and a millpond, or a windmill in an open field, its sails reaching out to catch the breeze. Though these are common sights, in picture books if not in real life, most people know little about what goes on inside. It is much like being inside a giant clock, midst a fascinating collection of wooden gears, pulleys and shafts that translate the power of wind and water to millstones, saws and pumps.

A drawing of a Dutch windmill in New York

Some waterwheels were turned by controlled flows of water from a dammed-up stream. Many on the North Shore, however, used the flow of the tides, and thus could be operated only at certain times of the day.

"We had probably the greatest concentration of tide mills on the eastern seaboard, and we have the greatest surviving concentration of windmills," said Robert McKay, director of the Society for the Preservation of Long Island Antiquities. "This is due in part because we don't have a lot of rivers to provide the kind of falling water that powered the Industrial Revolution in New England."

There are 11 surviving windmills on eastern Long Island built between 1795 and 1820. These are called "smock" mills, supposedly because they look like someone wearing a smock; the upper part moves, while the rest of the mill remains stationary. None of the "post" windmills built in the colonial era still exists. These were mounted on a large post, with the entire structure turned into the wind by moving a tail pole projecting from the rear.

In 1699, Adam Smith, the son of the legendary Richard (Bull) Smith, the founder of Smithtown, built a gristmill on a stream called Stony Brook. The original water mill and dam were washed out in a flood, being replaced in 1751. Now, 246 years later, that gristmill is not only standing, it is — after an extensive overhall a few years ago — the finest example of a working gristmill on Long Island.

No job too big or too small for the extraordinarily typical Dominy family

Little Shops of Craftsmen

BY MICHELE INGRASSIA
STAFF WRITER

From their little shops on North Main Street in East Hampton, the Dominy family presided over a remarkable domain. Between 1760, when they opened their doors, and 1840, when the last sales were posted, Nathaniel IV, Nathaniel V and Felix — father, son and grandson — turned out 90 clocks and nearly 900 tables, dressers, desks and chairs. They repaired watches and guns, built houses and windmills. On or off the workbench, no job was too big or too small. Nathaniel IV served as a town trustee, inspector of common schools, sealer of weights and measures. Nathaniel V was an overseer of the poor. Early in his career, Felix designed the arm-and-hammer symbol of the New York Mechanics Society; near the end, he covered the dome of the Montauk Lighthouse, using 220 feet of copper sheeting and 1,080 rivets.

Yet what was most extraordinary about this family of clock makers and cabinetmakers was how typical they were. At a time when a new nation was struggling to take hold, craftsmanship — especially rural craftsmanship — was about necessity more than art. And craftsmen did whatever else they had to to survive. As Dominy scholar Charles F. Hummel put it, "If the Dominys had to rely strictly on the production of clocks, they would have starved to death."

But money is just one measure of success. The Dominys, for all their precarious finances, left a priceless legacy: virtually every tool, every account book, every piece of shop equipment, more than 1,300 pieces in all. Discovered in a Southampton warehouse in 1957, the trove is one of the largest and most complete of the colonial era, and offers researchers an unrivaled look at the day-to-day workings of craftsmen from the peak of the handcraft era in the mid-1700s until its decline in the industrial revolution a century later.

"It was akin to what an Egyptologist would encounter unearthing the tomb of an ancient pharaoh," says Hummel, curator emeritus of the Henry Francis du Pont Winterthur Museum in Winterthur, Del., where the Dominy workshops have been re-created. "The survival of so much gives us a wonderful picture of the state of technology throughout the western world, because so much of what the Dominys were doing was similar to what craftsmen were doing in France, Germany and England."

Although they called them "manufactories," shops like the Dominys' were run on sheer muscle power, aided by simple tools and basic machinery. Large-scale equipment like the great wheel lathe demanded strenuous effort to turn a chair leg or a table base. Yet because craftsmen built towering clock cases one day and repaired delicate watches the next, they also demanded smaller tools. The Dominys amassed a prodigious array, including 37 different planes, 30 different bits and two dozen different files, some acquired from customers who paid their bills with gimlets and saws.

What those tools produced was as straightforward and utilitarian as the equipment itself. Surely the Dominys were worldly enough to understand the blossoming design community beyond East Hampton. But their clients were mostly farmers, who had no need for lavishly carved Philadelphia Chippendale chairs. "In colonial America and in the new republic, farm people spent money on what kept them in business — livestock, farm equipment and land, not clocks," says Hummel.

Dean Failey, senior director of American furniture and decorative arts at Christie's auction house, says that if any one piece embodies Dominy style, it's the splat-back chair, a simple piece they could produce quickly and in large numbers. Similarly, though Dominy tall clocks are unadorned, there is often a twist — say, a pewter dial engraved, "Death don't retreat to improve each beat."

As the 19th Century faded into a new era of assembly-line technology, handcraftsmen could no longer compete with factories turning out clocks faster and cheaper. But even before then the Dominys were losing ground to entrepreneurs such as Nathan Tinker of Sag Harbor, who opened a warehouse in 1823, shipped in ready-made furniture and advertised that he could supply "any article of household furniture" on short notice.

And that might have been the end of the Dominy story — another craft family felled by time and technology — except for Connecticut antiques dealer Rockwell Gardiner, who stumbled over some old tools during a 1957 buying trip to Ethel Marsden's shop in Southampton. What Gardiner suspected — and what Winterthur confirmed — was a trove of Dominy clock and woodworking tools.

Many had assumed the tools had vanished, if not when the Dominy house was sold in 1939, then surely when it was torn down in 1946 or when the adjoining clock shop was sold. But what Gardiner uncovered was just the first batch.

Robert M. Dominy, a great-grandson of Felix and one of the last Dominys to live in the family homestead, had loaned hundreds more tools to the East Hampton Historical Society in the 1940s and had effectively forgotten about them. But, Dominy said, soon after Winterthur bought the tools in Marsden's shop, he discovered that the East Hampton Historical Society had upped and sold its cache — *his* cache — to the museum.

"Someone said they thought I was dead," said Dominy, who is 81 and lives in Atlanta. When he showed up with ownership papers, the tools were returned to him and Dominy immediately gave them to Winterthur.

Three years later, Winterthur opened a Dominy wing, with detailed replicas of the Dominy shops, based on drawings made by the 1940 Historic American Buildings Survey and on Dominy family recollections. Just listen to Robert Dominy: "They put a door in the reconstructed shop, and I said, 'It's in the wrong place — it's four inches out of line.' So they moved it. They said, 'If that's the way it was, that's the way it will be.' " For in those details lie the lives of generations of craftsmen.

A clock built by Nathaniel Dominy IV (1737-1812); the dial says, "O trifle not, till time's forgot ..."

Newsday Photo / Bill Davis

WOOD FROM HONDURAS? NO PROBLEM

In the early 1790s, Sag Harbor merchant William Johnson Rysam asked Nathaniel Dominy V for a set of nine mahogany Windsor chairs. Problem was, Rysam wanted to use mahogany from his plantation — in Honduras.

"Rysam came to Dominy and said, 'I was wondering if you could build a wind-driven sawmill that I could ship to Honduras and set up there to cut the mahogany board,' " said Dean Failey of Christie's auction house.

Construction was no challenge for Dominy, who would build nine East End windmills around the turn of the century. But the rest of the adventure certainly was. After Dominy tested the mill on East Hampton's Study Hill, he dismantled it and shipped it to Sag Harbor, then loaded it onto Rysam's 202-ton brig, Merchant.

When the mill arrived in Honduras, Rysam reassembled it in his groves, sawed the mahogany, then shipped the boards back to Dominy — as if this were all a normal part of furniture-making.

"We think of the world as so isolated in that era," says Failey, "yet here are these chairs, signed and dated 1794 by Nathaniel Dominy, who is so proud of them." — **Michele Ingrassia**

Newsday Photo / Bill Davis

A Dominy Windsor chair; it and the clock are at the Custom House in Sag Harbor.

Craftsman and revolutionary Elias Pelletreau found success even in rural Southampton

A Reputation Forged in Silver

BY MICHELE INGRASSIA
STAFF WRITER

Newsday / Bill Davis

A pepper caster, spoons and a tankard made by Elias Pelletreau, now part of the Suffolk County Historical Society collection.
At left, the restored Pelletreau workshop (first built 1686) on Main Street in Southampton. It is open Wednesday to Saturday afternoons between July 4 and Labor Day.

Listen, my children, and you shall hear of the midnight ride of . . . Elias Pelletreau? Well, not exactly.

Few 18th-Century American craftsmen rivaled the myth and magic of Paul Revere, the Boston silversmith, Revolutionary patriot and muse for Longfellow's heart-thumping poem, "Paul Revere's Ride." Nevertheless, Pelletreau — Revere's Southampton-born contemporary and a revolutionary patriot in his own right — flourished, if not as Revere's artistic equal, certainly as one of the most prolific rural silversmiths of the era and Long Island's most important.

"Pelletreau was not a *great* artist, but he was significant," says Pelletreau scholar Dean Failey, senior director of American furniture and decorative arts at Christie's auction house. What distinguishes his work is not just art, but commerce. "He was one of a very, very small handful of silversmiths who were able to successfully carry on their craft in a nonurban setting. His ability to network was remarkable."

But Pelletreau was no Revere-lite. Like many upwardly mobile young men, this son of a successful Huguenot merchant was considered a worthy candidate for apprenticeship. "We talk about Little Italy and Chinatown today, but the Huguenot community was a very important part of 18th-Century New York," says Failey. "His contacts had everything to do with the fact that he was part of that community."

In 1741, at age 15, Pelletreau was sent from Southampton to New York to learn from Simeon Soumaine, the master goldsmith and fellow Huguenot. Unlike many urban apprentices, though, he left after his tutelage, returning home in 1750 to set up shop in the building attached to his father's house on Main Street. The one-room structure still stands, sandwiched between an antiques shop and the Southampton Chamber of Commerce.

During the next 30 years — including seven spent in Connecticut during the British occupation — Pelletreau crafted a steady stream of tankards, porringers and teapots for some of Long Island's most formidable families. Among them: Nathaniel Woodhull; David Gardiner, the sixth proprietor of Gardiners Island; his son, John Lyon Gardiner; merchant Samuel Townsend; and Dr. George Muirson, who later pioneered the Island's use of the smallpox vaccination.

To understand the magnitude of his success, it's important to note that working in revolutionary Southampton (population 2,792) would have been akin to couturier John Galliano setting up shop today in Cedar Rapids, Iowa: There wasn't a ready audience for grand designs. Rural markets typically demanded just a handful of pieces a year, few more adventurous than spoons. Silver was a luxury, after all, and customers tended to be urban, well-educated and well-traveled, a group with a taste for fashion and the money to indulge it.

But Pelletreau wasn't typical. His ledgers list more than 100 hollowware customers — urbane types who could have bought anywhere, and inward-looking locals who, as East Hampton preacher Lyman Beecher wrote in the early 1800s, "made no other journey during their whole lives" than the trip to church on Sunday. Part of Pelletreau's cachet reflected his status as farmer (he owned 125 acres), patriot (though too old to fight, he was made captain in the Southampton militia company) and benefactor (he reportedly loaned William Floyd money to travel to the first Continental Congress).

More important was his hybrid style, which mixed the fashionable and the solid, drawing from New York, where silversmiths were influenced by cutting-edge London, and New England, which defied trendiness. Some of his tankards, for example, were flat-topped New York style; others were dome-topped New England.

For the most part, though, this was straightforward design, devoid of the rococo flourishes raging in Europe. "What separates a straightforward piece from something we go oooh and ahhh over is an element of decoration, such as engraving," says Faily. Since Pelletreau was not an engraver or an embellisher, his legacy suffers.

Though Pelletreau surpassed local silversmiths and rivaled many New York contemporaries, even his best work falls short of pieces by top artisans such as Revere and New York's brilliant Myer Myers. "The best of Myers and the others goes one step beyond reducing an English form to American tastes and transforms it to something that soars," says Kevin Stayton, curator of decorative arts at the Brooklyn Museum, which mounted a 1959 Pelletreau show.

Where does that leave Pelletreau's legacy? Financially, his silver fetches respectable if not staggering prices today — about $2,000 to $3,000 for a porringer; $10,000 to $15,000 for a tankard and more than $20,000 for a teapot. Stylistically, there is much to praise. "A number of significant factors come together in Pelletreau: his French descent, the fact that his silver is very handsome, and his solid craftsmanship," says Stayton. "There was no one else on Long Island producing like that — and producing a full repertoire."

ROBERT H. PELLETREAU

"We had a lot of Elias Pelletreau's silver, but we gave it to the State Department," says Robert H. Pelletreau of Bellport, the 88-year-old great-great-great grandson of Long Island's most notable silversmith. Pelletreau donated the pieces — two porringers, a tankard, mug and bowl — in 1987, when his son, Robert Jr., became U.S. ambassador to Tunis. But what the family lacks in silver, it makes up for in luster: a line of descendants as distinguished as the most celebrated Pelletreau.

The family's Long Island roots date back to Elias' father, merchant Francis Pelletreau, who moved from New York to Southampton in 1717. This Pelletreau branch descends from Elias' older son, Elias, who, like his grandfather, was a merchant.

Newsday Photo / Bill Davis

The modern Pelletreaus begin with Robert S., a Suffolk County surrogate early this century and a lawyer who opened his Patchogue firm when he retired from the bench in 1935, at age 70. His son, law partner and now the oldest living Pelletreau — Robert H. — has been a prominent estates lawyer for more than a half-century.

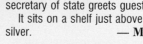

However, only Robert H. Pelletreau Jr. — the oldest of Robert's four children — has made his mark on a world stage. In 35 years in the foreign service — he retired this year — he served as ambassador to Bahrain, Tunis and Egypt and as undersecretary of state for Near East affairs, a post in which he figured prominently in the Israeli-PLO peace talks.

As for Pelletreau's silver, it's displayed in the John Quincy Adams drawing room, where the secretary of state greets guests.

It sits on a shelf just above Paul Revere's silver. **— Michele Ingrassia**

BY KATTI GRAY
STAFF WRITER

Long Island's colonial children keep busy just to help the family survive

Sun to Sun, All Work, Little Fun

In colonial Long Island, it was expected that all but the wealthiest and most feeble bodies would perform the tasks required for daily living.

Children — whether enslaved or free — were no exception. Like adults, they rose and retired with the sun, filling the daylight with chores: Harvesting clams. Digging clay to be fired into bricks. Retrieving well-water. Guarding cornfields from ravenous wildlife. Stoking hearths that burned around the clock, every day of the year — because fires were needed for cooking, cleaning and warmth and were difficult to ignite in the first place.

Often, children transformed work into play, telling stories or swimming off the coast at a time when toys were limited to wooden dolls or, for the well-to-do, tin boxes with exercise wheels for pet squirrels.

In what was a largely agrarian age, many lived on farms that at their smallest could average about 80 acres. It was a lot of territory to cover.

Other than general tidbits about the roles children played in commerce or household maintenance, historians say little else is known about the lives of young people.

"Couples married as much for economics as anything else back then. A woman alone could not run a homestead. A man alone could not. Together, and with children added to that mix, they could survive," said Barbara Kelly, curator of special collections at Hofstra University's Long Island Studies Institute.

Given this narrow understanding of colonial children, it is difficult to determine how adults measured a child's human worth back then, said Bonnie Thompson Dixon, executive director of the Long Island Children's Museum.

"What exactly was the value of a child? Was it another mouth to feed? An accident? Or were they brought into the world to help humans move to the next level, so to speak? That's a big question," she said.

What does seem clear, though, is that children were made to know their place as adults defined it.

"Whether you were a rich child or some other child, children really would never have spoken to an adult unless the adult spoke first," said Kathleen Kane, director of education for the Society for the Preservation of Long Island Antiquities. "Parents ate and the children waited for them to finish . . . Often, children ate separately and afterwards. Children weren't the main event of the family as they are today. They were expected to act like little grown-ups."

The Granger Collection

Young men work as indentured servants for an American colonial potter in an engraving from the 18th Century. Education and discipline were two perceived benefits.

Because of the status of children, no one wrote much of their lives. Much of the limited information available on colonial children has been gleaned piecemeal from such material as paintings from that period, letters — mainly adult observations — and other archives.

History that was passed down orally through generations of Indian families, and finally penned on paper, also provides glimpses of children who resided in the region long before English and Dutch immigrants arrived, said historian John Strong, an expert on Long Island's Indians.

As small children, Indians spent much of their time under the wings of women. As they became older, the boys would participate in rites of manhood during which they were deprived, for a time, of food or water but eventually were welcomed back into the fold as full-grown men.

Smaller children, along with their mothers, harvested the fields and set up wigwams during round-the-clock gatherings of crops.

"They played a very important role in the economics of these communities," Strong said.

"We do know their lives centered around family, gathering, hunting. But it was not structured in the way we have come to know work. The whole day was a mixture of socializing with your family. The notion of play and social activity was often not separate. You taught your children as they picked acorns. Your kids may be throwing acorns back and forth. The young boys, while they were hunting, were doing all the male-bonding that we talk so much about these days."

In addition, Indian children were known to have played with miniature bows and arrows, precursors to adult-sized tools they eventually would use.

So, manual labor was the norm for all children, who first served as apprentices of sorts in their own homes and often for actual employers later on.

What they learned at home, in shops, in the fields and on the waters often took the place of formal schooling, which was erratic in those early years. Believing ignorance was sinful, Purtians established some of the first schools. But this was long before public education became a legal right — and, even then, it was against the law for slaves to be educated even informally.

And with so much of the focus on a family's sheer survival, parents frequently considered churning butter, spinning textiles, tanning animal hides and so on as *the* life skills to teach their offspring.

"Some of these were very simple tasks — dipping candles, feeding the chickens, harvesting crops — but they were things that had to be done," said Kelly of the Long Island Studies Institute.

"But these were kids doing the work of grown-ups. They had both parents to watch, to imitate."

And the teaching did not end there. It also was common for adolescents, particularly those from white families of more modest means, to be temporarily hired out as apprentices to craftsmen. In part, this helped families meet financial ends. And it gave apprentices a future as adult wage-earners.

"In a manner of speaking, kids were chattel," Kelly said. "Certainly a father could and would sign away their child into service but that way a child learned. They were not being sold into bondage."

Parents even drew up legal contracts regarding the years and terms of their children's service to others.

"It may sound harsh," said Kelly. "But what we don't hear is the conversation between the father and craftsman that said this child goes to sleep at a certain hour, maybe that the child sleeps late, the warnings a

LEGACY

LEARNING ABOUT CHILDREN OF YESTERDAY

By sitting on a feather-filled mattress or trying on clothes of the 18th Century, children get to sense colonial life at the Joseph Lloyd Manor House on Lloyd Neck.

"It's very important for children to learn about history outside of the textbook," said Eleanor Ryder, a teacher at Medford Elementary School who takes fourth-graders to the house every year.

One Medford student, Diana Ortiz, 9, of Patchogue, said life as a colonial child was hard, especially for slaves. "The slaves didn't play too much, they just worked," she said. "To me it's sad."

Diana found the house's feather bed soft. She was less enthusiastic about a "potty chair" used in days before indoor plumbing. "I don't think people would like it," she said.

Vinny DePierro, 9, of Patchogue, learned that 1700s children didn't have TV. "They never really had fun, except when they had time," he said. Vinny thought working as a child and not going to school "would be a little boring." But he could envision himself in colonial times: "If I'm busy I'm fine," he said.

Students from Medford Elementary School try on colonial clothes at the Joseph Lloyd Manor House. From left, with instructor Lorraine Anderson, are students Vinny DePierro, Shawn Garrett, Shannon Lauritsen and Lauren Calvin.

father gives that tell of how much he cares for the child."

Some historians say apprenticeships not only taught a child how to perform physical work, but also aimed to ward off chances that a child would become self-indulgent.

"They also were disciplined by these mentors, these employers," Kelly said.

Life was hard, as much for children as any other group, historians say. For the poor and the enslaved, circumstances could be much worse. Slave children were often sold away from parents or, for example, made to stand all night to keep a fireplace going. Matches were not yet invented and starting a fire from stone flints or by striking sticks was a time-consuming, tricky proposition.

Poor children of all persuasions were at risk of becoming motherless because of diseases such as smallpox, or accidents. Younger women accidentally burned to death with some frequency; the swirls of fabric that made up their attire would catch fire as they tended to chores around the hearth or elsewhere. And if dad did not remarry, much of mom's work fell to the orphans she left behind.

Poor children whose families also lacked the means to buy or plant nourishing foods were most vulnerable to diseases such as whooping cough and chicken pox. This, before the introduction of penicillin, sulphur and other curatives.

"Usually, if a child made it past 2, they were all right," Kelly said.

That reality — and the fact that many in colonial times believed erroneously that mothers could not conceive while nursing their newest babies — led many families to bear lots of kids, she said. "In general, families were large by our standards, averaging seven to nine kids. Some people had 23 to 25, though that was unusual. But of that seven to nine, not all of them reached adulthood. Childhood diseases were wiping them out. Influenza would come and go. Smallpox would come and go."

Rich children lived in a starkly different manner. They learned to dance, recite poetry, play musical instruments.

The truly elite child rarely worked in the fields, and had leisure time. Wealthier families hired teachers who, in exchange for their services, accepted room and board as part of their pay. Sometimes, teachers slept on bales of hay inside barns.

Lloyd Manor in Huntington was among area compounds that had a stand-alone school on its grounds.

In some cases, wealthier neighbors also would pool resources to hire an instructor, perhaps build a small community school or have an itinerant teacher travel from one house to the next.

Literate farmers would teach their children what they could. And folklore was often handed down verbally and maintained as oral histories.

Textbooks, though, were scarce. The first few that appeared were small enough to fit in the center of an adult palm and were only a few pages in length.

Likewise, paper, then made of linen, was expensive. So, lessons generally were written with chalk on slate. Around children's necks hung a small board bearing the alphabet on paper laminated with the melted drippings from animal horns. "A" was for ape, "Z" for zebra and so on, the boards read. They were precursors to flashcards used in more contemporary classrooms.

"It's a way of life we have forgotten. But when we look at it, it's not all that alien," Kelly said. "It was not elegant living for children . . . But, back then, it was normal."

Newsday Photos / Bill Davis

A doll at the historic John Bowne House in Queens was brought to America in about 1630 and enjoyed by generations of Bowne children.

Bundling: Getting to Know Thee

Part of the courtship ritual for colonial teens looking to wed was the practice of "bundling," lying in bed together partially or fully clothed, sometimes with a board between them.

Sex was not the intent. The practice was a way to test the waters, so to speak.

Indeed, parents arranged for their offspring of marriageable age — from early to late teens — to participate in the practice, which dates back to at least the 1620s.

"People lived in farms that were separated by great distances," said Kathleen Kane, director of education for the Society for the Preservation of Long Island Antiquities. "So when somebody visited, specifically if they stayed overnight, bundling was the idea sometimes of putting a board between people who would sleep together — a man visiting someone's daughter that he was courting. It was a little bizarre but that was the basic idea and it was all under parental supervision. Despite all the Puritanical stuff, this was their reality."

Some scholars have said bundling offered privacy and warmth, especially in crowded houses.

After the Revolution, bundling would arouse the ire of critics and find less acceptance.

— Katti Gray

Medieval methods, and the need to expand, lead to a classic style of house

Evolution of the Colonial

BY DENISE FLAIM
STAFF WRITER

Picture a time machine, out of which jumps a century-tripping colonist from a Long Island of 300 years ago.

After mastering the exigencies of modern survival on Long Island — LILCO outages that wipe out outgoing answering-machine recordings, three-hour waits at The Source mall's Rainforest Cafe, and traffic, traffic everywhere — our visitor succumbs to the same primal need that's lured people here since the 17th Century:

Homeownership.

So, scanning our late-20th Century landscape, he drives past the high ranches, the boxy "Miami Vice" contemporaries, the neo-Victorians, and heads to . . .

Levittown?

"I think it's funny that the first great housing development after World War II was colonial," says Nassau County historian Edward Smits, referring to the Cape Cod cottage, which, along with the saltbox, was common on Long Island by the early 1700s. "And I think Levitt felt the cape was an efficient, simple house, which is also why it became the standard house in the colonial period."

But not by any means the only one. Or, for that matter, the first one. Like a Levitt house, which in its simplicity was fated to be a work in progress, the English colonial on Long Island went through a multi-step evolution — from early, experimental medieval adaptations to, more than a hundred years later, established styles that satisifed the colonial desire for New World order.

By the time the English started settling Long Island in the 1640s, the Dutch had already made their architectural mark from Queens and east to Oyster Bay. The wide-eaved, hipped-roof house that is universally known as the Dutch Colonial continued to be built long after Holland's political power waned in Long Island. Though intermingling between the two European building techniques sometimes occurred — with, for example, Dutch framing methods cropping up in English structures of the period — the two architectural styles never merged.

Initially, in that early settlement period, the English built what they knew: timberframe houses whose construction had been virtually unchanged in England since the Middle Ages. But they were short-lived on this side of the Atlantic. "They learned thatched roofs didn't work after trying them briefly in our harsh climate," explains Robert MacKay, director of the Society for the Preservation of Long Island Antiquities.

No examples of those very early, thatched-roof houses survive — in part because their builders hadn't quite grasped the concept of the starter home. "You make the assumption that people start out small," says architectural historian Zachary Studenroth, director of the Lockwood-Mathews Mansion Museum in Norwalk, Conn., and formerly preservation coordinator for the Society for the Preservation of Long Island Antiquities. "But when people first began to build, it seems some of them started off more ambitiously than climate and resources could support."

By the 1660s and '70s, colonists had tinkered with their medieval prototype long enough to hit on Long Island's first real house form — a two-story wood house, with two rooms on each floor grouped around a center chimney for heat conservation. Because they had been modified to suit the Long Island climate — for example, the abundance of wood dictated shingled roofs — many of these houses survive today.

But, Studenroth cautions, the longevity of these impressive houses is a direct product of their ambitiousness. And most Long Island colonists couldn't afford to build them any more than the North Shore groundskeeper of the 1920s could manage to live in an Oheka. "The norm for people of average means was a single cell with a chimney at one end of it, and maybe a ladder leading to a loftlike attic space," Studenroth explains. "And those humble little hovels are long gone."

What evolved from them was a vernacular form born of an impulse familiar to any modern Long Island homeowner — expansion. The saltbox became a conventional way to expand the two-room-over-two-room house by adding a lean-to, usually a kitchen, along the length of the back, and then sloping the roof down to meet the one-story addition. Viewed from the side, the house's profile resembled the old-fashioned salt-keeping container after which it was named.

The saltbox started appearing as a distinct style, rather than just an adaptation, around 1710 — about the same time the predecessor to our time-traveler's Levittown lodging started cropping up, too.

"We probably have more capes on Long Island than they have on Cape Cod," says Studenroth, adding that the style's migration here was a natural: "That kind of compact, land-hugging house was a very practical response to the sandy, windswept geography with which we associate the East End."

The one-story-plus-attic structure had all its principal rooms on the main floor: a formal parlor and bedchamber on either side of the central chimney and stairs, then a long kitchen centered against the back of the chimney. At each corner of the rear of the house, flanking the kitchen, was a small unheated room, used as a pantry or small bedchamber. The attic space above it promised the same possibilities for expansion — dormers, anyone? — that Levitt capitalized on 250 years later.

Today, the term "colonial" crops up relentlessly in real-estate ads, referring to houses with center halls, outside-wall chimneys and a scattering of pillars — actually, features of the more self-conscious and symmetry-obsessed Federal homes of the late-colonial period. But in its broadest sense, perhaps any modern house that captures the spirit of its colonial predecessor — a striving for comfort over chic, practicality over posturing, common sense over fashion dictates — can lay claim to that word.

LEGACY

VENERABLE ARCHITECTURE

Some examples of Long Island colonial architecture exist as museums today. Here are a few:

Early Colonial House: The Old House at Cutchogue, Cases Lane on the Village Green; 516-734-7122.

Colonial Cape Cod: Miss Amelia Cottage Museum, Montauk Highway at Windmill Lane, Amagansett; 516-267-3020.

Colonial Salt Box: Thompson House, 91 N. Country Rd., Setauket; 516-941-9444.

The Miss Amelia Cottage Museum in Amagansett was built around 1725 and relocated in 1790.

ONE FOR THE AGES

Because of 18th-Century Long Island's agricultural focus — and the lack of rich patrons to spur high-quality commissions — most of our colonial furniture wouldn't have made it into the Architectural Digest of the day.

But what it lacked in sophisticated flourishes, Long Island furniture made up for in practicality — sturdy Windsor chairs and gateleg tables in English homes, and the distinctive squat armoire, called a *kas,* and fold-down, built-in beds in Dutch ones.

Fittingly, those two European influences merged to form what Robert MacKay of the Society for the Preservation of Long Island Antiquities calls "Long Island's most recognizable antique furniture form" — the two-panel blanket chest.

"It has a very Dutch look to it," MacKay says of the chest, which has turnip-shaped or bracketed feet and a top that lifted off, "even though it was made by Quakers living in Nassau County." —Denise Flaim

Newsday Photos / Bill Davis

A double-paneled blanket chest, circa 1750, at the Old Bethpage Village Restoration

By George DeWan
STAFF WRITER

The characters and sights of Long Island intrigue a Maryland physician in 1744

A Magical History Tour

On a trip on horseback to New England in the summer of 1744, a 32-year-old doctor from Annapolis, Md., named Alexander Hamilton got a good taste of colonial Long Island:

He ate moldy cheese in Jamaica . . . got lost in the Hempstead Plains . . . met a man in Huntington who was both a shoemaker and a doctor . . . was entertained in Brookhaven by a 75-year-old sailor who stood on his head . . . was turned off by the desolation of the pine barrens . . . was charmed by pretty Long Island waitresses.

The Scottish-born Hamilton later wrote a journal about the trip, published as "Hamilton's Itinerarium." The Long Island section began on Tuesday, July 10, when, in the company of two Boston merchants, Benjamin Parker and Henry Laughton, he crossed the East River on the ferry:

We arrived a quarter after ten at Jamaica . . . We stopped there at the sign of the Sun, and paid dear for our breakfast, which was bread and mouldy cheese, stale beer, and cider.

They set out for Hempstead, and here follows a good description of the Hempstead Plains:

At four o'clock, going across this great plain, we could see almost as good a horizon 'round us as when one is at sea, and in some places of the plain, the latitude might be taken by observation at noonday. It is about sixteen miles long. The ground is hard and gravelly; the road very smooth but indistinct, and intersected by several other roads, which make it difficult for a stranger to find the way. There is nothing but long grass grows upon this plain, not above a foot high.

Hamilton then tells a story about getting lost.

We lost our way here, and blundered about a great while. At last we spied a woman and two men at some distance. We rid up towards them to inquire, but they were too wild to be spoke with, running over the plain as fast as wild bucks upon the mountains. Just after we came out of the plain and sunk into the woods, we found a boy lurking behind a bush. We wanted to inquire the way of him, but, as soon as we spoke, the game was started and he ran away.

The trio arrived at Huntington about eight o'clock in the evening, putting up at an inn called the Half-moon and Hart, run by an Irishman named Platt.

We had no sooner sat down, when there came in a band of the town politicians in short jackets and trousers, being probably curious to know who them strangers were who had newly arrived in town. Among the rest was a fellow with a worsted cap and great black fists. They styled him doctor. Flat [Platt] told me he had been a shoemaker in town, and was a notable fellow at his trade, but happening two years ago to cure an old woman of a pestilent mortal disease, he thereby acquired the character of a physician, was applied to from all quarters, and finding the practice of physic a more profitable business than cobbling, he laid aside his awls and leather, got himself some gallipots [small vessels used to hold medicines], and instead of cobbling of soales fell to cobbling of human bodies.

Leaving Huntington at 6:30 the next morning, they arrived at Brookhaven, or Setauket, about 2 p.m., where they had dinner at a place run by a man named Buchanan.

While we were at Buchanan's an old fellow named Smith called at the house. He said he was a-traveling to [New] York, to get a license or commission from the Governor to go a-privateering, and swore he would not be under any commander, but would be chief man himself.

He showed us several antic tricks, such as jumping half a foot high upon his bum, without touching the floor with any other part of his body. Then he turned and did the same upon his belly. Then he stood upright upon his head. He told us he was seventy-five years of age and swore damn his old shoes if any man in America could do the like.

At 5:30 p.m. they were off again, arriving at 8 o'clock at a house called Brewster's, where they put up for the night.

Thursday, July 12th. — When I waked this morning I found two beds in the room, besides that in which I lay, in one of which lay two great hulking fellows, with long black beards, having their own hair, and not so much as half a nightcap betwixt both them. I took them for weavers, not only from their greasy appearance, but because I observed a weaver's loom at each side of the room. In the other bed was a raw-boned boy, who, with the two lubbers, huddled on his clothes, and went reeling downstairs, making as much noise as three horses.

At 6 a.m. Hamilton set out again, riding 16 miles through what is now known as the pine barrens.

Here we passed thro' a plain of six or eight miles long, where was nothing but oak brush or bushes, two feet high, very thick, and replenished with acorns; and thinly scattered over the plain were several old naked pines at about two or three hundred feet s distance from one another, most of them decayed and broken. In all this way we met not one living soul, nor saw any house but one in ruins. Some of the inhabitants here call this place the Desert of Arabia.

Passing through Riverhead, he rode in the rain another 18 miles up the North Fork to Southold, where he put up at the home of a Mrs. Moore.

We ordered some eggs for dinner and some chickens. Mrs. Moore asked us if we would have bacon fried with our eggs; we told her no. After dinner we set out to inquire for a boat to cross the Sound.

At night the house was crowded with a company of patched coats and tattered jackets, and consequently the conversation consisted chiefly in damn ye Jack; and here's to you, Tom.

One of the crowd, "a comical old fellow," was asked what sort of entertainment the group might find at its next stop, Oyster Pond — now Orient — where they planned to take a boat across the Sound.

"Why truly," said he, "if you could eat such things as we Gentiles do, you may live very well, but as your law forbids you to eat swine's flesh your living will be but indifferent." Parker laughed, and asked him if he took us for Jews or Mahometans. He replied: "Gentlemen, I ask pardon, but the landlady informed me you were Jews." This notion proceeded from our refusing of bacon to our eggs at dinner.

At Oyster Pond, they stopped for breakfast at a place called King's.

Here we saw some handsome country girls, one of whom wore a perpetual smile in her face, and prepared the chocolate for our breakfast. She presently captivated Parker, who was apt to take flame upon all occasions . . . We put our horses on board ten minutes before three, and set sail with a fair wind from the Oyster Pond.

The Half-moon and Hart inn, in Huntington, also known as Platt's tavern, where physician Alexander Hamilton stayed in 1744. Based on building plans, the drawing was done for the Town of Huntington around 1982 by Henry J. Poh of East Northport. He said a gas station now occupies the site at Route 25A and Park Avenue.

In the 1600s, families dominate local boards that route roads and hand out land

In Charge at Town Hall

BY GEORGE DEWAN
STAFF WRITER

Early town governments on Long Island were often kept in the family. In Huntington, for example, only five families held the supervisor's job between 1694, when the first board of trustees was formed, and 1776, when the Revolution started.

"It was, essentially, government of the many by the privileged few," historian Geoffrey Rossano wrote in 1981 in the Quarterly of the Huntington Historical Society. This was a pattern repeated elsewhere. In Smithtown in 1763, of the 19 officials chosen at an annual town meeting, 12 were named Smith.

The list of Huntington Town trustees in the colonial period is dominated by the same family names, year after year. And those in power didn't always pass the jobs around: Some men held multiple town jobs. In 1749 the trustees chose Eliphalet Wickes for seven different jobs, including trustee, constable, town clerk and treasurer.

©1995, Anthony D'Adamo

Smithtown, 1736

"At a town meeting held at Smithtown the first Tuesday in April 1736, Ebenezer Smith [was chosen] Clerk, Platt Smith chosen Supervisor, Aaron Smith Constable, Job Smith and Richard Smith chosen assessors, Edmund Smith chosen Collector."
— **Town Records**

This is how town government began on Long Island. The foundations for today's governments in three Nassau and 10 Suffolk towns were laid in the late 17th and early 18th Centuries. Residents, no longer settlers, were now members of established local societies choosing the elite males among them to meet and make rules by which to live.

Huntington Town, which was settled in 1653, is one example. The early residents ran things for themselves at town meetings until the British conquest over the Dutch in 1664. In patents issued by three different governors-general, residents were given official title to the land. But, still under the Duke's Laws, which created New York's colonial government, communities had little authority.

Everything changed following the English Revolution of 1689, when new charters gave Huntington and other towns the powers of town corporations. In 1694 Huntington elected its first board of trustees. There were still town meetings, but their opinions were merely advisory to the board.

As the 17th Century ended, Huntington was a growing community of about 500. "There were at least four flour mills in operation, two or three saw mills, several tanneries, one or more brickyards, a town dock, a town school, a town church, and a fort and depository for arms and ammunition," wrote former supervisor Charles R. Street in his introduction to the 1888 publication of the Huntington Town Records.

Compared with today's multi-million-dollar town budgets, the annual spending by early 18th-Century Long Island towns was minuscule. Often, the business of the trustees did not involve spending money at all. One of their most important functions was granting parcels of land as the town expanded southward toward the Great South Bay (the southern section of the town was not split off as Babylon Town until 1873).

A plum job given out by the Huntington trustees was that of fence-viewer. A fence-viewer was responsible for inspecting new fences and settling disputes over trespassing by escaped livestock. He was paid a half-crown (2 shillings sixpence) per day, but it cost the town nothing, since the fee was paid by the owner of the fence.

In 1695 a problem arose with unauthorized tree cutting on the common land, and the new town goverment had to act. On March 24, in what was probably the first order ever made by the Huntington trustees concerning common lands, such cutting was banned, with the penalty the forfeiture of the trees, plus a fine of triple their value: "And it is ordered that whomsoever peeleth any standing trees for bark for their use of tanning: they shall forfeit five shillings for ever tree found so peeled."

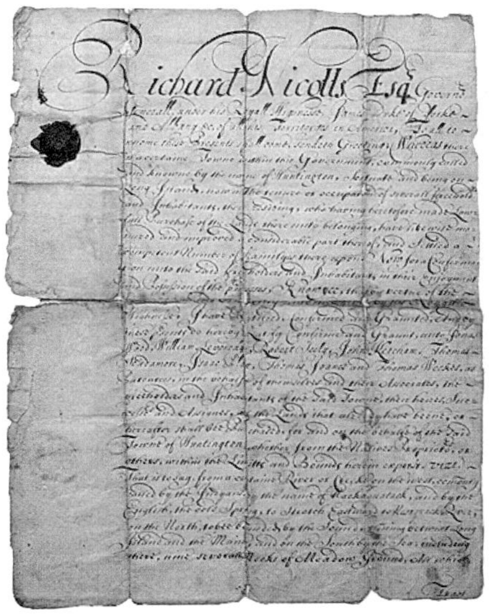

The Huntington patent of 1666, issued by Richard Nicolls, governor of New York; the document is held by the town clerk.

As the community grew, trustees became more involved in the need to improve paths that had become highways. They appointed John Ketcham as a layer-out of roads. The first record of the formal laying-out of a highway in the town was written by Ketcham on May 8, 1695:

Laide out by the survaiers of the towne of Huntington a highway beginnig at the head of the wigwam swamp [Cold Spring Harbor] six rods in width upland and so running by the swampe and banke side all most to the path of the beach.

No subject got the attention of the town board more than the highly contagious disease smallpox, which had ravaged Europe for centuries. The earliest attempt to control the disease was by inoculation of material from a skin lesion of an infected person into the skin of a well person. Though this can make a person resistant, it carried the serious danger of spreading the infection. The safer cowpox inoculation developed by Edward Jenner did not come into use until the turn of the 19th Century.

In 1760, Huntington was among those communities threatened. "Many persons here, who had been inoculated, died, and the affair caused great excitement, so that many stringent orders were made against inoculation, except under special conditions," wrote Street.

On New Year's Day, the trustees issued an order providing for a pox house in a remote part of town where inoculations by designated doctors could take place. All other inoculation was forbidden. Two such houses were actually opened, by Dr. Gilbert Potter and Dr. Daniel Wiggins. The town order had to be repeated again in 1763, when the disease spread again. Once again, in 1771, the order was repeated and expanded to prohibit Potter and Wiggins from inoculating someone from out of town.

By this time, another problem for the town fathers, and the entire colony, was making itself felt. That was the continuing escalation of America's war of words with the mother country. In 1774, the trustees issued the Declaration of Rights, declaring British taxes in the colonies to be unconstitutional.

War edged closer, and at the annual town meeting in 1775, trustees were selected and a vote was taken. Town records said: "May 2, 1775 at a general town meeting it was voted that there should be eighty men chosen to exercise and be ready to march."

LEGACY

AN EARLY FILE CABINET

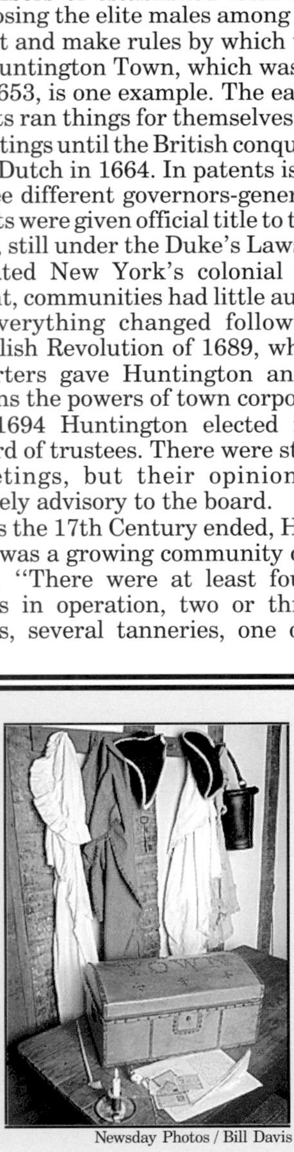

Newsday Photos / Bill Davis

There may have been a time in Huntington's early days when all official town records could be carried around in the town clerk's back pocket. But after the Revolution, a chest was needed, so in 1796, Town Clerk John Ketcham had one made. It can be seen at the Huntington Arsenal on Village Green. The tattered original leather covering of the pine box, which is about two feet wide and 10½ inches high, has been replaced, but the original brass decorations remain. Inside the box is a receipt from Obediah Johnes, apparently the maker: "Received in Huntington the 25th of April 1796 the sum of twelve shillings for a box for the town use."

Gossips, thieves and other criminals find harsh treatment under colonial laws

Crime and Punishment

BY ELLEN YAN
STAFF WRITER

On his way to a waterfront tavern one Saturday night, an Oyster Bay native named Adam Smith fell into bad ways.

He broke into the cabin of a boat moored at Peck's Slip, now part of South Street Seaport, slipping away with the captain's chest, bedding and 6 pounds in cash. He went into a nearby watering hole, where the bundle under his coat raised suspicion. The next day, he was arrested.

Smith, not yet 23, explained he had joined up with villainous folks despite having poor, honest parents who taught him the principles of Christianity.

But remorse didn't help. He was hung in front of the townspeople. Just like adultery and the dastardly filching of apples in Southampton, burglary was a capital offense in colonial times.

"The idea of punishment was not only to punish wrongdoing, but it was also intended to set an example to others," said Ted Burrows of Northport, a history professor at Brooklyn College. "There was really nothing standing between the community and lawlessness than its ability to inflict those kinds of exemplary punishments."

In colonial times, crime was defined by community morals. Gossiping, not going to church, and breaking a marriage proposal were crimes in some places. In one case, a servant went to court for making a face behind a landowner's wife. Fathering a child out of wedlock was against Southampton law, so servant George Wood was fined 10 pounds in 1641.

Beating up someone in East Hampton was punishable by a 10-shilling fine while beating up on someone's reputation cost more, 5 pounds. In Newtown, now part of western Queens, Isaac Gray accused Thomas Wandall of defaming him. "The plaintiff declares that the defendant charges him 'for wearing a scarf his cousin Richard lost.' "

Punishment came swiftly after verdicts: lopped-off ears, banishment and water-dunking. Others deemed guilty hunched for hours at the pillory, a wood plank with holes for the neck and wrists, while townspeople pelted them with food. Flogging could be a road show, with the convicted tied to the end of a cart and led to street corners to be whipped.

It wasn't enough to just brand someone. The disfigurement was best visible on the cheek or forehead — "T" for thief and "R" for rogue. A cross-like mark on the muscle of the thumb meant those branded had averted one execution because of their ability to read but could not be pardoned a second time if they committed another capital offense.

"Our ancestors were not squeamish," wrote Alice Morse Earle in her 1896 book "Curious Punishments of Bygone Days." "Truly long hair and wigs had their ulterior uses in colonial days when ear-cropping was thus rife . . . Life was dull and cramped in those days, but there were diversions; when the breeze might lift the locks from your friends or your lover's cheek and give a glimpse of ghastly hole instead of an ear, or display a burning letter on the forehead . . . "

Images from The Granger Collection

Engravings depict pillories and dunking, two public forms of punishment in the colonies. Shame was seen as an effective deterrent, so imprisonment was uncommon.

Southampton's public whipping post and stock — a plank with holes for the ankles and sometimes wrists — was at the village's center, currently trendy Job's Lane and Main Street. In 1641, the wages of the local whipper were 12 pence per whipping, to be paid by the whipped in money or work.

The punishment for each crime was not always stipulated by law, and colonists tried to suit the sentence to the crime. The tongue of a gossiping woman was kept out of her mouth with a wedge or "forked stick" at the pillory, said Southampton Town historian Robert Keene. "They kept it on there long enough to read the charges."

Spanking was too good for unruly Southampton children: "Rebellious children, whether they continue in Riot or Drunkeness, after due correction from parents, or whether they curse or Smite their parents Are to bee put to death," the law read. But although the death penalty was on the books for many crimes, it was not always handed down because of a shortage of labor.

Drunkenness was considered the most vexatious threat to community morals. Those who drank too freely were whipped or forced to sit with hangovers for hours in the stock.

The white settlers of Long Island drafted laws aimed at blacks, Indians and strangers. Some towns forced settlers to reclaim horses they had sold to Indians. Other laws required blacks to hold candles when they walked the streets at night, and slaves to carry written permission to leave their master's house or else be whipped.

A 1689 Hempstead Town meeting made it a crime to entertain or house any "unresident Person" more than 48 hours without official sanction or face fines. The next year, the town elected two men to "find any settled on ye towns Land without ye towns Consent and in ye towns behalfe to give notis to them forthwith to desert ye same otherwise they may Exspect to be sued."

Although different places had different laws, the justice system mirrored England's. People often represented themselves. Town courts met about once a month. There was a Court of Sessions for Suffolk and another for Queens and what is now Nassau; both met about twice a year and were composed of the towns' justices of the peace, the sheriff and other officials. The Court of Assizes, overseen by the governor, his designees and town magistrates, met yearly to hear important trials and appeals.

Problems plagued the fledgling justice system. Court proceedings were sometimes postponed because no one, from the sheriff to jurors and litigants, showed up. Collectors of court-ordered fines were known to keep the money. Judges as well as jurors were often unlearned in the ways of the law.

Bribes could be had, and Thomas Jarvis, a Suffolk justice of the peace who held court at his tavern, found himself on trial after allowing a litigant to buy liquor for the jury to sway its verdict, wrote Douglas Greenberg in his book "Crime and Law Enforcement in the Colony of New York 1691-1776."

Townspeople frequently flouted authority. They cursed judges and attacked constables trying to make arrests. Some men chosen as jurors or constables against their will preferred to pay fines rather than serve. In one election for constable, Greenberg wrote, a man charged that he had been "maliciously chosen he being unacquainted with the English dialect."

Imprisonment made little sense in a society that saw punishment as a community matter, said Eli Faber, a professor of history and criminal justice at John Jay College of Criminal Justice.

"Why bother to put people in an expensive institution that they can break out of?" he said. "Picture a person who commits fornication. He's going to be whipped in front of his mother, his sister. He's going to have to live with these people . . . If you lock people up, why would there be shame? Nobody would see them."

The colonies protest new taxes from George III and clash with British troops

On the Verge of War

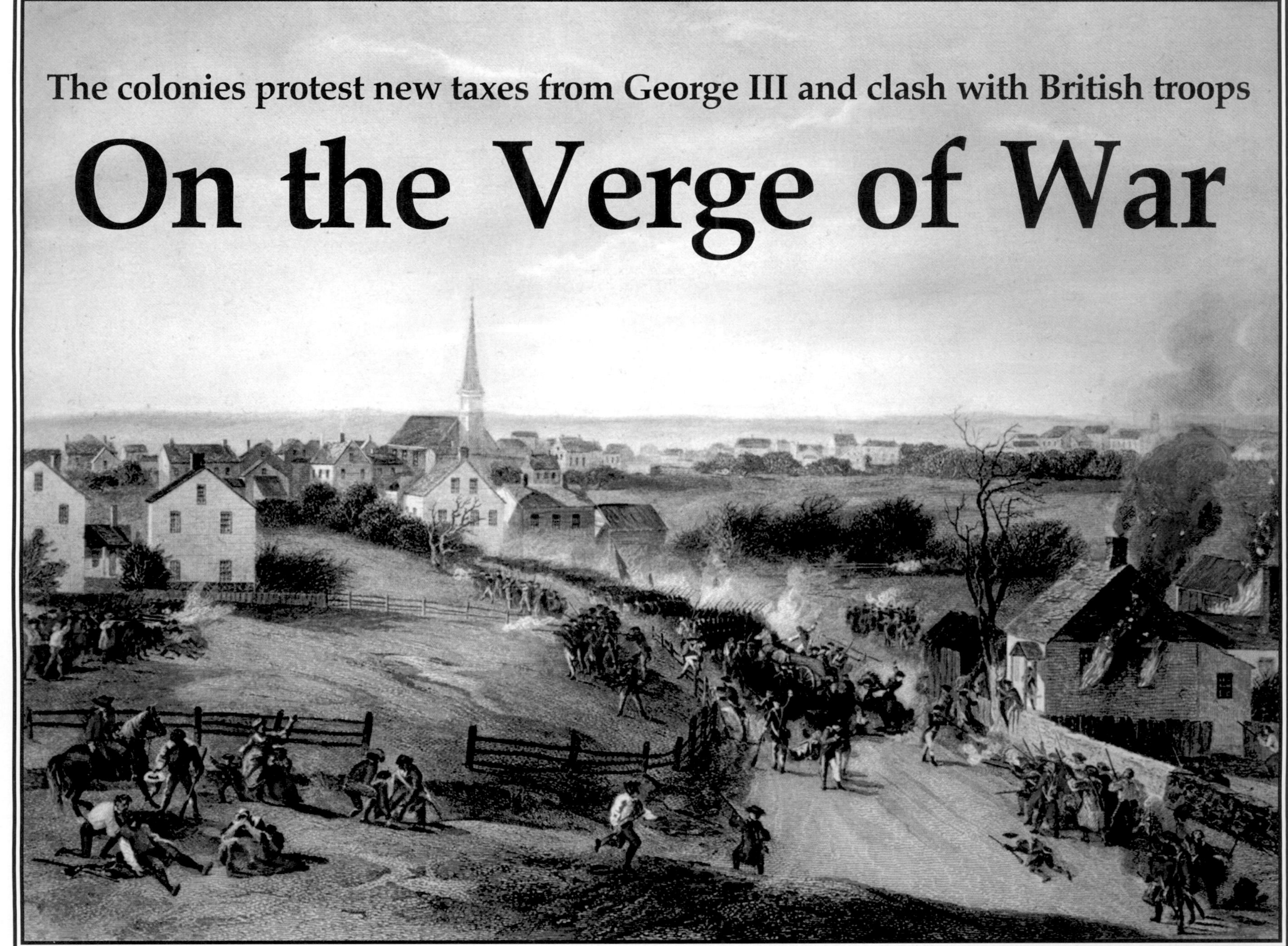

The Granger Collection

In a 19th-Century engraving, British troops retreat while exchanging gunfire with Americans at Concord, Mass., on April 19, 1775. The Revolutionary War was on and would last for eight years.

BY GEORGE DEWAN
STAFF WRITER

On a cool fall day in New York, Oct. 28, 1765, representatives of nine of the 13 colonies held an urgent session at Town Hall to rage against the Stamp Act, newly imposed by Great Britain.

As the clock ticked away the hours, the debate gathered steam and the noise in the hall became a tumult. Up stood the brilliant 41-year-old merchant from Charleston, S.C., Christopher Gadsden, to plead for a common front against Parliament and King George III:

There ought to be no New England men, no New Yorker . . . but all of us Americans!

Thirteen disparate colonies were taking small steps toward nationhood. For more than a century, Americans had been left pretty much free to develop their political, economic and social institutions as they pleased, with little interference from abroad. So when the British Parliament attempted to bring the colonies in line with other British institutions, rebellion was a natural outcome. Liberty was at stake.

In 1760, George III, age 22, ascended the British throne. Three years later, Britain's seven-year war with France ended, leaving the country financially drained. Much of its debt had been incurred on North American soil in clearing Canada, Florida and all the land east of the Mississippi of Frenchmen and Spaniards. Britain now saw the growing wealth of the American colonies as a source of income. And it was felt only proper that Americans should contribute to their own defense.

In 1765 the British Parliament passed the Stamp Act, the first direct tax levied on the American colonies. It went into effect Nov. 1.

The act required that all newspapers, pamphlets, legal documents, commercial bills, advertisements, school diplomas, liquor licenses and other papers issued in the colonies bear a stamp, the revenue from which was to be used to pay for the defense of the American colonies. It was immediately denounced throughout the colonies. Merchants boycotted British goods; stamps were confiscated and destroyed.

Alexander Flick, New York State historian in 1920-39, wrote:

It was a doleful day. Bells tolled the death of American liberty. Shops were closed; flags hung at half-mast; mourning costumes were donned by the people; newspapers printed a skull in the place where the stamp should have been; and protesting pamphlets appeared.

Since the colonists were not represented in Parliament, the cry of "No taxation without representation!" went up.

Faced with a loss of trade, and knowing that it could not be enforced, Parliament repealed the Stamp Act in 1766.

The colonies erupted in joyful celebration. To honor the king's birthday, the New York General Assembly, the colony's legislature, paid 1,000 pounds sterling to have a gilded equestrian statue of George III made in England, shipped to New York and erected on a 15-foot-high marble pedestal at Bowling Green.

At that point the colonists did not want to be separated from the mother country. They felt strongly, however, that they should have all the rights that their English cousins had. Events of the next decade, however, caused the seed of revolution to germinate, take root, grow and blossom.

In 1767, Parliament tried again, passing the Townshend Acts, designed to collect revenue from the colonies by imposing customs duties on their imports of glass, lead, paints, paper and tea. Protests followed, and

LI HISTORY.COM

To read the full text of Huntington's Declaration of Rights, see http://www.lihistory.com.

the Massachusetts Assembly was dissolved by the British for sending a circular letter to the other colonies urging solidarity. British troops, sent to enforce the laws, came up against a populace ready to fight.

The Americans had their supporters in England, especially among the Whig opposition in Parliament. Chief among them was the Dublin-born Edmund Burke, who rose in the legislature to add his brilliant voice to the pro-American, anti-Townshend forces. Burke said:

The people of the colonies are descendants of Englishmen . . . They are therefore not only devoted to liberty, but liberty according to English ideas, and on English principles. The temper and character which prevail in our colonies are, I am afraid, unalterable by any human art. We cannot, I fear, falsify the pedigree of this fierce people, and persuade them that they are not sprung from a nation in whose veins the blood of freedom circulates.

Most of the acts were repealed three years later. But the tea tax was retained, heightening the tension between British troops and angry colonists. On the evening of March 5, 1770, the so-called Boston Massacre took place. British troops, taunted by rock and snowball-throwing agitators, fired into the crowd: Three men were killed and two others later died of their wounds.

This is often said to be the first blood spilled in the Revolution. But New York City makes a prior claim. Almost three weeks earlier, on Jan. 5, antitax agitators clashed with British soldiers at a little rise on John Street known as Golden Hill, and one American was killed.

Three years later, in 1773, the tax on tea was still causing problems. At the Boston Tea Party, as it became known in the history books, colonists led by Samuel Adams and Paul Revere disguised themselves as Indians, boarded three ships in Boston Harbor loaded with 342 chests of tea and threw the cargo overboard.

"The dye is now cast," the king wrote to Lord North, the prime minister. "The Colonies must either submit or triumph."

In response to the Boston Tea Party, Parliament passed five new laws — Americans called them in derision the "Intolerable Acts" — limiting the freedoms of the colonists, especially in Massachusetts. Expressions of solidarity with the beleagured New Englanders came from across the colonies, including Long Island.

In a memorable meeting in Huntington held June 21, 1774, the town fathers joined the Patriot cause in support of "our brethren in Boston," passing what has become known as the Huntington Declaration of Rights. The document declared:

That every freeman's property is absolutely his own, and no man has a right to take it from him without his consent . . . that therefore all taxes and duties imposed on His Majesties subjects in the American colonies by the authority of Parliament are wholly unconstitutional and a plain violation of the most essential rights of British subjects.

But Long Island was divided in its feelings about the mother country. In predominately Dutch Kings County, residents seemed to regard the conflict as an English problem, preferring to ignore the oncoming revolution. In many parts of Queens, commercial ties with England were strong, as were ties with the Anglican Church, and towns like Hempstead, Jamaica and Oyster Bay made public their support for the king. Residents of the northern part of Hempstead, on the other hand, strongly supported the Patriot cause. But Patriot sentiment was strongest in Suffolk County. In fact, the war, when it came, was in many ways a civil war — between Loyalist and Patriot Americans — in addition to being a revolution.

There would be no turning back. On April 18 1775, the British commander at Boston, Gen. Thomas Gage, sent 700 elite grenadiers and light infantry troops to Concord, 16 miles away, to capture military supplies in order to prevent armed rebellion. While on the way the next morning, the British troops came upon a group of militiamen in Lexington, shots were exchanged, and eight Americans were killed. Then later that day at Concord, more shots were fired, and dozens more men were killed or wounded on each side. The king's troops fell back to Boston, where 10,000 British troops were massed.

This is how the war began. It would not end for eight years, the longest war in the nation's history until the Vietnam War.

Decades after Concord, Ralph Waldo Emerson would look upon the Battle Monument just erected there and write:

Here once the embattled farmers stood,
And fired the shot heard round the world.

The Granger Collection

New Yorkers protest the Stamp Act, in a 19th-Century engraving. The act, which required a stamp on printed materials, was passed in 1765 and repealed the next year.

The Granger Collection

Thinking that Americans should contribute to their own defense, England's George III, right, began taxing them in 1765. Above is an embossed Stamp Act stamp.

Painting by Allan Ramsay, c. 1767 / The Granger Collection

> not the growth of our climate: murmurs & Rebellion are the produce of Europe Americans disclaim them. on what instance pray are the Americans called Rebels? what have they done to deserve the name? they have asserted their rights, and are

Rare Book and Manuscript Library, Columbia University

"On what instance pray are the Americans called Rebels?" Charity Clarke wrote to a cousin in England in 1774. "What have they done to deserve the name? They have asserted their rights . . ."

Charity Clarke, a spirited New Yorker, writes of her resolve to win freedom

A Woman Ready to Fight

BY GEORGE DEWAN
STAFF WRITER

Charity Clarke was a young New York City woman with strong opinions about the growing tensions caused by Great Britain's tightening grip on its American colonies. A staunch defender of the American cause, she waged a rousing war of words with her cousin Joseph Jekyll, a London lawyer, in a series of letters written between 1768 and 1774.

"When there is the least show of oppression or invading of liberty you may depend on our working ourselves to the utmost of our power," Clarke wrote on Nov. 6, 1768. What had aroused her ire was the landing in Boston a month earlier of a garrison of British soldiers to quell increasing disorders brought about by the Townshend Acts, which put customs duties on a number of imports, including tea.

Clarke, who signed her letters, "Your friend and affectionate cousin," could nevertheless be ironic and slyly sarcastic when the occasion called for it:

What a pretty figure your expedition to Boston will make in history . . . They may now employ themselves in gathering of shells or what may please for they have nothing else to do . . . As to insurrections, we know of none. And unruly mobs we'll leave to England, they don't govern America.

These letters, which are owned by Columbia University, were written when Clarke, who was born in 1747, was just entering her 20s. They provide one American woman's first-hand look at the troubles that led to the American Revolution.

Charity Clarke brushed history in other ways. Her father, Thomas Clarke, named his property in lower Manhattan "Chelsea," for the soldiers' hospital near London, and thus gave a name to the Chelsea neighborhood of New York. She married Benjamin Moore, who later became the second Protestant Episcopal bishop of New York and president of Columbia College. Their only child, Clement Clarke Moore, a respected biblical scholar, is best-known for his poem "A Visit From St. Nicholas."

On March 31, 1769, Clarke echoed a general sentiment among Americans: They wanted an accommodation with Great Britain, not separation. One of the weapons being used by the colonies was a restriction on English imports, a tactic that caused some problems:

The attention of every American is fixed on England. The last accounts from thence are very displeasing to those who wish a good understanding between Britain and her colonies. The Americans are firm in their resolution of no importations from England. The want of money is so great among us that land sells for less than half price. The merchants have no cash to buy bills of exchange, which are now very low.

The following June, Clarke announced her readiness to join "a fighting army of Amazones" who would take to take to the hills, if necessary, to flee the oppressive British.

If you English folks won't give us the liberty we ask . . . I will try to gather a number of ladies armed with spinning wheels [along with men] who shall all learn to weave & keep sheep, and will retire beyond the reach of arbitrary power, cloathed with the work of our hands, feeding on what the country affords . . . In short, we will found a new Arcadia.

Worried about how her cousin might react to her scrappy letters, Clarke wrote in December, 1769, to wish that he be not offended:

I will not however rescind, no not even to possess your good opinion. They are my sentiments and I cannot help them, nor can I by any means think them seditious.

By Oct. 28, 1771, the Townshend Acts had been annulled, except for the tax on tea. But in the spring of 1770, five Patriots had died in the Boston Massacre, and anger was rising in the colonies. Charity Clarke wore her patriotism on her sleeve:

Unaffected patriotism & true virtue will I trust distinguish America in every age, and among every nation. So my dear Coz your fears are groundless. America still practices the though unboasted list of virtues, which the generality of English men have scarce an idea of.

King George III makes an interesting appearance in a letter of May 7, 1772. Whereas the king has become the symbol for everything wrong with late-18th Century British colonial policy, Clarke has sympathy for him, reserving her barbs for the policies of the British Parliament, and the barely competent prime minister, Frederick, Lord North.

How I pity the situation of our poor King, what with the death of his mother, the folly of his brother & the misfortunes (I hope not vices) of his sister. He has enough to overwhelm his heart with sorrow & embitter every enjoyment of life.

AP Photo

A portrait of King George III by the 18th-Century Swiss artist Jean-Etienne Liotard

That spring, the latest scandal in London was that the king's favorite brother, 29-year-old William, had been for six years secretly married to a widow with three children — when all along the king thought the woman was merely William's mistress. The king's youngest sister, 21-year-old Caroline — who had married her first cousin, the disreputable King Christian VII of Denmark, when she was 16 — had long been the mistress of Christian's court physician, Johann Struensee, who earlier in 1772 had been jailed for plotting against King Christian.

Months passed, and things in America got worse. The last pre-revolutionary letter is dated Sept. 10, 1774. A year earlier, the Boston Tea Party had inflated British temperatures, and Parliament passed acts limiting the freedom of the colonists, especially in Massachusetts. But for Charity Clarke, "rebel" was a misnomer:

In what instance pray are the Americans called Rebels? What have they done to deserve the name? They have asserted their rights, and are determined to maintain them . . . Great Britain stands ready to destroy her sons for inheriting her spirit.

Clarke was now in high dudgeon, writing like a pamphleteer.

What care we for your fleets and armies, we are not going to fight with them unless drove to it by the last necessity, or the highest provocation . . . Though this body is not clad with silken garments, these limbs are armed with strength. The soul is fortified by Virtue, and the love of Liberty is cherished within this bosom.

Then she attacked Lord North:

A proud, ambitious Minister governs in Britain. By his sophistry makes the King deaf to the remonstrances of his subjects, by his bribery obtains the majority of Parliament and by his power would spread tyranny to the western continent. But its inhabitants are not sunk in luxury, nor are they clouded by pomp. Their eyes watch over their liberty, observe every encroachment and oppose it. And is this their crime in your eyes, my Cousin? Do you condemn them for not being foolish enough to give away the property of their posterity? Surely you ought not to condemn America.

The final pages of this letter are missing. Thus, abruptly and in midtirade, ends Miss Charity Clarke's letters to her London cousin Joseph Jekyll on the eve of the American Revolution.

Puritan influences leave no room for decking the Christmas halls on Long Island

A Somber Yuletide

BY MOLLY MCCARTHY
STAFF WRITER

A roasted goose rests on the table. A Christmas tree, adorned with candles and strings of cranberries, takes up a full corner of the room. Stockings hang from the hearth, stuffed with presents. And perhaps a Tiny Tim-esque boy offers the season's toast: "God bless us every one!"

That's probably what most people picture when they envision how the earliest Europeans celebrated Christmas on Long Island — but they're wrong.

When Dec. 25 rolled around in the colonial 1600s and 1700s, most Long Islanders did what they did on any other day of the year. Women cooked or spent the day catching up on the wash. Men worked in the barns or, if weather permitted, in the fields preparing for the next growing season.

"You have to remember that Long Island during the colonial period was heavily Puritan," explained Alice Ross, a local historian who has researched the Island's early Christmas celebrations. "Puritans did not celebrate Christmas because they thought it was a very pagan ritual.

"People didn't walk around in the woods singing Christmas carols. The Puritans thought these things very severe." In fact, Ross added, Christmas is very rarely mentioned in letters, diaries or official documents of the day.

Christmas celebrations were actually declared illegal from 1659 to 1681 in New England, the hotbed of Puritanism, historian Stephen Nissenbaum noted in his recent book, "The Battle for Christmas," which chronicles the evolution of the holiday in America. If anyone was caught observing Christmas by drinking, partying or song, they were fined five shillings.

December was a slow month for farmers and other laborers of the day. The harvest was gathered, and often the weather was too severe to work outdoors. It was also the time of year when beasts were slaughtered and beer and wine were ready for consumption. In other words, a perfect time to eat, drink and be merry.

But Puritan ministers frowned on this behavior. In 1712, the Rev. Cotton Mather of Boston wrote: "The Feast of Christ's Nativity is spent Reveling, Dicing, Carding, Masking, and in all Licentious Liberty . . . by Mad Mirth, by long Eating, by hard Drinking, by lewd Gaming, by rude Reveling." Another minister, this one a 16th-Century Anglican bishop, made a statement that is not unlike remarks made about Christmas today: "Men dishonour Christ more in the twelve days of Christmas, than in all the twelve months besides."

So, when the founding fathers of Southold and Southampton left New England for the twin forks in 1640, they brought with them this Puritan suspicion of Christmas.

But, while the Puritans were busy punishing anything smelling of Christmas revelry, the Dutch introduced their own version of the holiday celebration to western Long Island in the settlement of New Netherlands.

"The Dutch celebrated St. Nicholas Day, on December 6, more than Christmas," said Harrison Hunt, supervisor of collections and historic sites for the Nassau County Department of Recreation and Parks. "Children would leave out their wooden shoes. That idea later evolved into hanging stockings on the mantel. And St. Nicholas was said to visit, later Santa Claus, and leave presents inside the shoes."

If the idea for stuffing stockings originated in Holland, Hunt said, the Christmas tree was undoubtedly a German import. The first Christmas trees on Long Island were said to be spotted in Cedar Swamp (now Old Brookville) during the Revolutionary War. Hunt said he has never seen any firm evidence documenting this claim by local historians.

If they did exist in that settlement along the North Shore, they were probably the work of Hessian soldiers enlisted by the British during the occupation of Long Island. By decorating a small fir tree, the German soldiers didn't feel so far from home, where it was an integral part of their Christmas observance.

Despite these early sightings of Christmas trees during the Revolution, historians suggest that the adorned arbor didn't become a part of the American Christmas tradition until much later.

Hunt supervises the historic home of William Cullen Bryant, Cedarmere, in Roslyn Harbor. He recently came across a letter written by Frederick Law Olmsted's wife, Mary, to Bryant's wife.

In the letter, dated in the late 1800s, Mary Perkins Olmsted marveled at how the Christmas holiday had changed and the celebrations grown since the two of them saw their first Christmas tree at the Bryant home in the 1840s.

"The Bryants were people on the cutting edge of things," said Hunt, "so they were probably among the first to adopt the Christmas tree as part of their celebration."

Nearly a decade after the Bryants tried out their first Christmas tree, New York State in 1849 designated Christmas an official holiday. But it took many more years for the holy day to evolve into the commercial extravaganza it is today.

Consider these recollections of Christmases past by a prominent Hempstead resident as told to a reporter for The Hempstead Sentinel in 1916.

During his youth in the 1850s, Richard Brower talked of sleigh rides with the ladies and presents of fruits and homemade candy and trees decorated only with candles.

"I don't think they made quite so much of Christmas as a time for interchange of gifts," Brower recalled.

"They didn't give us elaborate toys and we didn't wait for our parents to give us sleds. We made them — bob-sleds and double-runners — and we kept their runners shining bright."

A
VISIT FROM
ST. NICHOLAS.
BY
CLEMENT C. MOORE, LL. D.
With Original Cuts,
DESIGNED AND ENGRAVED BY BOYD.
New-York:
HENRY M. ONDERDONK,
10 John street.
1848.

CLEMENT CLARKE MOORE'S CLASSIC POEM

A scholar in Hebrew and son of an Episcopal bishop, Clement Clarke Moore was a religious man. He was born in Newtown (now Elmhurst) during the Revolution in 1779, and all his life opposed most democratic reforms, such as the abolition of slavery.

He is also the same man who sat at a desk one evening in 1822, put fountain pen to paper and created one of the most beloved Christmas tales of all time.

Some men will do anything for their children.

Drawing from Dutch traditions, the writings of Washington Irving and other sources, Moore wrote "A Visit From St. Nicholas," commonly known as " 'Twas the Night Before Christmas," in a single night. He never intended it to go beyond his own household.

But a young relative, Sarah Harriet Butler, copied the poem into her diary and her father sent it in 1823 to a newspaper in Troy, N.Y. After its publication, readers clipped and saved it. The tale soon became a classic.

An academic, Moore was somewhat embarrassed by the poem and would not admit he wrote it. That is, until some 26 years later, when a book-length edition was printed. (A facsimile appears above.)

Accompanying an illustration depicting a somewhat thinner version of the jolly old patron saint of children, the 1848 cover read: "A Visit From St. Nicholas," by Clement C. Moore.

LI HISTORY.COM

The full text of Clement Clarke Moore's "A Visit From St. Nicholas" appears on lihistory.com on the Internet.

"An Old-Fashioned Christmas," Dover Press

When is New Year's? For much of the 18th Century, Americans marked it in March

Resetting Their Calendars

BY GEORGE DEWAN
STAFF WRITER

It's time for a celebration, since Dec. 31 is the last day of the year and tomorrow is New Year's Day. Or is it?

If we were still in colonial Long Island — let's say we were in the year 1697 instead of 1997 — tomorrow would be just another work day. New Year's Day wouldn't arrive until March 25. In fact, today wouldn't even be Dec. 31; it would be Dec. 18.

If you are confused, you are not alone. Dates given for historical events in the American colonial period — including the ones used in "Long Island: Our Story" — are usually based on the older, Julian calendar, rather than the Gregorian calendar in use today. Britain and its American colonies did not change to the Gregorian calendar until 1752.

George Washington, for example, was born on Feb. 11, 1731, when the Julian calendar was in use. But that's not what they teach in school, where children learn that he was born on Feb. 22, 1732. Once again, old vs. new.

Early calendar systems did a poor job of making dates conform to the natural cycles of the Earth's rotation (a day), the moon's revolution around theEarth (a month) and the Earth's revolution around the sun (a year). Each successive reform got the calendar and the natural cycles closer and closer together, so that today, the calendar we use, the Gregorian, is off by only 26 seconds a year.

Until the reign of Julius Caesar, the Roman calendar was a mess. The calendar Caesar approved in 46 BC, known as the Julian calendar, had a year of 365¼ days, or 365 days and 6 hours. This led to a system with 365-day years for three years in a row, followed by a 366-day "leap" year. The problem is that a year is only 365 days, 5 hours, 48 minutes and 46 seconds long — that's how long it takes the Earth to revolve around the sun.

By the 16th Century, those 11 minutes, 14 seconds a year had resulted in a calendar that was 10 days out of whack. Enter Pope Gregory XIII, who brought the calendar in line with the real world by lopping off 10 days. The day following Oct. 4, 1582, became Oct. 15, and the 10 days in between disappeared. To prevent the same problem from coming up again — calendar creep, you might call it — he changed the leap year system with a wonderful bit of fine-tuning. He dropped the leap year at the end of every century, except for centuries that are divisible by 400. That includes the year 2000, by the way.

"The truly improved Gregorian calendar was quickly accepted throughout the Roman Catholic world," writes Harvard paleontologist Stephen Jay Gould in his new book, "Questioning the Millennium." "But in [Protestant] England, the whole brouhaha sounded like a Popish plot, and the Brits would be damned if they would go along."

Surprisingly, the British did go along for some time with one Rome-inspired variation on the calendar. It was an ancient custom in the Pope's executive office to begin the new year not on Jan. 1, but on March 25, the Feast of the Annunciation, when the angel Gabriel is said to have announced to the Virgin Mary that she would be the mother of Christ nine months later. Many civil governments, including England, adopted this practice for the legal dating of documents.

Thus, dates during the colonial period on Long Island and elsewhere in the colonies, under the Julian calendar, were off by 10 days up to 1700, and 11 days thereafter, until Britain's adoption of the Gregorian calendar in 1752. In addition, dates in January, February and through March 24 were at the end of the old year. That is, December, 1731, was followed by January, 1731. The year 1732 didn't arrive until March 25, New Year's Day. Historians usually distinguish between dates in the Julian and Gregorian calendars as Old Style and New Style, or O.S. and N.S.

These sorts of calendrical oddities lead to questions like this: Why, in Soviet Russia, was the anniversary of the October Bolshevik coup always celebrated in November? The answer: Russia did not convert to the Gregorian calendar until 1918 — and by then the Julian calendar was off by 13 days. The coup began on Oct. 24, 1917 (Old Style), which is Nov. 6, 1917 (New Style).

No new changes are expected in anyone's lifetime. The current calendar is off by only 26 seconds a year, so it'll be another 3,000 years before it's wrong by even one day.

Illustration ©1997, Anthony D'Adamo

Counting days in a year has been a challenge through the ages. In 1582, Pope Gregory XIII took scissors to the calendar, lopping off 10 days that the old Julian calendar had miscalculated. So when is Washington's birthday? Feb. 11 under the Julian system, Feb. 22 under the Gregorian.

Celebrating New Year's With a Bang

Colonists on Long Island were serious about their New Year's noisemakers.

Historian Gabriel Furman wrote in 1874 that on New Year's Eve and on the first two days of the new year, colonial Long Islanders would go from house to house with their guns, fire salutes, and then enjoy a spiced drink or a bite of sweets. Then the men of the house would join the visitors and proceed to the next home. After all the men of the community were together, they would go to a convenient spot for target practice and athletic events.

New York's colonial legislature voted in 1773 to ban the firing of arms on these three days, warning that "great damages are frequently done" in the celebrations. But the noisy tradition evidently continued. After the American Revolution, in 1785, the New York State Legislature revived the New Year's gun ban and extended it to prevent the firing of "guns, pistols, rockets, squibs and other fireworks" on Christmas Eve as well.

Descendants of the Island's early settlers tell their family stories

Knowing Their Roots

As the colonial chapter of "Long Island: Our Story" comes to an end, Newsday visits with descendants of some of the families whose roots on the Island go back to that period. Many of these families have spent countless hours researching their ancestors in town records, property deeds and other documents. Here, in their own words, are the stories pieced together by members of those families.

The Budds, as told by Marshall Budd of Dix Hills

The earliest mention of the Budd family was in France, where Jean Budd was a commander in Charlemagne's army in 900. In 1066 his descendants joined William the Conqueror in the invasion of England, where they founded the town of Rye.

John Budd, of Pirbright, England, married Katherine Brown, daughter of Sir Anthony Brown, the founder of the Montacue family that produced King Henry V. John Budd's son John came to America on June 26, 1637, aboard the Hector. The group wintered in Boston, then traveled to New Haven the following spring and arrived in Southold several years later.

John Budd was the first military officer to train a home guard to protect the community and was thereafter referred to as Lt. John Budd. In Southold he owned a piece of property at the east end of town known as Budd Pond. He built the Old House in Southold. When his daughter Anna married Benjamin Horton, he gave her the Old House as a wedding gift. Benjamin's brother Josiah Horton, a carpenter, moved the house from Southold to Cutchogue for about $25 in today's money. John Budd built a second house on Tuckers Lane in Southold which went to son John II when he went to Westchester about 1660. John Budd also bought a large tract of land in Westchester and changed the name of the town from Hastings to Rye. The only Budds from our line still on Long Island are me and my son, who also is named John.

Newsday Photo / Bill Davis

Marshall Budd

Another branch of the family in England was the Rev. Thomas Budd, a vicar of the Church of England. His son Thomas and family arrived in 1678 and settled in Burlington County, N.J. Descendant Edward G. Budd founded the Budd Co. of Philadelphia, which built electric passenger cars for the Long Island Rail Road.

Photo Courtesy of Anthony Seaman Murphy

Louise and Andros Seaman, great-grandparents of Kathy Seaman Murphy, in about 1920. Andros was keeper of the Point Lookout lifesaving station in the early 1900s.

The Seamans, as told by Kathy Seaman Murphy of Stony Brook

I am a descendant of the Seaman family. Capt. John Seaman settled here in approximately 1644. Although early accounts are contradictory, his name appears on various Indian land deeds and appears again as one of three signers for Hempstead Town, which was then an area roughly the size of Nassau County. With his enormous land purchases, his holdings were among the largest during the early years of settlement. He owned 2,200 acres. He was active in all aspects of town affairs and did much to foster further development — including that of propagation. He fathered 16 children! (Two wives.)

Newsday Photo / Bill Davis

Kathy Seaman Murphy

A Seaman woman, Jemima Seaman, married Elias Hicks, the famous Quaker preacher. There is a Seaman home at the Old Bethpage Village Restoration and one at the Milleridge Inn in Jericho. In the Freeport-Baldwin area, the family name is carried on in a prominent thoroughfare — Seaman Avenue — a school, a park and even an island in Middle Bay. There have been many outstanding citizens, community activists and public servants to carry the Seaman name. A famous court case, Seaman vs. Gore, brought by a Judge Seaman, went all the way to the Supreme Court and gave the state ownership of what is now Jones Beach.

In my own direct family line, my great-grandfather, Andros Seaman, was keeper of the Point Lookout U.S. Life Saving Service station starting in 1911. Andros had seven sons and one daughter. All the sons were in the Life Saving Service. Many grandsons would join the Coast Guard, serving at Short Beach, Gilgo and Fire Island. Those not in the service were all baymen.

The Cortelyous, as told by Jane Cortelyou Smith of Northport

Our family has lived on Long Island for 12 generations. Our ancestor Jaques Cortelyou came to the New World in 1652. Cortelyou Road in Brooklyn is named after him. He was a surveyor under Peter Stuyvesant and made the first official map of lower Manhattan.

He founded a town on Long Island on the "Bay of the North River" and named it New Utrecht. He built a house on the bluff that commanded a sweeping view across the Narrows to Staten Island and regularly traveled to Manhattan, perhaps as Long Island's first commuter. One of the villages now included in Brooklyn is Bushwick. This was another area of Dutch settlement that Jaques Cortelyou had an important part in starting.

The fifth-generation Jaques lived in the Old Stone House at Gowanus, also known as the Cortelyou House, a pivotal landmark in the Battle of Long Island. George Bruce Cortelyou, eighth generation and secretary of the treasury under Theodore Roosevelt, spent much of his life on his estate, Harbor Lights, in Halesite.

Our family moved to Briarwood, Queens, in 1945 and stayed until 1972. I married Robert Smith, a language teacher in the Huntington schools. My brother, Jaques Van Wyck Cortelyou, married Gale Windsor and settled in Smithtown. My other brother, Pieter Van Wyck Cortelyou, married Kathryn Thomas and settled in Saint James. Our children — my sons, Robert and Thomas; Jaques' daughters, Colette and Denise, and Pieter's daughter, Kathryn — are the 12th generation living on Long Island.

Stories Compiled by Bill Bleyer

Newsday Photo / Bill Davis

Jane Cortelyou Smith with a copy of the survey of lower Manhattan made by ancestor Jaques Cortelyou

Huntington Historical Society Photo

TIME MACHINE

PICTURING THE PAST AND PRESENT

Just the Latest Of Its Tenants

Life comes full circle sometimes, and so blue jeans are back at the crossroads of Huntington.

When it was built in the 1880s, the three-story structure above at Main Street and New York Avenue was a dry goods and general merchandise store run by O.S. Sammis, and it's a good bet that dungarees were on the shelves. Today the denim is offered by the Gap.

Through its life, the building has been a Swezey's furniture store, a Hartmann's full-service department store and a Snappy's shoe shop. Some residents still make plans to meet at "Hartmann's corner," says Mitzi Caputo of the Huntington Historical Society.

The center structure above is the George W. Conklin building, once a seed and grain store. The old photo, taken in the 1890s, shows a bell on top of the building. When it was rung, fire fighters came running — maybe even wearing their jeans.

Newsday Photo / Bill Davis

CHAPTER 4

The Revolution

From the near-disastrous Battle of Long Island to triumph and the end of a bitter occupation

An amazing personal story from the journal of a soldier, sailor, prisoner and patriot

Christopher Vail's Revolution

BY GEORGE DEWAN
STAFF WRITER

In the summer of 1775, with the news of Lexington and Concord fresh in their memories, the aroused American colonies stood on the threshold of revolution. Those who chose to fight in the new Continental Army stepped forward, one by one.

And so, a 17-year-old apprentice rope maker from Sag Harbor went to war.

I Christopher Vail of Sagg-harbour, Suffolk County and State of New York enlisted as a soldier in Capt. John Hulberts company . . . July 5, 1775.

This is one man's Revolutionary War story, an extraordinary seven-year odyssey told in an unpublished, 18,000-word account titled "Christopher Vail's Journal 1775-1782," a copy of which is owned by the Library of Congress.

Vail is everyman. And he seems to be everywhere. His is a Long Island story and more. He joins a militia troop in Bridgehampton. He marches to Ticonderoga, N.Y. He guards cattle at Montauk. He misses the Battle of Long Island by hours. He joins in whaleboat raids on a Long Island occupied by British troops. He sails on privateers that prey on British shipping, and is captured and imprisoned in Antigua. He's taken to London, and escapes. He goes to the Mediterranean, is captured and escapes again. He hides out in Portugal, crosses over into Spain and makes his way back to Salem, Mass. He's in New London, Conn., when the traitor Benedict Arnold torches the city. He once more goes to sea and is captured again and put aboard the notorious prison ship Jersey, where thousands die.

Vail was 17 when he enlisted for six months in Capt. Hulbert's company. First taking a boat to New York, the company marched north of Albany to Fort Ticonderoga, which had been taken from the British in the spring of 1775. They stayed a month. Vail's quiet first enlistment ended as his troop escorted British prisoners south, and he headed home to Sag Harbor, arriving Jan. 15, 1776.

Preludes To a War For Freedom

When the Declaration of Independence was announced in New York on July 9, 1776, jubilant citizens had second thoughts about the gilded King George III on horseback the city had erected 10 years before at Bowling Green.

Swarming around the 15-foot-high marble pedestal, the cheering New Yorkers toppled both George and his horse. The pieces were later melted down and cast into 42,088 lead bullets by the patriotic ladies of Litchfield, Conn.

Since the bloodshed at Lexington and Concord 15 months earlier, revolution seemed inevitable. On June 15, 1775, 43-year-old George Washington, Virginia planter, colonel in the Virginia militia and veteran of the French and Indian War, was appointed by the Second Continental Congress as head of the new Continental Army. Before Washington even had time to travel to Boston to take command of his ragtag army, militia there clashed with British troops at the Battle of Bunker's Hill. Although the British won the battle — which actually took place at nearby Breed's Hill — their losses were devastating. Almost half of their 2,200 troops engaged were killed or wounded.

The split between the colonies and the mother country was underlined on New Year's Day, 1776, when Washington raised the first national flag on a hill near Boston. It contained 13 alternating red and white stripes to represent the united colonies; it also displayed the British Union Jack in the canton (the field of stars would not be introduced until 1777).

From "The American Revolution, A Picture Sourcebook"

An illustration of King George III's statue being torn down in New York City after a reading of the Declaration of Independence, July 9, 1776

On St. Patrick's Day, 1776, Gen. Lord William Howe evacuated the British troops from Boston and headed to Halifax, Nova Scotia, where they could regroup and decide where to attack next.

In April, 1776, Howe got some wise, though unsolicited, advice from The Gentlemen's Magazine of London: "A letter to Gen. Howe recommends Long-Island, in the province of New-York, as the only spot in America for carrying on the war with effect against the rebels. 'It is,' says the letter-writer, 'one hundred thirty miles long, is very fertile, abounding in corn and cattle . . . in this fertile island the army can subsist without any succour from England or Ireland . . .' "

Washington had no trouble figuring out that New York would be the next target, and that is where he began moving his army. He wasn't certain of the point of attack, however. It might come directly on New York City, or Howe might begin his assault at Brooklyn Heights, thus gaining both the Long Island breadbasket as well as a jumping-off point to attack the city.

When, early in the summer, a huge armada of British ships loaded with troops began to mass off Staten Island, Washington knew that he would get his answer soon. — **George DeWan**

I enlisted again in a few weeks as a private in Capt. John Davis' company, and Wm. Havens 1st Lieut., in the continental service for twelve months, and was stationed at Montaug Point in order to guard a large quantity of cattle which was kept there belonging to several towns.

At that time there were about 1,000 cattle and about 2,500 sheep pastured on common land at Montauk Point. British warships were threatening Gardiner's Island as well as the mainland, where they would occasionally land to try to steal cattle to feed their troops.

But in that summer of 1776, the Royal Navy was concentrated in New York Bay, where the British were making plans to attack Brooklyn. The onslaught — known as the Battle of Long Island — began and ended on Aug. 27.

Nothing extraordinary happened until 27th of August 1776 when we were informed that the British had landed on the west end of the Island. We had our orders to march up the Island to reinforce our troops, and began our march immediately, and after marching 40 miles distance we were informed that the Island was captured after a hard battle was fought, and a great loss on our side. We immediately began our retreat to Southold where we obtained vessels and carried our company over the Sound.

Sometime that fall, Vail got his first taste of "whaleboat warfare," which would become common throughout the war. Whaleboats, loaded with Patriot soldiers, would be rowed, and sometimes sailed, across the Sound from Connecticut to attack British-held positions on Long Island. Some were minor skirmishes, others all-out battles, and there was plenty of bloodshed.

We at this time had information of a company of Tories that was stationed at Sautucut [Setauket] L. Island. We collected about 60 whale boats and manned them and cros'd over the Sound in a heavy blow from N. West in the night in company with the armed schooner Spy of 10 guns, Capt. Niles and arrived at the Island about 11 P.M. and divided our force so as to take their whole force by surrounding their guardhouse and head quarters at the same time. On our arrival at the guard house numbers fled to head quarters where the whole was taken. We killed 13 of the enemy and brought off 40 prisoners, and made prizes of two sloops — we had one man killed, none wounded, and the day following we returned to New Haven.

In May, 1777, Vail participated in one of the best-known raids on British encampments on Long Island. This was the brilliant attack on Sag Harbor, led by Lt. Col. Return Jonathan Meigs. With 234 men in 13 whaleboats, the raiders crossed over to Southold, carried their boats overland to Peconic Bay and then rowed to Sag Harbor. Six British were killed and 90 prisoners taken; Meigs did not lose a man.

We landed on the west of the port about half a mile and surrounded the village at once and proceeded down to their quarters where we completely succeeded in capturing the whole force except one man. We burnt all the coasting vessels which was all loaded and laid along side the wharf and a store that was 60 feet long that stood on the wharf.

Vail said that the British soldiers had just gotten their pay, and many had been eating and drinking heavily.

They remained went to drinking &c. [etc.] and all got pretty well boozey. When we arrived we took ninety nine Tories. Some had nothing but his shirt on, some a pair of trowsers others perhaps 1 stocking and one shoe and in fact they were carried off in their situation to New Haven.

A few days after the raid, Vail was discharged. But he kept coming back for more. For the next few months he joined in other whaleboat raids. A number of times they would sneak over late at night and board enemy sloops and take them back across the Sound as prizes of war. One of these raids, probably in 1778, was typical:

The next day went with our boats across the Sound, and landed at the Canoe place on L. Island and hauled the boats up in the bushes and marched up the Island about 20 miles to a place called Speonk where we took possession of 8 or 10 whale boats, and brought them off to New London.

Though there is no reason to question the truth of this account, it boggles the mind to imagine getting eight or 10 whaleboats from Speonk in southwestern Southampton to New London. They possibly headed south to the ocean, then east around Montauk Point.

That summer, 1778, Vail entered a new phase of his military service. He would for the next four years work as a seaman on armed ships searching for "prizes," that is, British or Loyalist vessels that were themselves on plundering missions. These were privateers, private

Please see VAIL on Next Page

DESCENDANT

CARL VAIL

When the 21-year-old blacksmith Jeremiah Vail left England and landed in Salem in 1639, he would begin a family line that would become an important part of Long Island's history. One of the patriarch's sons, John, had a great-grandson named Christopher Vail, whose Revolutionary War journal we can read today. Another son, Jeremiah Jr., had a great-great-great-great grandson named Carl Vail, who is 102 years old and lives in Southold, where Christopher Vail — his fourth cousin, three times removed — was born in 1758.

Carl Vail has seen a lot in his days. Born in 1895 in Peconic, he served as an Army private and earned the Purple Heart in World War I, and when he left the service he got a franchise to sell a new car called a Hupmobile. Selling cars became a career, and the Vail Motor Corp. in Riverhead is his legacy.

He knows all about Jeremiah Vail. But until recently Vail had never heard of his distant Revolutionary War relative, Christopher. When told in some detail about Christopher's 7-year odyssey, Vail listened intently until it was over, then said briefly, but with obvious satisfaction:

"That's pretty good, isn't it?"

Newsday Photo / Bill Davis

Carl Vail, Christopher Vail's distant cousin

LI in the Revolution

Some of the communities in and around Long Island and their roles in the American Revolution

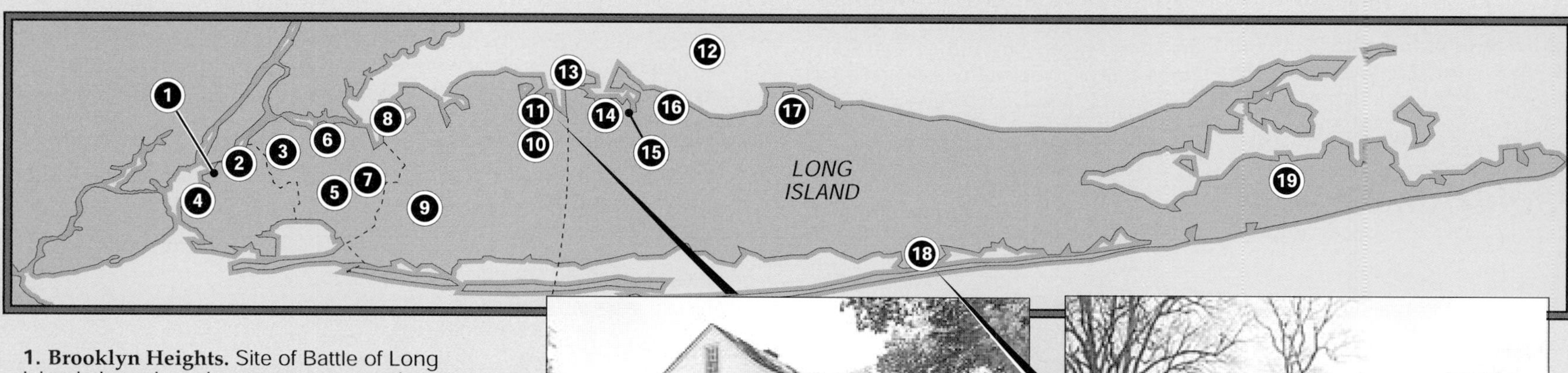

Newsday Photo

Newsday Photo

1. **Brooklyn Heights.** Site of Battle of Long Island, the only major engagement on Long Island during the Revolution. The British defeated Washington's troops, who managed to escape to Manhattan.

2. **East River.** Where British prison ships were moored.

3. **Queens**. Detachment of New Jersey Patriot militia marched through Queens in fall, 1775, seeking to disarm Loyalists.

4. **Brooklyn.** Home of Philip Livingston, a signer of the Declaration of Independence.

5. **Jamaica.** Stronghold of Loyalists

6. **Whitestone.** Home of Francis Lewis, one of the signers of the Declaration of Independence.

7. **Hollis.** Brig. Gen. Nathaniel Woodhull was mortally wounded here after being captured by the British.

8. **Great Neck and Cow Neck.** Patriot residents north of today's Old Country Road voted in 1775 to secede from Tory-led Town of Hempstead and to back the Continental Congress.

9. **Hempstead.** Heavily Loyalist, site of Battle of Hempstead Swamp in June, 1776.

10. **Norwich.** Group of Loyalists was disarmed here by Patriot militia in the fall, 1775.

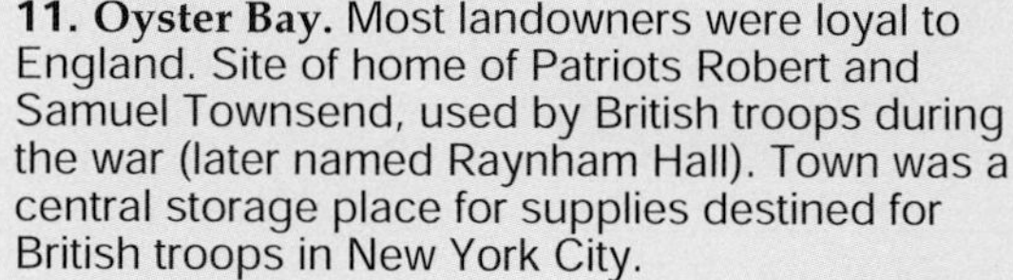

11. **Oyster Bay.** Most landowners were loyal to England. Site of home of Patriots Robert and Samuel Townsend, used by British troops during the war (later named Raynham Hall). Town was a central storage place for supplies destined for British troops in New York City.

12. **Long Island Sound.** Patriot privateers preyed on British shipping here. In addition, Caleb Brewster transported Patriot spy information across the Sound to Connecticut.

13. **Lloyd Neck.** Site of British Fort Franklin. Patriots in whaleboats raided the fort in September, 1779.

14. **Huntington.** Declaration of Independence was read, effigy of George III was exploded, July 23, 1776. Important British base during war.

15. **Halesite.** Nathan Hale landed here to begin his ill-fated mission to New York City.

16. **Fort Salonga.** Site of British Fort Slongo. Patriots raided the fort in October, 1781.

17. **Setauket.** Key link in Patriot spy ring. Loyalist forces replused a Patriot attack here in 1776.

18. **Mastic.** Home of William Floyd, a signer of the Declaration of Independence. Nearby is British-occupied Fort St. George, which Patriot Maj. Benjamin Tallmadge raided in 1781.

19. **Sag Harbor.** Center of British shipping. Patriots raided the port in May, 1777.

Newsday / Linda McKenney

One Man's Revolution

VAIL from **Preceding Page**

vessels sailing under a "letter of marque" from the American officials, allowing them to capture or destroy any enemy shipping they encountered.

In July, 1778, Vail signed on with the Warren, a 32-gun frigate. On Sept. 2 they ran into a hurricane while in the Gulf Stream, and the ship was upset, lying with keel out until she righted again. Men were blown off the topsail and drowned, and the Warren was battered.

At this time the whole horrizon was like a thick fog. The clouds and water all mixed together. And you could not hear a man which was standing along side of you and halloring as loud as possible. The sea at this time as smooth as a mill pond and no motion to it but as the wind got steady and blowed from the N.E. the sea at once rose to a mountain. At 8 P.M. the whole ocean seemed on fire. It was my trick at the wheel from 8 to 10 P.M. The sea that came tumbling after us looked to be half a mile high, and would brake a part of it on our gangway and go 30 feet over the bows. . . . The day following we took a brig laden with molasses from Jamaica bound to Halifax.

After the Warren sailed to Newfoundland and captured an English brig with a cargo of wine and fruit, Vail wound up in New London, where he stayed until Jan. 1, 1779. He then shipped out on the 10-gun sloop Revenge, bound for the West Indies. After

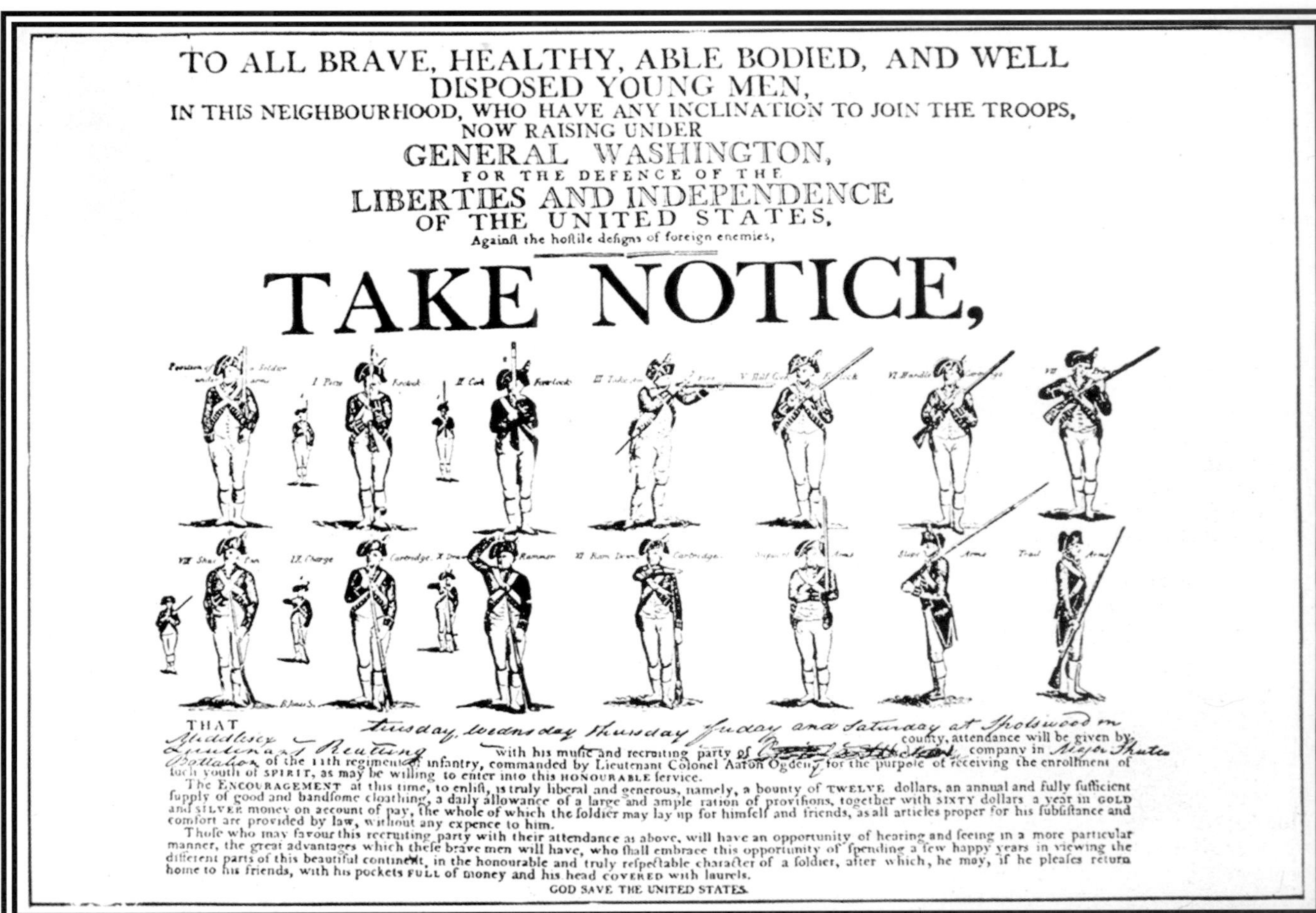

TO ALL BRAVE, HEALTHY, ABLE BODIED, AND WELL DISPOSED YOUNG MEN,
IN THIS NEIGHBOURHOOD, WHO HAVE ANY INCLINATION TO JOIN THE TROOPS,
NOW RAISING UNDER
GENERAL WASHINGTON,
FOR THE DEFENCE OF THE
LIBERTIES AND INDEPENDENCE
OF THE UNITED STATES,
Againſt the hoſtile deſigns of foreign enemies,

TAKE NOTICE,

THAT *Tuesday, Wednesday Thursday Friday and Saturday at Spotswood in Middlesex* county, attendance will be given by *Lieutenant Reuting* with his muſic and recruiting party of [illegible] company in *Major Shute's Battalion* of the 11th regiment of infantry, commanded by Lieutenant Colonel Aaron Ogden, for the purpoſe of receiving the enrollment of ſuch youth of SPIRIT, as may be willing to enter into this HONOURABLE ſervice.

The ENCOURAGEMENT at this time, to enliſt, is truly liberal and generous, namely, a bounty of TWELVE dollars, an annual and fully ſufficient ſupply of good and handſome cloathing, a daily allowance of a large and ample ration of proviſions, together with SIXTY dollars a year in GOLD and SILVER money on account of pay, the whole of which the ſoldier may lay up for himſelf and friends, as all articles proper for his ſubſiſtance and comfort are provided by law, without any expence to him.

Thoſe who may favour this recruiting party with their attendance as above, will have an opportunity of hearing and ſeeing in a more particular manner, the great advantages which theſe brave men will have, who ſhall embrace this opportunity of ſpending a few happy years in viewing the different parts of this beautiful continent, in the honourable and truly reſpectable character of a ſoldier, after which, he may, if he pleaſes return home to his friends, with his pockets FULL of money and his head COVERED with laurels.

GOD SAVE THE UNITED STATES.

National Archives

Gen. George Washington's call-to-arms as the United States prepared to wage war against the British

capturing a schooner from Surinam bound for Halifax, Vail boarded the prize to take it to New London.

On Feb. 13, the schooner was captured by the British and taken into St. John's, the capital of Antigua. He and his mates were put into a two-story stone prison. It would be his home for the next 11 months and 9 days.

Our allowance per day was 1/4 lb. salt beef and 3/4 lb. bread, and water that had been to Guinea and brought back again, and millions of worms in it. Sometimes they gave us puddle water, but seldom rain water. I have frequently weighed the beef and found it seldom to weigh over two ounces. And if a bony piece you may say there was none of it. We then pounded the bone and sucked the substance, as long as we could find any substance. We generally ate it raw, for if it was boiled it would not be over an inch square. And no substance in it . . .

One day in the dividend of our beef a bony piece fell to a poor Frenchman who immediately hauled up his shoulders and said no bone, no bone, *which in English is* no good. *An Irishman standing by and one of the prisoners says in reply*

Revolution Begins

Long Island

June 21, 1774. Town of Huntington passed Declaration of Rights.

Aug. 22, 1774. Col. William Floyd of Mastic was chosen as one of nine delegates to represent the colony of New York at the First Continental Congress.

United States

Dec. 16, 1773. Protesting the Tea Act, a group of men dressed as Indians boarded English ships in Boston Harbor and destroyed their cargo of tea. The incident became known as the Boston Tea Party.

March 31, 1774. Parliment voted to close Boston Harbor to punish Massachusetts for the Boston Tea Party. It was the first of five laws that Patriots called the "Intolerable Acts."

Oct. 10, 1774. The First Continental Congress adopted a declaration of rights that included the right to "life, liberty and property."

March 23, 1775. Patrick Henry delivered a speech against English rule in which he closed with the line, "Give me liberty or give me death."

April 19, 1775. British troops sent to capture arms in Concord met militia in Lexington. Eight Minutemen were killed in the first engagement of the American Revolution.

The World

May 10, 1774. King Louis XV died and was succeeded as king by his grandson, Louis XVI, who was later beheaded in the French Revolution.

May 20. Quebec Act by British Parliament expanded Quebec and gave French-Canadians the right to exercise their customs, laws and religion.

1774. Rules of cricket were first drawn up.

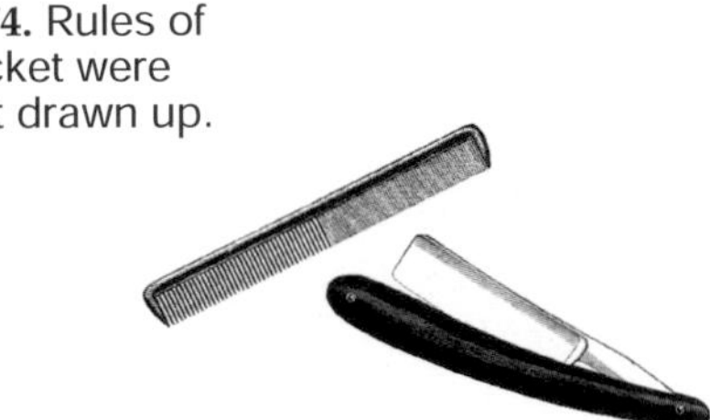

Feb. 23, 1775. Pierre de Beaumarchais' new comedy, "The Barber of Seville," was a great success in Paris.

Dec. 1773 | Jan. 1774 | Feb. | Mar. | April | May | June | July | Aug. | Sept. | Oct. | Nov. | Dec. | Jan. 1775 | Feb. | Mar. | April *to the Frenchman, by Jasus I think it is all bone . . .*

We tried every method that could be invented to make our escape but very few got off the Island after breaking out. If you did not leave the Island that night you was almost certain to be taken the next day, as there was 8 dollars a head allowed for every man that made his escape out of the prison . . .

Vail describes numerous attempts to escape, and although some men made it, he never did. One attempt failed when the guard they bribed took the money, then threatened to blow anyone's brains out who attempted escape. In another, they cut a hole through the roof, but the first man out was shot as he descended the wall with a ladder.

Our rooms that we was kept in was about 18 feet square and in each room stood 2 necessary tubs for our use which never was removed until filled which was very nauseus. We generally kept up good spirits. We sold our clothes, buckles, hats & in fact every thing that would fetch a cent. As for myself I had nothing to wear but a pair of trowses worn off up to the knee and no sleeves to my shirt, which was my complete prisoner uniform.

After a while, Vail began thinking about how to make prison life more livable. He hit upon a surprising solution.

I found there was no exchange of prisoners and no chance of escape, and I being as ragged as an Indian, neither bed nor bedding to lie down upon. And an empty stomach all the time, and a ravenish appetite. I began to think what was to be done in my present situation in order to relieve my wants.

I took the resolution of drawing figures on paper and staining them with my blood. I found I could make ready sale for my painting such as it was to children. And frequently in the course of the day could sell 6d worth which was a very great addition to my old allowance.

Unfortunately for Vail, another prisoner saw what he was doing, copied it and did it even better, so Vail lost all of his customers. He then found a piece of pine planking, and with his knife proceeded to carve small boats, which turned out to be a better business than blood-painting.

For one of them I had a dollar, and found my capital increasing. By this time I could have a dish of coffee in the morning bread and butter and at noon a yam with my beef & some left for supper.

After about eight months, someone took up a subscription for the relief of the prisoners at the Antigua jail. This provided for a twice-a-week additional ration of a pound of pork, a quart of rice and a quart of rum for each man.

And that added to our former allowance we lived tolerably well. They gave each man a shirt, trowses and blanket. I now began to grow rich, and had money on hand.

One day Vail was sitting at the front gate of the jail, with his legs hanging through the grating, when he saw a black woman with a servant girl. He called to the woman, who he understood was from New York and was the mistress of the captain of an English privateer. She asked what he wanted. He said he was from New York, too, and begged her to bring him some of the necessities.

She observed that she was very poor and went on to the market. About 4 in the afternoon as I still sat at the grates I saw the girl servant to the black woman coming toward the gaol with a very large waiter on her head, and soon after her mistress following. She came to the gaoler and demanded entrance. The door of the prison was unlocked and my black friend came into the room with a large waiter containing one quarter of a small pig, well roasted, a dish of cucumbers, 6 small loaves of bread and different kinds of vegitables with a pitcher of good punch. And about 20 cents in cash. All which I very thankfully received and selected my particular friend and sat down with a thankful heart. Nor never shall I forget the donor. She also gave me about 20 cents per week during my stay at this place.

Vail then opened a new line of business. He would buy a new blanket from an Antiguan for 20 cents, pay a tailor

Please see **VAIL** on **Next Page**

Finally Home, Vail Settles Down

Christopher Vaill (he dropped the final "l" as an adult) was born in Southold on May 7, 1758. As a youth he went to sea for a short time, and in the summer of 1775 he was an apprentice rope maker in Sag Harbor when he joined the militia at age 17.

Vail left the military for good in the summer of 1782, and the following November he married Mary (or Molly) Ann Everit in Norwich, Conn., where they settled. From the year 1789 he ran the packet boat Venus from Norwich to New York City. About 1810 he moved to Richmond, Va., where his son was a druggist, but he later moved back to Norwich.

Vail kept a diary during the war, but the journal, which has never been published and whose present location is not known, appears to have been written at a later date. A handwritten copy of the journal was made for a mid-19th Century project directed by archivist Peter Force, part of which was published as "American Archives." Force later sold all of his documents, including Vail's journal, to the Library of Congress.

"The American Revolution: A Picture Sourcebook"

An illustration of an American soldier during the Revolution

In 1832, Vail was awarded an annual pension of $79.33 by the U.S. Government under the newly passed Revolutionary Claim Act. He died May 27, 1846, at age 88. His wife died six years later. — **George DeWan**

July 5, 1775. Christopher Vail of Sag Harbor enlisted in the Suffolk County militia.

April 13, 1776. Gen. George Washington arrived in New York to command city's defenses.

Aug. 20, 1776. British troops landed near Gravesend Bay on Long Island.
Aug. 27. The Battle of Long Island.
Aug. 28. Brig. Gen. Nathaniel Woodhull captured near Jamaica, Queens, while driving cattle eastward out of the hands of the British.

Sept. 22, 1776. Nathan Hale was hanged as a spy in New York City.

June 15, 1775. George Washington was selected commander-in-chief of the Continental Army.

Jan. 10, 1776. Thomas Paine published "Common Sense," in which he called for the complete independence of the American colonies.

March 17, 1776. The British evacuated Boston following a siege by Continental troops.

July 4, 1776. The Declaration of Independence was adopted by the Second Continental Congress.

Dec. 26, 1776. Continental troops captured nearly 1,000 Hessian troops during the Battle of Trenton.

Jan. 2, 1776. The Hapsburg emperor of Austria, Josef II, enacted a series of sweeping legal reforms, including abolition of the death penalty and torture.

1776. An analysis of society's economic forces was published by the Scottish writer-philosopher Adam Smith. "An Inquiry into the Nature and Causes of the Wealth of Nations" suggested individual self-interest builds economies and that those interests should not be constrained by the government.
- Edward Gibbon published the first volume of "The Decline and Fall of the Roman Empire," shocking readers with a thesis of Christianity as the chief cause of Rome's decline.
- The Bolshoi Ballet was founded in Moscow.

May | June | July | Aug. | Sept. | Oct. | Nov. | Dec. | **Jan. 1776** | Feb. | Mar. | Apr. | May | June | July | Aug. | Sept. | Oct. | Nov. | Dec.

Newsday / Linda McKenney

One Man's Revolution

VAIL from **Preceding Page**

another 20 cents to make a jacket out of it, then sell the jacket for a dollar.

On Jan. 11, 1780, the prisoners were taken out of the jail to make room for some newly captured French seamen. Vail and the other prisoners were distributed aboard the warships in the British fleet, which were by then doing regular battle with the French Navy. The French had joined in the war on the American side in 1778. Vail was put aboard the 74-gun Suffolk. The problem for the prisoners was that the British expected them to participate in the fighting.

We had frequently been called to quarters and threatened several times to be punished if we did not take an active part but we always refused the orders and risqued the consequences. . . .

When the Spanish joined the French on the American side, pressure on the prisoners to take part in the British ship's battles grew. The captain even threatened them with flogging.

We told him that we were American prisoners of war and would not go to quarters. He ordered us to the quarter deck and asked us if we meant to raise a mutiny. On our return from the quarter deck I heard the boatswan observe damn them I like them better for their conduct. The next day came, the drum beat to quarters, but not one American started an inch.

On July 8, 1780, the entire gang of prisoners was ordered onto another warship bound for England as part of the protection for 40 merchant ships. On board were a number of disabled men, and when the prisoners again refused to do sea duty, junior officers took canes and crutches from the disabled and beat many of the prisoners unmercifully. Vail was later transferred to a British merchant ship, where the treatment was better. But living still was hell.

The whole stock of provisions on board except the flour had been condemned six months before as unfit for use but we had no other. It consisted of white bread, black beef, yellow pork, and bunches of sour oat meal and blue butter. The bread you could take it in your hand and crumble it all to atoms, and was full of weavels and worms. The beef all but rotten and black, the pork nothing but yellow rust and the oat meal not fit for hogs. The butter had not even a streak of light color in a firkin [a quarter-barrel]. Twice a week we had a plumb pudding and every day a good drink of grog. We frequently toasted the biscuit and put on the black butter and made it into toast. Other times made the oatmeal into mush, and put in the pickle of the beef and seasoned it. We lived in this manner until we arrived in England.

At this point Vail's status as a prisoner becomes confusing. He was allowed to go ashore at Falmouth, England, where he escaped. He signed onto the 20-gun privateer Amazon. He knew the Amazon would be looking for ships sailing under the flag of the French, who were American allies. But that, he reasoned, was better than being "impressed" (taken by force) to serve on a regular British warship. On Nov. 30, the Amazon sailed into port at Lisbon where Vail saw a chance for freedom.

I got liberty one day to go on shore at Lisbon. As soon as I landed I inquired for the French consul and went to his house. Found him a very agreeable old gentleman. He provided me a dinner and a bottle of wine.

The French consul also arranged for Vail to obtain both Portuguese and Spanish "passports." (Vail probably meant visas.) He gave Vail some money and sent him on his way by land, river and ferry to Cadiz, Spain, passing over the Portugal-Spain border at the Guadiana River.

The buildings in this country is very mean, the inhabitants poor and the living wretched. . . . The general living is cabbage and fish boiled together and plenty of olive oil added to it. We had plenty of bread and wine and cheap. My whole expense from Lisbon to Cadiz 300 miles did not cost me above $6.00. The houses of entertainment has no floors nor furniture. The traveller and his beast all put up together under the same roof.

After crossing the river into Spain, Vail took a boat down to Ayamonte, where the Guadiana spills into the Gulf of Cadiz. In this large town he got into a religious misunderstanding.

I was one morning in the market at this place when the host came along. The whole number of people in the market fell on their knees and went to prayers except myself. The Fryar . . . appeared very angry as I did not kneel, and I was unaquainted with their custom and religion. And on my return to the tavern where I put up I mentioned the circumstance to the landlord. He observed to me when I was in Rome I must do as the Romans do. I afterwards found him correct.

On arrival in Cadiz, Vail found an American agent, who told him to find a boarding house until an opportunity to leave presented itself. In February, the agent gave Vail $4 and put him aboard a French warship bound for Bordeaux. They never got there. They came onto a British warship, and after a vicious battle — with Vail manning a 12-pound cannon — limped back into Cadiz. He then found a ship bound for Salem, Mass., and he returned to New London May 5, 1781. He had been away for a little more than two years and four months.

In two days, Vail went back to sea. During the summer he was aboard the privateer Jay, which captured nine vessels, including two English privateers, and took them back to New London. After being refitted, the Jay was about to leave New London on Sept. 6 when Vail found himself involved in yet another historic revolutionary event — the burning of New London by the notorious traitor Benedict Arnold.

As a move to divert Continental troops away from their march on Yorktown, Va., Arnold proposed an attack on New London, an area he knew well since he was born and grew up in nearby Norwich, Conn. (the same small town in which Vail would spend most of his adult life and where he would later die). But Arnold did more than attack. He had his men put the torch to the city, and to nearby Fort Griswold, commanded by Lt. Col. William Ledyard.

The town was full of merchandize and in a short time after the British arrived nearly the whole town was in flames. . . .

The British finally succeeded and entered the fort. Col. Ledyard immediately delivered up his sword which they received and run him through the body and killed him with it. And a general massacre here took place. Every man run into the barracks to save himself but was pursued and murdered. I know of one man who told me they put the muzzle of the musket to his mouth and fired down his throat. The ball came out about 3 inches below the jaw. A cousin of mine in the fort had his skull cut open in 3 places, his back cut to the bone in 3 or 4 places and 10 bayonet wounds in his body. After the massacre was over 74 of our citizens, heads of families, within 4 miles laid dead. The wounded was all put into a wagon which stood at the fort on the top of the hill and then the wagon was set a rolling down the hill I suppose 50 or 60 rods where it brought up against a rock. The people told me the shock hurt them more than their wounds.

Three days later, Vail volunteered to go aboard the warship Dean, where he ran into more bad luck. Vail's ship was captured by two British frigates and he was taken to Wallabout Bay in New York Harbor. He was put aboard the dreaded prison ship Jersey, one of a number of British prison ships in which an estimated 11,500 Patriot soldiers would die. Vail describes the rotting food, crowded conditions with bodies piled upon bodies, lack of air, and death all around.

Here we suffered very much for food and fresh air. We were in No. 1150 on board and all put down between decks. At sun down there was as many people lay on deck as to touch each other all round the deck and as many hammocks as could sling over head. And the fore part of the ship full of sick prisoners with the fever. There was only one passage to go on deck at a time. And if a man should attempt to raise his head above the grate he would have a bayonet stuck in it. Many of the prisoners was troubled with the dis-entary and would come to the steps, and could not be permitted to go on deck, and was obliged to ease themselves on the spot. And the next morning for 12 feet around the hatches was nothing but excrement . . .

There was all kinds of business carried on. Some playing cards, others swearing, stealing, fighting, some dying &c. When a man died he was carried up on the forecastle and laid there until the next morning at 8 o'clock when they were all lowered down the ship sides by rope round them in the same manner as tho' they were beasts. There was 8 died of a day while I was there. They were carried on shore in heaps and hove out the boat and on the wharf, then taken across a hand barrow, carried to the edge of the bank, where a hole was dug 1 or 2 feet deep and all hove in together.

Vail was on the Jersey when he heard the news of the surrender of Charles Lord Cornwallis at Yorktown, on Oct. 19, 1781. This pretty much ended the war, although it would not become official for another two years.

We heard the firing of cannon from the Jersey for rejoicing and whenever our people fired the British would fire from their batteries so as to confuse that people should not be informed of Cornwallis capture.

Vail was soon released in a prisoner exchange. On his way up the Norwich River heading for Norwich, Conn., where he was planning to live, he came down with a fever.

I staggered and realed like a drunken man. I got to the house that evening. I soaked my feet in warm water and I soon lost my senses for 27 days . . . In about six weeks I was able to walk about and was asked whether I should go to sea any more. I told the person who asked me that I never would if I begged my bread from door to door.

But Vail's resolve weakened as soon as salt air refreshed his nostrils. In the middle of March, 1782, he was in New London, and he went to sea again. In a flurry of privateering activity off Montauk Point and Block Island Sound, his ships captured a number of prizes that were sailed back to New London. Vail ended his role in the Revolutionary War in the summer of 1782. He was 24 and would live to be 88.

This is how Christopher Vail ends his journal:

This was in August. After this I remained on shore until November when I got married and remained at home until the next spring, when peace took place.

Get a Copy of Vail's Journal

A complete copy of Christopher Vail's 18,000-word diary — along with the transcriber's historical notes — is available on the Internet at http://www.lihistory.com.

Or call 1-800-2FINDOUT (1-800-234-6368) 9 a.m. to 5 p.m. on weekdays to request a copy that will be mailed to you for a nominal charge.

One of the general's own guards joins the king's Loyalists in a wide conspiracy

The Plot to Kidnap Washington

BY GEORGE DEWAN
STAFF WRITER

A miserably bungled plot to kidnap George Washington and assassinate his chief officers led to the hanging of one of his special guards, the jailing of the mayor of New York, and a stepped-up search for Loyalists on Long Island.

One of these Loyalists was 18-year-old George Smith, who in June, 1776, took a Patriot musket-ball through the chest while hiding out in a Hempstead swamp two months before the Battle of Long Island. His was the first blood of the Revolution spilled on Long Island.

Smith was a mere foot-soldier in the Loyalist cause. There were almost a hundred plotters, including one of Washington's hand-picked Life Guards, and they reached high into Tory circles.

One was William Tryon, the colonial governor of New York, who so feared the city's Patriot rabble that he took up residence on a British merchant ship, the Duchess of Gordon, anchored in the harbor. Another was New York Mayor David Matthews, who would wind up in jail. A third was one of Long Island's most prominent Loyalists, 64-year-old Richard Hewlett, of what today is East Rockaway, who fled into hiding to save his skin until the British could rescue him.

The conspirators went into action shortly after Washington arrived in New York from Cambridge, Mass., on April 13 and began making plans to defend the city from the British, whose ships were expected during the summer. The Patriot hold on the area was precarious, because Loyalist sentiment was strong, especially in the city and in Queens County. The plotters were laying the groundwork for an insurrection that would help the British take control of New York.

"The general report of their design is as follows," read an unsigned letter to the Pennsylvania Journal published on June 26. "Upon the arrival of the British troops, they [the American Loyalists] were to murder all the staff officers, blow up the [ammunition] magazines, and secure the passes of the town."

(An apocryphal story making the rounds of the taverns where carousing Tories drank regular toasts to the king was that someone tried to get rid of Washington by poisoning his green peas. The general's housekeeper, suspecting foul play, threw the peas out in the yard, where the chickens who ate them promptly died.)

National Archives

A weak link in the plot was one of Washington's trusted Life Guards, an 18-year-old private named Thomas Hickey, ' . . . an Irishman and hitherto a deserter from the British Army.'

North Carolina Division of Archives and History

A portrait said to show William Tryon, colonial governor of New York, above; he plotted with others to capture Washington, at top, and kill his top officers.

A weak link in the plot, however, was one of Washington's trusted Life Guards, an 18-year-old private named Thomas Hickey, who has been described as "a dark-complexioned man of five feet six, well set . . . an Irishman and hitherto a deserter from the British Army." Hickey was himself jailed by American authorities for attempting to pass counterfeit notes, and he unwisely talked of the plot with a cellmate, another counterfeiter named Israel Ketchum, who was from Cold Spring Harbor.

Ketchum, seeing an opportunity to be set free, squealed on Hickey. The ex-guard was court-martialed and found guilty of mutiny and sedition. On orders of Washington, and with 20,000 Continental soldiers as spectators, Hickey was hanged on June 28 in a field near Bowery Lane. ("We are hanging them as fast as we find them out," a correspondent wrote to a friend in Boston.) Although other Life Guard members were also implicated, Hickey was the only one of the plotters to be executed.

On the morning of the execution, Washington wrote to the president of the Congress:

I am hopeful this example will produce many salutary consequences, and deter others from entering into the like traitorous practices.

With Hickey's revelations fresh in the air, a contingent of militia from Jamaica, Queens, was ordered to round up a list of Loyalist sympathizers hiding out in the woods, brush and swamps of Hempstead. At the top of the list was Richard Hewlett.

The militiamen marched along the trail that is now Merrick Road, heading toward what is today the eastern portion of Lynbrook. On June 22, they came to the home of one of the Loyalists, Isaac Denton, near the intersection of Merrick Road and Ocean Avenue. But he — like many of the Loyalists they were looking for — had disappeared. The militia decided to look in the nearby swamp, not far from today's Tanglewood Preserve. Nineteenth-Century historian Henry Onderdonk Jr., in his book, "Revolutionary Incidents of Queens County," related this story:

1776, on Saturday, June 22, party of Whig soldiers went to Hempstead swamp (at the head of Michael DeMott's mill pond) to take up some Tories who were hiding there. They made some resistance, and fired on the soldiers in the woods. The soldiers returned the fire, and wounded George, son of William Smith. They then called for quarter. The soldiers took six prisoners and put them in Jamaica jail.

Onderdonk said of George Smith:

He was attended by Dr. James Searing, from June 22 to 29, whose charge for dressing the wound, bleeding, basilicon [ointment], a plaster, cathartics, ivory tube to suck out the blood, and nine visits was £1.17.6. [One pound, seventeen shillings sixpence.] He recovered from the wound, but not from the fright. To the day of his death he would now and then start up in his sleep, and cry out: They're a-coming!

British and Hessians stun the Americans in the Battle of Long Island

The Patriots' First Big Test

BY GEORGE DEWAN
STAFF WRITER

On Flatbush Road, near the village of Brooklyn, 18-year-old Michael Graham looked death in the face. It was early in the afternoon of Aug. 27, 1776, and the Pennsylvania farm boy was facing a frightening British and Hessian onslaught.

In his application for a federal pension, Graham later wrote:

> *It is impossible for me to describe the confusion and horror of the scene . . . our men running in almost every direction, and run which way they would, they were almost sure to meet the British or Hessians. And the enemy huzzahing when they took prisoners made it truly a day of distress to the Americans.*

The Battle of Long Island was the first major military test for the Continental Army, and the army failed. The defeat would lead to seven years of occupation marked by the British taking over homes, leveling forests for firewood, demanding grains and cattle, and also by retaliatory whaleboat raids across the Sound.

Two months earlier, on the eve of the adoption of the American Declaration of Independence in Philadelphia, Gen. Lord William Howe was about to throw the largest expeditionary force in British history at the upstart rebels. Although the plan would ultimately fail, it was an attempt — with the aid of a British strike south from Canada — to cut off New England from the southern colonies, and perhaps win the war quickly.

The first all-out confrontation of the Revolutionary War was imminent.

Daniel McCurtin, a young Maryland rifleman on duty in lower Manhattan, was astounded at the British armada in New York Bay on June 19. "I declare, at my noticing this, that I could not believe my eyes," he wrote in his diary. ". . . In about 10 minutes the whole bay was full of shipping as ever it could be . . . I thought all London was afloat."

With little opposition, a formidable army of about 32,000 British troops assembled on Staten Island, where Loyalist support for King George III was strong. These included 7,800 tough Hessian mercenaries under Lt. Gen. Leopold Philip von Heister, recruited predominately from the German principality of Hesse-Cassel, soldiers-of-fortune who had a reputation for using the bayonet at close quarters.

At Brooklyn Heights, the main American defensive position of forts, trenches and redoubts ran from Wallabout Bay on the north to Gowanus Bay on the south, about a mile and a half in length. A couple of miles southeast of the Heights, in what is today Greenwood Cemetery, lay a ridge of hills, thick with trees and impenetrable brush, called the Heights of Guan, or Gowanus. This hill formation — with heights of up to 190 feet — is the western end of the 18,000-year-old glacial moraine that runs across the Island to Orient Point.

Early in the morning of Aug. 22, the British juggernaut was ready to move across the Narrows from Staten Island to Long Island. Thousands of troops, accompanied by guns, munitions, horses and other equipment of war, landed from Gravesend Bay north to Denyse's Ferry, now Fort Hamilton. Within days the British troops on the Island numbered about 20,000.

The British forces would be opposed by about 9,500 Patriot troops, both Continental regulars and militiamen. A small Long Island militia was composed of a 300-man Suffolk County regiment under Col. Josiah Smith of Moriches, and the 100 men of the Kings and Queens County regiment under Col. Jeronimus Remsen of Newtown.

The Americans, though outnumbered, were well dug in at Brooklyn Heights, as well as in forward positions at the ridge of hills. They were vulnerable to attack from the south only along the shore road following the curve of Gowanus Bay as well as four passes through the Gowanus Heights. Inexplicably, the farthest north of these, the Jamaica Pass, was left undefended, except for five mounted militia officers who were to give a warning if the pass were threatened.

A few light skirmishes took place soon after the British landed. But it was on Aug. 27 that the Battle of Long Island — or the Battle of Brooklyn, as it is sometimes called — began and ended.

The key to the British victory was a brilliant plan developed by Howe's second-in-command, Lt. Gen. Sir Henry Clinton. First, Howe positioned about half his army strategically near the three southern passes to give the impression that that was where the main attack would come.

Then, at 8 o'clock in the evening of the 26th, Howe gathered 10,000 British troops at Flatlands and began a long, stealthy march north along Kings Highway under a brilliant, almost-full moon. They jogged right to New Lots, now East New York, then marched north to the Jamaica Pass, which they reached about 2 in the morning. The five militia officers were captured without a shot being fired. Once through the pass, the British moved west on Old Jamaica Road, toward Bedford village. They planned to attack the left flank and rear of the Americans, while the remaining British forces attacked from the front.

The flanking movement worked to perfection. The assault began about 9 a.m., crushing the Americans left, right and center in a day of vicious fighting. Surprised and completely overpowered, the Americans who were not killed, wounded or captured escaped in confusion back to the lines at Brooklyn Heights. Many, however, were caught in a British-Hessian vise. "The greater part of their riflemen," Hessian Col. Heinrich von Heeringen wrote in a report, "were pierced to the trees with bayonets." Washington, meanwhile, had ordered reinforcements from Manhattan, but they arrived too late to get into the battle. By 2 p.m. it was over.

"A hard day this, for us poor Yankees!" Capt. Enoch Anderson of the Delaware regiment later wrote to his nephew. "Superior discipline and numbers had overcome us. A gloomy time it was, but we solaced ourselves that at another time we would do better."

Outflanked by the British

★ Patriot Troops
■ British Troops
⬟ Hessian Troops
Troop positions are at 8 a.m. Aug. 27, 1776; arrows represent troop movements at other times.

1. Thursday, Aug. 22:
British move 20,000 troops from Staten Island to Brooklyn, landing them from Denyse's Ferry (now Fort Hamilton) to Gravesend Bay. Five thousand of the troops are Hessian mercenaries (from a part of modern-day Germany).

2. Monday evening, Aug. 26:
Leaving Flatlands with 10,000 British troops, Gen. Lord William Howe, commander of all British forces, moves north to the lightly guarded Jamaica Pass. The plan is to move north through the pass, then west toward the left flank of the Patriot lines, linking up with troops farther west to trap the rebels in a pincer action.

3. Tuesday, Aug. 27:
The British plan is executed perfectly and Patriots retreat behind their defenses.

Newsday / Linda McKenney

From "Dictionary of American Portraits"

Gen. Lord William Howe led the successful effort to secure Long Island for the British.

BY GEORGE DEWAN
STAFF WRITER

Crushed in battle, nervous Patriot troops await a knockout punch

Days of Defeat

Brooklyn Historical Society

"The Battle of Long Island," a painting by Alonzo Chappel, shows American soldiers retreating across Brooklyn's Gowanus Creek after their defeat by British and Hessian forces on Aug. 27, 1776.

As he stood on a Brooklyn hill watching the first great battle of the Revolutionary War taking place below him, Gen. George Washington is reported to have said: "Good God! What brave fellows I must this day lose!"

The general was viewing the most stirring action of the one-day Battle of Long Island, Aug. 27, 1776. For heroism, nothing matched the actions of a band of close to 400 gallant men from Maryland led by 50-year-old American Brig. Gen. William Alexander, better known as Lord Stirling, a title he claimed in Scotland.

Outnumbered more than five to one, Stirling's men were defending the American right flank, protecting the massive retreat of American forces being threatened with annihilation. Six times they charged a superior British force holed up in the Vechte-Cortelyou House on Gowanus Road. Six times they were repulsed. When the effort finally collapsed, 259 American men lay dead, and another 100 or so were wounded.

Many accounts have Washington, impeccably dressed in his buff and blue uniform, moving back and forth among his troops, encouraging, goading, prodding. The 44-year-old general, as anyone who crossed him knew, was tough and single-minded, and could use language that would scorch the paint off a barn.

BATTLE OF LONG ISLAND

A special graphic appears on Pages 122-123

"If I see any man turn his back today, I will shoot him through," one unidentified private later claimed to hear Washington shout at his men. "I have two pistols loaded, but I will not ask any man to go further than I do. I will fight so long as I have a leg or an arm."

Not much that is positive can be said of the Long Island militiamen who fought in the battle. The small contingent from Queens and Kings Counties, assigned to picket duty guarding the Bedford Pass, were "spooked" by their British counterparts even before the major battle began, running helter-skelter to the safety of the American lines in Brooklyn.

Part of the Suffolk regiment, carrying a "Liberty" battle flag, surrendered to a massive Hessian force. Hessian Col. Heinrich von Heerington later wrote this account:

The captured flag, which is made of red damask, with the motto 'Liberty,' appeared with 60 men before [Col. Johann] Rall's regiment. They had all shouldered their guns upside down, and had their hats under their arms. They fell on their knees and begged piteously for their lives.

Col. Josiah Smith left a sketchy diary account of his Suffolk militiamen's participation. For the 27th, he wrote:

We wors alarmed aboute 2 in the Morning, and we had many Scurmishes and thay atemted to forse our Lines & they kild 1 of my men & we Suppose that we kild a number of them & we Drove them Back & Laie in the trenches all nite.

On the other side, there was joy. In a Sept. 3 letter published in England, a British officer wrote:

Rejoice, my friend, that we have given the rebels a damned crush . . . The Hessians and the Highlanders gave no quarters; and it was a fine sight to see with what alacrity they despatched the rebels with their bayonets after we had surrounded them so that they could not resist. Multitudes were drowned . . .

By mid-afternoon, the battlefield was still. With the acrid smell of gunsmoke hanging in the air, the combatants went about the grisly business of tallying up their losses. The numbers, especially those of the Americans, are not agreed-upon even to this day. The British and Hessians, by their own count, lost 63 killed, plus 316 wounded. About 300 Americans were killed, 650 wounded and at least 1,100 taken prisoner.

Aug. 27 ended with Gen. Lord William Howe's forces digging in. They were 600 yards from Washington's battered army, which was clustered behind its fortifications in Brooklyn Heights.

The following day, with their backs to the water, the American troops waited nervously for the superior British forces to storm the barricades. The attack never came. To this day, no one is certain why Gen. Howe chose not to follow up on his brilliant, crushing defeat of the Patriot forces 24 hours earlier. Perhaps he feared another Bunker's Hill, where victory would prove to be a bloody loss. Perhaps, as someone who actually opposed the war with the colonies, he felt that now peace could be negotiated.

If this had been the Trojan War, the poet Homer would have said that the gods were about to intercede. In fact, the intervenor was not Pallas Athena, but the weather. By midday, the sun had disappeared behind rapidly darkening, cloudy and rumbling skies. Cold winds blew in out of the northeast and soon torrential rains began to fall on Tory and Whig alike. Trenches filled with water and mud, clothes and boots became soaked through and gunpowder became useless. Most of the men had to sleep without tents that night.

Washington may not have slept much at all. In his mind a plan began forming to extricate his troops from this mess.

Newsday Photo / Bill Davis

THE OLD STONE HOUSE

Remains of the Vechte-Cortelyou House on Gowanus Road in Brooklyn were dug up in 1930 and the house was restored. The house was a British stronghold on Aug. 27, 1776, in the Battle of Long Island. American troops charged six times but failed to take control, and 259 died trying. Their action, however, enabled Patriot soldiers to regroup elsewhere in Brooklyn and then retreat to Manhattan. The house is open to the public noon to 4 p.m. on Saturdays.

The Battle of Long Island

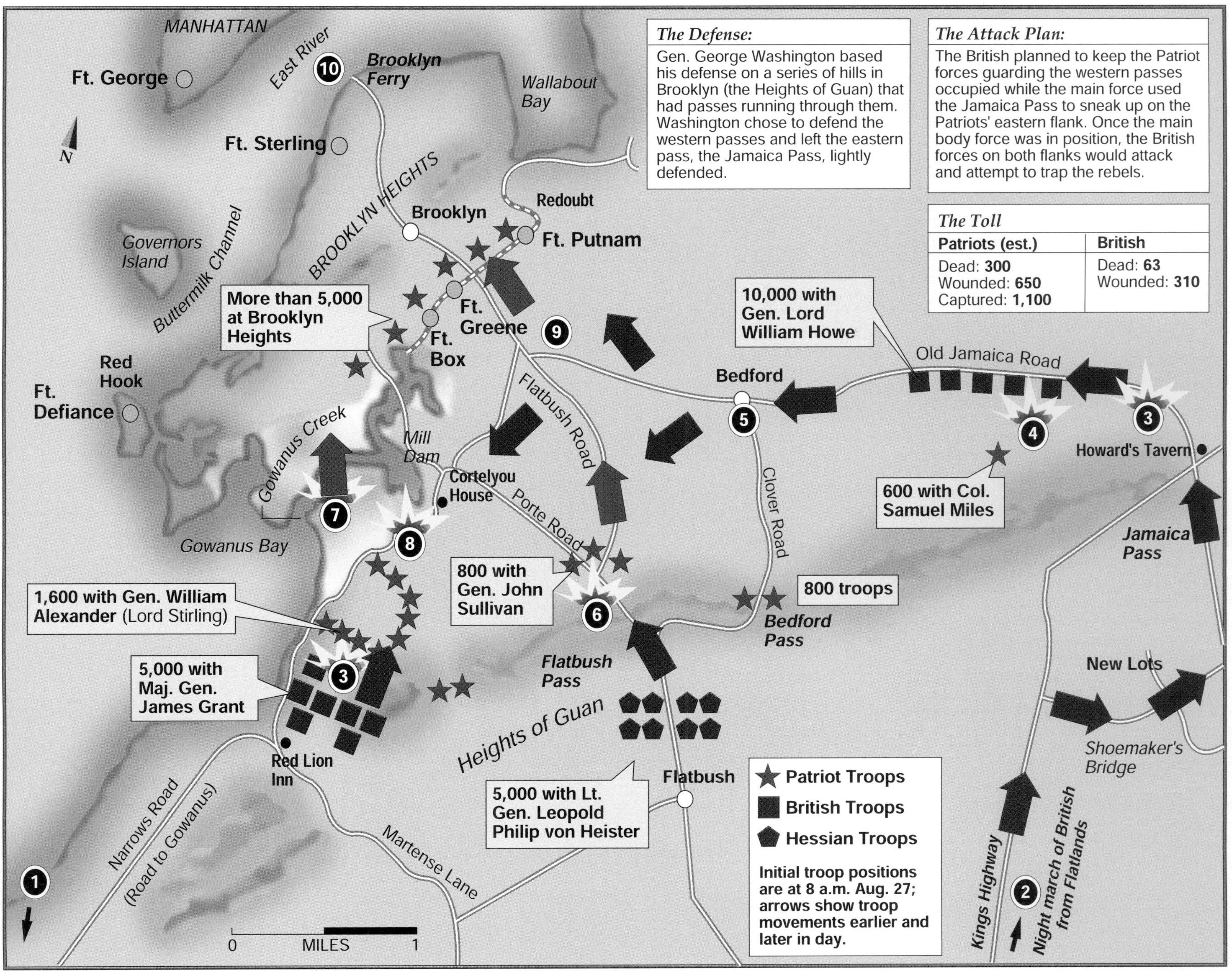
MANHATTAN
East River
Brooklyn Ferry
Ft. George
Wallabout Bay
Ft. Sterling
N
The Defense:
Gen. George Washington based his defense on a series of hills in Brooklyn (the Heights of Guan) that had passes running through them. Washington chose to defend the western passes and left the eastern pass, the Jamaica Pass, lightly defended.
The Attack Plan:
The British planned to keep the Patriot forces guarding the western passes occupied while the main force used the Jamaica Pass to sneak up on the Patriots' eastern flank. Once the main body force was in position, the British forces on both flanks would attack and attempt to trap the rebels.
The Toll
Patriots (est.)
Dead: 300
Wounded: 650
Captured: 1,100
British
Dead: 63
Wounded: 310
BROOKLYN HEIGHTS
Redoubt
Brooklyn
Ft. Putnam
Governors Island
Buttermilk Channel
More than 5,000 at Brooklyn Heights
Ft. Greene
Ft. Box
10,000 with Gen. Lord William Howe
Old Jamaica Road
Red Hook
Ft. Defiance
Bedford
Flatbush Road
Gowanus Creek
Mill Dam
Cortelyou House
Porte Road
Clover Road
Howard's Tavern
600 with Col. Samuel Miles
Jamaica Pass
Gowanus Bay
800 with Gen. John Sullivan
800 troops
1,600 with Gen. William Alexander (Lord Stirling)
Bedford Pass
Flatbush Pass
5,000 with Maj. Gen. James Grant
New Lots
Heights of Guan
Red Lion Inn
Shoemaker's Bridge
Flatbush
5,000 with Lt. Gen. Leopold Philip von Heister
Patriot Troops
British Troops
Hessian Troops
Initial troop positions are at 8 a.m. Aug. 27; arrows show troop movements earlier and later in day.
Narrows Road (Road to Gowanus)
Martense Lane
Kings Highway
Night march of British from Flatlands
0 MILES 1

1 *Thursday, Aug. 22, 1776.* British land 20,000 troops on Long Island from Staten Island. Five thousand of them are Hessian mercenaries (from a part of modern-day Germany).

2 *Monday, Aug. 26.* Gen. Lord William Howe, the British commander, leaves Flatlands with 10,000 British troops and begins his march to Jamaica Pass. With him are Lt. Gen. Charles Cornwallis and Lt. Gen. Sir Henry Clinton.

3 *Tuesday, Aug. 27, 3 a.m.* In response to an attack by British Major Gen. James Grant, Israel Putnam, in command of Patriot troops on Long Island, dispatches Brig. Gen. William Alexander, also called Lord Stirling, to take two regiments and defend the Gowanus road. Meanwhile, Howe's troops capture the five-man rebel patrol guarding Jamaica Pass.

4 *8 a.m.* Col. Samuel Miles spots the tail of Howe's column. With 230 men, Miles launches an attack against the rear baggage guard of Howe's column. Miles and 150 men eventually are captured. The rest of his troops and the other troops guarding Bedford Pass retreat toward Brooklyn Heights. Cornwallis' troops chase them in vain and begin firing on Ft. Putnam.

5 *9 a.m.* British fire two cannons from Bedford, signaling Grant's troops and the Hessians to launch all-out attacks. Grant delays his full attack, perhaps due to a lack of ammunition.

6 *Shortly after 9 a.m.* Patriot Gen. John Sullivan's men see Hessians advancing in front of them and British coming from the rear. Most of the Patriot troops withdraw to Brooklyn Heights. Cornwallis' troops stop firing on Ft. Putnam and attempt to cut off the retreating Patriots, but fail to reach them in time. Cornwallis then advances toward Stirling's positions.

7 *11:30 a.m.* Stirling sends most of his men retreating through the swamp. He keeps 250 Maryland troops behind to cover the retreat. Grant and his men pursue the retreating line through the swamp, but are driven back.

8 *11:30 a.m.-2 p.m.* Stirling and the remaining troops attack Cornwallis' troops six times near Cortelyou House and each time are driven back. Stirling surrenders at 2 p.m.

9 *After 2 p.m.* Howe, instead of attacking the rebel fortifications right away, opts to dig trenches and wait.

Wednesday, Aug. 28-Thursday, Aug. 29. Heavy rains make further battle impossible.

10 *Aug. 29.* As darkness falls, Gen. George Washington – with the help of the Marblehead and Salem regiments – begins moving his 10,000 men and their equipment into boats to cross the East River to Manhattan. By early Friday morning, under cover of a dense fog, the evacuation is completed.

Friday, Aug. 30. Howe's troops move behind the Brooklyn fortifications and find the Patriots have gone.

SOURCE: "The Battle of Brooklyn 1776"; First Division Museum at Cantigny; Cowle's History Group; "The British Army in America 1775-1783"; "George Washington's Army"; Long Island Historical Society; "Early Amerian Wars and Military Institutions"; "Rebels and Redcoats"; "Encyclopedia of American History"; Williamsburg Savings Bank; World Book Encyclopedia; "The Battle of Long Island"

The Soldiers

13th Pennsylvania Regiment

Background: In July, 1776, Washington issued his decision to create some uniformity in the army by clothing troops in a type of hunting shirt. He pointed out that this buckskin shirt (linen was also used) was cheap, convenient, cool in summer, and warm in winter. The Continental Army did not have a consistent uniform until 1781.

Uniform: In the Pennsylvania Regiment, the riflemen wore hunting shirts and trousers; the musket battalion wore a blue-and-red uniform.

Shoes: Generally, a buckle shoe that did not distinguish between left and right feet. they were worn alternately to save wear. Some soldiers wore Indian-type moccasins.

Equipment: Rifle, powder horn, hunting knife, hunting pouch and tomahawk; food pouch, canteen, knapsack

British 35th Regiment of Foot

Background: Arrived in Boston in 1775. Since 1701, the regiment wore the orange facing conferred on it by William of Orange.

Uniform: Plain white waistcoats. White shoulder belts, 2 3/4 inches wide. Enlisted men's buttons were pewter, displaying the number 35. Hats, laced with gold, silver or white, were often too small and were often fastened by sewing in pieces of tape close to the hair color, and fastening them at the back of the head. Winter gaiters were black and above the knee; in the summer, they came to mid-calf.

Shoes: Switched daily to prevent irregular wear.

Equipment: Musket, sword (for the sergeants and everyone in grenadier companies), bayonets carried at the waist, cartridge box hung from the left shoulder.

How They Fought

1. Soldiers line up shoulder to shoulder, two or three rows deep. (Muskets were not accurate at more than 60 yards, so the attackers advanced as far as possible before shooting.)

2. After firing several rounds, the two sides closed in for hand-to-hand combat with bayonets mounted on the ends of their muskets. In the early years of the war, the Patriots had few bayonets, which gave the British an advantage.

Newsday Graphic by Linda McKenney

Alive to Fight Another Day

After losing the Battle of Long Island, Patriot soldiers retreat to Manhattan

BY GEORGE DEWAN
STAFF WRITER

For Gen. George Washington, the task now was not to win the battle, but to save his army.

On Thursday morning, Aug. 29, 1776, Washington ordered that all available boats be brought across the East River to Brooklyn Ferry. For the operation he had in mind, the general had the good luck to have two regiments of expert Massachusetts fishermen available, from Marblehead and Salem.

In the afternoon, Washington called a meeting of his top generals, proposing a middle-of-the-night evacuation to New York City. They agreed. They had several reasons, including the loss of the Gowanus Heights, heavy losses in personnel, the worsening weather, and the division of the Continental Army between Brooklyn and Manhattan.

Darkness came. With three regiments manning the fortifications, acting as if preparing for an assault on the lines 600 yards away, Washington's exhausted troops began quietly filing away from their positions and down to the boats. With the wind still high and the water choppy, the first boats began to pull away from Brooklyn Ferry, the site of today's Brooklyn Bridge.

"We were strictly enjoined not to speak, or even cough, while on the march," Pvt. Joseph Plumb Martin would later write. "All orders were given from officer to officer, and communicated to the men in whispers. What such secrecy could mean we could not divine."

There were upwards of 10,000 men to carry off, and the process was a slow one. For Washington, success was keyed to the British not getting wind of the evacuation, which could have meant disaster.

And it did come close. A curious incident is related by the 19th-Century historian Henry Onderdonk Jr.:

It is said that Mrs. John Rapelye, who lived at the Ferry, suspected what was going on, and sent her slave to inform the British general of the preparations for a retreat by the American Army. The negro was apprehended by a Hessian guard, and not being able to make himself understood, was detained under guard till morning, when he was escorted to Head Quarters, and delivered his message just in time to be too late.

The weather also cooperated. Toward midnight, the rain and wind ended, but a heavy cloud cover remained. Then a heavy fog descended on the area, effectively masking the departing troops.

About 4 a.m. on Friday, Aug. 30, a British patrol noticed the absence of American pickets in front of the fortifications. A while later British soldiers screwed up their courage and went into the enemy lines — which they found empty. Racing forward to Brooklyn Ferry as the morning sun burned off the fog, they saw the last boats leave. Parting shots were fired. Four Americans were wounded, the only casualties of the evacuation.

"There never was a man that behaved better upon the occasion than General Washington," one soldier wrote to an unidentified newspaper on Aug. 31. "He was on horseback the whole night, and never left the ferry stairs till he had seen the whole of his troops embarked."

National Archives

George Washington directs a retreat after the Battle of Long Island, in an engraving by J.C. Armytage published around 1860.

It was a brilliant tactical maneuver on the part of Washington, a retreat that some military historians feel was every bit as outstanding as Gen. Lord William Howe's victory two days earlier.

Among the last Patriot soldiers to leave the lines was a freshly minted lieutenant from Setauket, 22-year-old Benjamin Tallmadge, who Washington would later put in charge of his Long Island spy ring. He wrote in a memoir:

In the history of warfare, I do not recollect a more fortunate retreat. After all, the providential appearance of the fog saved a part of our army from being captured, and certainly myself, among others who formed the rear guard. Gen. Washington has never received credit which was due to him for this wise and most fortunate measure.

Long Island was now in the hands of the British, and for the next seven years, the Island would serve them well. Ambrose Serle, private secretary to Howe, kept a journal, and on Sept. 6, he wrote:

The fleet & army are now exceedingly well supplied with fresh provisions & vegetables from Long Island, which is a pleasing circumstance both for the health & spirit of the troops. The Hessians, in particular, never fared so well before, and seem remarkably happy in their situation. Add to all this, the trees are so loaded with apples, that they seem to defy all the powers of a fair consumption.

The Retreat

Where the Patriot troops retreated to Manhattan and their defensive positions on that island.

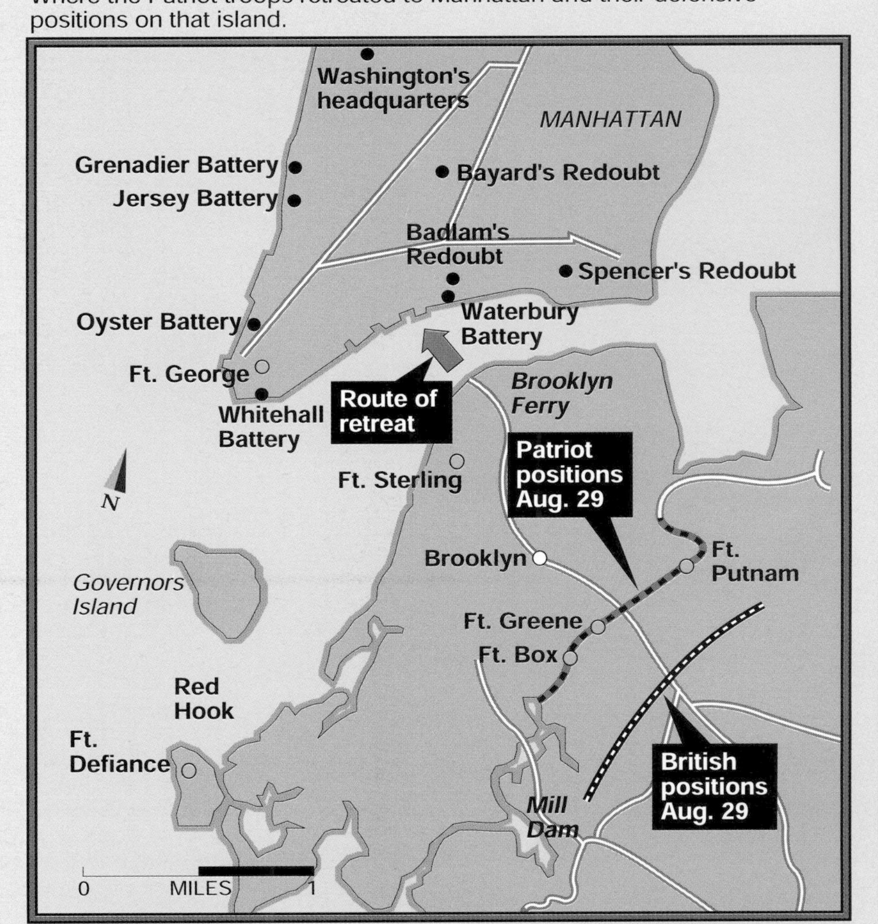

Newsday / Linda McKenney

ORIGINAL SOURCE

LET THE 'GOD OF ARMIES' DECIDE

On Sept. 7, 1776, the Pennsylvania Evening Post printed an unsigned, open letter to Lord Howe, commander-in-chief of his Britannic majesty's forces in North America. The letter-writer proposed a more chivalric way to determine the war's winner and loser:

Let your lordship select ten thousand of your best troops and officers, with your lordship at their head; draw them up on the extensive plains of Long Island [i.e., the Hempstead Plains], where you will have every opportunity of displaying your great abilities. Arrange them in whatever manner you please; then let an equal number of Americans form themselves in battalia, and let each army be provided in all respects equal, with trains of artillery, and all other offensive weapons; then, on a given signal, begin the attack, and leave the issue to the God of armies.

'God save us all,' Nathaniel Woodhull told his attackers . . . Or did he?

A Hero's Last Words

BY GEORGE DEWAN
STAFF WRITER

Schools are named for him, an honor reserved for heroes. Textbooks cite him as a model of patriotism during the Revolutionary War. Every Memorial Day, the American Legion stops at his gravesite in Mastic to pay him respect.

There is an often-told legend of his bravery in the face of death. When ordered by his British captors to say "God save the king!" Brig. Gen. Nathaniel Woodhull of Mastic replied defiantly, "God save us all!" At this, a furious British cavalryman slashed Woodhull with his saber, and the Long Island general died within days.

The tale of Woodhull's death has been boiled down to these four words: "God save us all!"

But he probably never uttered them.

Was Nathaniel Woodhull the Island's greatest revolutionary hero, whose ringing words of defiance as he faced death made him a martyr to the cause of liberty? Or are the stories of a soldier's final and agonizing days colored by the myth-making of hero-worshipping historians and journalists?

Nassau County Museum Collection, Long Island Studies Institute

The capture of Gen. Nathaniel Woodhull depicted in an 1800s painting

Woodhull was born of a well-to-do landholding family at Mastic on Dec. 30, 1722. He later married his neighbor, Ruth Floyd, sister of William Floyd, a signer of the Declaration of Independence. When he was 36, Woodhull joined the New York provincial forces as a major, to fight for the British in the French and Indian War. In August, 1775, on the eve of the Revolution, he was elected to the prestigious position of president of the New York Provincial Congress, the illegal Patriot governing body, which, in turn, appointed him head of the combined militias of Suffolk and Queens Counties.

On the eve of the Battle of Long Island — in August, 1776 — Woodhull went to war. But surprisingly, given his rank and stature, he was not sent to Brooklyn to defend against the British. Instead, he was ordered to put on his general's uniform and become a cattle herder. Ever the dutiful soldier, he complied.

Not that the assignment was unimportant. There were 100,000 head of cattle spread across Long Island from Queens to Montauk. In addition to the Island's prolific agricultural resources, these stock were crucial to the British as a source of food for their armies. Woodhull's orders were to drive the cattle east to keep them out of the hands of the enemy. His problem was that he had only 190 militiamen to do the job, and he never knew on falling asleep at night how many of them would still be around by morning.

The next stage of the Woodhull story — in fact, the final stage of his life — has taken on mythic proportions.

Records of the Provincial Congress show that late on Aug. 27, with only about 90 men remaining — and they were fast deserting — Woodhull's troops had driven 1,400 cattle out onto the Hempstead Plains and had 300 more ready to go. A severe thunderstorm drove the general to take refuge in a tavern run by Increase Carpenter, about two miles east of Jamaica in what is now Hollis. In a forlorn letter earlier in the day, Woodhull begged the Congress (now called the Convention of the People of the State of New York), for more troops.

The next day, he wrote again:

If you cannot send me an immediate reinforcement, I am afraid I shall have no men with me by tomorrow night, for they consider themselves in an enemy's country . . . I hope the Convention does not expect me to make bricks without straw.

It was the last letter Woodhull would write. A few hours later, a British cavalry patrol surrounded the tavern, and Woodhull was captured and mortally wounded. What exactly happened at Increase Carpenter's tavern is not certain, but the "God save the king" version of the story has been told time and again.

It was not until Feb. 28, 1821 — almost 45 years after the fact — that Woodhull the Martyred Hero was created. On that day, an anonymous ballad about the heroic death of Nathaniel Woodhull appeared in the National Advocate newspaper in New York. The ballad included the line "God save us all!" Though there is no evidence to support the story, it has been told to schoolchildren — and countless adults — for years.

Without regular repetition, such historical anecdotes have little staying power. In this case, Woodhull — who certainly had a splendid record up to that point — has had his name burnished by some of Long Island's best-known historians. Silas Wood, the Island's first historian, repeated the story in his 1826 history. A few years later, Benjamin F. Thompson, repeated the Silas Wood story almost word for word. Since then, popular histories have continued the "God save the king!" story — including three that are currently used with students either in grade four or in junior high school.

There have been plenty of skeptics, nonetheless. For example, in 1902, historian Peter Ross called the Silas Wood narrative of Woodhull's capture "one of the wonder tales with which the details of the incidents of every war are embellished." Another historian, W. H. Sabine, later wrote, "Someone had transformed the once unresisting victim into a martyred hero."

But there is no question that Woodhull was severely wounded by sword in the head and arm in the course of being captured. Some sources say he was caught trying to escape over a wooden fence. Others say he manfully and patriotically stood his ground, offered his sword in surrender — a common and honorable practice at the time — only to be brutally hacked at by British soldiers.

Woodhull was taken to Jamaica, where the wounds were dressed by a British surgeon, then, with other prisoners, moved to Gravesend and put on board a filthy prison ship in the harbor. Later he was taken to a house-hospital in New Utrecht. His gangrenous arm had to be amputated.

It was too late. Nathaniel Woodhull died on Sept. 20, 1776, at age 54. He was buried at his Mastic home. But the legend lives on.

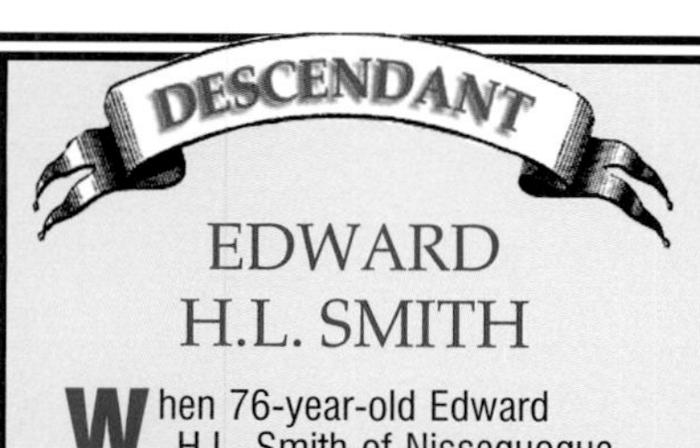

EDWARD H.L. SMITH

When 76-year-old Edward H.L. Smith of Nissequogue wanted to join the Sons of the Revolution years ago, he had to come up with an ancestor who had fought in the Revolutionary War. For him, it was easy, since Nathaniel Woodhull was his great-great-great-great grandfather.

"It's interesting, but by the time you go back eight or ten generations, you have all kinds of ancestors," says Smith, who worked for both the state and Suffolk County governments and twice ran for Smithtown supervisor. "Some of them do good, some are just ordinary people. I don't think it makes too much of an impression on people to have someone like this as an ancestor."

— George DeWan

NATHANIEL WOODHULL'S GRAVE

The graves of Nathaniel Woodhull and his wife, Ruth Floyd Woodhull, are in a small, fenced-in, private family cemetery in Mastic Beach that was once part of the Woodhull Estate. On Neighborhood Road between Lakeview and Whittier Drives, the cemetery is opened to the public once a year by American Legion Post 1533 during Memorial Day ceremonies. The epitaph says his death was "regretted by all who knew how to value his many private virtues, and that pure zeal for the rights of his Country to which he perished a victim."

Newsday Photos / Bill Davis

In Mastic Beach, the Woodhull cemetery is opened to the public once a year.

British officers make themselves at home during their 2,653-day occupation

Long Island's 7-Year Hitch

BY GEORGE DEWAN
STAFF WRITER

There is a knock on the door and the woman of the house hurries to answer it. In front of her stands a finely dressed British officer. "Well, madam," he says politely, "I've come to take a billet on your house."

The officer is not making a request. He's issuing an order that the British are taking over part of the house. For the family inside, the occupation has begun.

Such scenes were common on Long Island during the seven years of British occupation. They took over homes and churches and demanded food, livestock and fuel.

The impact of the occupation was described by the historian Silas Wood, who lived through it as a child growing up in Huntington.

"The whole country within the British lines was subject to martial law, the administration of justice was suspended, the army was a sanctuary for crimes and robbery. The officers seized and occupied the best rooms in the houses of the inhabitants. They compelled them to furnish blankets and fuel for the soldiers, and hay and grain for their horses. They pressed their horses and wagons for the use of the army. They took away their cattle, sheep, hogs and poultry, and seized without ceremony, and without any compensation, or for such only as they chose to make for their own use, whatever they desired to gratify their wants or wishes."

For 2,653 days, Long Island was occupied territory. Despite the apologists for the British and their Tory supporters, the consensus is that these were a tough seven years.

"In summer, the soldiers lay encamped in tents; in winter, in huts, or else billeted in farmers' kitchens," wrote Henry Onderdonk in "Revolutionary Incidents of Queens County." "Each family was allowed one fireplace, and the officers fixed the number of soldiers to be billeted in each house, which was usually from 10 to 20. They had three tiers of hammocks, one above the other, ranged

Please see OCCUPATION, Page 128

Newsday Photo, 1980

The interior of the Quaker Meeting House in Flushing. A marker outside tells how the British used it for a prison, hospital and stable during the Revolutionary War.

Occupation and Revolution

Long Island

May 24, 1777. Led by Lt. Col. Return Jonathan Meigs, Patriots in whaleboats crossed the Sound and successfully attacked the British fort at Sag Harbor.

Nov. 6, 1779. Loyalist Judge Thomas Jones of Fort Neck, Queens (now Massapequa), was abducted from his home by Patriots to be later exchanged for Patriot Major Gen. Gold Silliman.

United States

Oct. 17, 1777. British Gen. John Burgoyne surrendered to American Gen. Horatio Gates following the Battle of Saratoga. The surrender provided impetus for France and other European powers to enter the conflict.

Nov. 15. Continental Congress adopted the Articles of Confederation.

Feb. 6, 1778. France signed a treaty with the colonies and entered the war.

Sept. 23, 1779. The Bonhomme Richard, captained by John Paul Jones, defeated the British warship Serapis.

March 1, 1780. Pennsylvania became the first state to abolish slavery.

The World

Jan. 1, 1777. The Journal de Paris, the first daily newspaper in France, was published.

1778. The La Scala opera house opened in Milan.

Feb. 14, 1779. Capt. James Cook, who discovered Hawaii a year earlier, was killed by natives.

Aug. 10, 1779. French King Louis XVI freed the last remaining serfs.

Jan. 1777 | Mar. | June | Sept. | Dec. | Jan. 1778 | Mar. | June | Sept. | Dec. | Jan. 1779 | Mar. | June | Sept. | Dec. | Jan. 1780 | Mar.

Seeking Refuge From The British

BY GEORGE DEWAN
STAFF WRITER

When war came, one out of every six inhabitants fled Long Island.

On Aug. 29, 1776, with Long Island lost to the British and fear rampant from the East River to Montauk about what would happen to those who supported the Revolution, the New York Convention (formerly called the Congress) passed the following resolution:

Resolved, that it be recommended to the inhabitants of Long Island to remove as many of their women, children and slaves, and as much of their livestock and grain, to the main [i.e., mainland, or Connecticut] as they can; and that this Convention will pay the expense of removing the same.

Ardent Patriots on Long Island had two choices: Stay and pledge an oath of allegiance to the king or flee to Patriot-held territory, usually Connecticut. About 5,000 of Long Island's 30,000 residents chose to leave.

Courtesy of Jacqueline Pell Tuttle

This Rodman Pell painting depicted the exodus of Long Islanders at Southold, mainly to go to Connecticut, when British soldiers occupied the Island in 1776.

Here is how historian Henry Onderdonk noted the rapidly changing pace of events on Long Island, as people fled, leaving behind businesses, farms, valuable possessions and sometimes family:

"Sept. 7, 1776. It was reported that the enemy was trying to prevent the exodus of persons and cattle from Long Island."

"Sep. 15. Wharves at Sag Harbor crowded with emigrants."

On Nov. 12, the Convention approved paying 100 pounds sterling to Samuel Brown, owner of the sloop Polly, for five trips "from hence to Long Island and back to Guilford, bringing horses, cattle, sheep, hogs, people, household goods, &c. [etc.]"

The list of refugees included well-known names such as the family of William Floyd of Mastic, and the Southampton silversmith, Elias Pelletreau. But, by and large, it was made up of commoners, men and women of small means who felt they had more to lose by living under British rule than by moving to an uncertain future in Connecticut. Sometimes they were wrong.

"The refugees had a long and hard experience in Connecticut," wrote Frederic G. Mather in "The Refugees of 1776 From Long Island to Connecticut." Mather said that the people in Connecticut were friendly to the refugees, but often were in no position to help. Many refugees who brought large families with them found that as the war dragged on, they became so poverty-stricken that they begged to be allowed to return to Long Island and take their chances.

One of them was a Suffolk resident named David Weldon, who was living in East Haddam with his wife, his mother-in-law, six children and a cow. In April, 1780, Weldon sent a petition to the Connecticut General Assembly in Hartford, reading, in part:

Tho his [Weldon's] circumstances would be far from affleuent on said island but there is fish and clams and many other things that he may obtain for his family (in this day of trouble) that he cannot obtain here, where the cold hand of charity seems to slack. He promises your honours that he will take no active part against the United States, but wishes to live a quiet life in abscurity.

The petition was granted.

The refugees would return to a devastated Long Island, and it would take years to put their lives back together.

Sept. 23, 1780. British spy Maj. John Andre was captured by L.I.'s Benjamin Tallmadge, leading to the exposure of turncoat Gen. Benedict Arnold, who had conspired to surrender West Point to the British.

Nov. 23, 1780. Patriots captured Fort St. George in Mastic.

Oct. 3, 1781. Patriots from Connecticut attacked and burned Fort Slongo.

Spring, 1783. About 5,000 Loyalists, mostly from Queens, fled New York for Nova Scotia, Canada, to resettle.

Sept. 19. Loyalists – many of them Long Islanders – set out in 30 sailing ships to settle in Canada.

Dec. 4. Ten days after leaving New York City, British troops finally evacuated Long Island and the war officially ended.

Oct. 19, 1781. Gen. George Cornwallis surrendered to Gen. George Washington at Yorktown.

Sept. 3, 1783. United States signed peace treaty with Britain, ending the Revolution.

Dec. 24. Washington resigned his commission as commander-in-chief.

Nov. 29, 1780. Austrian Empress Maria Theresa died and was succeeded by her son, Joseph II.

March 13, 1781. Sir William Herschel discovered the planet Uranus.

March, 1782. Legislative independence was granted to the Irish parliament.

June 4, 1783. Montgolfier brothers, Joseph and Jacques, launched the first hot air balloon.

June | Sept. | Dec. | Jan. 1781 | Mar. | June | Sept. | Dec. | Jan. 1782 | Mar. | June | Sept. | Dec. | Jan. 1783 | Mar. | June | Sept. | Dec.

Newsday / Linda McKenney

British Occupation

OCCUPATION from Page **126**

round the room, and made of boards stripped from some fence or outbuilding."

One of the grossest abuses of power by the British and Loyalist troops was how they treated houses of worship, particularly Presbyterian churches and Quaker meetinghouses. Episcopal churches were usually left alone because they were the American version of the Church of England. In fact, St. George's Episcopal Church in Hempstead, where pro-British sermons were the norm, was regularly attended by the occupying troops.

The Dutch church in Jamaica was used as a storehouse, and its pews and floors were torn out and used for building huts and barracks for the soldiers. The Quaker meetinghouse in Flushing was used as a prison, then a hospital, and finally to store hay. The Presbyterian Church in Hempstead was first used as a soldiers' barracks, then later as a prison, and finally, the floor was ripped out and the building used as a riding school for the cavalry.

British and Loyalist troops stationed on Long Island had a twofold duty. First, they had to protect the Island from incursions by Patriot raiders from Connecticut. Throughout the war, the great nemeses of the occupiers were the so-called whaleboat raiders from across the Long Island Sound. As a result, the British built a series of forts at strategic places on the Island. These included Ft. St. George in Mastic, Ft. Franklin at Lloyd Neck, Ft. Slongo in Smithtown and others in Sag Harbor, Setauket and Brooklyn. These forts, in turn, were often the target of Patriot attacks.

One of the best-known Loyalist officers was Col. Richard Hewlett. In 1777, he occupied and fortified the Presbyterian church in Setauket, and when whaleboat raiders demanded his surrender that August, Hewlett gained a measure of fame by defying the Patriot commander and turning back his forces.

The second duty of the occupiers was to scour the Island for firewood, grain, cattle and sheep to feed the ever-growing demands of the British army, which numbered up to 20,000 men in and around Manhattan Island. As a result, prime Long Island forests became denuded and residents were constantly forced to turn over their crops and cattle to the British. In fact, in September, 1776, a matter of weeks after the British defeat of the Americans at the Battle of Long Island, the British commissary of forage, John Morrison, published a blank order form for Suffolk residents that could be used at will. It read:

> *You are hereby ordered to preserve for the King's use ——— loads of hay, ——— bushels of wheat, ——— of oats, ——— of rye, ——— of barley, ——— of Indian corn, and all your wheat and rye straw; and not to dispose of the same, but to my order in writing, as you will answer the contrary at your peril.*

DESCENDANT

JOHN HEWLETT

There are two reasons why John Hewlett knows quite a bit about the Revolutionary War on Long Island. First, he's a seventh-grade social studies teacher in the Half Hollow Hills School District. Second, Hewlett's great-great-great granduncle was the notorious Col. Richard Hewlett, the well-known Loyalist from the Rockaways who fled to Nova Scotia in 1783.

Does Hewlett, who lives in South Setauket, think his ancestor was a bad guy? "Definitely not," Hewlett responds quickly, pointing out that Richard Hewlett was a leading citizen of New Rockaway, an established farmer of a large piece of property, an active member of St. George's Church.

"The man did what he felt was right, and continued throughout his life to support the causes he believed in. He turned out to be on the wrong side. But he had every right to have taken the part that he did. He certainly wasn't alone."

— **George DeWan**

John Hewlett, above, holds a sword and a 1781 document signed by Richard Hewlett. At right is a document dated Sept. 10, 1781, in which Richard Hewlett gave power of attorney to his son Oliver. Hewlett protected his 264 acres in New Rockaway (now East Rockaway) from confiscation by the state by deeding it to Oliver, who had stayed neutral in the Revolution.

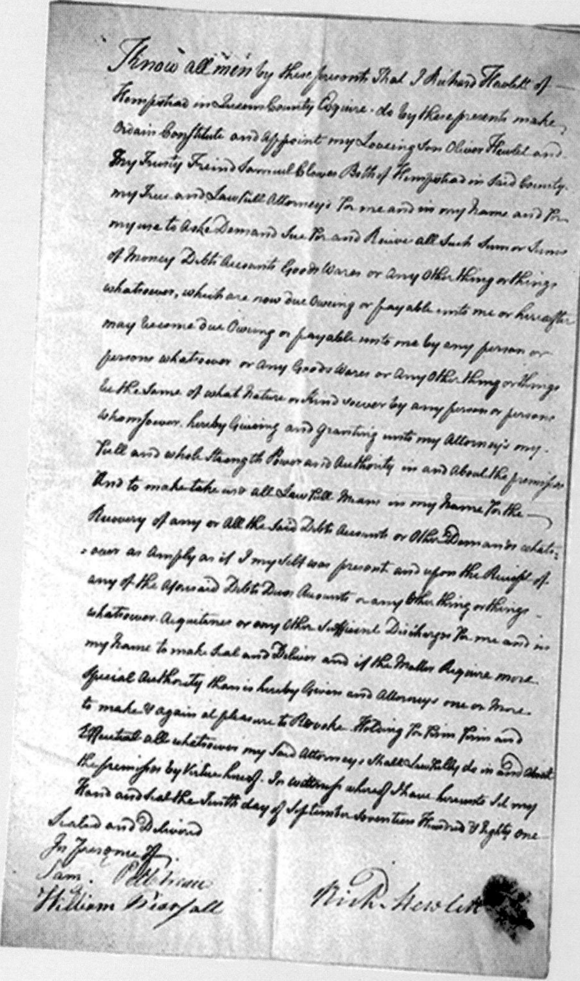

Know all men by these presents That I Richard Hewlett of Hempstead in Queens County Esquire do by these presents make Ordain Constitute and Appoint my Loving Son Oliver Hewlett and my Trusty Friend Samuel Clowes Both of Hempstead in Said County my True and Lawfull Attorneys for me and in my Name and for my use to Aske Demand Sue for and Recive all Such Sum or Sums of Money Debts Accounts Goods Wares or Any Other thing or things whatsoever, which are now due Owing or payable unto me or hereafter may become due Owing or payable unto me by any person or persons whatsoever or Any Goods Wares or Any Other thing or things be the Same of what Nature or Kind soever by any person or persons whomsoever, hereby Giving and Granting unto my Attorneys my Full and whole Strength Power and Authority in and About the premises And to make take use all Lawfull Means in my Name for the Recovery of any or All the Said Debts Accounts or Other Demands whatsoever as Amply as if I my Self was present and upon the Receipt of any of the Aforesaid Debts Dues Accounts or any Other thing or things whatsoever Acquitance or any Other Sufficient Discharge for me and in my Name to make Seal and Deliver and if the Matter Require more Special Authority than is hereby Given and Attorneys one or More to make & again at pleasure to Revoke Holding for Firm and Effectual all whatsoever my Said Attorneys Shall Lawfully do in and About the premises by Virtue hereof. In witness whereof I have hereunto Set my Hand and Seal the Tenth day of September Seventeen Hundred & Eighty one

Sealed and Delivered
In presence of
Sam. [illegible]
William Pearsall

Rich. Hewlett

Newsday Photos / Bill Davis

With Long Island's forests unable to meet the demand for firewood for the British army, the necessity to keep warm resulted in the discovery of a fuel supply in Queens that many Long Islanders had never heard of. It was called peat, the partially carbonized turf in common use as fuel even today in Britain and Ireland. The first turf was cut by British soldiers on the Newtown farm of William Furman, who was at first bewildered, then angered that they would ruin his land.

"So they cut it, regardless of his objections, and without paying him for it, as he was known not to be a loyalist, and had relatives in the American army," Furman's great-nephew, the historian Gabriel Furman, later wrote. William Furman quickly became a convert to the use of peat for fuel. He wrote:

> *It was truly a providential discovery for the Long Island people, who were beginning to be distressed for want of wood, which had nearly all been cut off by the British troops.*

To keep the peace on Long Island, more than 40 different units came and went during the war. They included red-coated British regulars, kilted Scottish Highlanders and German mercenaries called Hessians. But they also included perhaps a dozen green-uniformed Loyalist units, Americans loyal to the king.

"The English officers expected the utmost reverence from all who came into their presence," read one report. "If a farmer should meet one in the street and forget to pull off his hat he might expect a caning."

Although the occupying soldiers were all pretty much disliked across the board, Onderdonk reported that the Hessians might have made a better impression than the British. "The Hessians were more sociable than the English soldiers, and often made little baskets and other toys for the children, taught them German and amused them in various ways; sometimes corrupting them by their vile language and manners," he wrote.

Soon after the evacuation of Brooklyn by the Patriots, Loyalists were ordered to wear some sort of red badge in their hats, both as a protection and as a sign of loyalty. "They obeyed with ludicrous alacrity, and straightaway the loyal badge flamed from every hat and cap in the county," wrote historian Henry Stiles in "The History of the City of Brooklyn." "Many ladies wore scarlet ribbons, while all the negroes, of course, were royalists and bedecked their hats with scarlet rags; and females even dispensed with their flannel petticoats, in order to supply the unprecedented demand for cloth of the requisite hue."

Not everyone agreed that the British occupation was a bad thing.

It was reported in Gaines' New-York Gazette and Weekly Mercury on Feb. 17, 1777, that two companies of Tories and a dozen British officers were in Huntington. In a letter to the newspaper on that day, a "Gentleman who has lately been to Long Island" wrote harshly of the British and the Tory soldiers:

> *They are billeted on the inhabitants, all of them without pay, and have plundered, stole and destroyed to such a degree that the inhabitants must unavoidably starve in a little time for want of food. Sundrey of the principal men have been beat in an unheard of manner for not complying with their unrighteous requests, particularly good Doctor Platt and Mr. John Brush.*

But in an unsigned note immediately following the letter, the editor Gaines had his say:

> *The villainy and falsehood of the above paragraphs are too obvious to every person who knows of the state and conduct of His Majesty's troops, or of this city and Long Island, to need a remark. They were meant for the unhappy people in the back-country still in rebellion, and meant to dilude them."*

For all the hardships of the seven-plus years of the British occupation, the final injustice was dealt to Long Island after the war was ended in 1783. The State Legislature levied a tax of 37,000 pounds sterling on Long Island for not having been in a condition, as an occupied territory, to support the war effort.

LI HISTORY.COM

Past installments and enhancements to "Long Island: Our Story" are available on the Internet at Newsday's special site, http://www.lihistory.com.

With the colonies on the brink of revolution, political differences split a Long Island town

A Divided Hempstead

Newsday Photo / Bill Davis

St. George's Church, founded in 1702, as it stands today in Hempstead; situated in the part of town loyal to the king, the church was used for worship by British troops and their supporters.

By George DeWan
STAFF WRITER

In 1775, civil war erupted in the Town of Hempstead. It was a war of words between Loyalists in the south and Patriots in the north, but it was nasty enough to permanently split the town.

The issue came to a head that April when a Hempstead Town meeting controlled by those loyal to George III voted to swear allegiance to the king rather than support the Continental Congress. Outraged at the decision, Patriots in the northern part of the town, then part of Queens County, voted to support the Congress.

In September, the northern residents published their declaration of independence. Claiming they were in a "distressed and calamitous situation," they seceded from the Town of Hempstead, with a border to be a certain "country road," generally, today's Old Country Road. Soon after the war, the State Legislature made it official, dividing Hempstead Town into North Hempstead and South Hempstead, which became simply Hempstead in 1796.

This political split mirrored the antagonism in the colonies as a whole between American Loyalists (also known as Tories) who supported King George III and American anti-British Patriots (known as Whigs), who by this time were on the verge of revolution. Although estimates vary, as much as a fifth of the population in the colonies was thought to be Loyalist. But nowhere was Loyalist sentiment stronger than in Queens.

"Queens County was the stronghold of loyalism in New York," wrote State historian Alexander Flick in his book, "Loyalism in New York." "Its inhabitants were a standing menace to the American cause and an encouragement to the British. They caused the Continental Congress, the Provincial Congress and Gen. George Washington more anxiety and trouble than the loyalists of any other county." Queens County at that time included all of what is now Nassau County.

New York State, probably the most Loyalist state in the colonies, furnished 15,000 men to the British army and another 8,000 to local militias, according to one historian, and Long Island contributed undocumented thousands to these numbers. Seven of the military units that operated on Long Island, and especially harassed the heavily Patriot Suffolk County residents, were composed of Loyalists, rather than British soldiers.

Alarmed at Hempstead's refusal to support the Patriot cause, the Continental Congress in early 1776 ordered Col. Nathaniel Heard to take 500 or so of his New Jersey militia and disarm every dissenting Loyalist. Heard and his men cut a wide swath through Jamaica, Hempstead, Jericho and Oyster Bay, forcing 500 Tories to sign a loyalty oath and collecting a wide assortment of muskets, blunderbusses, swords and cutlasses.

The foray into Queens resulted in a famous piece of Loyalist doggerel making fun of Heard, sung to the tune of "Yankee Doodle":

Colonel Heard has come to town
In all his pride and glory.
And when he dies he'll go to hell
For robbing of the Tory.

One of the most prominent Queens Loyalists was Richard Hewlett, who was among the plotters in a bungled attempt in 1776 to kidnap Washington and assassinate his chief officers. Born in 1729 in Hempstead, Hewlett later moved to New Rockaway, which is now East Rockaway. Strong-willed and arrogant, he despised what he saw as the rabble that opposed the king. By 1777 he was a colonel of a regiment of Tory soldiers.

Early in 1777, Hewlett, with 260 men, took possession of the Presbyterian Church at Setauket, fortifying the church with a stockade and several cannons. On Aug. 22, about 500 raiders from across Long Island Sound moved in and demanded that Hewlett surrender. The following exchange is said to have taken place:

Hewlett: "Soldiers! Should we surrender?"

Men: "No!"

Hewlett: "Then I'll stick to you as long as there's a man left!"

As it turned out, little injury was done to either side, and the Americans retreated when several British ships appeared in the Sound.

It became clear early in the war that taking sides, whether Loyalist or Patriot, would have consequences well beyond the years of the war itself. The Loyalists found this out to their sorrow. After ratifying the Declaration of Independence, the Convention of the newly proclaimed State of New York decreed that all persons in the state owed allegiance to the laws of the state, and those who helped to make war on the state were guilty of treason. This meant Loyalists.

Those who chose Loyalism, including large numbers of Long Islanders, were to face severe penalties when the war was over. Personal property was confiscated, homes seized and reputations destroyed. Many of them fled to other parts of the world, never to return.

An Arranged Swap: Your Judge for Our General

Fairfield Historical Society

Loyalist Judge Thomas Jones was kidnaped by Patriots and held at the home of the hospitable Mary Silliman — even while her own husband was a prisoner of the British forces.

You took the general, so we'll take the judge.

It was common practice for the British and the Americans to exchange high-ranking prisoners during the war. But when the Patriot Gen. Gold S. Silliman was captured in the spring of 1779, the Americans held no one important enough to exchange for him.

No problem. The Americans went out and kidnaped a well-known Loyalist State Supreme Court judge, Thomas Jones of Fort Neck, which is now Massapequa.

Silliman, from Fairfield, Conn., was held prisoner at Flatbush. In the fall of 1779, two dozen whaleboat raiders crossed Long Island Sound, landed at Stony Brook, marched 60 miles through enemy territory and showed up at the front door of Jones' large mansion about 9 p.m. on Nov. 6.

It was Saturday evening and a weekend party was in full swing. When Jones opened the door, he was told the party was over. Jones said later that the raiders plundered the house, insulted his guests, drank his Madeira and took all of Mrs. Jones' clothes except those she wore on her back.

"They compelled [me] to march in two nights, through the woods, swamps, and morasses, and over hedges, ditches and fences, sixty miles on foot, and sleep two days in the woods, without fire, victuals, or drink (a little mouldy cheese and a hard biscuit, with a little water, given [me] by the party, excepted)," he wrote later.

Silliman's wife, Mary, put up Jones at her home for two or three days, after which he was interned at Middletown, Conn., until the next April, when the exchange was agreed upon. Ships bearing each of the men met in the middle of the Sound, whereupon the two dined together. Mrs. Silliman later received a note from Mrs. Jones, thanking her for her kindness to her husband, and enclosing as a gift a pound of green tea.

—George DeWan

Analysis shows the Hulbert banner did not predate Betsy Ross' design

Flag of a Different Stripe

BY GEORGE DEWAN
STAFF WRITER

As visitors swarmed into the New York World's Fair in 1940 they were stopped in their tracks when they came to the Long Island exhibit. They saw a ragged old American flag with the inscription: "The John Hulbert Flag — Original Stars and Stripes."

The Hulbert flag had been put there by the Suffolk County Historical Society, which insisted that it was America's first Stars and Stripes, even predating Betsy Ross'. Ever since the flag turned up in a Bridgehampton attic in 1927, the society maintained that it had been created in 1775 for a militia company led by John Hulbert of Bridgehampton. As recently as 1976 it was featured on a commemorative medal minted by the Suffolk Bicentennial Commission.

But Betsy Ross, don't move over yet. An expert analysis has concluded that the Hulbert flag is a newcomer. It was created no earlier than 1840.

"The materials used in the construction of this flag indicate the flag was constructed in the mid-19th Century, no earlier than 1840," wrote Fonda G. Thomsen, director of Textile Preservation Associates Inc. of Sharpsburg, Md., in her seven-page analysis. The report, done last summer for the historical society, was funded by Newsday as part of the "Long Island: Our Story" series.

Thomsen based her conclusion primarily on the fact that the type of thread used to sew large parts of the flag did not come onto the market before 1840. A more limited, non-laboratory analysis of the flag, done in Riverhead in 1972 by Grace R. Cooper of the Smithsonian Institution, reached similar conclusions.

The report by Thomsen would seem to consign the Hulbert flag story to a prominent spot in the museum of Long Island mythology.

Newsday Photos / Bill Davis

A new analysis shows the Hulbert flag, found in a Bridgehampton attic, was sewn no earlier than 1840. An earlier assertion put the flag's origins around 1775.

What sets the story apart from most other historical myths about Long Island is that we know exactly how it got started.

On June 19, 1927, an article in The New York Times said that the old flag had been discovered by a banker named William D. Halsey in the attic of the former Bridgehampton home of the late John L. Gardiner. Also found were "authentic documents" relating to Hulbert's company, though none of them mentioned the flag.

Halsey produced a letter he had received from Morton Pennypacker, a Philadelphia-born calendar salesman, then living in Kew Gardens, Queens, who was gaining a reputation as a collector and a historian of the revolutionary era. Pennypacker, who later became Suffolk County historian, asserted that the flag was the original Stars and Stripes, and it had been made in 1775 by members of Hulbert's company.

In a paper read before the New York State Historical Association in 1932, Pennypacker said that Hulbert formed a company of militia in Bridgehampton in July, 1775. After guarding cattle at Montauk for a month, Hulbert and his men were ordered to Ticonderoga, north of Lake George. So far, so good. But here is where Pennypacker's account and some of the facts part company.

While at Ticonderoga, Pennypacker said, Hulbert was ordered to march recently captured prisoners to the Continental Congress, in Philadelphia. It was "more than probable," he said, that the company displayed the flag in Philadelphia, and Congress was so pleased by its design that it was later used as the basis for the first Stars and Stripes.

The problem with this story, which went unchallenged at the time, is that Hulbert did go to Philadelphia, but he went alone. And no known document exists saying that Hulbert's company had a flag made.

A study of the documents Pennypacker cited shows that he drew conclusions that were pure conjecture; at other times he completely misrepresented the documents. Hulbert was ordered to have all the prisoners except the officers taken to Canaan, Conn., not Philadelphia. The officers were to be taken by Hulbert to Trenton, N.J., where they were quartered on Friday, Nov. 17. Hulbert reported alone to Congress the following Monday.

Although the Hulbert flag story seemed to undergo a metamorphosis from speculation to hard fact as the years went by, it did not lack critics. Among them were the Bridgehampton historian Ernest S. Clowes; the then-state historian, Alexander Flick, and Clarence Ashton Wood, an associate editor of the Long Island Forum. All are dead.

In 1927 Halsey said the flag had been found in the attic of the Gardiner home in Bridgehampton. But the story was slowly transformed into myth. Later retellings incorrectly had the flag being found in the attic of Hulbert's old house in Bridgehampton. Halsey, who purchased the flag in 1925 from the estate of Mrs. John L. Gardiner, later donated it to the Suffolk Historical Society.

In 1951, Pennypacker brought up a curious piece of information. He said that he — not Halsey — had found the flag and that he had discovered it in a former Hulbert home in Sag Harbor, not Bridgehampton. He said that, at the time, he was interested only in the documents, not the flag. This discrepancy has never been explained.

This leaves the historical society with an old flag, but not a Revolutionary War flag. Wallace Broege, society director, had hoped for a different verdict from Thomsen. But he was philosophical.

"We were disappointed," Broege said. "But the flag is still a treasure as far as we're concerned. We have an 1840-1850 American flag, which is not common."

Looking Deep Into the Threads

Fonda Thomsen spent two days poring over the Hulbert flag, thread by thread, stripe by stripe, star by star. By the time she was finished, there was very little she didn't know about it, other than the name of the person who made it.

The most complicated instrument in Thomsen's one-room building in Sharpsburg, Md., is an automatic binocular-zoom surgical microscope with a magnification power of 210. The work is more cerebral than technical, more Sherlock Holmes than FBI crime lab.

"It doesn't take a lot of high-tech," Thomsen said. "It takes experience looking at flags. It's like a fake painting. A good curator can look at it and say, 'No.' " Thomsen works with museums, historical societies and government agencies, primarily as a consultant on the preservation of flag collections.

"You try to determine what's original and what was added later," Thomsen said of the Hulbert flag. "You

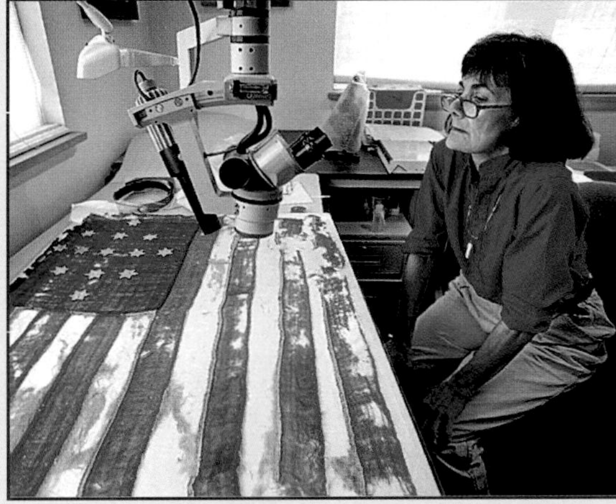

sample various materials and threads. Then you try to identify all the materials you have, make a list of fabrics and sewing threads. Look at them through a microscope, to see what they are, what period they are."

She rejected the need for dye analysis. Because both the red and blue sections were colored by natural dyes, madder and indigo, that have been in use for a long

Fonda G. Thomsen with the Hulbert flag; at right, she examines it under a microscope.

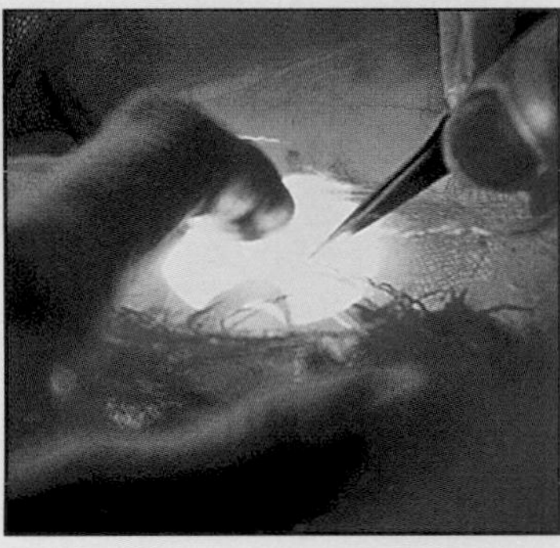

time, neither would date the flag.

When Thomsen puts an old flag, or an old textile of any kind, under her microscope, she is never sure what she is going to find. Peering through the microscope at the Hulbert flag, she was suddenly brought up short.

"Woo! There are little red things here," Thomsen exclaimed. "My God, they look like berries. Like little tiny seeds, from raspberries. Somebody was eating raspberries. It's in the wool."

Interesting, but no help in dating the flag.

— George DeWan

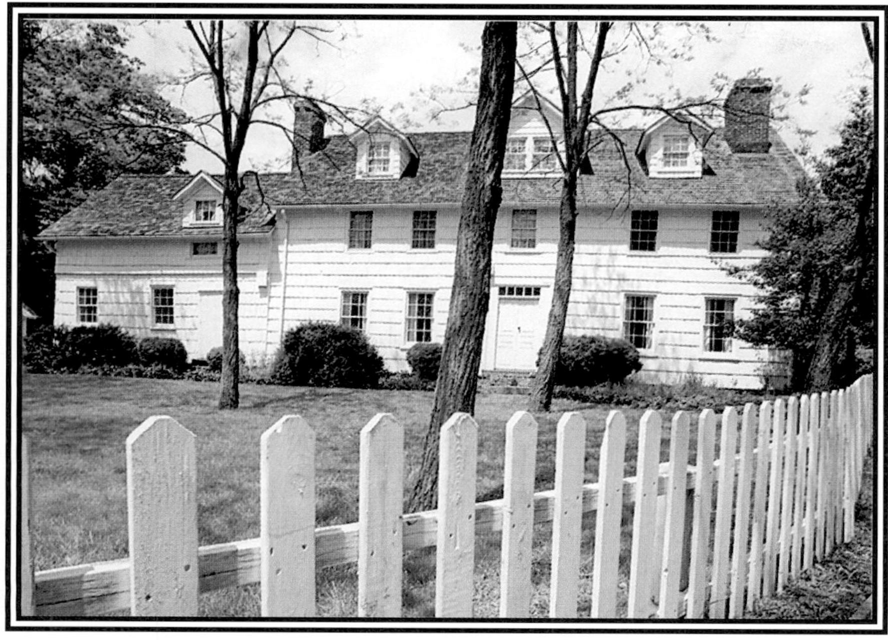

Newsday Photos / Bill Davis

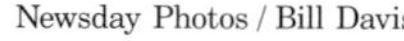

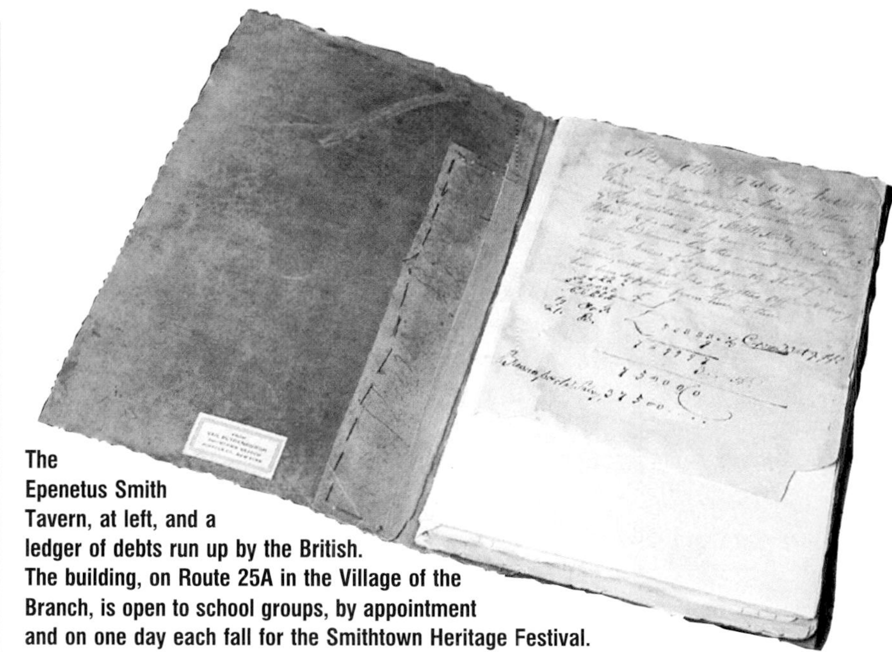

The Epenetus Smith Tavern, at left, and a ledger of debts run up by the British. The building, on Route 25A in the Village of the Branch, is open to school groups, by appointment and on one day each fall for the Smithtown Heritage Festival.

Before the British get the boot, they run up a tab by 'buying' booty from Long Islanders

Those Despicable Deadbeats

By George DeWan
STAFF WRITER

Lt. Col. Banastre Tarleton brought his Loyalist British Legion into Smithtown on a foraging expedition in November, 1778. He left town a few days later, despised and reviled as an arrogant and ruthless interloper. Also, a cheapskate.

Chief among those who spat on Tarleton's memory was tavern-keeper Epenetus Smith, who was left with an unpaid bill for £250 6s 11d (250 pounds, six shillings, 11 pence). Not only did Tarleton and his men drink Smith's rum, eat his food and sleep in his beds, they rode away with 40 gallons of rum, 42 sheep, five beef cattle, 16 turkeys, three geese, one hog, 40 bushels of Indian corn and a host of other items. They even took two petticoats and one silk handkerchief. And not a penny did they pay.

This was typical of how the British and Loyalist regiments treated the residents of Long Island, especially those in Suffolk County, where Patriot sentiment was strongest. It is true that the British sometimes paid for what they took, but often they did not.

What the British left behind was a paper trail of IOUs. Nowhere is this better documented than in a remarkably well-preserved 222-year-old account book kept by the innkeeper Epenetus Smith — known as 'Netus to his friends — a great-grandson of Richard (Bull) Smith, the founder of Smithtown. The account book has been preserved by the Smithtown Historical Society. Smith wrote boldly on the first page:

The following is an account of ye articles with which his Majesties Army has been supplied from time to time by ye Inhabitants of Smith=Town on Long Island; & for which they have received no reward at all. And however large this amount may seem, certainly know it falls greatly short of ye real value, with which his Majesties Officers & Army has been supplied from time to time.

The National Gallery

In the name of King George III, Lt. Col. Banastre Tarleton, left, took what he wanted and didn't bother to pay.

Some of the handwriting is hard to read, but the accounts by 53 claimants, sworn to before a judge, total more than 4,000 British pounds. Smith was by far the major creditor, with IOUs totalling 577 pounds.

But Smith was not the only object of Tarleton and his men. In a theft that seems to have cemented Tarleton's reputation as one of the vilest Britishers ever to have passed through Smithtown, they took 6,396 feet of board from the Presbyterian Church, valued at 127 pounds, 18 shillings four pence. In a wryly sarcastic bit of understatement, the judge who witnessed the oaths of debt, Gilbert Smith, wrote after this entry: "This is a fact too well known to want any attestation."

In Smithtown, the 24-year-old Tarleton was just getting warmed up, for he later would become a merciless cavalryman with a notorious reputation. In 1780, he earned the nickname "Bloody Tarleton" after allowing his troops to butcher men who had already surrendered at Waxhaws, S.C. Born of wealthy Liverpool parents, Tarleton was of below-average height, red-haired and muscular, and he gained a reputation as a brilliant tactician, but at any cost. "As a man, he was cold-hearted, vindictive and utterly ruthless," wrote historian Christopher Ward. "He wrote his name in letters of blood all across the history of the war in the South."

Both before and after Tarleton, 'Netus Smith's tavern was known far and wide for the quality of its food and drink and its overall hospitality. So it is no surprise to see some of the best-known names among the occupying British and Loyalist officers in Smith's book. Among them was Gen. William Tryon, who spent a good part of August, 1777, moving about Suffolk County, forcing residents to take an oath of loyalty to King George III. On Aug. 1 and Aug. 3, he ran up a bill for 27 pounds, 9 shillings sixpence for pasturing 40 oxen, the use of horses, and carrying away a ton of hay and three bushels of oats.

In addition to running the tavern, Smith was a member of the town board for four decades, then supervisor for two terms and town clerk for seven terms. Smith, who was born in 1723, was a rabid Patriot, and, despite his age, he enlisted as a "minuteman" on April 7, 1776. Although never paid for his losses during the Revolutionary War, he remained an innkeeper until he died in 1803

Another well-documented example of non-payment is right next door in Huntington. In the Appendix to Volume Three of the "Huntington Town Records," compiled in 1887, there is a 48-page list that is introduced: "A True Copy of Receipts Signed by Officers of The British Army &c. [etc.] as followeth not paid." The British took horses and hay, sheep, oxen, cattle, oats, Indian corn and wood, all for the use of his majesty's troops.

Many years later — 1976 to be precise — the flamboyant Huntington Town historian, the late Rufus Langhans, came up with a novel way to dramatize the Bicentennial. Dressed in white knee-length breeches, immaculate white hose, ruffled shirt, green fringed hunting jacket and black tricorn hat, he flew to London to present a bill for $15,000 to the British chancellor of the exchequer to cover 200-year-old unpaid debts incurred by British troops quartered in Huntington during the Revolution.

Langhans claimed to have found British IOUs totaling 7,132 pounds in a town vault, and he converted the amount to 1976 dollars. In fact, the total was 7,249 pounds, 9 shillings sixpence, and Langhans didn't discover it at all: It was first documented in a book published in the 1820s by the early Long Island historian from Huntington, Silas Wood, who lived through the Revolution as a young boy.

In 1976, not surprisingly, the chancellor rejected Huntington's demand. But then, a few weeks later, in a gesture of amicability notably absent two centuries earlier, two high school students from Huntingdon, England, presented the Town of Huntington with a token payment of three pounds, all in coins in a small, red drawstring bag. The payment was accepted and the town withdrew the claim.

At 1976 exchange rates, the payment amounted to $6.72.

By 1774, the town emerges as an energetic proponent of revolution

Huntington Takes On the King

BY GEORGE DEWAN
STAFF WRITER

Newsday Photo / Julia Gaines

Members of the Ancient and Honorable Huntington Militia, bearing arms and the town's red Liberty Flag, stand for inspection during a re-enactment near the Huntington Arsenal.

In 1775, no one was more active in the Patriot cause than Gilbert Potter of Huntington, a medical doctor who had served in the French and Indian War. Potter, who a year later would be named a lieutenant colonel in charge of the western regiment of Suffolk militia, wrote to Congress Dec. 10, begging for more than the 100 pounds of gunpowder it had allotted Huntington in September. He wrote:

I have exerted myself in my station. But if nothing is done by your House, I must be obliged to desist. But as to myself, as an individual, I am determined to live and die free.

The next month, 1,000 more pounds of gunpowder were sent to be stored in the Huntington Arsenal.

The town's finest moment in an ongoing war of words with Britain had come 19 months before. It was in the form of one of Long Island's most important revolutionary documents, Huntington's Declaration of Rights of June 21, 1774, putting the town in the vanguard in opposition to British repression. The town defiantly declared that taxation without representation was wrong. The resolution by the town fathers, sent to the king's representatives in New York, read, in part:

That every freemans property is absolutely his own, and no man has a right to take it from him without his consent . . .

That therefore all taxes and duties imposed on his Majesties subjects in the American colonies by the authority of Parliament are wholly unconstitutional and a plain violation of the most essential rights of British subjects.

With Long Island divided in its support for the British or the American cause, Patriot sentiment was strongest in Suffolk, and the Town of Huntington had showed an independent spirit that reached back into the early days of English rule. In 1670, only six years after England had wrested control from the Dutch, the governor's council in New York ordered the outlying areas to pay a tax to help pay for repairs to Fort James in the city. Since a promised Colonial Assembly had never been formed, Huntington, along with the towns of Flushing, Hempstead and Jamaica, refused. Huntington's reason, first and foremost, was "because we conceive we are deprived of the liberties of Englishmen."

Furious, the council denounced the Long Islanders' petitions as "scandalous, illegal and seditious." The colonial governor, Francis Lovelace, ordered the papers publicly burned in front of City Hall, and the men who wrote them prosecuted. But nothing more came of it.

More than a century later, on May 2, 1775, Huntington reactivated its militia. It was fast becoming a town where gunpowder replaced talk in the community's grievances against the king.

> **LI HISTORY.COM**
>
> To see a copy of Huntington's Declaration of Rights and to read its full text, see http://www.lihistory.com on the Internet.

On July 4, 1776, the Congress in Philadelphia adopted the Declaration of Independence. The British, having abandoned Boston, were massing troops on Staten Island, preparing for an attack at Brooklyn that would take place on Aug. 27.

The news of the newly adopted declaration reached Huntington July 23, and its public reading set off a wild celebration. In what is today called the Village Green, at the center of town, there was a Liberty Pole, a flagpole that residents used to stir up opposition to British policies, but as loyal subjects of the king. Thus, the flag was scarlet with a Union Jack in the canton. On one side was the word "Liberty," and on the other side, "George III."

Revelers ripped off the words "George III," cut away the Union Jack, leaving what has since been known as the Huntington Liberty Flag, a white "Liberty" on a red background. The Liberty Flag was carried as a Suffolk regimental battle flag at the Battle of Long Island. Hessian troops under Col. Johann Gottlieb Rall captured the flag and 60 militiamen.

Then, in the town's final insult to the king, an effigy of George III was stuffed with gunpowder, hung on a gallows and exploded. Later that evening, according to an account in Holt's N.Y. Journal, the town fathers and other worthy citizens drank 13 toasts to the heroes who had died at Boston, Lexington and Concord, and to "the free and independent States of America."

But no excess of patriotic spirit could stop the British occupation from coming. On Aug. 26, Lt. Col. Potter sent an urgent letter to Brig. Gen. Nathaniel Woodhull, head of the Suffolk militia. British ships carrying Redcoats were expected in Huntington Bay before morning.

Have not ordered any men from here as yet, but am mustering them to make as good opposition as possible. We must have help here. Everything possible for me, shall be done. I think General Washington should be acquainted. Our women are in great tumult.

The help did not come. Potter, with the pounding of British boots ringing in his ears, wisely fled to Connecticut. The conquering troops, 200 infantrymen and 100 mounted cavalry under Gen. Oliver DeLancey, arrived Sept. 1. Huntington became occupied territory. Huntington's male population ages 15 and above were given two choices: either sign an Oath of Loyalty and Peaceable Behavior or flee to Connecticut. A total of 549 men signed the oath, although it is uncertain how many really meant it.

Apparently the Huntingtonians did not completely give in to their British overlords. When a complaint was made that Col. J.G. Simcoe of the British Queen's Rangers gave no receipts for the cattle, sheep and provisions that he seized, Simcoe replied:

I did not give receipts to a great number of people on account of their rebellious principles, or absolute disobedience of the general orders. The inhabitants of Huntington came under both descriptions.

HUNTINGTON ARSENAL

The little red building that looks like a toolshed is at 425 Park Ave. in Huntington, right next to the entrance to the Cinema Arts Centre. It is, in fact, the only surviving colonial arsenal on Long Island.

When Congress sent 1,000 pounds of gunpowder to the Huntington Militia in early 1776, it was stored in the arsenal, a former granary then owned by Job Sammis. It was also used to store weapons and other military equipment. Today, the arsenal is open Sundays from 1 p.m. to 4 p.m., admission is free, and the public can view muskets, military clothing and listen to volunteers tell stories about the town's revolutionary past. A revolutionary soldier may even fire off his musket for you.

— George DeWan

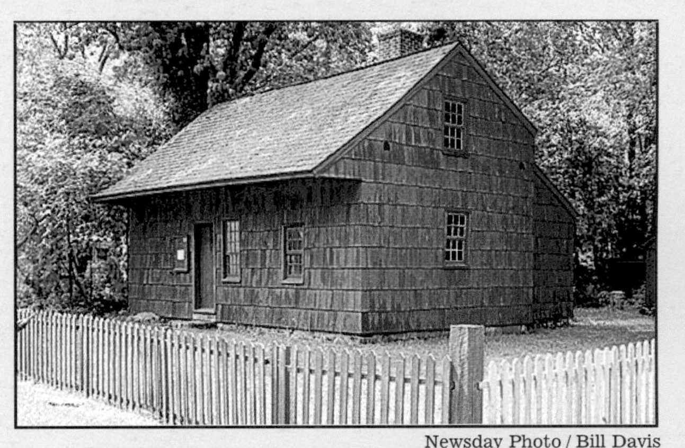

Newsday Photo / Bill Davis

The town bought the arsenal in 1974 to save and restore it.

Loyalist Benjamin Thompson tried to keep the town under his boot

The Man Huntington Loved to Hate

From "Memoir of Sir Benjamin Thompson"

Failing to gain a commission in the American army, Benjamin Thompson turned to the British.

BY GEORGE DEWAN
STAFF WRITER

If a Gallup Poll had been taken in Huntington in the winter of 1782-83, Benjamin Thompson would have been the unanimous choice for the most despicable man in town.

There is no question that Thompson — later known as Count Rumford — made his mark on Huntington's history, for his ghost lingers like an incubus among the time-worn gravestones in the Old Burying Ground on East Main Street. But his short and violent tenure in this bastion of rebel sentiment was a circumstance notable more for its curiosity than for its impact on the Revolutionary War, which was zero.

Here was a remarkable young man of 29, a Loyalist New Englander charged with keeping Huntington under his boot for the British occupiers. He was a future Bavarian count and a scientific genius who, in only a few months, managed to rub raw the festering wounds of American-British hostility. The reason none of Thompson's actions was necessary to the outcome of the war was that the British had long since given up, and its official end was merely a formality.

Thompson knew all this, but he persisted in his pigheaded goal of bringing Huntington to its knees.

Well before he got to this stage in his life, however, Thompson showed signs of scientific brilliance combined with an appalling sense of interpersonal relations. He had a knack of ingratiating himself with men of power but was completely without sensitivity to his peers and his inferiors. Born in Woburn, Mass., in 1753, he displayed an early aptitude for matters of science, and at age 18 he began the study of medicine. A year later he married a wealthy widow 14 years his senior, a marriage that would last only three years. But that marriage connection, and the fact that he looked handsome mounted on a horse, got him named a major in the New Hampshire militia.

Soon after George Washington took command of the Continental Army in 1775, Thompson applied for a regular commission, but was rejected, apparently because he was blackballed by his fellow officers from New Hampshire, who found him quite disagreeable. So he turned, without compunction, to the British, who were glad to have him, and he, them. Thompson went to London, and returned in 1781 as a lieutenant colonel in the British Army. The following March he saw some insignificant action in South Carolina. In September, 1782, with a provisional peace agreement about to be signed between the British and the Americans, Thompson was assigned to move his Loyalist regiment, the Kings American Dragoons, to winter quarters in Huntington.

The outrage was soon to come. On Dec. 5, 1782, the following item appeared in a Fishkill, N.Y., newspaper:

> *The enemy are fortifying Huntington. They have pitched on a burying yard and have dug up graves and gravestones, to the great grief of the people there, who, when they remonstrated against the proceeding, received nothing but abuse.*

This is the building project for which Thompson has earned the everlasting contempt of Huntingtonians. With no intent other than to gratify a malignant disposition, as one early historian put it, Thompson built a fort — Fort Golgotha, he called it, displaying the wit that often made him insufferable — in the center of the public burying ground. Gravestones were torn up and used to build ovens to bake bread for the troops. Historian Nathaniel Prime wrote in 1845 that he had talked with old men who were there at the time, and they had "seen the loaves of bread drawn out of these ovens, with the reversed inscriptions of the tombstones of their friends on the lower crusts."

Prime's father, Ebenezer, had been pastor of the Old First Church until he died in 1779, and Thompson placed Prime's tombstone in front of his tent, so that he could "tread on the old rebel" when coming and going. To provide lumber for the men's barracks, Prime's church was torn down, and then Thompson moved into the parsonage.

Having made himself *persona non grata* in less than seven months, Thompson at age 30 left Huntington and sailed for England on April 11. Although that ended the Huntington portion of his story, Thompson's remarkable life as a scientist was really just beginning

On his return to England, Thompson was knighted by King George III. He then set out on a tour of Europe, where he so impressed the Bavarians that they made him minister of war, minister of police and grand chamberlain of the court. He was also named a count of the Holy Roman Empire, choosing the title Count von Rumford (after the old name of Concord, N.H., where his former wife was from — which is a bit hard to understand, since he had separated from a woman whom he never wanted to see again, and, in fact, never did). In his 11 years in Bavaria he improved the living conditions of the army, abolished beggary by putting all the mendicants to work on public projects and laid out a beautiful park in Munich called the English Garden.

Thompson also continued his scientific experiments. He invented a kitchen range for army cooks. He invented a drip coffee maker. He improved the understanding of gunpowder, and made advances in the understanding of the effect of friction on heat. He lived his later years — he would die at Auteuil, near Paris, at 61 in 1814 — in England and France, absorbed in his scientific studies and writing scientific papers.

While in France, Thompson married Marie Lavoisier, the widow of the famous chemist, Antoine Lavoisier. That marriage, slightly less unhappy as the first, lasted only seven years, because, as one writer put it, *he* loved flowers and tranquillity, *she* loved dinner parties and entertainments. Marie should have known him in Huntington.

LEGACY

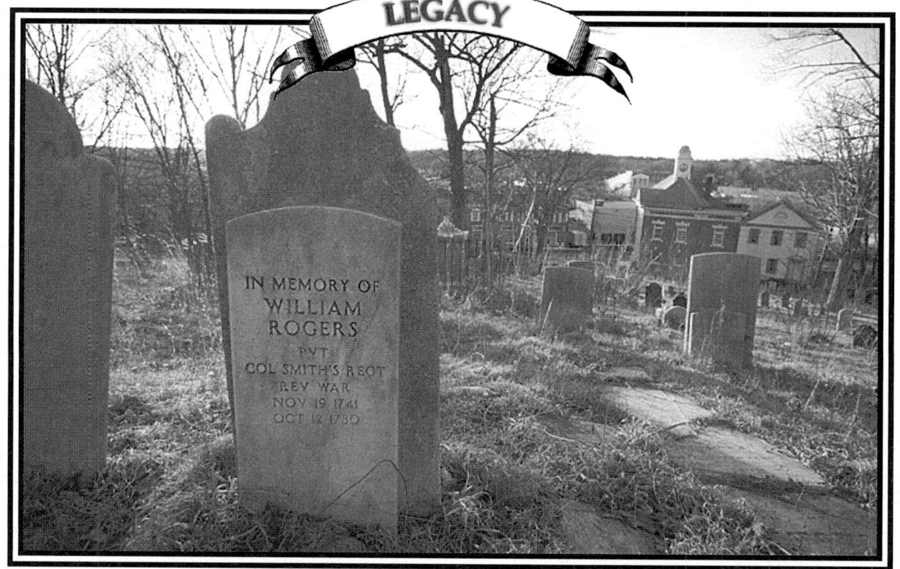

Newsday Photo / Bill Davis

A DESECRATED CEMETERY

British soldiers under Thompson's command dug up graves and transformed the Old Burying Ground overlooking Huntington into Fort Golgotha. Gravestones were used for ovens, and legend is that fresh-baked bread bore the reverse inscriptions of the stones.

How beautiful is death, when earn'd by virtue!
Who would not be that youth? What pity is it
That we can die but once to serve our country!
— Joseph Addison, 1713: "Cato," Act 4, Scene 4

He may never have said those famous words, but it was

Nathan Hale: Failed Spy,

The 1776 execution of Patriot spy Nathan Hale as illustrated in Harper's Weekly in October, 1880

BY GEORGE DEWAN
STAFF WRITER

In the pantheon of revolutionary heroes there stands a flaxen-haired, blue-eyed young man, a handsome former schoolteacher, fair of skin and athletic in build, full of hope and promise, fated for an untimely death. He was Nathan Hale.

A beautiful death, earned by virtue. Born in Connecticut but forever tied by history to Long Island, Hale was hanged by the British as a spy at the tender age of 21, left grotesquely suspended for three days as a lesson to the hated rebels, then cut down and cast into an unmarked grave somewhere on Manhattan Island.

Hale may not have been a very good spy, but he gets high marks for attitude. But the story of Nathan Hale has frustrating gaps, like a jigsaw puzzle with key pieces missing. Did Hale really say, "I only regret that I have but one life to lose for my country," just before the noose tightened around his neck? Was he captured in Huntington or in New York? Did he participate in a plot to burn down New York City?

Here is what is known. Born June 6, 1755, at Coventry, Conn., Hale grew up with eight brothers and sisters on a prosperous 240-acre farm. The Hales were ardent Patriots, and six of the boys took part in the Revolution. Nathan studied at Yale College, graduating in 1773. For the next two years he was a schoolteacher, but in July, 1775, he accepted a commission as a lieutenant in the Continental Army.

For more than a year he soldiered without distinction. He was at the siege of Boston until the British evacuated in March, 1776. He also was present at the Battle of Long Island that August, as a captain, though he engaged in no fighting himself. Hale felt frustrated, wanting to make a more significant contribution. He was about to get his chance.

After losing the Battle of Long Island on Aug. 27 and being forced back to New York, Gen. George Washington ranged his forces in Manhattan from the Battery to Harlem Heights. But he was in the dark about what the enemy, dug in on western Long Island from the Narrows north to Astoria, would do next. He asked Hale's regimental commander to find among his officers someone to volunteer as a spy.

Hale was fired up by the possibility. He immediately went to see a close friend, Capt. William Hull, who related what happened in a memoir published in 1848. Hale was excited but Hull tried to talk him out of it, telling Hale that his nature was "too frank and open for deceit and disguise . . . I ended by saying that should he undertake the enterprise, his short, bright career, would close with an ignominious death."

"I am fully sensible of the consequences of discovery and capture in such a situation," Hale responded. "But for a year I have been attached to the army, and have not rendered any material service, while receiving a compensation, for which I make no return."

Hale's last words to Hull were: "I will reflect, and do nothing but what duty demands."

Accompanied by Sgt. Stephen Hempstead, the new spy left camp at Harlem Heights about Sept. 12 and made his way to Norwalk, Conn., far enough from the city to avoid confrontation with the British while crossing Long Island Sound. He found an armed sloop to take the two of them to Huntington, landing somewhere on the beach near what is now Huntington Bay.

In a letter to a newspaper published in 1827, Hempstead described what happened next:

Newsday Photos

Because no portraits of Nathan Hale exist, artists guess at what he looked like. At left is a Hale statue at New York's City Hall; at right, a statue at Yale University, which Hale attended.

Capt. Hale had changed his uniform for a plain suit of citizens brown clothes, with a round broad-brimmed hat, assuming the character of a Dutch school-master, leaving all his other clothes, commission, public and private papers, with me, and also his silver shoe buckles, saying they would not comport with his character as school-master, and retaining nothing but his College diploma, as an introduction to his assumed calling.

This was Sept. 15 or 16. Hale's plan was to make his way westward back to the British lines. He assumed — incorrectly, as it turned out — that the main British forces were still in the neighborhood of Brooklyn Heights. He expected to relay information to Washington by retracing his steps back to Huntington and across the Sound.

No one knows what route he took, but Hale made his way to the western end of the Island, where he would have learned that the British had already taken most of Manhattan. All of Washington's troops had been pushed back to Harlem Heights, north of what is now 110th Street. At that point, since Washington already knew what Hale had been sent to find out, Hale could have gone back the way he came. But, consistent with a bravery that bordered on the foolhardy, Hale crossed over into New York, probably at Brooklyn Ferry, near today's Brooklyn Bridge. As he went, he secretly took notes of such his thought that counted . . .

Superb Patriot

LI HISTORY.COM

An account of Nathan Hale's capture and execution written by Stephen Hempstead, Hale's sergeant at the time, is available on the Internet at http://www.lihistory.com.

things as locations of troops and sketches of fortifications.

For the Americans, Hale had disappeared. Washington did not learn of his fate until the evening of Sept. 22. A British aide to Gen. William Howe, Capt. John Montresor, visited the Americans under a flag of truce to discuss a prisoner exchange. As an aside, Montresor mentioned that an American, Capt. Nathan Hale, had been hanged as a spy at 11 o'clock that morning. Hale's friend, William Hull, visited with Montresor, who gave him a lengthy account of what happened. Hull's memoirs give us most of what we know about Hale's last hours.

Montresor told Hull that when Hale was captured on Sept. 21 he was carrying concealed papers with sketches of fortifications and other information. Hale, as frank and open as Hull said he was — poor qualities for a spy — acknowledged that he was on a secret mission for Gen. Washington. Howe ordered him to be executed the following morning at 11. Hale asked to speak to a clergyman, and for a Bible, but both requests were refused. The best available evidence places the hanging at approximately the intersection of the present Third Avenue and 66th Street.

But are the last words attributed to Hale the ones that he actually said? Once again, not everyone agrees, but it is generally accepted that Hale, familiar with the English writer Joseph Addison, was paraphrasing a line from his play "Cato."

A 1777 newspaper article reported Hale as saying that "if he had ten thousand lives, he would lay them all down, if called to it, in defence of his injured, bleeding country." Four years later another newspaper story quoted Hale's last words as: ". . . my only regret is, that I have not more lives than one to offer in its service." Hull's 1848 memoirs give us the pithier version we know today: "I only regret that I have but one life to lose for my country."

Other parts of Hale's story are debatable. Although Washington always denied it, many people believe there was a plot to burn down New York City, after it was realized that it was going to be lost to the British. On the morning of the day Hale was arrested, a major fire broke out in lower Manhattan, destroying at least one-quarter of the city's houses. In a July 14, 1975, New York magazine article, historical novelist Thomas Fleming speculated that Hale was likely to have been part of the plot. But that remains speculation.

Whether Hale was captured in Huntington or in New York has been debated for more than a century. One belief is that he was apprehended after being betrayed at a tavern in what is now Huntington Bay, then put aboard the British ship Halifax and taken into New York to be hanged. What has been verified by British documents is that Hale was captured on the night of Sept. 21 and executed at 11 a.m. the next day. The question is whether a Huntington capture is consistent with that schedule.

A blue-ribbon panel appointed by Huntington Town to settle this issue reported in 1939 that it was impossible to prove one way or another. But Yale professor James G. Rogers, writing in George D. Seymour's 1941 book, "Documentary Life of Nathan Hale," gives what is probably the most complete analysis of all the conflicting stories. He rules out Huntington.

First, Rogers says, the ship's logs show that the Halifax was not near Huntington on Sept. 21. Second, based on the rate of cruise of sailships in those waters, the Huntington-to-Manhattan trip took more than a day. Thus, Hale could not have been transported into New York in time for his own hanging.

If not Huntington, then where? One possibility is upper Manhattan, near the boundary of the British and American lines, which Hale was trying to reach. Other sources suggest that it was somewhere on the western end of Long Island, between Hell Gate and Flushing Bay.

In the end, does it really matter if the puzzle is never completely solved? Like Paul Revere and Betsy Ross, Nathan Hale has become part of our national revolutionary drama. In the early part of this century, a writer named Watson Sperry wrote in The Hartford Courant:

When Sir William Howe ordered him to be strung up he no doubt meant to make an end to the young American captain, but in fact he made the beginning of him. From that moment young Hale passed from an engaging and capable personality into an enduring national symbol.

Hale's Travels

1. July 1, 1775. Commissioned as a first lieutenant in the First Connecticut Regiment. Sent to Cambridge as part of the siege of Boston. Later promoted to captain.

2. April 30, 1776. Landed at Turtle Bay (near East 45th Street) with other colonial troops.

3. May, 1776. Spent three weeks at Brooklyn Heights, participating in building of fortifications. Later returned to New York City.

4. August. Hale did not participate in the Battle of Long Island – he was posted behind the fortifications. Withdraws with the rest of the forces on Aug. 29.

5. September. Leaves camp at Harlem Heights with Sgt. Stephen Hempstead, a New London friend and one of his sergeants. They traveled to Connecticut, looking for an appropriate place to cross over to Long Island. Settled on Norwalk, Conn., where they were put in touch with Capt. Charles Pond, commander of the armed Colonial sloop "Schuyler."

6. Sept. 15. Pond's sloop sails from Norwalk.

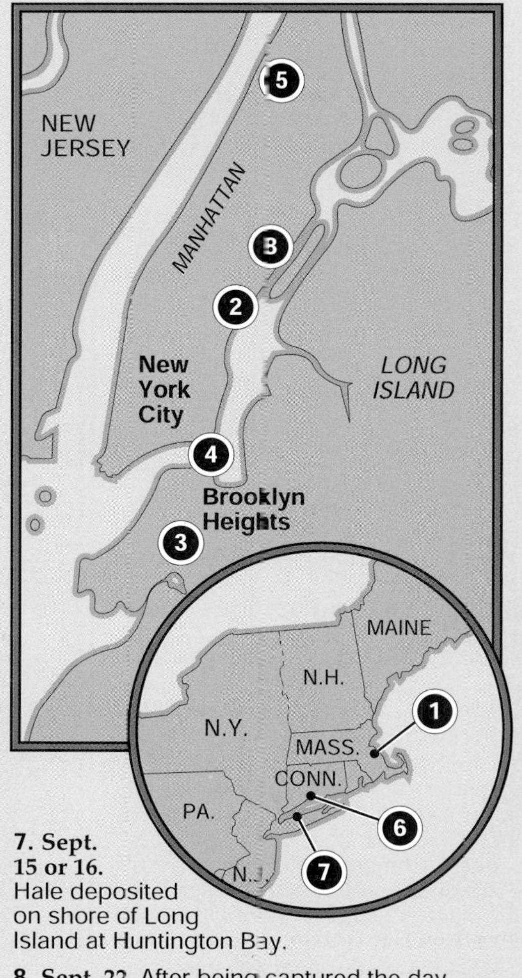

7. Sept. 15 or 16. Hale deposited on shore of Long Island at Huntington Bay.

8. Sept. 22. After being captured the day before, Hale is hanged at the intersection of the present Third Avenue and 66th Street.

Newsday / Linda McKenney

Newsday Photo / Bill Davis

NATHAN HALE MONUMENT

The Nathan Hale Stone in Huntington is no place to go for a history lesson.

On one of the boulder's brass plaques it states that Hale was "captured by the British on this shore Sep. 1776." The truth is that Hale was most likely captured in New York — not in Huntington.

The first Hale quote cited on the monument is: "I will undertake it." He is supposed to have said that when his colonel asked for a volunteer spy from among his junior officers. The remark was first published in 1856 and repeated often by popular writers — but there's no evidence that Hale ever said it.

The most famous Nathan Hale quote of all? Well, he most likely said something quite similar to it, and it has been refined over the years to this: "I only regret that I have but one life to lose for my country." But the plaque reads: "I only regret that I have but one life to *give* for my country."

In 1897, a private developer named George Taylor placed the memorial — a 45-ton boulder — at a spot where the beach meets the end of Vineyard Road, and named the area Halesite. Part of the original area later became the Village of Huntington Bay. This is roughly where Hale landed to begin his spying mission, a fact that everyone seems to agree is true. In 1976 the boulder was donated to the town and moved well inland to a grassy island in front of the American Legion hall, where Mill Dam Road meets New York Avenue.

There it stands, history set in stone.

— George DeWan

The Culper Spy Ring foils the British by delivering critical information to Washington

A Ruse Saves the French Fleet

BY GEORGE DEWAN
STAFF WRITER

Four years after the botched attempt at spying on the British ended with Nathan Hale's execution, Gen. George Washington needed his Long Island spies. In the summer of 1780, the British were threatening Rhode Island.

These are the men he turned to:

Benjamin Tallmadge . . . code name John Bolton.

Abraham Woodhull . . . code name Samuel Culper Sr.

Robert Townsend . . . code name Samuel Culper Jr.

Caleb Brewster . . . code name Agent 725.

Austin Roe . . . code name Agent 724.

A French fleet of seven ships-of-the-line, four frigates and more than 30 transports carrying 5,000 troops was about to sail into Newport, R.I., to assist its new American allies against the British. But Washington did not know what the British knew about the French fleet, and what they planned to do about it. He feared the worst.

"As we may every moment expect the arrival of the French fleet a revival of the correspondence with the Culpers will be of very great importance," Washington, who was camped in New Jersey, wrote on July 11 to his chief of intelligence, John Bolton. The message was even more urgent than Washington realized, since the French had arrived the day before.

On July 15, Bolton left his headquarters at Van Cortlandt Manor in Westchester to find Agent 725 in Fairfield, Conn. Agent 725 took some men and rowed his whaleboat across the Sound to Setauket. He could not find Samuel Culper Sr., the next link in the spy chain, so he took the message directly to Agent 724, the ring's courier. Taking his fastest horse, Agent 724 raced 55 miles into Manhattan and contacted Samuel Culper Jr.

Culper Jr. immediately moved around the city, where he was well known to the British as a merchant and a part-time journalist for Rivington's Gazette, a noted Tory paper. Along the waterfront he went, talking to shippers; then he stopped at coffeehouses and taverns, buying porter and rum for his British and Loyalist friends, asking questions and gleaning bits of information about the British plans. On July 20, he had the information he needed, and wrote a message in invisible ink to Washington.

With the message in his saddlebag, Agent 724 galloped the 55 miles back to Setauket and delivered it to Culper Sr. In haste and with a sense of great urgency, Culper Sr. composed a brief cover note to Agent 725:

Sir. The enclosed requires your immediate departure this day by all means let not an hour pass; for this day must not be lost. You have news of the greatest consequence perhaps that ever happened to your country.

The spy information was in Washington's hands by 4 p.m. on July 21, the fastest delivery of a dispatch the Culpers had ever made. Washington learned that the British, now under the command of Gen. Henry Clinton, had 8,000 troops about to embark at Whitestone to sail up the Sound to Newport and crush the French before they had a chance to organize.

Painting by Vance Locke, 1952

Culper Spy Ring member Austin Roe carries information for George Washington about British plans to intercept the French fleet. The painting is at the Setauket School.

With the British fleet just moving out, Washington had to act fast. He knew that one of Clinton's greatest fears was an American attack on New York, which the British had controlled since September, 1776. Since he did not have the manpower to mount such an attack, Washington resorted to guile. He and his officers drew up a plan for a fictitious, 12,000-man attack on New York, put the plan in an official pouch, and gave it to a man who would pose as a Tory farmer. The man delivered the pouch to the British, saying he had found it along the road.

Clinton fell for the ruse and called back the British fleet. He ordered a series of signal fires along the north shore of Long Island, passing the message to the fleet, which was off Huntington Bay, heading east at full sail. The fleet returned to New York. The French fleet at Newport was safe.

This was probably the most important achievement of Washington's Long Island spy connection, which became known as the Culper Spy Ring, or, sometimes, the Setauket Spy Ring. As befits the cloak-and-dagger business, their names and numbers were merely aliases.

Maj. Benjamin Tallmadge, 26 in 1780, was a native of Setauket and had been a friend and Yale classmate of Nathan Hale, whose death had affected him deeply. Abraham Woodhull, 27, was a Setauket farmer, a tall, thin, nervous man who appeared older than his years. Robert Townsend, also 26, was the purchasing agent for his father, Samuel Townsend, a well-known Oyster Bay merchant whose large home, later known as Raynham Hall, was being used as a British headquarters. Caleb Brewster, 28, was a daring, rough-and-tumble whaleboat captain from Setauket. Austin Roe was a 27-year-old Setauket tavern keeper.

There were others at various times in the spy ring. Two of them were women, one whose name we know, one whose name we don't. Anna Smith Strong, 40, known as Nancy, was Abraham Woodhull's neighbor in Setauket, and she used her laundry line to pass on messages between the agents.

The second was a mystery lady who lived in New York. Though her role seems to have been minimal, over the years writers have told the story of her torrid and star-crossed romance with the spy known as Culper Jr.

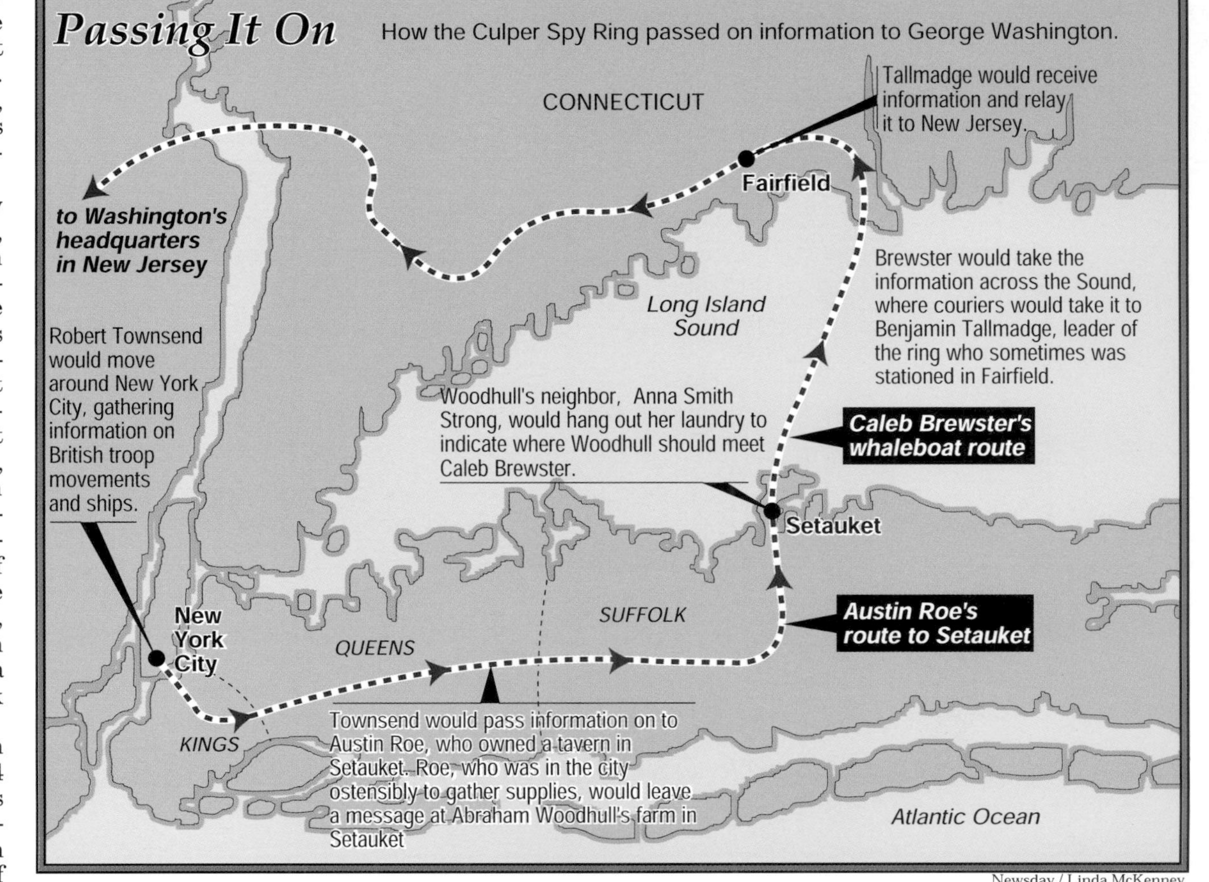

Passing It On
How the Culper Spy Ring passed on information to George Washington.
CONNECTICUT
Tallmadge would receive information and relay it to New Jersey.
Fairfield
to Washington's headquarters in New Jersey
Long Island Sound
Brewster would take the information across the Sound, where couriers would take it to Benjamin Tallmadge, leader of the ring who sometimes was stationed in Fairfield.
Robert Townsend would move around New York City, gathering information on British troop movements and ships.
Woodhull's neighbor, Anna Smith Strong, would hang out her laundry to indicate where Woodhull should meet Caleb Brewster.
Caleb Brewster's whaleboat route
Setauket
SUFFOLK
Austin Roe's route to Setauket
New York City
QUEENS
KINGS
Townsend would pass information on to Austin Roe, who owned a tavern in Setauket. Roe, who was in the city ostensibly to gather supplies, would leave a message at Abraham Woodhull's farm in Setauket
Atlantic Ocean

Newsday / Linda McKenney

Newsday Photo / Bill Davis

A rendering by Allyn Cox, for a mosaic at Ward Melville High School in East Setauket, shows Austin Roe ready to hand a message to Caleb Brewster in Old Field for delivery across Long Island Sound.

Based on Long Island, the Culper spies give the Americans a valuable edge

Washington's Eyes and Ears

BY GEORGE DEWAN
STAFF WRITER

Spying was risky business. Gen. George Washington wanted the newly recruited Culper Spy Ring to be aware of just how risky it was.

"There can be scarcely any need of recommending the greatest caution and secrecy in a business so critical and dangerous," Washington wrote from his New Jersey headquarters to his chief of intelligence, Maj. Benjamin Tallmadge, on July 10, 1779.

With the British controlling New York City, there was much that the commander in chief needed to know: The sizes and numbers of vessels in the harbor, and how they were protected; the number of men guarding the city, and how they were deployed; descriptions of forts and redoubts that had been built by the British, and whether pits had been dug in front of them "in which sharp pointed stakes are fixed"; and last, "The state of the provisions, forage and fuel to be attended to, as also the health and spirits of the army, navy and City."

The spy ring had begun its activities on a small scale in 1778, with Abraham Woodhull of Setauket, alias Samuel Culper, doing much of the snooping in New York. But his absences in Setauket started to become noticeable. In the fall he found Robert Townsend of Oyster Bay, who was his father's purchasing agent in New York, to take over that job. Townsend exacted a promise that no one, not even Washington, would ever know his real name. He took the spy name Culper Jr., making Woodhull Culper Sr. Townsend's real name was not learned until 1930, when Suffolk historian Morton Pennypacker, aided by a handwriting expert, matched Culper Jr.'s handwriting with Townsend's.

As Culper Jr., Townsend dug out most of the important information needed by Washington. He was not only a merchant, he also worked part time, without pay, as a journalist for Rivington's Gazette, a pro-British New York newspaper. And he became a silent partner in a nearby Wall Street coffeehouse run by the paper's owner, James Rivington. It was frequented by British officers eager to get their name in the paper, so they talked freely to Townsend.

Here is how the spy ring worked: Imagine a communications loop running from Washington's headquarters somewhere in New Jersey, across Westchester County, then Connecticut, then across Long Island Sound to Setauket. From there the loop would make its way into New York City, where British headquarters lay.

Sometimes, Washington would have a specific request, which would be sent around the loop into the city. Once gathered, the information would return in the reverse direction. At other times, Townsend in New York would come up with some vital information on his own, and send it on its roundabout way to the general.

Austin Roe, the Setauket tavern-keeper, made the 55-mile ride into New York at least once a week, sometimes more often. His cover story was that he needed to purchase supplies for his business. He would meet Townsend, and when the papers were ready, return to Setauket, where he would deposit the information in a box in the corner of one of Abraham Woodhull's farm fields.

After checking the drop-box, Woodhull would use a spyglass to keep a close watch on the clothesline of his neighbor across Little Bay. That was Anna Smith Strong, better known as Nancy, whose husband, Judge Selah Strong, had been imprisoned by the British in New York for "surreptitious correspondence with the enemy."

Woodhull was looking for Nancy Strong's black petticoat, which she would hang out only when she knew that Agent 725, Caleb Brewster, had arrived from Connecticut in his whaleboat. She would add to the line one to six white handkerchiefs, indicating in which of six coves Brewster was hiding. No one has ever figured out how Anna Strong knew when Brewster was in town, or where he was hiding.

Under the cover of night, Brewster would sneak through the British boats guarding the nearby waters and make his way across Long Island Sound to Fairfield, Conn., which was still controlled by the Americans. A courier would take the papers to Tallmadge, and Tallmadge would send them to Washington.

Toward the end of the war, Washington got impatient with waiting for a response to his questions. And British counterintelligence raised suspicions about the Setauket connection. The route was eventually shortened to go across the Sound near Cow Neck, the modern Port Washington.

From the very start, the general made clear that his standards were high. In a June 27, 1779, letter to Tallmadge, Washington enclosed 10 guineas to reimburse Culper Sr. for expenses, and then commented somewhat sharply — not an unusual trait for Washington — on his expectations for Culper Sr.'s successor in New York, Culper Jr.:

> *His successor (whose name I have no desire to be informed of provided his intelligence is good, and seasonably transmitted) should endeavor to hit upon some certain mode of conveying his information quickly, for it is of little avail to be told of things after they have become matter of public notoriety, and known to every body.*

Even the respected Tallmadge was not immune from the general's tongue. Within a week, Tallmadge's camp was attacked by the British, and in the ensuing battle, he lost his horse, most of his baggage, Washington's letter and the 10 guineas. Washington wrote to Tallmadge on July 5:

> *The loss of your papers was certainly a most unlucky accident, and shows how dangerous it is to keep papers of any consequence at an advanced post. I beg you will take care to guard against the like in the future. If you will send me a trusty person, I will replace the guineas.*

LEGACY

ANNA STRONG'S GRAVE

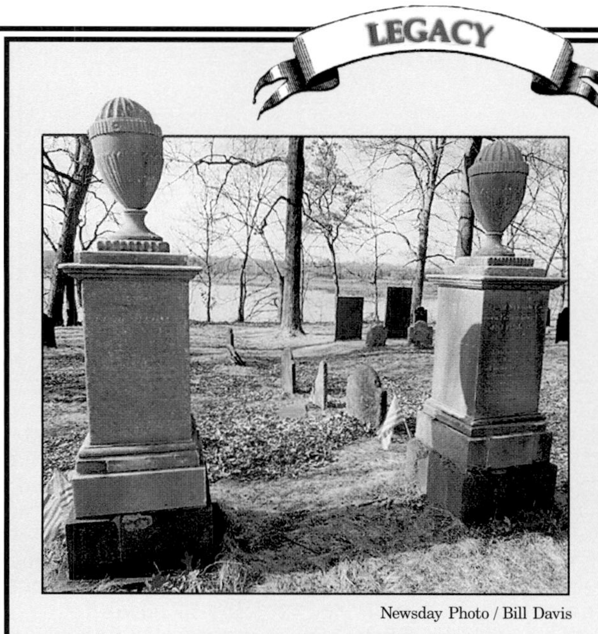

Newsday Photo / Bill Davis

Spy ring member Anna Smith (Nancy) Strong is buried with her husband, Selah Strong, in the St. George's Manor Cemetery on Strong's Neck, Setauket. First used for the burial of William Smith in 1705, the small, private family cemetery is on Cemetery Lane, off Dyke Road. It can be visited by the public.

How George Washington's intelligence gatherers enciphered their communiques

Crafty Codes of American Spies

BY GEORGE DEWAN
STAFF WRITER

Fearing that their messages might get intercepted by the British, the Culper spies quickly resorted to both secret code and invisible ink.

Here is the beginning of a coded letter sent by Abraham Woodhull, alias Culper Sr., to Gen. George Washington.

"729 29 15th 1779.

"Sir. Dqpeu Beyocpu agreeable to 28 met 723 not far from 727 & received a 356 . . . Every 356 is opened at the entrance of 727 and every 371 is searched, that for the future every 356 must be 691 with the 286 received."

Translated, it reads:

"Setauket August 15th 1779

"Sir. Jonas Hawkins [an early messenger] agreeable to appointment met Culper Jr. not far from New York & received a letter . . . Every letter is opened at the entrance of New York and every man is searched, that for the future every letter must be written with the ink received."

Though the codes used by the Culper spies were elementary by today's standards, they apparently were good enough for the Revolutionary War. It wasn't until 1939 that historian Morton Pennypacker revealed the Culper secret code system for the first time. He said that Maj. Benjamin Tallmadge, Washington's spy chief, prepared codebooks for four people: Washington, Abraham Woodhull, Robert Townsend, alias Culper Jr., and himself. He took hundreds of words from a commonly used dictionary of the day, then assigned numbers to each word.

All the spies, as well as other people important to the ring, also were given numbers. For example: Washington was 711; Tallmadge, 721; Robert Townsend, 723. Many places were given numbers: New York, 727; Long Island, 728; London, 746. There were numbers for the months of the year. And for each of the 26 letters of the alphabet, a different letter was substituted, a so-called substitution cipher.

Even more important to the spy ring was the use of invisible ink, called by Washington a "sympathetic stain," or "white ink." It had been invented by James Jay, a physician living in England, the brother of John Jay, who would become the first chief justice of the United States. The invisible ink was first used on a blank piece of paper, which, after the message was written, was inserted in a half-ream of new paper. By an earlier agreement, Washington knew by counting from the top of the half-ream how to find the page with the message. He would then use a second solution to make the message reappear. Later, thinking that carrying a blank piece of paper might invite suspicion, Washington ordered the invisible messages to be written between the lines of, or under, a regularly written message.

Spying was a risky game, and great chances were taken by all the members of the ring. In October, 1779, Culper Sr. wrote to tell the general about getting mugged on Long Island.

"It is too great a risque to write with ink in this country of robbers. I this day just saved my life. Soon after I left Hempstead Plains and got into the woods I was attacked by four armed men, one of them I had frequently seen in N. York. They searched every pocket and lining of my clothes, shoes, and also my saddle, which the enclosed was in, but thank kind Providence they did not find it. I had but one dollar in money about me. It was so little they did not take it, and so came off clear."

Though Washington was publicly a reticent man, he occasionally made clear his approval of the work of the Culper Spy Ring. Of Culper Jr., he wrote on Feb. 5, 1780: "His accounts are intelligent, clear and satisfactory . . . I rely upon his intelligence." In May, 1781, Washington recorded in his diary: "Of the Culpers fidelity and ability I entertain the highest opinion."

With the war officially ended in 1783, the Culper Spy Ring disbanded.

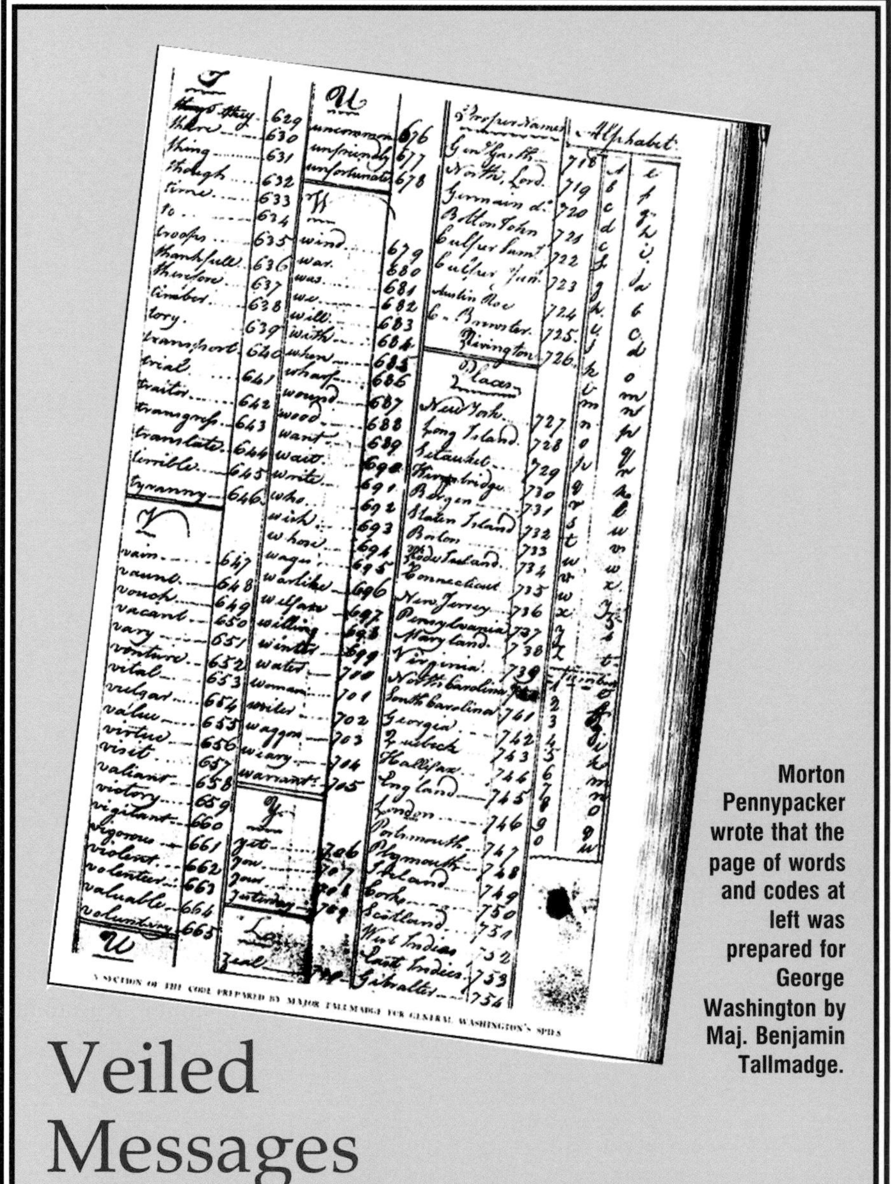

Morton Pennypacker wrote that the page of words and codes at left was prepared for George Washington by Maj. Benjamin Tallmadge.

Veiled Messages

Here is a sampling of the secret code used by Gen. Washington, Benjamin Tallmadge, Robert Townsend and Abraham Woodhull. Each had a book of hundreds of commonly used words that were assigned two- or three-digit codes:

Code	Translation		Code	Translation
15	advice		345	knowledge
60	better		347	land
73	camp		728	Long Island
121	day		349	low
156	deliver		355	lady
151	disorder		356	letter
178	enemy		371	man
745	England		727	New York
174	express		476	parts
230	guineas		585	refugees
286	ink		592	ships
309	infantry		660	vigilant
317	importance		680	war
322	inquiry		691	written
			708	your

Each letter had a substitute, for spelling words.

a = e	n = p
b = f	o = q
c = g	p = r
d = h	q = k
e = i	r = l
f = j	s = u
g = a	t = v
h = b	u = w
i = c	v = x
j = d	w = y
k = o	x = z
l = m	y = s
m = n	z = t

LI HISTORY.COM

All previous installments and enhancements to "Long Island: Our Story" are available on the Internet at Newsday's http://www.lihistory.com.

After Their Revolution Was Won

Here is what happened to the chief players in the Culper Spy Ring:

Benjamin Tallmadge (1754-1835) settled in Litchfield, Conn., where he became a merchant. He represented his district as a Federalist in the U.S. House of Representatives from 1801-1817. He died in 1835 at age 81.

Abraham Woodhull (1750-1826) returned to his farm. He served as judge of the Court of Common Pleas for six years, then was named a Suffolk County judge, 1799-1810.

Robert Townsend (1753-1838) returned to his Oyster Bay home, continuing his work as a merchant and helping to manage the estate of his father, Samuel Townsend.

Austin Roe (1749-1830) continued operating Roe's Tavern in Setauket. In 1798 he moved to Patchogue, where he founded Roe's Hotel.

Caleb Brewster (1747-1827), who settled in Fairfield, Conn., was pensioned by Congress for gallantry in action in a whaleboat raid. For many years he was the captain of a revenue-cutter (an armed government vessel used to prevent smuggling) in the New York area.

Anna Smith (Nancy) Strong (1740-1812) remained on Strong's Neck in Setauket after her husband, Selah, was released from a British prison in New York and took the children to Connecticut. At war's end the family was reunited in Setauket, where the family property was restored to its former status as St. George's Manor.

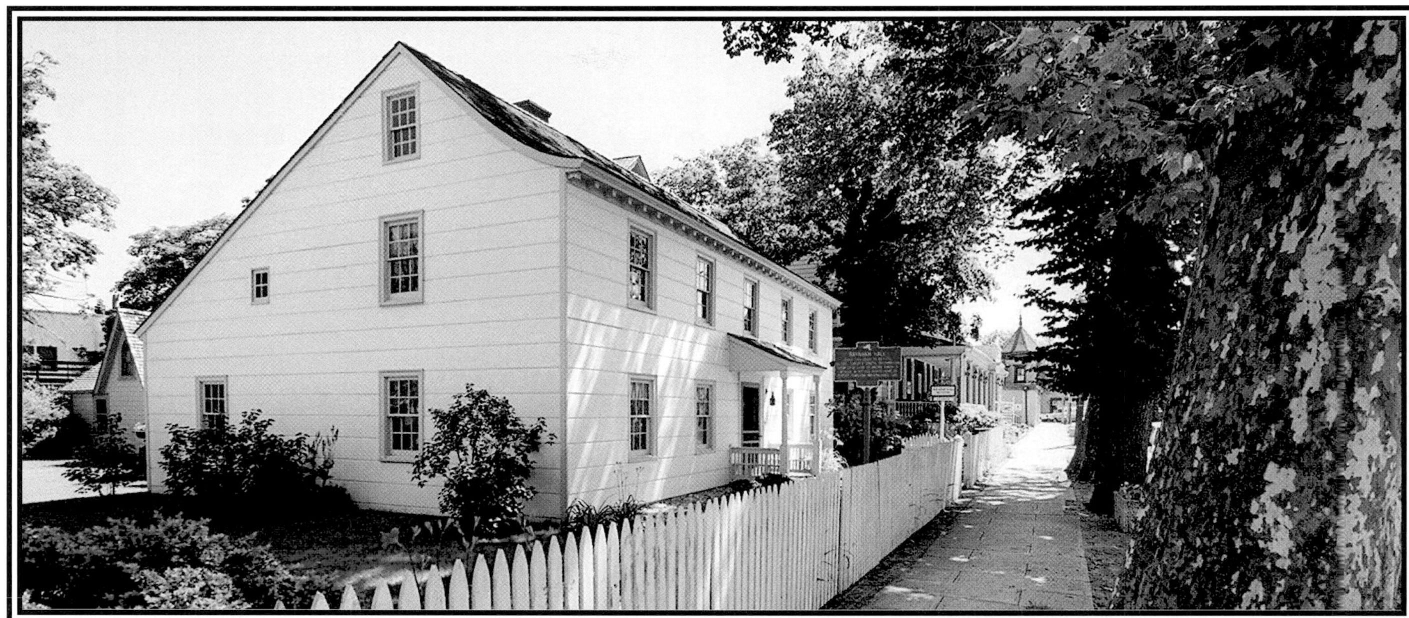

Raynham Hall, built in 1738, was home to the Townsends, including Robert Townsend, a member of the Culper ring that spied on the British for Washington. The hall, at 20 W. Main St., Oyster Bay, is open Tuesday through Sunday, 1-5 p.m.

Newsday Photo / Bill Davis

Unraveling the case of the Patriot spy who never was

The Mystery of Agent 355

BY GEORGE DEWAN
STAFF WRITER

Girl Who Spied for Washington
Died on Wallabout Prison Ship

Say Child Was
Born to Her in
Hulk of Vessel

This grotesque headline, sad and yet deliciously wicked, appeared in the Brooklyn Eagle on May 30, 1948. The Culper Spy Ring story behind it has been eagerly repeated ever since by writers who refer to the unidentified spy as Agent 355. Or the Mysterious Lady. Or Madame X.

Here is a mystery that lingered long after the story of the spy ring was pieced together. And there's more.

The father of the child, the lover of Agent 355, was said to be the lifelong bachelor Robert Townsend of Oyster Bay, known in the revolutionary spy business as Culper Jr. Agent 355, the story goes, was captured by the British and thrown aboard the prison ship Jersey, where she later died. But the lovechild survived and became a respectable citizen named Robert Townsend Jr. The problem is that the story, though widely believed, is not true.

Is this, then, an exculpation of Robert Townsend? Not exactly. Through some very nice detective work by two skeptical writers working independently of each other, Culper Jr. is still found to have a skeleton in his closet.

The fact is that Townsend did have a son named Robert Townsend Jr. born out of wedlock. But Robert Jr.'s mother was not in the Culper Spy Ring. She was Mary Banvard, an immigrant from Nova Scotia, who was Townsend's housekeeper in his New York apartment. Robert Jr. was not born until Feb. 1, 1784 — his mother was then 24 and Townsend 30 — after the war was over and the spy ring disbanded. The baby was raised by his mother, who later married someone else.

Part of the story appeared in the winter, 1993, edition of the Long Island Forum, in an article written by Estelle D. Lockwood of the Three Village Historical Society. Then, in 1995, in a detailed, three-part series that appeared in the New York Genealogical and Biographical Record (copyrighted by Dorothy Horton McGee, the Oyster Bay Town historian), writer Harry Macy seems to settle the question once and for all.

Supporters of the myth about the mother's death on the prison ship Jersey point to Robert Jr.'s connection to a memorial to those who died on the prison ships as proof that his mother was one of them. But the facts don't bear this out.

Raynham Hall Museum

This ink drawing of Patriot spy Robert Townsend was done by his nephew, Peter, in 1813.

Robert Jr. became a carpenter, but he developed a lifelong interest in politics and government and was elected to a term in the New York State Assembly in 1836. He joined the Tammany Society in 1807, Macy writes, and he was soon appointed to seven-member Wallabout Committee, which was planning the memorial — now known as the Prison Ship Martyrs Monument at Brooklyn's Fort Greene Park. As a member of this committee, Robert Jr.'s name was included on the cornerstone that was laid for the monument in 1808. But there is no evidence that his support of the memorial was anything more than civic duty.

It is the family scrapbook of Robert Jr.'s cousin, Solomon Townsend, that gave Lockwood proof that Robert Jr.'s mother was not the mystery spy. The scrapbook is owned by Raynham Hall Museum in Oyster Bay, the longtime Townsend family home. In it, Solomon writes that Robert Jr. was accepted in the family as Robert Townsend's son. But the mother, who Solomon did not name, was the housekeeper in the New York apartment, which Robert Townsend shared with his brother William, and another unidentified relative. In fact, Solomon suggests it was possible that William was the father of the boy, not Robert. However, Robert Townsend accepted the child as his responsibility, and paid for his education.

Macy, it turns out, was researching the story at the same time as Lockwood, and what he produced two years later is a lengthy genealogical record of Robert Jr. Macy found out the name of Robert Jr.'s mother, and detailed his political involvement that led to the creation of the memorial to the prison ship dead.

This seems to put to rest the legend of Agent 355, the spy who never was. The question is, how did it begin in the first place?

The answer lies with the former Suffolk County historian, Morton Pennypacker, who wrote a number of books and articles about the Culper Spy Ring. In a 1948 book, Pennypacker told for the first time the story about a bold female spy who bore Townsend's child and who later died on a prison ship, with the child placed in the care of an unidentified benefactor. The problem is that little evidence was presented by Pennypacker to back it up.

The only hint that there was even a woman involved at all is in a single line in a coded letter to Washington dated Aug. 15, 1779, by Culper Sr., Abraham Woodhull of Setauket. The line read:

I intend to visit 727 [New York] before long and think by the assistance of a 355 [lady] of my acquaintance, shall be able to out wit them all.

There was no Agent 355; the number 355 meant simply the word "lady" just as the code number 371 meant "man." There may have been a woman in New York who assisted Woodhull in some manner in the early stages of the spy ring. Nothing else is known of her.

The lady remains but a cipher.

PAUL TOWNSEND

Paul Townsend figures that in addition to being relatives separated by two centuries, he and Robert Townsend — the spy known as Culper Jr. — are brothers-under-the-skin.

"I've always enjoyed the fact that Robert Townsend was in business in New York City, and he wrote a column for Rivington's Gazette," Townsend said. "I'm a columnist and he was a columnist. I'm in business and he was in business."

Townsend, who is 78, is a columnist, editor and owner of the Long Island Business News. A former public relations consultant, the Bellport resident took over the paper in 1953 and made it into a major business force on Long Island.

Morton Pennypacker unraveled important stories of Long Island's history

Passionate About the Past

BY GEORGE DEWAN
STAFF WRITER

One of the Culper Spy Ring's deepest secrets eluded historical detectives for almost a century and a half. The real name of the spy known as Culper Jr. was not uncovered until 1939, and the sleuth was a dedicated amateur historian named Morton Pennypacker.

It was Pennypacker who discovered, with the help of a handwriting analyst, that the mystery spy was Robert Townsend. For 10 years, Pennypacker had searched for handwriting to compare to that in letters written to Gen. George Washington by Culper Jr. He finally came across "a chest of old documents" that was once the property of Robert Townsend of Oyster Bay.

"It was found that the paper upon which they were written was identical," Pennypacker wrote. "The same watermark, the same shade, the same weight, the same laid marks minutely varying one from the other on the same sheet, but corresponding exactly with all the little variations and flaws with other sheets among the Townsend Papers. The handwriting, looking so similar, was not declared identical until the world's greatest expert, Albert S. Osborn, had examined it."

That Pennypacker should make such a discovery was not surprising. Once he was asked by a reporter why he was such a passionate collector of books and documents having to do with Long Island history. The answer was simple — he was in love, he said.

"I'm doing this because I love Long Island and its history makers," Pennypacker said in a Dec. 4, 1923, interview in the Brooklyn Daily Eagle. "They were splendid men and women. If people knew how interesting it all is, there would be more of them following in my lines. I am passionately fond of the work, and it is more than a hobby — it is a love."

Although he was not a professional historian, Pennypacker, who died in 1956 at age 84, had a remarkable effect on Long Island history. He published a number of books and articles, but his most notable contribution was a collection of books, pamphlets, maps and historic manuscripts that became the foundation for the Pennypacker Long Island Collection at the East Hampton Free Library.

It is ironic that such a dedicated Long Islander as Pennypacker was not born or reared on Long Island at all. He was born Frank Knox Morton Pennypacker in Philadelphia on Aug. 13, 1872. The son of a merchant, Pennypacker was educated at home and never attended college. He learned the trade of printing, and for 18 years he and his brothers ran a printing plant in Asbury Park, N.J. He later took a job as a salesman with the Osborne Advertising Co. in New York, and moved to Kew Gardens, then Mineola and, eventually, East Hampton. He worked for Osborne from 1920 to 1952.

East Hampton Library

Ettie Hedges Pennypacker and husband Morton Pennypacker in 1946 portraits by William Whittemore; Ettie was the East Hampton Library's first librarian.

But it was Long Island history that attracted Pennypacker, and he began collecting Long Island materials during the 1920s, sometimes item by item, other times in entire collections from other collectors. As part of his job, he traveled all over the Island, and as his collection grew, he began looking for a public place to deposit it. In 1930, the East Hampton Library became the happy recipient of what turned out to be 7,314 items, of which 2,600 were books, the rest pamphlets, clippings, manuscripts, maps and other historical miscellany.

There were many attractions for Pennypacker in East Hampton. Not the least of these was Ettie Hedges, who had been named the library's first librarian in 1898 at the age of 19. In 1936, Hedges and Pennypacker were married, settling in the Hedges' old family house down the street from the library. It was the first marriage for both. She was 57; he was 63.

Pennypacker, who was Suffolk County historian from 1943 to 1954, is perhaps best-known for his books — "The Two Spies," about Nathan Hale and Robert Townsend, and "General Washington's Spies on Long Island and New York," an exhaustive study of the Long Island spy system.

His passion, however, may have led him to conclusions about other aspects of the spy ring that are historically troubling. In his 1939 book, Pennypacker told a completely undocumented story about how the Culper Spy Ring was instrumental in the capture in 1780 of Maj. John Andre, the British spy, as he was about to meet secretly with Gen. Benedict Arnold at West Point. The story gives much of the credit to Townsend's sister, Sarah (or Sally), whose Oyster Bay home was then occupied by the British.

In his 1953 book, "The Traitor and the Spy," historian James Thomas Flexner wrote, "The story is told in such detail that many documents would be needed for substantiation; Pennypacker cites no sources. Furthermore, the anecdote does not stand to reason."

A second Pennypacker story is equally suspicious. In 1948, he told, for the first time, a story about a mysterious female in New York City who not only assisted Townsend, but became his lover. She became pregnant, was arrested by the British and thrown aboard the prison ship Jersey, where she died. The baby, the story ends, survived as Robert Townsend Jr. Though the story has been retold and heavily embellished by subsequent writers, it has recently been shown to be totally untrue.

Pennypacker also was the first person to claim — incorrectly, it seems — that the so-called Hulbert flag predated Betsy Ross' flag as the first Stars and Stripes.

Pennypacker's reputation, however, is based primarily on his creation of the Long Island Collection in East Hampton, a treasure trove of local history.

THE LONG ISLAND COLLECTION

This collection is . . . the history of Long Island, the first of the first editions.
— Morton Pennypacker, Sept. 10, 1931

There is something for every researcher in the Long Island Collection housed in two recently remodeled rooms at the rear of the East Hampton Library on Main Street. Novels and poetry written about Long Island or by Long Islanders. Materials on the Quakers, agriculture, Long Island history, churches. There are maps, town records and fascinating old diaries and sermons by Long Island preachers. There is Vol. 1, No. 1 of Frothingham's Long Island Herald, the first newspaper published on Long Island, in Sag Harbor. There is even a book in Latin published in 1475, a few years after Johann Gutenberg introduced moveable type to Europe. The collection is open to the public from Monday through Saturday, 1-4:30 p.m.

East Hampton Library

Morton Pennypacker at work in an undated photograph

Benjamin Tallmadge, the revolutionary spy, soldier and hero from Setauket

Leading the Charge

BY GEORGE DEWAN
STAFF WRITER

Here is how William Patchin, a 19-year-old foot soldier from Connecticut, saw his commanding officer, Maj. Benjamin Tallmadge of Setauket:

He was a large, strong, and powerful man and rode a large bay horse which he took from the British. He was a brave officer, and there was no flinch in him. He was a man of few words, but decided and energetic, and what he said was to the purpose.

A confidant of Gen. George Washington, Benjamin Tallmadge was one of the most exceptional Long Islanders to come out of the Revolutionary War. Not only did he lead a number of important whaleboat raids from Connecticut to Long Island, he was chief of Washington's secret service. Also, his name will be forever linked with the British spy, Maj. John Andre, who was captured and hanged in connection with Benedict Arnold's treason.

This is quite a load to carry for a man who was only 22 when the Declaration of Independence was signed in 1776.

Descended from a line of Tallmadges who had their roots in England, he was born in Setauket Feb. 25, 1754, the son of a minister. By the time he entered Yale College at age 15, he already had learned Greek and Latin from private tutors. He was a classmate and friend of Nathan Hale's, and, like Hale, he became a schoolteacher in Connecticut. On June 20, 1776, he was appointed a lieutenant in the Connecticut militia.

Tallmadge was at the Battle of Long Island on Aug. 27, where his brother William was captured, later to die of starvation in a British prison. By the following April, Tallmadge had risen to the rank of major. He was, as he later put it, "full of ambition and panting for glory."

After one battle near Philadelphia in late 1777, the handsome 23-year-old major rescued a damsel in distress whom he had met at a roadside tavern called the "Rising Sun." He relates the story in his "Memoir of Colonel Benjamin Tallmadge":

After we had made ourselves known to each other, and while she was communicating some intelligence to me, I was informed that the British light horse were advancing. Stepping to the door, I saw them at full speed chasing in my patrols, one of whom they took. I immediately mounted, when I found the young damsel close by my side, entreating that I would protect her. Having not a moment to reflect, I desired her to mount behind me, and in this way I brought her off more than three miles up to Germantown, where she dismounted. During the whole ride, although there was considerable firing of pistols, and not a little wheeling and charging, she remained unmoved, and never once complained of fear after she mounted my horse. I was delighted with this transaction, and received many compliments from those who became acquainted with it.

Teacher, scholar, soldier, spy: Benjamin Tallmadge, George Washington's chief of intelligence and one of the most exceptional Long Islanders to fight in the Revolution

A John Trumbull Sketch From "The American Revolution, A Picture Sourcebook"

LI HISTORY.COM

In his memoirs, Benjamin Tallmadge details life at the front lines of the Revolutionary War. Excerpts of this document are available on the Internet at http://www.lihistory.com. To get a copy of the excerpts, call 1-800-2FIND-OUT, or send $5 to Newsday Library, 235 Pinelawn Rd., Melville, N.Y. 11747-4250.

But Tallmadge had more serious business ahead of him. Washington chose him as his chief of secret service, and as such he led the activities of Long Island's Culper Spy Ring. At the same time, he led attacks on Fort Franklin at Lloyd's Neck, Fort St. George at Mastic, and Fort Slongo at what is now Fort Salonga.

Tallmadge played a key role in the capture of the 30-year-old Maj. Andre in the affair of the turncoat Benedict Arnold in 1780. Arnold, who had taken command of West Point, conspired to surrender it to the British. The London-born Andre, a charming and personable man to whom both men and women were attracted, was chief of intelligence for the British, and an excellent officer. Tallmadge, too, would come under his spell.

On Sept. 23, 1780, after a secret meeting with Arnold behind American lines in Westchester County, Andre — who was using the alias "John Anderson" — was captured by three militiamen. He was taken to North Castle, where Lt. Col. John Jameson was in command of American troops. After Andre produced papers signed by Arnold, Jameson sent him on his way to West Point.

Tallmadge, who was operating out of North Castle, arrived later in the day and suspected foul play. Though he was Jameson's subordinate, he managed to have troops go out and bring "John Anderson" back. Andre revealed his true identity. Although Arnold got away, Andre, after a trial, was hanged as a spy at Tappan, N.Y., on Oct. 2, 1780.

In the days following Andre's capture and leading up to his execution, Tallmadge found himself drawn closer and closer to the major, finding him "a most elegant and accomplished gentleman." In his memoir, he explained his feelings further:

For the few days of intimate intercourse I had with him . . . I became so deeply attached to Major Andre, that I can remember no instance where my affections were so fully absorbed in any man. When I saw him swirling under the gibbet, it seemed for a time as if I could not support it. All the spectators seemed to be overwhelmed by the affecting spectacle, and many were suffused in tears.

But quickly, Tallmadge was thrust back into the turmoil of war, and three years later it was officially over. In 1784 Tallmadge married Mary Floyd, daughter of William Floyd of Mastic. He became a businessman in Litchfield, Conn., and then served from 1801 to 1817 in Congress. He married Maria Hallet of New York after the death of his first wife, and he died in 1835.

At age 23, Tallmadge was panting for glory. When he died at age 81, he was covered in it.

ORIGINAL SOURCE

RISKING HIS LIFE FOR HIS HORSE

It was not just damsels in distress that Benjamin Tallmadge liked to rescue when the bullets began to fly. His horse got the same treatment.

One of the last men to escape on the boats that ferried the Americans safely across the East River after the failed Battle of Long Island in August, 1776, Tallmadge had left his horse tied to a post at the ferry in Brooklyn. But then he had second thoughts, as he related in his memoir:

The troops having now all safely reached New York, and the fog continuing as thick as ever, I began to think of my favorite horse, and requested leave to return and bring him off. Having obtained permission, I called for a crew of volunteers to go with me, and guiding the boat myself, I obtained my horse and got off some distance into the river before the enemy appeared in Brooklyn. As soon as they reached the ferry we were saluted merrily from their musketry, and finally by their field pieces; but we returned in safety.

— George DeWan

Americans and British cross Long Island Sound to stage surprise raids

Whaleboat Warfare

BY GEORGE DEWAN
STAFF WRITER

At 1 p.m. on May 23, 1777, the Patriots began striking back at occupied Long Island.

Leaving Guilford, Conn., with 170 men in 13 whaleboats, escorted by two armed sloops, Lt. Col. Return Jonathan Meigs crossed Long Island Sound, skillfully avoiding armed British vessels. The raiding party landed about 6 p.m. on what is now Hashamomuck Beach in Southold, one of the narrowest points on the North Fork.

What took place early the next morning is commemorated on a granite monument near the Old Whalers' Church in Sag Harbor. The Battle of Sag Harbor was worth a monument.

Meigs and his troops — men like Elnathan Jennings of Southampton and Christopher Vail of Southold — carried their boats across 300 yards of land, reentered the water and rowed across Southold Bay and Shelter Island Sound, landing at midnight on the beach four miles west of Sag Harbor.

At 2 a.m., Meigs struck, taking the British, many of whom were drunk, completely by surprise. The raiders burned 12 brigs and sloops, killed six men and captured 90, then returned with their prisoners the same way they came. Without losing a man, they were back in Connecticut 25 hours after they left.

This was whaleboat warfare.

Long Island Sound, however, was a two-way thoroughfare. In fact, the first cross-Sound raid was made by the British. On April 25, 1777, Gen. William Tryon, the colonial governor of New York, led a 2,000-man force across the water to destroy part of Danbury, Conn. The sortie by Meigs was in retaliation for Tryon's raid.

These whaleboats were of the type used for offshore whaling, though many were probably built solely for the purpose of revolutionary warfare. They were fast, and they were double-ended, for two-way rowing and for better handling in rough surf. Light enough to be carried on men's shoulders, the boats could be fitted with a single sail, and usually carried a small, swivel cannon in front. Six or eight oars were standard.

Most of the Patriot raids were made in Suffolk County, where anti-British sentiment was strongest. British forts at Lloyd Neck (Fort Franklin), what is now Fort Salonga (Fort Slongo), Mastic (Fort St. George) and Sag Harbor were successfully attacked. However, a raid on Setauket was repulsed by the British. The British made later raids on Greenwich, New Haven, Fairfield, Norwalk and New London.

The Setauket School

Benjamin Tallmadge, sword raised, leads a raid on Mastic after reaching the Island with 80 men in 10 boats. The painting is by Vance Locke.

The most spectacular Patriot whaleboat raid was made on Fort St. George in Mastic in the fall of 1780, led by 26-year-old Maj. Benjamin Tallmadge, Gen. George Washington's spy chief. The strategically placed fort had been built a month or so earlier by Loyalist troops from Rhode Island at the Manor of St. George on Smith's Point. The triangular fort included two houses from the manor in two corners, and an additional fortification in the third. The fort served as a supply base for British forces.

At 4 p.m. on Nov. 21, 1780, Tallmadge and 80 men shoved off in their whaleboats from Fairfield, Conn., landing at 9 p.m. at Old Man's — now Mount Sinai. After a rain delay, they began their march the next day, arriving at the fort before sunup Nov. 23. With the prearranged cry of "Washington and glory!" three detachments attacked the fort, and it was quickly taken. But the main body of the British garrison was in the two houses. In a later memoir, Tallmadge told what happened next:

While we were standing, elated with victory, in the centre of the fort, a volley of musketry was discharged from the windows of one of the large houses, which induced me to order my whole detachment to load and return the fire. I soon found it necessary to lead the column directly to the house, which, being strongly barricaded, required the aid of the pioneers with their axes. As soon as the troops could enter, the confusion and conflict were great. A considerable portion of those who had fired after the fort was taken, and the colors had been struck, were thrown headlong from the windows of the second story to the ground. Having forfeited their lives by the usages of war, all would have been killed had I not ordered the slaughter to cease.

Tallmadge then had his men turn the fort's guns on a nearby ship, burning it to the water line. Then they destroyed the fort. By 8 a.m. it was over. Seven Loyalists were killed or wounded and 53 officers and men captured. Tallmadge lost no men, and only one was wounded.

"All things were now secured and quiet," Tallmadge wrote, "and I had never seen the sun rise more pleasantly."

Tallmadge was not finished. Taking a dozen men — including 33-year-old Caleb Brewster, who was Agent 725, the whaleboat captain in the Culper Spy Ring — and mounting them on Loyalist horses taken from the fort, Tallmadge headed for the 300 tons of hay stored at Coram. He sent the main body of troops with the prisoners back to the whaleboats. Reaching Coram in an hour and a half, Tallmadge's men overcame the guards, set fire to the hay, and went on to rendezvous with his troops. They reached the whaleboats at 4 p.m. on Nov. 23. By midnight they had crossed the Sound and were back in Fairfield.

Although Washington was pleased with Tallmadge's work, and Congress passed a resolution praising him, Loyalists saw the Battle of Fort St. George in a different light. Here is an excerpt from a Dec. 2, 1780, news report in the Royal Gazette, a Tory newspaper:

Mr. Isaac Hart of Newport in Rhode Island, formerly an eminent merchant and ever a loyal subject, was inhumanly fired upon and bayoneted, wounded in fifteen different parts of his body, and beat with their muskets in the most shocking manner in the very act of imploring quarter, and died of his wounds in a few hours after, universally regretted by every true lover of his King and country . . . A poor woman was also fired upon at another house and barbarously wounded through both breasts, of which wound she now lingers a specimen of rebel savageness and degeneracy.

LI HISTORY.COM

Past installments and enhancements to Long Island: Our Story are available on the Internet at Newsday's special site, http://www.lihistory.com.

THE FIRST PURPLE HEART

New Windsor Cantonment State Historic Site

The nation's first Purple Heart was won for bravery in whaleboat raids on Long Island.

The recipient of the medal, originally called the Badge of Military Merit, was 27-year-old Sgt. Elijah Churchill, who enlisted at Enfield, Conn. He was cited for bravery in the 1780 raid on Fort St. George in Mastic and then in the 1781 raid on Fort Slongo, in what is now Fort Salonga, Smithtown.

In creating the medal on Aug. 7, 1782, Gen. George Washington said it was for "any singularly meritorious action." It was not redesigned and reissued as the Purple Heart — for Americans killed or wounded in combat — until 1932.

Fort Slongo was a minor redoubt built on a hilltop near the Sound, and the whaleboat attack took place at dawn on Oct. 3, 1781. The British surrendered within minutes, but not before Churchill, who led the charge, was wounded, the only American casualty.

Churchill's Badge of Military Merit is on display at the New Windsor Cantonment State Historic Site near Newburgh. All that remains of the original fort is a fenced-in mound of earth in the backyard of a private home.

— George DeWan

Wanton Piracy on the Sound

Not all whaleboat raids on Long Island were made to help defeat the British. Some were made simply for pillage and plunder.

Long Island Sound, and to some extent Great South Bay, teemed with literally thousands of small craft looking for opportunities to pounce on any unsuspecting prey. It could be another boat carrying supplies into New York for the British, or it could be an inland homeowner with something valuable to steal and resell.

Much of this predation was legal, and often it was hard to separate the legal from the illegal. Gov. Jonathan Trumball of Connecticut issued hundreds of commissions allowing specific whaleboats and privateers alike to cruise in the sound, preying on Loyalist and British shipping. In the absence of any navy to speak of, this was a way to put such enemy boats out of commission. The booty was divided among the crew — their pay, so to speak.

One of these whaleboat captains, Peter Hallack, went too far, as did many others like him. On Aug. 11, 1788, Trumball sent this message to Halleck:

[S]undry persons belonging to your or one of your armed boats have, contrary to the tenor of your commission and bond, made descent upon the island of Long Island and plundered the inhabitants of their stocks and effects . . . and in particular have lately violently taken six oxen from Colo. Phineas Fanning . . .

Hallack apparently returned the oxen.

Despite Connecticut's efforts to control the whaleboat privateers, the practice got worse and worse, until, in 1781, the state revoked all the earlier commissions.

There was also something known as the "London" or "Illicit" trade, similar to a 20th-Century black market. Long Islanders who opposed the British publicly were privately stealing agricultural products and animals, and selling them to the British in occupied New York City. On the other hand, New York was well supplied with British imports — tea, pepper, silks and other luxuries — and these would be shipped out of the city on the pretext of being for Loyalist customers on Long Island. But often they would be smuggled across the sound in whaleboats to be sold at inflated prices to Patriots in Connecticut.

Courtesy of Jacqueline Pell Tuttle

Armies in whaleboats approach Long Island from Connecticut in a Rodman Pell painting

"What was undertaken, at first, in a spirit of adventure soon grew to a size both enormous and profitable," wrote Frederic G. Mather in his book, "The Refugees of 1776 from Long Island to Connecticut." For example, an owner of a Long Island store who wanted to get British goods to Patriot friends in Connecticut would import them from New York, then arrange to have the store robbed by whaleboat marauders. Or the owner of a boat would allow himself and his cargo — which belonged to someone else — to be captured. In either case, the confiscated goods would be sold and the profits divided among the plotters.

"The mixed bands which carried on the trade were composed of Whigs, Tories, Refugees, American and British soldiers, and camp followers from both armies," Mather wrote. "So that, whenever an investigation was ordered, it could not proceed far without hitting friends of the party, or the power, which was making the investigation. And there seemed to be no disgrace in the practice; for nothing popular is ever disgraceful."

As for the whaleboat activity on the Great South Bay, Thomas Jones of Massapequa, the well-known Loyalist judge, later wrote about it with contempt:

The rebels having nothing to fear, sailed down the bay as far as Rockaway, within 15 miles of the city, and destroyed all the wood boats, hay boats, coasters, canoes, and floats, belonging to the inhabitants on the south side of the island. They frequently landed, robbed the inhabitants of their furniture, linen, wearing apparel, money, negroes, rum, wine, sugar and salt; killed their cattle, hogs, sheep and poultry; and burnt their hay, their oats, wheat, rye and Indian corn.

Despite all the official efforts to stop the illicit trade and the plundering by the whaleboaters, it ceased only with the end of the war. No longer popular, it once again became disgraceful.

— George DeWan

Small relics tell the story of British strongholds from the Revolution

History Is Her Fort

BY MOLLY MCCARTHY
STAFF WRITER

A spent musketball embedded in a clear plastic block hangs from a wall in a church foyer. A red sandstone headstone of a long-dead soldier rests in the garden wall of a Victorian estate. And a corner of a back lawn rises into a grassy mound half the size of a tennis court.

They are hints of history, the subtlest traces of a dramatic episode in Long Island's past when American patriots, thirsting for independence, took up arms against their English rulers. They are reminders of the British forts that once dotted the Island's coastline.

Fort Franklin. Fort Slongo. Fort Setauket. Fort St. George. Sag Harbor Fort. Patriot raiders from Connecticut, slinking ashore from swift-moving whaleboats, targeted these strategic strongholds in hopes of weakening the enemy's grip on Long Island.

Helen Gurland with the remains of the British Fort Slongo in her backyard in Fort Salonga. The mound measures about 40 feet by 40 feet.

None of the forts has survived. Some, like Sag Harbor Fort and Fort St. George in Mastic, are marked by a simple stone monument or brass plaque. At Sag Harbor, a boulder placed in 1902 reads: "A British Fort near this spot was captured by the Americans under Lieut. Col. Meigs at the Battle of Sag Harbor, May 23, 1777." Tourists must take the monument's word that something important once happened there.

But there are other spots that boast more than a plaque or monument — that betray slight signs of a turbulent time.

Nearly 200 years after Maj. Benjamin Tallmadge led a raid on Fort Slongo, Helen Gurland was scanning real-estate listings for a new home. She was intrigued by an ad for a Fort Salonga ranch with a "historic site on the property."

The "historic site" turned out to be the remains of Fort Slongo. On Oct. 3, 1781, Tallmadge and his men killed two British soldiers, captured 21 more and burned the stockaded fort to the ground.

"It's not much of anything to look at," said Gurland, a science teacher at Friends Academy in Locust Valley who has lived in her ranch home since 1971. "It was really the house, in the end, and not the fort that made me buy it."

Bordered by a few trees and bushes, the fort's remnants are snuggled in a corner of Gurland's backyard. Rising about two feet from the rolling lawn, the sides of the embankment form a flat-top square. A small garden grows in its center.

But a dense stand of trees blocks any view of the nearby Long Island Sound. Gurland doesn't even bother bringing students to see it. "They'd stand there and say, 'Where's the fort?' "

Still, Gurland visited the Library of Congress to see the crude map Tallmadge used to find the fort. "The accounts say the rebels landed at Crab Meadow Beach, but that's an awfully long walk," Gurland says. Then she points out a depression in the woods behind the fort. "That could be the ravine they're talking about where the rebels came up."

FAST FORWARD

Yesterday's Events Making News Today

About 10 miles east of Gurland's home, a half-dozen worshippers gather for a noon service in The Caroline Church of Brookhaven, a 269-year-old building on the edge of Setauket's village green. Sitting on soft, red cushions in bright white pews, the parishioners recite the Lord's Prayer led by the church rector. In the summer of 1777, British soldiers, praying to God and the king, worshipped where the parishioners now stand.

The soldiers at Fort Setauket didn't have far to walk to reach the Caroline Church, then an Anglican church named for King George II's wife. It was only a few yards across the village green from the Presbyterian Church the British converted into a fortified outpost.

Rebels attacked the fort in August, 1777. But the Patriots soon retreated when word came that British ships were en route from Huntington. Although the Presbyterian Church burned after being struck by lightning several years after the war, the Caroline Church endured.

"Many of the congregants had to leave Long Island after the war because they were considered traitors," said David Elling, the Caroline's junior warden. "I'm eternally grateful to them for all their hardships. The church is there because of all the sacrifices those people went through."

During a renovation in the 1930s, a musketball was extracted from one of the church walls. The flattened chunk of lead was encased in plastic and hung in the foyer. The gold-lettered inscription reads: "Found embedded in church wall near Southwest corner in 1936. Doubtless a relic of Battle of Setauket of 1777."

Elling says the legacy is probably more doubtful than doubtless. "It could have been left 50 years later by a boy shooting at squirrels with his grandfather's gun. There is just no way of proving it."

At least two raids were carried out at Fort Franklin, situated on a high bluff on the western edge of Lloyd Neck with a clear view of Oyster Bay and Cold Spring Harbors. The first attack, run by Tallmadge in September, 1779, was an overwhelming success, although the fort was left intact. The second, tried two years later with a French garrison, was a bust.

A century after Tallmadge's victory, workers unearthed a cache of relics while digging a foundation for a summer mansion. They recovered musket shot and cannonballs and found the gravestone of a Loyalist soldier in a nearby field. All were built into the mansion's garden wall.

"As for other visible remains, there's really nothing," said Robert MacKay, director of the Society for the Preservation of Long Island Antiquities. "There are two embankments left that form the inner courtyard, but they had to cut into the berms during the restoration. They replaced it with clean fill. They're a little too perfect looking."

But, perhaps the most striking reminder of Fort Franklin is the site's commanding view. "It's one of the most dramatic views on Long Island," says MacKay. "If you think about the Revolution and the way the channel hugs the Lloyd Neck shore, you can control the channel and, hence, control the two harbors. And that was the raison d'etre for Fort Franklin."

Gathering up what remains of these few forts would make for a rather anemic exhibition. Yet the legacies are enriched by the people who come across them year after year. Nudged by a small remembrance of the past, they wonder what those days must have been like when war ruled Long Island.

Pushing a lawnmower over her misshapen back lawn this past summer, Gurland was struck by an idea. "I was thinking that this fall, on the anniversary of the battle, I should invite the neighborhood over for a get-together in the backyard," she said. "Many of them have never even seen the fort."

Newsday Photos / Bill Davis

The headstone of a Loyalist soldier, as well as cannonballs and musket shot found at the site of Fort Franklin in Lloyd Neck, have been built into a wall at a private mansion.

Blacks fought on both sides in the War of Independence, but gained little

Revolution's Unseen Rebels

Part of a 1996 sculpture by Ed Dwight depicting Revolution-era blacks, including one as a soldier.

If the Revolutionary War had been photographed, the participation of blacks would have been appreciated generations ago.
— **Ellen Gibson Wilson, "The Loyal Blacks"**

BY GEORGE DEWAN
STAFF WRITER

When the war came in the summer of 1776, Benjamin Whitecuff and his older brother, both free blacks, worked on their father's 60-acre farm near Hempstead. But they were on opposite sides of the war. Whitecuff became a spy for the British; his father and brother joined the Continental army.

Whitecuff was credited with saving 2,000 British troops in one engagement in New Jersey. One time at Cranbury, N.J., he was caught by Patriot troops and hanged, but after three minutes he was saved by a British cavalry unit. His father and brother, whose names are not known, were both killed in battle near Germantown, Pa.

This illustrates one of the era's best-kept nonsecrets: Blacks played an important role in the Revolutionary War. What is more, they fought on both sides, sometimes actually shooting at each other. Which is a great irony, since they presumably were fighting for the same thing — their own personal freedom.

In 1776, there were 500,000 blacks within a total American population of 2.5 million. About 5,000 blacks, the majority of them slaves, fought on the American side, about one-sixth of the total military. At least twice that number joined up on the British side, although the exact number is not known. Even though the first American death in the war was a black man, Crispus Attucks, killed at the 1770 Boston Massacre, blacks saw limited service on the Patriot side in the early years of the Revolution. After an extended debate in 1775, the Continental Congress — because of heavy opposition from southern colonies — forbade further recruitment of slaves and free blacks in the military, but allowed free blacks to re-enlist. As manpower needs became more acute, blacks were actively recruited.

The change was the result of a very early British policy of openly seeking blacks. "The number of blacks who fled to the British ran into the tens of thousands," Benjamin Quarles wrote in his book, "The Negro in the American Revolution." This included blacks on Long Island and in New York. "Most often Negroes worked as teamsters; at one time most of the drivers in the city's quartermaster department were runaway slaves, working for wages and housed in separate barracks . . . On Long Island — at Flushing and Jamaica — the British employed Negroes in the forage service."

Black men fought and died with the British at the Battle of Long Island in late August, 1776. Later that year, in a skirmish at Setauket, troops from Rhode Island took two dozen British prisoners, six of whom were black. The British actively recruited among Long Island blacks. "The Tories at Coram are beating up for volunteers to join our enemies," the Patriot Col. Henry B. Livingston wrote in the fall of 1776. "Negroes as well as whites are taken into pay."

Black Americans were used heavily by both sides as seamen. "The use of Negro sailors [by the Americans] was easily acceptable because there was nothing novel about it," Quarles said. "The waterways of the Atlantic coast bred black seafaring men as well as white."

The recruitment of free blacks by the Americans, especially in the North, became common by 1777. By 1779, slaves also were being recruited. Many enlisted, but they went into the military by other means as well. It was a common practice at that time to allow someone with a militia obligation to use a substitute, and many whites used black men — sometimes their own slaves — as substitutes. They served as soldiers and sailors, but also as cooks, servants, laborers, guides and teamsters.

On Long Island, as elsewhere, there were black slaves who saw the military as a way to gain their freedom. Early in the war, Maj. Gen. Edward Hand of Pennsylvania received a letter from a Long Island slave named Charles, who, with his wife and daughter, had fled from his master, but was captured by one of Hand's regiments and sold back into slavery. In his letter, Charles said that he was "ever ready under your honors command to fight against all enemys of the Honble. United States in defense of liberty and the rights of mankind." It is unlikely that Charles was taken up on his offer.

"Many slaves who came into British hands were merely victims of military force," Quarles wrote. ". . . Many more slaves, however, voluntarily deserted to the British. They had no particular love for England, but they believed that the English officers would give them their freedom."

But in neither the British nor the Patriot cause was military service a guarantee of freedom. Many who fought on both sides were forced back into slavery after it was over. The British, who had promised freedom to blacks who fought for them, did, however, ship thousands to Nova Scotia, London and the Caribbean.

Like thousands of other black Loyalists who fought on the losing side in the Revolution, Benjamin Whitecuff went to Nova Scotia after the war. Later, he ended up in London, where he and a number of ex-slaves unsuccessfully sought government pensions. The Loyalist Claims Commission said they had gained their freedom, and could expect no more than that.

FAST FORWARD

REMEMBERING BLACKS WHO FOUGHT IN THE REVOLUTION

The 5,000 blacks who fought on the Patriot side in the Revolutionary War are slated to get their own memorial on the Mall in the nation's capital, between the Lincoln Memorial and the Washington Monument. The Black Patriots Foundation must complete the raising of $9.5 million by Oct. 27 to pay for the Black Revolutionary War Patriots Memorial. Plans call for two complementary curved and sloping walls, one bronze and one granite, showing both historical text and relief figures of black men, women and children brought to this continent.

A rendering of the proposed Black Revolutionary War Patriots Memorial; artist Ed Dwight's mock-up sculpture at the top of this page would be enlarged for the site.

Jupiter Hammon of Lloyd Neck, subservient or subversive?

America's First Black Poet

BY GEORGE DEWAN
STAFF WRITER

A few years after the end of the Revolutionary War, America's first black poet sat in his slave quarters on Lloyd's Neck and composed an eloquent address to his brethren. He looked back at the war and the cause of liberty for which it was fought, and concluded that liberty should be not only be for whites, but for his fellow slaves as well.

"That liberty is a great thing we may know from our own feelings, and we may likewise judge so from the conduct of the white people in the late war," Jupiter Hammon wrote in his most important non-poetic work, "An Address to the Negroes in the State of New-York," published in 1787.

Then the 76-year-old man added a poignant message that might have been addressed more to his white masters than to his black brethren:

I must say that I have hoped that God would open their eyes, when they were so much engaged for liberty, to think of the state of the poor blacks, and to pity us.

It would be another 40 years before slavery would end in New York State. Curiously, while Hammon approved of liberty for his fellow slaves, he did not want it for himself. He seems to have felt that he was too old to make it on his own.

. . . for my part I do not wish to be free, yet I should be glad if others, especially the young Negroes, were to be free; for many of us who are grown up slaves, and have always had masters to take care of us, should hardly know how to take care of ourselves; and it may be more for our own comfort to remain as we are.

It has only been during the 20th Century that Hammon — who was born, lived and died a slave on Long Island — has been given credit for being the first black American poet. This honor had earlier been given to the remarkable and much better-known Phillis Wheatley, who had been abducted in Africa and sold into slavery, eventually becoming the star of Boston literary salons. But Hammon's first poem, a heavily religious work titled "An Evening Thought. Salvation by Christ, with Penetential Cries," was published in 1760, a full 10 years before Wheatley's work.

Hammon was born the son of slaves on Oct. 17, 1711, on the Lloyd estate at what was then called the Manor of Queens Village, on Lloyd's Neck. He was first owned by Henry Lloyd, then passed down to Joseph Lloyd, and finally, John Lloyd. It is not certain what work he performed, but he seems to have had a special status. He was taught along with the other children on the manor by a Harvard-educated schoolmaster. "Hammon was an intelligent and privileged slave, respected by his master for his skill with tools, and by his fellow slaves for his power as a preacher," Langston Hughes once wrote of him.

AN
ADDRESS
TO THE
NEGROES
In the STATE of NEW-YORK,
BY JUPITER HAMMON,
Servant of JOHN LLOYD, jun, Esq; of the Manor of Queen's Village, Long-Island.

"Of a truth I perceive that God is no respecter of "persons:
"But in every Nation, he that feareth him and "worketh righteousness, is accepted with him."— Acts x. 34, 35.

NEW-YORK:
Printed by CARROLL and PATTERSON
No. 32, Maiden-Lane,

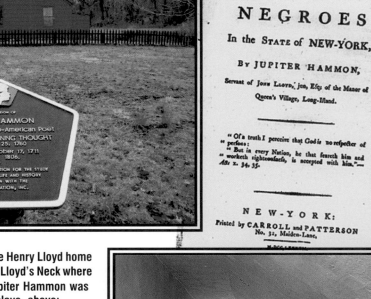

The Henry Lloyd home on Lloyd's Neck where Jupiter Hammon was a slave, above; at right are a copy of his 1787 statement about freedom, and a top-floor room possibly used by Hammon. Maintained by the Lloyd Harbor Historical Society, the home is open to the public by special appointment.

Newsday Photos / Bill Davis

LEGACY

VERSE OF JUPITER HAMMON

While in Hartford in 1782, Jupiter Hammon completed a poem that addressed slave children directly about the present life and the hereafter. It was titled "A Poem for Children with Thoughts on Death." Here are two stanzas:

Remember youth the time is
short,
Improve the present day.
And pray that God may guide
your thoughts,
And teach your lips to pray.

To pray unto the most high
God,
And beg restraining grace.
Then by the power of his word,
You'll see the Savior's face.

Apparently allowed to use the library at the manor, Hammon developed a strong control of the English language. Since there is no record of how he earned money, it is surprising to note that when he was 22, he purchased a Bible with Psalms from his master, Henry Lloyd, for seven shillings and sixpence.

When the war and the British occupation came in 1776, the Lloyds fled Long Island and took Hammon with them to Connecticut, living mainly at Hartford and New Haven. He published eight works in his lifetime, including four prose pieces. Half of his work, including a poem titled "An Address to Miss Phillis Wheatley," was published while he was living in Connecticut.

Hammon was writing primarily for a black audience, and his work was religiously evangelical. His themes were biblical, concerning themselves with prayer, salvation, Christ, God's love and life after death. Although he rightfully receives his due as the first black poet, his work has often been savaged by critics. In addition, he is often criticized for being submissive and subservient to the white masters. The black historian J. Saunders Redding has called Hammon's poetry "rhymed prose, doggerel, in which the homely thoughts of a very religious and superstitious man are expressed in very limping phrases."

But there is a more current, revisionist look at Hammon's work that attacks this negative view head-on. In her book, "Jupiter Hammon and the Biblical Beginnings of African-American Literature," Sondra A. O'Neale, the dean of the College of Liberal Arts at Wayne State University in Detroit, argues that, in fact, Hammon was really a subversive. For example, she says that when Hammon urged his fellow blacks to accept Christ, to become baptized and accept communion, he was, in fact, subtlely entreating them to enter into the colonial mainstream. For whites, this meant political enfranchisement and economic empowerment. The implication was that it could do the same thing for blacks.

By 1787, when he published "An Address to the Negroes in the State of New-York," Hammon had long since returned to his slave quarters on Lloyd's Neck. He was getting old. But the details of the rest of his life elude us. It can only be said that he died some time between 1790 and 1806, buried probably in a slave burial plot on the Lloyd property.

Hammon wrote in 1787:

Let all of the time you can get be spent in trying to learn to read. Get those who can read, to learn you; but remember, that what you learn for, is to read the Bible. If there was no Bible, it would be no matter whether you could read or not. Reading other books would do you no good.

LI HISTORY.COM

Another Hammon poem, "A Dialogue Entitled the Kind Master and Dutiful Servant," is available online and dramatizes an exchange between an owner and slave. For a copy, see http://www.lihistory.com on the Internet.

Nations at war shiver through the Northeast's hard winter of 1779-80

Frozen Ducks In the Kitchen

BY GEORGE DEWAN
STAFF WRITER

It was so cold the ducks froze.

The snow began to fall about the 10th of November, 1779, and continued falling almost every day until the middle of the following March. The Northeast virtually shut down. It was known as The Hard Winter, and may have been the coldest these parts have seen since the Wisconsinin glacier.

It was a world of ice. The rivers, creeks and streams on Long Island were frozen solid, as was Upper New York Bay. The East River and the Hudson River could be crossed by foot. British cavalry thundered from Manhattan to Staten Island. Long Island Sound was more ice than water.

As for the frozen ducks, the Long Island Loyalist judge, Thomas Jones, a sober man not usually given to tongue-in-cheek tall tales, passed along a "remarkable if true" story about a Staten Island farmer named Goosen Adriance:

"He went out in the morning upon his farm, which adjoins the water, and going along the shore, he observed a parcel of ducks sitting erect and in their proper posture," Jones wrote in his book, "History of New York During the Revolutionary War." The author continued: "He walked up to them, found them stiff, and as he supposed perfectly dead; he carried them home, threw them down upon the table in his kitchen, where a large wood fire was burning, and went into the next room to breakfast with his family. Scarce was the breakfast over when a great noise and fluttering was heard in the kitchen. Upon opening the door how great the surprise. The supposed dead ducks were all flying about the room."

According to weather historian David M. Ludlum, no winter before or since was as cold.

"Long Island Sound was almost completely clogged with ice, and people were able to cross from Long Island to the vicinity of Stamford on the Connecticut shore for several days," Ludlum writes in "Early American Winters: 1604-1820." "Some Hessian soldiers took advantage of this route in order to escape from their regiments."

Judge Jones, who lived at Fort Neck (now Massapequa), wrote in his book that 200 provision-laden sleighs, pulled by two horses each, escorted by 200 light cavalry, made the five-mile trip from New York to Staten Island. On Long Island, with British occupiers making demands for firewood, cattle and living space, already harsh conditions were made even harsher. Part of Long Island Sound became a highway of ice. "It was so strong, that deserters went upon the ice to Connecticut from Lloyd's Neck, upon Long Island, the distance more than 12 miles."

George Washington's troops were shivering in winter quarters at Morristown, N.J. — one writer said it made Valley Forge of the previous year look like a picnic. But his men occasionally sneaked across the frozen harbor and attacked British troops on Staten Island. The British hauled cannon across the ice from Manhattan to defend themselves.

Washington, an inveterate diary-keeper, has this entry for Jan. 6, 1780: "The snow which in general is 18 inches deep is much drifted — roads impassable." He was apparently referring to the new snowfall from a major storm on that date, since other records indicate there was already close to four feet of snow on the ground.

"In the woods it lay at least four feet upon a level,' Jones wrote. "It was with the utmost difficulty that the farmers got their wood . . . All the wood upon New York Island was cut down. The forest trees planted in gardens, in court yards, in avenues, along lanes, and about the houses of gentlemen by way of ornament, shared the same fate. Quantities of apple trees, peach trees, plum trees, cherry trees, and pear trees, were also cut down."

The New York Packet reported a thermometer reading of 16 below zero in the city. Current records of Central Park readings only go back to 1869, so this would beat the 15 below zero recorded in 1934. The severe cold reached up and down the coast from Maine to Georgia. Ludlum says that the Connecticut Courant in Hartford provided the most complete temperature record. And, due to the lack of sophistication of the newspaper's audience, the editor believed it was necessary to explain the nature of a thermometer and what its readings meant.

When springtime came, New York was depleted of wood. So on June 16, 1780, the new British governor, James Robertson, issued an order to "the inhabitants of Long Island" to furnish wood for the army barracks in the city, "to guard against the severities of a long winter." Their quotas: Kings County, 1,500 cords; Queens, 4,500; western Suffolk, 3,000 cords. The inhabitants of Southold, East Hampton and Southampton were required to cut 3,000 cords from the Smith and Floyd estates at Mastic. They were to be paid at varying rates, but it is not clear whether payments were ever made.

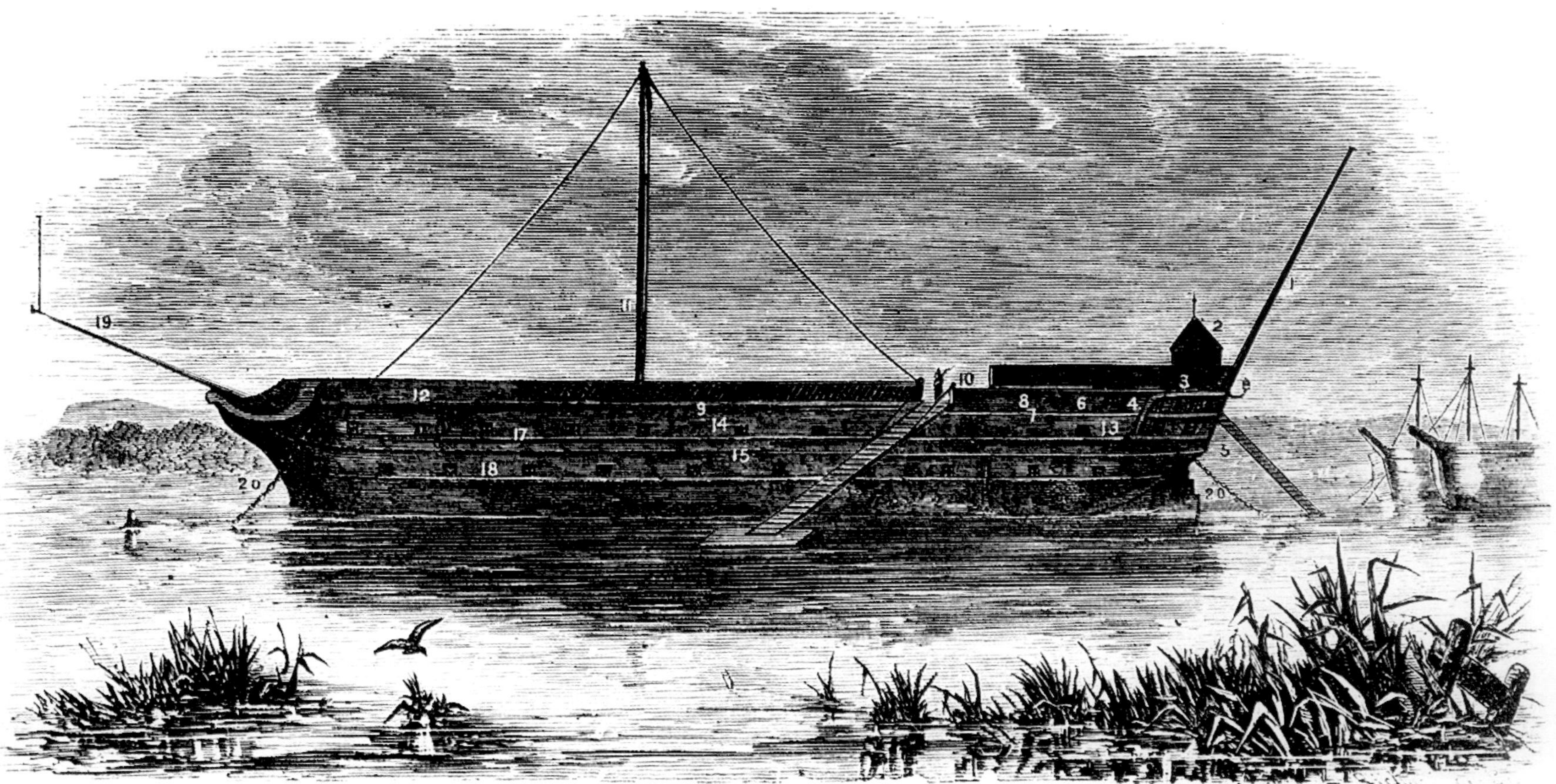

Brooklyn Historical Society

"Turn out your dead!" the British jailers would yell each day on rounds of the prison ship Jersey, anchored off Brooklyn.

BY GEORGE DEWAN
STAFF WRITER

Death, disease and injury were the fate of thousands held at sea by the British

The Wretched Prison Ships

More Americans died in British prison ships in New York Harbor than in all the battles of the Revolutionary War.

There were at least 16 of these floating prisons anchored in Wallabout Bay on the East River for most of the war, and they were sinkholes of filth, vermin, infectious disease and despair. The ships were uniformly wretched, but the most notorious was the Jersey.

Following the Battle of Long Island in August, 1776, and the fall of New York City soon after, the British found thousands of prisoners on their hands, and the available prisons in New York filled up quickly. Then, as the British began seizing hundreds of seamen off privateers, they turned a series of aging vessels into maritime prison ships.

There were more than a thousand men at a time packed onto the Jersey. They died with such regularity that when their British jailers opened the hatches in the morning, their first greeting to the men below was: "Rebels, turn out your dead!" Christopher Vail, of Southold, who was on the Jersey in 1781, later wrote:

When a man died he was carried up on the forecastle and laid there until the next morning at 8 o'clock when they were all lowered down the ship sides by a rope round them in the same manner as tho' they were beasts. There was 8 died of a day while I was there. They were carried on shore in heaps and hove out the boat on the wharf, then taken across a hand barrow, carried to the edge of the bank, where a hole was dug 1 or 2 feet deep and all hove in together.

Charles Allen Munn Collection, Fordham University Library

A sketch of starving men on the Jersey; inmates could wait, try to escape or join the British.

Few aspects of the war were documented as well as life on the prison ships, presumably because the experience, for those who survived, was forever imprinted in their memories. There are occasional reports of attempts by the British to treat prisoners humanely, but these are the exception. In 1778, Robert Sheffield of Stonington, Conn., escaped one of these ships, and told his story to the Connecticut Gazette. He was one of 350 men jammed in a small compartment belowdecks.

"Their sickly countenances and ghastly looks were truly horrible," the newspaper wrote on July 10, without identifying the ship. "Some swearing and blaspheming; some crying, praying, and wringing their hands, and stalking about like ghosts; others delirious, raving, and storming; some groaning and dying — all panting for breath; some dead and corrupting — air so foul at times that a lamp could not be kept burning, by reason of which the boys were not missed till they had been dead ten days."

There were 4,435 battle deaths during the Revolutionary War, according to the Department of Defense. One historian estimated that there were between 7,000 and 8,000 prison ship deaths, but other sources claim even more. A letter-writer from Fishkill in 1783 claimed that on the Jersey alone, 11,644 died. Although that figure is unlikely for the one ship, it is reasonable for all the prison ships together, and is cited regularly.

On his first day in captivity on the Jersey, Capt. Thomas Dring found himself surrounded by men suffering from smallpox. He had never had smallpox, and since there was no one there to inoculate him, he decided to inoculate himself.

"On looking about me, I soon found a man in the proper stage of the disease, and desired him to favor me with some of the matter for the purpose," Dring later wrote. ". . . The only instrument which I could procure, for the purpose of inoculation, was a common pin. With this, having scarified the skin of my hand, between the thumb and forefinger, I applied the matter and bound up my hand. The next morning I found that the wound had begun to fester; a sure symptom that the application had taken effect."

Built in 1735 as a 64-gun ship, the Jersey was was converted to a prison ship in the winter of 1779-1780. Virtually stripped except for a flagstaff and a derrick for taking in supplies, the Jersey was floated, rudderless, in Wallabout Bay, about 100 yards offshore of what is now the Brooklyn Navy Yard. Its portholes were closed and supplanted by a series of small holes, 20 inches square, crossed by two bars of iron.

The best prisoner quarters on the Jersey was a former gunroom, which went to captured officers. American sailors were kept in two compartments below the main deck. French and Spanish prisoners got the worst quarters, in the hold, and probably had the highest mortality.

Gen. George Washington heard many reports of poor treatment on the prison ships, and on Jan. 13, 1777, he wrote an indignant letter to the chief of the British forces, Gen. Lord William Howe. "You may call us rebels, and say that we deserve no better treatment," Washington wrote. "But, remember, my Lord, that supposing us rebels, we still have feelings as keen and sensible as loyalists, and will, if forced to it, most assuredly retaliate upon those upon whom we look as the unjust invaders of our rights, liberties and properties."

There were various ways to get off the prison ships. The British had a standing offer that any prisoner could be released immediately if he joined the British forces, and an unidentified number did so. Prisoners who carried money with them could buy their way off the ship. Others managed to escape. Also, prisoner exchanges were quite common, with officers exchanged for officers, seamen for seamen, soldiers for soldiers. But for vast numbers of prisoners, there were only two possibilities: death or the end of the war, whichever came first.

Even in the summer of 1782, when the the war's end was more a matter of diplomacy than fighting, the British made life hell for those on the prison ships. On the Fourth of July that summer, the prisoners began hanging flags, singing songs, giving speeches and cheering in a daylong celebration of independence. When they refused to stop when ordered, the guards came below on a reign of terror. Henry R. Stiles, in his book, "A History of the City of Brooklyn," described what happened next:

> *The helpless prisoners, retreating from the hatchways as far as their crowded condition would permit, were followed by the guards, who mercilessly hacked, cut, and wounded every one within their reach; and then ascending again to the upper deck, fastened down the hatches upon the poor victims of their cruel rage, leaving them to languish through the long, sultry, summer night, without water to cool their parched throats . . .*

At war's end, survivors were released, and the prison ships abandoned. In later years, bleached bones of the dead were constantly exposed to the tides and weather along the Long Island shore. And well into the next century, low tide regularly exposed the rotting timbers of the Jersey, the ship they called Hell.

LEGACY

Memorials To the Dead

The bones of the prison ship dead are no longer exposed, and the memory of the those who died in the floating prisons on Wallabout Bay is forever enshrined at the Prison Ship Martyrs Monument in Brooklyn's Fort Greene Park.

It took a while to get there, however. It wasn't until 1808 that the bones of many of the prison ship dead were given a proper burial near the Navy Yard in Brooklyn by the Tammany Society of New York. In 1873 the bones were re-interred in Fort Greene Park. The current monument was erected in 1908 by the Society of Old Brooklynites. Now, the Brooklyn group is planning to erect an eternal flame — actually, a stainless steel sculpture in the shape of a flame that would be gilded, like the flame of the Statue of Liberty — atop the column. — **George DeWan**

The Prison Ship Martyrs Monument in Brooklyn's Fort Greene Park and a stone at the base of the monument.

Newsday Photos / Bill Davis

Inside New York City's 'Loathsome Dungeons'

The British prisons in New York City were almost as bad as the prison ships on Wallabout Bay. Especially because they were run by the notorious Capt. William Cunningham, who, when he was about to be hanged for forgery a few years later, confessed to having starved to death thousands of American prisoners by selling their rations.

Prison space in New York was limited when the British captured the city in 1776. As the numbers of prisoners rapidly increased, the British turned every conceivable building into a prison: three sugar houses, several dissenting Dutch churches, Old City Hall, Columbia College for a while. They soon became jammed, and bad food and infectious disease took their toll.

"Here," wrote Henry R. Stiles in his history of Brooklyn, "in these loathsome dungeons, denied the light and air of heaven; scantily fed on poor, putrid, and sometimes even uncooked food; obliged to endure the companionship of the most abandoned criminals, and those sick with small-pox and other infectious diseases; worn out by the groans and complaints of their suffering fellows, and subjected to every conceivable insult and indignity by their inhuman keepers, thousands of Americans sickened and died."

In charge of all of this, as head of the military police, was the provost marshall, Cunningham, who Stiles calls "an Irishman by birth, and a brute by nature." He was hanged for forgery in London in 1791, and made a dying confession:

> *I shudder to think of the murders I have been accessory to, both with, and without, orders from Government, especially while in New-York, during which time there were more than 2,000 prisoners starved in the different churches, by stopping their rations, which I sold. There were also 275 American prisoners and obnoxious persons executed, out of all which number there were only about one dozen public executions, which chiefly consisted of British and Hessian deserters.*

— **George DeWan**

William Floyd and Francis Lewis, the two Long Islanders who took a stand for freedom

They Signed for Independence

Floyd, a Mastic landowner, had a lot to lose

BY GEORGE DEWAN
STAFF WRITER

On Aug. 10, 1776, William Floyd of Mastic sat down in his room at Mary House's Philadelphia boarding house and wrote a worried and urgent letter. It is not known to whom he wrote, but apparently the letter was to someone in New York City. A week earlier, Floyd and others in the Continental Congress had provoked King George III by signing the Declaration of Independence.

"Have you heard anything from my family?" Floyd wrote. "Have any of our friends got off the Island with their families, or what must they submit to? Despotism or destruction, I fear, is their fate."

Here was a conservative Long Island landowner who had a lot to lose in a war with the British. But when it came time to take a stand in 1776, William Floyd signed the most revolutionary of documents. And he paid: His family was forced to evacuate Long Island for the duration of the war.

A religious man and a successful businessman, Floyd was regularly called to participate in state and national assemblies. Except for one year, he served in the Continental Congress from 1774 to 1783. Born Dec. 17, 1734, Floyd had little formal education. His father, a wealthy man, died when Floyd was 18, and his mother died soon after, so the son took over management of the estate. It was a large and prosperous operation, producing cattle, sheep, grain, flax and wood for export to New York City. With 14 adult slaves in addition to indentured servants, Floyd was one of the Island's largest slaveholders.

His wife, Hannah, and their three children fled Mastic on a ship to Middletown, Conn., before the British occupiers moved down the Island. Although Mrs. Floyd often brought the children to live with Floyd in Philadelphia, she died unexpectedly in Connecticut in 1781.

Floyd and his Declaration signature

In 1783, Floyd returned to Mastic. It has been part of the Floyd legend that occupying British troops did extensive damage to the house and property. But there is no evidence this is true, according to Steven Czarniecki of the National Park Service, which manages the historic site.

In 1784, Floyd remarried. He served in the first U.S. Congress, 1789-1790, but did not win re-election. In 1803, at 69, Floyd deeded his Mastic estate to his son and moved his wife, Joanna, and two new daughters to property in Oneida County he had bought in 1784. He built a home similar to his Mastic home, at what is now Westernville, N.Y., where he died in 1821.

By history-book standards, Floyd was not a man of renown. Except for one thing: He was a "Signer," a mark of distinction held by only 55 other men.

Newsday Photo / Bill Davis

Never to Be Forgotten

Eight generations of Floyds lived at the **William Floyd Estate**, above, in Mastic since Nicoll Floyd built the original six-room house on 4,000 acres in 1724. By the 1970s, all but 613 acres of the original land had been sold. Today, the estate contains the 25-room Old House, 12 outbuildings, forest, fields and marshland and a cemetery that includes the graves of some Floyd slaves. The grounds are open from 9:30 a.m. to dusk for cross-country skiing, hiking and bird watching. Guided tours are given in the summer.

•

Floyd and Lewis also had major roads named for them. The name **William Floyd Parkway** was given to a short, two-lane road running from the Smith Point Bridge to Montauk Highway in the Town of Brookhaven. Today, as a four-lane divided highway, it runs 17 miles from Smith Point north to Route 25A near East Shoreham. **Francis Lewis Boulevard**, originally Cross Island Boulevard, was renamed in the 1930s. Today it runs about 10 miles from Whitestone south to the Nassau County line near Valley Stream.

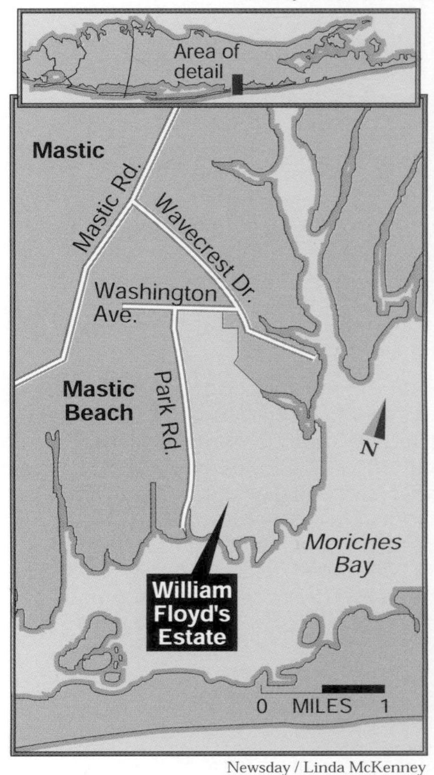

Newsday / Linda McKenney

Francis Lewis put patriotism before wealth

Francis Lewis was a Welsh-born merchant who spent the first part of his adult life making money and the second part spending much of it to help foment a revolution.

His was a remarkably eventful life. In his 20s he was shipwrecked twice off the coast of Ireland while on business. Later, he was captured in upstate New York during the French and Indian War and jailed in France. And, most painfully, during the Revolutionary War his Whitestone country home was destroyed by the British and his wife was captured and made prisoner in a filthy room in New York.

Born in Llandaff, Wales, in 1713 and orphaned at age 5, Lewis was raised by relatives. At 21 he inherited some land, sold it and invested the proceeds. When he was 25 he came to America and went into business with a New York merchant named Edward Annesley, whose sister, Elizabeth, he later married. During the French and Indian War, Lewis got a contract to supply the British forces in northern New York State. While at Oswego in 1756, he was captured by the French and imprisoned in France, and later released.

Returning to New York, he resumed his business. By 1765, having accumulated a considerable fortune, Lewis purchased a 200-acre estate at Whitestone and retired.

However, Lewis was rapidly becoming a protester against British trade restrictions and tax policy, and he was on his way to becoming a rebel. He joined the Sons of Liberty, a secret society formed to protest the Stamp Act, and he poured his money into supporting this and other like-minded groups. In 1775 he was elected to the Second Continental Congress in Philadelphia, and he was there when the Declaration of Independence was signed on Aug. 2, 1776.

National Archives

Lewis and his signature

Lewis paid dearly for his boldness. British troops went to his Whitestone estate, arrested Elizabeth and destroyed the home — Lewis himself probably would have been hanged if he had been there. His wife, in her late 50s and already in poor health, was freed after six months, but, physically devastated, she died two years later.

Lewis was about to take another familial hit. His only daughter, Ann, fell in love with a British naval officer. Infuriated, he refused to give his blessing. They married anyway, then sailed for England. One of his sons, Morgan, would become governor of New York in 1805, but Lewis would not live to see the inauguration.

When he died at age 89 in 1803, Lewis left only $15,000, and was buried in an unmarked grave in Trinity churchyard. Not poverty-stricken, but a long fall from the wealthy merchant of pre-Revolution days.

— George DeWan

How a Long Island teen broke the future president's heart

Madison's Unrequited Love

It had all the makings of a romance novel. Passion. Power. Betrayal. While he was tending to the business of a renegade colony, 31-year-old James Madison fell in love with 15-year-old Kitty Floyd, the daughter of William Floyd and one of the most beautiful women the future president had ever seen.

The affair of the heart was born amid affairs of state in a Philadelphia rooming house where the shy Virginian and the brown-eyed Long Island girl first met. As representatives to the Continental Congress, Madison and Kitty's father stayed at the house on Market and Fifth Street, owned by Mary House and run by her daughter, Eliza Trist.

When Madison first saw Catherine Floyd in 1779, she was just 12 years old and it is most likely that he regarded her only as the young daughter of his new friend, William Floyd of Mastic. But three years later, in the fall of 1782 after she had spent a summer in Connecticut, he saw her in a new light: She was almost a woman, and a lovely one at that. Although he was deeply involved in the turmoil of the era, Madison found time to fall in love. If Kitty's youth and nature made her a coquette, it did not seem to bother him.

One of those who promoted the romance was Madison's good friend and fellow Virginian, Thomas Jefferson, who also stayed at House's place on his occasional trips to Philadephia. After one visit that winter, Jefferson wrote to Madison on April 14, 1783 — in a letter composed in a numerical code they had devised — of his happiness about the match:

I desire [my compliments] to Miss Kitty particularly . . . I wished it [marriage] to be so as it would give me a neighbor [Kitty] whose worth I rate high, and as I know it will render you happier than you can possibly be in a single state.

On April 22, two days before Kitty's 16th birthday, Madison wrote back, also in code. He acknowledged, in his own stiff and formal way (his salutation to his good friend was "My dear Sir"), that marriage was in the works and that he was happy:

Your inference on that subject was not groundless Before you left us I had sufficiently ascertained her sentiments. Since your departure, the affair has been pursued. Most preliminary arrangements, although definitive, will be postponed until the end of the year in Congress. At some period of the interval I shall probably make a visit to Virginia. The interest which your friendship takes on this occasion in my happiness is a pleasing proof that the dispositions which I feel are reciprocated.

Madison and Kitty exchanged ivory miniature potraits of themselves by Philadelphia artist Charles Wilson Peale, and love was still in bloom when Floyd and his children left Philadelphia for New York on April 29. So immersed had Madison been in his work, he had not been away from Philadelphia for three years. But this time he accompanied his fiancée and her father on a two-day trip 60 miles to Brunswick, N.J., there to say bon voyage as the Floyds headed off to see their Mastic home for the first time in seven years.

The lovers never met again.

That summer, Kitty sent her fiancé a letter of rejection — sealed, according to family tradition, with a lump of rye dough. In Philadelphia, she had met a 19-year-old medical student named William Clarkson. While away from them both in the country quiet of Mastic, Miss Kitty decided that she loved William more than James.

Madison was crushed. And so he wrote his friend Jefferson again. This time, the letter was not in code. In the original, now in the Library of Congress, 13 lines were later inked out, but historian Irving Brandt, a Madison biographer, has reconstructed some of them in "James Madison: The Nationalist, 1780-1787." He begins the letter with two sentences that were not obliterated:

At the date of my letter in April I expected to have had the pleasure by this time of seeing you in Virginia. My disappointment has proceeded from several dilatory circumstances on which I had not calculated.

Then follow the inked-out 13 lines, part of which Brandt reconstructs as:

One of them was the uncertain state into which the object I was then pursuing has been brought by one of those incidents to which such affairs are liable. This (?) has rendered the time of my return to Virginia less material as the necessity of my visiting the state of New York no longer exists.

He ends the letter with a reference to "a profession of indifference at what has happened," apparently on Kitty's part.

Two years later Catherine Floyd married Clarkson, who eventually became a Presbyterian minister. In 1787, Madison became the Father of the Constitution. In 1794, at the age of 43, he married an engaging young widow, 26-year-old Dolley Todd. In 1809 he became president of the United States.

While Madison's star was rising, Kitty's was falling. In 1813, four years after Madison entered the White House, Kitty's husband died, leaving her a 46-year-old widow with three children Then, in 1817, her father wrote a will in which he accused her of squandering "considerable sums" of money he had given her, as well as a piece of land worth $7,000. Criticizing her as "not capable of taking care of property," he bequeathed her $70 a year.

Just before he died four years later, Floyd softened and gave Kitty a piece of land in Oneida County and an additional $1,000.

Pretty much forgotten, Kitty Floyd was living with a daughter in New York City when she died at age 65. She was buried in Greenwood Cemetery in Brooklyn.

Still, Madison never got over Kitty. When the fourth president of the United States was nearly 80 he came into possession of the two letters he had written about Kitty in 1783 to Jefferson. Madison was so upset in rereading his own words that he violently inked out the references to his early lost love as if to obliterate the memory.

James Madison and Kitty Floyd exchanged miniature potraits of themselves by Philadelphia artist Charles Wilson Peale in 1783. But in the spring of that year, she dumped the politician for a medical student.

Photos From the Library of Congress

BY GEORGE DEWAN
STAFF WRITER

Sarah Frost began her exile as a Loyalist seven months pregnant. She boarded the ship Two Sisters at Lloyd's Neck on May 25, 1783, with her husband, William, and their two children. On June 28 they arrived at the Bay of Fundy, at the mouth of the Saint John River, in Nova Scotia.

The sight that greeted them was intimidating: a few tents and small log shacks were overwhelmed by a rocky and wooded landscape.

"It is, I think, the roughest land I ever saw," Sarah wrote in her diary that day. "We are all ordered to land tomorrow, and not a shelter to go under."

Like other Loyalists, the Frosts disagreed with friends, relatives and neighbors over what was best for the future of America. Originally from Stamford, Conn., they had been driven from their home because of their British sympathies — Sarah's parents themselves were ardent Patriots — and took refuge for the remainder of the war near a British garrison on occupied Long Island at Lloyd's Neck.

When the British lost, there was nothing for most Loyalists to do but leave the country and head into an uncertain future. It was the largest exodus in American history, with estimates as high as 100,000, although there is disagreement over the numbers. Former New York state historian Alexander Flick estimated in 1901 that as many as 60,000 Loyalists left all of the colonies during and immediately following the war. Of these, 35,000 were inhabitants of the new State of New York, including Long Islanders. Many went to the British Isles, and some to the British West Indies. Most of those who left New York, however, went to what would become Canada, where British officials promised free land. This included Nova Scotia, which would not officially become part of Canada until the 19th Century.

"Many of them were driven out by persecution, others fled through fear, but most of them left at the close of the war because their cause had been lost," wrote Flick in "Loyalism in New York During the American Revolution." "They loved British institutions, were true to their oaths of loyalty, dreaded the scorn and contempt of their victorious brothers, hated republicanism, loved adventure, and wished to help preserve the integrity of the British Empire."

Photo by Bob Wilson

The obelisk at left marks the grave of Lt. Col. Richard Hewlett, in Queenstown, New Brunswick, Canada. After the American Revolution, he led a dozen ships carrying Long Islanders loyal to the British to Nova Scotia.

Thousands of Loyalists flee north to settle in Nova Scotia

A Long Island Exodus

Although Loyalists had been leaving America since the beginning of the war, the first major fleet left New York in the spring of 1783. The second fleet left in the fall, and it was under the command of Col. Richard Hewlett, the strong-willed and arrogant Queens resident who had commanded a battalion of Loyalist troops on Long Island. He had protected his 264 acres in New Rockaway (now East Rockaway) from confiscation by the state by deeding it to his son Oliver, who had remained neutral.

Now 54, Hewlett commanded a dozen ships carrying almost 2,500 Americans who had remained loyal to King George III to Nova Scotia. On the way, one of the ships foundered on rocks near Yarmouth, Nova Scotia, killing 99 of its 174 passengers. Hewlett, who settled up the Saint John River, named his settlement "Hampstead," for his Long Island birthplace, Hempstead, and he called the county Queens.

At the time of the emigration, the area of the Saint John River was part of Nova Scotia, but Loyalist influx of about 14,000 led Great Britain to create a new province, New Brunswick, with a capital at Fredericton. Many of the first settlers picked a site at the mouth of the Saint John River and named it Saint John. When it later became an incorporated city, its charter was modeled after that of New York City.

In New Brunswick, Hewlett lived as a farmer and received half-pay from the British army. He died in 1789 when he was 59. Only one of his sons, Joseph, remained in Canada. His wife, Mary, and a daughter returned to Long Island after his death.

This was a frontier, and these Loyalists braved frigid winters, sickness and loneliness for home as they carved out a new life from the wilderness. Some died of small pox during the first winter. Others returned to the United States and quietly eased themselves back into an American society that, as the years went by, began to forgive and forget. But most stayed, and many made their mark.

Long Island Loyalists were prominent in the Maritime Provinces. Edmund Fanning, who was born in Riverhead and commanded a regiment of Loyalist troops, later became lieutenant governor of Nova Scotia. Two brothers who had large estates near Hempstead — estates that were later confiscated by the state — also prospered in the new land: George D. Ludlow, who was superintendent of police for Long Island during the occupation, was appointed the first chief justice of the new province of New Brunswick. Gabriel G. Ludlow, who commanded a brigade of Loyalist Americans, was the first mayor of the City of Saint John.

While Patriot Americans felt that these Loyalist refugees were the scum of the Earth for not supporting the Revolution — they would refer to them disparagingly as Tories — Canadians count them among the solid founders of the nation. That they chose the king over rebellion was not, to some minds, a bad thing. William Kirby, a 19th Century writer and editor who was born in England, educated in Cincinnati, and who adopted Canada as his home, published a poem in 1877 that glorified the Loyalists who had braved the wilds of New Brunswick almost a century earlier. It includes these lines:

Not drooping like poor fugitives,
they came
In exodus to our Canadian wilds;
But full of heart and hope, with
heads erect
And fearless eyes, victorious in
defeat.

The Revolutionary War Comes to an End

While Long Islanders lived under the yoke of occupation, the war dragged on elsewhere. It would not end until the Treaty of Paris in 1783, long after the Americans, aided mightily by France, had worn down the beleagured British forces.

After being driven off Long Island and out of New York City in the fall of 1776, Washington struck back around Christmas, crossing the ice-choked Delaware River from Pennsylvania to win victories at Trenton and Princeton. But, as the pamphleteer Thomas Paine said at the time, these were the times that tried men's souls.

The year 1777 was crucial. The British defeated the Americans at Brandywine, took Philadelphia and resisted Washington's attack on Germantown. The Americans' first great victory of the war came in October at Saratoga, and it not only gave a huge psychological boost to the Patriot cause, it helped to bring in France on the side of the Americans. Washington and his men spent that winter at Valley Forge, Pa. There, a lack of food and clothing and miserable living conditions were offset only by the inspired training of the German Baron Friedrich von Steuben, who took a ragtag group of men and made them into an army.

The next year, France's treaty of alliance greatly aided the Patriot cause, especially because of France's superior naval power. The major part of the war, meanwhile, shifted to the South, where the British gained major victories, highlighted by the taking of Savannah, Ga., and Charleston, S.C.

The war would effectively end in 1781 at Yorktown, Va. British troops under Gen. Charles Cornwallis had been driven out of the Carolinas and into Virginia. The French fleet under Admiral Francois de Grasse bottled up the British fleet in Chesapeake Bay while an American and French army under Washington marched south to confront Cornwallis. For Cornwallis, surrounded and outnumbered, the jig was up. On Oct. 19, he surrendered.

The fighting was over, and the rebellion was successful. It would take until 1783 to get a peace treaty signed in Paris, but long before that, the British began making plans to evacuate America.

Defeated British and Loyalists board ships to leave the U.S.

America Celebrates Its New Freedom

By George DeWan
STAFF WRITER

As his boat was being rowed out into New York Harbor from the southern tip of Manhattan, Hessian Capt. Johann Ewald looked back on the land he was leaving after seven years of war. Slender and erect in his green coat and vest, with carmine red collar, cuffs and lapels, Ewald had been known for his compassion as well as his courage, but on this day he was just another defeated soldier who had survived.

Frustrated by cut ropes and a greased flagpole at the Battery, John Van Arsdale hammered cleats into the pole so he could fly the Stars and Stripes.

Illustration From Fraunces Tavern Museum

It was Nov. 25, 1783, evacuation day in New York City, which had been the headquarters for the British army since September, 1776. The harbor was filled with British sailing ships, jammed with 7,500 troops. They were going home, leaving America to its destiny.

Ewald chose to remember the moment, not with bitterness, but with magnanimity, as well as a touch of sadness. In his book, "Diary of the American War," he wrote:

On all corners one saw the flag of thirteen stripes flying, cannon salutes were fired, and all the bells rang. The shores were crowded with people who threw their hats in the air, screaming and boisterous with joy, and wished us a pleasant voyage with white handkerchiefs. While on the ships, which lay at anchor with the troops, a deep stillness prevailed as if everyone were mourning the loss of the thirteen beautiful provinces.

At 8 a.m., a detachment of 800 American troops marched down from Harlem Heights to take over the city as soon as the British officially left. That came at 1 p.m., when the British removed their last guards and took down the Union Jack at Fort George at the Battery. As thousands of wildly happy New Yorkers cheered and waved, two companies of Gen. George Washington's men were sent to raise the Stars and Stripes in its place.

There was a hitch, because someone on the British side — it is not known who — had greased the flagpole at Fort George and stolen the halyards. The planned 13-gun salute could not take place without an American flag flying in place.

"Three times a sailor-boy attempted its slippery length, only to descend in haste," wrote Henry P. Johnston in Harpers New Monthly Magazine in November, 1883. ". . . Boards, hammer, saw, and nails were sent for, and cleats cut out. The sailor-boy stuffed his pockets with the cleats; he nailed them on, and climbed as he nailed, until the top was reached, where new halyards were reeved, and the flag raised, amid cheers, by an artillery officer."

Winding down the war had been a long, tedious process. When Gen. Charles Cornwallis surrendered at Yorktown, Va., on Oct. 19, 1781, the war was effectively over. Little fighting was done in 1782. That November, a preliminary peace treaty was signed in Paris; it was ratified the following April by Congress, and officially signed in Paris on Sept. 3, 1783.

During this period, the Loyalist units on Long Island and elsewhere were disbanded. They were given the choice of receiving free transportation to safety in Nova Scotia or somewhere else out of the colonies, or to return to their old homes. Thousands chose the unknown trials of exile to the known problems of staying in a hostile environment.

On Long Island, the last military units to leave were in Queens As so often happens in wartime, warm relationships often developed between the occupying soldiers and the local young ladies. Here is an often-told but unverified story about a Hempstead lady and her kilted Scottish lover as it appeared in Onderdonk's "Revolutionary Incidents of Queens County":

"A Miss H., near Hempstead, had formed an intimacy with a Highlander, against the wishes of her friends. But when the British forces were about to evacuate the Island, she was missing. The distressed father expressed his apprehensions to the commanding officer that his daughter had eloped, and was now in the company of her lover. Forthwith the men were drawn up, and the father walked along the ranks, when he discovered his daughter in the guise of a soldier, by the whiteness of the skin where the garter is usually tied."

The British and Loyalist soldiers left Long Island in an orderly fashion, some with bands playing, others quietly marching toward New York and the ships. "On the evacuation of Flushing, in the morning there were thousands around, barns full," Onderdonk reported. "In the afternoon all were gone, and it seemed quite lonesome."

For the winners, however, it was time to cheer. In Jamaica on Dec. 8 there was a celebration of peace, with rifle volleys, an elegant dinner and band music. "After drinking thirteen toasts," the Independent Gazette reported, "the gentlemen marched in column, thirteen abreast, in procession through the village, preceded by the music, and saluting the colors as they passed. In the evening, every house in the village, and several miles around, was most brilliantly illuminated, and a ball given to the ladies concluded the whole."

Dec. 4: LI's Liberation Day

Although evacuation day in New York City was Nov. 25, 1783, Long Island would not get its freedom until Dec. 4. The Island was occupied longer than any other area in the 13 colonies during the Revolutionary War.

The British ships were carrying not only military men, but an unknown number of Loyalists fleeing the country. But the British did not have sufficient ships to carry them all, and a large number of Long Island-based troops were detained for nine days.

"This long delay was owing to the removal of so many loyalists, who dared not remain here after the passage of so many violent resolutions by whig meetings in various parts of the Union," 19th-Century historian Henry Onderdonk Jr. wrote. "Ships were sent for from the West Indies, and even Europe."

As the Loyalists were leaving Long Island at war's end, 5,000 refugees who had fled to Connecticut were returning. What they returned to was not always pleasant.

"The situation there was a tragedy," wrote Frederic G. Mather in his 1913 book, "The Refugees of 1776 From Long Island to Connecticut." "Nearly all the refugees were men of small means. They returned one by one; not in large groups, as was the case in New York. They found their properties wasted, and often destroyed altogether."

Those who were farmers, and this would have been the majority, found their lands abused by British occupiers. Valuable timber had been cut for firewood, wooden buildings destroyed for lumber, and homes damaged. In other cases, there was seven years of disuse, crops not planted and once-bountiful fields gone to seed and brush. And, of course, farm animals were gone: work horses and oxen stolen, and cattle, sheep and pigs long since fed into the bellies of the occupying British soldiers.

— George DeWan

With the war won, Benjamin Tallmadge celebrates in Manhattan and Setauket

Washington Says Thanks

BY GEORGE DEWAN
STAFF WRITER

The war was over, and Lt. Col. Benjamin Tallmadge was going home to Setauket. But first, he had to say goodbye to his general.

At midday in New York City on Dec. 4, 1783, the 29-year-old revolutionary hero made straight for the tavern at the corner of Pearl and Broad Streets run by Samuel Fraunces. The West Indian-born purveyor of fine food and wines had secretly aided the Patriot cause by passing along choice bits of British gossip to Gen. George Washington's spies.

A slight nod of understanding passed quickly between the two men. The colonel had been Washington's chief of intelligence, and he knew of Fraunces' contribution, which was to remain a secret. Tallmadge was joined by the rest of Washington's trusted officers, dressed in the best uniforms they could put together, boots polished, sabres hanging at their sides.

Washington was about to arrive for his farewell to his officers. In the Long Room, waiters had set out a massive buffet luncheon on linen-draped tables overflowing with joints of meat, seafood, vegetables, bread and butter and dozens of decanters of wine. But it lay untouched as the gathering officers waited nervously for the commander in chief.

Then the great man arrived, and the room became charged with emotion. Attempting to put the men at their ease, the general picked up a plate, put some food on it and sat down, bidding his men to do the same. Slowly, they complied. For an account of what happened next we turn to Tallmadge, the inveterate note-taker and memoir-writer who had begun the war as a freshly minted lieutenant at the Battle of Long Island.

After partaking of a slight refreshment, in almost breathless silence, the General filled his glass with wine, and turning to the officers, he said: "With a heart full of love and gratitude, I now take leave of you. I most devoutly wish that your latter days may be as prosperous and happy as your former ones have been glorious and honorable."

After the officers had taken a glass of wine, Gen. Washington said: "I cannot come to each of you, but shall feel obliged if each of you will come and take me by the hand."

General Knox being nearest to him, turned to the Commander-in-Chief, who, suffused in tears, was incapable of utterance, but grasped his hand; when they embraced each other in silence. In the same affectionate manner, every officer in the room marched up to, kissed, and parted with his General-in-Chief. Such a scene of sorrow and weeping I had never before witnessed, and hope I may never be called upon to witness again.

Sketches depict George Washington's farewell to his officers at the war's end, top; Fraunces Tavern, left, and Col. Benjamin Tallmadge of Setauket.

From "The American Revolution: A Picture Sourcebook" and the Litchfield Historical Society (Tallmadge)

Tallmadge continued:

Not a word was uttered to break the solemn silence that prevailed, or to interrupt the tenderness of the interesting scene. The simple thought that we were about to part from the man who had conducted us through a long and bloody war, and under whose conduct the glory and independence of our country had been achieved, and that we should see his face no more in this world, seemed to me utterly insupportable. But the time of separation had come, and waiving his hand to his grieving children around him, he left the room, and passing through a corps of light infantry who were paraded to receive him, he walked silently on to Whitehall, where a barge was in waiting.

We all followed in mournful silence to the wharf, where a prodigious crowd had assembled to witness the departure of the man who, under God, had been the great agent in establishing the glory and independence of the United States. As soon as he was seated, the barge put off into the river, and when out in the stream, our great and beloved General waived his hat, and bid us silent adieu.

Tallmadge had one more stop to make before settling in Litchfield, Conn., with his prospective bride, Mary Floyd of Mastic. He went home to Setauket, where he had been born in 1754, and where his father and Patriot friends had survived seven years of British occupation.

The people had determined that they would celebrate the occasion by some public demonstration of their joy. They therefore concluded to have public notice given, that on a day near at hand, they would have an ox roasted whole on the public green, to partake of which all were invited to attend.

As the honored guest, Tallmadge was made master of ceremonies.

When the ox was well roasted, the noble animal on his spit was removed to a proper place, and after a blessing from the God of Battles had been invoked by my honored father, I began to carve, dissect, and distribute to the multitude around me. The aged and the young, the male and the female, rejoiced to receive a portion, which, from the novelty of the scene, and being in commemoration of so great an event, obtained a peculiar zest. All was harmony and joy, for all seemed to be of one mind.

A Tory could not have lived in that atmosphere one minute. By sunset the whole concourse — a vast multitude — dispersed and returned to their own homes in quietness and peace.

Benjamin Tallmadge's war was over. It began with the saving of his horse after the Battle of Long Island; it ended with the roasting of an ox on the public green in Setauket. In between, all was glory.

LI's Boswell With a Camera

Hal B. Fullerton — photographer, farmer, ace publicist — was hired by the Long Island Rail Road in 1897 to promote the railroad and its destination: Long Island, not yet the chic resort area it would soon become. To market the Island as a good place to live and farm (and increase the railroad's freight revenue), he created a prize-winning model farm in Wading River, then set out to find the "10 worst acres on the Island." He settled on the scrubby sand of Medford, where he again raised spectacular crops.

Meanwhile, Fullerton photographed Long Island, compiling 2,500 pictures during three decades, one of the best pictorial records of that bucolic era. A bicycle aficionado, he would pedal around the Island with an 11-by-14-inch view camera, tripod, holders and other gear strapped behind.

But he became best known for setting up a media event in which Charles (Mile-a-Minute) Murphy, who in 1899 pedaled a bike a measured mile in 57.8 seconds behind an LIRR train. Though some suggested Murphy would have better demonstrated his speed (and his courage) had he been put in front of the train, the stunt made him and the railroad internationally famous.

— Rhoda Amon

Photos From the Fullerton Collection, Suffolk County Historical Society

A fishing boat is hauled ashore in East Marion in about 1902. Fullerton produced one of the era's best pictorial records of Long Island.

TIME MACHINE

PICTURING THE PAST AND PRESENT

A view of Lloyd Harbor, with a sailboat at rest, in 1902

The wreck of a ship in Amagansett, 1902, and a sentry on patrol with Company H, 71st NY Regiment, at Camp Black, which acquired the name during the Spanish-American War in 1898 and became Mitchel Field in 1918.

A view of Roslyn's Bryant Avenue and East Turnpike

The Suffolk County Fair at Riverhead

Yerk's Beach at Lake Ronkonkoma, which had cabanas and a sand beach

A view of the Halesite post office and a trolley that ran to Amityville

TIME MACHINE

PICTURING THE PAST AND PRESENT

Postcards From the Collection of Joel Streich

Straw hats on a warm day at the Sea Cliff station, which still stands today

Long Island in the Mail

The idyllic days of the trolley car, the horse and buggy and the steam engine that suggest a simpler way of life on turn-of-the-century Long Island were captured and preserved on postcards by the best photographers of their day.

The postcards often were printed in Germany, according to collector Joel Streich of Commack, a member of the Long Island Post Card Club. Many of the scenes from this period were photographed in black and white and then hand-colored by craftsmen. World War I ended the German production of the cards.

Streich said there are perhaps a dozen collector-dealers of postcards on Long Island. He says, however, that he and Charles Huttunen of Northport probably have the biggest collections of Long Island-oriented cards. They call their hobby "deltiology."

Huttunen, who has some 200,000 cards, was chairman of the Post Card Club's 21st annual show in March, 1998.

Newsday Photo

Joel Streich

CHAPTER 5

Building A New Nation

From the days of whalers

and the coming of the railroad

to "America's Poet" and the Civil War

Defeated as a general in 1776, Washington returns in 1790 as the nation's first president

An LI Victory Tour

BY GEORGE DEWAN
STAFF WRITER

George Washington bore disturbing memories of the last time he had been on Long Island. Fourteen years earlier his outmanned Patriot forces had taken a terrible pounding from the British at Brooklyn Heights. With the battle lost he had sneaked away from the Brooklyn shores under the protection of a dense fog, willing to wait until another day to win the war.

Roslyn Public Schools; Newsday Photo

Mill owner Hendrick Onderdonk speaks with George Washington in Roslyn in a 1937 mural by Robert Herbert Gaston.

Now it was April 20, 1790, and the 58-year-old retired general returned to Long Island as the first president of the new nation. Washington was a traveling man, and he liked to meet the people and see how they worked the land.

It was an exhilarating time, for Washington and for the people. A new Constitution had taken the disparate and prickly notions of 13 confederated states and fashioned a unified America, a land that was still mapping its destiny. The idea of newness was everywhere: America was a wilderness, and never again would so many things be done for the first time.

Washington sensed this in those days before he returned to Long Island. "I walk on untrodden ground," he had written to historian Catherine Macaulay Graham in January, not without an acute sense of his own place in history. "There is scarcely any part of my conduct which may not hereafter be drawn into precedent."

The Long Island that Washington would visit in 1790 was largely a place of serenity and quiet. "A traveller is forcibly struck with a sense of stillness, and sequestration from the world," Yale College president Timothy Dwight would write a few years later after a five-day visit to the Island. "Every place seems to him a retirement."

There were no newspapers yet on the Island, so news of the outside world was slow in coming. Benjamin Franklin had died on April 17, but few Long Islanders knew it. The more educated knew that the French had had their own revolution the previous summer, but keeping up to date was difficult. Although many people made their living along the coastal waters, Long Island was primarily a land of farms. Some of them were large and manorial, but more common were small family operations that often used indentured servants and slaves to keep things going. Crops and livestock were the main products, along with the abundant supplies of wood for both fuel and lumber that were shipped to New York via the Sound. Insular quiet was the natural order of things.

The previous fall, Washington had spent a month visiting New England. As a war hero and as the nation's No. 1 citizen, he found his travels were usually the occasion for pageantry, celebrations, fireworks, endless speeches and official ceremonies.

Stony Brook Community Fund; Newsday

Washington: His 1790 tour of Long Island was fairly quiet.

This trip would be different. From all available records, Washington's tour of Long Island, from April 20 to April 24, was as quiet as the countryside through which he traveled. Although a number of people came out to see him pass by, the trip was informal and low-keyed. He had with him his servants, and he traveled in an elegant, cream-colored coach, drawn by four magnificent gray horses. It carried him on a looping, 165-mile journey into south Brooklyn, to Jamaica, and along the South Shore to Patchogue. He then went north to Setauket, and turned back along the North Shore, stopping in Smithtown, Huntington, Oyster Bay, Roslyn and Flushing. He was back home in New York before sundown on Saturday the 24th of April.

"About 8 Oclock having previously sent over my servants, horses and carriage I crossed to Brooklyn and proceeded to Flat Bush . . . " So begins Washington's diary entry for the morning of April 20, 1790. He was passing through the territory where he had suffered perhaps his most ignominious military defeat, the Battle of Long Island, on Aug. 27, 1776.

In keeping with his taciturn character, the diary reveals little about what Washington felt, who he saw and what he talked about during his trip. But he gives a fair amount of detail about the look of the land and its agricultural potential.

His first stop was at New Utrecht, where he had a meal at the house of "Mr. Barre":

He told me that their average crop of oats did not exceed 15 bushls. to the acre but of Indian corn they commonly made from 25 to 30 and often more bushels to the acre but this was the effect of dung from New York (about 10 cart load to the acre) — that of wheat they sometimes got 30 bushels and often more of rye.

Washington commented constantly about the quality of the soil, which he found generally poor. The use of fertilizer was only beginning to take hold, and the western farms in Queens and Kings Counties were making the best use of horse manure from the nearby streets of New York City. Although Long Island was a land of farmers, few were aware of the new methods of crop rotation and fertilization that experimenters were developing. Old agricultural practices were ruining the land.

"The yields were not large, because an impoverished soil, inherited from colonial times, was scratched with shallow and unlevel furrows and constantly drained by an exploitative crop rotation," Ralph Henry Gabriel once wrote of that earlier period. Changes were on the way, however, but not in Washington's lifetime. It was more than change: A revolution in agriculture — both in tools and in methods — was on the way, and it would come to Long Island in the first half of the 19th Century.

Having left Brooklyn and passed through the hills to the plains of southern Brooklyn, Washington noted "rich black loam" in the productive farmland around Gravesend. But later he passed by the Hempstead Plains, barren of trees. "The soil of this plain is said to

Please see WASHINGTON, Page 160

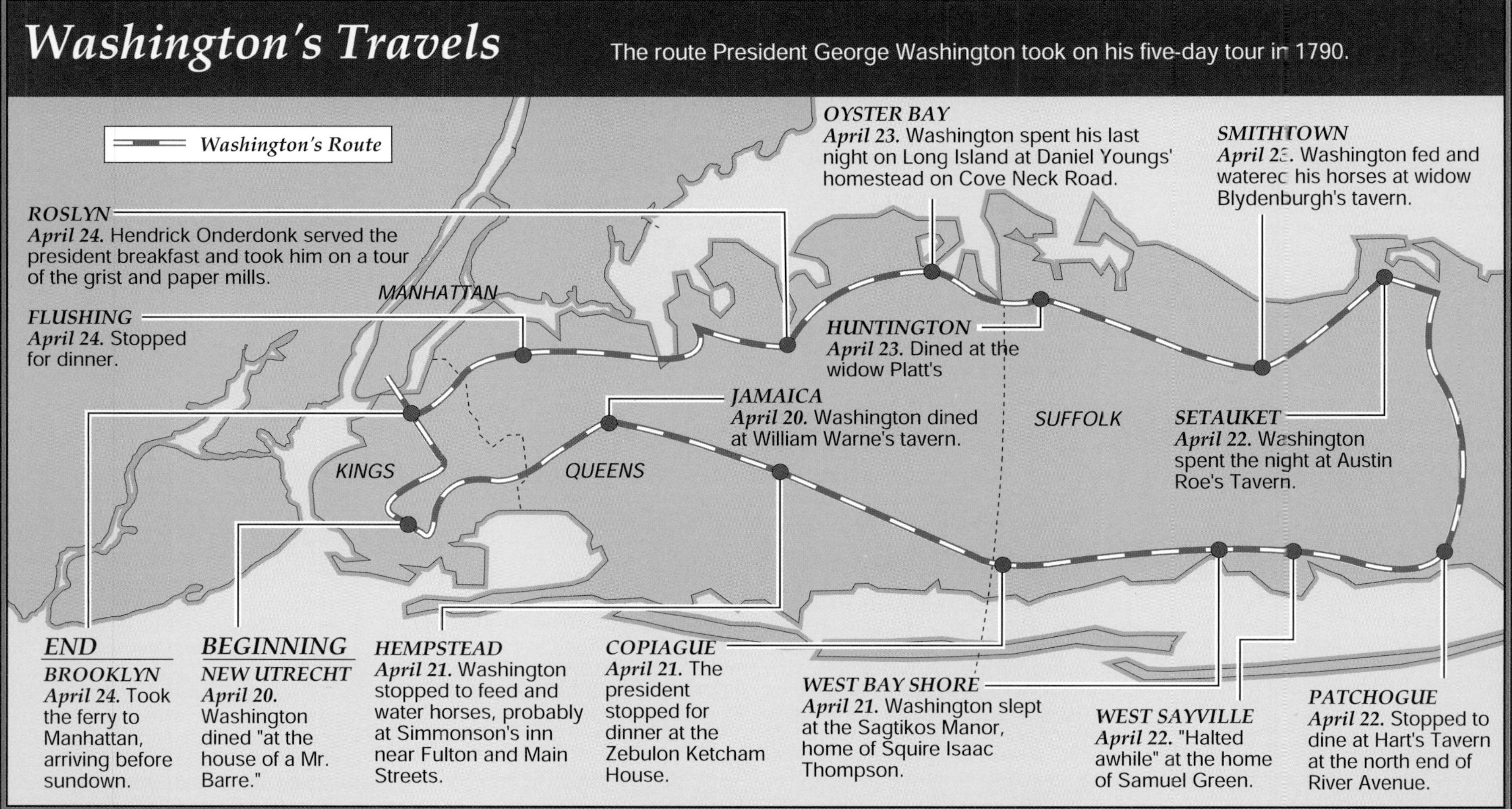
Washington's Travels
The route President George Washington took on his five-day tour in 1790.
Washington's Route
OYSTER BAY
April 23. Washington spent his last night on Long Island at Daniel Youngs' homestead on Cove Neck Road.
SMITHTOWN
April 23. Washington fed and watered his horses at widow Blydenburgh's tavern.
ROSLYN
April 24. Hendrick Onderdonk served the president breakfast and took him on a tour of the grist and paper mills.
MANHATTAN
FLUSHING
April 24. Stopped for dinner.
HUNTINGTON
April 23. Dined at the widow Platt's
JAMAICA
April 20. Washington dined at William Warne's tavern.
SUFFOLK
SETAUKET
April 22. Washington spent the night at Austin Roe's Tavern.
KINGS
QUEENS
END
BROOKLYN
April 24. Took the ferry to Manhattan, arriving before sundown.
BEGINNING
NEW UTRECHT
April 20. Washington dined "at the house of a Mr. Barre."
HEMPSTEAD
April 21. Washington stopped to feed and water horses, probably at Simmonson's inn near Fulton and Main Streets.
COPIAGUE
April 21. The president stopped for dinner at the Zebulon Ketcham House.
WEST BAY SHORE
April 21. Washington slept at the Sagtikos Manor, home of Squire Isaac Thompson.
WEST SAYVILLE
April 22. "Halted awhile" at the home of Samuel Green.
PATCHOGUE
April 22. Stopped to dine at Hart's Tavern at the north end of River Avenue.

Newsday / Linda McKenney

In Montauk, Lighting the Way for Sailors

BY GEORGE DEWAN
STAFF WRITER

Almost from its very beginning, the 80-foot-high lighthouse at Montauk Point was, in the words of an early visitor, "a landmark of the first importance." The lighthouse was born in the aftermath of the Revolutionary War, when it became clear that safe coastal navigation was essential to the new nation's economic well-being. President George Washington agreed with Congress that a series of lighthouses along the Eastern Seabord was a priority.

"Perhaps no building of this useful kind was ever erected on this side of the Atlantic in a spot where it was more necessary for the preservation of man," wrote Yale President Timothy Dwight on his 1804 visit to Long Island.

In 1795, Washington approved plans for a structure that would eventually rise 110 feet above the bluffs that mark the place where the eastern edge of Long Island meets the sea at Montauk Point. Opened in the spring of 1797, it was the first lighthouse built in New York State and the fifth completed by the U.S. government.

Legend holds that even before there was a lighthouse, before the white man came to claim the land, Montaukett Indians would build great fires at Montauk Point to call council meetings. And during the Revolutionary War, when the British occupied Long Island for seven years, the Royal Navy kept a huge fire burning on Turtle Hill — the Europeans' name for the bluffs that resembled the carapace of a huge turtle — as a signal beacon for their ships that were blockading Long Island Sound.

LI HISTORY.COM

For more on the Montauk Lighthouse, see http://www.lihistory.com on the Internet. You'll get:

- The proclamation in which George Washington called for the construction of Montauk's lighthouse.
- A video on the lighthouse's history.
- Photos that illustrate changes to the lighthouse.
- Profiles of other L.I. lighthouses.

National Archives Photo

An 1871 view of the Montauk Lighthouse. A brown stripe was added in 1900.

Now there stands on Turtle Hill a lighthouse that for two centuries has been a beacon for sailors navigating the treacherous waters that envelop the eastern end of Long Island. Sometimes the sea has won the battle, and the stories are legion of ships that have wrecked within range of the flashing beam that has a range of 24 miles.

In its lifetime, the lighthouse has progressed from smoky whale oil lamps to sophisticated modern lenses. Along the way, it has survived nature's onslaughts and human neglect. The bluffs on which it stands have been chewed at by erosion, and the tower has been buffeted by gales and hurricanes.

Built at a cost of $22,300 on what was originally a 13-acre site, the octagonal tower ismade of sandstone probably imported from Connecticut. By the middle of the 19th Century, the lighthouse was falling apart, and in 1860 it was completely overhauled rather than being torn down, as was originally planned. The wooden floors and windows were gutted and replaced by iron, and new iron decks and doors were installed. The most conspicuous change came in 1900, when the all-white lighthouse was given a horizontal brown band to distinguish it in daytime. Electricity and indoor plumbing weren't installed until 1938.

At one point, the lighthouse seemed doomed. In 1968, continued erosion threatened to topple it into the sea. But a major project turned things around, to the point where there has not been any major erosion in the control area for at least a quarter-century

The Coast Guard fully automated the lighthouse in 1987, installing a new type of low-maintenance lens that uses a 1,000-watt bulb in front of a parabolic mirror. The Coast Guard then leased the property to the Montauk Historical Society for 30 years. Although the beacon still flashes on top, the remainder of the lighthouse has become a museum.

Today, 110,000 visitors a year visit the end of Long Island, the end of New York State, to see the extraordinary view from the Montauk Lighthouse. It is an almost mystical place, where the rising sun bathes the cliffs in an orange glow, and the ocean's waves play a percussive symphony against the shore.

It is a place for poets. Walt Whitman knew this place well, as he tells us in "Specimen Days":

> *I . . . spent many an hour on Turtle Hill by the old lighthouse, on the extreme point, looking out over the ceaseless roar of the Atlantic.*

Washington's Return to LI

WASHINGTON from Page 158

be thin and cold and of course not productive, even in grass.'' Farther out on the Island he noted unproductive, sandy soil, scrubby oak trees and ''ill thriven pines.'' Only on his return along the North Shore did he note an improvement in the soils, especially around Oyster Bay.

This was sparsely settled country, and not without bumps and bounces.

''In many localities there were no roads, and where these did exist they were poor and frequently impassable; bridges were almost unknown,'' reads the introduction to a 1908 government reprinting of the New York State part of the 1790 federal census. ''Transportation was entirely by horseback, stage or private coach.''

Although the chief ''road'' on Long Island at this time was the Sound — the ocean to the south was usable, but dangerous — the beginnings of a real road system had been made. Already developed — though primitive and sometimes impassable in winter snow and mud — were South Country Road (now basically Route 27A), North Country Road (Route 25A) and Middle Country Road.

Washington spent April 20 journeying to Jamaica, where he spent the night at William Warne's tavern, ''a pretty good and decent house.'' He left at 8 the next morning, stopping in Hempstead to water and feed his horses. About 4 p.m. he had dinner at Zebulon Ketcham's house in what is now Copiague.

Over the years there has been much discussion of why Washington chose to make the trip to Long Island, and why he chose the stops he did. Part of the answer comes from his diary entry for Oct. 5, 1789, just before he made a one-month tour of New England:

> *Had conversation with Colo. [Alexander] Hamilton on the propriety of my makg. a tour through the Eastern states during the recess of Congress to acquire knowledge of the face of the country the growth and agriculture there of and the temper and disposition of the inhabitants towards the new government . . .*

When on the road, Washington liked to chat with the people and hold counsel with the notables, always keeping a keen eye out for agricultural practices. But an additional reason for his Long Island trip has been deduced by historians over the years. That was to meet and thank at least one, if not more, members of those Patriots on British-occupied Long Island who had risked their lives as spies for the Revolutionary cause.

Along the way, there were constant reminders of the recent war. After dining at Ketcham's, Washington headed for Isaac Thompson's Sagtikos Manor in Bay Shore, where he would spend the night. During the occupation, the manor had been used as a headquarters by British troops. A visitor to the manor today can see the room Washington slept in, as well as a nearby room said to have been used during the Revolution by Gen. Sir Henry Clinton, the British commander.

The next morning Washington headed north to Setauket, and on the way he passed by Coram (or, Koram, as he spelled it), in Brookhaven. In 1780, Washington had issued a special commendation to one of his favorite officers, Maj. Benjamin Tallmadge, who had led a sortie from across Long Island Sound to destroy 300 tons of valuable hay at Coram used as forage for British horses. Tallmadge had been Washington's chief spy, but if the president was reminded of him when he passed through Coram, he did not mention it in his diary.

If there is anything in Washington's sober diary commentaries that is likely to make a reader smile it is his understated entry for Thursday, April 22, where he stayed overnight in Setauket at the tavern of Austin Roe:

> *. . . thence to Setakit 7 mi. more to the house of a Captn. Roe which is tolerably dect. [decent] with obliging people in it.*

Thus does he camouflage an important agent in the so-called Culper spy ring. Setauket tavern-keeper Austin Roe regularly traveled to New York City to bring back secret messages to be transported across the Sound to be delivered to Washington.

Washington returned across the North Shore and met Revolutionary history at every stop. On April 23 he rested and watered his horses at the widow Blydenburgh's in Smithtown, where the arrogant and ruthless Lt. Col. Banastre Tarleton in 1778 led his band of Loyalist raiders on a foraging expedition. He dined at the widow Platt's in Huntington, where the menu, according to a 19th Century Fourth of July orator, included ''oysters, baked striped bass, a monster round of beef, stuffed veal, roast turkey, chicken pie, with all the vegetables of the season, and various kinds of preserves.''

There were more memories for Washington: On the shores of nearby Huntington Bay, in September, 1776, young Nathan Hale landed to begin his fateful spying trip to New York City. And as Washington headed west out of town after his big meal, he passed directly by the Old Burying Ground, where the infamous Lt. Col. Benjamin Thompson in the winter of 1782-83 had his Loyalist troops rip up gravestones and build a fort.

That evening, Washington slept at the Oyster Bay home of Daniel Youngs, on Cove Neck Road, across the road from a family cemetery where a future president, Theodore Roosevelt, would be buried. This was an odd choice of lodging, since Youngs had been a captain in the Loyalist Queens militia during the war; in other words, the enemy. As usual, Washington doesn't explain. The house is today owned by Charles Wang, the billionaire chairman and chief executive officer of Computer Associates International Inc. of Islandia.

Up earlier than usual, at 6 a.m. on the 24th, Washington had breakfast with Hendrick Onderdonk in Roslyn. The home is now the Washington Manor restaurant, and Onderdonk's grist and paper mill down the road is badly in need of repair. Onderdonk's paper was of the highest quality available in New York, and family tradition has it that Washington actually made a piece of paper while there.

Washington's Long Island trip was coming to a close. He had 30 miles to go and was in a hurry. He had dinner in Flushing and then headed for Brooklyn Ferry. ''Before sundown we had crossed the ferry and was at home,'' he wrote.

The Long Island that Washington saw was sparsely settled and little removed from its colonial days. But change was on the way as the 18th Century turned into the 19th.

Slavery was in full force in 1790, though it would be ended in New York State by 1827. Roads were still primitive, but the new century would see major developments in road-building. A half-century later there would even be a railroad running down the spine of the Island. Even though there was work to be done, there would be poets and painters to celebrate it.

Like the new nation, Long Island was about to begin building.

A New Nation

Long Island

1784. New York State Legislature fined Long Island for not taking a more active role in the American Revolution.

July 26, 1788. New York ratified the Constitution.

April, 1790. Washington toured Long Island.

March 2, 1793. Congress appropriated $20,000 to purchase a site and build the Montauk lighthouse.

1806. First turnpike built on Long Island, linking Jamaica and Rockaway.

1812. British squadron anchored in Gardiners Bay and later raided Sag Harbor.

1814. Steam ferry service began between Brooklyn and Manhattan.

Bettmann Archive Photo

1827. Slavery was abolished in New York State.

United States

Dec. 7, 1787. Delaware became the first state to ratify the Constitution.

April 30, 1789. George Washington was inaugurated president.

Dec. 15, 1792. Bill of Rights went into effect.

April 30, 1803. United States bought 828,000 square miles from France. The act is known as the Louisiana Purchase.

May 14, 1804. Meriwether Lewis, right, and William Clark began expedition to explore the Louisiana Territory.

June 18, 1812. Congress declared war on Great Britain, beginning the War of 1812. The conflict ended two years later.

Dec. 2, 1823. President James Monroe issued the Monroe Doctrine, which declared that any attempt by Europeans to colonize the Americas would be interpreted as an act of aggression.

The World

July 14, 1789. A French crowd stormed the Bastille prison.

Jan. 21, 1793. France's King Louis XVI was executed.

Dec. 2, 1804. Napoleon Bonaparte crowned himself emperor of France.

Oct. 21, 1805. British naval force commanded by Adm. Horatio Nelson defeated a combined French-Spanish fleet at the Battle of Trafalgar.

Sept. 16, 1810. Revolution broke out in Mexico. Four years later, the country declared its independence from Spain.

October, 1813. Simon Bolivar defeated the Spanish in Venezuela, the first of many Latin American countries that he would help lead to independence.

June 18, 1815. Napoleon was defeated by the Duke of Wellington at the Battle of Waterloo. The French emperor was exiled to the island of St. Helena.

1780 | 1790 | 1800 | 1810 | 1820

A Critic Gives LI One Thumb Up

BY GEORGE DEWAN
STAFF WRITER

Unlike the laconic Mr. Washington, Yale College president Timothy Dwight left a lengthy and occasionally critical record of a two-week visit to Long Island in the late spring of 1804.

He saw a quiet, inward-looking land, where farms and villages were far apart, and the people were friendly but unsophisticated. For the worldly Rev. Dwight — he was also a Congregational minister — the rustic Long Island countryside and its plain and pleasant people did not meet the exacting standards of New Haven academia. But as a picture of the Island at the beginning of the 19th Century, Dwight's account is unmatched.

Dwight's arrival from across the Sound with three Yale companions was enough to make a lesser traveler turn around and head for the comforts of home. Their sail-driven ferry left Norwalk, Conn., at 5 a.m. on the 14th of May, and due to feeble winds, they found themselves entering Huntington Harbor 16 hours later, when a thunderstorm broke out. They arrived at an inn in Huntington, drenched, hungry and exhausted, not getting to sleep until 4 a.m.

"The family arose with a great deal of good nature, and entertained us very kindly, and very well," Dwight wrote in "Travels in New-England and New-York," which was not published until 1823, six years after his death.

Heading for Setauket the next morning, the travelers stopped in Smithtown to dine. Unfortunately, the inn had run out of food. But there was food for the eyes in the person of the innkeeper's daughter, Phebe McCoun, about whom the 52-year-old man of the cloth waxed lyrical — more so than about any other sight in the journey. He seemed stunned to find such a jewel in such a sty.

We found a young lady about eighteen, of a fine form and complexion, a beautiful countenance, with brilliant eyes animated by intelligence, possessing manners which were a charming mixture of simplicity and grace, and conversing in language which would not have discredited a drawing-room or a court.

Convinced that the beautiful Phebe was destined to cast her radiance unappreciated in this dark backwater, Dwight was reminded of a line from Thomas Gray's "Elegy Written in a Country Churchyard," which he slightly altered to read: "Flowers are born to blush unseen / And waste their sweetness on the desert air."

When he reached Riverhead, on the Peconic River, then the county's administrative center, Dwight found it a dreary place.

The court-house, a poor decayed building, and a miserable hamlet, containing about ten or twelve houses, stand near the efflux of this river.

The legal business was pretty slow in 1804.

From this account of the court-house you will naturally suspect that the business of lawyers and sheriffs is not here in very great demand, nor in very high reputation. The suspicion is certainly well-founded . . . No lawyer, if I am not misinformed, has hitherto been able to get a living in the county of Suffolk.

New-York Historical Society

'No lawyer, if I am not misinformed, has hitherto been able to get a living in the county of Suffolk.'

— Rev. Timothy Dwight after his 1804 visit to Riverhead

Please see **DWIGHT** on **Next Page**

March 6, 1836. The Alamo was captured by Mexican forces.

1837. Long Island Rail Road began service to Hicksville.

1839. The Amistad was captured off Montauk.

Aug. 29, 1842. The British forced the Chinese to sign a treaty that ended the Opium War, opened up several ports for trade and ceded the island of Hong Kong to Britain.

April 30, 1846. Mexican-American War began with Mexicans besieging a fort in Texas. The war ended two years later with Mexico cedeing Texas, New Mexico and upper California to the United States.

1848. Revolutionaries wanting democratic reforms staged revolts throughout Europe. The revolts were put down by 1849.

1855. Walt Whitman published the first edition of "Leaves of Grass."

1855. Work began on constructing the Suez Canal.

Dec. 20, 1860. Following the election of Abraham Lincoln as president, South Carolina seceded from the Union.

March 17, 1861. Victor Emmanuel II became the ruler of a newly united Italy.

1861-62. Benjamin Willis recruited Company H, which became part of the 119th Regiment and fought in many Civil War engagements.

April 12, 1861. Civil War began when Confederate forces fired on Fort Sumter.

March 9, 1862. Ironclad warship Monitor launched from Greenpoint, Brooklyn.

1863. Civil War draft riot in Jamaica.

June 27-July 4, 1863. Gen. Robert E. Lee was defeated at the Battle of Gettysburg.

April 9, 1865. Lee surrendered his army to Gen. Ulysses S. Grant at Appomattox Courthouse, Va.

April 14, 1865. Lincoln was assassinated.

1830 | 1840 | 1850 | 1860 | 1870

Newsday / Linda McKenney

Census Snapshot: 1790

Total population

New York State = 340,120

County	Total population	Slaves
Kings	4,495	1,432
Queens*	16,014	2,309
Suffolk	16,440	1,098

Township populations

	Free People	Slaves	Total
Queens*			
Flushing	1,267	340	1,607
Jamaica	1,453	222	1,675
Newtown**	1,578	533	2,111
North Hempstead	2,189	507	2,696
Oyster Bay	3,716	381	4,097
South Hempstead	3,502	326	3,828
Suffolk			
Brookhaven	2,991	233	3,224
East Hampton	1,398	99	1,497
Huntington***	3,047	213	3,260
Islip	574	35	609
Shelter Island	177	24	201
Smithtown	856	166	1,022
Southampton	3,262	146	3,408
Southold****	3,037	182	3,219

*-Includes present-day Nassau County
**-Includes present-day Elmhurst and surrounding communities
***-Includes present-day Town of Babylon
****-Includes present-day Town of Riverhead

SOURCE: Bureau of the Census, "Heads of Families at the First Census of the United States Taken in the Year 1790"

Slaveholders	Kings	Queens*	Suffolk
Percent of white families holding slaves	61.1%	34.6%	17.7%

Families	Kings	Queens*	Suffolk
Avg. members per white family	5.6	5.7	5.1

Population Profile

Suffolk and Queens*

Americans were not asked about their ethnic or national background in the 1790 census. This ethnic profile of the 1790 census is based on an analysis of the surnames of the white population, according to Inter-University Consortium for Political and Social Research, a not-for-profit organization. "Slaves" and "Other" categories were added to complete the population.

*-Includes present-day Nassau County

Newsday / Linda McKenney

The U.S. Takes Its First Head Count

In 1790, when the first federal census was taken, there were 3,893,635 people counted in the United States, the number about equally divided between men and women. Of these, 694,264 were slaves.

New York State, with 21,324 slaves, was the largest slaveholding state in the North, and Virginia, with 292,627, was the largest slaveholding state in the Union.

Long Island had 36,949 people, of whom 4,839 were slaves. By contrast, New York, city and county, had 33,131 people, 2,369 of them slaves. The largest slaveholders on Long Island were: Suffolk County, William Floyd of Mastic (14); Queens, Samuel Martin of South Hempstead (17); and Kings, Jacob Bennet of Brooklyn (17).

The taking of a federal census every 10 years was required under Article I, Section 2 of the Constitution, to be used as the basis for apportioning seats in the House of Representatives. The 1790 census included five categories: (1) free white males of 16 years and older, including heads of families; (2) free white males under age 16; (3) free white females, including heads of families; (4) all other free peoples (this included free blacks as well as Indians); (5) slaves.

A Critic's Mixed Portrait of LI

DWIGHT from **Preceding Page**

After traveling up the North Fork and finding the land good and the people industrious and thrifty, Dwight felt obliged to make some general observations. The sum and substance is that he was not impressed.

The truth is, this country is not distinguished, like others through which I have travelled, by a succession of varieties, continually inviting the eye, and furnishing a fund of materials for observation. A general sameness spreads over its face; and in an excursion of twenty or thirty miles a traveler may be said, in a sense, to have seen it all.

But Dwight pressed on to the South Fork and the South Shore. Noticing its resemblance to Cape Cod and Martha's Vineyard. Noting the abundance of stones smoothed by years of having been washed by water, he made a conclusion that has been borne out by later geologic study:

It would seem to be a natural conclusion that the great body of this island, or perhaps more properly the materials of which it is composed, were at some former period covered by the ocean . . .

Looking closely at the soil, Dwight noted that in the short time since Washington had seen the soil depleted of nutrients, Long Islanders were beginning to do something about it. He was seeing the beginning of good agricultural practices that would continue throughout the century. New farm implements would come later, but for now, fertilizer was the key, and they went far and wide to obtain it.

Not content with what they could make and find on their own farms and shores, they have sent their vessels up the Hudson, and loaded them with the residuum of potash manufacturies; gleaned the streets of New-York; and have imported various kinds of manure from New-Haven, New-London, and even from Hartford.

When it came to fertilizer, Dwight was almost as rhapsodic as he was about Phebe McCoun:

In addition to all this, they have swept the Sound; and covered their fields with the immense shoals of white-fish, with which in the beginning of summer its waters are replenished. No manure is so cheap as this where the fish abound, none is so rich, and few are so lasting. Its effects of vegetation are prodigious.

Dwight traveled to East Hampton and farther out to Montauk, and commented on the "fantastical scenery." He found the East Hamptonites terribly isolated, living simple, quiet, self-contained lives: an island within an island.

The Yale president was struck by the hospitality of Long Islanders.

A traveller is received with an air of frankness and good-will which he cannot distrust, and which endears his entertainment much more than manners however polished, or accomodations however convenient. He feels that he has been received not only with civility, but with kindness; and leaves the house of his host with affection.

Traveling west, probably along South Country Road, now Montauk Highway, Dwight noted that the first settlement of any importance he saw after leaving Southampton came 60 miles later near the western border of Huntington Town. The flat expanse of the Hempstead Plains intrigued him, and he pointed out, with barely concealed disdain, that the plains was a great theater for horse racing.

Wherever this kind of sport prevails, no man, acquainted with human affairs, will expect any great prevalence of morals or religion.

Arriving in Jamaica, Dwight noticed the civilizing aspects of proximity to New York City.

This town, from its neighborhood to New-York, and from having long been a customary resort for the inhabitants of that city, has acquired a polish not visible in the towns further eastward. Its buildings and fences are neater, and the manners of its inhabitants have more of what may be called a city air.

All in all, the Rev. Dwight seemed to be of two minds about Long Islanders. He acknowledged their good points, their industriousness, frugality and thriftiness, their civility and kindness. On the other hand, Dwight concluded that Long Islanders were an insular and narrow-minded people. They traveled very little, exercised their minds very little and seemed little interested in expanding their horizons. Those who had shown some degree of talent soon left for New York City.

Such, it would seem, must, through an indefinite period, be the situation of Long Island.

'This town, from its neighborhood to New-York, and from having long been a customary resort for the inhabitants of that city, has acquired a polish not visible in the towns further eastward.'

— Dwight's comments about Jamaica, from his journal

The port once rivaled New York City's, attracting people from around the world

Sag Harbor's Heyday

BY STEVE WICK
STAFF WRITER

On a typical day in the early 1800s, the streets of Sag Harbor were the world's streets, teeming with people from places as exotic as the Fiji Islands, the Sandwich Islands, Madagascar, Ceylon.

Algonquian Indians walked around the waterfront clutching steel-tipped harpoons; Africans strolled the narrow streets speaking in languages never heard before in America. European businessmen brokered deals for whale oil; carpenters lugging tool bags negotiated for work in shipyards and on vessels that had sailed around the world. Ship captains who'd seen everything, been everywhere, stood at the bar in waterfront gin mills and told stories. And they were some stories.

This was Sag Harbor, Long Island's metropolis.

Soon after the English arrived on the South Fork in the mid-1600s, they discovered deep water on the bay side, where big ships could drop anchor and unload trade goods. Farmers from Sagaponack on the ocean side could ride there in their carts to meet incoming boats, and soon the broad meadow overlooking the deep harbor took on the name Sagaponack Harbor. Then it was shortened to Sag Harbor.

By the mid-1700s, houses were being built. Soon, Sag Harbor became a village of firsts — the first deep-water port in the region, the first U.S. Customs House on Long Island, the first great whaling community, the first newspaper on the Island, and perhaps the first place on the Island where milk was delivered to front doors. In contrast to the rest of Long Island, it was cosmopolitan, outward-looking and wide open. Ships that stopped in Sag Harbor after years at sea had crews of American Indians, Polynesians, runaway slaves from the South, Africans and aborigines from Australia. The working world of the sea was integrated.

It was the village's status as a busy port, where a polyglot of languages was spoken, that made it Long Island's window to the world.

"Sag Harbor in the early 1800s was like no other place in America," said Robert Keene, the Southampton Town historian who died recently. "But it began before then, with the growth of the ship-building industry in the late 1700s. Then, with the growth of the whaling industry, the village was remade again. It's really true that the world came to Sag Harbor, from all parts of the South Pacific, the Indian Ocean, Africa.

"The village burned down four times and was rebuilt four times, that will tell you something about Sag Harbor," he added. "In 1843, a history of New York State was published. In the Long Island section, it says there were only two places of any importance — Brooklyn on the west end and Sag Harbor on the East End."

In 1789, the U.S. Congress declared Sag Harbor a "port of entry" and set up a customs house to collect import duties. That year, according to Dorothy Zaykowski's "Sag Harbor — The Story of an American Beauty," the village "had more tons of square-rigged vessels engaged in commerce than even New York City." The first customs collector was John Gelston of Bridgehampton; the second was Henry Dering, who held the position for more than 30 years. He was succeeded by his son, Thomas.

Henry Dering was also the village's first postmaster. Sag Harbor's post office, one of the first on Long Island, was set up in Dering's house. Mail went back and forth between Sag Harbor and New York City by stagecoach. Delivery time: three days. Two years after the port of entry designation, in 1791, the first newspaper on Long Island, called Frothingham's Long Island Herald, was started.

During the War of 1812, British naval troops raided the village. There were no known casualties, but there was extensive property damage. Soldiers from surrounding villages arrived, and a pitched battle erupted on the waterfront. "Limbs were falling from trees, solid shot were screaming overhead, houses were being shattered and pandemonium reigned generally," wrote A.M. Cook of Bridgehampton.

The war devastated Sag Harbor's commercial fleet. "We formerly had twenty to twenty-five coasting vessels employed in southern trade and in carrying wood to market," wrote Rep. Ebenezer Sage. "Three or four of them remained . . ."

While slow to recover from the war, Sag Harbor went back to being a sophisticated community. But a fire — the first of four devastating conflagrations — erupted in the spring of 1817. The blaze, which started in a hay barn, roared along the waterfront, destroying dozens of homes and businesses. As a result of the fire, the village formed a fire department, the Otter Hose Company, which was the first volunteer company in New York State.

Rebuilding was slow, but by 1820 — on the eve of a boom that would come to Sag Harbor with the growth of the whaling industry — there were 150 houses in the village, one of the first circulating libraries on Long Island, and a thriving sea trade based in the harbor.

Seven years later, a businessman named Nathan Tinker took out an unusual advertisement in the Jan. 6, 1827, edition of the village's other newspaper, the Republican Watchman. "The subscriber offers to supply families in this vicinity with MILK, upon such terms as will add greatly to their convenience." Milk delivery — at a rate of four cents a quart — had arrived on Long Island.

For the three decades between 1820 and 1850, the whale trade brought Sag Harbor untold profits. It also helped transform America, because what the whalers really brought back in their holds was more than oil. It was light.

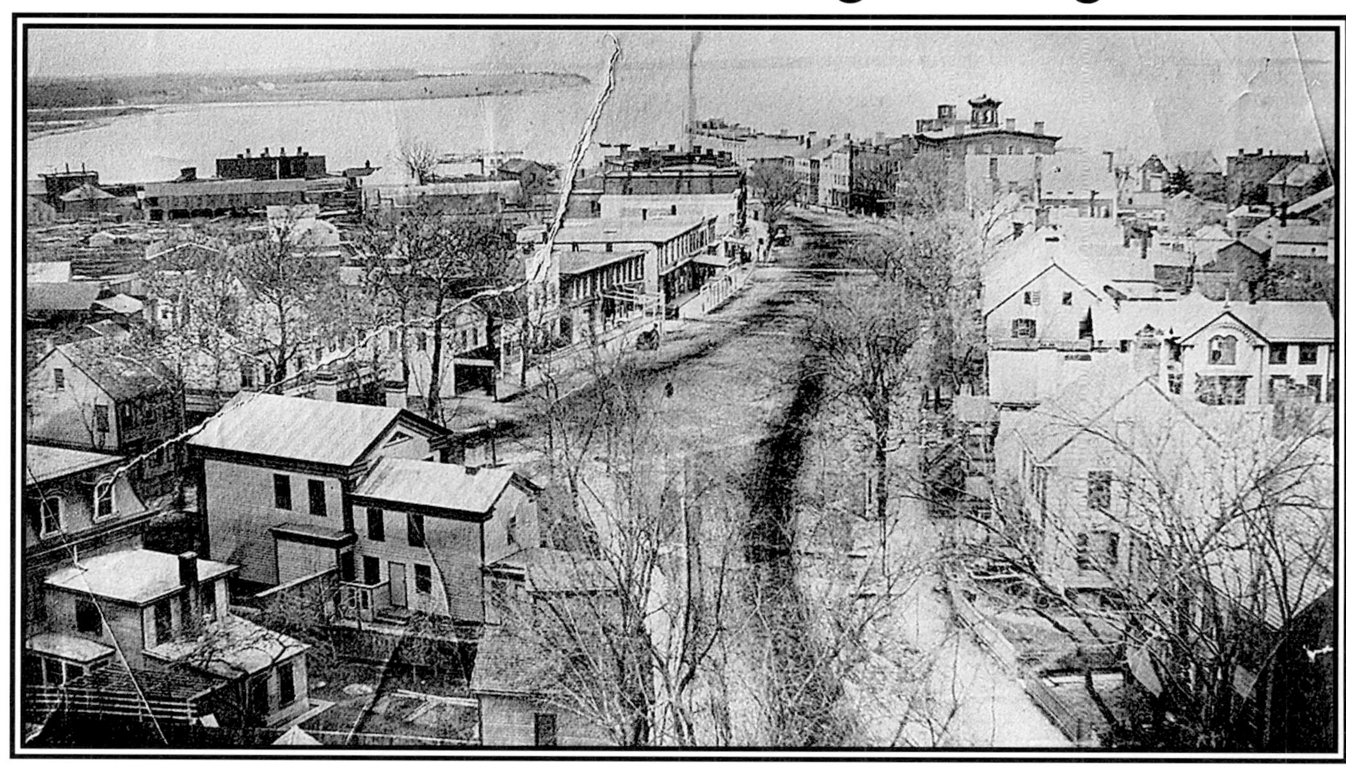

John Jermain Memorial Library; Newsday Photo

A view of lower Main Street in the village, about 1859. For the decades between 1820 and 1850, the whale trade brought untold profits.

Cooper's Inspirational Visit

It was whale oil that brought James Fenimore Cooper to Sag Harbor. He stayed long enough to get a book out of it.

Cooper, born and raised in upstate New York, came to Sag Harbor in 1819 after his marriage to Susan DeLancey, whose family owned land in Sag Harbor and on Shelter Island.

That year, Cooper bought shares in a whaling vessel, the Union, which sailed from Sag Harbor on its maiden voyage. He based two books — "The Water Witch" and "The Sea Lions" — on his experiences in Sag Harbor. The first few chapters of "The Sea Lions" are set in Orient Point, where Cooper also spent time.

If these books had modest success, his subsequent books made him a household name. In the mid-1820s, he published a series of novels, including "The Last of the Mohicans," that featured woodsman Natty Bumppo. According to Dorothy Zaykowski's "Sag Harbor — The Story of an American Beauty," it is believed that Bumppo was modeled after a celebrated Sag Harbor whaling captain, David Hand, who had lived a colorful life.

"Captain Hand had been a seaman and privateer and, before the age of twenty, had seen Washington, been a prisoner of war five times, and was one of the exchange of prisoners from the Jersey prison ship," Zaykowski wrote.

— Steve Wick

National Archives Photo / Matthew Brady

James Fenimore Cooper, whose contact with Sag Harbor resulted in two books

Island's first newspaper dishes a portion of humor, knowledge and . . . news

A Publisher's Ambitious Start

BY ANDREW SMITH
STAFF WRITER

On the afternoon of May 10, 1791, in an unassuming house on Main Street in Sag Harbor, David Frothingham finished setting four pages of type by hand, cranked his hand-operated press and hoped for the best.

The 26-year-old printer, recently arrived from Boston, was Long Island's first newspaper publisher. And its first editor. And its first reporter. And its first ad salesman. And its first paper boy.

For the next 7½ years after that Tuesday afternoon, Frothingham's Long-Island Herald would be Long Island's only newspaper.

In appearance and content, the Herald was typical for the time. It was a single sheet of durable rag paper, folded into four 8-by-17-inch pages. Page one of that first issue contained items on the value of a free press, on happiness, on religion, on how to prevent unhappy marriages: "1. Let every man who marries a person young enough to be his grand-daughter be deemed an ideot . . . "

And it featured Frothingham's introduction to his public.

The fledgling editor pledged to make the Herald "a useful repository of knowledge, humour, and entertainment; while Vice, the bane of society . . . though cloathed with the garb of authority, will be branded with every mark of infamy."

He chose as his motto a quote from Alexander Pope's "Essay on Man": "Eye nature's walks, shoot folly as it flies, And catch the manners living as they rise."

The year before Frothingham arrived, President George Washington had named Henry Packer Dering, scion of an East End mercantile family, collector of the new port of Sag Harbor. Like many prominent men of the time, Dering decided to establish a newspaper — giving himself a voice in the debate over how the nation should evolve and a tool to lobby the infant government.

But before he could have a newspaper, Dering needed someone to run it. His search for a printer led him to Boston, where he tried to convince Frothingham, a journeyman printer, to come to Long Island to publish a newspaper.

Frothingham's goal of providing Long Islanders with "knowledge, humour, and entertainment" was an ambitious one, but didn't leave much room for news. Amid the philosophical essays, poems and political treatises, news was confined to pages two and three, and the bulk of it was weeks-old articles reprinted from American and overseas newspapers. News of local events often was rendered tersely — if at all.

"It is with regret we inform the public, that in almost every town on this end of the Island it is very sickly, insomuch that in many families there are not well enough to take care of the sick," a typical grammatically twisted item read in its entirety.

Frothingham soon hired post riders to deliver the Herald to subscribers all over Long Island. It even had readers in New York, where it was shipped by boat. Indeed, it soon boasted advertisements from several city businesses. Other ads promoted ships sailing to New London, Conn., and New York, local dry goods stores and land for sale. Some notices sought the return of runaway slaves.

The Herald soon gained momentum, but financial success clearly eluded Frothingham. He charged the equivalent of one dollar a year for the paper but also accepted produce as payment. Although he didn't lack for readers, subscribers who paid their bills on time were somewhat scarce.

"The Printer earnestly requests all those indebted to him for Newspapers, to make immediate payment, as he is much in want of Money at the present time," Frothingham wrote in the June 8, 1795, issue. "It is impossible for him to wait on his subscribers at their houses, without neglecting other business."

Further hindering Frothingham was his difficulty in obtaining paper. He regularly asked his readers for old rags, the raw material for cotton paper. During paper shortages, Frothingham would reduce the size of the Herald or not even print it for one or two weeks.

Much of the news that did make The Herald was devoted to events in the nation and Europe. Certainly, with Sag Harbor's reliance on trade, that news was compelling. The revolution in France and war between France and Britain were as important to the port town of Sag Harbor as burglaries in Southampton.

The federal government's attitude toward France and Britain was watched carefully by Frothingham, Dering and the rest of Sag Harbor. When President John Adams and his administration negotiated treaties accommodating the British, the Herald reflected the local anger still remaining toward Britain. The Herald was suspicious, as well, of Federalists such as Alexander Hamilton who resisted sharing political power with citizens.

Coupled with his always precarious finances, however, Frothingham's anti-administration slant soon made publishing the Herald an unacceptable risk for his patron, Dering. The administration of John Adams won passage of the Alien and Sedition Acts in 1798, making it illegal to publish "any false, scandalous, and malicious writing . . . against the government of the United States."

With no fanfare, the last issue of the Herald was issued Dec. 17 that year.

A copy of Frothingham's Long-Island Herald, which was LI's only paper for 7½ years

East Hampton Library Photo

AN EDITOR FADES AWAY

David Frothingham's career — and perhaps his life — came to a tumultuous end soon after the Herald closed. What happened to him remains a mystery almost 200 years after he disappeared without a trace.

Two days after he printed the last issue of Frothingham's Long-Island Herald, he attended an anti-Federalist political rally in Bridgehampton. Aaron Burr, who was planning to run for president against John Adams in 1800, offered Frothingham a job at the Argus in New York, a paper owned by one of his supporters. He left his wife and six children at Sag Harbor to take the job. Frothingham's role at the Argus was limited to running the printing operation. Nevertheless, when the Argus reprinted in its Nov. 6, 1799, issue a letter alleging that Alexander Hamilton was secretly using British money to suppress a newspaper critical of him, Frothingham became a target.

Hamilton had Frothingham arrested for libel under the Alien and Sedition Laws. Even though the letter had appeared in several other papers and even though Frothingham had nothing to do with the decision to reprint it, he was sentenced to four months in jail and fined $100. He was never heard from again.

Some historians have suggested that Frothingham and other political prisoners were taken out West and killed in the waning days of the Adams administration. A Boston newspaper in 1814 reported that a David Frothingham was on a ship that sank at sea. And in 1822, another Boston paper said that Frothingham died on the Congo River in Africa.

A gravestone in Sag Harbor bears his name and the date 1814 but there is no body beneath the stone. — Andrew Smith

Newsday Photo / Bill Davis

David Frothingham's home on Main Street in Sag Harbor

In primitive classrooms, students learned about morals — and hauling firewood

The Hard Road to Learning

BY KATTI GRAY
STAFF WRITER

Imagine having to haul your own firewood to class, or risk being expelled for showing up without it.

Or arriving there sopping wet from a trek through rain or snow. As you and your classmates sit around the small, wood-burning iron stove at the center of a one-room schoolhouse, your damp woolens begin to smell.

The fire isn't quite warm enough, going out with such frequency that the fluctuations in room temperature cause your feet to itch painfully.

And if you get out of line, you're really in trouble. Corporal punishment is the norm, or you might have to sit in the dunce corner or the teacher could wash out your ear with a hot corncob.

Such was life in the classroom during the late 1700s to mid-1800s as the first community schools — private and public — began sprouting up across on Long Island.

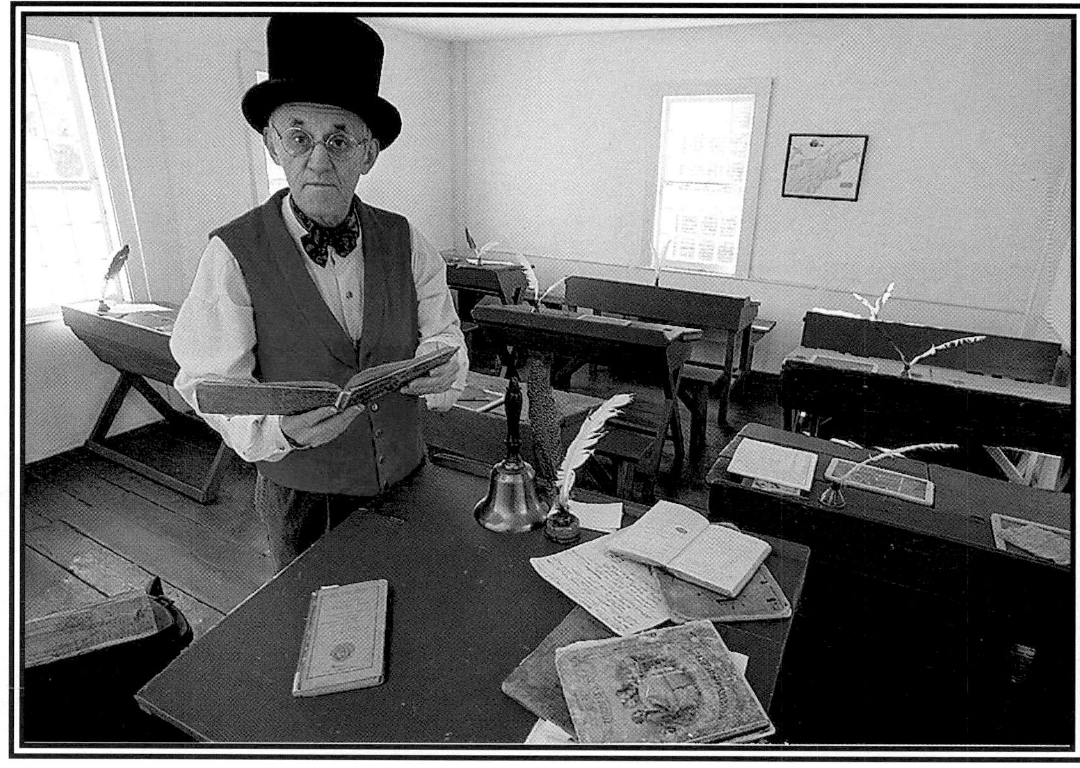

In period dress of a teacher, Hugh King stands in the Town House Museum, a one-room schoolhouse in East Hampton.

While offspring of the wealthiest families had been taught by private tutors ever since colonization began in the region, public education did not begin evolving until the early 1800s.

By 1836, almost every white child on the Island — far less is known about Indian and black children — attended school at a cost of $1.50 per year, according to Edna Howell Yeager in her book "Around the Forks." Some families still footed part of that bill based on the number of days their children attended school. By the 1870s and 1880s, the school year was being structured as we now know it, including the grading of student performance.

But for students attending schools that opened as the 18th Century was coming to a close, schools were places to learn the kinds of skills that helped out on the farm or in whatever occupation kept food on the family table.

"You went to learn enough math to help do the business ledger, enough reading to comprehend the Bible," said Hugh King, director of education for the Town House Museum, an East Hampton facility that initially doubled as a meeting place and as one of Long Island's first one-room schools. (The very first was the Red Creek schoolhouse, established in Southampton in the mid-1600s.)

"School was an extension of family. Manners were taught there. Reading lessons generally were moral lessons — what with all the Puritans and Presbyterians," he said.

"It was reading, writing, recitation. Spelling was a cornerstone subject, taught by rote. You said the word out loud and clapped your hand to each letter. Meanings of words were not important initially, since Webster's wasn't created until the 1840s."

The fact that students, who generally attended school through the age of 14 or so, would be formally taught represented a major shift in how they were perceived by adult society. "In the 1700s, the society thought children were evil and needed to be punished," King said. "In the 1800s — and they were by no means coddled then — philosophically, society began nurturing them."

The Rev. Samuel Buell helped lead that charge locally as one of the founders of Clinton Academy. Named for then Gov. George Clinton, it was the first private school chartered by New York State. That was in 1786, 17 years before legislators established common school districts statewide and almost a century before laws mandated school attendance for children aged 8 through 14. The first headmaster was William Payne.

LI HISTORY.COM

To read the diary of a New York schoolgirl in the mid-1800s, see http://www.lihistory.com on the Internet.

In the earliest schools, many teachers rented space in which to work. Usually, men taught boys and women, girls. And, as puritanism prevailed, instructors boarded with families who kept close watch on how teachers behaved outside as well as inside the classroom.

Initially, classes were segregated by gender. Boys generally enrolled from September through April after they were no longer needed for the harvest, while girls attended school from May through September. Clinton eventually would change that and become coeducational, preparing boys for college or vocational careers and training girls in areas such as social etiquette and spiritual reading.

Former Islip Town Historian Nathaniel R. Howell wrote in 1944 that the mother of Harriet Beecher Stowe had opened a boarding school for girls in 1799 in East Hampton. In 1834, another academy for girls was established in Riverhead, with instruction in areas including English, mathematics and Latin.

Whatever the academic subject matter, the focus on the soul was common in early schools.

The day began with a biblical reading. Other studies included geography, and history that was as much a mix of lore and legend as the truth. Much of it focused on the exploits of white men as pioneers and heroes, while members of other races were referred to as "savages'" or ignored altogether.

Math problems had to be calculated in the head, without the aid of fingers or other objects for counting.

"They thought the mind was a muscle," King said. "You had to use it."

Handwriting was practiced with quill and ink on paper that, because it was so expensive, was often recycled. A child might write, over and over: "Obey your parent" or "Be a good child."

Another popular subject was sewing, which was taught to boys and girls.

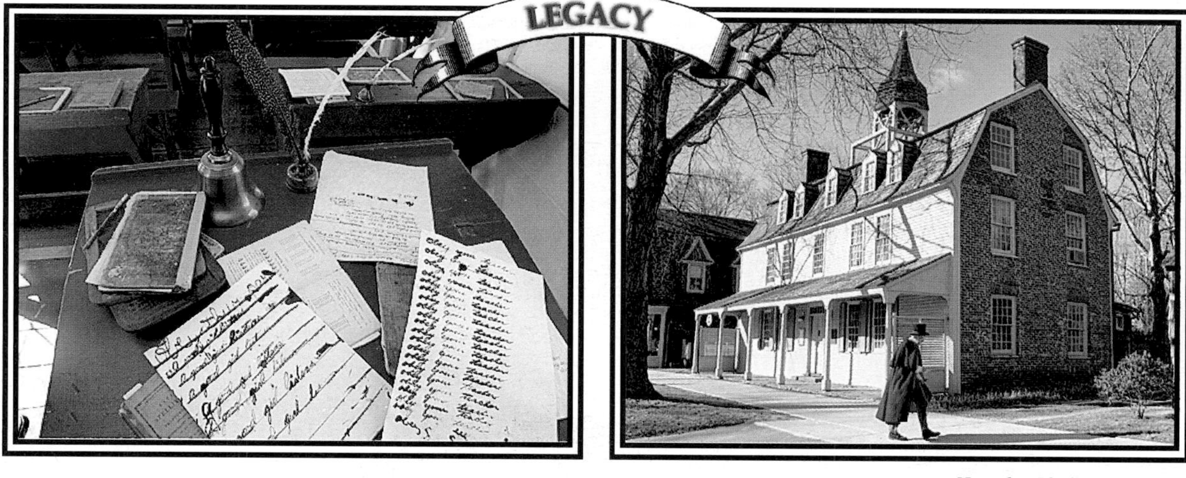

Newsday Photos / Bill Davis

The desk, left, of an 18th Century teacher in the East Hampton Town House. The Clinton Academy, right, was founded 1786 as the first private school chartered by the state. The Main Street buildings are open to the public between Memorial Day and Labor Day. A tour of both costs $4 for adults, $2 for children and seniors. Call 516-324-6850.

Lessons did not last more than 15 minutes. Often, there were not enough books. Sometimes teachers were barely out of their teens and, by today's standards, minimally educated.

"If you taught older children, sometimes the brightest child was smarter than the teacher," King said. "Six-year-olds would come and do the ABCs and then sit there for the rest of the day . . . I have to think that the people who did well in school enjoyed it. But those who had difficulty did not — just like today."

U.S. and British skirmish on the Sound in the War of 1812

War on the Waters

BY BILL BLEYER
STAFF WRITER

The partially submerged vessel that steamed out of New York and into Long Island Sound on June 19, 1814, was like nothing local mariners had ever seen. It was one of America's first submarines, a weapon designed to offset Britain's naval supremacy in the War of 1812.

Because of its curved, iron-clad deck, the vessel was named Turtle. But the way its maiden mission turned out, it should have been named Turkey.

The 23-foot semi-submersible — it sat just about even with the surface of the water — was bound for New London, Conn. The 12-man crew intended to use its five towed torpedoes — designed by steamboat inventor Robert Fulton — to sink British warships blockading the Sound. But one day out of New York, Turtle was caught in a gale and blown ashore in Southold. The crew and local farmers failed in an attempt to burn the hull and keep it out of British hands.

As a result, the hulk was still on the beach on June 26 when the British warships Maidstone and Sylph happened by. Despite fire from American militiamen — including 67-year-old Noah Terry, who climbed up on the submarine and defiantly waved his hat — the British landed and blew up Turtle.

Turtle's debut and destruction was the most unusual episode of the War of 1812 on Long Island. For the most part, it consisted of blockades and minor skirmishes. No Long Islanders are known to have lost their lives on local soil.

The United States declared war on Great Britain June 18, 1812, following more than a decade of the Royal Navy "impressing" or kidnaping crew members — including at least 20 Long Islanders — from American merchant vessels.

It wasn't until March 20, 1813, that eight warships sailed over the horizon to blockade Long Island Sound — one of two entrances to New York Harbor, a nautical highway for commerce, and site of several shipyards. It wasn't much of a contest — the British enjoyed a lopsided superiority in ships, and the few American men-of-war were drydocked in Brooklyn for repairs.

The closest the two navies came to a full-fledged battle in Long Island waters was in the summer of 1814 when Commodore Stephen Decatur sailed with the ships the United States, the Hornet and the Macedonian down the Sound toward the British. On June 1, Decatur, after receiving inflated reports of British strength, withdrew into the Thames River at New London. Although the Hornet escaped the next year, the United States and the Macedonian were bottled up for the rest of the war.

That left only privateers to confront the British in the region. The sloop of war Beaver, fitted out on the East End, captured 11 British prizes.

The blockade was porous. Many ships sailed to and from New York with impunity while some ports were virtually shut down. More than two dozen Long Island merchant ships were captured.

Weather dealt the British Navy its worst loss in the region. On Jan. 16, 1815, the Sylph ran aground near Southampton in a snowstorm. Only six of the 121 aboard were saved when fishermen launched a boat through the surf.

Britannia was not content to just rule the waves. British forces raided several ports, including Sag Harbor, sufficiently important and vulnerable to be guarded by a fort garrisoned by 3,000 soldiers. On July 11, 1813, about 100 British marines landed at the wharf and began firing cannons. "Houses were being shattered and pandemonium reigned generally," wrote A.M. Cook of Bridgehampton. With American militiamen converging on the town, the British only had time to set fire to one sloop before cannon fire from the fort drove them off. Americans led by Capt. David Hand extinguished the flames and recovered abandoned British weapons.

The same year two British warships sailed into what is now Port Jefferson Harbor after dark, captured seven merchant ships and fled. Fort Nonsense in Poquott opened fire on the British with its single cannon. When one of the captured ships ran aground, the British burned it.

Babylon thought the British were coming when a whaleboat approached in 1814. The story had begun months before when the American frigate Essex, commanded by Capt. David Porter, was captured off Chile. Porter and his crew were set free in a small boat, Essex Jr., after promising never to bear arms against the British again.

After 73 days at sea, they were stopped by HMS Saturn near the entrance to New York Harbor. The Essex Jr. was allowed to proceed but was stopped again for another search. Porter regarded this as a violation of the rules of warfare and decided to escape. The next morning he and 10 crew members pulled away in a whaleboat and escaped into the fog. They rowed for 60 miles, risked the dangerous surf in Fire Island Inlet and crossed Great South Bay to Babylon.

Residents suspected they were British spies. But after Porter produced his naval commission, the whaleboat was placed on a wagon, and captain and crew climbed aboard for a trip to the Brooklyn Navy Yard, where they were received in triumph.

Many Long Islanders, particularly on the East End, were hurt by the war long after it ended Feb. 18, 1815. Writing about Sag Harbor in 1814, the district's congressman, Ebenezer Sage, said that by the time the British were through burning and capturing vessels, only three or four of the port's fleet of 20 ships remained in sailing condition.

Even though the end of the war brought a boom in commerce, it would take two years after peace was restored for Sag Harbor's maritime trade to rebound.

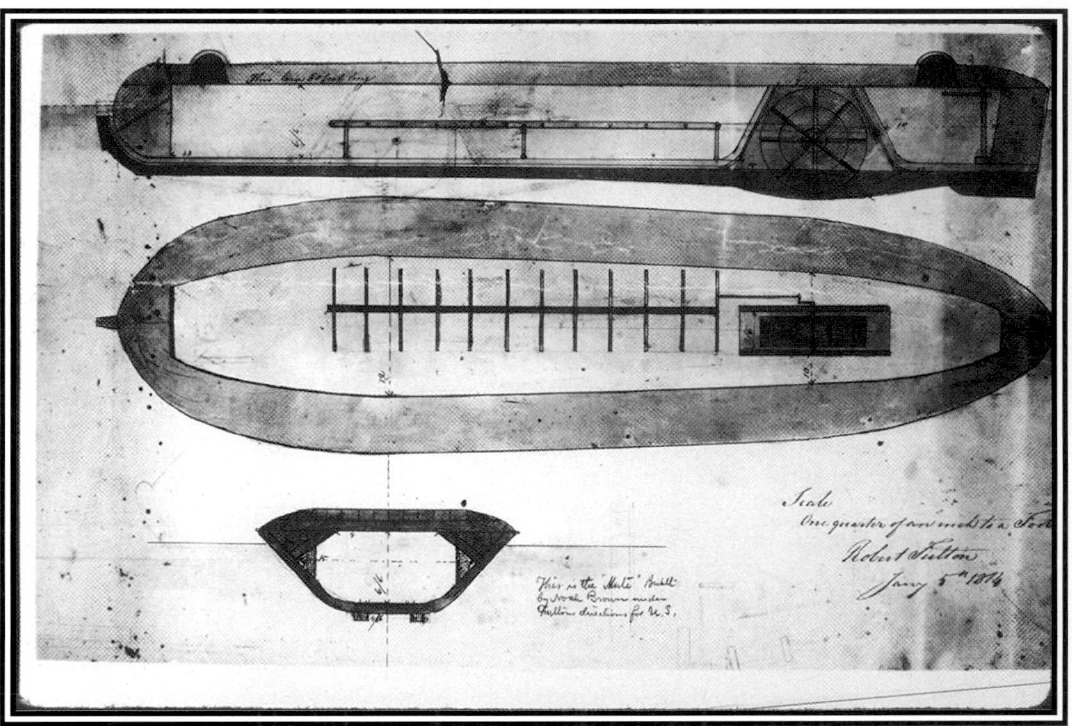

Naval Submarine Force Museum

Inventor Robert Fulton's plans for the Mute, a submarine he designed for the U.S. Navy, though it was not finished before the War of 1812 ended. An earlier U.S. sub, the Turtle, was blown up on Long Island by the British.

HIRAM CRONK DEAD.

Hiram Cronk, the last survivor of the War of 1812, died this morning at his home in Ava, near Rome, N. Y., aged 105 years.

Hiram Cronk, last surviving veteran of the War of 1812, in a Brooklyn Daily Eagle obituary in 1905.

1812: AMERICA IS AT WAR WITH ENGLAND AGAIN

The Treaty of Paris ended the American Revolution in 1783, but it didn't end hostility between the United States and Great Britain.

England was at war with France. American vessels sailing to French ports were seized and about 2,500 American sailors were "impressed" to serve in the Royal Navy. The British also incited Indian attacks against American frontier forts and settlements.

Although the American Army had only 6,000 men and the Navy less than 20 ships, Congress declared war June 18, 1812. Sentiment about fighting England varied by region. Generally the New England and Middle Atlantic states, which had the most shipping to lose, opposed the war while the southern and western states supported it.

The war that neither side wanted was ended by the Treaty of Ghent in late 1814, although fighting continued into the next year until the word got out. The treaty did not mention rights of seamen, but impressment ended, as did Indian incursions. By fighting the world's greatest maritime power to a standstill, the United States gained prestige.

Ninety years later, a postscript would be written on Long Island when the last veteran of the war was buried here.

More than 25,000 mourners jostled for a view of the body of Hiram Cronk lying in state on May 17, 1905, in New York's City Hall after he died at the age of 105. The procession to Cypress Hills Cemetery in Queens the next day halted traffic on the Brooklyn Bridge.

Cronk, an upstate shoemaker, was 14 when in 1814 he enlisted.

Plans for Cronk's funeral were made a year before his death when New York City officials decided to give him a full send-off, even though he had never set foot in the city.

— Bill Bleyer

Many of the best thoroughbreds can be traced to LI's 'great progenitor'

The Father of Racehorses

BY JOHN JEANSONNE
STAFF WRITER

Here is a dead horse you just can't beat: Messenger, whose ashes now lie near the driveway entrance to an estate in northern Nassau County. He lived from 1780 to 1808 — roughly paralleling the presidency of George Washington — and was the father of our country's racehorses.

He was "the great progenitor." He was the "founding sire" of harness racers, a distinctly American breed, and the most prominent contributor to the nation's thoroughbred stock. Among the chips off the Messenger block were Eclipse, Man o' War, Equipoise, Gallant Fox, Peter Pan, Kelso, Spectacular Bid, Riva Ridge, Swaps, Tom Fool — even Secretariat — not to mention harness superstars Hambletonian, Bret Hanover and Niatross.

He was, like so many of the humans of his day, an early immigrant who hit the only-in-America jackpot. In his native England, Messenger had had a modest racing career of 10 wins in 16 starts. But, once in the New World, with a new career standing at stud, he became the central figure in the fledgling nation's first popular spectator sport. And he played an enormous role in establishing Long Island, whose racing traditions dated to the country's first-ever racetrack in 1665, as the American cradle of turf and breeding.

Among Messenger's earliest progeny was a grandson, Eclipse, who in 1823 beat a North Carolina horse named Sir Henry in a celebrated North vs. South match race at Union Course in Queens — America's first "national" sports event. Attended by an estimated 50,000 from as far away as Virginia and Maryland, the duel "symbolized the onset of modern sport," historian Melvin Adelman declared in his 1986 book, "A Sporting Time."

Messenger first worked in Philadelphia in 1788 and wound up on Long Island, owned by Townsend Cocks (or "Townsend Cock," according to some references) on a farm in what now is the Matinecock section of Locust Valley. For more than two decades, Messenger was bred to English thoroughbreds, halfbreeds and even draught horses, his influence reaching well beyond what Maurizio Bongianni called the "zootechnical invention" of the trotter in a 1984 book, "Champion Horses."

In 1935, horse lovers at the Piping Rock Club in Locust Valley commissioned racing historian John Hervey to write a limited-edition history of Messenger, and erected a monument at his burial site adjacent to their club. A bronze-gone-to-green plaque, attached to a 2-foot-high stone, sits alongside Duck Pond Road, just east of the Piping Rock Road intersection and the 1671 Quaker meetinghouse where Messenger often grazed on the front lawn.

Museum of the City of New York

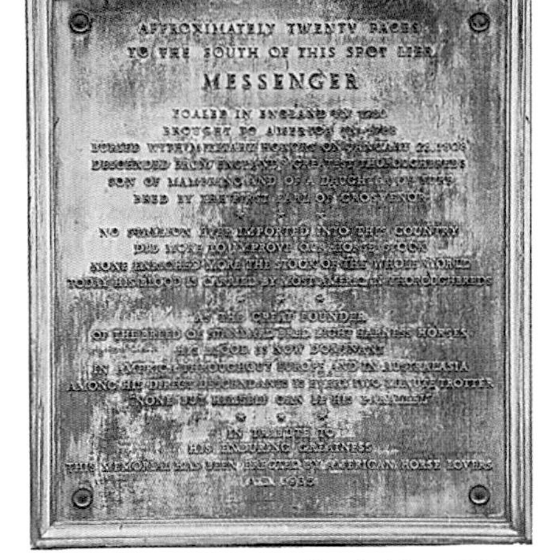

Newsday Photo / Bill Davis

Messenger in a Currier & Ives image from around 1880. At left is the plaque on a Locust Valley monument that honors the great horse, which lived from 1780 to 1808.

"Approximately Twenty Paces to the South of This Spot Lies MESSENGER," the plaque announces. "No Stallion . . . Did More to Improve Our Horse Stock / None Enriched More the Stock of the Whole World / 'None But Himself Can Be His Parallel' . . ." Across the two-lane country road from that marker in the ritzy, leafy neighborhood of sprawling estates is the old red barn where Messenger died, at 28, almost 190 years ago, and was buried, Hervey wrote, "with full military honors . . . in his holiday clothing."

About 1950, a textile executive named Harvey F. Raymond built the current mansion on a piece of Cocks' land. Messenger's burial site is near the north end of Raymond's long driveway — labeled on Hagstrom maps as Messenger Lane. When veteran sports publicist Joe Goldstein, then working for Roosevelt Raceway, created the Messenger Stakes in 1956 as part of harness racing's triple crown, he was told by Raymond that as many as 1,500 cars per year pulled into that driveway to inspect the historic spot. Raymond once had to decline a horse lover's request to dig up a piece of his lawn as a souvenir.

LI HISTORY.COM

Trace Messenger's "family tree" and learn the lineage of other great racehorses on the Internet at http://www.lihistory.com.

Long after his death, Messenger remained a hot sports topic, with his descendants dominating the harness and flat tracks and with baseball's emergence as the national pastime still decades in the future. In December of 1875, John H. Wallace's Monthly excitedly announced, "FOUND AT LAST! After a search of many years, we have an outline drawing of IMPORTED MESSENGER [and] we will soon be able to furnish every horseman throughout the country with an elegant and truthful likeness of the greatest horse that ever crossed the Atlantic!" Alas, it turned out that Messenger was not a beautiful animal, rather a powerfully built but heavy gray critter with an abnormally prominent windpipe. His head was large and heavy, his neck short, his shoulders low and rounded, his mane and tail thin.

Ironically, too, Hervey wrote that despite Messenger's status as the patriarch of trotters, there was no record of Messenger himself ever having been "broken to harness, or driven; it appears he never was systematically trotted," though he "possessed trotting action — the long, sweeping stride — accompanied by such strength, stamina and hardiness, together with much great speed . . ."

Over the years, harness racing has declined and most students of thoroughbred pedigrees have lost track of recent champions' connection to Messenger. But a computer search by the Lexington, Ky.-based Jockey Club can water and feed the Messenger legend: Messenger sired Miller's Damsel, who was the dam of Eclipse, who was the sire of Medoc, who was the sire of Melody, who was the dam of Florine, who was the dam of Aerolite, who was the dam of Spendthrift, who was the sire of Hastings, who was the sire of Fair Play, who was the sire of Display, who was the sire of Discovery, who was the sire of Miss Disco, who was the dam of Bold Ruler, who was the sire of Secretariat.

In the horse world, you can't beat that.

TROTTING'S FIRST SUPERSTAR

Messenger's great-granddaughter Lady Suffolk, known as "the old gray mare of Long Island," was the first trotting superstar when harness racing was the most popular spectator sport in America. Foaled in 1833 in Smithtown — she took her name from her native county — Lady Suffolk at first was a working horse, pulling a butcher and oyster cart, when Irish immigrant David Bryan bought her in 1838 for his livery stable.

The livery business was the nerve center of the transportation system, and Lady Suffolk had just begun her new job when William Porter, a horse-racing fan who in 1831 had started the nation's first weekly sports journal, happened to hire her for a trip from New York to Commack. According to historian John Hervey, Porter suggested that Lady Suffolk be tried at harness racing.

Most histories say she first raced in Babylon, and from 1838 to 1853, she entered 162 recorded races and probably at least double that number in impromptu challenges and exhibitions. Harness racing was then a major attraction at county fairs, and Lady Suffolk — much in demand — traveled through 17 states for races, almost always pulling her own racing equipment, driver and owner behind her between command performances.

— John Jeansonne

Smithtown Historical Society

A lithograph depicts Lady Suffolk in a mile race in 1849

Sag Harbor Whaling Museum; Newsday Photo

"Fire in the chimney" — what whalers called the effect of blood spurting through a whale's blowhole. The artwork, from the Sag Harbor Whaling Museum, is an aquatint done around 1830.

Hundreds of ships and thousands of men set sail from Long Island in the industry's heyday

In Search of Whales

BY STEVE WICK
STAFF WRITER

Just after sunrise on a cold December morning in 1845, the whaler Konohassett pulled up anchor in Sag Harbor and slipped into the falling tide that flowed into Gardiners Bay.

Soon, the ship passed the rounded bluff of Montauk. The lighthouse atop the bluff was the last thing the men aboard the vessel would see on Long Island as they headed out to sea; it would be the first thing they would see on their return trip.

Whenever that would be.

They would not be back until their crews had killed enough sperm whales, right whales and bowhead whales to fill barrels with oil that would make the ship's owners wealthy, lubricate machinery, and light homes, schools and businesses up and down the East Coast. America glowed because of the men aboard the Konohassett, and men on hundreds of other vessels who on this same morning prowled the world's oceans on a murderous intersection with whales. Since the first of the year, 26 other whaling vessels had left Sag Harbor, and none had yet returned.

The men aboard the 300-ton Konohassett represented a cross section of Long Island life and of America itself. Her captain was J.B. Worth, a white man from a Southold farm family; his crew was made up of white farm boys, Indians from reservations and shanty towns who spent their lives on the poor margins of society, and three black men — Reese Smith, Philip Smith and Solomon Ward — who came to the Konohassett because it was one of the few jobs they could get.

No work anywhere in America was so integrated, but it was harsh reality and not good intentions that brought crews together. "Whaling was the most dangerous job on the sea that has ever existed," said George Finckenor, curator of the whaling museum in Sag Harbor. "There was no romance associated with it at all — it was brutal. Few men wanted to do it."

To get men to work on whaling vessels, owners posted advertisements near port towns. The advertisements would read: "Chance of a Lifetime" or "Come See the World" or "Strong Whalemen Wanted." Because of the dangers, small pay and years at sea, whaling most often attracted men who could not find other work — Indians, former slaves, poor whites.

Ships' records tell the day-to-day stories of long voyages, of years at sea, of the killing and butchering of whales, and of other ships sighted and islands visited. But they also tell the stories of captains killed by whales, crewmen drowned or their limbs ripped off by ropes, of ships lost in ice floes, of ships wrecked on uncharted shoals. There are graves of Long Island and New England whalers on islands in the Atlantic and Pacific Oceans.

And there are monuments, too. There is a monument today in Japan to the men of the Manhattan, a Sag Harbor whaler whose crew included a former slave from Southampton and a Shinnecock Indian. It is one more

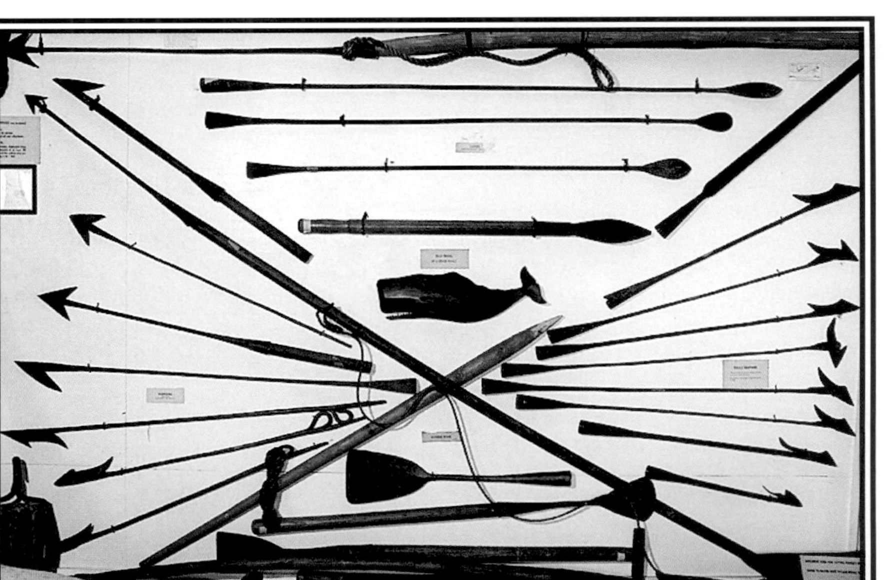

Newsday Photo / Bill Davis

Harpoons of many sizes are among tools on display at the Sag Harbor Whaling Museum.

monument than exists on Long Island to either Indians or slaves.

"These were men who went where no one had ever gone," said David Littlefield, a historian at Mystic Seaport in Connecticut.

The whaling industry, which brought millions of dollars in profits to Long Island in less than 30 years before the industry's sudden collapse in the 1860s, was documented in precise detail. Captains kept journals of exactly where their boats were, what they saw, how many whales were killed and how many got away. They even made pencil drawings in their journals of the whales they killed. Seen today, these handsome drawings stir the imagination, and evoke images of an extraordinary chapter in American history.

Captains were not the only ones to keep records. Whaling companies also kept detailed accounts of exactly how many barrels of oil were collected on journeys, along with how many pounds of whalebone; some crew members kept detailed diaries showing every event that occurred during months at sea. In one case, a woman from Orient, Martha Brown, kept a diary of her experiences on the Lucy Ann, in the late 1840s. She wrote of burials at sea, animal life sighted, and visits to exotic places with names like Three Kings Island. She lived out her life in an old Orient farmhouse; a photograph taken in 1905 shows a white-haired Brown greeting visitors in front of her house.

Aboard the Konohassett, Worth was like every other whaling captain — he kept a detailed journal. Five months after leaving Sag Harbor, the ship was in the South Pacific. There, in the dark of a spring night, Worth, half a world away from his Southold farm, coolly penned a one-paragraph comment.

May 24, 1 o'clock in the morning, ship K, under full sail before the wind, going at a rate of 5 knots, struck upon a coral reef which is not drawn on any chart. We are obliged to leave ship in our boats with a little bread and water.

* * *

By the mid-1840s, whaling was the second-largest industry in New York and New England, and the seventh-largest in the country. At its height, the industry employed more than 10,000 seamen, and thousands more worked as coopers, carpenters, rope and sail makers, and boat builders.

"In 1846, the height of whaling in the Northeast, there were 730 ships involved," Littlefield said. "While an exact dollar amount has been very hard to pin down, it involved tens of millions of dollars in profits that were spread out to crewmen, captains, ship owners, agents and everyone involved in the support industries. It was a massive business."

The business made Sag Harbor a bustling port town and home to a U.S. customs house that kept records of every ship and every ship's cargo. More than 60 whaling ships called Sag Harbor home; much smaller fleets worked out of Greenport and Cold Spring Harbor. To the north, New Bedford, Mass., was home to the largest whaling fleet on the East Coast. There, Herman Melville set his novel "Moby Dick," about a white whale's destruction of a ship and its captain — a story inspired by the real-life sinking of a ship by a sperm whale.

Sag Harbor's maritime history can be read in its streets — they lead directly to the harbor.

"If a visitor were dropped into Sag Harbor blindfolded, he would know immediately by the directions of the streets that he was in a place different from nearly every other community," said Robert MacKay, director of the Society for the Preservation of Long Island Antiquities. "In Long Island communities, streets were built around a commons area, or ran parallel to the water, not perpendicular to the water."

In the 1600s and 1700s, whaling had been a shore business, with spotters on the ocean beaches seeing whales offshore, then calling for crews to man dories that would chase and kill them. The dead whale would be towed to the beach, where its thick blubber would be stripped off with long poles that looked like spades. It was ugly, bloody work, the carcass laid bare down to the bones.

TALES OF WHALES AT TWO MUSEUMS

Long Island was a major whaling center in the 19th Century and the reasons why it was so are on display in two local museums.

Cold Spring Harbor Whaling Museum: Main Street (Route 25A), Cold Spring Harbor, 516-367-3418. The four-room museum features memorabilia including a 30-foot whaleboat (one of a dozen in the world), harpoons, scrimshaw and a diorama of the whaling port in its 1850 heyday. There is also a biology and conservation gallery. The "Cold Spring Harbor: Time Measured by the Tide" exhibit focuses on the harbor community from 1799 to 1913 and will be open through June. The museum also sponsors weekend lectures, films, programs and family activities. It is open 11 a.m.-5 p.m. year-round daily, June to Sept. 1, then closed on Mondays (except holidays). Fee: $2; ages 6-12 and over 65, $1.50.

Sag Harbor Whaling Museum: Main and Garden Streets, Sag Harbor, 516-725-0770. This museum is in a striking Greek Revival structure that visitors enter through the jaw bones of a whale. Artifacts include paintings, log entries, scrimshaw, harpoons and other items associated with the industry that once made Sag Harbor Long Island's foremost whaling port. It is open 10 a.m.-5 p.m. Monday-Saturday, 1-5 p.m. Sunday, mid-May-September. Fee: $3, $1 ages 6-13, $2 over 60.

Photo by Pat West

Newsday Photo / John H. Cornell Jr.

The whaling museums in Cold Spring Harbor, left, and Sag Harbor.

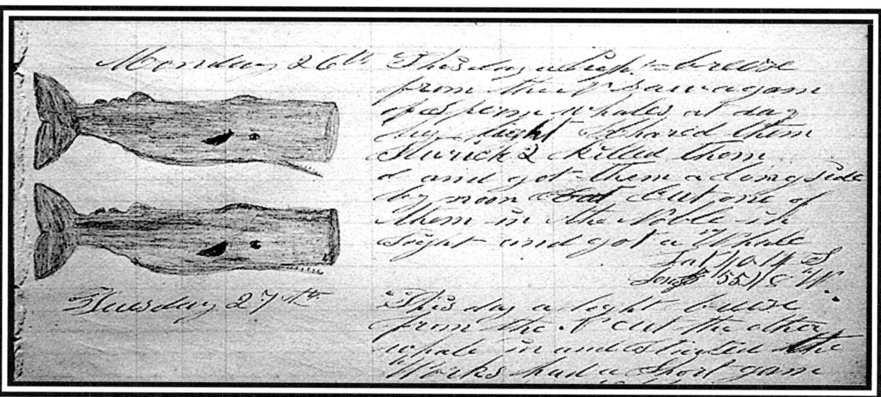

Thursday 27th This day a light breeze

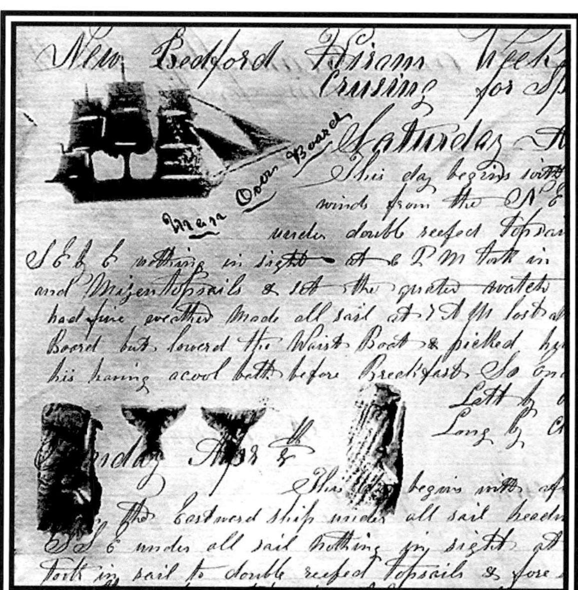

New Bedford

Cruising for

Saturday

This day begins with

winds from the

under double reefed topsa

nothing in sight at 6 P M took in

and Mizen topsails & set the

had fine weather Made all sail

Board but lowered the Waist Boat & picked

his having a cool bath before Breakfast

under all sail nothing in sight

took in sail to double reefed topsails & fore

Newsday Photos / Bill Davis

Log pages from the John Jermaine Library in Sag Harbor and the Sag Harbor Whaling Museum, left, show how whalers recorded their activity. Above, a page of the bark Mary Gardiner between 1859 and 1861 shows that two sperm whales were slain in the North Atlantic on a particular day. At left, a log page shows whales that were taken and those that got away. See the "Man Over Board" note near the drawing of a ship.

The thick, rubbery blubber would be taken to a "tryworks," where it would be boiled in large vats, and the oil poured into barrels. The bones would be shipped to manufacturers for use in such items as shoehorns, gentlemen's collars, umbrella stays and hoops in women's dresses.

"When the tryworks were going, everyone in town knew it," MacKay said. "The smell was just awful. You see in many town's earliest records laws that said tryworks had to be well away from where people lived."

Before Europeans arrived, the Indians of Long Island hunted whales from dugout canoes. The Algonquian people were masters at chasing whales from dugout canoes, and killing them with long spears. The Indians used the whale parts both for food and in ceremonies.

But by the early 19th Century, shore whaling was long dead. Whales were no longer coming in close to the shore, and because of the great distances traveled to hunt them, large ships were outfitted to be away for months, even years. "It has always been believed that whale populations had diminished to a point where people no longer saw them from the shore," said Littlefield. "Now there's some thinking that suggests the whales had gotten smart and traveled by different routes so as to avoid hunters."

By the 1820s, large ships were being constructed on the Long Island waterfront for use in the round-the-world whale trade. Whale oil — particularly the fine oil found in the heads of sperm whales — was highly prized for candles and as a lubricant for machinery, in particular machines used in the textile industry. The sperm whale was the whale of choice for hunters: After killing one, they would sever its head with long, pole-like axes and drain the oil out of a large cavity. Right whales and bowheads were valued only for the oil in their blubber.

After the crew spotted a whale, dories were dispatched to chase them across the open ocean. A man armed with a harpoon stood in the front of the dory, a huge coil of rope laying at his feet. When he was alongside the whale, the man plunged the harpoon into the whale's chest, hoping to strike the lung or heart. Whalers had a term for when blood shot out of a blowhole, which indicated the animal had been struck in the lungs — "fire in the chimney."

"You can imagine coming up alongside a huge whale in a small dory when blood was shooting out the blowhole," said Finckenor "But that's what the whalers wanted — to kill it quickly. Otherwise, the whale could pull the dory for miles and if the harpoon pulled out, the whale was lost. And many times the whale would dive hard and because of its size and weight overturn the dory it was attached to. Whales were also known to turn on the dories and attack them. Sperm whales had that reputation."

Once the whale was dead, it was towed alongside the ship, where it was butchered. As the blubber was being cut off the carcass, the ship floated in a sea of blood churned by sharks feeding on the carcass.

"The man doing the cutting stood on a wood plank that jutted out from the boat," Littlefield said. "He held a long spade in his hands and as he cut up the whale, the blubber would be pulled up onto the boat by blubber hooks and block and tackles. If the man fell off the plank, he would have to hope a crewman would get him out

Please see **WHALING** on **Next Page**

Another Trip Over, They're Deeper in Debt

Before Lewis Temple, a black man from New Bedford, Mass., invented the toggle harpoon, the killing of whales by men in small dories was a difficult and dangerous proposition.

"The toggle harpoon made it much easier to strike the whale and hold on to it," said George Finkelnor, curator of the Sag Harbor Whaling Museum. "Before that, harpoons often pulled out and the whale got away."

Because whaling was a job of last resort, many blacks and Indians found employment in the industry. There are accounts of many whaling vessels with crews made up mostly of blacks, with Long Island Indians — Shinnecocks and Montauketts, mostly — hired on as harpooners.

An account ledger called the Pigskin Book shows the extent to which at least one whaling company depended on Indians. The book lists accounts kept by Indians who worked for the Smith family of Brookhaven, and runs from 1696 to 1721. The book is in the collection of the Bellport-Brookhaven Historical Society.

The book lists the number of whales taken in a season, as well as the pay — and debts — of Indians involved in the venture. It is structured in the form of modern-day spread sheet, John Strong, a historian at the Southampton Campus of Long Island University, has written. "It shows that none of the men whose names appear in the account book ever ended a season out of debt," he said. "The result of a season of arduous and dangerous labor was higher debt."

The book lists dozens of Indian names, what goods they bought on credit, how much they were owed by the company, and their share of the oil gathered. This is from a sample page:

Name	share (oil)	share (bone)	value (pounds)*
Pumpsha	7 barrels, 8 gal.	54 lbs.	17:04
Quogue	6 barrels	45 lbs.	14:05
Wamahow	4 barrels, 13 gal.	24 lbs.	10:00
Natutamy	3 barrels, 19 gal.	23 lbs.	08:06

* In British pounds; 17:04 represents 17 pounds, 4 shillings

— Steve Wick

From "America Explored," Viking Press, 1974

Indians on Long Island often killed whales for meat. Later, whaling companies hired many of them as harpooners.

Chasing Whales

WHALING from **Preceding Page**

before the sharks got him."

If going to sea had a romantic attraction to 19th Century men and women, the butchering of the whales was anything but that.

"It's always been believed that there was something glamorous about going to sea and being on a whaling vessel," MacKay said. "People go to places like Sag Harbor and see the handsome captain's house with the white picket fence around it and think the whole enterprise was somehow romantic. But it was an ugly, mean affair."

Mean and difficult enough to make it hard to find crews. "In many cases," Littlefield explained, "a ship would leave, say, New Bedford, with only a small crew. The first stop would be the Azores islands, which were traditional sperm whale grounds, then south to the Cape Verde Islands. At these places, crews would be filled out so that on some whalers most of the crews were from these islands."

The pay was absymal. What a ship brought back in terms of profit depended on how much oil and bone it collected — and, specifically, how much sperm oil, which was more valuable — and what price it brought at the time. For example, oil prices ranged from a few cents a gallon some years to more than $2 a gallon in the 1860s, when whaling was scaled back because of, among other things, the Civil War.

"Traditionally, the profit was divided into thirds," said Littlefield. "One third went to the owners and agents, one third went to upkeep of the ship, and one third went to the captain and crew. The captain would get a larger share of that one-third than a crewman. Some crewmen got one-two hundredth, or one-two hundred and twenty-fifth. A captain might get a tenth, or a sixteenth. But if you were at sea for two years or more, the money was not much."

Of the 26 Sag Harbor whalers that sailed in 1845, one, the American, suffered the loss of its captain (a man named Pierson) and three crewmen, who were killed by a whale. The surviving crew mutinied in the Sandwich Islands — now called Hawaii. The ship was condemned and never returned to Sag Harbor.

Marine Museum Photos

Above, Gabriel Edwards, left, and Everett J. Edwards are dwarfed by the jawbone of a right whale, the last whale killed off Long Island, on Feb. 22, 1907. Right, Capt. Josh Edwards

Then there is the story of the Konohassett. Captain Worth's journal tells the story of hitting the coral reef, "which is not drawn on any chart," and of abandoning the ship with only bread and water to survive on.

Records at the John Jermaine Library in Sag Harbor say that the boat had hit "Pell's Reef," and that the crew built another ship from the wreckage of the Konohassett, salvaging timbers, pitch, sails, nails and a single drill. Eighteen days later, the new boat, the 22-foot Konohassett Jr., was launched, with Worth and six others aboard. After 42 days at sea, the little boat sailed into the Sandwich Islands.

There, Worth boarded a larger ship and sailed back to Pell's Reef, where he picked up the rest of his crew — "no lives lost, a remarkable feat," according to one account.

Months later aboard another ship, Worth and his crew rounded the familar bluff of Montauk Point, and saw the light atop it. They were home, at long last.

* * *

Events conspired to cripple the whaling industry, which peaked in the 1840s. The discovery of gold in California in 1848 — the same year a Sag Harbor whaler became the first to ever sail through the Bering Strait and into the Arctic Ocean to kill bowheads — caused a flood of men who otherwise might have worked on whalers to go west; in addition, owners of vessels that had been used to hunt whales found it more profitable to carry passengers to California.

Several Long Island whaling vessels sailed to California and never returned. One was the Niantic, which was left to rot on a San Francisco dock in 1849. A fire in 1851 burned it to the waterline, and a hotel was built on top of it. A section of the Niantic's hull was excavated in 1978 — a small piece of Long Island history, far from home.

When the last whaling vessel sailed out of Cold Spring Harbor in 1858, the glory days of whaling from that village had faded. The following year, oil was discovered in Pennsylvania, and overnight a new — and close-to-home — supply of oil was in the marketplace. Two years later, the beginning of the Civil War all but killed off any remaining vestiges of whaling.

"Whalers in the open ocean came under attack from Confederate raiders," Littlefield said. "It now became even more dangerous to go to sea. Most ships just stayed at home."

In 1866, one of the last Sag Harbor whalers, the Ocean, sailed to sea and was never seen again. The very last Sag Harbor whaler was the Myra, which sailed in 1871. Three years later, the Myra came to an inglorious end, breaking up off Barbados, her wreckage scattered across the ocean floor.

While the market for whale oil died in the 1850s, the market for baleen — whalebone — lived on until 1908. That year, a new type of women's dress was invented that did not need thin strips of whalebone to keep it billowy. And corsets, which used stays made of baleen, went out of fashion, too. And with it, an industry died.

The last whale hunted off Long Island was killed Feb. 22, 1907, by a group of aging East Hampton whalers, such as Josh Edwards. It was towed to an Amagansett beach, where a group of men, using tools they had not used in decades, cut off the blubber. But there was no demand for whale oil, so their work was an exercise in nostalgia.

The whale was itself a relic. Its bones were shipped to the Museum of Natural History in New York, where they were reassembled and hung from a ceiling as part of a display.

A Wife Copes on a Whaling Ship

Pregnancy is among her adventures

BY BILL BLEYER
STAFF WRITER

When her husband, Edwin, sailed for the Pacific as captain of the whale ship Lucy Ann on Aug. 21, 1847, Martha Brown of Orient went along. It would be more than two years before she saw Long Island again — years of love and loneliness and happiness and hardship.

"If Quince Groves and moon light nights are incentives to make love," she wrote as they cruised the Pacific, "surely moon light nights on ship board are doubly so."

But five months later, the moonlight had lost its glow. "I have been sick most of this week and by dint of hard labour have only made one shirt with short sleves," Brown wrote on March 25. "I have catched as many colds as there is days in the week, and nights to, for all what I know, and have come to the conclusion that if I go on deck and open my mouth I am sure to get a new addition."

It was unusual, although not unheard of, in the 1800s for women to sail with their husbands on whalers and other vessels engaged in coastal or international trade. At least 48 of the women hailed from Long Island. The journeys were arduous but the alternative, especially for the wives of whalers, was up to several years at a time of separation from their mates.

Martha Brown left a more detailed, earthier record of her impressions than many of the wives, and the ups and downs of her voyage chronicled in her journal, while typical in many ways, were also more pronounced.

At the start of the voyage, 26-year-old Martha Brown was convinced that sailing on the Lucy Ann had been the right decision, even though it had meant leaving behind her 2-year-old daughter, Ella. But her mood sank the longer the voyage dragged on. On March 8, 1848, in the South Pacific, she wrote: "It appears you can have no Idea how warm, or how hot rather, it is. There is heardly a bit of comfort to be taken but on deck, and that we have not had the privalage of enjoying untill today for it has rained every half hour for a week."

Part of Brown's discomfort undoubtedly stemmed from the fact that she was pregnant — a situation that would result in a most trying experience. Being in "circumstances," as Brown put it, and with meager medical care available aboard ship, it was decided that she would be put ashore in Honolulu to have the baby, which wasn't due for five months. She was stranded for seven months, one of 600 non-Hawaiians on the island. She knew no one, and her husband left her with so little cash that she couldn't afford to live in town with the other foreigners. As a result, she rarely got to see her "whaling sisters," as she called other whaling wives. "This is not my home and I do not know of one here that I can call friend," she wrote in her first entry ashore on April 30.

On Nov. 5, a week before her husband returned to pick her up, Brown wrote, "Oh Edwin, how can I longer await your return? Day after day passes away, and night succeeds night, but I am not permitted to clasp the object of my fondest affection . . . They say absence strengthens love. Be it so."

Oysterponds Historical Society

Martha Brown's fascination quickly turned to fatigue.

But when her husband returned, Martha didn't let the moonlight wash out her resolve. On the voyage home she left a message for her husband in the ship's logbook: "Adieu to Whale grounds and now for home and right glad am I. And now my Dear, alow me to inform you that this is the last time you are to leave, or visit these waters . . ."

Capt. Brown didn't take the hint. He sailed again at least twice before settling down as a farmer in Orient at age 39.

If Martha Brown had a tough time, other sailing wives had it worse. When Malay crew members mutinied aboard the trading ship Frank N. Thayer in the South China Sea in 1885, they tried to murder Capt. Robert Clarke of Quogue. His wife, whose first name has not been recorded, tackled a seaman who had cut open Clarke's chest. She pushed his lung back inside his body, then held off the mutineers with pistol fire long enough for her to bandage her husband's wound and organize an escape. They sailed 200 miles in a small boat to St. Helena, and the captain survived.

Cold Spring Harbor Whaling Museum

Life on a whaler was hard. Above, an E.F. Tufnell painting of the Alice, a ship that sailed from Cold Spring Harbor in 1858 and returned in 1862.

LI HISTORY.COM

Relive four months of 1848 through the journal of Martha Smith Brewer Brown on the Internet at http://www.lihistory.com.

Some sailing women never returned. The wife of Capt. Ernest L. Arey — her first name also has been lost — died with her husband and child within sight of their Quogue home when the coastal schooner Nahum Chapin ran aground in the winter of 1897.

"The conditions varied greatly," said Michele Morrisson, director of the Three Village Historical Society. "The women who sailed with deep-water merchants served as hostesses in luxurious cabins. The whaling wives had a miserable time, because they were on a ship with a crew of 30 men, many of them of questionable character. A whaling voyage could extend up to seven years away from home." Trading ships traveled from port to port, giving the women a break and company.

One thing that kept Brown and other women on whaling voyages was the occasional chance rendezvous at sea — called "gamming" — with another ship carrying a captain's wife, or a stop in a foreign port with an enclave of American families.

Women first went to sea because they could. With the coming of the Industrial Revolution, changes in technology freed women from domestic chores. The women sometimes left children with relatives, so they wouldn't be separated from their husbands. Some sailed with other motivations as well, such as preventing the sailors from getting drunk or getting too familiar with native women or to spread the Christian gospel.

The crews had mixed feelings about having women on board, using the term "hen frigates" to describe vessels carrying wives. The women's presence reduced the tendency toward violent discipline, but it also made the crews lonelier because they were not allowed to bring their spouses.

While whalers' wives had private accommodations, they were rarely spacious. The Lucy Ann was only about 100 feet long, so Martha Brown was restricted to very cramped quarters in the stern.

On small coastal cargo schooners, like the one Carrie Davis of Orient sailed on, conditions were also cramped. But at least the voyages lasted only days or weeks.

On a larger ship with a substantial crew, women had no role other than captain's wife; on smaller coastal schooners women often were an integral part of the crew. Davis was one of the three crew members on the Ellis as it cruised Long Island Sound. The cabins and galley were her domain, and her life at sea was little different than life at home.

"Today," Davis wrote of one Saturday as the ship lay at anchor in Norwich, Conn., in March, 1878, "cooked steak and potatoes for breakfast, knead bread, made Oyster pie for dinner, made a doz stickies, thirteen sugar cookies, two pans of wheat bread, a pan of biscuit and two pans of sweet meal bread, prepared nearly a lb. of suet for shortening, boiled some sauce for tomorrow, besides other work."

When an LI ship sailed into Tokyo's bay, it was met with curiosity and hostility

A Cold Welcome in Japan

BY BILL BLEYER
STAFF WRITER

When he sailed into the Pacific in 1845, Southampton sea captain Mercator Cooper was looking for whales — not for an excuse to visit Japan.

In those days, Japan was a dangerous destination for American sailors. The last time an American vessel had visited the feudal nation, eight years earlier, it was driven off by cannon fire. Some foreign sailors shipwrecked in Japan had been killed. Except for one Dutch trading outpost, Japan had been closed to foreigners since the beginning of the 17th Century. Most traders and missionaries, too, were seen as undermining the culture.

But Cooper knew an opportunity when he saw one.

Cooper had taken the sailing ship Manhattan out of Sag Harbor on Nov. 9, 1843, on a whaling voyage to the Pacific. When he stopped at St. Peters Island near Japan, he was seeking water and firewood. In addition, his log entry for March 15, 1845, reads: "we found 11 Japan men that had been cast away" or shipwrecked. "We took them on board." The next day, "we fell in with a Japanese junk with her stern stove in and 11 men on board." These sailors also were rescued.

He sailed to the coast and put four of the refugees aboard a Japanese craft to tell the shogun of Jeddo, as Tokyo was then called, that he intended to sail into the bay to deliver the rest of the refugees.

On April 18, a barge arrived carrying an emissary of the emperor. The Manhattan had official permission to proceed. "About three hundred Japanese boats with about 15 men in each took the ship in tow," Cooper wrote. ". . . they towed us into a bay . . . and they formed their boats around the ship with a guard of about three thousand men. They took all our arms out to keep till we left. There were several of the nobility came on board to see the ship. They appeared very friendly."

But only to a point. A Japanese interpreter made it clear that any American attempting to leave the ship would be killed. He communicated this by drawing a sword across his throat.

The Japanese visitors showed great curiosity about everything on the ship, particularly Pyrrhus Concer, a crewman from Southampton who was the only black on board, and a Shinnecock Indian named Eleazar. These were the first dark-skinned people the Japanese had ever seen and they wanted to touch the men's skin.

On April 20, Cooper listed the provisions provided by the Japanese, who refused payment: water, 20 sacks of rice, two sacks of wheat, a box of flour, 11 sacks of sweet potatoes, 50 fowl, two cords of wood, radishes and 10 pounds of tea. The officials "thanked us for fetching them here. The Emperor sends his compliments to me and thanks me for picking up their men and sends me word that I must not come again."

The Manhattan sailed the next day. "We hove up our anchor and about 300 boats took us in tow," pulling the ship 20 miles out to sea. In all the confusion, Cooper retained a large chart of the waters around Japan that had been salvaged from the sinking junk. It would come in handy later for the U.S. Navy.

The ship continued whaling along the coast of Russia and the next year sold its cargo in Amsterdam. After a voyage of two years, 11 months and five days, the Manhattan returned to Sag Harbor on Oct. 14, 1846.

Cooper's visit to Japan had little immediate impact. The following year, two American Navy ships sailed into the same bay and were ordered to depart. The reception was more tempered when Commodore Matthew Perry arrived with four U.S. warships on July 8, 1853, and presented a list of demands. When he returned the following February, the Japanese agreed to better treatment for American shipwrecked-sailors and trading rights.

Two monuments mark the accomplishments of Cooper and the Manhattan. One was erected in Tokyo in 1972. The other stands in Southampton Cemetery on Windmill Lane across from the captain's house.

New Bedford Whaling Museum

A portrait of seaman Mercator Cooper, circa 1835

DESCENDANT

DEBORAH COOPER KENDRICK

Deborah Cooper Kendrick feels like Mercator Cooper was a member of her immediate family, not a renowned ancestor.

"We grew up with his story and lived with things he brought back, like a shell collection he had put together over the years," said Kendrick, a 55-year-old former legal secretary who is the whaling captain's great-great-granddaughter. The Southampton resident, whose late father was a local judge named Mercator Cooper Kendrick, said she and her cousin, Douglas Degroot, are the only descendants of Cooper still living on Long Island.

"Most of what was important in regard to his trip to Japan has gone to the whaling museum in New Bedford [Mass.]," she said. This included paintings and lacquerware and an ivory chess set that were gifts from the ruler. "We still have some scrimshaw and the shell collection."

Newsday Photo / Bill Davis

Kendrick

The captain's house at 81 Windmill Lane is owned by Rogers Memorial Library and is used for a computer lab, meeting and storage space, and apartments. Kendrick would like to see it restored as a museum house.

— Bill Bleyer

PYRRHUS CONCER

When the Manhattan dropped anchor in Japan in 1845, one of the crewmen attracted more attention than the captain. Pyrrhus Concer was the first black man the Japanese had ever seen and they all wanted to touch his skin.

The color of Concer's skin was not an issue among his colleagues, however, because whaling attracted culturally diverse crews.

Concer, who was named Pyrrhus after a Greek king, was born into slavery on March 17, 1814. He was owned by the Pelletreau family and worked as a farmhand. Freed when he turned 18 in 1832, he began shipping out on whaleships, working up to the key position of boat steerer. That meant not only that he steered the whaleboat but that he gave the *coup de grace* to whales with a lance after they were harpooned.

With the whaling industry dying off, Concer went to California in 1849 to prospect for gold. He returned to Southampton a year later and married. When Southampton turned into a summer colony after the Civil War, Concer ran a sailboat ferry across Lake Agawam, charging a nickel a trip.

When he died Aug. 23, 1897, at age 84, the Southampton Press called him "one of the most respected residents of the village." Because there were no churches in Southampton serving black congregations, Concer had become a member of the First Presbyterian Church. He left the church several hundred dollars for youth programs, and his bequest is still generating income for those programs.

His contributions are marked by a monument on Pond Lane across the street from his house, now a private home, and an obelisk over the grave of Concer and his wife, Rachel, at the old North End Cemetery in Southampton. It is inscribed:

THOUGH BORN A SLAVE
HE POSSESSED THOSE
VIRTUES, WITHOUT WHICH,
KINGS ARE BUT
SLAVES.

— Bill Bleyer

LEGACY

Left, New Bedford Whaling Museum; Above, Newsday Photo / Bill Davis

Left, a Japanese artist's view of the visitors. Above, Pyrrhus Concer's memorial is on Pond Lane in Southampton.

An actor, writer, producer and ambassador best known for 'Home, Sweet Home'

Payne's Sweet Song

BY PETER GOODMAN
STAFF WRITER

John Howard Payne was a theater critic at age 14, a playwright soon after and then a child star. He was a friend of Washington Irving and Charles Dickens, a staunch defender of the Cherokee Indians as they were forced from their homes in Georgia to Oklahoma on the "Trail of Tears" and a diplomat who died at his post as American consul general in Tunis.

But what brought him the greatest fame were the words he wrote in London for a little song in the operetta "Clari, or the Maid of Milan."

It was called "Home, Sweet Home."

The melody wasn't Payne's — the music was by British composer Henry Rowley Bishop, who may have borrowed it from a tune he heard in Sicily — but the combination of notes and lyrics was a show-stopper. It turned into the first blockbuster hit ever written — not that Payne or Bishop ever got any royalties.

And what was the "lowly thatched cottage" that beckoned the lonely wanderer in the song? Was it the house at 33 Pearl St., Manhattan, where Payne's father ran a school for a few years? Or was it the cedar-shingled saltbox on the East Hampton village green owned by the writer's grandfather, Aaron Isaacs?

Payne himself claimed to have been born in New York. That's what he wrote in his memoirs — published in London in 1815, when the great man was all of 24 years old. But the partisans of East Hampton dismiss that as self-serving: New York was a much better address in those days.

East Hampton is where the Home Sweet Home Museum is, right next to St. Luke's Episcopal Church. The house was built around 1670, probably by a man named Robert Dayton. By 1740 or so, it was owned by Aaron Isaacs, a Jewish peddler who found his way from New York to what was then called Maidstone, who grew prosperous, married Mary Hedges, member of a founding family, and converted to Presbyterianism — "What was he supposed to do? He was surrounded by Puritans," exclaimed museum director Averill Geus.

Nevertheless, Isaacs kept his business records in Hebrew, and among his grandson's treasured possessions was a seal ring with a Hebrew inscription.

The Isaacs had 13 children, of whom the fifth, Sarah, took a business trip with her father to New London, Conn. There she met a widower named William Payne, whom Isaacs brought to East Hampton to teach in the newly founded Clinton Academy, the first secondary school in New York State.

The question of John Howard Payne's birthplace is a murky one. In 1791 the family moved to New York to set up a school, and their fifth child, John Howard, was born that June 9. "He could have been born in a rowboat going to Shelter Island," Geus said. "Nobody knows."

Wherever the blessed event took place, there's little doubt that Payne spent significant parts of his early life at his grandfather's house, being frightened by the geese on the green and roaming among the thatched houses.

It was in New York that the 14-year-old Payne — a clerk by day and a theatergoer by night — published the first issue of The Thespian Mirror, a weekly journal of theater criticism. Not content with working 12 hours a day and writing a weekly magazine, Payne wrote and produced his first play, "Julia; or The Wanderer, a comedy in five acts," at the Park Theater on Feb. 7, 1806.

The play caused an uproar — it's full of double entendres about the heroine, a 16-year-old orphan besieged by rakes, one of whom says "Damme" several times. "Julia" got only one performance, and Payne earned virtually nothing.

Wealthy patrons gave him a scholarship to Union College in upstate Schenectady. But he yearned for the stage, and on Feb. 24, 1809, at age 18, made his debut at the Park Theater as Young Norval, the hero of John Home's "The Tragedy of Douglas; or The Noble Shepherd."

Payne was an immediate success — he appeared in five other plays that season, and earned the immense sum of $1,400 in a performance of "Romeo and Juliet."

The succeeding years were a roller coaster of fame and failure. He toured the United States, attended one of Dolly Madison's White House parties, and in 1813, during the War of 1812, sailed to England — where he was immediately arrested and jailed for two weeks until his passport was cleared.

Payne stayed in Europe for the next 20 years, acting, writing, producing, visiting Paris and becoming an important member of the English literary world. It was in his play "Brutus" that the tragedian Edmund Kean became a tremendous star in 1818.

Payne himself was thrown into debtors' prison after a bad season running the Sadler's Wells theater. There he wrote another play whose profits got him out of jail.

In Paris during 1822, Payne saw a ballet entitled "Clari; or the Promise of Marriage" and quickly wrote some dialogue. Composer Bishop saw the ballet, too, and suggested they turn it into an operetta. Payne was living at the time in the very elegant Palais Royal, but he was writing letters to his siblings in New York about "my yearnings toward Home."

Newsday Photo / Bill Davis

Dictionary of American Portraits

The Home Sweet Home Museum, above, and John Howard Payne; Aaron Isaacs, grandfather of Payne, lived in the house around 1740. The museum is at 14 James Lane, East Hampton. It is open by appointment during the winter months. In other seasons, it is open 10 a.m. to 4 p.m. Monday through Saturday, 2 to 4 p.m. Sundays. Call 516-324-0713.

And so, on May 8, 1823, "Clari; or the Maid of Milan" premiered at London's Covent Garden theater. It was a hit, and publisher John Miller issued sheet music for "Home, Sweet Home" separately. It sold as many as 100,000 copies in the first year; Payne was paid about 100 British pounds for "Clari," and got nothing for the song.

As playwright, producer and literary figure, Payne continued high in the public's eye for the rest of his life. At one point he carried a discreet torch for Mary Wollstonecraft Shelley, author of "Frankenstein." He loved her but she loved Washington Irving, who was not interested.

Payne returned to America in 1832, toured the country in triumph, traveled with John James Audubon, lobbied Congress to keep the Cherokees from being forced from their ancestral home (the Georgia Guard, a sort of pre-Civil War Ku Klux Klan, held him prisoner for a few weeks in 1835 — one of his captors whistling "Home, Sweet Home" at the time), and eventually was appointed consul general in Tunis, a post he occupied twice in the period from 1843 until his death in that city on April 9, 1852.

The song itself lived on — during the Civil War the armies of both sides, encamped on the battlefield, would sing it together at night. Jenny Lind sang it during her tour of America; Adelina Patti sang it for President Abraham Lincoln in the White House.

In 1883, financier William Wilson Corcoran, founder of the Corcoran Gallery, got Payne's body exhumed and brought to the United States. It arrived first in New York, for one procession, and then, in a massive ceremony attended by President Chester A. Arthur and Gen. William T. Sherman, was interred in Washington's Oak Hill Cemetery.

And that had never been his home.

HEAR 'HOME, SWEET HOME'

At 19, the diva Adelina Patti was already acclaimed on two continents when she sang "Home, Sweet Home" at the White House for Abraham and Mary Lincoln in 1862. In mourning for their son, Willie, who had died of typhoid fever, the Lincolns were moved to tears and asked for an encore. As the 20th Century began, both Patti and "Home, Sweet Home" were still renowned.

To hear the popular recording she made, call (516) 843-5454 or (718) 896-6969 and enter category 4663, or visit http://www.lihistory.com on the Internet.

International Portrait Gallery

Soprano Adelina Patti

Slavery Died A Slow Death

In New York, the Revolutionary War fails to inspire a strong quest of freedom for all

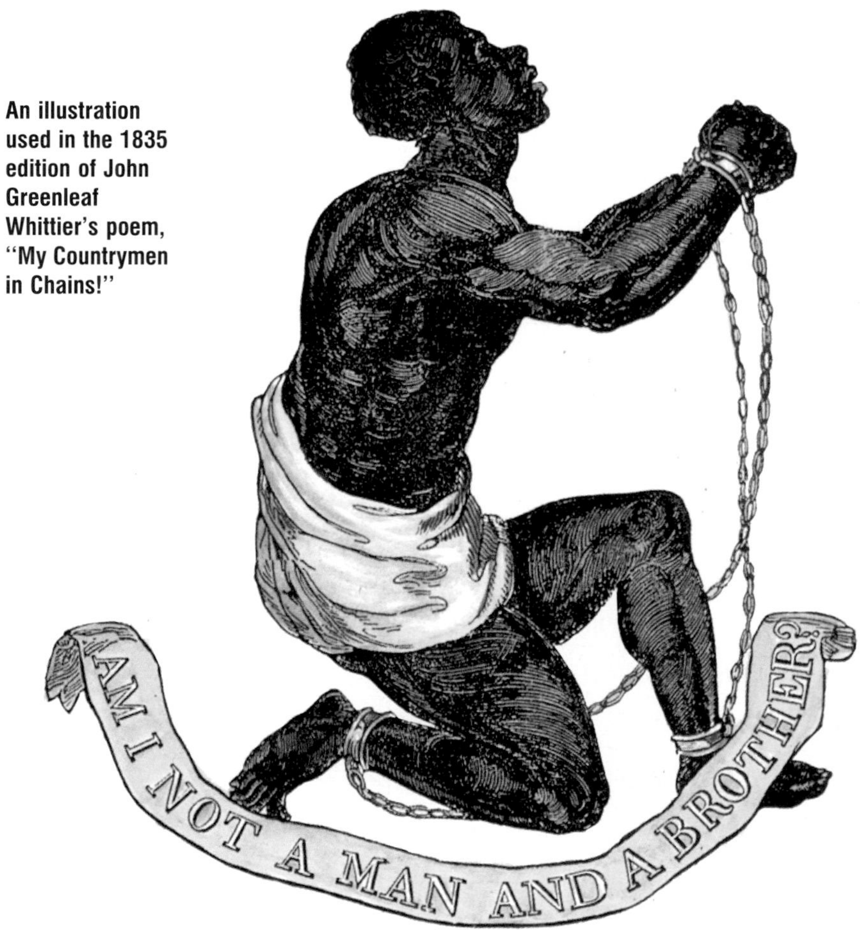
AM I NOT A MAN AND A BROTHER?

An illustration used in the 1835 edition of John Greenleaf Whittier's poem, "My Countrymen in Chains!"

The Granger Collection

BY GEORGE DEWAN
STAFF WRITER

On the Fourth of July, 1827, two centuries after it began, slavery ended in New York State.

The end did not come overnight, with a great thunderclap of insight that the owning of one person by another was morally wrong. The largest slave state in the North ended slavery only gradually — as did the other northern states — during a period of three decades, and only after a great debate.

Slavery was allowed to die a slow death in New York because such gradualism protected the economic interests of slaveowners, according to David N. Gellman, a lecturer in early American history at Northwestern University. Gellman, an expert on the abolition movement in New York State, was asked recently whether the policy of gradually freeing slaves had been a success.

"It certainly beats the Civil War, if that's the alternative," Gellman said. "Unquestionably, from a moral standpoint, you would have to say no. But it's a human institution, and it's not easy to dislodge. It's a problem of political give and take, though it seems appalling that real human beings should be subject to this give and take."

With the exception of the Quakers, antislavery sentiments in New York did not appear with any great force until after the Revolutionary War. Even then, the "all men are created equal" rhetoric of the Declaration of Independence, and the winning of the war itself did not lead to a quick decline in slavery. Slaveholders on Long Island and up the Hudson River Valley did not want to part with an important source of labor.

But antislavery politics began to take hold after the war. The New York Manumission Society, with many of its members Quakers, was organized in 1785 with the purposes of securing legislation to end slavery in New York, monitoring compliance with laws relating to slavery and educating blacks. That same year, the Legislature narrowly defeated a bill that would have provided for gradual abolition of slavery in the state.

Despite this defeat, a law was passed banning the importation of slaves, and, three years later, banning their export. "No one ever seriously proposed immediate abolition in New York," Gellman said. "It was not politically viable. There were too many counties in New York where slaves made up a sizeable percentage."

One of the biggest problems for authorities was that, in violation of the law, slaveowners — aware that total abolition of slavery in the state was on its way — were selling their slaves in the South, where there was a ready market. Documentation of this practice is sketchy, but historians agree that it happened often, as did kidnaping of free blacks to be sold into southern slavery. In his 1966 book, "A History of Negro Slavery in New York," Edgar J. McManus says that an analysis of census figures shows an extremely sharp drop in the growth rate of New York's black population after 1800. Many blacks must have left, he concludes, and few left voluntarily.

"The conclusion is inescapable that the exodus was largely the work of kidnapers and illegal traders who dealt in human misery," McManus writes.

The abolitionists favoring gradualism achieved their first major victory in 1799, when the Legislature passed An Act for the Gradual Abolition of Slavery. It provided that all children born to New York slave mothers after July 4 of that year would not be slaves. However, these same children would be required to serve the mother's owner until age 28 for males and age 25 for females.

The law thus kept the new children from slavery and created them as a type of indentured servants. Slaveowners got to keep their laborers. The children had to be registered with the town clerk.

As the 19th Century began, the system of slavery on Long Island and elsewhere in New York was in turmoil, because of abolitionist pressures and a growing antislavery attitude among nonslaveholders and the politicians who represented them. Many slaveowners began freeing their slaves: Manumission in wills became common. But the selling of slaves continued, and the following advertisement from the Suffolk Gazette, May 13, 1805, illustrates how little concern there was for separating mothers from their children:

> *FOR SALE: A Negro woman, in every respect suitable for a farmer — she is 25 years old, and will be sold with or without a girl four years old.*

Running away became common, indicating a gathering resistance to slavery. Runaways were usually male, usually young and they were often skilled in English. The following advertisement appeared on Sept. 26, 1793, in The Connecticut Gazette:

> *RAN-away from Nathan Pierson, on Long-Island, the 16th instant, a negro man named TITE, about 5 feet high, thick set, about 20 years old, very likely; had on when he went away a light coloured homespun coating coat, spotted calico trowsers, large smooth plated Buckles. He plays on the Violin and fife. Whoever will take up said negro and confine in the the gaol in New-London, shall have TEN DOLLARS reward, and all necessary charges, paid by EBENEZER DOUGLAS, Gaoler.*

Because of the changing conditions of the institution of slavery, the work force on Long Island farms became a mixture of slaves, free blacks, Indians, indentured servants and the farmer's own children. In a diary kept in the first decade of the 19th Century, Samuel L. Thompson of Setauket, a prosperous farmer as well as a medical doctor, notes all types working together. A female slave named Rose joins a male slave named Killis digging post holes. A freed black slave named Jacob is hired to cart a load of hay. Thompson's son Franklin works side by side with his slaves Robin, Cuff, Sharper, Killis and Jack, as well as free blacks named Walter, Amos, Ginne, Sib and Dick.

There was no turning back from the commitment made in 1799. In 1817, the Legislature passed the law that ended slavery in New York State, to take effect 10 years later, on July 4, 1827. A loophole in the law that allowed transients to bring slaves into New York for a nine-month period, and part-time residents to bring their slaves into the state temporarily, was closed in 1841.

For some New Yorkers, slavery was an embarrassment. At the 1821 state constitutional convention, there was an amendment proposed making slavery not only illegal, but unconstitutional. Some members opposed the amendment, not wanting to draw attention to this shameful episode in the state's history. One was 66-year-old Rufus King, a U.S. senator from Jamaica.

"If we omit to mention it in our constitution," King said, "it may hereafter be forgotten that slavery once existed in the state."

Grand Celebration !
THE ABOLITION OF THE SLAVE TRADE
GENERAL ORDER.

A poster invites people to a parade circa 1827, the year slavery was outlawed in New York State.

The New-York Historical Society

The state's newly freed slaves cope with a landscape still pocked with restrictions

Freedom: Then What?

BY GEORGE DEWAN
STAFF WRITER

James Williams was an 18-year-old slave on the Ichabod Brush estate in Huntington when his owner died in 1809. In his will, Brush freed Williams and willed him $200. Despite the ex-slave's many attempts to get his legacy, Brush's executors refused to give it to him, claiming he was a drunkard and unable to manage his affairs.

Williams moved to New York City, but he never forgot his legacy. In 1817, when he was 26, he hired a lawyer and sued the executors, denying their claims and asking for his $200. The former slave won, receiving not only the $200, but interest of $103.16.

By fleeing the Island to seek a new life in the city, Williams did what a number of freed Long Island slaves had done. New York City by 1810 had the largest concentration of free blacks in America: At 8,137, they outnumbered slaves in the city by a 5-1 ratio. Williams said in court papers he would use the money to return home to his friends and relatives in Demerara, a coastal river settlement in South America that later would became part of Guyana.

As two centuries of slavery slowly ended in New York State in the first three decades of the 1800s, the lives of formerly enslaved black men, women and children changed drastically. Some, like Williams, fared better than others. Several became landowners. Many freed slaves came together to form communities and to found black churches. Many others, however, became outcasts, gathering in bleak shantytown poverty, depending on charity to survive.

Whites, too, were adjusting to a new reality. While the majority of whites supported emancipation of blacks from slavery, many had reservations about former slaves participating fully in white society. Northern states began passing laws that restricted free blacks, especially in politics. "Everywhere in the North the condition of the free Negro worsened as slavery passed from the scene," writes Edgar J. McManus in "A History of Negro Slavery in New York."

Former slaves were now citizens, and, for the adult males, at least, they had the potential to become voters. In New York, the Democratic-Republicans (the forerunner of today's Democratic Party) in power did not have the support of free black voters. The result was a series of voting restrictions on free blacks that culminated in changes in the state Constitution at the 1821 constitutional convention.

"New Yorkers meeting in 1821 to rewrite their state's constitution swept away most of the restrictions to the white male franchise," Northwestern University historian David Gellman wrote in his recent doctoral dissertation. "At the same time, the delegates imposed property requirements on potential black voters which excluded most African Americans otherwise eligible."

The law that freed all slaves as of 1827 perpetuated one great affront against black children. Although the children of slaves born on or after July 4, 1799, were legally free, the new law continued to require them to serve their mother's owner as indentured servants. This meant that although slavery was banned after 1827, blacks could be kept in servitude until as late as 1848: They were never slaves, but neither were they free. An example of this was Pyrrhus Concer, a black man born in Southampton in 1814 who historians and his own gravestone have said was a slave. He was not a slave, but was required to work for the Pelletreau family. At age 18, he was released and began going to sea on whaling ships.

The black slave woman Isabella who became the abolitionist Sojourner Truth, born in Ulster County about 1797, bore five children who were indentured under this law. One of them was Peter, born in 1821. Taking only an infant daughter with her, Isabella walked out on her owner, John Dumont, in the fall of 1826. Within a few weeks Dumont sold Peter, who was 5 years old, to one of his in-laws. Young Peter was resold, and resold again, the last time illegally out of state to an Alabama planter, where the child was enslaved. It took a lawsuit, paid for by Ulster County Quakers, to retrieve Peter from Alabama and return him home in 1828.

Many ex-slaves found themselves unable to do anything but stay right where they were, on white men's farms. They continued to work for their former owners, probably doing the same jobs, for minimal pay. Indebtedness to the former owners for the staples of food and clothing was common.

Smithsonian Institution Photo, 1864

Abolitionist Sojourner Truth, born in Ulster County about 1797, walked out on her owner in 1826.

"Pervasive white racism, almost universal on Nineteenth century Long Island, forced African-Americans into low-wage work and made it extremely difficult for them to accumulate capital and obtain land or other productive property," writes Grania Marcus in "Discovering the African-American Experience in Suffolk County: 1620-1860." "Ex-slaves' often marginal economic and social status meant that they sometimes became the financial responsibility of the town in which they resided."

An Englishman named Marshall Field wrote about the poverty-stricken remnants of slavery on Long Island after an 1854 visit to the United States:

> *I must mention that in Flushing and Jamaica, both in Long Island, there are two colonies of Free Africans, of about three hundred and two hundred respectively, left by the abolition of slavery. They are in the most degraded and wretched condition, living on a few clams (oysters) gathered by the shore, and by begging. They are ignorant, wragged, forlorn and ready to famish in the midst of surrounding abundance for the want of the necessaries and comforts of life.*

While widely dispersed as slaves on individual farms, freed blacks often came together as a form of solidarity. In her new book, "Making a Way to Freedom: A History of African Americans on Long Island," Lynda Day, professor of African studies at Brooklyn College, says that in the first half of the 19th Century, black people formed communities in Huntington, Bellport, East Hampton, Mastic, Greenport, Westbury, Jamaica and Eastville in Sag Harbor. Also, in Success (now Lake Success), Smithville (North Bellmore) and Newtown (Elmhurst).

"As slavery began to die out on Long Island, African-Americans established their own settlements, self-help organizations and churches," writes Day. "Though life was precarious in many ways for the freedmen, they still built stable families and communities in Kings, Queens and Suffolk Counties."

No longer tied by the slave code to an owner who did as he pleased with them, former slaves worked out new arrangements to earn their bread and raise their families. As the century progressed, jobs opened up in the whaling and fishing industries, as well as in the fast-growing business of brickmaking.

Gradually, then, slavery ended in New York State, and the focus of the abolitionist debate shifted to the South. There, it would take the Civil War and the 13th Amendment to end slavery, immediately and for good.

The Granger Collection

LI HISTORY.COM

"The Negro's Complaint" and "To a Slave Holder" are two antislavery poems published in The Suffolk Gazette in 1804 and 1807. They can now be found on the "Long Island: Our Story" Web site on the Internet at http://www.lihistory.com.

A woodcut from around 1840 shows an abolitionist freeing a slave from chains, from an antislavery almanac.

From campground meetings to the rise of the African Methodist Episcopal Church

A Crusade to Praise

BY BOB KEELER
STAFF WRITER

Deep in the woods of Setauket, for the community of Indians and African-Americans that had grown together in the years after the first slaves arrived on Long Island in the 17th Century, the options for worship were few.

One choice was to pray in churches controlled by the white families they served, such as the Caroline Church or Setauket Presbyterian. Another was to gather in the woods, at campground meetings led by itinerant preachers.

The memory and the practice of that campground worship lingered into the early 20th Century. "My grandmother and my aunts all talked about how they met in the woods, sang songs in the woods," said Theodore Green, 70, whose curiosity as a child led him to a lifelong study of the history of his family and his Setauket community.

One of his ancestors, Titus Sells, of combined Indian and African-American heritage, was born in 1772. About that time, a distant event struck the spark leading to the creation of a religious movement that would provide a new option for black communities in Setauket and across Long Island: the African Methodist Episcopal Church.

In 1777, an itinerant Methodist preacher took the Gospel to a group of slaves in the Delaware woods. One of them was Richard Allen, 17, who had been born into a slave family once owned by a Philadelphia lawyer and later sold to a Delaware farmer. The farmer eventually sold Allen's mother and three siblings, and he never saw them again.

Allen embraced the Gospel and returned often to the woods to meet with the preacher. Later, Allen bought his freedom for $2,000 and began to preach. He gravitated to the Methodist movement, before it became a separate denomination in 1784, because its leader, John Wesley, abhorred slavery.

In the late 1700s and early 1800s, slavery began losing its hold in some parts of the North. There, some slave owners didn't find it as economically crucial as it was in the South, and they took to heart the revolutionary ideology of equality.

"So they began to set their slaves free," said Lawrence Little, who teaches African-American history at Villanova University and wrote his dissertation on the African Methodist Episcopal Church. "You begin to have not large numbers but significant numbers of free black Americans. What begins to happen is you start to see racism set in."

That is what happened to Allen, after he had been invited to preach at the nation's first Methodist church, St. George's in Philadelphia. His presence built up black attendance at the predominantly white church, but the church's leaders forced black members to sit toward the back or to stand, then rejected Allen's requests for permission to start a black church.

The friction boiled over when a white church trustee asked Allen and two other black men to move from the place where they knelt in prayer at St. George's. Trustees tried to lift Allen's friends from their knees. "By this time the prayer was over," Allen recalled, "and we all went out of the church in a body, and they were no more plagued by us in the church."

Later, Allen established his own church in Philadelphia, which became known as Mother Bethel, the parent church of his movement. There, in 1816, Allen called a meeting of black churches. The delegates launched a new denomination, the African Methodist Episcopal Church, electing Allen the first bishop.

Racism within the very walls of the church was hardly unique to Philadelphia. "The white Methodists of New York had much the same attitudes," Little said. The result of racism in New York was the creation of another denomination, the African Methodist Episcopal Zion Church, which elected James Varick as its first bishop in 1823.

"If Varick and Allen had seen eye to eye, it would not have been a different denomination," said the Rev. Lillian Frier Webb, pastor of Mt. Olive AME Church in Port Washington. The two men differed over geographical expansion strategy. "It was not theological or doctrinal. It was just regional."

The two denominations quickly reached Long Island. "In Nassau County, it runs neck and neck with Mt. Olive in Port Washington and Salem in Roslyn," Webb said. Macedonia AME Church was founded in Flushing in 1811. Bethel AME Church, now in Copiague but originally in Amityville, claims to be the oldest AME congregation in Nassau and Suffolk. It started in 1814, even before the creation of the denomination itself.

The movement reached Setauket at about the same time that the Town of Brookhaven decided to establish a black cemetery there in 1815. "We have no deed for that first church," Green said. But he believes his godmother, Caroline Moore, 93, the oldest member of the congregation, who has told him that the first church was at that cemetery on Christian Avenue.

That church is believed to have been an AME Zion church, but it later became an AME church. The first building for which the community has records went up in 1848, at Lubber Street and Christian Avenue. In 1874, the community erected the present church, at Locust Avenue and Christian Avenue. Fire heavily damaged it and destroyed valuable records in 1909.

As it celebrates a 150th anniversary during Black History Month, the Setauket church can look back on overcoming hard times. Though the rise of industry brought manufacturing jobs to Setauket starting in the late 1800s, the low wages did not allow many blacks to buy homes. So the population was transient and the church was poor. In 1941, a fading, handwritten record shows, one week's contributions amounted to less than $3.

Providentially, the woods surrounding the church were filled with blueberries and other fruits, and the congregation used them for income. "The church sold an awful lot of blueberry pies," Green said.

Despite economic hardship, AME churches have played a crucial role in developing black leadership, starting at a time when the only place black people could vote was in church elections. "It was in the house of God where they had their first opportunity to use their talents and skills," said the Rev. Gregory Leonard, pastor of Bethel AME Church in Setauket.

The congregation is still small, about 100 people, but still essential. "This has been pretty much the only Afro-American house of worship in the Three Village area for a good little while," Leonard said. It also attracts people from Middle Island, Centereach and Selden. And he sees hopeful signs for its future.

"More and more people are moving into this area — Afro-Americans," Leonard said. "Our arms are always open."

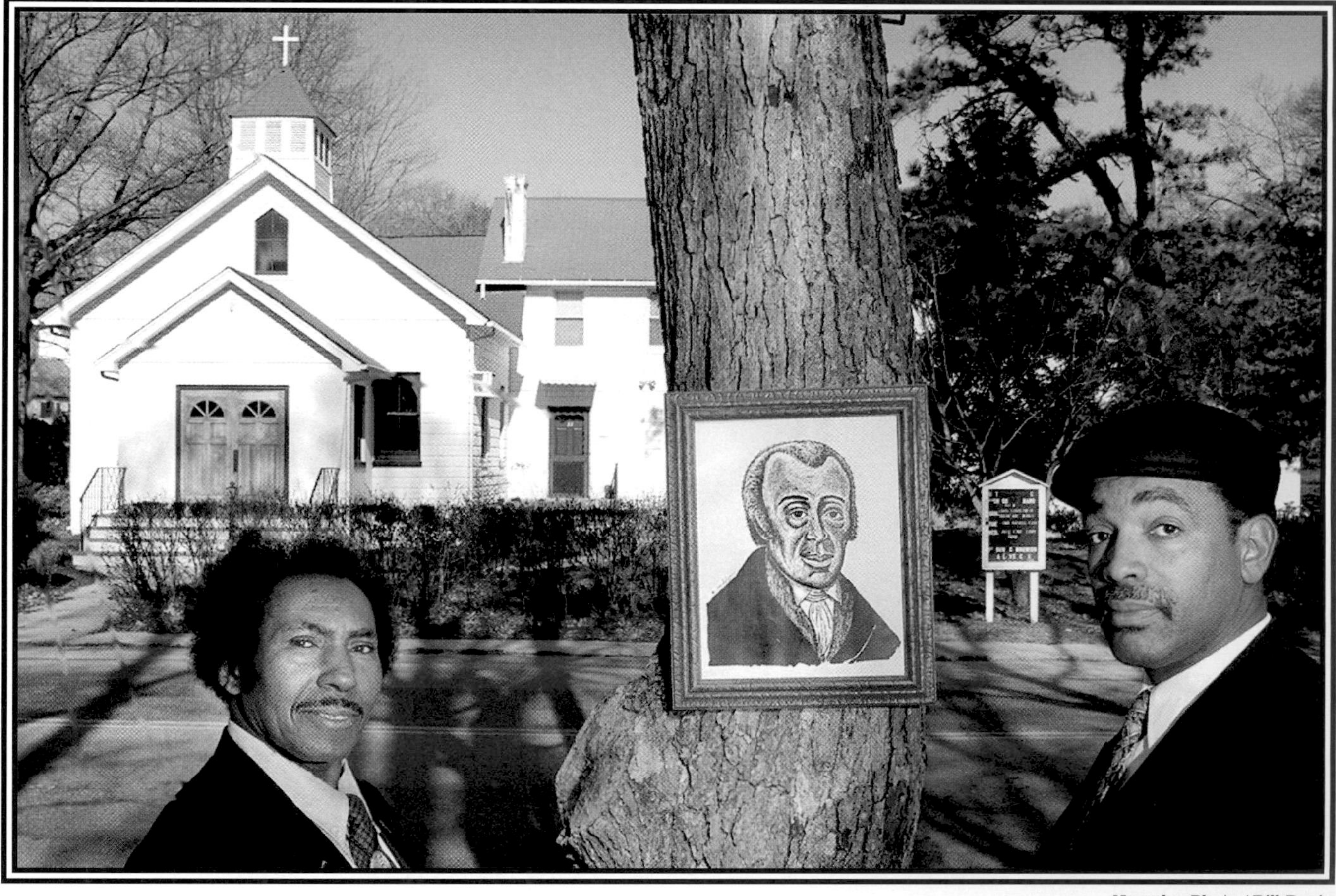

Newsday Photo / Bill Davis

Theodore Green, left, and the Rev. Gregory Leonard stand in front of the Bethel AME Church in Setauket with a portrait of Richard Allen.

> '. . . and we all went out of the church in a body, and they were no more plagued by us in the church.'
>
> **— Richard Allen, founder of the African Methodist Episcopal Church, on an early 1800s incident in a white church**

Traversing Long Island wasn't easy when four-wheel drive meant a stagecoach

Horsepower Was Just That

BY SIDNEY C. SCHAER
STAFF WRITER

On a pleasant Friday afternoon in August of 1835, Gabriel Furman, a lawyer with a sense of history, got off a stagecoach and found himself walking leisurely eastward along the South Country Road somewhere between Patchogue and Moriches.

Later, the bookish attorney, who already had published a history of Brooklyn, described his musings as he walked ahead of the stage.

". . . Here you need give yourself no uneasiness about being left by the stage, as is the case of some of the go-ahead parts of our country — in this particular region the middle of the road is sandy, and the driver, like a considerate man, gives his horses an opportunity to rest, so that they may the better travel through this piece of heavy road . . . After walking for some two or three miles upon the green sward at the edge of the road, gathering and eating berries as you strolled along, until you tired, you would find the stage a short distance behind you . . . "

Sands Point Preserve

NOTICE!

The Subscr[illegible] ishes to inform [illegible] ublic generally that he [illegible] on and after the [illegible] run a weekly STAGE from Moriches to Sag-Harbor, for the conveyance of Passengers &c.

Stage will leave Moriches every WEDNESDAY morning, and Sag-Harbor every THURSDAY morning at 8 o'clock.

All Packages &c., entrusted to his care will be promptly attended to.

If very stormy on Wednesdays, Stage will not leave till the next day.

LEWIS G. TERRY, Proprietor.

Moriches Bay Historical Society; Newsday Photo

A John Evers painting, circa 1864, of the stagecoach arriving at the Sammis Tavern at Main and Fulton Streets in Hempstead, and a handbill advertising the stage going between Moriches and Sag Harbor

Furman was a municipal court judge in Brooklyn who served in the state Assembly and ran unsuccessfully as a Whig for lieutenant governor. His account of his trip from Brooklyn to Montauk was part of a manuscript about the history of Long Island found among his papers years after he had died in the 1850s in poverty. It was eventually published posthumously in 1875.

While Furman offers a detailed record of the actual route of the regular mail-stage, which left Brooklyn every Thursday about 9 a.m., stopping in Hempstead for dinner, with the first layover in Babylon, and a second layover in Quogue, he fails to identify either of the inns he stayed at. He reports that on the last day of the trip, stagecoach passengers ate breakfast in Southampton before making the final leg of the trip through a forest en route to Sag Harbor for lunch and arriving in East Hampton by sunset.

It mattered, perhaps, that the trip was at the beginning of August, and not in the middle of the winter. Even though it took nearly nearly three days to travel a distance of 110 miles, "most pleasant days they were, and no one has ever tried this mode of journeying through Long Island who had pleasure in view, who did not wish to try it again."

It was indeed the era of the stagecoach, although on Long Island the preferred means of travel was by boat on Long Island Sound, or along the Great South Bay. Unlike the rest of the growing nation, the Island remained insular, according to Nathaniel Prime, whose 1845 book, "A History of Long Island" describes the Island as *terra incognita* to almost the whole world.

"The roads of Long Island are exceedingly numerous and difficult for strangers," wrote Prime, who suggested that the local population were not great travelers to begin with.

"After a heavy rain, if only a single carriage has preceded you to open the ruts, you may get along with tolerable speed; provided [which is matter of great doubt] your wheels fit the track. But in a time of drought, the sand in many places is so fine, deep and fluid, that you may travel for miles with the lower felloe [rim] of your wheels constantly buried out of sight."

Still Prime suggested there were some decent roads in Kings and Queens Counties, clearly having evolved as Long Island began to grow in the first part of the 19th Century. The most explosive growth was in Brooklyn, which more than tripled its population in 15 years, growing from 20,535 in 1830 to 68,691 in 1845. At the same time, stagecoaches became more comfortable and functional, tied to delivering both parcels and people.

And because the Island's three main east-west routes had evolved from colonial times, the stage routes followed them, and so did the development of inns, to serve travelers as well as the local community. The earliest known route meandered across Long Island and dates back to before the Revolution when, in 1772, three innkeepers — Samuel Nicholls of Hempstead, Benjamin Havens of Setauket and Nathan Fordham of Sag Harbor — developed a scheme to build a stagecoach that would stop at their taverns and also include a stopover at the Epenetus Smith Tavern in Smithtown.

By 1817, the Long Island Star, published in Brooklyn, was listing 16 stagecoach routes and their proprietors. Some trips, such as from Brooklyn to Jamaica, were simple one-day affairs. The coach left Jamaica at 7 a.m. It left Brooklyn at 4 p.m. for the return trip.

The trip to Hempstead was longer, with a stage leaving Brooklyn at night, about 9 p.m., and making the turnaround the following day.

In Hempstead, a traveler might have stayed at the old Sammis Tavern, which once stood at the northeast corner of Fulton Avenue and Main Street. The tavern, which opened in 1660, served as a base for British soldiers during the Revolution and eventually became a stage stop.

The Sammis Tavern eventually was torn down, but a structure that housed an inn and stage stop in Center Moriches survives, and offers a poetic glimpse backward to a time when horses pulled coaches across the dirt roads of Long Island.

The mist still rises in the morning where the two-story Terry / Ketcham Inn stands at the bend of Montauk Highway in Center Moriches heading toward the Hamptons. The inn began as a simple wooden cottage in 1693. Eventually two fireplaces were added. Then came a second story, two front doors and several reconstructions. Both Thomas Jefferson and James Madison purportedly stayed at the inn, and by the 1800s, it had become a stop along the Brooklyn-to-Sag Harbor route. Long after stagecoaches stopped running, someone thought to call it the Stage Coach Inn. In 1989 it was almost destroyed by fire.

Led by local architect Bert Seides, the Ketcham Inn Foundation is working to restore it so that future generations can see its gradual transformation from a residence to a travelers' waystation.

And possibly our historian from 1835 Brooklyn, Gabriel Furman, might have stopped there on that late Friday afternoon for some refreshment.

Perhaps it is a simple coincidence of history that while Furman was waxing poetic about his trip in what one historian called the "step-lively era" of stagecoach travel, the future was already under construction. The Brooklyn & Jamaica Railroad, the line that would become the Long Island Rail Road and relegate the stagecoach to local deliveries of passengers, was being built. Furman was one of the founders of the railroad.

Railroad investors use Long Island as a rail-sea shortcut to Boston — but

The Coming of the

BY SIDNEY C. SCHAER
STAFF WRITER

To some, the idea seemed like an impossible dream.

Travelers who wanted to go from New York to Boston would no longer have to devote a minimum of 16 hours by steamer, or several days aboard an out-of-date 5-mph stagecoach. Instead, they would have breakfast in New York and get to Boston in just 11 hours, in time for supper.

The idea was for them to go by way of Long Island. Mostly by train.

As the plan was envisioned in 1834, passengers from Manhattan would catch the South Ferry to Brooklyn, where a train would take them 96 miles across the wilds of Long Island all the way to Greenport. There, a steamboat would ferry them across Long Island Sound to Stonington, Conn. In Stonington, a New York, Providence & Boston Co. train would be waiting to carry them to Boston.

The idea may have seemed simple, but it took 10 years to achieve.

Delayed by a national economic crisis in 1837 and by nervous investors wary of a new, untested technology, by competing interests and a shortage of funds, the Long Island Rail Road finally rumbled toward its destiny in the summer of 1844.

The LIRR's founders had hoped to tie the completion of the main line to the celebration of Independence Day, 1844. Instead, they had to settle for a later date to link Long Island's two extremities by rail. On Saturday, July 27, three trainloads of celebrants departed from Brooklyn at 8 a.m., and traveled at an average of 30 mph nonstop to Greenport — the first train arriving in an unheard-of three hours and 45 minutes.

LI HISTORY.COM
To see LIRR artifacts — a timetable, fare schedule and newspaper dispatch — and to learn more about the early railroad, see http://www.lihistory.com on the Internet.

It was still an era of lyrical prose even if life was beginning to speed up and the correspondent for the Brooklyn Daily Eagle — who was among the 500 celebrants gathered in Greenport to mark the railroad's completion — described the trip this way: "The interior of old Suffolk, which until that day, has been sacred to the gambols of wild deer . . . has been disturbed only by the sharp crack of the huntsman's rifle, or the low rumble of the village coach as it plodded on at the rate of five miles an hour was saluted for the first time by the shrill whistle of the locomotive; and the iron horse with its lungs of brass and sinews of steel, came dashing along at a furious rate, puffing volumes of smoke and flame from its nostrils, and warning the people, who gazed in astonishment that . . . the prediction of the seers and prophets like [Robert] Fulton was accomplished."

Leading the contingent of train riders to Greenport was the railroad's fourth president, George B. Fisk. Accounts of the day reported that James Sprague, mayor of Brooklyn, made the trip, and the mayor of New York was invited but was not on the train. Champagne and hyperbole flowed in Greenport that Saturday. John A. King of Jamaica, who would become New York's first Whig governor and was a founder of the LIRR's precursor, the 11-mile-long Brooklyn & Jamaica Railroad, toasted the occasion with champagne, saying, "Railroads and steam engines, the Promethean inventions of modern days." Another speaker, John McCoun, perhaps spoke more about the meaning of what had been accomplished: "The eastern extremity of Long Island, this day made a neighbor of New York and Brooklyn."

Preston Raynor, a young man at the time, would write down his recollections years later in 1917. He had grown up in a house in Manorville near the place where the railroad made one of its two refueling stops. On the big day, Raynor worked with others cutting

A diagram from about 1835 shows the type of engine first used by the Long Island Rail Road. The LIRR's first two engines were named the Ariel and Post Boy, both built by the M.W. Baldwin Locomotive Works.

Nassau County Museum Collection, Long Island Studies Institute suddenly lose their market to competition

Iron Horse

wood to fuel the train's locomotive. His brother Edgar crowded aboard the first or second train for the ride to Greenport. But Raynor's group, hoping to grab a space on the last of the three trains, missed out.

"When the third train came, it did not stop and I with the others got left," he reported. "That was the first and only train that did not stop at Manorville for the next 14 years."

The refueling stop put Manorville — once called Punk's Hole, or the Manor of St. George — on the map, and historian Nathaniel Prime, writing in 1845, still found it amazing: "Had a man, 30 years ago, ventured to predict that this spot was destined to become a daily stopping place for the refreshment of hundreds of travelers between New York and Boston, he would have been considered a madman, and possibly might have been bound with cords, for fear he might do injury."

Two days later, regular service began, and by August the profitable Boston route was operating.

An impossible dream had been realized. But in three short years a faster route that would take travelers all the way to Boston by train would make the LIRR's original purpose both obsolete and irrelevant.

Instead of being a long-distance hauler, the LIRR would be forced to look to Long Island for its business — traversing a route that would come to haunt its founders.

* * *

The Long Island Rail Road was organized at the dawn of the age of railroading. It was the seventh railroad chartered in the United States — conceived less than a decade after the opening of the Erie Canal in 1825, which made New York City the region's pre-eminent port. Other cities on the East Coast had to cope with "Erie Fever" and one solution was a new transportation technology pioneered in England — the steam locomotive. In the first half of the 19th Century, railroads would gradually supplant canals, as it became apparent that they weren't subject to winter shutdowns.

By 1832, when the Brooklyn & Jamaica Railroad was begun, there were only 229 miles of track laid throughout the country. Because the technology of railroad building was still in its infancy, straight, flat routes were preferred. The route through Connecticut seemed unthinkable in the 1830s because of hilly terrain and because major rivers would need to be crossed. It was in this period that the Long Island Rail Road Co. was born. The route went straight through the Island's undeveloped center. It was a civil engineer's dream.

"It is entirely free from navigable rivers, without a bridge for a hundred miles and with grades of an average of less than 10 feet per mile, having six curves only in 80 miles, and with its eastern termination in one of the most beautiful harbors to the ocean," the railroad's engineer, James J. Shipman, wrote in a report to the board of directors.

Maj. David B. Douglass, the chief civil engineer of the Brooklyn & Jamaica Railroad, who was hired as a consultant for the new line, was equally encouraging: ". . . The public mind is quite familiar with speeds of 20-30 miles per hour and numerous locomotives in various parts of our country are wheeling daily over their respective tracks, at these rates, without a murmur of alarm or disapprobation . . . only eleven and one half hours will be required for the entire journey from New York, or Brooklyn to Boston."

The route began at water's edge in Brooklyn, at Atlantic Street (now Atlantic Avenue), and moved along an 11-mile right-of-way that extended from the village of Brooklyn through what it is now East New York, then crossed into Queens near the Union Race Course and continued to Jamaica.

The right-of-way was already in place — built by the Brooklyn & Jamaica Railroad, which was chartered by the state and empowered to raise $300,000 to finance its construction. The LIRR founders decided to lease Brooklyn & Jamaica tracks and two new locomotives and to extend the route another 85 miles to Greenport at a cost of $1.5 million. They stopped at a place just south of Jericho when the money ran out, and named the community Hicksville, after one of the railroad's founders, Valentine Hicks.

Hicks was a member of a historic

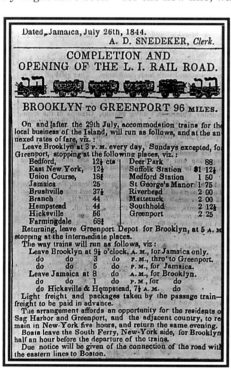

Please see **LIRR** on **Next Page**

Dated, Jamaica, July 26th, 1844.
A. D. SNEDEKER, *Clerk.*

COMPLETION AND OPENING OF THE L. I. RAIL ROAD.

BROOKLYN TO GREENPORT 96 MILES.

On and after the 29th July, accommodation trains for the local business of the Island, will run as follows, and at the annexed rates of fare, viz.:

Leave Brooklyn at 3 P. M. every day, Sundays excepted, for Greenport, stopping at the following places, viz.:

Bedford,	12½ cts	Deer Park	88
East New York,	12½	Suffolk Station	$1 12½
Union Course,	18¾	Medford Station	1 50
Jamaica	25	St George's Manor	1 75
Brushville	37½	Riverhead	2 00
Branch	44	Mattetuck	2 00
Hempstead	44	Southhold	2 12½
Hicksville	56	Greenport	2 25
Farmingdale	68¾		

Returning, leave Greenport Depot for Brooklyn, at 5 A. M. stopping at the intermediate places.

The way trains will run as follows, viz:
Leave Brooklyn at 9½ o'clock, A. M., for Jamaica only.
do do 3 do P. M., thro' to Greenport.
do do 5 do P. M., for Jamaica.
Leave Jamaica at 8 do A. M., for Brooklyn.
do do 1 do P. M., for do
do Hicksville & Hempstead, 7½ A. M. do

Light freight and packages taken by the passage train—freight to be paid in advance.

The arrangement affords an opportunity for the residents of Sag Harbor and Greenport, and the adjacent country, to remain in New-York five hours, and return the same evening.

Boats leave the South Ferry, New-York side, for Brooklyn half an hour before the departure of the trains.

Due notice will be given of the connection of the road with the eastern lines to Boston.

Courtesy of David Morrison, LIRR

A timetable printed the day before the first run of the LIRR from Brooklyn to Greenport in 1844

FAST FORWARD

1830s Decisions Still Shape the LIRR

BY SIDNEY C. SCHAER
STAFF WRITER

More than 150 years have passed since the Long Island Rail Road reached Greenport, but to many of today's commuters the planners of that route were on the wrong track.

Some of the problems confronting travelers on Long Island can be traced to the decisions made in the 1830s when the LIRR was routed across the spine of Long Island through its least populated areas.

The railroad's investors, including Cornelius Vanderbilt, perceived their railroad as a bridge for its profit-making New York-to-Boston service. The purpose was to simply get people across Long Island, rather than to serve the people living here.

"They made a huge miscalculation and built a railroad to nowhere," says planner Lee Koppelman.

Even today, some of the railroad's critics argue that the mind-set created by that original east-west route has never noticeably changed. The LIRR accomplished one thing by linking the length of Long Island to New York City, but it has never succeeded in accommodating the needs of travelers who want a railroad that links Long Island's North and South Shores.

The LIRR accomplished one thing by linking the length of Long Island to New York City, but it has never succeeded in accommodating the needs of travelers who want a railroad that links Long Island's North and South Shores.

"It was probably a mistake," says Long Island Rail Road historian Vincent F. Seyfried, characterizing the original decision to locate the railroad's path along the flattest, least populated section. He said there were technological as well as economic reasons for the decision. "There were limits involving the technology available at the time . . . locomotives that had difficulty climbing grades and going around curves."

From the outset, the railroad's founders rejected two alternative routes that would have linked the small but thriving communities of Long Island's North Shore and chose the route that is now the railroad's main line.

But with the advent of a competitive all-rail route from New York to Boston, the LIRR in 1850 went into receivership. Although it reorganized, the line continued to struggle.

Because the Long Island Rail Road of the mid-19th Century couldn't afford to move swiftly enough to serve Long Island, it spawned a set of competitive railroads built through Queens, and into what became eastern Nassau County.

Two other railroads, the Central, built by department store magnate A. T. Stewart, and the South Side Rail Road, built to serve communities not reached by the LIRR, also came into existence. The competition was fatal.

"The sharpness and bitterness of the rivalry was so intense, that whatever competition could reach, business was done at ruinous rates and sooner or later all the systems became financially embarrassed," explained a brief history published by the LIRR on its 100th anniversary in 1934.

Eventually all these interlacing lines were consolidated under the Long Island Rail Road's banner.

According to current LIRR President Tom Prendergast, that legacy also shapes the service offered today. "Most railroads were built following corridors of population," he says, "but it is also true that railroads historically have created corridors of population as well."

Still, a century and a half after it was built, the railroad's original route — the 96 miles of Main Line — serves only 12.5 percent of all westbound peak morning traffic. It ranks fourth behind the Babylon, Port Washington and Port Jefferson branches in the number of commuters who use it to travel to New York City.

The Long Delay at Hicksville

BY SIDNEY C. SCHAER
STAFF WRITER

The longest delay in the annals of Long Island Rail Road occurred on a stretch of track five miles long between Hicksville and Farmingdale. It took the railroad nearly four years to travel the distance.

The delay occurred in 1837 when the railroad arrived in Hicksville and ran out of money. Its next stop had the inelegant name of Hardscrabble. As the line waited to push forward, a real estate speculator from Buffalo, Ambrose George, began purchasing land in the area. He decided that if his project were to prosper, the first thing that had to go was the area's name. Who, he wondered, would want to go to Hardscrabble? So he changed the name to the more bucolic Farmingdale.

By the time the railroad finally arrived in October, 1841, on its bumpy journey to Greenport, Farmingdale not only became the line's new Long Island terminus but what had been a tightly knit little farming community at the eastern edge of what was then Queens County was about to be transformed.

In preparation for the railroad's coming, George opened a small general store, and named one of the streets after his daughter, Elizabeth. In 1841, there were two trains a day, and the railroad also scheduled a Sunday train, much to the chagrin of some of Long Island's more Sabbath-minded residents.

Hardscrabble had become a memory. And now Farmingdale was a transportation hub. The 1841 schedule noted that stagecoaches would take passengers from the train to Islip, Babylon, Patchogue, Oyster Bay and South and West Neck.

The community also would become a key stop for the railroad, where steam locomotives could refuel and get water. And it would catch the eye of an inveterate traveler named Walt Whitman.

In an account of a trip to Greenport that appears in "Walt Whitman's New York," America's most celebrated poet writes: "At Farmingdale, anciently known under the appellation of 'Hardscrabble,' you begin to come among the more popular specimens of humanity which old Long Island produces. (Though we ought not to have overlooked the goodly village of Jericho, two miles north of Hicksville — a Quaker place, with stiff old farmers, and the native spot of Elias Hicks.) Farmingdale rears its towers in the midst of 'the brush' and is one of the numerous offspring of the railroad, deriving no considerable portion of its importance from the fact that the train stops here for passengers to get pie, coffee, and sandwiches."

Whitman recognized what would be one of the LIRR's central contributions to Long Island: the building of communities.

A year after reaching Farmingdale, the railroad had moved another 13 miles eastward and created a new terminus called Suffolk Station, which eventually became the core of Central Islip. And in 1851 a group of reformers started a utopian village called Modern Times, eventually evolving into the community known today as Brentwood.

The Main Line

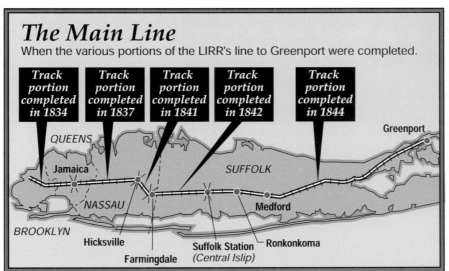

When the various portions of the LIRR's line to Greenport were completed.

Track portion completed in 1834
Track portion completed in 1837
Track portion completed in 1841
Track portion completed in 1842
Track portion completed in 1844
QUEENS
Jamaica
NASSAU
BROOKLYN
SUFFOLK
Greenport
Medford
Hicksville
Farmingdale
Suffolk Station (Central Islip)
Ronkonkoma

Newsday / Linda McKenney

The Coming Of the LIRR

LIRR from **Preceding Page**

Long Island family. His cousin Elias was a noted Quaker preacher who helped found the community of Jericho. Valentine Hicks, postmaster of Jericho from 1826 to 1839, had grown rich as a shipowner in New York. He also saw a chance to increase his wealth by having the railroad's route cross through the spine of Long Island, where he and relatives had large holdings, instead of following a much more northern route nearer the established communities of Long Island's North Shore.

Hicks became president of the railroad during the Panic of 1837, which dried up investment capital. It took four years before a successor, Brooklyn businessman George B. Fisk, was able to jump-start the railroad's construction beyond Hicksville.

It mattered that the men behind the railroad ranged from investors who saw the Boston route as a big profit-maker to people such as James Huggins Weeks, an Oyster Bay native who moved to Yaphank to manage family holdings, especially timber. Weeks saw the railroad as both a wood-buying customer and as a much cheaper way to ship to New York.

To get to Yaphank and beyond to Greenport, the LIRR had to borrow $100,000 from New York State. And it had to negotiate a reduction in the annual payment it was making to the Brooklyn & Jamaica line. Stockholders upset with what they saw as a lack of progress often held chaotic meetings. In a history of the railroad published in 1898, Elizur B. Hinsdale, a former general counsel of the line, wrote: "At almost every meeting of the board, resolutions were passed forfeiting the stock of stockholders for nonpayment of assessments."

"Boroughs of Brooklyn and Queens," 1925

George B. Fisk, the fourth president of the Long Island Rail Road, oversaw construction of rails from Hicksville to Greenport. At right, a poster announces a produce freight train for use by Long Island farmers in 1841.

FARMERS
Marketmen,
Gardeners, &c.
Long Island
RAIL ROAD.
A FREIGHT TRAIN
WILL LEAVE
Hicksville and Hempstead,
EVERY
SATURDAY MORNING,
In time to arrive in market by
daylight, with every description of freight: Vegetables, Grass, Fish, Clams, Meats and Market Truck generally.
N. B. A Ferry Boat will leave the South Ferry for Fulton Market, on the arrival of the Cars with passengers and freight, at the same rates as charged at Fulton Ferry.
☞ To commence on the first of June.
N. B. Sheds will be erected at Hicksville, where Horses can be kept during the day without charge to the owners.
Brooklyn, April 1, 1841.

Courtesy of David Morrison, LIRR

Nor trains exempt from accidents. One account of a famous early derailment appeared in the Long Island Democrat published on May 4, 1836.

"As the train of cars attached to the two locomotive engines on the Brooklyn and Jamaica Railroad was passing Wyckoff's Lane, at a rapid rate, a cow standing across the track was caught under the wheels, which threw the engine off the rails, and the rear locomotive, not being able to stop in time, ran foul of the front cars causing considerable damage. The train was going to Brooklyn to bring up engaged passengers to the Union Course Races, which commenced yesterday. Persons to the number of about two thousand were thus disappointed in their ride to the sporting ground, and were compelled to 'foot it' or return to their homes greatly chagrined. Hundreds of disappointed pedestrians were seen plodding their way toward the 'scene of merry strife' with violent imprecations on their tongues against the negligence or ignorance of the engineers."

By 1840, when a Saturday snowstorm in December created service delays between Brooklyn and Jamaica, not only were passengers left waiting at the depot in Brooklyn, but they immediately organized what may have been the first commuter council to complain to the railroad's president.

The new line was learning to deal with problems that still confront it today — accidents, weather and time. Early schedules failed to show when trains would arrive at intermediate stops, but that changed. Eventually, a table of times would be required, since trains sharing the same track had to know precisely each other's locations.

By 1841, the railroad had reached 32 miles to Farmingdale, was charging 62½ cents as its highest fare, and had revenues of about $60,000, according to its annual report.

A year later, the railroad had finally passed through Queens County, which included present-day Nassau, and arrived in Suffolk. It reached Deer Park in March and what is now Brentwood in June, 1842. A month later, the line reached Suffolk Station, now Central Islip.

It wasn't until June of 1844 that trains were steaming into Yaphank and work crews were rushing to finish the

LEGACY

A LONG-LOST TUNNEL IN BROOKLYN

In the same year that the Long Island Rail Road reached Greenport, a tunnel grew in Brooklyn.

The tunnel was the outgrowth of the LIRR's technical problems and protests from Brooklynites about the noise, soot, fumes and smoke created by primitive locomotives.

The technical trouble concerned an incline at the foot of Atlantic Avenue, where the route started. The LIRR's predecessor, the Brooklyn & Jamaica Railroad, got over the hurdle with horses that pulled the train up Cobble Hill. But in 1844, the LIRR received permission to construct a tunnel that would in effect lessen the grade at the journey's beginning and allow steam locomotives to do the job.

The Atlantic Street tunnel, according to Appleton's 1854 traveler's guide, extended 2,750 feet from Columbia to Boerum Streets, was 30 feet below street level and cost the company $96,000 to build. It was finished in December, 1844. For the next 17 years, the LIRR used the tunnel.

But a committee was formed by Brooklyn residents who didn't like steam locomotives, period. They argued that in Manhattan, the Harlem and the Hudson River Railroads were not permitted to run their locomotives into the "settled and improved parts of the city."

Eventually the tumult over steam locomotives reached such a pitch that the Long Island Rail Road gave up part of its Brooklyn route and built another route through Woodside, Queens, into Hunters Point, which became its western terminus in Long Island City. The tunnel was sealed in 1861 and abandoned.

More than a century passed before the tunnel would be rediscovered in 1981 by Bob Diamond, a Brooklyn railroad buff who used long-forgotten blueprints and dug his way in. The tunnel is still closed.

One description of a ride through the tunnel was offered by Walt Whitman years after it had been sealed shut. In "Walt Whitman's New York," he wrote: "The old tunnel, that used to lie there under ground, a passage of Acheron-like solemnity and darkness, now all closed and filled up, and soon to be utterly forgetten . . . The tunnel dark as the grave, cold, damp, and silent. How beautiful [to] look at earth and heaven again, as . . . we emerge from the gloom!" — **Sidney C. Schaer**

Brooklyn Historical Society

A drawing of the Atlantic Avenue tunnel built in 1844; it served trains in Brooklyn until 1861.

final miles of track to Greenport.

But another crisis arose — a shortage of rail. A shipment of English forged rails from Liverpool had been delayed. Just west of Punk's Hole, the railroad substituted about three miles of so-called snakehead rails — flat bars of iron, 3 inches by three-fourths inches, spiked to the timbers — until the forged rails arrived.

On July 27, 1844, champagne flowed in Greenport as the railroad made history.

A year after service to Greenport and Boston got under way, historian S. Prime, in his 1845 "History of Long Island," included a brief chapter on the LIRR: "It is impossible to divine the amazing changes, which this improvement will effect on both the intellectual and secular interests of the eastern parts of the island." Prime added: "The necessary consequence is that locomotion, at least to any distance from home, is almost unknown on Long Island. The writer has heard men sixty years of age say that they were never 20 miles from the spot on which they were born . . . seclusion from distant parts instead of making them restless, seems to have confirmed the habit of staying at home."

And then, commenting on the route, Prime wrote: ". . . The site of this road is through the most sterile and desolate parts of the island. After leaving Jamaica, you scarcely see a village or a farm of good land."

It was almost as if Prime were prescient about the line's fate. The LIRR's original route — tied to the New York-Boston connection — would haunt the railroad. "The principal villages, as well as the best land, are to be found on the sides of the island," he wrote.

Railroad travel was still a novelty, as this 1847 account of a trip to Greenport makes clear in the Brooklyn Eagle: "At half past one o'clock yesterday afternoon, I started on the L.I. railroad from the South ferry on my way to the eastern section of 'old Nassau.' The usual splutter which precedes a start attended us, of course. Little boys with newspapers, friends taking leave, women uttering 'last words,' Emerald Ladies with peaches . . . and small fry with various wares, surrounded the cars; and these, with the assistance of the furious steam pipe, and certain obstreperous iron work that certes seemed to have some rickety disorder, made up a sceen that would make the fortune of a melo-drama, if brought in at the close of an act — but which I was glad enough to escape from, I assure you."

But the novelty and excitement of railroad travel weren't enough in the end to save the line from facing financial disaster.

By the end of 1848, the Long Island Rail Road had been supplanted; what investors and engineers believed to be inconceivable in the 1830s became a reality with the opening of the New York, New Haven and Hartford link to Boston. The LIRR's fate was sealed when one its most famous investors, Cornelius Vanderbilt, realized that the future lay with the all-railroad route. Vanderbilt withheld his steamer from the Long Island connection; he also was an investor in the New Haven line. Built with a mission that no longer was profitable, the LIRR ended up a railroad that went nowhere.

Now the line would have to find its market on Long Island. Instead of taking people east on a route to Boston, it would evolve into the nation's largest commuter railroad — shuttling Long Island's population to and from New York City.

But that did not happen without a struggle. In March, 1850, the line went into receivership. In its "Report upon the Wild Lands of Long Island," a committee of the railroad ruefully noted: "When the Long Island Rail Road was constructed and completed in 1844, it traversed an almost unbroken wilderness, in which there was scarcely a dwelling and hence the name of 'the Long Island Barrens' was applied to this extensive territory."

It would take a while for those wild lands to be tamed, and to this day, some remain almost as undeveloped as when the railroad first laid its tracks there.

By 1850, the LIRR was coping with nearly a lost market and debts of nearly $500,000. In its report to stockholders, several months before it went into receivership, the line pinned its hopes on the future growth of Long Island:

"The time is not far distant when all the advantages of healthfulness, proximity to the city, and convenience of access will increase the population of Long Island; the beneficial effects of which will be felt in the increased revenue of the railroad."

And indeed it would. But it would not happen overnight.

EXPIRES October 31st 1868
Long Island R. R.
COMMUTATION TICKET, No.
1056
TO BE USED BY F. J. Richardson
Between Queens
and Hunter's Point.
Charlick
TREASURER.
NOT TRANSFERABLE.

NOT TRANSFERABLE.

This Ticket is good for One Hundred Passages, if used before the date of expiration according to agreement signed by holder. It is only good when the margin is punched by Conductor and on detachment of one of the Coupons by him, upon each passage.

The Company will not issue a duplicate of this ticket, under any circumstances.

Queens Borough Public Library

An 1868 Long Island Rail Road commuter pass for 100 trips

A building boom in Port Jefferson launches the county as a center of ship construction

Shipshape in Suffolk

BY BILL BLEYER
STAFF WRITER

Schools are closed. The people of Port Jefferson are wearing their best clothes as they flock to the harbor where every ship is adorned with flags, bunting and streamers.

It's not a national holiday. On the contrary, it's a common occurrence in 19th-Century Port Jefferson. It's a launching day in Long Island's busiest shipbuilding town.

As soon as a bottle of champagne is broken over the bow and the craft splashes into the harbor, the guests enter the boat-building shed for a party. It's a big christening because most of the adult males in the village of 300 work in ship construction.

Port Jefferson Historical Society Photo

The bark Carib under construction in Port Jefferson in 1868, toward the end of the building boom

From the late 1700s to 1884, 327 wooden vessels were built in the community. This represented about 40 percent of the more than 800 ships that went down the ways in Suffolk County, the state's largest shipbuilding center outside of New York and Brooklyn. By 1840, shipbuilding had become a major Long Island industry, based almost entirely in Suffolk. By 1855, there were 25 yards employing 419 workers. Twelve of those shipyards were in Port Jefferson. Ship construction was also a major industry in Northport and Greenport, but vessels were going up in almost every deep protected harbor along the North Shore and around Peconic Bay.

Skilled craftsmen were needed. First a one-sided model was carved, then lumbermen cut trees and sawyers turned them into the proper-shaped timbers. Shipwrights using hand tools such as augers, mauls, saws, hammers and adzes worked from the keel up attaching frames and planking. Shipsmiths forged the iron spikes, pins, rings and other fittings. Blockmakers made the pulleys used in the rigging. Caulkers pounded oakum, a fiber like unraveled rope, into the seams to make the hull watertight. Mastmakers built the masts. Finally, riggers completed the rigging and sailmakers made the acres of canvas sails.

None of this was going on in Drowned Meadow, as Port Jefferson was first called, until John Willse, a farmhand from New Jersey, began building vessels in 1796 in what is now Poquott. It was the start of a shipbuilding dynasty. A year later, he purchased land on the southeast corner of the harbor and built six ships. By 1809, Willse had hired Richard Mather as an apprentice. Five years later, Mather had married Willse's daughter and constructed five sloops to become the community's largest shipbuilder.

Among the ships of note from the village's shipyards were the schooner Edward L. Frost, built in 1847 and the first American ship to bring cargo from Japan in 1856 after trade had been established by Commodore Matthew Perry.

By the 1870s, the whaling industry had died and the boom years were over for wooden sailing ships. The tide had turned to steamships and iron-hulled vessels, which required larger yards and more machinery than was available in Port Jefferson. In 1900, only three major shipyards were left, surviving by building recreational vessels or doing repair work.

In 1901, the hamlet held its last big christening for a wooden ship. The schooner Martha Wallace was more than 200 feet long — the largest sailing ship ever built on Long Island.

The outbreak of World War I temporarily resuscitated the dockyards as the government financed the construction of steel-hulled military vessels. Between 1917 and 1919, the number of shipyard workers mushroomed from 250 to more than 1,100. But government contracts dried up with the end of the war, closing the shipbuilding era in Port Jefferson.

For a while, shipyards continued to operate on a small scale in other harbors such as Greenport, Huntington and Oyster Bay. Now there are only a handful of yards left, building and repairing small commercial vessels and pleasure boats.

The Water World Begins to Pick Up Steam

Traveling by boat from Long Island to Manhattan or Connecticut was no joyride in colonial times. The earliest ferries were rowboats or sailboats at the mercy of tide and weather.

The adventure of crossing the East River or Long Island Sound became more predictable in the 1700s when some ferries were powered by horses walking on treadmills that turned the paddlewheels. But this faster and more reliable service was not without risk. In 1741, a horse-powered ferry to Connecticut operated by Thomas Jones of Oyster Bay capsized in a storm, drowning Jones, 10 passengers, including six slaves, and six horses.

In 1814 Robert Fulton and his backer, Robert Livingston, initiated a steam-powered ferry between Manhattan and Brooklyn. The Nassau carried its first passengers on May 10. "This noble boat surpassed the expectations of the public in the rapidity of her movements," The Long Island Star reported breathlessly. "Her trips varied from five minutes to twelve minutes, according to tide and weather . . ."

On the first day of business, the company, which advertised a $10 annual commutation ticket, carried 549 passengers. The new ferry, the newspaper said, is "a sure harbinger of the future . . . prosperity of Long Island." It was: The improved access to Brooklyn spurred its development into a suburb.

The Nassau's debut was not entirely rosy. The Star noted that "Mr. Lewis Rhoda (chief engineer of Wm. Fulton's works) accidentally got hurled into the machinery . . . which cut off his left arm a little below the elbow, and broke his neck. He expired in about three hours after."

The Long Island Sound steamboat United States in 1827, and a copy of the first Fulton Ferry ticket

The Nassau represented a key step in steam-powered transportation for Long Island. On March 21, 1815, Capt. Elihu Bunker piloted the first powered vessel through the rocks of Hell Gate on the East River and into Long Island Sound. Bunker's 134-foot Fulton could only travel as far as New Haven — at 8 mph. Eventually bigger, faster steamboats would travel farther east and carry millions of passengers until World War II.

For travelers who had endured the five-day, jarring trip by stagecoach to Boston, the steamboats created an epoch of elegance and speedy transportation. When on June 15, 1835, the Connecticut arrived in Providence and was met by a train instead of just stagecoaches, the trip to Boston could be made in less than 24 hours.

Cornelius Vanderbilt dominated the steamboat scene from 1835 until he got into railroads 15 years later. He owned so many steamboats that the newspapers began to refer to him as The Commodore.

Steamboats also carried goods and passengers to and from Long Island ports. In 1829, the Linnaeus began service to and from Glen Cove. By the early 1850s, regularly scheduled steamboats operated to Lloyd Neck and Port Jefferson. Steamers sailed on the Sag Harbor-Greenport-Orient-New York route beginning in 1859. And the Bridgeport and Port Jefferson Steamboat Co. was formed in 1883, providing regular service across the Sound that still continues.

— **Bill Bleyer**

Steamer, "American Steam Vessels," 1895; Ticket, Harper's Weekly, 1872

New Haven Colony Historical Society

A mural depicts the courtroom scene in U.S. District Court, New Haven, Conn. The captives, who rebelled and took control of the Amistad, were taken there after they came ashore at Montauk.

An ex-president battled a sitting president in a case settled by the Supreme Court

Captives Of The Amistad

BY GEORGE DE WAN
STAFF WRITER

From the weather-beaten, black-hulled schooner anchored off Culloden Point a boatload of parched and hungry black men paddled to the Long Island shore to look for food and fresh water. Their arrival on American soil at Montauk touched off a debate about slavery that would pit an ex-president against a sitting president and would not end until it reached the U.S. Supreme Court.

The date was Aug. 25, 1839. The ship was the Amistad.

The men were from Sierra Leone, West Africans who had been borne across the great ocean to Havana, Cuba, in a brutalizing Portuguese slave ship. Sold there at a slave auction and transferred to the bowels of the Amistad ("Friendship," in Spanish), where they were chained like wild animals, the 49 men and four children had released themselves through a bloody insurrection on the high seas.

The Africans' few hours on Long Island would be the last freedom they would know for 1½ years. Their leader was a tall, muscular man in his mid-20s whose name in his native Mende tongue, spelled phonetically, was Singbe-pieh, but who would become known as Cinque (pronounced "sin-KAY").

It was not long before a U.S. Navy brig, the Washington, appeared and seized the Amistad and all its men and children. They were taken to New London, Conn., a state where slavery would not become illegal until 1848.

Two Spanish-speaking slaveholders, José Ruiz and Pedro Montes, who were being held on the ship by the Africans, told the Coast Guardsmen the story. They had bought the Africans as slaves in Havana, a Spanish possession. While in the Amistad for transport to another part of the island, the Africans, led by Cinque, broke free, killing the captain and the cook. Promising to sail the Amistad to Sierra Leone, Montes and Ruiz headed east by day and then altered course by night, without the Africans realizing that the ship was actually heading up the East Coast.

In Connecticut, the captives initially were charged with murder and piracy. But the legal issues later centered on attempts to have the captives returned to the two Spanish slavers, which landed them in U.S. District Court.

Newspaper publicity about the captives galvanized abolitionists in New York, who formed a committee to provide for their defense, a committee that included a strong Christian missionary element. The formidable Connecticut attorney Roger Baldwin agreed to represent them as chief defense counsel.

At issue in the January, 1840, trial were two international treaties. First was a reciprocal agreement of 1795 between Spain and the United States under which each pledged to return any ships or goods of the other found on the high seas. Citing this, U.S. government attorneys, supported by the Spanish embassy, argued that the U.S. courts had no jurisdiction and that the captives should be returned to Ruiz and Montes as their property.

Baldwin, however, cited an 1817 treaty between Spain and Great Britain that outlawed the importation of slaves into Spanish colonies after 1820. Thus, the Amistad captives were imported illegally, Baldwin said, and were not slaves, but free men. After listening to a week of testimony, District Judge Andrew T. Judson sided with Baldwin and ordered the captives freed.

This should have been the end of it. But President Martin Van Buren, supporting the Spanish position, ordered the decision appealed to the Supreme Court. He was seeking re-election and did not want to lose the votes of the slaveholding South.

The president's actions angered former President John Quincy Adams, then serving in the House of Representatives. He agreed to assist Baldwin with the Supreme Court appeal. For the 73-year-old Adams, it would be a platform for him to attack Van Buren.

On Feb. 22, 1841, the Supreme Court arguments began, and the attorney general and Baldwin laid out the same opposing cases that had been made in New Haven. Then Adams turned his oratorical guns on Van Buren. It was, he said, nothing more than a question of justice vs. injustice. The Supreme Court upheld the District Court decision.

The Amistad Africans were free. But the abolitionists who supported them wanted to save their souls as well as their bodies. For almost nine months the Africans studied the Bible, hymn-singing and the English language, so that they could return to Africa to spread the Christian faith. On Nov. 27, 1841, Cinque and his friends, along with some Christian missionaries, sailed for Freetown, Sierra Leone, on the ship Gentlemen.

Adams, a meticulous man, had one more detail to attend to. He asked the marshal of the District of Connecticut to amend the 1840 federal census so that the Africans would appear as free men, not slaves.

'Amistad' Fact and Fiction

Steven Spielberg's 1997 movie "Amistad," while powerfully evocative, is flawed by questionable history.

The movie leaves the impression that this case laid the legal groundwork for overturning slavery, awakening Americans to its horrors and leaving political Washington searching for a solution. It did nothing of the sort: Amistad came and went, while the illegal international slave trade prospered and slavery remained embedded in the social system of the South. In fact, the U.S. Supreme Court's Amistad decision affirmed that slaves were property; the Amistad Africans were free to leave because they were *not* slaves.

And there are other discrepancies as well:

- The movie says that seven of the nine justices were southern slaveholders. Fact: Five of the Supreme Court justices were southerners, and four of them were slaveholders.
- When the Africans land on Long Island, they see ice forming on pools of water. Fact: They landed on Aug. 25.
- Cinque visits Adams' house in Quincy, Mass. In Adams' greenhouse, he is moved almost to tears by seeing an African violet. Fact: Cinque never visited Adams' home, and the African violet is native to East Africa but not Sierra Leone in West Africa.
- In the Supreme Court scene, Cinque sits right behind Adams. Fact: Cinque was never there; he was under arrest in New England.
- The movie leaves the impression that the U.S. government paid to have the Africans returned to Sierra Leone. Fact: President John Tyler, Martin Van Buren's successor, refused such a request.
- Roger Baldwin, who first defended the Amistad captives, is represented as a young, inexperienced real estate lawyer. Fact: He was almost 50, successful both as a lawyer and a politician, and would become Connecticut governor in 1844.

— George DeWan

New Haven Colony Historical Society

A portrait of the slave leader Cinque by Nathaniel Jocelyn

Foundered ships, rescue tragedies led to the creation of lifesaving stations

A Lifeline For Sailors

BY BILL BLEYER
STAFF WRITER

Fog clouded the shore as the Bristol, a three-masted vessel out of Liverpool, neared New York with a crew of 16 and 100 Irish immigrants on board. The bark ran aground on the shoals off Long Beach. As the ship lay helpless in the surf, the wind gusted and a giant wave smashed the lifeboats and snatched the hatches off the deck.

It was Nov. 21, 1836, and the only help available was from fishermen who rowed out from shore twice and rescued 32 people. But when they returned for a third load, breaking seas overturned their boats. By the next morning, 84 people had drowned and only a fragment of the Bristol was visible above the waves.

Such tragedies were not uncommon in the early 19th Century when there was no Coast Guard to rush to the aid of foundering vessels. There were hundreds of shipwrecks over the centuries along the approaches to New York, and if fishermen or other ships couldn't get to the scene, the death toll could be staggering.

Less than two months after the Bristol disaster, the Mexico, also carrying Irish immigrants, ran aground in the same area with the loss of all but eight of the 128 aboard.

These and other tragedies sparked a public outcry for a government-funded rescue network, but it was private industry that forced the issue.

Companies that insured ships knew they could recover most of the cargo if help got to a wreck quickly. So the industry pressured Congress, which in 1848 came up with $10,000 to build lifesaving stations in New Jersey and Long Island. These were small equipment huts to be used by volunteers. The Jersey stations went on line in 1848. Eatons Neck is believed to have been the first Long Island station — starting operations on March 3, 1849. The stations were overseen by the new U.S. Life-Saving Service.

Newsday Archive

A drawing of the wreck of the three-masted Mexico off Long Beach in 1837, with the loss of 120 lives. The event spurred creation of a network of East Coast lifesaving stations.

The volunteer efforts paid off immediately. In the winter of 1850, nearly 300 lives were saved by the Long Island stations, and over the decades the lifesavers plucked more than 100,000 people off foundering ships.

Because equipment in the huts was often stolen, the government began to hire keepers for $200 a year. By 1871, it was clear the volunteer system was running into trouble. Some keepers lived miles from their stations and volunteers were not always available. So the government allocated funds to hire crews. There were 32 Long Island stations including one on Fishers Island.

Despite their oilskin suits, the lifesavers were usually drenched and nearly frozen. Frequently, boats swamped in the surf. But the rigorous training usually prevented disaster. According to Van Field of Center Moriches, author of the 1997 book "Wrecks and Rescues on Long Island," the only Long Island lifesaver to perish was a crewman in Southampton who drowned while trying to cross an inlet in a rowboat at night.

The early stations were equipped with a galvanized lifeboat, mortar and shot for throwing lines to ships, a manila hawser, lanterns, shovels, axes, a speaking trumpet and a wagon for carrying equipment along the beach. Later the crews were given rockets, a cannon called a Lyle gun for firing lines to ships and a breeches buoy — a ring suspended from a pulley with trousers attached to it. Survivors climbed into the breeches and were pulled to shore by a line that ran above the waves.

At least that was the theory. It didn't always work. In January, 1891, the Bellport lifesaving station responded to the stranded schooner Otter. One crewman was rescued with the breeches buoy apparatus. What happened to the next seaman is described in the official Life-Saving Service report:

"He had placed himself snuggly in the buoy, when his weight caused the hawser to slip down . . ." The line jammed and the lifesaving crew tried pulling the seaman back onto the ship to free the line. "This was repeated two or three times . . . meanwhile the poor fellow in the buoy, unable to climb out, was being smothered by the seas tumbling onboard in rapid succession, until at last he was dashed out of the buoy." The man died, as did another crewman who only got one leg into the buoy before a sea washed him away.

When they weren't responding to a wreck, the crews stood watches from the stations and patrolled the beaches at night or in bad weather.

"Night patrol was a lonely duty, two and a half miles to the half-way house through sand. Often through deep grass and snow," wrote J. Sim Baker, who joined the Life-Saving Service in 1911 and was stationed at Fire Island. "Sometimes forced at high tide to wade gullies through which the sea poured after every breaking wave."

The Life-Saving Service continued until 1915 when it and the Revenue Cutter Service were merged to form the current agency that performs rescues along the coastline: the U.S. Coast Guard.

LEGACY

LIGHTHOUSES OF LONG ISLAND

Lighthouses were so important to the growing commerce of America that the ninth law adopted by the fledgling United States in August, 1789, provided for the government to build and maintain the aids to navigation.

Initially, all lighthouses had keepers. As the lighthouses were automated in this century, the keepers were removed. The last lighthouse on Long Island to be automated was Montauk in 1987. Over the years, 19 lighthouses would be built on Long Island and offshore islands and shoals. They were, in order of construction:

Montauk, lighted 1797.
Eatons Neck, 1799, renovated 1868.
Little Gull Island, off the North Fork, 1806, rebuilt 1868.
Sands Point, 1809, keeper's house added 1868, deactivated 1922.
Old Field Point, 1824, rebuilt 1868, discontinued 1933, and reactivated 1991.
Fire Island, 1826, rebuilt 1858, discontinued 1974 and relighted 1996.
Plum Island, 1827, rebuilt 1869, discontinued 1978.
Cedar Island, near Sag Harbor, 1839, rebuilt 1868, discontinued 1934.
North Dumpling, north of Fishers Island, 1849, rebuilt 1871 and 1980.
Execution Rocks, Long Island Sound off Sands Point, 1850, reconstructed 1868.
Huntington, 1857, rebuilt and relocated 1912.
Horton Point, Southold, 1857, discontinued 1933, relighted 1990.
Shinnecock Bay, 1858, discontinued 1931, demolished 1948.
Long Beach Bar (Bug Light), Orient, 1870, discontinued 1945, burned 1963, rebuilt 1990.
Stepping Stones, 1877, Long Island Sound, north of Great Neck.
Race Rock, off Fishers Island, 1878.
Cold Spring Harbor, 1890, deactivated 1965 and relocated to Centre Island shore as a private art studio.
Coney Island, 1890.
Orient Point, 1899.

The Horton Point Lighthouse in Southold was built in 1857, discontinued in 1933 and relighted in 1990.

Newsday Photo / Bill Davis

Long Island Sound's worst steamboat fire produces dramatic stories of survival

The Wreck of the Lexington

BY BILL BLEYER
STAFF WRITER

Stephen Manchester stood at the wheel of the Lexington on a freezing winter night when the cry of "Fire!" sounded above the chuffing and clanking of the great steamboat.

The pilot spun around and confronted flames spilling out from around the smokestack. Instinctively, Manchester cranked the wheel — hoping to head the 205-foot wooden vessel to the Long Island shore — four miles and more than 20 minutes away.

He was too late. Before the eastbound Lexington could complete the turn toward Eatons Neck, the tiller ropes burned through. The ship plowed on out of control at about 13 mph toward the northeast — and disaster.

Before the night of Jan. 13, 1840, was over, all but four of 143 passengers and crew aboard one of the era's premier steamboats would be dead. They would be victims of flames or bone-chilling water in Long Island Sound's first and worst steamboat fire. Ironically, the survivors owed their lives to the cargo of cotton bales that had fueled the fire but also served as makeshift rafts.

SHIPWRECKS OF LONG ISLAND

A special graphic appears on Pages 186-87.

Despite a cold spell that left sheets of ice on the Sound and kept its competitors in port, the 5-year-old Lexington, pride of the Navigation Co.'s Stonington Line, had sailed at 4 p.m. from Manhattan. It was bound for Stonington, Conn., carrying 150 cotton bales, some of them stored near the smokestack.

By the time dinner was served off Sands Point at 5:30 p.m., the temperature had plummeted to near zero and the wind was gusting.

When the alarm sounded two hours later, Capt. George Child sprinted to the freight deck, where the fire started. While some crew members worked to start a fire pump, the captain organized a bucket brigade. But the cotton-fed fire was already out of control, and Child shouted to passengers to take to the three lifeboats.

But the flames kept crewmen from shutting down the boilers. As a result, the Lexington was still speeding through the waves and the lifeboats capsized as soon as they hit the water, throwing the occupants into the sea.

Chester Hilliard, a 24-year-old ship captain traveling as a passenger, also heard the shout of "Fire!" and ran out on deck. After waiting 15 minutes for the boilers to peter out, he led deck hands and passengers in throwing bales overboard to serve as rafts. Hilliard and ship's fireman Benjamin Cox nudged the last bale, about 4 feet long, 3 feet wide and 18 inches thick, into the water and climbed onto it. It was about 8 p.m. Minutes later the center of the main deck collapsed, killing everyone there.

"We were sitting astride of the bale with our feet in the water," Hilliard told the coroner's inquest a week later. "It was so cold as to make it necessary for me to exert myself to keep warm, which I did by whipping my hands and arms around my body. About four o'clock [in the morning], the bale capsized with us." Hilliard and Cox climbed back aboard but eventually Cox could no longer hold on or even speak. "I rubbed him and beat his flesh," Hilliard said. Then a large wave jarred the bale. "Cox slipped off and I saw him no more." About seven hours later, a Capt. Meeker of the sloop Merchant spotted Hilliard waving his hat and rescued him.

The Mariners' Museum, Newport News, Va.

Lithographer Nathaniel Currier, then 26, gained fame when this depiction of the burning of the Lexington caused readers to snap up copies of the New York Sun within days of the 1840 fire. He later was a partner in the Currier & Ives picture agency.

LI HISTORY.COM

Two survivors' accounts and the findings of an inquest held after the deadly fire are available on the Internet at http://www.lihistory.com.

After Hilliard abandoned the Lexington, about 30 others remained on the bow with Manchester. The fire died down by 10:30 p.m. after consuming the center of the ship. Around midnight, Manchester was convinced the Lexington could not stay afloat much longer. The pilot joined two or three others on a makeshift wooden raft that immediately sank from their weight. Manchester climbed aboard a floating bale occupied by a man who gave his name as McKenny.

McKenny died about 3 a.m. That was about the time the Lexington should have arrived in Stonington. It was also when the hulk plunged 140 feet to the bottom northwest of Port Jefferson, carrying all those still aboard to their deaths.

"My hands were then so frozen that I could not use them at all," Manchester told the inquest. But when he saw the Merchant, he raised a handkerchief between his hands and Meeker plucked him off the bale. It was noon — an hour after the Merchant had rescued Hilliard.

Two hours later, Meeker spotted a third bale supporting fireman Charles Smith, who had escaped just before the ship sank.

The most amazing survival story was that of David Crowley, the mate, who went over the side with a bale of blazing cotton. He drifted for 43 hours after he left the Lexington, coming ashore nearly 50 miles to the east, at Baiting Hollow. He managed to stagger almost a mile to the nearest house and knock on the door before collapsing. Crowley kept the bale as a souvenir until the Civil War, when he donated it to be used for Union uniforms.

The inquest jury lambasted the Lexington's owners and crew: "Had the buckets been manned at the commencement of the fire, it would have been immediately extinguished." The jury said that with better discipline, the lifeboats could have been launched successfully. And the jury condemned "the odious practice of carrying cotton . . . on board of passenger boats, in a manner in which it shall be liable to take fire."

Despite those findings, "there didn't seem to be any response to it" by the government, said Edwin Dunbaugh, author of two books on Long Island Sound steamboats. It was not until the steamboat Henry Clay burned on the Hudson River a dozen years later that new safety regulations were imposed.

The Lexington disaster proved to be a boon for Nathaniel Currier, a young man who made colored engravings. The New York Sun asked him to make an image of the fire for a special edition. It was one of the first illustrated news stories, and it made Currier famous.

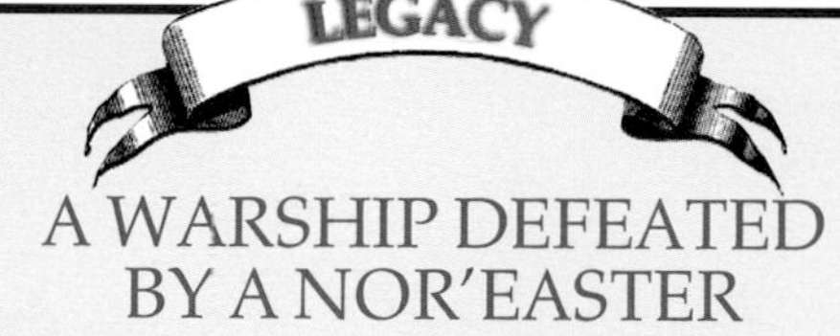

A WARSHIP DEFEATED BY A NOR'EASTER

The traces of Long Island's most historically important shipwreck lie buried in Block Island Sound north of Montauk.

On Jan. 24, 1781, during the American Revolution, the 74-gun British man of war Culloden was caught in a nor'easter and tried to clear Montauk Point to ride out the storm in the Atlantic. Blinded by snow, the pilot thought the ship had cleared the point and turned south. The ship went aground at what is now Culloden Point, north of the community of Montauk.

All 650 crewmembers survived and salvaged cannons and equipment before burning the ship to the waterline.

Today, after acquiring 14.3 acres of shoreline property adjacent to the wreck, the Town of East Hampton and Suffolk County are moving ahead with plans for Long Island's first underwater park at Culloden Point. A committee has been formed to plan facilities for scuba divers and terrestrial visitors. The wreck owes its importance to its connection to the Revolution, the artifacts it has yielded and the fact that it is the only underwater site in Long Island waters protected by state law.

— **Bill Bleyer**

Suffolk County Historical Society

The Royal Navy's Culloden, destroyed off Montauk

Claimed by the Sea

Twenty Prominent Long Island Shipwrecks

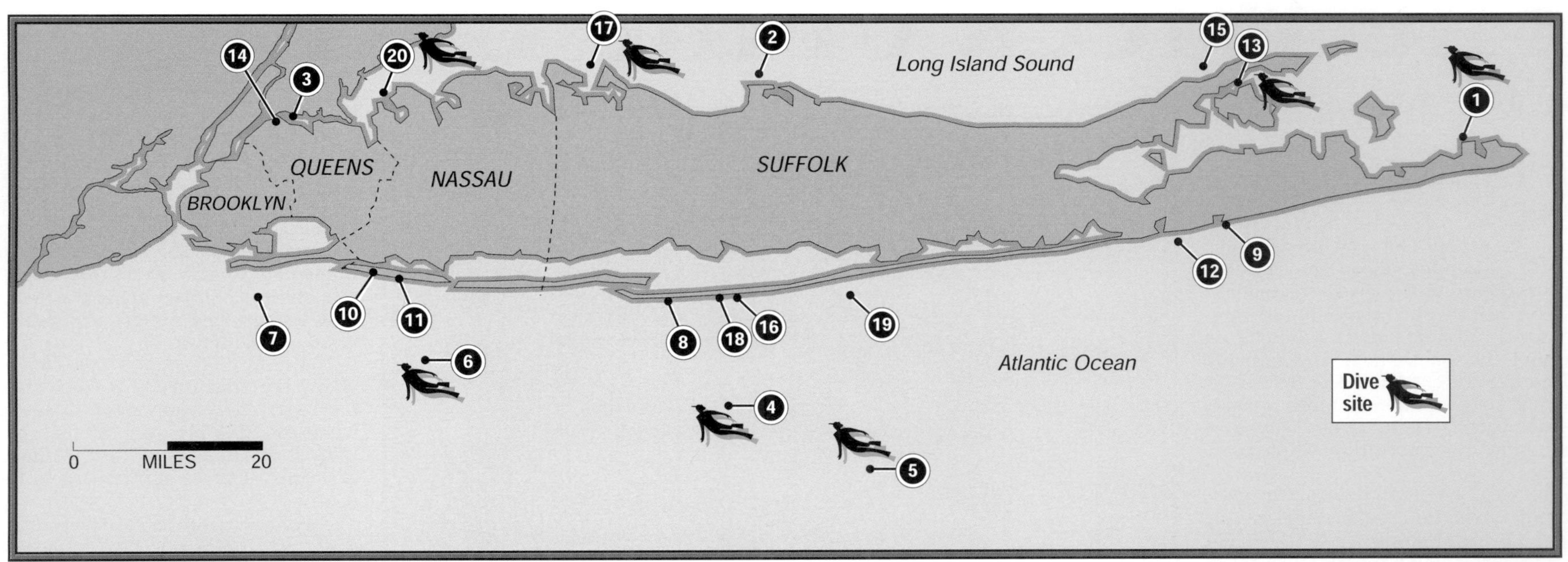

Department of the Navy

1. ***Culloden.*** British man-of-war ran aground in a storm Jan. 24, 1781. Burned to waterline after crew of 650 removed most guns and supplies. All survived.

Steamship Historical Society

4. ***San Diego:*** Navy cruiser sank July 19, 1918, after hitting a mine laid by German U-boat. Only major U.S. warship lost during World War I. Of the 829 crew members, six died.

Mariners' Museum Photo

5. ***Oregon:*** Cunard liner sank March 14, 1886, after colliding with a schooner that also sank. Nine aboard schooner died; all 845 on Oregon were saved.

Mariners' Museum

2. ***Lexington:*** Steamboat burned Jan. 13, 1840, and sank the next morning. Four of 143 passengers and crew survived.

Mariners' Museum

3. ***General Slocum:*** Worst marine disaster in local waters. On June 15, 1904, an excursion boat with 1,525 passengers and 23 crew ran aground at North Brother Island. Only 407 survived.

Courtesy of Hank Keats

6. ***Lizzie D.:*** Tugboat carrying Prohibition booze sank in October, 1922, killing crew of eight.

National Archives Photo

7. Turner: Destroyer sank Jan. 3, 1944, after explosion believed to have been caused by improper cleaning of anti-submarine weapon; 138 crew members died, 163 survived.

8. Prins Maurits: Long Island's first recorded shipwreck, March 6, 1657. Dutch ship carrying colonists to Delaware ran aground. Crew of 16 and 113 passengers got ashore in lifeboat and was saved by Indians.

East Hampton Free Library

9. Circassian: Square-rigger sailing from Liverpool, England, to New York Dec. 11, 1876, ran aground. After passengers and crew of 47 were rescued, salvage company put 20 crew members and 12 local workers, including 10 Shinnecock Indians, back aboard to try to save the ship. But another storm hit Dec. 29, breaking up the ship and killing 28, including all the Shinnecocks.

10. Bristol: Bark carrying 100 Irish immigrants and crew of 16 was stranded in fog Nov. 21, 1836. Boats from shore rescued 32; 84 people drowned.

Newsday Archive

11. Mexico: Bark carrying 112 Irish immigrants and 16 crew members grounded and broke up Jan. 2, 1837. Only eight survived.

12. Sylph: British 22-gun sloop of war wrecked Jan. 16-17, 1815. Only six of 121 aboard were rescued.

Department of the Navy Photo

13. Ohio: Seventy-four-gun ship of the line launched in 1820 was being scrapped in Greenport Harbor in April, 1884, when a storm wrenched it loose from mooring. Ship was burned to reduce obstruction to shipping but bottom of hull remains below the sand and silt.

14. Hussar: Twenty-eight-gun British frigate sank after hitting rock Nov. 23, 1780. Eight to 10 sailors drowned out of 200-member crew.

Newsday Archive

15. Commodore: Side-wheel steamboat traveling from New York to Stonington, Conn., became stranded on sandbar in a gale on Dec. 27, 1866. Crew got drunk and took only lifeboat ashore. Captain and 92 passengers were rescued the next day after a farmer retrieved the lifeboat.

Long Island Maritime Museum

16. Louis V. Place: Three-masted schooner was wrecked Feb. 8, 1885. Crew of eight could not handle rescue lines from lifesavers and climbed into rigging. When storm abated two days later, only two were left alive and one of them died in the hospital.

Northport Historical Society Photo

17. Gwendoline Steers: Tugboat sank with all nine aboard on the night of Dec. 30-31, 1962, in winds of more than 95 mph

18. Elizabeth: Bark wrecked July 19, 1850. The 10 victims of the 22 aboard included Margaret Fuller, author and advocate of women's rights.

19. "The Money Ship": Vessel, whose real name is unknown, came ashore in fall of 1816. Only captain and a boy, carrying Spanish silver coins, were rescued. Wreck drifted east to Shinnecock, where people began finding silver dollars on the beach.

Steamship Historical Society Photo

20. Maine: Excursion steamer sank Feb. 4, 1920, after becoming stuck in ice. No one was injured but the estimated 59 aboard were stranded for three days without heat or water. After salvage of equipment, wooden superstructure burned.

Newsday / Linda McKenney

Early years on Long Island inspire the creative genius of an American literary giant

The Paumanok Poet

By George DeWan
Staff Writer

When in his old age, often painfully bedridden in his Mickle Street house in grimy, run-down Camden, N.J., Walt Whitman talked endlessly with his young friend Horace Traubel, who became his Boswell.

America's greatest poet and Long Island's finest gift to the world of letters had one request:

"Be sure to write about me honest: whatever you do, do not prettify me: include all the hells and damns."

In his poetry and prose, and in the millions of words that others have written about him, the good gray poet comes down to us unprettified, with all the hells and damns intact. Whitman, whose "Leaves of Grass" rattled the establishment when it was first published in 1855, wrote a poetry that was loose and free, sensual and demonic, where rhyme was usually absent and the self-conscious "I" was ever-present.

I celebrate myself and sing
myself . . .

From Montauk on one end of the island he called Paumanok to New York and Brooklyn on the other, Whitman celebrated the world that gave birth to his genius: the thundering ocean waves pounding on the sandy Island shores, the rolling hills where he hiked in search of birds and butterflies and the throbbing energy of the expanding metropolis to the west that attracted him like a magnet. Over this island he rambled with an absorbing purpose: When the time was right, the poetry burst forth in an effusion of strange, wonderful and often perverse language that sought a connection with the universe.

I sing the body electric,
The armies of those I love
engirth me, and I engirth them ...

But before the thunderclap that was "Leaves of Grass," the first version of which did not come until Whitman was 36, there were years of apprenticeship. He was a schoolteacher on Long Island, a printer, a carpenter, the founder of the Huntington weekly newspaper The Long-Islander, and for years an editor and writer on at least 10 newspapers on Long Island and in New York City.

During the remarkable Civil War period of his life, Whitman volunteered as a nurse in hospitals surrounding Washington, D.C., that had been hurriedly constructed to house the Union wounded. He walked like a bearded saint among the bloodied, crippled bodies, comforting young men ravaged by war's destruction, talking to them, writing letters home for them, bringing them candy, writing paper, fruit juices and tobacco, and dressing their wounds, both real and psychic. It was a defining moment in Whitman's middle life, one that drew from him richly imagined, elegiac poetry lamenting the mutilation of fragile human bodies and the loss of an assassinated president he had grown to love.

Returning, resuming, I thread
my way through the hospitals,
The hurt and wounded I pacify
with soothing hand,
I sit by the restless all the dark
night, some are so young,
Some suffer so much, I recall the
experience sweet and sad . . .

In his free time, Whitman wandered the streets of the capital, occasionally seeing a weary President Abraham Lincoln moving about. And when Lincoln was shot at Ford's Theater, came this:

When lilacs last in the dooryard
bloom'd,
And the great star early droop'd
in the western sky in the night,
I mourned, and yet shall mourn
with ever-returning spring.

Whitman's life and his writing were a mass of contradictions, and the "myself" in the poetry is not always the real-life Walt. In the great poem that anchors "Leaves," called "Song of Myself," his first-person hero is "one of the roughs," a swaggering, earthy fellow of simple pleasures, "turbulent, fleshy, sensual, eating, drinking and breeding . . ." But, though he was 6 feet tall, 200 pounds, burly, with big hands and feet, Whitman was both physically and emotionally a tender and sensitive soul, more likely to be charmed by a butterfly than a barroom brawl — and probably one who never did any breeding, since he was more attracted to men than to women.

The man who sings the song of himself boasts of being a healthy, swaggering, gutsy imbiber of life. But Whitman was not completely well by his mid-40s, according to a major biographer, the late Paul Zweig of Queens College.

"In 1855 and 1856, he sang out about his 'magnetism' and his radiant bodily health and offered to pull his readers — and all of America — up to his gigantic level," Zweig wrote in "Walt Whitman: The Making of the Poet." "It is an astonishing combination of poetic genius, street theater and fraud. And something else, too: a feeling of power, a genuine physical aura which was the outreaching form of Whitman's egotism."

Do I contradict myself?
Very well then I contradict myself,
(I am large, I contain multitudes.)

In the middle of the summer of 1881, when he was 62, Whitman returned for the last time to the place where he was born in Huntington. It set off a flurry of memories. The poet walked to the Whitman family burial hill above an apple orchard, sat on a grave, took out pencil and paper and made notes. A year later he published the autobiographical

National Archives

Walt Whitman sat for this portrait by pioneer photographer Mathew Brady around the 1860s.

WALT WHITMAN, HIMSELF

To hear a recording of Walt Whitman reading "America," call 516-843-5454 or 718-896-6969 and choose category 3880 from a touch-tone phone.

On the Internet: A link to more than 300 of Whitman's poems and "Leaves of Grass" is available on the Internet at http://www.lihistory.com.

THE WHITMAN BIRTHPLACE AND JAYNE'S HILL

Though Walt Whitman left his West Hills birthplace when he was 4 years old, the two-story, cedar-shingled house built by his father about 1816 remains an important historic attraction in the middle of Route 110 commercialism. The **Walt Whitman Birthplace State Historic Site and Interpretive Center** is located at 246 Old Walt Whitman Rd. in South Huntington. The site contains not only the old house, with period furnishings, but also a new building with exhibits that trace the poet's development. There are audiovisual shows, guided tours, a research library and a museum shop. Open 1-4 p.m., Wednesday-Friday; 11 a.m.-4 p.m., Saturday-Sunday. From Memorial Day to Labor Day, open daily, 11 a.m.-4 p.m. Admission, $3 adults, discounts for seniors and children. Call 516-427-5240.

Nearby is West Hills County Park, where Whitman liked to hike up to **Jayne's Hill**. At 400.5 feet above sea level, it is the highest point on Long Island. A Suffolk County "green key" pass is required. Call 516-854-4949 for fee information.

Walt Whitman Birthplace Association; Newsday Photo

The Whitman family home as it appeared in 1902, above, and the museum today

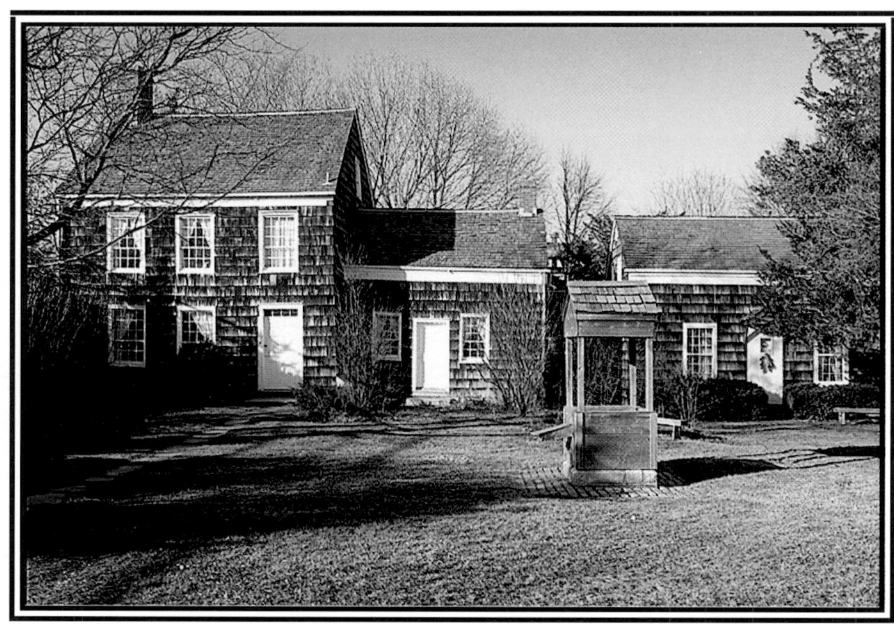

Newsday Photo / Bill Davis

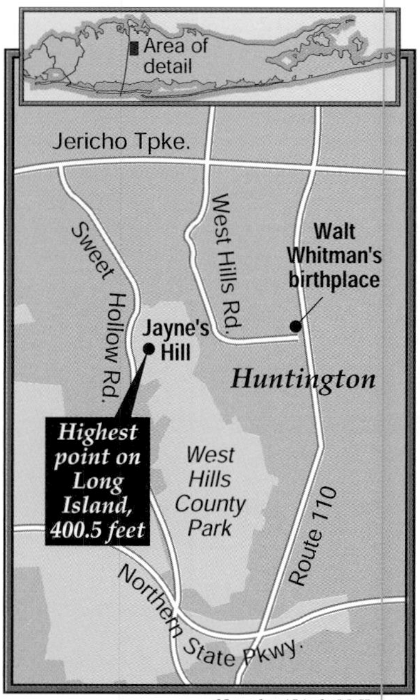

Newsday / Linda McKenney

"Specimen Days," his most lyrical and evocative prose work:

"Rode around the old familiar spots, viewing and pondering and dwelling long upon them, everything coming back to me . . . The successive growth stages of my infancy, childhood, youth and manhood were all pass'd on Long Island, which I sometimes feel as if I had incorporated. I roam'd, as boy and man, and have lived in nearly all parts, from Brooklyn to Montauk Point."

One image leads to another, and Whitman's thoughts travel back to his days of hiking to the top of nearby Jayne's Hill, the highest spot on Long Island. He remembers eel-spearing on the frozen Great South Bay, gathering seagulls' eggs in the summertime, sailing around Shelter Island and down to Montauk Point, picnicking on Turtle Hill beside the old lighthouse, wandering through the Hempstead Plains, making friends with baymen, farmers, fishermen:

"As I write, the whole experience comes back to me after the lapse of forty and more years — the soothing rustle of the waves, and the saline smell — boyhood's times, the clam-digging, barefoot, and with trowsers roll'd up — hauling down the creek — the perfume of the sedge-meadows — the hay-boat, and the chowder and fishing excursions . . . while living in Brooklyn (1836-'50) I went regularly every week in the mild seasons down to Coney island, at that time a long, bare unfrequented shore, which I had all to myself, and where I loved, after bathing, to race up and down the hard sand, and declaim Homer or Shakespeare to the surf and sea-gulls by the hour."

Walter Whitman Jr. — he became "Walt" when "Leaves of Grass" was published — was English on his father's side, Dutch on his mother's, with family lines going back to the mid-1600s. For the Whitmans, life was strained. Walter Whitman Sr. was a quiet and brooding Huntington carpenter, given to fits of depression, who moved regularly from home to home as he failed and failed again to provide for his family. Walt's mother, Louisa Van Velsor, came from a nearby, Quaker-influenced family that bred horses.

Whitman was the second of nine children. One died in infancy and three of five brothers and one sister had severe problems. One was mentally handicapped, and eventually institutionalized. Another died of tuberculosis and alcoholism at age 36, and his wife became a prostitute. A third died in the Kings County Lunatic Asylum. A sister was, according to some sources, a lifelong hypochondriac, and by others, a borderline psychotic whose artist husband died in a mental institution.

Walt was born May 31, 1819, in the two-story West Hills house that his father had built in Huntington. Just before his fourth birthday, the Whitmans packed up and moved to a rented house in Brooklyn. It was there that Walt spent his childhood, though the family moved constantly as the father had mixed success in finding work. At age 11, the boy's schooling ended, as he went out to work full time, first as a clerk. When the father moved the family back to Long Island in 1833, Walt stayed in Brooklyn, although he often visited his family in places like Hempstead and West Babylon. Some of these summer visits were occasions for joyous romps on the beach or in the woods, where Walt got back in touch with the natu-

Please see **WHITMAN** on **Next Page**

A Whitman Sampler

Walt Whitman spent many days, man and boy, on Long Island, and memories of those days suffuse his poetry. It is the poetry of an Island whose sandy beaches, boiling surf and flocking shore birds inspired him. Here are some examples:

An excerpt from
"Starting From Paumanok"

Starting from fish-shape
Paumanok where I was born,
Well-begotten, and rais'd by a perfect mother,
After roaming many lands, lover of populous pavements,
Dweller in Mannahatta my city, or on southern savannas,
Or a soldier camp'd or carrying my knapsack and gun, or a miner in California,
Or rude in my home in Dakota's woods, my diet meat, my drink from the spring
Or withdrawn to muse and meditate in some deep recess,
Far from the clank of crowds intervals passing rapt and happy,
Aware of the buffalo herds grazing the plains, the hirsute and strong-breasted bull,
Of earth, rocks, Fifth-month flowers experienced, stars, rain, snow, my amaze,
Having studied the mocking-bird's tones and the flight of the mountain hawk,
And heard at dawn the unrivall'd one, the hermit thrush from the swamp-cedars,
Solitary, singing in the West, I strike up for a New World.

"From Montauk Point"

I stand as on some mighty Eagle's beak,
Eastward the sea absorbing, viewing (nothing but sea and sky),
The tossing waves, the foam, the ships in the distance,
The wild unrest, the snowy curling caps — that inbound urge and urge of waves,
Seeking the shores forever.

MORE ON PAGE 191

Long Island's Walt Whitman

WHITMAN from **Preceding Page**

ral beauty of Long Island.

A child said "What is the grass?"
fetching it to me with full hands;
How could I answer the child? I do
not know what it is any more
than he . . .
I guess it is the handkerchief of the
Lord . . .

Taking a job as a printer's apprentice at the Long Island Patriot in 1831, when he was 12, Walt began his early career as a journalist. New York City became his mecca, a roaring, bawdy town where child prostitutes, dandies, drunkards and scavenging pigs vied for sidewalk space. Whitman explored this great metropolis, embroiled himself in Democratic politics and drank in the music of its opera halls and the rhythms and sounds of its cacophonous streets.

"Mannahatta!" Whitman would later write. "How fit a name for America's great democratic island city! The word itself, how beautiful! how aboriginal! how it seems to rise with tall spires, glistening in sunshine, with such New World atmosphers, vista and action!"

Off and on for the next quarter-century, Whitman either edited or wrote for a number of daily or weekly newspapers in the New York area, including a short period of editing the Brooklyn Eagle. In the spring of 1838, just before his 19th birthday, he bought a printing press and type in New York City and lugged them to Huntington, where he founded a weekly newspaper, the Long Islander. Although he sold the paper after about a year because he was restless, the experience left a vivid impression, as he later noted in "Specimen Days":

"I bought a good horse [a white mare named Nina], and every week went round the country serving my papers, devoting one day and night to it. I never had happier jaunts — going over to south side, to Babylon, down the south road, across to Smithtown and Comac, and back home. The experience of those jaunts, the dear old-fashion'd farmers and their wives, the stops by the hay-fields, the hospitality, nice dinners, occasional evenings, the girls, the rides through the brush, come up in my memory to this day."

About this same time, Whitman earned his bread by teaching in country schools around Long Island. But it was not a calling he especially liked, and he kept returning to journalism. He was also writing, but nothing memorable. Poetry, short stories, even a bad novel, "Franklin Evans," the story of a Long Island country rube who comes to the big city, falls under the spell of evil liquor, and saves himself only through temperance. (Whitman later called the novel "damned rot.") It was putting words together, and Whitman was under the spell of words.

"A perfect writer," he once wrote, "would make words sing, dance, kiss, do the male and female act, bear children, weep, bleed, rage, stab, steal, fire cannon, steer ships, sack cities,

Walt Whitman Birthplace Association; Newsday Photos

Not Shy Before a Camera

Portraits through the years, from left: In the 1840s when Whitman was teaching; in 1855, from the book "Leaves of Grass"; and in 1878, around age 57.

Teaching School Among the 'Bumpkins'

BY GEORGE DEWAN
STAFF WRITER

Teaching school on Long Island was not always a happy time for Walt Whitman. But to make ends meet as a young man, he taught for short periods in schools all over the place. In at least one of them, he may have gotten himself into deep trouble.

Although as an old man he fondly reminisced about his teaching days, Whitman earlier complained bitterly about life in the sticks with backwoods yahoos.

"I believe when the Lord created the world, he used up all the good stuff, and was forced to form Woodbury and its denisens, out of the fag ends, the scraps and refuse," the 21-year-old Whitman wrote to a friend, Abraham Leech, in the summer of 1840, when he was teaching at a one-room schoolhouse in Woodbury. In a series of letters that summer, he referred to Woodbury as "Devil's Den" and "Purgatory Place," and characterized the residents as "coarse gumpheads," "brutes," and "contemptible ninnies."

"I am sick of wearing away by inches, and spending the fairest portion of my little span of life, here in this nest of bears, this forsaken of all Go[d]'s creation; among clowns and country bumpkins, flat-heads, and coarse, brown-faced girls, dirty, ill-favoured young brats, with squalling throats and crude manners, and bog-trotters, with all the disgusting conceit, of ignorance and vulgarity."

Though fascinated with these Woodbury letters, scholars have taken them with a grain of salt. Here was a young man, away from the bustle and camaraderie of the city he loved, forced into the countryside to earn a living; a budding writer, trying out the language, being outrageous for effect, trying to make the words swagger, bluster and dance a literary jig. An editor of a selection of Whitman letters, Edwin Haviland Miller, writes: "Beneath the caustic commentary and the posturing and self-pitying emerges a picture of a very lonely young man."

Having left school himself when he was 11, Whitman first stood in front of a classroom of children when he was only a teenager himself. Off and on for five years, between the ages of 17 and 21, the future poet was a schoolmaster in at least 10 Long Island schools. When he was later established as a writer, Whitman took a special interest in the subjects of teaching and children's education, and from him we learn a lot about 19th-Century local schools.

"There are still left some old-fashioned county schoolhouses down through Long Island, especially in Suffolk County," Whitman wrote in the Brooklyn Daily Times on April 27, 1858. "The 'studies' pursued in this temple, are spelling, reading, writing, and the commoner rules of arithmetic, with now and then geography and 'speaking,' and perhaps in more ambitious cases, in addition to these branches, a little grammar, surveying, algebra, and even Latin and French."

These country schools were sometimes open year-round, with the year divided into three-month quarters, and teachers were often hired a quarter at a time. They were paid, Whitman said, about $40 or $50 a quarter, plus board. "Sometimes the teachers 'board round,'' he wrote. "That is they distribute and average themselves among the parents of the children that attend school — they stop two or three days in one place, a week in another, and so on."

Teaching in those days was often a quick stop on the way to somewhere else. "The teachers of these Long Island country schools are often poor young students from some of the colleges or universities, who desire to become future ministers, doctors or lawyers — but, getting hard up, or fagged out with study, they 'take a school' to recuperate, and earn a little cash, for future efforts," he wrote. "They are apt to be eccentric specimens of the masculine race — marked by some of the 'isms' or 'ologies' — offering quite a puzzle to the plain old farmers and their families."

Records are skimpy on Whitman as a schoolteacher. In only a couple of instances do we have any evaluation of his performance, one negative, and one extremely positive. An old man named Sandford Brown in West Hills told an interviewer in 1890 that Whitman had been his first teacher, although Brown didn't identify the school. "He warn't in his element," Brown was quoted as saying. "He was always musin' and writin', 'stead of tending to his proper dooties."

Whitman seems to have been much more successful in Little Bay Side, near Flushing, in the winter of 1839-1840. In 1894, Whitman's friend Horace Traubel interviewed a man named Charles A. Roe, who had been Whitman's student when he was a boy of 10. Whitman seemed to have been, at age 20, an instinctive progressive educator, abandoning rote instruction and never using corporal punishment. He engaged children in long conversations, played word games with them and engaged them in "mental arithmetic."

Roe said that the students "were all deeply attached to him, and were sorry when he went away." At one period later in life Whitman would affect the

Walt Whitman Birthplace Association; Newsday Photos

Above, circa 1883, holding a butterfly prop; and in 1887 in a George Cox photo taken when Whitman was about 68 years old

charge with cavalry or infantry, or do any thing that man or woman of the natural powers can do."

The mature Walt Whitman was about to emerge. It all came together in the spring of 1855, when Whitman published on his own a 95-page book that he called "Leaves of Grass." It contained 12 untitled poems, but Whitman kept revising, rearranging, deleting and adding new material until he died in 1892, by which time the ninth edition of "Leaves" was 426 pages long and contained 417 poems.

I hear America singing, the
varied carols I hear . . .

Whitman was ready for America, but America was not necessarily ready for Whitman. "In 1855, Whitman felt America needed him, and he was there to supply the need," writes David S. Reynolds in his 1996 cultural biography, "Walt Whitman in America." "He firmly believed his country would absorb him as affectionately as he had absorbed it. It was not long before he knew that he was terribly mistaken."

"Leaves" was not a complete failure, but the first edition sold only several hundred copies and the reviews were sharply divided. There was one extraordinary accolade, however, that has had literary critics buzzing ever since. One of the people who was given a first copy was the poet and essayist Ralph Waldo Emerson, one of Boston's leading intellectuals. On July 21, 1855, Emerson wrote Whitman a letter that has been called the most famous letter in American literary history.

"I find it the most extraordinary piece of wit and wisdom that America has yet contributed," Emerson said of "Leaves." ". . . I greet you at the beginning of a great career . . ." Whitman, no slouch at self-promotion, used the letter as a publicity tool for subsequent editions of the book.

Though a number of critics applauded the new poet, many Americans were not ready for Whitman's odd-sounding free verse. They were even less ready for his unbuttoned, freewheeling celebration of the body, of the robust human appetite for sex, both heterosexual and homosexual. They were simply not ready for Walt Whitman's gargantuan, offbeat appetites. There was, for example, New York journalist Rufus Griswold, who wrote that "Leaves of Grass" was "a mass of stupid filth."

Through me forbidden voices,
Voices of sexes and lusts, voices
veil'd and I remove the veil,
Voices indecent by me clarified
and transfigur'd.

Emerson himself once proposed that Whitman clean it up a little, but Whit-

Please see **WHITMAN** on Next Page

Walt Whitman Birthplace Association; Newsday Photo

Whitman taught at this school at Woodbury Road and Jericho Turnpike, Woodbury. An unhappy young man, he called Woodbury "Purgatory Place" and its residents "coarse gumpheads."

dress of a foppish dandy, but as a schoolteacher he was conventional, Roe said. Whitman "always dressed in black — dressed neatly — very plain in everything — no attempt at what would be called fashion . . . He was never sick; did not smoke; never, that I saw or heard of, drank any liquors. As to his eating, I never knew him to have any peculiar habits."

Whitman was thrust into teaching as a result of two disastrous fires that devastated New York City in 1835, virtually destroying, among other things, the printing and publishing industries. Out of work with thousands of others, Whitman took his first teaching job in June, 1836, in Norwich (now East Norwich). Over the next five years — with a year out to found The Long-Islander and then abandon it — he took quarterly teaching jobs on the Island. They included schools in Babylon, Long Swamp (Huntington), Smithtown — where he stayed for two quarters and became an active member of the local debating society — Jamaica, Little Bay Side, Trimming Square (now parts of Garden City and West Hempstead), Woodbury and Whitestone.

Notably absent from this list is Southold. Whether or not Whitman taught there for a term in the winter of 1840 is a puzzlement. Whether or not Whitman was accused of sodomy with one of his schoolboys, tarred and feathered and run out of town is equally perplexing.

Whitman never mentioned teaching in Southold. But Southold Town historian Wayland Jefferson, citing conversations with old-time residents, wrote a booklet published in 1939 that contained the Whitman-in-Southold story, including the tarring and feathering. In early January, 1841, Whitman, according to Jefferson, was denounced as a Sodomite from the pulpit of the First Presbyterian Church by the Rev. Ralph Smith, who referred to the Locust Grove school where Whitman taught as the Sodom School, and the name stuck. In 1966, Katherine Molinoff of Smithtown, an English and journalism professor at both Hunter College and C.W. Post, wrote a booklet expanding on the Jefferson story with interviews from a number of Southold residents who had heard the stories for years.

The current Southold historian, Antonia Booth, was asked recently how the community felt about the story. "People here seem to believe it," she said. "Not in a ga-ga, Looney Tunes sense, either. The community believes that he taught here. I'm not sure that the community believes that he was . . . what would you call it? I've never seen any proof that he sodomized little boys or anything."

So, Walt Whitman taught all over Long Island. Maybe even in Southold.

A Whitman Sampler

"Paumanok"

Sea-beauty! stretch'd and
basking!
One side thy inland ocean
laving, broad, with copious
commerce, steamers,
sails,
And one the Atlantic's
wind caressing, fierce or
gentle — mighty hulls
dark-gliding in the
distance.
Isle of sweet brooks of
drinking-water — healthy
air and soil!
Isle of the salty shore and
breeze and brine!

Excerpt from **"As I Ebb'd with the Ocean of Life"**

As I ebb'd with the
ocean of life,
As I wended the shores
I know,
As I walked where the
ripples continually
wash you Paumanok,
Where they rustle up
hoarse and sibilant,
Where the fierce old
mother endlessly cries
for her castaways,
I musing late in the
autumn day, gazing off
southward,
Held by this electric self
out of the pride of which
I utter poems,
Was seiz'd by the spirit
that trails in the lines
underfoot,
The rim, the sediment
that stands for all the wa-
ter and all the land of
the globe.

Excerpt from **"Crossing Brooklyn Ferry"**

Flow on river! flow with
the flood-tide, and ebb
with the ebb-tide!
Frolic on, crested and
scallop-edg'd waves!
Gorgeous clouds of the
sunset! drench with your
splendor me, or the men
and women generations
after me!
Cross from shore to shore,
countless crowds of
passengers!
Stand up, tall masts of
Mannahatta! stand up,
beautiful hills of
Brooklyn!
Throb, baffled and curi-
ous brain! throw out
questions and answers!
Suspend here and every-
where, eternal float of
solution!
Gaze, loving and thirsting
eyes, in the house or street
or public assembly!
Sound out, voices of
young men! loudly and
musically call me by
my nighest name!

MORE ON NEXT PAGE

Laurels, Brickbats From the Critics

BY GEORGE DEWAN
STAFF WRITER

From the publication of "Leaves of Grass" in 1855 right up to the present, Walt Whitman has had his critics. Some loved his poems, some hated them; rarely were they in-between. Here is what some have written:

Editor **Charles A. Dana**, the New York Tribune, July 23, 1855: "His words might have passed between Adam and Eve in Paradise, before the want of fig leaves brought no shame; but they are quite out of place amid the decorum of modern society . . ."

An anonymous critic, later identified as **William Swinton** of the New York Daily Times, on Nov. 13, 1856: "In detailing these pictures he hangs here and there shreds and tassels of his wild philosophy, till his work, like a maniac's robe, is bedizened with fluttering tags of a thousand colors. With all his follies, insolence, and indecency, no modern poet that we know of has presented finer descriptive passages than Mr. WALT WHITMAN."

Writer **Henry David Thoreau**, Dec. 7, 1856: "We ought to rejoice greatly in him. . . . He is awfully good."

Anonymous, in the London Critic, April 1, 1856: "Walt Whitman is as unacquainted with art as a hog is with mathematics."

Anonymous, in the Cincinnati Commercial, Jan. 1, 1860: "Never, since the days of Rabelais, was there such literature of uncleanness as some portions of this volume exhibited."

Novelist **Henry James**, in the Nation, Nov. 16, 1865: "It has been a melancholy task to read this book; and it is a still more melancholy one to write about it."

Anonymous, in the New York Tribune, Nov. 19, 1881: "The chief question raised by this publication is whether anybody — even a poet — ought to take off his trousers in the market-place."

Orator **Robert G. Ingersoll**, speaking at Whitman's funeral, March 30, 1892: "He walked among men, among writers, among verbal varnishers and veneerers, among literary milliners and tailors, with the unconscious majesty of an antique god."

Novelist **Willa Cather**, 1896: "If a joyous elephant should break forth into song, his lay would probably be very much like Whitman's famous 'Song of Myself.' "

Poet **Ezra Pound**, 1955: "He is America. His crudity is an exceeding stench, but it is America. . . . He is disgusting. He is an exceedingly nauseating pill, but he accomplishes his mission."

Novelist **D.H. Lawrence**: "This awful Whitman. This post mortem poet. This poet with the private soul leaking out of him all the time. All his privacy leaking out in a sort of dribble, oozing into the universe."

Poet **Randall Jarrell**, 1952: "They might have put on his tombstone WALT WHITMAN: HE HAD HIS NERVE. He is the rashest, the most inexplicable and unlikely — the most impossible, one wants to say — of poets. He somehow is in a class by himself, so that one compares him with other poets about as readily as one compares 'Alice' with other books."

Painter **Vincent Van Gogh**, 1888: "He sees in the future, and even in the present, a world of health, carnal love, strong and frank — of friendship — of work — under the great starlit vault of heaven a something which after all one can only call God — and eternity in its place above the world. At first it makes you smile, it is all so candid and pure."

Then there was the Argentinian short-story writer and poet **Jorge Luis Borges** who, instead of writing criticism, wrote a poem. Titled "Camden 1892," it was translated by Richard Howard and Cesar Rennert. Here is an excerpt:

The old man lies
Prostrate, pale, even white in his decent
Room, the room of a poor man. Needlessly
He glances at his face in the exhausted
Mirror. He thinks, without surprise now,
That face is me. One fumbling hand touches
The tangled beard, the devastated mouth.
The end is not far off. His voice declares:
I am almost gone. But my verses scan
Life and its splendor. I was Walt Whitman.

A Whitman Sampler

From "There Was a Child Went Forth"

There was a child went forth every day,
And the first object he look'd upon, that object he became,
And that object became part of him for the day or a certain part of the day,
Or for many years or stretching cycles of years.

* * *

The hurrying tumbling waves, quick-broken crests, slapping,
The strata of color'd clouds, the long bar of maroon-tint away solitary by itself, the spread of purity it lies motionless in,
The horizon's edge, the flying sea-crow, the fragrance of salt marsh and shore mud,
These became part of that child who went forth every day, and who now goes, and will always go forth every day.

A Whitman Bibliography

Few American writers have gotten the attention of other writers as has Walt Whitman. Here is a sampling:

David S. Reynolds, **"Walt Whitman's America: A Cultural Biography."**

Henry M. Christman, editor, **"Walt Whitman's New York: From Manhattan to Montauk."**

Justin Kaplan, **"Walt Whitman: A Life."**

Bertha H. Funnell, **"Walt Whitman on Long Island."**

Gay Wilson Allen, **"The Solitary Singer: A Critical Biography of Walt Whitman."**

Philip Callow, **"From Noon to Starry Night: A Life of Walt Whitman."**

Paul Zweig, **"Walt Whitman: The Making of the Poet"**

James Woodress, **"Critical Essays on Walt Whitman."**

Horace Traubel, **"With Walt Whitman in Camden,"** five volumes.

— George DeWan

Long Island's Walt Whitman

WHITMAN from **Preceding Page**

man later told his friend Traubel that he would have none of it. "If I had cut the sex out I might just as well cut everything out," Whitman said. And later, he added, "Damn the expurgated books! I say damn them! The dirtiest book in the world is an expurgated book."

Those who feel that "Leaves of Grass" is a dirty book — or at least a homoerotic book — might point to lines like these from the poem "When I Heard at the Close of Day":

For the one I love most lay sleeping by me under the same cover in the cool night,
In the stillness in the Autumn moonbeams his face was inclined toward me,
And his arm lay lightly around my breast — and that night I was happy.

When the Civil War ended in 1865, Whitman stayed on in Washington after obtaining low-paying government jobs that gave him the freedom to continue his revisions of "Leaves of Grass." But in 1873 he was partially crippled by a stroke, and was taken in by his brother George, who was then an inspector in a Camden, N.J., pipe foundry. He was not an easy guest, since he liked to spend his days working on his poems and entertaining numerous guests from far and wide who came to pay their respects.

Walt Whitman Birthplace Association; Newsday

George Washington Whitman as a soldier; he took in his brother the poet after Walt suffered a stroke in 1873.

The best-known story from that period concerns the day in 1882 when the great Irish author and wit Oscar Wilde, then only 28, came to visit the master. "I come as a poet to call upon a poet," Wilde said. Whitman opened a bottle of his sister-in-law's homemade elderberry wine and offered Wilde a drink from a dirty glass. Wilde later said that he would have drunk it even if it had been vinegar.

Whitman, however, wanted to be on his own, and in the spring of 1884 he bought a house in a workingman's neighborhood at 328 Mickle St. for $1,750. It was near the railroad tracks, and freight and passenger trains rumbled by on a regular basis. He called it his "shanty," and he lived there for eight years, slowly getting weaker and weaker, less and less able to take care of himself. In addition to Traubel, nurses became his regular companions.

With the end of his life nearing, Whitman began thinking about his own memorial. He chose Camden's Harleigh Cemetery as the site of a Massachusetts granite mausoleum that would contain not only his remains, but those of a number of family members as well. He was delighted with the effect, and visitors came round to visit the tomb even before Whitman was buried there.

On the evening of March 6, 1892, Walt Whitman died. He was 72.

Seventy years later, across the highway from the cedar-shingled house where he was born in Huntington, developers built a shopping mall and put Walt Whitman's name on it. Purists who visit the house love the old place but feel the commercial setting is deplorable. Walt, however, might have gotten a chuckle out of it. A company once produced a Walt Whitman cigar, and when he saw his picture on the box, Whitman, a nonsmoker, laughed and said: "That is fame!"

William Sidney Mount's artful imagery captures the flavor of 1800s American life

Elevating The Everyday

By Julia Szabo

The Museums at Stony Brook

William Sidney Mount's self-portrait was done in 1832. His scenes of fellow Long Islanders busy with everyday life were used even on bank notes.

These days, an artist's success is measured in work exhibited in galleries and museums. But for 19th-Century painter William Sidney Mount, his widespread popularity was solidified not by exhibitions but by engraved reproductions.

Especially on bank notes.

Banks issued their own notes in those days, and the Setauket painter's farmer — the central figure in his work, "The Long Island Farmer Husking Corn" — was picked up by engravers.

"The image of the farmer was juxtaposed with George Washington and the pyramid with the eye in it — all these incredibly potent national symbols," said Deborah Johnson, president and chief executive of the Museums at Stony Brook, repository of Mount's paintings, drawings and papers. "So Mount's imagery quickly became recognized as being symbolic of national life. And as those bank notes were circulated, the American people became familiar with Mount's imagery."

And with Mount himself.

Popularizing the common American as a hero worthy of art, Mount became something of an American hero himself. His fame grew as his paintings were reproduced in popular engravings and gift books, collections of short stories written by American authors and illustrated by American artists. "Well-known writers would create stories around Mount's pictures," Johnson said. "So therefore, Mount's paintings influenced native literature and the storytelling of American life."

Born in Setauket in 1807, Mount got his start as apprentice to his brother Henry, a sign and ornamental painter in New York City. William Mount became a professional artist about 1830, achieving distinction for his genre paintings — scenes of everyday life that depicted his fellow ordinary Long Islanders at work and at play. At that time, depicting common folk engaged in the pursuit of happiness was unheard of in fine art; only figures out of history, myth, literature or the Bible were considered worthy of representation.

Similarly, for the serious young American artist, it was considered a requirement to travel to Europe — the birthplace of civilization! — to study painting. Not for William Sidney Mount; Long Island was his muse. No Europe-worshipper, he spent most of his time at his Setauket birthplace, the Hawkins-Mount Homestead, where he painted the scenes of agrarian life he saw around him. The work widely regarded as his masterpiece, "Farmers Nooning" (1836), depicts a languid, typically all-American scene of field hands breaking for lunch, yet the subjects are rendered with an attention to detail previously reserved for portraits of noble Europeans. In spirit, the painting is pure democracy.

At home, in the Setauket-Stony Brook area, Mount was a local hero as well. An accomplished violinist, he was often invited to play the popular jigs, waltzes and reels of the time for parties and dances. "Everybody knew him," Johnson said. "He had a reputation, and people enjoyed being around him. They were very proud of him."

Mount even patented an instrument called The Cradle of Harmony, a violin he designed to be more audible over the boisterous foot-stomping typical of hoedowns such as the one he depicted in his painting, "Rustic Dance After a Sleigh Ride."

"His love for music competed constantly with his love for art," Johnson said. "In fact, there were times when he became so involved with his music and designing his violin that he didn't paint for a year at a time." Mount's two great loves meet in "Catching the Tune," his portrayal of a fiddler not unlike himself.

Although little is known about his private life, it appears that Mount, who never married, was appreciated by his contemporaries for his sense of humor, too. "He had a subtle and pointed wit which is apparent in his paintings," Johnson said. "His paintings can be quite funny. For instance, in 'Bargaining for a Horse' you notice an interesting detail: The horse's ears are turned up and toward the two Yankees, as if he's listening to their negotiations."

Though he only occasionally left the Island for brief forays to New York City, Mount's fame traveled far and wide. "During the 1840s and '50s," Johnson said, "there was about a 10-year period where his paintings were sent to France and made into lithographs by the house of Goupil, a major printing and lithography firm in Paris. The firm stated in a press release that Mount was the first American artist to be recognized as an original talent, and not a derivative talent. He was the visual artist who really crystallized for Europeans what the people of the New World were all about."

Mount died in 1868, of pneumonia contracted on what would be his final trip to New York City. Toward the end of his life, he was eclipsed by another great American painter: Winslow Homer, whose favorite subject was the sea. But by the time of his death, William Sidney Mount's place in history was secure. For in his heyday — the quarter-century between 1830 and 1855 — he was our visual ambassador, painting scenes that proudly represented our country and its people, both at home and all over the world.

Julia Szabo is a freelance writer.

DESCENDANT

'THAT'S MY GREAT-GRANDMOTHER'

New York State Historical Association, Cooperstown; Photo by John Bigelow Taylor

In William Sidney Mount's painting "Eel Spearing at Setauket," a woman in a large hat stands in the bow of a rowboat poised to strike with a long spear.

"That's Rachel Holland Hart; she's my great-grandmother," says Theodore Green, 70, a retired construction worker who's spent his whole life in Setauket. "My mother's maiden name was Hart.

"My great-grandmother lived not too far from where I am now. She worked on Strongs Neck for the Strongs. She was their housekeeper. She's buried in Setauket. My mother said she loved the water. When we were small we fished in the same area for eels. There's still plenty there now. The area behind her in the painting — that's the Strong's property — looks about the same, but the house has been modified."

Green also knows who's paddling the rowboat for his great-grandmother. "That's Thomas Strong, who I think was nicknamed Judd."

Newsday Photo / Bill Davis

Theodore Green

A color reproduction of the painting is mounted in his den, a present from the New York State Historical Association in Cooperstown. His sister was visiting the upstate village and saw the painting on the wall of the museum and said, "That's my great-grandmother." A museum staff member heard her and got more details on the family, and the museum gave her several color copies of the 1845 painting. Hart was not the first of his forebearers to live in the area. "We go back to the late 1600s that I have records for," Green said.

— **Bill Bleyer**

Suffolk County Historical Society Photo

Picking cranberries in Riverhead, about 1900. The berries were brought from Cape Cod to the Sayville-Patchogue area at the end of the Civil War.

With careful cultivation, a living and a way of life grew

Farming Takes Root

BY BILL BLEYER
STAFF WRITER

Local farmers didn't impress John Johnston when he toured Long Island in 1860.

"The greater part of the farmers appeared to be at least a half century behind the age," the upstate farmer sniffed in a letter published in Country Gentleman and Cultivator magazine. "The land I think is excellent . . . but a good deal of it badly cultivated, or not cultivated at all, having been tilled as long as it would bear crops."

Unfortunately, Johnson was right when it came to western Long Island. In the late 1700s, some of that soil was depleted and fertility was declining on the rest of the Island as well.

As a result of poor farming methods, farmers were left with declining wheat yields after the turn of the century. In contrast, there is strong evidence that eastern Long Island retained its more fertile soil and farmers quickly embraced techniques to keep it that way.

As it was in colonial times, farming was more than the backbone of the local economy — it was a way of life for about one of every five residents.

Working alone or in pairs, farmers tended an average 18 acres of crops on a 100-acre farm. They spent as much time fertilizing as they did cultivating and harvesting. And they rotated crops.

The largest cultivated crop was Indian corn, totaling 773,549 bushels a year on the Island, followed by oats and potatoes, according to the 1840 census. Farmers also produced wheat, hay, rye, barley, flax, cucumbers, cauliflower, pumpkins and cranberries. They raised livestock as well. There were about 15,000 horses and mules, 42,395 cattle, 73,326 sheep and 50,412 pigs. Later, farmers would raise ducks.

The animals provided farmers a valuable byproduct: manure. It was so highly prized as fertilizer that it showed up in an estate inventory appraised for almost as much as a 2-year-old horse.

Ezra L'Hommedieu, a wealthy Southold farmer and state legislator, experimented with using seaweed and shells to improve soil fertility. Soon, other farmers also turned to seaweed and shells as well as fish, ashes and bonemeal.

Northville farmer Noah Youngs spent 11 days carting dung and four days plowing it into the soil before planting wheat, he noted in his 1822 diary. He also worked three days collecting seaweed and in the spring he spent more than 36 days repairing nets and catching menhaden, a bait fish, for fertilizer.

East End farmers practiced crop rotation — alternating potatoes, corn, buckwheat and oats with wheat, grass and clover. They also were quick to add equipment. Youngs owned a threshing machine by 1835. Reapers began to show up before 1855.

Farm communities were self-sufficient. Farmers produced almost everything they needed, with the exception of molasses, sugar, salt, spices, rum, iron and lime, said Justine Wells, Riverhead town historian. Most farmers worked at other trades; one of Wells' ancestors, for example, was also a coffin-maker.

Many farmers on eastern Long Island bartered with neighbors or sold their products locally because the limited New York City and Brooklyn markets were supplied by farms in western Long Island, New Jersey and along the Hudson River. The two products these farmers did ship to the city were cordwood and charcoal. Youngs' diary records 38 days spent cutting and transporting cordwood.

U.S. Department of Agriculture Photo / Scott Bauer

The Hessian fly, a scourge of wheat, supposedly came over with Hessian troops.

The Long Island Rail Road's arrival in Greenport in 1844 expanded farmers' access to city markets. Hay to feed city horses became East End farmers' biggest cash crop.

Wheat was a major crop for a brief time starting in colonial days. But when President George Washington toured Long Island in 1790, he saw little wheat "on acct. of the fly." He was referring to the Hessian fly, so named because supposedly it came from Europe with grain imported with Hessian mercenaries during the Revolution.

First detected in Brooklyn in 1779, the fly eventually spread as far as California. But it stopped destroying local fields after a Flushing farmer named Underhill obtained a southern strain of wheat that proved resistant.

By the end of the century, wheat was being produced more cheaply in the West. Long Island farmers then shifted to potatoes. Potatoes went on to become the premier crop in Riverhead for more than a century.

Cauliflower and strawberries also became important crops. Cranberries from Cape Cod were introduced at the end of the Civil War, first in the Sayville-Patchogue area and later in Calverton and Manorville.

But it was ducks and pickles that would join potatoes as Long Island's most famous exports. Farmers raised White Pekin ducks around Moriches and Riverhead. Farmers in Greenlawn grew cucumbers, which were cured into pickles at several area processing plants.

Whatever they grew, 18th-Century farmers relied heavily on "hard hand-work," said Kenneth Wells, 77, a 10th generation Riverhead farmer. And so did their descendents. "When I grew up, we didn't have a tractor; we had horses," he said. "The hoe was the main tool."

SUMMER OF '16 WAS COOL, BUT NOT *THAT* COOL

It was so cold that on Long Island there was frost every month of the year, including July and August.

It was so cold that on July Fourth, Long Islanders celebrated Independence Day wearing mittens and overcoats.

It was so cold that the corn crop failed.

That's the myth in history books about the weather of 1816, which has become known as The Year Without a Summer.

The myth was not entirely unfounded. Because of widespread cold outbreaks that have been linked to the effects of ash from the eruption of Mt. Tambora in Indonesia in 1815, sunspots and natural climatic fluctuations, summer was cooler than usual. And there were harsh effects, including extensive crop failure in northern New England, because of unseasonable frosts.

On Long Island, it was cool and crop yields were lower because of a shorter growing season. But over the years, accounts of the most severe New England weather somehow drifted into Long Island lore without any apparent historical basis.

"I've never come across anything that discusses real problems during 1816 out on Long Island," says William R. Baron, a history professor at Northern Arizona University in Flagstaff who has done extensive studies of New England weather during the period.

There are no regular weather records for Long Island during that time. However, Baron said that cold Canadian air masses that settled over the Northeast during June, July and August of 1816 were moderated elsewhere along the coast by relatively warm ocean waters. This especially would be true for Long Island.

The few agricultural reports from the period note shortages of hay and a shortfall in the corn crop, but no other signs of distress.

Still, accounts of "havoc and privation" on Long Island during the summer of 1816 persist. No less an authority than naturalist Robert Cushman Murphy wrote in 1964 of the "appalling" summer on Long Island, repeating, among other things, the old tales of a frost in every month and a frigid July Fourth.

Actually, on July 10, 1816, the Long Island Star, published in Brooklyn, contained the following report on New York's Independence Day celebration: "The weather was uncommonly fine."

— **Phil Mintz**

Julia Gardiner married the 10th U.S. president, John Tyler.

Tyler, Newsday Archives; Gardiner, Courtesy of Gardiner Family, Newsday Photo

At 24, Julia Gardiner charmed a president and enjoyed a brief tenure as first lady

A Long Island Social Climber

BY STEVE WICK
STAFF WRITER

When she was single, one newspaper called her "the Rose of Long Island." When she was married, she was "the Lovely Lady Presidentress."

Her name was Julia Gardiner, and she was born on the island that still bears her family's name in East Hampton. Lion Gardiner, the first Englishman to settle on Long Island, was her ancestor.

By all accounts, she was the spoiled daughter of socially prominent parents who was courted by men both on Long Island and in Washington. At one time she was dating two congressmen, three Supreme Court justices and a naval officer.

When she was 24 years old, she married the widowed president of the United States, John Tyler, and soon demonstrated a certain flair. She ordered 12 young women in white dresses to follow her wherever she went. And she apparently goaded a New York Herald Tribune reporter into referring to her as "the Lovely Lady Presidentress" and "her serene loveliness."

Julia Gardiner Tyler of East Hampton was some first lady.

Her journey to the White House begins on Gardiners Island, where she was born in 1820. Her father was David Gardiner, a state senator and a man of wealth and political connections; her mother was Juliana, the daughter of rich New York Scotch immigrants.

"Julia was my grandfather's sister," said Robert David Lion Gardiner, who lives in East Hampton and Palm Beach, Fla. "She was known far and wide for her beauty. I heard about her when I was growing up. My father knew her quite well."

When she was 20, Julia and her sister, Margaret, took a "grand tour" of Europe, stopping in England, France and Italy. "In London, Julia was courted by a nobleman who wanted to marry her," said Gardiner. "She went on to Rome, where she met a prince who wanted to make her his princess."

After the tour, she went to Washington, where she made the social rounds. In January, 1842, she met President John Tyler at a White House party. Tyler had assumed the presidency in 1841 after the death of President William Henry Harrison, who succumbed a month after taking the oath of office. The following September, Tyler's wife, Letitia, died in the White House of a stroke.

That fall of 1842, Julia dated a number of men, including Rep. James Buchanan, who was later elected president, another congressman, Francis Pickens, three Supreme Court justices and a naval officer. The following Feb. 7, she visited Tyler in the White House. According to "First Ladies: The Saga of the Presidents' Wives and Their Power," by Carl Sferrazza Anthony the invitation was to play cards.

"By evening's end," according to the book, "the president, thirty years her senior, was chasing Julia down the stairs and around tables." A few weeks later, he asked her to marry him. She did not immediately give him an answer and, the book states, her mother opposed the marriage because Tyler was not rich enough.

On Feb. 28, 1844, Julia and her father joined Tyler and 400 others for a cruise on the Potomac on the USS Princeton. The event of the day was to be the firing of the Princeton's big gun — the Peacemaker, the largest in the Navy.

At 3 p.m., the boat was off Mount Vernon, George Washington's plantation. "They were going to fire it in a salute to Washington," said Gardiner. "A minute or two before it was to be fired, Julia and the president went below to have a glass of champagne. Just as they left the deck, the huge gun exploded."

Among the dead were the secretary of state, the secretary of the Navy and Julia's father, David. "The president should have been up on the deck for the firing of the gun, but he was below with Julia drinking champagne. She saved his life," Gardiner said. "She had a knack for being in the right place at the right time."

The following June, Julia Gardiner and Tyler were married in a secret ceremony in a Fifth Avenue, New York, cathedral. "I have commenced my auspicious reign," Julia Tyler wrote after the wedding, "and am in quiet possession of the Presidential Mansion."

She became the first first lady to pose for a daguerreotype, and the first to hire a press agent. She was also the first first lady to dance at a White House party, and wherever she went she was accompanied by 12 "maids of honor," six on each side, all dressed alike.

A reporter for the New York Herald — who was said to be in love with Julia and coined the phrase "Lovely Lady Presidentress" — wrote in one dispatch that Julia was "the most accomplished woman of her age," and possessed a "spirit of youth and poetry, love and tenderness . . . "

Tyler did not seek re-election, so Julia was first lady for only seven months. The couple then retired to his plantation near Richmond.

While there is no hard proof, Gardiner is certain that, as president, Tyler and his wife visited the Gardiner house on Main Street in East Hampton and toured Gardiners Island.

"When I was growing up, my family called our home the summer White House," he said. "And to this day, there is a hitching post on the curb in front of the house on Main Street that I was told was put in for the president's messenger when he came with telegrams."

When the Civil War broke out in 1861, Julia was an ardent supporter of the South. Her stepson, John Alexander Tyler, fought with Robert E. Lee; her brother, David, was a colonel in a New York regiment. President Tyler died in 1863, and as far as Gardiner knows, Julia never returned to East Hampton or Gardiners Island. She died in 1889 and was buried in Richmond.

John Alexander Tyler married Sally Gardiner — another of the East Hampton Gardiners — and his elaborate grave marker is in the Gardiner family plot in East Hampton.

ANOTHER FIRST LADY'S L I UPBRINGING

Anna Symmes Harrison, the wife of President William Henry Harrison, was not born on Long Island but her roots were here.

In a Long Island Historical Journal story published in 1993, Natalie Naylor has written that Anna's parents, Anna Tuthill and John Symmes, were from Mattituck. Their oldest daughter, Maria, was born in Mattituck in 1762. After that, the family moved to a farm near Morristown, N.J., where Anna was born in 1775.

Anna's father brought her to Southold to live with her grandparents during the chaos of the Revolution. She attended Clinton Academy, a private school in East Hampton. She later moved with her father to what was then called the Northwest Territory — Indiana and Ohio — where she met Harrison, who was later elected president of the United States.

Harrison died of pneumonia a month after his inauguration. His successor was John Tyler, who took Julia Gardiner as his second wife. There is no record that Anna Harrison ever came back to Mattituck.

— **Steve Wick**

Why does Queens have so many cemeteries? Answers go back to mid-1800s Manhattan

The Cemetery Belt

BY RHODA AMON
STAFF WRITER

Under cover of darkness the creaking horse-drawn wagons are loaded onto the ferry. Once across the river, they lumber through the sleeping countryside, finally coming to a halt on Queens hillsides where graveyard workers unload their strange cargo — thousands of skeletons and coffins exhumed from Manhattan churchyards.

By daylight the only sign of the nocturnal operation will be fresh mounds on the hills and meadows that have been converted into burial grounds.

The wagon trains of the dead — triggered by a law that turned burials into business — kept rolling from the 1850s until the early 1900s, transporting bodies to western Queens, which became known as the Cemetery Belt. More than 35,000 bodies were transferred to Cypress Hills Cemetery alone.

Today more than 5 million of the departed, including the famous and the infamous from Mae West to Lucky Luciano — almost triple the live population of Queens — are buried in 29 Queens cemeteries — four Catholic, three Protestant, 14 Jewish and eight nondenominational.

The Queens land rush began in 1847, after the state Legislature passed the Rural Cemetery Act. Before that, burial was mostly in churchyards or on family farms, where servants and slaves were interred beside their masters. The new legislation "commercialized death for the first time," said historian Vincent F. Seyfried of Rockville Centre. It authorized nonprofit corporations to buy land, open cemeteries and sell plots to individuals for money. The law stipulated that no organization could acquire more than 250 acres in one county, but land dealers got around that by buying land straddling two counties. Cypress Hills, two thirds in Queens, one third in Brooklyn, is one of 17 cemeteries that form a sea of headstones along the county line.

By the 1830s, immigration from Ireland and central Europe was already overcrowding Manhattan neighborhoods and land prices were soaring. Manhattan had a population of 202,589; Queens had 9,049 in an area more than four times the size of Manhattan. Church and backyard gravesites were no longer sacrosanct. "Many were sold, tombstones removed and housing placed on top of graves," said Queens historian Jeffrey Gottlieb.

In 1832 and again in 1849 a cholera epidemic swept Manhattan, which was using well water. The many deaths exhausted the graveyards. Many suspected that disease was being washed down from the gravesites into the drinking water. In 1852 the Common Council of New York City (then consisting of only Manhattan) passed a law prohibiting any more burials.

The churches looked to rural Queens. St. Patrick's Cathedral trustees purchased land in Maspeth in 1846, and the first body was interred in Calvary Cemetery in 1848. "By 1852 there were 50 burials a day in Calvary, half of them Irish poor under 7 years of age," Gottlieb reported. By the 1990s there were nearly 3 million graves in Calvary Cemetery.

Newsday Photo / Bill Davis

A forest of monuments, with the Empire State Building in the background, crowds Calvary Cemetery, where the first burial, in 1848, was followed by innumerable others.

Cypress Hills was the first nonsectarian cemetery corporation organized in Queens. The land scramble was on. Although most Queens cemeteries were founded by legitimate church groups, land speculators got into the act, buying cheap farmland to turn into profitable burial grounds.

The first Cypress Hills burial in 1848 "made the land tax-exempt," said Kurt T. Kraska of Ridgewood, author of a "History of Cypress Hills Cemetery and Its Permanent Residents." From 1854 to 1856, more than 15,000 bodies were transferred from churchyards in Manhattan and Williamsburg. Wooden coffins had decayed, leaving only skulls and bones to be exhumed. Unidentified bones were buried in mass graves, said Kraska, a City Transit Authority electrician who became fascinated with cemetery history when growing up in the cemetery belt.

When Union Cemetery closed in Brooklyn in 1897, more than 20,000 bodies were moved to Cedar Grove Cemetery in Flushing. "The curious crowd had abundant opportunity to study the contents of the graves," reported the Brooklyn Eagle. The remains were moved at midnight to "prevent the work being turned into a sideshow," Kraska said.

Churchmen pooled their resources to establish bigger and better cemeteries. The Rev. Frederick William Geissenhainer, pastor of St. Paul's German Lutheran Church in Manhattan, bought 225 acres in Middle Village in 1852 for a cemetery to serve Lower East Side immigrants. Members decided to call it the Lutheran Cemetery although it was open to all faiths. It became the final resting place for the 1,021 victims of the excursion boat General Slocum, which burned and sank during a Manhattan Sunday School outing in 1904. Today, it's the All Faiths Cemetery and most of its interments are Italian with some Hispanic, African-American and Jewish, said chief executive officer Daniel Austin.

The 19th-Century Queens communities grew rapidly. Picnicking families would come on the Astoria-Yorkville ferry, which, signs on the terminal proclaimed, was the "shortest route to St. Michaels, Lutheran, Calvary, Cypress Hill, Mt. Olivet and Mt. Zion Cemeteries." Restaurants, saloons and beer gardens flourished. The cemetery is "the principal industry of the people in the vicinity," reported W.W. Munsell's 1882 "History of Queens County."

But tensions developed over "the endless funeral processions that were wearing out the roads. Some roads were not even paved," historian Seyfried said. "Worse, the cemeteries were exempt from taxation."

There were also outcries about the high cost of dying, particularly when Calvary raised its price to $10 per plot. "A whole funeral might cost $10 in Cypress Hills," Seyfried said. Lutheran Cemetery originally charged $2.50 for a burial, $7 for a plot. Bridges, tunnels, subways — all the construction of a fast-growing city took its toll of churchyards. Graves dislodged by the Williamsburg Bridge were moved to Queens cemeteries.

With the improved access, especially with the completion of the Queensboro Bridge in 1909, thousands of city dwellers moved to the once-isolated Queens communities. "The churches themselves began to follow their congregations to Queens," said Queens County historian Henry Ludder. When the Queensboro Bridge opened in 1909, the Queens population soared, although it never came close to the numbers of dead. Today there are more disinterments than reinterments as families moving to other areas take their departed with them.

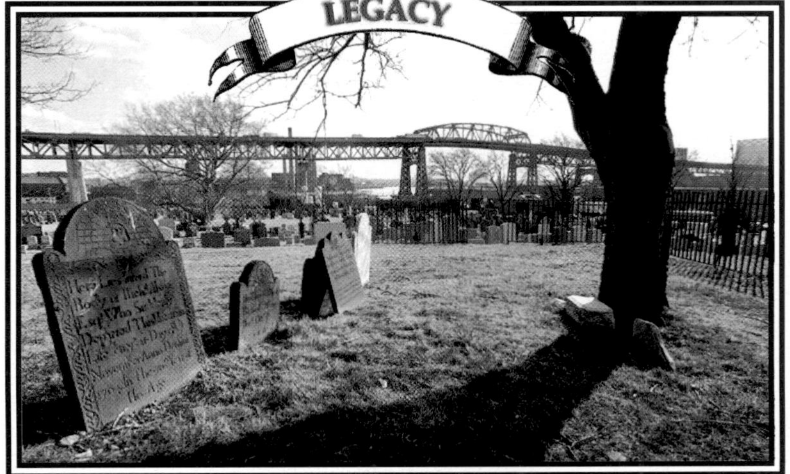

Newsday Photo / Bill Davis

COLONIAL ERA FAMILY CEMETERY

The Alsop plot of colonial times exists as a cemetery within a cemetery at Calvary. In the background is the Kosciusko Bridge. Six of these family graveyards are preserved as city landmarks, according to Stanley Cogan, president of the Queens Historical Society. But some colonial graveyards in Queens remain overgrown and neglected. Cogan founded the Queens Family Cemetery Alliance to safeguard the old graveyards.

Modern Times, the notorious and short-lived utopian village that preceded Brentwood

An Experiment in Anarchy

BY ELIZABETH MOORE
STAFF WRITER

British and French philosophers exalted it. New York intellectuals argued about it. And riders on the Long Island Rail Road gawked out the windows as they passed Modern Times, the notorious Suffolk County settlement where there were no police, money, fences or laws. Where women went about in bloomers. Where free-love escapades were rumored to be behind every cottage door.

Actually, the anarchist village of 150 was never as wanton as outsiders imagined, and it never lived up to its aim of an entire economy based on barter. It lasted only from 1851 to 1864 before its name was changed to Brentwood. But in that short time, it managed to leave a more mundane legacy as one of the first suburbs created by the railroad. And if some of the radical mores that led to its undoing wouldn't raise an eyebrow nowadays, others foreshadowed domestic partnership laws and sexual freedoms still evolving.

All of which might have comforted settlers like Charles Codman, who near the end of his life in 1900 picked up a pencil and described the people of Modern Times:

"If they were lacking in Capital they were flush in Enthusiasm . . . they were willing to sacrifice much in building an Equitable village which should be an example of Harmony and Justice; which should be a bright and shining light to all the world . . . They hoped that . . . the sacrifices of pioneering in the howling wilderness would be but of short duration, sure to be followed by enduring peace and plenty."

Codman said his fellow pioneers believed that "the long dreams of the millennium" were imminent in Suffolk County. "They felt . . . that the ideals of prophets, philosophers and poets of all ages were near at hand — Yea, already located in the 'Pine Barrens' of Long Island, N.Y."

The Revolution had pulled the plug on history. The wide-open continent offered room for every kind of social experiment, and a parade of idealists — from Shakers to Quakers, pietists to perfectionists — had founded scores of model communities to usher in the golden age. Others, like Ralph Waldo Emerson, argued for nonconformity, while Emerson's friend Henry David Thoreau protested his taxes and dropped out of society at Walden Pond.

Brentwood Public Library; Newsday Photo; Above, From "Josiah Warren: The First American Anarchist," 1906

Anarchist visionaries: Stephen Pearl Andrews, left, and Josiah Warren founded the nonconformist Modern Times on cheap forest land along the new railroad in Suffolk in 1851.

"That government is best which governs not at all," Thoreau wrote in 1849.

At about that time, a philosopher-inventor named Josiah Warren was coming to the same conclusion while surveying the wreckage of New Harmony, the Indiana socialist community he'd lived in.

Warren and a fellow visionary named Stephen Pearl Andrews decided some cheap forest land along the new railroad in central Suffolk would make a perfect place to experiment with anarchy, an approach no one had yet tried. Warren's only covenant for the settlement of Modern Times would be anathema in today's Long Island: Nothing could be sold for a penny more than it had cost. The land was there for homes, not real estate investments.

He printed "A Card to the Public" in Horace Greeley's New York Tribune, and American dreamers arrived from all over: A contingent of Yankees from a failed Boston community. A covered wagonload from Ohio. A dentist from New York. The estranged wife of an Englishman.

The settlers bought one-acre lots in Warren's woods for about $18 and began ripping up stumps, planting gardens and erecting houses of home-made brick. Some were skilled craftsmen, fewer were skilled farmers, but they all excelled at talk. Many were fleeing failed marriages, hungry to reinvent their lives in a remote place whose motto was "mind your own business."

They planted pine trees and cedar hedges along the lanes, and many kinds of fruit trees, so that, as one city father put it, "the wayfarer may not have to demean himself by begging at our door." Women cut their locks short and men grew theirs long as a badge of nonconformity. They bartered goods and services through a "time store" using "labor notes" based on the corn standard.

In the evenings, Modern Timers sang, staged plays, danced and held lectures in the "Archimedian Hall" of William Dame's house, which the Yankee carpenter had designed in an octagon, like Modern Times' schoolhouse, for more efficient use of space. There, Codman recalled, they jawboned about every kind of reform. "From . . . Abolition of Chattel Slavery, Woman's Rights, Vegetarianism, Hydropathy (and all the pathies), Peace, Ante-Tobacco, Total Abstinence, to the Bloomer Costume."

The pioneers were usually tolerant, if cool, toward the string of nuts and faddists drawn by the news of their free-living town: the blind man who paraded naked in the street, the woman who wore men's clothing, the young fellow who set up house with three ladies, and the woman whose "theoretical speculations about diet" led her to subsist on beans without salt until she wasted away and died.

But residents were upset when feminist divorcee and free-love lecturer Mary Gove Nichols moved in and promptly announced that anyone thinking of moving to Modern Times must be dedicated to free love and "willing to be considered licentious."

In the end, Modern Times' pioneers cared more for ordinary happiness than a life in the radical vanguard, says State University at Stony Brook historian Roger Wunderlich. He said monogamy, not bed-hopping, was the norm. Men and women living "in sin" usually married each other as soon as pending divorces became final.

Most also earned real currency outside the village — like dentist-phrenologist Edward Newberry, who commuted by train to his Manhattan office. And the pioneers passed on Warren's educational theories, opting to set up a conventional public school district.

When the Civil War broke out, this anarchist haven showed its patriotism with a brass band and 15 volunteers. This was finally too much for Warren, who abandoned his social experiment for good sometime after October, 1862.

Well pleased with the pretty village they'd built but tired of the notoriety, Modern Times' citizens toned down their costumes and in 1864 renamed the haven Brentwood after a decorous English suburb. And as the healthful forested land rose in value, they took what the traffic would bear, Wunderlich says, going on to lives of getting and spending in the best Long Island tradition.

"The fundamental mistake we made," Codman wrote, "was in thinking that even a small percent of those who are clamorous and insistent for Justice are honest and in earnest — they are not."

Codman's millennium never arrived. "Alas! . . . that I shall have passed without a glimpse of the 'promised land' . . . and my query is Will anyone see it? — Is it only a Chimera?"

REMINDERS OF MODERN TIMES

LEGACY

An 1857 "labor for labor" Modern Times promissory note. At left, an octagonal schoolhouse used from 1857 to 1907 at Fourth Street and Third Avenue in Brentwood, and the same building today, awaiting restoration on the grounds of Brentwood High School.

Currency and Old Photo, Brentwood Public Library; Right, Newsday Photo / Bill Davis

The 104 men of Company H fought in the bloodiest conflicts of the Civil War

Long Island Marches Off To Battle

BY STEVE WICK
STAFF WRITER

John Carman was in Fairfax, Va., a lonely soldier a long way from home, when he sat down and wrote his sister a letter.

Dear sister i now write you a few lines informing you that i am well and sincerely hope these few lines wil find you all the same. I received your letter the 1st and it done me a great deal of good to hear from you. We are encamped at fairfax court house at present but doe not know how long we shal stay here ... i am tiered of a soldiers life and i want to get to Long Island.

He dated his letter Oct. 3, 1862, addressed it "Mrs. Valentine Smith, Merrick Post Office, Long Island," and sent it on its way.

That fall, Carman's infantry unit — Company H of the 119th New York Volunteers — was a month old. The 119th had been formed in New York City late that summer and was composed mostly of German immigrants. Wanting a company of his own, a Roslyn attorney named Benjamin Willis coaxed 104 men who lived in and around Hempstead to join together, and they became Company H.

The regiment's 1,000 men left New York City in early September, sailed on a steamer to New Jersey, where they boarded a train that took them to Harrisburg, Pa., Baltimore and then Washington, D.C. By early October, when Pvt. Carman wrote his letter to his sister, the regiment was bivouacked around the Fairfax County Courthouse in Virginia. And there, Company H of the 119th New York did what soldiers have always done — they waited impatiently for orders.

As Company H settled in that October, the war between the North and South — between those states that called themselves free and those states which to protect their peculiar institution of slavery voted to quit the Union and fight — was 18 months old. For the men of the 119th, the worst was yet to come. Slaughter on a scale never seen before in America would soon unfold on farm fields from Tennessee to Pennsylvania. And Carman, 21 years old and a vegetable farmer back in Merrick, would see much of it for himself.

In all, the 119th, with 104 young men from Long Island carrying the banner of Company H, would participate in more than a dozen engagements. They would see, feel and experience the bloodiest days of the Civil War. Company H would bury its own in ground up and down the East Coast. And its survivors would come back to Long Island, far different from what they were when they left, to restart their lives.

From Brooklyn, a burgeoning city of 266,000, all the way east to the

Nassau County Museum Collection, Long Island Studies Institute

Roslyn attorney Benjamin Willis formed Company H of "everyday Long Islanders — farmers, baymen, laborers of all stripes" — in the Hempstead area and became its captain.

Innovative Monitor Was Born in Brooklyn

BY BILL BLEYER
STAFF WRITER

The Confederate ironclad vessel Virginia had already rammed one frigate and sunk another with cannon fire. Now it lumbered into Hampton Roads, Va., on March 9, 1862, to continue its rampage through the Union fleet blockading the Rebel coast.

The Virginia — which would be better remembered by its original name, the Merrimack — steered for the Union warship Minnesota. Suddenly, the Virginia's crew was surprised by a low-profile vessel that looked like a cheesebox on a shingle emerging from behind the Minnesota.

The Confederate decimation of wooden warships was over. The strange ship was the product of a Brooklyn shipyard, and it would revolutionize naval warfare. It was called the Monitor.

Concussions from cannon fire knocked crewmen senseless but did little injury to either vessel. The only notable damage was sustained by the Virginia when it rammed the Monitor. Taking on water and with the tide dropping, the Confederate ironclad broke off the world's first clash of armored vessels after four hours. Although the Union claimed victory because the Virginia had withdrawn, the fight was a draw.

The battle of the ironclads ushered in a new era of naval design. Although warships of the time were equipped with steam engines and more effective cannon, they were not radically different than those in the War of 1812. The man responsible for the sea change was an engineering genius named John Ericcson. The Swedish-born Ericcson had produced a series of innovations including a steam locomotive that traveled at an unheard of 60 miles an hour, but his most impressive work was perfecting a screw propeller to replace ship paddlewheels.

The Civil War gave him the chance to test his design for the ultimate warship. A Korean admiral had fabricated oar-powered, metal-topped "turtle ships" in the 16th Century, and Britain and France armor-plated warships in the 1850s. What set the Monitor apart was its radical design, including the first turret.

Ericcson might not have gotten his break if the Confederate navy had not decided in 1861 to salvage and armor-plate the Merrimack, a Union ship scuttled when federal troops abandoned Norfolk Navy Yard. After President Abraham Lincoln learned of the Confederate plan, a meeting was arranged with the 58-year-old temperamental inventor.

Critics insisted "Ericcson's Folly," also derided as "the iron coffin," would never float. But Ericcson promised Lincoln it would float "like a duck." Replied Lincoln: "All I have to say is what the girl said when she stuck her foot into the stocking: It strikes me

Company H Goes to War

Company H of the 119th New York Volunteers was formed by Roslyn lawyer Benjamin Willis. Its 104 members were recruited in Hempstead in 1862 and began fighting in the Civil War the next year. Here are 14 encounters they were involved in, including the pivotal Battle of Gettysburg and the March to the Sea. Casualty figures were not available for all incidents.

1. Chancellorsville, Va., May 1-3, 1863. Confederate Gen. Robert E. Lee's most brilliant victory. Casualties: 17,000 Union; 13,000 Confederate. Company H had four killed, five wounded, one captured.

2. Gettysburg, Pa., July 1-3, 1863. Key Confederate loss. Casualties: 23,049 Union; 28,063 Confederate. Company H had two killed, seven wounded, one who died later of wounds and six captured.

3. Wauhatchie, Tenn., Oct. 28-29, 1863. Casualties: Union, 76 killed, 339 wounded, 22 missing; Confederates, 460 killed.

4. Tunnel Hill, Ga., Nov. 24, 1863. The hill was the eastern end of a fortified Confederate position on Missionary Ridge, captured the next day.

5. Missionary Ridge, Tenn., Nov. 25, 1863. Casualties for the two days: Union, 753 killed, 4,722 wounded, 349 missing; Confederates, 361 killed, 2,160 wounded, 4,146 missing.

6. Rocky Face Ridge, Ga., May 8-10, 1864. Company H's first fighting in the successful Union campaign to capture Atlanta. The Atlanta campaign lasted from May 1 until Sept. 2, 1864. Each army suffered 30,000 to 40,000 casualties.

7. Resaca, Ga., May 14-15, 1864. Casualties: Union, 6,000; Confederate, 5,000.

8. Cassville, Ga., May 19-22, 1864. Skirmishes during the Confederate retreat to Atlanta.

9. New Hope Church, Ga., May 25-27, 1864. A preliminary engagement leading up to the Battle of Kennesaw Mountain. Casualties: Union, 3,100; Confederate, 500.

10. Pine Knob, Ga., June 19, 1864. Company H had five killed, five wounded and one death later from wounds. Another engagement before the Battle of Kennesaw Mountain, which fell to Union troops on June 27.

11. Peach Tree Creek, Ga., July 20, 1864. Casualties: Union, 1,600 killed or wounded; Confederate, 2,500 killed or wounded.

12. March to the Sea, Georgia, Nov. 15-Dec. 21, 1864. Union army lost 2,200 men but destroyed the state's ability to support the war.

13. Siege of Savannah, Ga., Dec. 9-21, 1864. March to the Sea was completed when the Union took the seaport.

14. Bentonville, N.C., March 19-21, 1865. Battle led to negotiations for the surrender of Confederate Gen. Joseph E. Johnston. Casualties: Union, 1,645; Confederate, 2,606.

SOURCE: Company H, 119th New York Volunteers Historical Association; "The Civil War Dictionary"; "Historical Times Illustrated Encyclopedia of the Civil War"; "The Encyclopedia of Military History from 3500 B.C. to the Present"

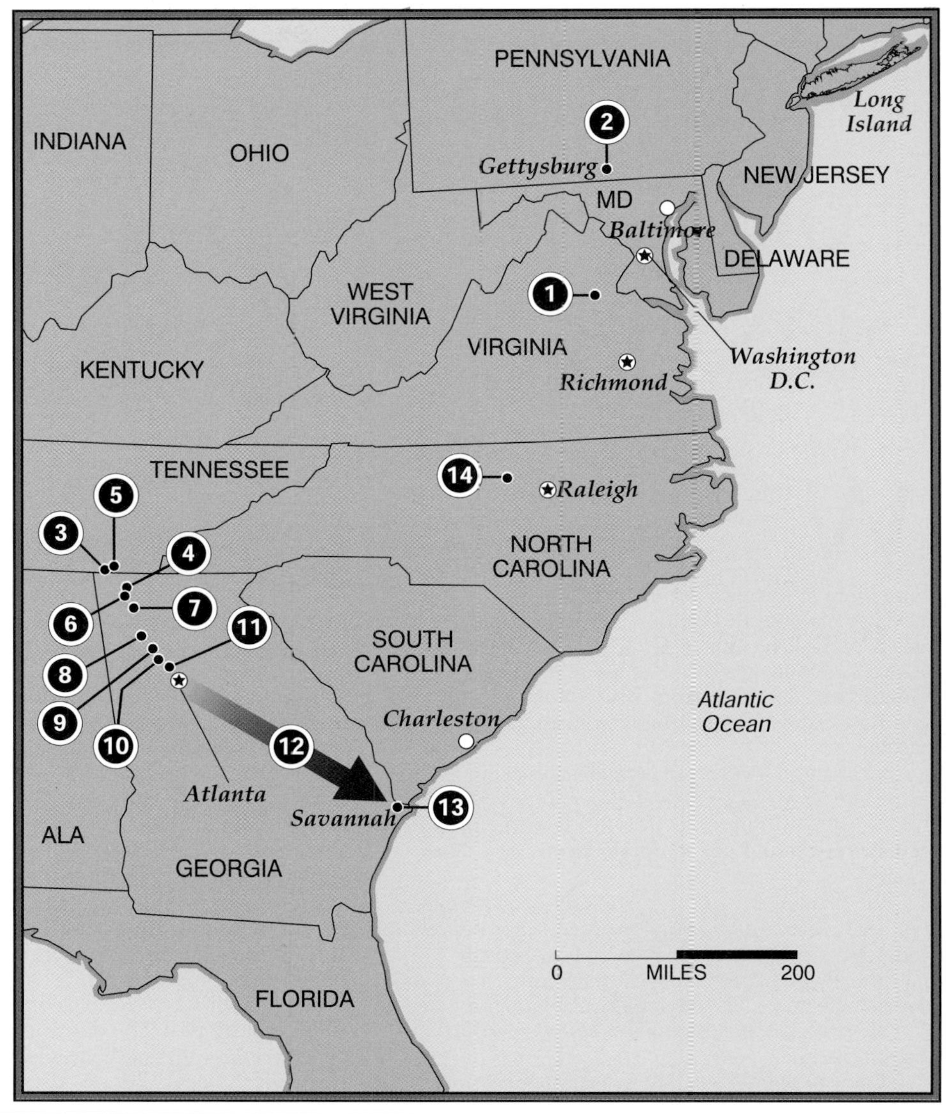

Newsday / Linda McKenney

tiny farming hamlets on the North and South Forks, the beginning of the war in April, 1861, was a distant alarm. Within months, what began as an effort by the southern states to become independent led to pitched fighting on the battlefield. And in New York, as in every other northern state, thousands of young men rallied 'round the flag.

Hundreds from Long Island enlisted in dozens of companies that were themselves attached to dozens of regiments and militia units. Some went because they wanted to help end slavery; others went because they wanted to keep their country together, and others simply wanted to see what it was all about. Hundreds of others on Long Island signed a document called a Certificate of Exemption on Account of Having Furnished a Substitute, which meant, in short, that they bought their way out of service and stayed home.

Some on Long Island, including Henry Reeves of Greenport, an influential newspaper publisher, were labled Copperheads — open supporters of the South and secession. Confederate flags were seen flying on Long Island, and men spoke in favor of the South's cause. On top of that, when President Abraham Lincoln instituted a draft in 1863, hundreds rioted against it. Those riots began in Manhattan and spilled over into Queens County (which then included what is now Nassau County). For the most part, these draft riots took on the form of pogroms — rioting Irish immigrants hunting down free blacks and murdering them.

Long Island would never see a battle. The nearest fighting was at the Pennsylvania farming community of Gettysburg, in July, 1863, where over three days nearly 50,000 men were killed or wounded — a number about 7,000 greater than the population of Suffolk County in 1860. John Carman and the 119th would be there. Carman would survive to march with Gen. William Tecumseh Sherman as

Please see **WAR** on **Next Page**

U.S. Navy Photos

The Union's Monitor, left, vs. the Confederacy's Virginia in the world's first clash of armored vessels, which lasted four hours and ended inconclusively. At right, the officers of the Monitor, whose radical design revolutionized naval warfare

there's something in it." Three days later Ericcson and his partners had a $275,000 contract.

The keel was laid Oct. 25, 1861, at Continental Iron Works in Greenpoint, Brooklyn, a shipyard owned by Thomas F. Rowland. The ship was 172 feet long with five layers of one-inch iron plates. Its rotating turret contained twin 11-inch cannon. The Virginia was 262 feet long and carried 10 cannons, but none were as large as the Monitor's and they could not rotate. The Monitor had forced-air ventilation (which could not keep the interior temperature from reaching 150 degrees), and even a toilet flushed by compressed air.

The Monitor was launched into the East River on Jan. 30, 1862, with Ericcson standing near the stern to show his faith in his invention. A reporter noted it showed "not the slightest intention of sinking."

On Tuesday, March 4, commanding officer John Worden and his 58-man crew received orders to head south. Five days later, they met the Virginia head on and made history.

After the standoff, neither side wanted to risk its prototype in a return engagement. In May, with federal forces advancing, the Confederates blew up the Virginia. The Monitor sank in a gale off Cape Hatteras, N.C., on New Year's Eve with the loss of 16 officers and men. The wreck was discovered in 1974 and declared the Monitor Marine Sanctuary.

As the war dragged on, Ericcson built a fleet of improved monitors — several of them in Rowland's shipyard. Other navies copied his ideas.

Rowland's ironworks is long gone. But the ship and its inventor are commemorated in Greenpoint by Monitor Street and the John Ericcson School.

Divergent Foes Of Slavery

BY JOYE BROWN
STAFF WRITER

William Cullen Bryant earned laurels as a poet and newspaper editorial writer. Sojourner Truth drew fame as a traveling preacher and women's rights activist.

They worked in the North, spreading word of their opposition to slavery as the Civil War loomed. Hundreds of miles away in Georgia, Ward Lee, Tom Johnson, Katie Noble, Uster Williams and Lucy Lanham worked reluctantly as slaves.

Bryant and Truth never met each other; nor did they ever meet the southern slaves. Still, incredibly, all have ties to Long Island, where abolitionists had a stronghold before the Civil War.

The influential Bryant, Massachusetts-born, well-educated and literary-minded, was a renowned poet long before he reluctantly lowered his sights, at age 32 and desperate for pay, to become a newspaperman. "Contempt is too harsh a word for it, perhaps, but it was far below respect," he would recall.

He became editor of the New York Evening Post and during the war chided President Abraham Lincoln for moving too slowly in freeing southern slaves. Bryant, who lived on a magnificent estate, Cedarmere, in Roslyn, was more an emancipationist than an abolitionist.

He was against exporting slaves to Africa because the United States would lose good workers. He also was a strong believer in states' rights. As such, before the Civil War, he advocated against the spread of slavery into annexed areas rather than abolishing the existing slavery in the South.

Personally, however, he had long abhorred the "accursed institution" of slavery. In a poem, "The African Chief," he described the anguish of a prisoner who could not convince his captors to free him:

His heart was broken — crazed his brain;
At once his eyes grew wild
He struggled fiercely with his chain,
Whispered, and wept and smiled.

But where Bryant imagined the plight of the enslaved, Sojourner Truth looked no further than her own life. Truth, a slave in upstate Ulster County from age 12 to 30, could not read or write. Her first language was Dutch, not English. Yet, the imposing, spiritual woman, her accented voice as uniquely low as her 6-foot height was unusually high, went on to become one of the most ardent opponents of slavery.

Port Jefferson Historical Society

Four hundred of about 600 on board survived the voyage of America's last slave ship, the Wanderer, which was built in Setauket.

With her fiery style and fearsome execution, Truth gained a reputation for bringing about conversions during her camp meetings. In 1843, she left New York City and walked through Queens, east to Huntington, drawing crowds at each stop along the way. When she published a narrative of her life, renowned abolitionist Harriet Beecher Stowe recommended it to readers. Later, they became friends.

During the Civil War, Truth glorified black soldiers, and in urging them on, came up with her own version of "The Battle Hymn of the Republic":

We are done with hoeing cotton, we are done with hoeing corn;
We are colored Yankee soldiers as sure as you are born
When massa hears us shouting, he will think tis Gabriels horn
As we go marching on.

Drawing, Photo From the National Archives

Sojourner Truth decried slavery on a trip to Huntington. William Cullen Bryant, emancipationist, lived in Roslyn.

Bryant and Truth both had occasion to meet Lincoln, Bryant in 1862 and Truth two years later. Bryant and Lincoln enjoyed a good relationship. After Lincoln's assassination, Bryant declined an offer from Lincoln's friends to write a biography of the president. Truth, despite the glowing recollections in her narrative, received a far different reception.

She and a fellow abolitionist, who was white, were kept waiting for more than three hours as Lincoln joked with male visitors. When Truth went before Lincoln, he became tense and sour. He called Truth "Aunty, . . . as he would his washerwoman," the abolitionist, Lucy Coleman, would recall. She rushed Truth from the room.

Long after their meetings, Truth, along with Bryant, continued their work. And after the war, she went on advocating women's rights and black empowerment; he advocated sufferage for free blacks and took the lead in founding the National Freedman's Relief Association.

Their work directly aided freed slaves, including Lee, Johnson, Noble, Williams and Lanham in Georgia. The five were among 400 (of about 600) who survived the voyage of America's last slave ship, the Wanderer, which brought them from the Congo to the United States in 1858 — more than half a century after importing African slaves had been banned.

The ship was built in Setauket as a pleasure yacht that was to be "bigger, better and faster" than any other ship. It was sold to a cotton broker from Savannah, Ga., who returned the ship to Port Jefferson for alterations. Afterwards, the owner told authorities he was going on a pleasure cruise but stole into the Congo to kidnap slaves instead.

The last enslaved Africans were sold in the South. In the early 1900s, they were photographed and interviewed by anthropologists, who later wrote of their language and memories of Africa in a professional journal.

In several places, the authors referred to their subjects as "the savages." In 1904, about 40 years after the Civil War and the Emancipation Proclamation, one of the slaves, Ward Lee, begged for assistance to get home.

To the Public:
Please help me . . . One year ago, it was revealed to me to go home back to Africa and I have been praying to know if it is God's will . . .

History does not note whether Lee made it.

Eventually, the Wanderer was confiscated for illegally importing slaves. But the owner and crew were never punished. During the Civil War, the ship was seized by Union forces, who converted it to a gunboat.

Once the war was over, the vessel was used in the fruit trade. In 1871, it ran aground in Cuba — and was declared a total loss.

LI Marches Off To Battle

WAR from **Preceding Page**

he blazed his way across Georgia to the sea; he would march with the other survivors of Company H in the huge victory parade in Washington, D.C., after the war ended in April, 1865. He would return to his Merrick farm, where he died in 1919 — one of 35,000 men from Long Island who served and fought in the Civil War.

The vast majority of those 35,000 were from Brooklyn. But approximately 3,000 men from Queens and Suffolk Counties enlisted. They came from every walk of life, from members of old families to just-off-the-boat immigrants. They were doctors, lawyers, blacksmiths, sailors, farmers, cigar makers, carpenters, teachers, politicians, laborers of all kinds and failures of all kinds. Women left their homes to work as battlefield nurses; Walt Whitman, who was born in Huntington, left for Virginia to work as a nurse after he heard that his brother had been injured. What he saw changed this poet forever.

The hot flame of war also drew black Americans in extraordinary numbers. More than 800 blacks from Brooklyn, Queens and Suffolk enlisted, and for them, there were no philosophical discussions as to why they should fight — it was to end slavery, finally, no more excuses, and to contribute to a country they believed in even as it shortchanged them in every conceivable way. These black soldiers put their lives on the line for an idea — freedom for everyone.

No black man born on Long Island who was of enlistment age was a former slave, for that institution ended in New York in the 1820s. But they knew former slaves; many of their mothers and fathers were former slaves, and they knew the South was home to hundreds of thousands of slaves. They had seen the human face of slavery when runaways hid out on Long Island. Simply put, a Confederate victory meant slavery would continue; a Union victory meant it would end.

Many Long Islanders were killed, including sets of brothers, and an unknown number were taken prisoner, deserted and were never seen again, or were reported missing in battle. At least five soldiers from Long Island were taken prisoner and incarcerated at the notorious Confederate prison camp at Andersonville, Ga. Four died there — Jonathan Miller of Glen Cove, and Samuel Vernon, Cornelius Remsen and James Butler, all of Oyster Bay. The fifth, Josiah Brownell, of Glen Cove, survived and wrote a brief account that was published in 1867 by the Glen Cove Gazette.

Brownell, who worked as a house and sign painter, enlisted in 1862 in Company C, of the Second New York Cavalry, which was called the Harris Light Cavalry. The unit took part in the battles of Manassas, Antietam, Fredericksburg, Gettysburg and the Wilderness. According to his account, Brownell was captured at the Battle of the Wilderness, in May, 1864, and shipped to Andersonville, which held more than 30,000 Union soldiers in a crowded, filthy environment. More than 12,000 died, nearly all of disease and malnutrition.

When he returned to Glen Cove, he wrote a brief account titled, "At Andersonville — A Narrative of Personal Adventure at Andersonville, Florence and Charleston Rebel Prisons." It sold on Long Island for 25 cents a copy.

"We think of the Civil War as something that happened in the South, where the fighting occurred, but the war deeply affected many Long Island families," said Harrison Hunt, a Nassau County resident who is writing a book about Long Island during the Civil War. "Long Island was very representative of the North as a whole. We had factories, maritime interests, farming and other businesses, and there were divided opinions. But when the war began, you find support behind saving the Union. People felt the South had tried to get its way for too long and had now crossed the line — they couldn't just walk out of the Union, this is what people thought."

One of the smallest political minorities was the Copperheads — northern supporters of the South and secession. Their most prominent mouthpiece was Henry Reeves, the publisher of the Republican Watchman newspaper in Greenport, who spoke in favor of slavery and white supremacy and believed the South had the constitutional right to go its own way. During the war he was arrested and jailed for treason, but after 1865 he became a leading political figure on Long Island.

Soon after the war began, in April, 1861, recruitment drives sprang up across Long Island. The war, some said, would be over in 90 days, and young men signed up in droves. The 14th Brooklyn quickly recruited 1,000 men, including a number from Suffolk County; the 15th Regiment, in Queens, recruited all over what is now Nassau County. Company C, of the 74th New York Volunteers, was recruited in Flushing and communities to the east. While the 119th Regiment was filled in Manhattan, Benjamin Willis formed

New York Volunteers Historical Association

John Carman, a member of Company H of the 119th New York Volunteers, came from a vegetable farm in Merrick.

Company H in Hempstead and became its captain.

The 48th New York recruited heavily in Huntington; the 127th New York recruited in Huntington and Southold; Company C of the 102nd New York was filled with men from Oyster Bay and Cold Spring Harbor. Recruitment posters were nailed to trees, poles and on buildings where the public gathered. While posters were different for each regiment, they had common themes, such as the one used to win recruits to the 127th Regiment. Across the top the words, "PATRIOTS, COME FORWARD!" were emblazoned. It read, in part:

"In the present critical state of our country, will young men still wait to be drafted? Come voluntarily, young men, and choose your associates in the performance of a most sacred duty. Who would not rather be a Volunteer than a drafted man in such a glorious cause?"

Black recruitment became legal after 1863, and regiments were formed quickly. The 26th U.S. Colored Troops included blacks from Long Island, as did the 20th U.S. Colored Troops and the 4th Rhode Island Colored Troops. Two black men from Oyster Bay who joined the 20th were Simon Rappaljae and David Carll, both of whom survived.

Rappaljae had unique bloodlines — he could trace his rich ancestry back to Sarah de Rapelje, the first Dutch child born in New York, in 1625, and to freed blacks and Matinecock Indians. He lived in a house on what was once called Poverty Hollow Road, and is now called Mill River Road. A letter he wrote to his wife, Bertha, dated Sept. 11, 1864, was found in a wall of the house. It read in part:

You must keep good spirits. I think I shall get home once more. Give respects to all my friends. Tell them I am well. We have some good news from the war. Our folks has taken Atlanta with 25000 prisoners. Today our regiment has fired 100 guns as cheers for it. Write soon and let me know the news around home . . .

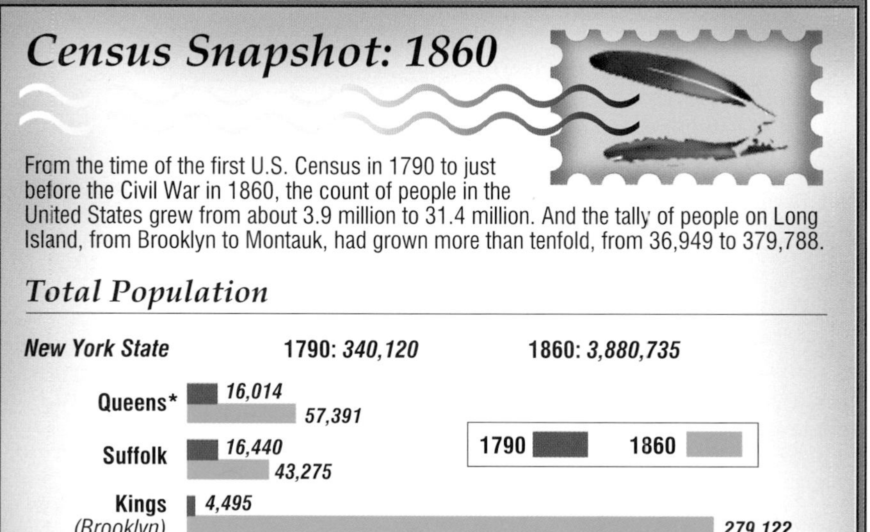

Census Snapshot: 1860

From the time of the first U.S. Census in 1790 to just before the Civil War in 1860, the count of people in the United States grew from about 3.9 million to 31.4 million. And the tally of people on Long Island, from Brooklyn to Montauk, had grown more than tenfold, from 36,949 to 379,788.

Total Population

New York State	1790: 340,120	1860: 3,880,735
Queens*	16,014	57,391
Suffolk	16,440	43,275
Kings (Brooklyn)	4,495	279,122

Town Populations

Queens*	1790	1860
Flushing	1,607	10,189
Jamaica	1,675	6,515
Newtown***	2,111	13,725
North Hempstead	2,696	5,419
Oyster Bay	4,097	9,168
Hempstead	3,828	12,376

Suffolk	1790	1860
Brookhaven	3,224	9,923
East Hampton	1,497	2,267
Huntington****	3,260	8,924
Islip	609	3,845
Riverhead*****	NA	3,044
Shelter Island	201	506
Smithtown	1,022	2,130
Southampton	3,408	6,803
Southold*****	3,219	5,833

1860 Racial Breakdown

	White	Black	Mulatto**
Queens*	54,004	3,120	267
Suffolk	41,477	1,345	453
Kings	274,123	4,022	977

* Queens included present-day Nassau County until 1898.
** The racial descriptions used in the 1860 Census, black and mulatto, were grouped under the heading "free colored." In addition, in New York State, 140 American Indians were counted in the 1860 Census; 3,785 "retaining their tribal character" were not included in the total state population.
*** Present-day Elmhurst and surrounding communities
**** Huntington included present-day Babylon until 1873.
***** Southold included present-day Riverhead until 1792.

SOURCE: "New York State Population," 1987; Bureau of the Census reports for 1790 and 1860.

Newsday / Linda McKenney

One black man — Joachim Pease, who wrote on his enlistment papers that he was from Long Island, but did not specify a town — won the Congressional Medal of Honor for bravery on a U.S. Navy vessel that battled a Confederate raider off the coast of France. A Huntington white man who led black troops, George Brush, also won the medal.

Historians familiar with Long Island's role in the Civil War say they have no exact count of war dead. But there are solid indications that many died. For example, Company H of the 119th had a full complement of 104 men when Carman wrote the letter to his sister in October, 1862; by July, after the battle of Gettysburg, Company H had 60 men. Historians say Company C of the 74th New York Volunteers was decimated — by the spring of 1863, there was none left.

By all appearances, Company H was a cross section of Long Island. "The regiment was recruited in Manhattan and was made up mostly of German immigrants," said Gary Hammond, the historian for the Company H, 119th New York Volunteers Historical Association, which has re-created the life and times of the company. "But when Willis put together his company, it was everyday Long Islanders — farmers, baymen, laborers of all stripes.

"Willis felt strongly about preserving the Union," Hammond added. "He really cared about the country staying together. Willis came back and ran for Congress. He died in 1886."

The history of Company H continues with the historical association, but there are living links — generation to generation, strung together like the beads on a necklace. A Theodore Tupper of East Rockaway was an original member of the company, and survived to come home. His grandson, Theodore Tupper, of Massapequa, is a member of the association. He has another claim to historical distinction — he survived the Japanese attack on Pearl Harbor in 1941.

The last survivor of the company died in 1936 His name was Benjamin Sprague. He was a bayman from East Rockaway. He was born in 1847, and was married in 1864 to a woman named Mary Adeline Denton when he returned to Long Island on a furlough. She died in 1914.

They had three daughters and two sons. One of the girls lived in Island Park and died in 1958. A grainy photograph taken shortly before Sprague's death shows him posing with his grandson, William Pearsall.

In the photograph, Sprague proudly wears his history — the blue uniform of Grand Army of the Republic.

Treasured Letters From the Front

BY STEVE WICK
STAFF WRITER

In the doldrums of a hot summer day, Aug. 6, 1861, a soldier named John Burton wrote to his friend Elizabeth Velsor, who lived with her family on a farm in Westbury. He wasn't much of a speller, and surely he didn't know the function of a period. But he had a great deal to write about.

I take the presant opportunity to write a few lines to you to let you know that i am well and in wat part of the world i am i am now in the land of cotten were i wished to be long befor i got here but now i have got here i have wished I was back not because i am afraid but because they will not let us go a head they ceep us pend up in camp . . . the place were we are incamped is a very pretty place it is on the side of a hill and we are about half a mile of the city of alexandria and close by forte ellsworth we have the guns right over us and they are ranged . . . so as to land right into the city so as to burn the city . . .

Perhaps wanting to explain himself, he wrote her again four months later:

I came to be a soldier to fight for my countrys flag and i shall always try to do the best I can i try to be always ready for any duty that i am caled upon to do and have never had any trouble but it is a hard life to live . . . I should liked to have bin home when you was their and should like to get home for a week now but they will not give any furloughs . . .

During the four years of the Civil War, letters crisscrossed America in numbers never seen before in the history of the country. Regimental mailmen, Union and Confederate, processed tens of thousands of letters a week; train cars filled with bags of letters went north, south, east and west, to every city, every farm town. Few things were as important as the mail — troop trains were attacked, mail trains were left alone. Because a letter wasn't just a letter — it was flesh and blood reduced to words. The letter represented life in a landscape of death.

Soldiers wrote on stationery they'd brought with them, along the margins of newspapers, on whatever they could find, and sent it on its way, certain it would arrive. Dozens of Long Island soldiers wrote hundreds of letters. Their families wrote back, telling them how the hay harvest went, who had a baby, who had died, who had enlisted. A collection of these letters is kept at the Nassau County Historical Museum.

A few days after fierce fighting in Pennsylvania, a young captain from Roslyn, Benjamin Willis, wrote down what he had seen.

On July 1, about 5 a.m., we started on the road to Gettysburg; marched hastily over rough and muddy roads through a drenching rain, reaching there about 12 o'clock that day, a distance of 11 miles. At this time the First Corps had already been engaged for some time, and had commenced to retire. We continued the march through the town and took positions on the right of the road leading from Gettysburg to Chambersburg, in an orchard, where we for a short time halted, being subjected meanwhile to a severe cannonade of the enemy. Here one company [H] was ordered to deploy as skirmishers, which they did in handsome style, having instructions to prevent the enemy from advancing to a large barn and several buildings to our right . . .

"I . . . feel it is right for me to be here and try and feel content. I believe in doing what the Conscience says is right . . . I enlisted to help save our country and I believe that the President has done what he thought is right and I am agoing to stand by him . . ."

— Henry Prince, from letters to his parents

On March 23, 1862, a soldier from what is now Nassau County, Isaac Van Nostrand, wrote to an unidentified friend.

i have sat down to Write you a few lines to let you Now that i am Well . . . i have seen a Nuf of the War Now and i am Comming home in a few Weeks . . . i hope these few lines Will find you all Well . . . you say that you Ant seen My Wife in Some time if you go and see hur i dont think you Can do hur Eny hurt . . .

Edwin Valentine, Company E, of the 127th New York Volunteers, was from Huntington, where the other members of his company were recruited. In an undated letter, sent from South Carolina, he showed how much he craved news from home.

I will send you A news Paper that is printed down here As soon as I can get it . . . As I have got mutch more news To tell you this time. I will try And write more the next. you must give my love to all The folkes and tell them all to write to me. and you must Do the same. give my love to Aunt ruth and grandmother when You see them. it is getting near Time for dress parade so i guess That I will close my letter so Good buy till the next time. please write soon. You must excuse me for making you pay the postage on this letter but my postage stampes is played out.

Valentine was mustered in on Oct. 1, 1862; he died five weeks later, on Nov. 13.

In Southold, Henry Prince's family followed his every move. He wrote several letters a week, telling his family what he had seen and where he was. By the volume of his letters, Prince was a letter writer first and a soldier second. Here are excerpts from a number of his letters to his parents:

Dec. 20, 1862: I have but little faith in our government. The soldiers are Patriotic, would fight better if our Generals were better.

Jan. 1, 1863: I wish you all a happy New Year. A good many of the co. have gone out on passes. I thought I would remain in camp and enjoy myself by writing and meditation. I would like very much to be with you today, but feel it is right for me to be here and try and feel content. I believe in doing what the Conscience says is right . . . I heard today that Benny Prince is dead. [Benny was Henry's cousin; he was killed in Georgia in December, 1862, at age 20]. His father must feel very bad. I feel anxious to hear from Maria Tuthill. I am afraid she is not long for this world. I feel that she must not die before I return home, if I ever do.

March 23, 1863: As for war news, you know as much as I do . . . I believe the North are becoming more united. I hope the Copperheads [northern supporters of the Confederacy] will have to close their mouths, or crawl in the dirt and spit forth nothing but dust . . . I enlisted to help save our country and I believe that the President has done what he thought is right and I am agoing to stand by him and the government three years unless sooner discharged. I believe that the North will Conquer.

May 3, 1863: . . . as I write there is a battle going on across the river. We were left behind. If we had been called on, some of the Regt would probably, before the sun sets, lay cold in death. I wish the war might end. It seems cruel to slaughter so many men, yet I believe our cause is just and if it is God's will, we ought not complain. The innocent must suffer for the guilty in this world. The reward will come hereafter. I will stop for the present. With much love to all, from your son,

Henry

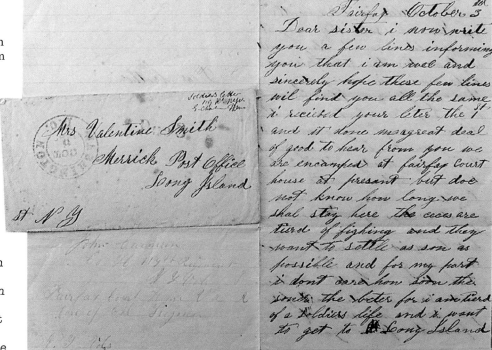

LI HISTORY.COM

See the Civil War through the eyes of a young Southold farmer who enlisted in 1862 and kept a journal of his experiences. Three years of entries are available on the Internet at http://www.lihistory.com.

New York Volunteers Historical Association

A letter from John Carman, one of many sent by soldiers who saw death in faraway places

Long Islander Joachim Pease was one of the bravest of the Navy's sailors

In the War For Liberty

BY STEVE WICK
STAFF WRITER

His name was Joachim Pease, and sometime after the start of the Civil War, he enlisted in the U.S. Navy.

History does not tell us much about him, except that he was born on Long Island, won a Congressional Medal of Honor for extraordinary bravery aboard a naval vessel, and he was black.

"When he enlisted, all Pease wrote on his papers was that he was born on Long Island," said Lynda Day, a historian at Brooklyn College and the author of "Making a Way to Freedom — A History of African Americans on Long Island," which was published last year.

"At the start of the Civil War, blacks were not allowed to join the Army," she said. "But they were allowed to enlist in the Navy, which Pease did. Unfortunately, nothing has been found to say whether he survived the war, or ever came back to Long Island."

At the beginning of 1863, the Emancipation Proclamation, which freed slaves in the Confederate states, went into effect. At almost the same time, President Abraham Lincoln signed an executive order allowing blacks to enlist in the Army in segregated units. By early spring of that year, black regiments were being set up — the first was the 54th Massachusetts Regiment and others followed in Rhode Island and New York.

Eager to join the fight, five black Long Islanders traveled to Boston and enlisted in the 54th Massachusetts, according to Long Island historian Harrison Hunt. (The movie "Glory" celebrates the story of the 54th Massachusetts.) More than 800 black Long Islanders enlisted in various regiments. It is not known how many died and did not come home; Hunt said the number could have been as high as 100. Nationwide, more than 178,000 blacks enlisted; 24 — including Pease — won the nation's highest award, the Congressional Medal of Honor.

"Blacks were allowed in the Navy from the start of the war because they had a long history of serving on ships, particularly in the whaling industry," Hunt said.

After Lincoln's order allowing blacks to enlist in the Army, recruitment posters appeared across New York and Long Island. While whites had many reasons to enlist, blacks felt an urgent need to help kill the institution of slavery, once and for all. A recruitment poster reads, in part:

MEN OF COLOR, TO ARMS! NOW OR NEVER!

This is our golden moment. The government of the United States calls for every able bodied Colored Man to enter the Army for the three years' service, and join in fighting the Battles of Liberty and the Union. A new era is upon us. For generations we have suffered under the horrors of slavery, outrage and wrong; our manhood has been denied, our citizenship blotted out, our souls seared and burned, our spirits cowed and crushed, and the hopes of the future of our race involved in doubts and darkness. But now the whole aspect of our relations to the white race is changed. Now therefore is our most precious moment. Let us Rush to Arms! Fail now and Our Race is Doomed on this the soil of our birth. We must now awake, arise, or be forever fallen . . . What is life without liberty? We say that we have manhood — now is the time to prove it. A nation or a people that cannot fight may be pitied, but cannot be respected.

Pease's exact enlistment date is not known — nor his hometown on Long Island — but it was soon after the beginning of the war. What is known are the events of June 18, 1864, when the naval vessel on which Pease served as a seaman, the frigate Kearsarge, got into a fight with a Confederate raider, the Alabama, off the coast of France.

Pease was in charge of one of the Kearsarge's cannons. A Confederate shell hit near him, killing or wounding a number of men around him. But Pease kept loading and reloading the cannon. According to "Negro Medal of Honor Men,' published in 1967, "Acting Master David Summer, Pease's superior officer, personally congratulating him, said, 'You sustained your reputation as one of the best men on the ship.' " Summer nominated Pease for the Congressional Medal of Honor.

Records of Medal of Honor winners say Pease "exhibited marked coolness and good conduct and was highly recommended by his divisional officer for gallantry under fire."

There is nothing today on Long Island that honors Pease's memory, or the memories of the 800 other blacks who fought in the Civil War.

"I hope one day we can find out where he was from, and whether he came home or not," Day said.

U.S. NAVY
THE CONGRESSIONAL MEDAL OF HONOR
"For conspicuous gallantry and intrepidity at the risk of life, above and beyond the call of duty..."
JOACHIM PEASE
1864

The National Archives

A poster featuring Joachim Pease, winner of the Congressional Medal of Honor in 1864.

Walt Whitman Birthplace Association; Newsday Photo

The 107th U.S. Colored Infantry, of Kentucky, at Fort Corcoran in Arlington, Va., in 1865

Caught Up In Anti-Draft Riots

In mid-July, 1863 — 10 days after Gen. Robert E. Lee's troops were defeated at Gettysburg — a murderous rebellion erupted in the streets of Manhattan.

Called by historians the anti-draft riots, street fighting by huge crowds made up largely of Irish immigrants turned into vicious attacks on free blacks, police and firemen, and on federal troops that rushed to New York City.

It was the third summer of the war. With no end in sight, President Abraham Lincoln instituted a draft. "Immigrants were angry that the draft fell harder on them," said Lynda Day, a historian at Brooklyn College who has written a book on black history on Long Island. "Rich people could buy their way out of the draft, the poor couldn't."

Newspaper accounts of the riots show whites, including police and firemen, were attacked, buildings set ablaze — including entire blocks — and telegraph lines cut. But the hunting down of blacks, and the torching of the Colored Orphan Asylum on 44th Street by the mobs shows the rampage was not just about the draft. Eleven blacks were killed by rioters.

A letter from a Westbury woman, Ruth Velsor, to her sister-in-law, shows how the mob attacked a black man named Jim, who narrowly escaped death and fled to Long Island. She wrote:

The times are quiet in the city but they are going to draft again, but there are so many troops in the city now that they will keep the mob down if they try that again . . . the colored man that drove cart for Townsend Jackson had a narrow escape . . . he was going up to the stable the same as usual to take care of the horses and fix to go down town, when the mob started after him and he run in a stable and hid and the mob went right to Townsends stable and they hunted farely for him but did not find him . . . Townsend found him 2d day afternoon about five o'clock, but they were two other colored men with him and they did not see Townsend so they would not let him in, and about ten o'clock he went again and then they let him in they saw him out of the window and came down and opened the door. Then he went home again to get them something to eat and started again on horse back he thought he would go farther around for fear some one was watching him and he came upon the mob and they tooke him to be some officer and started for him and struck at him and cut his horse face with the blow that was ment for Townsend so he did not get there and the next day the man ventured around to the stable and Jim was there and they got him on a cart and turned a box over him and started for the 34th street ferry and got him across and put him on horseback and told him to ride for his life . . .

— **Steve Wick**

A Jamaica teen enlists and covers battles for readers back home

The Fighting Editor

BY ANDREW SMITH
STAFF WRITER

Michael Shaw thirsted for battle, glory and fame when the Civil War began. Thanks to his job in the print shop of the Long Island Democrat, a weekly newspaper in Jamaica, he got all three.

Shaw, 18 or 19 when war broke out in 1861, had been a cheerful, well-liked apprentice at the Democrat for more than two years. When he enlisted in Company B of the Excelsior Brigade's Third Regiment that June, he talked the editor, James Brenton, into making him the paper's "Fighting Editor."

With the advent of the telegraph and reliable mail service, the Civil War was the first in which newspapers could tell readers about battles relatively soon after they happened. Most newspapers relied on letters from local soldiers for war correspondence.

"They wanted to have lively first-hand accounts of what happened at the front," said historian Vincent F. Seyfried, an expert on Long Island newspapers. Brenton relied on Shaw and a handful of other Jamaica soldiers for war news.

For a year — until Shaw's parents objected — Shaw's memoirs of Army life appeared in the Democrat. Sometimes naive, sometimes horrifying and sometimes poignant, Shaw's candid account made the war real for readers.

For months, Shaw waited impatiently for battle at a camp in Maryland, complaining about the food and wondering, melodramatically, whether he would survive the war.

In the Jan. 21, 1862, issue, Shaw said he hoped he wasn't writing too often about too little, "but as I have nothing but this wood pile to guard, which shows no disposition to run away, I may as well do it, if only to murder time."

Finally, in May, he saw his first significant battle at Williamsburg, Va. In the May 20 issue, he wrote:

"It was the first regular engagement I have been in, and I must confess to strange thoughts crowding on my brain. Home, friendship, and a thousand things rushed on my memory . . . I ask you when the groans of the wounded still ring in my ears and ghastly forms crowd before my eyes — limbs without bodies, and bloody bodies without limbs — gore of men and horses mingling in one common pool — friend and foe locked in a death grip and dabbled with each others blood! This is not fancy, it is actual fact and I can't get over it all at once.

"We are now advancing on to Richmond, driving the enemy before us."

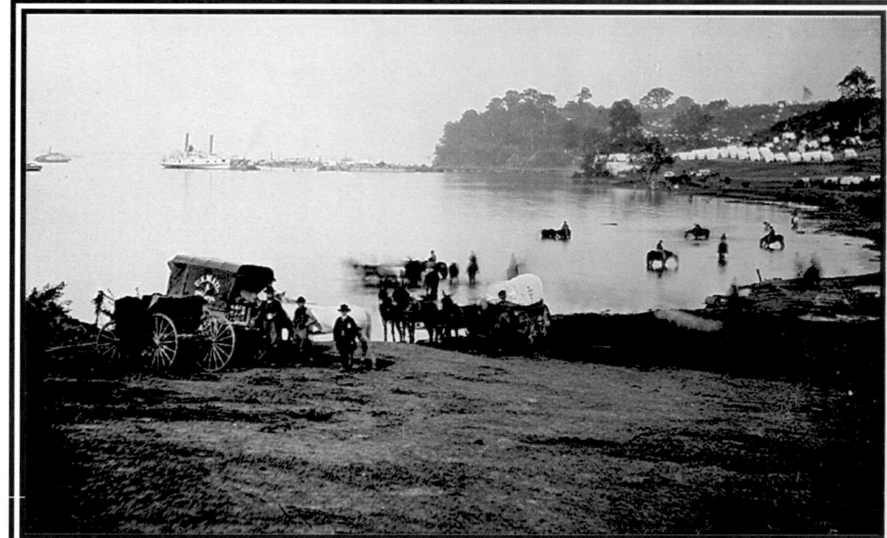

National Archives Photo / Mathew Brady

A mail wagon waits at a Union Army camp on the James River, in Virginia. The mail allowed newspapers to print accounts of Civil War battles soon after they happened, relying on soldiers' letters for details.

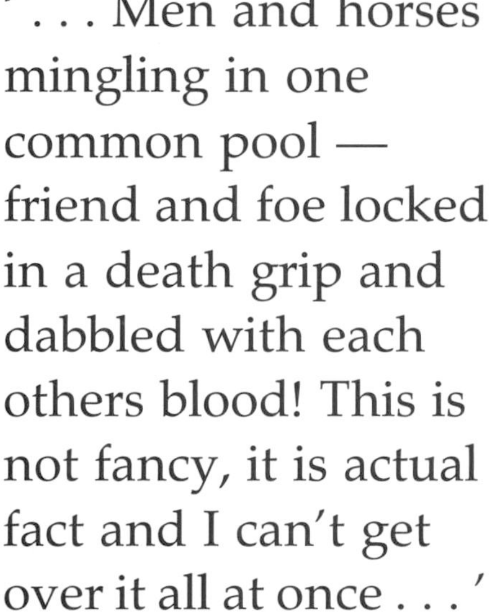

'. . . Men and horses mingling in one common pool — friend and foe locked in a death grip and dabbled with each others blood! This is not fancy, it is actual fact and I can't get over it all at once . . .'

— Michael Shaw, reporting his first battle

A few months later, he wrote of feeling uneasy firing into rebel lines:

"I do not know that any one was hurt for I shut my eyes and turned away, not wishing to see a fellow creature in agony on my account."

Brenton obviously loved the drama of Shaw's dispatches and pressed him for more. Shaw was aghast at the request, replying:

"I want to know what you think I am made of, and how you suppose it is possible for me to sit down, and coolly write a letter detailing all the circumstances connected with a battle, as soon as I come out of it, and while my hands are yet red with the blood of the poor fellows I have just been assisting to slaughter . . . Excuse me if I find it impossible to communicate with you fully, and at once."

Shaw's correspondence abruptly disappeared in August, 1862. For months there was no explanation, but in May, 1863, Brenton explained that Shaw's family had asked him to publish no more of his letters.

Two months later, another notice appeared: "Our 'Fighting Editor' Wounded." Shaw had been shot in the shoulder during the Battle of Gettysburg. Brenton wished his former apprentice well and lauded his bravery in action.

Shaw was discharged from the Army in June, 1864, and a relieved Brenton welcomed him back:

"He has performed his duty faithfully, and we are glad to see him 'at home' once more."

LONG ISLAND IN MOURNING FOR LINCOLN

Men cried in the street. Churches, businesses and private homes were draped in black for a week. Newspapers, even those that routinely had excoriated President Abraham Lincoln as barely fit to govern, had thick black lines of mourning between their columns.

Long Island came to a stunned halt at the news of Lincoln's assassination.

Like the rest of the nation, Long Islanders had barely begun to celebrate the end of the long, brutal Civil War when Lincoln died on Saturday, April 15, 1865, the morning after he was shot in Washington. Telegraphs flashed the news to Long Island within hours.

"Men cannot speak with each other without tears flowing or evidently suppressed," reported the Queens County Sentinel, published in Hempstead. "As soon as the news of the President's death reached our village the bells of all our churches were tolled."

Emotion reached a peak on Wednesday, April 19, the day of Lincoln's funeral. Businesses stayed closed.

"Last Wednesday will long be remembered by our citizens," wrote the Long Island Democrat, a virulently anti-Lincoln paper based in Jamaica. "The tolling bells, the flags at half-mast, and the houses draped in the symbols of woe, marked the deep and solemn feeling of every citizen in our midst."

In Sag Harbor, the day began with a salute of cannon fire. A solemn parade moved through the village to the Presbyterian Church.

Jamaica merchant J.S. Seabury spoke for all of Long Island when he hung a portrait of Lincoln above his door, with a sign that read, "And all the people wept over him."

— Andrew Smith

Photo Courtesy of Vincent F. Seyfried

Black bunting is draped on first-floor windows at the Howard House Hotel in East New York, Brooklyn, following the assassination of President Abraham Lincoln. The photo from April, 1865, is one of the earliest showing a Long Island Rail Road locomotive.

At College Point, industrialist Conrad Poppenhusen built a legacy that endures

The Benevolent Tycoon

BY RHODA AMON
STAFF WRITER

In College Point, Poppenhusen is not just a funny name. This north Queens community has a Poppenhusen Institute, Poppenhusen Avenue, Poppenhusen Library and Poppenhusen Monument. And, a century after his death, every schoolchild here knows who Conrad Poppenhusen was.

Today the institute, where thousands of immigrants learned the arts and a vocation, is the most significant reminder of a benevolent tycoon who came to College Point in 1854 and built a rubber factory — and a town.

And, most remarkable in that day of public-be-damned robber barons, Poppenhusen built homes for his workers, drained the marshes, paved roads, brought clean running water into the community, and constructed a cobblestone causeway and a railroad.

The German immigrant donated $100,000 and land for the construction of the institute as a gift to the people of College Point on his 50th birthday in 1868. He endowed another $100,000 to pay teachers' salaries and operating costs for the educational-cultural center, where workers and their children studied English, learned a trade and were introduced to art, music, theater, literature, history. It was open to all races and creeds.

That same year Poppenhusen also built the Flushing-Whitestone Railroad. This would lead eventually to his consolidating the Long Island Rail Road and becoming the line's president — something that would ultimately be his undoing.

In 1868, the Poppenhusen Institute was College Point. It served as the village hall — Poppenhusen was a justice of the peace and at one time was president of the village trustees. It was the first home of the Congregational Church, the College Point bank, the public library, the firehouse, even the jail (the two cells in the basement can still be seen by visitors). At the institute, Poppenhusen established the nation's first free kindergarten.

The institute was to be run by the Conrad Poppenhusen Association, which was incorporated with this high-minded purpose:

"The protection, care and custody of infants; the advancement of science and art, with such equipment as may be useful for that purpose; and the improvement of the moral and social conditions of the people."

Today, 130 years later, the Poppenhusen Institute is still a community-cultural center. A five-story Victorian edifice with tall arched windows, it towers above the small houses of its working-class neighborhood.

It fell on hard times in the 1970s and came within a razor's edge of being demolished in 1980. But College Point residents formed The Concerned Citizens for the Poppenhusen Institute, and after a three-year court battle worthy of Poppenhusen himself, won the right to continue to exist. It is primarily funded by city and state grants.

"If we lost it, I would have left the community," said Susan K. Brustmann, a leader in the court fight, now the institute's executive director.

Poppenhusen was a 19th-Century Horatio Alger story who started at age 10 doing accounts in German and English for his father, a textile trader in Hamburg. His father died when Conrad was 14, leaving him to support his mother and pay off his father's debts.

Poppenhusen Institute; Newsday Photo

Poppenhusen Institute

Conrad Poppenhusen, at left with his family, formed the American Hard Rubber Co., above, on the College Point waterfront. Poppenhusen's beneficence endeared him to his workers.

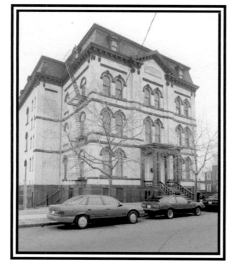

Newsday Photo / Julia Gaines

When his employer, H.C. Meyer, offered him an opportunity to manage a small business in the Williamsburg section of Brooklyn, Poppenhusen, then 25, married and penniless, sailed for the new world in 1843. He became a partner in the firm of Meyer and Poppenhusen, manufacturing brushes, combs, buttons and corset stays, all from whalebone, which was becoming scarce. The alternative was natural rubber, which had a tendency to turn sticky, especially in hot weather.

Then Poppenhusen met Charles Goodyear, who had invented a vulcanization process for hardening rubber and needed capital to turn his invention into profit. The two reached a deal in 1854 whereby Poppenhusen would have sole rights for several years to the use of Goodyear's invention. Goodyear would found the company that bears his name.

Searching for a larger manufacturing base, Poppenhusen came upon College Point, a small community on the East River. Waterfront land could be bought cheap.

Poppenhusen's Enterprise Rubber Works was soon swallowing up smaller companies to become the American Hard Rubber Co. College Point became known as the "rubber capital of the Northeast." It also was a lively seaside resort.

Like Henry Ford, Poppenhusen introduced new cost-cutting techniques. Needing ever more workers, he recruited immigrants when they stepped off the ship at New York piers. A cradle-to-the-grave employer, he organized a mutual benefit association to assure workers' sick benefits and even death benefits — unheard-of practices in those days. The company employed more than 1,500 workers at its peak.

During the Civil War, Poppenhusen's rubber works flourished with war orders for flasks, cups and uniform buttons. Poppenhusen encouraged his workers to enlist and made provision for the families left behind. Their jobs were waiting when they came back and other veterans joined the ranks. After the war, immigrants, particularly German and Irish, poured into town. "Many Irish learned German passably well, so there was no serious language barrier," wrote Robert A. Hecht in his "History of College Point, N.Y." Poppenhusen imported German teachers for his growing kindergarten. He donated $30,000 to build the First Reformed Church, opened a library and took all his employees and their families, 1,000 people, by special trains to the nation's centennial celebration in Philadelphia in 1876.

Fascinated by trains, he bought railroads. In 1870 he acquired the North Shore Railroad, which ran from Long Island City to Flushing, and extended it to College Point. He invested $3 million to $6 million in the consolidation of several existing lines into the Long Island Rail Road. His three sons, lacking their father's business acumen, plunged recklessly into the railroad-buying act. Poppenhusen was stuck with a hodgepodge of stations, rolling stock and tracks, and the recession of 1873-78 made matters worse.

In 1877 the line went into receivership. Poppenhusen was bankrupt.

He returned to Germany in 1878 and tried to recoup his lost fortune, returning several times to his College Point mansion, where he died in 1883. The mansion was demolished in 1905, after the death of his second wife. The factory limped along until the 1930s when it moved to Butler, N.J., and eventually folded. Plastics were replacing hard rubber.

In 1884, the townspeople erected a monument on College Point Boulevard, inscribed "To the memory of the benefactor of College Point." But the Poppenhusen Institute, a national landmark where children come to learn music, dance and karate and view an exhibit of American Indian life 1,000 years ago, remains his most enduring legacy.

POPPENHUSEN INSTITUTE

The Poppenhusen Institute, 114-04 14th Rd. in College Point, has two original jail cells and a restored grand ballroom where town meetings were held. The five-story institute also houses the first free kindergarten in the United States and a fire department exhibit with an original hose wagon and a replica of a firehouse. The institute is open from 9 a.m. to 5 p.m. Mondays-Wednesdays and 1 to 9 p.m. Fridays. Call 718-358-0067 for an appointment. Admission is free, but there is a $3 charge for the Native American Museum, which focuses on the Matinecocks of College Point.

A symbol of the Algonquian past, Stephen Pharaoh inspires today's Montauketts

An Indian Named Pharaoh

BY STEVE WICK
STAFF WRITER

His name was Steven Pharaoh, and he was the embodiment of everything that ever was on Long Island and everything that would never be again.

In 1879, Pharaoh lived in a small house on the high, rocky moraine at Montauk Point. On maps of the day, this place was called Indian Fields, and was home to a small number of Montaukett families whose ancestors had lived on this same spot for thousands of years. It was a place of memory and history — for Pharaoh, it was all he had ever known.

That year, Pharaoh was 60 years old. As a child he had been bound as an indentured servant to an East Hampton family; he had worked as a hunter, fisherman and whaler. Some said he sailed to California in 1849 to look for gold; in the early 1860s, when he was in his 40s, he enlisted as a soldier in the Civil War.

He was said to have walked all over the South Fork and Long Island. He boasted of walking to Brooklyn and back in a single day. For a small fee, he'd walk letters to homes miles apart. His white neighbors in East Hampton nicknamed him "Talkhouse," for reasons now lost to history. Talkhouse Pharaoh was a local celebrity.

But he was much more than that. Tall, bone thin, his long black hair cascading over his shoulders, Pharaoh was the living symbol of Long Island's Algonquian past — a past that by 1878 had all but faded into oblivion. That year, a suit was filed by two East Hampton residents trying to force the sale of Indian Fields. Pharaoh and his half-brother, David Pharaoh, had joined to fight the sale in court. Then David died, leaving Talkhouse Pharaoh to fight alone.

The next year, in that place, Pharaoh sat at the intersection of fate and history. What little remained of the Algonquians' world was about to be replaced by a new and emerging Long Island. Even as the tiny Montaukett community was fighting to stay at Indian Fields, 80 miles to the west, in the Hempstead Plains, a New York City businessman had already built a planned community called Garden City. Within seven years the Brooklyn Bridge would open, and Long Island would never be the same.

Seeing Pharaoh as a unique figure, circus promoter P.T. Barnum displayed Pharaoh as "The Last King of the Montauks," as if he were the only survivor of a dead race. East Hampton businessman I.G. Van Scoy felt the same way, and in 1867 had posed Pharaoh for a portrait, which was then sold as a memento. The photograph shows Pharaoh dressed in a long frock coat, white shirt and frilly bow tie, seated in a chair, clutching a long walking stick in his right hand. Pharaoh looks like a man who has suddenly found himself lost in a familiar place.

"Talkhouse Pharaoh was born in a wigwam at a site called Molly's Place near Three Mile Harbor," said John Strong, a history professor at Southampton Campus of Long Island University. "Steven had that presence that struck everybody who met him. That's why people sought him out for photographs. He was the ideal type. So when he died, people thought there were no more Montauketts anywhere."

Suffolk County Historical Society

The Montaukett Indian Steven (Talkhouse) Pharaoh sits stiffly for his photograph in 1867.

The name Faro appears on deeds marked by the Montauketts' Xs in the mid-1600s. Later, the name was reconfigured into "Pharaoh," probably by English settlers who wanted to give the family a regal-sounding name that would confer on them the status to sell off land.

"Growing up, I'd hear stories about Steven Talkhouse. He was quite the man, an exemplary man. No one had a bad word about him," said John Fowler, a Montaukett who can trace his lineage back to the 17th Century. "We look at him today as someone who represents what we were."

Today, the tiny Montaukett community is seeking federal recognition that would grant them what would otherwise seem obvious — recognition that they are still on Long Island and can seek redress for what they consider past wrongs. To supporters of the effort, Talkhouse Pharaoh is an inspiration, a guiding light.

"We look at him and are inspired by his life," said Robert Cooper, the recently elected chief of the Montauketts. "In honoring our history, we honor his memory." Cooper said he dreams of a tall statue being made of Talkhouse Pharaoh that would stand at Indian Fields, which is now part of parkland owned by Suffolk County.

Over the generations after English settlers arrived, the community of Montauketts who lived at the site were gradually diminished, losing their land base and their culture. By the 1790s, very little of their language had survived, and to save what was left, a word list was compiled by John Gardiner, who employed Indians on the island that bears his family's name. It is a short list, but it's all there is.

The changing character of Montauk Point can be seen in maps. Early maps of the region show the words Indian Town or Indian Fields at the place where the Indians lived. As a distinct community, Indian Fields survived on these maps well into the mid-1800s. Then the reference was gone.

That summer of 1879, Steven Talkhouse Pharaoh, immortalized in one of the earliest photographs ever taken on Long Island, was found dead on a wooded path in Montauk. It is not known who found him, or what he died of. He was buried on a plot overlooking Lake Montauk, where generations of Montauketts had been buried.

The community known as Indian Fields did not survive long after Pharaoh's death. In October, Brooklyn businessman Arthur Benson, who dreamed of deepwater ports and railroad facilities, bought Montauk Point at an auction. Needing clear title, and evidently not wanting the Montauketts living in the middle of his dream, Benson's agent offered small amounts of money to the Indians to induce them to leave.

After 500 generations of occupancy, they were the very last Montaukett families that would ever live at Indian Fields.

New York State Museum, Albany

A detail of an 1880 painting by E.L. Henry entitled "King of the Montauks" shows David Pharaoh, half-brother of Steven, traveling in eastern Long Island. He fought in court to save their land.

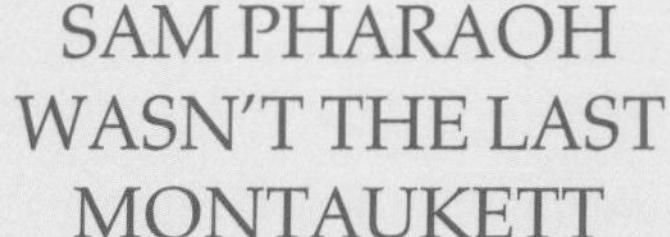

SAM PHARAOH WASN'T THE LAST MONTAUKETT

In 1927, when Steven Talkhouse Pharaoh's nephew, Sam Pharaoh, died, The Bridgehampton News carried this story under the headline "INDIAN PRINCE IS FROZEN TO DEATH."

Sam Pharaoh, the last of the royal family of the Montaukett Indians and a descendant of Wyandanch and other Indian chieftains on Montauk, is dead. His body was found on a grassy knoll near Three Mile Harbor, frozen to death, and had apparently been there for a week or more.

This last descendant of a truly noble line was laid to rest at East Hampton on Friday . . . The last of the Montauketts was the son of David Pharaoh and Maria Banks . . . Sam's father, King David, up until the time of his death, was an honest citizen and a worthy king. For years he had tried to regain possession of the Montauk acres . . . but without success.

Sam Pharaoh was not the last Montaukett. Today, his descendants are still trying to reclaim part of the land that once belonged to their ancestors.

— Steve Wick

On Long Island, re-enactors remember the soliders and fight the battles of the 1860s

Keeping the Civil War Alive

BY BILL BLEYER
STAFF WRITER

The shrill rebel yell echoed across the muddy field as a handful of Confederate infantrymen emerged from the woods with their muskets crackling. Company H of the 119th New York Volunteers formed ranks and advanced to confront the enemy.

With some of their comrades falling from Rebel fire, the Yankees marched with weapons shouldered until their captain ordered a halt. "Commence firing," he shouted. Flames jetted from Union muskets and now the men of the Company B, 57th Virginia, began dropping.

"You got me, you Yankee scum," one Confederate yelled as he crumpled. The smell of gunpowder filled the cold February day until a final Union volley left all seven Rebels dead or wounded.

At which point, the audience applauded until the casualties got to their feet and dusted themselves off.

This clearly wasn't Gettysburg. The soldiers on the field at the Nassau County Museum of Art in Roslyn were Civil War re-enactors, weekend warriors who bring history to life.

The boys in blue were members of the Company H, 119th New York Volunteers Historical Association (Box 738, Melville, N.Y. 11747). They portray members of the same company, which was formed in 1862 in Hempstead and fought in more than a dozen engagements from Gettysburg to Atlanta. The re-enactors have "fought" on some of the same battlefields and appeared in the movie "Glory." The boys in gray were re-enactors from Company B, 57th Virginia Infantry (246-35 87th Ave., Bellerose, N.Y. 11426), headed by Ray Pickett of Bellerose, a great-great-grandnephew of Confederate Gen. George Pickett, who led the famous charge at Gettysburg.

Yesterday's Events Making News Today

Since the Company H group was formed by Nassau County Museum staff members in 1980, it has grown to about 50 members, including women who play civilians.

"When we started, we didn't want to just fire muskets at people," said Jim McKenna, an association founder who is now its chairman. "We wanted to relive history."

Association historian Gary Hammond, who works with McKenna at Old Bethpage Village Restoration, matches each enlistee with an original Company H soldier. The matches are based on similarities such as occupation. And that's just the beginning.

Mark Adler, an Oceanside electrician who has portrayed harness-maker Alfred Noon of Roslyn for 17 years, said, "I sent to the National Archives to get his military and pension papers and I researched him so well that I found his granddaughter, who knew him, living in Ronkonkoma."

The re-enactors can become very attached to their alter egos, said McKenna, who portrays Sgt. John Cornelius, a Hempstead stableman. Cornelius was wounded at Chancellorsville in 1863 and recuperated in time to fight at Gettysburg two months later.

"I still go to John Cornelius' grave every year and make sure a flag is kept there," McKenna said.

If a Company H veteran were to return, he'd feel right at home in the ranks. The re-enactors study Civil War drill and battle maneuvers — with officers, sergeants and musicians taking training courses at places like Gettysburg.

Their obsession with accuracy is most evident in the re-enactors' uniforms and weapons. The company's expert, Jim Lennon of Levittown, said it costs at least $1,500 to purchase high-quality reproductions of everything from rain ponchos to underwear. The most expensive item is an Italian-made Springfield musket reproduction that goes for more than $500.

Like most re-enactors, Lennon, who portrays Merrick farmer John Carman, has been fascinated by the Civil War since childhood. Many members collect Civil War artifacts. Lennon's interest is the life of "the common everyday Joe." So he studies diaries and journals. He made a pilgrimage to Maryland to learn how clothing was made in the 19th Century so he could make his own shirts and overcoats.

Don Effinger of Deer Park, who portrays Joseph Denton, a farmer and bayman from Hempstead, is a student of Civil War cuisine. Before each encampment, he spends 90 minutes making a batch of hardtack biscuits, the rock-hard and often bug-infested staple of the Civil War soldier's diet. Effinger's hardtack is fresh, therefore softer, and he occasionally stretches authenticity by adding historically inaccurate flavorings such as garlic.

The re-enactors are so passionate about the war that many go to more than a dozen events a year to play soldier. "This is putting what you read into practice," Lennon said.

"I just like how it was Americans versus Americans, cousins against cousins, fathers against sons," said Kevin Sheehan, a 13-year-old from Long Beach who joined two years ago to be a drummer boy.

"When there's thousands of men on the field and you're in the mist of battle you forget who you are," said Adler, who started as a private and is now the captain. Even though the muskets and cannons fire blanks, he said, "you can just start to feel the bullets whizzing over your head and the shells exploding. At some really large events, they'll have ground charges exploding near you and shells exploding overhead. Last September we were at the 135th anniversary of Antietam and there were 17,000 men on the field and over 100 cannon. The ground was shaking like an earthquake."

While the musket and cannon fire is simulated, the bayonets are real, so they remain in their scabbards during simulated combat. So far Company H hasn't needed a surgeon. "We've had some minor stuff," Adler said. "Somebody got poked in the eye, and one fellow had his musket discharge accidentally and the blast burned his fingers a little bit."

Newsday Photo / Bill Davis
Members of Company H, 119th New York Volunteers Historical Association, drill at the Nassau County Museum of Art in a re-enactment.

A SOLDIER'S STORY

His name was Henry Prince, and he was a farmer's son from Southold.

Soon after his 23rd birthday, Prince heard a speech given by a charismatic recruiter named Steward Lyndon Woodford. Afterward, Prince signed a ledger in the Southold Presbyterian Church enlisting in Company H of the 127th New York Regiment of the Union Army. It was Aug. 21, 1862.

That month, the Civil War was 16 months old. Over the next 11 months, armies of the North and South would clash on the battlefield, at places that still resonate deeply in American history — at Antietam, Fredericksburg, Chancellorsville and Gettysburg.

Over the course of the next 2½ years, Prince would write letters to his parents telling them where he was, what he had seen, and asking about life on the farm. He also wrote in a leather-bound diary, which he kept in his knapsack.

His letters and diaries are the most extensive of any Civil War veteran from Long Island. They provide a unique portrait of one man and one town at an extraordinary moment in history. That summer, 109 men from Southold enlisted; 29 would not come home. Prince would be one of the lucky ones.

Newsday Photo
Southold's Civil War monument

Staff writer Steve Wick's feature story about Henry Prince that first appeared in Long Island Life, begins on the following page.

One Soldier's Story

BY STEVE WICK
STAFF WRITER

THE MEMORIAL STANDS on a curve in the road near the American Legion Post, a silent piece of granite atop a patch of freshly cut grass. Cars pass it day after day, year after year, and it seldom attracts a visitor.

But those who stop to admire it are rewarded, for this monument on Route 25 in Southold speaks for itself. On its four sides, in long columns, are names of local men who fought in the Civil War — 83 names, including several pairs of brothers, and multiple sets of cousins.

They were 83 men from a small town at the eastern end of Long Island. Men who on their enlistment papers said they were farmers, fishermen, mariners, butchers, laborers, carpenters, teachers and students. Men who were barely 20 years old, and men who were approaching 40, with children at home. Men whose family histories were, by the start of the war in 1861, more than 200 years old in this old English town — men with names like Horton, Tuthill, Booth, Case and Wells. And men whose histories in America had begun when they got off a boat a few years before.

Perched on the granite pedestal rich with names is the concrete statue of a soldier. Clutching the barrel of his rifle with both hands, he is the vision of a man who has seen men die, seen whole regiments slaughtered in the course of a long, bloody day.

"When you look at the records, you can see that many of the enlistment dates are the same, or just a few days apart," says Southold Town historian Antonia Booth. In an old ledger she keeps in her office are the names of dozens of men who enlisted on one day — Aug. 21, 1862 — and formed the heart of a new regiment, the 127th New York, Company H. "They went to the Presbyterian church in Southold on that day and heard a call for enlistment and signed up."

On Long Island, monuments to American wars and to those who fought in them are as ubiquitous as church steeples and baseball fields. They honor soldiers from the Revolution to Vietnam. Some are grand, flooded with light at night, towering over the land around them, unveiled with great fanfare and speeches by politicians and veterans. Others are small, weatherworn and off the beaten track. They sit by roads and in town parks, seldom attracting more than a few curious people. These monuments have stories, too, but not many people know of them, or look at the names carved on them, never connecting the flesh-and-blood histories of men who lived in their towns and went off to war to people who might live there today.

This is the story of one of those monuments, the Civil War memorial in Southold. It was erected in 1887 with great fanfare, parades and speeches. In a town that was then nearly 250 years old, the day of the unveiling was one of the biggest in its long history. On that day, hundreds of people stopped what they were doing and walked or rode in their buggies to stand around the monument and hear all 83 names read out loud. As they listened, drums played and bugles sounded, and the sweet music floated across the surrounding farmland like the ringing of church bells. On that day, everyone knew someone whose name was carved in granite.

Suffolk County Historical Society

Farmer-turned-soldier Henry W. Prince.

Beyond being a biography of a war memorial, this is also the story of one of those 83 names, a young farm boy who enlisted in the U.S. Army that summer of 1862. His name is carved on the south side of the pedestal, third from the top — H. W. Prince. By the time the war ended in 1865, Henry Prince would know that 29 men from his hometown — out of a total of 109 who enlisted — had been killed.

Prince was one of the lucky ones. He came home.

* * *

Late in the summer of 1862, when the war was going badly for the North, a charismatic man named Stewart Lyndon Woodford came out from Brooklyn to drum up support for the war. Accounts say he was a powerful speaker, and dozens of men of enlistment age came to hear him sermonize on why they should fight for the Union. Woodford had a reason to come to Southold — his mother, Susan, was a Terry, who were among the first Europeans to settle there. His ancestors were buried in the handsome cemetery that sat next to the church.

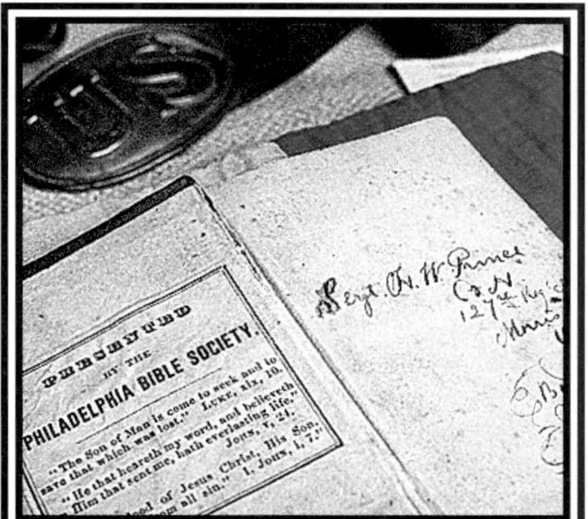

Newsday Photo / Bill Davis

On the first page of one of his diaries, Prince notes the places he has been.

On Aug. 21, dozens of men lined up to sign the enlistment ledger. One of them was Edward Foster Huntting, whose grandfather, the Rev. Jonathan Huntting — a tall, square-shouldered preacher remembered as having a stern countenance and a grave demeanor — had for 22 years been the church's minister. Another enlistee that day was Prince, who was 23 years old and bored with farm chores. Over the next two weeks, as Woodford crisscrossed the town, 109 men enlisted.

By all accounts, Prince was an ordinary young man fated to witness history up close. His father, Orrin, was a fisherman who, when his son was 10, bought a 30-acre farm that sat on a bluff overlooking Long Island Sound, just east of the Horton's Point Lighthouse. Even as he farmed his new land, Orrin continued to fish, running seine nets in the Sound and bay so he could catch enough bunker to use as fertilizer on his fields.

The family grew potatoes, wheat, corn, oats, rye and barley. The young Henry cut wood, husked corn, hauled manure and bunker to the fields, and helped with the butchering. Many days he would accompany his father fishing and helped him set his seine nets. When he was 17, he went to work in a Brooklyn grocery store that sold the Prince farm's potatoes. But after two winters in Brooklyn, he came home.

Even as a teenager, Prince was a prolific writer. Boxes of his diaries, journals and letters are part of an extraordinary collection housed at the Suffolk County Historical Society in Riverhead. At 14, he wrote his first entry: "Henry W. Prince's diary begun 28th Apl., 1854, Southold, L.I., State of New York." Two weeks later, while visiting his great-grandfather's farm in Orient, he recorded an eclipse of the sun. He wrote almost up to his death in 1925 — writings that chronicle his life on a farm, as a fisherman, Civil War soldier, town businessman, elected official, banker and small-town man with a keen eye. Perhaps no man of his time on Long Island ever wrote down so much about what he saw, what he heard, and how he felt.

All of his writings were collected by Helen Prince, who lives in Southold and whose husband was a descendant. She organized the collection, prepared indexes to help researchers, and enclosed Prince's precious Civil War letters — written in ink on folded paper while he sat in camps across the South — in folders for their preservation.

Prince first met Woodford when he spoke in Orient that summer of 1862. Prince went again to hear him at the Presbyterian church on the night of Aug. 21, and this time Henry was one of 23 young men to walk up to the altar and ink his name on enlistment papers. They and others formed the nucleus of a new company — H, which was affiliated with the 127th New York Regiment. A few days later he traveled to Manhattan to be sworn in. From there, he wrote home, addressing his letter, "Good Morning, Mother."

"I now must go to head quarters at 814 Broadway, from there to Staten Island and the future with our God," he wrote. "I expect we will go to Virginia, so do not think it strange if it is a week or 2 before you hear from me. I think the Rebellion will soon be

This article first appeared in Long Island Life on May 25, 1997.

A farm boy's letters bring history to life

crushed. Don't worry about me. I have the same protector as if I was Home. Give my love to all, from your Son, Henry."

Life in the Army was a shock to a young man used to eating well and living comfortably. At a camp on Staten Island, wrote Helen Prince in an introduction to a published collection of Prince's letters, "they were marched to a large cookhouse, and after waiting their turn by companies, were given a cup of tea and a slice of bread . . . They slept at night in crowded rows on a hard barracks floor, the tiers of bunks, three high, not sufficient for their number . . . The men were soon issued their clothing, which consisted of overcoat, pants, blouse, two woolen shirts, two pair of woolen drawers, two pair of heavy woolen socks, heavy cowhide shoes, woolen blanket and a rubber blanket with a slit in the middle so it could be worn as a cape when it rained."

Within a few days, Prince was aboard a crowded train en route to Washington, D.C., and the bloody war beyond.

Just before Christmas, Prince wrote home, boasting that he had met a large group of "Southold friends," including Oliver Vail, who was now an Army captain. Even as he told his parents he had been promoted to corporal, he said he was losing faith in the war effort.

"I have but little faith in our government," he wrote. "I am afraid we are ruined soldiers, are getting very tired of this war. The soldiers are Patriotic, would fight better if our Generals were better. It is not the men's fault, but

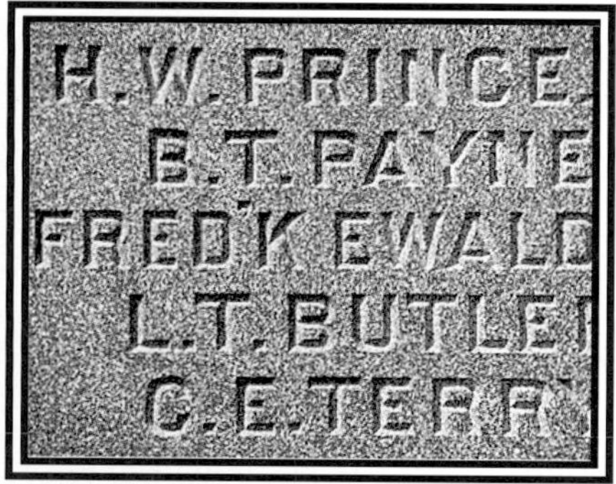

Prince's name is among those of 83 local men on the memorial.

there is a wrong somewhere. But I trust something will yet be done."

Throughout the fall and into early winter, Prince stayed in a camp in Virginia, close to Washington. Occasionally, according to his letters, his company was rousted out of its boredom and sent chasing rebel troops, but there were no conflicts. All the while, he wrote home, telling his family everything he saw, from the farm animals to the weather. In return, he received letters and fat packages from his family.

In a long letter to his parents dated Jan. 1, 1863, he wrote that he spent New Year's Day eating smoked eels his mother had mailed from Southold, and he wondered out loud if they had spent the day at a friend's house, as they always did. And he brought up a subject evidently dear to his heart — slavery.

"Today, Lincoln's Proclamation goes into effect," he wrote, referring to the Emancipation Proclamation, which freed slaves — on paper, at least — in the Confederate states. "I am afraid it will not do much good as our armies don't seem to succeed very well. I trust something will be done by spring, but see very little to encourage us. I put very little confidence in men. The North is desperately wicked as well as the South, but Slavery is a curse."

On Nov. 17th, having been moved for months around the South like a pawn in a bloody game, Prince wrote his mother from South Carolina: "As this is my 24th birthday, I will devote part of the day in writing to you. I can hardly realize that I am so old. 24 years ago today I expect you felt proud of your Boy Baby. Do you rejoice today that he is a soldier in his country's service? Many changes have taken place since my first birthday. God only knows how many of us that are alive today will see 24 years more. All is in the dark."

Nine days later, Company H celebrated the nation's first Thanksgiving — named a national holiday on orders of President Lincoln — with a shooting competition. In a letter written in early January, 1864, he wrote his mother how happy he was with the Christmas gifts she had sent him — an orange, a pear, some candy and a shirt.

And later that month, he informed his mother that blacks would soon be allowed to fight in their own regiments. "I believe it right and I am glad the Negro can fight for his freedom," he wrote. A few days later, in another letter home, he said his company had attended a poetry reading, "followed by a debate about the white man's treatment of the Negroes compared to that of the Indian. The Negro was considered to have fared better."

By midsummer, 1864, Prince was writing home to ask about the family's potato crop. He was bored stiff, writing home every few days as well as jotting down his thoughts in his journal. On Aug. 15, he wrote that he had received a copy of the funeral service back in Southold of a soldier with whom he had enlisted on that day in August, 1862 — Edward Huntting, the preacher's grandson. He was killed Feb. 20, 1864, two months shy of his 21st birthday. The town ledger kept in Booth's office in Southold reads "his body was left on the field and nothing more is known of it. This was his first (and last) battle."

Late in the fall, still in South Carolina, Prince, in a letter to his mother, said he yearned for a "glorious peace," and he said he missed "my native Isle and those I love." Then the second national Thanksgiving came around, and he noted that he ate sweet potatoes and chicken. In a letter back to him, his

Newsday Photo / Bill Davis

Route 25 memorial to Southold's contribution to the war.

parents told him his aunt in Southold had died and the year's potato crop was dismal, portending a hard, cash-poor winter. The year 1864 was nearly over.

Soon, the 127th — with Woodford, the man who had traveled to Southold to recruit troops, as its commander — was sent into action against rebel forces guarding railroad lines near Charleston. The regiment now included the 55th Massachusetts, a black regiment. Blood was being shed, and Prince saw it and wrote about it both in his journal and in letters home. In one hot battle, the 127th lost 57 men; Company H lost three.

In early December, four members of Company H were killed and 24 wounded in another fight. In a letter to his parents, Prince wrote of a "terrible but glorious victory . . . Thanks to Divine Providence that I am alive this morning." For years, Prince's family kept a pair of drawers with a bullet hole through them that he was wearing on the day of the fight.

By February, the war nearly over, Prince wrote his mother that he had met General William Tecumseh Sherman, whose troops had burned their way into the deep South, who he said "looks more like a farmer than so good a general." And he mentioned the death of another Southold soldier, George Latham, of Orient, who, like Prince, had enlisted on Aug. 21, 1862. The Lathams still farm in Orient.

The war ended while Prince was stationed in Charleston. He was there when he heard, on April 19, that Lincoln had been assassinated. By June, Prince wrote "To All at Home" that he would soon be returning. He was mustered out of the Army on June 30 and boarded a steamer for New York.

On July 10, Prince set foot in Southold for the first time in nearly three years. On the 15th, he and his father went fishing.

* * *

It took a few years to get his bearings, but soon Henry Prince was earning a good living as a traveling salesman. In November, 1867, he married a Mattituck girl, Jenny Wells. Their first child, Anna, was born in 1870. Soon, he and his brother, Orrin, bought a general-merchandise store in town.

With so many dead in a small town — 29 in less than three years,which meant funerals averaged one a month — the war's effects on Southold were not easily forgotten. In 1883, a group called the Ladies Monumental Union began to raise funds for the purchase of a monument. It took four years to reach their goal of $1,800, the purchase price of the statue and granite pedestal — four years of potluck suppers, plays and concerts, with anyone giving $50 or more getting his name published in the local newspaper.

Town records show that the group wanted a monument that had a base five feet square and a pedestal eight feet in height, to be made of "the best Maine granite" Atop that the soldier's figure was to be six feet high.

It was unveiled on May 30, 1887, 22 years after the war had ended. Hundreds of people showed up on that day, including Prince, his wife and their three children An honored guest was a 97-year-old veteran of the War of 1812 — Samuel S. Vail, who arrived in a carriage, an American flag draped across his lap. The name of his nephew, Oliver Vail, was carved near the bottom of a long list of names on the west side of the pedestal.

After a parade, a canvas shroud covering the statue was pulled down by Edith Prince, Henry's daughter, who was to live until 1980.

When the applause died down, speeches were delivered, and then each of the names were read out loud, one after another, a long, slow roll call.

Queens Borough President's Office

TIME MACHINE

PICTURING THE PAST AND PRESENT

Something Is Missing

Perhaps the most monumental structure to dominate the intersection of Jamaica Avenue and Parsons Boulevard, Jamaica, is not shown in either of these photos. It was the elevated subway tracks that ran down the avenue from 1918 to the late 1970s. In the background of the top photo, taken in about 1910 along Jamaica Avenue, are the spires of the Dutch Reformed Church, which still exists. The building in front housed the Jamaica Beef Co. In its place, the recent photo shows the Joseph P. Addabbo Federal Office Building, which dates from 1989. The 11-story building houses the Social Security Administration's Northeast Program Service Center and has a payroll of about 1,450 employees.

Behind the building on the right is Grace Church, built in 1862. Today, the area is anchored by York College and the Jamaica station of the Long Island Rail Road.

THEN & NOW

Newsday Photo / Ken Sawchuk

CHAPTER 6

City And Suburb

From the building of the Brooklyn Bridge to the summer White House at Sagamore Hill

The magnificent Brooklyn Bridge becomes the last great work of an age

Gateway to a Century

BY DREW FETHERSTON
STAFF WRITER

On the sunny afternoon of May 24, 1883, an ironmaker and political reformer named Abram Hewitt stepped to a podium to formally present the great new bridge over the East River to the mayors of New York City and Brooklyn.

The multitude that had assembled to celebrate the bridge's opening stretched far beyond the reach of Hewitt's voice. It filled adjacent neighborhoods to the rooftops, filled the decks of steamboats that almost carpeted the river, filled the deck of the bridge itself.

Hewitt, who had been been a government watchdog on the project, and who became New York's mayor in 1887, compared the structure to the pyramids. "The cities of New York and Brooklyn have constructed, and today rejoice in the possession of, the crowning glory of an age memorable for great industrial achievements."

In a sense, Hewitt missed the Brooklyn Bridge's significance: The splendid, soaring structure was less the crowning glory of his age than the cornerstone of the next, of the half-century in which America would become the most powerful nation on the planet and the envy of the world.

Still, Hewitt had every right to be impressed. He was describing what was then the longest suspension bridge in the world, a bridge whose stone towers were taller than every building in New York City except for the slender steeple of Trinity Church. Its four great cables each contained enough wire to stretch from New York to London. The project had taken more than 15 years to complete, had cost several lives and $15 million, had killed its designer and crippled his son.

And the bridge was, as Hewitt said, the last great work of an age. Willard Glazer, in his 1886 book "Peculiarities of American Cities," noted, "With the completion of this bridge the continent is entirely spanned, and one may visit, dry shod and without the use of ferry-boats, every city from the Atlantic to the Golden Gate."

Except for the swift and turbulent East River, all of the waters that flowed between the oceans had been spanned before John Roebling and his son, Washington Roebling, began work on the bridge. For Long Island, the bridge was a stimulant for growth — allowing easy access to the great marketplace of New York City and the nation beyond.

But the Brooklyn Bridge was more than a mere link in a transportation system. It was also a catalyst for change. When it opened, a correspondent from Harper's Magazine wrote: "The wise man will not cross the bridge in five minutes, nor in twenty. He will linger to get the good of the splendid sweep of the view about him."

Among the sights, he wrote, were "the marshes, rivers and cities of New Jersey stretching to Orange Mountain and the farther heights; the Palisades walling the mighty Hudson . . . And when he takes his walks about New York he can scarcely lose sight of what is now the great landmark which characterizes and dominates the city . . . "

Within a few years, the long vista stretching miles into New Jersey would be blocked by the great metropolis that replaced the three- and four-story City of New York, and the bridge would stand in the shadow of immense buildings. The modern world that it had helped to create would come to view the Brooklyn Bridge as an esthetic rather than an

National Archives Photo

The base of the center span of the Brooklyn Bridge as it appeared in 1881; the view across the East River is toward Manhattan.

LI HISTORY.COM

All installments and enhancements are available on the Internet at Newsday's http://www.lihistory.com.

Harper's Weekly, 1872

Brooklyn's Fulton Ferry, site of the Brooklyn Bridge, as it looked in 1750: Ferries were crowded, sometimes dangerous, and not always reliable in stormy weather.

Collection of Archibald S. Alexander Library, Rutgers University

John Roebling, left, was chosen to design and build the bridge, but never saw its completion. He died of tetanus in 1869, and his son, Washington Roebling, right, took over the project.

engineering triumph.

The idea of an East River bridge had been around long before there was technology to build one; legislation authorizing such a link was introduced in Albany in 1802.

Nine years later, an eccentric visionary named Thomas Pope offered to span the East River between Brooklyn and New York with what he called his Flying Pendant Lever Bridge, a timber rainbow that would soar 223 feet above the swift-running water.

Pope — whose business card identified him as an "architect and landscape gardener" — said the bridge could be built of wood alone to keep costs low.

Doubters he dismissed as being "under the influence of one of two things: namely, a total ignorance of the invention, or a contemptible opposition to its success." His confidence was not matched by any public enthusiasm. He left town to try his sales pitch — again unsuccessfully — in Philadelphia.

It was not that New Yorkers and their Long Island neighbors didn't want an East River bridge. Everyone was acutely aware of the dangers and incoveniences of crossing the river by ferry.

Commerce between the city and the Island had long before made the ferry service a lucrative, government-regulated business. The problem was that population had quickly outstripped technology: When Pope arrived, people were crossing just as they had in 1679, when the Dutch missionary Jasper Dankaerts made the trip "in a rowboat, as it happened, which, in good weather and tide, carries a sail."

Nathaniel S. Prime, in his 1845 "History of Long Island," recalled a time, early in his century, when the ferries offered "oar-barges for foot-passengers and sprit-sail boats for horses and carriages." Prime recalled times when he "waited from morning to night on the Brooklyn side, in a northeast storm, before any boat ventured to cross to the city." Ice and storms claimed boats, goods and lives with depressing regularity.

But no one quite believed that Pope could deliver the graceful cantilever bridge — with revenue-producing warehouses, stores and houses built into its stone abutments — for the $144,000 he said it would take. They instead put their faith in new horse-powered paddle-wheel boats that made their appearance in 1814, and the steam-powered marvels that followed almost immediately.

Steamboats made matters worse, in a manner now familiar to road planners: They encouraged the growth of Brooklyn, which quickly became the first suburb of New York as well as a prospering city in its own right.

In the 50 years after Pope proposed his bridge, the population of Kings County increased from about 8,000 to nearly 300,000. The ferry boats were crowded, carrying 32.8 million passengers in 1860 and 41.4 million in 1865. And the boats were still liable to be delayed by wind, fog or ice.

They could be dangerous, too. During the morning rush of Nov. 14, 1868, the

Please see **BRIDGE** on **Next Page**

Roebling's First Dream: The Queensboro

BY DREW FETHERSTON
STAFF WRITER

John Roebling was enthusiastic.

"No other part of the East River offers a locality so favorable to bridging," the great engineer wrote to the New York businessmen who proposed building a span to link Manhattan and Long Island.

But the East River bridge that so interested Roebling was not the Brooklyn Bridge that would be the cornerstone of his enduring fame. This span — proposed in 1856, more than a decade before the Brooklyn Bridge project took form in 1867 — was what would become the Queensboro Bridge.

Roebling had been thinking about an East River bridge since 1852. He quickly concluded that Blackwells Island — now Roosevelt Island — would make a perfect steppingstone for crossing the swift stream. One could build two bridges of manageable size — from Manhattan to Blackwells Island, and from the island to Long Island City — rather than one very long span.

It was far from an original idea. In October, 1836, a Jamaica weekly newspaper, the Long Island Democrat, reported that "a project has been lately started, to build a suspension bridge over Long Island Sound near Hallet's Cove or Ravenswood." The cove is near the north end of Blackwells Island; Ravenswood is near the center.

Such a link, the editor wrote, "would soon

Please see **QUEENSBORO** on Page **216**

Newsday Archive

The Queensboro Bridge under construction: This was the East River bridge that first interested John Roebling.

Gateway To A New Century

BRIDGE from **Preceding Page**

ferry Hamilton collided with the Union as the latter was about to leave its slip on the Manhattan side. A news report spoke of "the crashing of timbers and the shrieks of the people . . . Among the shouts of men who were endeavoring to preserve order were the shrieks of the injured who were under the timbers." The accident injured 20 and killed a boy.

Yet when the bridge project first stirred, it attracted scant attention. The Jan. 7, 1867, edition of the Brooklyn Eagle noted, halfway through a column of Albany political doings, that State Sen. Henry C. Murphy of Brooklyn had introduced a bill "to construct a bridge over the East River . . . sufficiently high over the river to enable the largest ships to pass under. The entire length to be somewhere in the neighborhood of three thousand feet; the work to be undertaken by a private company, and then the two cities to have the option of buying at the actual cost. The measure meets with general favor."

The Eagle, which Murphy had founded in 1841, moved on quickly to legislation concerning a proposed parade ground in Flatbush.

But the harsh winter of 1866-67 spurred public support for the bridge. "There were days in that season when passengers from New York to Albany arrived earlier than those who set out the same morning from their breakfast-tables in Brooklyn for their desks in New York," Harper's Magazine noted. The river at times was so blocked with ice that intrepid souls could only cross it on foot.

By the end of May, Murphy's bill was law, the New York and Brooklyn Bridge Co. held its first board meeting, the Eagle was openly enthusiastic and John Roebling had been selected to design and build the bridge for an estimated $7 million, not including the cost of land for the approaches.

Frank Leslie's Illustrated Newspaper

Huge caissons were used in building the bridge. Visitors, left, wait for air pressure to equalize before climbing into a caisson, right.

Roebling, 60, had considerable experience in building bridges. In 1866, he finished the Cincinnati suspension bridge, with a 1,057-foot main span, over the Ohio River, and in 1855 completed an 821-foot suspension bridge over the Niagara River gorge. He had also been consulted, in 1856, by a group that hoped to build an East River bridge to Queens over Blackwells — now Roosevelt — Island.

Experience was an excellent qualification then in bridge-building, which was a far from fully developed art. Throughout the 19th Century, and well into this one, many bridges fell down. In 1854, winds blew down the Wheeling Bridge, a 6-year-old, 1,010-foot suspension bridge over the Ohio River. Roebling had been an unsuccessful candidate for the Wheeling job.

He had been studying the possibility of building an East River bridge for more than a decade: One account suggests he thought of the idea in 1852, on the deck of an ice-bound Brooklyn ferry.

Now he had his chance. He first examined three possible routes for the bridge. Even then, Roebling foresaw other bridges over the river — the next, he thought, would probably go to Williamsburg, and the third would cross to Long Island City over Blackwells Island. History would prove him correct.

Chatham Square and Canal Street were examined, but Roebling chose a site next to City Hall as the landing place for the Manhattan end of the bridge — it was, he reasoned, far enough downtown to be little affected when the future Williamsburg bridge was built.

The Brooklyn end was sited in deference to geography, on the low ground where Brooklyn Heights abruptly fell away. The span would be 1,595.5 feet, suspended between masonry towers 276 feet, 8 inches tall. The suspension cables would be set in huge stone anchorages, each 102 feet by 132 feet, each rising about 90 feet — which made them taller than most buildings in New York City at the time. The Manhattan anchorage covers the spot on Cherry Street where George and Martha

Taking Shape

Long Island

1869. Alexander Stewart purchased 7,000 acres and established Garden City.

1870. St. John's College established in Brooklyn.

1870-72. The Steinway piano factory was established in Astoria.

1874. Prospect Park, designed by Frederick Law Olmsted and Calvert Vaux, was finished.

May 24, 1883. After 13 years of construction, the Brooklyn Bridge opened.

United States

March 30, 1867. United States bought Alaska from Russia for $7.2 million.

May, 1868. President Andrew Johnson was acquitted of impeachment charges.

July 28, 1868. The 14th Amendment, which granted citizenship to blacks, was passed.

Oct. 8-11, 1871. Chicago fire killed more than 250 people. It destroyed an area of 3 1/2 square miles and left nearly 100,000 people homeless.

June 25, 1876. Sitting Bull and his Sioux Indians defeated Gen. George Custer and the 7th Cavalry at the Battle of Little Big Horn.

March 7, 1877. Alexander Graham Bell received the first U.S. patent for the telephone.

July 2, 1881. President James Garfield was shot in a Washington, D.C., railroad station by a disgruntled office seeker.

The World

March 15, 1867. Austria and Hungary are united under one monarch.

1869. Leo Tolstoy finished "War and Peace."

Nov. 17, 1869. The Suez Canal opened.

May 10, 1871. France and Germany signed a peace treaty to end the Franco-Prussian War. Under the terms of the treaty, Germany took possession of the provinces of Alsace and Lorraine.

Nov. 13, 1871. An expedition led by U.S. journalist Henry Morgan Stanley found David Livingstone in Central Africa.

July 13, 1878. A treaty signed at San Stefano took a large portion of the Ottoman Empire in Europe and divided it among the Russians, Austrians and British.

March 13, 1881. Czar Alexander II was killed by a bomb in St. Petersburg.

1865 — 1870 — 1875 — 1880

Washington lived in 1789 and 1790, when he was president and New York was the capital.

John Roebling never saw any of this built: On June 28, 1869, he was looking over the Brooklyn tower site from the adjacent wooden ferry slip. The pilings shifted as a boat nudged its way into the slip. Roebling's right foot was caught between two beams and partially crushed. Tetanus developed and he was dead within a month. His son, Washington Roebling, 32, took over the project.

The towers would stand in the river, which dictated the way they would be built. The river bed was filled with loose mud, silt and stones, which would have to be removed so that the tower foundations would stand on firm ground or bedrock.

To reach this foundation level, the towers were built on caissons, which are basically wooden boxes, open at the bottom. As the towers rose atop the caissons, laborers removed the muck from within. The caissons thus sank lower and lower until they found a firm foundation.

Caissons had been used since about 1850 — indeed, as Washington Roebling assumed command, they were being used to construct bridges over the Mississippi River at St. Louis and the Missouri at Omaha.

But nothing of the scale of the Brooklyn Bridge caissons had ever been attempted. The top of the Brooklyn caisson was 102 feet by 168 feet — almost three times the size of an original Levittown building lot. The Manhattan caisson was 172 feet by 102 feet. Its top was 22 feet thick, built of huge timbers of dense southern pitch pine. The walls were 8 to 9 feet thick at the tops and tapered to 8 inches at the iron-shod bottom edge. The bolts and metal bracings alone weighed 250 tons. They were three times the size of the caissons being used in the Mississippi bridge project. Each was divided into six sections by sturdy bulkheads. Headroom within them was 14 feet.

These massive structures were built at the Webb & Bell shipyard in Greenpoint, towed four miles downriver, and positioned between carefully placed pilings. The great stone blocks of the towers were placed on their backs, and they began their journey toward bedrock.

The caissons functioned like diving bells. Compressed air was pumped into them to keep them from simply sinking into the muck. As depth increased, so too did the air pressure. Workers entered and left through an air lock.

An illustration shows how master mechanic E.F. Farrington made the first crossing on the Brooklyn Bridge via a chair suspended on a rope between the two towers in 1876.

Harper's New Monthly Magazine, 1876

Conditions in the caissons were hellish and dangerous. Compression made the air hot and extremely humid, so there was always a haze and the temperature never fell below 80 degrees. Illumination came from calcium lights — the famous "limelights" of the theater. Every object quickly acquired a slimy coating of mud.

A Harper's Magazine journalist wrote of a visit to the caissons, describing the air lock as "an iron can or jar of large size, sufficient for a dozen men to stand in erect . . . like meats for preservation." When compressed air was let into the lock, "the compression of the common air . . . in the chamber develops an oppressive heat, like that of an oven, while the increasing density of the air begins to be painfully felt in pressure upon the organs of respiration, and particularly in the ears."

One visitor "was so much overcome by the heat . . . that he insisted on being let out before the lock was filled." The relatively cooler air of the caisson came as a relief.

Inside the caisson, pulses speeded up, then slowed to as few as 15 beats per minute. It was difficult to speak and impossible to whistle because the muscles of respiration were unequal to the task. The tongue felt slow and cumbersome, the skin itched, noses bled easily. Deep voices became shrill trebles, a powder blast — used to pulverize boulders — had the sharp crack of a pistol shot.

But all of that was merely discomfort. A far more dangerous foe lurked in the gloomy recesses of the caissons: Under pressure, the bloodstream dissolved enormous quantities of gases. When a worker returned to normal pressure through the airlock, this overload of gases came out of solution and formed bubbles in the bloodstream, causing excruciating pain and damage to the joints.

It was called caisson disease or "the bends," but it wasn't understood. It was supposed that pressure merely drove the blood deeper inside the body, leading to congestion in the spinal cord and brain. Medical opinion of the day could only suggest that workers should eat and rest well.

Caisson disease crippled even Washington Roebling, who thereafter had to direct construction from his home in Brooklyn Heights, with the considerable assistance of his wife, Emily Warren Roebling.

The Brooklyn caisson was filled with concrete in March, 1871, after a fire damaged it at a depth of about 43 feet in the river bed, in ground that was considered firm enough to support the tower. The Manhattan caisson was built, and moved into place in November. Work continued there until May, 1872, when the caisson reached a depth of 78.5 feet. Caisson disease by that time was so severe that several workers died. Roebling stopped digging, concluding that the sand below would sup-

Please see **BRIDGE** on **Next Page**

1890. Biological laboratory was established in Cold Spring Harbor.

1892. The Shinnecock Hills Golf Club opened.

1897. The Brooklyn Museum was opened.

1898. Camp Black, near Mineola, and Camp Wikoff, near Montauk, served as training grounds for troops in the Spanish-American War.

1898. Queens became part of New York City.

Jan. 1, 1899. Nassau County was established.

Oct. 28, 1886. The Statue of Liberty was unveiled in New York Harbor.

April 22, 1889. The Oklahoma land rush started with the firing of a starter's gun.

May 18, 1896. In Plessy vs. Ferguson, the Supreme Court ruled that racial segregation was legal if equal facilities were offered to both races.

Feb. 15, 1898. The battleship Maine exploded in Havana harbor, killing 260 seamen. The Spanish-American War started three months later.

Aug. 12, 1898. Spain agreed to peace terms, ending the Spanish-American War.

Feb. 26, 1885. At the Congress of Berlin, the European powers divided up Central and East Africa.

1891. Arthur Conan Doyle published "The Adventures of Sherlock Holmes."

April, 1896. Athens hosted the first modern Olympic Games.

Sept. 19, 1899. Alfred Dreyfus, the Jewish officer who claimed that he was wrongly convicted of espionage, was formally pardoned by the French government.

1885 1890 1895 1900

Newsday / Linda McKenney

Roebling's First Dream

QUEENSBORO from Page **213**

make Hallet's Cove rival Brooklyn in population."

In the following two years, the bridge proposal acquired form in articles published in The Family Magazine: It would have three 700-foot suspension spans — the center one would cross Blackwells Island — and a 45-foot-wide roadway. It was to be 120 feet above the water, and the Manhattan end would be somewhere between 65th and 75th Streets. It would cost between $500,000 and $600,000.

Nothing happened, though, until the financiers approached Roebling and invited him to design a bridge over Blackwells Island.

Roebling obliged with drawings of a very slender bridge composed of two 800-foot suspension spans linked by a 500-foot cantilever section over the island. The roadway would be a mere 22 feet wide (the inner roadway on the Queensboro Bridge is about 51 feet wide), and would be flanked by two 6-foot-wide walkways outside the suspension cables. The cost, Roebling said with typical precision, would be $1,216,740.

But the project stalled, and Roebling in 1857 wrote to Abram Hewitt, an industrialist who would become New York's mayor in 1887, suggesting that a bridge be built to Brooklyn. Hewitt caused the letter to be published in New York.

Hewitt, who later became a government watchdog and trustee of the Brooklyn Bridge project, credited the Civil War with making that bridge possible, since it "accustomed the nation to expenditures on a scale of which it had no previous conception."

Newsday Archive

Mayor George B. McClellan rides in the first car in a procession at opening ceremonies for the Queensboro Bridge on March 30, 1909. The toll booth was on the Manhattan side.

Political corruption followed, Hewitt said: "In the city of New York . . . the government fell into the hands of a band of thieves, who engaged in a series of great and beneficial public works, not for the good they might do, but for the opportunity which they would afford to rob the public treasury."

One of the great public works born of corrupt impulses, according to Hewitt, was the Brooklyn Bridge, which the Tweed Ring infiltrated in a quest for patronage jobs and outright graft. Powerful politicians thus had a vested interest in that project.

They had no such interest in the Blackwells Island bridge, and the results were predictable: Although the Queens bridge company received its state charter on the same day as the Brooklyn group — April 16, 1867 — the span across Blackwells Island remained a paper dream while the Brooklyn Bridge became granite-and-steel reality.

The Blackwells Island bridge was of particular interest to a series of top executives of the Long Island Rail Road, which hoped to run trains from its Sunnyside yard across the bridge, to link up with the New York Central tracks.

But the project was beset by delays. In 1877, the bridge's most powerful backer, piano maker William Steinway, stepped down as chairman of the New York and Long Island Bridge Co., to be replaced by William Rainey, a steamship operator who agreed to invest $30,000. The bridge would bring the ruin of his hopes and his health during the next two dozen years.

It wasn't until March 25, 1881, when the Brooklyn Bridge was nearing completion, that the New York and Long Island Bridge Co. awarded a $6.4-million contract to a Philadelphia company to start work.

"It is only when the narrow East River is crossed and free, open, high, healthy Long Island is reached that the poor man's land is found, a place of refuge from tenement life," Rainey wrote a few week later. "Give these cheap-home seekers a chance, and they will gravitate to it as by a natural law."

Work began on the first pier in the Queens side of the river, but the venture ran out of money even before the Brooklyn Bridge opened in May, 1883.

Construction resumed in 1895, but litigation and the death of Austin Corbin, president of the Long Island Rail Road and a prominent backer, halted it almost immediately. The *coup de grace* came in 1901, when the city decided to build the bridge itself.

Rainey was a guest at the opening ceremonies for the bridge in 1909. The ailing 84-year-old swallowed whatever bitterness he felt and pronounced it "a grand bridge, much grander than the one I had in mind. It will be of great service to thousands in the years to come." He was dead within a year. In 1912, the city acquired land that would have been the Queens end of his bridge, and named it Rainey Park.

As Rainey had foreseen, the bridge helped turn Queens into a boom town, with real estate development spreading like ripples in a pond from the plaza at its end. When the bridge opened, Queens' population was 275,000; it grew to 469,000 by 1920 and topped a million by 1930.

A herald of this expansion was to be found in the person of Elizabeth Augenti, 19, who was chosen "Queen of the Queensboro Bridge" for the opening ceremonies. Augenti worked for Long Island Guarantee Trust, a bank that was assembling tracts of land for development. Her job was to pose as a buyer of modest means, to keep the bank's price low.

Gateway To A New Century

BRIDGE from **Preceding Page**

port the tower.

By July, 1876, both towers were finished. By then, the project had survived a bad national financial panic in 1873, and the strong scent of scandal from having powerful politicians — including the notorious Tammany leader William M. (Boss) Tweed — as major shareholders in a venture that was mostly financed with public money. Brooklyn had subscribed to $3 million worth of bridge stock and New York had agreed, rather grudgingly, to put in half that amount. The cities would later take over the whole project, and their respective outlays would more than triple.

But scandal and the slow pace of construction had hardly dampened public enthusiasm for the bridge. On Aug. 25, 1876, shortly after a loop of three-quarter-inch-diameter rope had been run around pulleys in the anchorages and over the two towers, E.F. Farrington, the bridge's master mechanic, became the first person to cross the river dry-shod.

He did so in a boatswain's chair, a board seat suspended by ropes at its corners. As he rose from the Brooklyn anchorage, Harper's Magazine reported, "his surprise was great, on looking down . . . to see the housetops beneath him black with spectators, the streets far below paved, as it were, with upturned faces . . . With the rushing rope hissing and undulating like a flying serpent through the air, the boom of cannon far below announced to [Farrington] that his intended private trip was a public triumph."

As he neared the end of his 22-minute journey, "the cannon roared, and the myriads of spectators swung their hats and cheered with wild excitement, while all the steamwhistles on land and sea shrieked their uttermost discordance."

Years of work followed, spinning the four giant cables (each made up of 5,434 small steel wires), building the river and side spans and approaches to a total length of 5,989 feet. In all, the bridge cost $15,099,263.56, according to a book-balancing done shortly after it was completed. Of that sum, about $3.8 million went to acquire land, so the construction cost was about $4.3 million over the original estimate of $7 million.

The labor of the men who built the bridge was cheaper than the stone that went into the structure: Labor costs were $2.4 million, while $2.1 million went for granite and $668,000 for limestone. Daily wages ranged from $1.75 for a laborer to $4 for a blacksmith or mason. The cost in workers lives isn't known — no records were kept — but estimates range from 20 killed to 40.

When it opened — on May 24, 1883, under a great shower of fireworks and a similarly extravagant outpouring of oratory — it cost a penny to walk across the pedestrian promenade and 10 cents to drive a one-horse wagon on the roadway. The original toll structure reflects a very different time: It cost 5 cents for a cow or horse to cross, 2 cents for a hog or a sheep.

Cable-driven railway cars started service in September, 1883; within two years, ridership had more than doubled, from 16,500 to 36,500 riders, and the cars were running 24 hours a day.

The cities grew and changed. In 1869 Brooklyn, with 400,000 inhabitants, had less than half the population of Manhattan. When the bridge opened, Brooklyn had 580,000 inhabitants; by 1898, this had grown to nearly 1 million. By 1930, Brooklynites outnumbered Manhattanites.

By then, other bridges spanned the East River — the Williamsburg in 1903, the Manhattan and Queensboro in 1909 — and the number of people who crossed the Brooklyn Bridge diminished, despite elimination of pedestrian tolls in 1891 and vehicle tolls in 1911. The peak year was 1907, when 426,298 crossed; by 1930, this number had dwindled to 171,110.

But its importance as a symbol never faltered. It became the subject of poetry, of song, of painting and photography. Its Gothic towers came to be as revered as those of the great medieval cathedrals.

Which proves that Hewitt was not wrong in all of his pronouncements on the day the bridge opened. He noted that it was "more than an embodiment of the scientific knowledge of physical laws." It was, he said — recalling the genius that had imagined and designed it, and the suffering that had been the human cost of its construction — "a monument to the moral qualities of the human soul."

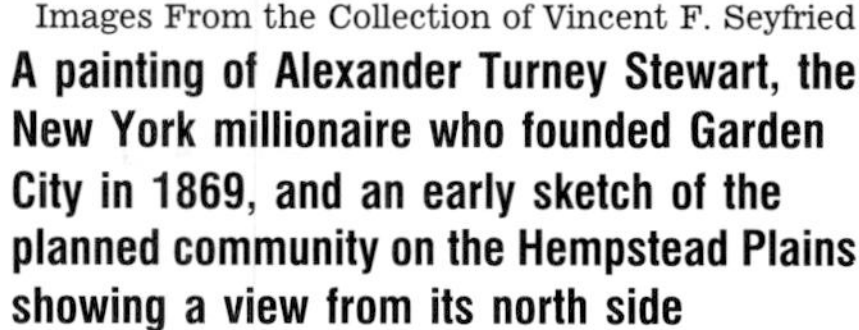

Images From the Collection of Vincent F. Seyfried

A painting of Alexander Turney Stewart, the New York millionaire who founded Garden City in 1869, and an early sketch of the planned community on the Hempstead Plains showing a view from its north side

Grazing land gives way to Garden City, one of the earliest planned developments

Home on the Plains

BY RHODA AMON
STAFF WRITER

In 1823, Alexander Turney Stewart was a 22-year-old immigrant sleeping in a room behind his dry goods store to save money. By 1848 he was a millionaire with a large marble store in Manhattan. In 1869 he founded a city.

It was a time when great fortunes could be amassed. It was also an Age of Idealism, when a perfect planned Eden also seemed achievable. Stewart bought what was left of the vast Hempstead Plains and created Garden City. He was one of the earliest developers to envision a model city on the open fields of Long Island.

To the west, Cord Meyer Jr., heir to his father's sugar-refining fortune, was visualizing a model community along Queens Boulevard that he would call Forest Hills. Twenty years later — but still a half century ahead of Levittown (and Betty Friedan, too) — developer Helen Marsh was creating a model village in western Nassau that she would call Belle Rose.

In the 1860s, on the Hempstead Plains where cattle still roamed, anything seemed possible. The plains, common pasturage for more than a century, were finally offered for sale in 1867. Charles T. Harvey of upstate Tarrytown, a backer of the New York City "El," put in a bid of $42 an acre, but no one knew what Harvey had in mind — an enormous cemetery or a jail?

Out of the blue came New York merchant Alexander T. Stewart with a dazzling offer of $55 an acre and a plan for a settlement with roads, buildings and homes. Harvey tried to outbid him, but Hempstead Town was sold on Stewart. For $395,328.35 cash he got 7,170 acres extending from Floral Park to Bethpage. The money was used to build a town poorhouse, purchase a town hall and to support the public schools.

The man with the vast fortune and the fire in the belly to build his own town was not an imposing figure. He was a small man with thin red hair and beard and a mild unassuming manner that belied his hard-driving business acumen.

He was born of Scotch Protestant parents in Lisburn, Northern Ireland, in 1801, a few weeks after his farmer father died of tuberculosis. His mother remarried two years later and emigrated to America with her new husband, leaving her young son to be raised by his grandfather, John Torney. Torney sent the boy to a small English academy, hoping to prepare him for the ministry, but Stewart had other ideas. In 1818, two years after his grandfather died, he sailed for America.

He tried school teaching for a couple years, then made a quick round trip to Belfast in 1822 to claim a $10,000 inheritance and make his first business purchase: a package of Irish lace trimmings and muslin. He married Cornelia Clinch, daughter of a wealthy New York ship chandler, and began his merchandising career.

The schoolteacher quickly learned the tricks of his new trade and reportedly invented the "remnant sale." He would buy up the stock of competitors ruined by fire, add his own leftovers and hold a sidewalk sale. By the time he was ready to buy part of the Hempstead Plains, Stewart had built the world's largest retail establishment — his six-story Great Iron Store (later Wanamaker's). He had worldwide purchasing outposts and was said to own more New York City real estate than any man except William Astor. He also amassed a large art collection that he displayed in his Fifth Avenue mansion. A staunch supporter of the Union during the Civil War, he was tapped for secretary of the Treasury by the Grant administration in 1868, but not confirmed because of his great business interests.

Long Island historian Vincent F. Seyfried notes that Stewart was not a philanthropist on the scale of an Andrew Carnegie — perhaps he was not as burdened with guilt as the robber barons of his day. During the Irish potato famine of 1848, Stewart sent a shipload of provisions to his native Lisburn, and invited young people to take passage free on the returning vessel — 139 came and Stewart found jobs for them all. He sent a similar shipload to the textile workers of Paris during the Franco-Prussian War and $50,000 to the victims of the great Chicago fire.

But his whole heart was in his municipal plan, and he was adept at promoting it. Harper's Weekly predicted that the "Hempstead Plain, hitherto a desert, will be made to bloom like a rose . . ." Only The World in 1870 cautioned against Stewart's being a one-man "landlord, mayor and alderman, in fact the whole municipality."

Stewart and his architect, John Kellum, laid out the town and graded 16 miles of streets and avenues. It included a central park bordered by a railroad station, stores, homes and a hotel. He built a railroad connecting his town with the city and with his brickyards in Farmingdale. He built a waterworks. He bought out the stock of the historic Prince Nurseries in Flushing and hauled 30,000 trees to his town.

Home-building was temporarily slowed by Kellum's death in 1871, but Stewart pushed on. The first 12 "fine villa residences" cost $17,000 each and rented for $1,200 annually. He also built $5,000 cottages to rent to his workmen at $300 a year.

Nothing was sold; all stores and homes were leased. Stewart was determined to keep control of his community. The village was slow to fill up, possibly because Stewart's insistence on retaining ownership of everything went against the American ethos of individual home ownership.

He died in 1876, his dream village uncompleted. Almost 100 houses had been built but half were vacant. The undeveloped areas would become Levittown and Bethpage. Stewart had no children. His widow endowed the Episcopal Cathedral of the Incarnation as a memorial to her husband, making Garden City a cathedral town. Then a strange thing happened: Stewart's body was kidnaped before it could be moved to a crypt of the cathedral. A century later the body snatching remains a mystery.

One story holds that Judge Henry Hilton, Stewart's executor, declined to pay the $200,000 ransom demanded by the ghouls but deluded Cornelia Stewart into believing the body had been recovered. Another unconfirmed account had the widow negotiating on her own and recovering the body for $20,000.

After Cornelia Stewart's death in 1886, a bitter court battle between her heirs and Hilton resulted in the formation of the Garden City Corp. in 1893, with her heirs as directors. They voted to sell rather than rent the houses and stores, and Garden City boomed. Famed architect Stanford White redesigned the Garden City Hotel and it became a center of Long Island society.

Whether or not Stewart's body lies in its crypt, the handsome well-planned community that he created remains his enduring monument.

From slave to entrepreneur, Samuel Ballton lived a life of struggle and triumph

The Reign of the Pickle King

BY BETH WHITEHOUSE
STAFF WRITER

It's nice to imagine an August day when the sun tackled the brim of Samuel Ballton's cap, tumbling onto his arms and his work clothes, leaving his face in the shadows.

It had been a pickle harvest like no other in the late 1800s. And how farmer Samuel Ballton might have looked, sitting in front of his house in Greenlawn, would have captured the essence of his life: some of it in sunshine, some of it in shadows.

The richest men in Greenlawn might well have been congratulating Ballton. Charles D. Smith slapping him on the back, perhaps. Alexander Gardiner shaking his head in awe.

And they weren't just rich men. They were rich, *white* men.

Samuel Ballton had been born a slave on a Virginia plantation. But he'd bested his northern friends in their own pursuit. Ballton had grown one million and a half pickles. One million. And a half! In one summer. Around Greenlawn they were calling him The Pickle King. Yes, pickles made Greenlawn famous. But Ballton had grown the pickles.

His wife, Rebecca, would have been there, too. Taking a break from her quilting, perhaps, to congratulate him or tease him for being too proud. Ballton would have turned his face, with its thick mustache and sideburns, to greet her. Rebecca knew Samuel like no one else. For she'd met him in the days of the shadows.

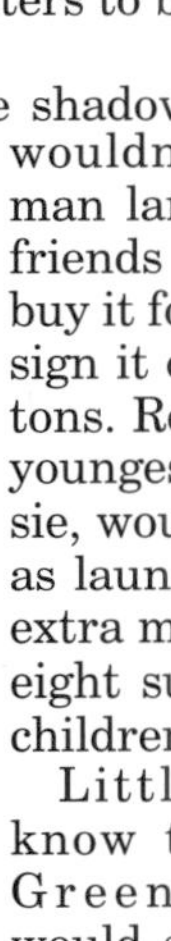

Centerport-Greenlawn Historical Association; Newsday Photo

A pickle processing plant near the railroad in an undated photo

Ballton had been born on New Year's Day in 1838. While Dixie revelers who threw back too much moonshine would shake their hangovers within days, Ballton was born with a headache that wouldn't go away for almost 30 years — he was born a slave.

He fell in love with Rebecca, a slave on a neighboring farm, and the sweethearts married in April of 1861, the same month the Civil War broke out. The young groom — on the slight side at just over 5-foot-7 — was soon hired out by the plantation to a Confederate detail working on the railroad in the Blue Ridge Mountains. One night, he and five other slaves hid flour and bacon under their shirts and fled north.

Ballton snuck back and forth over enemy lines to visit Rebecca. Once, when he was caught, he told the Rebel soldiers he missed his "massa" and was on his way back to his plantation. Calling him a "good nigger," they let him go. Ballton would tell the Brooklyn Eagle newspaper about this in a 1910 interview. He said that it had been one of the proudest moments of his life when he helped Rebecca escape to freedom with him.

In 1864, Ballton left his family in Alexandria, Va., and enlisted in the Fifth Massachusetts Cavalry — Colored of the Union Army and helped to secure his own permanent freedom. He saved his cavalry sword, and kept it along with the family Bible after The War Between the States ended in 1865.

Ballton used his new freedom to move to Greenlawn in 1873, when he was 35 years old. It was a typical Long Island town then. One hotel. One general store. One butcher shop.

In those days, the 4-inch green cucumbers grown in Greenlawn were called pickles even before they were processed and flavored with such tastes as dill or jalapeño, and sent off in wooden barrels to New York City grocery stores. Sure, pickles weren't a crop that could keep, not like the southern tobacco. But people pickled vegetables to hold them through the winter when fresh vegetables weren't available. Pickles were fine with Ballton, even though the processing plants that went up near the Long Island Rail Road tracks in the 1880s made the air smell something awful.

Ballton got his start with some of Greenlawn's wealthiest men. Smith was his first farm employer. Then he worked as a sharecropper for Gardiner, a descendent of the famous East End family, on his 600-acre estate west of the hamlet. With a cloth bag of seeds over one shoulder, he dropped seeds into holes he made with his toes.

On that day of the banner crop in the late 1800s, Ballton probably watched as his pickles were counted in the traditional way — workers grabbing two in one hand and three in the other to make five with each toss, and making a chalk mark on the side of the barrel for each five counted.

Ballton had always been driven and hatched a plan to earn even more money by buying pickles for a Boston pickle house, being paid a dime for each thousand. He also obtained personal loans from wealthy farmers like Gardiner. With that he bought property, recruiting former slaves and carpenters to build houses that he sold to farmers.

Sure there would be more shadows: Some people wouldn't sell a black man land, so his white friends would have to buy it for him, and then sign it over to theAlltons. Rebecca and their youngest daughter, Jessie, would have to work as laundresses to make extra money to feed the eight surviving Ballton children.

Little did Ballton know that six of his Greenlawn houses would still be standing along Boulevard Avenue, Taylor Avenue and Smith Street nearly 100 years later, and that his granddaughter, Berenice Easton, daughter of Jessie, would still live in one in 1998.

Berenice's sister, Virginia, would make a tape recording about her grandfather in 1982, several years before she died. "He could figure in his head better than I could do it on paper," she would say of the grandfather who never went to school a day in his life yet learned how to read and write. Others in the modern era would also admire Ballton. "They don't make houses like this anymore," said the engineer who checked out one of the Ballton houses when Bill and Helen Shaw bought the place in the 1970s.

Four years before his death, Ballton would take Greenlawn residents to task in a letter to the Long Islander newspaper, saying he had contributed to the development of Greenlawn's two thriving butcher shops, fine ice cream parlor and booming department store. Had other residents had "a little more grit and spunk, Greenlawn would be quite a little more advanced than it is," he would write.

By the time of Ballton's death on April 30, 1917, the 79-year-old man would live in a home estimated to be worth $5,500 and wired for electric lights. He would still be a devoted member of the William Lloyd Garrison chapter of the Veterans of the Grand Army of the Republic, and march each year in local veteran parades. Ballton would be buried in the black section of the Huntington Rural Cemetery on New York Avenue.

When the Pickle King died, the death of the pickle industry would be imminent as well. By the 1920s, a disease called "white pickle" blight turned cucumbers white and hard and stunted their growth at 2½ inches.

During his life, Ballton would never be a man who sat still for long. So it's nice to imagine that on a hot August day in the late 1800s, he was content to set for a minute, and soak up the sun's kindly rays.

Centerport-Greenlawn Historical Association; Newsday Photo

A painting of Samuel Ballton, who helped Greenlawn prosper through pickle production

A murder case with everything: sex, spurned love, mutilation and two lemons on the beach

'The Kelsey Outrage'

BY GEORGE DEWAN
STAFF WRITER

On Sept. 5, 1873, there was a funeral in Huntington for Charles Kelsey's legs. While the Second Presbyterian Church on Main Street was filled to overflowing, Kelsey's casketed legs — actually, the lower half of his body, from the second vertebra down — were left outside on the church lawn. Two ministers disagreed on whether the remains inside the coffin were really those of Kelsey. They were.

For the sleepy little village of about 2,500 people, "The Kelsey Outrage," as it came to be known, produced one of the most sensational murder cases Long Island had ever seen. It had all the ingredients: sex, mutilation, spurned love, tar-and-feathering, a missing body that later turned up floating in Oyster Bay Harbor — half of it, at least — murder charges against two leading Huntington citizens, and two lemons found on the beach.

Ten months before the funeral, Charles G. Kelsey was alive. But Nov. 4, 1872, was the last day of his life. All because of his infatuation with a plump and saucy young orphan, Julia Smith, who lived with her grandmother, Charlotte Oakley, in a large mansion on Main Street.

A well-educated, prosperous farmer in his 30s, an occasional teacher and a pedestrian poet, Kelsey had a terrible crush on Smith, who was just out of her teens. The long-haired, goateed Kelsey had met Smith as a teenager at their church, the Second Presbyterian, where he often taught Sunday school. The thought of the young lady taking up with an older man, a poet, no less, mightily displeased Oakley and other church members. It was said that Smith would put a lantern in the window to signal Kelsey when the coast was clear.

Smith turned fickle, however, switching her attentions to 25-year-old Royal Sammis, a member of a locally prominent family. They became engaged to be married.

Kelsey persisted, writing long and bitter love letters, filled with his poetry. In an incident that was said to have triggered the tar-and-feathering, Julia's aunt, Abby Smith — as she later told the story — traded bedrooms with her niece as a trap. One night Kelsey slipped through the window, lay down on the bed and placed his hand on Aunt Abby's breast, mistaking it for that of his beloved. She screamed and Kelsey escaped through the window.

The next evening, walking home from a political rally, Kelsey passed by the Oakley house, and he saw a light in the window. Coming closer, he was immediately accosted by a group of masked men in Oakley's backyard.

The assailants threw Kelsey to the ground, roughly cut his hair and beard and stripped him naked. After covering his body with hot tar, they dumped feathers over him, and exhibited him to the women who had gathered outside. Then released, he staggered up Spring Street to the house he shared with his sister, Charlotte. From that point on, Kelsey was missing.

The story was picked up by newspapers and spread far and wide. Huntington became known as "Tar Town." Residents lined up in two opposing factions, with the "Tars" supporting the punishment of Kelsey, the "Anti-Tars" opposing it.

The day after the tar-and-feathering, a fisherman found a blood-soaked shirt, a necktie and two lemons on the shore at Lloyd Neck, looking out over Cold Spring Harbor. After days of hearings, Justice of the Peace William Montfort charged three men with riot and assault: Royal Sammis, Claudius Prime and Dr. George Banks, who was a member of the Huntington School Board.

The search for Kelsey was halted for the winter. In the spring, the town trustees approved a reward of $750 to anyone finding his body.

In June, 1873, Julia Smith married Royal Sammis. The Brooklyn Eagle, in its Sept. 25 edition, referred to Sammis as the ringleader of the Tar group, and sneered at the newly married couple:

"No other American woman will grudge her the possession of such a husband as Royal Sammis, and he, on his part, may take comfort in the certainty that no American man will envy him his wife."

On Aug. 29, two men fishing in Oyster Bay Harbor between Moses Point and Plum Point spotted the lower half of what turned out to be Kelsey floating in the water. The legs were encased in a pair of black pants which were later identified as probably Kelsey's, and attached to the pants was a gold watch chain that was identified as his. On cutting off the trousers, tar and feathers were found still on the legs. The genitals had been hacked off.

A coroner's inquest in Oyster Bay began building a case against Sammis, Banks and others. Doctors testified that Kelsey had been alive when mutilated, and that he died from blood loss due to the emasculation. On Oct. 25, the coroner's jury concluded that Kelsey had been murdered, but it did not specify by whom. It said, however, that Sammis, Banks and four others "aided, abetted and countenanced by their presence the committal of the gross outrage and inhuman violence upon the person of Charles G. Kelsey."

Meeting in Riverhead on Nov. 7, a Suffolk County grand jury indicted Sammis and Banks for riot and assault. A few hours later, the grand jury indicted Sammis and his 19-year-old brother, Rudolph, for second-degree murder.

Then the story took one of its more bizarre twists. About the time of the grand jury indictments, the town board decided to pay the reward to the fishermen, but they offered only half of it, since only half of Kelsey's body had been found. The board later relented and paid out the entire $750.

The court cases against Kelsey's assailants dragged on and on. In October, 1875, a jury in Riverhead found Royal Sammis and George Banks not guilty of the riot and assault charges. The murder charges against the two Sammis brothers were never brought to trial. The upper half of Kelsey's body was never found.

As for the lemons on the beach, Charlotte Kelsey testified that she had asked her brother to buy them on his way home from the political rally.

Newsday Photo / Bill Davis

Huntington Historical Society; Newsday Photos

The barn, top, where Charles Kelsey was tarred and feathered, with illustration at left. Kelsey, illustrated above without a beard, was murdered because of his infatuation with Julia Smith, right, whose future husband, Royal Sammis, was accused of being one of the assailants.

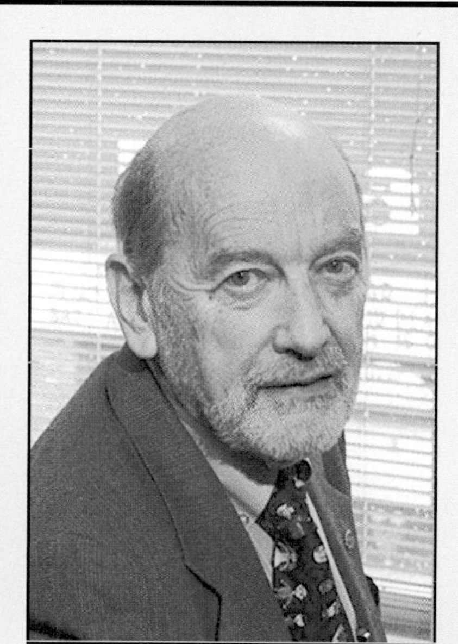

Newsday Photo / Dick Kraus

DESCENDANT

QUENTIN SAMMIS

Quentin Sammis, the owner of a major real estate-insurance business in Huntington, is the best-known member of one of the town's most prominent families. The alleged murderer Royal Sammis was his fourth cousin, twice removed.

"I want to disassociate myself from that story," Sammis said in a recent interview. "In everybody's ancestry there's a closet you don't want to open, somebody who's in jail or somebody who did something. "This is one of the things I don't like to talk about because it's not a very pleasant story."

Nassau County Museum Collection, Long Island Studies Institute

Shellfishermen work the Great South Bay from catboats about 1900 — the oyster industry's peak. Then overfishing, contamination and the opening of the Moriches Inlet struck.

South Shore shellfish were welcomed internationally and brought prosperity home

The Oyster Was Their World

BY BILL BLEYER
STAFF WRITER

In the closing days of the 19th Century, the streets of West Sayville were paved not with gold, but with oyster shells.

There was no oyster rush of speculators hoping to get rich quick in the shell game. But the prized taste of Great South Bay bivalves made them an international luxury and created a multimillion-dollar industry that made shellfish entrepreneurs rich and provided a living for thousands of others who dredged the bays and toiled in canning factories.

No one profited more than Jacob Ockers, "the Oyster King." The oystermen were primarily Dutch immigrants. Ockers, who was born in Holland in 1847 and brought to America three years later, began working on his father's oyster schooner when he was 8, and had his own boat before his 17th birthday.

Ockers ascended the oyster throne by buying shellfish and shipping them to New York City by water. In 1876 he set up an oyster processing plant in Oakdale and became the largest dealer of Blue Point oysters. The Blue Points were so highly valued that in 1908 the state Legislature passed a law defining them as oysters that had spent at least three months growing in Great South Bay. Ockers eventually controlled beds as far away as New Jersey and Massachusetts. Over time, he purchased in full or in part 10 schooners, becoming the first dealer to export large quantities of oysters to Europe — shipping 30,000 barrels there annually in the 1890s.

Shellfishing had begun centuries before with the Indians and expanded in the early 1800s as settlers dug oysters and clams from shallow water using open boats and long, iron-toothed rakes known as tongs. Rowboats gave way to sloops, and by 1890, there were 25 oyster processing factories known as shanties in Bay Shore, Oakdale, Sayville, Blue Point and Patchogue. The oysters were shucked and sent in wooden barrels to the city, first by boat and in the late 1860s by the Long Island Rail Road.

Not all of Great South Bay was equal when it came to supporting shellfish. Oysters and clams would set, or reproduce, better in the eastern part of the bay but would grow faster and fatter in the western part. The key was that the western end was saltier. Not only did the seed oysters grow better in the fresher water, but it discouraged the oyster's enemies such as drills and starfish.

About 1847, baymen began to use the east bay as a source of seed oysters they transplanted to the west bay. About this time Brookhaven Town officials began to lease two-acre underwater lots for $2 a year. To prevent poaching and the taking of undersized oysters, the towns began issuing licenses and appointed inspectors known as "toleration officers."

Historically, Long Island's baymen have had trouble tolerating government intervention. The most dramatic exception occurred in 1861 when they asked for help. Shellfishermen along the south shore of Queens and Brooklyn were incensed that competitors from New Jersey were digging clams along the New York shore under cover of darkness. When the clamdiggers' request for state intervention was ignored, they patrolled the beds with shotguns, and battles ensued. Ultimately the baymen notified the state that they were seceding. They organized the "Rockaway Republic" with Gil Davis as governor. New York Gov. Edwin Morgan sent the militia to arrest Davis. He was never caught but the poachers were scared off by the troops.

By the time of the Civil War, baymen had swapped their tongs for dredges — steel nets with teeth that scraped the oysters off the bottom. By 1901, all the local oystermen had boats with power dredges.

The Great South Bay oyster industry received a boost in the 1870s when Connecticut shellfishermen developed a system of growing seed oysters they shipped to Long Island for sowing. The industry's high point came in the 20 years bracketing the turn of the century when more than 150,000 barrels of oysters a year were being shipped from the shanties along the bay.

But overfishing, contaminated runoff and nature swamped the oyster business. On March 4, 1931, a new inlet opened opposite Moriches and within a few years, as the salinity increased, all the best seed beds had been wiped out by predators. Baymen switched to clams, and, on the East End, scallops. The 1938 hurricane swept about a third of the bay's oysters and clams off their beds and buried them in deep water where they died — taking some of the shellfishing companies down in the process.

Not all large-scale oystering took place on the South Shore. Oyster Bay and other North Shore harbors also supported an industry until overfishing and pollution took their toll. Only one holdout remains — Frank M. Flower & Sons Co. of Bayville and Oyster Bay.

Its history begins in 1876 when William A. Flower staked out three acres of oyster beds in Mill Neck Creek, an arm of Oyster Bay. His son Frank added a fleet of power dredges about the turn of the century. Frank's sons Allen, Butler and Roswell built a base in Bayville around 1940 and in 1962 a hatchery was added to grow seed oysters and clams. The company, now owned by three longtime Flower employees, continues to cultivate and harvest oysters and clams from its leased beds, making it Long Island's only surviving traditional oyster company.

LEGACY

Photos Courtesy of Bob Doxsee Jr.

Doxsee employees shuck oysters, left, around 1900. Above, James Harvey Doxsee

THE DOXSEE SEA CLAM CO.

James Harvey Doxsee was running his family's Islip farm in 1865 when two men rented a waterfront site from him to can seafood.

Doxsee thought the business so promising that the next year he and brother-in-law Selah Whitman bought the small factory. A year later, their operation became the first Long Island company to can hard-shell clams.

In 1900, the Great South Bay harvests had tapered off, so James' oldest son, Henry, set up an operation in Ocracoke, N.C. That branch of the business still produces clam broth under the Doxsee name.

The Islip cannery closed in 1905. John Doxsee, another of James' sons, began setting fish traps in the ocean, from Islip and later from Meadow Island near Freeport. In 1933, John's sons, Bob Sr. and Spencer, began installing fish nets in the ocean and moved to a new plant in Point Lookout. The company shifted to dredging for surf clams in 1944.

The Doxsee Sea Clam Co. still produces chopped clams for restaurants and prepared retail seafood under the name of Off Shore Seafood.

Doxsees remain at the helm. Bob Jr., 67, is president, and daughter Beth handles sales. — **Bill Bleyer**

The tiny Tuthills of Orient were said to resist the sideshow life offered by P.T. Barnum

They Were Big on Dignity

BY IRENE VIRAG
STAFF WRITER

You might think that Addison Tuthill would have been impressed when P.T. Barnum himself, the greatest showman of his time, came all the way to the little hamlet of Orient on Long Island's North Fork just to see him.

As the story goes, Barnum, the impresario behind such stellar attractions as the double-jointed India-rubber man, wanted Addison Tuthill, a Lilliputian Long Islander, to join his show. There is no record of what he offered, but at some point he would give Addison a 22-inch-long gold-handled walking stick and a pocket watch the size of a quarter.

Legend holds that Addison wasn't the least bit tempted. Nor was he awed by Barnum's added attraction, General Tom Thumb, the little man who boasted that he had kissed 2 million women "including the Queens of England, France, Belgium and Spain." Never mind that Tom Thumb had rolled down the Champs Elysees in a miniature gilded carriage drawn by tiny ponies. Or that his wedding to a little woman named Lavinia Warren, in 1863, jammed Broadway from Ninth Street to Union Square.

Addison Tuthill was a small man in stature only. He had a large sense of dignity and, it is said, was appalled by the general, who danced the jig and the hornpipe in Barnum's traveling show. As for Tom Thumb, he seems to have been jealous of Addison, who at 33 or 34 inches tall was at least a half-foot tinier than the man billed throughout the world as the smallest human alive. Perhaps it is only a tall tale, but the story is that the meeting of the midgets turned into a fistfight.

No one knows how the contest ended but one thing is for certain — Addison Tuthill never put himself on public exhibition. Such a display would have been as out of character for Addison as it would have been for his equally diminutive sister, Emma, or their three slightly taller aunts, Cynthia, Lucretia and Asenath. They were the tiny Tuthills of Orient, descendants of a founding family, and they refused to take the low road to fame and fortune that ran through sideshows and circuses. Instead, they lived lives of quiet dignity in the everyday world that is perhaps the most difficult stage of all for anyone who is different.

Oysterponds Historical Society

The Tuthills of Orient: Emma, far left, and Addison, above, stood less than 3 feet tall. Their aunt Cynthia, in a 1832 painting, was 4 feet tall.

Emma was born in 1840, and Addison a year later. Their parents and siblings were normal in stature. But their father's three sisters were known as "the small sisters." As children, Emma and Addison would hide beneath the dining room table when vistors showed up and play with their miniature Parcheesi or checker sets or read their tiny Bibles in the shelter of the crocheted tablecloth.

Portraits, personal belongings and old records offer clues to the way the tiny Tuthills looked and lived. Addison was a gentleman farmer who raised potatoes, turnips and Brussels sprouts and delivered fresh eggs to his neighbors. Emma and her aunts were expert seamstresses — Emma stood on a chair to measure her clients. It is said that the tiny Tuthills walked single file on the lanes of long-ago. Addison in the lead, a neat man in a dark three-piece suit who grew a mustache in his mature years, followed by Emma, who wore a straw hat decorated with ribbons and pink roses and stopped to greet the women whose Sunday dresses and wedding gowns she had sewn.

Sometimes their aunts accompanied them as they strolled past the shoe shop and the schoolhouse and the white two-story inn where the stagecoach stopped. Cynthia with her long dark hair fastened stylishly high on top of her head with a tortoise shell comb. Lucretia with a monogrammed cotton chemise under her hand-stitched black taffeta blouse. Asenath holding a New Testament in one hand and a church psalmist in the other.

Dignity was important to all the tiny Tuthills, and it wasn't always easy to maintain. Men of the village frequently teased Addison and there is a story of a woman relative who tossed the adult man in the air as if he were a child.

The tiny house where Addison and Emma lived no longer exists, but a house built by a relative for Cynthia and Lucretia after Asenath died still stands in the village. The current owners, Susan and Tom Madigan, who bought the small Cape in 1983, found out later who had lived in it.

"There are no vestiges left of that time," said Susan Madigan. "The ceiling in the living room was low but that's not unusual for a house that age. Of course, no one could stand up in the attic where the women did their sewing." And her husband recalled bumping his head on the low doorjambs before the ceiling was raised and the house renovated.

Until recently, some of the tiny Tuthills' belongings — Lucretia's sewing box, an oil painting of Cynthia with rings on every finger, Asenath's silver thimble, Emma's monogrammed stockings, Addison's miniature Parcheesi chips — were on view in a museum that was once the stagecoach stop. The Oysterponds Historical Society packed away the tiny artifacts to make way for a new exhibit on life in an early 19th-Century boardinghouse.

The little people of Orient might not be upset that their lives are no longer on display. When Addison died at 52 in his sleep on July 16, 1894, from heart trouble and pneumonia, he was the last of the tiny Tuthills. His obituary did not mention his size or his visit from P.T. Barnum. Instead, it noted his remarkable memory and patience, his studiousness as a boy, his belief in an afterlife — the qualities that distinguished Addison Montgomery Tuthill in his time and place.

DESCENDANT

LAURA RYDER

When they were little girls in Orient, Eloise and Laura Luce played dress-up with the women's clothes that were stored in their grandmother's attic. The clothes not only were from another time but they were almost the right size. They had been made and worn by the girls' ancestors, the tiny Tuthills.

When she had children of her own, Eloise Norklun dressed her 3-year-old son in an outfit belonging to her great-grandfather's brother, the man she calls "Uncle Addie."

"We took a walk up Village Lane in Orient," says Eloise, now an 83-year-old great-grandmother who lives in New Brunswick, Canada. "He was wearing Uncle Addie's high silk hat and carrying the cane from P.T. Barnum. People couldn't believe what they were seeing. Oh, he made a big hit that day."

Eloise and Laura grew up in the house built for Addison's small aunts. They say that Addison, his sister, Emma, and their three aunts were the only little people ever born to the family. "Everyone in Orient knew them," says 81-year-old Laura Ryder, also a great-grandmother, who still lives in the village. "They were cute little people. They were Orient's tiny treasures."

— **Irene Virag**

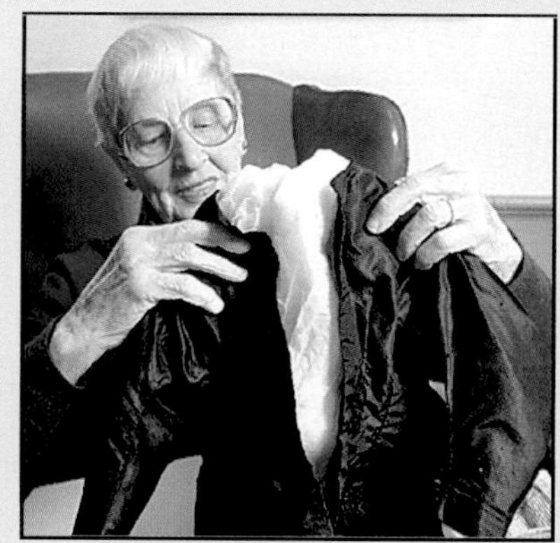

Laura Ryder holds a jacket that belonged to her great-great-aunt Emma Tuthill, and a pair of Emma's gloves.

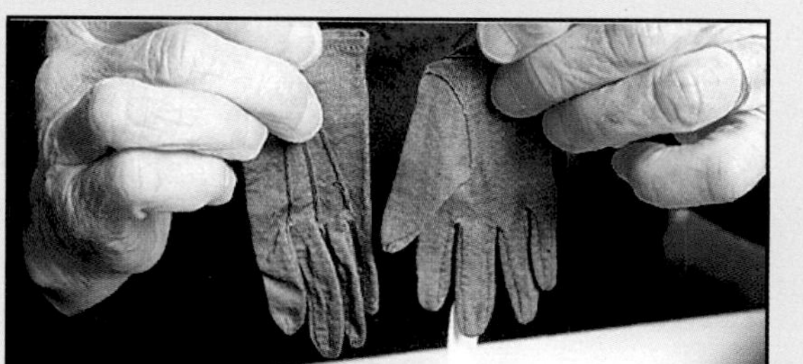

Newsday Photos / Bill Davis

Cooper Family Photo

Shinnecocks and Montauketts fight to regain areas taken in questionable deals

Lost Indian Lands

BY STEVE WICK AND THOMAS MAIER
STAFF WRITERS

Real estate promoters and local officials eager to bring the railroad to the East End of Long Island used questionable and possibly illegal means to break leases with Indians in Southampton and East Hampton towns a century ago and strip away their rights to 14,500 acres of prime real estate.

The breaking of leases with the Shinnecock and Montaukett Indians, in 1859 and the early 1880s, appears today to have been accomplished by deceit, lies and possibly forgery, a Newsday examination of historical and legal records shows. While the Indians themselves raised these issues at the time, their protests were dismissed in the courts.

In the case of the Shinnecocks, an 1859 petition that asked the state Legislature to pass legislation breaking a lease that covered the Shinnecock Hills may have contained forged names, names of dead Indians and minors.

"I remember the day when Capt. Louis Scott, Austin Rose and Capt. Jeter Rose drove on the reservation," a Shinnecock named David Killes testified under oath before a U.S. Senate subcommittee hearing in 1900. Killes said one of the men told his father ". . . the petition is going to Albany tomorrow and he said to my father, 'Are you going to sign it?' He said, 'I told you I would never sign it.' He said, 'Luther (my uncle), are you going to sign it?' He said, 'I will never sign it.' But they forged the names and put them on."

In the case of the Montauketts, an East Hampton man later admitted under oath in court that he had lied when he told the Indians that if they signed away their rights to land at Montauk Point, they still could return during summer months. But according to testimony before the same subcommittee in 1900, they were barred by force from returning, and Montauketts alleged that at least one of their homes was burned to the ground.

The breaking of the leases is not only important to historians but resonates today. The Montauketts have filed a notice of intent with the federal Bureau of Indian Affairs asking for recognition of their tribal rights. If they win recognition, the Montauketts say they will file a court case alleging fraud in the loss of their lands at Montauk Point, which today are mostly maintained as parkland by Suffolk County and New York State.

In Southampton, the Shinnecocks say they are assembling historical documentation in preparation for filing for federal recognition of their tribal status. Today, nearly all of the Shinnecock Hills are incorporated in two world-class golf clubs that sit on land worth millions of dollars.

Both the Shinnecock and Montaukett land deals were motivated by the expansion of the Long Island Rail Road in the

Montauketts in the 1924 photo at left filed a lawsuit to reclaim land; the suit was dismissed. Top row, from left: Charles Fowler, John Fowler, Pocahontas Pharaoh and Sam Pharaoh; bottom row, from left, Marguerite Fowler, George Fowler and Maria Pharaoh Banks. Maria, widow of a deceased chief, gave up her right to live at Montauk's Indian Fields in the 1880s in exchange for $100, an annual annuity, and promises — later broken — that she could return in the summer.

mid-1800s. At that time, the railroad ran through the middle of Long Island from Queens to Greenport, but not along the South Shore. Hoping to induce officials to extend tracks farther east, many towns along the South Shore right-of-way floated bonds to help defray costs. Committees of businessmen, farmers, fishermen, elected officials and real estate promoters were formed in each town to lobby the Long Island Rail Road to extend its tracks from Queens to Babylon, Islip, Patchogue and east to Sag Harbor, then the most populous village in Suffolk County.

"It is certainly of vital interest that this road be constructed," the Sag Harbor Express editorialized in 1859. The year before, an official Suffolk County map had shown a proposed rail line leading from Riverhead to Southampton. "With the inauguration of this road our property will be doubled in value," the newspaper said.

But to reach the village — or any place on the South Fork, for that matter — a rail line had to cross the Shinnecock Hills, which was Indian land locked away for centuries under the terms of a lease signed in 1703 with the town trustees. The Shinnecocks used the high and rolling hills — among the most striking parcels of land on the East End — to hunt, cut wood and graze livestock.

"It was impossible for the railroad to come to the South Fork without crossing Shinnecock land," said John Strong, a history professor at the Southampton Campus of Long Island University. "The Shinnecocks could not legally sell a right-of-way because they did not own the land, they leased it. And the lease was good for 1,000 years. For the railroad to come, it had to cross Shinnecock land, so some kind of an arrangement had to be struck with the Shinnecocks or the lease had to be broken."

The Indians lost 3,500 acres of the Hills in the winter of 1859, when a group of investors that included leading citizens of Southampton proposed to break the 1,000-year lease in exchange for giving the Indians title to Shinnecock Neck, a tract of approximately 750 acres where the Indians today maintain a reservation. Saying they had a petition signed by 21 Shinnecocks in support of the proposition, the investors got the state Legislature to pass a bill authorizing the swap.

Only days after this petition arrived in Albany, records show, a second petition signed by another group of Shinnecocks reached the Capitol, alleging that the first petition was a forgery. The Legislature ignored the second petition. As a tribe, the Shinnecocks received no money for the exchange, nor did they approve it, although a federal law passed in 1790 required congressional as well as tribal approval for Indian land deals.

Records filed in the Suffolk County clerk's office in Riverhead show the investors held the land for two years, then sold it to a larger group that included themselves and others with the same last names. They then sold a 66-foot-wide

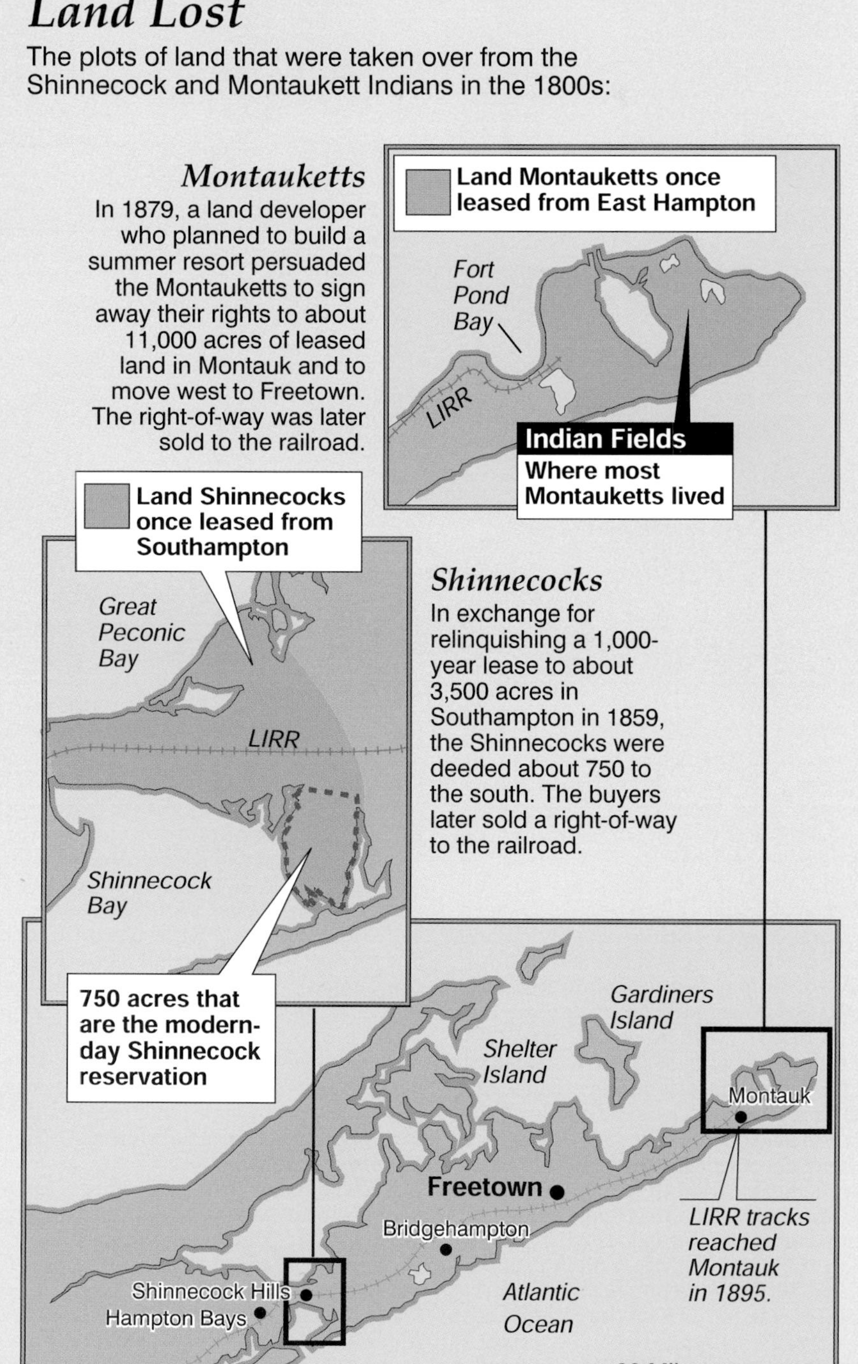
Land Lost
The plots of land that were taken over from the Shinnecock and Montaukett Indians in the 1800s:
Montauketts
In 1879, a land developer who planned to build a summer resort persuaded the Montauketts to sign away their rights to about 11,000 acres of leased land in Montauk and to move west to Freetown. The right-of-way was later sold to the railroad.
Land Montauketts once leased from East Hampton
Fort Pond Bay
LIRR
Indian Fields
Where most Montauketts lived
Land Shinnecocks once leased from Southampton
Great Peconic Bay
LIRR
Shinnecock Bay
750 acres that are the modern-day Shinnecock reservation
Shinnecocks
In exchange for relinquishing a 1,000-year lease to about 3,500 acres in Southampton in 1859, the Shinnecocks were deeded about 750 to the south. The buyers later sold a right-of-way to the railroad.
Gardiners Island
Shelter Island
Montauk
Freetown
Bridgehampton
LIRR tracks reached Montauk in 1895.
Shinnecock Hills
Hampton Bays
Atlantic Ocean
20 Miles

Newsday / Steve Madden

Collection of Vincent F. Seyfried

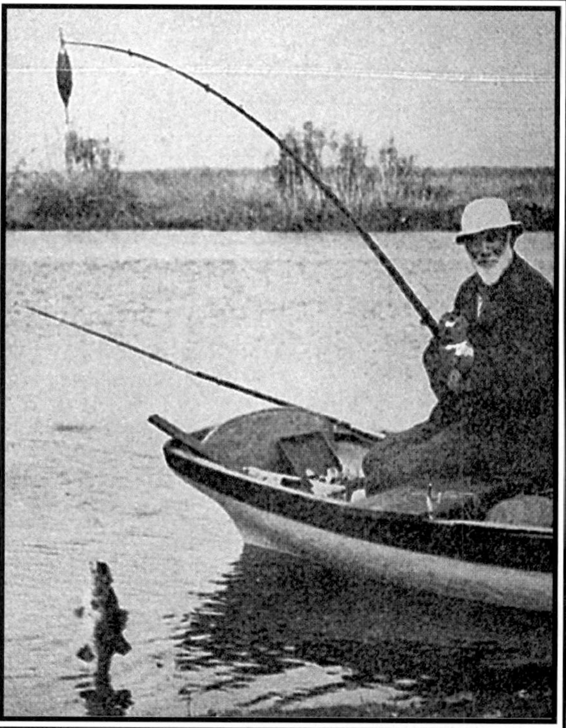

Long Island Rail Road president Austin Corbin, above, planned to build tracks through Indian lands. Arthur Benson, right, who bought much of Montauk Point in 1879, fishes in Fort Pond. He dreamed of an exclusive summer colony along the ocean, connected by railroad to New York City.

Courtesy of East Hampton Library

right-of-way to the South Side Railroad Co., which would later merge with the LIRR. In 1869, tracks were laid across the Shinnecock Hills, connecting New York City to Sag Harbor. Land values soared.

By the mid-1880s, the Hills were sold to an enterprise called the Long Island Improvement Co. One of the company's five directors was Austin Corbin, president of the Long Island Rail Road. Newspaper accounts say that Corbin and his investors — including the president of Brooklyn Gas and Light Co., Arthur Benson — planned to build a hotel and a large summer colony on the site. Those plans never materialized, but within a few years, Corbin's land company started the Shinnecock Hills Golf Club on the site. Today, Shinnecocks work as groundskeepers at the club.

It was a similiarly grand dream — involving Corbin and Benson — that helped push the last group of Montauketts off leased land at Montauk Point, where the Indians were objects of curiosity for newspaper writers and tourists traveling to see the lighthouse.

In 1879, Benson bought approximately 10,000 acres reaching from Napeague to the point for $151,000 from a private group of East Hampton residents. Benson dreamed of an exclusive summer colony along the ocean, connected by railroad to New York City.

But smack in the middle of the point, on a tract of land called Indian Fields, the Montauketts were living under the terms of an East Hampton Town lease that granted to them residency and other rights "in perpetuity." In order for Benson to have clear title to the point — and also so that he would not have an impoverished Indian community inside a ring of expensive homes — he had to persuade the Montauketts to sign away their rights to the land and then move away. As was the case at Shinnecock, there appear to be no records showing that the Montauketts ever were approached as a group and asked to agree to the sale.

Benson hired the town's assessor, Nathaniel Dominy, to induce the Montauketts to move to homes he would provide in the Freetown section of East Hampton. Dominy offered the Montauketts as little as $10 each for signing individual deeds that gave ownership of Indian Fields to Benson. According to court testimony, Dominy also told the Indians they could return to Indian Fields whenever they wanted, a statement he later admitted was a lie.

The transcript of the U.S. Senate subcommittee hearing shows that hardball tactics were used against reluctant Montauketts. One Montaukett testified at the hearing that the houses at Freetown that Benson gave the Indians as an inducement to relocate were no better than pig pens.

After gaining title to the property, Benson recouped part of his investment by selling a huge tract to the railroad — whose president was Corbin — for a right-of-way. He also sold other large pieces to Corbin individually. By 1890, according to newspaper records, the land at Montauk Point had soared in value and was worth between $3 million and $4 million. Records and newspaper accounts show that Corbin and Benson became partners in a grand scheme to turn Fort Pond Bay into what Corbin called a "nationally significant" deepwater port where cross-Atlantic steamships could dock. The dock would be connected to

Please see LAND on Next Page

Indians Fight For Lost Land

LAND from **Preceding Page**

Manhattan by extending Corbin's Long Island Rail Road to Montauk.

If both Indian groups go to court, fraud will not be easy to prove. Official records of the Shinnecock Tribal Trustees, which have been kept by the Southampton Town clerk since the town's earliest history, are missing for the period immediately surrounding the 1859 land swap. Those records could possibly prove what contacts, if any, the original investors had with the tribe itself; they could also possibly substantiate the arguments made in the second petition that the names on the first were forged. There are also questions today as to how private investors in both towns managed to gain control of the land.

And, of course, witnesses to both events are long dead, their legacies kept alive in the memories of their descendants.

"We intend to do what we can to answer these questions," said the Rev. Michael Smith, a Shinnecock who is minister of the Presbyterian Church on the Southampton reservation. "It's important the truth be told."

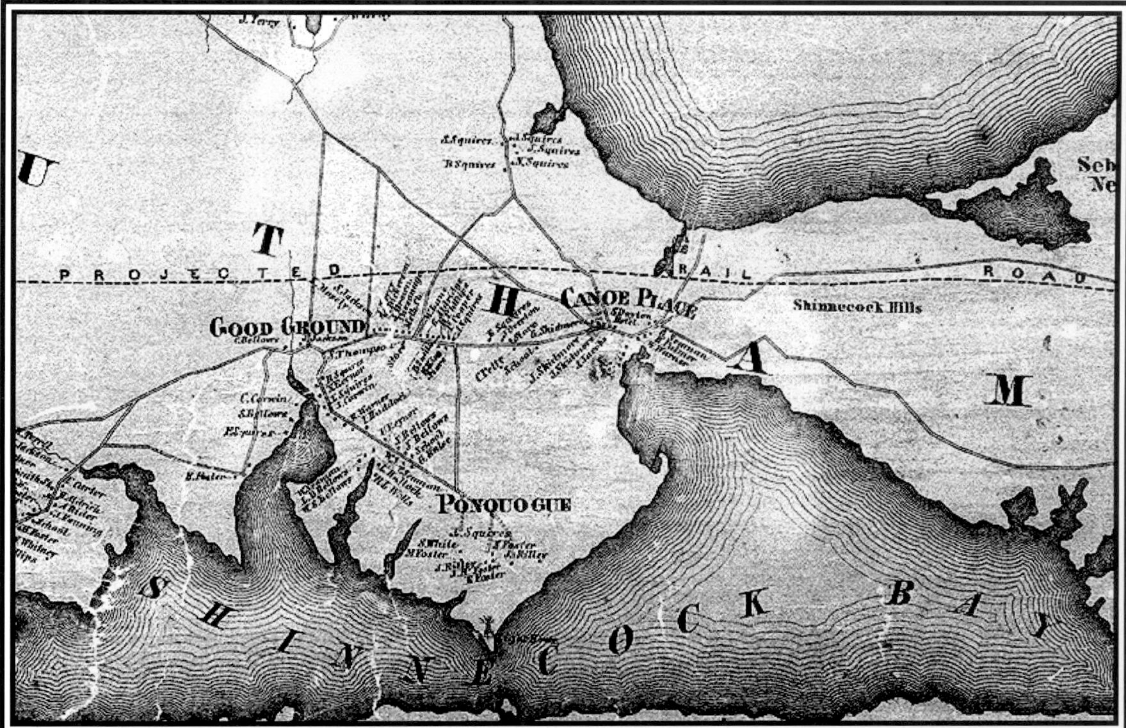

The Chace map of 1858 shows railroad tracks crossing Shinnecock Hills years before they were laid. A 1,000-year lease signed in 1703 allowed the Shinnecock community to live and farm the land east of Canoe Place. But in the late 1800s, developers saw the Indian community as a barrier when they proposed the railroad.

Suffolk County Historical Society; Newsday Photo

Shinnecock Hills

Soon after their arrival in Southampton in 1640, the English began making land deals with the Indians. The Shinnecocks' land base shrank as the English took more and more farmland and woodland. Soon, the only Indian villages in the town were on both sides of the narrow strip of land that separated Peconic Bay from Shinnecock Bay, a spot called Canoe Place. Today, the Shinnecock Canal passes through this narrow waist of land.

In 1703, the town trustees wrote a lease they said would be good for "one thousand years." It was signed by the trustees, who under the terms of the Dongan Patent — which governed land matters in New York — had the authority to negotiate with the Indians. Three Shinnecocks signed it — Pomguamo, Chice and Mahmanun — but the lease says it was approved by them "and their people."

The lease allowed the Indians to live, farm and cut wood on all of the land east of the Canoe Place, bounded by Peconic Bay on the north and Shinnecock Bay on the south. The eastern boundary ran from Shinnecock Creek north to the bay. This was the entirety of the Hills. In exchange for signing the lease, the Shinnecocks were paid 20 pounds in English money.

By 1859, the clamor to bring the railroad to the South Fork had risen to a crescendo. The year before, an official map of Suffolk County called the Chace map was published. For the first time, a county map showed a proposed railroad line from Riverhead to Southampton.

"The railroad was seen by everyone as progress," said Vincent F. Seyfried, the historian for the LIRR. "It allowed products to go back and forth and connected the towns to New York City. It was the future for these towns."

Apparently beginning in the fall of 1858, the Proprietors of the Trustees of the Common Lands of Southampton — a private group of investors not affiliated with town government — began approaching the Shinnecocks with the express purpose of breaking the lease. According to records, the proprietors were among the town's most influential families — Edwin Rose, David Rose, Austin Rose, David Hedges, Jeremiah Hedges, Enoch Halsey, Isaac Osborn, Erastus Foster, Seldin Foster, Edwin Post, George Post and Jon Fithian.

According to the testimony taken by the U.S. Senate subcommittee in 1900, individual Shinnecocks were approached by some of these men, asking them to sign a petition to the state Legislature that would legalize the breaking of the lease.

One Shinnecock, Eugene Johnson, testified: "In 1859 they circulated a paper among the Indians to get their signatures, agreeing to divide the reservation from the hills. Very few of the Indians signed it. The major part of them refused to sign it." One of the Shinnecocks who testified, James L. Cuffee — whose name appears on the petition — said his name was forged.

Under oath, Cuffee testified: "Mr. Rose came out . . . on the Neck and tried to get all the names signed to it that they could. He came to me at that time. I was trustee on the Neck and I told him no. I would not sign anything of the kind, and he went to several others to my knowledge — I do not know how many — but he could not get the majority of them. They would not sign it."

But the petition — which was entered into evidence at the Senate subcommittee hearings — reads as if the Shinnecocks themselves wanted to give the Hills to the proprietors because of disputes over livestock grazing. It reads, in part:

"Your petitions further show that of late years various disputes have arisen between the said Indians and the trustees of the proprietors of common lands of the town of Southampton in regard to their respective rights under the several deeds and leases, and that to put an end to these differences they have consented to an arrangement with the said trustees by which they are to surrender their lease to certain portions of these lands, and the trustees are to reconvey to the said tribe the residue."

It contains 21 Shinnecock signatures, 10 of which are a simple X. The name James L. Cuffee appears twice. The name Wickham Cuffee appears also as Wicks Cuffee.

Within days of this petition being sent to Albany, a second petition was written, this one signed by 12 Shinnecocks, including James L. Cuffee. It reads, in part: ". . . we depose that said names . . . were forgeries . . . some of the names purporting to be names of signers were not signed by the parties bearing the name in the petition; that others of the signers, or pretended signers, who had a right to those names signed were dead, and buried for years; that others were never known to the tribe, nor did they ever belong to the tribe; that the others . . . were minors . . ."

Today, there are no town or tribal records to show who was alive or dead as of that date, or even who was a Shinnecock. The records of the Shinnecock Tribal Trustees are missing for that period. "There is so much that is lost," said Michael Smith, adding — as the Shinnecocks in 1900 also testified — that there are no indications the community itself approved the breaking of the lease.

"If the breaking of the lease was entirely above board, why didn't they ask the tribal government to approve it?" he said. "If this is a good petition, why are names repeated twice?"

Testimony at the Senate hearing showed that, once the lease was broken and the railroad extended, the value of the Hills soared to more than $3 million. Testimony also showed that Shinnecocks were barred, sometimes by force, from returning. One Shinnecock testified that his elderly Indian aunt "got banged pretty nearly to death for cutting a stick of basket wood."

Records on file in the Suffolk County clerk's office in Riverhead show that the proprietors sold the Hills in 1861 for $6,726, or approximately $2 an acre — well below the value of surrounding land in the town — to a group that included themselves and family members. There are Roses, Fosters and Posts on both lists. Records in Southampton Town, along with newspaper accounts, said the proprietors retained the railroad right-of-way, which they sold after the 1861 sale for $500. In two years, more than $7,000 had changed hands, none of it ending up with the Shinnecocks. By the spring of 1870, rail service to Sag Harbor had been inaugurated.

Accounts in a Southampton newspaper called the Sea-Side Times show that the arrival of the railroad in Southampton Town began a period of enormous change. In 1881, Corbin — who had developed the summer resort at Manhattan Beach in Brooklyn — became president of the LIRR. During the summer of 1882, he brought what were described as his real estate partners — a British investment firm called the American Improvement Co. — to Shinnecock Hills.

Describing one excursion of Corbin and the investors, the newspaper wrote: "They stopped on some of the elevations on Shinnecock Hills and prospected the sight of a contemplated summer hotel." The same story said: ". . . at Shinnecock Hills, the company proposes to lay out a large park of 500 acres, the arms of which should be lined with cottages — those fronting the sea in villa style, and those inland surrounded by small farms of from two to five acres in extent. Those improvements will cost $3.5 million."

A story in the Brooklyn Union-Argus that summer of 1882 said: "Mr. Corbin's plans for the development of Long Island are so comprehensive that practical people . . . may be inclined to consider them as merely imaginative. But Mr. Corbin is backed by almost limitless foreign capital."

In March, 1884, a company in which Corbin was one of the directors, the Long Island Improvement Co., bought the Shinnecock Hills for an undisclosed price — newspaper accounts say the price was hundreds of thousands of dollars — from a group that included some of the original proprietors who had broken the lease in 1859, one of whom was Austin Rose. Newspaper stories and land records show that one of Corbin's partners on the Hills was Arthur Benson, the Brooklyn Gas and Light Co. president, who in 1879 had bought Montauk Point from the Proprietors of East Hampton — also a group of private investors — and was planning a huge summer resort there.

In 1891, the Long Island Improvement Co. opened the Shinnecock Hills Golf Club on the site and a grand clubhouse designed by Stanford White was completed the next year.

"You come out on the train and you see that Stanford White house when you stop at the Shinnecock station," said

10 Unforgotten Names in Granite

BY STEVE WICK
STAFF WRITER

On the Shinnecock Indian Reservation in Southampton stands a small granite memorial with 10 names etched on it.

It is not in a public place, so the only people who see it are the residents of the reservation, who keep the weeds at bay and plant flowers to brighten the memorial. They have not forgotten the names of the 10, who died in the cold surf not far from the reservation on a bitter December day in 1876.

"Every December we have a church service in which we remember those who died," said the Rev. Michael Smith, pastor of the reservation's Shinnecock Church. "Many people on the reservation are related to those 10, so it's still fresh."

The Shinnecock men listed on the memorial died aboard a freighter called the Circassian. The ship was en route from Liverpool, England, to New York Harbor, when it foundered in a storm on a sandbar at Mecox, east of the reservation. The ship's holds contained more than 1,000 tons of such items as bricks, lime, bleach and rags, according to "The Shinnecock Indians: A Culture History," published in 1983.

The Circassian left England in early November with 36 men aboard and was soon in the teeth of a winter storm. En route across the Atlantic, the ship picked up the captain and crew of a boat it found foundering in heavy seas. It was not a good omen. Still hundreds of miles from New York, the freighter's riggings were covered with layers of ice and the storm was worsening.

Wind and sea raged as the ship neared Long Island. On the night of Dec. 11, the Circassian struck a sandbar. Flares shot into the dark sky as the freighter foundered a few hundred yards from shore, at the eastern edge of Mecox Bay, near the tiny farming hamlet of Bridgehampton.

Suffolk County Historical Society; Newsday Photo

The wreck of the Circassian, on which 10 Shinnecock Indians died, was illustrated in Harper's Weekly.

Soon, rescuers from a nearby lifesaving station discovered the ship. But as dawn broke, attempts by the rescuers to launch dories into the surf were rebuffed by huge, icy waves. After repeated attempts, a line was successfully fired to the freighter with a mortar. The line landed on the ship's deck and was tied by the crew.

Then, at mid-morning, as the storm subsided, rescuers reached the freighter in dories. After several hours, the crew was safely ashore. Now, the business of unloading the cargo and towing the ship off the sandbar began.

A company brought in to unload the cargo hired a group of Shinnecocks, most of whom had served on whaling vessels and were eager for the work. The men agreed to stay aboard the Circassian until all the work was done and the ship was free of the sandbar. But then, on Dec. 29, another storm approached. According to the Shinnecock book, some men left the boat, including an Indian named Alfonso Eleazer, but the others were ordered by an official of the salvage company to stay aboard and ride out the storm.

"There are stories handed down from generation to generation . . . that pistol threats had to be used to encourage the men to stay with the ship," according to the book. "No matter the reason, they stayed."

That night, the ship broke in half in a gale. Some men scrambled up the rigging to safety. Unable to reach the Circassian because of the storm, people on the beach could hear the Shinnecocks aboard the ship singing Christian hymns. By the morning of Dec. 30, the ship was in pieces, the men aboard tossed into the icy sea. Only four men made it to the beach alive.

Of the 32 men who had stayed aboard, 28 died, including all 10 Shinnecocks. Their names are carved on the memorial: Lewis Walker, John Walker, David W. Bunn, J. Franklin Bunn, Russell Bunn, William Cuffee, Warren N. Cuffee, George W. Cuffee, James R. Lee, Oliver J. Kellis.

LI HISTORY.COM

The Circassian's last days were detailed in the records of the U.S. Life-Saving Service. This moving account is available on the Internet at http://www.lihistory.com.

David Goddard, a Southampton archivist hired by the golf club to research its history. "It was done that way by the improvement company to attract development. Corbin had always had his hand in two places — the development of huge resorts and the expansion of the railroad."

Montauk Point

They were a small group in the 1880s, perhaps no more than 20 people. They lived in small houses on rocky land overlooking salt water. They fished, hunted, cut wood, tended livestock and chickens, and worked for white families in East Hampton.

Tourists on their way to the 18th-Century lighthouse at the tip of Montauk Point passed by their little Indian community. Often the visitors would stop and look them over as if they were sideshow attractions. The only thing missing was a billboard telling tourists to turn left at the dirt road if they wanted to see "The Last Village of the Montauk Indians."

Corbin and Benson had big dreams for this same land. Their plan, which would produce millions in new revenue for Corbin's railroad, was to construct an international seaport at Montauk's Fort Pond Bay. They envisioned British merchant ships docking to avoid New York's crowded harbor — reducing their voyage across the Atlantic by 120 miles.

The story begins in 1879, when Benson bought approximately 10,000 acres of Montauk Point from the proprietors for $151,000. He surprised onlookers by plunking down a 10 percent deposit in cash pulled from his pocket.

But although Benson now owned the land, he did not have unrestricted rights to it — there was the matter of the lease given to the Montauketts in 1703. That lease was for approximately 11,000 acres of Montauk Point, and covered residency, hunting and fishing rights "in perpetuity." A year before the auction at which Benson bought the property, a local judge had ruled that it was legal for the trustees to sell tracts at Montauk Point, but the tribe's rights to use the same land had to be protected as spelled out in the old lease.

After buying the land, Benson began building summer resort homes, including some designed by Stanford White. Soon, his friends were conducting English-style fox hunting on the high plains. One of his summer guests was Corbin, who promised to build a giant railroad terminus at this new port and to ship passengers and freight on his LIRR trains to New York at 60 mph. He would eventually travel to England and raise $5 million for a syndicate he controlled with investors from London and Boston.

Corbin was not one to shrink from a challenge. By 1881, he had gained control of the money-losing railroad — that year, it lost $136,000 — and began to pull it out of receivership and toward profitability. After purchasing other rail systems running through Brooklyn and Queens, Corbin was dubbed by the press as "the King of Long Island." He bought a luxurious home in Babylon, where he entertained President Chester A. Arthur and his son in 1882.

Please see LAND on Next Page

Newsday Photo / Bill Davis

Robert Cooper, near the Montauk Lighthouse. He and other Montauketts are determined to see their community receive federal recognition as a tribe. If that happens, they plan a legal fight to recover some of their ancient lands.

Indians Fight For Lost Land

LAND from **Preceding Page**

But Corbin and Benson acted cautiously in informing both the Montauketts and the white townspeople of their plans. In September, 1882, some East Hampton residents expressed alarm about his plans for a railroad through the town. Even as Corbin was suggesting he would extend the line to Montauk, he was already deep in plans to do it.

In October, 1882, the Hempstead Inquirer published an account of a meeting that took place between "Mr. Benson, the proprietor of Montauk, and the representatives of the Long Island Railroad and others interested in the establishment of a fast line of steamers between Europe and Montauk." But the same account said that Benson had "declined an offer of $100,000 for the right of way to Fort Pond Bay and land for a depot."

Two months later, the newspaper indicated that Benson had a change of heart. He was now "willing to sell his land" to the railroad, but with no indication of when such a future deal would take place.

But land records reviewed by Newsday show that Benson had already signed an agreement, in January, 1882, for a railroad right-of-way with a company called the Montauk Association, which was controlled by Corbin. After an initial payment of $18,235, Benson privately joined in Corbin's Montauk development efforts. Their agreement included a promise by Corbin, as court records would later show, to buy more of Benson's land.

But the Montauketts at Indian Fields were a crucial stumbling block to these grandiose plans. To help secure the rights to this land, Benson enlisted the help of Nathaniel Dominy, the East Hampton Town assessor, whose family had known the Montauketts for a long time. Dominy agreed to act as Benson's agent in trying to persuade the Montauketts to sign away their rights and move to small lots in the Freetown section of East Hampton. Letters written back and forth between the two men show that Dominy was being paid for his services, and that Benson pushed him hard when some Montauketts balked at giving up their rights at Indian Fields and relocating to Freetown.

First, Dominy and Benson focused on Maria Pharaoh — widow of deceased chief David Pharaoh — who worked as a midwife in East Hampton. Together, they tried to persuade her to sign a written agreement that Benson had prepared. Dominy promised that Benson would pay her $100 outright and an annual annuity of $240 if she would sign. Dominy also offered to relocate her home from Indian Fields to Freetown. As he would later testify in a court proceeding, Dominy assured Pharaoh that she could return to Indian Fields in the summer months.

Maria signed the deed in the spring of 1885. Also signing was her brother George, and her son Wyandank, who because he was a youngster, received only $10. In the next few years, other Montauketts who had rebuffed Dominy's initial offers slowly followed their example, each for $100 in cash and a small plot in Freetown. There was no returning after that. Testimony at the U.S. Senate subcommittee hearings in 1900 indicated that at least one house at Indian Fields was set ablaze, and newspaper accounts show that Benson leveled the houses there as soon as deeds were signed.

By 1886, Corbin had lined up much of his investment money for his international shipping and rail plan, and began lobbying Congress and Albany for legislation to open the new seaport at Fort Pond Bay. He also wanted to establish a U.S. Customs office on the site. In addition, he pushed hard for federal approval to carry the mail on ships out of Montauk.

In the meantime, Corbin continued to buy up land around Montauk. To show off the viability of his Montauk rail plans, he made a test run from Long Island City to the new train station at Amagansett, covering the 110 miles in 109 minutes.

In 1895 — by now, Benson had died — Corbin and his partners bought 4,000 acres of the original 10,000 from Benson's widow and his son, Frank, for $200,000. Just 16 years before, Benson had bought the entire 10,000 acres for $151,000. A court case brought by the Montauketts later revealed that Corbin planned to buy more Benson family land at Montauk. Meanwhile, Corbin's LIRR planned to invest hundreds of thousands of dollars in the railroad and other improvements. At Montauk and Shinnecock, Corbin was investing both as an individual and as the president of the railroad.

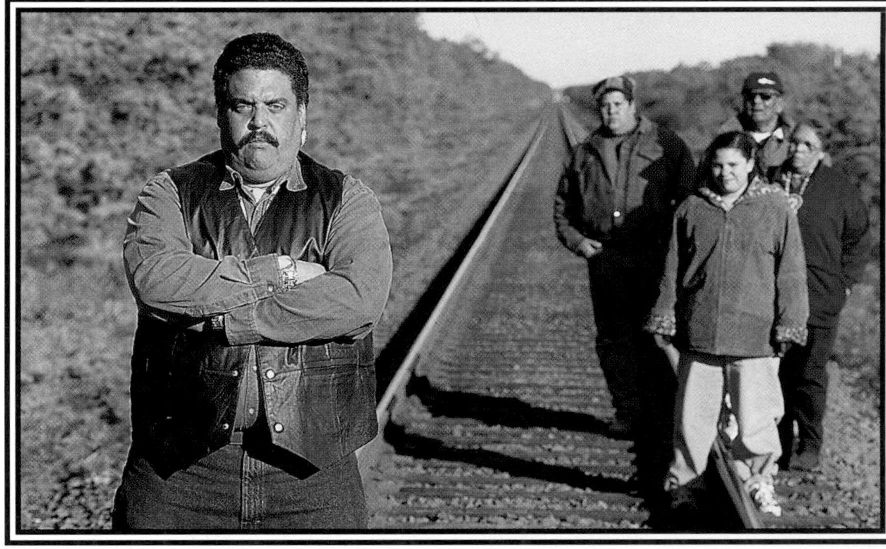

Newsday Photo / Bill Davis

Montaukett Robert Pharoah on LIRR tracks in Montauk; at rear, his daughter Tami, and, from left, his cousin, Frederick; Frederick's father, Bill Pharoah, and Bill's sister, Carolyn Pharoah.

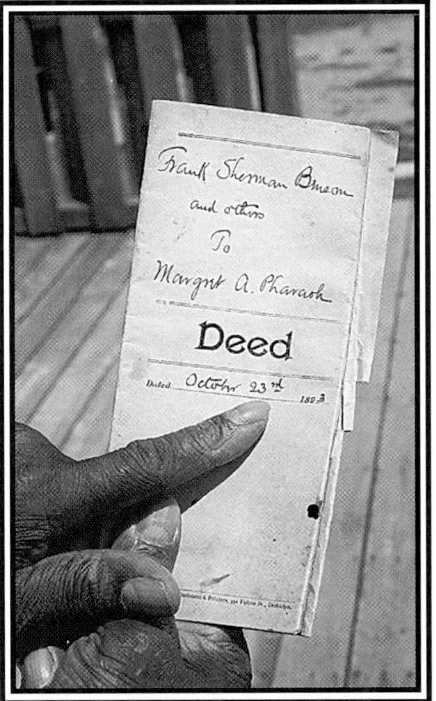

Newsday Photo / Bill Davis

A deed to a Freetown site was given to Margaret Pharoah and others in exchange for their Montauk Point land, about 1890.

At a Montaukett community meeting in that summer of 1895, the Indians decided to hire a lawyer to contest the Benson purchase of their ancestral land, which they said had been done without the tribe's approval.

In the meantime, Corbin proceeded full speed with his plans for the Fort Pond Bay development. He arranged for a bill to be introduced in the U.S. Senate that would establish a duty-free port at Fort Pond Bay. And, in March, 1896, he began building docks at Fort Pond Bay, with a new steel pier. But that summer, fate intervened.

While vacationing in New Hampshire, Corbin went for a ride with his grandson in a horse-drawn wagon. At one point, the horses bolted when Corbin raised a sun umbrella into the air and the carriage plummeted down an embankment. The coachman was killed and Corbin and his grandson suffered fractures. Corbin died later that day, leaving an estate estimated at between $25 million and $40 million.

Though some early construction would be finished, Corbin's ambitious plans for Montauk essentially died with him. But his rapid build-up of the LIRR across Long Island is still considered the railroad's golden age.

For the Montauketts, their lawsuit contesting the sale of their lands dragged on for years. Gradually, some questionable aspects of the deal came to light.

At the U.S. Senate subcommittee hearing in 1900, several Indians testified, as did Dominy, and a number of leases and other documents were entered into evidence. Dominy spoke at length of his efforts to push the Montauketts off Indian Fields, saying at one point that he paid one "lame" Indian child named Ephraim Pharaoh just $10. He also said that, at the time, the boy was a cook in the Dominy household.

The testimony from the Montauketts was bitter and emotional. One man, Eugene Johnson, said Montauketts who tried to return to Indian Fields after Benson bought the property were arrested or removed "by force." Another Montaukett, Nathan Cuffee, said Benson and Dominy promised, in moving the Indians to Freetown, to either relocate their homes or build new ones.

"The understanding or the promise by Mr. Benson to those people was that he was to build them comfortable homes, with so much land to accompany each house," Nathan Cuffee testified. "And I have been in the houses, every one of them, without exception, and most of the houses, except one, are built of plain pine boards, stood on end, without any chimneys to them, without any plastering; just such a pen as I would build for a pig."

In 1909, the Montaukett lawsuit finally went to trial. Now in his 80s, Nathaniel Dominy took the stand. Referring to Maria Pharaoh, he was asked by the tribe's lawyer: "Did you tell her that after she moved away, and was given this deed, that she could move back?"

"I told her this," Dominy replied. "I venture to say . . . I told every one of them."

Instead of trying to defend the deal with the Montauketts, the lawyers for the Benson estate argued that the Montauketts had intermarried with blacks and thus diluted their "Indian blood." After a year of deliberation, Judge Abel Blackmar in Riverhead State Supreme Court threw out the Indians' case, saying that the Montauketts no longer existed as a tribe. Inside the packed courtroom, 75 Montauketts sat in stunned silence. Later, the New York Court of Appeals affirmed Blackmar's ruling.

Robert Cooper — who recently was elected chief of the tribe in a disputed vote — and his cousin, Robert Pharaoh, say they are determined to see the Montauketts' rights as a tribe recognized by the federal government. If the government grants recognition to the tribe, they say they will launch a legal effort to have some of their lands returned. Today, much of the land at Montauk Point comprises county-owned parkland along with private homes.

"I would call it coercion, a land fraud — leading people with promises that never happened," says Pharaoh. "These were people with very little money, who worked as domestics and were victimized from the time they lost their lands until they passed away."

Scholars and legal experts interviewed by Newsday seem to agree with this assessment. "The law says that you can't negotiate directly with individual Indians and that you must deal directly with the tribe," declares John Strong.

By modern legal standards, experts say, a court could overturn this land deal because of the evidence of false promises to the tribe. "You'd have a real shot at overturning on the basis of fraud, especially when the buyer was promising they could return but was already interested in the selling the property to the railroad," says Anthony P. Gallo, chairman of the Suffolk County Bar Association Real Property Committee. "I'd say this was a fraudulent act perpetrated on the Indians."

On a recent afternoon, Robert Pharaoh stood on an overlook of Montauk Highway and gazed toward the small cemetery where his ancestors are buried. Beyond the cemetery, the land sweeps majestically to the sea. The railroad tracks can be seen in the distance, a reminder of what happened a century ago.

"I come here and draw strength from this place," he said. "My ancestors know what happened isn't right."

Collection of Vincent F. Seyfried

Queens Borough Public Library, Long Island Collection

In the late 1860s, several lines served the Island, including the South Side Railroad. One of its locomotive engines is at left. Above is the station at Sag Harbor, circa 1900. To compete with South Side, the LIRR completed a branch there in 1870.

After discovering Long Island, the LIRR pulls ahead by absorbing other lines

Getting On Track

BY SIDNEY C. SCHAER
STAFF WRITER

In the 1850s, the Long Island Rail Road was the little train that couldn't.

The line had rolled into receivership after its reason for being—express train and steamboat service to Boston — vanished a few years after its birth. That happened in 1848 when the New York, New Haven and Hartford Railroad completed an all-land route along the southern New England coast.

While the LIRR had originally showed little interest in the real estate it crossed on its way to its last stop at Greenport, it was clear by the end of the Civil War that the line's only hope for getting back up to speed lay with serving future development on the Island.

After the war ended in April, 1865, a decade-long railroad building boom began with communities throughout Long Island pleading for train service.

By 1867, rails had been laid along the South Shore from Jamaica to Babylon. But unfortunately for the LIRR, the tracks belonged to another line — an upstart enterprise called the South Side Railroad. Also filling the vacuum left by the LIRR were other railroads, such as the Flushing and North Shore line and the Central Railroad of Long Island. At one point, passengers could embark at three separate terminals in Hempstead.

The tumultuous decade was marked by fevered construction, cutthroat competition, fare wars and duplication of service that left the competing railroads — including the LIRR — exhausted. Eventually, all would be amalgamated under the banner of the LIRR during the tenure of Austin Corbin, a land entrepreneur who ran the railroad until his death in an 1896 carriage accident.

Corbin was preceded by a cast of colorful characters. The most significant was Oliver Charlick, a former New York police chief who had briefly gone west during the California Gold Rush. There was also Conrad Poppenhusen, the tycoon who turned College Point into the rubber capital of the Northeast. And there was Alexander T. Stewart, the Manhattan department store mogul who built a railroad to serve Garden City, his model suburban community on the Hempstead Plains.

Charlick became the LIRR's 11th president when associates including former New York Mayor Henry Havemeyer assumed control in 1863. It became Charlick's task to rebuild the LIRR's customer base. Already suffering from the all-rail link to Boston, the line lost more riders when it was forced to abandon its Brooklyn terminal when the city outlawed its smoky steam locomotives in 1861. The LIRR relocated the terminal to Hunters Point in Long Island City.

Charlick reigned for 12 years as communities clamored for service, most vocally along the South Shore, where residents were forced to trek to the center of the Island to catch a train.

He was not a sympathetic listener. Elizur Hinsdale, who later became the LIRR secretary and general counsel, wrote in the first LIRR history, published in 1898, that "numerous negotiations and schemes were projected for building [LIRR] branches to the south, but for some reason Oliver Charlick and his associates failed to comprehend the growing importance of that section of the Island, nor did they believe it possible for it to escape from their control." That blind spot allowed the South Side to be built, but the newcomer lacked a route west of Jamaica.

So in 1867, representatives of the newly completed South Side Railroad met with Charlick. They tried to convince him that both lines would benefit if the LIRR allowed the South Side to share the Long Island City terminal.

After listening to his competitors, Hinsdale wrote, Charlick remained "obdurate." It wasn't the only time. Charlick became so upset when residents of Cold Spring Harbor pushed for an extension from Syosset through their community that he simply bypassed it. Cold Spring Harbor now has a station, but the area where the tracks veer inland around the Huntington area is still known as Charlick's Curve.

Bizarre incidents ran along the twisting track to a consolidated Long Island Rail Road. In 1871, Hempstead residents were unhappy that LIRR service for their community was provided by a roundabout connection off the main line at Mineola. So they arranged to have the South Side build a branch from Valley Stream. One of the South Side's suppliers, named Pusey, briefly was elected president of the resulting New York and Hempstead Plains Railroad. When its directors ousted him in a financial dispute, Pusey sought to foreclose on the railroad.

Not content with legal action, Pusey literally took matters into his own hands. On Jan. 8, 1872, he attempted to take control of the line's Hempstead property. He fired shots at a locomotive attempting to pick up morning commuters. When the engineer abandoned his post, the passengers ran the train themselves to Valley Stream.

As the South Side's passenger count rose — it would jump from 246,000 to more than 600,000 in 1872 — the LIRR finally realized it could lose the entire South Shore if the rival line expanded east of its Patchogue terminal. As a preemptive strike, Charlick authorized construction of a branch to Sag Harbor, which was completed in 1870.

By the mid-1870s, the competing railroads were mired in a web of leases and foreclosures. Poppenhusen, the driving force behind the expansion of the Flushing and North Side Railroad, had agreed to operate Stewart's Central Line. The latter began in Flushing, crossed the LIRR's main line and then almost ran parallel to it though Garden City, Hempstead and Bethpage before reaching Babylon. Poppenhusen managed to gain control of the now-failing South Side and then the LIRR. But his subsequent efforts to consolidate other competing lines failed.

Austin Corbin, who had been developing real estate in Brooklyn, led investors in an 1880 takeover of the LIRR. For the next 16 years, he pruned and expanded — and also made a profit. Corbin extended the railroad to Montauk; he died just before it reached Port Washington in 1898.

Under Corbin's guidance, the consolidated LIRR, which in 1845 owned only 98 miles of track, entered the 20th Century with almost 400 miles of rail. Corbin's railroad continued the process of creating and serving communities on Long Island, and it was poised for its historic entrance into Manhattan through tunnels leading to a mammoth Pennsylvania Station.

David D. Morrison / LIRR

Oliver Charlick, the 11th LIRR president, was supposed to bolster the line's customer base.

With help from the LIRR and physics, Charles Murphy rode a mile in a minute

Superman on a Bicycle

BY BETH WHITEHOUSE
STAFF WRITER

Faster than a speeding bullet! More powerful than a locomotive! Those lines were made famous by Superman, but they were earned by a real person: Charles M. Murphy, a man from Brooklyn who rode his bicycle faster than a Long Island Rail Road train.

The year was 1899. The whole country was in the midst of a biking frenzy. Murphy, a blond-haired, blue-eyed, mustache-wearing 29-year-old, boasted he could bike a mile in a minute, if he were fronted by a charging train that would eliminate wind resistance and create a vacuum.

It was a publicity stunt, of course. But it also had athletic chutzpah: A lone man, on a regular bicycle, riding the equivalent of 60 mph behind a train, as fast as a car flying down the Long Island Expressway today. In the jaded 1990s it might be greeted with a shrug. But a hundred years ago, well, it was bold.

Hal B. Fullerton, a public relations man for the LIRR, heard Murphy speak at a meeting of the League of American Wheelmen, a biking club. Fullerton jumped at the idea. If Murphy did it, he would drag the name of the Long Island Rail Road with him for a worldwide public relations ride.

That was important, because the Jay Lenos of the day used the LIRR for stand-up comedy fodder. "Audiences and readers got the distinct impression that a young man embarking on the LIRR at Patchogue for New York was a decrepit graybeard before he reached Jamaica," wrote Fullerton's daughter Eleanor F. Ferguson in her book "My Long Island," republished in 1993.

So Murphy and Fullerton devised a scheme that became the most sensational sporting event of the era, according to a plaque and photo display commemorating the race that hangs in the Babylon LIRR station.

It was front page news in The New York Times that Mile-a-Minute Murphy, as he was dubbed, rode a mile in 57.8 seconds. The reporter wrote that Murphy had proved that "human muscle can, for a short distance at least, excel the best power of steam and steel and iron." The Brooklyn Eagle called the feat "the most plucky and wonderful performance ever accomplished by any athlete."

The ride took place Friday, June 30, 1899. Rail workers prepared a nearly three-mile stretch of lonesome line in a place called Maywood, between Farmingdale and Babylon. They laid out wood plank between the railroad tracks for Murphy to bike on.

Suffolk County Historical Society Photos

Charles (Mile a Minute) Murphy, above, practicing for his record-breaking run. He completed a mile riding behind an LIRR train in 57.8 seconds, below, possibly reaching 70 mph at the height of his run.

On the day of the race, the weather was clear and cool. Thousands of spectators lined the track, abutting the open fields. An engine was attached to an observation car. Fifty reporters and VIPs sat in the car, which had a hood extending out to cover the rider and a white plank of wood attached for Murphy to focus on as he rode.

"The hood, of course, broke the force of the wind, so he was able to pump like mad," said Vincent F. Seyfried, a Long Island Rail Road historian. "It was set up to favor the bicyclist."

Murphy, at 5-foot-7 and 145 pounds, wore blue woolen tights and a thin blue jersey with long sleeves. Murphy's wife sat near the tracks with her young son.

At 5:10 p.m., Murphy held the handlebars of his Tribune Blue Streak. As the run began, the railroad's superintendent reportedly wailed, "The poor man will be killed!"

"Outside, there was just a whiz and a rush and a cloud of dust," the Times wrote of the run. "No eye could follow the stroke of his legs on the pedals."

Observers thought that Murphy could have gone even faster had the train been able to. Six times he hit the observation car and was knocked back. Reporters said this gave Murphy the impression that the wood plank was flying up in pieces as he rode over it. He had probably hit 70 mph at the height of the run. It was a world record.

"I was riding against hope," said Murphy in his own account, as published in Ferguson's book. "I expected the worst — for the first time I realized that the eyes and minds of people thought my ride was impossible, but the sight of agonized faces on the rear platform yelling, holding out their hands, sent a thrill of determination through me."

Murphy's wife is said to have laughed as he passed by, knowing he was meeting the challenge.

But then came the moment of truth — as the train neared the end of the plankway. One thing that worried Fullerton was how to stop Murphy so he wouldn't plunge into the halted train. The engineer blew the whistle. Fullerton and another man leaned over the platform and lifted Murphy up and over the rail. Murphy clamped his toes in the toe tips of his bicycle, wrapped his legs around it and fished it up with him. "In that fraction of a second, a few men lived ages," wrote the Brooklyn Eagle.

The place erupted into pandemonium. People hugged. Kissed. Fainted. Went into hysterics.

Murphy later became the first motorcycle policeman in Nassau County. "I don't think his achievement revolutionized railroading or did much to change cycling, but it made a hero of Murphy and he became known all over the world as Mile-a-Minute Murphy," wrote Ferguson. "He lived on this fame the rest of his life." Murphy died in 1950.

As for the railroad, any impact was difficult to determine, wrote Charles L. Sachs in "The Blessed Isle: Hal B. Fullerton and His Image of Long Island 1897-1927." Said he: "For Fullerton (and probably his superiors at the time), the wild public relations value — demonstrating the railroad's technical ingenuity and speed and its commitment to a large sporting constituency — was probably considered well worth the effort and expense."

If nothing else, it was a day when a man became a superman, when a man kept up with a train using nothing more than the power of his legs.

Nassau County Museum Photo, Long Island Studies Institute

These women out for a ride on East Broadway in Roslyn, circa 1900, joined the sport that created a frenzy across the nation.

LATE-1800s BIKE CRAZE OVERTAKEN BY THE AUTO

On the day papers reported the success of Mile-a-Minute Murphy, they also reported:

- That a man had cycled the world on his bicycle.
- That a 10-year-old boy had left Lincoln, Neb., on a bike determined to pedal 4,100 miles in 80 days.
- That Patchogue was in the midst of a three-day meeting of the New York State Division of the League of American Wheelmen, which would end with a bike parade.

In the late 1880s, a bicycle mania swept the country. A new type of bicycle had recently been marketed, replacing the tall, old-fashioned bikes with the huge front wheels. The new bikes were called safety bicycles because they had front and back wheels of similar size and were closer to the ground. In 1888 they got pneumatic tires.

Bicycle clubs mushroomed across Long Island. In 1897, the Long Island Rail Road ordered six baggage cars specially rigged to transport bicycles. In 1898, the LIRR published a pamphlet called "Cyclists' Paradise," with maps of Island cycling paths.

By the early 1900s, the craze ended with the coming of the automobile. — Beth Whitehouse

Although far apart, Sag Harbor and Glen Cove both had early Jewish communities

Long Island's Founding Jews

BY STUART VINCENT
STAFF WRITER

After Sag Harbor's heyday as a whaling center passed in the late 19th Century, the village fathers searched for new industries to revive the community. They persuaded a New Jersey manufacturer to relocate his watch-case factory to the East End port. One unanticipated result was the establishment of a Jewish community and Long Island's first synagogue in 1896.

At about the same time at another Long Island port to the west, Jewish settlers in Glen Cove worked as peddlers and shopkeepers in the growing city. They held services in private homes for 20 years and, in 1897, founded Tifereth Israel, Nassau's first synagogue and Long Island's oldest continually operating, year-round congregation. Like many Jewish and Christian congregations on Long Island, both congregations were founded by European immigrants drawn here by the prospect of jobs. Although there were several other early Jewish communities on Long Island, including Lindenhurst and Setauket, the great wave of Jewish immigration did not occur until well after the turn of the century.

The earliest records of Jews on Long Island mention Aaron Isaacs, an 18th-Century merchant and part owner of a Sag Harbor wharf who was among those who fled to Connecticut when the British occupied the Island during the Revolutionary War. A German immigrant, he died in 1798 in East Hampton after converting to Christianity and fathering several children, according to a centennial history of the Sag Harbor congregation written by Nancy Solomon.

But Sag Harbor's Jewish community was not established until a century later, after village officials persuaded a man named Joseph Fahys to relocate his watch-case factory there from New Jersey. Fahys, a Christian, brought with him 40 to 50 Jewish immigrants who had just arrived at Ellis Island. The factory was built in 1882 and by 1900, according to Solomon, it employed 100 Jewish men, mostly of Polish, Russian and Hungarian descent.

In 1883, the Polish and Russian Jews formed the Jewish Association of United Brethren of Sag Harbor and, in 1890, paid $50 for property for a cemetery. Hungarian Jews formed their own cemetery association, the Independent Jewish Association, and bought land adjacent to the United Brethren cemetery.

In 1896, Nissan Meyerson, a member of the Brethren, paid $350 for the land on Elizabeth Street on which the synagogue still stands. The formal dedication of what was called Temple Mishcan Israel took place in 1898. Hungarian Jews held their own High Holy Day services at the local Engravers Hall.

Solomon's history relates a colorful, though undocumented, tale that the congregation received its first Torah from Theodore Roosevelt. The story goes that Roosevelt acquired the prayer scroll in 1898 for use by Jewish soldiers when the Rough Riders were quarantined for yellow fever at Montauk. When they left, he supposedly donated the Torah to the congregation.

By the turn of the century, the synagogue was in financial straits. In January, 1918, the mortgage was foreclosed for nonpayment of a $1,295 debt. Three congregation members bought it back at auction for $1,400. The congregation vowed never again to take out a mortgage on its property.

In May, 1918, the 52 men of the Russan-Polish and the Hungarian communities united to form the newly renamed Congregation Adash Israel. Two years later, on Dec. 8, 1920, during Chanukah, the congregation burned its mortgage and celebrated its unity with a parade through the village.

Gertrude Katz — whose parents, Phillip and Nettie Rosenstein, opened a women's clothing shop in 1930 — still lives in the village. She said she doesn't recall any of the anti-Semitism that touched other communities during her childhood. "There were Italians, Irish. We were all first- or second-generation. Basically, we were all insecure . . . Everyone was concerned with putting bread in their mouths and a roof over their heads."

Being such a small community, however, Sag Harbor's Jews faced social isolation, Solomon said. Katz' mother had kosher meat delivered from Patchogue two or three times a week. Margaret Bromberg, another long-time member, said she attended Sunday school in Riverhead, carpooling with children from other Jewish families.

Not all East End communities were as hospitable to Jews as Sag Harbor. "Bigotry and discrimination were not confined to children alone," Solomon writes. One man interviewed for the synagogue's centennial history told of how, a few months before his family moved to Bridgehampton in 1933, a cross was burned near their farm.

During the Depression, the community could no longer afford even a part-time rabbi. By the early 1940s, the ritual bath, or mikvah, was boarded up and the synagogue was used only for the High Holy Days. In 1948, a somewhat revived congregation changed its affiliation to the Conservative movement and its name to Temple Adas Israel, which remains today. In 1975, it became a Reform congregation.

When Sag Harbor turned into a summer playground, the synagogue found itself filling up with vacationers. For 18 of the past 19 years, Rabbi Paul Steinberg, vice president and dean of Hebrew Union College in Manhattan, has been the congregation's part-time rabbi — traveling to Sag Harbor each weekend between May and October to lead Friday night sabbath services.

Early Photo, Temple Adas Israel; Newsday Photo / Bill Davis

Above, members of the first synagogue on Long Island on Elizabeth Street in Sag Harbor, and below, the current temple on the same site. It was first called Temple Mishcan Israel and today is called Temple Adas Israel.

During the time Adas Israel was being formed, Jews in Glen Cove had been holding services in local homes. They secured a Torah now known as the Bessel Torah after Isaac Bessel, who with his wife, Esther, settled in the area of the city known as The Hill in the 1880s and ran a horse farm. The Bessel Torah is still used today. The earliest Jewish settler in the city was Samuel Sandman, who arrived in 1868, followed by Barney Friedman, who ran a general store and arrived in the early 1870s.

Bernard Singer arrived in Hicksville in 1898 after emigrating from Lithuania, but he moved to Glen Cove a few years later after encountering anti-Semitism. He peddled sewing supplies from a cart and then from a horse and wagon. In 1901, he opened a store on School Street, later moving it to Glen Street. The store survived almost a century; it closed last month.

"When you're living in a mobile society as we are, it's very difficult to have multigenerational families [in one place], but Glen Cove seems to have that . . . ," said David Zatin, who chaired last year's centennial celebration. He is Bernard Singer's great-grandson.

The small congregation bought its first home — a former opera house on Continental Place — in 1900. The sanctuary was a converted dressing room, although for High Holy Day services the opera hall itself was used.

That building was razed in 1926 and a new synagogue built on the site. In 1955, the congregation bought 14 acres on Landing Road and built a new home and school.

Rabbi Jason van Leeuwen, who since 1995 has led what is today an egalitarian, Conservative congregation, said Tifereth Israel has endured through the efforts of dedicated members, such as the late Arthur Buxenbaum, who for decades served as *gabbai*, assisting the rabbi in planning services, and as keeper of the minyan, ensuring the presence of the minimum 10 persons needed to hold a prayer service. He died in October.

Historical Society of the Westburys; Newsday Photo

An archival photo shows St. Brigid's, Nassau's first Catholic church. The church on the left was built in 1894. The smaller structure dates back to 1851 and was dedicated in 1856.

Having met prejudice, churches take root in Westbury, Glen Cove, Sag Harbor

A Catholic Presence on LI

BY STUART VINCENT
STAFF WRITER

'Probably we shall never know if Long Island was visited by St. Brendan or other Irish seafarers between the Sixth and Ninth Centuries . . ."

So mused Msgr. John Sharp as he began his centennial history of the Diocese of Brooklyn (1853-1953), which at the time of the book's publication in 1954 encompassed all of Long Island from Coney Island to Montauk Point. In fact, even after the Dutch colonies of New Amsterdam and Breuckelen were founded in the early 1600s, little is known of the early Catholics because anti-Catholic sentiment forced them to maintain a low profile.

The first Catholic who laid eyes on Long Island was probably Giovanni da Verrazano, a Florentine explorer who in 1524 sailed into New York Harbor beneath the spot where a bridge would one day bear his name. But Catholics who lived in the colonies were not granted the freedom to practice their religion until the English took over in 1664. Even then, it was a brief respite.

After King James II declared himself a Catholic in 1674, he granted religious liberty to all in New York, "provided they give no disturbance to the public peace." He appointed New York's first Irish politician, Sir Thomas Dongan, who became governor in 1683. Dongan sailed from Nantucket to Long Island, then traveled the length of the Island to New York. His chaplain, the Rev. Thomas Harvey, may have celebrated the first mass on Long Island during the journey. Harvey did offer the first mass in New York on Bowling Green on the site of the former Custom House.

Soon after arriving in New York, Dongan issued the Provincial Charter of Liberties, which stated that no one "which profess faith in God by Jesus Christ shall at any time be any ways molested, punished, disquieted, or called in question for any difference in opinion or matter of religious concernment . . ."

Glen Cove Public Library; Newsday Photo

An undated photo of Glen Cove's St. Patrick's Church, which was built on a hill in 1854

But in 1688, James II was forced to flee his throne by the English Protestants. Anti-Catholic sentiment dominated the colonies for the next century. That didn't change until after the Revolutionary War in 1784, when a New York law outlawing priests was repealed. The following year, the Roman Catholic Church in New York was incorporated and the cornerstone was laid for the first Catholic church in Manhattan, St. Peter's.

In 1822, the cornerstone was laid for St. James in Brooklyn, now the cathedral for the Diocese of Brooklyn. Flushing village in Queens hosted that future borough's first Catholic mass in 1826 in a Main Street shop, and St. Michael's Church was dedicated there in 1842.

The first known mass in what is now Nassau County was said in 1840 at the home of Barney Powers in northern Uniondale by the Rev. James O'Donnell from St. Paul's in Brooklyn. Four adults and three children attended. "Money was collected for a church, but only enough was raised to build a shed," according to an 1882 Queens history.

It wasn't until 1850 that Nassau's first Catholic church was born when New York Archbishop John Hughes formed a society to raise money for a sanctuary. The next year, they bought land on what is now Post Avenue in Westbury for what would become St. Brigid's Church.

Sharp noted that a wooden frame for the church was built, but Alfred Peck, who is writing a history of the church for its 150th anniversary, said the first church was a converted farmhouse. In any case, Sharp wrote that 600 Catholics came to the first mass in 1851. St. Brigid's was dedicated by Bishop John Laughlin, first bishop of Brooklyn. (It would be just over a century — 1957 — before the Diocese of Rockville Centre would be created.)

But St. Brigid's didn't have a resident pastor until 1892, and was served until then by pastors from St. Patrick's Church in the more populous Glen Cove, which led to a friendly dispute between the two parishes as to which is the "mother church" of Nassau County.

Glen Cove's claim goes back to 1854 when the Rev. Patrick Kelly oversaw the building of a wooden church atop a hill on Glen Street. St. Patrick's parish was established two years later. "The first Catholics here were Irish Catholics. They came for the [Duryea corn] starch factory, and some of them were farmers, too," said Msgr. John McCann, the current pastor of St. Patrick's.

But Glen Cove's Catholics didn't wait for a church to be built to say their first mass. Mary Ford, who came to Oyster Bay from Ireland in 1850, wrote in a letter that in 1850, she and others from Oyster Bay "came over to Glen Cove in a party of four or five and went down to a place called Garvies Point and held mass on a rock by a mulberry bush."

The new St. Patrick's parish went far beyond the city limits. The Rev. James McEnroe, who took over as pastor in 1858, was a circuit-riding priest. Galloping through the countryside on a white horse, his area included Sea Cliff, Oyster Bay, Roslyn, Mineola, Farmingdale, Massapequa, Garden City, Bethpage, Hempstead, Freeport and Bellmore.

Suffolk's first parish was St. Andrew's in Sag Harbor, established in 1859, followed a year later by another St. Patrick's, in Huntington. But masses had already been said for decades in those and other communities such as Smithtown, Greenport and Riverhead.

No priest was known to have set foot in Sag Harbor prior to 1832, but an Irishman named Michael Burke organized Sunday services at his home as early as 1829 for 15 families — 14 Irish and one Portuguese. Priests said mass in the whaling center in the early 1830s and the mission was adopted by St. James' Church in Brooklyn about 1835. When the local Methodist congregation outgrew its church soon afterwards, Burke arranged to buy it for $1,052.50 through a third party, who was Protestant. Because of anti-Catholic feelings in the village, according to the parish history, he believed the Methodists were unlikely to sell their church to "papists."

The Rev. Joseph Brunemann became St. Andrews' first resident pastor in 1859, when the parish was established.

The name St. Patrick's — reflecting the Irish population — is repeated throughout Suffolk. St. Patrick's, Smithtown, began as a mission chapel in 1841, becoming a parish in1952. St. Patrick's, Huntington, opened in 1849, becoming a parish in 1860.

Babylon hotel workers step up to the plate to become unofficial world champions

First Black Team a Big Hit

BY JOHN JEANSONNE
STAFF WRITER

Town of Babylon Historian

The first U.S. black pro baseball team was composed of Hotel Argyle employees. Their sponsor billed them as Cubans because of a belief that whites would not go to see blacks play. The hotel, left, was built in 1882 as an era closed, and it was torn down in 1904.

Babylon Historical and Preservation Society; Newsday Photo

Babylon's Argyle Hotel was a white elephant. It was built too late; the area's booming resort-hotel era was coming to an end near the turn of the century. It was built too big; its 350 rooms and 14 cottages never were more than one-third occupied. Within the Argyle's short 22-year existence, it was sold, boarded up for almost a decade and finally razed in 1904.

But as a diamond in baseball's historical rough, the Argyle endures forever. It was from its staff of waiters and porters that America's first black professional baseball team was formed in 1885. It was on the Argyle grounds where that team, originally called the Athletics of Babylon, so dominated local white teams that a white New Jersey promoter bankrolled them as the "Cuban Giants" and sent them on the road to become the Harlem Globetrotters of their time and their sport.

From Argyle headwaiter Frank Thompson's first team, which won all 10 of its games against white Long Island clubs that first summer, came the "world colored champions" of 1887 and 1888: Among them, George Parago, Ben Holmes (Homes, in some records), Shep Trusty, Arthur Thomas, Clarence Williams, Frank Miller, Billy Whyte (or White), George Williams, Abe Harrison, Ben Boyd, Jack Fry, and a man whose last name, Allen, is all that survives in the sketchy records of the time.

Not a Cuban among them. But Trenton businessman Walter Cook devised the Cuban Giants tag based on racial realities of the day; it was believed that white crowds would sooner pay to see Latinos than blacks play ball, so players were instructed to "bound onto the field chirping pidgin *Espanol* and cackling loudly, in a gross parody of everybody's idea of how Hispanics acted," according to Mark Ribowsky's 1995 "Complete History of the Negro Leagues."

He wrote that, in spite of "reams of attention in the press . . . it takes a leap of the imagination to believe that anyone who came to see them perform was really conned" by the Cuban ploy. And plenty went to see them play. According to Jules Tygiel, a historian of black baseball, the Cuban Giants toured the East in a private railroad car, consistently drawing sellout crowds, and were so financially and artistically successful that they spawned a handful of imitators in the 1890s: the Lincoln Giants from Nebraska, the Page Fence Giants from Michigan and the Cuban X Giants in New York.

Pitchers for the Cuban Giants earned $18 a week, infielders $15, outfielders $12 — salaries equivalent to what those men were paid for their hotel jobs.

It is not entirely clear, based on incomplete accounts at the time, whether the team originated as simply an after-hours diversion for the black Argyle employees, or as part of the hotel's planned amusement for its white vacationers.

At the time, Babylon was just beyond the crest of its resort era, which had been sparked by the arrival of the Long Island Rail Road in 1867. First as the gateway to Fire Island's hotels and beaches — the words "Fire Island" were written as large as "Babylon" at the original Babylon station — the village began to accommodate the stream of summer visitors from New York City with the construction of more than a dozen hotels.

The Argyle was the last of these hotels, funded by a syndicate headed by LIRR president Austin Corbin and built on the former estate of Brooklyn railroad magnate Electus B. Litchfield. Litchfield's sprawling property, called Blythebourne, included a large mill pond that would become Argyle Lake, and took on its new name because the group of hotel investors included the son of the Duke of Argyll.

Also, at that time, base ball (two words, then) had gone beyond a recreational activity to become America's No. 1 spectator sport. The Aug. 22, 1885, edition of Babylon's South Side Signal reported that a game on the Argyle grounds, between the National Club of Farmingdale and the Athletics of Babylon, was won by "the employees at the Argyle Hotel," 29 to 1.

Some accounts say that the team then "went professional" under a white promoter named John F. Lang, who arranged for the club to play an exhibition against the New York Metropolitans of the big league American Association. The Metropolitans won, 11-3, but the Argyle workers soon knocked off Eastern League champion Bridgeport, apparently the event that caught promoter Cook's eye.

Within two years, the non-Cuban Cubans "had attained a level of notoriety that gave them the right to pick and choose which white teams they would play," Ribowsky wrote. In 1888, the black Indianapolis Freeman newspaper reported, "The Cuban Giants, that famous base ball club, have defeated the New Yorks, four games out of five, and are now virtually champions of the world. The St. Louis Browns, Detroits and Chicagos, afflicted with Negro phobia and unable to bear the odium of being beaten by colored men, refused to accept the challenge."

Art Rust Jr., in his history of the black man in baseball, wrote that the Cuban Giants had the best black pitcher (Trusty) and best long-ball hitter (Sol White) of the 1880s, and White later wrote in his own history of black baseball that the Cuban Giants "were heralded everywhere as marvels of the baseball world."

By 1897, the Cuban Giants began to be done in by their legacy: Among the black teams that imitated them, the come-lately rival Cuban X Giants beat the Cuban Giants two of three games in a publicized showdown series and, losing their control and even their identity, the Cuban Giants began calling themselves the Genuine Cuban Giants. Their impact further dwindled with the creation of more-formal leagues.

But their inheritance goes on, in last year's 50th anniversary of Jackie Robinson's entry into the big leagues and this month's vote to put Larry Doby, the American League's first black player, into the Hall of Fame. Not to mention the general — if slow — integration of professional sports.

In modern-day Babylon Village, lumber from the old Argyle Hotel exists in several of the homes built on the former hotel grounds, just as the Cuban Giants live on in the big-league timber of every current black player.

Eastern towns of Queens win the fight to separate after six decades of wrangling

Nassau's Difficult Birth

BY GEOFFREY MOHAN
STAFF WRITER

If Nassau County has anything approaching a Bunker Hill, a solitary stone marker in front of a Waldbaums on Jericho Turnpike will have to do.

The granite stone commemorating the founding of the Long Island Bible Society makes only a scant reference to the courthouse that stood here, at what was once the geographic center of Queens County. But it was here in Garden City Park, more than a century ago, that bitter words over replacing that structure divided a county that once stretched from the East River to Cold Spring Harbor.

That tiff over a $100,000 expenditure touched off a secessionist fever in what then were the easternmost towns of Queens — Oyster Bay, North Hempstead and Hempstead — that would outlast the Mexican-American War, the Civil War and the Spanish-American War. The torch of secession flamed for six decades — passing from father to son, and dividing brother against brother.

It gave a new national political party called the Republicans a foundation on Long Island, and created the modern zeitgeist of Nassau County as a place striving to be everything that its neighbors to the west are not.

But to say secession from Queens was just about a courthouse would be like saying the American Revolution was just about tea. This was about taxes, about the collision of urban and rural values. And it was about bare-knuckled political ambition.

For every eloquent speech on civic benefit that graced these battles, there were a dozen more masking pecuniary motives. Newspaper editors sought prestige, circulation and political office, while land speculators, hotel owners and turnpike investors angled for profits from a new courthouse, or even better, a whole new county.

In the end, the prized courthouse went west, to Long Island City, and some 30 years later, the western towns went to New York City. The enraged eastern towns finally got their county at the turn of the century — and built their own courthouse at Mineola.

It was a twisted path that led to that moment, one that was strewn with compromise, shady horse trades and bad blood.

* * *

The old Queens County Courthouse in Garden City Park wasn't much to fight over. A wooden building, two stories tall, it stood virtually alone at the northwestern edge of the Hempstead Plains, accessible by dirt roads and eventually the Jericho Plank Road.

It was a rough-and-tumble affair, commissioned in 1785 for 2,000 pounds after British troops tore down its predecessor in Jamaica, which would never forgive the slight.

"The court of Queens county is at all times the least orderly of any court I ever was in," an assistant attorney general wrote in 1799. "The entry of the court-house is lined on court days with the stalls of dram sellers and filled with drunken people, so as to be almost impassable."

By the 1830s, editorial writers from both sides of the county lampooned the isolation of Queens' seat of justice.

"They chose the very umbilical point, the actual navel of the county, from the elevated summit of which the majestic dome looks abroad, in lonely majesty, and overlooks, and looks down upon, nothing," one wry editorialist wrote in 1835.

By then, prisoners frequently escaped with minimal effort, punching holes through walls or skulking away when left in the hallway for exercise.

"There is not a single secure room in it, nor a single apartment in which a prisoner can with safety be confined, should the said prisoner attempt to escape, or have the smallest assistance from without," a grand jury reported in 1838.

Queens needed a courthouse, and both Hempstead, the most populous town at the time, and up-and-coming Jamaica wanted it badly.

The Hempstead Inquirer was the first to suggest, on Oct. 17, 1833, that the "whole establishment, sheriff and all" be transplanted to Hempstead, "where there are a profusion of public houses for the accommodation of the numerous people who attend."

The paper got an immediate "hold on a bit, neighbor" from the Long Island Farmer, published in Jamaica, which preferred "taking it up and setting it down in this village."

Hempstead scoffed. Jamaica was a nice little village, and soon would be linked by rail to Brooklyn, but, Hempstead was on a course to "outshine Jamaica all intents and purposes," according to the Inquirer.

It didn't. By the end of the Civil War, Jamaica was laced with rail lines and its population outstripped Hempstead, which had just one branch of the Long Island Rail Road to link it with the rest of Queens.

The center of gravity of Queens had shifted from the parsimonious, mostly Whig (later Republican) farmers of the east, toward the merchants and manufacturers of the west, a Democratic bailiwick. By 1870, when Long Island City broke from Newtown, the west — which also included Jamaica and Flushing — had a 4-3 dominance on the Board of Supervisors.

Jamaica and its western cohorts were

Decades to a New County

1830s — Agitation grows to replace old Queens Courthouse in Garden City Park.
1840s — Population grows in western Queens; talk of annexation to Brooklyn or Manhattan begins.
1850s — First Republican county committee is formed, helping unite farmers in the east.
1860s-1870s — Eastern forces push State Legislature to divide Queens, but fail.
1872 — Decision to build new courthouse in Long Island City worsens Queens' east-west rift.
1877 — Eastern secessionists' bid to split Queens fails in Albany.
1894 — Queens referendum supports annexation to New York City.
1896 — Consolidation of western Queens is approved; takes effect in 1898.
1898 — Bill creating Nassau County is approved in Albany.

Meanwhile, the World Changed

1836 — Having defeated Mexico's forces, Gen. Sam Houston is sworn in as president of the republic of Texas.
1842 — The Opium War ends with the complete victory of Great Britain over China, which was forced to open ports to trade.
1848 — After two years of fighting, Mexico cedes Texas, New Mexico and California to the United States.
1861 — Fort Sumter in Charleston, S.C., falls to Confederate forces, touching off the Civil War.
1871 — A peace treaty is signed to end the Franco-Prussian War, in which France surrendered Alsace and Lorraine to Germany.
1885 — Fifteen European nations agree on the partition of Central and East Africa; the Congo is the prize, going to King Leopold II of Belgium.
1898 — The Spanish-American War ends with Spain giving up Cuba, Puerto Rico, Guam and the Philippines to the United States.

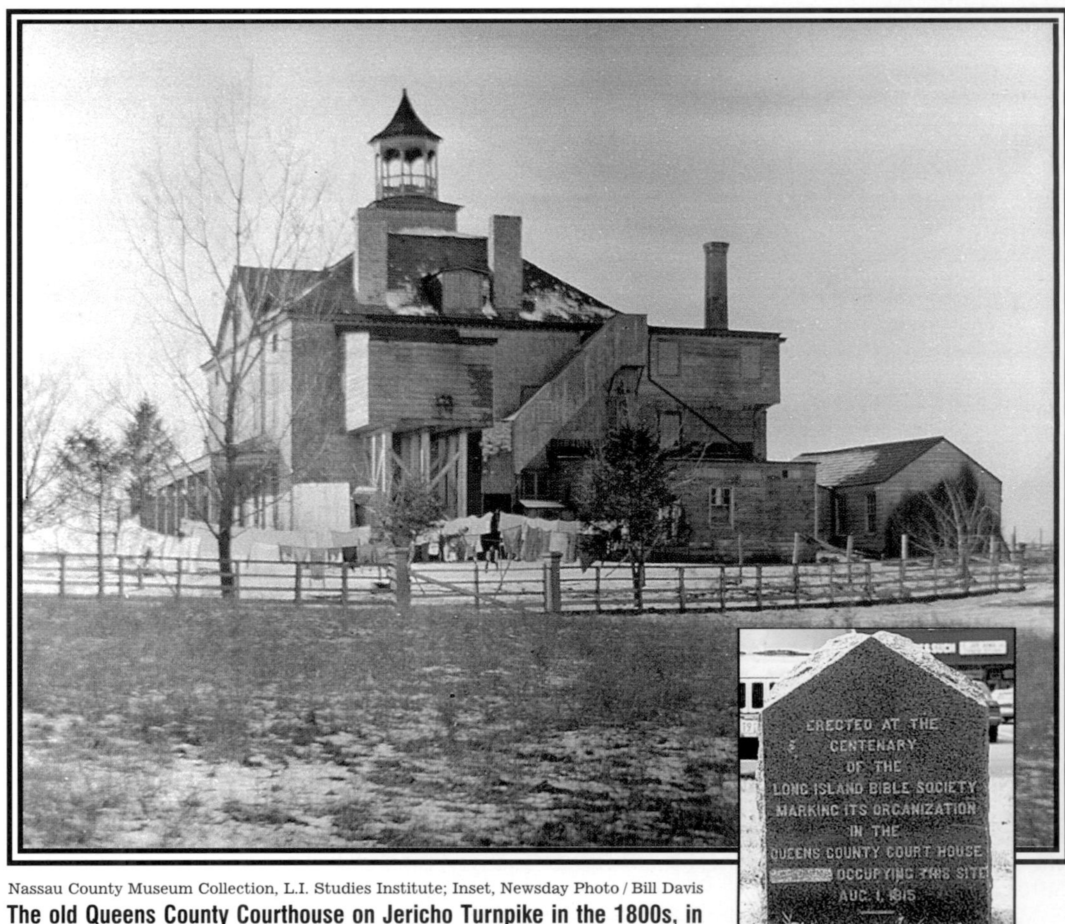

Nassau County Museum Collection, L.I. Studies Institute; Inset, Newsday Photo / Bill Davis

The old Queens County Courthouse on Jericho Turnpike in the 1800s, in what is now Garden City Park, and the stone that marks the spot today.

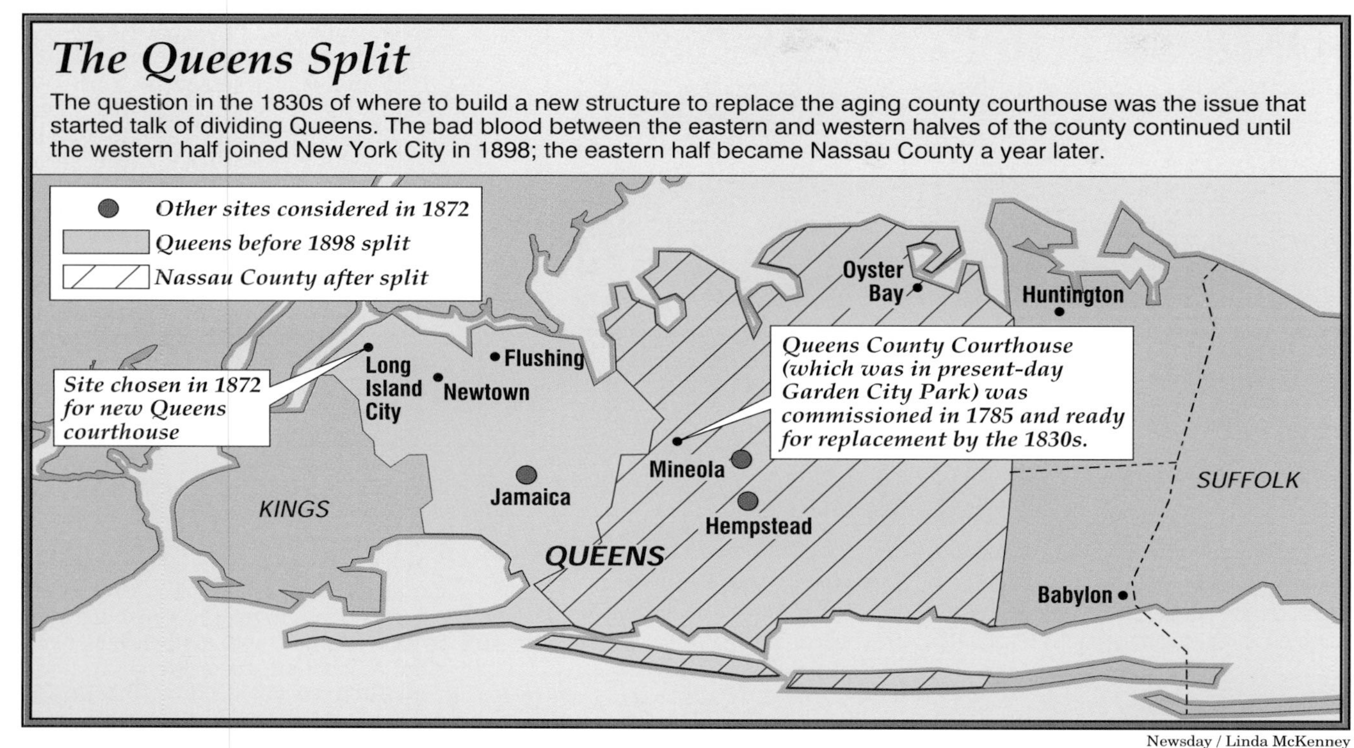

The Queens Split

The question in the 1830s of where to build a new structure to replace the aging county courthouse was the issue that started talk of dividing Queens. The bad blood between the eastern and western halves of the county continued until the western half joined New York City in 1898; the eastern half became Nassau County a year later.

Newsday / Linda McKenney

free-wheeling towns with liberal attitudes toward alcohol, and were rapidly filling with immigrants. At least since the 1840s, there were rumors that Newtown, Flushing and Jamaica would be annexed to Brooklyn or Manhattan.

The Queens Sentinel, published in Hempstead, was the first to suggest dividing the county to solve the courthouse debate. Its plan called for taking Huntington, which then included Babylon, from Suffolk County and adding it to Hempstead, North Hempstead and Oyster Bay.

"The western towns are closely united in their sympathies with the office of New York and Brooklyn and a great proportion of the crime which fills our jail, and which is on the increase, comes from this direction," The Sentinel explained on Nov. 3, 1859.

Jamaica and Hempstead each tried to hustle bills through the state Legislature to get the courthouse. Each was stymied. And so it went for decades.

The courthouse machinations only served to lay bare the deep differences between east and west. Three times — in 1869, 1876 and 1877 — the same parties working for a courthouse in the east tried to leap over the narrower issue and convince the state to divide Queens. Three times, they failed.

Each attempt was marked by clamorous meetings, mostly in inns and hotels. Innkeeper John A. Searing hosted one, and championed the cause, particularly if a new county meant a courthouse in Mineola, where he ran his establishment.

William T. McCoun, who had organized the first Republican county committee in 1854, and helped vault the party's candidate, John Alsop King, into the governor's office, also took a leading role.

To secessionists, members of the Democratic-controlled Queens Board of Supervisors were profiteers benefitting from the labor of honest farmers.

"They reap their richest harvests in large and overgrown counties, and will make a desperate fight to keep the taxpayers of the three eastern towns in a condition where they can compel them to pay tribute in the way of large salaries, and for schemes of local aggrandizement," The Glen Cove Gazette wrote.

Benjamin D. Hicks, a scion of the Island's original Quaker families, joined the movement in 1870, at the age of 34, when he moved from Manhattan to Westbury. Unlike many of his fellow secessionists, Hicks would never hold public office, though he rubbed shoulders with Republican governors from King through Frank S. Black, who signed Nassau into existence in 1898.

Opinionated but a born facilitator, Hicks led the secession movement for the next 30 years, through bruising and mostly losing battles in the Assembly.

His most painful lesson came at a time when the east seemed to have won the narrower fight over the courthouse. But it would explode in betrayal and fire up the embers of secession.

Four decades after the topic first arose, the Assembly passed a courthouse bill palatable to the eastern Queens towns in 1872. It allowed the supervisors to choose a site within three months. But if they were still stalemated, the courthouse would go to Mineola by default.

As the time ran out, the supervisors met in Pettit's Hotel in Jamaica on Aug. 2, 1872. Mineola advocates such as Supervisor Henry D. Remsen of North Hempstead needed only to stall as factions squabbled over Hempstead, Jamaica and the upstart Long Island City.

Seven votes were taken, all stalemating between eastern and western choices. The board took a 15-minute break. When it returned, Remsen again voted for Mineola, but abruptly changed his mind and endorsed Long Island City — creating a 4-2 majority for that community not far from the East River.

Remsen never publicly explained his decision, which touched off much speculation. Some viewed it as a spite to Hempstead. "There are some queer phases of this question yet to be made public, which we shall not at present dwell upon," the Inquirer wrote. It never quite elaborated.

Secessionists were spitting mad over

Please see **QUEENS** on **Next Page**

FAST FORWARD

The Mineola Mets: An Amazing What-If

BY IRVING LONG
STAFF WRITER

The Mineola Mets? The LaGuardia Expressway? Who knows what might have happened if the county now known as Nassau had not split from Queens a century ago.

"Maybe the secessionists made a mistake," said Rep. Peter King (R-Seaford), who was born in Queens. "Imagine if we were still a part of New York City: the Mineola Mets, the Seaford Subway, Mayor Mondello and a plethora of potholes for Al D'Amato to fill."

King was one of a number of elected officials who were asked to conjecture just how life would have been different, for them and for their constituents, if the two counties had not gone their separate ways.

The secession issue may still be a difficult one for politicians. A few declined to speculate, including Nassau County Executive Thomas Gulotta and Queens Borough President Claire Shulman. Others faced up to the what-if question with tongue-in-cheek bravery.

"I wouldn't have all this conflict, deciding whether to be a Rangers fan or an Islanders fan," said Rep. Gary Ackerman, a Democrat whose

> 'Imagine if we were still a part of New York City: the Mineola Mets . . . Mayor Mondello and a plethora of potholes for Al D'Amato to fill.'
>
> **— Rep. Peter King**

Fifth Congressional District embraces parts of Queens, Nassau and Suffolk. "I would save a lot of money, in that I wouldn't have to buy both the Queens and Nassau editions of Newsday . . . I wouldn't have to worry about my constituents having different area codes."

Ackerman added: "I would have had 73 less mayors to deal with." And he hypothesized that Rudolph Giuliani wouldn't be mayor of New York City because he would have been unpopular with Nassau voters.

"Probably somebody from Great Neck would have been mayor of New York City," Ackerman said. He suggested "Bob Rosegarten, the mayor of Great Neck Plaza."

Both Ackerman and County Legis. Bruce Nyman (D-Long Beach) agreed that property taxes would be lower in Nassau County if it were a part of the city. "Children in Nassau County would probably be going to school in Flushing," Nyman said, "so our property taxes would be lower, but our bus ride would be longer. And we would have a city income tax. I would be a city councilman, I guess. And New York City would have more council districts than Washington has congressmen."

Nyman, who collects old postcards, says he has one from the 1890s — a few years before the split — which was mailed from Long Beach and which is postmarked "Queens, N.Y."

He saw two more possibilities to ponder. If Nassau were still a part of Queens, he said, "Joey Buttafuoco would have been tried in the city, and the Long Island Expressway would have been called LaGuardia Expressway."

A County Divided

QUEENS from Preceding Page

the location, sure that it would one day be part of the competing metropolises of Brooklyn or Manhattan.

"If the people of the eastern towns really wish to avoid taxation for the erection of a public building upon a site which is manifestly destined to be the part of another county, they should awaken to a sense of duty and make a strenuous effort to effect a division before that expensive edifice at Long Island City has progressed much further," the Hempstead Inquirer pleaded on July 25, 1873.

Hicks and the secessionists rekindled the Sentinel's idea of forming a county with Huntington and Babylon. The two towns would add enough land area and population to pass constitutional tests for a county, they reasoned. And besides, those western Suffolk towns would eagerly set themselves free of the East End powers who held court in distant Riverhead. But residents of the two towns were split about leaving Suffolk. In February, 1877, a public vote on the measure won narrowly in Babylon, but lost dramatically in Huntington.

The Hempstead Inquirer and Huntington's Long Islander, both run by Republicans, nonetheless championed the cause.

But Democrats attacked from the flanks. The Farmer, a pro-Democratic paper in Jamaica, teamed with the major East End newspapers, including the Watchman of Greenport. The Watchman's publisher, Henry A. Reeves, also was a county supervisor and a Democrat of the southern school who had written editorials supporting the Confederate cause.

"Finding that a county could not be formed out of the three eastern towns of Queens county," The Sag Harbor Express wrote in February, 1876, "the projectors of the uncalled for scheme have concluded to invade old Suffolk so as to bring about their nefarious work."

Longtime secessionist Townsend D. Cock of Locust Valley, once a supervisor from Oyster Bay and now in the State Senate under the Republican flag, introduced a bill for secession of a new county, at first called Ocean, but later changed to Nassau, the name the British had once applied to the entire Island.

The bill died in the Assembly, and was revived the following year.

Led by editor-and-supervisor Reeves, the Suffolk Board of Supervisors opted to lobby against the bill — with dissenting votes only from the supervisors from Huntington and Babylon, Stephen C. Rogers, and Charles T. Duryea, both also Democrats.

Rogers promptly lost his next election in Babylon, and was replaced by Elbert Carll, who opposed joining the new county and squared off against Duryea when it came time to lobby in Albany.

The debate in Albany was eloquent and barbed.

John M. Crane, one of the opponents from Jamaica, told an Assembly committee the division was ". . . a scheme, born of discontent, nursed by a spirit of retaliation, if not of revenge, strengthened, supported and sustained by an overmastering, I had almost said, unhallowed, political ambition."

He pilloried the eastern towns for being "quite willing to avail themselves of the excellent roads — macadamized and other — which have been made, and are maintained at the expense of the western towns, exclusively over which to transport their agricultural products to the New York markets."

So what is at the bottom of the whole argument for division, Crane asked. "I answer, in a word, Politics!"

Crime, taxes and spendthrift policies were behind it, the secessionists countered.

They argued that the western towns of Queens ran up annual expenses of $129,805, compared to $13,980 in the east, while the east paid $2.2 million in taxes on personal property, compared with $1.3 million in the west.

The western towns also were responsible for "two-thirds of the paupers and criminals" consigned to the jail in 1875.

When the final vote was taken in Albany on May 18, 1877, the bill lost by a dozen votes, 55-43.

A dejected Benjamin D. Hicks, in a long public letter blamed the defeat on "selfish politicians, both on Long Island and at Albany, who justly fear that the success of our struggle for independence will jeopardize their hold upon the public offices and perquisites."

"On our Island the opposition to a new county came principally from a few well-known office-holders and place-seekers of Suffolk County, and from a like class of politicians in one or two towns of Queens County . . . I would respectfully recommend that when either of the gentlemen above referred to, is a candidate for office, that the friends of Nassau strenuously oppose his nomination in convention."

The assemblyman for Queens, Democrat George E. Bulmer of Long Island City, made a speech against dividing Queens, and no doubt was one of the men Hicks had in mind. Five months later, in October, 1877, Bulmer failed to get his party's renomination.

Huntington and Babylon would arise again as potential partners in the Nassau County movement, but Hicks and other leaders were gunshy. It was hard enough to fight western Queens without antagonizing the political powers of the East End. And Hicks was assured by state judicial officials that a new county would pass constitutional tests without adding the Suffolk towns.

With Democrats holding a virtual lock on political power, the secessionists would not get another try until Queens was asked to vote on an "advisory" referendum on consolidating with Brooklyn, Manhattan and the Bronx to form a "Greater New York City" in 1894.

The idea of a Greater New York had been in the air since the 1840s. Manhattan and Brooklyn, then locked in civic rivalry, had little interest in adopting the expenses of rural parts of Queens. And those rural areas had long since made their animosity toward the cities known.

The map of the proposed Greater New York that came out of the Legislature in 1894 embraced only the western towns of Queens, with just a small wedge of western Hempstead, including Inwood, Lawrence, Bellerose, Elmont and all of the Rockaways. (See story on next page.)

North Hempstead, Oyster Bay and the rest of Hempstead were excluded from the vote.

With the exception of the nearly bankrupt Long Island City, which voted overwhelmingly for consolidation, Queens had favored annexation by a slim, 51-percent majority.

At first, no one seemed to take the prospect seriously. The Farmer, from Jamaica, referred to the referendum as "a sentimental expression for consolidaton on some terms or other, at some future time or other."

But a Republican boss, Thomas C. Platt, pushed a consolidation bill through the Legislature in the spring of 1896, and Gov. Levi P. Morton, also a Republican, signed it in May. New York, as it is now known, would come into existence on Jan. 1, 1898.

What was left was a strange political creature, unique in the country, and on untested constitutional ground. A Board of Supervisors still ruled all of Queens, but could not levy taxes on the part that was in New York City. And that was the part that held the majority of votes on the board.

A tax revolt brewed. On Dec. 17, 1897, a group of the old secessionists gathered to form the Tax-Payers' Non-partisan Association of Queens County. Among them were Hicks and former Assemb. James Pearsall, who had pushed the secession bill of 1876 and lost.

A relative newcomer, P. Halstead Scudder, descendant of the Scudder family of Northport, made a lengthy speech that earned him a leadership position next to Hicks, some 30 years his elder.

"It is probable that there will be extra trouble when the outskirts of the greater New York are in our midst," Scudder warned. "Provision against impending danger is wisdom."

It was Scudder who summarized the eastern towns' options in a meeting that is Nassau's equivalent of the Continental Congress. About 300 residents met on Jan. 22, 1898, at 3 p.m. in Allen's Hotel, Mineola. Hicks chaired and moderated.

Scudder laid out the options, including annexation to New York, to Brooklyn, and including Huntington and Babylon in a new county. He rejected all except that of forming Nassau only from the non-city remnants of Queens.

Charles E. Shepard, the editor of the Long Islander, in Huntington, tried to convince delegates to include his hometown, but others prevailed, among them Pearsall, who had seen his bill go down in flames 20 years earlier.

J.B. Coles Tappan of Oyster Bay offered the resolution to create Nassau, which passed. The delegates chose Scudder to head a contingent to Albany.

It would bring him face to face in opposition to his younger brother, Town-

SOME OF THE PLAYERS

Benjamin D. Hicks: A scion of the Island's original Quaker families, he led the secession movement for 30 years during the late 1800s.

Townsend D. Cock: Republican state senator from Locust Valley who introduced a bill for secession in the 1870s; his effort failed.

Frank S. Black: Republican governor and a friend of Hicks who signed the bill that created Nassau County in 1898

Nassau County Historical Society Photos

George Wallace: Republican assemblyman who introduced the county bill to the state Assembly and Senate on Feb. 17, 1898.

send Scudder, a Democrat and hired counsel for the Queens Board of Supervisors, which was dead-set against dividing their county.

The Scudder brothers appeared together in front of the Board of Supervisors on March 3, 1898. They never addressed each other, though the conflict emerges in their replies to questions from the supervisors.

Townsend Scudder told the anti-secession supervisors that division would "deprive the western towns of the share of county taxes from the eastern town toward county expenses," according to the Farmer's transcription of events.

"P.H. Scudder had come prepared for any such objection, and gave figures to show that the additional expense on the borough towns would not exceed $5,000," the Farmer wrote.

Jamaica's supervisor challenged Halstead Scudder about whether the county bill had been submitted to a popular vote. Halstead insisted it wasn't necessary, and would only delay the matter.

But Townsend Scudder quickly suggested he could draft a provision for an election and lobby for its inclusion in the bill. To which his brother rebutted that there "was no desire for a vote that he heard of."

Republican Assemb. George Wallace — former editor of the Southside Observer in Rockville Centre — introduced the county bill on Feb. 17, 1898. It passed the Assembly and Senate the following month.

On April 27, a large delegation went to see Republican Gov. Frank S. Black, who allotted very little time for discussion. Black was a friend of Hicks.

Hicks waited patiently as Townsend Scudder took most of the allotted time.

Scudder began by saying the Board of Supervisors of the more-populous part of the county did not want the division, that it would be expensive, and that the new county would have no public property except Barnum Island off the South Shore — worth about $25,000.

He argued that with the nation at war — Teddy Roosevelt and his Rough Riders were fighting the Spanish in Cuba — it was an inopportune time to create a new county.

When Scudder finished, Hicks politely assured the governor that the Republican taxpayers of the eastern towns favored the measure. Black signed the bill the next morning.

By June, Halstead Scudder had become counsel to the new Nassau County Board of Supervisors, where blood proved thicker than politics. On at least one occasion, the elder Scudder rose to his younger brother's defense when the new board attempted to renege on decisions Townsend Scudder had made with the pre-Nassau board.

The first order of business for the new board included erecting a much-contested courthouse, on land owned by A.T. Stewart's Garden City Co.

On July 13, 1900, a slim Theodore Roosevelt, the Republican governor of New York, and recently named vice presidential candidate, stepped to the podium at Mineola to lay the cornerstone of the new courthouse.

Men once divided in their loyalties now rubbed elbows near the dais. Hicks, 64 years old and retired from public life, took a seat in the front row. His foster son, Frederick Cocks Hicks, ran the festivities.

Nearby was Hicks' old adversary, Townsend Scudder, now Rep. Scudder, representing a district comprising the same county he once spoke against. The lifelong Democrat had run on a platform of "Long Island First, Last and All the Time."

Roosevelt was introduced by former Queens District Attorney William J. Youngs, who likewise had once opposed the formation of Nassau.

Roosevelt never mentioned the men who had fought to create Nassau. He spoke instead of nonpartisan morality and decency.

"The public servant must be decent, upright and honest," he said. "The average citizen must be a good husband and father, but he must also observe honesty and decency and honor in public life."

Benjamin Hicks died six years later, and Halstead Scudder in 1909. Townsend Scudder went on to a long career as a judge on the state bench through the 1930s.

In 1903, a tinsmith repairing the roof of the Queens County Courthouse in Long Island City touched off a spark. The building, which had been built amid such controversy 30 years earlier, burned to its foundation. It was rebuilt in 1910.

That same year, flames also claimed the old Queens County courthouse in Garden City Park, which had become an asylum and then fallen into disuse.

Five years later, members of the Long Island Bible Society placed a black granite marker on the site, to commemorate their organization's founding "in the Queens County Courthouse . . . occupying this site."

The stone still stands, an anachronism in an asphalt meadow, dimly reflecting the image of passing cars.

Nassau County Museum, Long Island Studies Institute

A new Queens County Courthouse, in an undated photo, was built in the 1870s in Long Island City. Its location fueled the secessionists, who wanted it for what is now Nassau County.

SLICE OF QUEENS DELIVERED TO NASSAU COUNTY

Lawrence, Queens? Cedarhurst, Queens?

It almost happened. When the activists pushing for a Greater New York City drew a map of the proposed metropolis before the consolidation vote in 1894, they dropped a plumb line from the southeast corner of the town of Flushing (about present-day Floral Park) through the middle of a channel that is now part of Atlantic Beach.

The line cleverly eliminated from the vote the rebellious eastern Queens, which had made its opposition to the consolidation movement clear for decades.

But it also placed parts of Inwood, Lawrence, Cedarhurst, Elmont and Bellerose, and all of the Rockaways in Greater New York City.

"It wasn't a very deep slice," said Vincent F. Seyfried, a Queens historian and author. "It didn't take any village. This was all open fields."

Hempstead got everything but the Rockaways back within a year of the formation of New York City. Seyfried suspects the remaining area was returned as a consolation prize for the loss of the Rockaways, though he and other local historians say there is scant historical explanation of the land transaction.

"I suspect it was the usual political quid-pro-quo," Seyfried said. — **Geoffrey Mohan**

Nassau County Museum Photos, Long Island Studies Institute

Gov. Theodore Roosevelt was present, above, for the laying of the cornerstone of the Nassau County Courthouse in 1900. The building is shown at right in an undated photo.

LEGACY

Brooklyn's Thirsty Hunt for Water

Queens and Nassau supplies were tapped

BY BILL BLEYER
STAFF WRITER

The City of Brooklyn was running out of water.

In the mid-19th Century, the city's population was soaring and wells were running dry or becoming contaminated. Engineering studies convinced city officials that the way to go lay to the east in Queens, which then included what is now Nassau County.

So private companies and then the city itself began acquiring land in Queens. Wells were drilled, ponds enlarged and streams diverted to create a water supply network, according to a 1992 study by historians Richard Winsche and Harrison Hunt.

Those efforts would alter the landscape of Long Island. But the water network would turn out to be a boon for the suburbs in ways no one could anticipate. It set the scene for a major roadway that spurred development and population growth. And it preserved open space for the state park system.

But the short-run impact in Queens was severe: The water table dropped, wells dried up, mills lost their power source and the oyster industry was undermined because of changes in salinity.

The initial attempt to quench Brooklyn's thirst began with the formation of private water companies in 1852. Within six years, the Nassau Water Co. had acquired a string of South Shore ponds from Jamaica to Hempstead. Brooklyn bought out Nassau Water in 1857. The following year a reservoir was built in Ridgewood.

But by 1870, Brooklyn's population had grown to 400,000. The city needed another reservoir and bought 557 acres in Hempstead that included three mill ponds.Construction began the following year on a 22-foot-high dam that Brooklyn water commissioners estimated would form a reservoir containing a billion gallons of water. They ignored earlier engineering studies that showed much of this water would disappear into the permeable sand. Ultimately, the reservoir — now part of Hempstead Lake State Park — could only contain a third of its estimated capacity.

And Brooklyn was still swelling. By 1880, its population had soared to almost 600,000, precipitating a new water shortage. This was met by sinking new wells in Queens. Then the Brooklyn Bridge opened in 1883, unleashing a new housing explosion. By 1890, the population had reached 800,000.

Now the city fathers decided to extend their conduits east from Rockville Centre to Massapequa. All of the more than 300 properties acquired in Queens between 1853 and 1887 had been obtained through negotiated purchases. In 1887, Brooklyn politicians pushed for a shortcut. They lobbied for a bill in Albany that would give them the right of eminent domain to acquire land in Queens and Suffolk.

The Hempstead Inquirer blasted Brooklyn for "sapping . . . the very life-blood of Queens County." The newspaper noted that "Long Island is not blessed with much more than enough to supply her own needs."

Queens County officials attempted to block further encroachment by Brooklyn or at least to regulate the amount of water taken. But Brooklyn had more political clout and the legislation passed.

The 10-mile extension to Massapequa began in 1889. Two miles east of Rockville Centre, a 400-million gallon reservoir was constructed. To help the water along, a large pumping station was erected on the Freeport-Baldwin border. The Milburn Pumping Station in Freeport turned out to be one of the most extraordinary and beautiful industrial structures ever built on Long Island. Frank Freeman, a Brooklynite and a master of Romanesque revival architecture, was commissioned to design the 300-foot-long pumping structure.

Newsday Photos / Bill Davis

The Milburn Pumping Station in Freeport as it looks today: By 1907 it was supplying about 85 percent of the 145 million gallons consumed in Brooklyn each day.

Work began on the conduits and pumping station in 1890. By the end of the next year, the pumping station was almost completed and its equipment was tested. Unfortunately, there was still a gap in the pipes at Rockville Centre and the huge surge of water inundated workers. But a week later the pumping station was pushing water to Brooklyn around the clock. By 1907 the system was supplying about 85 percent of the 145 million gallons a day consumed in Brooklyn.

The creation of Greater New York City in 1898 put the New York City Board of Water Supply in control. By 1917, a new Catskill aqueduct started 12 years before was supplying most of the city's water.

In the 1920s the city began paying Nassau County $80,000 a year in taxes for the water system property. To cut their tab, city officials suggested building a highway above their pipeline. The state Legislature authorized the plan, and the result was Sunrise Highway. It was dedicated on June 8, 1929.

The city also dedicated 2,200 acres in Nassau to the Long Island State Park Commission in 1925. This land would be transformed into the Southern State, Meadowbrook, Wantagh and Bethpage Parkways and Valley Stream and Hempstead Lake State Parks. While the city retained the right to pump water, its dependence on the old system continually dropped until it was used only in emergencies, the last time in a 1965-66 drought.

In 1977, when the system was obsolete, Nassau gained ownership of the pumping station. The county obtained the property around the station and 1,750 additional acres of watershed land four years later. The remaining water system property was purchased by the county in 1986.

Nassau considered using the pumping station for its public works department or an aviation museum. In 1986 it was sold to developer Gary Melius, who had restored the Otto Kahn mansion in Cold Spring Hills. A 1985 fire that destroyed much of the building has stalled restoration plans, but Melius is still hoping that he can convert the building into a nursing facility.

The Milburn station, once one of L.I.'s most beautiful industrial structures, around 1910

Nassau County Museum Collection, Long Island Studies Institute; Newsday Photo

Immigrants toiling in Port Washington's sand pits help create Manhattan's canyons

Shifting Sands and Fortunes

BY RHODA AMON
STAFF WRITER

The story is told of the Italian immigrant in the late 1800s in New York who learned three things on arrival: "First, the streets aren't paved with gold. Second, they aren't paved at all. And third, you're expected to pave them."

The thousands of immigrants who came to work in the sand mines on the Port Washington peninsula could claim to have a hand in paving the streets of Manhattan as well as building skyscrapers, bridges and subways. From the late 1860s through the 1980s, more than 200 million tons of sand were dug from the peninsula and ferried to the concrete mixers of the burgeoning city.

The story of Cow Bay Sand, as it was called, began 20,000 years ago when the glaciers that formed Long Island retreated, leaving mounds of glacial sand and gravel. This is not the powdery stuff found on beaches but a mixture of grain sizes and shapes. "It has life in it . . . just the right combination of coarse and fine grains for making concrete," sand miner Al Marino told Elly Shodell for a Port Washington Library oral history called "Particles of the Past, Sandmining on Long Island 1870s-1980s."

Another factor was cheap transportation. The Port Washington peninsula juts into Long Island Sound 17 miles east of Manhattan. By the 1920s, 50 barges a day left Hempstead Harbor delivering thousands of yards of sand.

Sand mining started in 1865 on the western rim of the peninsula and moved to the eastern shore, where tall bluffs stretched for almost three miles. The work was low-paying and dangerous, and miners were recruited from Nova Scotia and Europe.

Pockets of sand mining developed all over Long Island, in Huntington, Northport and Oyster Bay, but Port Washington was the major center.

While the industry fed the local economy, there were outcries against the gouging of the land. In the '50s, when the post-World War II building boom caused a spurt in sand mining, Francis Wood, a Newsday reporter who lived in Port Washington, wrote a series called "The Rape of Long Island." "We're being gouged, chewed, gobbled up, torn, flattened and shoveled away — in broad daylight," Wood wrote.

Large sections of Port Washington were leveled, according to geodetic surveys. "Port Washington before sand mining probably resembled present day Sea Cliff with 80-foot cliffs dropping off at the water's edge," local historian Mitch Carucci wrote in a study of peninsula sand mining.

Early sand mining had minor impact. The sand was shoveled onto wheelbarrows to schooners and scows beached at low tide. The vessels would return with a load of horse manure for peninsula farmers. As technology advanced in the 1900s, sand was moved on rail cars to the processing area, later by giant conveyors tunneled under West Shore Road to waiting barges. Movie companies used the sand canyons for western desert scenes.

Suffolk County Historical Society Photo

Diggers work in the Glenwood Landing pit in 1897. The sand they dug up would be used to make concrete for the burgeoning city to the west. The last pit closed in the 1990s.

Sand mining became Nassau County's largest industry. As many as 800 workers were housed in barracks on the Port Washington sand banks. Some brought their families to live in company-owned cottages rented for $3 to $5 a month. Marino recalled that his father rented small houses to immigrant families who would buy their groceries from his store. The Goodwin-Gallagher Sand Co., once the largest in the world, built a school for miners' children in 1916.

The work was no picnic. Death from cave-ins was a constant threat. When an accident occurred, usually on sand cliffs cut back too sharply, all work stopped and men would come running from all the sand banks to dig for hours for the victims.

Though townspeople didn't want the jobs, resentment against foreign labor surfaced. In 1908, Italian workers staged a walkout demanding an increase of 25 cents over their $1.50 for a 12-hour day. The strike was broken in five days when the sheriff deputized 150 firemen and the sand companies hired 50 men from the Federal Detective Agency in New York City. Strikers were arrested, fired and fined $10 to $40 for "disorderly conduct." Polish replacements were brought in.

Meanwhile, once-deep Hempstead Harbor was filling with silt discharged from the sand washers. Political influence was charged as town officials ignored residents' protests. The sand companies, who occupied half the shore by 1909, were granted 25-year leases to build docks and charged $25 to $100, an "absurdly low figure even in those days," Carucci said.

Francis Wood in 1956 found that town ordinances to govern the sand companies were ignored and permit fees were never collected. "You can't stop a man from digging a hole on his own property," then-North Hempstead Town Attorney James Dowsey Jr. told Wood. "But what if a man digs a hole a couple of miles wide and 100 feet deep?" Wood inquired.

If Town Hall was silent about sand mining, so were local newspapers. Another industry, housing, was taking hold, and sand mining didn't fit into the promotion of a tranquil suburban community. The sand companies themselves realized the potential profit in real estate development. Gallagher sold property to Miami Beach developer Carl Fisher for 20 exclusive summer homes.

Residents who complained about harbor damage as early as 1893 were told they would have the shore back in 25 years.

"The Rape" that began in the 1860s would continue for some 125 years, until the sand banks were exhausted. The last company turned out the lights in the early 1990s.

Newsday File Photo / Bill Davis

Talk about sand traps! Leftover pits such as this one in Port Washington are being developed as parkland containing golf courses, nature trails, athletic fields and a privately owned senior life-care community.

FIGURING OUT HOW TO FILL UP ALL THOSE EMPTY SPACES

The "green monster," the giant sand-washing facility that loomed over West Shore Road, came down in 1996, symbolizing the close of Port Washington's sand-mining century. But a long controversy over what to do with the leftover sandpits was still wide open.

Now the debate is almost over. Plans by the Town of North Hempstead for an 11-story waste incinerator on a Hempstead Harbor sand-mining site brought an avalanche of protest and brought down a long-time Republican administration. The 460-acre property, which, according to current Democratic Supervisor May Newburger, has been a financial drain since its purchase in 1988, is being developed as parkland with golf courses, nature trails, athletic fields and a privately owned senior life-care community.

Nassau County owns more than 200 largely undeveloped acres at the north end; an industrial park and a condo development have replaced sand canyons, while town and county beaches line the shore. Older flattened areas have sprouted houses, shops, schools and a marina.

Changing times also are symbolized by a 41-acre sandpit in Port Washington North that has returned to woodland. **— Rhoda Amon**

The first convenience foods feed LI's appetite for innovation

What's Cooking? Plenty

BY ALICE ROSS

The Civil War had ended, and Long Islanders were looking backward as well as forward. On one hand, they were hungry for peace and normalcy and reached for tradition, and what better way to do so than with food? Plebian hasty puddings and samp porridges of the colonial past, mainstays on the postwar table, were further glorified by the patriotic fervor of the 1876 centennial.

And yet the Industrial Revolution stirred an appetite for innovation. Long Island Rail Road extensions spurred the growth of villages and hamlets along their tracks, delivering stock to general stores and food to new residents.

Homemakers bought newfangled commercial products and indulged their passion for specialized utensils such as geared cast-iron peelers and grinders, and the common agateware that arouses nostalgia today.

And now the first convenience foods appeared — canned items, packaged baked goods, sweet snacks and drinks.

Flour, sugar and spice had become readily available and inexpensive, encouraging home cooks to enlarge their baking repertoires. Elaborately filled and frosted layer cakes took their place as high-status items alongside the more conventional yeasted loaf cakes or gingerbreads.

Kitchen cookstoves worked overtime, filling pantry shelves with voguish canned and pickled specialties in glass Ball jars, invented in the late 1850s. Dressed salads, particularly chicken salad — *de rigueur* at elegant gatherings — spiced the culinary scene, reflecting fascination with foods eaten out of season and rich sauces.

A homemaker intent on upgrading her table may have turned to the writings of Sara Josepha Hale, editor of the matriarch of women's magazines, Godey's Lady's Book, or to the new newspaper columns written by celebrity cooking teachers. And then there were cookbooks.

The expanding publishing industry brought out great numbers of encyclopedic cookbooks at affordable prices. One didn't need to be affluent to keep one or two alongside a notebook of handwritten recipes. Long Island homemakers commonly consulted cookbooks written by Maria Parloa ("Appledore Cookbook," 1872), Marion Harland ("Common Sense in the Household," 1872) or Mrs. Croly ("Jennie June's American Cookery," 1878), which became local standbys for the old faithful and new high-fashion dishes. Within a few years, the enterprising church women of Sound Avenue in what is now Riverhead would write Long Island's first fund-raising cookbook, "The Practical Cook Book," published in 1886.

The social business of Long Island's women demanded good food in abundance. Town women, blessed with more leisure than their farm sisters, used social rounds to maintain family and work duties, to network with neighbors, and for volunteer work. Drop-of-the-hat hospitality demanded the exchange of treats, often at the afternoon tea table. Their diaries tell us that Saturday was the regular baking day, but if one ran short of the requisite stock of breads, pies, doughnuts, cakes and cookies, a weekday might also be needed.

Therina King, writing in her diary in Miller Place in July, 1879, noted that she offered visiting relatives "pork, potatoes, beets, and blackberry pie for dinner, for tea bread, biscuit, soft sugar cake, ginger nuts [cookies], prunes, dried apples, and smoked beef." When neighbor Charlotte Davis came to help with the farm work in September, 1880, Therina served "roast ducks, beef, potatoes, sweet potatoes, turnips, apple crust, grapes, watermelon, & tea for dinner . . . for tea we had wheat and rye bread, baked apples, pear preserves, smoked beef, chocolate cake, and ginger nuts."

Apparently the balance between tradition and fashion fed Long Islanders well during this period. Although it would seem that their work was hard and demanding, the budding Victorians likely looked back on more primitive times and enjoyed what seemed to be newfound ease and luxury.

The recipes presented here offer a taste of the past. They represent what was old and new on Long Island tables in this post-Civil War era, and are offered largely as originally written.

Alice Ross is a food historian.

LEGACY

Newsday Photos / Bill Davis

Chicken salad with celery garnishes and a celery glass: Celery became chic because it could be purchased out of season.

The large quantity of celery and the celery leaf garnishes in the following recipe from 1886 were then high fashion, as celery was one of the new out-of-season foods one could buy.

Today, you may wish to reduce the amount of celery, and substitute lettuces. This is how the recipe appeared in Long Island's first fund-raising cookbook, "The Practical Cook Book."

Chicken Salad

"Boil [or roast] chicken until tender; when cold cut in small pieces and add twice the quantity of celery cut with a knife, and one cold boiled egg sliced and thoroughly mixed with the other ingredients.

"For dressing put on the stove [and warm] a sauce-pan with one-third pint of vinegar and one teaspoonful of butter; beat one egg [extra-large] with one teaspoonful of mustard, one of pepper, one-half teaspoonful of sugar and one-quarter teaspoon of salt; when thoroughly beaten pour slowly into the vinegar or until it thickens.

"Be careful not to cook too long or the egg will curdle. When cold, mix the salad. Garnish the top with slices of cold boiled egg and the edges of the salad dish with celery leaves."

Makes 4 to 6 servings

Gingersnaps, a popular cookie then and now, cool on a Victorian wire rack.

Traditional Gingersnaps With a Bite

Adapted from Gladys Howell, Recipe Collection, Southold, 1875

1 cup butter
1 cup mild molasses
1 cup sugar
2 tablespoons cider vinegar
6-8 tablespoons powdered ginger, or to taste
1 teaspoon baking soda
½ teaspoon salt
3 cups flour

Cream butter with molasses, sugar and vinegar. Add ginger, baking soda and salt. Add 3 cups of flour, or enough to make a sticky dough. Drop in teaspoonfuls onto a greased pan, allowing for spreading. Bake at 350 degrees for 12-15 minutes, or until the surface cracks. Remove to wire rack to cool and harden. Makes 4 to 5 dozen.

Therina King's diary is at the Miller Place-Mount Sinai Historical Society. Howell's recipes are in the collection of Mary Mooney-Getoff, Southold. "The Practical Cook Book" is in the collection of Estelle Evans, Riverhead.

In his Corona factory, Tiffany spins colorful confections in glass

Gilding the Gilded Age

BY MICHELE INGRASSIA
STAFF WRITER

It seemed to be the arrogance of youth: As a teenage artist studying in Europe in the 1860s, Louis Comfort Tiffany was drawn to the medieval windows of Chartres Cathedral, haunted by their jewel-like colors and boldly wrought designs. But for the brash young New Yorker, their beauty wasn't enough. "He wanted," says William Valerio, curator of the Queens Museum of Art, "to make glass that was even *more* beautiful than the great cathedrals of France."

Tiffany's legacy is that he surpassed even his own braggadocio. From 1893, when the chapel he created for the World's Columbian Exposition in Chicago earned him international acclaim, until the late 1920s, when the looming Great Depression reduced him — at least temporarily — to a symbol of the despised Gilded Age, Tiffany reigned as the foremost artist of the art nouveau and arts and crafts movements. From his factory in Corona, he produced thousands of windows, lamps and vases, pieces that transformed glass from utilitarian object to work of art, as dazzling as any of the gems at Tiffany & Co., his father's famous jewelry store.

"He loved art and believed people would have a better quality of life if they surrounded themselves with good quality objects," says Donald Davidson, retired curator of the Morse Museum of Art in Winter Park, Fla., whose Tiffany collection is world renowned. "What made him different was his creative approach. He decided that glass was something that could be explored, that he could paint *with* glass, not *on* glass."

Ironically, Tiffany yearned to be a painter. In 1867, he planted himself in the studio of American landscape artist George Innes. A year later, he set off for Paris to observe painter Leon Bailly. He toured Morocco and Egypt, taking in the rich patterns and supersaturated colors that would eventually echo in his glass and interior designs.

But it was the windows of Chartres and the mosaics of Ravenna, Italy, that beckoned Tiffany to abandon landscapes. In an era when most window artisans painted designs on colored glass, Tiffany began experimenting in the early 1870s, hoping to duplicate the iridescence of ancient glass. It was Tiffany who, in 1881, registered a patent for the opalescent windows he created by adding metal oxides, rather than pigments, to the molecular structure.

Newsday File Photo
Louis Comfort Tiffany, who yearned to be a painter and made glass into a work of art

What distinguished Tiffany's Favrile, or handmade, glass wasn't just color — he produced 5,000 hues — but its ever-changing forms. Tiffany Studios, opened in 1893, developed scores of new patterns — drapery glass, mottled glass, confetti glass, jeweled glass among them. In audacious combinations, Tiffany could create designs never before dared, be it a dragonfly with ruby red cabachon eyes or fields of pansies more brilliant than nature's own.

Not surprisingly, he proved to be an unrelenting taskmaster to the workers who took delicate paper designs and cut them in glass, rimmed them with copper and soldered them into three-dimensional reality.

"He had a walking stick, and he'd walk through the factory," says Nancylee Dikeman, whose father-in-law, John, was foreman of the lamp department, and whose husband, Fred, became one of the country's foremost restorers. "He'd tap a lamp with his stick and say, 'This one is nice. This one is nice.' Then he'd take the cane and just wipe the others onto the floor."

Worse, he could be a snob. Although he dreamed of a Tiffany in every house and he saw his colorful lamps as the antidote to the cold, bare lightbulb, his pieces were actually grand adornments for even grander houses. The Rockefellers were his customers; so were the Astors and the Rothschilds. Dikeman recalls their visits to the Manhattan showroom, "where they could sit and have tea or coffee and choose which base they wanted with which shade."

In 1881, when Mark Twain became popular and prosperous enough to buy a mansion in Hartford, Conn., he hired Tiffany's design firm to craft everything from windows to woodwork. A year later, President Chester Arthur paid him $15,000 to renovate the White House.

Of all Tiffany's designs, perhaps none was grander than Laurelton Hall, the 85-room mansion that he built for himself in 1905 on 850 acres overlooking Cold Spring Harbor. From the outside, it evoked the mystery of the Orient; inside it exploded with color, from the blue glass dome of the three-story hall to the fountain vase that changed hues depending on the time of day.

But like the house, destroyed by fire in 1957, Tiffany's glory seemed far more brittle than his glass. By the time he died at age 85 in 1932, the Depression had tarnished the Gilded Age, art deco had supplanted art nouveau, and Tiffany was, Donaldson says, "a joke." The business finally fell into bankruptcy.

"It wasn't until the Museum of Contemporary Crafts in New York did a big Tiffany exhibition in 1958 that Tiffany was rediscovered," says Donaldson. "The show took the town by storm."

In the 40 years since, the challenge has not only been how to find a genuine Tiffany — lamps can sell for tens of thousands of dollars, windows for millions — but how to duplicate one. No one has perfected the depth of Tiffany's color and kaleidoscopic effect of his glass, but each year the copies improve.

"The way people are replicating them, the Tiffany lamp may well be like the '32 Ford," says Donaldson. "There are more '32 Fords on the road today than were ever made in Michigan, thanks to fiberglass kits. One day, it may be the same with Tiffany."

Alastair Duncan Collection, Queens Museum of Art
Workers around the year 1900 at Corona's Tiffany Studios, which developed new patterns such as drapery glass, mottled glass and confetti glass

Newsday Photo / Bill Davis
A restored Tiffany window, "St. John the Evangelist," at St. Mark's Episcopal Church

LOOKING FOR JEWELS IN CHURCH'S ASHES

When fire broke out in St. Mark's Episcopal Church in Islip on Dec. 5, 1989, it threatened not just a crisis of faith, but an artistic crisis as well: Of the 20 stained glass windows in the 150-year-old church, eight were the work of Louis Comfort Tiffany.

Fortunately, the process of rescuing them began even before the arson fire was out. As the blaze soared through the roof, Rector Jerome Nedelka stood with firefighters, trying to guide their hatchets and hoses away from the precious panels. "You try to be gentle," he says, "but how gentle can you be?"

Several windows were smashed. The "Recording Angel," a 5,500-piece panel, was among many encrusted with soot. Virtually untouched, however, was "St. Mark," an early ecclesiastical figure window by Tiffany, who was a sometimes worshiper at St. Mark's and a friend of many parishoners, including William K. Vanderbilt, who financed the construction of the church.

Like the rescue of St. Mark's, the salvaging of the Tiffanys owed itself to the community. For three weeks, legions of volunteers sifted ashes looking for jewel-like slivers. "There was no heat, everything was wet and temperatures were in the 30s," Nedelka says. "Still, they got 97 percent of the glass."

In the end, it fell to East Marion glass restorer Jack Cushen to bring the windows back to life in a six-month, $250,000 project. "You should have seen those poor windows hanging there after the fire," Cushen says. "It's amazing how wonderful they came out."

— Michele Ingrassia

Newsday Photo / Bill Davis

Collection of Vincent F. Seyfried

Two Stanford White designs: above, the Garden City Hotel as it looked in 1898; at left, the octagonal Wetherill house above Stony Brook Harbor in Head of the Harbor.

Stanford White, designer of elegant Long Island houses for the Gilded Age

The Architect of Desire

BY RHODA AMON
STAFF WRITER

Stanford White, one of America's most famous architects, married into Long Island history — though he was less than an ideal husband.

In 1884, White, who designed some of the most opulent structures on Long Island, wed Bessie Smith, a descendant of Smithtown founder Richard (Bull) Smith. Twenty-two years later, still married, White was shot to death on the roof of Madison Square Garden by the jealous husband of his former lover, a teenaged showgirl.

With his untimely end in stark contrast to his ebullient lifestyle and rich architectural legacy, White is summed up by his great-grandaughter as a gifted, complex and, ultimately, tragic figure. "He didn't want to hurt anyone," said writer Suzannah Lessard. "At the same time he had a destructive side, an inability to not do what he did." Her 1996 book, "The Architect of Desire: Beauty and Terror in the Stanford White Family," chronicles the generations of descendants who continue to live in and near Box Hill, the Saint James house Stanford and his wife bought as a summer home in 1886.They also had a home in New York City, where he was born in 1853.

During his heyday, White designed about 40 luminous Long Island structures, including the old Garden City Hotel and the Harbor Hill mansion in Roslyn, and set a standard for beauty and opulence for generations of architects. In the late 1880s, White became the darling of the nouveaux riches, who discovered Long Island as a fox-hunting, polo-playing, yacht-sailing haven.

"They wanted to live like the nobility of Europe, with huge estates secluded behind gates," said Lessard. White cultivated them, partied with them and fulfilled their wishes by creating baronial "cottages" for them. (White himself never became rich; during his last years he was deep in debt.)

Yet with his passion for beauty and elegant interiors, he epitomized the Gilded Age, which would start to fall apart after World War I. That age, with its large houses set back on great gated estates, ironically, set the stage for Long Island's "suburban sprawl," Lessard said. Instead of developing a system of clustered villages, Long Island grew sprawling developments of homes surrounded by as much private property as possible.

One of White's first efforts on Long Island was a Montauk Point enclave of shingled houses with wide porches. The East End had not yet emerged as a chic destination when, in 1882, eight wealthy sportsmen approached White's New York City firm, McKim, Mead & White, to create a hunting and fishing colony on a bluff at the easternmost tip of Long Island.

Stanford White

The Montauk houses were among the earliest of the Shingle Style summer places of 10 to 30 rooms, popular in the late 1800s. The firm built seven cottages and a clubhouse, and the owners were determined to keep it exclusive. One owner, corporate lawyer Harrison Tweed, would clear the area of intruders by strolling naked on the beach. Now, only five cottages remain, all listed in the National Register of Historic Places.

Tragically, two of White's most trend-setting creations have been lost. "If you were to list the 10 greatest losses to Long Island in the 20th Century, you would include the old Garden City Hotel and Harbor Hill in Roslyn," said Robert B. MacKay, director of the Society for the Preservation of Long Island Antiquities.

White redesigned the 1871 Garden City Hotel, making it U-shaped with parallel wings. Reopened in 1895, the hotel was gutted by fire four years later. Undeterred, White directed the rebuilding, making it larger and grander with a vertical tower adapted from Independence Hall in Philadelphia. It became the center of Island society, frequented by Vanderbilts, Morgans, Astors. The hotel slid into decline and was demolished in the 1970s.

It would take White five years to complete Harbor Hill, the huge stone French château he built on 600 acres in Roslyn Harbor for silver mining heir Clarence Mackay. Until then, the resort homes of the late 1800s were built Shingle Style on a smaller scale.

"After Harbor Hill, architects began tearing down houses, or building masonry envelopes around them," said Robert MacKay, co-author of "Long Island Country Houses and their Architects, 1860-1940," published in 1997. "From then until 1914, really large mansions were built in the European style."

To furnish the château, White scoured Europe for treasures, bringing back shiploads of tapestries, paintings and medieval armor for Mackay's world-class armor collection. The Mackays entertained in their showplace, climaxed by a glittering party with 1,200 guests in 1924 for the prince of Wales (briefly Edward VIII and later the duke of Windsor), who reportedly said, "I am impressed with the grand scale of hospitality on Long Island." Unfortunately, the mansion was demolished in 1947. All that's left is an elegant gateway on Roslyn Road, now the entrance to a swim club.

What is still intact, however, is White's last project, the 1906 Trinity Episcopal Church on Northern Boulevard in Roslyn, commissioned by Katherine Duer Mackay, and modeled after medieval English parish churches.

LI HISTORY.COM 

A list of remaining White-designed structures — some of which are not open to the public — is available on the Internet at http://www.lihistory.com.

White's work also can be seen in the Shingle Style Shinnecock Hills Golf Clubhouse, the first golf clubhouse in America.

The game was so little known in the United States at that time that a businessman bringing golf clubs from Scotland was stopped by a customs agent who didn't believe a game could be played with "instruments of murder."

Lessard can recognize her great-grandfather's style. The work of his partner, Charles McKim, was "monumental. Stanford's work had a lightness." Their company, McKim, Mead & White, one of the nation's most influential architectural firms, trained hundreds of young architects, some of whom may have contributed designs credited to the flamboyant White.

The trial of his murderer, millionaire playboy Harry Thaw, was on a par with the recent O.J. Simpson trial. The scandalous sex triangle shocked a nation still clinging to Victorian virtue. New York's 14 newspapers fed on the lurid details — which included details of White pushing his lover, Evelyn Nesbit, naked on a red velvet swing. Thaw's two trials gave ample opportunity to savor the exposure of the "satin-lined sins of the rich." The first trial ended in a hung jury. At the second one, he was found not guilty by reason of insanity and was committed to a mental institution — from which he later escaped. (He was recaptured in Canada, pronounced sane in 1915 but was recommitted after he horsewhipped a teenaged boy.)

"The public was repudiating the excesses of the rich, and they mistakenly thought Stanford White was one of them," Lessard said.

Protests by nonwhites end a policy of exclusion at a new school in Amityville

A Blow for Integration

BY JOHN HILDEBRAND
STAFF WRITER

It was the pride of Amityville — a formidable, Victorian-style building of rich red brick, topped by an 80-foot bell tower. When the school opened in the winter of 1895, it advertised the community's growing wealth in unmistakable terms, with arched entryways, a white marble drinking fountain and curved staircases of dark-stained wood.

For all this ornamentation, however, it was clear to Charles Devine Brewster and his neighbors in North Amityville that the Amityville Union School fell far short of its promise. Brewster's own son had been barred from classes on opening day, on the ground that the school, located barely a mile from his home, was reserved for whites only.

On the night of Feb. 28, the father arrived at a school board meeting — by sleigh and in the midst of a near-blizzard, according to a story passed down by descendants. Brewster's message was blunt: Either the district would close its segregated one-room schoolhouse in North Amityville and admit nonwhites to the new building, or the district would face a boycott. Headlines were immediate. "Color Line Drawn in the Amityville Public School," said the Brooklyn Daily Eagle. As word of the parents' protest spread, additional demonstrations erupted in Hempstead, in Jamaica, Queens, and elsewhere — an embryonic civil-rights movement that would still echo 60 years later.

Protesters included black business owners, stung by the fact that their growing prosperity was not reflected in their legal status.

"I and my father and mother have paid taxes in Jamaica for 80 years," said one protester, Samuel Cisco, the owner of a successful scavenger business. Yet, Cisco added, his own children had been turned away from a white school, while "Irishmen, Italians and Dutchmen, who have been here only three months, can go in there, although covered with dirt."

While such frustration ran deep, it said something about the social attitudes of the times that it often took whites completely by surprise.

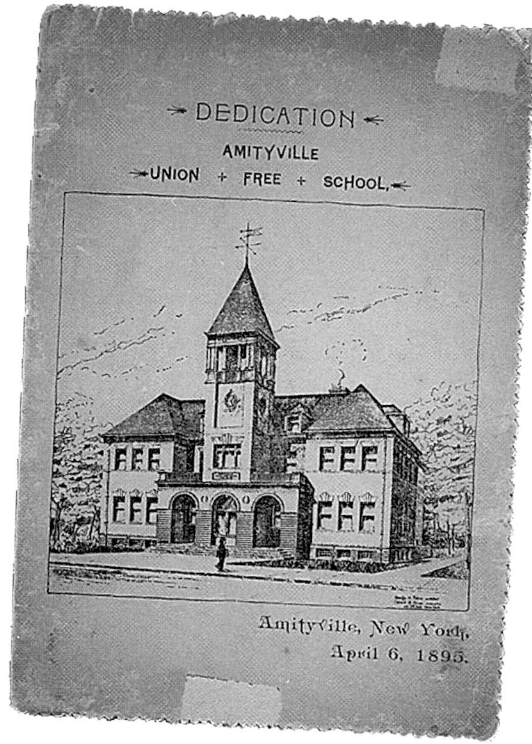

Amityville Historical Society; Newsday Photo

Amityville's Victorian-style building of red brick with an 80-foot bell tower was formidable, and, initially, for whites only.

"It seems strange that in several Long Island localities the colored people are 'kicking' so vigorously in regard to school matters," wrote a correspondent for the South Shore Signal, a Babylon newspaper. The writer was certain that blacks generally took "but little interest in educational matters."

This touched the issue of racial identity. Many North Amityville protesters regarded themselves, not as blacks, but as descendants of Indians who had fished and farmed on Long Island since time immemorial. The issue was complex, because there had been intermingling among American Indians, blacks and whites since colonial times.

What was perfectly clear, however, was that the Brewsters, Devines, Fowlers and other families of North Amityville took great pride in their heritage and possessed a long tradition of education.

Amityville Historical Society; Newsday Photo

A 1907-08 class at the Amityville school, which was opened in 1895, reflects the integration that followed the closing of a "colored" school in North Amityville.

For nearly 60 years before the threatened boycott, these families had maintained a local school — first with support from a Quaker charity, then with their own taxes.

Now, those same taxes would help pay for Amityville's grand new school, used today as an administration building. Brewster and his neighbors argued that their families had been promised access to the school, in return for their votes in favor of its construction.

Initially, the protesters' threats of boycott met resistance, including hints that any students skipping school would be tossed into a truants' home. But within a few days, protesters were invited to submit a petition to the board, requesting closure of the "colored" school. This was done, and in August, the old school was closed by unanimous vote of 40 residents attending the district's annual meeting.

Elsewhere on the Island, resistance to integration was far stiffer. In Jamaica, seven black parents, including Cisco and his wife, were arrested for refusing to send children to an all-black school. The protesters fought back in court, and sometimes got charges dismissed. Peace was restored to Jamaica in 1900 when a progressive new governor, Theodore Roosevelt, signed a law abolishing segregation in urban districts.

Thus vanished three separate black schools in Jamaica, Flushing and Hempstead. Two rural districts upstate continued to segregate, as did Roslyn on Long Island. Roslyn finally closed its all-black school in 1917, in response to parents' pressure. The two other holdouts shut their doors in 1933 and 1943, respectively.

By then, however, school segregation was reappearing, first in Manhattan and Brooklyn, then in other communities. This racial division was even more stubborn than the old, being based primarily on housing patterns rather than on overt government restrictions.

The forces for integration had won some memorable early skirmishes, to be sure, but the school wars were just beginning.

FAST FORWARD

AMITYVILLE STRUGGLES TO KEEP RACIAL DIVERSITY

As days grow warmer, teenagers black and white hang out on the front steps of Amityville Memorial High School, or shoot hoops together in impromptu matches.

Though they often live in separate neighborhoods, Amityville students today experience integration each day in school. But just how long this 3,000-student system will remain racially diverse is anybody's guess.

"The schools are struggling," said Diane O'Neill, a district secretary who is white and who has a son and daughter at the high school. "But I would like to see this remain an integrated district. That's one of the strengths of Amityville."

During the past 20 years, the student majority has shifted from two-thirds white to two-thirds black. Hundreds of students, mostly whites, have transferred to nonpublic schools. A volunteer group, Parents for Public Schools, is trying through personal contacts to coax back such students.

Meanwhile, reading scores lag below state standards, and backlogged repairs in aging buildings total an estimated $16 million. A new superintendent, Dean Bettker, hopes to improve scores through after-hours tutoring, while repairing buildings through passage of a bond issue.

Despite problems, district residents who once fought to keep schools racially diverse insist their work was not wasted. A 1960s lawsuit integrated the district's Northeast Elementary School, which formerly was virtually all-black because of segregated neighborhood housing.

"It gave a certain generation of our children a chance to enter into the mainstream," said Dorothea Devine of North Amityville, a former officer in the National Association for the Advancement of Colored People.

— John Hildebrand

As president, Theodore Roosevelt spent summers at his beloved Cove Neck mansion

The White House on the Hill

BY GEORGE DEWAN
STAFF WRITER

Theodore Roosevelt was a two-fisted rancher in the Dakota Badlands, a corruption-hunting police commissioner in New York City, a guns-blazing Rough Rider in Cuba, a corporation-taxing governor in Albany, a trust-busting president in Washington, a big-game hunter in East Africa and a fearless explorer in the malaria-infested Amazon jungle in Brazil.

But home was Sagamore Hill.

Photo by C.J. Duprez; Newsday Archive

The indomitable T.R. grew to love Long Island, where he combined national and family matters.

For the large Roosevelt family, the rambling, 23-room mansion on 95 acres on Cove Neck in Oyster Bay, overlooking Long Island Sound, was a sanctuary. "After all, fond as I am of the White House and much though I have appreciated these years in it, there isn't any place in the world like home — like Sagamore Hill," Roosevelt wrote in June, 1906, to his 14-year-old daughter Ethel.

And for seven summers all roads led to Oyster Bay.

From 1902 to 1908, President Theodore Roosevelt's Sagamore Hill was the summer White House, the focal point of world affairs, where the 26th president combined the nation's business with his family's recreation. Momentous events happened there: In the summer of 1905, Roosevelt mediated a settlement of the war between Japan and Russia, for which he received the Nobel Peace Prize, the first Nobel ever awarded to an American.

Folksy events as well: At the end of his first summer as president, Roosevelt held an open reception where 8,000 people showed up on the great lawn to drink lemonade, eat gingersnaps and shake hands with the president. It was like a county fair. After the receiving line had gone on for two hours, a woman commented, "Mr. President, how tired you must be!"

"Not a bit!" Roosevelt responded in his high-pitched voice, his prominent teeth snapping. "It takes more than a trolley car to knock me out, and more than a crowd to tire me." He continued shaking hands for two more hours.

Although he was born sickly and had to build himself up physically, Roosevelt was to prove such durability many times over, including surviving an assassin's bullet in the chest in 1912. At Sagamore Hill, Roosevelt was able to pursue the strenuous life that he advocated. And the children and their relatives and friends were his partners, as was sometimes his wife, Edith. There were romps in the woods, horseback riding, hiking, tennis, pitching hay, chopping wood, rowing in Cold Spring and Oyster Bay Harbors and overnight camping trips with a half-dozen boys.

"The boys are sufficiently deluded to believe that the chicken or beefsteak I fry in bacon fat on these expeditions has a flavor impossible elsewhere to be obtained," he wrote to a friend.

Roosevelt's hyperactive relaxation was legendary. The Chicago Tribune once ran a six-panel cartoon titled "The President is resting at his home in Oyster Bay." These were the six captions: "He first chops down a few trees . . . After which he takes a brisk stroll of twenty miles . . . And rests a moment or two . . . Then has a little canter cross country . . . He then gives the children a wheelbarrow ride . . . By which time he is ready for breakfast."

When Roosevelt was playing with his children, he was like a child himself, and Sagamore Hill was usually overrun with Roosevelt kin, many of whom lived nearby. They treated him like one of the gang.

"I am rather disconcerted by the fact that they persist in regarding me as a playmate," Roosevelt wrote to his sister-in-law Emily Carow on Aug. 6, 1903. "This afternoon, for instance, was rainy, and all of them . . . came to get me to play with them in the old barn. They plead so hard that I finally gave in, but upon my word, I hardly knew whether it was quite right for the President to be engaged in such wild romping as the next two hours saw."

"I love all these children and have great fun with them," he added in a later letter, "and I am touched by the way in which they feel that I am their special friend, champion, and companion."

Affairs of state often had to give way to affairs of the family. One July afternoon the president was in the library, meeting with a visiting dignitary to discuss Cuba. At the door of the library appeared a group of boys dressed in old clothes and sneakers. "Cousin Theodore," one of them said, "it's after four."

"By Jove, so it is," Roosevelt said. "Why didn't you call me sooner? One of you boys get my rifle." Turning to his visitor, he said, "I must ask you to excuse me. We'll finish this talk some other time. I promised the boys I'd go shooting with them at four o'clock, and I never keep boys waiting. It's a hard trial for a boy to wait."

Roosevelt's love of children was only one side of a many-sided man. He was a complex, multidimensional figure who, in retrospect, reveals himself in different ways, depending upon on which surface the light is focused. "There was so much of him," biographer Edward Wagenknecht once wrote.

"The historical Theodore Roosevelt fits into no foursquare format," Roosevelt biographer Edmund Morris said at Hofstra University's 1990 conference on the former president. "No matter how large the confines of the study, he always requires extra space, added dimensions."

Critics have a wonderful time with Theodore Roosevelt because he presents such a huge target. The popular image of him is reflected in a handful of scenes. One is with the Rough Riders in Cuba in 1898, leading a charge that helped win the battle for Santiago in the Spanish-American War. Another is the big-game hunter in the American West, or later in East Africa, whose thirst for blood sport seemed to know no bounds. And third, as president, the peacemaker, the conservationist, the trust-buster, the man who said it was wise to talk softly and carry a big stick. The public came to know him as Teddy. He never liked the nickname, but the newspapers used it anyway.

Unlike that other great 19th-Century Long Islander from nearby Huntington, Walt Whitman, Roosevelt was not born on Paumanok. But once he found it, he never let it go.

One of four children, the son of a well-to-do merchant — also named Theodore — Roosevelt was our only president born in New York City. That was on Oct. 27, 1858, in a brownstone at 28 E. 20th St. The family traced its lineage back to Klaes Martensen van Rosenvelt, an immigrant from Holland who settled in New Amsterdam about 1644.

"I was a sickly, delicate boy, suffered much from asthma, and frequently had to be taken away on trips to find a place where I could breathe," Roosevelt wrote in his autobiography. Just before his 12th birthday, his father took him aside and said, "Theodore, you have the mind but you have not the body, and without the help of the body the mind cannot go as far as it should. You must make your body. It is hard drudgery to make one's body, but I know you will do it."

"I'll make my body," young Theodore answered.

"So began a course of exercise that continued for the rest of Roosevelt's life," writes H.W. Brands in his new biography, "T.R.: The Last Romantic." "He lifted weights, practiced gymnas-

LI HISTORY.COM

See entries from Roosevelt's diary from 1884, read his 1905 inaugural address and link to archival photos and writings on the Internet at http://www.lihistory.com.

LEGACY

Still a Presence at Sagamore Hill

BY BILL BLEYER
STAFF WRITER

It was almost as if Theodore Roosevelt were still alive.

Even after his death in 1919, his larger-than-life presence continued to attract visitors. They came — the famous and the ordinary — in a steady stream to T.R.'s grave and then to Sagamore Hill. The prince of Wales, Queen Marie of Romania and King Albert of Belgium. And once a year from 1920 into the 1940s, the president's closest friends would make a journey they called "the Roosevelt Pilgrimage." Fellow politicians and hunting friends and journalists, they would place wreaths at his grave and celebrate his memory on Jan. 6, the anniversary of his death.

Newsday Photo / Bill Davis

Sagamore Hill today: Efforts have been made to re-establish its historic appearance.

And people whose lives he had touched by simply being Teddy Roosevelt came, too, often uninvited, and asked to see the house. Boy Scouts and townspeople and journalists, too. "They would knock on the door and Mrs. Roosevelt would generally receive them, usually dressed all in white or all in black for mourning," said John A. Gable, executive director of the Theodore Roosevelt Association.

Edith Roosevelt lived on in the Victorian mansion in Cove Neck for more than a quarter century until her death at age 87 in 1948. There were frequent visits from four of her children living nearby and their children. Ted and Kermit had their own houses in Cove Neck; Archie lived in Cold Spring Harbor, and Ethel lived in Oyster Bay hamlet.

Within months of T.R.'s death, the newly formed Roosevelt Memorial Association — later renamed the Theodore Roosevelt Association — approached his widow with a proposal to buy the house. The group wanted to turn it into a museum and build a presidential library on the grounds, both novel concepts at the time.

But Edith Roosevelt wanted to stay in the house where she had raised a family and leave it to her eldest son. But Ted, a brigadier general who won the Congressional Medal of Honor for leading an assault on D-Day, died in France of a heart attack during World War II. Later, the association approached her again and she agreed that the group should be allowed to buy the house after her death. In 1950, the 23-room mansion with its contents and surrounding 83 acres was purchased by the association. After three years of restoration that brought the cost of the project up to $400,000, it was opened to the public on June 14, 1953, at a ceremony featuring President Dwight D. Eisenhower and former President Herbert Hoover.

The Theodore Roosevelt Association also purchased Theodore Jr.'s adjacent Old Orchard home for $115,000 after his wife's death in 1960.

The association operated Sagamore Hill as a museum until 1963 when the house and Old Orchard were donated to the National Park Service along with an endowment. Old Orchard opened as a museum in 1966.

When the association acquired Sagamore Hill, the house was a little run-down. But there had been only minor alterations over the years. Electricity had been added and rooms repainted or repapered. Mrs. Roosevelt had removed the tin ceiling in the parlor. Before the house was opened to the public, the first of several major restoration projects was completed.

One 1985 project resulted in the mustard yellow and green exterior color scheme being replaced by blue-gray and gray. This was designed to reflect the appearance of the house from the later years of T.R.'s presidency until his death. In 1993, the house was closed for six months to allow many of the rooms — which reflected different periods of the Roosevelts' life at Sagamore Hill — to be restored to a more unified and historically accurate appearance of the house as it was from 1901 to 1919. Today, Theodore Roosevelt's presence still pervades Sagamore Hill. Visitors can see such remembrances of the nation's 26th president as his Rough Rider hat, sword and binoculars hanging from elk antlers in the North Room, the bronze rhino in the front hall where Edith used to put her hat and the boys left phone messages, and the family's presidential china set on the dining room table as if dinner were about to begin.

The grounds have changed over time as well. Trees have grown up around the house, almost entirely blocking the panoramic views T.R. loved of Oyster Bay and Long Island Sound. When the Roosevelts were in residence, much of the property was used for farming or allowed to grow into meadows. Now the Park Service maintains manicured lawns, although there have been recent efforts to re-establish the estate's historic appearance — including outlining T.R.'s old tennis court in the woods.

More changes are coming. The antiquated exhibits in the Old Orchard Museum will be redone by the year 2000. A contract has been signed to connect Sagamore Hill to the Oyster Bay Water District so there would be water service for firefighting. Currently, drinking water comes from local wells and firefighters would have to draw their water from Oyster Bay Harbor.

The Park Service also hopes to replace the old wiring in the mansion. That would allow installation of upgraded lighting to improve visitors' ability to see into the rooms without damaging fabrics.

Meanwhile, the famous and the ordinary still make pilgrimages to Sagamore Hill, to walk in the rooms where Theodore Roosevelt comes alive. Last year, there were 96,500 pilgrims.

Sagamore Hill National Historic Site Photos / National Park Service

Roosevelt addresses a crowd in 1917 from a porch at Sagamore Hill; in his library, skins cover the floor. Visitors also can see such remembrances as his Rough Rider hat, sword and binoculars hanging from elk antlers in the North Room.

tics on equipment set up in a specially remodeled room in the house on 20th Street, took lessons in wrestling, rode horseback, hiked, climbed, swam, rowed and generally engaged in just about every form of physical activity imaginable, in hot weather and cold, rain and shine, days and sometimes far into the night."

Roosevelt's first love was natural history, and early on he plunged into the study of plants and animals with the vigor with which he attacked virtually everything he attempted. He became a voracious reader and constructed in his bedroom his Roosevelt Museum of Natural History, which, because of the sounds and odors, was later banished to a back hall upstairs.

His zoological studies were helped by summer excursions to the country, first in New Jersey, then later to Oyster Bay, which his grandfather and then his father found to be a splendid vacation spot. In 1874, Theodore Sr. rented a summer house in Oyster Bay, and the 16-year-old began a love affair with Long Island that continued until the day he died. In his autobiography, he proudly notes that it was recorded in an obscure journal that he had captured a fish crow and an Ipswich sparrow on the shore at Oyster Bay. And up on Cove Neck, there was a special hill he wandered, noting the birds and other animals, looking out over the Sound, and daydreaming.

While at Harvard College, Roosevelt studied the natural sciences but his choice of a career began to drift toward public service. He was abetted in this by the first love of his life, 17-year-old Alice Hathaway Lee, the cousin of a classmate who was part of Boston's social set. The romance took its course while Roosevelt finished college, and in 1880 they were married. Roosevelt began law school at Columbia University, but he dropped out to run, successfully, as a Republican for the New York State Assembly, when he was 23.

A few weeks after his wedding, Roosevelt thought about his favorite hill in Oyster Bay, and he conceived the idea

Please see **ROOSEVELT, Next Page**

White House On the Hill

ROOSEVELT from **Preceding Page**

of buying the property and building a mansion for Alice and their family, which he expected would be large. He purchased 155 acres on Cove Neck early in 1883 for $30,000, keeping 95 acres for himself and selling the remainder to relatives. By the summer, Alice was pregnant, and Roosevelt found himself on top of his hill, pacing the ground with architects and planning the solid, three-story, many-bedroomed house that would anchor him on Long Island for the rest of his life. He would name it Leeholm, in honor of the wife he adored.

"I wished a big piazza, very broad at the n.w. corner where we could sit in rocking chairs and look at the sunset," he later wrote. "A library with a shallow bay window opening south, the parlor or drawing-room occupying all the western end of the lower floor; as broad a hall as our space would permit; big fireplaces for logs; on the top floor the gun room occupying the western end so that north and west it look[ed] over the Sound and Bay."

Before the building contract could be signed, a double tragedy struck. In the ninth month of her pregnancy, Alice was living in a house on West 57th Street with her mother-in-law, Mittie Roosevelt, who was sick in bed with what turned out to be typhoid fever. Alice herself was not feeling well, and it later turned out that she was suffering from Bright's disease, an inflammation of the kidneys, a sickness that had not been detected earlier.

On Feb. 12, 1884, Alice Lee Roosevelt was born in New York City while Roosevelt was in the Assembly in Albany. Not long after celebrating his firstborn with his fellow legislators, he received a second telegram saying that his wife was seriously ill. He arrived at the house Just before midnight on the 13th. When he took Alice into his arms, she barely recognized him. At 3 a.m. on St. Valentine's Day, Mittie died. Eleven hours later, Alice died.

In his diary for Feb. 14, 1884, Roosevelt wrote only this: "The light has gone out of my life."

"With the exception of two brief, written valedictories to Alice — one private, one for limited circulation among family and friends — there is no record of Roosevelt ever mentioning her name again," Roosevelt biographer Edmund Morris wrote in "The Rise of Theodore Roosevelt. ". . . Ironically, the name of another Alice Lee — his daughter — was sometimes forced through his lips, but even this was quickly euphemized to 'Baby Lee.' Although the girl grew to womanhood, and remained close to him always, he never once spoke to her of her mother. When, as ex-president, he came to write his autobiography, he wrote movingly of the joys of family life, the ardor of youth, and the love of men and women; but he would not acknowledge that the first Alice ever existed."

Curiously — since he had no immediate plans to live there — two weeks after the funeral, Roosevelt signed a contract with John A. Wood and Son, carpenters of Lawrence, for the construction of the 22-room house on the hill in Oyster Bay for a total cost of $16,975 — the spacious, museum-like North Room was added 20 year later. He put Alice in the care of his unmarried sister Anna, known as Bamie, and when the house was completed, in 1885, she would take care of it for him.

Theodore Roosevelt Collection, Harvard College Library

The future president as a 21-year-old member of the sculling team at Harvard. While at college, he studied the natural sciences but his choice of a career began to drift toward public service.

Roosevelt immersed himself in work. He finished his term in the State Legislature, and then headed to Dakota Territory, where he had earlier purchased two ranches. He raised cattle and he hunted and killed enormous numbers of wild animals, some of whose stuffed heads today hang from the walls of Sagamore Hill. But he kept returning East to keep his hand in, for politics drew him like a magnet. And when he wasn't doing politics, he was writing books, something he did for the rest of his life: biographies of Gouverneur Morris and Thomas Hart Benton, a history of the War of 1812, a multivolume history of the winning of the West, narratives of his hunting exploits in the West and in Africa, and many more.

The resume is awesome. Roosevelt was a state assemblyman, 1882-1884. He was defeated for mayor of New York City in 1886. A member of the U.S. Civil Service Commission, 1889-1895. President of the New York City Board of Police Commissioners, 1895-1897. Assistant secretary of the Navy, 1897-1898. Commander of the First U.S. Volunteer Cavalry Regiment, known as the Rough Riders, summer, 1898. Governor of New York, 1898-1900. Vice president, March-September, 1901. President of the United States, September, 1901-1909.

The big house in Oyster Bay would not remain empty for long.

Despite his feeling after the death of Alice that he would never marry again, Roosevelt did just that on Dec. 2, 1886. He married Edith Kermit Carow, an old friend from childhood days with whom he had often spent time during those golden Oyster Bay summers of their youth. The following spring, they moved into the house on the hill. The name Leeholm became a memory, just as did the name Alice Lee. Roosevelt called the place Sagamore Hill — named for a Matinecock Indian sagamore, or sub-chief, named Mohenas, whose people once owned the land that made up the original Oyster Bay settlement.

Roosevelt was about to get a houseful of children to play with. In the order born, they were: Theodore, known as Ted (1887); Kermit (1889); Ethel (1891); Archibald, known as Archie (1894), and Quentin (1897).

As police commissioner, Roosevelt would commute to Oyster Bay via the Long Island Rail Road. Even when the family lived in the governor's mansion in Albany and in the White House, Sagamore Hill was the place they returned to whenever possible. When his children weren't with him, he constantly kept in touch by writing letters. On Aug. 25, 1903, when the summer White House was at Sagamore Hill, 16-year-old Ted was away on a hunting trip: He wrote:

"On Sunday, after we came back from church and bathed, I rowed mother out to the end of Lloyd Neck, near your favorite camping ground. There we took lunch and spent a couple of hours with our books, reading a little and looking out over the beautiful Sound and at the headlands and white beaches of the coast. We rowed back through a strange, shimmering sunset."

A visitor to Sagamore Hill today might be startled to walk into a house that is so masculine in its decor — with the one possible exception of Edith's drawing room, where softer colors, French tapestries, elegant rugs and Sevres porcelain dominate. Otherwise, there is a profusion of elephant tusks, bearskin rugs — including snarling heads — and uncountable mounted heads of American and African buffalo, white-tailed deer, elk, bison and antelopes.

"Theodore took more pride in those game-heads than in any of the books he had written or the political achievements that had already carried his name across the continent," wrote his friend Hermann Hagedorn in "The Roosevelt Family of Sagamore Hill." "They meant manhood to him, manhood won at a price: tokens of triumph of character over physical inadequacy, testimony to daring, strength, endurance, straight aim and steady nerves, none of them innate, all laboriously acquired."

With an energy level that never seemed to run down, Roosevelt went at his playing full tilt. Even if it meant an occasional broken bone or bloody wound. One day he was out riding when his horse tumbled at a fence, and he returned home dripping with blood. Young Alice fled screaming, but Edith took it in stride. The story is told of the day the windmill that pumped their water jammed, and Roosevelt climbed up to see what was wrong. Unexpectedly, the wheel started, hitting Roosevelt in the head. The wound to his scalp bled profusely, so much that he could barely see when he entered the entrance hall, where he met Edith.

"Theodore," Edith said evenly, "I wish you would do your bleeding in the bathroom. You'll ruin every rug in the house."

Although there were Secret Service agents guarding him when the Summer White House was at Oyster Bay, they didn't follow him everywhere. He once took Ted and two cousins on an overnight horseback ride to visit relatives in Sayville, a good 30 miles away. A heavy rain was falling, and no one recognized the president until they neared Sayville late the next morning. After an overnight stay, they reached home by lunchtime the following day.

They were greeted by Edith. "I am glad to see you safely home, Mr. President," she said.

The New York World was delighted. "Now that the President has proved by actual experience that the trip from Oyster Bay to Sayville and back can be

Newsday Archive

Theodore Roosevelt Collection, Harvard College Library

Roosevelt with his oldest son, Theodore Jr., who was born in 1887. At right, his first wife, Alice Lee Roosevelt. They were married for four years, and when she died, he wrote in his diary: "The light has gone out of my life."

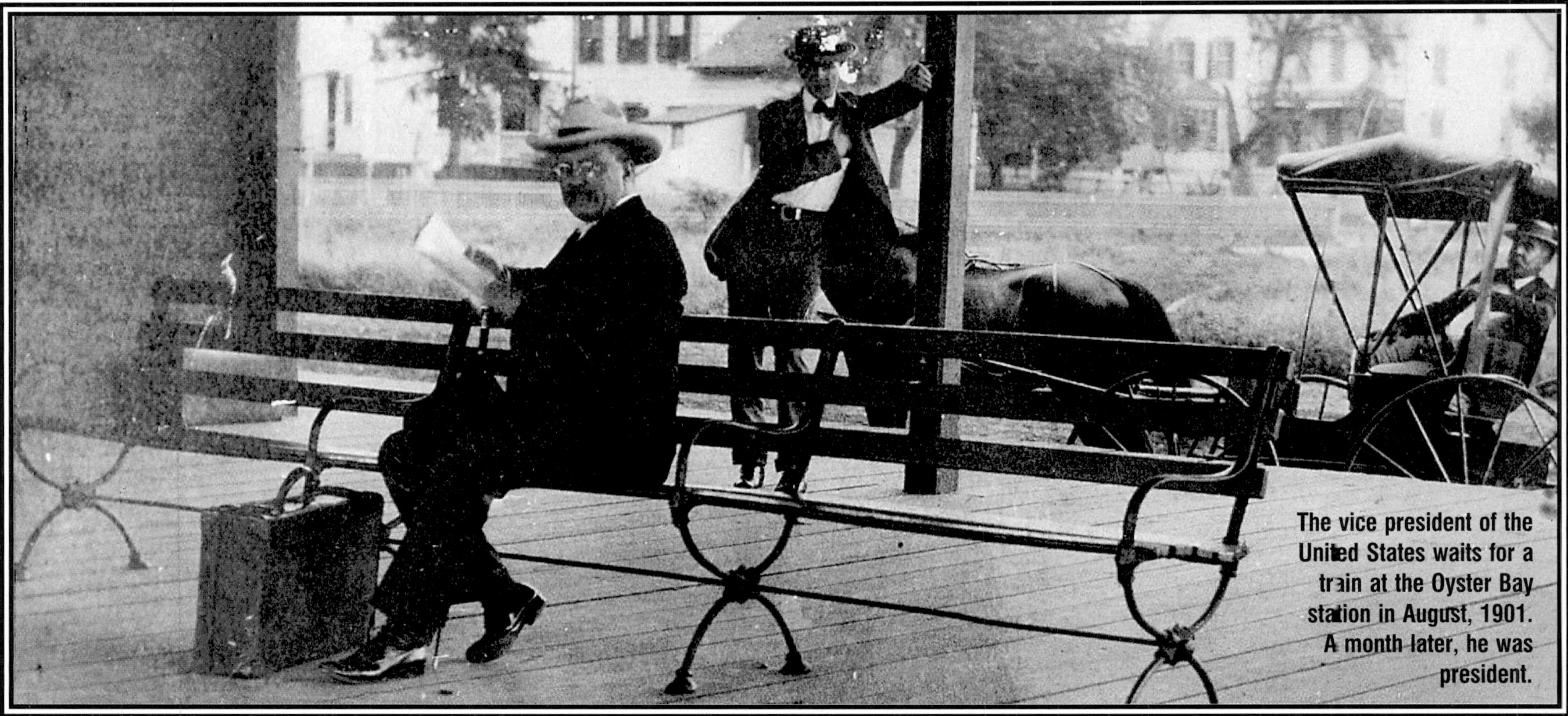

The vice president of the United States waits for a train at the Oyster Bay station in August, 1901. A month later, he was president.

Theodore Roosevelt Association Photo

made on horseback," the newspaper editorialized, "with what new discovery will he next thrill a waiting nation?"

Until he became president, there were no telephones at Sagamore Hill. If anyone wanted to contact them, a phone call was made to a drugstore in Oyster Bay. A boy on a bicycle would then take the message up the hill. The press of presidential business, however, ended the telephone holdout. After Roosevelt succeeded to the presidency upon the assassination of President William McKinley in September, 1901, a brand new telephone was installed at Sagamore Hill; to reach the president you called Oyster Bay 67.

No single international crisis focused as much attention on the summer White House as did the Russo-Japanese War. Since 1904, Japan and Russia had been vying for supremacy in northeast Asia, and attacks back and forth had worn down both sides in lives and in finances. By late spring of 1905, the Japanese appeared to have the upper hand. But the western powers, including Roosevelt, were determined to see the affair end with power balanced between the two, rather than one nation overwhelming the other.

Ignoring Congress and bypassing his secretary of state, who was sick, Roosevelt became the mediator. By subtle and persistent jawboning, he got the two nations to agree to a peace conference in Portsmouth, N.H. Before that, negotiators from both countries met separately with Roosevelt at Sagamore Hill. Then, on Aug. 5, Roosevelt had the presidential yacht Mayflower anchored in Oyster Bay, and there, before heading for Portsmouth, the envoys met each other for the first time, at lunch. In his biography, "Theodore Roosevelt: A Life," Nathan Miller describes the tricky protocol arrangements that Roosevelt had to deal with.

"Protocol and precedence threatened to end the conference before it got under way," wrote Miller. "Which delegate would sit on the presidential right? Which ruler would be toasted first? Who would enter the dining saloon first?"

Roosevelt solved all these problems, Miller says, by taking both representatives by the arm on either side of him and steering them into the room together. From a round table, he served them a cold buffet luncheon that was eaten standing up. And then, champagne glass in hand, he proposed a toast to which he would allow no reply: "To the welfare and prosperity of the sovereign and people of the two great nations, whose representatives have met one another on this ship."

While the negotiations went on in New Hampshire, Roosevelt monitored the proceedings from Oyster Bay. But he took an afternoon off to try something new. Without the knowledge of reporters, he had himself taken out into Oyster Bay to a rounded steel shell called the Plunger, one of six submarines owned by the Navy. Squeezing in through the hatch, he spent the next three hours on the sub, about an hour of it submerged. He even took the controls himself for a while. He was thus the first American president to ride in a submarine. Just after he left office, he became the first president to fly in an airplane, taking a 3-minute, 20-second flight at about 50 feet at a St. Louis air show in 1910.

The Portsmouth negotiations were difficult, but on Aug. 29 the telephone rang at Sagamore Hill. An agreement had been reached. "This is splendid!" Roosevelt declared. "This is magnificent."

In a 1904 election-night statement that he later came to regret, Roosevelt said he considered his 3½ years in office as a full term, and would not run again for president, thus honoring the two-term precedent set by George Washington. When he left the presidency in 1909, Roosevelt went home to Sagamore Hill. But now it was a full-time residence. Or, as full-time as any place could be for someone as active as Roosevelt. He soon left with his son Kermit on a year-long safari to Kenya, where they killed, by Roosevelt's count, 512 animals, large and small. Many critics objected to what they saw as game butchery. He responded by saying that every animal killed

Please see **ROOSEVELT, Next Page**

AN UNBROKEN LONG ISLAND LINK

Theodore Roosevelt was the first of his clan to live on Long Island year-round. Four of his six children followed suit as adults, and some grandchildren and great-grandchildren still live here.

T.R.'s eldest son, Theodore Jr., lived in a mansion named Old Orchard near Sagamore Hill until his death in Normandy of a heart attack during World War II. Archie lived in Cold Spring Harbor until he moved to Florida a few years before he died in 1979. Ethel married Richard Derby and continued to live in Oyster Bay until her death in 1977. Kermit lived in New York and Oyster Bay until he joined the Army in World War II; he killed himself while stationed in Alaska.

Two of T.R.'s 17 grandchildren have Long Island connections. Kermit's son J. Willard Roosevelt is a composer living in Orient. Nancy Roosevelt Jackson lives in Manhattan but still owns her father Archie's old house in Cold Spring Harbor.

Of the 34 great-grandchildren, Melissa Morgan, Nancy Jackson's daughter, is an assistant Brooklyn district attorney who lives in Cold Spring Harbor with her husband, Jim, and three children. — **Bill Bleyer**

Newsday Archive

The president and Edith at home in 1907 with their children, from left, Quentin, Ethel, Kermit, Theodore Jr. and Archibald. Two of T.R.'s 17 grandchildren have L.I. connections. Kermit's son J. Willard Roosevelt lives in Orient. Nancy Roosevelt Jackson of Manhattan owns father Archie's house in Cold Spring Harbor.

Above, in an undated photo, Roosevelt keeps time by a barn at Sagamore Hill as his children race. At right, Roosevelt's son Quentin at Nassau County's Hazelhurst Field in 1917. A year later, he was killed flying in World War I, and the airport was renamed Roosevelt Field in his honor.

Sagamore Hill National Historic Site; Newsday Photos

White House On the Hill

ROOSEVELT from **Preceding Page**

was either used as food for his large retinue or for scientific purposes, that is, for museums, except for "about a dozen" returned to Sagamore Hill as trophies.

On his return, unhappy with the conservative direction of the administration of President William Howard Taft, Roosevelt bolted the Republicans to form the Progressive Party, the so-called Bull Moose Party, to run again for president in 1912. With Taft and Roosevelt splitting the Republican vote, the election was won by the Democrat Woodrow Wilson.

Back at Sagamore Hill, Roosevelt continued to write magazine articles and books, especially his autobiography. By July, 1913, he had spent more time living continuously at Sagamore Hill than he had spent living in any one house since he was a child. He had time to think back on the richness of his life.

"There are many kinds of success in life worth having," Roosevelt wrote in his autobiography. "It is exceedingly interesting and attractive to be a successful business man, or railroad man, or farmer, or a successful lawyer or doctor; or a writer, or a President, or a ranchman, or the colonel of a fighting regiment, or to kill grizzly bears and lions. But for unflagging interest and enjoyment, a household of children, if things go reasonably well, certainly makes all other forms of success and achievement lose their importance by comparison."

But he was getting restless. So he proposed a seven-month, 1,500-mile expedition, again with Kermit, through Brazil, to explore an Amazon River tributary called Rio Duvida, River of Doubt. To those who said it was too dangerous for a 55-year-old, he replied, "I have to go. It's my last chance to be a boy."

It was dangerous, more so than Roosevelt imagined. Boats overturned, food supplies ran low, a man drowned, another was murdered and Roosevelt badly injured a leg, which became infected and led to a high fever. He also contracted dysentery and malaria, at one point having to be carried in a litter. Once more, he survived, though he was 57 pounds lighter and his health was permanently damaged. The Brazilian government, in his honor, renamed the river Rio Roosevelt.

With Wilson in the White House trying to keep the United States out of the war that had begun in 1914 in Europe, Roosevelt the interventionist found a prime target. He pushed hard for American entry into the war — once referring to Wilson as a "lily-livered skunk" — and when the United States entered the war in 1917, he went personally to see Wilson with an offer to recruit and lead a volunteer force into battle, just as he had done in the Spanish-American War.

Biographer Brands thinks that Roosevelt was looking for one last chance at heroism. "The romantic notion of death in battle held an irresistible appeal for him," he writes, "the more so as he felt old age coming on and the prospect of increasing enfeeblement."

Wilson turned Roosevelt down, saying that volunteers would seriously interfere with the creation and deployment of an effective regular army. So Roosevelt turned to his four sons as surrogates, and, as the former president, he had some pull as to their assignments. "With their enthusiastic assent," Brands writes, ". . . he eschewed safe staff positions, aiming instead to place his boys precisely where he wanted to be: amid the fiercest fighting."

So Roosevelt stayed at Sagamore

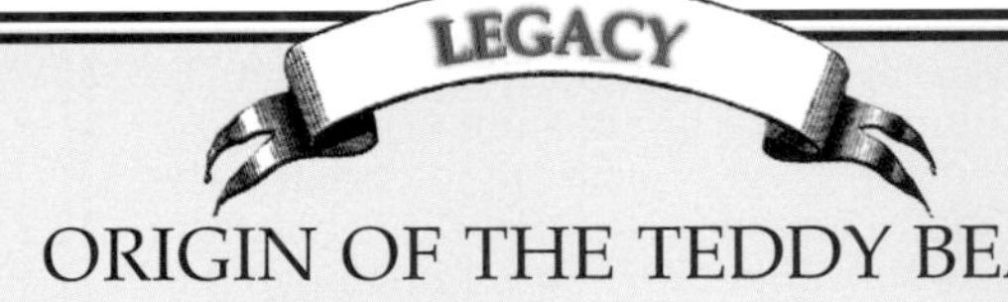

LEGACY

ORIGIN OF THE TEDDY BEAR

There were toy stuffed bears before Theodore Roosevelt came along, but no one called them Teddy Bears.

Not until the president went on a bear hunt.

Roosevelt was in Smedes, Miss., on Nov. 14, 1902, when a guide spotted an old female bear. The hunting party's dogs attacked the bear and a guide roped it to a tree.

T.R. was invited to shoot the helpless creature. Hunter or not, he declined the unsportsmanlike opportunity. Instead, he told a guide to put the bear out of its misery.

Newspapers reported the bear facts the next day. But that Sunday's Washington Post published a cartoon by Clifford Berryman titled "Drawing the Line in Mississippi." It depicted T.R. in a hunting outfit turning his back and refusing to shoot the bear.

Berryman began to use the bear in all of his T.R. cartoons, turning it into a cute cuddly creature with big ears.

Now the story switched to the wilds of Brooklyn, where Rose and Morris Michtom, Russian immigrants who owned a candy store where they sold handmade stuffed animals, began turning out stuffed cubs labeled Teddy's Bear. As the demand increased, the family hired extra seamstresses and rented a warehouse. Their operation eventually became Ideal Toy Corp.

"They claim to have written to T.R. for permission and to have received a response from T.R. saying, 'I don't know what my name may mean to the bear business but you're welcome to use it,' " said John A. Gable, executive director of the Theodore Roosevelt Association. "Alas, the letter was lost."

DRAWING THE LINE IN MISSISSIPPI

Theodore Roosevelt Collection, Harvard College Library

A 1902 cartoon shows T.R. refusing to shoot a bear. The event inspired creation of stuffed cubs called Teddy's Bears.

The Michtoms were not the only toymakers noticing the interest in stuffed bear cubs. The German Steiff family, the world's premier stuffed animal-maker, turned its own stuffed bears into Teddy Bears about 1905. The two companies argued over who had the first Teddy Bear. But Gable said, "One can trace it back and indeed show that the Michtoms were making bears earlier."

Regardless of who was first, the bears were wildly popular. In 1907, Steiff made 974,000 Teddy Bears. "Soon you had Teddy Bear dishes and books by Seymour Eaton where everything rhymes," Gable said.

A historical marker now commemorates the site in Mississippi where all the excitement began.

— **Bill Bleyer**

LEGACY

AT REST, AT LAST, ON A HILLTOP IN OYSTER BAY COVE

Newsday Photos / Bill Davis

The grave site of Theodore and Edith Roosevelt in Youngs Memorial Cemetery

Two days after his death, Theodore Roosevelt was interred on a hilltop in Youngs Memorial Cemetery in Oyster Bay Cove not far from his home. The grave was marked by a granite headstone containing just his name, the dates of his birth and death — Oct. 27, 1858, and Jan. 6, 1919 — and the presidential seal.

A plaque on a nearby rock bears T.R.'s own words: "Keep your eyes on the stars and keep your feet on the ground."

It is no coincidence that 26 steps lead to the grave. Roosevelt was the nation's 26th president.

Previous generations of Roosevelts had been buried in Brooklyn, but T.R. and his second wife, Edith, purchased a plot at the 17th-Century cemetery with a view of his beloved Oyster Bay.

For about a year after his death, the grave was guarded around the clock because of the crush of visitors. Then an 8-foot-high black wrought-iron fence was erected around the grave and its surrounding flagstone path and plantings.

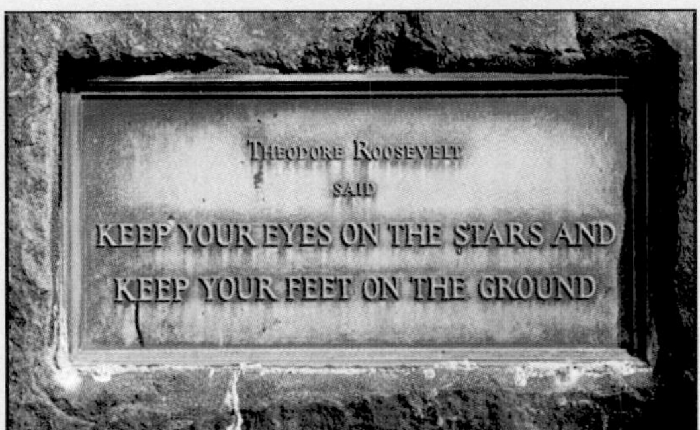

A plaque near the site bears his own words.

After her death, Edith was placed to his right, and her dates — Aug. 6, 1861, and Sept. 30, 1948 — were added to the headstone.

Soon after T.R.'s death, his cousin, W. Emlen Roosevelt, and his wife, Christine, purchased the remaining property on the southern end of the cemetery for a family section that now contains 25 graves, including those of two of Theodore and Edith Roosevelt's children, Ethel and Archie.

T.R.'s other children are buried elsewhere. "The Roosevelt motto was 'Bury them where they fall,' " said John A. Gable, executive director of the Theodore Roosevelt Association. So sons Quentin and Ted Jr., who died in World Wars I and II, respectively, are buried side by side in Normandy. And Kermit, who committed suicide in Alaska during World War II, is buried there. Roosevelt's eldest child, Alice, who was a famous Washington gossip and pundit, is interred in Washington. She died in 1980 at age 96.

— Bill Bleyer

Hill, and he and Edith hung in the entrance hall the small flag, blue stars on a white background, that showed he had sons in the service. Theirs had five stars: one for each of his four sons, plus one for Ethel's husband, Richard Derby, a medical doctor. "We boys thought it was up to us to practice what Father preached," Quentin told a friend.

Unable to go to the front himself, Roosevelt spent much of his time writing his opinions about the war, and how it was being handled by Wilson and the Democrats — badly, he felt — for monthly magazines as well as the daily Kansas City Star. Wilson felt the lash of Roosevelt's tongue, but he generally kept quiet. "I really think the best way to treat Mr. Roosevelt is to take no notice of him," he wrote to a friend. "That breaks his heart and is the best punishment that can be administered."

Roosevelt was about to get his heart broken in a way that no words could accomplish. Ted and Archie, then 30 and 23, were commissioned as Army officers and sent to France. Kermit, who was 28, took a commission in the British Army and was sent to Mesopotamia (now Iraq) with a motorized machine-gun unit. Derby, Ethel's husband, was assigned to an Army hospital in France, and Ethel went along as a nurse. Even Ted's wife, Eleanor, went to France, the first woman to be sent overseas by the YMCA, to organize canteens for men on leave. And the youngest, Quentin, 19, fascinated by the new airplanes, enlisted in the Army's air squadron, and, after earning his wings, was shipped off to duel with German airmen.

In addition to worrying about his sons, Roosevelt had recurring health problems. Although he had kept it a secret for most of his life, a doctor at Harvard had told him he had a weak heart, and to avoid too much exertion — advice he seems to have immediately and permanently ignored. He had occasional stomach trouble, insomnia, chest colds and asthma. He was hospitalized for a recurrence of the problems with the leg that had been injured in Brazil, and an inflammation in his left ear eventually led to deafness on that side. He was already blind in his left eye, due to an injury received in 1904 while boxing at the White House.

Sagamore Hill was almost empty. "They have all gone away from the house on the hill," Edith wrote to her sister, Emily.

The boys were in harm's way. Quentin got pneumonia, but recovered. Archie was wounded in the left leg and arm by shrapnel and given the Croix de Guerre by the French. Ted, promoted to lieutenant colonel, was decorated for "conspicuous gallantry" after being gassed, and was later wounded in the leg. Kermit, who had received the British Military Cross for gallantry in action, got a discharge so he could join the American forces, where he was made a captain in an artillery regiment.

It was Quentin who Roosevelt worried about the most. In early July of 1918, Quentin wrote that he had downed his first German plane, and there was celebration on the hill. But on July 17 an Associated Press reporter drove up to the house from Oyster Bay and told Roosevelt that Quentin's plane had been shot down behind enemy lines. He would soon find out that Quentin was dead. It is Quentin for whom Hazelhurst Field in Garden City was renamed Roosevelt Field in 1919.

"Roosevelt never got over Quentin's death," writes Brands. Or, as Roosevelt's close friend, Hermann Hagedorn, wrote at the time, "The boy in him had died." Occasionally, when Roosevelt thought no one else was around, he could be heard to say, softly, "Poor Quinikins!"

The father wrote his own tribute to the son: "Only those are fit to live who do not fear to die; and none are fit to die who have shrunk from the joy of life. Life and death are parts of the same Great Adventure."

But he wrote little else about him. "There is no use in my writing about Quentin; for I should break down if I tried," he said in a letter to Kermit on Aug. 14. "His death is heartbreaking."

Nassau County Museum Collection, Long Island Studies Institute

Roosevelt, a lame duck president, is greeted by a well-wisher as he approaches a polling place to vote in Glen Cove in the 1908 election, when William Howard Taft defeated William Jennings Bryan.

On Oct. 27, 1918, when the end of the war was only three weeks away, Roosevelt turned 60. Persistent infections had bothered him since the Brazil episode, and he had been diagnosed with inflammatory rheumatism. On Nov. 11, the day the armistice was signed ending the war, he was admitted to Roosevelt Hospital in New York with pain wracking his body. He remained until Christmas Eve.

"Well, anyway, no matter what comes, I have kept the promise that I made to myself when I was twenty-one," he said to his sister Corinne from his hospital bed. "I promised to myself that I would work up to the hilt until I was sixty, and I have done it. I have kept my promise, and now, even if I should be an invalid — I should not like to be an invalid — but even if I should be an invalid, or if I should die, what difference would it make?"

At Sagamore Hill, he began making a slow recovery, and began writing again. On Jan. 5 he worked for a while, then sat on a sofa, reading and looking out the window at the waves on Long Island Sound. Edith sat nearby, silently playing solitaire. She finished a game, then, as she rose to go Theodore spoke gently to her:

"I wonder if you will ever know how I love Sagamore Hill."

At 4:15 the next morning, Theodore Roosevelt died in his sleep of a coronary embolism.

Epilogue

It was late May, 1904, a fine spring day in Washington, D.C., almost three years into Theodore Roosevelt's first term as president. For the children, the eagerly awaited summer vacation was about to begin. Out of an open White House window Edith heard her 10-year-old son Archie singing joyously to himself as he swung back and forth under a magnolia tree.

"I'm going to Sagamore, to Sagamore, to Sagamore," Archie cried with delight. "I'm going to Sagamore, oh to Sagamore!"

After a 'bully fight' in Cuba, Roosevelt and his men land in Montauk as heroes

The Rough Riders Return

BY GEORGE DEWAN
STAFF WRITER

It was summer, 1898, and Teddy Roosevelt and his Rough Riders were coming home.

Flush with victory over the Spaniards in Cuba and threatened with diseases and fevers that were decimating its ranks, the Fifth Army Corps fled the malaria, dysentery and yellow fever of the southern climates for the breezy beaches of eastern Long Island. When Roosevelt disembarked at Fort Pond Bay in Montauk on Aug. 15, the press was out in force to meet him.

"THE ROUGH RIDERS LAND AT MONTAUK" read the headline in The New York Times for Aug. 16, 1898. The publicity was just as in Cuba, where Roosevelt and his men had upstaged the entire American Army that had fought valiantly to take Santiago's San Juan Heights in what Secretary of State John Hay later called "A splendid little war."

"How are you feeling, Colonel?" was the first shouted question as Roosevelt walked down the gangplank from the troopship Miami.

"Well, I am disgracefully healthy," Roosevelt responded, according to The Times. "Really, I am ashamed of myself, feeling so well and strong, with all these poor fellows suffering and so weak they can hardly stand. But I tell you, we had a bully fight."

While thousands of other equally weary heroes of the short but brutal war to drive Spain out of Cuba arrived at Montauk both before and after the arrival of the Rough Riders, the newspapers often focused on the colonel, who was being mentioned as a Republican candidate for governor, and his men. Out of about 29,500 men who passed through Camp Wikoff, only 1,137 were Rough Riders, officially known as the First U.S. Volunteer Cavalry.

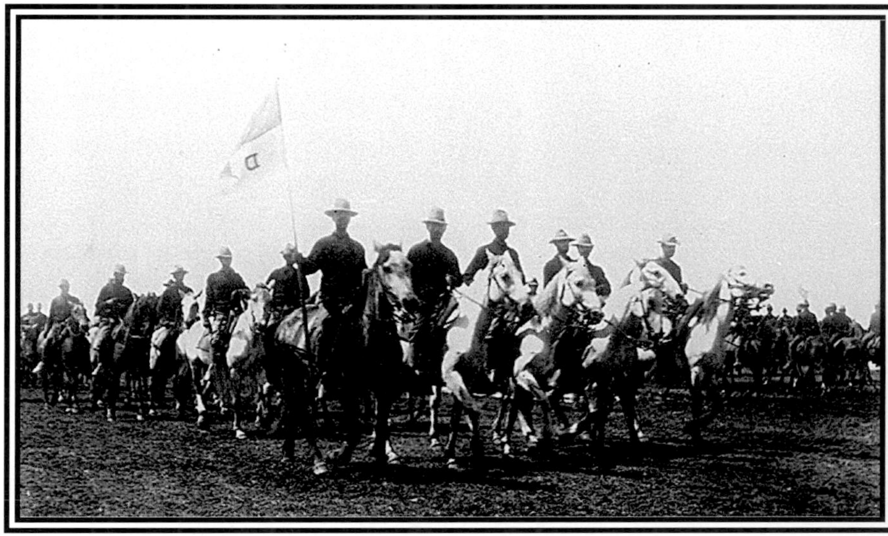

Fullerton Collection, Suffolk County Historical Society

Rough Riders in Montauk, 1898: T.R.'s regiment had upstaged the whole American Army.

"They dominated the coverage," said Jeff Heatley, whose book, based on newspaper accounts, "Bully!: Col. Theodore Roosevelt, the Rough Riders & Camp Wikoff," is to be published next month. "Everyone was focusing on Roosevelt. The Rough Riders were huge heroes. The others just didn't get any coverage."

This year, Suffolk County is sponsoring a series of events to commemorate the centennial of the Wikoff encampment: on May 30, a museum display at Third House at Theodore Roosevelt County Park in Montauk; Sept. 5-7, Rough Rider days at Deep Hollow Ranch, Montauk; Sept. 18-20, at Theodore Roosevelt County Park, a reunion of descendants of Spanish-American War veterans, and an encampment by Rough Rider re-enactors.

The camp, named for Col. Charles Wikoff, the first American officer killed in Cuba, had been recently opened for rest and recuperation of men who either fought in Cuba or had waited in Florida staging areas. The battle at Santiago, Cuba, had been short but tough, but equally hazardous were the tropical conditions that virtually laid waste the Army. In addition to typhus, malaria and dysentery, there were the beginnings of yellow fever. And the troops that were disembarking at Montauk — the sickest were sent elsewhere — were a sorry lot.

Pale and emaciated, men stumbled and fell as they exited the ships, and many had to be carried off on stretchers. When they got to the camp, all of them had to be sent to a detention section, that was essentially a five-day quarantine to weed out those with communicable diseases, especially yellow fever.

Death tracked the Army up from the battlefields of Cuba. It struck on the transport ships, and it struck over and over at Wikoff. Official statistics listed 263 deaths at Wikoff, but Heatley, who studied death records in the East Hampton Town clerk's office, has identified 341 soldiers and 15 others, with typhoid the main cause of death, followed by malaria and dysentery. There were two deaths from yellow fever.

In his book "The Rough Riders," Roosevelt wrote that he could always get free time to ride through the countryside. "Galloping over the open, rolling country, through the cool fall evenings, made us feel as if we were out on the great Western plains and might at any moment start deer from the brush, or see antelope stand and gaze, far away, or rouse a band of mighty elk and hear their horns clatter as they fled."

On Sept. 13, the day before mustering-out, officers went to Roosevelt's tent at 1 p.m. and summoned him outside. The Rough Riders were grouped there but a number of other troopers were on their fringes. At their center was a rough pine table with an object on it covered by a horse blanket.

"As lieutenant colonel of our regiment, you first made us respect you," Trooper William S. Murphy said as the men's spokesman. "As our colonel, you have taught us to love you deeply, as men love men." Murphy then pulled away the blanket to reveal a 2-foot-high bronze statue by Frederic Remington titled "Bronco Buster."

His voice faltering at the start, Roosevelt said he was touched and pleased, that he was proud of the regiment beyond measure. "Outside of my own immediate family," he said, "I shall always feel that stronger ties exist between you and me than between me and anyone else on earth."

Then, Roosevelt took notice of the black soldiers from the Ninth and 10th Cavalry, often known as the Buffalo Soldiers, who fought bravely alongside the Rough Riders in Cuba. "The Spaniards called them 'Smoked Yankees,' but we found them to be an excellent breed of Yankees."

On Sept. 15, the Rough Riders' regimental colors were taken down for the last time. "So all things pass away," Roosevelt said to his newspaper friend Jacob Riis. "But they were beautiful days."

DAD WAS A ROUGH RIDER

Newsday Photo / Bill Davis

Ted Powers with medals of his father, Albert, a corporal

The letter is fragile, almost disintegrating at its folds, and Helen Fraas of Westbury opens it gingerly.

"Sir, the bearer, Mr. Albert Powers, was a corporal in my regiment. He was wounded in our first fight while doing his duty . . . He was an excellent man . . . " The document is signed "Very respectfully, Theodore Roosevelt."

Powers, Fraas' grandfather, was a Rough Rider. The letter of recommendation written by Roosevelt at the end of the Spanish-American War helped him get jobs as a postal worker, immigration inspector at Ellis Island and finally a watchman on the Williamsburg Bridge.

Powers was born in Ireland in 1868. He came to Philadelphia with his father and was apprenticed to a plumber there, said his son Ted — named after T.R. — who is 92 and a resident of a Staten Island nursing home. "When he was 18 years old, he enlisted in the cavalry," Ted Powers said. He served for eight years, breaking horses and fighting in Indian wars, including the infamous engagement at Wounded Knee.

After leaving the Army and prospecting for gold in New Mexico, he walked 65 miles to enlist in the Rough Riders. During the charge up San Juan Hill, "his left arm was shattered by a Spanish sniper," his son said.

The family has newspaper clips of Albert Powers visiting the White House. One clip quotes the president as saying, "Why, I know him. He was in the Rough Riders."

Albert Powers was buried at the national cemetery at Cypress Hills Cemetery in Brooklyn after he died of a heart attack at 60.

Ted Powers said he got to meet his namesake, Theodore Roosevelt, but he was too young to remember it. "I was on my father's horse and my father took me over to him during a parade and I shook hands with him." — **Bill Bleyer**

BY BILL BLEYER
STAFF WRITER

Thousands of city patients are sent to LI for fresh air and productive work

Caring For The Mentally Ill

As the 19th Century came to a close, city institutions for the mentally ill were overflowing. The hospitals were little more than warehouses, and treatment and therapy were negligible. Progressive doctors argued that the solution lay to the east — to Long Island where patients could breathe fresh air and be productive in fields or workshops.

Their recommendations resulted in a system of three major state hospitals on Long Island that would serve hundreds of thousands of patients and create new communities for tens of thousands of workers.

The philosophy that these hospitals represented was best described in 1895 by Dr. George Smith, the first director of a new facility in Central Islip. He summed up his treatment regimen as "O & O and R & R."

The initials stood for "occupation and oxygen" and "rest and recreation."

The first hospital was built in a quiet farming community that would become Kings Park. In 1885, officials of what was then the City of Brooklyn established the Kings County Farm on more than 800 acres to care for the poor and the mentally ill.

"At the time, 32 male and 23 female patients were moved to three hastily constructed wooden houses . . . where the stresses and unhealthy conditions of city life would be alleviated, thereby assisting in their cure," Kings Park Psychiatric Center historian Leo Polaski wrote in a recent history.

While Brooklyn patients were going to Kings Park, mental hospitals in Manhattan also were overflowing. In 1887, the city purchased 1,000 acres of pine barrens in Central Islip. The first 49 male patients arrived at the New York City Farm Colony in 1889 and were put to work building the hospital. They were joined the following year by 40 female patients who handled household tasks.

As new buildings went up at Kings Park, so did the patient population. Soon, overcrowding eroded patient care and there were complaints about patronage, waste and graft. Protests by the medical staff and the public spurred the state to take over both the Kings Park and Central Islip facilities in 1895.

At the turn of the century, Kings Park in just 15 years had grown to 2,697 patients and a staff of 454 — giving the hospital a larger population than the rest of the Town of Smithtown.

Photos From King Pedler, Kings Park Heritage Museum

Above, patients engage in an arts and crafts session at the Kings Park facility's solarium, circa 1920. Below, a view of residential buildings at Kings Park as they looked around 1915.

By 1928, overcrowding both in the city and on Long Island brought state approval of a third institution in Suffolk that would become the largest psychiatric hospital in the world. Pilgrim State — named after mental health pioneer Dr. Charles Pilgrim — was built on more than 1,057 acres in Brentwood. It opened on Oct. 1, 1931. Eight years later, the state bought 875 acres to the west and built Edgewood State Hospital. It was operated as a federal military hospital during the war and returned to the management of Pilgrim in 1946. It was closed in 1971.

In the early years of Kings Park and Central Islip, about half the employees were Irish immigrants. "We had a bus that used to go from the hospital to the docks in Manhattan and pick them up," said Central Islip's historian, Muriel Remsen. During World War II, when many employees joined the armed forces, Central Islip recruited black workers from the Carolinas, which led to cultural changes in the community.

All the hospitals prided themselves on being self-sufficient farm communities. At Kings Park, the three wooden houses grew into more than 150 permanent buildings, including a bakery, laundry, amusement hall, bandstand, library, furniture repair shops and nursing school.

At Central Islip, where doctors early in this century helped isolate the bacteria that caused syphilis, patients held a variety of jobs. "They made their own shoes, they made their own bricks, they made their own park benches, their own water fountains, birdbaths, their own clothing, mattresses and brooms," said Remsen. A fire department was organized in 1907 with 10 volunteer employees.

Pilgrim even had its own courts. Central Islip, Pilgrim and Kings Park built their own railroad spurs. Central Islip had five miles of track on the grounds and its own locomotive and special hospital car to carry patients from Long Island City to the hospital and back.

Life for patients and staff was highly regimented. Central Islip employees lived on the grounds and were not allowed to leave the property, even during their off hours. They had to wear ties or buttoned-up blouses on duty — even when they were bathing patients — and were forbidden to bicycle around the grounds. Staff and patients did get eggs, oysters or clams once a week and poultry twice a month. Because there was a farm, there were plenty of vegetables.

For therapy and to raise money for hospital activities, the patients were encouraged to engage in crafts. The birdhouses and toys they made at Central Islip were sold to the public once a year, and the variety shows produced by the patients until the 1960s always drew sellout crowds from the community. Central Islip patients were given their own garden plots and competed for produce prizes at county fairs.

Over time the philosophy of "O & O and R & R" gave way to new techniques. Insulin shock therapy was used at Pilgrim in 1936 and electric shock therapy was introduced in 1940. Prefrontal lobotomies were performed there beginning in 1946. Drug-based treatment arrived in the 1950s, starting with Thorazine, and patient populations began to decline. Kings Park's peak came in 1954 with 9,300 patients. Central Islip had its maximum patient population — 10,000 — in 1955. And Pilgrim topped out at 15,000 in the late 1950s.

Drug therapy combined with a push to "decentralize" psychiatric patients into community facilities or outpatient treatment lessened the need for the mammoth complexes. Kings Park and Central Islip closed in 1996, with most of their remaining patients transferred to Pilgrim Psychiatric Center, which now serves 1,200 inpatients.

In Central Islip, most of the hospital grounds have been taken over by New York Institute of Technology, court buildings, senior housing, a business park, a public elementary school and other facilities. The Kings Park facility is up for sale by the state.

The empty brick hospital buildings left behind seem stark and Dickensian now, relics of a less enlightened age. But former employees say the institutions were pleasant places. King Pedlar, who worked at Kings Park and lived on the grounds for 31 years, recalled that "the biggest thing that struck me was that the outside of the buildings had a scary, dismal look, but when you went inside, there was such a cheerfulness. When you're inside, you really don't notice the bars. It wasn't a snake pit kind of a place. The whole place was like an oasis."

Inventor Lewis Latimer, a son of slaves, made the light bulb a practical device

Recognizing A Luminary

BY RHODA AMON
STAFF WRITER

Were it not for a modest 28-year-old draftsman-inventor, Alexander Graham Bell might not have gone down in history as the inventor of the telephone. And Thomas Alva Edison might have accumulated a lot fewer than his 1,093 patents.

Bell's telephone application, expertly drafted by young Lewis Latimer, was registered hours before an application by another inventor, Elisha Gray, in 1876. Latimer went on to become a key player on the Edison team and a major pioneer in the development of electric lighting.

The son of runaway slaves, Latimer didn't rate a mention in "Edison, the Man," the 1940 film starring Spencer Tracy. Nor was he acknowledged in "The Story of Alexander Graham Bell" in 1939, in which Don Ameche played the title role.

But 70 years after his death, Latimer's name is getting the recognition that eluded him during his lifetime. His frame house in Flushing, declared a New York City landmark in 1995, is being restored as a house-museum to illuminate his life and work. To save it from demolition, the house was moved from Holly Street to 137th Street, in the shadow of Latimer Gardens, the housing project named for him.

His granddaughter, Winifred Latimer Norman of Manhattan, a retired social worker and leader in restoring the house, was recently visited by the founders of the Latimer Society of Chelsea, Mass., where Latimer was born. They wanted her help in establishing him as a role model for the town's young people.

A more appropriate role model would be hard to find.

Lewis Howard Latimer was born in 1848, the youngest of the four children of George and Rebecca Latimer. His father, born to a white Virginia stone mason and a slave, fled north in 1842 and became a cause celebre for anti-slavery leaders when he was recaptured and put on trial. After serving a jail term, he fought for laws to prevent the capture of fugitives.

But George Latimer was never to fully enjoy freedom. He moved his family from one place to another to avoid being recaptured under the Fugitive Slave Law of 1850. He struggled to support them. Finally, when Lewis was 10, he left them.

"Perhaps George felt that his celebrated status as a runaway slave would make him an obvious target for slave hunters," Norman speculates in a biography of her grandfather. "They might throw the whole family into jail."

Latimer was sent to the Farm School, a Massachusetts institution that "bound out" young apprentices. He fled, rejoined his mother in Boston, and at 13 got a job as an office boy.

In 1864, when the ban on black enlistees in the Civil War was lifted, Latimer at 16 lied about his age and joined the Navy. Home again after the war and facing competition from immigrants pouring into Boston, he acted on a tip from a black office worker: Crosby and Gould, patent lawyers, were looking for an office boy "with a taste for drawing."

He got $3 a week and his first toe-hold in the Industrial Revolution. The office boy saved his small salary to buy drawing tools and a second-hand book, studied at night, watched the draftsmen at work and politely asked the head draftsman if he could do some drawings. Eleven years later Latimer was head draftsman at $20 a week (still $5 less than white draftsmen were paid). He also had his first patent, for the invention of an improved toilet for trains.

Soon after Alexander Graham Bell made his first telephone call, he asked Crosby and Gould for help in patenting his invention. Thus began the collaboration with Latimer that was to affect millions of lives. It didn't change Latimer's life. As the nation wallowed in the depression of the late 1870s, he left his position, worked at odd jobs, relocated to Bridgeport, Conn., and finally landed a draftsman job in a machine shop. Here Hiram Maxim, founder of the U.S. Electric Lighting Co. and Edison's arch rival, walked into Latimer's life.

Newsday Archive

Lewis Latimer, a Renaissance man from Flushing

Maxim reportedly said, "I never saw a colored man making drawings. Where did you learn?" Hired on the spot as a draftsman, Latimer soon displayed his ability as an inventor by improving Edison's 1878 light bulb. Edison's filament — the slender wire that the current heats to incandescence — lasted only a few days. Latimer invented a long-lasting carbon filament and made electricity affordable to millions. He oversaw the installation of electricity in the streets and buildings of New York, Philadelphia, Montreal, London.

It's not clear how many of Latimer's ideas were credited to his employers. "Hiram Maxim was known to be especially quick to steal the credit for other people's ideas," Norman wrote. Leaving Maxim in 1883, he was soon recruited by Edison.

In 1890 Latimer published "Incandescent Electric Lighting, A Practical Description of the Edison System," one of the first guidebooks to understanding electric lighting. He accumulated patents for an arc lamp, a cooling and disinfecting device, a locking rack for coats, hats and umbrellas.

By 1906, he had moved his family from Brooklyn to a 2½-story house in Flushing, where, for the next two decades, he and his wife, Mary, entertained the leaders of New York's black community. Deeply concerned with the problems of his race, he corresponded with Frederick Douglass, Booker T. Washington and other activists.

"He was a Renaissance man," Norman says. "He taught himself French and German so he could read publications in those languages. He was a musician, an artist, a poet."

In later years he was a patent consultant and a member of the Edison Pioneers, a select group of men and women who had worked with The Wizard. He was a founder of the Unitarian Church in Flushing.

Lewis Latimer died at age 80 in 1928. He had followed his own advice written early in his career: "Good habits and good manners are powerful means of advancement that rarely fail to bring reward."

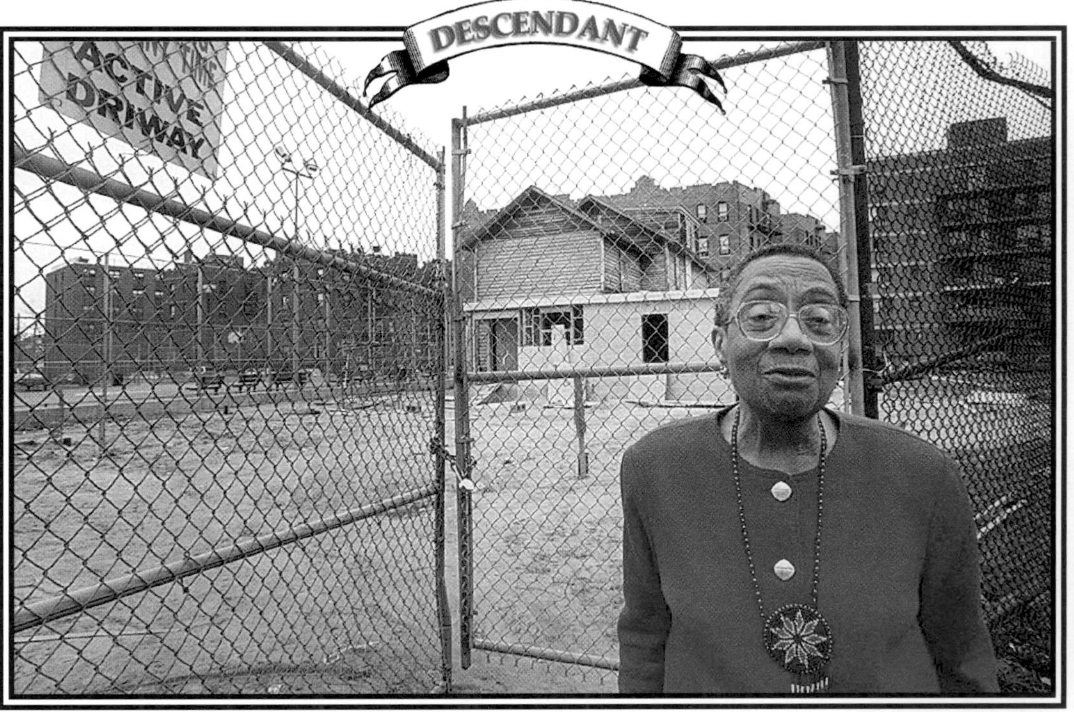

Newsday Photo / Bill Davis

Winifred Latimer Norman, at the 137th Street site of her grandfather Lewis Latimer's home in Flushing

RESTORING HER GRANDFATHER'S HOUSE

Winifred Latimer Norman at 83 is immersed in the restoration of her grandfather's Flushing home. "My brother and I used to play in the attic of that house," she recalls.

She grew up with a sense of family pride. Her father, Gerald F. Norman, taught at Long Island City's Bryant High School, "the first African-American high school teacher in the state," she says. Her mother, Jeanette, was a concert pianist. Her brother, Gerald, was an administrative judge.

Norman attended the Jamaica Training College, "an experiment in coed education for teachers." When the college folded during the Depression, she was transferred to Hunter College, where she got her education degree. "Jobs were scarce — I decided I better get more education." She earned master's degrees from New York University in 1938, and from Hunter in 1964.

The retired social worker is active with United Nations committees on religious freedom and aging. She is vice-chairwoman of the Latimer Fund, which is helping to restore the 1880s Latimer House. — **Amon**

Cutchogue Library Photos

Skipper Frank Cable, left, stands in the conning tower of a Holland submarine tied up at New Suffolk. Right, workers who tested the subs pose in front of Holland's North Fork factory.

John Holland's persistence at America's first sub base leads to improvements

Submarines in LI Waters

BY BILL BLEYER
STAFF WRITER

It didn't take long for submarine builder John P. Holland to decide that New York Harbor wasn't the best place to test his designs. While the protected waterway was calm enough, Holland's hope of working without interference was continually torpedoed by heavy ship traffic, curious citizens, and snooping by Navy vessels and foreign spies.

So in the spring of 1899, Holland dispatched Charles Morris, chief engineer of the Holland Torpedo Boat Co., to the Greenport area to look for a new test site. Morris recommended a tiny resort community on Cutchogue Harbor, and Holland leased a shipyard.

The Fulton, a Holland submarine tested in New Suffolk.

The operation expanded and New Suffolk became the home of America's first submarine base.

Holland, a small man who wore rimless glasses and bowler hats and seemed in constant motion, was born in Ireland in 1840. He immigrated to the United States at 33 and became a parochial-school teacher in Paterson, N.J.

His first working submarine, called simply Boat No. 1, was launched in Paterson in 1878. Rebuffed by the Navy, he turned to the Irish Republican Brotherhood, a group devoted to Irish independence, which anted up $6,000 for the 14-foot, one-man vessel.

But when the submersible was launched for its first test, no one remembered to insert two drain plugs. The boat sank; there were no injuries, and the craft was salvaged.

The inventor's sixth design — the Holland — was a breakthrough. Launched at Elizabethport, N.J., on May 17, 1897, it was 53.3 feet long and could travel at 7 nautical mph submerged and 8 on the surface. It had one torpedo tube and a gun for shooting dynamite charges and carried a crew of five. A gasoline engine powered the Holland on the surface and an electric motor did the job submerged; this dual power system was an innovation copied in subsequent submarines until the nuclear era.

Holland began testing the craft in early 1898 from his base in Perth Amboy, N.J. Morris reported that, "She goes like a fish and dives better than one." With the Spanish-American War looming, both U.S. Navy vessels and Spanish spies watched the ship perform. Assistant Secretary of the Navy Theodore Roosevelt recommended that the Holland be purchased for use in the anticipated war. The Navy demurred, leaving the inventor to continue his tests from a new site in Brooklyn.

When Morris suggested that the boat be reconfigured to put the rudders behind the propeller instead of in front of it, an entrepreneur named Isaac Rice went for a test ride and agreed to foot the bill — and more. He bought out Holland and established the Electric Boat Co. Soon afterward, Holland and his new boss arranged for the Holland to be towed down Long Island Sound and around Orient Point to New Suffolk.

The Holland was expected to reach Port Jefferson the first night out. But Morris noted in his diary that the towboat crew had brought along a large supply of beer and got so drunk that he decided to stop for the night in Huntington Bay. The two vessels reached New Suffolk the next day. The Long Island Traveler newspaper reported that on June 8 the submarine had reached Greenport, where "many pairs of curious eyes gazed at the strange craft as she came up the harbor . . . The members of the crew have strict orders not to allow any visitors on board."

Morris had leased the Goldsmith and Tuthill Shipyard for $10 a month. The arrival of the Holland created a boom for local businesses. "The folk of this sleepy little town saw a chance to make some quick money by raising the rates on room and board," Morris noted.

Before New Suffolk, Holland had always been the captain for trial voyages. But Rice beached him. Frank Cable, a young electrician trained by Holland, became the new skipper. Part of the reason may have been Holland's absentmindedness — he once got lost while walking the two-odd miles from the Cutchogue train station to New Suffolk.

A three-mile test course was marked by buoys in Little Peconic Bay. The Holland took naval officers and VIPs on demonstration runs. Most were uneventful. But on July 23, 1899, one of the passengers was Clara Barton, the feisty 77-year-old founder of the American Red Cross.

Barton scolded Holland for inventing what she called "a deadly instrument of war." Holland replied that submarines could act as a deterrent to future conflict.

The most memorable test run occurred Oct. 11, 1899, with two U.S. senators on board. A gasket failed and exhaust fumes overcame crew and guests. The Holland glided unmanned into the dock. Employees ashore secured the vessel and revived those aboard. From then on, skipper Cable carried caged mice along. "When the mice died, it was time to go ashore," he said.

Despite the Holland's good performance, the Navy still wouldn't buy it. So the company decided to send the vessel to Washington to sell itself. The 500-mile trip — made through inland waterways because no insurance company would underwrite an ocean voyage — generated banner headlines and curious crowds. After an overhaul in the Washington Navy Yard, the Holland was put through trials in the spring of 1900 in front of VIPs including Adm. George Dewey, hero of the Spanish-American War. Its performance convinced the Navy to purchase the Holland. It paid $150,000 even though the company had invested $236,615

With a Navy crew aboard, the Holland proved itself against surface vessels in maneuvers off Newport, R.I., and was commissioned into the Navy as the Holland on Oct. 12, 1900. Lt. Harry Caldwell became the U.S. Navy's first submarine captain.

The Navy agreed to purchase six new submarines patterned on the Holland. Five of them — the Adder, Moccasin, Porpoise, Shark and Fulton — were tested in New Suffolk until Electric Boat moved to Groton, Conn., in 1905. Now part of General Dynamics, it's still there building nuclear submarines.

The Holland, later renamed SS1, served as a Navy training vessel until 1910. Later, it was a traveling exhibit and a park display before it was purchased for $100 in 1930 and broken up for scrap.

In 1904, John P. Holland left Electric Boat and set up a new company. He built two submarines for Japan that year but continued opposition from his former employer and the Navy thwarted his efforts. He lived unnoticed in East Orange, N.J., until his death in 1914.

Holland was called the "Father of the Modern Submarine." His principles were adopted in U.S., English, German, Russian and Japanese submarines.

The boatyard in New Suffolk is now vacant except for one building that was used by Holland. But the only indication that it served as America's first submarine base is a historical marker at First and Main Streets.

At 1900, Long Islanders still look to their heritage, but the future is coming into view

As Century Turns, Out With the Old

BY STEVE WICK
STAFF WRITER

As the end of the 19th Century approached, Long Island began looking at itself, impressed by where it had been and awed by where it was going.

The past was still visible in the distance, and the future was around the corner.

"I think people still thought of themselves as the descendants of the Puritans and pioneers who had settled Long Island," said Roger Wunderlich, a historian at the State University at Stony Brook.

"Long Island still retained its pristine ambiance. It was easy to look around and see the past. By 1900, I think, in many ways most Long Islanders still thought of themselves the way they did a generation or two earlier. But the die was cast for the future."

So much of what had been the norm for so many generations was disappearing, as a new Long Island began to emerge on top of an older one. Whaling, which once connected Long Island to the world, had vanished. Farm life at the western end of the Island, where Dutch settlers had first put down roots, was fading away, acre by acre.

New York City's exploding population was pushing east like a modern-day glacier, reshaping the landscape all over again. But, still, the broad middle of Long Island was a series of small, tidy towns that ran east, all the way to the end. And while a new sophistication was growing, aging Civil War veterans wearing their Grand Army of the Republic uniforms still marched in Fourth of July parades, and patriotic speeches often featured reminders of Long Island's occupation by the British during the Revolution.

But as the century ended, every township on Long Island was connected by rail lines to New York City. More than 50,000 people each day rode ferries back and forth between Long Island and jobs in Manhattan. The formation of Nassau County in 1899 had given western Long Island its own identity and sense of purpose. Slowly, the North Shore of Long Island was being transformed into a separate and distinct "Gold Coast" of wealth and privilege. Summer colonies were cropping up on both shores.

In many ways, a bell was ringing in the future, and all Long Island had to do was answer it.

In 1900, the Pennsylvania Railroad assumed ownership of the Long Island Rail Road and almost immediately commenced plans to dig tunnels under the East River that would allow train service to move directly from Long Island to Manhattan. Perhaps nothing in Long Island history would have such a profound influence on the future as the construction of these tunnels.

"They transformed Long Island from rural to suburban," said Wunderlich. "They changed Long Island forever. It made it possible for people to live in Nassau County and western Suffolk and hold a job in New York City."

With the end of the century, newspapers began publishing stories of where Long Island had been, and what people could expect in the future. Political and social clubs held open houses on Dec. 31, 1899; churches held special midnight services; New York's young governor, Theodore Roosevelt, held an open house in Albany, and long lines wrapped around the Capitol building. And there were lively discussions as to whether the 20th Century began on Jan. 1, 1900, or one year later, on Jan. 1, 1901. Many writers to newspapers thought the century began in 1901. And they were right.

Across New York City and Long Island, there were celebrations remembering huge services held 100 years before — on Dec. 31, 1799 — in honor of George Washington, who had died on Dec. 14. On that day, flags were at half staff, businesses were closed. One newspaper, on Dec. 30, 1899, wrote: "One hundred years ago today New York was in deep mourning for the death of George Washington. It was Washington's funeral day in this city, and a parade of an elaborate and novel character had been arranged by the municipal officials, in which every civil and military society took part."

One hundred years later, as Long Island prepared to greet the 20th Century, people still celebrated Washington in a big way. Perhaps Long Islanders still thought of themselves, even in 1899, as deeply grounded in colonial-era history.

Nassau County Museum Collection, Long Island Studies Institute

A cartoon from an 1899 issue of the Nassau County Review asks, as we do now: Exactly when *does* a century end?

In 1900, Suffolk County had a population of 77,582, nearly double its 1860 population of 43,275. In the first population count in the new Nassau County, there were approximately 55,000 residents in 1900. Queens County had grown tremendously in those same 40 years — from 57,391 to 152,999.

As the century ended, there were speeches galore on what the future held. Many newspaper writers predicted America would become the dominant nation in the world. "The year 1900 will stand marked in our national history as a period of unprecedented commercial and financial prosperity," one newspaper proclaimed.

Public officials confidently predicted a growth in the railroad and textile industries, that exports would set records, and farmers would become prosperous.

"The future has no clouds," a federal official was quoted as saying.

Census Snapshot: 1900

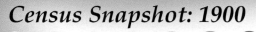

110 Years of Growth: From 1790, when the first U.S. Census was taken, through 1900, the population of the United States grew from nearly 3.9 million to 76.2 million. And the number of people on Long Island, from Brooklyn to Montauk, grew from about 37,000 to 1.45 million, with the majority in Kings County. Nassau County, which was formed in 1899, had its first census in 1900.

Total Population

New York State 1790: *340,120* 1900: *7,268,894*

	1790	1900
Queens*	16,014	152,999
Nassau		55,448
Suffolk	16,440	77,582
Kings (Brooklyn)	4,495	1,166,582

Town Populations

Nassau	1790	1900
North Hempstead	2,696	12,048
Oyster Bay	4,097	16,334
Hempstead	3,828	27,066

Suffolk	1790	1900
Babylon**		7,112
Brookhaven	3,224	14,592
East Hampton	1,497	3,746
Huntington	3,260**	9,483
Islip	609	12,545
Riverhead***		4,503
Shelter Island	201	1,066
Smithtown	1,022	5,863
Southampton	3,408	10,371
Southold	3,219***	8,301

*-Included present-day Nassau County until Queens joined New York City in 1898.
**-Huntington included present-day Babylon until 1873.
***-Southold included present-day Riverhead until 1792.
SOURCE: "New York State Population," 1987; The World Almanac

Newsday / Linda McKenney

Hits and Misses In a Forecast For the 1900s

Grandiose predictions for the 20th Century were made in the Dec. 30, 1900, edition of The Brooklyn Eagle. Among the predictions were these:

- "Liquid air" will "banish poverty from the earth."
- Advertising "will be in future the breath of life in commerce."
- Compressed air and electricity will "revolutionize present modes of transportation."
- "Cheap and speedy transportation" will decentralize populations and eliminate the horse and buggy. Trains will travel at more than 100 mph.
- Churches will become more "spiritual and practical."
- Mail will be delivered to homes in pneumatic tubes.
- "Artificial light" will cut the crime rate; suburban life will expand due to growth of "rapid transit"; houseflies will disappear, and the telephone and telegraph will become commonplace.
- "The journal of the 20th century will not be the newspaper." Instead, information will be passed along by "applied electricity."
- "All business will be done at home."
- Automobiles and airships will be the "20th century vehicles."
- Man will "live longer and be happier, owing to use of plant foods only."
- Science will find the means to bring the dead back to life. **—Steve Wick**

Northport Historical Society Photo

TIME MACHINE

Northport's Old Row

One of the remarkable things about Main Street in Northport Village is how much remains the same after nearly a century.

The photo above, taken with the photographer's back to Northport Harbor, appears to be an Independence Day parade of Civil War veterans around 1905, according to Dick Simpson, a founder of the Northport Historical Society Museum.

Even today, as seen in the photo at right, there are similar points of reference. Trolley tracks remain embedded in Main Street, although the trolley provided rides to the local train station only from 1902 to 1924. Most prominent in the scene is the row of five three-story buildings on the left. The first, partially cropped out, was built in 1871 and for decades was a general store. The pointy-roofed structure at the far end went up in 1891. Then in 1894-95, architect Albert V. Porter designed three buildings to fill the gap. The narrow building with the stepped top and arched entrance held the Bank of Northport. At center came a wide building that around 1910 would have a nickelodeon, and beyond that a light-brick building was used by the First National Bank.

THEN & NOW

Today, the row's occupants include a florist, jeweler, real estate-insurance office, cafe, delicatessen, sweet shop, nail salon, liquor store and dance studio. "They're tremendous," Simpson says of the buildings. "I don't think that anywhere else in town we have such a series of buildings that old."

Newsday Photo / Bill Davis

"Huckleberry Frolic" is an oil-on-canvas painting made in 1937 by J. Theodore Johnson; it hangs in the Garden City Post Office.

Newsday Photos / Bill Davis

TIME MACHINE

PICTURING THE PAST AND PRESENT

Painted in 1938 by William Gropper, this mural depicts air-mail service; it is located in the Freeport Post Office.

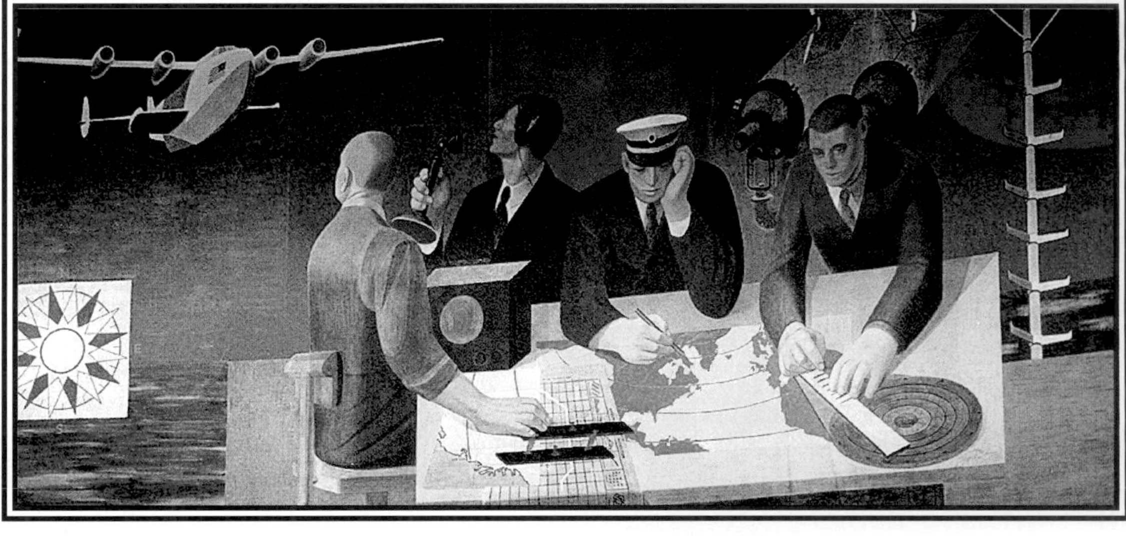

Above is part of the 360-degree mural by James Brooks in LaGuardia Airport's Marine Air Terminal.

The WPA Artists' Enduring Legacy

The Great Depression left deep scars on those who struggled to survive, but it also produced enduring works of beauty.

The federal Works Progress Administration, which lasted from 1935 to 1943, provided employment to about 700,000 workers and their dependents in New York City alone. Among them were writers, musicians and artists. The latter created about 10,000 works nationwide, including murals that still adorn numerous public buildings in the metropolitan area. The program employed such noted painters as Raphael Soyer, Stuart Davis and Jackson Pollock.

At right, a Victor White work in the Rockville Centre Post Office depicts village history.

CHAPTER 7

The Modern Era

From the arrival of the automobile to the birth of the United Nations

Sportsman William K. Vanderbilt II's cup race paves the way to the future

The Age of the Auto

BY SYLVIA ADCOCK
STAFF WRITER

Vanderbilt, Vanderbilt Museum; Race, Nassau County Museum Collection, Long Island Studies Institute

The 1908 Vanderbilt Cup race, above, was held on a circular route that included Jericho Turnpike and the new Long Island Motor Parkway, which was built by Vanderbilt, left.

As dawn began to break over the Hempstead Plains on a frosty October morning, the clustered crowds along Jericho Turnpike watched the great racing cars line up in their starting order.

The racecourse was ready. Street-sprinkling carts had covered the roads with 90,000 gallons of petroleum to keep the dust down. William K. Vanderbilt II had arrived from the Garden City Hotel in his trademark white Mercedes, and a half-dozen men pushed the first car, a red Mercedes, to the starting line.

At 6 a.m., the starter yelled "Go!" and the red car lurched forward. The crowd roared. An overly imaginative newspaper reporter wrote of "a crash of exploding oil" and flames reaching out from the sides of the car. Two minutes later, the next car was off.

It was Oct. 8, 1904. The age of the automobile had arrived on Long Island.

The Long Island Rail Road had run full trains all night long to bring the curious to the Vanderbilt Cup Race, the first international auto race in the United States. "Almost everyone who could afford a holiday took it," one newspaper reported, and some onlookers arrived on horses that "chafed impatiently on the bit, as if longing for a test of speed with these new things that man had made to take their place."

The first Vanderbilt Cup Race was not just a test of race cars, it was an event that would popularize the automobile like no other. Drivers from all over the world fighting for a silver Tiffany cup for nearly 300 miles excited the imaginations of the horse-and-wagon populace. And the races that followed would leave a legacy: the first concrete highway in the United States was built after the 1906 race left a spectator dead and Vanderbilt was forced to establish a private road. Called the Long Island Motor Parkway, it also was the first highway designed exclusively for automobiles and the first to use overpasses and bridges to eliminate intersections.

When a New York newspaper reporter asked Thomas Edison for his thoughts on the first Vanderbilt Cup Race, the inventor said he wouldn't be surprised if someone got killed. In that same interview, he had another, more prescient prediction that went beyond the race itself: "In time the automobile will be the poor man's wagon," Edison said. "He will use it to haul his wood, convey his farm freight, get to and from the post office and for the family for church."

That might have seemed far-fetched in 1904, when automobiles were still the exotic playthings of the rich. But years later, the easy ownership of automobiles would create and define modern suburbia, a sprawling universe where it would be nearly impossible to live without one. Cars would bring newfound freedom, making life easier. At the same time, they would bring traffic jams, making life more difficult. Most of all, they would make this century very, very different from the last.

But as the 20th Century was dawning, the road ahead was uncertain. And the day of the first Vanderbilt Cup race had not come without obstacles.

When word got out that Vanderbilt and some of his wealthy friends planned to close off public roads to hold a race, there was a public outcry. "In order that the speed-madness monomaniacs may drive their man-maiming engines at an excessive and illegal pace, the residents and taxpayers of the island are bidden to keep off the road," the New York World fumed. "It is an extraordinary condition of affairs when a coterie of idlers, rich men's sons and gilded youth can take possession of public highways."

The cup race would last for hours, as race cars covered 10 laps on a triangular route that included Jericho Turnpike, Bethpage Turnpike and Hempstead Turnpike — all roads used by farmers to take their produce to market. Shortly after the Nassau Board of Supervisors approved the route, the farmers went to court to try to block the race, but failed to convince a judge that the supervisors' action was illegal.

Tensions mounted as the racing teams flocked to Long Island, and a chauffeur for the Pope Toledo Co. who was testing the course was thrown out of his car and killed when he nearly collided with a farm wagon near Hicksville. Residents were outraged when signs were posted saying, "Chain your dogs and lock up your fowl" on the day of the race. "Farmers Will Carry Pistols to Auto Races," one headline warned.

On the day of the race, bent nails were scattered on parts of the course but no one brought a gun. The farmers ended up offering parking spots for $25 — a huge amount of money — and went through the crowds selling coffee and sandwiches. One fatality marred the race: Carl Muessel, a mechanic for a French team, was thrown from a race car near Franklin Square and fractured his skull.

When the race was over, George Heath, driving a French 90-hp Panhard, took the cup. He completed the course in 5 hours, 26 minutes, 45 seconds. His average speed was 52 mph.

The crowds were attracted by the exotic machines and the thrill of speed. Albert Clement of France described to a newspaper reporter what it felt like to go more than 60 mph: "When you first start, the ground seems to be rising up in front of you, as if to hit you in the face . . . You haven't time for anything but the thrill, and the watching of the long narrow road in front. You haven't time to see what's on one side or the other."

The onlookers seemed a bit bloodthirsty. During the second race, in 1905, a huge crowd gathered at an S curve near Albertson, "attracted by the possibility of witnessing something in the way of a death-defying accident," The New York Times reported. They were rewarded for their efforts, as "two of the most sensational smash-ups of the day occurred at

LI HISTORY.COM

Leaf through some pages from the official 1904 program to see profiles of cars and drivers, view a map of the track and browse auto advertisements. On the Internet, see http://www.lihistory.com.

this point."

The turning point came in 1906. This time, it wasn't a racer who was killed, but a spectator. Vanderbilt had hired men to keep order and spent thousands installing wire fencing to hold back the crowds, who would run out onto the road to get a better look at an approaching car. But some spectators brought wire-cutters, and at 9 a.m., the crowd broke through the fence at Krug's Corner in Mineola, the intersection of Willis Avenue and Jericho Turnpike, just as Elliott Shepard's 130-hp Hotchkiss was approaching. Shepard slammed into the knot of people, killing Kurt Gruner of Passaic, N.J., who left a wife and two children. Two small boys were also injured, and the newspapers proclaimed it a miracle that more were not killed.

"I am deeply distressed that the contest should have been marred by any fatalities, but I am sure it was unavoidable," Vanderbilt said after the race. At the Garden City Hotel that day, the young millionaire and his friends decided to build a toll road that could be used as a racecourse. Before long they had formed a corporation with stock of $2.5 million and a board of directors that included such notables as John Jacob Astor and Harry Payne Whitney.

"The Long Island Motor Parkway is a necessity," said the 1906 prospectus. "The use of the much-frequented highways of the Island by motorists is becoming irksome." The new road was expected to greatly increase property values so much that property owners were asked to donate strips of their land for the right-of-way.

In a massive public relations campaign, Arthur R. Pardington, the parkway corporation's vice president, went from town to town speaking about the advantages of the new road. In an article for Harper's magazine, Pardington wrote that it would be "the modern Appian Way for the motorist."

The reaction on Long Island was mixed. A Melville farmer donated rights to his land and convinced a few landowners around him to do the same. A Dix Hills farmer donated a strip of his farm. But others resisted. "Mr. Pardington thinks landowners ought to give their land to millionaires for their pleasure," said one letter-writer to the Long Islander newspaper in Huntington. "And I think the millionaires should pay for what they want." Another complained that the parkway was "an experiment to cut an island practically in two separate parts."

The parkway route ended up snaking across the Island, twisting and turning around spots where Vanderbilt couldn't get the land he wanted.

Construction began in June, 1908, using a new paving method of reinforced concrete. Two layers of heavy crushed stone were laid upon the roadbed, separated by a sheet of wire mesh. A thin, soupy mixture of cement and sand from Jones Beach was poured over the stones and the surface was brushed for texture.

Please see VANDERBILT, Page 259

A Desire Named Streetcar

BY SYLVIA ADCOCK
STAFF WRITER

Long before the automobile took over Long Island, when the century was very, very young, a network of streetcars took Long Islanders from place to place with clanging gongs and whistles that announced their arrival.

For a brief time, the trolley had its day in the sun.

Electric trolley cars rumbled on tracks along heavily traveled roads such as Northern Boulevard, New York Avenue and Jericho Turnpike, drawing their power from electric wires overhead. The network was extensive. You could take a trolley from Elmont to Hempstead. From Roslyn to Mineola, Garden City to Freeport, Amityville to Babylon, Huntington to Farmingdale. For only a nickel, with service as often as every 15 minutes.

And then the trolleys vanished, almost overnight. The tracks in the roadbed were paved over, the trolley poles that held the electric wires were taken down, the trolley drawbridge over Alley Creek in Queens was dismantled, and it was as if they'd never been here. As quickly as they came, it seemed, they were gone.

Their story began in the 1890s, as "trolley fever" swept the country. In cities everywhere, electric trolleys began replacing horse-drawn carts. This new form of conveyance was what planners today would call "light rail." Unlike railroads, which were designed for longer trips, trolleys made short hops with frequent service, often carrying folks from one neighborhood to the next.

The first electric trolleys arrived on Long Island in 1898 in Babylon and Huntington. As early as 1871, a horse-drawn cart ran on tracks down Fire Island Avenue bringing passengers from the Babylon railroad station to the ferry dock, where they could catch a steamboat to Oak Island. In 1898, the Babylon Railroad, as the service was called, replaced the horse-drawn cart with a new electric trolley. That same year, the Long Island Rail Road bought out a similar horse-drawn service that ran along New York Avenue from the train station to Halesite, called the Huntington Railroad. The LIRR immediately put up overhead electric wires and began trolley service along the route, later extending it south to Amityville.

It was after 1900 that traction companies began to build a booming network of trolley tracks. In 1902, one company started a line that would extend from Brooklyn to Freeport along the South Shore, and then north to Mineola from Freeport. When the workers laying trolley tracks on Franklin Avenue in Garden City reached the LIRR tracks, there was trouble. The railroad, fearing grade-crossing accidents and competition from the trolley lines, balked. But the trolley finally got permission to cross, and the route — from the county courthouse to South Shore beaches — was immediately popular. A brass band met the trolley in Freeport on its first run.

In 1907 another traction company built a network of rails along the less populated North Shore, from Flushing to Roslyn and then north to Port Washington and south to Hicksville. A concrete retaining wall was built alongside Northern Boulevard just north of the Roslyn clock tower to keep soil off the tracks. Today, the wall still hugs the road, which is called Old Northern Boulevard.

Another line ran from Patchogue to Holbrook. The Suffolk Traction Co. planned service to Port Jefferson, but although tracks were laid in that village, the battery-powered cars never ran. The Long Island Rail Road also operated small train-station-to-village trolley lines in Northport, Sea Cliff and Glen Cove.

Nassau County Museum Collection, Long Island Studies Institute

A streetcar on Main Street in Mineola, above, in 1913; below, a horse-drawn trolley in Babylon in an undated photo

Babylon Historical and Preservation Society

The trolley's finest moment was in 1914. But things started going downhill after World War I began. For one thing, the war drove up prices for materials the traction companies needed — coal for fuel, copper for electric wires and steel for rails.

But what hurt the trolleys most was the fact that they weren't allowed to raise their fares. The traction companies had made agreements with villages to charge a base fare of 5 cents, and the villages wouldn't let them increase it. Keeping employees was difficult because the traction companies couldn't match the pay of munition factories.

And then there were the automobiles. Production had been suspended during the war, but once it was over, people began buying Ford's Model T. Buses also began to compete on the trolley routes. The buses, which didn't need overhead power lines and miles of track, were much cheaper to operate. In 1921, traction company representatives appeared before Hempstead Village officials, complaining that the new buses were robbing them of their passengers, pulling up to the curb in front of the trolleys to pick up a waiting throng of passengers.

By the late 1920s, most of the traction companies had gone out of business, and private bus lines bought out the trolley routes. The last to go was the LIRR's Huntington line, which ran from the train station to Halesite until 1927. Remnants of tracks remain in Northport.

But some things don't change. Perhaps today's LIRR commuter could sympathize with a passenger who took a trolley daily from Port Washington to Hicksville. "Almost invariably, I have the pleasure of listening to the stale jokes, ribald songs and comment on passengers," he wrote to a local newspaper. "Three or four regular riders at night seem to think they own the car. Is there no remedy?"

FAST FORWARD

Discoveries Of a Road's Scholars

BY SYLVIA ADCOCK
STAFF WRITER

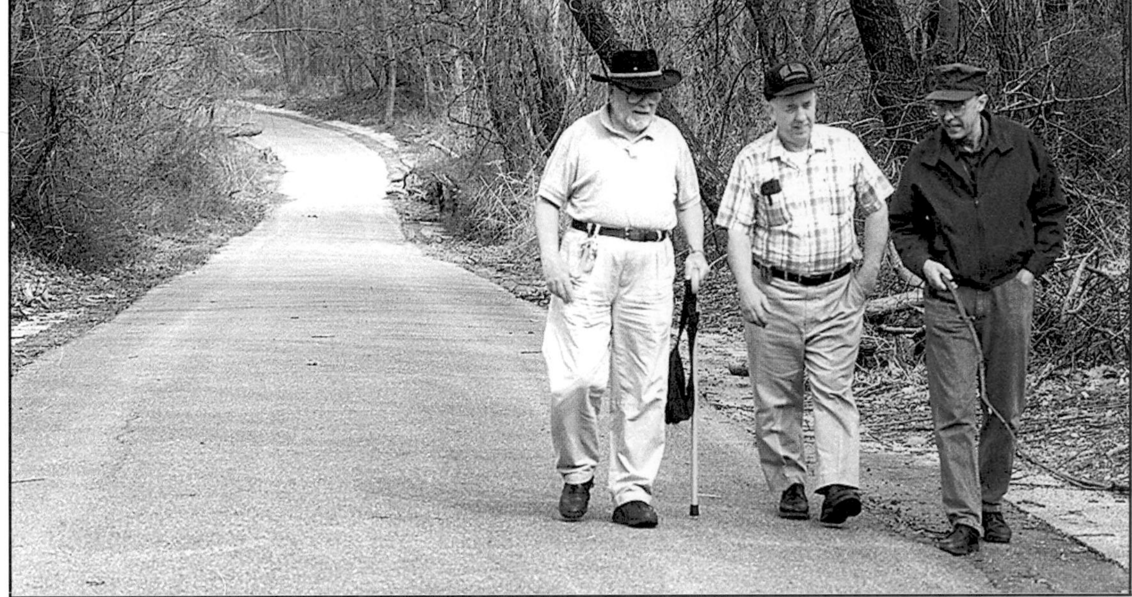

Newsday Photo / Daniel Goodrich

From left, Bill Donnelly, Dale Welsch and Robert Miller walk on the old parkway near Springfield Boulevard in Queens.

Dale Welsch remembers the moment when he discovered the Long Island Motor Parkway.

Growing up in New Hyde Park, Welsch loved to explore strips of a deserted roadway not far from home. One day, near Old Courthouse Road, he and his friends discovered a tiny bridge that seemed to go nowhere.

"We came back all excited that we had found this mystery bridge and a road under it, and we asked my father what it was," Welsch said. "We took him up there, and he said, 'Why, that's Motor Parkway.' "

The more Welsch learned about the parkway, the more he wanted to know. "It was like a hidden treasure," he said. For years, the 60-year-old plumber has been faithfully retracing the route of the original road, joined by a small but dedicated army of buffs.

They think the Long Island Motor Parkway never really got its due from the history books. The Bronx River Parkway usually gets credit for being the first parkway in the nation. "But it was started three years after the Long Island Motor Parkway was finished," said Robert Miller, a librarian in the Queensborough Public Library who is the unofficial parkway historian. Miller began tracing the parkway in the 1960s after he read an article in a local historical journal. "I thought, I wonder what's left? So I borrowed my father's car, strapped a bicycle on it and went out looking."

The patches of pavement run through backyards in Levittown, alongside an apartment complex in Manhasset Hills, behind Roosevelt Field Mall and show up as bike trails in Alley Pond Park. In Lake Success, a road leading to the Great Neck school district's athletic fields is an original section, and another well-preserved segment runs through backyards behind the American Legion Hall in Albertson.

Much of the parkway has vanished since William K. Vanderbilt II gave it to Nassau, Suffolk and Queens Counties in 1938. Suffolk kept 12 miles as a roadway, but Nassau sold much of the road to the Long Island Lighting Co. for a right-of-way for the utility's electric power lines. The parkway buffs, armed with old maps, use the giant electric towers as one clue that the parkway may be nearby.

"It's almost a cultlike following," said John Ellis Kordes, a Garden City historian who put together an exhibit on the parkway for the Garden City Chamber of Commerce.

Keeping what's left of the old road isn't easy. It's vanishing, bit by bit, every year. Last year, Al Velocci of New Hyde Park learned that houses were going up on a tract of land in Searingtown containing 200 feet of the old road. Velocci apprached the developer and asked him to try to save the parkway. But the developer said he had no choice. The old pavement was bulldozed and today houses sit where the parkway once ran.

"It wasn't considered a landmark so there wasn't anything the town could do about it," Velocci said. "That's what happens. You end up losing bits and pieces of it."

Into the 20th Century

Long Island

Sept. 14, 1901. Theodore Roosevelt was inaugurated president. His home in Oyster Bay then became the summer White House.

1901. Guglielmo Marconi sent the first wireless radio message from Babylon.

Oct. 8, 1904. The first Vanderbilt Cup race was held.

1917-18. Soldiers bound for World War I trained at Camp Mills in Garden City and Camp Upton in Yaphank.

United States

Sept. 6, 1901. President William McKinley was shot in Buffalo. He died eight days later and Theodore Roosevelt was sworn in as president.

Dec. 17, 1904. Orville and Wilbur Wright made their first successful flight.

April 18, 1906. An earthquake shook San Francisco and made more than 500,000 people homeless. The quake was the most damaging in U.S. history.

April 6, 1909. Robert Peary reached the North Pole.

Aug. 15, 1914. The Panama Canal officially opened.

April 6, 1917. President Woodrow Wilson signed a joint resolution of Congress proclaiming a state of war with Germany.

The World

Aug. 14, 1900. Allied troops defeated the Boxers and relieved their siege of the diplomatic quarter in Beijing.

Oct. 7, 1908. Austria-Hungary annexed Bosnia-Herzegovina. The area's population had favored union with Serbia.

Feb. 12, 1912. China's last emperor, Pechie, a 5-year-old boy, abdicated, ending 267 years of imperial rule.

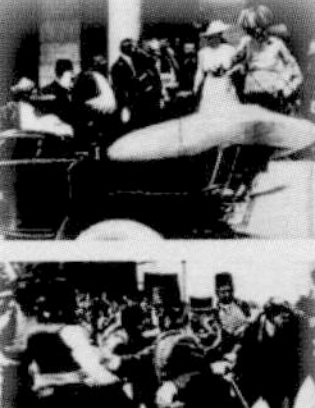

June 28, 1914. A Serbian nationalist shot and killed the heir to the Austro-Hungarian empire. The assassination set off a chain of events that led to the beginning of World War I in early August.

Nov. 7, 1917. The Bolsheviks, led by Vladimir Lenin, took over the Russian government.

Nov. 11, 1918. Germany agreed to an armistice, ending World War I.

1900 1905 1910 1915 1920

The Motor Parkway

In 1938, William K. Vanderbilt II turned his Motor Parkway over to Queens, Nassau and Suffolk in lieu of back taxes. The longest stretch of parkway remaining is 13 miles in Suffolk; smaller pieces remain elsewhere – on bike trails, in backyards and behind shopping centers. Here's how Vanderbilt's Motor Parkway looked in the late 1920s:

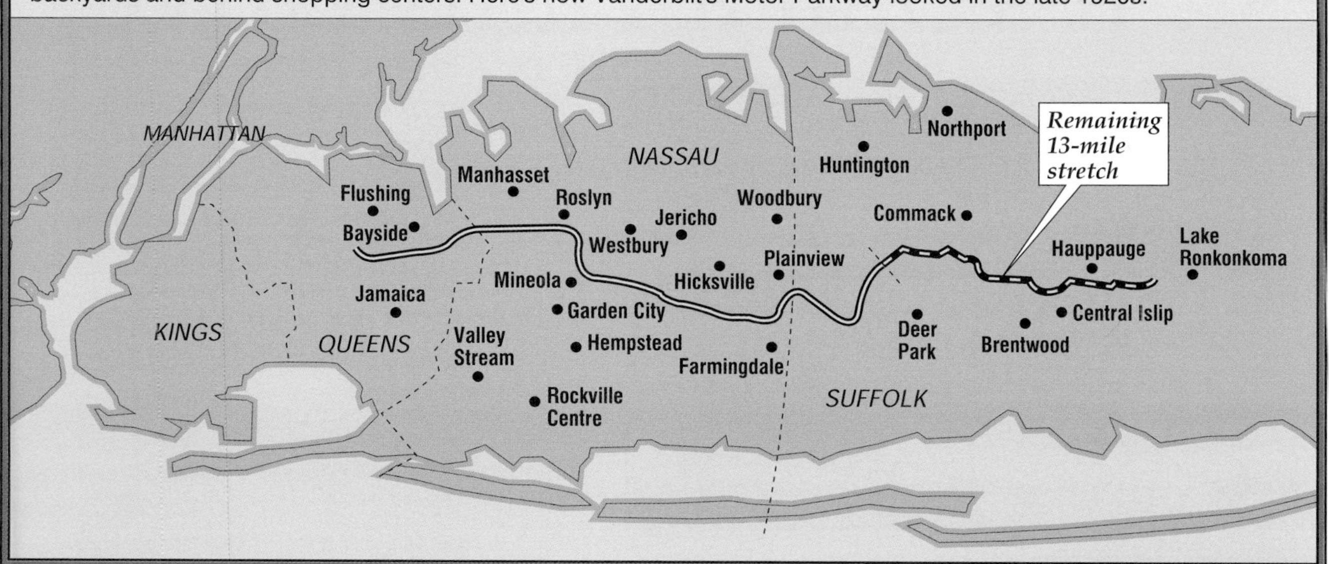

Newsday / Linda McKenney

Vanderbilt Museum; Newsday Photo

Drivers from all over the world competed for the Vanderbilt Cup, made of Tiffany silver.

A Road Leads To the Future

VANDERBILT from **Page 257**

By October, nine miles of the roadway were open, from the Westbury area to Bethpage. Bridges and overpasses avoided intersections with other roads, a feature that had been used only on the traverse roads through Central Park.

The 1907 race was suspended but in 1908 cup races were held on a circular route that included Jericho Turnpike and the nine miles of the new parkway. As cars became more powerful, the number of accidents mounted. A planned 30-mile racing loop in Riverhead had never been built, so Vanderbilt still had to use some public roads for the races. After the 1910 race, when four were killed and 20 were injured, Scientific American called it the "Vanderbilt Cup Race Slaughter." Automobile manufacturers and race-car drivers declared the race unsafe and refused to return. Indianapolis, not Long Island, became the auto racing capital.

The motor parkway would never again be a racetrack. But it continued to be used as a testing ground for leading car and tire manufacturers, including Packard and the U.S. Rubber Co.

By 1910, it stretched for 43 miles from Lakeville Road in Great Neck to Ronkonkoma, and in 1911 Vanderbilt extended it west to Springfield Boulevard in Queens. The parkway had 65 bridges. Its 12 toll lodges were designed in the French Provincial style by John Russell Pope, who designed the American Museum of Natural History in Manhattan. Where the road ended at Lake Ronkonkoma, Vanderbilt built an inn called the Petit Trianon, also designed by Pope.

In early years the parkway toll was $2, a hefty fee in those days. Auto traffic was still relatively light, as few could afford the tolls, much less to own an automobile. Vanderbilt reduced the tolls to $1.50 in 1912, and to $1 in 1917.

The parkway's popularity increased in the 1920s as car ownership became more affordable. After 1924, 150,000 cars traveled on the motor parkway each year, some on their way to East End vacation spots, some out for a Sunday drive. A parkway brochure in 1925 advertised the picnic spots at the parkway's end: "Shaded grove for basket parties. Free boating. Duck dinners $2."

In 1926 Vanderbilt poured more money into the parkway, building a two-mile extension to Horace Harding Boulevard in Queens, and a two-mile spur to connect the road to Jericho Turnpike in Commack. He also widened the roadway from 16 to 22 feet. But traffic began to wane in the 1930s as the Depression slowed car-buying. In 1933, the toll was reduced to 40 cents.

The biggest blow to Vanderbilt's parkway came in 1929, when Robert Moses began construction of his Northern State Parkway. Vanderbilt had approached Moses about buying the motor parkway for his new road. Moses rejected the proposals, saying the motor parkway was badly constructed. "A white elephant for the last 20 years," he called it.

In 1933, when the Northern State opened from Queens to Mineola, Vanderbilt knew he'd been beaten. In 1938, he turned the road over to the state in lieu of back taxes. In a brief speech at the Nassau County executive's office, Vanderbilt reflected on the parkway's histo-

Please see **VANDERBILT, Next Page**

1922-24. F. Scott Fitzgerald wrote "The Great Gatsby" while living in Great Neck.

May 20, 1927. Charles Lindbergh left Roosevelt Field on the first nonstop solo flight across the Atlantic Ocean.

1929. Grumman Aircraft was founded in a rented garage in Baldwin.

1930-31. The Big Duck was built in Riverhead.

Sept. 21, 1938. Hurricane caused severe damage on the East End, killing 70.

1939. Pan Am began overseas air flights from Manhasset Bay.

June 13, 1942. Germans landed from submarine in Amagansett. All four eventually were captured.

1945. Miracle Mile shopping center opened along Northern Boulevard in Manhasset.

April 7, 1927. First successful demonstration of a television took place.

Oct. 29, 1929. More than 16 million shares were sold on the New York Stock Exchange – the start of the Great Depression.

March 1, 1932. Charles Lindbergh's baby was kidnaped. The body was found May 12.

Dec. 7, 1941. Japanese forces bombed the U.S. military facilities in and around Pearl Harbor.

Aug. 6, 1945. A U.S. plane dropped an atomic bomb on the Japanese city of Hiroshima. Another bomb was dropped on Nagasaki three days later and Japan surrendered.

Jan. 30, 1933. Adolf Hitler became chancellor of Germany.

May 6, 1937. The airship Hindenburg exploded while landing in New Jersey. Thirty-five passengers and crew died.

Sept. 1, 1939. German troops invaded Poland, beginning World War II.

June 6, 1944. Allied troops landed in Normandy in the biggest combined land, sea and air operation of all time.

May 8, 1945. Germany surrendered, eight days after Hitler had committed suicide.

1925 1930 1935 1940 1945

Newsday / Linda McKenney

Road Test: It's Still a Hard Drive

BY TOM INCANTALUPO
STAFF WRITER

Take your hat off to the drivers of the Vanderbilt Cup. But put it back on again if you ever ride in a car like the ones they drove.

Bring earplugs, too, because 600 or more cubic inches of engine with the muffler deactivated sounds like the furies of hell unleashed — even when you're just moseying along a back road in Huntington in Walter McCarthy's 1910 Simplex, a car of the type that ran in the Vanderbilt.

To say it drives, sounds and rides like a truck would be unfair to the trucks so many of us drive nowadays. It's an open car that exposes the driver to the elements, and by our pampered standards, it rides hard, it steers hard and it's not easy to brake.

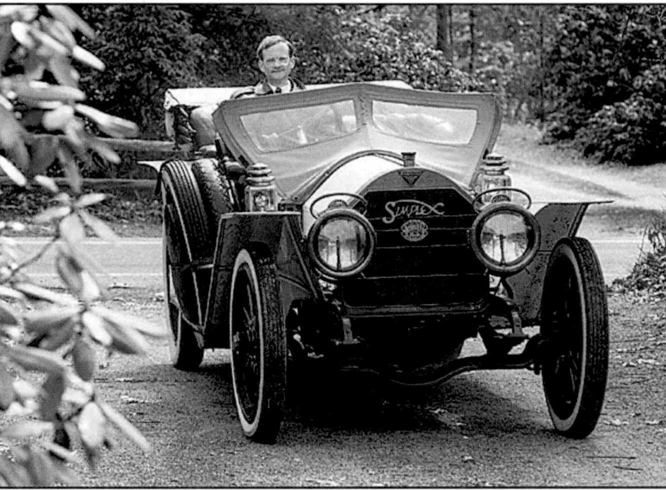

Newsday Photo / Bill Davis

Newsday automotive writer Tom Incantalupo tools around in a 1910 Simplex, a car of the type that ran in the Vanderbilt Cup races.

To those of us who consider lack of air conditioning "roughing it," it's difficult to imagine five hours of hard driving behind the wheel of this Simplex and tougher still to imagine driving it at speeds of up to 100 mph that were sometimes attained during the Vanderbilt race.

One has to settle nowadays for a car "like" those that drove for the cup because the only car in existence known to have competed in the race — a Locomobile that won in 1908 — is in the Henry Ford Museum in Dearborn, Mich.

But several Simplexes did compete, and a ride in McCarthy's four-passenger car offers a hint of the skill, the courage and, maybe, the recklessness that was required to drive very fast in the early years of this century.

At 4,450 pounds and 16 feet long, the Simplex is about the same weight and just 4 inches longer than a Ford Explorer. Its seating position is about the same height, though the driver sits in the right seat, not the left.

But no modern sport utility vehicle is as difficult as the Simplex to drive. Steering has no power assist and a ratio so tight that the wheel moves only three-quarters of a turn "lock to lock." So, changing direction takes some muscle.

The clutch's spring pressure requires an energetic push of the pedal to disengage it. Clutch, brake and accelerator pedals are in the same positions as in modern cars, relative to the driver. So is the four-speed shifter, whose H-pattern is familiar and whose gears engage easily without clashing.

Although modest compared to many cars that raced in its day, the four-cylinder engine's cubic inch displacement is about twice that of most V-8s in modern cars or light trucks. But the technology is early 20th Century and, even accounting for differences in how horsepower is calculated now, the engine probably produces about half the 300 hp that a modern V-8 of about 300 cubic inches typically produces.

McCarthy, a retired teacher, restored the Simplex in his Huntington home and drives for fun, even though many cars today can out-accelerate it.

And all of today's cars can out-stop it as well. The Simplex' drum-type brakes act only on the rear wheels and its narrow tires have a fraction of the grip of modern ones. On the road, McCarthy suggests augmenting the mechanical foot-operated system with the handbrake, a handle to the driver's right.

There are springs; we saw them. But you'd hardly know it from the car's ride.

The Simplex' fuel economy supports the truck analogy; McCarthy says he gets about 10 miles to the gallon on the road. The car was built in Manhattan and cost $5,750 new, said McCarthy. David Brownell, technical editor of the collector magazine Hemmings Motor News, says it could easily be worth more than $200,000.

McCarthy has another, race-prepared, Simplex under restoration. It lacks fenders, as well as the four-passenger version's folding top and its canvas and plastic half windshield.

Now, that's roughing it.

THE VANDERBILT TOLL LODGES

It looks like a doll's house, a tiny two-story stucco cottage with a steep shingled roof and a covered canopy that left plenty of room for automobiles.

In the heart of Garden City stands the last remaining toll lodge from the Long Island Motor Parkway — or at least, the last one that hasn't been modified until it is unrecognizable. The toll lodge is the home of the Garden City Chamber of Commerce, which in 1989 moved the tiny house from its original location on Clinton Road to Seventh Avenue.

There were 12 such toll lodges, all designed by John Russell Pope, who also designed the American Museum of Natural History in Manhattan. The employees lived in the houses and were on call 24 hours a day. They stood in a tiny vestibule and collected tolls from cars entering under a canopy in what must have been America's first drive-through. On the main floor is a working fireplace and a tiny kitchen. Upstairs were two bedrooms where the family slept. The Garden City toll lodge was built in 1911, and William K. Vanderbilt II later modernized the homes, adding electricity.

When Vanderbilt turned the roadway over to the state in 1938, he offered the lodges to the employees for $500. The Garden City toll collector bought the house, reared his three children in it, and sold it in 1977. Today the Garden City Chamber of Commerce maintains a tiny museum with displays on the Long Island Motor Parkway in the basement of the toll lodge.

— Sylvia Adcock

Newsday Photo / Bill Davis

A toll lodge now used by the Garden City Chamber of Commerce; foreground, Motor Parkway toll permits

A Road Leads To the Future

VANDERBILT from **Preceding Page**

ry. It owed its existence, he said, not to any hope for profit, but "to the enthusiasm of a group of motorists, who 30 years ago felt the need for an express highway where high speed could be permitted with safety."

In all, Vanderbilt spent $10 million building and improving the Motor Parkway. Neither he nor his investors ever made a cent of profit. On Easter, 1938, the roadway was shut to traffic and the toll lodges were offered for $500 to the tollkeepers, who had reared their families in the tiny four-room houses.

Queens County chose to use its small portion of the roadway for bike trails in Alley Pond Park. Nassau gave its portion to the Long Island Lighting Co. for a right-of-way. Today, there are only tiny stretches of concrete remaining, running through backyards and vacant lots. Only Suffolk County kept part of the road in use, calling it the Vanderbilt Motor Parkway.

"Think of the time it will save the busy man of affairs," Pardington had said at the groundbreaking ceremony in 1908. "Speed limits are left behind, the Great White Way is before him, and with the throttle open he can go, go, go and keep going, 50, 60 or 90 miles an hour until Riverhead or Southampton is reached, in time for a scotch at the Meadow Club, a round of golf and a refreshing dip in the surf, and all before dinner is served, or the electric lights begin to twinkle."

Garden City Toll Lodge Museum Photo

Workers build one of the 65 bridges on the Long Island Motor Parkway, circa 1908.

A household in Oyster Bay is stricken, and the trail leads to the cook, Mary Mallon

Dinner With Typhoid Mary

BY RIDGELY OCHS
STAFF WRITER

Poor Mary Mallon.

Of all the bizarre and melancholy fates that could befall an otherwise ordinary person, hers has to be among the most sad and peculiar.

Like millions before and since, she came to this country from Ireland, seeking a better life. Instead, she was forced by public health officials to live for a total of 26 years on a tiny island in the East River, isolated from and shunned by her fellow humans. And while she was not the only one of her kind, her name became synonymous with disease and death.

She was Typhoid Mary, and her story really begins on Long Island.

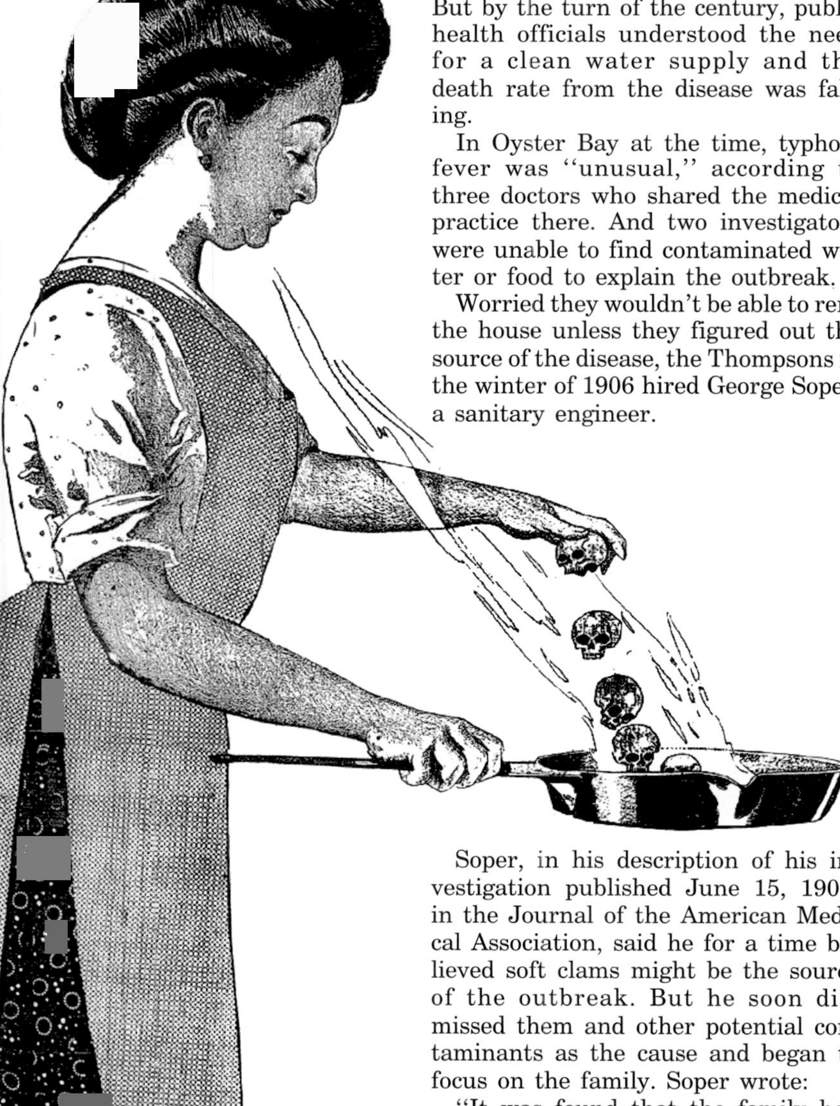

Mallon as she was portrayed in an illustration in the June 20, 1909, edition of The New York American

In the summer of 1906, Mallon, who was born in 1869 in County Tyrone and emigrated to the United States in 1883, was working as a cook for a wealthy New York banker, Charles Henry Warren, and his family. The Warrens had rented a house in Oyster Bay for the summer, described as "large, surrounded with ample grounds, in a desirable part of the village," from Mr. and Mrs. George Thompson.

From Aug. 27 to Sept. 3, six of the 11 people in the house came down with typhoid fever, including Mrs. Warren, two daughters, two maids and a gardener.

Typhoid fever, caused by the bacteria *salmonella typhi*, is spread through water or food supplies. In the 19th Century, typhoid fever, which causes headache, loss of energy, upset bowels and a high fever, was a scourge, especially in cities, killing about 10 percent of sufferers. But by the turn of the century, public health officials understood the need for a clean water supply and the death rate from the disease was falling.

In Oyster Bay at the time, typhoid fever was "unusual," according to three doctors who shared the medical practice there. And two investigators were unable to find contaminated water or food to explain the outbreak.

Worried they wouldn't be able to rent the house unless they figured out the source of the disease, the Thompsons in the winter of 1906 hired George Soper, a sanitary engineer.

Soper, in his description of his investigation published June 15, 1907, in the Journal of the American Medical Association, said he for a time believed soft clams might be the source of the outbreak. But he soon dismissed them and other potential contaminants as the cause and began to focus on the family. Soper wrote:

"It was found that the family had changed cooks on August 4. This was about three weeks before the typhoid epidemic broke out . . . She remained in the family only a short time, leaving about three weeks after the outbreak occurred . . . The cook was described as an Irish woman about 40 years of age, tall, heavy, single. She seemed to be in perfect health."

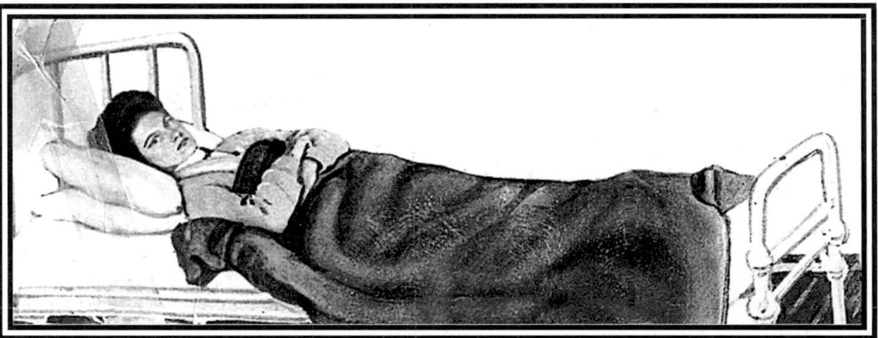

UPI / Bettman-Corbin Photo

Mary Mallon, an Irish immigrant, shown in an undated photo, unwittingly spread typhoid fever; she was a carrier but not ill herself. Mallon was kept in isolation for 26 years.

This cook was Mary Mallon, and Soper became convinced she was a healthy carrier of the disease. This meant she had at some point had a mild case of typhoid, which she still carried and could spread, although she herself was not affected. Soper was the first to identify a healthy typhoid carrier in the United States.

Although his deduction was undoubtedly brilliant, his handling of Mallon was not.

"I can't help feeling that if that initial encounter had been different, the whole story could have been different," said Judith Walzer Leavitt, a professor of the history of medicine at the University of Wisconsin and author of the book "Typhoid Mary, Captive to the Public Health" (Beacon Press, 1996).

Soper tracked Mallon down in March, 1907, to the home on Park Avenue in Manhattan where she was a cook. Appearing without warning, Soper told her she was spreading death and disease through her cooking and that he wanted samples of her feces, urine and blood for tests.

In a later description, Soper wrote: "It did not take Mary long to react to this suggestion. She seized a carving fork and advanced in my direction. I passed rapidly down the narrow hall, through the tall iron gate."

Unable to get any lab samples from Mallon, Soper reconstructed her work history: Within the previous 10 years, the cook had worked for eight families. Seven had had typhoid outbreaks, including the Park Avenue home in which she was working. Twenty-two people had become ill and one had died of the disease, Soper said. One of the epidemics occurred at Sands Point in 1904, and four servants were infected.

Convinced by Soper's data, the New York City health inspector in March, 1907, carried Mallon off, screaming and kicking, to a hospital, where her feces did indeed show high concentrations of typhoid bacilli. She was moved to an isolation cottage on the grounds of the Riverside Hospital, a hospital for infectious diseases on North Brother Island, between the Bronx and Rikers Island.

She stayed there for three years, in relative isolation. It was during that time that she was dubbed Typhoid Mary. Described as intelligent but capable of "almost pathological anger" by the head of Riverside Hospital, Mallon despised the moniker and protested all her life that she was healthy and could not be a disease carrier: She apparently could not accept that unseen and unfelt "bugs" could infect others. As she told a newspaper: "I have never had typhoid in my life and have always been healthy. Why should I be banished like a leper and compelled to live in solitary confinement . . . ?"

After three years, she was allowed to go free as long as she stayed in touch with the health department and did not work with food.

For a time she worked washing clothes. But, apparently unable to earn enough money, she disappeared from health department view and returned to cooking. She resurfaced again in 1915, using the name Mrs. Brown and working as a cook in Sloane Maternity Hospital in Manhattan. During her three months there, she had spread typhoid to at least 25 doctors, nurses and staff, two of whom had died.

She was sent again to North Brother Island, where she lived the rest of her life, 23 years, alone in a one-room cottage. She was certainly not the only known typhoid carrier: In 1938 when she died, a newspaper noted there were 237 others living under city health department observation.

But she was the only one kept isolated for years, a result as much of prejudice toward the Irish and noncompliant women as of a public health threat, Leavitt believes.

She labored in the hospital as a domestic worker and toward the end of her life, she worked in a bacteriology lab on the grounds, washing bottles.

She also had a cottage industry making and selling goods to hospital employees. In fact, according to Leavitt, who quotes the son of two employees, she baked and sold cakes.

LI was part of the turf where radio pioneers Marconi and Tesla fought for fame

A Battle Over The Air Waves

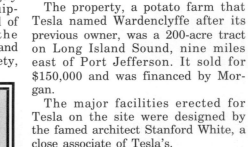

Newsday Archive

Guglielmo Marconi, above, set up a wireless "radio shack," left, at Virginia Road and Fire Island Avenue in Babylon in about 1902 to communicate with ships.

BY ROBERT COOKE
STAFF WRITER

As the 20th Century was dawning, two pioneers in the birth of electronics — Guglielmo Marconi and Nikola Tesla — were locked in an almost neck-and-neck race to develop radio as a "wireless" communication system, a revolutionary development destined to radically alter the path of history.

The younger Marconi eventually won the laurels, including the 1909 Nobel Prize in physics, for inventing radio, even though Tesla eventually prevailed in a U.S. Supreme Court decision affirming that Marconi had infringed on his patents.

Part of the battle was fought on Long Island, where Tesla set up a large research and manufacturing facility in Shoreham, and Marconi's company established some of the first ship-to-shore radio relay stations.

As for the invention of radio communications, it is clear that the brilliant, Tesla had demonstrated transmission of pulsed radio signals through the air in 1893, during a lecture in St. Louis. Others, in Europe as early as 1842, also had sent detectable signals over relatively short distances. But it was Marconi, a native of Italy, who cobbled together several toy-like inventions to create a viable system.

In fact, in 1901 Marconi finally succeeded in transmitting a coded message — the three-dot Morse code symbol for "S" — all the way from Cornwall, England, to St. John's, Newfoundland. That essentially clinched it for Marconi, who is considered the father of radio.

In contrast, despite his enormous achievements, Tesla finished his life in poverty. Though he lived for years in New York City's posh Waldorf-Astoria Hotel, and created the major research and manufacturing facility in Shoreham, legal battles, personal conflicts and professional jealousies eventually drained his money and sapped his effervescence.

During the years of wrangling, neither side cared much for niceties: According to Tesla biographer Marc Seifer, he even referred once to Marconi as a "parasite and microbe of a nasty disease," although not by name.

In any case, the name Marconi is now almost synonymous with radio, while Tesla — who produced many inventions of huge significance, especially the use of alternating current to run machinery — essentially sank into obscurity. Only recently have biographers begun to resurrect the quixotic inventor's story. Two important ones are "Wizard," by Marc J.

LI HISTORY.COM
Learn about 15 influential people in the history of radio, get important dates in radio history and read notable quotes about Marconi's invention on the Internet at http://www.lhistory.com.

Seifer (Birch Lane Press, 1996), and "Tesla, Man Out of Time," by Margaret Cheney (Dorset Press, 1981).

In all, it took more than half a century of legal maneuvering, courtroom battles and public wrangling before the Supreme Court affirmed that Tesla, not Marconi, was actually radio's inventor. In 1943, the court affirmed that Marconi had infringed on Tesla's patent, a judgment that arrived belatedly, just three months after Tesla's death.

In England, too, Marconi's priority was vigorously contested by the friends and supporters of Oliver Lodge, who demonstrated "wireless telegraphy" in 1894.

These bitter struggles over the origins of radio came at a tumultuous time in the history of technology, and was joined by some of the biggest names in science and invention. Into the competition between Marconi and Tesla came America's most famous technological wizard, Thomas Edison, plus the well-known inventor of the air brake, George Westinghouse.

Ironically, Tesla originally came to the United States in 1884, to work in New Jersey for Edison. Tesla once recalled that, "I was thrilled to the marrow by meeting Edison." While working with Edison, Tesla advanced his own ideas about alternating current vs. direct current electricity.

Eventually, Tesla and Westinghouse were united, via the pocketbook, after Westinghouse bought the

Babylon Historical and Preservation Society; Newsday Photo

rights to Tesla's brilliant discoveries using alternating current to run electric motors, incandescent lights and other devices. Edison, wedded to his own competing direct current system, was in Marconi's corner in the brouhaha over radio.

On Long Island, Tesla's imprint was far deeper than Marconi's. Tesla's big laboratory still stands in Shoreham, and Tesla actually spent much time on Long Island, some of it commuting back and forth to the city.

Marconi's impact here was largely through the installation of equipment. According to Natalie Stiefel of Sayville, who is involved in the Friends of Long Island Wireless and the Rocky Point Historical Society,

"The first Marconi station on Long Island was built at Sagaponack in 1902, for communication with ships nearer New York than Marconi's station at Nantucket Island."

Old news reports also indicate the first radio message to Long Island came from a departing steamship, the Wilhelmader der Grosse, on June 20, 1902.

A second Marconi station for communicating with inbound and outbound ships was set up several months later, a "radio shack" on Fire Island Avenue in Babylon. The facility also served as a training site for Marconi wireless operators.

A third station — at Seagate, in Brooklyn — was set up to make the last communication with ships before they docked in New York, or the first radio link for ships leaving the harbor.

The Babylon shack was used only briefly, but it was salvaged as a historical artifact and stored for years at Rocky Point. It was finally restored, and now sits in front of the Frank J. Carasiti Elementary School, on the road renamed Marconi Boulevard.

Tesla, who ran his own laboratory in New York City for years, won substantial backing from famed industrialist J.P. Morgan. He then moved his work to a big laboratory on Long Island, in the area now called Shoreham.

The property, a potato farm that Tesla named Wardenclyffe after its previous owner, was a 200-acre tract on Long Island Sound, nine miles east of Port Jefferson. It sold for $150,000 and was financed by Morgan.

The major facilities erected for Tesla on the site were designed by the famed architect Stanford White, a close associate of Tesla's.

Tesla's ultimate goal was to create a "world telegraphy center" that included his laboratory, a huge radio transmitter system, plus manufacturing facilities to make his oscillators and vacuum tubes.

Unfortunately, Tesla's dreams for Wardenclyffe never fully matured. Deep in debt and living on credit at the Waldorf-Astoria, the inventor was finally forced to sign over his big property to the hotel's owners, who in 1917 ordered that the tall radio tower be dynamited and the steel be sold for scrap.

Suffolk County Historical Society

Dover Publications

Nikola Tesla, above, erected a radio tower, left, in Shoreham that was dynamited in 1917 to help pay his debts.

THE ISLAND'S FIRST TELEPHONES

In 1881, Henry A. Roberts installed a private telephone line in his Glen Street drugstore, making Glen Cove the first community in Nassau and Suffolk to have phone service, although it only reached to neighboring Glenwood Landing.

Roberts had five subscribers, but two years later, the New York & New Jersey Telephone Co. bought out his system and installed an 18-line switchboard. Roberts' drugstore became the first central office east of Flushing. G.A. Roullier, a Flushing civil engineer, got the first Queens switchboard that same year.

During 1879, J.L. Haigh, who manufactured wire for the Brooklyn Bridge, communicated from his Brooklyn factory to his downtown Manhattan office over lines strung across the half-finished span. "Haigh was the first paid phone subscriber in both Brooklyn and New York," said Willard Elsasser, a retired telephone technician and founder of the Telephone Pioneer Museum in Commack.

By 1889, Flushing had 65 phones, Glen Cove had 17. The telephones were mostly in stores, the switchboards in homes where the housewife was the operator, according to Ralf Krause, curator of the telephone museum at 445 Commack Rd., which holds an open house on the first Sunday of each month. Elsasser tells of the first phone in Rockville Centre — in a barbershop back room shared with a bathtub. "Baths cost 25 cents and when someone was in the tub, all telephone service was tied up."

— **Rhoda Amon**

AT&T Photo

This is a 1907 version of the telephone; similar types remained in use through the 1930s.

From gas to LILCO's electricity, it took more than flicking a switch

Let There Be Light!

BY DAN FAGIN
STAFF WRITER

From the beginning, Long Islanders haven't had much good to say about the colorful entrepreneurs who labored to light up the countryside.

Capt. David Congdon was the first. A Sag Harbor native who combined a sense of civic virtue with a keen instinct for making a fast buck, he closed his steamboat line in 1858 and decided that what his village needed was gas lighting. Not the whale oil lanterns that had dimly lit its streets for years, but a system of gas mains to show the world that Sag Harbor had a future beyond the dying whaling industry.

Congdon bought a machine to distill gas from rosin and arranged for pipes to be laid along Main, Jefferson and Suffolk Streets. On Dec. 8, 1859, when he turned on the gas, the whole village showed up to gape and cheer in the glow of the light that turned night into day. The story of Congdon and of the region's other lighting pioneers was told in "Lighting Long Island," a self-published book by James W. Carpenter.

As Carpenter told the story some 40 years ago, it didn't take long for public acclaim to evaporate. Soon after the lights went on, The Sag Harbor Press grumbled:

"Think of this ye men of olden time. To what have your children degenerated! Truly no more can we boast of the simplicity and rusticity of the East Enders. The charm is forever broken, and the Community which has abandoned so far the customs of the 'good old times' as to introduce gas for lights, is ripe for anything."

Within three years, Congdon had given up. He was tired of dealing with complaints that gas leaking from his lights was damaging the elm trees on Main Street, and with criticism from the state Legislature that his rates — $7 per thousand cubic feet — were too high.

Meanwhile, 80 miles away in Hempstead, another attempt at gas lighting wasn't faring much better. By 1859, a group of merchants led by grocery-owner Seaman Snedeker had finally sold enough stock to build a small coal-gas plant on Clinton Street. On Jan. 23, 1860, the group turned on the gas and began offering service from dusk to midnight. Chaos followed. The system was frequently shut down for repairs. The boiler exploded during the winter of 1871-72, and soon after it was repaired, Hempstead fired its only lamplighter when he demanded an increase in his monthly wage of $12.50.

Similar woes plagued the other Long Island villages that experimented with gas mains, so when the news reached the Island in 1882 that Thomas Edison was lighting up downtown New York with electricity, local merchants clamored for similar systems.

Babylon was the first on Long Island to electrify Edison-style, with a central station and a network of wires. Generating power from a small waterfall that served an old mill on Sumpwams Creek on the east edge of town, the Babylon Electric Lighting Co. turned on the juice on a Monday evening, Nov. 24, 1886. Eight stores were lighted and there were three street lights.

Electricity proved safer and more reliable than coal gas, but Hempstead, Riverhead, Oyster Bay — the first community to go electric in Nassau County, in 1891 — and the other villages that introduced Edison's Magic Candle to Long Island found that financial insecurity was still a big problem.

The electric companies were mostly hand-to-mouth operations, where investors staffed the tiny generators and an unpaid bill or two could force a shutdown that darkened the whole village. The only exception was the gold-plated Roslyn Light and Power Co., started in 1890 by a group of Wall Street barons who wanted to illuminate their country homes.

LILCO Photos

Above, an independent crew lays a gas main in Babylon in the early 1900s. Below, LILCO's first line crew in the 1910s; the company soon became a target for reformers and ratepayers.

Throughout the Island, there was still plenty of grumbling about the newfangled lights. During the Spanish-American War in 1898, Southampton entrepreneur Harri Micah Howell ran into trouble when villagers feared the nighttime electric service he proposed would be a beacon for marauding ships of the Spanish fleet. Howell calmed those fears by offering to sweep a searchlight across the beach

A young New York City engineer, Ellis Laurimore Phillips, surveyed the chaos and saw opportunity. He was a builder, too, and thought that what Long Island needed was a single interconnected grid powered by a few giant electric plants. And if those plants could be built by E.L. Phillips & Co., well, all the better.

On New Year's Eve in 1910, a group of New York City investors incorporated the Long Island Lighting Co. Six weeks later they heard a presentation from Phillips, who proposed purchasing four small electric companies in Sayville, Amityville, Northport and Islip for $308,672.15. Phillips, who became the company's general manager at $200 a month, closed the deal on June 11, 1911, and LILCO was in business.

Phillips' first move was to hire his own company to build a 500-kilowatt power plant in Northport for $61,000. Soon, LILCO was gobbling up other electric and gas companies, first in Suffolk, then Nassau, and finally the Rockaway peninsula in Queens.

But LILCO's rapid growth and high rates, and public outrage over Phillips' self-dealing and princely pay ($5,000 a year by 1915), made the company a target for government reformers as well as unhappy ratepayers.

In fact, local politicians and the state Public Service Commission were assailing LILCO's rates and its top management 50 years before the company ever thought about building a nuclear power plant at Shoreham.

En route to an LI picnic grove, a steamboat catches fire, and more than 1,000 lives are lost

The General Slocum Disaster

BY BILL BLEYER
STAFF WRITER

The Mariners' Museum, Newport News, Va.

A fire aboard the General Slocum on June 15, 1904, turned into the worst maritime disaster in the New York area's history.

As she waited on deck for the excursion steamer General Slocum to leave lower Manhattan for a Long Island picnic grove, Mrs. Philip Straub had a premonition of disaster. Just before the gangway was removed, she rushed ashore. A man she confided her fears to grabbed his wife and five children and followed.

It was a wise decision. Within an hour, flames would race the length of the 264-foot vessel. Screaming passengers would leap into the East River with their clothes on fire, only to be dragged down as their garments, and even lifebelts, became waterlogged. Others would be thrown against cabin walls so hot that the boiling paint seared their skin.

A dozen tugs, two fireboats, a police boat and more than a hundred other vessels would join the rescue effort — some of them catching fire as they came alongside the Slocum. Charred bodies would surround the flaming ship and litter the shoreline. The Slocum would burn to the waterline, killing more than a thousand passengers and crew in the worst maritime disaster in the New York area's history.

The disaster occurred on June 15, 1904. From its first summer afloat in 1891, the ship, named for Civil War hero Henry W. Slocum, was star-crossed. In the years before the fire, the paddlewheel steamboat managed to run aground six times and collide with four other vessels.

Five weeks before the disaster, the Slocum was checked by the U.S. Steamboat Inspection Service, which certified its 13-year-old lifebelts as "up-to-date and of good quality." The inspectors never checked the fire pump and hoses or noticed that the six lifeboats were stuck to the ship by a thick coat of paint.

St. Mark's Evangelical Lutheran Church, which served primarily German immigrants in lower Manhattan, chartered the aging Slocum for its 17th annual excursion to the Locust Grove Picnic Ground on Eatons Neck. With the exception of the captain and chief engineer, the Slocum's 35 crew members were inexperienced. The day before the St. Mark's trip, men from the church delivered three barrels of glasses. After they were unpacked, a deckhand stored the barrels filled with packing hay in the forward cabin, even though it was illegal to have loose hay aboard.

At 9:20 a.m., the Slocum headed up the East River from its Third Street dock with 1,331 passengers, more than 500 of them under the age of 20. As the band played, children danced on the deck and passersby waved from the shore. But when the ship reached Astoria, onlookers waved frantically for a different reason — they could see smoke coming from the portholes.

The story of the disaster is recounted in "The Burning of the General Slocum," a 1981 book by Claude Rust of East Rockaway, whose grandmother died on the ship.

Newsday Photo / Alan Raia

A memorial at Lutheran All Faiths Cemetery, Middle Village, where 61 victims are buried

A boy ran up to deckhand John Coakley and cried, "Mister, there's smoke coming up one of the stairways." He opened the cabin door and the smoldering hay in the barrels burst into flame. It was 10 a.m.

Twelve-year-old Frank Perditsky ran to the deck below the pilothouse and yelled up to Capt. William Van Schaick, "Hey Mister, the ship's on fire!" The captain dismissed the warning as a prank. "Get the hell out of here and mind your own business!"

Searching for something to smother the flames, Coakley grabbed two bags of flammable charcoal. Finally he located the first mate, Ed Flanagan, who wasted several minutes by going to see the chief engineer before calling the captain and deploying a fire hose. But when the water pump was turned on, the rotted and kinked hose burst.

As soon as the captain looked out the pilothouse door and saw flames leaping up from the port side and passengers hurling themselves over the rail, he decided the strong following current and the gas plants on the nearby Bronx shore left him only one choice for a place to beach. "Put her on North Brother Island," he told the pilot.

The island, near today's LaGuardia Airport, was only three minutes away. Passengers with their clothes on fire vainly sought safety. Some tried to pull loose the wire mesh holding life preservers to the ceilings. "Some of them we could not budge, and others pulled to pieces and spilled the crumbs of cork all over our heads," recalled Annie Weber, who escaped over the side on a rope.

The Slocum grounded on a rocky ledge with its stern still in deep water. The captain, his hat on fire, scrambled over the rails along with passengers. Anna Frese, 14, would remember that "my father told me to jump, but I could not get my hand off — it was baked on the rail with the paint." When she managed to free herself, "I had to be careful to clear the paddlewheel, as people were being caught [in it] and died; so I tried to jump out far enough, and I struck a rock and broke all my front teeth."

As the medical staff of hospitals on the island aided some victims, a few people on shore or in boats took advantage of them — stripping them of their jewelry or demanding money before pulling them out of the water.

The death toll was ultimately set at 1,021. An inquest determined the fire was started by a cigarette or match tossed into one of the barrels. The inquest jury indicted the captain, first mate, officers of the steamboat company and a steamboat inspector.

But only the captain was convicted — of not holding fire drills, not training the crew properly and not maintaining fire apparatus. Sentenced to 10 years, he was paroled after 3½ years when 250,000 people signed a petition to President William Howard Taft.

What was left of the Slocum was converted to a barge. It sank in a 1911 gale near Atlantic City.

The Slocum's victims are memorialized by two monuments. One is in Tompkins Square in Manhattan, near where St. Mark's was located. The other is at Lutheran All Faiths Cemetery in Middle Village, where 61 unidentified victims were buried. That monument was unveiled a year after the fire by 1½-year-old Adella Wotherspoon, the youngest person to escape. The New Jersey resident, who lost two sisters and two cousins in the fire, is one of the two Slocum survivors known to still be alive.

"I just know what I was told by my parents," she said recently. "I was on the ship with my mother and father, two sisters and two cousins and an aunt and uncle. My mother was very badly burned on her upper left side so I assume she had hung on to the railing until she couldn't hold on any longer and dropped into the water with me in her right arm.

"The men stayed on board looking for the other four children until their clothes burned off and then they jumped overboard. We were reunited on the island."

Every year on a weekend in June, the Organization of the General Slocum Survivors holds a memorial service at the cemetery.

Workers in a perilous craft create a web of East River tunnels to speed LIRR commuters

The Manhattan Connection

By Drew Fetherston
STAFF WRITER

On the frosty morning of Dec. 28, 1892, Pietro Rocco was about to shave the first customer in his Long Island City barber shop when there was a sudden brilliant flash of light and a shattering explosion.

"I thought of a volcano or an earthquake," Rocco said later. "I heard a scream from my wife at the instant of the shock." Rescuers found Rocco dazed and bloody. His wife was dead in the apartment behind the shop at 27 Jackson Ave. Three neighbors were dead, another was dying and scores were injured.

Eighty-seven pounds of dynamite, which workmen had been thawing in a steambox, had exploded in a vacant lot at Vernon Avenue and 50th Avenue. The blast wrecked several buildings, set fire to others on Jackson Avenue, and postponed a direct rail link between Manhattan and Long Island for almost 20 years.

The explosion ruined the New York and Long Island Rail Road Co., which was using the dynamite to blast a tunnel under the East River to carry the Long Island Rail Road tracks into Grand Central Terminal. The 100-foot-deep shaft and its short length of tunnel were abandoned for almost 13 years.

But a great age of public works arrived with the turn of the century. When it ended — about the time America entered the First World War — Manhattan sat at the center of a web of tunnel and bridge links, and suburbs were blossoming around the railroad's stations on Long Island.

The agent of change was the Pennsylvania Railroad, which acquired the Long Island Rail Road in 1900. Alexander Cassatt, who became the Pennsylvania's president in 1899, decided to build a series of railroad tunnels from the New Jersey Meadowlands through Manhattan and out onto Long Island. Two tunnels would cross the Hudson River; four would cross the East River.

The keystone of this vast project would be a monumental railroad terminal on the west side of Manhattan: Pennsylvania Station. In Long Island City, the tracks would join those of a new connecting railroad that would carry trains north over a new East River bridge at Hell Gate and thence to New England.

A.J. County, a top Pennsylvania executive, predicted the tunnels would "open to the people in the thickly populated Borough of Manhattan the residential sections of Long Island."

From the first, Pennsylvania Station drew the most attention. It was one of the greatest public buildings ever built in this hemisphere, an architectural triumph whose soaring marble-lined spaces left visitors in awe until crass commerce pulled it down in the 1960s. "Through it one entered the city like a god," the architectural historian Vincent Scully wrote of the old station. "One scuttles in now like a rat."

But great as the station was, it was dwarfed — in scale and technical difficulty if not in esthetic value — by the railroad tunnels. The four East River tunnels would cost $70 million — $20 million more than the Manhattan, Williamsburg and Queensboro Bridges combined. Each tube, with an outside diameter of 23 feet, was lined with cast-iron rings which were then covered with concrete. They ran a distance of 4,000 feet under the river, then an additional 2,000 feet underground to emerge near the Sunnyside rail yard. Each cast-iron ring was 2½-feet wide and weighed more than 11 tons. The rings were held together with 1.5 million iron bolts.

New-York Historical Society Photo

Rapelje Family Photo

The monumental Pennsylvania Station, above, was the hub of the vast tunnel project. Some of the workers who made it happen are shown circa 1905 in a subway tunnel that would link Long Island City with Manhattan.

Work on the East River tunnels began in May, 1904. One of the first problems was finding skilled workers. In October, 1907, The Engineering Magazine noted that while Britain had "a class — it might almost be called a race" of skilled tunnelers, "it has been necessary in New York to train men to their work, and to produce from the rawest material, more or less skilled tunnel builders."

Recruits faced harsh and dangerous work. Underwater tunneling was still a new and imperfect craft: The first such tunnel had been completed in 1843, beneath the Thames in London, and only a dozen or so others had been built by 1900. The Pennsylvania tunnel excavations were pressurized to keep them from collapsing, which meant that tunnelers could be crippled or killed by gas bubbles in their blood when they returned to the surface.

Ground conditions ranged from solid rock, which had to be drilled and dynamited, to mud and quicksand. All were dangerous: On April 25, 1906, two workers were killed in a blasting accident. Less than two months later, two more workmen were killed when the compressed air blew out the 8 feet of soft ground overlaying the tunnel. A geyser of water shot out of the river; the men's bodies later were found floating nearby.

When the tunnels began carrying trains in 1910, it became possible to commute to a Manhattan workplace from a Long Island home. The railroad ferries to 34th Street and James Slip in the Wall Street area disappeared, replaced by a swift transit under the river. The number of passengers carried by the LIRR surged. In 1915, the railroad carried 43 million; by 1928, that had risen to 114 million.

Work on the tunnel doomed by the 1892 explosion resumed in 1905, after the Interborough Rapid Transit Co. bought it as a link in a 41-mile subway system in Queens and Manhattan.

The first streetcar rolled through the completed tunnel in September, 1907, but it emerged to find a changed political climate: New York State was fighting the IRT's monopoly, and refused to sanction the tunnel's opening.

It lay unused until June, 1915, by which time the city had bought it and the IRT had agreed to operate it. The tunnel, which was a powerful force in the development of Queens, now carries the IRT's Flushing Line subway trains.

FAST FORWARD

GRAND ENTRY FOR LIRR COMMUTERS?

If current plans come true, Long Island Rail Road commuters may once again enter Manhattan's streets through the colonnaded facade of a landmark terminal designed by McKim, Mead & White, the famous turn-of-the-century firm of architects.

It wouldn't be Penn Station, of course, but the huge General Post Office building, built in 1913 to face the railroad terminal across Eighth Avenue.

Like Penn Station, the post office was built over the railroad tracks that run west to New Jersey and east to Long Island.

A federal transportation bill making its way through Congress includes $315 million to convert the post office to a railroad station. The "new" station would handle Long Island Rail Road, New Jersey Transit and Amtrak trains.

The conversion would confer on commuters the famous commendatory phrase, carved above the columns and originally intended for mail deliverers: "Neither snow nor rain nor heat nor gloom of night stays these couriers from the swift completion of their appointed rounds."

— Drew Fetherston

Cradle of Aviation Museum Photo

Henry Walden, credited with flying the first American monoplane, with Walden IX in an undated photo. In his day, creativity and courage were more important than an engineering degree.

Risking life and limb, they turn LI into a buzzing center of innovation in aviation

Fliers Take Wing

BY LAURA MUHA

Dawn tinged the sky over the Hempstead Plains as dentist Henry Walden, cigar clamped between his teeth, climbed into his homemade airplane and opened the throttle.

The engine roared and the rear-mounted mahogany propeller whirled furiously. Walden's two assistants, gripping the tail to prevent the plane from shooting forward, grimaced as they were hit in the face by a spray of engine-lubricating castor oil. Their hair and dusters, caught in the propeller wash, streamed straight out behind them. A boy standing nearby made the sign of the cross.

It was Aug. 3, 1910, barely 13 months since pioneer aviator Glenn Curtiss had taken off from a nearby field, becoming the first person to successfully fly a plane on Long Island. But in that short time, the treeless grasslands of central Nassau — formed by a glacial outwash thousands of years before — had become a well-established airfield. On almost any day of the week, amateur aviators like Walden flocked there to test the principles of aerodynamics in airplanes that were little more than motorized box kites.

A 26-year-old New Yorker, Walden had already had some success: During a test run in December, 1909, his wood-and-fabric airship had risen a few feet off the ground and traveled just over 10 yards, becoming the first American monoplane — an aircraft with one set of wings instead of two — to fly.

But on that flight and subsequent ones, Walden had been able to stay aloft no more than a minute before the plane's one-gallon gas tank ran dry. And most people didn't count that as a legitimate flight. Some even dismissed Walden as a crackpot, the common perception of aviators as their era began.

On this day, with a new 10-gallon tank mounted on the wing above his head, Walden was determined to prove them wrong.

With a thrust of his arm, he signaled his assistants to let go. The plane raced across the grass, shaking violently as it picked up speed. The Long Island Motor Parkway, called "the graveyard" because downward air currents caused so many crashes there, loomed ahead.

Walden checked the legs of his pants. The fabric flapped stiffly from his calves — a sign he'd reached flying speed. He pulled the steering wheel toward him. The earth dropped away.

He was soaring over the parkway when suddenly and unexpectedly, the plane seemed to stop moving. A downdraft! Frantically, he clutched the steering wheel as the horizon came up to meet him.

Then everything went black.

How much time passed, Walden couldn't say. But gradually, he became aware of voices — fuzzy at first, then louder and clearer. "A feeble throbbing in my temples grew more distinct," he would write later. "A heavy weight seemed lying on my chest. My head, hands and feet seemed fastened to the ground on which I lay . . . I wanted to talk but couldn't bring a syllable out."

He'd fractured his ankle and collarbone, torn several ligaments and broken three ribs, one of which had punctured a lung. His plane was totaled. But to Walden's joy, news of his crash appeared on the front page of the New York Evening Journal under the headline "WALDEN AIRSHIP FALLS." Now people would *have* to believe he'd flown.

"I had a harrowing experience and I was in pain, but . . . [it] turned out to be the happiest day in my youthful life," he wrote. "My 'failure' turned into a complete success."

In the next few years, Walden would build nine more airships, survive at least a dozen more crashes, perform at numerous air shows and establish

---

LI HISTORY.COM

Through two centuries, Long Islanders have been at the forefront of advances in the way the world travels.

A special section looks at "Pioneers in Motion," including Elinor Smith Sullivan, who was a world-class pilot while in her teens; the two main founders of the Grumman Aeronautical Engineering Co.; and William K. Vanderbilt II, whose cup races brought Long Island the first U.S. toll highway.

To read about these pioneers, see http://www.lihistory.com on the Internet.

Freeport Historical Society

Elinor Smith Sullivan

EARLY AVIATOR TELLS HER STORY

Elinor Smith Sullivan, the pioneering pilot who flew 26 hours over Long Island in 1929, recounts "the worst flight of my life" in a recent recording. Call 516-843-5454 or 718-896-6969 and enter category 2359 from a touch-tone phone. The recording also is available on the Internet at http://www.lihistory.com.

For more on the life of Elinor Smith Sullivan, please see Page 394.

CHAPTER 7 THE MODERN ERA

A Craving For Speed, Danger

Some people thought early fliers were romantic heroes reaching for the sky. Others thought they were fools risking their necks. The truth probably lies somewhere in between. The fact is, early aviation was a bloody business, with crashes occurring frequently.

"Once, we had seven deaths in seven days," recalls George Dade, 85, of Glen Head, who grew up in an apartment at Curtiss Field in Mineola, where his father worked. "And it wasn't unusual to have three crackups at the same time."

Engines were unreliable and planes were fragile; it wasn't unusual for a wing to break off or a throttle to jam at a critical moment. And since runways weren't paved, a rut in the ground could cause a plane to flip on landing. In June, 1928, well-known aviator Viola Gentry crashed in the Hicks Nursery in Old Westbury when the plane in which she and another flier were trying to set an endurance record ran out of gas and nosedived into a field. She survived with serious injuries but her copilot died.

Some pilots developed creative ways of surviving crashes. Joshua Stoff, curator of the Cradle of Aviation Museum at Mitchel Field, says early fliers have told him of settling in treetops or flying between trees, trying to snag the plane's wings on the branches to slow down the force of impact.

Given the danger, why did so many people want to fly? "In any generation there are people who crave speed, crave danger, crave life on the edge, and they [early pilots] were like this," says Peter Jakab, curator of early aviation at the National Air and Space Museum in Washington, D.C.

In fact, some pilots considered crashes something to brag about. "The guy who turned upside down and got a scar on his face was proud to show it to his friends," says Dade. "It was a badge of honor — if you lived to tell about it."

As a teenager, Dade made a living scraping wrecks off the field, loading them onto his father's flatbed truck and hauling them to the "bone yard" — an area behind one of the hangars where mangled planes were dumped. "I suppose in my day I brought 100 or more crackups back to the field," says Dade.

To the public, such crashes were part of the draw of early aviation. "People would go to the aviation meets to see people crash much the same way they go to the Daytona 500 today," says Jakab.

— **Laura Muha**

Three Long Island plane crashes: above, a 1929 Fleet on Post Avenue in Westbury; left, a Curtiss Jenny mail plane, an an unknown location in about 1920; below, a Fleet in an unidentified field circa 1934, with the man in the foreground wearing overalls from the Roosevelt Field Service Hangar

Cradle of Aviation Museum Photos

three airplane manufacturing companies — exploits he describes in an unpublished 117-page autobiographical manuscript now in the collection of the Cradle of Aviation Museum at Mitchel Field.

More than just the story of one man's passion, the document provides a remarkable glimpse into the dawn of the aviation age on Long Island — an age in which the cluster of airfields surrounding Mineola would host some of the most significant events in aviation history: the first air mail flight; the first "blind" flight in which the pilot took off, navigated and landed by instruments; the setting of numerous speed, altitude and endurance records; the founding of one of the first flying schools, and the epochal 1927 takeoff of Charles Lindbergh as he set out on his transatlantic flight.

The businesses that sprang up in the wake of such activities also would transform what had been a largely rural suburb into a dynamic hub of the aerospace industry — an industry that would shape the Island's destiny for nearly a century.

LI Studies Institute, Nassau County Museum

Henry Walden, a dentist with the heart of a flier, commands the Walden VII circa 1910.

"It just kept building on itself," Joshua Stoff, curator of the aviation museum, says of the development of flight on Long Island. "The lunar module, which took men to the moon in the 1960s, would not have been built here had not aviators been flying on the Hempstead Plains in 1910."

In those days, creativity and courage were far more important than an engineering degree when it came to building and flying airplanes. Yes, there were professionals out there laying the foundation for what would become the aviation industry. But for every Orville Wright or Glenn Curtiss — who founded Long Island's first airplane manufacturing company — there were dozens of people like Henry Walden: backyard tinkerers who cobbled together airplanes using nothing more than their wits and parts from the local hardware store.

Born Nov. 10, 1883, in a small town in Massachusetts, Walden spent part of his childhood in Romania, where his father, a builder, had a contract to lay out a series of roads. While there, the boy saw a hot-air balloon demonstrated in a park — a demonstration that ended in tragedy when a gust of wind slammed the balloon into a wall on lift-off, killing the balloonist.

Despite the disaster, Walden would recall the event as one of the formative experiences of his life. "The [idea of] sailing through space fascinated me," he wrote. "It strcke a cord within me, probably inborn, which I can definitely trace to tendencies, experiences and developments in my later life."

Walden and his best friend, Emmet, soon began making 10-foot-tall tissue-paper balloons of their own, following directions in a magazine. Their early models inflated but refused to fly; the kerosene lamp they were using as a heat source wasn't efficient enough.

Undeterred, the boys soaked a length of wick in kerosene and suspended it from crosswires attached to a hoop at the base of the balloon. To their joy, the wick burned hotter than the lamp, pro-

Please see **FLIERS, Next Page**

Long Islanders watch one of the frail craft at an air meet in an undated photo.

Nassau County Museum Collection, Long Island Studies Institute

FLYING MACHINES AS MASS ENTERTAINMENT

By 1911, hundreds of people were flocking to the Hempstead Plains every week to gape at the "man-birds" who defied gravity in their flying machines.

Bleachers were set up along the fence that lined the field, and for a dime, spectators could buy guidebooks that described the fliers' latest exploits. "Clifford B. Harmon has the distinction of being the first aviator here to carry a woman passenger," one account read. "He was accompanied by his wife in a ten-minute flight on June 29th." The books also included fill-in-the-blank scorecards, so fans could keep track of who was setting what record.

"It was a really big thing to come out and watch the planes get off the ground," recalls George Dade, 85, of Glen Head, who grew up in a converted barracks on Curtiss Field. "People would be all dressed up in their Sunday best."

Hanging out at the field became so popular, in fact, that an entire industry soon sprang up around it. At the Airport Diner, spectators and pilots alike could down 20-cent plates of hot dogs and beans and nickel glasses of Coca-Cola. And bystanders who were brave enough could plunk down $5 and go up for a 15-minute ride in an airplane. "If they gave the guy an extra $5, he'd do a loop or a spin," recalls Dade, who sold flight tickets at Curtiss Field in the 1920s.

Not everyone thought that was such a great idea.

"You had situations where the man was all for it and the wife didn't want to pick her feet off the ground," recalls Dade, adding that very occasionally, it was the other way around. Dade said he would always try to reassure the reluctant parties by telling them that he'd never known anyone to be injured — as a passenger.

"But most of them had their arguments before they got to me!" he says, laughing. **— Laura Muha**

LI Fliers Risk Life and Limb

FLIERS from **Preceding Page**

viding more lift.

"What a flame," Walden wrote. "In the blink of an eye the bag began to take its form . . . ten feet high . . . What a bulk of roaring heat that was . . . Then it began to tug . . . It really tugged. The mooring released, we let go . . . and off went the balloon, hoop, wick, kerosene and all . . . Our work was a complete success."

The boys made a new balloon and organized a demonstration for their friends, charging pen-nibs and buttons as entry fees. Sure enough, that balloon sailed off, too — and was such a hit that the boys set off a third the next afternoon. But this one refused to fly, and as they tried to coax it into the air with a pole, a friend dashed into the yard, yelling. "Run . . . run . . . the cops . . . the cops . . .

"Forgetting all about the balloon, we dropped the pole and ran," wrote Walden. "We jumped the fence back of the barn eluding our pursuers, ran to the rear of Emmet's house, ran into it and made for the bedroom. There, we sneaked into the shelter of their large twin bed, or rather under it and there we lay."

As it turned out, the previous day's balloon had settled on a lumber yard in a nearby town and burned it down. Worse, in their haste to escape the police, the boys had forgotten about the balloon they'd been about to set off. It had settled on the family's wooden well — and burned that down, too.

"What a mess . . .," wrote Walden. His father received a bill for the damages, Walden received a spanking — and his youthful career as a balloonist came to an end. But his dreams of flying did not. "Riding my bike in open spaces, I immagined to have wings on and wished it was true."

Returning to the United States at the turn of the century, Walden studied dentistry at Columbia University. He graduated in 1906 and set up a practice in Manhattan.

While he was in dental school, an event occurred that would change aviation forever: Brothers Orville and Wilbur Wright made the first machine-powered flight at Kitty Hawk, N.C. Although their 1903 accomplishment was at first largely ignored by the public — probably, Wilbur speculated, because no one believed it was true — by 1908, a growing number of people were trying to duplicate the brothers' success.

That summer, Walden read a newspaper article about the newly formed Aeronautic Society of New York, a group with a membership roster that included scientists, mechanics, millionaires — or, as Walden put it, "dreamers bound by one great object and moved by one great ideal . . . to achieve practical flight." He paid $10 and joined the club.

The society provided members with work space at the old Morris Park racetrack in the Bronx. Arriving there for the first time, Walden was astonished at the array of strange-looking contraptions members were working on: a bicycle with a propeller mounted on its rear; a triplane, which had three sets of wings; and a machine called an ornithopter, which beat the air with its wings like a bird.

Looking at them, Walden felt as if he'd finally found his calling. "It all became part of me, and I became part of all . . . That was the beginning of my aviation career."

Before long, Walden was devoting more time to building planes than to cleaning teeth. He hired an elderly dentist to cover his practice, appearing only when patients insisted on his personal services.

The first two planes he designed — both biplanes — were failures. So for his third, Walden decided to try something different: a plane with one set of wings instead of two. Similar monoplanes had been flown in Europe on several occasions, but most people believed them to be dangerous. Walden, however, said he became convinced of the rightness of the design by studying birds. "I'd think, 'God only gave it [a bird] two wings. He must know what He's doing.' "

To avoid the three-hour round trip to Morris Park, Walden rented a loft a block from his dental office and, with the help of his cousin Henry and a mechanic named Radu, began building the plane.

Six months later, when it was finally ready for testing, a new problem arose: how to get it out of the loft. Eventually, Walden and his helpers decided to disassemble the airship and lower the parts through the window to a waiting truck. All went well until they got to the wings. "They were about one half of an inch too wide to pass them through. We had miscalculated the thickness of the window frame."

Obviously, there was only one solution: Hack out the window and worry about damages later.

It took five hours for Walden to transport the plane to a vast field adjacent to the Mineola Fair Grounds. Glenn Curtiss had moved his base of operations there from Hammondsport, N.Y., in July, 1909; the Aeronautic Society, whose lease at Morris Park was about to expire, had soon followed. Almost overnight, the area had become a center of aviation — albeit a primitive one.

"We housed our disassembled plane in [a] creaky shanty . . . about thirty by forty feet in size," Walden wrote. "A few panneled windows faced the Old Country Road and a very large door opened to the fields. A few broken panes and a little round coal stove were to keep us warm for the rental of $7 per month. . . . A frozen water outlet was the sole additional accomodation. The wide and apparently endless field was there and that was what we wanted."

Nassau County Museum, Long Island Studies Institute Photo

The British dirigible R-34, the first airship to cross the Atlantic, is hauled in at Roosevelt Field on July 6, 1919. The 600-foot-long airship, piloted by Royal Air Force Cmdr. G.H. Scott with a crew of 30, reached a top speed of 62 mph during the 108-hour trip from Scotland.

George Dade Collection

Planes arrayed at Roosevelt Field in the early 1920s were used for sightseeing, exhibitions and training. A decade earlier, amateur aviators began flocking to the plains area to test the principles of aerodynamics in airplanes that were little more than motorized box kites.

On Dec. 9, 1909, after a week's work reassembling the plane, Walden and his assistants rolled it from the shed to attempt what they called "grass-cutting": driving the plane along the ground to test the engine and steering. "I had no intentions to fly that morning," Walden noted.

As he rolled across the grass, however, he opened the throttle — and the plane unexpectedly took off, rising to fence-post height. "I do not know exactly how it happened but . . . [it] was a wonderful sensation," Walden wrote.

Until, that is, he realized the shed lay dead ahead.

"Quickly I pushed the tail into the positive angle . . . The wheels were on the ground again as I slapped the foot brake into it and stopped short a few feet before I reached the shed. Henry [his assistant] almost fainted."

Thus ended the maiden voyage of the first American monoplane.

Walden made a series of successful flights in the little airship before it was destroyed in his August, 1910, crash. But even that didn't slow him down: Against his physician's wishes, he was soon back at the airfield, leaning on crutches as he supervised the dismantling of the wreckage.

Until his accident, Walden had been planning to participate in the Third International Air Tournament, scheduled for Oct. 22-30, 1910, at Belmont Park Race Track. Such meets were becoming an increasingly popular form of entertainment for the public and this one was expected to be the biggest ever, drawing fliers from all over the United States and Europe. Walden was bitterly disappointed when he realized that neither his body nor his plane would be in any shape to compete.

Still, he managed to attend every day, joining an estimated 10,000 who crammed the bleachers and cheered the daredevil pilots in their flimsy flying machines as they raced around pylons, performed stunts and set records for altitude (9,714 feet) and speed (70 mph). "It was bewildering to see the advancement in aviation in a mere couple of months," Walden wrote. "Such rapid progress could not have been anticipated even in the spring of that year."

The meet also marked a turning point for aviation, as Walden pointed out. "The world began to realize that planes had come to stay. We were no longer ridiculed. We became heroes with some, adventurers with others and just curiosities with most."

Shortly after the meet, Walden — whose reputation as a legitimate aviator had been established by his crash — teamed up with an English flier named Capt. George Dyott to form the Walden-Dyott Aeronautic Co.

They erected a corrugated iron hangar at the Hempstead Plains field, bought two new engines and, with a third engine salvaged from his earlier wreck, began building monoplanes. Business was slow.

"We did consummate one deal although it did not involve an actual sale," Walden wrote. "The United Dressed Beef Company held a convention . . . and paid us the sum of $300 to hang one of our monoplanes off the center of their ceiling for the duration. A large basket had to replace the usual aviator's seat and various parts of beef were to hang from it. It was intended to prophesize a futuristic delivery of perishable victuals . . . The exhibit was a colossal success and gave us a great deal of publicity, but no sales were made."

By spring of 1911, the partners decided to disband their company. Dyott received two of the monoplanes, which he later sold in South America; Walden got the hangar and the third plane, which wasn't quite complete.

Perhaps realizing it was time to become more fiscally responsible — he'd recently become engaged to his longtime sweetheart — Walden went back to dentistry, but didn't give up on aviation entirely.

Typically, he'd work in his dental office from 10 a.m. to 8 p.m., then make the hour-long trip to the Hempstead Plains on his motorcycle. There, he'd work on his latest airship by the light of a kerosene lamp until about 1 a.m., fall asleep on a cot in the hangar, and get up again at 5 a.m. to test his latest design. In those days, most flights took place at dawn or dusk, when there was less wind to buffet the fragile planes. Then he'd head back to the city to work.

For the next few years, Walden kept up that grueling schedule, sinking nearly all the money from his dental practice into airplane parts and appearing at air meets around the country, competing for cash prizes that would enable him to keep his avocation alive.

At one meet, he was coming in for a landing when another plane took off directly into his path. Caught in the propeller wash, his plane flipped and the left wing hit the ground. Walden was thrown 50 feet ahead of the plane, which somersaulted across the ground and landed on top of him. "Walden Falls Before 25,000 at Aviation Meet," the New York Evening Mail proclaimed.

In 1912, Walden and one of his star pupils, Frank Fitzsimmons, traveled to Maine to demonstrate one of the dentist's planes at the state fair. Fitzsimmons asked to do the flying, and Walden agreed. But as Fitzsimmons took off, the engine stalled.

"His left wing dipped . . . and the plane started into a spin," wrote Walden. "I don't know how I lived through it . . . A fraction of a moment seemed endless."

The plane fell into an alley beyond the field. Incredibly, Fitzsimmons suffered nothing more than two broken legs. But Walden was so shaken that he began rethinking his commitment to flying. "I never shirked at my own risk, of which I was always aware, but it was hard to think of others crippled or killed with tools of my own creation.

It was time, he decided, to quit flying, and concentrate on laboratory work.

In 1915, he developed and patented the first radio-controlled missile, a model of which is in the Smithsonian Institution. And when the United States entered World War I, he formed another airplane manufacturing company in partnership with the owners of a New Jersey lumber mill, and made aircraft wings, stabilizers and fins for the government.

In 1919, Walden and his wife were divorced; he eventually remarried and moved to Great Neck. In 1929, he formed a third company, Walden Aircraft, in Long Island City. But by then, aviation was becoming big business and it was hard for such a small company to compete. Three years later, he closed the plant and went back to tinkering in the workshop adjacent to his dental lab.

The result: More than 80 patents for a variety of devices, among them motion-picture and still cameras that made pictures appear three-dimensional; a mechanical lighting unit for medical photography; an artificial heart, which was used for research purposes at Mt. Sinai Hospital; an ink-refiller for ballpoint pens; a vegetable slicer for home use, a coffee-packing machine and an animated electric sign that flashed news bulletins on what used to be the Times Tower in New York City's Times Square — a precursor to the famous Times Square "Zipper."

Walden died of cancer in 1964 at age 81 — which was probably remarkable in itself, considering the dangers every aviator faced in those early years of flying. "Of the 16 original pilots who flew out of Mineola, he was the only one who died at home in bed," Richard Walden of Williamsburg, Va., one of three sons, says of his father.

But Walden's fame didn't end with his death. Five days later, his family was notified that he'd been elected to the Aviation Hall of Fame in Dayton, Ohio.

Walden may have written his own eulogy in his autobiography. "I cannot help but feel a little pride in whatever minute contribution my work added to aviation."

Laura Muha is a freelance writer.

Tens of thousands of draftees train at Camp Upton for trench fighting in World War I

From LI to Over There

BY GEORGE DEWAN
STAFF WRITER

In the summer of 1917, the largest city on Long Island was created out of 10,000 acres of mosquito-infested scrub oak and pine in central Brookhaven. Not long after the First World War ended, the city disappeared.

This was Camp Upton, built in an uninhabited area northeast of Yaphank to prepare 40,000 draftees at a time to go to war. Among them was the soon-to-be-famous 77th Infantry Division, made up of New Yorkers. During the war, more than a half-million men passed through the camp, either for training or as a short-term stop either going overseas or returning home.

Fame of another sort came to Camp Upton in 1918 when a Russian-born, 29-year-old draftee from the Lower East Side named Irving Berlin was inducted. In the beginning, he scrubbed floors, did K.P. and guard duty with his buddies. But after he put on a show in May for the camp commander — getting help from about 70 of his entertainer friends from New York, including Al Jolson, Eddie Cantor, Will Rogers and the chorus girls from the Midnight Frolic — Berlin was promoted to sergeant.

Instead of going to battle in Europe, Sgt. Berlin stayed and wrote a musical, "Yip, Yip, Yaphank," with a hit song that became a classic, "Oh! How I Hate to Get Up in the Morning." The show was produced in August, 1918, at New York's Century Theatre, with an all-male cast from the camp, many of them in drag.

That, however, was a diversion. Camp Upton, named for Civil War Maj. Gen. Emery Upton, was engaged in deadly serious business. The camp was one of the Army's 16 newly created cantonments, but in September, 1917, it was only about one-third built when the first draftees arrived. The trees and tangled undergrowth had been cleared and a rail spur connected the camp with the Yaphank station of the Long Island Rail Road, but the first draftees found themselves put to work as laborers.

"Nothing was there; we even had to cut the stumps out," Morris Gutentag of Oakdale, an infantryman in the 77th who was wounded and taken prisoner by the Germans, said in a Newsday interview in 1981, when he was 86. "We didn't have no rifles, nothing whatsoever. Broomsticks. We learned about it with broomsticks for about two or three weeks, until we got our rifles. The carpenters were working day and night to finish the barracks for us."

Modern trench warfare was what the 16-week training program was designed to teach. "Trench raiding, scouting, trench building and operations of all kinds which may be called for in actual combat will be duplicated at the camps throughout the night hours," The New York Times reported.

The Brooklyn Eagle reported that the men from eastern Long Island "were a fine looking set of fellows, well-built and with a freshness of face and quietness of manner that contrasted with the men who arrived from the city." And one of the camp officers was later to recall that the recruits included ". . . the gunman and the gangster, the student and the clerk, the laborer, the loafer, the daily plodder, the lawyer, men of muscle and men of brain."

The new doughboys at Upton not only got uniforms and rifles, they also got Bibles, courtesy of the American Bible Society. One recruit later wrote to a friend: "The Bible is printed on nice, thin paper and is excellent for rolling the makings of a cigarette. In fact, I have smoked through the New Testament as far as Second Corinthians."

The Bible Society's president, James Wood, later commented, "Let us hope he read before he smoked."

One of the innovations the government came up with was to hire professional boxers as athletic trainers for the men. Assigned to Upton was lightweight champion Benny Leonard. Learning rudimentary boxing skills would, a government announcement said, "teach them confidence, aggressiveness, shiftiness on their feet and the boxer's coordination of eye and hand. This will make these men better bayonet fighters."

The 59-year-old former President Theodore Roosevelt came out to Camp Upton in November, 1917, to give the boys a pep talk, and he got a rousing reception when he attacked isolationists who opposed the war. "The nation that won't fight when its women and children are killed stands on a level with the man who won't fight when his wife is knocked down or his daughter kidnaped," Roosevelt said.

The heavily decorated 77th Division gained recognition for its valor during 68 days of combat in campaigns at Baccarat, Oise-Aisne, Aisne-Marne and Meuse-Argonne. The so-called Liberty Division — with its insignia a Statue of Liberty in gold with a "7" on each side on a blue background — lost 2,275 men killed and 4,934 wounded.

There were other World War I training camps on Long Island. Hazelhurst Field in Garden City became one of four U.S. aviation schools, and it was where Roosevelt's son, Quentin, earned his wings. He was later shot down and killed over Germany, and the airfield was renamed Roosevelt Field. South of Stewart Avenue in Garden City, the Army opened Camp Mills as an embarkation center for troops about to go overseas.

At 11 a.m. on Nov. 11, 1918, the war ended. For a while, Camp Upton served as a demobilization site for veterans. When deactivated, a public auction in August, 1921, saw everything removed from the base. The scrub oak and pines were allowed to grow wild again.

The wilderness was brought back to life in 1940, on the eve of America's entry into World War II. A new camp was built for use as an Army induction center. Later it was converted into a convalescent hospital. When the war was over this time, however, the site was not allowed to go to seed. In January, 1947, Brookhaven National Laboratory was born there as a research center for the peaceful uses of atomic energy.

Brookhaven National Laboratory Photos

Bayonet practice, above, was part of training at Camp Upton. In his off-hours, draftee Irving Berlin had time to pen the popular song "Oh! How I Hate to Get Up in the Morning."

A MISSILE FLIES OVER THE BAY

The first successful guided missile was launched out over Great South Bay from a small airfield in Copiague in March, 1918. Developed by Sperry Gyroscope Co. founder Elmer Sperry and his son Lawrence, the "aerial torpedo," as it was then called, was developed too late to be used in World War I, but it was the forerunner of the devastating guided missiles of later wars.

Sperry was asked by the government to explore the idea of using his gyro-stabilizer on a pilotless, radio-controlled plane that would be loaded with explosives.

"The flying bomb test of March 6, 1918, marks the first entirely successful flight of an automatic missile in this country, if not in the world," Rear Adm. Delmar Fahrney and Robert Strobell, deputy curator of the National Air Museum, wrote in Aero Digest magazine in July, 1954.

— George DeWan

Nassau County Museum Collection, L.I. Studies Institute

Elmer A. Sperry with a gyroscope, around 1928

German U-boat blamed for mining the only major U.S. warship lost in World War I

The Sinking of the San Diego

BY BILL BLEYER
STAFF WRITER

As the armored cruiser San Diego slowly capsized within sight of Long Island, Capt. Harley Christy jumped from the tilting bridge, descended a ladder to the deck, slid down a rope and then walked over the rolling hull as if he were a lumberjack on a floating log, stopped for a moment to salute his vessel, then dropped eight feet into the Atlantic.

In keeping with tradition, the captain was the last man to leave the 504-foot ship. As a lifeboat picked up Christy, the more than 1,200 crew members in boats, on rafts or in the water cheered their skipper. And as the San Diego sank stern first into the flat sea, the men sang "The Star Spangled Banner" and "My Country 'Tis of Thee."

Steamship Historical Society, University of Baltimore

WZ-Bilddienst, Wilhelmshaven, Germany

The U-156, left, is believed to have caused the sinking of the San Diego, above, the only major U.S. warship to be lost in World War I.

The San Diego was the only major U.S. warship lost in World War I. And its sinking on July 19, 1918, only 8 miles south of Fire Island, showed how brazen and effective German U-boats could be.

Most of the historical evidence indicates that a mine laid by the German U-156 took the lives of six crewmen and sent the San Diego to the muddy bottom 110 feet below.

When the United States declared war on Germany in 1917, the Germans developed larger submarines capable of crossing the Atlantic. In 1918, a foreign navy began attacking American shipping along the U.S. coastline for the first time since the War of 1812. During the six-month campaign, six U-boats destroyed 91 vessels between Newfoundland and North Carolina.

On its cruise to North America, the U-156 sank 36 vessels. Ironically, on the way home the submarine was sunk by an American mine in the North Sea.

The San Diego, the U-156's biggest victim, was commissioned in 1907 as the California. Renamed the San Diego in 1914, it became a convoy escort during the war. On July 18, 1918, it left Portsmouth, N.H., for New York.

The next day dawned warm and hazy with the cruiser steaming along the South Shore in state-of-battle readiness. At about 10 a.m., a lookout spotted a small object moving on the surface. Thinking it might be a submarine periscope, the gun crews fired several rounds until the target disappeared. It was the first time the San Diego's guns had been fired at a suspected enemy.

The ship was cutting through the calm sea at more than 15 mph when it was rocked by an explosion, and a column of water erupted along the port side. The San Diego immediately listed 10 degrees. It was 11:05 a.m.

The explosion blew a hole in the hull at the port engine room, killing two seamen instantly. Another crewman oiling the port propeller shaft was never seen again.

Christy rang for full speed on the undamaged starboard engine and turned toward shore, hoping to beach the ship. But the rush of water into the hole flooded the remaining engine and left the San Diego without power, preventing an SOS. Although the U-156 was already off the New England coast, crew members again thought they saw a periscope and began firing at it.

C.E. Sims, an 18-year-old seaman who became an engineer in Islip, wrote maritime historian Henry Keatts years later that he heard the explosion while he was on the bridge. "I looked aft and saw a huge column of smoke about a hundred feet high. There was no panic. There was an officer who stood on the ladder with his hand on his holster. I remember he said 'If anyone jumps before abandon ship is given, I'll shoot him.' "

When the captain gave the order, the crew struggled to launch the lifeboats manually. As the ship heeled, the smokestacks broke loose, one of them fatally crushing a sailor in the water. Another crew member died when a life raft fell on his head. A sixth sailor drowned after becoming trapped inside the crow's nest.

Christy dispatched a small boat to shore to contact the Navy. Two hours later, it sailed through the surf at Point O'Woods. Rescue vessels were soon on their way to help survivors and search for the sub. The ships dropped depth charges on a target that turned out to be the San Diego.

In 1957, the government sold the hulk to a New York salvage company for $1,221. But in 1961, before work began, environmentalists, divers and fishermen formed a group to save the wreck. The Navy agreed to cancel the contract.

The San Diego became Long Island's premier dive site, attracting thousands of divers a year and taking the lives of six who became disoriented inside the silty hull. Artifacts from the ship can be seen at the Intrepid Sea-Air-Space Museum in Manhattan and the Maritime Industry Museum at the State University Maritime College in the Bronx.

The Navy has been trying to discourage divers from taking artifacts from the ship in recent years, saying the San Diego is still government property and a war grave. Earlier this year the wreck was put on the National Register of Historic Places in a further effort to preserve what's left.

NOW 97, HE RECALLS BEING A TEEN IN THE TRENCHES

Seventeen-year-old Richard Fredey lied about his age to enlist in the Marines in World War I.

He was shipped to France in time for the war's last offensive. The 97-year-old East Quogue resident recalled that he arrived at the front in the Argonne Forest on Nov. 1, 1918. "We went over in the early morning under what was called a rolling barrage. From then on there was contact pretty regularly for the next eleven days." His left knee was permanently injured by a shell fragment.

"Every morning for six or seven days we were gassed. They shelled the gas in usually during the night. You'd get a whiff of it and put your mask on."

The son of an Alsace-born chef had to subsist on canned survival rations. "It was cold, damp and very rough; everyone had dysentery and body lice. We lived like animals."

Newsday Photo / John H. Cornell Jr.

Richard Fredey

After the war, Fredey followed his father and uncles into the hotel-restaurant business. During World War II he enlisted again, and was commissioned a Marine first lieutenant. He took part in the invasion of Okinawa and was awarded a Bronze Star and a Purple Heart after receiving a shrapnel wound in his neck. After Japan surrendered, he returned to the hotel business and stayed in the reserves, commanding training units in Miami and Smithtown before retiring as a colonel in 1964.

Fredey said his experiences in 1918 had a positive impact. "I was so grateful for my survival that I made pledges to do things." He said he still keeps those pledges, waking up every day feeling optimistic and grateful to be alive, thinking what he can do to make others feel better and doing something to improve himself. "War changes your whole life." **— Bill Bleyer**

From Port Washington, March King John Philip Sousa sent music all over the nation

The Sound Of America

BY PETER GOODMAN
STAFF WRITER

John Philip Sousa might not have spent much time on Long Island, but he loved the time he spent.

In 1921, answering a query from a friend about whether he wanted to sell Wilbank, his Mediterranean-style mansion overlooking Hempstead Harbor, Sousa replied: "I have to live somewhere, and the North Shore is so near Paradise that I have no idea of ever renting or selling my place."

The March King was already rich and famous when he came to Sands Point in 1914. Sousa's family — J.P., wife Jane, son J.P. II and daughters Jane Priscilla and Helen — had been living in New York hotels for more than 20 years before he bought the mansion.

The Port Washington peninsula remained Sousa's home from then until his death in 1932, and daughter Jane lived in Wildbank until she died in 1958. The North Shore, filled with wooded estates occupied by the royalty of an expanding, confident, industrial nation, was a good place for a musician who embodied as well as anyone the peak of late 19th-Century American society.

For Sousa was a self-made man of tremendous talent and energy, a real all-American, from his many variations of mustache and beard to his love for shooting and partiality to the manly art of boxing. He was a full-blooded patriot born in 1854 in Washington, D.C., of a Portuguese-Spanish father and a Bavarian mother. At 60, he was already the composer of music that sounded like America, especially the thrilling martial notes of such marches as "The Stars and Stripes Forever," "Manhattan Beach" and "El Capitan."

His Sousa Band was probably the most successful and popular musical organization in the country in its time — but that very success kept him from spending much time on Long Island. The band toured incessantly, crossing and criss-crossing the nation by train, sometimes giving two concerts a day, and spending the summers giving daily and nightly performances at places such as Willow Grove Park outside Philadelphia and Manhattan Beach in Brooklyn. It engaged in several European trips and a round-the-world tour in 1910-11.

When he did come back to the spacious house on a cliff overlooking the water, he would spend part of his time composing or ensconced in his library. Sousa was an avid rider and sportsman who didn't motor into town to pick up his mail. He would saddle a favorite mount, such as Aladdin or Patrician Charlie, and head for the post office, which in those days was at the foot of Main Street where it begins to curve south along Manhasset Bay.

He never did bring the Sousa Band to Long Island — the money was in New York and points west, according to Floyd Mackay, announcer and emcee at Port Washington's Sousa Bandshell, where they still have band concerts on summer evenings. But Mackay and his wife, June, treasure the stories they heard from her uncle, D.P. (Webb) Walker, who worked at the post office and knew Sousa.

"He was a rather generous sort of person," Mackay said, "involved in the community but not overinvolved." Sousa, among his many clubs and associations, was an active Mason, and Walker chatted with him once about his becoming master of the local lodge. "He said, 'Yes I am, and if you pick up a few musicians, I'll conduct them for you,' " Mackay recounted.

But there's no indication Sousa ever did lead a Masonic band in Port Washington; there were reports that he led a community band in Port Washington once, and he was, according to Mackay, scheduled to conduct the school band two weeks after he died.

He also liked baseball. His band would play other bands on the road and Sousa sometimes pitched the first inning — and he sponsored a Sousa Band team in Nassau County in the 1920s.

Another of his favorite activities was trapshooting — he was, according to Paul E. Bierley's biography, "John Philip Sousa, American Phenomenon," one of the best shots in the country. Naturally, Sousa was friendly with Theodore Roosevelt, who lived at Sagamore Hill on the next peninsula east. They would often go shooting together, or discuss politics and world affairs.

Sousa came by his nationalism virtually by birth, for his parents lived in a section of Washington known as the Navy Yard, only a block and a half west of the Marine Barracks. His father, Antonio, was a trombonist in the Marine Band, and young John grew up hearing military music — and watching the streams of troops and wounded pass through the capital during the Civil War.

U.S. Marine Corps Photo

John Philip Sousa, composer of "The Stars and Stripes Forever," "The Washington Post" and other marches, in his uniform as the director of the Marine Band

LI HISTORY.COM 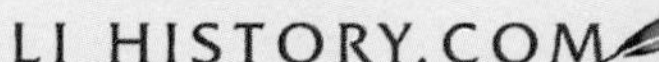

To learn more about the composer and to listen to scores of sound clips from his career, see http://www.lihistory.com on the Internet.

The boy enlisted in the Marine Corps at the age of 14, as an apprentice musician. A violinist, he spent his teenage years playing for the government during the day and with local orchestras at night. In 1880, at the age of 26, he was named director of the Marine Band — and promptly grew a beard to appear as old as the veterans he was conducting.

In his 12 years as leader, he reformed the band, adding new music, including his own work, raising standards and tightening discipline. The band's reputation grew, and it began to tour. The band even made some pioneering cylinder recordings, but Sousa found the work boring and let an assistant lead during the sessions.

Finally, he left the Marines and formed a partnership with manager David Blakely; his own Sousa Band gave its first concert in Plainfield, N.J., in September, 1892. During the next 40 years, the Sousa Band became the *ne plus ultra* of wind-powered musical organizations, and one of the finest ensembles of any kind. Sousa re-upped during World War I, commissioned at the age of 62 as a lieutenant in the Naval Reserve, to train and lead military bandsmen. His Band Battalion, called the Jackie Band, raised more than $21 million in war bonds and other funds.

He was a businessman as well as a musician and, as a founding member with Victor Herbert of the American Society of Composers, Authors and Publishers (ASCAP), fought to ensure that composers and performers got paid for their work.

The grand old bandmaster never retired. "When you hear of Sousa retiring, you will hear of Sousa dead," he told reporters in his latter years.

And he was right: Early in the morning of March 5, 1932, the day he was to conduct the Ringgold Band of Reading, Pa., in its 80th birthday concert, Sousa suffered a heart attack and died at age 77. He was buried in his native city of Washington, D.C., on March 10 after a service in the Marine Band Auditorium.

Wildbank remained in family hands until it was sold in 1965. The current owners, Peter and Bridgette Hirsch, say the house has been completely renovated and, except for a plaque on the wall and a section of wallpaper, "no part of the house is Sousafied."

Newsday Archive

Sousa and his band in Hamburg, Germany, on May 30, 1900, during a European tour. His base was Manhattan until he moved his family to Sands Point in 1914. He described the place as "near Paradise."

A 25-year-old unknown pilot named Lindbergh departs LI on a transatlantic gamble

Flying Against the Odds

BY LAURA MUHA

On May 12, 1927, an obscure airmail pilot named Charles Lindbergh taxied a wood-and-aluminum monoplane to a stop on the muddy grass at Curtiss Field in Mineola.

Immediately, a crowd of reporters and photographers surrounded him.

"Look this way, will ya!"

"Tell us something about your flight from California."

And the question on everybody's mind: "When're you going to start for Paris?"

In those days, the idea of a New York-to-Paris flight was front-page news. Since 1919, when New York hotelier Raymond Orteig had announced a $25,000 prize for the first person to fly nonstop between the two cities, three teams had attempted the trip. Two had crashed on takeoff. One was missing at sea.

Now Lindbergh, a 25-year-old unknown, was taking a crack at the prize.

George Dade Collection

Charles Lindbergh and the Spirit of St. Louis at Mineola's Curtiss Field on one of the days in May, 1927, that storms delayed his trip to Paris. Just after daybreak on May 20, his plane was rolled to Roosevelt Field for the historic flight.

"He was taking a calculated risk," says Bob Van der Linden, an aviation historian with the Smithsonian Institution. "Perhaps it took someone 25 years old to have the guts to do it; he didn't realize he was mortal yet!"

The only child of a teacher and an attorney who was later elected to Congress, Lindbergh grew up on a farm in Little Falls, Minn. Fascinated by airplanes, he dropped out of the University of Wisconsin to enroll in flying school, then spent a year barnstorming.

In 1924, he enlisted in the Army's Air Service training school, graduating with a commission as a second lieutenant in the reserves. A few months later, he was named chief airmail pilot for St. Louis-based Robertson Aircraft Corp.

In his Pulitzer Prize-winning 1953 book "The Spirit of St. Louis," Lindbergh said he first thought of entering the transatlantic race in 1926, while making a mail run in a decrepit biplane and musing on what he could do in a better aircraft. "Possibly — my mind is startled at its thought — I could fly nonstop between New York and Paris," he wrote.

Such a trip wouldn't be easy. First, he'd need a plane powerful enough to get off the ground carrying 2,600 pounds of fuel — the amount he thought was necessary to cross 3,600 miles of ocean. Such a plane would cost at least $10,000 — money he'd have to raise quickly, since teams headed by famed aviators Clarence Chamberlin and Richard Byrd were planning New York-to-Paris attempts the following spring.

Lindbergh convinced a group of St. Louis businessmen to invest $15,000 in his trip, but buying an airplane proved more difficult. In "The Spirit of St. Louis," Lindbergh wrote that the manufacturers of his first choice, a Wright-Bellanca, refused to sell unless they could select the pilot; in frustration, he turned to obscure Ryan Airlines Inc. of San Diego.

Working with engineers there, Lindbergh designed a single-engined monoplane in defiance of conventional wisdom, which held that multiple engines were necessary on long trips because of the likelihood of mechanical failure. He also decided to save weight by flying without a navigator, radio or parachute.

Lindbergh spent two weeks testing the plane — named Spirit of St. Louis in honor of his investors — in California. Then he flew to Long Island, where he spent a week attending to details: overhauling the engine, dashing into Manhattan to get a passport, installing a specialized compass and checking his supplies, which included little more than an inflatable raft, a hacksaw blade, a ball of string, some flares, a bag of sandwiches and a special cup that could convert the moisture from his breath into drinking water.

As for a toothbrush or a change of clothes, he figured he'd buy them in Paris if he made it that far, and if he didn't, he wouldn't need them anyway. He was so determined to keep his load as light as possible that he even trimmed the margins from his maps to save a few ounces.

But to Lindbergh's chagrin, storms over the Atlantic repeatedly delayed takeoff, increasing the likelihood that Byrd or Chamberlin — both on Long Island gearing up for their own flights — would beat him to Paris.

Finally, on the night of May 19, while driving to Manhattan to see a Broadway show, Lindbergh stopped to call the weather bureau — and learned the storms were unexpectedly clearing.

Instantly scrapping his theater plans, he headed for the airfield and ordered preparations for takeoff. Then he returned to the Garden City Hotel in a vain attempt to get some sleep.

Just after daybreak on May 20, his plane was rolled from a hangar at Curtiss Field and towed to adjacent Roosevelt Field, which had a longer runway. A crowd, alerted by the action, gathered on the muddy, violet-dotted field.

"It was a damp, blustery, uncomfortable morning," recalls Anne Condelli, 81, of Garden City, who was 10 at the time of Lindbergh's flight. "There were people milling around, filling the plane with gas, wishing him well."

Her brother, Kenneth Van de Water, remembers the suspense as Lindbergh's plane lumbered down the runway. "He kept going and going and couldn't get off the ground," recalls Van de Water, 78, of Lexington, Va. "There were several times as he went down the runway that the plane bounced."

Finally, the Spirit of St. Louis lurched into the air. When it cleared the telephone wires at the far end of the field, a cheer went up from the crowd. It was 7:54 a.m.

Lindbergh was on his way.

Laura Muha is a freelance writer.

CORRIGAN FINDS A WAY TO FAME

AP Photo

Douglas Corrigan in Dublin in 1938; his announced destination was California.

When Charles Lindbergh arrived on Long Island to prepare for his transatlantic flight, mechanics discovered the spinner — a cap that fits over the propeller hub — had cracked, and replaced it with a new one.

The original, on display at the National Air and Space Museum in Washington D.C., was signed by all Ryan Airlines employees who worked on the plane — including Douglas Corrigan, who 11 years later would earn a place of his own in aviation history.

It all started on July 10, 1938, when, to the disbelief of the press and public, Corrigan piloted a rattletrap, 9-year-old plane nonstop from California to Roosevelt Field in 27 hours, 50 minutes.

A week later, he left Long Island, ostensibly to return to California — but instead arrived in Dublin, Ireland, 28 hours later, claiming he'd gotten lost. The feat earned Corrigan public adoration and the nickname "Wrong Way."

When he returned to Long Island, he was surrounded by autograph seekers, and honored at a dinner at the Roosevelt Field Inn. — **Laura Muha**

After a daring journey across the Atlantic, he lands in the center of public adulation

Lindy Flies Into History

BY LAURA MUHA

In the sun's glare above the Atlantic, Charles Lindbergh struggled to stay awake.

His eyes felt like stones, and his eyelids kept shutting against his will.

"I *must*, I *will* become alert," Lindbergh told himself, in a conversation he recounted in his 1953 book, "The Spirit of St. Louis." He stomped on the floorboards of his plane, threw his weight against the seatbelt to jar himself. Nothing helped.

It was just after 7:30 a.m. on May 21, 1927 — almost 24 hours since the 25-year-old airmail pilot had taken off from Roosevelt Field in an attempt to become the first person to fly nonstop between New York and Paris.

In those days, before jet engines and radar, it was a perilous trip — more than 33 hours over water, with only the sun, stars and a compass to navigate by. Two other aviators had died en route, and many people believed Lindbergh would meet the same fate.

Now, it looked as if they might be right. Lindbergh's plane edged downward until it was barely 100 feet above the waves, and he couldn't concentrate long enough to bring it under control.

"Can I hold on to consciousness? I must hold on . . ." He pushed his head out the window, forcing himself to breathe deeply until his eyes refocused and his mind cleared. He nosed the plane skyward.

Still, it wasn't until Lindbergh spotted the coast of Ireland later that afternoon that excitement wiped away the final traces of sleepiness. Paris was only a few hours away. "Yesterday I walked on Roosevelt Field; today I'll walk on Le Bourget," he told himself.

On the ground, the radio crackled with the news that the young American had been spotted over Ireland . . . then England . . . then France. Austin Wilkins, of Augusta, Maine, was on a college tour of Paris when he heard of Lindbergh's approach and rushed to Le Bourget, joining 100,000 others who jammed the roads leading to the airfield.

"We saw this little tiny flicker overhead, this little light," recalls Wilkins, now 94. "We could hear the sound of the motor, and finally we saw him circle the field three times . . . He landed at the upper end of the airport."

UPI Photo

Confetti pours onto Broadway on June 13, 1927, as Lindbergh receives a boisterous welcome.

It was 10:22 p.m. Paris time — 33 hours, 29 minutes and 30 seconds after Lindbergh's take-off from Roosevelt Field.

With a roar, the crowd broke past steel fences and military guards. In his 1927 bestseller, "We," Lindbergh describes what happened next: "I started to climb out of the cockpit, but as soon as one foot appeared through the door I was dragged the rest of the way without assistance on my part.

"For nearly half an hour I was unable to touch the ground, during which time I was ardently carried around . . . in every position it is possible to be in."

Lindbergh spent two weeks touring Europe, then returned to the United States aboard a Navy cruiser dispatched by President Calvin Coolidge. At Roosevelt Field, 60,000 people turned out to greet him — some showing up as early as midnight to secure spots for his 4:05 p.m. arrival.

"Roosevelt Field has entertained great crowds before, but Colonel Lindbergh — was the magnet that attracted the banner attendance of any event ever held in this county," the Brooklyn Daily Eagle reported on June 17, 1927. "The likes of it will never again be seen here."

In the folowing years, Lindbergh's celebrity never dimmed. Troubled times lay ahead — the 1930 kidnaping and murder of his first-born son; accusations that he was a Nazi sympathizer when he opposed the United States' entry into World War II. He was an isolationist, but not a Nazi sympathizer, some historians say.

In his later years, Lindbergh traveled around the world to promote conservation of natural resources.

But to most, he would always be the young man in the plane who had crossed the Atlantic — something his daughter, Reeve Lindbergh of Vermont, says he could never understand.

"To him, it was in the past," she said recently. "If you asked him about the flight, he'd say, 'Read my book.' He'd taken the flight, he'd written the book, and by golly, he was finished with it!"

Lindbergh died of lymphoma in 1974, at age 72.

Laura Muha is a freelance writer.

AVIATION'S PRODUCTIVE PARTNERSHIP

Before Charles Lindbergh left for Paris, Harry Guggenheim, a North Shore multimillionaire and aviation enthusiast, visited him at Curtiss Field.

"When you get back from your flight, look me up," said Guggenheim, who later admitted he didn't think there was much chance Lindbergh would survive the trip.

Lindbergh remembered and did call upon his return. It was the beginning of a friendship that would have a profound impact on the development of aviation in the United States. The two decided Lindbergh would make a three-month tour of the United States, paid for by a fund Harry and his father, Daniel, had set up earlier to encourage aviation-related research.

"Lindbergh was seen by literally millions of people as he flew around the country," said Richard P. Hallion, historian for the Air Force and the author of a book on the Guggenheims. "Airmail usage exploded overnight as a result," and the public began to view airplanes as a viable means of travel.

That year, Lindbergh spent a month at Guggenheim's Sands Point mansion, Falaise, while writing "We," his best-selling 1927 account of his trip.

Two years later, he was visiting Guggenheim when he read an article about Robert Goddard, a Massachusetts scientist trying to build something called a rocket. At Guggenheim's suggestion, Lindbergh went to see Goddard — and when he realized how innovative the scientist's ideas were, convinced Daniel Guggenheim to pledge $100,000 to further Goddard's work.

"To this day, you cannot design and build a spacecraft of any kind without infringing on one or more of Goddard's patents," said Hallion.

— Laura Muha

Newsday Photo, 1963

Harry Guggenheim

UPI Photo

Charles Lindbergh and his wife, Anne, in 1929. He spent a month at Harry Guggenheim's Sands Point mansion.

THE LINDY HOP

The moment that Charles Lindbergh landed in Paris, he became a celebrity. Towns and babies were named after him as was the Lindy hop, a popular dance of the time.

Hundreds of thousands of letters and gifts poured in from all over the country: a diamond stickpin, an amethyst ring, commemorative wallpaper and a horned toad that was dead on arrival.

Merchandisers cashed in on the "Lucky Lindy" popularity. There were Lindbergh picture puzzles, Lindbergh tapestries, Lindbergh souvenir beanies, and Lindbergh gum dispensers.

An estimated 5,000 poems and songs were written in his honor. One song, called "When Lindy Comes Home," included the following lyrics: "He's a coming, He's a coming; Hear the drumming, Rum-tum-tumming . . . Oh! Say what a day from Gotham to Nome, When Lindy comes back, From across the foam."

— Laura Muha

With Gold Coast parties and bathtub gin, Long Island epitomizes the Roaring '20s

F. Scott Fitzgerald Country

BY DAVID BEHRENS
STAFF WRITER

It was, suddenly, the Jazz Age.

It was the beginning of a decade of Prohibition and apparent prosperity: a time of jazz bands and petting parties, high-stepping flappers and college boys with hip flasks.

On Long Island, there were rumrunners and dealers in bathtub gin, gaudy parties on the grounds of fabulous Gold Coast estates, rowdy gatherings in neighborhood speakeasies and big-name entertainers in flashy nightclubs, where ordinary men and women brushed shoulders and clinked glasses with the famous and the notorious. There were also thousands of work-a-day people who went to work-a-day jobs, worried about their children's future and hoped to save up for the latest Ford.

It was the Roaring '20s on Long Island, which became a microcosm of the nation's revolution in manners and morals. F. Scott Fitzgerald had memorialized the era with his 1922 best-seller, "Tales of the Jazz Age," the year before he rented a house in Great Neck and began work on his best-known novel, "The Great Gatsby."

In the wooded villages of the North Shore, the affluent life was celebrated in the mansions of more than 500 estates. Some played host to grandiose dinner-dances where hundreds of guests transformed brightly lighted landscapes into a weekend playland. These scenes of newly won opulence and excess later found their way onto the pages of "Gatsby," a story of the American Dream gone awry.

At the same time, off the shores of Long Island, fleets of rumrunners fought a deadly battle with the Coast Guard and with each other, smuggling ashore the most precious cargo of the decade: illegal alcohol.

And along the byways of the South Shore was a string of roadhouses, nightclubs and speakeasies that turned Merrick Road and Sunrise Highway into what columnists called Glitter Alley and The Great Light Way, a scene to rival Broadway's Great White Way.

Here, shop girls on dates and college boys on vacation danced the Charleston, sharing the scene with an odd mixture of businessmen, show business figures, politicans such as New York City Mayor Jimmy Walker and gangsters such as Jack (Legs) Diamond. All came to imbibe illicit drink, to dance, and to listen to the latest sounds in blues and jazz.

International News Photos

This scene on a Southampton beach in 1919 was a sign of changing times: Even some "nice" girls used swear words and slang, smoked in public and sampled the illicit pleasures of drink.

Clubs along Merrick Road, such as the famed Pavillon Royal, which opened in 1924, featured the nation's best-known bands. Legendary entertainers such as Texas ("Hello, suckers") Guinan, Guy Lombardo, Eddie Duchin and Rudy Vallee drew customers from Long Island, New York City and across the nation.

At some clubs, champagne sold for $100 a bottle. On the strip, bandleader Paul Whiteman introduced a singing group called The Rhythm Boys featuring then-unknown Bing Crosby. Other show business favorites included comics Ken Murray and Victor Moore and singer Sophie Tucker, billed as the "Last of the Red Hot Mamas."

"Everyone in show business flocked there," Tucker, who lived in Freeport for a time, had told a local reporter. The small village boasted a famous private club, The Lights Club on Fairview Avenue, organized by George M. Cohan. Entertainment started at midnight and ran until dawn, with Al Jolson, W.C. Fields and Eddie Cantor among the regulars.

Great Neck also boasted its share of celebrities. In 1926, the local weekly engaged in some unabashed name-dropping with a letter from author Gene Buck. The village, he wrote, "has more truly noted people within its domain than any other community of its size in the world." He cited such residents as New York World publisher Herbert Bayward Swope, composer Oscar Hammerstein, and actors Ed Wynn, Frank Craven and Ernest Truex.

In another issue, the Great Neck News noted with pride: "Our Ring Lardner of East Shore Road wrote the scenario for 'The New Klondike' at the Rivoli next week." Film director Henry King of Elm Point had just made "Stella Dallas," starring Douglas Fairbanks, the paper reported.

Along Suffolk's North Shore, other well-known residents were spotted. Marion Davies had a hideaway in Halesite, courtesy of her patron, publisher William Randolph Hearst, and actresses Lillian and Dorothy Gish could be spotted cycling about town. And gambler Nicky Arnstein, Fanny Brice's husband, allegedly ran a dice game at the Halesite firehouse's annual fundraiser.

For the ordinary wage-earner, there was the local speakeasy. A large pitcher of beer cost $1.50 at Fred's Roadhouse in Wantagh or Otto's Silver Wave in Freeport, and bathtub rye, a homemade blend of rotgut alcohol, water and flavorings, was on sale at Old John's Shack in the Bellmore woods. On Sunrise Highway, speakeasies served shots of gin for 50 cents, while a motherly looking woman on Old Country Road sold "guaranteed Scotch" from her Garden City home.

A social revolution challenging accepted American traditions was certainly under way, historian Frederick Lewis Allen observed in his account, "Only Yesterday: An Informal History of the 1920s."

In the forefront of this rebellion were the children of ordinary American families. In communities across the country, young women bobbed their hair, painted their faces with rouge, slipped

Please see **ROARING '20s, Next Page**

The '20s Roar On Long Island

ROARING '20s from Preceding Page

on short sleeveless dresses, rolled down silk stockings below the knee and kicked up their heels on countless dance floors. By 1920, The New York Times reported that "the American woman . . . has lifted her skirts far beyond any modest limitation." Hemlines nine inches above the ground!

The more racy flappers stashed their girdles in the cloakrooms of popular dance places, complaining that men wouldn't dance with corseted women. Even "nice" girls used swear words and slang, smoked in public and, somewhat less openly, kept up with the menfolk drink for drink. And everyone seemed to be dancing: fox-trots at afternoon tea dances, high-kicking Charlestons into the early morning hours.

So it seemed.

But there was also an ambivalence about the changing times and a good deal of moderation. In the villages of Long Island, old values seemed to persist, regardless of pressure from the trendy culture. As recorded in local newspapers in the mid-'20s, day-to-day social life did not seem so different from the prewar era:

Mrs. Dudley B. Fuller Jr. of Franklin Court, for instance, entertained at dinner on Saturday night and took her guests to a theater party at the Community Club, the Hempstead Sentinel reported.

Little Hamilton Bishop was the host at a movie party on Wednesday for 11 of his friends, all members of Hammy's Gang in Garden City. "They all rejoiced at the performance of Charlie Chaplin in 'The Pilgrim,' " the social column noted. And Miss Janet Addison gave a bridge party on Friday, presenting favors of "artistic guest-room sewing bouquets" to her guests.

For many, doing the Charleston was just a wonderful exercise, not a change of lifestyle or values.

Gladys Barry, for instance, loved to dance. As a teenager in the early 1920s, she still remembers those special Saturday night dates, taking the train from Bay Ridge into Manhattan to Charleston at such hot spots as the Pennsylvania Grill and the Roosevelt Grill. "But I don't think I was conscious of any revolution. At that age you were just living at the moment and having a good time," Barry, who is 89 and lives with her husband in Franklin Square, said in a recent interview.

Everyone was aware of the speakeasies, of course, and like so many, she smoked in public. "My parents didn't object. That's what young people were doing and we just went along with the trend. Life was a lot of fun, but none of us drank. We'd play tennis a lot and we had parties afterward — with soda and peanuts."

Married in 1931, she and her husband moved to Garden City. Prohibition was still on but at her wedding in a private club, "there was all kinds of liquor . . . No one told us it was illegal."

Nassau and Suffolk Counties were still a network of small rural communities. In Nassau, the population had edged just over 126,000 by 1920. Suffolk's population was about 110,000.

Village merchants were pleased about growing retail sales and fretted over downtown traffic problems. People wondered how the local school football team would fare and, like everyone else, they were concerned about "The Problem of the Younger Generation," a frequent topic in the nation's magazines.

In small towns, people worried about all the craziness. Some tried to ban the new dances when they became too suggestive or "promoted carnality," as a few religious leaders warned. The new dancing had become a "syncopated embrace," as a college journal described the trend.

The newly resurrected Ku Klux Klan joined the chorus of critics, taking a law-and-order stance to lure recruits on Long Island. The hate-mongering KKK supported Prohibition and criticized the "loose morals" of the era. In its heyday, historians estimate that membership exceeded 25,000, about one out of every eight Long Island residents.

The mystique of the automobile also provided parents with a new set of anxieties, especially on Long Island, where new roads were in demand and under construction. For young couples, the car provided both transport and an escape from the critical eye of neighbors, relatives and chaperons. If petting and other sexual explorations at parties did not sully men's reputations, the more modern woman concluded, she, too, no longer needed to be preoccupied with her image.

So a decade of stunning change was unfolding — even in small villages where the phenomenon of social revolution was denied, condemned or reinterpreted.

On April 19, 1923, for instance, readers of the Hempstead Sentinel were reassured by the curious lead story on Page One. The headline seemed to promise that the more things change, the more they stay the same.

Typical Modern Girls Winners
In Home Baking Contest

"The modern girl is vindicated," the author announced. "In spite of the fact that she may dress differently, have her hair bobbed, dance to jazz time and superficially appear to be indifferent to household activities, under the surface she is as good as was her grandmother and her mother . . . and probably even does things better."

The litmus test, the writer contended, was the annual bread-baking contest at Hempstead High School on a recent Saturday. A panel of judges decided that "the modern girl not only can but did bake many batches of homemade bread and it was the finest lot of bread anyone could wish for."

The winner was Miss Dorothy Davidson, "a thoroughly modern girl" who walked away with the first-prize money — $15 in gold — for the best loaf in town. "She is 17 years old and she is one of the prettiest girls to be found in all of Hempstead," the reporter gushed.

Dorothy was both athletic and theatrical, starring just the week before in the high school production of "Daddy Long Legs." And like so many young people, she loved to dance.

"We are going to let our readers in on a secret," the story went on. "The night before the contest, Miss Davidson was going to a dance. So before she went out, she had to mix the dough for her bread. After getting it all ready to 'set' overnight, she went out to the dance and didn't get home until — well, it was long after midnight."

The moral of the story?

Miss Davidson was able to arise early enough the next morning to get her bread in the oven in time for the contest. Scott Fitzgerald's women might dance until dawn, the Sentinel seemed to be saying, but Long Island's bright young women still returned dutifully to hearth and home.

Skimming through the national magazines in the '20s, readers might have guessed that the libertines had captured the country. Zelda Fitzgerald, wife of the author, had expressed the view that the modern woman had "the right to experiment with herself as a transient, poignant figure who will be dead tomorrow." But the fatalistic message apparently did not reshape family life in the villages of Long Island.

Olive Darling, in her 80s now and a Suffolk resident, remembers her hometown of Port Jefferson as "just a sleepy little village where everyone knew everyone and everyone's business."

A high school student in the late '20s, she remembers people talking about the changing times. "About Prohibition and the gangsters and Texas Guinan and her speakeasies, about bootleggers killing each other or getting put in jail."

But her girlhood world in Port Jefferson was surrounded by farm country. It was an adventure to get into the family Buick, she recalled, to make the long drive to Patchogue for serious shopping.

Small-town life just seemed to go on as always, she said in a recent interview. "And I loved those times. I loved

Princeton University Library Photo

F. Scott Fitzgerald and his wife, Zelda, in 1920. They lived in the Great Neck area, which became West Egg in his novel "The Great Gatsby."

Gladys Barry, left, who lives in Franklin Square, with a friend in 1924: Barry partied but wasn't "conscious of any revolution."

Oh, Those Flabbergasting Flappers!

BY JULIA SZABO

It was back-to-the-future time in Paris last month. At the fall, 1998, ready-to-wear shows, the fashion news was that two top designers — Karl Lagerfeld for Chanel and John Galliano for Dior — had dressed models to look like Roaring '20s heroines right out of a novel by F. Scott Fitzgerald. As a result, fashion mavens everywhere were heralding the return of flapper style.

Which essentially means a style of dress best suited to young, thin women with the measurements of pre-adolescent boys.

"When people talk about flappers, they're talking about the mid-to-late 1920s," explains fashion historian Valerie Steele, chief curator of the Museum at the Fashion Institute of Technology in Manhattan. She described the style of the day as "slim, unconstructed dress with a skirt that was — more or less knee length — and straight. Instead of being fitted at the waist and curvy at the hips and bust, it was straight-up-and-down, as if the wearer's figure were 20-20-20."

Back in the Victorian days, younger, skinnier women padded out their bosoms and hips. No longer: The new physical ideal was the flapper with, dress historian Anne Hollander explains, "no waistline, and as minimal a bust and bum as you could manage."

It's hard to imagine such a style packing shock value today. But back in the 1920s, when the idea of women with bare, unstockinged legs was brand new, flapper chic raised eyebrows — and then some. "It was much more radical than women burning their bras in the '60s," Steele says. "People were really shocked in the '20s. They really worried about the androgynous boy-girl look — they complained that women weren't women anymore."

Along with the new ideal came a new, and equally shocking, hairstyle. "In addition to their flat chests and bare legs, flappers tended to have short hair," Steele says. "Before, women prided themselves on having long hair that they would put up in elaborate coiffures. But flappers scandalized their parents by cutting their hair as high as their ears, in very short hairdos called bobs, often dyed and marcel-waved into flat, head-hugging curls and accessorized with wide, soft headbands.

"Some fathers and husbands sued hairdressers who bobbed their daughters' or wives' hair," Steele says. "And flappers wore makeup, which was also scandalous, because, previously, cosmetics had been reserved for whores and actresses. Flappers would even put on their lipstick in public!"

Freeport Historical Society

A 1920s postcard shows off the flapper-style dress: Here was "the first youth revolution, long before the '60s and the miniskirt."

This was a style of dress the wearer could move in with much greater freedom than had been afforded her by the corsets and crinolines of centuries past. And move flappers did, executing the steps of a vigorous dance craze called the Charleston. Complementing the flapper's state of perpetual motion was the decoration on her short, straight dress: It was covered with beads and beaded fringe that moved and made noise as she shimmied about on the dance floor to the sounds of what Fitzgerald called the Jazz Age.

The fast-and-loose look was significant as a response to the changing social and cultural climate that spawned it. "It was the first youth revolution, long before the '60s and the miniskirt," Steele says. "Young people were very indignant after World War I, and felt the older generation had just murdered millions of young boys. So they stopped obeying conventional rules and invented their own liberated culture: driving their own cars, and drinking, and petting with people they weren't married to. And, for the first time in history, older women started copying younger women. In the late 19th Century, younger women wanted to look like grownups. Now, for the first time, everyone wanted the thinness and relative bosomlessness of early adolescence."

In Hollywood, flapper style was embodied by actress Clara Bow, a k a The It Girl. As historian Hollander explains, Bow was positioned on the sex-appeal spectrum somewhere between America's Sweetheart and The Vamp. "She was very cheeky, very mobile, perfectly adorable and not dangerous," Hollander says. "She got jobs and was on her own." As with most styles aimed directly at the young and thin, women endowed with less-than-perfect legs had a hard time keeping up. "If you had a good figure, you didn't mind the short skirts," says Maude Bouvier Davis, who came of age in the flapper era. "My twin sister Michelle and I had good figures, so we didn't mind them at all. But if you didn't have good legs, you were really out. We had a wonderful friend who was rich as Croesus and she wore the fashions, though she never should have — she didn't have the figure, and she had these big piano legs. But she wanted to be in fashion. I admired her courage."

In an ironic twist, more zaftig women wore corsets to achieve the fashionably "natural," uncorseted look. "Women who had bigger bosoms tended to wear flattener brassieres to achieve the fashionable straight-up-and-down look," Steele says.

It's not surprising, in our age of super-young, super-thin supermodels, that this look should be back in vogue again. It's arguable that flappers made possible Kate Moss and her ilk by ushering in fashion's enduring fascination with youth and a thin physique that is still difficult for most women to achieve.

But according to Susan Penzner, who owns a vintage-clothing store in Sag Harbor called At Haven's House, the style never really went away. "The narrow, sheer chiffon dresses with beading are hard to find in good condition," Penzner says, "and when I get really beautiful ones, they fly out of the store. People love to wear them to weddings, and there's always a costume party with a 1920s theme."

Julia Szabo is a freelance writer.

playing basketball and tennis and I had the most wonderful time in school, dancing in all the musicals, doing the Charleston at the school dances."

Later, her friends would patronize a bootlegger who sold homemade brew from his house near Port Jefferson. But the young people of her community were "not the kind of kids F. Scott Fitzgerald wrote about," she said.

The older generation, of course, fretted over magazine articles about all the daring young people. "But compared to kids today, my God!" she exclaimed. "Girls might have gone joy-riding in cars, staying out late with boyfriends . . . But I think every gal in our school was a virgin when they graduated. Oh, there was one girl who got pregnant before graduation. And there was some necking here and there. But I didn't know anyone who drank in high school.

"Everyone smoked cigarettes. That was quite chic then. It was a secret for a while and my parents were not very happy when I told them."

After graduation, she went to college in Virginia — one of the few women in her class to go on with her education — then worked for National Geographic magazine. There, she found that "old fashioned" notions prevailed.

"I was fired from my first job with the magazine — because young ladies were not supposed to get into auto accidents at two o'clock in the morning. We were not supposed to be out at that hour. Can you believe it! But my fellow workers protested and I was rehired. I thought it was hilarious."

She did not marry until she was in her late 20s and returned to Port Jefferson to run a small antique shop, the 1812 House. "Most people got married early but I had things to do. I was a liberated person before anyone knew what the word meant. Not that I was shacking up with anyone, but I was self-supporting. So I married when I was damn good and ready."

Olive Darling was not alone. By 1920, more women than ever before were earning wages outside the home. That year, after a long struggle, women had won the right to vote with the ratification of the 19th Amendment. On Long Island there were ads for jobs for women in small factories, shops and the phone company. New appliances made household chores less exhausting, and in many villages there was a boom in bakeries and delis, offering faster food and freedom from kitchen duties.

Adventure was in the air: On Long Island, Roosevelt Field became the nation's most famous airfield after Charles Lindbergh took off for Paris in 1927. On better roads, summer residents of the Hamptons made the drive from Manhattan in five or six hours. Large movie houses were opening in Great Neck, Hempstead and other villages. And on stage and screen and in modern literature, there was a new frankness in both language and theme, with James Joyce, Marcel Proust and Virginia Woolf setting new standards.

Many works reflected postwar feelings of disillusionment and cynicism. Ignoring the national ban on alcohol had become the fashion of the times. But in villages such as Hempstead, many people put the emphasis on good old American commercialism.

A 1923 Hempstead Sentinel editorial observed: "There were probably more

Please see **ROARING '20s, Next Page**

The '20s Roar On Long Island

ROARING '20s from **Preceding Page**

than 5,000 people in Hempstead last Saturday night in the business district, both for shopping and pleasure."

A survey counted 78 motor cars parked in the downtown district, not including four horse-drawn vehicles. Several thousand patrons attended shows at the two theaters, while "stores were crowded with shoppers and sidewalks literally flooded with pedestrians." With a population of about 6,300, Hempstead had become "a magnet for shoppers and pleasure-seekers," the editorial pointed out with a hint of self-satisfaction, a quality of small-town life Sinclair Lewis satirized in his 1922 novel, "Babbitt."

On the North Shore, however, the older generation was preoccupied with the "flaming youth" of the era. In 1926, the Great Neck News expressed disdain over "a disgraceful scene of rowdyism in front of the lunch wagon near the railroad station." Two young men were found sprawled near the depot, the News reported, while another drunken pair were in the diner, "using disgraceful language."

Just then, an auto rumbled down Middle Neck Road with another load of drunken young men. "This was nigh on to 3 a.m.," the reporter scolded.

The revelers were fugitives, perhaps, from one of F. Scott Fitzgerald's stories about the carefree generation. In 1920, at age 24, Fitzgerald had become a cultural hero with his first novel, "This Side of Paradise," defining the postwar social revolution. The petting party was an accepted fact of life for the new generation, he wrote, while the mothers of the nation had no idea "how casually their daughters were accustomed to be kissed."

The author's life on Long Island was documented in 1949 in "The Far Side of Paradise," by biographer Arthur Mizener. The Fitzgeralds rented a modest stucco house at 6 Gateway Dr. in Great Neck Estates in 1922, beginning a tireless whirl of party-going while Fitzgerald worked in a room above the garage, rewriting his only play, "The Vegetable," and starting a novel about a man named Gatsby.

Great Neck was transformed in the novel into West Egg, where newly rich Gatsby rented an estate. Across an inlet, Sands Point became East Egg, land of old money and home of his impossible love, Daisy Buchanan, a dream girl modeled after Fitzgerald's wife, Zelda.

Working only casually on "Gatsby," Fitzgerald wrote lighthearted sets of rules for the inevitable weekend house party guests. One guideline noted: Visitors in search of liquor were requested not to break down doors, "even when requested to do so by the host and hostess." Driving a secondhand Rolls-Royce and employing three servants, Scott and Zelda claimed they needed at least $36,000 a year for living expenses.

Fitzgerald went on the wagon in 1923, knocked out a dozen magazine stories to pay his bills and departed for Europe the following summer. In France, Fitzgerald hoped to drink less and write more — and in 1925, "Gatsby" was completed.

His classic work was not designed to tell the full story of Long Island's privileged. In the Hamptons, for instance, many wealthy families lived in a more decorous style, throwing grand but tasteful parties when their daughters were married. Among the most celebrated debutantes of East Hampton and Manhattan were the Bouvier twins, Maude and Michelle.

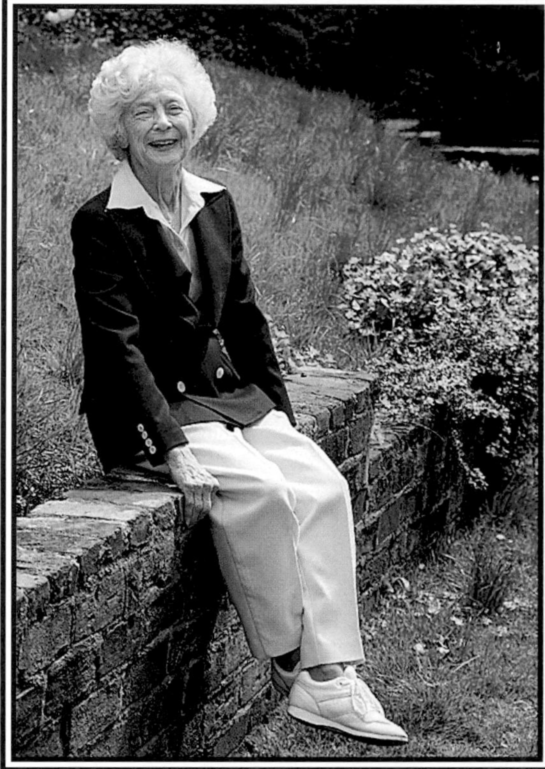

Newsday Photo / Bill Davis

Olive Darling Photo

Olive Darling today, at her Suffolk County home, recalls growing up in Port Jefferson as tame compared to the life youngsters lead now, "and I loved those times." Darling, at left above, and friends dressed for a costume party circa 1920.

Maude Bouvier Davis, now 93, sighs when she recalls the Hamptons in the 1920s: "It was Arcadia," she said in a recent interview. Her memory of the Jazz Age is still a vivid picture of a woodland paradise.

In later years, her brother Jack would become even more famous when his daughter, Jacqueline Bouvier, married John F. Kennedy and, in 1961, became the nation's first lady. But Maude and Michelle had brilliant weddings of their own at Lasata, the family's estate on Further Lane in East Hampton.

For Michelle's wedding in the summer of 1926, a flower-decked altar was erected on a terrace and 200 guests were seated on the lawn. Two years later, on a stormy Labor Day, Maude was married to stockbroker John E. Davis in Lasata's spacious living room. The scene is described in a history of the family by Maude's son, John H. Davis, whose work, "Jacqueline Bouvier: An Intimate Memoir," was recently published in paperback.

"Maude remembers that just as she said, 'I do,' the sun streamed through the great French windows," Davis wrote. Then, the wedding party streamed onto the terrace where a jazz band struck up a Charleston. Bridesmaids and ushers bobbed up and down to the beat, Davis wrote, while Michelle, the matron of honor, led the dancing like a high-stepping Rockette.

In 1923, when the twins were 18, their photos appeared often in the society sections of New York newspapers. "Oh, my," Maude Davis sighed again, "those debutante parties at the Ritz Carlton!" But Maude did not find the Roaring '20s to be an exceptional time: "We were doing all the usual things. We went to boarding school at Miss Porter's. We went to coming-out parties at Sherry's. We did all the things debutantes did."

She was aware, of course, of Prohibition and the young men who carried their whiskey in hip flasks. "Oh, everyone smiled at things like that," she said. "But my twin and I were probably the most stupid innocents in East Hampton. We never drank or smoked. I don't know why . . . We were from an old family in New York. We didn't worry about keeping up with the Joneses. We *were* the Joneses. But we had a wonderful time, just dancing and singing at parties."

Certainly there were "wild girls" in her set. "They were smoking and drinking and doing all kinds of things, running around without a chaperon." When she and Michelle went to parties, a maid rode in their taxi with their escorts. "My God, you couldn't come home alone with a man at two in the morning!," she said.

"I remember one Princeton house party. My date's roommate escorted a beautiful actress. Later, she and I went back to this very nice house where we were staying. And, my gosh, I was mortified! She got up and went out with another man and didn't come back until 6 in the morning. And her poor date was paying all the expenses."

In East Hampton, they were surrounded by gorgeous houses with immaculate lawns, and miles of corn fields and potato farms. They'd play golf and tennis and swim in the surf off the Maidstone Club, or go horseback-riding, cantering by windmills and saltbox mansions and salt marshes in the distance. And on Saturday nights, there would be dinner-dances at the Maidstone Club in formal dress.

Those were the Roaring '20s as Maude Davis remembers them. But then, the roar became a moan for many Americans. Illusions of unending prosperity slipped away in late October of 1929, when investors began to sell off their stock market holdings. On Oct. 29, stockholders sold off more than 16 million shares, many bought on credit, plunging prices by 40 percent before Thanksgiving Day. With the stock market crash of 1929, the nation's inflated sense of well-being abruptly ended: The Great Depression was just around the corner.

John H. Davis Photo

A 1926 painting of the Bouvier twins, Michelle, left, and Maude, among the most celebrated debutantes of East Hampton and Manhattan. Their niece was Jacqueline Bouvier Kennedy.

A rumrunning boat and cargo ashore on Fire Island in 1930: The Atlantic Ocean off Long Island was known as Rum Row during Prohibition, the period from 1920 to 1933 when alcohol was banned in the United States.

Nassau County Museum Collection, Long Island Studies Institute

Rumrunners Run Around LI

BY BILL BLEYER
STAFF WRITER

Hijacking on the high seas, gun battles on the highways, federal agents pouring evidence into funnels in their vest pockets, public officials on the take, gangsters torturing innocent victims with red-hot potato mashers. Dutch Schultz. Izzy and Moe. The real McCoy.

All that was happening on and around Long Island during the tumultuous time called Prohibition. A nickname for the Atlantic waters bordering the Island summed it all up: Rum Row.

For the 13 years that America was supposed to be dry after the Volstead Act went into effect in 1920, Long Island was the right place at the right time for rumrunners. It was close to New York City and had 1,180 miles of coastline with lots of out-of-the-way creeks and deserted beaches. It also featured both cops and Coast Guardsmen perfectly willing to accept bribes or even unload cargoes.

The booze came from Canada or the Bahamas on schooners or freighters that hovered just outside American waters with prices posted in the rigging. The most famous occupant of Rum Row was captain William McCoy, who bought a schooner named the Arethusa and turned it into a floating liquor store with free samples and a machine gun on the deck. While many suppliers offered watered-down liquor, McCoy developed a reputation for selling high quality stuff at fair prices. Buyers would seek out the Arethusa to get "the real McCoy," giving birth to the expression.

The first rumrunners who brought the booze ashore were enterprising fishermen in their own boats. Soon they were joined by other entrepreneurs in faster boats. The Freeport Point Boatyard built more than 30 rumrunning boats, and it also built 15 Coast Guard vessels designed to catch them.

"They knew the Coast Guard boats were going about 26 miles an hour so they made the rumrunning boats to go near 30 loaded," said Fred Scopinich Jr., 71, whose father and uncle ran the boatyard. "They were making rumrunners for *everybody*" — from cops and elected officials to gangster Dutch Schultz, who set up shop in Patchogue. It was no secret what the boats would be used for, especially when a boat like the Maureen was equipped with three surplus aircraft engines and a bulletproof pilothouse.

Most of the booze was unloaded at a dock or beach and trucked to speakeasies on the Island or in New York City. Occasionally it was brought ashore by seaplanes or carried away on LIRR freight trains.

The bottles were often removed from the case and transported wrapped in straw inside burlap bags for easier handling. Some rumrunners put salt and cork in the bag. If they were being intercepted, they threw the bags overboard. When the salt dissolved, the bags resurfaced for retrieval.

No Long Island community thumbed its nose at Prohibition more than Long Beach. City historian Roberta Fiore said that one police commissioner, Moe Grossman, organized all rumrunning in the city. Municipal employees reportedly used the light in the clock tower of the old City Hall to signal rumrunners when it was safe to land. In 1930, five Long Beach police officers were charged with offering a bribe to a Coast Guard officer to allow liquor ashore.

"You could tell the Volstead Act was not being enforced," said Greenport village historian Jerome McCarthy. "There were several rumrunning boats tied up at the railroad dock, and the Coast Guard boats would be tied up on the other side of the dock and the crews would talk to each other." In Freeport, rumrunners and government agents gathered every afternoon at Otto St. George's restaurant to make small talk and drink illegal booze. Coast Guard Capt. Frank Stuart was accused of taking $2,000, the equivalent of a year's pay, to let fishing boats land liquor in Montauk. And in 1932 the Coast Guard officer in charge of the Georgica Station in the Hamptons was sentenced to a year in jail for aiding rumrunners.

UPI Photo

Moe Smith, left, and Izzy Einstein, Prohibition agents, check out a still they confiscated during a raid in 1923.

Not everyone was on the take. Roland Baker, a 92-year-old retired Patchogue police officer, remembers that "there were a lot of bootleggers around here. They would offer police officers $25 when they were off-duty to come at night and help unload liquor down at a creek, but I didn't get involved in that."

In 1923 famous Prohibition agents Izzy and Moe raided the Nassau Hotel in Long Beach and arrested three men for bootlegging. Postal clerk Isidor Einstein and cigar store owner Moe Smith were hired by the federal government even though they looked nothing like Elliot Ness, but they had great imagination and a gift for impersonation. Once Izzy talked his way into a speakeasy by "portraying" himself. "I'm a Prohibiton agent," he proclaimed. "I just got appointed." Everybody laughed until he busted them. The two boys from Brooklyn collected evidence by pouring booze into a funnel in Izzy's vest pocket that was connected via a rubber tube to a flat bottle hidden in the lining.

For honest enforcement personnel like Izzy and Moe, it was a dangerous profession. Gun battles between agents and tommy gun-toting gangsters were common. "Coast Guard Shot In Rum Seizure," reads the headline in the Center Moriches Record of May 12, 1932.

Dutch Schultz was the most infamous gangster bootlegging on Long Island, but there were lesser lights like Charles (Vannie) Higgins and Larry Fay. Competition was spirited. Sam Grossman of Brooklyn was dumped along a quiet road in Brightwaters with three bullets in his head. The body of Arthur (Happy Whelan) Waring was found by a clammer in the same area, trussed to a lawnmower.

Gangs whose hooch was hijacked took a sober attitude. In 1931, Thomas Farrell Jr. and Jacob Antilety, both 21, were walking in Southampton when they were kidnaped by mobsters who accused them of stealing booze. They were tortured all night with a heated potato masher applied to their feet before being released.

Booze that wasn't seized by the law made its way to speakeasies, which weren't very hard to find. Long Island's most famous speakeasies included Frank Friede's in Smithtown, Texas Guinan's in Lynbrook and the Canoe Place Inn in Hampton Bays, where bootleggers could rub elbows with notables including New York Gov. Al Smith. There were no peepholes or secret passwords as depicted in the movies.

"It was all very open," Jack Greaney of Massapequa, whose father owned speakeasies, said recently. "Prohibition wasn't a very popular law."

Stung by anti-Semitism, Otto Kahn moves to LI and constructs 127 rooms

His Home *Was* a Castle

Newsday Photo / Bill Davis

Done in the style of a French chateau for financier Otto Hermann Kahn, the 127-room, 62,000-square foot mansion called Oheka was completed in Cold Spring Harbor in 1919.

Aerial View From Gary Melius, Oheka Castle; Newsday Photo / Bill Davis

An aerial view circa 1920 shows the gardens and the golf course; above, the ornate library.

BY BILL BLEYER
STAFF WRITER

Otto Hermann Kahn was a rising figure in the banking industry and a generous patron of the arts. But to his wealthy neighbors in Morristown, N.J., in the early 1900s, Kahn had an overriding fault: He was Jewish.

Shunned by social and cultural organizations, Kahn was blackballed even by a golf club whose members he allowed to play on his private course. In anger, he sold the estate and moved briefly to London, where he had lived before without experiencing anti-Semitism. Then, in 1914, when his standing in the banking world rivaled that of the great J.P. Morgan, he made a statement that no one could ignore. He purchased 443 acres in Cold Spring Harbor and built a castle called Oheka.

The estate proclaimed his stature as a financier and philanthropist whom Will Rogers called "The King of New York." Surpassed only by George Washington Vanderbilt's 250-room Biltmore in Asheville, N.C., it remains the second largest house ever built in the United States. When it was completed in 1919, Oheka — the name drawn from letters in Kahn's name — would contain 127 rooms and 62,000 square feet. Enrico Caruso would sing arias and Arturo Toscanini would conduct symphonies in the great ballroom. And in 1941 Orson Welles would film the exterior and gardens to serve as the home of Charles Foster Kane in "Citizen Kane."

Gary Melius, Oheka Castle

Otto Kahn in about 1920

Kahn was no Kane, but like the protagonist of the film, he enjoyed a privileged upbringing. Born in Germany in 1867, the banker's son was tutored privately at home and learned to play the piano, violin and cello. At 16, he became an apprentice at an investment firm. Ten years later, after a career stop in London, he was in New York working for the banking firm Speyer & Co.

Kahn hit the ground running in the United States and never left the fast track. In 1896, he married Addie Wolff, daughter of Abraham Wolff, a partner in the banking firm of Kuhn, Loeb and Co. Kahn had arrived in the states with all of his possessions in one suitcase. Only three years later, the newlywed had accumulated enough money to take a year-long honeymoon in Europe and buy an extensive art collection that included paintings by Rembrandt and Matisse.

Wolff offered him a partnership at Kuhn, Loeb, where Kahn spent the rest of his career. The bride's father commissioned a 100-room home on more than 140 acres in Morristown for the couple, who also made do with a townhouse in Manhattan. A blaze in the Morristown mansion destroyed many pieces of art, and Kahn would insist that all his future homes be fireproof.

A small, dapper man rarely seen without a gold-tipped ebony cane, Kahn preferred discussing the arts to talking about Wall Street. He donated large sums to charity, saying "I must atone for my wealth." He joined the board of the Metropolitan Opera Co., which he reorganized and saved from bankruptcy. As the opera's chairman, Kahn brought Caruso and Toscanini to the New York stage.

Kahn, who also had homes in Manhattan, Wisconsin, Florida and the Adirondacks, reportedly spent more than a million dollars for the Cold Spring Harbor property. He wanted his dream house to tower over the rest of Long Island, so workers spent two years piling up dirt with horse-drawn wagons to provide the proper setting. The house was designed by William A. Delano, one of the Gold Coast's premier mansion builders. Olmstead Brothers, the firm founded by Central Park designer Frederick Law Olmstead, planned the bridle paths and gardens.

The result was a five-story chateau patterned after the castles of France. It boasted a sweeping marble staircase in the entrance hall, a 2,500-square-foot ballroom with a ceiling nearly 60 feet high, 20 lavish bedroom suites and 49 fireplaces. As one might expect of a castle, there was a secret room off the library entered through a panel in one of the bookcases.

Several large airshafts ran through the foundation, allowing fresh air to move through the house and keep it cool even on the hottest summer days. Because gratings covered the conduits' openings on the hillside, rumors circulated that Kahn was keeping lions and tigers in the basement.

One of the finest 18-hole golf courses in the country was constructed on the grounds, even though Kahn showed little flair for the sport. The golf course and the stables make up today's Cold Spring Country Club. The estate included one of the largest greenhouse complexes in the country (now Otto Keil Florists), a gatehouse (now a real estate office), formal gardens with reflecting pools, fountains and statuary, a working farm and dairy, an indoor pool, tennis courts, an airstrip and a racetrack.

Kahn, his wife and four children moved into their new place in 1919. A private railroad spur and station was available for the family, their employees and guests. Kahn, who finally gained much of the social acceptance he craved, frequently had 50 or 60 dinner guests and sometimes the dining room was filled to its capacity of more than 200. Another rumor was that each egg in Kahn's Easter egg hunts contained a crisp $1,000 bill.

On March 29, 1934, Kahn suffered a fatal heart attack. He was 67. The funeral service was held in the ballroom at Oheka and Kahn was buried in St. John's Cemetery in Laurel Hollow. Kahn's widow could no longer maintain the estate and its 126-person staff, and it would endure future incarnations as a retreat for New York City sanitation workers and a government training school for merchant marine radio operators.

In the late 1940s, an upscale housing development was constructed on 256 acres. In 1948, Eastern Military Academy bought the mansion and 23 acres around it. Before going bankrupt 30 years later, the school bulldozed the gardens, subdivided rooms and painted over the paneled walls.

When the cadets marched out of Oheka, vandals moved in and set more than 100 fires. But Kahn's insistence on fireproofing paid off — the concrete, brick and steel shell resisted the onslaught. In 1984, Mineola developer Gary Melius purchased the estate for $1.5 million and poured $14 million into a partial restoration. After five years as lord of the manor, Melius sold the estate for $22 million, but continued to manage it — renting the mansion for weddings and other functions.

Last December the Town of Huntington approved Melius' application for a historic-zoning designation that will allow him to complete the restoration and convert the building into a luxury health spa by 2005. If that happens, Otto Kahn's castle may return to a semblance of its former splendor.

When a fashionably attired corpse washed ashore, the DA and the press knew what to do

A Body of Evidence on LI

BY STEVE WICK
STAFF WRITER

She was a lovely corpse.

Her nails were painted a bright red, her silk dress an expensive design she might have worn to a society party in New York City. And although her hair had been tossed around in the surf, you could still see the outlines of a fashionable cut.

The body was lying in a pile of seaweed on a deserted stretch of sand in Long Beach when five Nassau County detectives arrived. It was the morning of June 8, 1931. That day's edition of the Nassau Daily Review said:

Police today were seeking to identify the body of a young woman, about 24 years old, expensively dressed and apparently of a wealthy family, who was washed ashore at the foot of Minnesota Avenue, West Long Beach, early this morning . . . She had dark brown hair, apparently hennaed, well manicured nails, finished in a bright red polish, and perfect teeth.

By noon, Nassau County Police Insp. Harold King believed the dead woman was Elizabeth Wardwell, the daughter of an upstate bank president, who had been reported missing. But by the following morning, King also was trying to determine if the dead woman was Catherine Hill, 26, of Provincetown, Mass.

It would be another two days before a name was finally attached to the corpse: Starr Faithfull, the well-to-do daughter of a Manhattan society couple. STARR FAITHFULL fit perfectly into a splashy headline, over stories filled with talk of murder and cover-up, political intrigue, wild partying on cruise ships, Manhattan society affairs and mysterious diary entries.

"This was one of those cases that grabbed people's attention," retired Nassau County chief of detectives Ed Curran said recently. "When I came on in 1946, the old-timers were still talking about it."

Today, the only way to reconstruct the events that followed the discovery of Faithfull's body is to read newspaper accounts. The principals in the case — from King to the then-Nassau District Attorney Elvin Edwards, who said from the get-go that Faithfull had been murdered and boasted two days after the body's discovery that an arrest was imminent — are all dead. Edwards' voluminous records on the case have never been found.

Yet the case of Starr Faithfull, her life and death as told across the pages of New York's newspapers, is still intriguing today. In some ways, it was 20th Century Long Island's first big crime story. Or was it a crime story?

Within a day of Faithfull's body washing up on the beach, District Attorney Edwards had seized the story by the throat and was squeezing hard for all it was worth. A story on June 9 in the Nassau Daily Review — with a headline that read MALE COMPANION OBJECT OF HUNT — said Edwards had determined that the victim "had been subjected to physical violence before her body was thrown into the ocean."

Nassau County Museum Collection, Long Island Studies Institute

Starr Faithfull, whose death in 1931 inspired plenty of headlines but no indictments

His statement that the death was the result of "foul play" was based on bruises on her body, the story said. Police sources were quoted as saying Faithfull — "an aspiring writer" who apparently never wrote anything — had been kidnaped from her home in Manhattan and brought to Long Beach, where she was killed and her body tossed into the surf. This story also noted — in a way that suggested it meant something to the case — that Faithfull's next door neighbor in New York was the mayor, James J. Walker.

By June 10, two days after Faithfull's body washed up on the beach, the headlines screamed: GIRL'S KILLERS KNOWN; HUNT LEADS TO BOSTON. Under this headline in the Nassau paper, was another: DISTRICT ATTORNEY, MAINTAINING SECRECY, ANNOUNCES MEN SOUGHT FOR STARR FAITHFULL MURDER WELL KNOWN.

The first paragraph of the story read: "Seeking two men he has labelled 'the murderers of Starr Faithfull,' whose body was found at Long Beach early Monday morning, District Attorney Elvin Edwards was in Boston today."

Asked if Faithfull might have committed suicide, Edwards was quoted as saying, "Do you think I would be working like this if it were a suicide?" The story went on to say that Edwards "told reporters he was looking for two men who were with Faithfull Friday morning, when she was last seen. He expects an early arrest. He said he knew the names of the men and that one played an important role in New York political circles."

What did Edwards mean by "political circles"? Was he referring to the mayor, Jimmy Walker? "Sources" told the newspaper that Edwards and his investigators had grilled crewmen on a cruise ship docked in New York Harbor because of reports that a drunken Faithfull had been taken off the boat a few days before her death. "As attendants were placing her in a small boat, she screamed: 'Kill me. Throw me overboard.' "

Edwards had a new theory, too, according to the account. "Edwards' theory is that Miss Faithfull was murdered in New York and carried to Long Beach by taxicab. He believes her assailants placed her in a row boat during the night and carried the body out to sea . . . Edwards has secret information to support his belief."

On June 12, the Nassau paper trumpeted: STARR FAITHFULL DIARY MAY REVEAL BLACKMAIL — SLAYERS HIRED TO END CAREER. The story said investigators had learned that Faithfull had frequented "underworld haunts" and "revelled in the company of known killers and desperate criminals. The investigation also revealed her wide knowledge of men whose shady character and nefarious deeds would make them unwelcome in her plutocratic drawing room."

Edwards would ask for indictments that morning, the paper said. A source — presumably Edwards himself — told the paper that Faithfull's diary centered on "men, men, men — all sorts of men in all walks of life." And the source said she met her killers at a party aboard a cruise ship, the Franconia.

But newspapers of the next day, June 13, downplayed virtually every point made in the papers of the day before. The grand jury probe was a "disappointment," the Nassau paper said. Three days later, on June 16, Edwards told reporters he had been "deliberately and generally misquoted" by the newspapers.

On June 15, Edwards told reporters he was searching for a Chicago gang leader named "Blue," and his blond girlfriend, who he said had partied in New York with Faithfull the night before she disappeared. Ten days later, on June 25, Edwards' investigators questioned New York publisher Bennett Cerf, who said he had been at the party and had seen Faithfull.

But all this was talk, and by June 26, three weeks after the death, a small story in the Nassau paper said the case would soon be closed. The next day, Faithfull's father was quoted in the newspapers as saying Edwards was afraid to make arrests because "big" people were involved.

And that was that. Case closed.

FAST FORWARD

U.S. Postal Service

Two vestiges of 1920s Long Island retain commercial and historic value for the U.S. Postal Service, which issued these Gatsby and Lindbergh stamps nationwide on May 28 as part of a sheet of 15 first-class stamps representing that decade.

For Alva Erskine Smith Vanderbilt Belmont and other suffragettes, 'Failure is impossible'

LI's Rebels With a Cause

BY KATHY LARKIN AND JOYCE GABRIEL

'Brace up, my dear. Just pray to God. *She* will help you."

That advice, which still might raise eyebrows today, was offered decades ago to a weary suffragette protester by Alva Erskine Smith Vanderbilt Belmont of Long Island, New York and Newport. The recommendation was typical of Vanderbilt Belmont, a dark-haired dynamo who pursued votes for women as vigorously as she had vaulted up the social ladder.

As a 30-year-old bride, she had outwitted society matriarch Carolyn Schermerhorn Astor — better known as "the" Mrs. Astor — who considered Alva nouveau riche despite her marriage to William K. Vanderbilt, and snubbed her. The then-Mrs. Vanderbilt gave a costume ball in her $3 million Fifth Avenue replica of a chateau. To secure her daughter's place at the ball, Astor was forced to come calling on the woman she had scorned.

Vanderbilt Belmont embraced women's suffrage with the same wit and determination. So did many other women with brains, education and money enough to make a difference in a battle that stretched back down the years to the mid-19th Century, when women's suffrage was entwined with abolition. In 1848, in upstate Seneca Falls, anti-slavery activists Lucretia Mott and Elizabeth Cady Stanton joined forces to fight for the women's movement with activists such as Susan B. Anthony. The two causes later split.

In the crucial two decades before Aug. 26, 1920 — when Congress finally passed the 19th Amendment to the Constitution, following the lead of many states including New York — other prominent women joined their sisters to pick up banners, march, protest, even get arrested. As Natalie A. Naylor, director of the Long Island Studies Institute at Hofstra University, points out, wealthy socialities with summer homes on the Island rallied to the cause. So did many women of Long Island's founding families such as Lisabeth Halsey White, who, in 1915, headed the Southampton League of the Congressional Union fighting for the 19th Amendment.

By 1909, Vanderbilt Belmont — who had a home in Oakdale, now Dowling College; another in Uniondale, where she launched the unsuccessful Brookholt Agricultural School for Women, and a third in Sands Point, built in the 1910s after the 1908 death of her second husband, horse-mad millionaire Oliver Hazard Perry Belmont — was deep into the women's movement. She gave the remainder of her life and much of her money to it.

On Aug. 24, she opened her palatial Marble House in Newport, R.I., modeled on Marie Antoinette's Petite Trianon, to periodic suffragette meetings, hanging its marble halls with great purple and gold banners carrying the last words of Susan B. Anthony: "Failure is impossible." Addressing that first gathering, Vanderbilt Belmont declared: "The wife should not be the unpaid servant of the husband, but both must be equal."

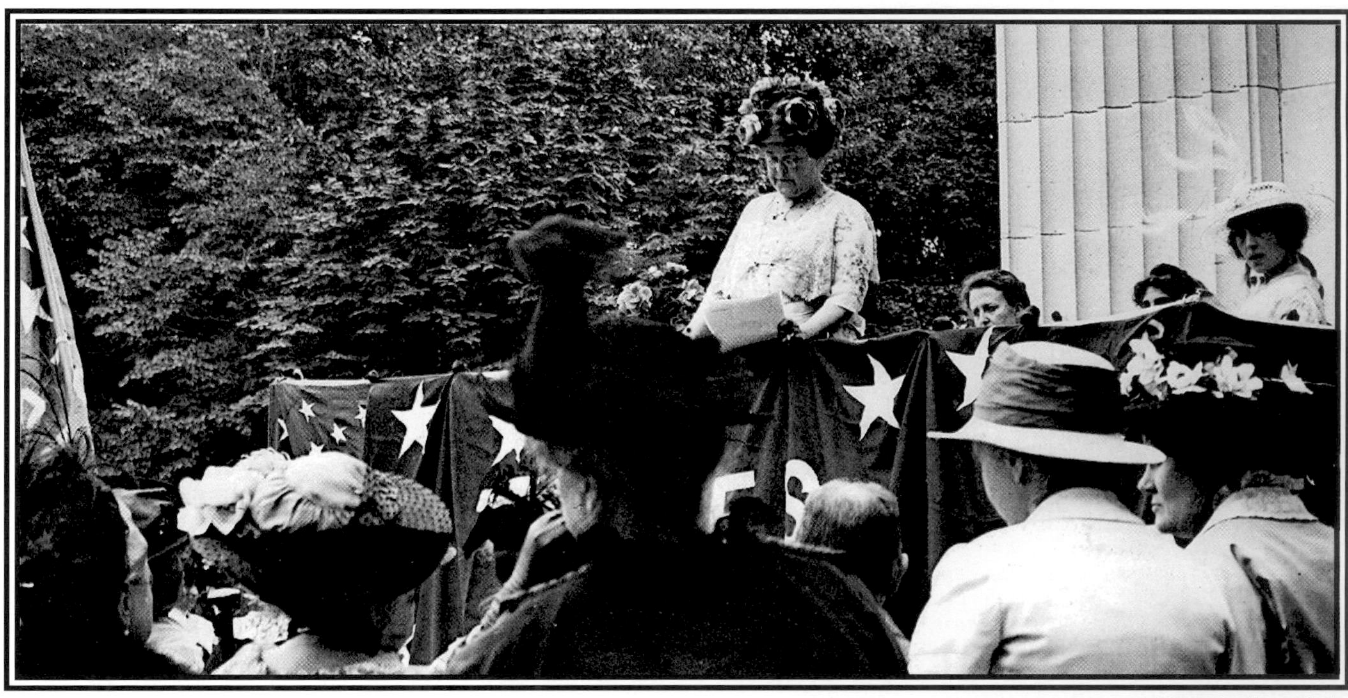

Brown Brothers Photo

Alva Erskine Smith Vanderbilt Belmont, addressing a meeting at her home in Newport, R.I., was among LI socialites who joined the cause.

That same year, she rented the 17th floor of a Fifth Avenue building as headquarters for her own Political Equity League and for the National American Woman Suffrage Association. She later broke with that group and its conservative leader, Carrie Chapman Catt, to head the National Woman's Party, made up of radical feminists who picketed Congress and the White House, went on hunger strikes and courted arrest. And she marched in the great 1912 Women's Vote Parade down Fifth Avenue at sunset, wrote a feminist operetta with party-giver Elsa Maxwell and had only women pallbearers when she died on Jan. 26, 1933, in France.

In 1911, Vanderbilt Belmont's path had crossed with that of another militant — Rosalie Gardiner Jones, descendant of Long Island's Jones, Livingston and Gardiner families and a lifelong resident of Cold Spring Harbor. Together with other suffragette leaders, the two harangued a crowd at the corner of Wall Street and Broadway, while ducking a barrage of eggs and tomatoes.

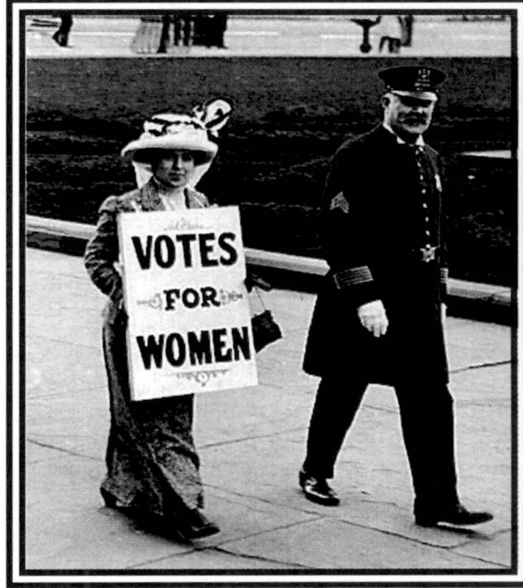

UPI Photo

A marcher in a 1920 suffrage parade in Brooklyn

A debutante who had been presented at the Court of St. James's, a girl with three brothers, a graduate of Adelphi College and Brooklyn Law School, Jones was smart, aggressive and, at 28, smitten with the idea that a woman was as wise as a man. She was also venturesome and commanding — traits that earned her the nickname "General."

With English suffragette Elisabeth Freeman, she crisscrossed Long Island in a horse-drawn wagon painted suffragette yellow and marked with names of all the states that had already granted women the vote. The march ended in May, 1912, in a mass meeting on Main Street in Huntington.

In December of that year, Jones gathered her troops for a 125-mile march from 242nd Street in Manhattan to the Legislature in Albany. For 13 days, the small army plodded through snow, rain and mud. Followers fell out and it was a small band of survivors that finally presented its petition to Gov.-elect William Sulzer. The press made "General" Jones and her parade headline news across America.

Jones — who, at 44, married U.S. Sen. Clarence Dill (D-Washington) and later divorced him — died alone and almost forgotten at 95 in a Brooklyn nursing home. Her ashes were scattered near her mother's crypt in Cold Spring Harbor.

But she and other feminists shattered barriers for generations to come. Writer Elizabeth Oakes Smith of Patchogue, who never lived to see women vote, was a powerful speaker for women's rights. So were Katherine Duer Mackay, who served on the Roslyn public school board from 1905 to 1910; Harriet Burton Laidlaw of Sands Point, and Helen Sherman Pratt of Glen Cove. Add Irene Davison of East Rockaway, who marched with Jones, and three-times-married Ida Bunce Sammis Woodruff Satchwell of Huntington, who became one of the first two women members of the state Assembly in January, 1919, about a year after New York had granted women the right to vote.

Kathy Larkin is a staff writer. Joyce Gabriel is a freelance writer.

WOMEN GO TO THE HEAD OF THE CLASS

In 1914, the battle for a woman's right to be her own person reached into the classrooms of Long Island. Records at the Seaford Historical Society show that when valedictorian Elsie Eldert rose to welcome parents and friends to the eighth-grade graduation class at Seaford Public School, she devoted a good part of her remarks to the topic of the day.

"We think we are a little smarter than last year's class and at least we know we are larger, and intent to carve our name far above the class of 1913," she said. "We are sorry that we have not more men in our class, but in these days, the young ladies must have their rights and good men are scarce."

The class colors, she explained, were yellow and white. "These colors are suggestive of Women's Rights as we often see in the city . . . big bows of white and yellow and just below is this sign 'Suffragette Headquarters.' " Choosing the same shades, she pointed out, "shows that we are up to the times. We do not intend to take a back seat, but will strive . . . for greater victory and success."

— Kathy Larkin

A stormy night, a faulty switch and death on the Shelter Island Express

The Great Pickle Works Wreck

BY BETH WHITEHOUSE
STAFF WRITER

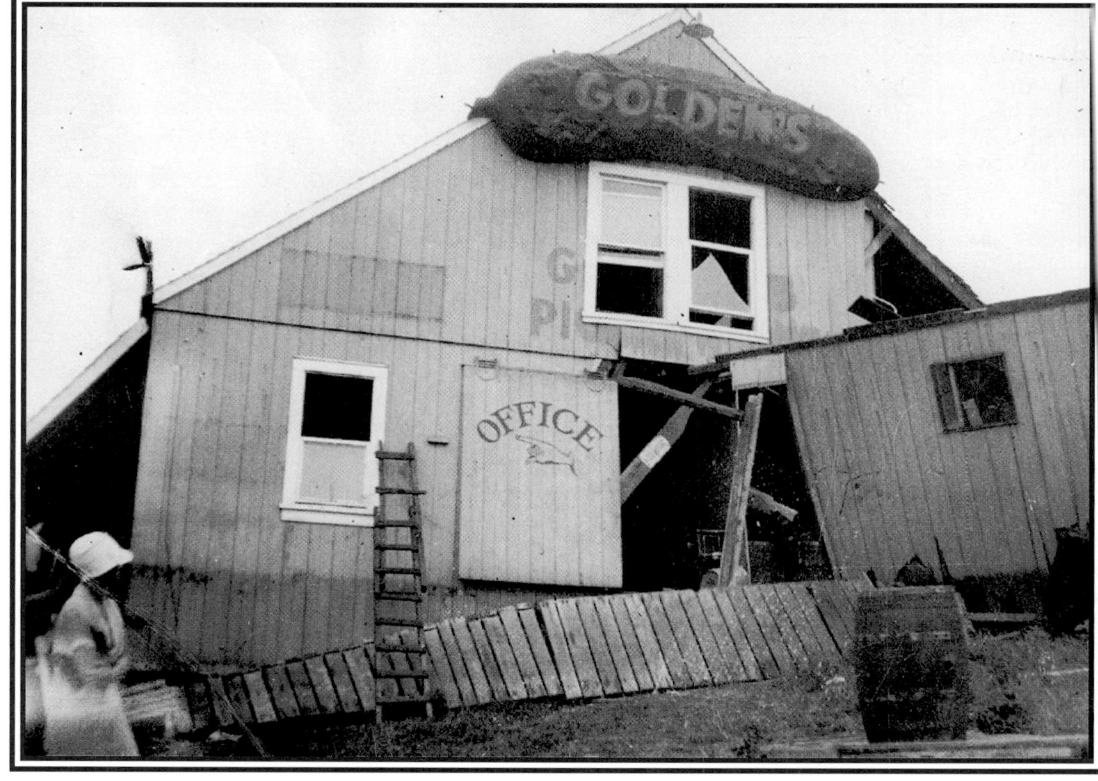

The Shelter Island Express derailed on Aug. 13, 1926, and slammed into Golden's Pickle Works in Calverton. Six people were killed, including two young children and their mother.

Photos From Collection of Ron Ziel

Gloom taunted the August night in 1926 even before the train crashed. Torrential lightning and rainstorms had plagued New York since at least the day before. The train was running 17 minutes late. And, if the power of superstition be respected, it was Friday the 13th.

As the yuppies of the era headed to the East End for a summer weekend escape from the city, the Long Island Rail Road had its most deadly Suffolk County crash in history. The Shelter Island Express plowed into a pickle factory in Calverton.

Six people were killed, including two young children and their mother, in what soon became known as the Great Pickle Works Wreck.

And one death was more horrific than the next. Harold Fish, a stockbroker and a member of an aristocratic New York family, was thrown from the posh parlor car into Golden's Pickle Works and trapped by twisted steel from the wreckage. Tons of salt from damaged barrels on an upper floor poured down on him like sand through an hourglass, smothering him as he yelled for help and struggled to push the salt away from his mouth.

Rescue workers couldn't cut away the steel quickly enough to get him out. Others managed to help another man in a similar position by cupping their hands above his mouth and catching the salt, which was used in the pickle brine, and tossing it aside as rescuers struggled to free him.

LIRR engineer William Squires and fireman John Montgomery were pinned against the boiler in the locomotive's engine room, crushed by tons of coals that tumbled out of the coal tender as the engine fell to its side off the tracks. The steam pipes burst, hitting them with blasts of 600-degree superheated steam.

"When they reached the body of one of the crew, they pulled him out and his legs stayed in the coal pile. He was like a lobster. Steamed," said railroad historian Ron Ziel of Water Mill, who has written six books about the Long Island Rail Road.

The wreck happened at 6:08 p.m. Engine No. 214 was leading the two-engine Shelter Island Express to Greenport with more than 350 passengers. The express traveled only on Fridays, taking people to weekend holidays. Accounts say it was traveling from 40 to 70 mph when it jumped a switch leading to the pickle works. The first engine fell to its side, while the second flew toward the factory with the train behind it, news reports said.

The Pullman parlor car, which was called Easter Lily, was directly behind the second engine, and every passenger who died in the wreck had been seated in that luxury car, with its chairs that swiveled and a waiter who served drinks. There was a smoker car and five day coaches on the train as well.

Decades ago, Ziel spoke with witnesses to the wreck, who told him the damaged train looked like a black worm. They said there had been the sound of a tremendous crash, and then dead silence.

The others killed were Mrs. George A. Shuford of Biltmore, N.C., and her two children, George A. Jr., 3, and Dorothy, 1. The two children were crushed in the parlor car wreckage. Their mother was pinned beneath the car for more than six hours, but was awake.

"Patiently and without a whimper Mrs. Shuford lay in the rain until the workmen had cut her free," reported The Brooklyn Daily Eagle. Workers cut through the steel around her with torches. Before she was extricated, she ate a sandwich and had coffee, The Eagle reported. But six hours after she reached Southampton Hospital, she was dead of internal burns suffered from inhaling steam. She had been assured her children were fine, The New York Times said, and still thought they were at the time of her death.

Shuford, an only child, had been with her parents in the parlor car. She had been visiting them for a couple of weeks. Her father, Charles A. Angell, was the head of a Brooklyn contracting firm and a well-known resident of Shelter Island. With Shuford as well was her maid, who also was pinned in the wreckage and had to have her left leg amputated to get her out.

Pictures from the day of the wreck show the pickle works caved into itself, with the almost comical giant sign shaped like a big, green pickle, still hanging above the attic windows. "Golden's," it said on the pickle.

There were various explanations for the wreck, from tampering with the track switch to its mechanical failure, said Vincent F. Seyfried, a Long Island Rail Road historian. "Probably no one could really pin it down," he said. "It's tough to reconstruct exactly what happened."

The most popular theory is that the disaster was caused by a missing cotter pin on the switch. A switch facilitates the movement of the train from one track to another. A nut and bolt fasten the control rod to the switch. The cotter pin keeps the nut from unscrewing and falling off.

In this case, investigators said that the cotter pin had not been replaced, perhaps during maintenance. Investigators surmised that when the first engine passed by the split where the main track divided from a side track leading to the pickle factory, the vibration of the passing locomotive caused the nut to work loose. The second engine then jumped off the main track toward the factory.

"For one lousy little piece of metal that, if stretched out, would have been 4 inches long, those people got killed and they had a terrible wreck," Ziel said.

About 300 rescuers worked by floodlights and flashlights and flashes of lightning to help the injured and to try to save the dying. The mud from the storms made their work slow and painstaking, newspapers reported.

The pickle factory was demolished and never reopened. The train locomotives, both more than 20 years old, were hauled to the scrap yard.

There's no sign now that the wreck ever took place. And life goes on.

In 1976, on the 50th anniversary of the Great Pickle Works Wreck, Ziel went to Calverton and hung a black wreath on a telephone poll near where the wreck occurred. And he took a picture as a modern LIRR train — with the same name, the Shelter Island Express — passed by his makeshift memorial.

This LIRR engine, the second of two pulling the train, crashed into the factory.

Born as a creature of commerce, the Big Duck grew to symbolize Long Island

It's a Tall Tail, but True

BY STEVE WICK
STAFF WRITER

In 1931, when Long Island was mired in the Depression, a Riverhead duck farmer named Martin Maurer had an idea he hoped would promote his business.

It was a big idea.

He decided to construct a 20-foot-tall concrete duck at the edge of his farm on West Main Street. It would be painted white, like the Peking ducks he raised, with a long orange beak. A door in its belly would open into a small shop, where Maurer would sell eggs and processed ducks.

Maurer's farm is long gone, but his Big Duck sits by the side of the road in Hampton Bays, at the edge of a Suffolk County park, an icon for a part of Long Island's history that has all but disappeared. It also is a symbol of the Island itself. Generations of people traveling to the East End for day trips or vacations passed the Big Duck on Route 24 and knew, as soon as they saw it, that their trip was almost over.

Newsday Photo / John H. Cornell Jr.

The Big Duck appeared unflappable in 1988 when it was removed from its second home, in Flanders, and escorted to Hampton Bays to perch near the entrance of Sears Bellows County Park.

Children still scream "There it is!" as they pass it; many families have bets on who will see it first; people stop to have their pictures taken in front of it. It is a concrete duck, a unique piece of roadside folk art, but it also is a keeper of family memories.

"It reminds people of their past," said Barbara Bixby, who works in the tiny gift shop inside the duck. "People walk into the shop and they are all smiles, as if all these memories have come back for them. It affects people of all ages. People honk their horns as they pass it. The word 'pilgrimage' comes to mind — people come to the Big Duck."

Maurer's idea didn't come out of nowhere. He had traveled to California and had seen big hats over restaurants, diners that looked like railroad cars and a giant coffee pot. He hoped the idea would work in Riverhead. It did. Maurer's Big Duck not only transformed his business, but put Riverhead on the map of America.

Today, there is only one duck farm left in the five East End towns. But there is still Maurer's Big Duck — glass-eyed, noble, sitting tall for an industry that barely exists on Long Island.

"It has become a major part of our heritage on Long Island," said Lance Mallamo, director of Suffolk County's Division of Historic Services. "I was there recently and a woman got out of her car with some kids, and she said, very seriously, 'Children, this is the Big Duck.' It's special. In our family when our kids were young, the person who saw it first would get a prize."

Sixty-seven years after it was built, the Big Duck sits at the edge of Sears-Bellows County Park. The small shop — which sells "duckabilia" — is operated by a group called Friends for Long Island's Heritage.

When it was built, the Big Duck joined dozens of roadside wonders across the country, looking like giant hats, or hot dogs, or milk bottles. Today, the story of the Big Duck — how it was built, and became a tourist attraction — is taught in some architecture schools.

"The Big Duck was the forerunner of 'duck architecture,'" Mallamo said. "Any building shaped like its product is called a duck."

It all began with one man's simple idea.

Like dozens of other duck farms in Riverhead, Maurer's farm sat alongside water — in his case, Upper Mill Pond. More than 30,000 white ducks waddled around the farm on their short journey from birth to death to dinner plate. All around Maurer, from Calverton to Aquebogue, were hundreds of thousands of ducks on more than 70 other farms. Riverhead sat at the epicenter of Long Island's duck universe.

Maurer hired a local builder, George Reeve, to help him build a duck covered in concrete. According to the Long Island Forum, Reeve — who had built barracks at nearby Camp Upton during World War I — asked his wife, Ella, to roast a chicken so he could study its skeleton.

Reeve hired two local brothers, William and Samuel Collins, to help with the design and construction. For additional inspiration, the brothers procured a live duck, which they tied to their front porch so they could study it. History does not tell us if their model lived on in honor or wound up in orange sauce.

When the head was complete, someone had a brilliant idea for what to use for eyes — a pair of tail lights from a Model T Ford. When it was completed that June, the Big Duck was 20 feet tall, 18 feet wide and 30 feet long. It had a little tail, and from the way it was built, appeared to be sitting on a nest. The Riverhead News, in a story that month, said, "Motorists passing through Riverhead now have something to remember us by; it is a big duck . . . and naturally it is attracting much attention."

Indeed. In November, 1932, a national magazine, Popular Mechanics, published an article on the duck. Maurer, seeing interest building in his creation, took out a design patent from the federal Patent Office. The Big Duck remained on Maurer's farm for only five years. In 1936, it was moved to Flanders, where it continued to serve as a place to buy eggs and processed ducks. In 1988, the 30-ton bird — facing possible extinction by a wrecking ball — was moved again and bought by Suffolk County. Not only has the Big Duck become a Long Island fixture, it also is acknowledged roadside art. Call it art ducko.

INTO THE 1950s, BUSINESS WAS JUST DUCKY

In its heyday, the Long Island duck industry was the marvel of the world. Of the eight million ducks produced nationally, more than six million per year came from Long Island.

"From the 1920s through the 1950s, we were the American duck business," said Doug Corwin, whose family owns Crescent Duck Farm in Aquebogue. Crescent is the last duck farm in Riverhead, where there once were dozens.

Through the 1950s, there were more than 70 duck farms on creeks and ponds throughout Brookhaven and the five East End towns. Today, according to Suffolk County officials, there are four duck farms left on Long Island. Still, the industry today is estimated to be worth approximately $18 million a year.

In the 1960s, county officials sought to close duck farms because of such environmental concerns as water pollution. Dozens were closed and the property was acquired by the county. Some of that land today is county parkland.

"I'm 39, and I remember 30 or 40 duck farms when I was a kid," Corwin said. "On every creek in Riverhead. Through the late 1950s, Long Island produced about six million ducks. Today, with the few farms left, we still produce about 2.5 million ducks.

"The East End was perfect for the duck industry. The climate was perfect, the land was perfect, there were farms all around. It wasn't to last. But we still produce a superior product."

— Steve Wick

Certified Duck Farm in East Moriches, pictured in 1957, had some 8,000 ducks.

Newsday Photo

'The wild ape' holds Smithtown hostage! Citizens are terrified! No one is safe!

Too Much Monkey Business

BY JOE HABERSTROH
STAFF WRITER

There was an ape on the running board.

That's what Bud O'Berry saw after he felt his father's car rock from the rear that afternoon as it was parked on Long Beach in Smithtown, near Pig Creek.

Bud O'Berry was 10 years old. He had looked back when the Willys-Overland touring car lurched.

Now he was face-to-face with the wild ape of Smithtown.

"His face was about a foot from mine," wrote O'Berry, who eventually became town historian and who died in 1987.

The boy and the ape blinked at each other.

Then Bud screamed.

The wild ape leapt from the running board and fled into the nearby woods.

"I think the poor ape was more frightened than I was," O'Berry wrote.

In that summer of 1918, as the world's geopolitical map prepared to dissolve and then reform with the climactic battles of World War I, a wholly different kind of alarm held sway in gentle Smithtown. A 90-pound primate — an adult chimpanzee, perhaps, and fleet of foot — had possibly escaped from a ship docked at nearby Port Jefferson Harbor and was on the loose. Whatever its precise biological classification, the intruder was known as "the great ape."

While no 1918 newspaper accounts exist to detail the wild ape's activities, older Smithtown residents have passed down the key information, and town financial records indicate with indisputable specificity that a local man was paid on Aug. 22, 1918, for the ape's apprehension and execution. Bud O'Berry's notebooks also have proven accurate over the years, agree former town historian Brad Smith, and Noel Gish, a Hauppauge High School teacher who has written a history of Smithtown.

"I can tell you that my daddy had a mind like a steel trap," said O'Berry's daughter, Ruth Ann O'Berry, who lives in Florida.

The lush and rolling landscape that distinguishes northern Smithtown to this day apparently provided the ape the necessary staging area for its general campaign of harassment.

From its leafy cover, the furry terrorist threw rocks and also reportedly attacked livestock.

"It was said that he could throw stones with deadly accuracy and that he killed many dogs in this manner," according to O'Berry's account. "It was also said that he would attack women and children in the same manner. The stories were so bad that women and children were afraid to venture out of the house unless the men of the house were present."

The wild ape ruled Long Beach, and this riled residents because it was a prime clamming spot. The Long Beach peninsula between Smithtown Bay and Stony Brook Harbor also provided a popular and breezy respite on those hot summer days.

Town leaders eventually placed a price on the head of the wild ape, and men with guns soon took to the woods.

One of those men was Norman O'Berry, proprietor of a gas station in St. James. O'Berry went hunting for the ape one day in August with his friend William Smith, their wives, and Bill Smith's sister, Annie. Also along was young Norman Jr., who was called Bud.

The Willys-Overland was a large open car and second in popularity in that era only to the Ford Model T. The elder O'Berry headed to Long Beach, and he parked the car on the sandy embankment between Pig Creek and Long Beach. Modern visitors would recognize this area as along Long Beach Road and just west of the town-operated marina.

"After hunting for an hour or so, my father and Bill came back and decided to go clamming as it was low tide," Bud O'Berry wrote.

The two men went splashing in the shallows opposite the creek.

The boy sat in the rear seat of the car probably in the shadow of the car's opened roof, which was pulled back and piled accordion-style atop the back seat.

"I felt the car go down . . . as someone stepped on the running board. I turned and looked and there was the ape standing on the running board, his face about one foot from mine."

This is where Bud screamed.

Norman Sr. and Bill Smith heard his cries and came running. By the time they got back to the car, the ape had scampered off across the sand and into the trees.

Just a few days later, a man named William Clark apparently succeeded in killing the ape.

Nellie Moseley, 87, who has lived in Smithtown her entire life, described Clark as a handyman whom she never saw "in anything but work clothes. He was a shuffling man. He lived on Meadow Road. He was well known."

At its meeting of Aug. 22, 1918, the Smithtown Town Board, as it did at every meeting, authorized the release of varying amounts of public funds.

Among the vouchers authorized, recorded in the flowing handwriting of Clerk Frank Brush:

"Wm. C. Clark, killing ape (wild) . . . $16.90."

FRANK BUCK'S ANIMAL KINGDOM OF EAST MASSAPEQUA

Joshua Soren Collection

Frank Buck poses with a simian friend in 1940.

When it came to exotic creatures, Frank Buck didn't monkey around. But his monkeys did.

On Aug. 22, 1935, 150 swinging simians hightailed it from Buck's jungle camp, situated just off Sunrise Highway in East Massapequa. They escaped by crossing a plank inadvertently left across a moat.

Frank Buck — the legendary big-game hunter and animal exhibitor, owner of the 40-acre Frank Buck Zoo, the man internationally famous for his motto, "Bring 'Em Back Alive" — wanted nothing more than to bring his monkeys that way.

The escapees left parts of two counties in rhesus pieces, scattering and chattering their way through local streets and, with no consideration for human commuters, stopping a Long Island Rail Road train. None of the monkeys had tickets.

The incident is a furry asterisk on the career of Buck, who in the 1930s was one of the most famous men in the world.

"He was a colorful guy, sort of an icon," says Carol Giannattasio of Massapequa, who never met Buck (she was only 2 when he died, at age 66 in 1950) but whose mother met him in Indiana.

Giannattasio got to know the native Texan through screenings of his films — including his most famous, the 1932 film "Bring 'Em Back Alive" — and reading his books.

Here's some of what she knows about Buck:

- He traveled the world but was terrified of airplanes. "He went everywhere by boat." In 1929, Buck and a boatload of his animals were caught in "the mother of all typhoons." Buck saved the creatures by "lashing them to the deck."
- When it came time in 1934 to open his grass menagerie, a sprawling outdoor exhibit that was among the first to feature cageless animal enclosures, Buck stopped here.

"He and a man named T.A. Loveland leased land from a man in Amityville who already had a lion house," Giannattasio says, adding that the Frank Buck Zoo was "south of Sunrise Highway, where Sears just left."

The zoo, which closed in the 1950s, had thousands of animals, including a 28-foot-long python that went to the Museum of Natural History when it died. The zoo also had monkeys. The ones that got away in 1935 were captured. Frank Buck brought 'em back alive. — **Jerry Zezima**

How planner Robert Moses transformed Long Island for the 20th Century and beyond

The Master Builder

BY GEORGE DEWAN
STAFF WRITER

One day in 1926 Robert Moses took several architects and engineers across the bay and onto a deserted sandbar called Jones Beach, where the quiet was broken only by the harsh squeals of the seabirds and the rhythmic pounding of the Atlantic waves. They looked around in disbelief as the animated, 37-year-old Moses spun a magical, futuristic vision of what would be one of the grandest bathing beaches in the world.

"It was the scale of the thing — nothing like this had ever been done in public recreation in America," one of the architects would recall later. "Here we were on an absolutely deserted sand bar — there was no way even to get there except by boat — and here was this guy drawing X's on the back of an envelope and talking about bathhouses like palaces and parking lots that held ten thousand cars . . . We thought he was nuts."

He was not nuts. He was Robert Moses.

Decades later, in a quiet moment when his years were winding down and most of his monument-building was behind him, Moses was asked what he was proudest of. "That's easy," he replied. "Jones Beach."

"Let us have no illusions about Jones Beach as we found it," Moses told the Freeport Historical Society in 1974. "It was an isolated, swampy sandbar accessible only by small boats and infrequent ferries, inhabited by fishermen and loners, surf casters and assorted oddballs, and beach combers trying to get away from it all . . . The tales told of a lovely, primitive, paradised wilderness with indestructible dunes were fiction."

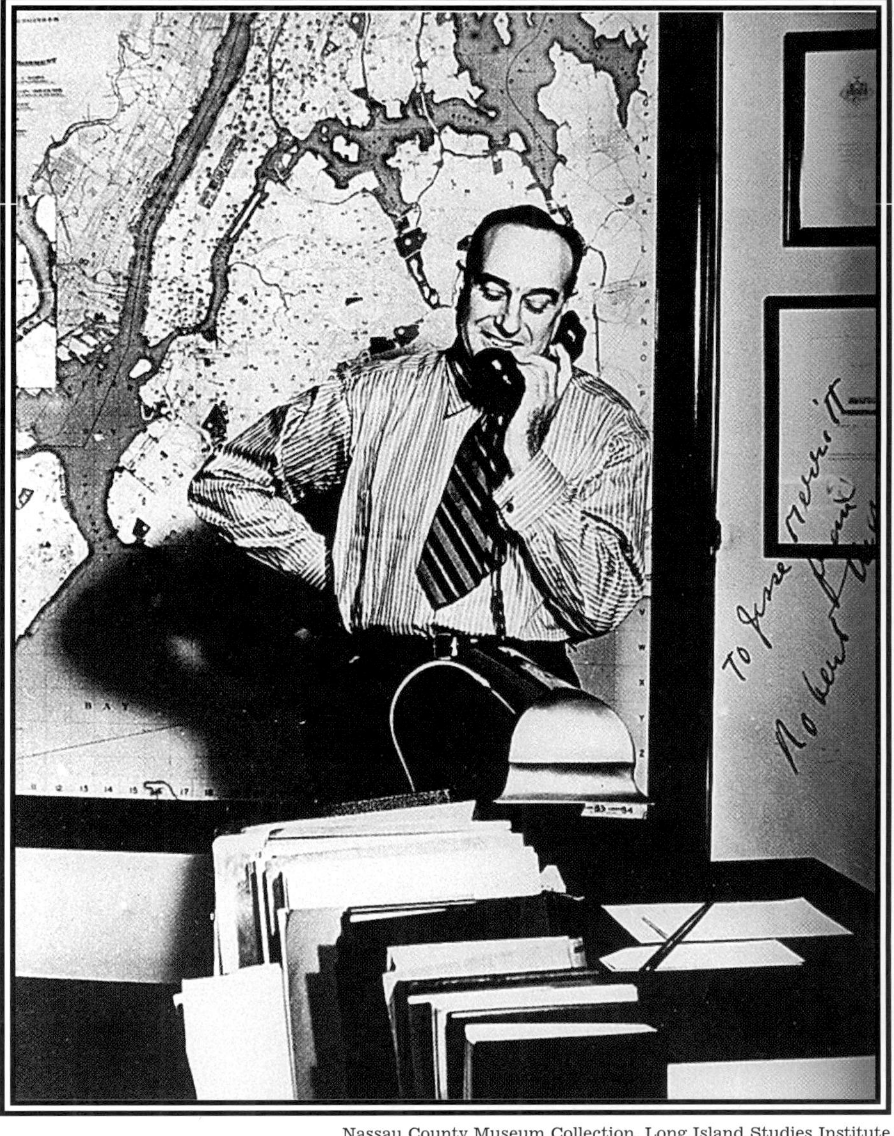

Nassau County Museum Collection, Long Island Studies Institute

Robert Moses: Though never elected to any office, he was among the state's most powerful men.

Before there was Robert Moses, there was an emptiness. The master builder filled this void with billions of dollars worth of bridges, tunnels, parkways, expressways, power projects, public housing, sandy beaches, concert halls and tens of thousands of acres of parkland.

Moses did as much to promote the use of the automobile as Henry Ford. For this, commuters, nature lovers, sand-worshippers and passionate autoists are forever in his debt. And also for this, critics who promote public transportation will never forgive him.

Whoever lives on Long Island or in New York City has been touched by Robert Moses. He was a builder, and his monuments are everywhere. There are the magnificent state parks, the parkways and expressways, and the cat's cradle of superhighways that moves traffic in and out of New York City. There are the mighty bridges and tunnels that tie the metropolitan area together, allowing motorists to move — sometimes at the pace of a snail — through, in and around the metropolis. In addition, there are Shea Stadium, Lincoln Center, the United Nations and the New York Coliseum. Also, huge New York City middle- and low-income housing projects. And, of course, both the 1939 and 1964 World's Fairs.

The public works projects that bear Moses' imprint — including upstate dams, superhighways and state parks as well — stagger the imagination. Between 1924 and 1968, according to Robert A. Caro's 1974 book, "The Power Broker," Moses developed projects costing $27 billion, which, adjusting for inflation, is about $125 billion today.

"More than any other single individual, this one man shaped Long Island as we know it, in its modern form," Caro said last week in a telephone interview. "He shaped it for the better, and a striking example is Jones Beach. And for worse, a striking example of which is the Long Island Expressway, which did not have to be built the way it was built. The building of the Long Island Expressway, the zoning policies with which he influenced communities, and the systematic starving of mass transit condemned Long Islanders to traffic jams for the rest of their lives."

"He in a sense, created the park system for Long Island," Lee Koppelman, executive director of the Long Island Regional Planning Board, said in an interview. "Certainly, the major jewel in the crown was Jones Beach, which is one of the finest beaches to be found in the world."

Koppelman says Moses ignored the fact that the superhighways he was building to carry people to his parks were destined to become jam-packed commuter roads, contributing to suburban sprawl. "Every time he extended a major road," he said, "all it did was create more traffic."

Moses has been criticized for not paying more attention to mass transit as an alternative to highways and automobiles, and is today blamed for much of the congestion on his own highways. He responded that mass transit was other people's business, not his.

The national flower is the concrete cloverleaf, city planner Lewis Mumford once said in derision. But Mumford, Moses' bitterest critic, knew success when he saw it. "In the 20th Century, the influence of Robert Moses on the cities of America was greater than that of any other person," he said.

"Anyone in public works is bound to be a target for charges of arbitrary administration and power broking leveled by critics who never had responsibility

Images and Maps From Long Island's Past

LI HISTORY.COM

Newsday's Internet site, lihistory.com, features photographs of every community and detailed maps published in the early 1900s. Expanding what was already the largest online archive of Long Island history, Newsday digitized more than 500 photos from a 1909 collection, "Long Island To-day," such as the one at right. The maps and photos are linked to the capsule histories written for "Our Towns," the special section published in February. To see the online exhibition, visit http://www.lihistory.com.

The Jamesport train station around 1900

Robert Moses' Legacy

Roads and parks in the metropolitan area in whose creation or reshaping Robert Moses played a dominant role as a government official from 1924 to 1968.

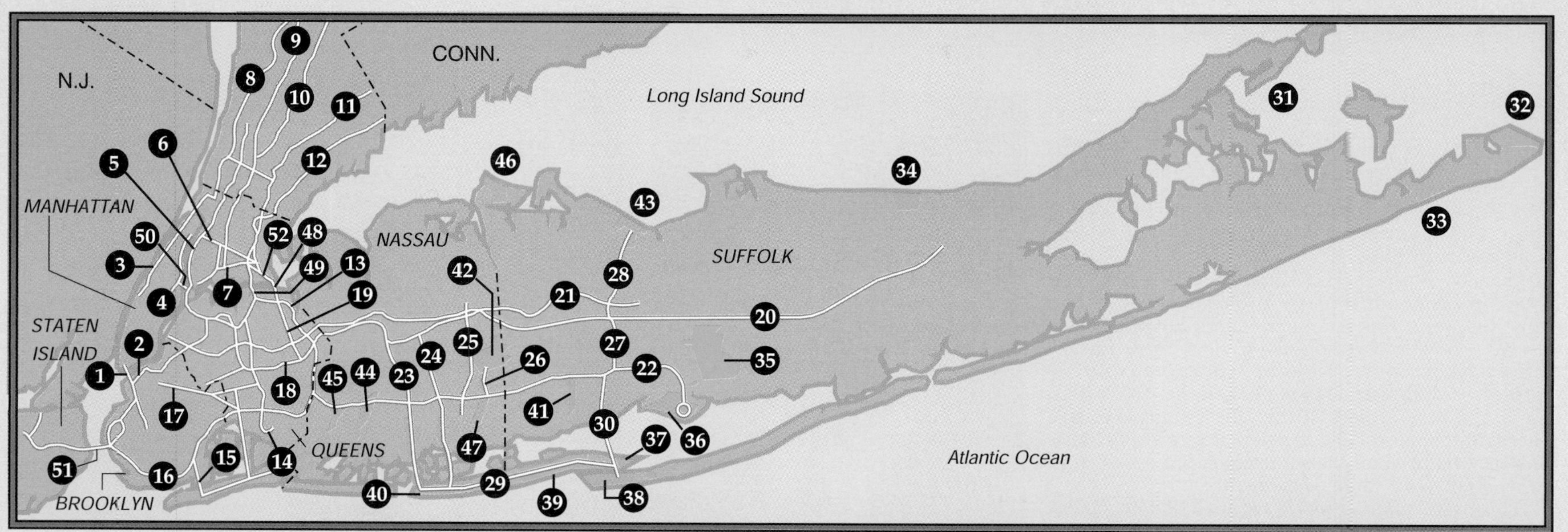

1. Brooklyn-Battery Tunnel
2. Brooklyn-Queens Expressway
3. Henry Hudson Parkway
4. Harlem River Drive
5. Major Deegan Expressway
6. Cross-Bronx Expressway
7. Bruckner Expressway
8. Saw Mill River Parkway
9. Sprain Brook Parkway
10. Bronx River Parkway
11. Hutchinson River Parkway
12. New England Thruway
13. Cross Island Parkway
14. Van Wyck Expressway
15. Marine Parkway and bridge
16. Belt Parkway
17. Atlantic Avenue
18. Grand Central Parkway
19. Clearview Expressway
20. Long Island Expressway
21. Northern State Parkway
22. Southern State Parkway
23. Meadowbrook State Parkway
24. Wantagh State Parkway
25. Seaford-Oyster Bay Expressway
26. Bethpage State Parkway
27. Sagtikos State Parkway
28. Sunken Meadow State Parkway
29. Ocean Parkway
30. Robert Moses Causeway
31. Orient Beach State Park
32. Montauk Point State Park
33. Hither Hills State Park
34. Wildwood State Park
35. Connetquot State Park
36. Heckscher State Park
37. Captree State Park
38. Robert Moses State Park
39. Gilgo State Park
40. Jones Beach State Park
41. Belmont Lake State Park
42. Bethpage State Park
43. Sunken Meadow State Park
44. Hempstead Lake State Park
45. Valley Stream State Park
46. Caumsett State Park
47. Massapequa State Park
48. Throgs Neck Bridge
49. Bronx-Whitestone Bridge
50. Triborough Bridge
51. Verrazano-Narrows Bridge
52. Throgs Neck Expressway

SOURCE: "The Power Broker," by Robert A. Caro; Long Island division of State Office of Parks, Recreation and Historic Preservation

Newsday / Linda McKenney

for building anything," the 86-year-old Moses responded to Caro in 1974. "I raise my stein to the builder who can remove ghettos without moving people as I hail the chef who can make omelets without breaking eggs."

Born of prosperous Jewish parents on Dec. 18, 1888, in New Haven, Conn., Moses grew up in New York City, where the family lived on East 46th Street, just off Fifth Avenue. He received degrees from Yale University, Oxford University and a doctoral degree in political science from Columbia. By this time, at 6-foot, 1-inch tall, he was athletic and broad-shouldered, an outdoorsman and a fine swimmer.

Thus intellectually armed, Robert Moses was loosed upon the world. Cultured, educated, sophisticated and not in need of a wage-paying job, he moved into New York City life with the passion of an idealist and a reformer. Registered as a Republican, he would make his friends and his enemies not on political grounds, but on personal ones. In 1914, one of these new friends was Frances Perkins, who would later become U.S. secretary of labor under President Franklin Roosevelt.

"He was always burning up with ideas, just burning up with them," Perkins later said. "Everything he saw walking around the city made him think of some way that it could be done better."

Moses was then only 25. The big ideas about making things work better would keep coming for the next 60 or so years.

Just before his 30th birthday, Moses fell into an opportunity that would change his life. In 1918, Democrat Al Smith had just been elected governor of New York for a two-year term (the length of terms at that time), and Smith asked Moses to become chief of staff for a new commission that was to reorganize the state administration. In the process, Moses became notoriously expert at drafting legislation, especially at writing a bill in which he could hide clauses that would further his own interests.

Telling other people how to reorganize their lives was a natural for someone with the talent and chutzpah of Moses. More important to Moses' career, however, was the beginning of a lifelong friendship with Smith, the poorly educated, gruff-voiced Irishman from the Lower East Side who virtually willed himself to become a great debater, one who could have his audience laughing one moment, crying the next.

Defeated for re-election in 1920, Smith won back the governorship in 1922, and he made Moses his right hand man, a sort of unpaid adviser. Moses jumped at the chance because it gave him his first taste of political power, a taste that would grow to a gargantuan appetite as the years went by. Smith was the only man Moses would ever call "governor." All others, and this included Franklin D. Roosevelt down to Nelson Rockefeller, Moses called by their first names.

State Office of Parks, Recreation and Historic Preservation

In 1929, Lt. Gov. Herbert Lehman and ex-governor Al Smith, left and center, officially receive Heckscher Park from mining magnate August Heckscher, who donated money to buy the land. The sprawling East Islip site was a major block in the system of L.I. parks that Moses would build.

In these years, one subject kept bubbling to the surface when Moses was on the prowl for problems to solve. Moses began thinking that the state should be getting involved in the planning and control of huge parks, well beyond the capacities and imaginations of the local town and county governments. One of the places he began thinking about was Long Island, with its vast open spaces.

In the summer of 1921, a friend invited him and his wife, Mary — they had married in 1915 and had two children — to weekend vacations in Babylon. It was the beginning of a lifelong love affair with the village, the Great South Bay and the entire South Shore. The next year, they rented a bungalow in Babylon for the summer, and later they would buy a house on Thompson Avenue, where their backyard was edged by Carl's Creek, which led to the bay.

Moses prowled around Babylon Town Hall. He was surprised to learn that in 1874 the City of Brooklyn, before it became part of New York City, had bought up water-carrying properties that ran the length of Nassau County and part of Suffolk. It was a hedge against a future water supply problem, a problem that never arrived,

Please see MOSES, Next Page

A Close-Up View, Warts and All,

By Tom Morris

I first met Robert Moses on a hot summer day in 1952. He was a big, talkative man with bronze-hued skin and flashing gray eyes set in a craggy face, hair tousled after swimming, the one recreation that was a lifelong obsession with him.

Usually, Moses swam in the creek behind his house on Thompson Avenue in Babylon Village, but when the water was too murky there he knew — as always — how to get things done. He'd phone ahead, throw a bathrobe over his swim trunks, hop into his big black chauffeured limousine with the "NY 2000" plate, and be delivered within five minutes to the waterfront home of old friends Rogers and Mary Howell, who lived on the same creek but a half-mile away, where the water was cleaner.

The master planner would swim a half hour, chat a half hour, take a Scotch, then disappear back into the limo.

I had dropped in on the Howells with a friend when we ran into Moses sitting in the screened-in porch that looks out on the canal. I was 23, a summer reporter for Newsday. Moses was 63, at the peak of his legendary career. I don't remember the conversation except that he was pleasant to begin with — and even more so when he learned that, summer job or not, I was working for a newspaper. Throughout his career, Robert Moses cultivated journalists.

On another Sunday morning when the limo apparently wasn't available, I saw Moses striding briskly along West Main Street in his bathrobe toward the Howells' place. Even now, the image lingers, seeming to catch the human side of this giant of public works with the well-deserved reputation for arrogance, vituperation, even tyranny in pursuit of his goals.

I thought about the man in the bathrobe during a long interview 20 years later. We were in his Randalls Island office beneath one of his great works — the Triborough Bridge.

To make a point, he pounded a fist on his desk, swiveled his big chair right up to me, stuck his face into mine, waggled an emphatic finger, and said, "Listen to me, chum. These ecologists are Johnny-come-latelys. In my day we called it 'conservation.' At Jones Beach, if we waited for the environment enthusiasts, the whole goddamn place would be covered with small cottages by now."

At the end of his career, Moses was still crusty.

We were never socially friendly, but during the next 27 years after that meeting at the Howells I would encounter him professionally many times and wonder at his complex and enigmatic personality.

Mary Howell, 80 now, said recently, "We were great friends because he had known me since childhood. He taught me how to swim when I was 5, but once he exploded at me right in my own living room."

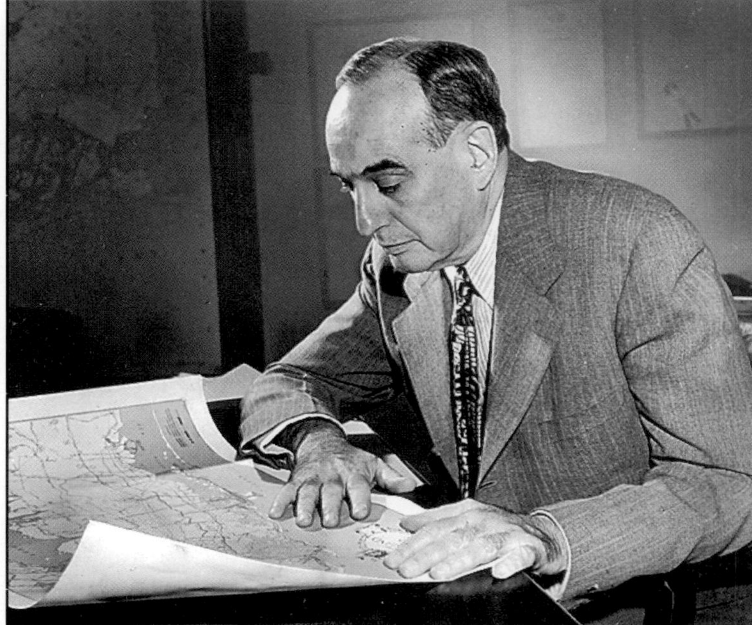

State Office of Parks, Recreation and Historic Preservation

Robert Moses as a gubernatorial candidate in 1934, left, and at work in 1947. He rose at 7 a.m. and pushed himself 16 hours or more a day, including Saturdays. But he tried to keep Sundays free to be with his wife, Mary, and their two daughters.

She had dared to suggest that, when he built the Ocean Parkway through Gilgo Beach in the 1930s, he should have installed a modest bridge so that tidal ocean water could get into Great South Bay to help cleanse it.

"Well, he was furious at that. He shouted at me, 'Mary, how could you say that? You don't know what you are saying. We know what we are doing. Where did you get your engineering degree?' Then just as fast, he cooled off and was nice as can be."

One stop on my rounds as a fulltime reporter for Newsday in the 1950s was Long Island State Park Commission headquarters at Belmont Lake State Park in North Babylon. Once in a while, Sidney Shapiro, a top Moses aide, would usher me into the great man's inner sanctum, the big room where he sat, tie pulled down, sleeves rolled up, snapping orders like an impatient general, pacing up and down, arms flailing, talking almost incessantly, a dynamo whirling around a huge table filled with blueprints and papers.

I was assigned to cover the opening of the Captree Causeway bridge across Great South Bay in June, 1954. After the ribbon-cutting, many of the anointed repaired to the Marine Dining Room at Jones Beach for one of those lavish, taxpayer-footed luncheons for which Moses was renowned — and that might have been the envy of a Roman emperor.

I sat with Moses for an hour at that event, though he worked the room off and on like a master politician. With the bridge in place, he said, his cherished road down Fire Island was "absolutely inevitable." Anyone who disagreed, he said with a scowl, "belongs in one of those tall brick places in Central Islip."

I told him I thought he was going to have fits with rich opponents on Fire Island. He got angry. "Your head is in the sand. That road will be built." It never was. The Fire Island National Seashore was established in 1964 instead.

One summer morning in 1959, I talked to Moses for two hours aboard the park commission cruiser Sea-Ef, moored near his house. This time he was the core of cordiality. He was sprawled out in a large green wicker chair in the cockpit, wearing old khakis, a faded plaid shirt and an oversized fedora hat.

I asked him some personal questions that might normally make him snort fire. He wasn't into golf, tennis or movies ("No time for that crap."), seldom went to the theater, disliked modern art and "dimwits" who couldn't write a simple letter, including some engineers he dealt with. ("We'd be better off if they were taught by crotchety old newspaper rewrite men.") He said he loved swimming, fishing, boats, beach picnics, baseball, gin rummy and all sorts of reading, from the 18th-Century poets he devoured as a Phi Beta Kappa at Yale to good whodunits.

For most of his life, Moses lived in Manhattan, notably at Gracie Square on the East River, but he owned the large old house in Babylon for almost 50

Moses, The Master Builder

MOSES from **Preceding Page**

so that the land lay undeveloped. A perfect place for a highway, Moses thought.

The almost-deserted barrier beaches, Fire Island and Jones Beach, separated by a narrow inlet, fascinated him. Moses would often take his old motorboat out through the reeds in the bay and pull up at Jones Beach, where he would sit and think and marvel at the possibilities for this almost virgin spit of sand.

"Sometimes, when Bob Moses stepped out of his boat onto Jones Beach, he could not see another human being," Caro wrote. ". . . He had returned to it a hundred times, pushing and pulling his little boat through the reeds, to sit lonely on the beach with wind rustling his hair, drinking in the wild, desolate scene."

There were millions of people longing to escape the sweltering New York City streets, if only for a day's relaxation, Moses thought. And Long Island could be that vacation haven. All it would take would be a road to get them there. A large part of the right-of-way was already owned by the city. One property even went all the way down to Great South Bay, directly across from Jones Beach.

"That was the idea behind Jones Beach and the Southern State Parkway," Moses told Caro. "I thought of it all in a moment."

Suddenly, Moses' imagination took off, as he began thinking about the possibilities for the rest of Long Island, as well as the rest of New York State. Moses never learned to drive, but he had himself chauffeured all over the Island, and everywhere he went, he saw other potential state park sites.

And he wanted not just one highway, but many, to get people to these parks. "He wanted 124 miles of parkways," Caro wrote. "And he wanted the parkways to be broader and more beautiful than any roads the world had ever seen, landscaped as private parks are landscaped, so that they would be in themselves parks, 'ribbon parks,' so that even as people drove to parks they would be driving through parks."

In 1923, Gov. Smith offered to make him president of the Long Island State Park Commission, which didn't even yet exist. Moses took on the job of writing the legislation to create it. As one of the craftiest writers of legislation in the state, he gave the commission and its president broad powers, especially in the area of condemnation and appropriation of private land.

A battle soon erupted over acquisition of the the old Taylor estate in East Islip — choice property that would eventually become the huge Heckscher State Park, fronting on Great South Bay. There came a prolonged legal battle with the members of the posh Timber Point Club, who feared having city riff-raff engaged in unspeakable sexual escapades in the sylvan glades next to their finely manicured golf fairways. At a hearing in New York to settle the issue, Smith bantered and joked with both sides, trying to get them together.

# of an Arrogant, Endearing Man

At Bridge, Office of Parks, Recreation and Historic Preservation; Portrait, Newsday Photo / Audrey C. Tiernan

Moses observes the construction of the Captree Causeway in about 1964. At right, Moses as a guest of honor in front of the Jones Beach tower on the beach's 50th anniversary in 1979. He called Jones Beach his proudest achievement.

years. His parents paid for it after he and his first wife, Mary Sims Moses, found it in 1921. A professional building now occupies the site.

He guarded his personal life as much as he could from the scrutiny given his vast public enterprises. He tried to keep Sundays free to spend with Mary, who died in 1966, after spending several years in a wheelchair as a result of arthritis and arteriosclerosis, and their daughters, Barbara and Jane.

But even on Sundays, friends said, he frequently would slip away during the afternoon to a private room with his omnipresent yellow legal pad in hand. He was a severe workaholic, rising at 7 a.m., pushing himself 16 hours or more a day, including Saturdays, and his subordinates almost as hard.

Most of his old friends are defensive of his memory, still angry at what they consider the rough treatment of Moses by Robert A. Caro in his Pulitzer-Prize winning 1974 biography, "The Power Broker."

Marian Ritz of Bellmore, who worked 37 years for Moses and became his chief secretary, said, "It was grossly unfair to a great man who did so much for so many."

Grace Farrington, 80, a girlhood friend of his daughter Jane, frequented the Moses summer place from age 17 on. "It was like my second home. I saw him on and off the rest of his life. We never saw the terrible temper. He was just a wonderful guy who loved the beach and the water and his job."

Moses hated mechanical things, friends said. Though sort of a klutz around the house, he liked to cook big bacon-and-egg breakfasts on Sundays for family and visitors. Once out of the office, he liked to party informally.

But work was an addiction. It energized him. One close Moses friend who asked not to be named, referring to personal problems that both of Moses' daughters developed as adults, said, "He was not around most of the time they were growing up. I feel he was more interested in his business than his family. Sad, very sad."

Work so preoccupied him that he was indifferent to clothes: baggy, rumpled suits were a hallmark. He was almost totally unable to handle his personal finances though he thoroughly understood public authority funding schemes and oversaw expenditures of billions of dollars in public funds.

Moses was not wealthy. Much of the public work he did was unsalaried. He was often strapped for personal cash. He lived for years on money doled out by his domineering mother, and once borrowed $20,000 from her to speed up a Jones Beach contract.

Isabel Gallagher of Babylon, who with her late attorney husband, Frank, was socially close to Robert and Mary Moses, remembers Moses as "one of the most charming and intriguing of men. You knew of his power but he did not flaunt it among friends."

He had no son and was grief-stricken when Jane's 21-year-old son, handsome, devil-may-care Christopher Collins, whom "Gramps" Moses dearly loved, was killed in an out-of-state car wreck one week before Moses' 80th birthday in late 1968.

Moses, at 77, married Mary Grady, secretary to aide George Spargo, within a month of his first wife's death. There were published rumors that Moses and Mary Grady had long had an affair, but Moses loyalists, including Marian Ritz, say it was untrue. Mary Grady Moses died in 1993.

One of the few charitable causes to which Moses lent his name was Good Samaritan Hospital in West Islip. He chaired its first five fund-raising balls from 1963 to 1967, and in the first year arranged to have New York Mayor Robert F. Wagner attend and Guy Lombardo and his Royal Canadiens play for 700 guests at the Southward Ho Country Club in Brightwaters, of which Moses was a member.

Retired hospital executive Ted Shiebler recalled, "Moses could part the waters in all he did."

During an interview with Moses in 1972, I visited the house he rented on Oak Beach. We could see Robert Moses State Park and Ocean Parkway and the Captree Causeway from the windows. The man who had planned them talked for three hours about everything from politics to poetry, waved off questions about a comeback, showed pictures of his grandchildren, and during a walk on the beach said he thought his work would be remembered for 100 years.

I accompanied him to the Brightwaters estate of Landon Thorne, one of his millionaire friends, where he swam a half-hour in the glass-enclosed pool surrounded by lush tropical vegetation, showing even at 83 the powerful crawl that made him captain of the swimming teams at Yale and Oxford so many years earlier.

We lunched almost three hours at LaGrange Inn in West Islip. He had brandy and soda, oysters, hashed brown potatoes, vegetables, rice pudding and espresso coffee. He talked with as much gusto as he ate, mostly about his joy as a younger man walking and sailing the barrier islands, the start of a public mission that would change the face of Long Island forever.

Moses died July 29, 1981. He was 92. I attended the crowded funeral at St. Peter's Episcopal Church in Brightwaters.

As the hymns swelled, I could not help but think how fitting was the line from Sophocles that Robert Caro had used to introduce his book about this great man: "One must wait until the evening to see how splendid the day has been."

Tom Morris, a Newsday reporter and editor for 42 years, retired in 1995.

But when one club member testified that he feared East Islip would be "overrun with rabble from the city," the laughter died abruptly.

"Rabble?" Smith said angrily. "That's me you're talking about!" Smith picked up his pen and signed the form authorizing the state taking of the land.

Neither was Moses himself keen on the "rabble" from the city using his Long Island parks, which he designed for the middle class, auto-owning people. Although he denied it, the bridges on the parkways had been built too low to accommodate buses so that poor people without cars, especially minorities, could not get to parks and beaches. Caro said that he was told this privately by one of Moses' right-hand men, Sid Shapiro, who later himself became head of the park commission.

"He doesn't love the people," his old friend Frances Perkins later said, according to Caro. "It used to shock me because he was doing all these things for the welfare of the people . . . He'd denounce the common people terribly. To him they were lousy, dirty people, throwing bottles all over Jones Beach . . . He loves the public, but not as people."

Jones Beach itself was owned in sections by the Towns of Hempstead, Oyster Bay and Babylon. And they did not want to give it up. In a 1925 referendum, Hempstead residents opposed selling the land to the state by a vote of 12,106 to 4,200. "It looked like we'd lost Jones Beach," Moses later told Caro. "It looked absolutely hopeless."

Well, not exactly. The power broker-to-be went to see the man who already had the power in Nassau County. Moses held a series of meetings with Republican Party boss G. Wilbur Doughty. It is not known what transpired at those meetings, but a new referendum the following year reversed the earlier vote, and the town ceded all its Jones Beach rights to the park commission. The neighboring towns soon fell into line.

Creating Jones Beach was a monumental task. Surveys showed that the mean level of the beach was only two feet above sea level, meaning that high waves during storm periods would inundate the beach. That was not a problem for the beach itself. But farther back, where buildings, parking lots and the incoming parkway were to be built, the land had to be 12 feet higher than that. Huge floating dredges were brought into the bay, and over a period of several months they pumped more than 40 million cubic yards of sand out of the bay bottom and onto the beach.

The vision that Moses laid out for his unbelieving engineers in 1926 soon became a reality. In June, 1929, Heckscher State Park opened. The Southern State Parkway opened in July. And on Aug. 4, in a howling sandstorm that ruined the paint on automobiles and choked carburetors, Jones Beach, in all the magnificence that Moses had planned, was opened as 25,000 cars rolled across the Wantagh Causeway.

"This is the finest seashore playground ever given the public anywhere in the world," one visiting Englishman exalted.

That same year, there were problems brewing with the planned Northern State Parkway. The whole project had

Please see **MOSES** on **Next Page**

Moses, The Master Builder

MOSES from **Preceding Page**

stalled over the direct route that Moses originally planned, because it ran straight through some of the most valuable property on Long Island, the estates of some of society's richest and most famous people.

When banker Otto Kahn found that the parkway was scheduled to go straight through the 18-hole private golf course he had recently built on his property in Cold Spring Harbor, he asked Moses for a meeting. Kahn offered to secretly donate $10,000 for new surveys, Caro wrote, providing they came up with a route that did not touch his property. Moses accepted the money. When Caro tried to ask Moses about this, Moses refused to ever talk to him again.

When attorneys for the Nassau estate owners found out about the Kahn-Moses deal, Caro wrote, they threatened a messy public battle over the issue. What happened next is not certain, but within a few weeks, Moses announced a change in the parkway route, one in which the road avoided the homes of the wealthy landowners.

State Office of Parks, Recreation and Historic Preservation

The Triborough Bridge during construction in 1934; Moses consolidated his power as head of the Triborough Bridge and Tunnel Authority.

When World War II ended, Moses was in his 50s and heavily involved with building projects in New York City, primarily through the Triborough Bridge and Tunnel Authority, for which he had an office on Randalls Island. The Cross-Bronx Expressway, the Major Deegan and the Bruckner Expressways had yet to be built, as did the Throgs Neck Bridge and the awe-inspiring Verrazano-Narrows Bridge.

Something was happening in these postwar years, however, that planners had been predicting for years. As prosperity returned to the nation, millions of new automobiles moved onto the nation's highways. Many planners had theorized that new roads, instead of relieving congestion, would generate new traffic and more congestion. They were right.

Moses' new highways competed directly with mass transportation like the Long Island Rail Road, and many rail commuters were seduced by the idea of getting to work in the city by driving on the parkways. What Moses had built as a roadway for the city masses to get to his parks turned into rapidly clogging commuter highways. The postwar LIRR peak ridership, for example, was 116,000 a day in 1946; by 1973 this had dropped to 57,000.

A singular event occurred on Long Island in 1955 that experts feel could have helped turn around the growing congestion of the roadways. That was the year construction started on the Long Island Expressway, a commercial highway that Moses had first proposed in 1936. Planners like Koppelman have argued for years that, by refusing to get involved with local zoning boards to control building along the parkways and the expressway, Moses was a key contributor to the "suburban sprawl" that has developed on Long Island.

Koppelman and Caro agree that when the Long Island Expressway was built, the state should have acquired enough right-of-way to build mass transit tracks down the middle. "Every other metropolitan area in the entire nation, except New York, has combined some form of mass transit built into their arterial network," Koppelman said. "If we had had down the center median some form of mass transit, we would not have the congestion."

What the planners mean is that drivers on the expressway, when they exit, do not mind driving another quarter-hour to get home. And this leads to sprawling developments all over the Island. But men and women arriving on high-speed transit would want to be within walking distance of their neighborhoods. As a result, high-density development would take place primarily along the central corridor in which the expressway ran.

One academic who disagrees, in part, with Caro and Koppelman is Columbia University urban history professor Kenneth Jackson, who says that there were larger forces at work, and that Moses was merely a product of his times. He argues that postwar national policy, reflected in the 1950s creation of the interstate highway system and federally backed low-cost mortgages, would have encouraged suburban sprawl on Long Island regardless of Moses.

Rerouting a Parkway

Robert Moses' original planned route for the Northern State Parkway and how it was changed after several wealthy local landowners complained.

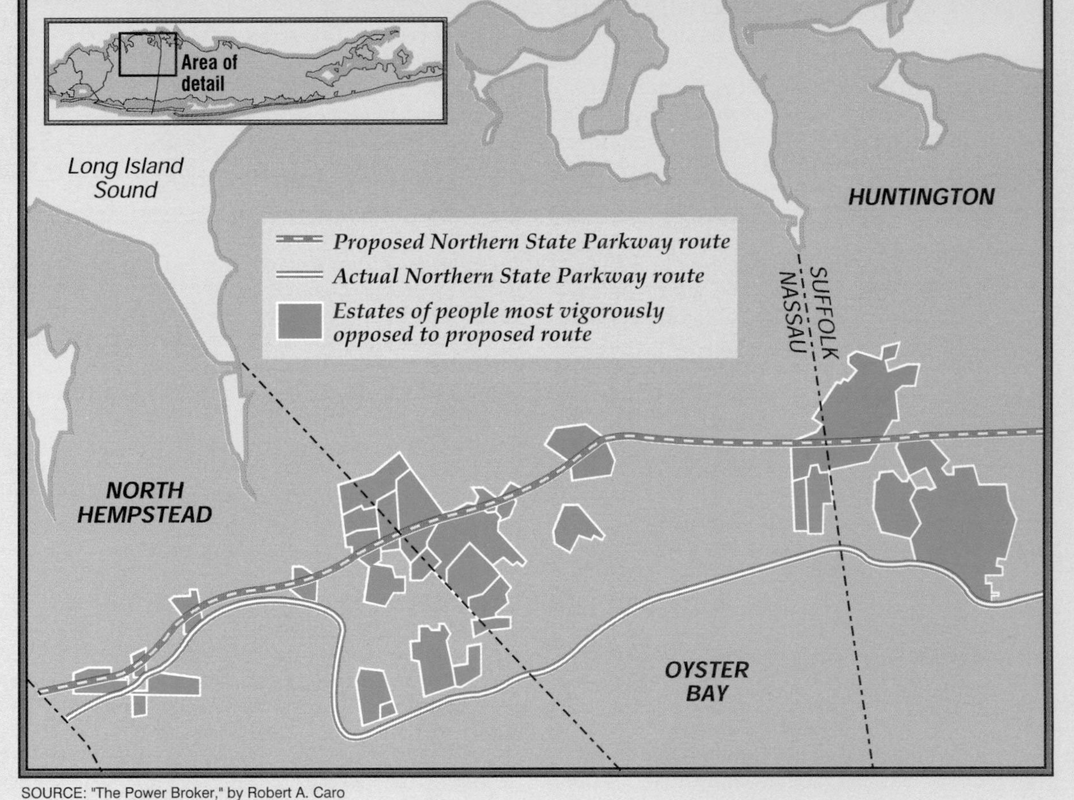

SOURCE: "The Power Broker," by Robert A. Caro

Newsday / Linda McKenney

Moses heard the criticism, and he occasionally responded to it. At a 1962 ribbon-cutting ceremony when the LIE first crossed the Nassau-Suffolk border, he defended his vision, and he did it eloquently.

"I have, with many others, been falsely charged with neglect, lack of vision, and general obtuseness in road building and with failure to anticipate the march of population to the suburbs," said Moses. "There will be squawking no matter what we do. We must face at once the demands of those impatient for new facilities and the anguished cries and curses of those who want to be left alone, who, like Canute, can command the waves to halt on the beaches and, like the Indians, keep the new settlers in the blockhouses."

One person who has a family story to tell about Moses and the Northern State Parkway is Mineola attorney John V. N. Klein, formerly Smithtown supervisor and Suffolk County executive. "My father, before I was born, used to live in Lake Success, with my mother," Klein said recently. "He came home one day and said that some guy

Jones Beach, The Marvel By the Sea

BY BILL BLEYER
STAFF WRITER

When Jones Beach opened Aug. 4, 1929, visitors marveled at the elegance of Robert Moses' nautical vision. A trip to the new state park was more than a day at the seashore; it was a voyage.

The water fountains were operated by miniature ships' steering wheels, the trash cans were hidden inside ship funnel ventilators and the employees were dressed like sailors.

The 2,413-acre state park featured swimming in the ocean surf, in a bay and in heated pools, and a variety of other activities. Patrons — and there were 1.5 million of them during the first full year of operation in 1930 — could also enjoy handball courts, deck tennis and shuffleboard courts, an outdoor roller rink, archery, softball, fishing docks, rowboat rentals, an 18-hole pitch-and-putt golf course, dancing, and other sports and entertainment programs. There were even solaria for nude sunbathers and electric bottle warmers for mothers caring for their babies.

As time and tide have washed across the beach over the decades, much has changed. The nautical water fountains and uniforms, the nude sunbathing and the bottle warmers are long gone, and other facilities and programs have been lost to budget cuts or changing times.

Among the things eliminated were handball courts, archery ranges, and umbrella, beach chair and rowboat rentals. The outdoor roller rink, unused for a decade, may be converted to lighted volleyball courts. Parking Field 9 was closed in 1977 because of beach erosion.

But other facilities and programs have been added as the park operation expanded. Since Gov. Franklin D. Roosevelt dedicated Jones Beach, the West End complex has been developed with two large parking fields, although West End 1 was closed in 1991 because of budget cuts. A pool was added in the East Bathhouse in the 1960s.

The 8,200-seat Jones Beach Theatre was added in 1952 — at first presenting musicals and then shifting to rock concerts. For this summer, the theater's seating capacity is being expanded to 14,354. The pitch-and-putt course has also been expanded and a miniature golf course was opened in the late 1970s. Basketball courts were added.

Joseph Lescinski, the Jones Beach superintendent, said the crowds have changed as well. When the beach first opened, most visitors came from New York City. Now there is a mix of city and suburban users. "Our weekday crowd tends to be primarily a Long Island crowd; our weekend crowd tends to be a mix of Long Island and the city."

In a typical year, the park attracts 7 million to 8 million people — about 5 million of them during the summer. The single-day attendance record was set on July 4, 1995, when about 275,000 hit the beach. On an average sunny July Sunday, the park attracts 150,000 to 200,000.

The parking fee, initially 50 cents weekends and 25 cents weekdays, has risen to $5. The park is run by about 75 year-round permanent employees with about 850 to 900 seasonal workers in the summer. The peak staffing back in the early '60s was about 2,000 employees. On Jones Beach's first opening day, three parking fields were open for 10,000 cars. Now there are a dozen that can accommodate 23,500 cars.

The history of Jones Beach and the other Long Island state parks is chronicled in a permanent exhibit called "Castles in the Sand," in the East Bathhouse. It displays photographs and memorabilia from the early days of the park system. There are maps and plans from park construction projects, old uniforms worn by employees, and videos of the park in the 1940s and 1950s, including snippets from a movie titled "The Girl From Jones Beach."

The exhibit is open April 1 to June 19 from 10 a.m. to 4 p.m. seven days a week; from June 20 to Sept. 7, noon to 8 p.m.; Sept. 8 to Oct. 12, 10 a.m. to 4 p.m., seven days a week; and from Oct. 13 to March 31, Saturdays, Sundays and holidays, 10 a.m to 4 p.m. The admission is $1.

Newsday File Photo
A view of Jones Beach State Park in 1949, with its landmark tower and plenty of parking spaces for thousands of cars

State Office of Parks, Recreation and Historic Preservation

Newsday Photo / Phillip Davies
At left, the West Bathhouse at Jones Beach during construction in about 1930; above railings and funnels on the boardwalk reflect the park's nautical theme. In a typical year, the park attracts 7 million to 8 million people.

named Moses was going to put a parkway through his property. To which my father said, 'Over my dead body.' He was half right. Moses put the parkway through my father's property, but fortunately my father didn't die."

Given all the power that Moses had and all the monuments he caused to be built in metropolitan New York, it sometimes comes as a surprise to realize that on a few proposed projects — a very significant few — he was defeated. And some of the defeats ate at him until the day that his heart finally gave out and he died at Good Samaritan Hospital in West Islip early in the morning of July 29, 1981, when he was 92.

Two Moses defeats were of significance to Long Islanders. He wanted Ocean Parkway to extend beyond Jones Beach to the eastern end of Fire Island, but that idea died when the Fire Island National Seashore was created in 1964. A more explosive issue was Moses' proposal for a cross-Sound bridge to run from the village of Bayville in Oyster Bay to the City of Rye in Westchester County. He described the proposed bridge as " . . . spidery and unobstrusive as to be at most times eerie and almost invisible . . . a gossamer thread over an arm of the sea." But Gov. Nelson Rockefeller, who at first supported the plan by Moses, then a consultant to the Metropolitan Transportation Authority, changed his mind and killed the idea in 1973.

Moses' career effectively ended on March 1, 1968, when the MTA came into existence with William Ronan as its head.

Recently, Koppelman — a man who, after saying something that irritated Moses many years ago, received a letter from him that began "Dear Nincompoop" — was asked for an assessment of Moses, adding up the good and the bad.

"For me," Koppelman said, "those parks are so priceless that I can live with the shortfalls. I d have to say, yes, he was an absolute positive force for Long Island."

BY DREW FETHERSTON
STAFF WRITER

Suffolk County Historical Society Photo
Immigrants, such as these Italian men who worked on the Long Island Rail Road around 1900, often took manual labor. The Island also has seen waves of immigrants from Eastern Europe, Greece, East Asia, Central and South America, and the Caribbean.

Arrivals from Poland, Italy and nearly everywhere else change the face of LI

Waves Of Immigrants

In 1884 a 44-year-old Polish immigrant farmer named Frank Fafinski stepped ashore in Manhattan from the Ellis Island ferry.

The sturdy Fafinski caught the attention of a Baiting Hollow farmer named DeFriest, who had come to the ferry to look for workers. He hired Fafinski and Adam Danowski, another Polish farmer who had arrived on the same ship, on the spot.

When Fafinski and Danowski began work, they were a novelty in Riverhead Town: At that time, there was only a handful of Poles who, like themselves, had been hired at the ferry dock and come to Suffolk County to begin their new lives.

Most of the land then was owned and farmed by descendants of the earliest English settlers. (Fafinski went to work for one of them, John Young, after a season with DeFriest.) The same families controlled politics and capital.

But great changes were afoot by the time Fafinski stepped off the boat, and the decades thereafter would see Long Island enriched by immigrants from scores of cultures from every segment of the globe. By the 1930s, New York City had become a melting pot and ethnic communities were spreading across Long Island. In 1933, the Queens public schools had students representing more than 50 nationalities.

The old English dominance had begun to erode in the 1840s, when a famine in Ireland and political upheaval in central Europe sent thousands of Irish and Germans fleeing to America. Many never went beyond New York or Brooklyn, but some found their way out to the Island.

Irish had been farming in the East End for a generation when Fafinski arrived; Calverton had enough Irish residents to be dubbed Dublin unofficially.

When a developer in the early 1870s offered lots at $50 to $100 in a place he called Breslau, enough immigrants responded to give the place — now Lindenhurst — a population of 1,000 and a distinct Germanic flavor.

Poles followed the same paths when they began to arrive in large numbers after 1880. They formed small but distinct communities in Greenpoint and Bay Ridge in Brooklyn and Maspeth and Elmhurst in Queens. Polish Catholic churches trace the eastward movement of the people: St. Casimir's in Brooklyn, founded in 1875, was followed by St. Adalbert's in Elmhurst in 1892, St. Joseph's in Jamaica in 1904, St. Josephat's in Bayside in 1910.

Fafinski and Danowski both wrote home of Long Island's charms and opportunities. Anton Danowski, Adam's brother, arrived in 1887. He worked for $12 a month and lodging on a Baiting Hollow farm, then moved to Southampton, where the pay was $18 a month.

When he had saved $500, he proposed to Mary Sadowska, who lived with her family in Jamesport. She brought a $100 dowry to the marriage — enough for the couple to buy a farm, also in Jamesport, where they would rear 15 children. When he retired, Danowski owned two farms, a large one in Jamesport and a smaller one in Aquebogue.

By that time, the Polish presence in the East End was pronounced. On June 5, 1905, Bishop Charles E. McDonnell of the Diocese of Brooklyn, which comprised all of Long Island, visited Riverhead to perform the sacrament of confirmation for more than 200 young Polish-Americans. After that, the bishop and an assemblage of clergy climbed into carriages and, escorted by six parishioners on horseback, drove to the new Polish church, St. Isidore's, to bless its bell.

"Polish people drove many miles to be present at the affair," wrote a correspondent for the Brooklyn Eagle. "They came in all sorts of conveyances; many on bicycles and a very large number, too poor to hire a wagon and having none of their own, walked many miles . . ."

In 1931, a newspaper article noted that "Polish immigrants have earned the money to buy and pay for 60 per cent of the best farms in Suffolk."

At the same time, other immigrants were changing the faces of Long Island. This century has seen waves of immigrants from Italy, Eastern Europe, Greece, East Asia, Central and South America and the Caribbean. Most came to New York City, whence some left for Long Island.

Traces of these succeeding waves are evident in the Island's Roman Catholic churches: In 1891, the Brooklyn diocese had 23 German parishes, three Italian, two Polish and one each of French, Lithuanian, Bohemian and Scandinavian.

By 1921, 21 more parishes with Italian congregations had been added, as well as 15 more Polish congregations, 10 German, four Lithuanian, one Spanish and three Greek. By the early 1920s, Greek immigrants left Manhattan to establish a colony in Astoria that endures to this day.

This process has made a minority of the Island's old landed gentry. In Nassau, 13,533 residents said they were of undiluted English ancestry in the 1990 U.S. Census, while 199,642 said they were of pure Italian ancestry. Other major groups in Nassau were Irish, 99,808; German, 64,580;, Russian, 44,993, and Polish, 40,918.

The pattern was the same in Suffolk, where the 22,444 of pure English stock were overshadowed by 211,019 Italians, 102,650 Irish, 79,646 Germans and 32,887 Poles. In Queens, the 7,996 residents of English stock were outnumbered even by the borough's 10,060 Romanians, 40,437 Greeks and 9,067 Arabs.

THE TASTES AND SOUNDS OF POLAND

When he gets together with his friends in Riverhead, Edward Harris speaks the language that is part of his heritage.

"In our household Polish was spoken within the confines of the house, mainly because my parents didn't speak English," said Harris, whose family name has been anglicized from Hareza. "The law was that you spoke Polish at home but you could speak anything you wanted when you went outside. That was how I learned Polish."

Harris' father came to the United States in 1912 and eventually made his home in Riverhead, where he farmed and his wife worked as a housekeeper. The Harezas had seven children, all of whom still live in the Riverhead area. Four of the Hareza brothers served in World War II, and Edward became a career Navy officer. He later worked for Grumman, and is now retired.

Harris and his friend, Frank Sendlewski, whose grandfather came to Riverhead in the 1880s, keep their culture alive through the Polish Museum, the annual Polish fair and the Polish Civic Association. Of his pioneering forebears, Sendlewski said, "They were pretty great people."

Harris had this to add: "Once you're in a Polish neighborhood, you're bound to preserve the culture. You talk alike, think alike and eat alike. If you can't cook *kabusta* [cabbage], kielbasa, or *golumbki* [stuffed cabbage] properly, you're in trouble around here."

— **Georgina Martorella**

Newsday Photos / Bill Davis
At left, Frank Sendlewski with photos of early arrivals from Poland who settled in Riverhead. Above, from left, are Bozenna Urbanowitz Gilbride, a Holocaust survivor; Edward Harris and Anelia Kobylenski, all of whom have links to Poland. Behind them are immigrant photo identification cards on exhibit at the Riverhead Savings Bank.

In the early 1920s, white robes and burning crosses are seen in many villages

The KKK Flares Up on LI

BY DAVID BEHRENS
STAFF WRITER

On a balmy June evening in 1923, more than 25,000 men and women assembled in a rolling meadow to hear the message of the Ku Klux Klan. The speakers, dressed in their familiar white robes and pointed hoods, warned that Jews and Catholics were a danger to the nation. And a Protestant minister on the rostrum branded the Catholic Church "a political party in disguise."

The rally did not unfold in Mississippi or Alabama or any of the former states of the Confederacy. The site was East Islip, on the South Shore of Long Island. The Ku Klux Klan was alive once again.

Most Americans who have seen or read "Gone With the Wind" associate the Ku Klux Klan with the years after the Civil War. The Klan had been founded by Confederate Army veterans in 1865 to perpetuate the culture of white supremacy in the South.

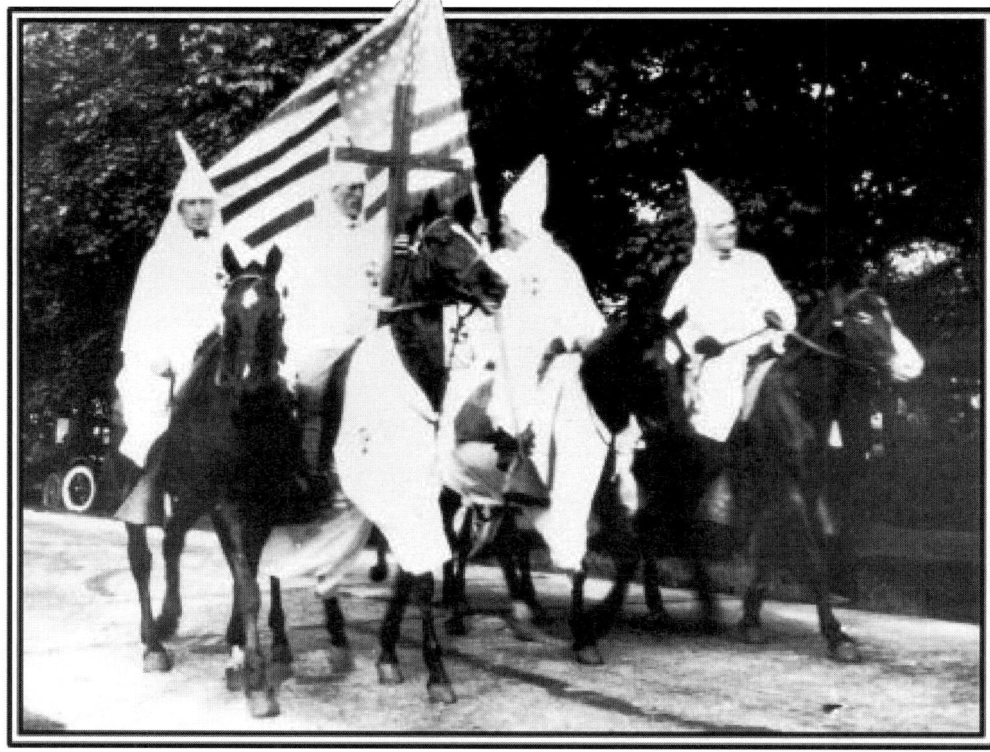

Frank J. Cavaioli and April Walker Photo

A Ku Klux Klan parade in Huntington in the 1920s

In the Reconstruction era, the hooded, white-robed night-riders terrorized former slaves, burned crosses, destroyed homesteads and lynched countless black Americans. The reign of terror subsided when Democrats regained political control in the South and used poll taxes and other means to exclude blacks from voting or running for office. The riders of the Klan, seemingly, galloped off into oblivion. But galvanized by the great waves of immigration from Europe about 1900, a new generation of Klansmen sprung up in Georgia in 1915 and spread to the North.

On Long Island, the "new" Klan adopted a law-and-order stance to attract recruits, backed Prohibition and criticized the "loose" morals of the times. By the early '20s, men in white robes were burning crosses once again, this time at rallies on the outskirts of dozens of Nassau and Suffolk villages. Within a few years, historians estimate, one out of seven to eight Long Island residents was a Klan member — about 20,000 to 25,000 men and women.

Challenging the bootleggers, the Klan organized armed patrols to intercept illegal liquor along the shores and roads of Long Island, usually acting without police authority. After one skirmish, when rumrunners killed a Southampton constable, Ferdinand Downs, 2,000 Klansmen attended the officer's funeral.

In contrast to its 19th-Century tactics, the Klan was hardly clandestine in the 1920s on Long Island. Often, respected clergymen and public officials openly supported the Klan and attended its rallies. On Sept. 20, 1924, for instance, the Klan drew 30,000 spectators to a parade through Freeport — with the village police chief, John M. Hartman, leading a procession of 2,000 robed men.

African-Americans were no longer the sole focus of the Klan's message of hate on Long Island, because black citizens comprised only 2 percent of the population. Catholics and foreign-born

Wagner Collection, Queensboro Public Library

KLORERO
MINEOLA FAIR GROUNDS
MINEOLA, LONG ISLAND
JULY 3, 4, 5, 6, 1926

Nassau County Museum Collection, L.I. Studies Institute

Klansmen in Wantagh in the 1920s. Historians say about one in seven to eight L.I. residents was a Klan member. Above, a KKK booklet published for a 1926 convocation in Mineola.

Americans were a much more visible target. By 1920, foreign-born residents had grown to 20 percent of the population. In Nassau, the number had increased in two decades from 11,004 to 25,998. In Suffolk, the figure rose from 14,650 to 23,888. These new immigrants constituted "the greatest threat to the American way of life," the Klan claimed.

Thousands of Long Islanders were drawn to the rallies to witness the fiery spectacle and to listen to the incendiary speechmaking.

On the night on Oct. 12, 1923, for instance, the Klan put on a pyrotechnic spectacular, burning crosses in a dozen villages across Long Island. Crosses were burned through the year in more than a score of villages including Freeport, Mineola, Bay Shore, Babylon, Riverhead, Huntington, Sayville, Garden City, Valley Stream and Hempstead. After an open-air meeting in Northport, a weekly newspaper observed: "A large percentage of the members of the Knights of the Ku Klux Klan of this village do not care whether people know who they are or not."

Klan activities drew scant criticism from officials and private citizens alike. Many Long Island churches eagerly accepted money and other gifts from the Klan, and hardly anyone raised questions of political correctness when school boards welcomed the donation of American flags by KKK members.

Among prominent Klan members were James Zegel, the U.S. Treasury agent in charge of Bay Shore's Prohibition-enforcement office who headed the Klan's Islip "klavern," or chapter. He held the title of Grand Exalted Cyclops. Maynard Spahr, popular pastor of a Methodist Episcopal Church, also held the grandiose title in Brookhaven.

Church trustees openly conceded that the Klan's appearance in a community boosted attendance at Sunday services, and many ministers in the early 1920s were reluctant to ignore the opportunity. When Lynbrook Klan members presented the Church of the Nazarene in East Rockaway with a new silk American flag and a purse of gold, Pastor Paul Hill thanked the 40 Klansmen for their generosity, the Nassau's Daily Review reported. A West Sayville clergyman, Andrew Van Antwerpen of the First Reformed Church, permitted a hooded Klansman to address his congregants. And William Norris, a Presbyterian pastor, exhorted members of his church in Bellport to vote for pro-Klan candidates.

The founding of one of Long Island's first klaverns, in Freeport, was memorialized on Sept. 8, 1922, in the Daily Review, which carried a banner headline about the meeting at Mechanics Hall on Railroad Avenue. About 150 new members were greeted by seven robed Klansmen, the newspaper reported.

Journalists were permitted to sit in briefly because, as a "Mr. Smith" explained, their editors would surely "twist and distort" the true story. From the rostrum, Jews were the target of the robed speaker. "He was attacking the Jew — as an individual, habits, politics and method of living . . . He stated that two-thirds of the advertising in the papers was controlled by Jews," the Daily Review reported.

Another account of a Klan presence ran in the Nassau Daily Review-Star when Klansmen staged a 1925 Memorial Day celebration in Hicksville, attracting 5,000 spectators: "A thousand men and women marched from a field east of Hicksville through the streets of the village and back to the field . . . in robes and hoods but with faces uncovered," the newspaper reported.

While membership was spurred by the rising number of foreign-born residents, the Klan's theatrics especially attracted older citizens, said Frank J. Cavaioli, a professor at the State College of Technology at Farmingdale. Speaking at a Long Island history conference in the 1980s, Cavaioli suggested that the Klan's melodramatic activities served "as a counterweight to the dullness of life on rural Long Island."

But by the mid-'20s, interest in the Klan cooled and cross-burnings became less frequent. Rivalries within the Klan's leadership had taken a toll and, politically, the Klan had begun to slip. In 1926, when anti-Klan candidates won election in Greenport, Babylon and Sag Harbor, The New York Times observed: "Long Island seems to be recovering from its belief in the Ku Klux Klan . . . Thus has good sense returned to Long Island."

Montauk Library Collection; Newsday Photo

Carl Fisher in about 1925: The 1929 stock market crash ended his ambitious plans for Montauk.

Carl Fisher created Miami Beach, but his plan to duplicate the feat on LI ended in ruin

The Mogul Of Montauk

BY STEVE WICK
STAFF WRITER

Carl Fisher was a blustering, cigar-chomping promoter. Above all, he was a dreamer.

Born in rural Indiana in 1874, Fisher was only 12 years old when he began making money by staging downhill sled races to advertise a dry-goods store. He dropped out of school and opened a bicycle shop at 17. His goal, he told friends, was to be a wealthy inventor. He was a multimillionaire while still in his 30s.

The invention that made him rich was a device that allowed gas to be compressed into tanks. Fisher parlayed the profits into a business that manufactured automobile headlights. Once, he advertised the business by filling the tires of a stripped-down Stoddard Dayton with helium, attaching it to a balloon and flying it over Indianapolis. He dreamed big. By 1915, he was rich enough to help start the Indianapolis Motor Speedway.

Fisher is best known as the man who, with John Collins, created Miami Beach out of a mangrove swamp. In 1910, Fisher and his wife, Jane, bought a house in Miami. Inspired by the potential of the area, he helped pay for the construction of a wooden bridge that connected Miami to the ocean beach; soon, he was clearing wetlands, pouring sand from the ocean floor onto the beach, and building luxurious hotels and homes for the wealthy. It was Fisher's genius that transformed the beach into Miami Beach.

In 1926, Fisher turned his attention to Montauk Point.

That year — just as land prices began to plummet in Florida — Fisher and four partners purchased 9,000 acres on the Montauk peninsula for $2.5 million as part of a grand plan to turn it into the Miami Beach of the North — an exclusive, expensive summer resort two hours east of New York City.

Fisher's vision was to turn the high, rocky moraine into a place where the "best" people — meaning the wealthiest and most socially prominent — kept second homes, and where they could fish, hunt and swim. "Miami in the winter, Montauk in the summer" became his slogan.

"His idea was to turn a very sleepy little community that was home to a small group of fishermen into the Miami of the North," said Peg Winski, author of "Montauk — A Century of History," published in Southampton in 1997. He saw the same potential in Montauk that he had seen years before in Miami's mangrove swamp. "There was really nothing here when he arrived," Winski said. "He wanted to build a hotel, golf courses, yacht clubs, beach clubs and expensive homes."

Between 1926, when he arrived at Montauk, and the beginning of the Depression three years later, Fisher — who maintained an office in Port Washington — built enough to leave his legacy today. One of his first constructions was Montauk Manor, an elegant 178-room hotel, with a dining hall that sat 500 guests. It opened July 4, 1927, and 25,000 guests showed up. The Manor is a condominium complex today. He also built a seven-story office tower he called the Carl Fisher Building, which still exists just off Montauk Highway, the marina complex at Star Island; the string of Tudor-style stores along Montauk Highway, and a mansion for his family that overlooked the ocean. And he built beach clubs and stables that still stand.

"The Montauk that tourists see today is in large part the vision of Carl Fisher," Winski said.

If Long Island throughout its history had always been a place where people could dream big, Fisher was in his element. Soon after buying the land, he employed more than 800 workers who built roads, planted nurseries, laid water pipes and built houses. Overnight, Montauk had become a factory town.

To improve Montauk's appeal to deep-sea fishermen, Fisher had a dredge cut a channel at the northern end of Lake Montauk to connect the lake to the sea. Boats could now dock at Star Island and the Montauk Yacht Club and motor out to the open sea in minutes. Fisher had Tudor-style homes built on the hillsides overlooking the lake, and he donated land for churches. Polo fields were put in, as were a theater and tennis courts.

But the 1929 stock market crash, and the earlier collapse of land prices in Florida, helped put Fisher out of business. Work on dozens of projects was halted, and the plans for others scratched. In 1932, his Montauk Beach Development Corp. went into receivership.

"He loved this place," said Peggy Joyce, the president of the Montauk Historical Society. "But the Depression three years after he arrived put an end to his plans. I've always wondered what Montauk would look like today had the Depression not put him out of business."

"He spent millions and millions at Montauk," said Jerry Fisher, the developer's cousin and author of a book about him called "The Pacesetter." "A hurricane hit Miami in 1926, and that hurt him financially, but the Depression finished it. His Montauk bonds came due and he couldn't pay them. He loved Montauk. He thought big and he acted big."

On July 15, 1939, Fisher, 65, died of a stomach hemorrhage in a Miami Beach hospital. His estate was valued at $52,000 — a tiny fraction of his worth in the mid-1920s, estimated at more than $50 million.

His dream of a Miami of the North died with him.

Montauk Library Photo

WORKS BY FISHER ADORN MONTAUK

Carl Fisher *is* Montauk.

During a brief window in the 1920s, Fisher began to transform Montauk into an exclusive resort. Between 1926 and 1930, a year after the stock market crash, Fisher built the Tudor-style Montauk Manor (at left), a seven-story office building, the Montauk Yacht Club and the original Montauk Golf Club. For his family, Fisher built a huge, three-story, white-columned mansion overlooking Lake Montauk. His mansion was heavily damaged by fire in 1990, but has been remodeled. His manor was closed from the 1960s until the 1980s, when it became a condominium complex. The lobby looks today the way it looked when Fisher built it. It has slate floors, large fireplaces and handsome woodwork.

"You walk into the lobby and you see exactly what Fisher did," said Joan Lycke, a trustee of the Montauk Library.

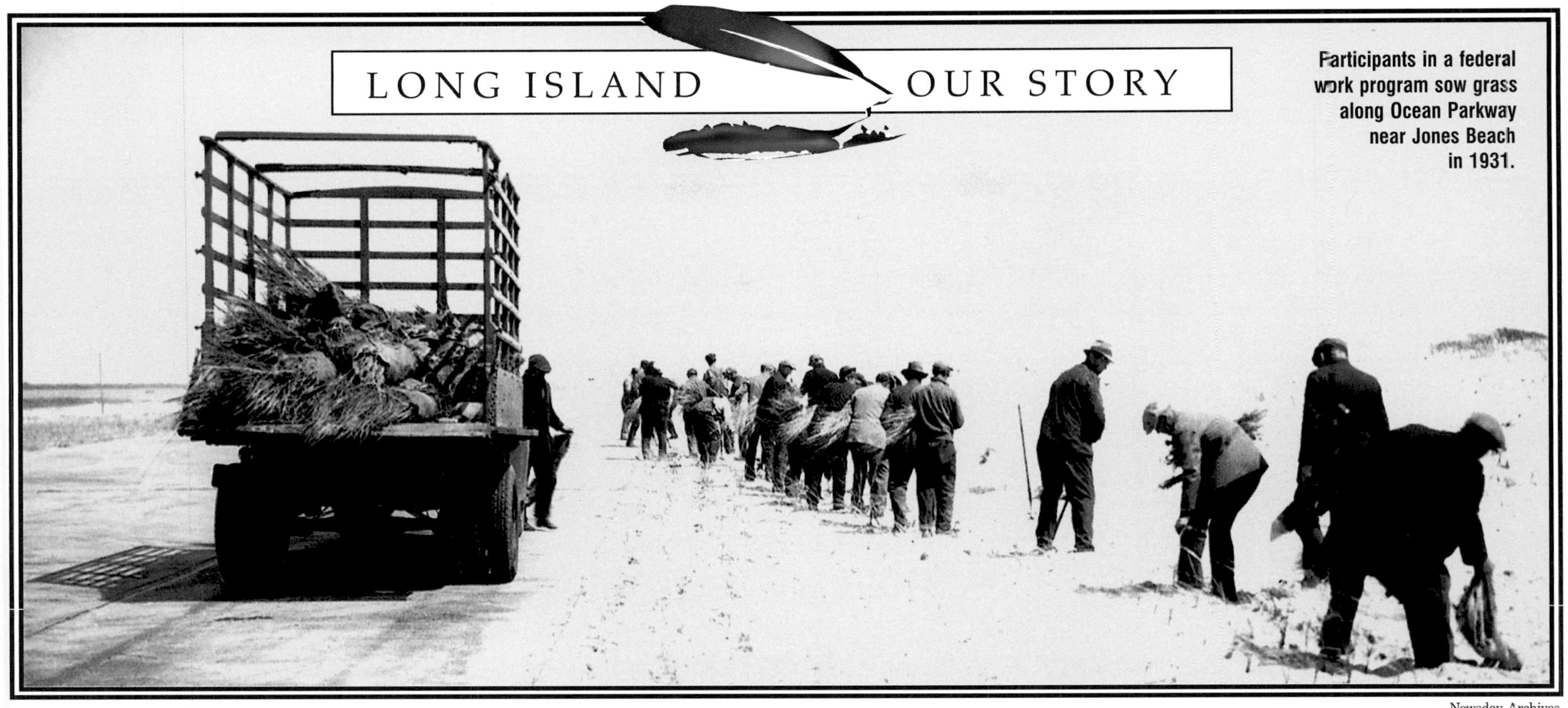

Participants in a federal work program sow grass along Ocean Parkway near Jones Beach in 1931.

Newsday Archives

Four Long Islanders tell how they scraped by, often by raising their own food

Surviving The Depression

BY GEORGE DEWAN
STAFF WRITER

Things were hitting bottom in September, 1933, when Queens resident Albert H. Amend wrote in a small notebook:

"We are flat cold stony broke and no place in the world to get any money. Have been living mainly on boxes of food from the Red Cross and received the last one yesterday as they have stopped giving them out. We owe 6 months rent. Resources all drained. I wonder what will happen now? God help us."

This was the middle of the Great Depression. Living with his wife and three children in Sunnyside, Amend was then 35, a scenic artist for vaudeville and stage shows. He was helped with jobs through the theater project of the WPA, the federal government's Works Progress Administration.

The stock market crashed in the fall of 1929. As the economic downturn began, banks failed, businesses went under and Americans saw jobs harder and harder to find. The Depression hit the nation the hardest in 1932-1933, when unemployment reached 25 percent. It took World War II, which began in Europe in 1939 and drew in America in 1941, to pull the nation out of its slump.

In the more rural Long Island setting, families seem not to have been as hard hit as families in urban areas, where soup kitchens and bread lines were common. There was land to grow vegetables and raise chickens and pigs on, and there were the bays and the ocean that gave up great amounts of fish, clams and scallops. But, even so, money was scarce, clothes were patched and shoes were worn long after the soles had given out.

It was not an easy time, but people survived. Here are four of them:

Daniel T. Smith, 89, of Southold: "If you had any ambition at all, you could go out and get a lot of your food. If the farmers were digging potatoes, a lot of the small potatoes would be left in the field, so you could go out and pick them up. There are a lot of ways to take care of yourself in the country. In the city you couldn't go out in the street and pick up a few potatoes, or find any clams."

After graduating from Southold High School in 1928, Smith got a certificate in horticulture from the New York State School of Agriculture (now the State College of Technology at Farmingdale) in 1931. The new skills got him and his family through the Depression. To add to his meager income, his wife, Margaret, sold baked goods from a front-yard stand.

"We were lucky," Smith said. "You squeezed every nickel you could get ahold of. And you knew there were a lot of people who didn't have a nickel. You probably hear a lot of people say, 'Oh, the Depression was terrible.' Well, it wasn't any fun. But if you had any ambition, you'd go out and find some work, and everybody got by."

Richard Willis, 71, of Commack: Willis grew up on Thurston's Creek in an area in Queens called Hungry Harbor during the Depression. The community was Springfield Dock, and it lay just about where the JFK Airport terminal is today.

Willis' father worked at the Brooklyn-Manhattan Transit Co., the BMT, as a maintenance man. "He came home one day in 1932 and said to my mother, 'I've just taken another pay cut.' Which meant that for a family of six we were going to live on $10 a week. I think he was making $23. That's when the Depression really hit."

The family raised chickens, and grew vegetables. Willis and his brother slept on the floor in the living room, next to an old potbellied stove. "The only way we could keep the newly hatched chickens alive was to bring them in and put them in a wire enclosure near the stove. So we went to bed and woke up to the sound of those chickens."

"Our clothing was the biggest problem. We managed to eat because we grew our own vegetables. Our clothing we considered pretty much of a disgrace. They were handed down to us. My father had some co-workers with older children. Often we were taunted in school: 'What garbage can did you get those clothes from, Willis?' "

"It was so bad, one family, the boys in the family combed their hair with a kitchen fork. That's how bad it was. Combs cost two cents. That's the way it was in the Depression, and everybody down there was in the same situation."

Emma Mae King, 76, of Springs: Her father, Florus W. Miller, was a fisherman who lived in Springs, near East Hampton, but was lured to Freeport in 1926 by a cousin, a builder, who promised him six days a week of work as a carpenter. The family prospered in Freeport, bought a new house and a new car. Then came 1929.

"In Freeport, when the market crashed, everyone was out on the sidewalks. They were moaning, groaning and crying."

In May, 1930, her father sold the house and moved back to Springs. "He raised chickens, had a garden, and he got a cow and a pig. He always butchered the pig, and we ate that. So we had eggs and chickens to eat, and milk from the cow. My mother was quite a sewer, so she made most of the clothes my sister and I wore."

"He was a proud person. He said, 'I'll make the money; I won't go on welfare.' He didn't ever apply for welfare, and he worked his bloody head off. To my father, it was kind of a disgrace to go on welfare, even if he had to work 12, 15 hours a day."

"I do remember having my father buy us nice shoes for church. We'd wear them until they had holes in them. My mother would put cardboard in the bottoms. We didn't think anything about it."

Betty Bezas, 85, of North Babylon: Born in Greece in 1912, she married a Greek-American mathematician, Zachary Bezas, who had a good job with a New York bank, and they settled in Brooklyn in 1928, where they bought a house near Coney Island. She said he belonged to the Sheepshead Bay Country Club, wore expensive clothes and was an avid bicyclist.

"When he lost his job, he went and dug cemeteries at Pinelawn to support his family. When the banks closed and everything went to pot, my husband had some property here on Long Island, in Wheatley Heights. When we lost the house and he said he was going to be a chicken farmer, everybody laughed."

The first building they built was a chicken coop. "We divided it in half. I had my daughter and myself in one half, and the chickens in the other." They sold eggs and broilers, delivering them to a market in Garden City, a business that lasted until the beginning of World War II, when her husband went to work for Republic Aircraft.

"We never took it hard, that we were poor. This was something that happened. We always said, we reached the bottom. You can't go lower than this. We made the best out of it. We never said we were poor."

Willis, Bezas, Newsday Photos / Bill Davis; King, Newsday Photo / John H. Cornell Jr.

From left, Richard Willis of Commack, Emma Mae King of Springs, and Betty Bezas of North Babylon, holding a picture of herself at age 15, when she married and moved to Brooklyn

Nassau County Museum Collection, Long Island Studies Institute

Nazi adherents parade at Camp Siegfried in 1937. Ostensibly a summer camp, its true intentions were suggested in a brochure promising, "You will meet people who think as you do."

In 1936, a seemingly bucolic Yaphank retreat makes Nazism a homegrown concern

Hitler's LI Legion

BY DAVID BEHRENS
STAFF WRITER

In the summer of 1936, the still-distant threat of Nazism cast an unexpected shadow across the hinterlands of Long Island.

That spring, Adolf Hitler had been preparing for war. His newly mobilized troops rolled into the Rhineland, unopposed by the Allies. It was the first of a series of Nazi military adventures setting the stage for World War II.

On Long Island, Nazism invaded Yaphank in the form of a summer retreat called Camp Siegfreid.

Located on a wooded lakefront near the mid-Suffolk village, the camp was ostensibly a summer place for youngsters and a weekend campground for adults. In reality it was more dangerous — a project sponsored by the German-American Bund, which had been established to promote Hitlerism in this country.

Fritz Kuhn, center foreground, and others of the German-American Bund meet Hitler at the 1936 Olympics in Berlin. Kuhn was quoted as predicting he would be "America's Fuhrer."

At the time, supporters of Hitler and Italian dictator Benito Mussolini boasted that under fascism, the trains ran on time. That summer, the bund's "Camp Siegfried Special" would also roll on time, pulling out of Penn Station at 8 a.m. every Sunday, bringing thousands of bundists from the greater New York area and other cities to the Yaphank depot.

At first, Long Island merchants reacted happily to the influx of potential customers, and many businesses took out ads in the bund's national newspaper. One farmer turned his fields into a parking lot for 500 cars, at 25 cents a car. Visitors were even invited to march through the village on the way from the Yaphank station to the camp.

The scene, at first, was more bucolic than bullying. When the lakefront campsite opened in mid-1935, it was known, innocuously enough, as the "Friends of New Germany Picnic Grounds," sponsored by the so-called German-American Settlement League.

But the following summer, the name was changed to Camp Siegfried, after the legend of the medieval Germanic warrior, one of the heroic myths adopted by the Nazis.

In the camp brochures, images of sylvan riverbanks and shaded woods were shown. Just another summer resort for adults and children, said Ernest Mueller, president of the German-American Settlement League. No barracks or weaponry here, he said, denying rumors. But one brochure promised: "You will meet people who think as you do." And on weekends, like-minded adult campers arrived in the martial uniform of the German-American Bund: black breeches and boots, gray shirts and black ties.

The bund, organized in 1936, had evolved from a series of nationwide German-American groups formed after World War I. The Free Society of Teutonia was organized in 1924, followed by the Friends of the Hitler Movement and the Friends of the New Germany.

Carrying flags emblazoned with swastikas, the emblem of the Nazi movement, older bundists and young campers paraded in uniform — showing off stiff-armed salutes and singing the "Horst Wessel Song," a Nazi anthem. Later, it was discovered that plans to commit espionage and sabotage in the future were also discussed covertly.

"We remain oblivious to the Nazi prototype that existed in our own backyard," Marvin Miller wrote in "Wunderlich's Salute," the first history of the bundist movement on Long Island, published in 1983. Miller, a Long Island high school teacher in the 1970s, decided to begin the project when he discovered that no history of the camp existed in book form.

Miller, now 63, recounted the experience of Murray Cohen, a Brooklyn high school student who rode the "Camp Siegfried Special" to Yaphank in 1937. Photographs Cohen secretly took at the camp were later published by PM, New York's liberal afternoon daily in the 1940s. On the train, Cohen

On Streets Paved With Acrimony

BY DAVID BEHRENS
STAFF WRITER

When Camp Siegfried opened in the mid-1930s, its pro-Nazi founders attempted to memorialize their movement by naming the streets of German Gardens, an adjoining subdivision, after the Third Reich's most notorious leaders.

The tributes to the Nazi hierarchy included a Hitler Street, a Goering Street and a Goebbels Street. The lakefront camp, organized by the German-American Bund in 1935, is long gone and so are the street signs in the subdivision that was laid out at the same time.

But the street names live on in the archives of Suffolk County.

Over the years, residents have voiced occasional protests, and a number of town and county resolutions have been passed, calling for the removal of the offending names from the subdivision maps in the county clerk's office.

Other residents have protested any erasure of the traces of Nazism from the historical record, arguing that the street names on the original maps serve as a healthy reminder of the horrors of a half-century ago.

The actual street signs were removed by the Town of Brookhaven in 1940, and the byways in German Gardens were renamed. "By then, many of the original signs had been stolen by collectors, after World War II broke out in Europe in 1939," said Marvin Miller, author of the first history of the bund's role on Long Island, in a recent interview.

In the mid-1940s, Brookhaven's Town Board passed several resolutions calling for the removal of the pro-Nazi names from the original subdivision maps, Miller said. But town officials found they apparently had no power to change the records.

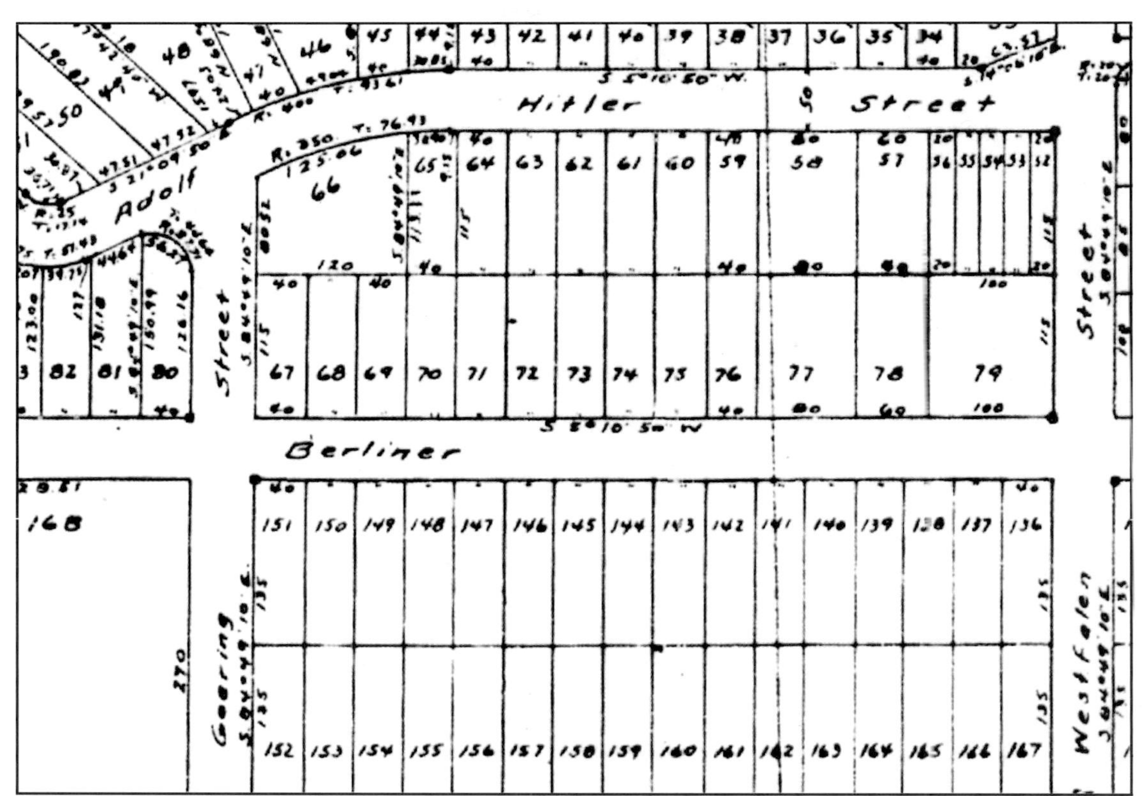

A map for German Gardens shows streets named for German leaders; some want to erase the names from the map.

In 1995, the issue arose again when Suffolk lawmakers passed a "sense of the Legislature" resolution, sponsored by Herb Davis (R-Yaphank). It called for the removal of pro-Nazi references on the subdivision records.

However, the resolution was not carried out, according to the county clerk's office, because the required authorization has not been approved by the state Legislature. Without such approval by the legislators, the clerk's office must follow the mandates regarding subdivisions of the New York State Real Property Law. "So far, we have heard nothing from the state Legislature," said a spokeswoman for the clerk's office.

Preservation of the original documents has been welcomed by Miller, a retired social studies teacher at Commack High School. Earlier this year, he called for the county Legislature to rescind its 1995 resolution.

Public opinion was divided in 1995 on the question of rewriting history. At the time, Miller called the Legislature's resolution "an inappropriate act of historical revisionism . . . denying not only Yaphank's youngsters but also teachers from gaining information about the area's past."

Davis had differed, arguing that the 50th anniversary of the end of World War II was an appropriate time to erase the reminders of Nazism. Original subdivision maps could be filed in county archives, he suggested.

At the time, many newer Yaphank residents expressed surprise at the village's connection with the Hitler regime. A few German Gardens residents recalled recently that, unexpectedly, the controversial old street names did show up in parentheses, next to the newer names, when they bought their homes and received maps of their lots.

"I thought it was kind of interesting," Yaphank resident Maggie McCutchen said in 1995. "I think they should leave it, really. It's part of history. I'm glad they changed the street names but I don't see what difference it's going to make if they take it off the map."

chatted with Mueller while, in the background, uniformed bundists sang Nazi anthems. One of the stanzas from the "Horst Wessel Song" includes the chilling lines:

When Jewish blood drips from the knife
Then will the German people prosper.

Henry Hauck, a Yaphank volunteer firefighter, ran the inn and restaurant at the camp. Around the inn flowers were planted in the shape of a giant swastika while a large photo of Hitler decorated a wall of the restaurant. There were free dances on Friday nights and Linden beer sold for 10 cents a glass. But every weekend, bundists were asked to contribute money to the Nazi cause. At least $123,000 in German bonds were sold at the camp, Miller reported.

Another $3,000 was raised to support the German Winter Relief Fund. About 70 contributors signed a "Golden Book" that Karl Weiler, a camp official, later presented to Hitler at the 1936 Olympics in Germany. Hitler reportedly urged Siegfrieders to keep up the *kampf* — the struggle — in the United States. While weapons were not on display, on one weekend, a group of bundists posed happily beside a fake cannon, figuratively "aimed" at Rep. Samuel Dickstein, a Democrat from Manhattan who headed a committee investigating the bund.

At the camp, Fritz Kuhn, a U.S. citizen who headed the bund, predicted that someday he would be "America's Fuhrer," Miller wrote. Activities included more than sports and sunbathing. There were recorded operas by Richard Wagner, Hitler's favorite composer, and anti-Semitic lectures by Walter Kappe, the camp's propaganda chief. Kappe argued that Jews were the founders of international communism. The Friends of the New Germany in America would become "what the Storm Troopers were in Germany," he promised.

By 1937, up to 40,000 bundists would arrive on Sundays to celebrate Nazism in America, while young Siegfrieders lined up to greet them as the train pulled into Yaphank. A large contingent of

Please see NAZIS, Next Page

Bundists at Camp Siegfried pose beside a fake cannon, figuratively aimed at Rep. Samuel Dickstein, a Democrat from Manhattan who headed a committee investigating the bund.

UPI File Photo

An undated photo at Camp Siegfried shows the swastika and the salute, familiar Nazi symbols, on display. When the Nazis invaded Poland in 1939, the campground was out of business.

Retreat Hides Nazi Realities

NAZIS from **Preceding Page**

Nazis also marched through the village of Lindenhurst that year. Some threats of violence came from members of American Legion posts, who threatened to break up the camp but were dissuaded by Suffolk District Attorney Robert Vunk.

Soon after, Miller wrote, Kappe was ordered to return to Germany to work on plans to land spies on the coast of Long Island. In the early days of the war, four would-be saboteurs were captured after landing near Amagansett — three turned out to be former Siegfrieders.

Two years later, the pastoral scene at Camp Siegfried began to fade. That summer, Mueller and five others were indicted in Riverhead on charges that the German-American Settlement League and Camp Siegfried were part of the bund, which required members to swear an oath of allegiance to Hitler. The state contended, therefore, that the German-American Settlement League had violated state law by failing to file its list of members, who had sworn loyalty to a foreign power.

Years later, Mueller told Newsday that the bund had "stolen" the camp from the German-American Settlement League, requiring its members to join the Nazi organization. Mueller, who died in 1966, is buried in Yaphank. In his book, Marvin Miller suggests the camp was probably a Nazi agency from the start, using the names of Nazi leaders for map designations, such as Himmler Street and Hitler Street.

Mueller and the others went on trial in Riverhead, where a witness named Willie Brandt testified that he had sworn his "loyalty and obedience" to Hitler. Then, a 45-year-old shipping clerk named Martin Wunderlich took the stand and demonstrated the stiff-armed Nazi salute used at the camp.

"That is an American salute?" asked Assistant District Attorney Lindsey Henry.

"It will be," Wunderlich said, in a warning that sent chills through the jurors, who returned a guilty verdict. The outcome was a victory for the prosecution, headed by Henry, who was the father of future Suffolk District Attorney Patrick Henry. The decision, however, was later set aside and never taken to the State Court of Appeals. But by then, the issue was moot. In the summer of 1939, the camp had lost its liquor license and many of its followers — and when the Nazis invaded Poland in September, the woodland campground was deserted and out of business.

In Camp Siegfried's heyday, bundists paraded with their swastika banners, and Kuhn spoke of the camp as part of "Germany in America."

But in the end, Kuhn was disgraced as a thief. Just before the war, he was convicted of grand larceny for pocketing money earmarked for the Riverhead trial. Stripped of his citizenship, he spent the war in a detention camp with about 40 Siegfrieders.

Then, in 1945, he was deported to West Germany and sentenced to 10 years in prison for his prewar Nazi activites. Kuhn died in 1951 in Munich. "Who would have known it would end like this?" he said to one of his jailers just before he died.

The "Camp Siegfried Special" is welcomed as it pulls into Yaphank station. The train would leave Penn Station at 8 a.m. on Sundays, carrying thousands of bundists from the New York area and other cities.

Growing Up With Subtle Anti-Semitism

BY DAVID BEHRENS
STAFF WRITER

During his formative years on Long Island, Jack Ain did not experience many blatant incidents of anti-Semitism. Just a few cross-burnings now and then, he says.

Growing up in Glen Cove and later in Sea Cliff in the 1920s and 1930s, Ain and his parents, immigrants from Poland, were familiar with the burdens of minority status in this country.

His father, Julius, came from Poland in 1911, living for a time on Manhattan's Lower East Side, where he learned the plumbing trade. In 1913, he moved to Glen Cove to work on the new St. Patrick's Catholic Church. His son Jack was born two years later.

"That year, when the church work was done, the man who hired him wouldn't give him any other job because he was Jewish," said Jack Ain, now 83 and one of the leaders of Temple Tifereth Israel in Glen Cove. "No one would hire my father, so he worked for a time as a peddler, a tree trimmer, anything to get by."

Newsday Photo / Bill Davis

Jack Ain, who grew up in Glen Cove and in Sea Cliff

In 1927, when Jack was 12, his parents moved to Sea Cliff, where he was graduated from high school in 1933, one of four Jews in a class of 35. "Anti-Semitism was subtle, but I remember the feelings. When I was 12, I joined a Boy Scout troop that met at a Methodist church. I had a lot of friends, mostly boys who were not Jews. Everyone was very friendly. Then, when I was 14, all of a sudden, they all disappeared."

Most of the scouts signed up with a youth group connected with the church and Ain was no longer included in their activities. "I don't think it was overtly anti-Semitic but if you were Jewish, you knew you would be accepted only up to a certain point. Then you were told you didn't belong. It was not something anyone ever apologized about."

The Jewish population on Long Island was relatively small, even in the late 1930s. There were fewer than 18,000 Jews in Nassau County and fewer than 4,000 in Suffolk. In Queens, the number of Jews had just reached 100,000.

There were small Jewish communities in Huntington, Patchogue and Farmingdale, Ain remembers. Roslyn had only six Jewish families in the early '30s, he said, while Sea Cliff's Jewish community totaled about 30 families, many attending Sabbath services in Glen Cove. Jews were just beginning to settle in the Five Towns, while Jewish celebrities such as Eddie Cantor and the Marx Brothers had bought summer homes in Great Neck.

"In the '30s, Jews were not readily admitted to medical schools or engineering colleges," he said. But in the fall of 1933, the year Adolf Hitler took power in Germany, Ain was accepted at Clarkson College in upstate New York. "I remember people trying to dissuade me, as a Jew, from pursuing an engineering career. They'd say: 'You won't get a job as an engineer.' I was aware of this at the time." He ignored the advice and went on to a successful career as a mechanical and industrial engineer.

Back on Long Island, Ain remembers, Jews were not welcome in many of Long Island's popular and prestigious country clubs. "It was an unwritten rule," Ain said. "Some clubs might have a token member, but most didn't countenance Jews."

So the Jewish communities founded their own clubs, such as the Glen Oaks Country Club and the Glen Head Club on Cedar Swamp Road, where the membership was primarily Jews from Great Neck and Roslyn.

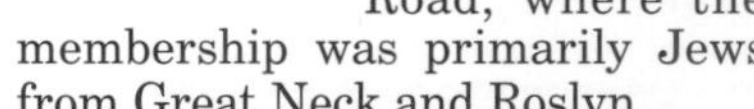

Members of the "restricted" North Shore clubs offered swimming privileges at beaches on Long Island Sound, but Jews were excluded. "There was never any question about it — that Jews were not welcome. It was not written out in their charter. Everyone understood that it was a gentleman's agreement," Ain said. Later the phrase inspired the best-selling novel of the same name by Laura Z. Hobson and Elia Kazan's pioneering film on anti-Semitism.

While the Ku Klux Klan had lost its potency on Long Island in the early '30s, Ain does remember some of the cross-burnings in North Shore communities. "But we felt we could stand up against them," he said. In college, he and his Jewish friends were more concerned about events in Central Europe and Hitler's rise to power. "We all wondered what would happen. But we never guessed the direction it was going to take."

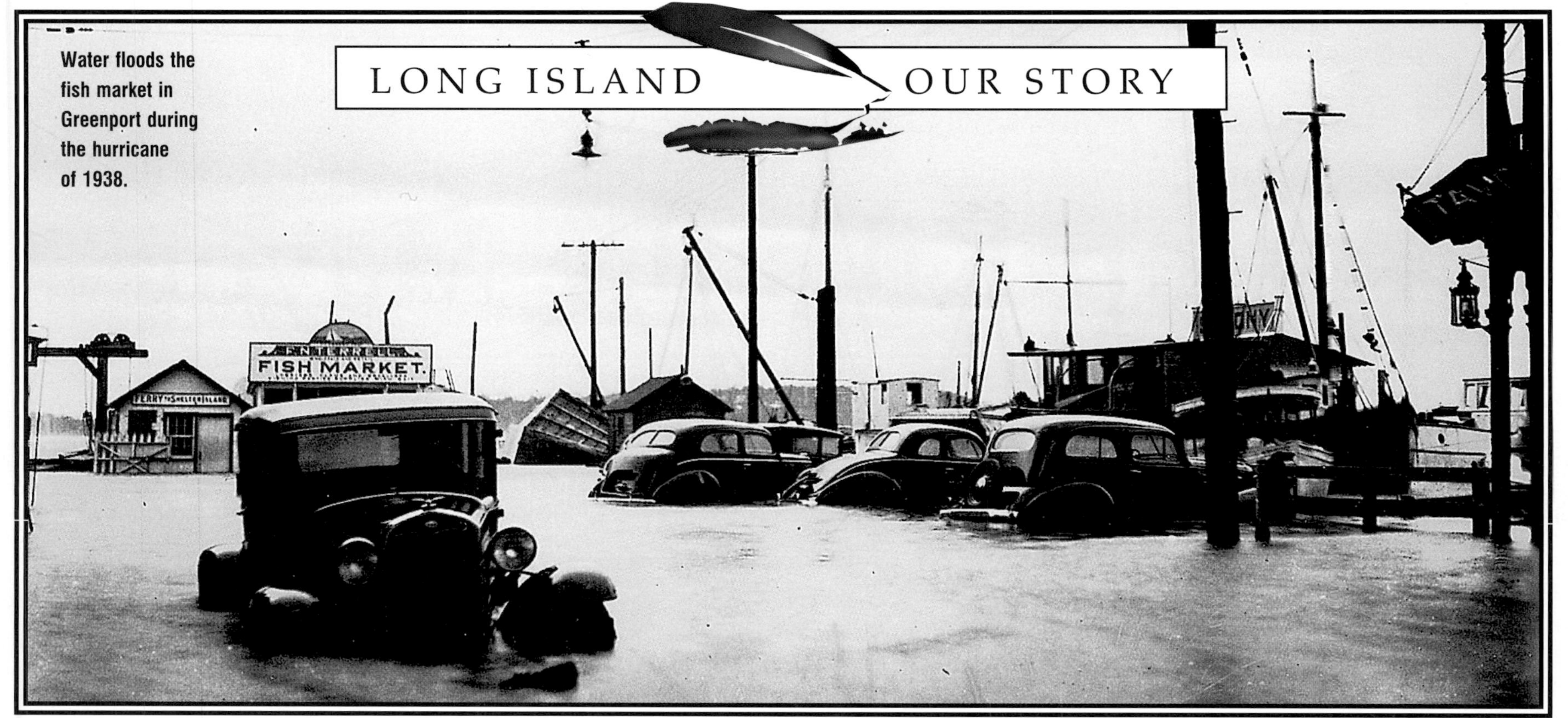

Water floods the fish market in Greenport during the hurricane of 1938.

Suffolk County Historical Society Photo

With howling winds, a hurricane slices through LI, claiming more than 50 lives

The Great Storm of '38

BY TOM MORRIS AND BILL BLEYER

It came without warning, with a ferocity without equal in modern Long Island history — the hurricane of Sept. 21, 1938.

More than 50 people died across the Island that Wednesday — 29 of them at or near Westhampton Beach. In little more than three hours, winds believed to have reached more than 125 mph drove 15-foot-high breakers onto the East End's South Shore, burying streets within a mile of the ocean under as much as 6 feet of water.

Only 26 battered shells of houses remained of the 179 summer places that stood between Quogue and Moriches Inlet. Two Coast Guard stations were destroyed, including Moriches, where the dozen crewmen had to flee in motor whaleboats just before their station was swept away.

Pat Shuttleworth of Quogue, now 70, was 10-year-old Patricia Driver, attending a children's party on Dune Road in Westhampton Beach. She was one of 17 adults and kids who survived only by cramming into the tiny attic of a two-story house and praying for help as the thundering water reached almost to the attic and a large section of the house was wrenched away by the raging torrent.

"The adults knew this was a life and death situation for all of us," Shuttleworth recalled recently. "They chopped a hole in the roof of the attic so we could holler or signal if we saw anyone to help us. It was very dark and noisy with howling wind and rushing water. We thought our last moment had come."

All 17 were rescued about 6 the next morning, the children reunited with distraught parents who'd been told the night before that everyone on the barrier beach probably had died. Many had, including a man who was killed when his garage blew onto him, and the bodies were laid out on a country club lawn in Westhampton Beach the next day.

In one case, more than a dozen people survived after clinging to a floating rooftop for three hours as it was swept from Westhampton Beach to Quogue.

Decades later, survivors have vivid memories of the storm. Ria Del Bene, 78, a lifelong Westhampton Beach resident, was 18 and "very nosy" when the wind and tide became ominous in early afternoon. She ventured alone away from her home in the village.

"I saw something that terrified me," she recalled recently, "a tidal wave rolling up Moniebogue Canal, which is just south of Main Street. The water backed away toward the bay then came roaring back up toward Main Street. I knew I had to get out of there. It was already a rushing river on Main Street where I was standing on some steps. I was nosy but not nuts. I ran home."

Mary Fritchie of Quogue, 78, then an 18-year-old domestic at a summer home on the north side of Dune Road in Quogue, told of escaping with a cook in a "long scary walk" through knee-deep water after the pickup truck they hoped would take them to safety conked out, flooded to the floorboards.

"We went out of the house to tie up a family boat on the bay side and suddenly saw the ocean coming right toward us. It was whizzing around both sides of the house. You don't realize until later how scared you are at such a sight. We knew we had to get out."

The 1938 hurricane was the worst in recorded history on Long Island in terms of fatalities and property damage, estimated at about $6.2 million, in 1938 prices, between Jones Inlet and Montauk Point.

Lee Koppelman, Long Island Regional Planning Board executive director, figures a similar hurricane now would cause upward of $6 billion in damage.

The maximum wind recorded Sept. 21, 1938, was 96 mph, according to the U.S. Army Corps of Engineers, but in the chaos little recording apparently was done.

The regional board says the sustained wind likely reached about 125 mph, with higher gusts, on the East End between 3 and 5:30 p.m., based on eyewitness accounts and study of the aftermath.

At the time, there was no radar or weather satellite warning system. The Coast Guard that day was expecting no worse than a seasonal nor'easter.

Lillian Morton, 78, of Islip, was dating her future husband, Thomas Morton, then 22 and an enlisted Coast Guardsman assigned to the Moriches station.

"He always told me they did not know it was a big hurricane coming," Morton, whose husband died four years ago, said recently. "It was so bad the men wanted to leave but the [commanding officer] vowed they were going to stick it out. Fortunately, he came to his senses just in time. They left in their motor boats just before the station was washed away."

The storm surge left water more than 6 feet deep on Westhampton Beach's Main Street almost a mile north of the bay.

In Montauk, the hurricane ravaged more than 80 fishing boats and 100 houses. Two fishermen drowned trying to save their trawler. Flooding cut off Montauk for two days.

Shortly after 30 people were asked to leave a movie theater in Greenport, the building collapsed in the teeth of the tempest. On Fire Island, two died in Saltaire, where 127 houses were wrecked and 300 people stranded until rescued by the Coast Guard. At Ocean Beach, 300 houses were splintered, along with 91 at Fair Harbor.

Western Long Island was not spared. Gilbert C. Hanse of Babylon, now 84, was an assistant fire chief when he helped rescue several people from flooded, battered houses at Oak Beach. "I will never forget seeing 30, 40, maybe 50 people standing on roofs or porches waving sheets or towels or anything they could to attract our attention," said Hanse, who later became mayor of Babylon.

Hanse and a fellow fireman, the late Teddy Tuddenham, rescued at least eight elderly people before the water on Ocean Parkway flooded Hanse's car. John Tooker, a bayman noted for his poetry, died at nearby Captree Island, entangled in a fish net while trying to secure a boat.

On the North Shore, Robert Pryde of Oyster Bay died at Asharoken when a large wave lifted the boat he was trying to save and dropped it on him.

The only known fatality in Queens was a hitchhiker who drowned in Whitestone while trying to swim away from the stalled car in which he was riding.

By 5:30 p.m., the great hurricane was almost finished with Long Island. Gale winds whined into the night and by 10 p.m. the skies were clear.

Tom Morris is a freelance writer. Bill Bleyer is a staff writer.

UPI Photo, 1938

The storm blew a path of destruction through Fire Island. In Saltaire, for example, 127 houses were wrecked.

Grudge shooting in 1939 causes a sensation in controversy-scarred Long Beach

A Cop Kills the Mayor

By Bill Bleyer
STAFF WRITER

Long Beach Mayor Louis F. Edwards had just walked out of his brick and stucco house on West Beech Street with his police officer bodyguard, James Walsh. Officer Alvin Dooley was on duty in a police booth on the corner 200 feet away. He left it and headed toward them. The three men came together on the sidewalk at 10:10 a.m. on Nov. 15, 1939.

"Hello Alvin," the mayor said.

"Good morning, Mr. Mayor," Dooley answered. Then he pulled out his .38-cal. service revolver and started shooting.

Edwards grappled with Dooley before falling with a bullet in his stomach. Walsh tried to run but a slug tore through his buttocks and stopped near his left kidney. A third shot grazed a passing postman in the arm. As the mayor lay bleeding, Dooley fired two more bullets into him. "You'll never get off the sidewalk you ———," he growled just as Edwards' wife, Claire, ran screaming from the house.

Edwards died in a police car on the way to the hospital. The next day, newspapers trumpeted the shocking story of assassination in Long Beach, an act so brazen that it seemed inconceivable even by the standards of the shorefront city where gambling and political corruption were rampant.

The 47-year-old mayor, father of five children, had come to Long Beach from Altoona, Pa. President of the Metropolitan Refining Co., he had promised to clean up the city and run it like a business.

Dooley was a 38-year-old Long Beach native. He had been a sickly youth who developed slowly mentally and physically. By the time he was 20, his body had filled out and he achieved his childhood dream of becoming a cop and gaining respect.

He was assigned to the motorcycle squad and polished his Harley-Davidson constantly. The job won him more respect, as did his unanimous election to the presidency of the Patrolmen's Benevolent Association after seven years on the force. Family and friends said the PBA was the most important thing in his life and he was obsessed about keeping political interference out of the union. For that reason, he kept the PBA funds in an out-of-town bank.

His immediate supervisor, Sgt. Bertram Wolff, said later that "Al Dooley was a quiet, peaceful, decent man who had everybody's respect." Dooley's record was virtually spotless, and he was known for giving out more summonses than any other cop.

His life began to unravel when city politicans to whom Edwards was obligated wanted the PBA account moved from a Rockville Centre bank to one they owned in Long Beach. Dooley resisted.

Calling it an economy move, Edwards cut the size of the motorcycle squad from four officers to two: Dooley ended up back on foot patrol. Soon afterwards, a woman complained to the mayor that Dooley had been discourteous. Although she quickly changed her story and admitted she had exaggerated, Edwards insisted on holding a hearing. Dooley was exonerated. Later his lawyer, famous defense attorney Sam Leibowitz, said the veteran officer felt humiliated and decided the mayor was out to get him.

Long Beach Historical and Preservation Society Photos

Before the fusillade: Officer Alvin Dooley, left, killed Mayor Louis F. Edwards after the mayor successfully maneuvered to remove him as head of the Patrolmen's Benevolent Association.

Dooley's anger at the mayor escalated when Walsh defeated him as PBA president in a Nov. 1 election. Edwards had actively supported his bodyguard, arm-twisting the membership. After the vote, Dooley went home to his mother and cried uncontrollably. "They beat me," he kept saying.

The night before the shooting, Dooley was out drinking until nearly 4 a.m. with fellow cops who ribbed him about his falling fortunes. When he came on duty at 8 a.m., other officers at headquarters noticed that his eyes were bloodshot. Nonetheless, he was assigned to the police booth on the corner of East Beech Street and Jackson Boulevard.

Tax Rate Will Be Slashed Under New 'Tight' Budget

Long Beach Life

KEEP AMERICA OUT OF WAR

D. A. TO ASK CHAIR FOR MAYOR'S ASSASSIN; WALSH HAS 'FIGHTING CHANCE' TO SURVIVE

MAYOR KEEPS PROMISE AS 20 PT. REDUCTION IS EFFECTED FOR 1940

CITY MOURNING DEATH OF MAYOR

WAIVES EXAMINATION; INDICTMENT EXPECTED BY GRAND JURY TUESDAY

STARK TRAGEDY FOR MAE DOOLEY

A Martyr
An Editorial

FUNERAL TODAY; BODY IN STATE

Governor Will Appoint Temporary Mayor Here

The killing led to days of headlines in Long Beach Life, such as this one on Nov. 17, 1939. Officer James Walsh, who recovered from his wounds, was the mayor's bodyguard. Walsh, with the backing of Edwards, had defeated Dooley for leadership of the local police union.

Two hours later, he killed the mayor.

After the shots were fired, Walsh crawled back into the mayor's house and called the police department, gasping, "The mayor's been shot." Dooley walked to the car of Frank Coombs, manager of the nearby Fleetwood Apartments, and reportedly said "I just killed that bastard." Then he walked to headquarters and told Lt. Leo Nolan "I just killed the mayor."

Cops in the room thought he was kidding until Councilman Teddy Ornstein walked in demanding justice. Dooley pointed the gun at Ornstein and threatened to shoot. When Police Chief Edward Agnew arrived, Dooley yelled, "I'm sorry I didn't get you too." Nolan told Dooley to hand over the gun and the officer complied meekly.

Dooley's arrest cards, still on file at police headquarters, state that he seemed moderately intoxicated. The desk blotter entry made by Nolan noted that Dooley had a half-pint bottle of Old Mr. Boston Rocking Chair Blended Whiskey that was about three-quarters full in his pocket.

Nassau County Police Insp. Harold King rushed Dooley into a car for the drive to county police headquarters in Mineola as crowds gathered, shouting "Hang him" and "Let's get him." Meanwhile, 500 residents gathered at City Hall, where the flag was lowered to half mast and the clock was stopped and turned back to the time of the shooting.

Edwards was buried in Cypress Hills Cemetery, and his pallbearers included U.S. Sen. Robert Wagner. Walsh, 38, had three blood transfusions and recovered sufficiently to testify at the trial. He retired on disability a few months after the shooting.

Dooley pleaded not guilty. The murder trial began in January, 1940. Dooley was defended by Leibowitz and prosecuted by Nassau District Attorney Edward Neary, who demanded the death penalty. Leibowitz argued that his client was not guilty because of temporary insanity. "Gentlemen, Edwards drove Dooley insane," Leibowitz argued in his opening. "This unfortunate man on trial was so intoxicated and so bereft of reason that he didn't know that what he was doing was wrong."

The prosecution introduced the transcript of Dooley's discussion with detectives. Asked when he decided to shoot the mayor, Dooley had responded: "when he gave me that phony 'Hello.' "

Liebowitz called psychiatrists to back up his insanity defense. One witness, Dr. Clarence Bellinger, testified that Dooley suffered from a "paranoid trend coupled with pathological intoxication." The jury deliberated 11 hours and then on Feb. 8 found him guilty of second-degree manslaughter. Dooley was sentenced to 10 to 20 years for manslaughter plus an additional five to 10 years for being armed with a dangerous weapon. After serving 15 years, he got a job at The Daily News. But he continued to drink and later was arrested for child molestation. He died in prison.

After the shooting, Jackson Boulevard was renamed Edwards Boulevard in honor of the mayor. His large house still stands. The police booth was demolished in the 1940s.

Mayor LaGuardia's complaint leads to an airport; but soon, another is needed

Major Airports Take Off

BY RHODA AMON
STAFF WRITER

Less than 40 years after the Wright brothers got an apparatus that looked like a box kite off the ground at a North Carolina site called Kitty Hawk, New York City opened what was then the world's greatest commercial airport on the marshlands of North Beach in Queens.

LaGuardia Field was dedicated Oct. 15, 1939, by a jubilant Mayor Fiorello H. LaGuardia, whose determination built it. Once occupied by the Gala Amusement Park, the site was transformed in 1929 into a 105-acre private flying field. The field was named Glenn H. Curtiss Airport after the pioneer Long Island aviator and later called North Beach Airport. Until 1939, air travelers from the city or Long Island — like Jean Steward of Sea Cliff, who took her first flight to visit relatives in Louisville, Ky., in 1935 — had to motor to and from an airfield in Newark, N.J. "My father wanted me to have the experience of flying," Steward said recently.

But LaGuardia himself wanted to land closer to home. The feisty mayor refused to leave a returning plane at Newark, claiming that his ticket read New York.

He considered Floyd Bennett Field, which had been reclaimed from marshland on Jamaica Bay in 1930, but the Brooklyn field was too distant from central Manhattan to attract commercial flights.

In 1937, after years of negotiations with the federal government, ground was broken for a new, enlarged airport at the LaGuardia site to be built by the city and the New Deal's Works Progress Administration. The work went quickly, considering it involved filling in 357 acres of marshland and constructing six immense hangars. The field opened to commercial traffic in December, 1939.

Not everyone was as enthusiastic as LaGuardia about the project — some regarded it as a $45-million boondoggle. But the public thrilled to the prospect of air travel. Families flocked to the airport on weekends just to watch the gleaming silver airliners take off and vanish into the blue or swoop majestically down onto the field. A dime got you through the turnstiles to a crowded observation deck. The turnstile dimes, plus parking fees, soon added up to $285,000, The New York Times reported two years later. With other yearly

Cradle of Aviation Museum

Above, an aerial photo shows LaGuardia Airport in 1940, a year after it was built. Below, an undated photo shows the marsh that eventually was transformed into Idlewild Airport.

State Office of Parks, Recreation and Historic Preservation Photo

revenues of $650,000, the LaGuardia "white elephant," as its opponents dubbed it earlier, soon was operating in the black.

The field also added a new population estimated at more than 10,000 — pilots, stewardesses, mechanics, other airline personnel — to Long Island's North Shore. But the war raging in Europe put a damper on plans to make LaGuardia an international airport. A seaplane terminal opened in March, 1940, without its prospective tenants: British Airways, Air France, Lufthansa. Never mind, the four-engine Pan-American Clippers that first took off from a seaport at Port Washington in 1939 were dramatic enough to draw thousands of dimes into the turnstiles.

The great international airport was yet to come. With LaGuardia quickly reaching its capacity, construction began in 1942 at the site of the Idlewild Golf Course in southeast Queens. It involved filling in acres of marshy tidelands on Jamaica Bay. Planned at first for 1,000 acres, Idlewild Airport grew to five times that size. It was dedicated in July, 1948, as New York International Airport, rededicated in December, 1963, after the death of the president, as John F. Kennedy International Airport and henceforth known as JFK. But some neighborhood diehards still refer to it as Idlewild.

Though the two Queens airports have been operated since 1947 by the Port Authority of New York and New Jersey, Mayor LaGuardia continued to be their most vociferous promoter.

But even a visionary like LaGuardia could not have foreseen the heights that air travel would reach. In 1945, while he was still mayor and with Idlewild Airport still uncompleted, LaGuardia predicted that someday more than 10 million passengers per year would pass through its gates. Today close to 30 million a year pass through JFK.

He was more on target in predicting that 40,000 men and women would be employed in operation, maintenance, traffic, transportation, sales, food and other airport activity.

LaGuardia died in 1947, the year before his dream of "the world's finest airport" was officially opened by President Harry Truman.

LaGuardia Airport also has continued to grow — mostly as a domestic airport. The Central Terminal Building, opened in 1964 to serve most of the airport's scheduled domestic airlines, twice has been enlarged.

The original airport terminal building, once called the Overseas Terminal, was built near the bay to accommodate the flying boats that dominated international air travel in the '30s and '40s.

Now called the Marine Air Terminal, it was designated a New York City historic landmark in 1995. Today the terminal is used by commuter airlines, air taxis, private aircraft and a private weather service. It boasts the largest mural created under the New Deal's Work Progress Administration's art program: "Flight," by James Brooks, completed in 1942.

A shuttle service, begun by Pan Am Airways in 1986 and purchased by Delta Air Lines when Pan Am ceased operations in 1991, operates hourly to Boston and Washington.

And it is not unusual for corporate types to commute daily to American cities from LaGuardia Airport or to take weekly hops to foreign cities from JFK. That's a commute Mayor LaGuardia may not have foreseen.

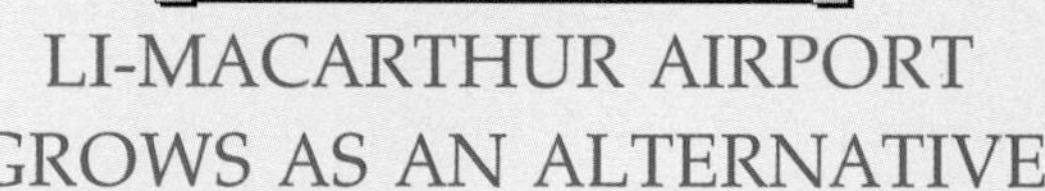

LI-MACARTHUR AIRPORT GROWS AS AN ALTERNATIVE

Long Island-MacArthur Airport proves that, if you build it, they will come. Tucked into central Suffolk, the airfield has been growing with the Island's population. It generates 1.1 million passengers a year from local industries and from Nassau-Suffolk residents who would rather not buck the traffic and hassle of getting to Kennedy and LaGuardia Airports or driving all the way to Newark Airport.

Outside of the Queens airports, MacArthur in Ronkonkoma is the only regional field on Long Island served by major scheduled jet carriers. The Islip Town-owned airport began in 1942 as a World War II defense-plane landing area. Lockheed Aircraft built the first hangar at the airport in 1944, and, after taking back the airport from the Army Air Corps at the close of the war, Islip built a terminal in 1949.

Allegheny Airlines was the first commercial airline to operate out of MacArthur, offering to Long Island its Boston-Philadelphia-Washington route in 1960. The Douglas MacArthur terminal was completed in 1968 in time for the spurt in regional airport usage, which was triggered by airline deregulation in the 1970s.

Despite local opposition concerned mostly with noise pollution, MacArthur continues to pull passengers. It is now in the midst of a $13-million renovation.

Long Islanders can now board flights of American Airlines, USAirways Express, Northwest Airlink, Airtram Airways, and Delta connections called Business Express and Delta Express. Comair, another Delta connection, is to begin service to Cincinnati from the airport on June 1.

— **Rhoda Amon**

The Trylon tower and the Perisphere globe stand above statues and the Lagoon of Nations at the 1939 World's Fair

Newsday Archives Photo

Before war strikes, hope for a better tomorrow draws millions to Queens' 1939 World's Fair

A Rosy View Of the Future

BY DAVID BEHRENS
STAFF WRITER

For a fleeting moment, the 1939 New York World's Fair held out the promise of a bright and easy future.

The theme was "The World of Tomorrow," a message of boundless optimism that came at a perfect moment in American history: that slim wedge of time between the sorrowful era of the Great Depression and the tragic years of World War II, just around the corner.

The symbols of the future were the gleaming-white Trylon and Perisphere. The Trylon was a 700-foot tower overlooking the Perisphere, a 200-foot-wide globe rising 18 stories above its reflecting pool. Bathed in floodlights, the modern design became the most famous symbol since the Eiffel Tower dominated the Paris Fair of 1889.

Inside the Perisphere, visitors rode on one of two moving belts around the interior, peering down on Democracity, a diorama of urban and exurban life in the future, as if seen from an airplane. "A symbol of a perfectly integrated futuristic metropolis pulsing with life and rhythm and music," the guidebooks read. Radio commentator H. V. Kaltenborn delivered the narration during the 6-minute circuit.

Much of the fair was devoted with reverence to the marvels of science, present and future, and the man-made achievements of the 20th Century. In retrospect, the message became one of the great ironies of the fair, with the nightmare of World War II and the atomic age just ahead.

Futurama, the General Motors exhibit, was the fair's most popular venture. Visitors queued up for hours, waiting for another glimpse of tomorrow. Riding in plush easy chairs on a moving belt, visitors saw a vision of the ultramodern city of 1960, where radio-controlled cars zipped along expressways, guided by beams on a 14-lane motorway. Steering would become an old-fashioned affectation in the midst of high-rise buildings and sleek suspension bridges. Writing about the fair, historian and futurist H.G. Wells saw the World of Tomorrow as a demonstration of "what can be done with human life today."

Claire Jay, a Freeport resident, was almost 12 when she made her only trip to the fair. It was "East Rockaway Day at the fair," she recalled recently. "We walked for hours. We'd see the Trylon wherever we went and we used it as a guidepost. There were fountains everywhere, lit up at night with colored lights. It was absolutely thrilling. It gave you a fairyland sort of feeling," she remembers as if it were yesterday.

A gust of wind blew away her best hat, a coral straw Easter bonnet that ended up in the Perisphere's reflecting pool. But a glimpse of the World of Tomorrow was worth the loss, Jay said. She was old enough, even then, to appreciate all the innovative structures.

"My parents had been terribly hurt in the Depression and my father, a carpenter, was out of work from 1932 until 1936. By 1940, he had been working for several years. Things were better. I was old enough to appreciate the struggle my parents had gone through. So just making the trip, seeing what life could be like, was a miracle."

Later, she and her family walked past the brightly lit Lagoon of Nations and into the Court of Peace, where 60 nations had built halls to celebrate a world at peace, another of the fair's great ironies. Only Germany, Spain and China were missing among the major nations.

By 1940, Nazi troops had already overrun Czechoslovakia and invaded Poland and their pavilions were draped in black. The Soviet Union spent millions on its hall, featuring a giant figure of a Russian worker holding aloft a red star. But in 1940, the hall was closed after the Soviet Union was branded the aggressor for its invasion of Finland.

Despite the shadows of war, more than 45 million admissions were recorded. Many visitors wore buttons that read "I Have Seen the Future." Or they sported the lapel pin shaped like a pickle, a freebie from the Heinz exhibit.

There were stars of every variety: Billy Rose's Aquacade featured America's most famous swimmer, Eleanor Holm, his wife. There was music by composers Kurt Weill and Aaron Copland, productions by Mike Todd and sculpture by Alexander Calder. And there were curiosities galore. Elsie, the Borden trademark, was the bovine biggie at the company's exhibit of the "Rotolactor," a mechanical milking device. There also was a talking Plymouth at the Chrysler exhibit and Electro, Westinghouse's talking robot. The GM-X, an experimental car from General Motors, as pointy-nosed as a fighter plane, also was on display. There was a simulated trip to the moon and a block-long diorama of New York, three stories high, twinkling in Con Edison's City of Light.

There were many other firsts: the first public demonstration of nylon, Lucite and Plexiglas; the first 3-D movie, the first use of fluorescent lighting. And at the RCA pavilion, there was the first demonstration of a new idea, a radio with pictures: television! On April 30, 1939, Franklin Roosevelt gave the opening day address and became the first president to appear on TV.

In the 1920s, the marshy site of the fair had become a monumental dump. The idea of a World's Fair on 1,200 acres along the Flushing River was proposed in 1935 as an economic boost to counter the lingering effects of the Depression. A nonprofit corporation was founded and $27 million in bonds were sold.

So the brilliant 1939 fair sprang out of the marshland, and in those innocent times, millions of visitors were convinced that the World of Tomorrow would be filled with joy and hope.

IN 1964, A LESS OPTIMISTIC MOOD

'Peace Through Understanding" was the theme of the 1964 New York World's Fair, symbolized by the Unisphere, the 140-foot-high steel sphere that still dominates the fairgrounds, now Flushing Meadows-Corona Park.

The Unisphere was ringed with brightly colored fountains in a style reminiscent of 1939. But the dominant mood of the new fair was set by industrial exhibits and a number of inventive amusements.

Beset by Cold War anxieties and nuclear nightmares, many fairgoers no longer shared the optimism of 1939 about scientific progress, the "wide-eyed hope at the future of modernity and the blessings of the Machine Age," critic Robert Rosenblum observed.

Amusing scenes and good food were the order of the day. Among the most popular exhibits were Sinclair's World of Dinosaurs and Walt Disney's "It's a Small World" at the Pepsi Pavilion. Another popular spot was the African Pavilion, which featured Nigeria's Babtunde Olitunji and his drummers. Halls opened by dozens of nations, with eateries serving ethnic specialties, drew enormous crowds. For many visitors, it was their first Belgian waffles.

— Behrens

The Unisphere dominates the event.

UPI Photo

Albert Einstein spent summers on LI, sailing and pondering world-shaking issues

Little Peconic Bay and E=mc²

BY GEORGE DEWAN
STAFF WRITER

The most famous summer vacationer in Southold history was the German-born genius who created the world's most famous equation. His name was Albert Einstein.

After theoretical physics, Einstein's second love was sailing, and Little Peconic Bay enchanted him. In the summer of 1939, Robert Rothman, the present owner of Rothman's Department Store in Southold, was 12. His father, David, then owned the store.

"Einstein came in and asked, did we sell sundials," Rothman said recently. "My father took him out to the back yard and showed him sundials. " 'No,' he said. 'No, no. Sundials,' and pointed to his feet"

The 60-year-old Einstein got his sandals, and he liked them so much that Rothman's father sent him a new pair for the next two years when the scientist was summering at upstate Saranac Lake. "It was very kind of you to send me again this year a pair of my favorite sandals," Einstein wrote to Rothman. "I cannot wear them yet because those you have given me last year are still of kingly elegance. I wear them always in the sailboat and out."

An avid sailor, if not always an artistic one, Einstein once called Little Peconic Bay "the most beautiful sailing ground I ever experienced . . . " In the summers of 1938 and 1939 he rented a cottage on Old Cove Road, now called West Cove Road, on Nassau Point, on the bay. Einstein spent many hours alone in the little sailboat he called Tineff (Yiddish for "worthless"), occasionally running aground, sometimes capsizing, often just drifting, and always doing what he did best, which was thinking.

Southold Historical Society Photo by Reginald Donahue

Einstein in Southold: The avid, if awkward, sailor was said to be enchanted by Little Peconic Bay.

On Aug. 2 of that summer, Einstein, at the request of fellow physicists, signed the famous letter to President Roosevelt, alerting him to new developments in nuclear physics that could lead to powerful weapons, and hinting that the Germans might be working on an atomic bomb. It was a letter that Einstein would later regret sending.

Since 1933, Einstein had lived in Princeton, N.J., where he was a professor at the Institute for Advanced Studies. In the summer of 1934, he shared a rented house with a friend in Watch Hill, R.I. In later summers, he spent time in Old Lyme, Conn., and Saranac Lake. In 1937, the summer after his second wife, Elsa, died, he rented a home on the water in Huntington. Also that summer, he occasionally visited friends at Nassau Point, near what was then called Peconic — now Cutchogue.

Einstein had little contact with most of the other residents in and around Nassau Point. But in 1939 he became a close friend of Rothman's father, who, like Einstein, played the violin. "He suggested they might like to play," Robert Rothman said. "My father knew a few others who were reasonably accomplished musicians. They came down, went into the living room and started playing together. They might have played every week, frequently, the whole summer."

Well out of the mainstream of physics by this time, Einstein had not given up what would ultimately be a failed quest for his own holy grail, a unified field theory. This would, in Einstein's words, "reduce to one formula the explanation of the field of gravity and of the field of electromagnetism." Other scientists, meanwhile, were getting closer and closer to unlocking the secrets of the atom.

But it was Einstein who, unfairly, was to get the unwanted label, "father of the atomic bomb." This judgment was based primarily on the theoretical work, including the Special Theory of Relativity, which he had published in 1905 while employed as a low-grade technical officer in the Swiss Patent Office. Out of this theory came the most famous equation ever written, the equation that defines the equivalence of mass and energy: $E = mc^2$. Because "c" represents the speed of light (186,282 miles per second), this meant that huge amounts of energy were locked up in minute particles of mass.

But that was only in theory. Practically, he did not believe that it was possible to release this enormous energy by bombarding the nucleus of the atom. Some experimental physicists thought otherwise, however. One of them was the Hungarian refugee Leo Szilard, who had produced a nuclear chain reaction in a laboratory at Columbia University. He and others feared that Germany might be working on an atomic bomb.

When Szilard and fellow physicist Eugene Wigner journeyed to Nassau Point in mid-July of 1939, they knew what Einstein did not know — that recent developments in nuclear fission made an atomic bomb possible. They wanted to get the ear of the U.S. government, and they knew that Einstein would not be ignored. They brought him up to date, and the great scientist was surprised.

"*Daran habe ich gar nicht gedacht!*" Einstein said — "I never thought of that!"

After a second visit, a letter to the president was drafted by Szilard. Einstein's final version, dated Aug. 2, 1939, said, in part: "[I]t may become possible to set up nuclear chain reactions in a large mass of uranium, by which vast amounts of power . . . would be generated. This new phenomenon would also lead to the construction of bombs . . . "

The letter is widely credited with setting in motion the Manhattan Project, the government effort to build an atomic bomb. The bureaucratic process was a long one, and the project did not begin until December, 1941. World War II effectively ended in August, 1945, with atomic mushroom clouds over Hiroshima and Nagasaki.

Later, Einstein had second thoughts about the famous letter.

"I made one great mistake in my life — when I signed the letter to President Roosevelt recommending that atomic bombs be made," Einstein told chemist Linus Pauling in 1954. "But there was some justification — the danger that the Germans would make them."

EINSTEIN'S MUSCLES AND MORALS

The English author and physicist C. P. Snow recalled driving to Nassau Point in 1937 to visit the 58-year-old Albert Einstein.

"What did surprise me was his physique," Snow wrote in Commentary magazine in 1967. "He had come in from sailing and was wearing nothing but a pair of shorts. It was a massive body, very heavily muscled: he was running to fat around the midriff and in the upper arms, rather like a footballer in middle age, but he was still an unusually strong man. . . ."

"Mostly we talked of politics," Snow continued. "The moral and practical choices in front of us, and what could be saved from the storm to come, not only for Europe but for the human race. All the time he was speaking with a weight of moral experience which was different, not only in quantity but in kind, from anything I had ever met. By this time he had lost any intrusion from his own ego, as though it had never existed. It was something like talking to the second Isaiah."

— George DeWan

LI-built planes give America superiority in the skies over Europe and the Pacific

The Wings of War

BY GEORGE DEWAN
STAFF WRITER

They had fearful and aggressive names like Wildcat and Hellcat, Avenger and Thunderbolt, and they lived up to their deadly image in the skies over Europe and the Pacific. Stamped with the label "Made on Long Island," these winged agents of destruction played a major role in winning World War II.

After the Japanese attack on Pearl Harbor on Dec. 7, 1941, Long Island, the cradle of aviation, turned its attention to making America the arsenal of democracy. The production of fighter planes by Grumman and Republic was a major part of that effort.

On Feb. 20, 1942, Navy Lt. Edward H. (Butch) O'Hare flew his Grumman Wildcat fighter plane into a forest of Japanese bombers attacking the carrier Lexington in the Southwest Pacific, his .50-cal. guns blazing. In just a few minutes he shot down five of them. Ecstatic workers at the Grumman Aircraft Engineering Corp. plant at Bethpage, where the airplane was made, took up a collection and sent O'Hare 1,150 cartons of cigarettes.

"You sort of tingle all over," O'Hare, who would win the Medal of Honor for his heroics and later be killed in action, said of being in an aerial battle. "You are dry as dust and thirsty. You don't have time to consider the odds against you. You are too busy throwing bullets."

One of the Grumman workers was George Burkhardt of Wantagh, a metalworker, the first 50-year-man with the company. "It gives you a tremendous charge," Burkhardt, 84, said recently when asked how it felt to hear that a Grumman plane was beating up on the Japanese. "It made us feel like we were right in there. We weren't being shot at, but we were producing planes that were desperately needed."

Down the road from Grumman, where the Republic Aviation Corp. at Farmingdale was making the legendary P-47 Thunderbolt for the U.S. Army Air Forces, there was also cheering for reports of heroes and air aces. The applause went both ways, as the pilots raved about the Grumman and Republic planes they were flying. The two leading World War II fighter aces in Europe flew the P-47: the Long Islander Francis S. Gabreski and the Oklahoman Robert S. Johnson.

The Pennsylvania-born Gabreski, who worked for Grumman after the war, is now 79 and lives in Dix Hills. He had 28 confirmed kills, and destroyed three more German planes on the ground. "The P-47 was one of the most durable, well-built airplanes," he said last week. "My tribute is to the people at Republic who built it. They built a great airplane that had the survival benefit built into it like a tank."

In his book, "Thunderbolt!," Lt. Col. Johnson — who also had 28 confirmed

Please see WAR on Page 307

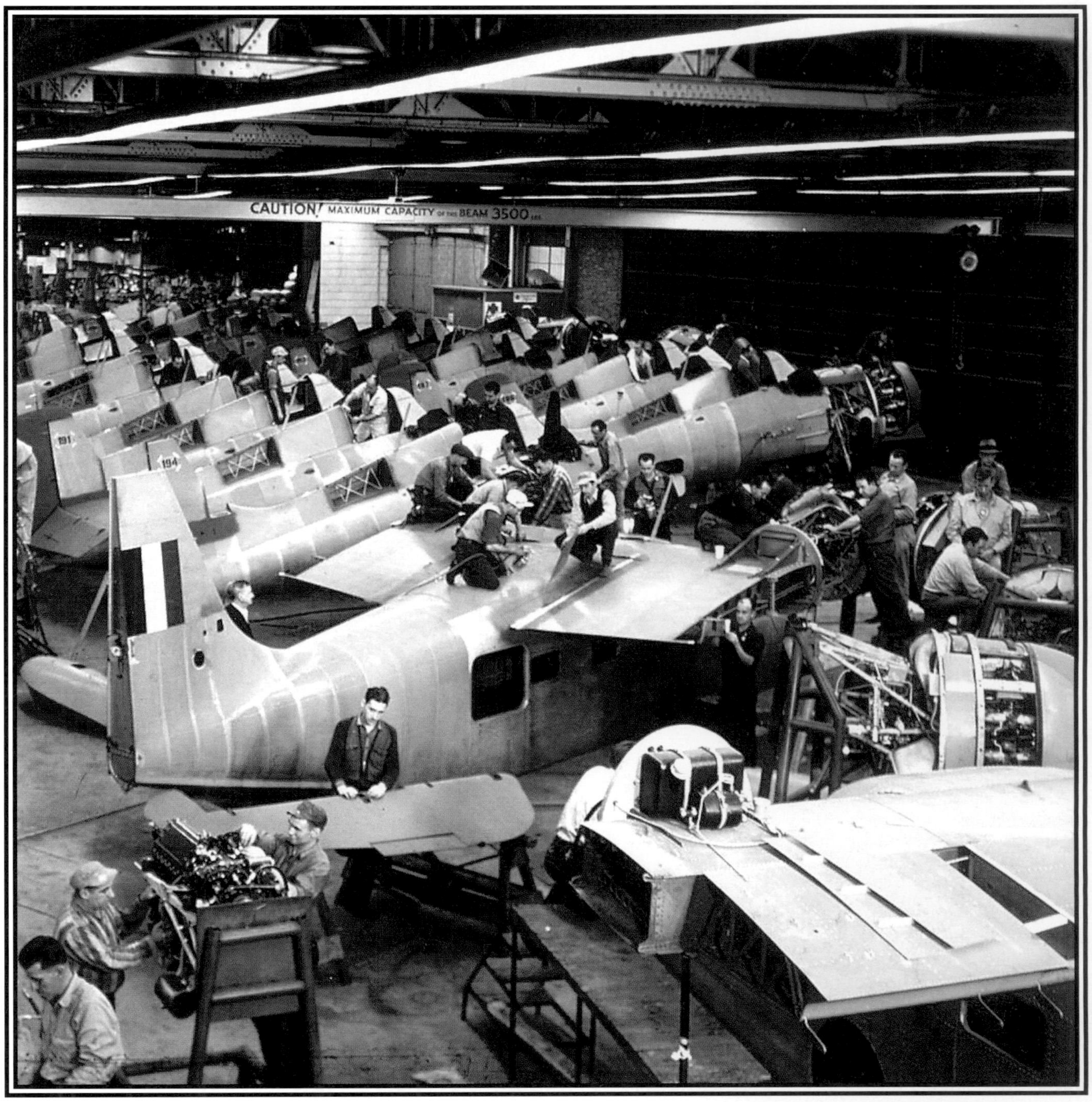

Northrop Grumman Photo

A Grumman plant in 1942. One thing the Grumman and Republic planes had in common was that they were sturdy aircraft that could survive devastating attacks.

LI HISTORY.COM

Newsday Photo / Don Jacobsen

Graves at Pinelawn National Cemetery

Remembering Those Who Died

The first online memorial dedicated to the 5,000 local members of the armed forces who died in World War II has been compiled by Newsday and is now available on the newspaper's Internet site. Names include those who served in the Army, Army Air Corps, Navy, Marines, Coast Guard and reserves.

Also available online is the "Long Island: Our Story" forum, where veterans and those who worked on the homefront can share their stories of service and sacrifice. For the memorial and the forum, see **http://www.lihistory.com.**

Serving On The Home Front

Making sacrifices on LI

BY DAVID BEHRENS
STAFF WRITER

'Don't you know there's a war going on!"

The phrase echoed everywhere, directed at neighbors who griped too loudly or too often about the growing demands on the home front. Once again, veterans of the Great Depression had to do without.

There were shortages of butter, coffee, sugar, beef and other staples of everyday life. Rationing would remain in place for the duration. In the towns and villages of Long Island, lights were dimmed and — when the sirens sounded — turned off in response to simulated air raids. Soon enough, gold stars, signifying that a family member had died in the service, would begin to appear in America's front parlors.

With the nation embroiled in global combat, World War II evoked a heady sense of unity at home.

Remembering Pearl Harbor was the order of the day. Families responded to one war bond drive after another, while collections of scrap metal, tin cans, newspapers and cooking fats for the war effort were persistent reminders of the national crisis.

Home front patriots responded by planting "victory gardens" to produce their own vegetables. In Garden City, appropriately enough, Joe and Gladys Barry were among many neighbors who planted their vegetable patch right on the front lawns of residential Kensington Road. In Oceanside, Ruth Fortin's father served as an air raid warden.

There were many adjustments: dealing with crowded buses and trains, gasoline shortages, even the miserable quality of professional baseball when the stars enlisted. Many did succumb to the lure of the black market and when acquisitions were too obvious, neighbors scolded with that recurring refrain: "Don't you know there's a war going on!"

There was much to complain about at home but even more to be grateful for. Though more than 300,000 Americans were killed in the war, the nation's civilian population was essentially unscathed during the war years. But for those who doggedly served at home, these times never would be forgotten.

Newsday Photo / Bill Davis

Ruth Fortin, who would watch troop convoys pass by

Ruth Fortin, still an Oceanside resident, remembers the first fearful months of the war. Newspapers and radio broadcasters supplied a daily diet of bad news: the fall of Manila. Execution of prisoners of war in the Pacific. Enemy submarines sinking ships off Long Island.

Beachgoers would stroll on the Long Beach boardwalk, Fortin recalled. "But we wouldn't swim there because the water was full of debris from torpedoed ships — life preservers, broken crates, huge pieces of wood, floating oil slicks."

Fortin, now 74, was graduated from Oceanside High in 1940. Living near South Nassau Communities Hospital, she remembers a cow pasture where the emergency room now stands. In Oceanside, she had not worried at first about a local attack. "But then a group of saboteurs who landed on Long Island were captured and, well, we wondered about such things. My father told us: 'Make sure your mother keeps the radio on all the time.' "

U.S. Department of Defense Photo

Long Island civilians are on the lookout for enemy airplanes. Lights were dimmed and — when the sirens sounded — turned off in response to simulated air raids.

On Dec. 7, 1941, it was her father who had told her about the news from Pearl Harbor. She and a cousin were about to leave for Rockville Centre to see a Deanna Durbin movie at the Fantasy Theater. They took a walk instead and met two soldiers on the street. "When we told them the news, they just ran for the bus to their base in Mitchel Field. We were too upset for a movie that day."

For many young people, sitting in eerie darkness during recurring air raid drills became a shared experience. Teresa Weiss, who grew up in Queens, remembers the night she and a girlfriend were caught in a blackout while waiting for the bus. "The sirens went off and everything went black. The bus had just pulled up and we were told to get in. Everyone sat in the dark for 15 or 20 minutes until the all-clear sounded," said Weiss, now 74 and a Huntington resident.

After graduation from high school in 1942, she took on the duties of a mature woman. Living with her father, stepmother and two younger brothers, she served as a "mother hen" on the home front, until she married her sailor-husband in 1944. For everyone, she said, the future seemed uncertain. "We weren't sure what was going to happen. Hitler had done so much damage in Europe, people thought we might have a heck of a fight if the Nazis ever landed here."

A sense of suspicion also lingered in the air. "You felt you had to be careful. Like the posters in the post office said, 'Loose Lips Sink Ships.' You could never be 100 percent sure your neighbors weren't spies."

At 18, she worked in Manhattan for Metropolitan Life Insurance. "I'd take the subway in, care for the house at night, cook the meals and do the shopping, trying to stretch all the coupons on everything that was rationed," said Weiss.

Her stepmother, an executive secretary, worked late, so Teresa made supper for her brothers and her father. Feeding a family of five was a job in itself. "We were allowed just so much butter, just so much meat. Finding a half pound of bacon, that was like looking for gold. So we had lots of vegetable meals. I'd make potatoes and vegetables and a salad and that was dinner."

At home in Garden City, Gladys Barry was the mother of two small children. Her husband, Joe, a salesman, commuted to his job in Manhattan on the Long Island Rail Road and made rounds by bus or on foot. At home, Gladys was in charge of coping with the wartime shortages.

"We just got used to the shortages," said Barry, now 89 and living in Franklin Square. "It was hard to buy meat so you took what you could get. We all felt patriotic, of course. But butter was the thing we missed the most. You cooked with Crisco and Spry. And then there was the gas rationing, which was horrible. Three gallons a week!"

She and her husband hardly used their Buick except to shop for groceries, but there were long lines at the local gas station. "The word would get

Please see HOME on Page 311

Form OPA R-501 UNITED STATES OF AMERICA
OFFICE OF PRICE ADMINISTRATION
GASOLINE RATION CARD A
Nº 3363583 -B
BUY UNITED STATES WAR BONDS AND STAMPS
THE ACCEPTANCE AND USE OF THIS CARD CONSTITUTE AN AGREEMENT THAT THE HOLDER WILL OBSERVE THE RULES AND REGULATIONS GOVERNING GASOLINE RATIONING AS ISSUED BY THE OFFICE OF PRICE ADMINISTRATION
OWNER'S NAME Leonard Witham
STREET ADDRESS 80 Washington Ave.
CITY OR POST OFFICE Oceanside STATE N.Y.
MAKE Nash BODY STYLE Coupe
VEHICLE REGISTRATION NO. 8T 7688 STATE OF REGISTRATION N.Y.
(SIGNATURE) Leonard Witham
READ INSTRUCTIONS ON REVERSE SIDE OF THIS CARD
ONE UNIT | ONE UNIT | ONE UNIT | ONE UNIT | ONE UNIT | ONE UNIT | ONE UNIT

Above, the gas ration card issued to Leonard Witham, Ruth Fortin's father. At right, cars line up for gas in Franklin Square in 1942. Its scarcity meant that cars were used only when necessary.

Newsday Photo

LI's Own Rosie the Riveters

BY BETH WHITEHOUSE
STAFF WRITER

Josephine Rachiele kept her World War II in a shoebox for years: metal caked with dirt. A chunk of a P-47 Thunderbolt that had crashed during a test flight on the East End. A soldier lugged it to Babylon for Rachiele. "Here's one of your P-47s," he said.

One of her P-47s. Rachiele riveted together the parts of those fighter planes, covering the metal with silver dots that lined up like rhinestones on a denim country-western jacket.

Rachiele held onto that chunk of plane for years, keeping it in the family's basement until her brother, thinking it was junk, threw it away. She held more tightly to a letter from Frank Colombo, a family friend who didn't make it back from the front lines of Europe. "Are you still holding on to your job at Republic? We see many a plane going over to give the Germans hell," he wrote her. And she saved the letter she wrote him in 1945, sent back coldly stamped "deceased."

She had written of how big-band leader Tommy Dorsey visited the Republic Aviation plant in Farmingdale. A black-and-white glossy photo shows Rachiele with dark hair and a wide smile, perched on the wing of a P-47 with Dorsey below. "We had a lot of fun that night. And the music was right in the groove," she wrote.

When America went to war, so did Josephine Rachiele. Sure, she never left Long Island. But in 1943 she gave up her job in a coat factory to go work at Republic Aviation, to become one of the legions of women nationwide dubbed Rosie the Riveter. Thousands of women worked in Long Island defense industry plants such as Republic and Grumman, making war planes while the men who normally would have held the jobs went off to fly them.

"I wanted to do something for my country," Rachiele said. "Some of the boys where I worked were drafted, and I decided I had to help."

Virginia Maryweathers Gordon, of Lakeview, echoed Rachiele's patriotism. Her first husband was in the Army during the war, and she worked at Grumman as a riveter on the tail section of the F6F Hellcat. "I felt that I was doing something to help out."

Gordon is now 77. Rachiele is 74, white-haired and living in West Babylon. But back in the 1940s, just into their 20s, they put on coveralls and pulled their hair back in bandannas so it wouldn't get caught in machinery. They worked with partners. One of the women would use a rivet gun to shoot the rivet through a hole marked on the airplane part. At the same time, the partner would buck the rivet — stand on the other side with a steel bar wedged against the part. The rivet would slam into the steel bar, which would flatten it on the other side. Rachiele said her hands would vibrate.

Badge, West Babylon Public Library; Above and Below, Northrop Grumman Photos

Above, women work on a Hellcat assembly line in Bethpage during World War II. At right, Virginia Maryweathers Gordon at Grumman, circa 1943. Below, Josephine Rachiele's ID badge from 1944, when she worked at Republic Aviation.

Rachiele flinched at the loud noise inside Republic's cavernous Building 17, noise so loud that now, 55 years later, she has hearing loss she believes started in those days. She would work 10-hour days five days a week, and eight hours on Saturday, carrying in her lunchbox three or four sandwiches.

Rachiele earned 60 cents an hour, making far more in a week than the $10 she had earned at the coat factory and spending most of it on clothes. By the time the war ended, she was making 90 cents an hour. Republic brought in bands to boost morale, and offered monthly bonuses if the workers produced more planes.

It didn't bother Rachiele that she was making fighter planes. Sometimes she would go outside during her lunch break and marvel at them all lined up and shiny. They had room in the cockpit for only the pilot. The planes weighed 13,500 pounds each, could go 433 miles per hour, and were armed with eight machine guns and one 500-pound bomb.

"What a sight to see all the planes lined up," she said. "They looked so beautiful." Rachiele got into a P-47 once when she was years older and at an air show. "I said, 'I want to get in that airplane just to see what it feels like.' I had a hard time getting in it. I don't know how those men did it."

The plant newsletter did a story on Rachiele and her two sisters, Sarah, who sharpened drills in the same building, and Theresa, who was an executive secretary at the plant. They were called the Home Front Sisters.

They would go home each night and write letters to the boys at war — boys such as Frank Colombo. Their father, Biagio, was a volunteer auxiliary police officer. In the neighborhood, people were required to cover windows with shades so no lights shined out at night, in case enemy bombers reached American soil and were searching for a target. Biagio carried a billy club and would knock on doors and let people know if light was peeking through. The family had a victory garden to grow vegetables in the backyard, so that mass-produced vegetables could go to the men overseas. Once in a while the girls would dress up on a Saturday and go into Manhattan to see a show with other girls from the plant.

This was Josephine Rachiele's World War II.

Theresa and Sarah both now live in Florida. But Josie stayed on Long Island. She has since been featured in books, and people have asked her for her autograph at air shows. "When they find out that I was a riveter during the war, they say, 'A Rosie, a real Rosie?' They never came in contact with a real Rosie the Riveter because most of them are young." They ask to have their pictures taken with her.

When the war ended, she gave up her Republic job so a returning soldier could have it. But a year and a half later, she returned to Republic. She loved it. She worked there for more than 40 years. "We proved we could do the job as well as men — maybe better," she said. Many a Rosie the Riveter found she liked working outside the home.

"Women were in the work force who previously would not have been," said Natalie Naylor, co-editor of a book called "Long Island Women: Activists and Innovators," published in March by Hofstra University. "World War II started the big shift and increase in women going into the paid work force, particularly in nontraditional jobs."

Along the way, Rachiele got married, and later divorced. She never had children. Rachiele is vice president of the local P-47 Alumni Association and treasurer of the Long Island-Republic Aviation Historical Society. Her apartment is filled with models and photographs of planes, and even a salt and pepper shaker set shaped like airplanes. Sometimes she'll go to Pinelawn Memorial Park in Melville to visit Frank Colombo's grave. And she'll think back to the war years, when a sign hung over the door inside the plant saying, "Keep That Line Rolling."

"During the war we had incentive to make more planes for our country," she said. "After the war it was a job. It was just a job."

Listening for News of the Boys

BY RHODA AMON
STAFF WRITER

Every night for three years, while her children were asleep and her husband was at work, she would listen on the shortwave radio to the strange cool voice of Axis Sally, the German counterpart of Tokyo Rose.

In her propaganda broadcasts in English, Sally would give the names, serial numbers and home addresses of American GIs, some wounded, who had been captured by German forces. Irene Walters, in her Patchogue home, would jot down the information and then write postcards to the families to let them know their boys were alive. Her war effort, begun in 1942 when she accidentally tuned in Axis Sally, continued until war's end.

"I always wrote the postcards the same night; sometimes I would be up until 3 or 4 in the morning," Irene Walters, now 87, recalls. "My son would drop them off at the post office the next morning on his way to school." It was not easy. The serial numbers were recited so fast, she sometimes missed a number. And she had to be up at 6 to make breakfast and get her children off to school. "I never put down what was wrong with the boys, if they were hospitalized — just that they were alive," she says. She had two brothers serving overseas, "and I would want to know that about them."

The grateful responses poured in, more than 1,000. Many said that the only information they had from the War Department was that their sons or husbands were "missing in action." The father of one POW sent her a map of *stalags* in German-occupied territory "so I could pinpoint where the boys were." One of them, now in his 70s, wrote that he had come upon her postcard in his late mother's effects. Would she still have his mother's response? She found it in the large tin cookie box where she's kept all her wartime correspondence for more than a half century. He sent her a Christmas tree made of dollar bills, about $12. It's on her living room wall. "Oh my, I wouldn't touch that money," she says.

Her husband, George, who worked nights for the Brooklyn Times, died 35 years ago; her son, a couple of years later. She has a daughter, three grandchildren and three great-grandchildren.

She's lived in the same house in Patchogue for almost 70 years, now with a TV set in the living room. "We traded the old radio set when TVs came out," she says, regretfully. "It was such a good radio."

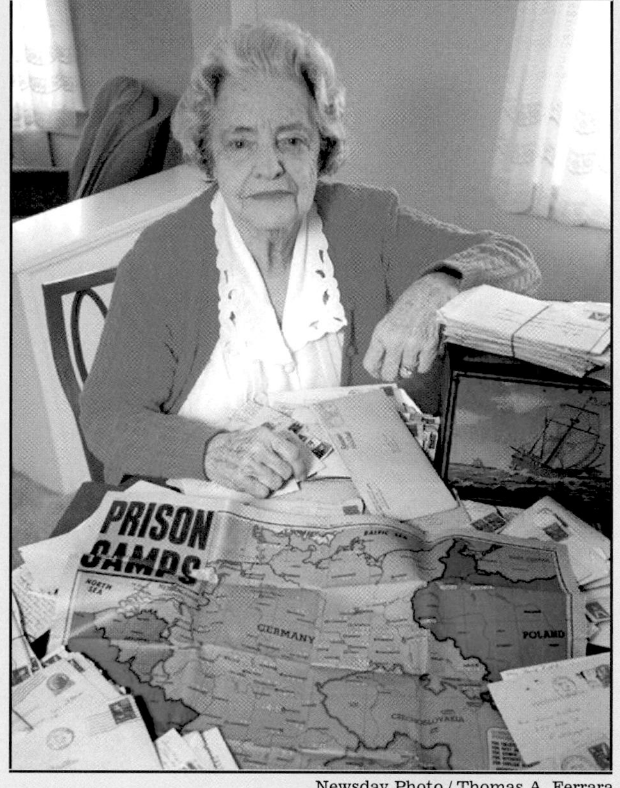

Newsday Photo / Thomas A. Ferrara

Irene Walters, of Patchogue, monitored German broadcasts to learn about U.S. captives. She kept families' thank-you letters.

LI's Sturdy Wings of War

WAR from Page 304

kills — tells a harrowing story of limping home to England after being virtually destroyed in midair by a German Focke-Wulf. Almost blinded, he made it back to the English airfield, got out and looked at his Republic-built Thunderbolt P-47.

"The Thunderbolt has brought me home," he wrote, almost in wonder. "Battered into a flying, wrecked cripple, she fought her way back, brought me home . . . My awe and respect for the fighter increase as I walk around the battered machine."

Johnson describes the damage: 21 gaping holes and tears from exploding 20-mm. cannon shells, hundreds of bullet holes through the wings, fuselage, tail and propeller, three cannon shell dents in the armor plate an inch from his head, cannon shell holes in both wings and the rudder, the exit canopy smashed and jammed. "The airplane had done her best."

One thing the Grumman and Republic planes had in common was that they were remarkably well-built, sturdy aircraft that could survive devastating attacks and return to base.

Stories are told and retold of Grumman Wildcat heroics early in the war at Guadalcanal, in the Solomon Islands, where the Japanese were building a major airfield from which they planned an attack on Australia. In August, 1942, the U.S. Marines, with later help from the Army, launched a surprise invasion, and they were able to take and hold the island only with the aid of Navy and Marine Wildcat air support.

One Wildcat pilot crashed head-on with a Japanese fighter in midair. The Japanese plane crashed; the American plane landed safely. In the first two months, one Marine squadron shot down 95 Japanese planes. Then, along came Marine Capt. Joe Foss, a Wildcat sharpshooter who soon bagged 26 Japanese planes, the first pilot to equal Capt. Eddie Rickenbacker's World War I total.

"Grumman saved Guadalcanal," Secretary of the Navy James Forrestal later told Grumman workers.

The Hellcat was an even better plane than the Wildcat. During the Battle of the Marianas in June, 1944, one Hellcat squadron shot down 177 Japanese planes within two weeks without losing a plane. They earlier had shot down 10 enemy aircraft, so their squadron leader, Cmdr. William A. Dean, wired home the following message, referring to Japanese Prime Minister Hideki Tojo:

"Tojo say Roy Grumman Public Enemy No. 1. Score 187 to 0 not good for Honorable Sons."

To which company founder Leroy Grumman replied: "Grumman Men and Women say Bill Dean Grumman Company's No. 1 worst customer. Score 187 to 0 not good for their business."

Just before the war there were no more than 5,000 people working at Long Island airplane plants, a figure that soared to at least 90,000 during the war, a large part of them women entering the work force for the first time. More than half of that peak employment figure represented Grumman and Republic employees, but there were smaller aircraft, or aircraft-related, industries scattered from one end of the Island to the other.

War-related industries mushroomed. Newspaper want-ads suddenly were filled with jobs in Long Island defense industries. In late 1942, Sperry Gyroscope advertised: "WOMAN WAR WORKERS. 23 to 35 years. High School education required." And in late 1944, Aerial Products Inc. of Merrick advertised: "Girls! Women! Housewives! 18 Years and Over. No Experience Required."

Sperry Gyroscope Co. Inc. of Lake Success was a major builder of airplane components, including artificial horizons, bombsights, automatic pilots, radar, gunsights, and armor-plated ball turrets for B-17 and B-24 bombers. The Brewster Aeronautical Corp. of Long Island City produced a fighter plane in the early part of the war, but it did not perform well.

The Ranger Aircraft Engine division of the Fairchild Airplane Manufacturing Co. produced engines in Farmingdale. There were also Columbia Aviation Corp. in Valley Stream, which produced military amphibian planes, and the Liberty Aircraft Products Corp. in Farmingdale.

A well-known company was Dade Brothers Inc. of Mineola, which picked up thousands of newly built airplanes at Bethpage and Farmingdale and hauled them by truck to ports such as New York or to the West Coast to be shipped overseas by the military. The company also built troop gliders. But smaller industries subcontracted to build radios, propellers, gun parts and electrical parts.

There was also a large amount of military activity on Long Island during the war. Camp Upton in Brookhaven was reopened, first as an induction center and later as a military hospital. Roosevelt Field was operated by the Navy as a shipping center, and Floyd Bennett Field in Brooklyn was a major naval aviation base. Mitchel Field, the Air Defense Center for New York City, was one of the largest air bases in the country, and was used both as the departure point for bomber squadrons going to Europe and a reception area for wounded men returning.

In 1942, Civil Air Patrol squadrons were established at Westhampton Beach and Roosevelt Field.

WORLD WAR II: THE COMBATANTS

The common wisdom is that World War II was the last good war. Americans were united in the belief that the cause of the Allied powers — the United States, Great Britain, France, China and Russia — was a just cause. Opposing them were Germany, Italy and Japan, the Axis powers, so-called because of a perceived political "axis" between Rome and Berlin.

The war began on Sept. 1, 1939, when Germany invaded Poland. But the decade of the '30s had seen the flowering of German leader Adolf Hitler's desire for *lebensraum* (living space), Mussolini's grandiose Fascist plans for recreating the Roman Empire, and the Japanese desire for domination of East Asia.

For the United States, the war began with the surprise Japanese attack on Pearl Harbor on Dec. 7, 1941. Hostilities ended Aug. 14, 1945, when the Japanese gave up, and on Sept. 2, the surrender agreement was signed. Almost 60 million people died in the war, more than half of them civilians.

— George DeWan

Please see **WAR** on Page 309

A Wing And A Plan

A mysterious proposal for underground LI hangars

BY MICHAEL DORMAN

Lt. Col. Anthony Cristiano, director of support for the 106th Rescue Wing of the Air National Guard, was sitting in his airport office in Westhampton Beach about five years ago when an airman plopped a flock of papers on his desk. The papers looked official and were accompanied by maps, charts and engineering sketches.

"I found these in a Dumpster," the airman said.

"What do you mean, you found them in a Dumpster?"

"I just happened to see them. They didn't look as if they belonged there. So I decided to bring them to you."

Neither Cristiano nor the airman had any way of knowing it, but the discovery of those papers at Francis S. Gabreski Airport would eventually bring to light a baffling mystery: Did the United States once plan to make a Westhampton Beach air base the Northeast's first line of defense against possible attacks by Nazi warplanes?

The chief document was a 13-page engineering plan for constructing a system of underground bunkers capable of holding 1,000 fighter planes that could swiftly be sent aloft to combat Nazi planes. The document was entitled "Engineering Brief for the Construction of a Major Military Airplane Base on Eastern Long Island, New York." It was dated December, 1940, and signed by two prominent Westhampton Beach engineers of the time, Hermon Bishop, later Suffolk public works commissioner, and E. L. North, later a high-ranking state engineer.

There is no evidence that such a plan was implemented. Bishop and North are dead. The mystery they left behind concerns why they drew up the complex engineering brief, whether the government ever asked them to do so, whether the government ever seriously contemplated building such a base and how the brief wound up in the Dumpster more than a half-century after it was prepared.

"I'll tell you this much," said Bishop's grandson, also named Hermon Bishop and also a Westhampton Beach resident. "My grandfather was a very practical man. He never would have spent the time drawing up those plans unless someone asked him to do it." Bishop said his grandfather was a longtime friend of President Franklin D. Roosevelt and often took Roosevelt on fishing trips from Westhampton Beach. It was possible, he said, that an invitation to draw up the plans had come through the Roosevelt connection.

North's son, Lee North of Brightwaters, remembers his father doing "runway and other work" at the Westhampton Beach Air Force Base, now Gabreski Airport, owned by Suffolk County. "I do remember blueprints and think they had to do with, at least in part, some underground facilities," Lee North said. But that is the extent of his recollection.

At the time the engineering brief was prepared, the United States was still a year away from entering World War II. But there were fears at the time that Great Britain would soon fall to the Nazis and that Adolf Hitler would then attack the United States.

Newsday Photo / Bill Davis

Lt. Col Anthony Cristiano shows the plans, which were found in a Dumpster.

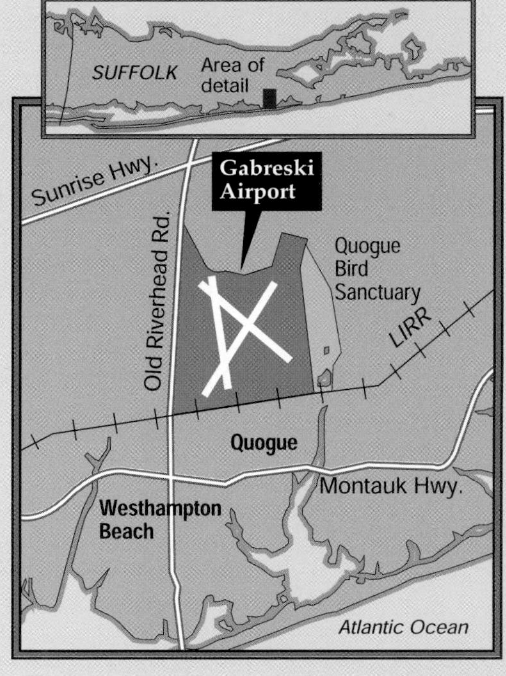

Newsday / Linda McKenney

News reports of the period showed German warplanes subjecting London and British military installations, such as a huge naval base at Southampton, to blitzkrieg bombing attacks. One Nazi raid on Dec. 9, 1940, pounded London with bombs for more than eight hours.

It was against this background that the engineering brief — no matter what its elusive genesis — was prepared. "The project hereby submitted is for the design and construction of a major military airplane base, located on eastern Long Island, New York, so planned on natural terrain as to permit extensive bomb-proof and fire-proof hangars to be constructed underground," the brief said.

There were then two small private airports on the site, which did become a World War II air base — but without underground bunkers. The engineering brief said the property was large enough "to allow the construction of bomb-proof hangars capable of safely sheltering at least 1,000 various type planes."

One section of the brief explained: "It has been shown that the first essence of military air strategy is a secure base from which to operate offensive and defensive air power; that bomb-proof and fire-proof shelter must be provided at the base for planes . . . that the base must be so strategically located as to enable its planes to intercept an invading air force. It is the purpose of this project to insure a major stronghold for the defense of the United States' industrial Northeast, the city of New York and its adjacent unprotected flying fields."

The brief emphasized the base would occupy a strategic position for national defense. "A patrol radius of only 500 miles from the project will include all of New England, New York, Pennsylvania, New Jersey, Delaware, Maryland and Virginia, which comprises over 60 percent of the industrial area of the United States."

Details down to where the base would obtain its electricity (from LILCO) and water (from the Quantuck Water Co.) — as well as a $17,746,300 construction budget — were included in the brief. The plan called for building two U-shaped underground hangars 200 feet wide and 2,200 feet long. "A salient feature of the hangars is that the planes may be warmed up inside the hangars and emerge into the open at flying speed. There are at this time no properly defended or sheltered air bases in existence for the protection of the United States' industrial Northeast. It seems, therefore of vital importance that a major underground camouflaged military base be constructed in this strategic location."

But although an air base was established on the site, it was not underground or camouflaged. Organizations from the Defense Department to the Franklin D. Roosevelt Library at Hyde Park, N.Y., to the National Archives reported they could find no references in their files to an underground base at Westhampton Beach.

Thus, the mystery remains. Nobody has been found — in Westhampton Beach or elsewhere — who can explain the existence of the engineering brief prepared by Hermon Bishop and E. L. North.

"But it's hard to believe they would have done all that work on their own," Cristiano says. "Somebody in the government must have asked them to do it."

Michael Dorman is a freelance writer.

LI's Sturdy Wings of War

WAR from Page 307

But the heart of the war production effort was at Grumman and Republic. Their contributions to the wartime and postwar national defense effort helped energize the Long Island economy and gave women a much larger role in the work force.

Created in a Baldwin garage by Leroy Grumman and his partners in 1930 and moved to Bethpage in 1937, Grumman was a small-time producer of military and nonmilitary aircraft on the eve of WWII, when it had only about 1,000 employees — a number that would increase to more than 25,000 before the war's end. Its specialty was carrier-based aircraft, and the folded wings of the F4F Wildcat, and its successor, the F6F Hellcat — doubling the carrying capacity of the aircraft carrier — may be the most distinctive feature of a WWII Navy plane at rest.

In the early years of the air war in the Pacific, the Japanese Zero fighter, a lighter, more maneuverable plane than anything it was up against, had the upper hand, especially since Japan had excellent pilots who were willing to die in a plane that had little protection for the pilot. But the Grumman Wildcat held its own.

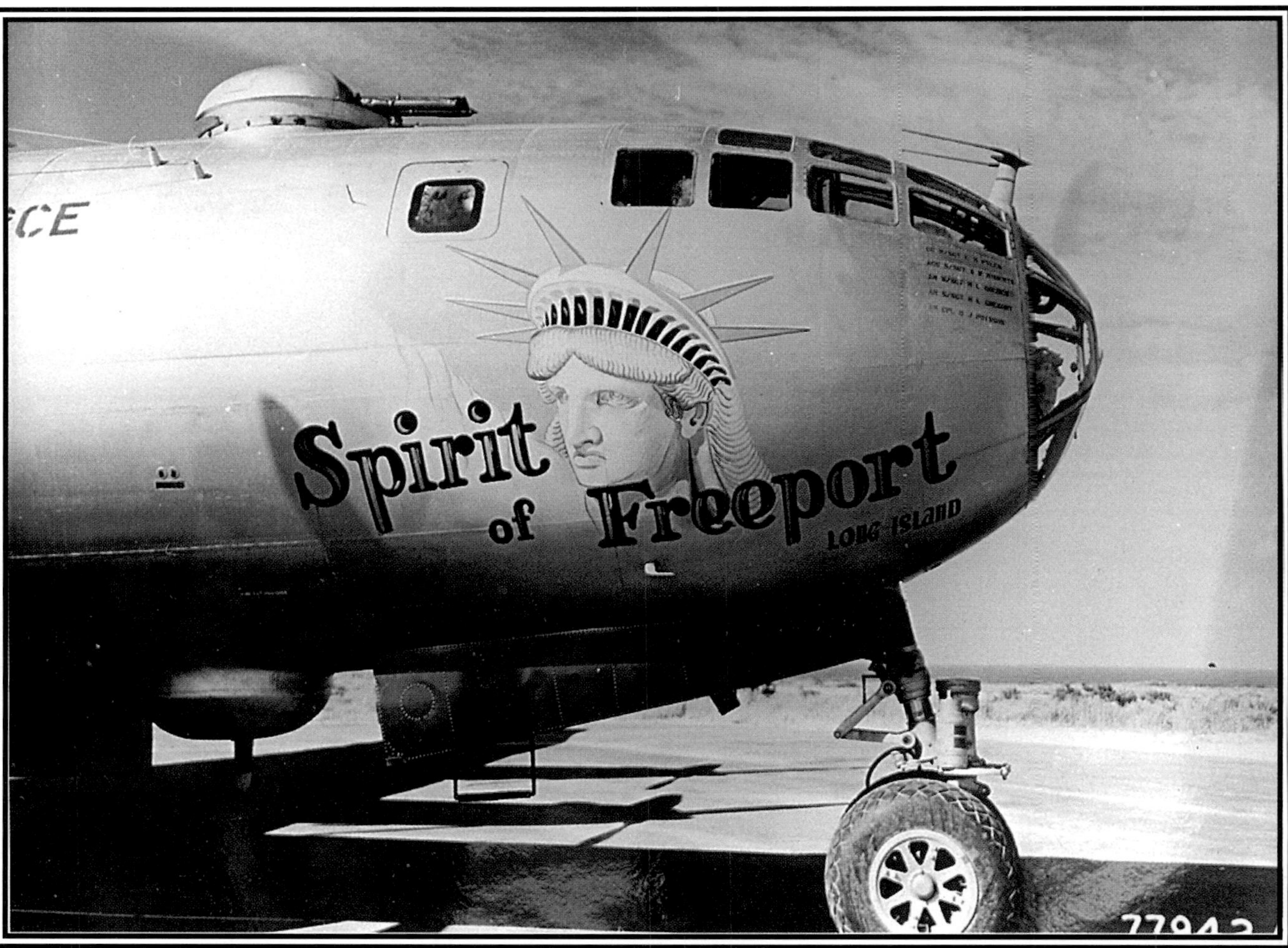

Nassau County Museum, Long Island Studies Institute

According to legend, this B-29 was dubbed Spirit of Freeport because it had been paid for through the sale of war bonds in that community.

"The name 'Grumman' on a plane or part has the same meaning to the Navy that 'sterling' on silver has to you," Vice Admiral John S. McCain told a labor conference in Washington, D.C., in 1942.

But a better plane was needed. When Butch O'Hare, now promoted to lieutenant commander, went to the White House in April, 1942, to receive his Medal of Honor from President Franklin D. Roosevelt, the president asked him: "Butch, what kind of fighter plane do you need to beat the Japs?" O'Hare replied: "Something that will go upstairs faster."

He would soon get what he wanted. Grumman's vice president, Leon (Jake) Swirbul, flew to Pearl Harbor to talk to Navy pilots. What they wanted, he learned, was "a plane with more speed and more climb."

By late 1942 the Hellcat was in production, and by war's end Grumman would produce 12,270 of what was considered the best Navy fighter plane in the war. That same year, Grumman began producing the TBF Avenger, the biggest carrier aircraft of the war, one model of which was flown by future President George Bush. Because of production needs at Bethpage for the Hellcat, production of the Wildcat and Avenger was later moved to General Motors facilities in New Jersey.

During the first five months of 1944, the Hellcat was officially credited with destroying 444 Japanese planes in air combat, and another 323 on the ground, with a loss of only 71 American aircraft. Then, in one of the war's greatest air battles, the Battle of the Marianas, June 19-20, 1944, known as "The Marianas Turkey Shoot," at least 350 Japanese planes were shot down by Hellcats, with American losses put at 30.

"Between Dec. 7, 1941 (attack on Pearl Harbor), and August 14, 1945 (victory in Japan), Grumman's 24,000 employees delivered a record 17,013 aircraft, more than any other U.S. manufacturer," wrote Joshua Stoff, author of "The Aerospace Heritage of Long Island." " . . . Navy records show that Grumman planes accounted for two-thirds of all enemy aircraft destroyed over the Pacific during World War II — a total of almost 6,000 Japanese planes."

Grumman was a very special place to work in those heady war days. One of the first problems faced was the loss of men to the war, with 5,000 having gone into the service by the end of 1943. More than 8,000 women were hired to replace them and expand the operations. Not only were the women riveters, but they did a host of other jobs. In 1943, three women test pilots were hired, the first women test pilots of military aircraft in the United States.

Most of these new employees had to be trained, and a 10-week course was set up, sponsored jointly by the New York State Department of Education. "These men and women — butchers, housewives, Wall Street brokers, gas station proprietors, farmers, clerks, policemen — were about 90 per cent Long Islanders, and most of them had never set foot in a factory before," Grumman said in a 1945 brochure. Operations were extended to satellite plants in Syosset, Amityville, Lindenhurst, Babylon and Port Washington.

Daniel Pflug of Hempstead, now 78, worked at Grumman until January, 1943, when he went into the service. The men did not object to women co-workers, he said, but those who were classified 1-A as fit for service knew that their days were numbered. "When they started bringing in women, we got drafted," he said in an interview. "When they came in one door, we went out the other."

Employee relations and morale were good at Grumman, and much of the credit went to Swirbul, who was production manager. He was a considerate man, but his methods were also aimed at reducing absenteeism.

Nursery schools were set up. Free turkeys were given out at Christmas.

Northrop Grumman Photo

In 1943, workers pose with a Grumman TBF Avenger, the biggest carrier aircraft of the war.

Wartime Employment

At the end of the 1930s, there were about 5,000 people working in Long Island airplane plants. The figure reached to almost 90,000 during the war. Here's how employment levels changed for the Grumman Corp., just one of several Long Island military contractors.

Year	Employees
1938	750
1939	900
1940	1,000
1941	2,000
1942	6,500
1943	19,500
1944	25,000
1945	21,500
1946	5,000
1947	6,000

SOURCE: Northrop Grumman; "Long Island: People and Places Past and Present"

Please see **WAR** on **Next Page**

An LI Pilot Exults On A Distant Island

BY TOM MORRIS

Andrew Jagger is smiling, his fists raised in triumph as he excitedly describes how he has just shot down a Japanese fighter plane. The 1944 photo of the World War II hero, then a 26-year-old Navy ensign from Southampton, hangs in the National Air and Space Museum in Washington, D.C., and is one of the most enduring images of the war.

"The reason I think the photo became so popular was it showed so much emotion," said Jagger, who will be 80 next month. "I guess I was a happy guy telling all about it."

Beginning in 1940, Jagger worked briefly for Grumman, helping design fighter planes while developing a passion to fly them. "I just loved those planes," he recalled from his home in Virginia Beach, Va. "As part of my prewar work at Grumman I sat in them in the hangars and really got the bug to fly them."

He won his wings at Jacksonville, Fla., and was called to active duty in 1941. He would rise to the rank of commander.

Ironically, he never flew a single Grumman plane in combat, although the Bethpage-made fighters dominated the Navy's arsenal. Instead, Jagger's hundreds of combat hours were spent at the controls of the F-4U Corsair, a large, noisy fighter bomber produced by Chance-Vought and nicknamed "Whistling" Death by Japanese pilots. He was credited with two official and two unofficial kills of Japanese Zero fighters.

In 1942, Jagger was assigned to the USS Bunker Hill as an initial member of the legendary "Jolly Rogers" fighter squadron, with its skull-and-crossbones insignia. He said its 154 certified kills of enemy aircraft set a Navy World War II record, but 14 of its about 40 pilots were killed.

The Corsair squadron, he said, was the only one in the Navy not flying Grumman planes. Marines were the only other group flying Corsairs. "That was the irony for me. I wanted to fly Grumman aircraft."

Still, the young pilot's derring-do leapt to national attention two years later when a national magazine published the photo of him at Bougainville Airstrip in the Solomons animatedly telling another officer about his kill of a Zero over Rabaul, a large Japanese naval center.

Jagger doesn't recall the photo being taken. When it made him famous, "I was the most surprised one in the world to think it could happen to me, a little, unimportant ensign."

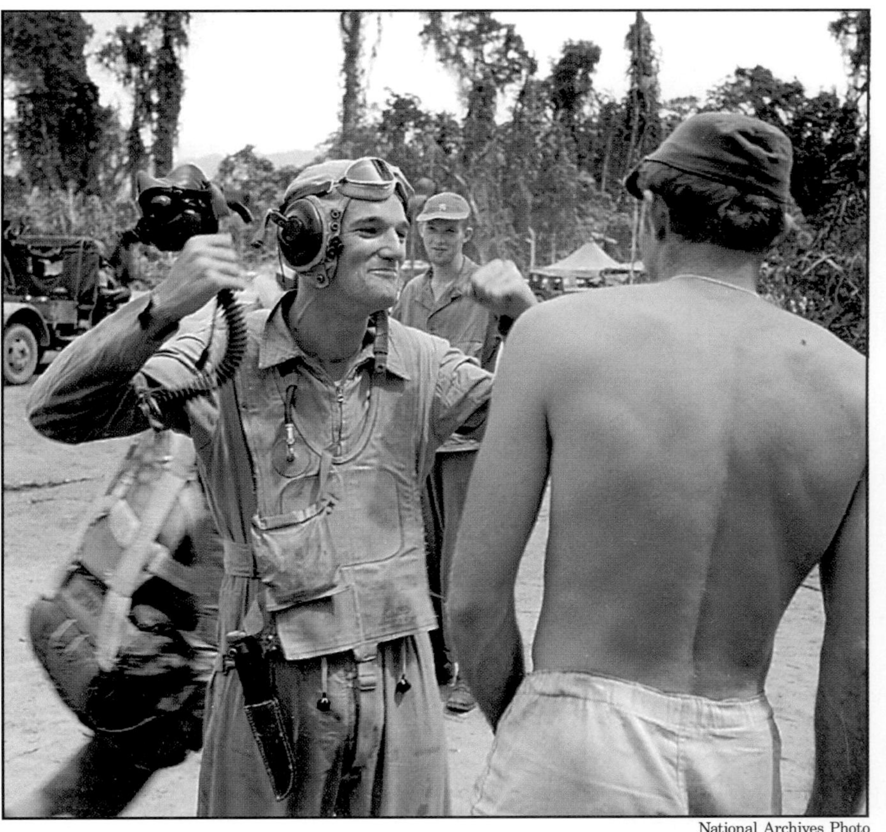

National Archives Photo

In 1944 in the Solomons of the Pacific, Ensign Andy Jagger of Southampton describes downing a Zero over a major Japanese naval center. He worked for Grumman before the war, but never flew a Grumman plane in combat.

The photo was put on display when the National Air and Space Museum opened 10 years ago. It is "the most frequently reproduced picture of a Navy pilot in World War II," said Kim Riddle of the Smithsonian Institution.

Some of his squadron's dogfights in the Corsair came as part of escorting bombers against Rabaul. But many of its kills, he said, resulted from the attack missions for which the Jolly Rogers yearned — and lobbied the brass to get.

"I wanted combat," said Jagger, a man with a large shock of gray hair and an infectious smile. "In a land-based outfit we got far more combat than we would have on a carrier — we frequently flew two missions in one day."

Jagger was usually the last pilot in a four-plane division, a spot pilots called "tail-end Charlies." The Zeros, he said, usually hit them first with machine guns as they attacked from the American formation's rear. "I was so lucky. I thank the good Lord for that. My plane was hit several times but I was not wounded. There were times I could actually see the tracers from a Zero's two wing guns zooming right by each side of my head, yet they all missed me. I was never shot down, but sure was shot up. My Corsair was full of holes several times. Being shot at helps your memory a great deal. It gives you something to remember."

Jagger married Betty, an Iowa girl who was then a Navy nurse in Norfolk, Va., at Easter, 1944, "as soon as I got back from the Pacific." In 1946, he rejoined Grumman after leaving the Navy but was recalled in 1953 for the Korean War and was a flight instructor in Pensacola, Fla., before leaving the Navy again in the mid-1950s to rejoin Grumman. He left Bethpage in 1973, when he retired as the firm's senior system safety engineer.

Tom Morris is a freelance writer.

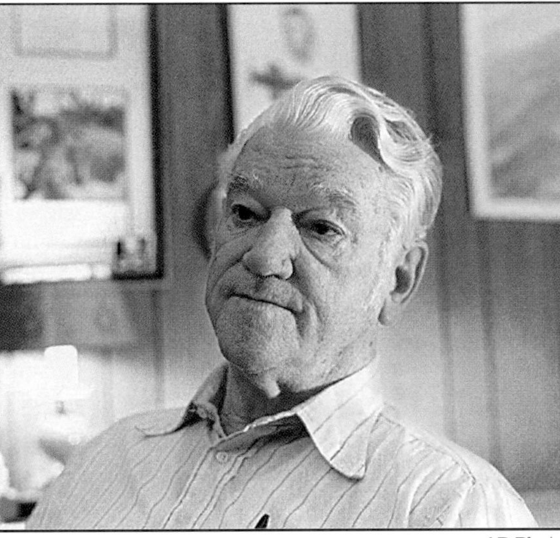

AP Photo

Andy Jagger, now 80, at home in Virginia Beach, Va.

LI's Sturdy Wings of War

WAR from **Preceding Page**

Swirbul set up a "green truck" service to cruise the parking lot and fix flat tires. But the truck crew also ran employee errands, fixed leaky faucets at employees' homes, checked to make sure the gas was turned off and closed windows if a rainstorm was threatening. He also built baseball and softball diamonds, and organized a company band to play for dancing at lunchtime. Maybe most important, he set up a bonus system, based not on an employee's individual performance, but on the total output of the plant.

Republic Aviation in Farmingdale did not take a back seat to Grumman. Begun in 1931 by Alexander de Seversky as the Seversky Aircraft Corp., in the '30s the company produced a number of planes for the Air Corps, the predecessor of the Army Air Forces, but financial problems led to a reorganization in 1939. A new name was needed, and a major requirement was that it have no more than eight letters, so that painting over the old Seversky signs would be easier. Thus, Republic was born.

Republic's focus was primarily on the P-47 Thunderbolt, and the company had an extraordinary production record for the plane, which was universally acclaimed as a workhorse. Although there were many other great American fighter planes in WW II — such as the North American P-51 Mustang, the Lockheed P-48 Lightning and the Vought Corsair — 15,630 Thunderbolts were produced, more than any other American plane. Republic had 5,900 employees in 1941, a number that increased to more than 24,000 in 1944, making it almost the same size as Grumman.

The Thunderbolt made its first flight on May 6, 1941, becoming the first all-metal fighter to fly at 400 miles per hour, an exotic speed for a propeller-driven plane in those days. Within a week of Pearl Harbor, the plant was on three shifts a day.

Designed by the brilliant chief engineer Alexander Kartveli, an immigrant from Soviet Georgia, the P-47 racked up awesome statistics in Europe: 546,000 combat sorties; 12,000 enemy planes destroyed or damaged; 86,000 railroad cars destroyed; 9,000 locomotives, and 6,000 armored vehicles and tanks destroyed. The Thunderbolt served in the air forces of the United States, Great Britain, France, Russia, Brazil and Mexico. Republic opened a second production plant in Evansville, Ind., and additional P-47s were manufactured by Curtiss-Wright in Buffalo.

The work was intense, according to 73-year-old John Weeks of Centereach, who in 1942 went into the Coast Guard. "You worked seven days, and got the eighth day off," Weeks said recently. "I was a young boy at the time. I was awed by all the aircraft. I would have worked 40 hours a day."

Weeks said morale was good at Republic. Each morning, the workers

LI Medal of Honor Winners

Since its creation in 1861, the Congressional Medal of Honor, has been awarded only 3,408 times. During World War II, five of 440 medals, the nation's highest military award, were awarded to local residents, according to the Congressional Medal of Honor Society and government records. World War II recipients were:

ANTHONY CASAMENTO, a Marine corporal from West Islip. On Nov. 1, 1942, at Guadalcanal in the British Solomon Islands, the 21-year-old Casamento was wounded 14 times leading a machine gun section whose members were all killed or seriously wounded by Japanese forces. Nonetheless, Casamento manned a machine gun and "despite the heat and ferocity of the engagement . . . repeatedly repulsed multiple assaults . . . thereby protecting the flanks of the adjoining companies and holding his position until the arrival of his main attacking force." He was cited for "conspicuous gallantry and intrepidity at the risk of his life above and beyond the call of duty." He had to wait 38 years for the medal, which was given by President Jimmy Carter in 1980 after Casamento led his own fight to find battlefield eyewitnesses and win support in Congress and from the American Legion and Sons of Italy. He picketed the White House in his wheelchair for 51 days in quest of the award. His war injuries left him partially paralyzed. The honor, said Carter, "was a long time in coming but heroism such as his is never diminished by the passage of time." Casamento died of cancer in 1987. A park in West Islip is named in his honor.

BERNARD J. RAY of Baldwin, an Army first lieutenant. He intentionally killed himself by wrapping his body in explosives and blowing a hole in a wire barrier in an encounter with German forces at Hurtgen Forest near Schevsenhutte, Germany, on Nov. 17, 1944. His citation reads: "By the deliberate sacrifice of his life, Lieutenant Ray enabled his company to continue its attack, resumption of which was of positive significance in gaining the approaches to the Cologne Plain." Ray, Brooklyn-born and Baldwin-raised, was a platoon leader with Company F, 8th Infantry. The American attack came in bitter cold in rugged woods laced with mines and wire barricades. The company was taking heavy casualties and was blocked by the wire. Ray set out to blast it apart on his own. He armed himself with explosive caps, field torpedoes and a length of highly explosive primer cord he wrapped around his body. He dashed alone to the barbed wire, but was severely wounded by a mortar shell. It seemed as if his self-imposed mission would fail. Then he made what his citation called "a supremely gallant decision." He hastily wired together his ammunition, body wire and all, and pushed the charger plunger.

THEODORE ROOSEVELT JR., of Oyster Bay. Army Brig. Gen. Roosevelt, eldest son of the 26th president, died four months after showing exceptional valor in helping to lead the first wave of Americans up the beach on D-Day, June 6, 1944. The medal was awarded Sept. 28, a month before his death. His commanding officer, in an unusual move, declared Roosevelt to be a battle casualty, although he survived the invasion and was stricken sometime later with a heart attack. After two oral requests to be among the first troops ashore at Normandy were rejected, the 56-year-old Roosevelt's written plea was approved. His citation says he "repeatedly led groups from the beach over the seawall and established them inland." He showed "complete unconcern at being under heavy fire," inspiring the troops "to heights of enthusiasm and self sacrifice." His "precise, calm and unfaltering leadership . . . contributed substantially" to establishment of the beachhead in France. Roosevelt grew up at Sagamore Hill in Oyster Bay, served in both world wars, was elected to the State Assembly, wrote seven books and worked as an investment banker.

JOSEPH E. SCHAEFER, of Richmond Hill. At age 22, Army Staff Sgt. Schaefer was an infantry squad leader when his 12-man unit came under attack at daybreak, Sept. 24, 1944, near Stolberg, Germany. One of three American squads at a key crossroads retreated and another was captured, leaving Schaefer's alone to hold the position. During the next 12 hours, Schaefer and his men, positioned in a house, repulsed two attacks, including a charge with hand grenades and flamethrowers. In a third try, Germans came from two directions: directly at the house, where he chose "the most dangerous" door position, and stealthily along a hedgerow. His citation says, "Recognizing the threat, Schaefer fired rapidly at the enemy before him, killing or wounding all six; then, with no cover whatever, dashed to the hedgerow and poured deadly accurate shots into the second group, killing five, wounding two others, and forcing the enemy to withdraw . . . In all, single-handed and armed only with his rifle, he killed between 15 and 20 Germans, wounded at least as many more and took 10 prisoners," thus "stopping an enemy breakthrough." Schaefer also won several other medals during a 23-year Army career that included service in the Korean War. Later, he spoke modestly of his exploits. Schaefer died at 68 of lung cancer in March, 1987. Four months earlier, a portion of Forest Park in Queens had been dedicated in his honor.

CHARLES W. SHEA of Plainview. Army 2nd Lt. Shea had just arrived at the front on May 12, 1944, when his unit was sent to capture a hill held by the enemy near Mount Damiano, Italy. The Americans took heavy casualties from three enemy machine guns. Shea realized his men were entering a minefield, ordered them to take a safer route, then continued by himself up the terraced slope under heavy fire. Lobbing grenades toward the first gun, he forced four enemy soldiers to surrender, and sent them to the rear. He sneaked up behind a second gun, capturing two soldiers after a fire fight. His citation says Shea then crawled toward the third gun, "suddenly stood up and rushed the emplacement and with well directed fire from his rifle he killed all three of the enemy machine gunners." His valor "was an inspiration to the officers and men of his company," who continued the attack, the citation says. Shea later spent 30 years as a deputy New York City commissioner for veterans affairs. He died in April, 1994, at age 73.

would be greeted by a recording over the loudspeaker system of Spike Jones' nonsense song, "Der Fuhrer's Face," followed by Kate Smith singing "God Bless America," after which they went to work.

Did he have any problem working with women on the assembly line? "No, none. It was very enjoyable to work beside a nice lady. They smelled nice. They looked nice. There was none of this sexual harassment like today."

Not all Long Island aircraft production companies were as successful as Grumman and Republic. The Brewster Aeronautical Co. of Long Island City produced the Brewster Buffalo in 1939, and by the time America got into the war, it was beaten so badly by Japanese Zeros that American flyers were calling it a flying death trap. Although it had some success in the Finnish Air Force against the Russians, the plane has not gotten very good grades from air historians. The company also had administration problems, and was shut down by the government in 1944, its bad reputation intact.

"When it comes to candidates for the worst fighter of World War II, one airplane usually leads the list," wrote Daniel Ford in Air & Space magazine for June-July, 1996. "There are two books entitled 'The World's Worst Aircraft,' and the Brewster Buffalo is the only fighter from an era to rate a chapter in both."

The downside of Long Island's airplane production story came as the war ended. Tens of thousands of workers were no longer needed, and the separations were often abrupt. Joseph A. Stamm, the Grumman purchasing agent and one of its founders, told an interviewer in 1971, when he was 71, that it was a sad time for him.

"I was called into a meeting, and there was a telegram: Terminate this and terminate that and the other thing. It was tough for everybody. I used to walk away from the place at 7 or 8 o'clock at night, feeling really down. I had to tell them there was nothing more, and I'd see them walking down the road feeling quite dejected. Except that I felt twice as dejected as they did. Because I don't like to be a hatchet man, but we have to be on occasion, and that was my job."

Staff writers Drew Fetherston and Irving Long contributed to this story.

Serving On The Home Front

HOME from Page 305

out about a delivery and you'd have to wait an hour or two before you'd get to the pump."

Air raids were barely a reality for most Americans, but there were vivid newsreel films of London and other cities under attack. "Sitting through our blackouts, we felt for the people over there. At home, we had to do with what we had, but there was no bombing here," Barry said.

But the changed look and feel of Long Island villages made a greater impact. Talking about the neighborhoods of Queens and the small villages along the Nassau border, Teresa Weiss remembers, her girlfriends would call communities such as Ozone Park and Valley Stream as "ghost towns" — all the young men had gone off to war. "All you saw were women and older men," she said.

But life went on. Young women took jobs in war plants. In downtown shops, older women took the place of men. At the time, 12 million American women had entered the workplace.

In summer, people crowded onto buses bound for Jones Beach and other parks. A popular gathering place was the Roadside Restaurant on Long Beach Avenue in Oceanside. "It was a huge place for hamburgers and people came by the busloads to dance under the stars," Fortin said. They would listen to the tunes of the war such as "The White Cliffs of Dover."

Young people also congregated on the Long Beach boardwalk, where arcades were open in the summer, covered with blackout canvas. "A lot of off-duty sailors from Point Lookout would hang out there, hoping to just sit and have a conversation with a girl. They were very lonely," Fortin said.

At night, Long Island villages were dark and quiet. The few cars on the roads had the top half of their headlights painted over and street lights were also browned out. "We'd walked long distances with absolutely no fear," Fortin said. "We knew the town drunks wouldn't bother us."

She remembers an elderly woman who was hired by a Hempstead store because so many young women were at Grumman or other war plants. In Hempstead, where she worked for the phone company, Fortin watched convoys of trucks pass by on their way to troop ships. "We'd wave and cry and the boys would wave back." Later, she and her friends took part in a USO program at a Mitchel Field hospital.

"We'd sit and talk to the wounded men. Some would slip in and out of consciousness. A few could dance. It took a lot of stamina for us because it was so sad, seeing how awfully wounded they were. Some had terrible emotional problems, like one fellow I danced with who could not talk."

Fortin had dated a soldier for two years before he was shipped overseas. "But I always had an early curfew. My father didn't like the fact there were so many soldiers around and I was dating one of them."

After the war, Fortin met a veteran on a blind date. They wed in 1947 and bought a home in Oceanside.

It seemed unlikely that Alicia Patterson's creation, Newsday, would survive

The Little Paper That Could

BY BOB KEELER
STAFF WRITER

The creator of America's most successful tabloid newspaper, the New York Daily News, warned Alicia Patterson that conservative Long Island readers would never accept a tabloid. That advice came from her father, Joseph Medill Patterson, the man she had always tried to please more than anyone else.

Another adviser, an immensely wealthy businessman whose philanthropies ranged from funding the start of modern rocket science to guiding the construction of the Guggenheim Museum, urged Alicia to get serious about her life. He advised her to learn how to run a small newspaper, so she could eventually play a leadership role at her father's Daily News. That was the counsel of her third husband, Harry Frank Guggenheim, who was so serious about it that he stood ready to bankroll her little starter newspaper.

A third influential businessman, the shrewdest collector of newspapers on the North American continent, made the enterprise possible by failing in a rare attempt to start up a paper of his own. He did not give Alicia advice, but in effect, he did give her a chance.

That was S. I. Newhouse, who launched the Nassau Daily Journal in a converted auto showroom in Hempstead on March 1, 1939. He shut it down on March 10, fearing that a labor dispute over delivery of the paper might engulf his more substantial Queens-based properties, the Long Island Press and the Long Island Star-Journal.

This serendipitous failure happened less than four months before Harry and Alicia were married, on July 1, 1939. They learned about the availability of this plant while they were on their honeymoon in Roswell, N.M., visiting Harry's rocket-scientist protege, Robert Goddard. The news came in a telegram from a close friend and colleague of Alicia's father, Max Annenberg, who was helping them search for a paper.

But the telegram caught Alicia, 32, in a self-doubting mood. "I had terrible inferiority feelings," Alicia said. "I didn't think I had anything."

Though she strove to show her father that she could be as plucky as any son, demonstrating courage as a record-setting airplane pilot and a hunter of exotic big game, she had a poor journalistic resume. Her one attempt at daily newspaper work, as a young reporter for the Daily News, had ended in humiliation: She fouled up a story, incurring a libel suit, and her father fired her.

"On the arrival of Max's telegram, Alicia balked," Harry wrote later. "She wanted, at that moment, to give up the whole idea." But the stern, practical and mature Harry, 48, insisted. "I refused to be shaken by her plea to forget all about it. I told her that we had started this job and we would have to finish it."

So Alicia said yes, and the newlyweds began moving forward. On a personal level, starting a newspaper in Nassau County made sense, because that's

Newsday Archive Photos

Left, pilot Alicia Patterson with her father, Joseph Medill Patterson, publisher of the New York Daily News. Above, Alicia and her husband, Harry F. Guggenheim, at their Sands Point estate, Falaise, in the 1950s.

where they'd be living — in Falaise, the Norman-style mansion that Harry had built with his second wife, in Sands Point. But they also wanted to make sure the venture made good business sense. So they asked William Mapel, a former reporter and editor who now had his own public relations firm, to check it out.

Surveying the area, Mapel and his assistant, Stanton Peckham, detected great enthusiasm for a new competitor to the only daily newspaper serving the county, the Nassau Daily Review-Star. They also decided the county had immense growth potential.

On Jan. 23, 1940, Mapel and Peckham submitted a report, modestly predicting: "By the end of the second year the paper should have a paid circulation in Nassau County of 15,000 copies daily." (By the end of the decade, it had reached 100,000.) On April 5, 1940, Harry agreed to buy the equipment of Newhouse's defunct paper and take over the lease of the former auto dealership at 283 Main St.

To Newhouse, the sale did not seem like a permanent defeat, because Alicia did not appear to have a long attention span. "I thought she'd see it as a toy, something to play with for a while, and that eventually I'd be able to buy it back from her," Newhouse said. That view didn't recognize her fierce drive to show her whole family, steeped in newspapering for a century, that she could be as good a journalist as any of them.

The next few months were a mad scramble: hiring a staff, including several from her father's Daily News; converting the press to print a tabloid; buying used office furniture, and coming up with a name — in a contest. Finally, Alicia pushed the button, and the first edition rolled off the presses on Sept. 3, 1940. Some embarrassing errors marred the first paper, prompting her to admit: "I'm afraid it looks like hell."

In an editorial the next day, Alicia apologized. "Newsday, we discovered, was just like a child, and as with our favorite youngsters, it refused to be at its best in its first public appearance. So, if you will pardon a not-too-good pun, even if we err again, we will not be discouraged, for tomorrow also will be Newsday."

The sloppy start provoked gallows humor on the new staff. "We were taking bets on how many days it would last," said one of Alicia's young reporters, Virginia Sheward. "That's how bad it was. It was a horror."

But the little tabloid survived, despite such hurdles as Alicia's emerging disagreement with Harry over politics. Little more than a month into Newsday's life, they ran opposing pieces on

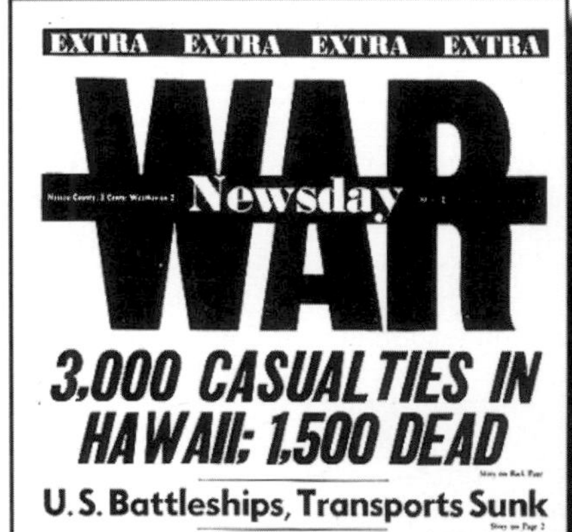

EXTRA EXTRA EXTRA EXTRA

WAR

Newsday

3,000 CASUALTIES IN HAWAII: 1,500 DEAD

U.S. Battleships, Transports Sunk

Japs Force Landing at Malaya

Congress Called to Act at Noon

Britain Declares War on Japan

Report Big Naval Battle Now On

Mitchel Field Ready for Action

Nassau Seizes Aliens in Roundup

Newsday's Dec. 8, 1941, edition reports Japan's surprise attack on Pearl Harbor.

the Franklin Roosevelt-Wendell Willkie race for president: Alicia supported Roosevelt; Harry backed Willkie. That pattern continued, as Harry used his majority ownership to try to exert more influence on the editorial side.

Later, Alicia also disagreed sharply with her father over Roosevelt, which didn't help their relationship. Joseph Medill Patterson's staff helped her in many ways, but he didn't give her the encouragement she would have liked. Asked by a colleague how she was doing, he said: "Oh, she's all right. She's got a little paper out in Hempstead, but it isn't going anywhere."

Running that little paper, Alicia had to overcome a lot. America's entry into World War II drained her young staff, for example, and removed Harry from the scene for naval duty, forcing her to run the paper herself.

Somehow, she overcame. After the war was over, the rise of Levittown started an eastward migration that launched Newsday into a long period of sustained growth.

Not only did she prove her father wrong about the potential for a Long Island tabloid, but she also showed he had been mistaken to predict that Newsday wasn't going anywhere. For a series of stories on a corrupt union leader, William DeKoning, Newsday won its first Pulitzer prize in 1954 and Alicia's face appeared on the cover of Time magazine.

She lived to enjoy this first taste of glory and to fight further battles with Harry over the presidential elections of 1956 and 1960. But shockingly she didn't live to celebrate Newsday's 25th anniversary, dying at age 56 after ulcer surgery in 1963. By then, however, Newsday was on the way with a circulation of nearly 400,000. One of her editors, Jack Mann, summed her up this way: "She was the greatest newspaperman I've ever known."

In 1942, four would-be saboteurs paddle ashore from a U-boat off Amagansett

The Nazi 'Invasion' of LI

BY STEVE WICK
STAFF WRITER

At 8 on the evening of June 12, 1942, the German U-boat Innsbruck completed its 15-day journey across the Atlantic Ocean. As darkness descended, the submarine settled quietly to the sandy bottom a few hundred yards off the Amagansett beach.

After midnight, the U-boat rose to the surface and began to move closer to the beach. The Nazi "invasion" of Long Island was about to begin.

That month, the war in Europe was 21 months old. The powerful German war machine controlled much of Western Europe right up to the English Channel, and had attacked east into the Soviet Union. The United States had entered the war the previous December, after the Japanese attack on the American naval base at Pearl Harbor.

Sticking out into the Atlantic for more than 100 miles, Long Island was, at its eastern end, sparsely populated; German submarines had been spotted on the surface not far from shore. Its miles of beaches invited trouble, as did its nearness to New York City. Two years before, in 1940, a German-American recruited by the Nazis — who was also working with the FBI — had set up operations in a house in Centerport where he was to send radio messages to Germany. And a large Nazi spy ring had been broken in Brooklyn before the start of the war.

But the Nazi threat was to take on a whole new dimension when, on the foggy night of June 12, four men carrying explosives and tens of thousands of dollars in cash paddled from the Innsbruck to a deserted stretch of Amagansett beach and walked ashore.

As they did, John Cullen, a 21-year-old Coast Guardsman who happened to be at this exact spot on the beach as part of his routine beach patrol — talk about being in the right place at the right time — saw their shadows through the night fog. Must be fishermen, he thought, and as he walked up to the four men — Richard Quirin, George Dasch, Ernest Burger and Heinrich Heinck — he told them to accompany him back to headquarters.

"How old are you?" Dasch asked Cullen in English.

"Twenty-one," he answered. "What's that got to do with it?"

"You got a mother and a father? You want to see them again?"

Ignoring the question, he noticed one of the men dragging a box over the beach. "What's in the bag, clams?" he said.

"You don't know what this is about," Dasch said. Dasch reached into his pocket and produced a wad of cash. He thrust $260 into Cullen's hand. "Forget you ever saw us."

Cullen backed into the fog and was soon running as hard as he could to Coast Guard headquarters three miles away. "They're German," he breathlessly told his duty officer when he ran in.Within minutes, a group of Coast Guardsmen armed with rifles returned to the beach but found nothing suspicious. But while standing on the beach, something happened: The ground vibrated. Peering out to sea, they thought they saw the outlines of a U-boat stuck on a sandbar, its diesel engines revving hard. Maybe, maybe not. Unsure, the searchers left and returned at dawn to scour the beach.

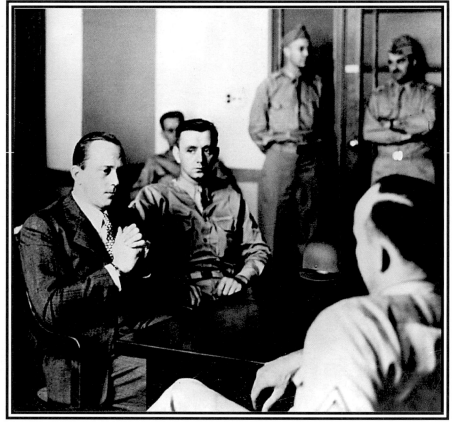

International News Photo

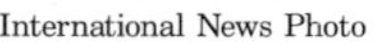

Newsday File Photo; AP Photo, 1948

Nazi agent Heinrich Heinck, shown above dressed in a suit during his sabotage trial in Washington, D.C., was sentenced to death. Near left is George Dasch, a German who turned himself in to the FBI and received a 30-year sentence. He spared the life of Coast Guardsmen John Cullen, far left, when they came face-to-face on an Amagansett beach.

International News Photo

Buried proof of saboteurs: A German hat, along with explosives, found in Amagansett

Meanwhile, the four Germans walked across farm fields to the Amagansett train station, where they caught the 6:57 to New York City.

As the Germans were comfortably riding west across the length of Long Island, Cullen and the other searchers looked for physical proof of a landing. They found it when Cullen spotted a pack of cigarettes. Next to it was a wet trail across the sand, as if something heavy had been dragged; near it was a patch of wet sand. Poking a stick into the sand, one of the men hit a hard surface. Minutes later, they had uncovered all the proof they needed that Long Island had been invaded by saboteurs — a canvas bag containing German uniforms, and tin boxes that held explosives, detonators and disguised bombs.

When their train reached Jamaica, the four Germans bought suits, got shaves and boarded a train for Manhattan, where they checked into hotels.

For reasons not known today, Dasch then did the incredible — he told Burger that he was going to call the FBI and turn himself in. Two days after walking ashore at Amagansett, Dasch did just that, telling an agent who answered the phone in New York that he was going to go to Washington and personally inform J. Edgar Hoover.

After arriving in Washington, Dasch spilled his guts to the FBI. And he dropped a bombshell — that four other Nazi saboteurs had landed at the same time from a second submarine on the coast of Florida. Two weeks after the invasion began, all eight Nazis were under arrest. It was over before it began.

In Washington, President Franklin Roosevelt decided all eight would be tried before a military tribunal. He wanted them all dead, he admitted in a memo to his attorney general. In the courtroom, all of the Germans said they had no intention of carrying out their orders to blow up installations.

And Cullen, the man who'd been in the right place at the right time, took the stand and testified that Dasch was the man he'd met on the beach. After his testimony, Cullen ran into J. Edgar Hoover in the hallway.

"Congratulations," Hoover said. "You were a help."

All were found guilty. Six were sentenced to die in the electric chair. Dasch, the whistleblower, received a 30-year sentence; Burger, who also cooperated, was sentenced to life in prison. On Aug. 8 1942, the six were executed, their bodies buried in a pauper's grave

Three of the four men who had landed in Amagansett — Burger, Heinck and Quirin — had been associated with Camp Siegfried in Yaphank, according to Marvin Miller. Miller, now 63 and a retired Long Island schoolteacher, wrote "Wunderlich's Salute," the first history of the the German-American Bund on Long Island. Miller said that seven of the eight who landed in the United States were members of the bund, which was established to promote Hitlerism in the United States. The bund sponsored the camp, a summer retreat that attracted thousands of bundists from throughout the metropolian area.

When the war was finally over, Cullen worked on Long Island as an insurance adjuster, a door-to-door salesman, and a sales representative in the milk business.

Burger and Dasch were paroled by President Harry Truman in 1948 and returned to Germany. In 1952, Dasch told a reporter he had been treated badly in Germany, where he was perceived as a traitor. He wanted to return to the United States, he said.

He also said he'd spared Cullen's life on the beach, as he was under orders by his superiors to kill any witnesses. "I saved that kid's life," he said.

In an interview in 1992, Cullen said he was lucky. Dasch, he said, "wasn't really a bad guy. If he was, I wouldn't be here."

Long Island marks V-J Day with quiet remembrances of those who didn't come home

It's Official: Peace at Last

BY DAVID BEHRENS
STAFF WRITER

On Sunday, Sept. 2, 1945, Americans commemorated the official end of World War II with the first observance of V-J Day — "Victory Over Japan." On Long Island, as in many other places throughout the nation, it was a quiet holiday of thanksgiving.

That Labor Day weekend marked the end of almost four years of loss and sacrifice for the nation. More than 300,000 Americans in the armed services had died in Europe and the Pacific arenas — and there was a sense of collective relief when the impending invasion of Japan was unexpectedly canceled by the advent of the atomic age.

In the towns and villages of Long Island, the boisterous celebrations came three weeks earlier.

In early August, America's secret weapon — the atom bomb — devastated the cities of Hiroshima and Nagasaki and rumors of peace began to circulate. Still, many Americans feared that the final battle of Japan was inevitable. Then, on the evening of Aug. 14, the rumors were confirmed: Japan's army had agreed to lay down its arms. Throughout the Pacific, the fighting ceased.

That night, more than 2 million people poured into Times Square, turning the plaza into one great back-slapping, jitterbugging, hugging-and-kissing reunion. In such villages as Port Washington, auto horns, fire sirens and church bells sounded the good news. Residents lined the streets in a "writhing spectacle of elation," the village weekly observed. In Glen Cove, shopkeepers went home early, hanging out signs that read: CLOSED FOR PEACE.

By Sept. 2, when the instruments of surrender were signed on the deck of the battleship Missouri in Tokyo Bay, officially marking the war's end, V-J Day turned out to be a day of reflection.

There were block parties and a few small parades as well as "solemn community ceremonies," as Newsday reported. People relaxed at the beaches that Sunday or traveled to New York to see the Brooklyn Dodgers and New York Giants split a doubleheader. Baseball was not yet televised.

Movies such as "The Corn Is Green" with Bette Davis, "Thrill of a Romance" with Van Johnson, and "Son of Lassie" with Donald Crisp and Peter Lawford were playing at the local theaters. On Broadway, theatergoers could choose among "Carousel," "Life With Father," "Oklahoma!" or newcomer Leonard Bernstein's "On the Town." There were Sunday services of thanksgiving and there were the inevitable political speeches.

More than 2,000 people assembled at Floral Park's Village Hall Sunday night to hear a speech by Mayor Fred Heidtmann, who paid tribute to the dead — 48 men from the village. "I don't like to think of this as a day of victory. We fought to protect our people," he said.

In Oyster Bay, Judge Percy Stoddard told an audience of 150: "This was no time for rejoicing — too many families have gold stars in their windows." The stars signified the loss of a relative in the armed services.

At a somber turnout in Glen Cove, Rep. Leonard Hall, later the Republican Party's national chairman, reminded the audience that thousands of servicemen would be needed in the future for occupation duty in Japan and Germany.

Others still mourned their dead at home. Some families waited for relatives to return from the armed forces. Many were still a long way from home.

Al Silver, a Massapequa Park resident who had survived the Bataan Death March and 44 months in a prisoner-of-war camp, found himself wandering about downtown Tokyo on V-J Day, looking for U.S. patrols to take him home. Frank Puglisi, a 23-year-old Marine, was on the captured island of Peleliu that Sunday, more concerned with die-hard Japanese snipers than a victory celebration, the West Babylon resident recalled recently.

But there were cheerful moments, too, the first signs of the return to suburban normalcy. At Morgan Memorial Park in Glen Cove, a 2-year-old named Linda Lee Lewis won the beautiful-baby contest. There was a water carnival that afternoon and, at night, more than 1,500 danced at a block party on Elm Avenue.

The three-day holiday had begun with blue skies and temperatures in the 80s. The weather turned cool and gray on V-J Day and the movie theaters were jammed. But more than 100,000 fans turned out at the Belmont and Aqueduct racetracks, and, despite threatening weather, Jones Beach and other Long Island beaches were packed.

The government had announced an increase in supplies of butter, canned salmon, ice cream and whipping cream, but meats would continue to be rationed, except mutton, kidney and tripe. For the first time since 1941, there was plenty of gasoline for the prewar roadsters, and the highways were filled with Sunday drivers on the first weekend of peacetime.

Newsday Photo

Confetti flew at Fulton and Main Streets in Hempstead on Aug. 14, 1945, after it was confirmed that Japan would surrender, ending World War II.

LI HISTORY.COM

Learn more about the Long Islanders and New Yorkers who fought the epic battles of World War II and were on hand for surrender and victory. On the Internet, see http://www.lihistory.com.

V-E DAY: THE FIRST TASTE OF VICTORY

The nation celebrated its first taste of victory on May 8, 1945, when President Harry Truman proclaimed V-E Day. In a radio broadcast, the president announced that the German armies had signed surrender papers the day before in a schoolhouse in Reims, France.

The nation was still stunned by the death just a month before of President Franklin Roosevelt, leader of the nation through the Great Depression and the war years — and V-E Day was a sober celebration in most towns and villages.

The memory of the war dead, said Nassau County Executive J. Russel Sprague, "should serve to make our observation of 'Victory Day' one of prayer and thanks." Long Island churches and synagogues held special services that evening, and Newsday reported that worshipers had sought "divine guidance to carry them through the difficult days ahead until victory in the Pacific had been won."

Some schools held assemblies to commemorate the day; others dismissed their students soon after Truman's broadcast. In Hempstead, thousands of students marched through the village to the beat of the high school band. No more blackouts, people chanted. No more air raid drills. At Mitchel Field, a brief V-E Day ceremony was held on the parade grounds, with an address by Maj. Gen. Frank O. Hunter, commander of the First Army Air Force. Many stores closed early that day, and war plants such as Republic, Sperry and Grumman sent employees home early.

At the time, families were still placing gold stars in their windows, marking the loss of loved ones. Many had expected the war to go on for months, perhaps years, until Japan was defeated. Then came the atom bomb. **— David Behrens**

Butch didn't notice World War II, and that was just fine with humans seeking normalcy

A Shaggy Dog's War Story

BY DAVID BEHRENS
STAFF WRITER

By the end of World War II, many Americans sensed that nothing would ever be the same again. But in Glen Cove, there was Butch — and everyone hoped that Butch would never change.

Butch was normalcy. Butch was the epitome of everyday life. Butch was everyone's favorite character. He hadn't even noticed the war go by.

Butch was a 240-pound St. Bernard. When peace came in the fall of 1945, Butch was still on his own tour of doggy service. When he needed to snooze, he'd take a nap on the sidewalk at the corner of Glen and School Streets, one of the town's busiest intersections. When he needed to escape the bustle of afternoon shoppers, he'd slip into the lobby of the Cove Theater and take another nap.

When hungry, he'd stroll over to the Big Ben Market, where the butcher always had a handout ready, even in the grim days of meat shortages and ration books. When restless, he'd get on the Long Island Rail Road for a ticketless ride to Oyster Bay, where another of his favorite butchers was never surprised to see him. Butch was fed by everyone, sheltered by many and, so it seemed, loved by all.

He was a big floppy monster of a St. Bernard, a forever-puppy-ish canine. Owned by a young sportswoman named Ann Miller, Butch was allowed to roam, to sleep where he wanted, to scrounge snacks to his heart's content. And as he went his own way, he captured the heart of his town.

For many a member of the armed forces who returned to Long Island after the war, Butch was, perhaps, a reminder of the small-town America they had left behind.

In the evening, stepping off the train at the Glen Cove station, there would be Butch, sleeping beside the potbelly stove in the ticket office. Shoppers at the local five-and-dime store would have to step over Butch, resting in the doorway.

He might be spotted at the Village Tavern, having a cool dish of water. Or he might be snacking at the Blue Ribbon Restaurant or O'Rourke's Diner, just across the street from the Big Ben Market. At night, he might choose the Western Union Office.

On March 25, 1946, six months after the end of the war, Butch made Life magazine. A weekly at the time, Life devoted three pages of photos to Butch and his wanderings around Glen Cove.

One of the headlines read: "Glen Cove's favorite beggar is a huge St. Bernard named Butch." Describing Butch's life, the magazine reported, "He prefers a vagrant life in town, making his own living from his regular round of meat markets, grocery stores and bars."

Even Mayor Arthur Aitkenhead was sought for a comment.

"Butch is a most unusual dog," the mayor responded. "He has the keys to the city. He has been our town character for some years now. He is very gentle and is loved by everybody." Certainly, it was hard not to love Butch. Even if he almost killed you, as Edward Russell attested.

Newsday File Photos

Butch, who had the run of Glen Cove and was a walking symbol of small-town life, counted Mayor Arthur Aitkenhead among his friends.

Russell was a movie projectionist in Glen Cove in the 1940s. Years later, he told this story to his grandson, Dan Russell, Glen Cove's current town historian:

One summer evening, after work, he had gotten into his open convertible without glancing into the back seat. Driving along a wooded street, he was startled by a groan from behind him. And in the mirror, he saw a giant form rising up — a giant form in a fur coat.

It was Butch. He had simply chosen another spot for a nap and was just stretching his sleepy bones after being so rudely awakened. The car swerved off the road and just missed a tree, but neither car nor driver nor St. Bernard was injured. Butch just strolled away, perhaps looking for the nearest diner and heading back to the depot.

At the station, on another occasion, Butch had almost become the target of a police team. Believing that burglars had holed up in the ladies' room at the depot, officers stormed the place with guns drawn, broke down the door and were ready to use reasonable force. But it was just Butch who strolled out into the sunlight.

On the streets of Glen Cove, Butch remained a fitting and reassuring symbol, a reminder that peace was at hand — and the Cold War had not yet begun.

Butch's tradition was carried on by Teddy, his son, also known as Butch II, according to historian Russell. And years later, the Glen Cove Lions Club put up a 20-pound marker honoring the memory of Butch, who died a few years after the war's end. With a profile of the St. Bernard sculpted in bronze, it was inscribed, simply enough: "Our Butch . . . He belonged to all of us."

It had been placed — where else? — at the railroad station.

But in 1969, some heartless soul stole the marker and its theft remained a mystery until 1981, when it turned up in the basement of an old house in North Merrick. It was found by the new tenants, who returned the tarnished plaque. Deciding to take no chances, the Lions Club donated the memorial marker to the Glen Cove High School, where it now rests in the school's main office — recalling a time of war when a big St. Bernard remained a small community's steadfast symbol of the simple, happy life.

Butch makes his rounds with Mary Terese Radgowski, age 11. He was allowed to roam, to sleep where he wanted, to scrounge snacks to his heart's content. And as he went his own way, he captured the heart of his town.

The World Came To Long Island

The small Village of Lake Success played a big role in the launch of the United Nations

By David Behrens
STAFF WRITER

In the years just after World War II, a series of historic decisions was made at the United Nations.

On May 14, 1948, the Security Council approved a proclamation recognizing Israel's independence. In early 1950, the Soviet delegation headed by Foreign Minister Andrei Gromyko staged the first walkout in UN history, to protest Taiwanese representation in the world organization. Later that year, on June 27, the Security Council approved the use of military force — principally U.S. troops — in the Korean War.

These actions, monitored around the world, took place in a small Long Island community.

The Village of Lake Success, on the Nassau side of the border with Queens, served as home to the Security Council from 1946 to 1951. The council operated from a cavernous factory building on Marcus Avenue that had housed part of the Sperry Gyroscope Co. during World War II.

The United Nations had been founded at a meeting in San Francisco in April, 1945, just before the war in Europe ended. That summer, the newly formed UN Secretariat found temporary shelter in the Bronx, on the Hunter College campus of what is now Lehman College, while the General Assembly met in London.

The search for a permanent home for the UN focused at first on small towns in Westchester and in Connecticut. Several sites in Connecticut's Fairfield County were considered, but the selections aroused vigorous opposition in neighboring communities.

Then New York Mayor William O'Dwyer, anxious to keep the UN in the area, offered the New York City Building at the site of the 1939 World's Fair in Flushing Meadows as a temporary meeting place for the General Assembly. The Sperry plant, just 20 minutes away by limousine, was suggested as an interim home for the Secretariat and Security Council.

Just southeast of Little Neck and Douglaston, the Lake Success area had been the home of the Matinecock Indians, one of the communities of the Algonquians, in precolonial times. The village name, in fact, had been derived from one of the Matinecock chiefs, Sacut.

In 1945, the decision on the future site of the Security Council was made, ultimately, at the grassroots level. The proposed conversion of the Sperry building had evoked vigorous protests in Lake Success, then a community of fewer than 1,200 residents.

As the official village history reads: "A group of usually tranquil citizens . . . rose up in opposition" — some in fear of losing their homes, some in fear of a decrease in the taxes Sperry paid. Earlier, residents had fought the arrival of Sperry and its application in 1941 to build a large defense plant to make planes and naval equipment, including its well-known gyroscope. Opponents argued against locating big industry in the quiet neighborhood. But with the approach of World War II, pressure from the federal government overcame the opposition.

In 1945, Lake Success Mayor Schuyler Van Bloem stepped in on behalf of the UN. "The mayor was afraid that Lake Success' image might be hurt if the UN was rejected," village historian Sylvia Bareish recounted in a recent interview.

Nassau County Museum, Long Island Studies Institute

The Union Jack flies beside flags of other nations in 1950 at the Sperry Gyroscope Co. building in Lake Success, then the temporary headquarters of the United Nations.

So the mayor named a committee of citizens to study the proposal, Bareish said, and after meeting with UN officials, the group recommended that residents put the question to an advisory ballot.

"In the unofficial referendum, the vote was 102-70 to invite the UN to Lake Success for a temporary stay," Bareish said. And on Valentine's Day in 1946, the General Assembly approved the relocation.

As a result, Lake Success' official history states: "The people of the Village were acclaimed all over the world as progressive, liberal Americans interested in furthering of peace." And for five years, the flags of the member nations were on display along the entranceway to the UN building.

The Security Council meets in the Sperry building in January, 1947.

> **LI HISTORY.COM**
> A list of historical milestones and the full text of the UN charter are available on the Internet at http://www.lihistory.com.

Renovation was still under way when the UN moved into part of the former Sperry building on Aug. 16, 1946. The first Security Council meeting came 12 days later, on Aug. 28. From the start, the Cold War was on the table. One of the first issues was a border dispute between Greece and Albania.

The vote to approve UN military involvement in Korea was the most dramatic event during the Security Council's years in Lake Success. With the world stunned by the prospect of another global war less than five years after V-J Day, the council's chamber was filled to capacity, while another 5,000 visitors had to be turned away, Newsday reported the following day.

The former defense plant had been partitioned to create office space for the Secretariat, the UN's administrative wing, while the Security Council met in a former conference room. During those years, UN drivers ferried delegates and staff members to and from the General Assembly hall in Queens, creating perhaps the world's first look at limousine diplomacy.

In 1947, the UN took possession of the Van Nostrand Homestead on the Sperry site and converted the former 18th-Century guesthouse into a nursery school for children of the UN Secretariat's employees.

During the postwar years, housing was difficult for most Americans. In Queens and on Long Island, nonwhite delegates found conditions especially difficult. Because of discrimination, "it was almost impossible for UN people to find housing," Sylvia Fuhrman, a Queens resident and a special representative of the UN secretary-general, said in 1989.

To solve the shortage of living space, the UN arranged construction of a number of housing projects, such as Parkway Village in Queens, with more than 600 units. About 40 percent of the UN's almost 35,000 employees now live in Queens.

In the spring of 1951, the UN moved to its current home along Manhattan's East River. Celebrating the organization's 50th anniversary in 1995, former employees gathered in the Lake Success building that once housed the Secretariat.

By 1995, the Sperry building was back in the business of defense, occupied by Loral Defense Systems-East to build navigation equipment for the Trident submarine. Today Lockheed Martin occupies the plant, making submarine systems, said a public relations officer at the company's Maryland headquarters.

"Fascinating," he said, "we didn't know the UN had been there."

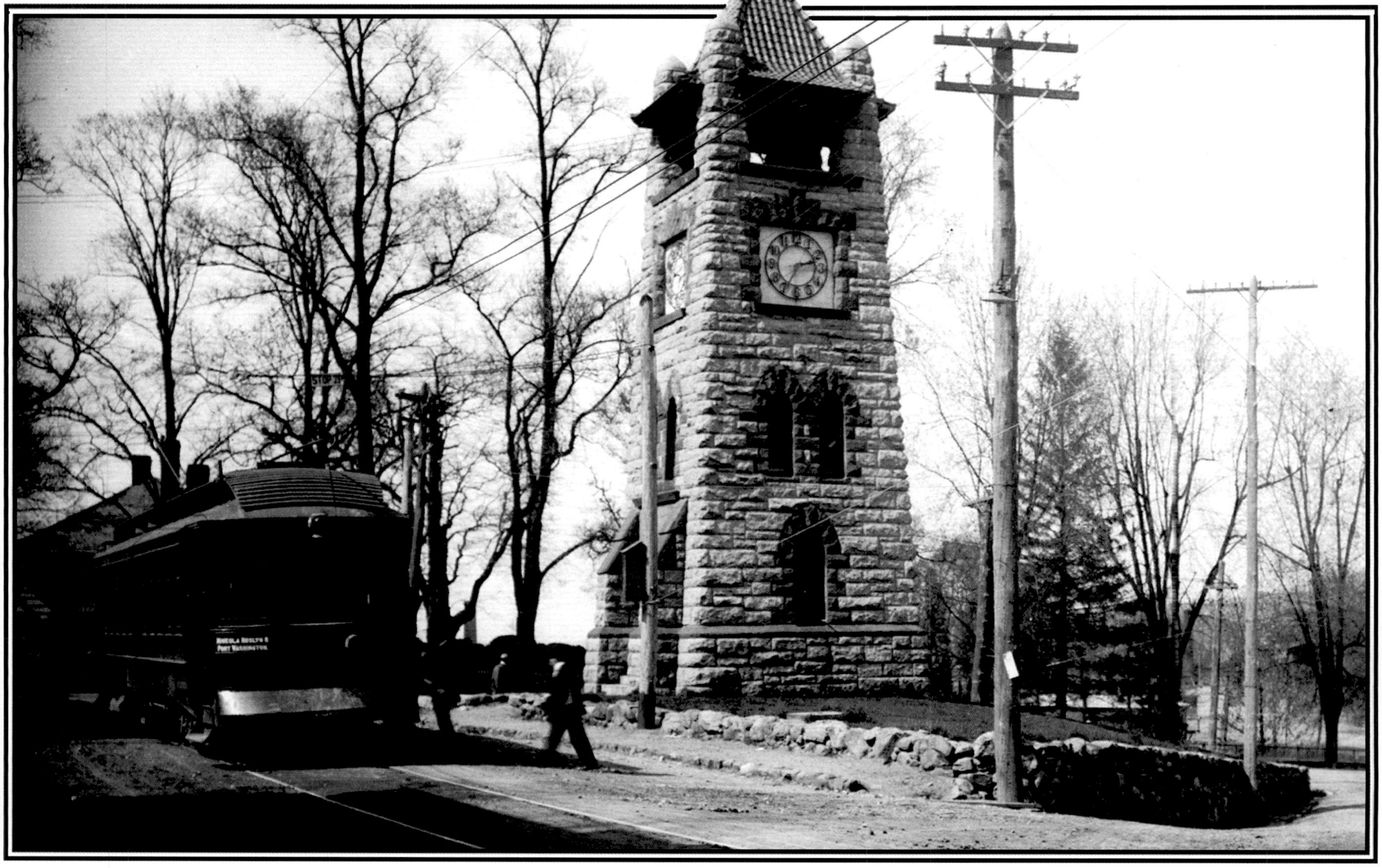

Nassau County Museum Collection, Long Island Studies Institute

TIME MACHINE

PICTURING THE PAST AND PRESENT

Newsday Photo / Bill Davis

A Tower of Strength

For more than a century, it has stood on Old Northern Boulevard, a witness to changing times and seasons in the Village of Roslyn. The old clock tower, seen above in a circa-1912 photo, and today, at left, remains resolutely the same, ringing out the time each hour.

The 44-foot tower was built in 1895 for $7,000 in memory of Ellen Eliza Ward, a twice-widowed longtime resident whose estate was valued at $3 million when she died in 1893. The tower was given to Roslyn by her children and heirs, Virginia, Robert and William Stuart. While alive, Ellen Ward had contributed generously to her church, Trinity Episcopal, and to the village, which she gave a granite drinking fountain and a fire truck.

THEN & NOW

It's not surprising that the tower has endured. Built from granite with red sandstone trimmings, its brick-lined walls are 2 feet, 6 inches thick. The bell weighs 2,700 pounds.

The clock, made by the Seth Thomas Manufacturing Co., is operated by large weights that drop slowly. Historical accounts tell that one of the clock's keepers was named George Washington. He was the son of a man who was born a slave. Washington cared for the clock for several years until his death in 1959.

In the 1960s a local building owner called the tower an eyesore and wanted it removed. But over time its many defenders have proudly restored the landmark. On July 18, 1995, the tower was deeded to the village.

UPI File Photo

TIME MACHINE

PICTURING THE PAST AND PRESENT

Confusion Flies High Over Lindbergh Flight

If there had been a Bob's Store in Westbury on May 20, 1927, Charles Lindbergh would have gone through the express lane.

On that historic day, long before Roosevelt Field had hangers instead of hangars, Lucky Lindy began his takeoff on the first transatlantic airplane flight from what is now the checkout area at Bob's.

Considering how long it took to get airborne, Lindbergh could have shopped till he propped.

Josh Stoff, curator of Nassau's Cradle of Aviation Museum, told Newsday that Lindbergh's plane, the Spirit of St. Louis, got rolling at Bob's, continued through Marshall's and lifted off between the garage at Fortunoff and the back of Cozymel's restaurant.

IT HAPPENED HERE

On May 19, 1997, to mark the 70th anniversary of Lindbergh's flight, Nassau County officials and historians unveiled a monument to his historic achievement outside the entrance to Fortunoff.

In what becomes a legend most, however, there is also some confusion: The monument contradicts a state historical marker at the Roosevelt Field Shopping Center — specifically, at the bottom of an escalator outside the Disney Store — signifying that Lindbergh took off from where the mall now stands.

The confusion may stem from the fact that Lindbergh didn't take off from the modern Roosevelt Field; he took off from the original one.

"In 1929, the people who owned Roosevelt Field bought out Curtiss Field and renamed the whole thing Roosevelt Field," Stoff said at the unveiling.

There is no doubt, however, about where Lindbergh landed: Paris. As yet, there is no Bob's Store there. — **Jerry Zezima**

Newsday Photo / Bill Davis

Charles Lindbergh, second from left above, gets ready to board the Spirit of St. Louis at Roosevelt Field to begin his historic flight to Paris in 1927. At left: Two men study a monument to Lindbergh outside Fortunoff in Westbury. The monument is situated on the spot where Lindbergh is said to have lifted off. Below: A map shows the aviator's takeoff route.

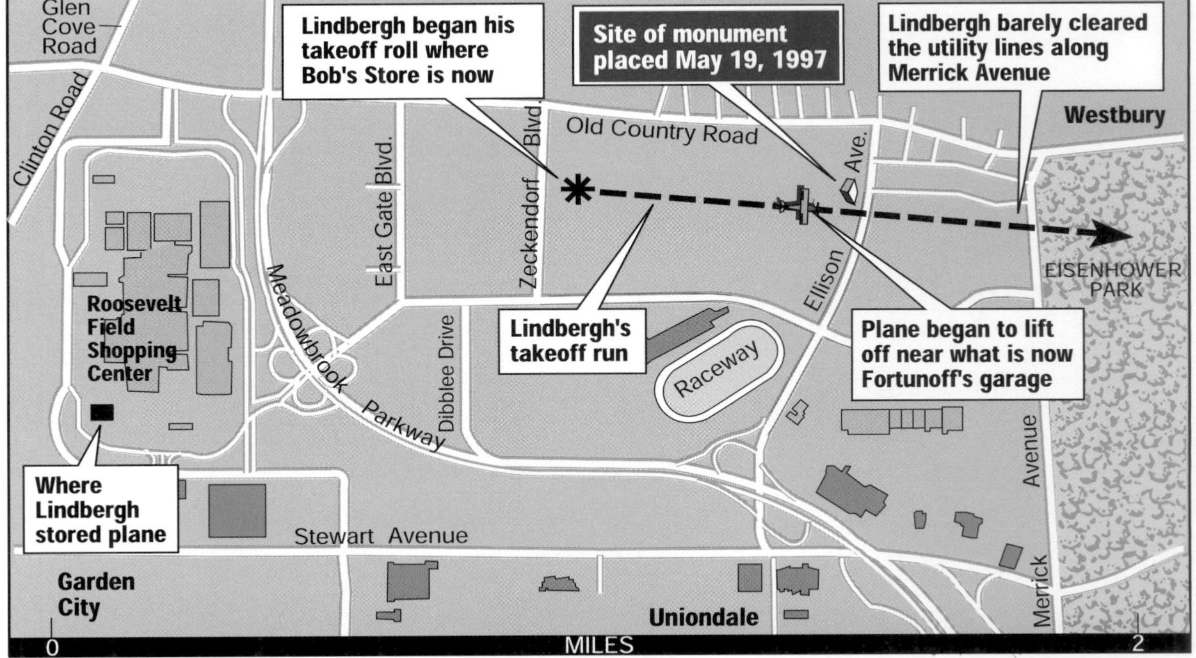

Newsday / Philip Dionisio

CHAPTER 8

The Growth Of Suburbia

From the building of Levittown to the landing on the moon

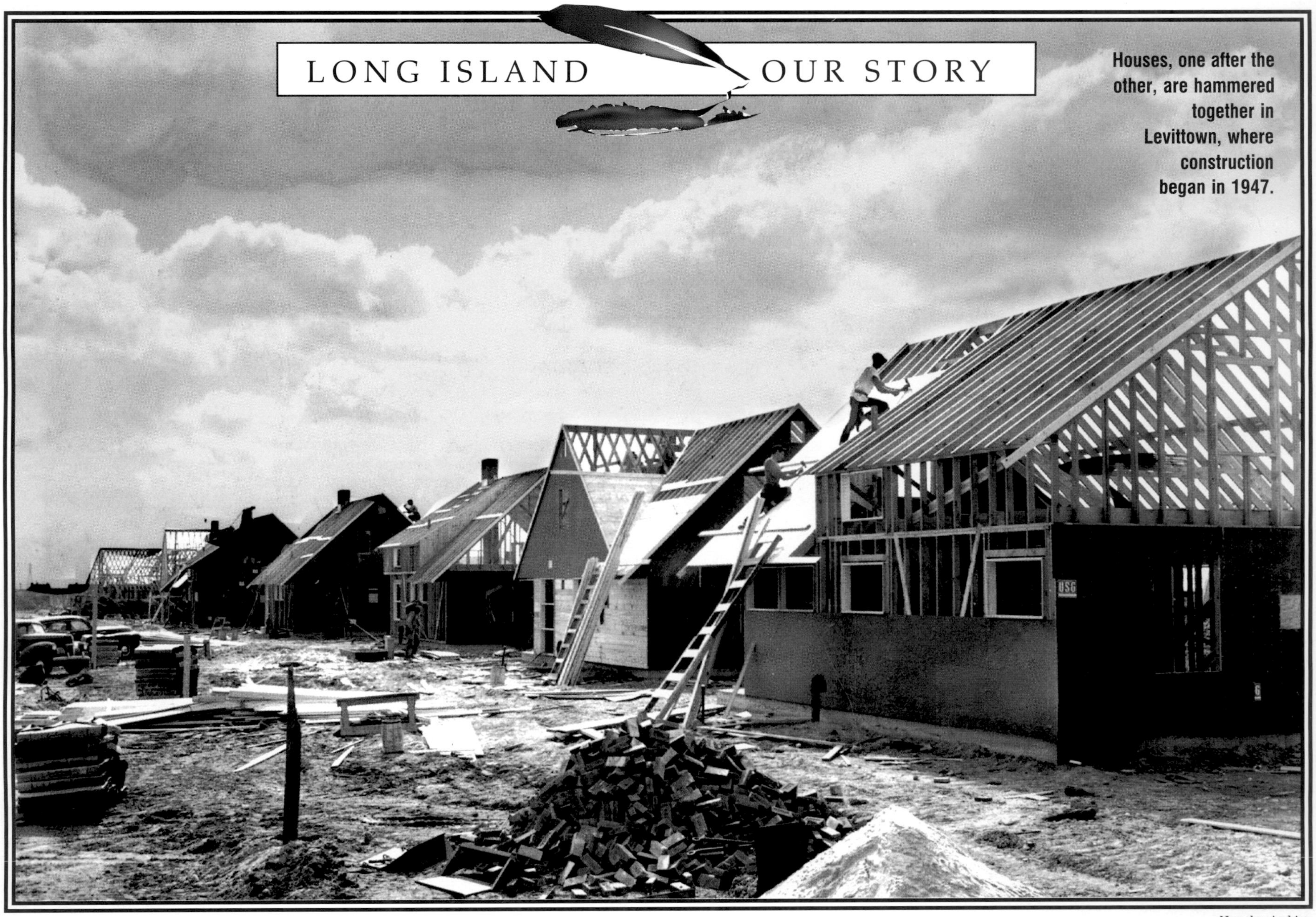

Houses, one after the other, are hammered together in Levittown, where construction began in 1947.

Newsday Archive

Veterans head east to claim a home of their own, creating a place called suburbia

The New Frontier

BY DAVID BEHRENS
STAFF WRITER

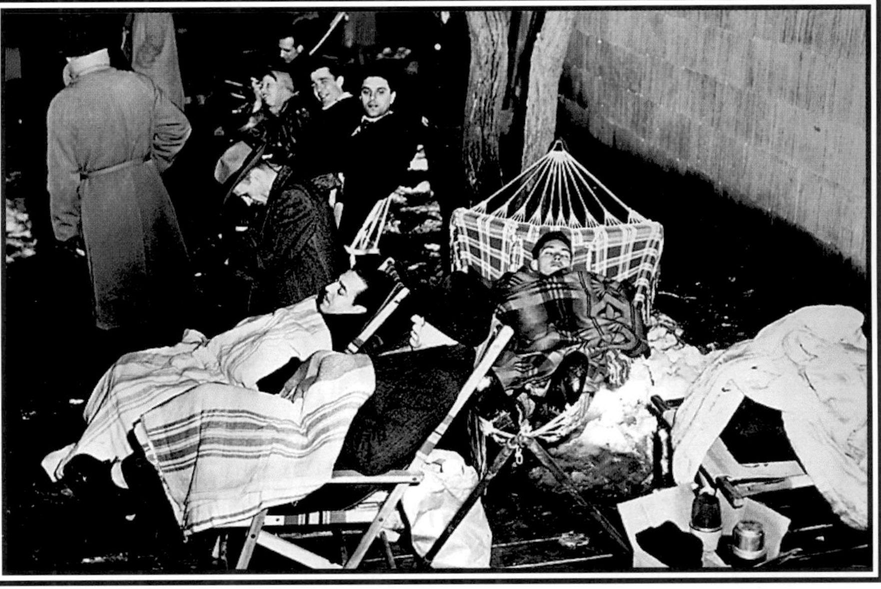

Newsday Archive

Veterans camp out in Levittown in 1947 in the hope of obtaining one of the new homes. More stories on builder William J. Levitt and the beginnings of his creation start on Page 403.

In the years after World War II, Long Island had become a frontier once again.

In the 1950s, builder Andrew Monaco would stand on the edge of the frontier looking across a vast expanse of farmland. Fields of potatoes, corn and wheat. He could almost see the future in as-yet unbuilt subdivisions: New homes. Men going to work. Children on their way to school. Little League fields. Nearby shopping centers.

"We had a vision of it," Monaco, now 80 and still involved in the business of building homes, recalled a few days ago.

Soon, an entry road into the property would be built and utilities run to the edge of the tract. Then two or three model homes would go up. A split-level, a ranch, a Cape Cod. Modern kitchens with built-in ovens. "On opening day, you usually got the feeling whether you had a success or not — which of the models would sell," Monaco said. "Then you'd extend the roads as the lots were sold."

Along this new frontier, a generation of settler-families transformed many of the villages and hamlets of Nassau and Suffolk — for better or worse — into a predominant American form: the sprawl called suburbia.

These settlers would establish patterns that reverberate profoundly into the present — a preoccupation with home ownership, a veneration of local government, an acceptance of pervasive racial segregation, and a toleration of jumbled residential and commercial development.

The 1950s and early '60s were a time of familial togetherness and social homogeneity, a time when most women stayed home to raise children and men found new fields of combat on the traffic-jammed highways of the expanding look-alike suburbs. There was also something Jeffersonian in the air.

"It was an old ideal," says Long Island historian Barbara Kelly, "a return to Jefferson's vision of the yeoman-farmer owning his home and a piece of land of his own."

The image of the yeoman-commuter was etched everywhere, in newspaper and magazine ads, on television and in motion pictures. The message sounded loud and clear — and inexpensive: You too can own a single-family home in the suburbs. Then you can hop on the Long Island Rail Road or zip down the nearby highway to your job in the city.

Pulling Up the Welcome Mat

By Samson Mulugeta
STAFF WRITER

In 1959, Eugene Burnett, a black veteran and a sergeant on the Town of Babylon police force, decided his growing family needed a bigger and better home.

A white broker drove the North Amityville resident to Wheatley Heights, which at the time had virtually no black residents. As they pulled up to one house, a white woman who lived across the street came running toward them, Burnett recalled recently. "She lay in the middle of the street, shouting at the broker, 'Judas! Judas! Judas sold Jesus for 30 pieces of silver!' "

To prevent him from buying the house, a neighborhood association purchased it, Burnett said. But a few months later, Burnett bought a house nearby. "We moved in the middle of the night, and I stayed up all night with my gun," Burnett said. "In those days, they would burn you out."

'We moved in the middle of the night, and I stayed up all night with my gun. In those days, they would burn you out.'

— Eugene Burnett, recalling his move to Wheatley Heights in 1959

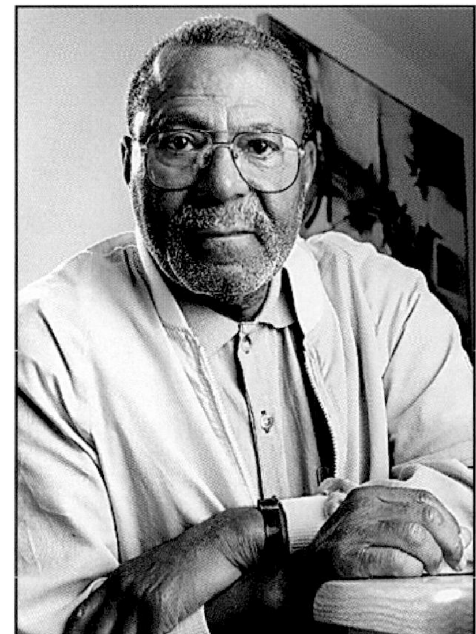

Newsday Photo / John Paraskevas

A veteran who left the Army in 1949, Burnett, 69, was one of many GIs turned away from Levittown. He settled in the Ronek Park development in North Amityville, where all races were welcome. But when it came time to buy a larger home, he once again faced racial barriers.

Now, Wheatley Heights stands out as an integrated hamlet with a population that is almost 60 percent white, with the balance a mix of African-Americans and Hispanics. The community has 5,000 residents.

The task of keeping the racial mix has not been easy, residents say. In the postwar years, some real estate brokers began steering prospective homeowners from the area. In response, civic activists took them to court — and won. For more than a decade, Jerome Finocchiaro, who is white, and Sandy Thomas, who is black, have worked together as president and vice president of the Concerned Taxpayers of Wheatley Heights and Dix Hills.

"We're just a nice middle class, integrated community with the highest median family income in the Town of Babylon and one of the lowest crime rates," said Finocchiaro, a resident for 25 years. (Last year, the median family income was $74,749.)

Much has changed in the nearly 40 years since Burnett moved to Wheatley Heights, which has successfully carved out an identity separate from predominantly white Huntington in the north and predominantly black Wyandanch to the south. Unincorporated and without an official name for most of this century, the community got its own post office and postal designation in the mid-1970s.

One thing has acted like a glue to keep the community together: the Half Hollow Hills school district, whose 7,000 or so students come from Wheatley Heights and surrounding areas. The highly regarded school district sent 91 percent of its 1996 graduates to college.

Burnett is proud of the system that graduated his three children, who went on to become a medical doctor, a pharmacist and an architect. But he is still embittered toward William Levitt, the builder of Levittown, because integrated Wheatley Heights — with its good schools and high quality of suburban life — is an exception on Long Island rather than the norm. "That's the legacy Levitt left us," Burnett said. "Most blacks and whites live in different worlds."

It was the right message for thousands of returning servicemen in search of a decent place to begin long-delayed family life.

When Bill and Marie Baum moved to Long Island in 1949, they were surrounded by young people. "It seemed wonderful to have so much support," Bill Baum reflected. "We were all the same age, with the same situations, the same backgrounds. Looking back, maybe it did influence our lives. But at the time, we weren't even aware of it."

Pat and Kay Catapano waited until the late '50s to make their move to the suburbs, buying a house in East Northport on the eastern fringe of suburbia.

"I was making a good living as a civil engineer," Pat, now 79, said recently. "We had watched the transition: a lot of couples moving from Brooklyn to Queens, then from Queens to Valley Stream and Malverne and the like. I said to my wife, 'Let's wait and make one big jump and then everyone else will have to catch up to us.' I knew what I wanted and I didn't want a Levitt house for $7,999. I didn't want to move once and then move again."

By the time they did move, the Catapanos would add a pair of 8-year-old twins and a 10-month-old girl to the Baby Boom on Long Island.

Through the years of the Great Depression and the war, America had placed its biological urges on hold. By the late '40s, the number of marriageable people had swelled with men and women from age 20 into their early 30s. Predictably, says historian Kelly, "The nation's dammed-up reproductive cycle just burst."

By the 1950s, Long Island's rate of growth was the highest in the nation. In 1960, Nassau County's population rose to 1,300,171, compared to 406,748 in 1940. In Suffolk, the 1960 figure of 666,784 was more than three times the prewar total of 197,255.

After Levittown, there were babies everywhere. By the '60s, children abounded, with 40 percent of Long Island's citizens under the age of 21.

The focus was on the care and feeding of children. Adults devoted long hours to attending PTA meetings, organizing Little League. Fathers managed teams, mothers chauffeured kids from ballet to ballfield. Hundreds of new schools opened, and neighborhood playgrounds were built throughout Nassau and western Suffolk.

New York City native Pat Catapano recalls the stunningly different street scene. "In Brooklyn or Queens, there were always kids out on the street, playing by themselves no matter how bad the weather. On Long Island, everything was organized in leagues for the kids." There was little attention paid to facilities for older people. "There were just young people with children in the neighborhood."

There was also traffic everywhere. Construction of the Long Island Expressway had begun in 1953 and crossed the Suffolk border in 1962. Ten years later, the road reached Riverhead. The expressway and the Northern and Southern State Parkways had heightened the suburban dream: A working man could move swiftly along new roads between work and home.

Newsday Photo / Bill Davis

Home builder Andrew Monaco: "On opening day, you usually got the feeling whether you had a success or not."

But for tens of thousands of daily commuters, the postwar dream would turn into a nightmare. Lost in the excitement of this idealized "World of Tomorrow," — the promise of the 1939 World's Fair — were unheeded warnings from urban planners that the new highways were likely to create more traffic rather than less. And they did.

But the future looked so bright in the early postwar years. With the passage of the Serviceman's Readjustment Act of 1944 — better known as the GI Bill of Rights — 5.5 million veterans were able to obtained low-cost federal housing loans by 1960. The legislation, approved by Congress just a few weeks after D-Day, created the biggest building boom in the nation's history as well as enabling tens of thousands of former GIs to attend college.

For the first time, government-supported housing for working class Americans was in place. By 1997, more than 248,000 home loans under the 1944 legislation were made to veterans on Long Island — 165,522 in Nassau and 83,105 in Suffolk.

The GI Bill certainly reshaped the Long Island of the future, said Kelly, curator of Hofstra's Long Island Studies Institute. With low-cost loans, veterans were able to buy inexpensive single-family homes with a bit of greenery, she said. "You suddenly had a whole new cohort of people who were college-educated and landown-

Please see SUBURBIA on Page 323

To the Malls, Bearing Money

BY MICHELE INGRASSIA
STAFF WRITER

When 6-year-old Lois Sabatella moved to Valley Stream in 1955, Green Acres was just being built, a gleaming 300-acre retail nirvana that beckoned from Sunrise Highway. It didn't take long before she was hooked. Every Saturday, from puberty to prom, she would curl her hair in rollers, tie a kerchief around her head and hop on the Elmont Road bus to the hippest hangout around, eager to snap up 29-cent records at Sam Goody's, 79-cent mascara at Woolworth's and $2.98 school shoes at A.S. Beck.

"We couldn't wait for Saturday," says Sabatella, now 49, her enthusiasm undiminished by the decades. "There were thousands and thousands of teenagers there. It was *the* place to be — the WMCA 'Good Guys' would broadcast from the mall; so would WABC. And we all had allowance money to spend — around $3 a week in those days — and when you had a birthday, you got money, too. For $10, you went home with a pocketbook and makeup and even had money left for lunch."

Nassau County Museum Collection, Long Island Studies Institute

In search of good buys and entertainment, shoppers stroll through Roosevelt Field, circa 1958.

It was the dawn of the modern retail age, when suburbanites turned shopping into leisure sport and malls into theater, a magnet for every teenager with birthday money and every housewife with a few hours to spare. And who could blame them? After decades of Depression-era poverty and wartime shortages, legions of GIs and their brides fled Mom's attic for 800 square feet of subdivision heaven. Suddenly, they had the bucks to furnish their nests and the time to do it.

"My father lived through the Depression, and when he moved from Corona to Long Island, he didn't want anything old in the house," says Amy Kraker, owner of Village Green, a Port Washington shop that sells the sort of vintage dishware that once filled her parents' kitchen.

Postwar Long Islanders hungered for all things modern — television sets, spun aluminum pitchers, New Look dresses and enough chrome to trim a squadron of B-52 bombers. And storeowners clamored to satisfy them. Between 1940 and 1970, when baby boomers filled suburban homes and schools faster than they could be built, Nassau and Suffolk annual retail sales soared from $270 million to $6.8 billion — staggering, considering that, even in 1970, median family income on the Island scarcely topped $13,000.

No matter. In 1956, three regional shopping centers opened in Nassau County — Green Acres, Roosevelt Field in Garden City and Mid-Island Plaza in Hicksville. But main streets, like downtown Hempstead, and community malls, like the Lake Success Shopping Center, were thriving, too, as certain a measure of the exploding consumer madness of the '50s and '60s as the Davy Crockett caps and Hula Hoops that boomers were demanding. By the time the Arab oil embargo and runaway inflation burst the spending bubble in 1973, retail space in Nassau had ballooned to 8 million square feet, nearly six square feet for every man, woman and child in the county. The pattern was set.

"The weekly shopping trip became fairly standard early on," says Barbara Kelly, curator of the Long Island Studies Institute at Hofstra University. "People thought of it as going shopping because they needed new curtains for the basement windows when, in reality, the windows were perfectly fine with the old curtains."

Still, shopping-as-entertainment didn't begin with the mall. "Even a few hundred years ago, people were getting off the farm, going to the general store and interacting with storekeepers and other people," says Hofstra University marketing professor Joel Evans. Shopping took on its modern persona at the turn of the century when respectable New York City women were permitted to go out unescorted, as long as they confined themselves to the Ladies Mile, the Manhattan retail district between Broadway and Sixth Avenues, from Union Square to 24th Street.

Overnight, women had an excuse to meet friends for lunch, to saunter over to Siegel-Cooper for the feather boas and A.T. Stewart for the dry goods. As stores blossomed and advertising expanded beyond snake oil, woman-as-domestic turned into woman-as-consumer.

And when the urban consumer became the suburban consumer, it was only logical that the great department stores would follow, abetted by a growing highway system that allowed retailers to stock their eastern outposts in days rather than weeks. Arnold Constable opened in Hempstead in 1936, followed by Bloomingdale's in Fresh Meadows in 1949, Abraham & Straus in Hempstead in 1955 and the first mall linchpins the following year — Macy's and Gimbel's at Roosevelt Field, Gimbel's at Green Acres and Gertz at Mid-Island Plaza.

Of course, before there were malls, there was Hempstead. For decades, "the Hub" was the center of transportation and shopping on Long Island, supporting not just Arnold Constable and A&S, Grant's and Woolworth's, but scores of mom-and-pop operations in an era when Mom and Pop still mattered. Even more important, Hempstead housed the county's largest bus terminus, making it a quick trip from as near as Garden City (before Garden City took over the carriage trade) and as far as Jamaica (whose own downtown dominated Queens).

"You have to remember how important the bus was," says Hempstead Village historian James York. "When Nassau started to expand, many GIs didn't have a job, much less an automobile." But as the bus gave way to the car and the downtown gave way to the mall, shopping began to change. By the 1960s, though, no downtown could compete with the malls' ever-growing array of card stores and shoe stores, their parking fields and their newfangled traditions (the department store Santa-turned-mall Santa, the indoor arts-and-crafts shows).

Spending Spree

Americans' purchases of audio-video equipment and automobiles increased dramatically after World War II.

Hitting the Road

Purchases of new and used automobiles (in billions of constant 1992 dollars):

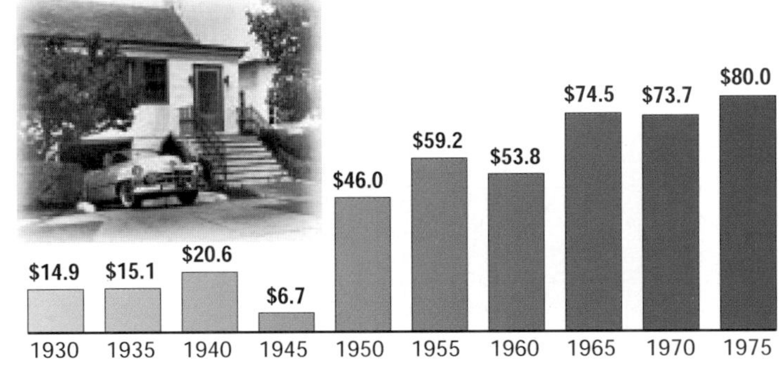

Sight and Sound

Purchases of audio and video equipment, such as radios, TVs and musical instruments (in billions of constant 1992 dollars):

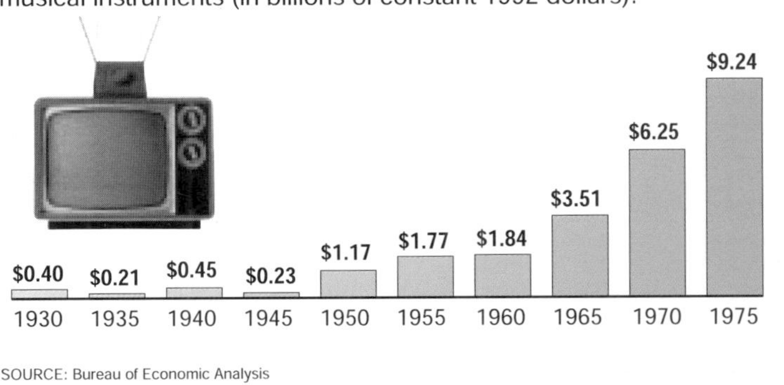

SOURCE: Bureau of Economic Analysis

Newsday / Linda McKenney

The modern shopper wanted to be entertained. And she wanted to buy — anything "modern" and "new." This was the era of wash-and-wear, of polyester shirts and Orlon sweaters, the age of Pyrex and Melmac and Bakelite. Even more, it was the dawn of television. Between 1950 and 1960, the number of American households with TVs soared from 4.6 million to 45.2 million, and retailers couldn't stock enough of them.

Of course, in the days before electronics, appliances cost a fortune. In 1957, a sewing machine fetched $400, a Kenmore washer $218, a Sears bench saw $75. But there were bargains in low-tech: The man in the gray flannel suit could pick up a new one at Wallach's for $59.75. His wife could snap up a mink-collared cashmere coat at Arnold Constable for $89, though, for many, even that was a bit steep. But Long Island was always a bargain-hunter's paradise — girls' sundresses for 97 cents, women's loden coats at E.J. Korvette for $7.97.

Even so, modern shopping was less about price than a dream — the quintessentially suburban dream of reinventing yourself daily. "After the war, people looked forward to new and exciting things," says Lois Sabatella, who came to Valley Stream from South Ozone Park and now lives in Plainview. "I remember going to Gimbel's with my mother so she could shop for a dress for Saturday night because people went out on Saturday night.

"And, as teenagers, someone was always having a party in their basement, so we'd buy a new top for $1.99 or a new piece of fake jewelry or new makeup," added Sabatella, who went from shopping at Green Acres to managing the Littman Jewelers there. "You always had a purpose for coming to the mall. Even if you didn't want to buy, it was enough to just window shop."

The New Frontier

SUBURBIA from Page 321

ers, who prior to World War II would have been high-school-educated and renters."

The loan program, administered by the Federal Housing Administration, guaranteed developers with up-front financing to mandate affordable housing. Returning GIs could obtain low-interest mortgages with little money down. By 1950, the government had pumped $20 billion into the building industry and helped to redefine the nation's postwar middle class.

But the business of building subdivisions was always risky, recalled Andrew Monaco, now living in Fort Salonga. In the early '50s, even with many homes built under the GI Bill, Monaco said, "There was still a great deal of anxiety, as there is today. Many of us had limited cash, so we always worried if our homes would sell."

As a developer, Monaco estimates his company, Pinewood Manor Inc., built more than 2,000 homes on Long Island, including a series of New England Village subdivisions. "We put them up in Hauppauge, Stony Brook, Centereach, so many, many more."

As subdivisions spread across Nassau and into Suffolk, dealers of autos and appliances followed the new consumers. Shopping malls sprang up everywhere. In 1956, Roosevelt Field Mall opened in Garden City, and Green Acres Mall in Valley Stream, and Broadway Mall, formerly Mid-Island Mall, in Hicksville. The Walt Whitman Mall opened in Huntington in 1962, and seven years later, the Smith Haven Mall opened in Lake Grove.

With a new frontier growing out of control, the challenge was met at the grass roots level by village and town agencies and suburban school boards — but often, not very well. Suburban problems were becoming clearer and local political jurisdictions were failing to meet them. Lack of strong zoning policies led to the ugliness of suburban sprawl and the dullness of cookie-cutter subdivisions.

"Through the 1950s, zoning was archaic, planning was virtually nonexistent and developers could to do what they wanted," recalled Lee Koppelman, longtime director of the Long Island Regional Planning Board. By 1960, the first remedial steps were taken. "But by then, the horse was out of the barn. Nassau and Suffolk had 19th-Century governments at the same time that their growth rate was approaching the 21st Century. The two fastest-growing counties in the country were led by the slowest-thinking politicans, still living in the past."

History might have been reshaped, Koppelman said, if the electorate had been aware of the inadequacy of the political system. But the newly arrived settlers remained "totally oblivous" that the population explosion was the problem. "Or they might have elected people to address the new problems, instead of officials who'd keep taxes down, who'd keep factories out, who'd keep 'other' people out."

Census Snapshot: 1950-1970

Baby Boom and Beyond: The population of the nation and Long Island grew dramatically in the 1950s, '60s and '70s. The U.S. population grew from 151.3 million in 1950 to 203.3 million in 1970. And the number of people on Long Island, from Brooklyn to Montauk, grew from about 5.2 million in 1950 to 7.2 million only 20 years later.

Total Population

	1950	1960	1970
New York State	14,830,192	16,782,304	18,241,391
Queens	1,550,849	1,809,578	1,987,174
Nassau	672,765	1,300,171	1,428,838
Suffolk	276,129	666,784	1,127,030
Kings (Brooklyn)	2,738,175	2,627,319	2,602,012
Nassau Towns			
North Hempstead	142,613	219,088	235,007
Oyster Bay	66,930	290,055	333,342
Hempstead	432,506	740,738	801,592
Nassau Cities			
Glen Cove	15,130	23,817	25,770
Long Beach	15,586	26,473	33,127
Suffolk Towns			
Babylon	45,556	142,309	204,256
Brookhaven	44,522	109,900	245,135
East Hampton	6,325	8,827	10,980
Huntington	47,506	126,221	200,172
Islip	71,465	172,959	278,880
Riverhead	9,973	14,519	18,909
Shelter Island	1,144	1,312	1,644
Smithtown	20,993	50,347	114,657
Southampton	16,830	27,095	36,154
Southold	11,632	13,295	16,804

SOURCE: "New York State Population," 1987; The World Almanac

Newsday / Linda McKenney

"By 1960, there were at least a thousand subdivisions, big and small, maybe more," says Bob Wieboldt, executive director of the Long Island Builders Institute. Suddenly, potato fields had become potentially expensive property for home sites.

In the 1950s, a potato farmer could sell off his land for $5,000 an acre, Wieboldt said. In turn, developers could build four to five houses on this acre, selling the houses and land for a total of $60,000 to $75,000. "If you wanted to buy a developed lot to build your own house, a quarter acre might cost you $3,000, or $6,000 for a half acre, so the value per acre was up to $12,000." Today, he noted, a half-acre lot in a subdivision might cost a home-builder $40,000 or more.

This stunning rise in the cost of land would summon greedy dreams of overnight fortunes and lead inevitably to political corruption. Rezoning land for commercial use was another of the suburban roads to wealth.

In the late 1960s, Suffolk County was rocked with land scandals in the Towns of Islip, Brookhaven and Babylon in which corrupt public officials manipulated rezoning powers for their own profit. A three-year investigative effort by a team of reporters led to indictments and brought Newsday its second Pulitzer Prize in 1970.

Today, the legacy of those boom days and the fast-and-loose zoning practices is still visible along arterial roads such as Hempstead and Jericho Turnpikes with their endless succession of service stations and fast-food restaurants, and a jungle of neon signs.

Despite the sprawling ugliness, for some young people, life in the suburbs seemed like a block party.

Raised in Rockville Centre, historian Doris Kearns Goodwin recalled her suburban childhood last year in a loving memoir, "Wait Till Next Year." Her tree-lined street was filled with playmates in the 1950s, she remembers, and she and her best friend ran a string across a narrow driveway to pass notes between their second-floor bedrooms.

It was a time when every house seemed like a part of an extended family, Goodwin said during a visit to her old block last fall. "We didn't have to knock on the doors. We just raced in, gathering up our gang, as if the block was one big house. There was no need for play groups or day care or camp. There was always someone home and we knew the inside of their houses as well as our own."

At the time, Goodwin was a drop-dead fan of Jackie Robinson, who broke baseball's color barrier with the old Brooklyn Dodgers. But in most Long Island communities, old and new, almost everyone who owned or rented a home was white. And the de facto segregation would establish housing patterns which have persisted to this day.

Diversity was barely in the political language in those days and hardly anyone fretted over ethnic homogeneity. Black residents often voiced complaints but they were ignored or generally unheard in white communities.

In a 1961 interview with a black resi-

Please see SUBURBIA on Next Page

Pat and Kay Catapano at home in East Northport. They had been married in 1948, and lived in the upstairs apartment of her parents' two-family house in Queens. They considered a Levittown-type solution but decided to skip the first rush to the suburbs. In 1958, they bought their first home in East Northport and they still live there.

Newsday Photo / Bill Davis

The New Frontier

SUBURBIA from Preceding Page

dent, for instance, Newsday reported that the woman resented the fact that, "I might drive past a house that was for sale and know that I couldn't buy it because I'm a Negro. Nobody likes to be told where you must buy."

With major Supreme Court decisions in the offing, some builders might have attempted to break the old color barriers. But the opportunity to change history was ignored.

One of suburbia's master builders, William J. Levitt, for instance, made no secret of his view on the racial status quo when Levittown opened on Oct. 1, 1947.

In his contract with the earliest Levittown home buyers and renters, Clause 25 spelled out a "white only" policy in no uncertain terms: "The tenant agrees not to permit the premises to be used or occupied by any person other than members of the Caucasian race."

"The plain fact is that most whites prefer not to live in mixed communities," Levitt stated at the time. "This attitude may be wrong morally and some day it may change . . . I hope it will. But it is unfair to charge an individual with the blame for creating this attitude or saddle him with the sole responsibility for correcting it. The responsibility is society's."

Until society is willing to confront these racial issues, Levitt said, "it is not reasonable to expect that any builder should or could undertake to absorb the entire risk and burden of conducting such a vast experiment."

A half century later, Lynda R. Day, an assistant professor of Africana studies at Brooklyn College, finds Levitt guilty of poor business judgment. "If he didn't think the houses would sell if African-Americans moved in, he was wrong. I think they would have. I think people were ready to move from Queens and Brooklyn. They had the money and they wanted the houses."

One of the African-American veterans who was rebuffed by Clause 25 was Eugene Burnett, a Wheatley Heights resident whose Levittown application was rejected. "Levitt had a moment in history to set an example for the rest of Long Island but he didn't seize it . . . He is the reason why Long Island is now so segregated," Burnett, a former Suffolk County police sergeant, said recently.

Exclusionary policies — written and unwritten — slowed the growth of Long Island's non-white population from the 1950s to the present.

In Nassau County, for instance, the black population was just over 13,000 in 1940, or about 3 percent. In 1960, despite the population explosion, nonwhite residents totaled only 42,132, still 3 percent. Suffolk's nonwhite population in 1940 was 8,700, or about 4 percent. In 1960, the figure rose to 34,787, about 5 percent. Today, the old patterns of segregation persist, even as the nonwhite population has slowly risen to just over 408,000, or 18 percent of the bi-county population of 2.6 million.

Newsday Photos / Bill Davis

Bill and Marie Baum moved to Huntington Bay in 1953 after renting in Levittown.

For many of the white settlers on Long Island, race was not a conscious issue in the 1950s. But in middle-class communities, residents did note how similar they were to their neighbors — and most of them seemed to like the idea.

Bill and Marie Baum, who bought a house in Huntington in 1953, after renting a Cape Cod house in Levittown, recalled that the makeup in their neighborhood seemed natural. For the women of Marie Baum's generation, with their growing entourage of preschoolers, it was a memorable time. "We were all so excited to be together — it was like a big party. We were only too happy to have a safe place for the children to play."

Bill and Marie were members of a bridge group that gathered once a month. They were all in their 20s or early 30s. Most of the men were former GIs who commuted to jobs in New York City. By 1949, most of the women had had their first or second child.

"There were 12 of us, meeting in each other's homes — and someone was always having a baby," Marie, now 73 and living in Huntington Bay, recalled. "Every month somebody else would announce a pregnancy. After a while, we were afraid to show up. I'd walk in and say, 'Who's pregnant tonight?' We ended up with 33 children!"

Most of their friends also moved on to larger houses, another Long Island pattern. But their group has retained their friendships for more than four decades, attending the weddings of each other's children over the years. In 1953, the Baums had come a long way from the Bronx, where they once

Toward Modern Times

Long Island

1946. United Nations began meeting in Lake Success.

1947. William Levitt built houses in what is now Levittown, beginning the postwar housing boom on Long Island.

Aug. 11, 1947. Construction began on the first peacetime nuclear reactor in the United States at Brookhaven National Laboratory.

1951. Roosevelt Field closed as an airfield.

1957. Ebbets Field was sold to build a housing development. The Dodgers left Brooklyn for Los Angeles.

United States

April 3, 1948. President Harry Truman signed the Foreign Assistance Act, which contained the Marshall Plan – a $5.3 billion recovery program for Europe.

April 22, 1954. Sen. Joseph McCarthy (R-Wis.) began hearings that would probe alleged Communist influence in the Army.

Sept. 24, 1957. President Dwight Eisenhower sent 1,000 Army paratroopers to protect nine black students who were to attend Central High School in Little Rock, Ark.

Aug. 21, 1959. Hawaii became the 50th state to join the United States.

The World

Oct. 16, 1946. Nine former Nazi leaders were hanged following the Nuremberg trials.

April 4, 1949. The North Atlantic Treaty Organization (NATO) came into existence.

June 25, 1950. North Korean troops invaded South Korea, beginning a conflict that would last until 1953.

Oct. 4, 1955. The Soviet Union launched Sputnik I, the first Earth satellite.

May 5, 1960. A U-2 plane on a spy mission was downed over the Soviet Union.

1946 | 1948 | 1950 | 1952 | 1954 | 1956 | 1958 | 1960

shared a tiny apartment. But more than 40 years later, Marie Baum remembers the friendly but still rueful reception they received when they moved eastward. "The residents who grew up there called us 'the new people who ruined Huntington,' " she said.

When Pat and Kay Catapano moved to East Northport, they heard no such criticism. They were, after all, pioneers.

They had been married in 1948, when the housing shortage in Brooklyn was so acute they lived in a furnished room with a hot plate for 15 months. Then Kay became pregnant with their twins and they decided to move into the upstairs apartment of her parents' two-family house in Queens. They considered a Levittown-type solution but decided to skip the first rush to the suburbs.

In 1958, they bought their first home in East Northport for $18,250, an exact figure that Pat Catapano has never forgotten — and he and his wife still live there.

At the time, the Long Island Expressway had not yet reached the Nassau-Suffolk border, but the Catapanos enjoyed the serenity of country roads. Like other settlers, they instantly felt the lure of this new space age — the delight of living space.

There was never a doubt about the rightness of it. "People would come out to visit, they'd stay for the weekend. It was too far to come for the day. There was hardly a car on Larkfield Road in those days," he remembers. "Now the traffic is horrendous."

Their subdivision was called Lenard Homes, where buyers chose one of the number of model homes on display. Pat and Kay selected a split-level. "It was expensive at the time. Another company was putting up homes for $14,000 in Deer Park Avenue. But we were relatively young and, I told my wife, 'We'll make it.' "

Like the Baums, the Catapanos found advantages in the shared interests of the neighborhood. "All of us had children; that was the nice part of it. We all had the same worries: having good schools, trying to meet the mortgage payments, making a living, getting the kids into college, doing the best we could. We didn't really think about social problems until the late '60s and '70s."

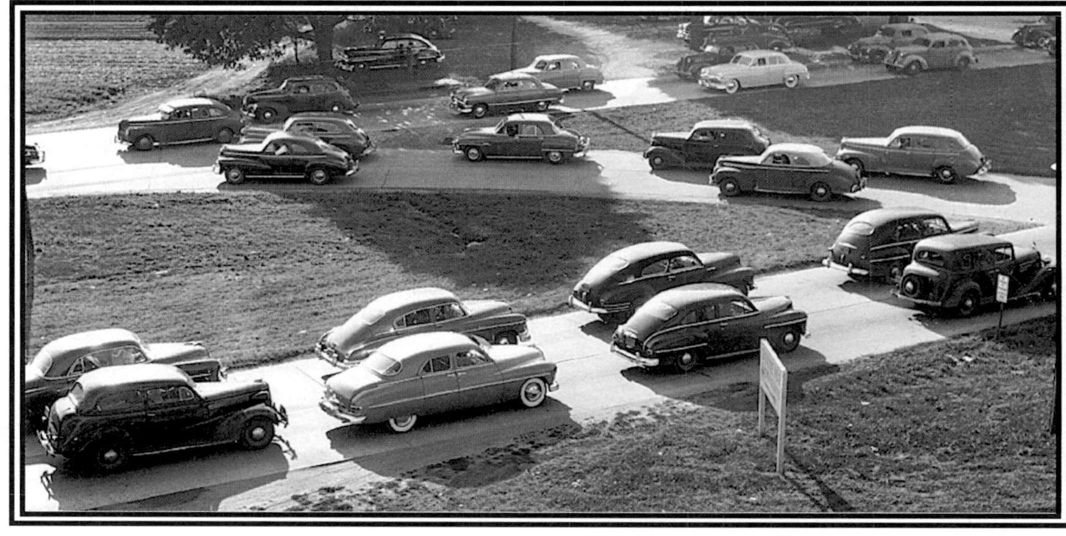

Newsday Photo

Cars and roads have changed but not the congestion: A traffic jam occurs in 1951 near Levittown.

Years later, as Long Islanders grew older, there would be taxpayer rebellions in the 1980s and '90s, protesting school budgets and the high cost of education. But in the euphoric '60s, Pat Catapano recalled, he paid only $123 a month, which covered mortgage, insurance and taxes, including school taxes. "I don't think anyone started complaining about taxes until the '70s."

His neighbors were friendly but not too friendly. Everyone knew each other and shared an occasional cocktail. "But if anyone needed help, we were there," he said. "Because we had the same problems: How are the kids doing? Are the grubs eating your lawn? Are you planning to paint your house?"

That feeling of camaraderie vanished later. Children grew up and moved on. Now there are new neighbors with children. "I see the school buses come down the streets again. A new generation. I see mothers doing the things our wives did," he said. But then, in 1958, there were no people in their 70s and 80s who lived down the block.

Catapano had grown up in a Brooklyn apartment above a store with a shared bathroom in the hall. "But I worked hard all my life — and I was very fortunate," he reflected. Like many others, he felt he had traveled a long way to suburbia — and he has loved where the road has taken him.

Author Alice Hoffman, who grew up on Long Island, drew upon her childhood experiences to examine the magic and the mistakes of suburban life in one of her best-selling novels, "Seventh Heaven."

The work is set in the 1950s in a community similar to her own hometown of Franklin Square, where Hoffman was the only child on the block whose mother was divorced. Her closest friend was not permitted to visit her house since her friend's father thought a divorced mother, even a social worker, might be a bad influence. In the novel, Hoffman's heroine, Nora Silk, is also the only divorced mother on the block. There, the wives on the block refuse to talk to their divorcee neighbor.

A few decades later, of course, single parents would become commonplace on Long Island.

Hoffman also remembers the magic in this era, as new suburbs sprawled along the Southern State Parkway. "Most children feel the magic of the place they grew up. Only they've forgotten. For me, Long Island was enchanted," Hoffman said in a Newsday interview.

Like her heroine, she was mesmerized by summer evenings when children captured fireflies in glass jars, playing games on safe streets late into the warm evenings.

"The kids had a community. All the houses were new and they looked alike, as if they all had been put under a spell," she said. The fathers disappeared during the day while the mothers stayed home and baked cookies, Hoffman remembered. "And that was kind of magical too."

1961. Throgs Neck Bridge opened, connecting Long Island to the Bronx.

1962. Cold Spring Harbor Laboratory was formed with the merger of the Biological Laboratory and Carnegie Station.

1964. Verrazano-Narrows Bridge opened connecting Long Island with Staten Island.

July 20, 1969. The Grumman-built lunar module landed on the moon. About 6 1/2 hours later, Neil Armstrong stepped out of the module and became the first person to set foot on the moon.

1971. The Counties of Nassau and Suffolk were designated a Standard Metropolitan Statistical Area, the first SMSA in the United States without a central city.

April 12, 1973. The Long Island Lighting Co. received a license from the Atomic Energy Commission to begin construction of the Shoreham nuclear power plant.

Nov. 22, 1963. President John F. Kennedy was assassinated in Dallas.

July 2, 1964. President Lyndon Johnson signed the Civil Rights Act of 1964.

April 4, 1968. The Rev. Martin Luther King Jr. was assassinated at a Memphis, Tenn., hotel. Two months later, Democratic presidential candidate Robert Kennedy also was assassinated.

May 4, 1970. During an antiwar demonstration at Kent State University, four students were killed when National Guardsmen fired into the crowd.

June 17, 1972. Five men were caught burglarizing Democratic headquarters, which was located at the Watergate complex in Washington, D.C.

Aug. 9, 1974. President Richard Nixon resigned the presidency because of the Watergate affair.

Oct. 28, 1962. Soviet Premier Nikita Khrushchev agreed to halt construction of bases in Cuba and remove rockets already there, ending the "Cuban Missile Crisis."

March 8-9, 1965. More than 3,500 Marines landed in South Vietnam, the first U.S. combat troops sent to the country.

Aug. 13, 1966. Cultural Revolution began in China.

June 28, 1967. Six-Day War ended with Israel taking control of a unified Jerusalem, the West Bank, Gaza Strip, Golan Heights and the Sinai peninsula.

Sept. 5, 1972. Terrorists killed 11 members of the Israeli Olympic team at the Summer Games in Munich.

April 30, 1975. Saigon, the capital of South Vietnam, surrendered to Communist forces.

1962 | 1964 | 1966 | 1968 | 1970 | 1972 | 1974 | 1976

Newsday / Linda McKenney

Fed by the GI Bill of 1944, the Island's postwar demand for higher education explodes

The Hunger for Learning

BY GEORGE DEWAN
STAFF WRITER

In early 1945, Nicholas Vogel was piloting a P-47 Thunderbolt on bombing and strafing missions in Europe until he was shot down over Dusseldorf and thrown into a German prison camp. The following September, with World War II ended, he was registered at Hofstra College under the new GI Bill.

The explosion of population on Long Island following the war and well into the next two decades produced a huge demand for higher education. Small colleges like Hofstra and Adelphi expanded rapidly, and new ones were created to satisfy a growing hunger for education beyond high school.

The so-called GI Bill of Rights — officially called the Servicemen's Adjustment Act of 1944 — which made free college education available to more than 15 million war veterans, played a major role in satisfying that hunger. It changed the face of college campuses, on Long Island and across the nation.

Vogel is one of thousands whose lives were changed by the GI Bill. He is now a professor emeritus of accounting at Hofstra, which opened as a college in 1935 and is now a university.

"The government picked up the tab for my college education," Vogel, a 71-year-old Hempstead resident, said recently. "It jump-started me in my whole professional activity." When he returned to teach accounting and business law at Hofstra in 1949, he found that most of his students were on the GI Bill.

"They were dedicated, they had a goal," Vogel said. "They were going to achieve that goal one way or another. I don't know of anyone I was associated with who didn't appreciate that government help. You didn't see many of them flunking out."

Barbara Kelly, curator of the Long Island Studies Institute, said although Long Island colleges existed before the war, it was in the postwar boom years that higher education took off. "The growth rate was incredible, and that is due to the GI Bill," she said. "Suddenly, you have older men and women who are veterans. The whole nature of higher education shifts. Earlier, it was a way of extending your childhood. After the war it was a way of preparing you for life."

Although the GI Bill for World War II veterans expired in 1956, its effects continued. A whole generation of parents with college education developed, and they wanted their kids to go to college as well. And the wives of GI Bill recipients went back to school themselves, after their children were older. All of this spiraling demand for higher education caused rapid expansion in old schools and created new ones.

"The GI Bill was temporary, but it opened the floodgates," said Kelly. "There's a whole difference in who's going to college. That difference is going to stick long after the GI Bill is over."

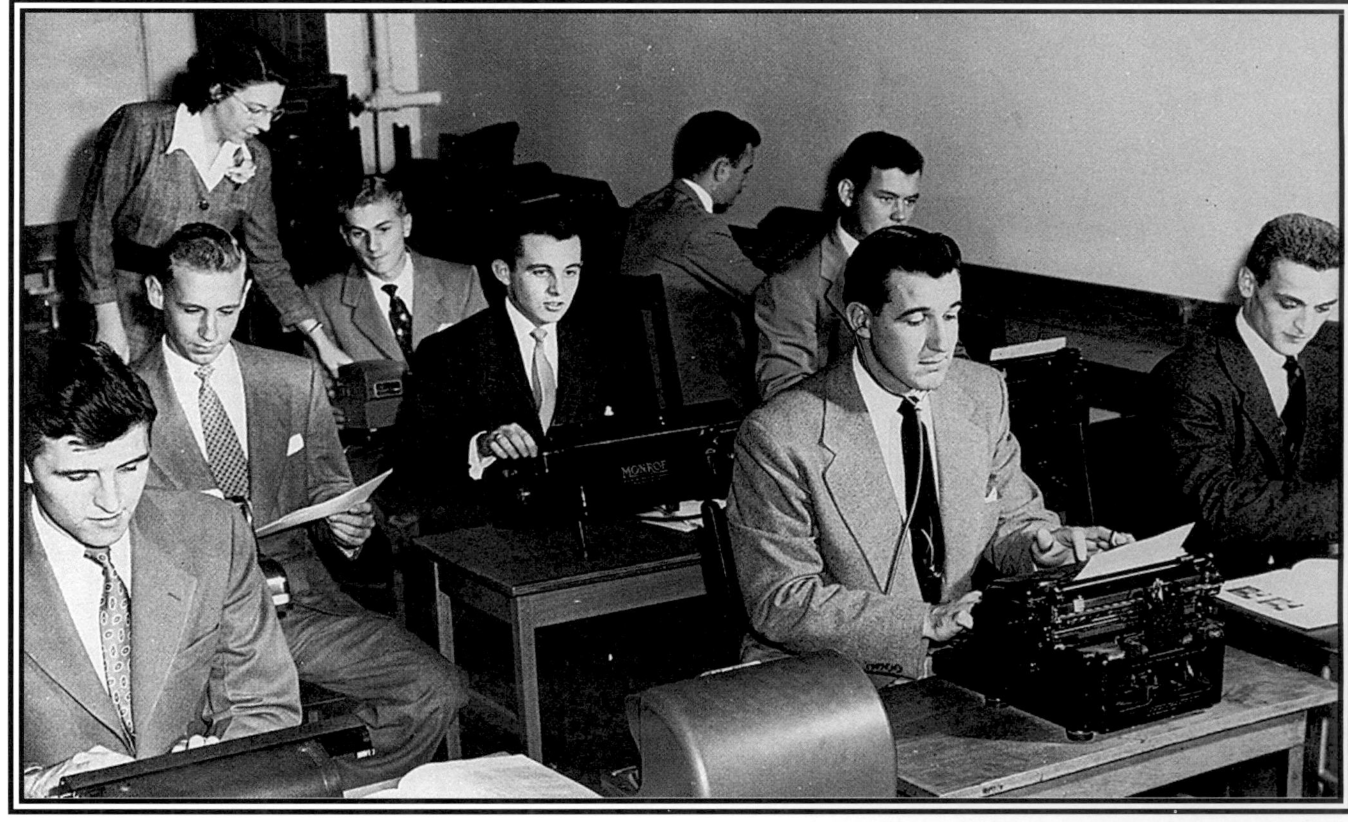

Adelphiana Collection, Swirbul Library, Adelphi University; Newsday Photo

After World War II, men entered Adelphi in Garden City for the first time, a result of the surge in college attendance created by the 1944 GI Bill.

"We were built by the GI Bill," said Long Island University president David Steinberg. "In those days we were solely at the Brooklyn campus. The first wave of those soldiers came through Brooklyn, and we grew to 10,000. We knew we needed to follow where industry was moving, where Grumman was, and the shopping centers."

Founded in Brooklyn in 1926, Long Island University opened the C.W. Post campus in Brookville in 1954, followed by Southampton College in 1963. "We followed the GIs out," Steinberg said. "Long Island is the only place in America that was settled west to east."

By the time the benefits ended in the summer of 1956, about 7.8 million out of 15.4 million World War II veterans had used the bill for post-high school education: 2.2 million for college, 3.5 million in technical schools, 1.4 million in job training and 700,000 in farm training.

One veteran who used everything the bill had to offer was Brooklyn-born George Merritt, who got out of the Navy in 1946, and bought his Levittown house in 1955 with a government-backed loan, also part of the legislation. He used his school benefits to attend the McAllister School of Embalming in New York City.

"I wouldn't have been able to go to school without the GI Bill," Merritt said. "My father worked in defense plants and got laid off at the end of the war. Without the GI Bill I would have been a garbage man, living in Queens in an apartment."

Higher education on Long Island grew as the Island grew. Adelphi University, begun as a tiny Brooklyn college in 1896 and later moved to Garden City, was a small school for women when World War II ended. With veterans streaming onto college campuses, Adelphi quickly became coeducational, and one of those men was Sam Gaynor, now 71 and living in Jackson Heights. He got a degree in business education. "The GI Bill was a lifesaver," he said. "I couldn't have gotten a college education without it."

The demand for higher education in the state led to the creation of the State University of New York in 1948, the SUNY system, making New York the last state in the union to have a state university. This led on Long Island to new four-year colleges — at Stony Brook, 1957, and Old Westbury, 1968 — and two-year community colleges in Nassau and Suffolk Counties in 1959 and 1960. Also, what began in Farmingdale in 1912 as a school of agriculture became a SUNY college campus. And Empire State College, a SUNY school in Saratoga, opened a Long Island campus at Old Westbury in 1971.

Most of today's private Long Island colleges and universities did not even exist at the end of World War II. Dowling College, begun in 1955 as part of Adelphi University, became a four-year school on its own in 1968. Five Towns College opened in Dix Hills in 1972. Molloy College in Rockville Centre was established in 1955, New York Institute of Technology in Old Westbury in 1955. Polytechnic University in Brooklyn opened a campus in Farmingdale in 1961. St. Joseph's College, with a main campus in Brooklyn, opened a branch campus in Brentwood in 1971, later moving to a site in Patchogue. Briarcliffe College opened in Bethpage in 1966. The Jacob Fuchsberg Law Center of Touro College opened in Huntington in 1980.

Two schools with older roots are: The U.S. Merchant Marine Academy, established in Kings Point in 1942, and the Webb Institute, the oldest school devoted to naval architecture and marine engineering, dates back to 1889.

There are about 150,000 students in Nassau and Suffolk colleges and universities. But Steinberg, president of Long Island University, says one of his chief concerns is that graduates of Long Island's highly rated high schools are going elsewhere to college. "The presumption is that schools are better elsewhere," he said. "I refuse to believe that."

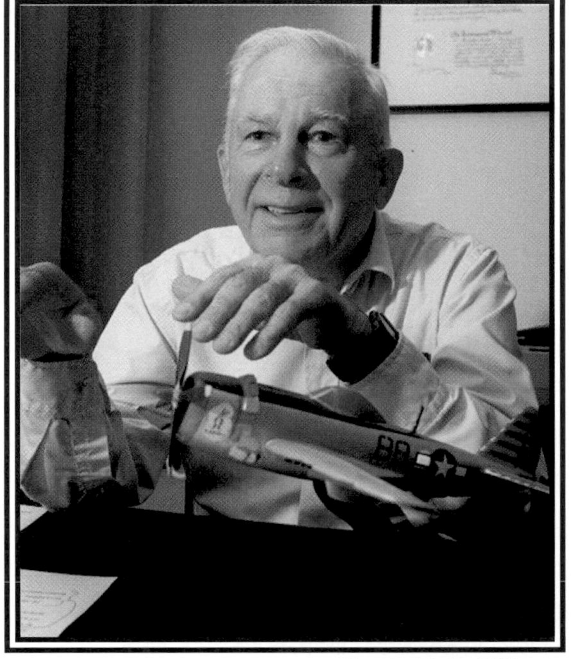

Newsday Photo / Bill Davis

Nicholas Vogel, now a professor emeritus at Hofstra, is one of thousands who attended college on the GI Bill.

Developer Zeckendorf's new idea produces a mighty mall at Roosevelt Field

A Shopping Giant Arrives

BY RHODA AMON
STAFF WRITER

On a chilly day in late April, 1955, five men, handsomely garbed in topcoats and felt hats, dug shovels into a deserted airfield on the vast Hempstead Plains. They were about to change Long Island's style of living and shopping. They were breaking ground for the mammoth Roosevelt Field Shopping Center.

The men, all big shots, were Nassau County Executive A. Holly Patterson, Hempstead Town Supervisor Harold Herman, Roosevelt Field president Herbert I. Silverson, Macy's president Wheelock H. Bingham and, most imposing of all, developer-tycoon William Zeckendorf.

The site chosen for the first such project on Long Island was billed as the place from which Charles A. Lindbergh began his landmark flight across the Atlantic in 1927. Actually, it wasn't. Lindbergh took off from a field in Westbury where Fortunoff now stands.

Newsday Photo

On a barren Roosevelt Field in 1955, construction commences on Macy's largest suburban store in the East.

The shopping center was sited in an area that had once been Curtiss Field. Curtiss and Roosevelt Fields were united in 1929 as one big Roosevelt Field. It had been "the largest, the premier aviation field in the world," according to Joshua Stoff, curator of Nassau County's Cradle of Aviation Museum. As many as 10,000 spectators would jam the roads to Roosevelt Field, to watch the aerial antics of the early fliers.

A half century later, 50,000 shoppers would jam the Roosevelt Field Shopping Center for the opening of Macy's largest suburban store in the East.

In the '30s, the airfield was already pressed by development. The eastern portion was given over to auto racing, later Roosevelt Raceway. World War II curtailed civilian aviation and the field was increasingly hemmed in by housing developments.

Webb & Knapp, the then-powerful real estate firm headed by Zeckendorf, took controlling interest in the floundering airfield in 1950, and Herbert I. Silverson, a company director, became president of Roosevelt Field Inc.

Silverson, now 87 and a California real estate consultant, recalled the debate over how to develop the huge space. "Some of our people wanted to build a lot of housing. I knew that growing suburbs need jobs, and they need shopping." After the flying ended in '51, the firm replaced the old hangars with industrial plants in the northeast corner, fronting Old Country Road.

The public was making other uses of the obsolete airport. "There were drag meets on weekends. One man was using a runway to teach his wife how to drive," Silverson recalled.

In 1954, when the Jones Beach State Parkway Authority was planning to extend Meadowbrook Parkway to connect Northern and Southern State Parkways, Webb & Knapp donated 48 acres so that the extension would cut through the airfield. "When they gave us a cloverleaf in the middle of it, we had our shopping center," Silverson said, "the largest in the country."

The center, which some have called Long Island's premier shrine to consumerism, was built at a cost of $35 million. It began in 1956 as an open-air mall, with space for 11,000 cars.

Designed by architect I. M. Pei, it was to be more than a shopping center. "We put in an ice skating rink, the first for a shopping center," Silverson said. There was also a 400-seat community theater, an art gallery, space for auto and boat shows. By the end of '56, Webb & Knapp had developed more than 300 acres, including the shopping and industrial areas, restaurants, bowling alleys, a hotel, a medical building.

Silverson left Webb & Knapp in 1958, convinced that the firm was overextended with nationwide projects. His last act as president was to sign on a Gimbel's store.

Not everyone welcomed the commercial development. The upscale-planned village of Garden City, which would have preferred one-family houses, agreed to a 55-acre office building complex west of the shopping center. Villagers were assuaged with a 72-foot wide buffer along Clinton Road, called Hazelhurst Park.

But they still resent the "gigantic commercial development" sharing their Garden City mailing address, according to local historian-photographer John Ellis Kordes. "The Roosevelt Field Mall has no relationship to Garden City and pays no taxes to the village," he said.

Roosevelt Field also was blamed for the decline of neighborhood retail areas, especially Hempstead Village, once the shopping hub of Long Island. Families could now drive to one-stop shopping at Roosevelt Field.

The mall did not take off in the early '60s. In fact, it lost nearly $8 million total over '62 and '63. The turnaround came in 1968 when the shopping center was enclosed. But Zeckendorf's empire had collapsed, and the property was sold to a combine for $35 million.

Corporate Property Investors of Manhattan, owners since 1973, expanded the center over two decades. In 1993, a second story was introduced. In 1996, the upper level was completed and 70 more stores added, including a food court. Now with 260 stores and increasingly upscale, it's the seventh largest mall in the country and the third most successful in sales per square foot.

In a deal to be closed in mid-1998, Roosevelt Field, along with the Walt Whitman Mall in Huntington, was scheduled to become part of the Simon DeBartolo Group of Indianapolis. "We consider Roosevelt Field a crown jewel," said spokeswoman Billie Scott.

Silverson, who moved to California in 1966 as consultant to another real estate tycoon, Harry Helmsley, revisited his "field of dreams" last year. Though Webb & Knapp went down the drain, he reflected, "Roosevelt Field got better and better over the years."

WILLIAM ZECKENDORF: PLANNER, DREAMER

Newsday Photo, 1960

William Zeckendorf did business on the move, here speaking on a car phone.

To the young, Zeckendorf is a boulevard cutting from Old Country Road to the Roosevelt Field Shopping Center. To another generation, William Zeckendorf was a flamboyant real estate magnate who changed the look of Long Island in the post-World War II years.

"He was a great planner, a dreamer," said Herbert I. Silverson, who worked with Zeckendorf on the development of Roosevelt Field, "but he was overenthusiastic, overzealous, over-everything."

Zeckendorf was "a tank-sized man" with an unquenchable appetite for big real estate deals, according to Associated Press writer Hal Boyle. In a 1956 story, Boyle described a power breakfast at which Silverson put down a proposal by Broadway showman Billy Rose for a million-dollar enclosed ice rink-amusement area at Roosevelt Field as "lame brain." Zeckendorf approved Rose's scheme, declaring, "to do less than the ultimate is to do nothing."

"Zeckendorf engaged in a real-life game of Monopoly involving some of the most prestigious properties in the United States, including the United Nations site, the Chrysler Building and the Chase Manhattan Plaza in Manhattan and Denver's Mile High Center," Newsday's T.J. Collins wrote in 1976 in Zeckendorf's obituary. Under his leadership, Webb & Knapp, based in Manhattan, built $3 billion worth of commercial projects in 20 years.

The bubble burst in 1963, and the firm was forced to sell Roosevelt Field. Zeckendorf, who lived in Manhattan, also resigned as board chairman at Long Island University, after 25 years during which the student body grew from 800 to 18,000 and campuses were developed in Brookville and Southampton. He died in 1976 at age 71. — **Rhoda Amon**

During a Thanksgiving eve rush in 1950, one train hits another, killing 78 riders

The LIRR's Worst Crash

BY MICHAEL DORMAN

It is Thanksgiving eve, 1950, in Manhattan's bustling Penn Station.

Dolores Barnes, 30, and her husband, John, 31, meet as they do every night after finishing work — she as a manicurist, he as a transport company expediter. Right on schedule, they board the 6:09 train for Hempstead. They plan to spend the evening at their Levittown home preparing the next day's turkey dinner with Dolores Barnes' mother, visiting from Havana.

John Steinheuser, 21, and Bernard Bahn, 31, usually take earlier trains. But both are running late this night, so they catch the first available Hempstead train — the 6:09.

Among others meeting at the station are George Brown, 46, a purchasing director from Baldwin, and his 18-year-old son, Stephen, coming home from college for the holiday. They catch the 6:13 train for Babylon.

AP Photo

Emergency crews and others gather at the scene of the 1950 tragedy; a train that had stopped in Queens was rammed by one bound for Babylon.

When the Hempstead train approaches Jamaica — passing signal block J in Richmond Hill — engineer William Murphy reduces speed to 15 mph. Then, for some reason, the air brakes lock. Murphy can't release them. The train rolls to a stop. Murphy tries repeatedly to get it moving again, but it will not budge. The 6:09 is stalled out there in the darkness.

It is 6:32. The train bound for Babylon, after leaving Penn Station four minutes behind the Hempstead train, now comes barreling down the tracks at about 65 mph.

Suddenly, with a cataclysmic boom, it slams into the rear of the stalled train — precipitating the worst train wreck in Long Island history, the worst in New York State history and the worst in the nation since 1943. The shuddering impact sends the front of the onrushing train plunging down the middle of the other train's last car — cutting it in half lengthwise as if sliced by a giant cleaver and driving it 15 feet into the air.

In moments, death, destruction and chaos descend on the lonely trackside. Dolores Barnes is dead. John Barnes is dead. George Brown is dead. Stephen Brown is dead. John Steinheuser is dead. Bernard Bahn is dead. Seventy-two others are either dead or dying. Those who survived offered anguished accounts. Harold Rosenberg, 34, was riding in the last car of the Hempstead train. "I saw a terrific red flash and felt a jolt like an atom bomb," he told a reporter. He fell to the floor. He was bleeding from the mouth and nose.

"People were lying all about, screaming in pain," Rosenberg said. "Others beat frantically at doors and windows, which were jammed shut. Seconds later, neighbors from across the way arrived at the scene with ladders and jimmied open the doors and started to take out the injured."

Arthur Kearney, 28, a tax analyst, said the crash came seconds after the conductor on the Hempstead train signaled the train was ready to go if Murphy could get it moving. "Just when he gave two short peeps on his whistle, the train from behind hit us," Kearney said. "It threw me up against the roof. The lights went out. Women started screaming. The chap behind me was either unconscious or dead. I managed to crawl to a broken window on the left side of the train. I looked out and found myself about 15 feet above the ground. In the train under us, all I could see was parts of bodies, arms and legs protruding from the windows. I took a chance and dropped to the tracks below, just between two third rails."

Robert Kopple of Roslyn said, "The front of the train that struck us looked as though it was wearing an overcoat — the rear car of our train."

Within minutes, fire trucks, ambulances and police cars — sirens screaming — raced to the scene. Searchlights were hastily erected. Heavy railroad wrecking equipment was dispatched to pry victims from the twisted remains. When the ambulances proved insufficient, station wagons were pressed into service to carry survivors to hospitals. In some cases, there was not time to reach the hospitals. Surgeons converted a nearby house into a makeshift operating room — working under an unshaded light bulb on a kitchen table covered with a sheet.

Those less seriously injured were wrapped in blankets and placed on stretchers near the tracks. Many lay side by side with the dead.

Emergency calls went out for blood donations. By midnight, nearly 1,000 donors appeared.

Days later, six local, state and federal agencies launched investigations. Hearings produced sharp criticism of both railroad policies and the performance of LIRR employees. There was testimony that the railroad — with government approval — had abandoned using an automatic safety device that would have cut the Babylon train's speed to 15 mph and reduced the disastrous crash to a slight bump. The Queens district attorney's office at first faulted the stalled train's engineer for failing to order his brakeman to flag down the Babylon train, but a few weeks later blamed the Babylon train's engineer for disregarding a stop-and-proceed signal. Years later, an LIRR official who was on the stalled train said a flagman had been dispatched.

In an exhaustive report, the state Public Service Commission ordered sweeping reforms — among them placing a conductor or brakeman with the engineer in the front car of every electric train and tightening physical requirements. "The consummation of the steps taken by this and other agencies should reduce to a minimum the consequences of human imperfection," the commission said.

That confidence aside, accidents would nonetheless continue to occur on the Long Island Rail Road. But, to date at least, none would be nearly so deadly as the night of horror on that doomed stretch of tracks in Richmond Hill.

Michael Dorman is a freelance writer.

ANOTHER 1950 DISASTER

Newsday Photo

Looking through the wreckage in Rockville Centre

Only nine months before the Richmond Hill collision, another disaster struck the Long Island Rail Road.

On Feb. 17, 1950, a train bound for New York and an eastbound train headed for Babylon collided head-on in Rockville Centre. Thirty-two people were killed and more than 100 seriously injured. The collision occurred in a "one-track gantlet" used at different times by eastbound and westbound trains. Authorities said the eastbound train ran through a stop signal.

Days later, the railroad — under fire — installed tripping devices in the gantlet to stop trains automatically and avert head-on collisions. A grand jury investigated the collision and issued a report accusing the railroad of giving inadequate consideration to safeguarding the public. The report recommended needed reforms — including installation of additional safety equipment, use of greater care in gantlet operations and more frequent physical examinations.

Such reforms, however, were not sufficient to prevent the Richmond Hill disaster. — **Michael Dorman**

Local controversies reflect the Wisconsin senator's zealous hunt for Communists

McCarthy's Shadow on LI

BY MICHAEL DORMAN

Henry Steele Commager, one of the nation's leading historians, was invited in 1956 to speak on the American presidency at Sewanhaka High School in Floral Park. But the speech was abruptly canceled when several school board members described Commager as "too controversial."

The board members raised questions about Commager's loyalty to the United States on the ground that he had signed a petition several years earlier seeking a Christmas amnesty for 16 convicted low-level Communists.

"I was told that I was considered too controversial a speaker," Commager said at the time. "Anybody could be controversial if you don't like the way he parts his hair. I don't think a speaker can be too controversial, especially in a school. If he weren't controversial, he would be boring."

Nonetheless, the school board refused to back down, even though no evidence was presented against Commager. He would maintain his eminent reputation until his death this year at the age of 95. That he was purportedly controversial was enough to put him on the board's blacklist. Critics of the decision noted that a year earlier the board had ignored four clergymen's protest against what they called a "one-sided" program in which all the speakers were supporters of Sen. Joseph McCarthy (R-Wis.).

McCarthy gave the language a new term, McCarthyism, springing from his investigations of purported communism and subversion throughout the country. Many charged that such investigations, by McCarthy and others, were witch-hunts victimizing innocent Americans. Whatever the truth about McCarthy, allegations of disloyalty played a significant role on Long Island in the 1950s. The Commager affair was one of many such incidents that erupted periodically across the Island.

In 1951, a Long Island school board election campaign was preoccupied with a dispute over purported Communist influence in the Island Trees district in Levittown. A former school board member, John Donellon, charged that an anti-Communist publication had identified the incumbent board chairman, Oscar Baruchin, as a signer of two petitions for Communist candidates in 1941 Queens elections. Donellon, spokesman for a group called the Independent Citizens Committee, also contended that Baruchin had been active in the Northern Boulevard Tenants Association. He said the association was affiliated with the New York Tenants Council — which he described as a Communist-front organization.

The allegations touched off an uproar at the board meeting. Baruchin said he could not recall signing any petitions such as those Donellon described and that he was certain his tenants association was not affiliated with any Communist front.

When the school board election finally took place at the end of the meeting, a Unity Committee slate — organized by Baruchin — won a clean sweep.

Two years later, a movie titled "Limelight" made by Charlie Chaplin — world-famous for his role as a tramp in baggy pants and bowler hat — opened across the country. When it appeared in Huntington, American Legion members picketed the theater over what they called Chaplin's "un-American" leanings. Chaplin was British.

In 1951, five Long Island clergymen were listed by the House Un-American Activities Committee as supporters of a supposedly pro-Communist document known as the Stockholm Peace Petition. All either denied signing it or said they had no idea it was Communist-inspired. The most outspoken was Rabbi Roland Gittelsohn of the Central Synagogue of Nassau County in Rockville Centre, a former Marine Corps chaplain and a member of former President Harry Truman's Committee on Civil Rights.

"My signature was never appended to the petition," Gittelsohn said. "It is my strong opinion that no committee of Congress or any other agency should release such a list on any matter without first checking the veracity of the signatures with the people involved."

That same year, the American Legion was involved in a dispute about Ernest Melby, dean of the New York University School of Education, who spoke at a meeting called by the Garden City Parent-Teacher Association. The local American Legion post, describing Melby as "controversial," asked that the invitation be withdrawn. But the PTA refused.

The executive committee of the William Bradford Turner American Legion Post charged that Melby had been vice chairman of the National Council of American-Soviet Friendship, purportedly regarded as subversive. Melby said the Soviet Union was a World War II ally of the United States during his tenure in 1943.

A PTA committee wrote the American Legion post's executive committee after Melby's talk: "Your committee made no charges against Dr. Melby save that he was a controversial figure. We believe we have proved it."

Michael Dorman is a freelance writer.

LEGACY

THE ROSENBERGS' GRAVES

Newsday Photo, 1975 / J. Michael Dombroski

AP Photo

Above, the Farmingdale gravestones of Ethel and Julius Rosenberg, who were executed for giving atomic-bomb secrets to the Soviet Union. At right, the Rosenbergs during their 1951 espionage trial in New York federal court.

The graves lie in Wellwood Cemetery, just off Wellwood Avenue in Pinelawn.

Evergreen ground cover shrouds the two graves. A large brown rabbit hops unhurriedly by on a recent afternoon. Three well-tended shrubs partially conceal the graves from the eyes of passersby.

But the persistent will discover a large gray headstone marked "Rosenberg" and two footstones reading "Ethel Rosenberg, born Sept. 25, 1915, died June 19, 1953. Julius Rosenberg, born May 12, 1918, died June 19, 1953." There is nothing in the grave markers to reflect that those identical death dates came about because the two people buried there were spies executed for giving atomic-bomb secrets to the Soviet Union.

Evidence produced at their 1951 federal court trial reflected that Julius Rosenberg was a central figure in widespread espionage activities from at least 1943 to 1950. Ethel Rosenberg's brother, David Greenglass, who had worked at the New Mexico laboratory where the atomic bomb was developed, was among the witnesses who implicated Julius Rosenberg in the delivery of atomic secrets to the Soviets. There was evidence that Ethel Rosenberg had typed some of the secret papers passed to Soviet spies.

The issue of the Rosenbergs' guilt or innocence became a political lightning rod. Controversy continued after they were executed in the electric chair at Sing Sing Prison in Ossining, N.Y. When the hearses carrying their bodies to the cemetery turned off the Southern State Parkway at Wellwood Avenue, demonstrators were waiting and shouting such imprecations as "dirty Commies" and "bury them in Russia." State troopers collected license-plate numbers of those there to honor the Rosenbergs — saying they wanted to "augment our subversive files." Speakers paid tribute.

Now, there is silence at the graves. Two small stones repose on each of the footstones — left as remembrances by mourners unknown.

— **Michael Dorman**

AP Photo, 1989

Henry Steele Commager: The historian was invited to speak at a Floral Park school in 1956 — and then disinvited when officials expressed concern about a petition he signed favoring clemency for low-level Communists.

UPI Photo, 1965

Roland Gittlesohn: The Rockville Centre rabbi was one of five L.I. clergymen listed by a congressional committee in 1951 as supporters of the supposedly pro-Communist Stockholm Peace Petition. He denied having signed it.

A socialite shoots her husband, and the killing is called a case of mistaken identity

A Slaying In High Society

BY MICHAEL DORMAN

The night began for the Woodwards with a glittering party in honor of the duchess of Windsor. It ended with a blaze of gunfire — an act of violence that would fascinate the nation for weeks and inspire two best-selling novels.

William Woodward Jr., 35, was the handsome, dark-haired owner of the top-rated racehorse Nashua and a member of a renowned racing family that had saddled three Kentucky Derby winners. His wife, Ann, four years his elder, was a beautiful blond former actress and model who had transformed herself from a Kansas farm girl into a sophisticated socialite.

Woodward's mother, Elsie Ogden Cryder Woodward, was regarded as the reigning figure in New York society. So it hardly seemed surprising that William and Ann Woodward would be among the 58 guests invited to the party honoring the duchess on Oct. 30, 1955, at the Locust Valley estate of Edith Baker, widow of a wealthy banker. One subject of discussion at the party was a wave of burglaries sweeping North Shore mansions.

Guests at the party would say later that the Woodwards seemed in good spirits. William Woodward had only a few drinks. His wife, a teetotaler, drank nothing. They left about 1 a.m.

After driving to their 43-acre Oyster Bay Cove estate, they retired to separate bedrooms across a corridor on the first floor of their mansion. Because of the recent outbreak of burglaries, they had taken to sleeping with weapons beside their beds. William Woodward had a revolver; his wife had a double-barrel, 12-gauge shotgun.

About 3 a.m., Ann Woodward said, she was awakened by the barking of her dog and what she took to be the sound of a prowler. She would give this account of the ensuing events:

Hearing the noise, she turned on a night light, grabbed the shotgun and ran to the door of her room. She threw open the door and spotted a figure in the doorway of her husband's room. Without a word, she fired the shotgun across the corridor — cutting loose two blasts almost simultaneously. And then, too late, it dawned on her that the figure in the doorway was not a prowler.

"Almost immediately, I realized it was my husband," Ann Woodward told police. "I ran to him and fell on the floor beside him."

She picked up a telephone and shrieked for help. A telephone operator could not make out what she was saying, but called the police.

When officers arrived, they found Woodward dead near the doorway to his room. He was nude. Woodward had been struck in the head and face by one blast of No. 7 shotgun pellets, ordinarily used for duck hunting. The other blast had struck the bedroom door.

Ann Woodward told police her husband must have heard the same noise that roused her and must have arisen to investigate. But the officers discovered he had not taken his revolver. They found the gun in a table near his bed. The Woodwards' children — William 3rd, 11, and James, 7 — had slept through the gunfire. They were taken to their paternal grandparents' home. Ann Woodward went to Doctors Hospital in Manhattan, where she was described as unable to answer further questions.

The news media jumped on the Woodward story like white on rice. It had all the elements: glamorous, socially prominent people with headline names. Wealth. Power. Violent death. And, above all, mystery. Had Woodward's shooting really been an accident? Or was it murder?

If it was murder, a possible motive soon surfaced — adding the titillating element of sex to the brew. A private detective, hired by Ann Woodward to shadow her husband periodically for seven years to see if he was cheating on her, went to the police. He said she provided him with the names of a dozen women she suspected of trying to wreck her marriage. Police began tracking down the women.

Concurrently, society figures circulated reports that William Woodward's relatives had opposed his marriage to Ann. Those reports were bolstered when the family hired a private detective to conduct his own investigation of the shooting. Conflicting stories surfaced on how much money Ann Woodward would receive from her husband's fortune, but the family lawyer said she would get millions.

Newsday Photo / Tom Maguire

William Woodward Jr. and his wife, Ann, arrive at the 1955 Belmont Ball. He was part of a renowned racing family; she was an actress who had become a sophisticated social figure.

When Ann Woodward emerged from the hospital, after missing her husband's funeral, she was questioned by detectives and told she would be called before a grand jury. While she was waiting to testify, police came upon a witness who supported her prowler story — a burglar who reported being in the Woodward mansion at the time of the shooting and hearing the shotgun blasts.

"His name was Paul Wirths," says Edward Curran, then a Nassau detective and now president of the state retired police officers' association. "He'd been driving us crazy. We knew his M.O., we knew what crimes he was committing, but we just couldn't catch him."

Wirths was arrested in a Suffolk case. "The police out there turned him over to us," Curran says. "We wanted to talk to him, as well as other burglars, about the Woodward case. We took him to the Woodward house. He told us: 'I was in the house. I heard the shots.' " Wirths said he immediately fled and took refuge in a barn.

Police were skeptical at first, but Wirths told them he had broken a tree limb while climbing into a mansion window and had hidden briefly in a closet containing a safe. "We checked and found the broken tree limb, the closet and the safe," Curran says. "You couldn't do much better than that."

Ann Woodward appeared before the grand jury three weeks after the shooting. She testified for only 25 minutes, and the grand jury quickly cleared her. Some said she received preferred treatment because of her station, but others contended Wirths' story assured she would walk.

After a suitable mourning period, she resumed her participation in the social whirl. Years later, her story provided the underlying themes for two novels — Dominick Dunne's "The Two Mrs. Grenvilles" and Truman Capote's "Answered Prayers."

The questions about her husband's death never faded. In 1975, friends say, she was shown an advance copy of Esquire magazine excerpts from Capote's forthcoming book. In Capote's version of the story, the character based on Ann Woodward was guilty of murder.

Not long afterward, the same year, some say because of anguish over Capote's account, Ann Woodward killed herself in her Park Avenue home. She took with her the answers to any lingering questions about just what happened at her North Shore mansion on the night of that glittering party honoring the duchess of Windsor.

Michael Dorman is a freelance writer.

AP Photo

UPI Photo

In 1955, two Woodward children on their way to see their mother, who was hospitalized after the shooting. At right, she comes home after police questioning.

AP Photo

GOP strongmen: At left, Nassau's first county executive, J. Russel Sprague, in 1949; at right, W. Kingsland Macy, the Suffolk party leader who worked through all levels of government, in 1932

LI's suburbs produced two Republican bosses whose political imprint remains

A Legacy of Kings

BY MICHAEL DORMAN

When Americans talked about big-time political bosses at the dawn of the 1950s, they usually thought in terms of powerful city machines. Two organizations leaping instantly to mind were the remnants of Tom Pendergast's Kansas City dynasty — which propelled Harry Truman on the road to the White House — and Frank Hague's Jersey City machine.

Not nearly so well known nationally, but every bit as dominant, were two suburban organizations. Both were Republican and between them they tightly controlled Long Island politics — J. Russel Sprague's powerhouse machine in Nassau and W. Kingsland Macy's in Suffolk.

Both of these barons of the ballot box would end their reigns during the 1950s. Their departures would signal a sea change in Long Island politics. A new generation of political leaders would seize control of the Island's Republican Party. And genuine two-party government perched just over the horizon.

But the swan songs of J. Russel Sprague and W. Kingsland Macy left an imprint on Long Island politics still visible today. An even more enduring impact can be discerned in the way Sprague and Macy held and wielded power — establishing campaign organizations, political strategies, debts of gratitude and voter loyalties lasting for generations.

Sprague's Nassau organization lasted longer than Pendergast's or Hague's, indeed longer than any political machine in the nation. It was founded by Sprague's uncle, G. Wilbur Doughty, immediately after Nassau split from Queens and became a separate county in 1898. Under Doughty's leadership, the Republicans dominated Nassau politics from the start. "I play politics 365 days a year," Doughty once said.

Such representation occasionally carried him down curious byways. In 1920, a grand jury indicted him on charges of conspiring to obstruct justice by tipping off gambling houses to impending raids. But the charges were dismissed.

The next year, a scandal erupted over a Nassau stolen-car ring. Among those sent to prison was a local detective, Carman Plant. Word reached the Doughty machine that Plant, imprisoned at Sing Sing in upstate Ossining, was threatening to connect the Doughty organization with the scandal. Doughty, Lt. Gov. Jeremiah Wood and Assemb. Thomas McWhinney of Lawrence paid Plant a secret visit.

But reporters soon learned about the clandestine visit. "Why, Doughty and McWhinney were old friends of Plant," the lieutenant governor told them. "It's perfectly natural they should want to talk to each other. I just went along because we were all there at the same time." The story and the scandal faded into history. And Doughty went on playing politics 365 days a year.

Under Doughty's tutelage, his nephew, Russ Sprague, began working his way up through the Republican machine. Three years after taking a law degree from Cornell University in 1910, Sprague became police justice in Lawrence and also served in party offices.

Doughty made plain he wanted Sprague to inherit his jobs as Nassau Republican leader and Hempstead Town supervisor. When Doughty died in 1930, Sprague easily took over the supervisor's job but was forced to fight for control of the Republican organization. The New York Times, in 1932, described Sprague's power this way: "In Sprague, his admirers see a second Doughty. When he is absent from a meeting of the [county] board of supervisors, the board, as a rule, defers action on every important matter until he is present."

Sprague's power, aside from his inheritance from Doughty, derived largely from his attention to the nitty-gritty of traditional politics. No hand was ever too grimy for him to shake. No meeting was too inconsequential for him to attend.

He made the decisions on everything from choosing candidates to the wording of campaign advertisements. If someone's child wanted a summer job, it was Sprague who would grant it. But that family had better be loyal to the Republican machine — supporting it financially and working for its candidates. Some lifelong Democrats who moved to Nassau from New York City decided soon after arrival to register and vote Republican for fear of incurring the Sprague machine's displeasure. And the machine thus built an ever more dominant lead over the Democrats in both voter registration and election results.

It was Sprague who served as architect of the current Nassau form of government — except for the county legislature established in 1996. He directed a drive in 1936 to install a county charter providing for a county executive. After voters approved the charter, Sprague was elected Nassau's first county executive — taking office in 1938.

Associates said one of Sprague's more far-sighted decisions involved ensuring that the East Meadow property originally known as Salisbury Park — now Eisenhower Park — would be preserved for recreational use. The late Forrest Corson, long an aide to Sprague, once explained: "A Catholic group wanted the land for a cemetery and so did a Jewish group. Then Russ said, 'We're going to save it for all the people who're still alive.' And he did." When the county park was dedicated in 1949, Sprague was initially scheduled to hit the first ball on the golf course. "Like hell," he said. "I'm not going to hook it over the fence over there for everybody to see."

Please see BOSSES on Page 333

A Vote for Ethnic Americans

Italian and Irish families begat political leaders

BY MICHAEL DORMAN

Two fathers, two sons: One father becomes Nassau County district attorney, his son Nassau County executive. The second father becomes Suffolk County district attorney, his son Suffolk County executive.

The stories of the Gulotta and Cohalan families are woven tightly into the fabric of Long Island public life. And both represent the rise of ethnic Americans in the Island's politics during the last half-century.

Aside from providing Suffolk a district attorney and a county attorney, the Irish-American family of John P. Cohalan Jr. and Peter Fox Cohalan has produced five State Supreme Court justices — more than any other family in state history.

Newsday Photo

State Supreme Court Justice John P. Cohalan Jr. in 1976, with his son, Peter Fox Cohalan, who was then Islip Town supervisor and would later become Suffolk executive

In Nassau, Frank Gulotta was in the vanguard of Italian-Americans achieving power in the Nassau Republican organization. And, on becoming district attorney in 1949, he was the first of his heritage in Nassau history to hold countywide office. And it was Gulotta, ailing and straining forward in a wheelchair, who swore in his teary-eyed son Thomas as county executive in 1988.

John P. Cohalan Jr. was born in 1907 in New York City into a family of Democratic judges. His father and grandfather were State Supreme Court justices, as was an uncle.

After graduation from Fordham University Law School, Cohalan moved to Suffolk and switched from Democrat to Republican. He worked his way through the county's Republican ranks, becoming district attorney in 1956. Perhaps his most celebrated case was the prosecution of serial killer Francis Henry Bloeth, who murdered three people in 1959. Bloeth was sentenced to life imprisonment.

Cohalan was considered one of the state's more scholarly prosecutors. He once wrote a 2,000-line poem in dactylic hexameter called "The Saga of Aaron Burr." It sought to remedy what Cohalan considered Burr's neglected place in history. He often spiced his judicial rulings with literary references. In 1965, Cohalan rejected a request by a 16-year-old boy to change his middle name, Percy, the subject of ridicule. "The name Percy has an ancient and honorable background," Cohalan said in his decision. "It is the diminutive of Percival, Sir Percival of Arthurian legend. And his counterpart is the Parsifal of Wagnerian opera."

In 1963, Cohalan followed his forebears onto the State Supreme Court bench. He served on the court's Appellate Division from 1974 until retiring in 1983. Cohalan died in 1988.

His son, Peter Fox Cohalan — who had followed him into public service and became Suffolk County executive — said, "The proudest moment in my father's life was when he coached LaSalle to an 8 and 0 football season in 1932 and was named Long Island high school coach of the year and state preparatory school coach of the year." The elder Cohalan, who had been a star athlete at LaSalle Military Academy in Oakdale and Manhattan College, also took pride in his brother Neil's role as the first coach of the New York Knicks.

"My father played a major role in guiding my life," Peter Fox Cohalan said. "When I was a kid — probably from the time I was 8 to 14 — he made me memorize poetry and history every day. Then he quizzed me at night. It gave me a tremendous ability later in life to remember what I needed to know."

But the younger Cohalan did not always follow his father's advice. "Interestingly, he discouraged me from going into public life. After I finished law school, he wanted me to stay in private practice longer than I did." Cohalan instead took the advice of a family friend, then-Suffolk Sheriff Frank Gross. "He told me to go for it."

Gulotta Family Photo

As wife Betsy and son Thomas James watch, Thomas Gulotta is sworn in as a member of the Assembly by his father, State Supreme Court Justice Frank Gulotta, in 1977.

So Cohalan ran for election as a Republican in 1971 as Islip Town supervisor and won the first of two terms. In 1979, Cohalan was elected county executive. He was re-elected four years later. In late 1986, Cohalan resigned to run for a State Supreme Court seat. He won — perpetuating the family tradition.

There was no such family tradition of public life sustaining Frank Gulotta when he entered government service as Lynbrook village counsel and a zoning board member in the late 1930s. "Both his parents were immigrants from Italy," Thomas Gulotta said. "He always worked hard to engender respect in the community."

Frank Gulotta, born in Brooklyn in 1907, took a law degree from St. John's University, became an assistant Nassau district attorney in 1938, then enlisted in the Army and won three battle stars for World War II service in Africa and Italy. After the war, Gulotta returned to the prosecutor's office. When District Attorney James Gehrig resigned to seek a judgeship, Gov. Thomas E. Dewey appointed Gulotta as his successor. He won three elected terms, beginning in 1949. In 1956, in the biggest case of his career, Gulotta prosecuted Angelo LaMarca in the kidnap-murder of 33-day-old Peter Weinberger. LaMarca was executed.

Gulotta left the district attorney's office when elected to a State Supreme Court seat. While being screened by the Queens Bar Association for the judgeship, Gulotta confronted the sort of prejudice against Italian-Americans that was prevalent throughout his career. One lawyer asked him during the screening procedure: "Mr. Gulotta, are you or have you ever been a member of the Mafia?"

"The Mafia?" Gulotta replied. "What's that?"

He later rose to presiding justice of the Appellate Division. He died in 1989.

"Neither he nor my mother ever tried to influence my choice of a career," Thomas Gulotta said. "For a time, I thought I wanted to enter the medical profession. But I thought I could serve people better in law than medicine."

After graduation from Columbia University Law School in 1969, Thomas Gulotta became an aide in the Assembly. In 1976, Nassau Republicans nominated him for an Assembly seat, and he quickly became one of the party's leading vote producers. Some attributed his popularity to his scrupulous attention to individual voters' concerns. One politician said Gulotta would stand for as long as 20 minutes, listening to a constituent's problems.

In 1980, chosen to run by Nassau Republican chairman Joseph Margiotta, Gulotta was elected Hempstead Town presiding supervisor. Eight years later, he became county executive. He has retained that office ever since.

Gulotta attributes whatever success he has achieved largely to his parents. "Both my mother and father worked very hard to provide better opportunities for their children than perhaps they enjoyed," he said.

Island Ruled By GOP Kings

BOSSES from Page 331

Another Sprague associate was Joseph Carlino, a successor as county Republican chairman who became speaker of the Assembly and now is a leading lobbyist. "Sprague was an unusual and remarkably intelligent man," Carlino said. "He had the vision to foresee the postwar boom, the potential political power of the suburbs, the need to bring Italians, Irish, Jews into a Republican county organization that had been dominated for decades by WASPs."

Perhaps not coincidentally, all Sprague's more recent successors as Republican chairman have been Italian-Americans — Carlino, Edward Speno, Joseph Margiotta and Joseph Mondello.

A Sprague contemporary, the late Brooklyn Republican leader John Crews, said, "A handshake from him was as good as a surety bond from Lloyd's of London. Most fellows are a nickel a pailful when it comes to a bona fide commitment."

One newspaper reporter who covered Sprague for Newsday recalls him as "a good-looking man, always beautifully turned out. And he always had his nails buffed."

In the early 1950s, there were revelations that Sprague had secretly owned stock in several enterprises controlling operations at Roosevelt and Yonkers Raceways. Since the county executive oversaw dealings with Roosevelt Raceway, critics saw conflicts of interest. When it was disclosed that Sprague had made nearly $400,000 on raceway stock that had cost him nothing, the public uproar led him to retire from his position as Republican national committeeman from New York. And the first major crack developed in the Nassau machine.

There was a power struggle between Sprague and Republican national chairman Leonard Hall of Oyster Bay, with whom Sprague had worked closely on presidential campaigns after helping persuade Gov. Thomas E. Dewey to run for the White House in 1944 and 1948 and Gen. Dwight D. Eisenhower to run in 1952. Later in 1952, the challenge to Sprague's authority and continuing discontent over the raceway scandal led him to retire as county executive. But he kept his job as Republican chairman.

After his retirement as county executive, Sprague hand-picked a protege, A. Holly Patterson, to succeed him. Patterson also took over later as Nassau Republican chairman. But many said it was Sprague, operating behind the scenes, who still made major decisions for both the party and the county.

By the late 1950s, profound change was clearly in the wind in Nassau politics. Sprague would live to see some of that change, although perhaps uncomfortable with it. But, even after his death on April 17, 1969, the lingering effects of J. Russel Sprague's political dynasty would continue to reverberate across Long Island's political landscape.

There would be increased centralization of power in the Nassau County government, in contrast to Suffolk, where the towns wield more authority. There would also be increased power at the top of the Nassau Republican Party — accompanied by a broadening of participation at lower levels.

As former Nassau Republican chairman Joseph Margiotta recently put it: "Russ Sprague made a very lasting impression on the way the Nassau Republican organization is structured to this day. In Suffolk, the Republican executive committee consists of the county chairman and the 10 town chairmen; there is much more emphasis in Suffolk on the towns. In Nassau, all of the 60-odd zone leaders are on the executive committee. Sprague set it up that way because his theory was that one person in every community and hamlet — the zone leader — would keep in touch with the people and issues and deliver the vote . . . I was a committeeman under Sprague and, when I was county chairman, I used to seek his advice. He was brilliant."

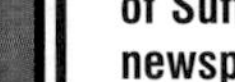

Nassau County Museum Collection

G. Wilbur Doughty, left, paved the political way in Nassau for his nephew, J. Russel Sprague. W. Kingsland Macy, right, enhanced his political power through his chain of Suffolk weekly newspapers.

AP Photo, 1936

Newsday Photo

A. Holly Patterson, left, with his predecessor as Nassau executive, J. Russel Sprague, in 1958

In Suffolk, W. Kingsland Macy — generally known as King but sometimes derisively called "the Kingfish" — held an iron-fisted grip on Republican politics for almost a quarter-century. Tall and patrician, he came to politics from a world of privilege. After attending the Groton prep school, Macy was graduated in 1911 from Harvard. He was a staunch conservative in both politics and attire — devoted to high starched collars long after they went out of style. He came from a family that had become wealthy through whaling and shipping interests. After college, Macy bought a seat on the New York Stock Exchange.

But he found his true calling when he gained political prominence by fighting unsuccessfully to prevent Robert Moses from creating Heckscher State Park in Islip Town, where Macy lived. Elected Suffolk Republican chairman in 1926, Macy exerted tight control over both the party machine and the county board of supervisors. This control was enhanced by his ownership of a politically influential chain of Suffolk weekly newspapers.

Swiftly broadening his sphere to include statewide politics, Macy defeated old-guard Republicans in a bitter struggle and was elected state Republican chairman in 1930. He quickly purged opponents on the Republican state committee, but evidently had more foes than he thought. In 1934 he was dumped as state chairman.

Macy would undertake further ventures into both state and national politics, but would never forget that his power was based on Long Island. And his control of the Suffolk machine would grow more pronounced. "He was an absolute czar," the late Newsday reporter Bob Pfeifle once said. "A sparrow couldn't fall and you couldn't have a job without his blessing."

The Suffolk Republican leader was elected first as a state senator, then in 1946 as a congressman representing all of Suffolk and part of Nassau. He also served as chairman of the Suffolk County Water Authority.

At one point, Macy tried to spread his sphere of political influence into Nassau. Sprague beat back Macy's incursion. There was bad blood between them for the rest of their careers.

All his power did not seem sufficient for Macy. He repeatedly became embroiled in losing power struggles with Gov. Dewey and other GOP leaders. And troubles confronted him in Suffolk. A gambling scandal burst into the headlines. Then there were charges of questionable financial dealings by the Macy-dominated Suffolk Water Authority.

Even more serious problems arose when Macy ran for re-election to congress in 1950. Editors of Newsday — competing with Macy's weekly newspapers and opposed to his stranglehold on Suffolk politics — determined to defeat him. Their campaign reached beyond traditional editorial-page criticism. Newsday managing editor Alan Hathway actually directed the campaign waged by Macy's opponent, a Republican turned Democrat named Ernest Greenwood.

A political amateur, Greenwood was a likable, intelligent emigrant from England. He had been headmaster of the Dwight School in Manhattan. To make up for Greenwood's political inexperience, Hathway drilled him on how to make a speech and how to campaign.

Then the race was thrown into turmoil by an unexpected development — the so-called "Hanley letter." Early in 1950, Dewey announced he would not seek another term as governor. Lt. Gov. Joe Hanley was the leading candidate to succeed Dewey. Macy, still feuding with Dewey, contributed heavily to Hanley's campaign. But then Dewey decided to run after all and was re-elected. For the record, Hanley claimed he had bowed out of the campaign voluntarily to clear the way for Dewey. But, in a "Dear King" letter to Macy, Hanley said Dewey had persuaded him to run for the U.S. Senate instead and had promised him a state job if he lost the Senate race. Hanley did run unsuccessfully for the Senate.

But the Democrats somehow got their hands on the Hanley letter. There was a national furor over charges that Dewey had bought Hanley off and that Macy himself had leaked the letter to expose Dewey's supposed treachery.

The election campaign against Greenwood reflected that if Macy still controlled the Republican machine, he no longer controlled his congressional district. On election night, the results were so close that no winner could be declared. It was not until almost two weeks later that the Suffolk Board of Elections completed its official canvass and announced the startling decision: Greenwood had won the congressional seat by 138 votes. That same day, with many members of the Republican County Committee in open revolt, Macy announced he was resigning as leader. Thus, he no longer held either of the jobs that had served as the base of his power.

But Macy wasn't finished yet. He spent the next 16 months fighting in the courts and in Congress to overturn the results of the congressional campaign, claiming he had been the victim of election fraud and other irregularities. In the end, however, he lost all his appeals.

Macy was succeeded as county Republican leader by County Clerk R. Ford Hughes. But many of those Macy had recruited and nurtured in the county organization remained in power. The political organization he had painstakingly constructed survived, if only to be taken over later by a new generation of Republicans. Nassau County Executive A. Holly Patterson and other leading Republicans continued to make pilgrimages to seek his counsel. But then, on July 15, 1961, Macy died.

When J. Russel Sprague died almost eight years later, both kings of Long Island politics were gone. The kings were dead, but their political legacies live and breathe to this day in the party clubhouses, halls of government and courthouses from the Queens line to Montauk.

Michael Dorman is a freelance writer.

It took about 20 years and 81 miles of six-lane road to create Robert Moses' LIE

A Link to 'All of Long Island'

BY SYLVIA ADCOCK
STAFF WRITER

For years, Long Island's parkways lived up to their names. The ribbons of roadway filled up with cars on weekends and through the summer as city residents headed for the country.

But after World War II, something changed. The Northern State and Southern State still got jammed on the weekends, but now cars were jamming the roads on the weekday rush hours as well. As more and more Long Islanders began to use the highways to get to work, the word parkway nearly became obsolete.

By 1950, state officials began to take notice of the traffic.

"Most of the state highways now show practically the same congestion on ordinary weekdays," wrote Joseph Darcy, then Long Island's district engineer for the state Department of Public Works, noting that the parkways were becoming commuter roads. "We cannot solve our problem just by widening and improving existing highway routes. The ultimate solution will come only by the building a new, modern expressway or throughway on entirely new locations."

The traffic jams continued as Long Island — and the nation — became more dependent on automobiles. Even the 1950 edition of the Levitt house had a new feature: the carport. And the idea of the one-car family quickly became outdated. Mom may have been staying home with the kids, but she needed her own car to get around. From 1949 to 1952, traffic on the Southern State Parkway doubled.

One year later Newsday carried the headline, "Super-Expressway to Link All of LI," and the Long Island Expressway was born, sprung from the fertile brain of master builder Robert Moses. The plans for the road, first called the Central Motor Expressway, were ambitious. A six-lane expressway rolling down the middle of the Island, routed through open land whenever possible, stretching for 81 miles. Trucks would be allowed, a move that would eventually deal a blow to the Long Island Rail Road's freight operation.

And in typical Moses fashion, by the time the plan was made public, work on the expressway had already begun near the Queens-Midtown Tunnel.

It was, Newsday said in an editorial, "the first concrete action taken by a governmental agency to recognize that Long Island is more than New York's playland." Indeed, the Island had grown up.

"One of the things the LIE did for Long Island was to put us on the map," said Barbara Kelly, curator of Hofstra University's Long Island Studies Institute.

There was little opposition. "The general attitude was that growth was good," said Lee Koppelman, now director of the Long Island Regional Planning Board. "There were no NIMBYs." And if there had been, it wouldn't have made much difference.

An undated photo looks west toward construction of the Long Island Expressway at the Route 110 interchange in Huntington Town. The six-lane expressway, which crossed the Nassau-Suffolk line in 1962, reached the end of the road in Riverhead in 1972.

Newsday Photo

Today, the state is required to perform studies that assess the impact on a community before building or expanding roads. But no such requirement existed when the LIE was built. The new highway was a foregone conclusion.

Koppelman remembers a few sparsely attended public hearings convened by a state official who made it clear he had no intention of changing the plans. "He would caution the audience that his job was to listen, and that they had to understand that notwithstanding anything they have to say, this is what the state is going to do," Koppelman said.

"People would get up and say, 'What is this? Russia?' and go home."

Work was slower than expected. Moses promised that the highway would be finished by 1958, and later revised it to 1961. But by 1957, it only stretched as far as Bayside. In 1958, it hit Roslyn Heights. It touched the Nassau-Suffolk line in 1962. By the time the "last exit" sign went up in Riverhead, it was 1972.

And by the time the road was finished, it cost $280 million, relatively cheap considering that today the cost would be closer to $64 billion.

Everywhere the road went, it brought changes. In all, 10,000 homes were demolished or relocated. The highway created a wall that effectively divided some communities. In Plainview, a new fire station had to be constructed. In Hauppauge, the school district was cut in half. "Now you had to run your buses to hell and back just to get from one segment of the community to another," Koppelman said.

Land prices soared. New housing tracts and industrial parks sprang up in Suffolk, transforming forever the open countryside. Trucks roared down the highway and backed up to loading docks at new shopping centers. The population in the Melville-Half Hollow Hills area increased by 200 percent.

"Come to close-in Commack, just 30 minutes from New York on the new Long Island Expressway," said one ad, vastly understating the travel time.

And as fast as the road could be built, the lanes filled with cars. In 1967, a Long Island Regional Planning Board study estimated that it would take 18 lanes to keep traffic on the LIE flowing freely.

Critics later accused Moses of shortsightedness, contending that he should have realized that the population increases spurred by the LIE would quickly make its six lanes obsolete. "I've been charged with neglect, lack of vision and general obtuseness in road building," he said shortly before his death in 1981. But, he said of the LIE, "Where would we be without it?"

THE LONG ROAD TO IMPROVEMENT

Newsday Photo / Bill Davis

HOV lane construction, shown near Exit 61 in Holbrook, is projected to continue until 2004.

Calls for improvements to the Long Island Expressway date back to the early 1960s, before the highway had even reached Riverhead.

Plans to double-deck it never got off the ground. A campaign to run trains down the median fizzled. It wasn't until 1994 that the first major expansion of the LIE was completed: a 12-mile stretch of HOV lanes in Suffolk County.

The high-occupancy vehicle lanes are restricted to carpoolers (or anyone with a passenger in their car) during rush hours. This summer, another eight-mile stretch will open from Exit 40 in Jericho to 49 in Melville. By 2004, expect to see HOV lanes stretching for 40 miles, from the Queens line to Exit 64 in Medford.

Do they work? That depends on whom you ask. Carpoolers, of course, are big fans. The state Department of Transportation touts the fact that the HOV lanes move more people in afternoon rush hours than any of the regular lanes.

But many people on Long Island can't carpool. And some experts say that HOV lanes can't erase congestion. As more cars shift to the HOV lanes, the additional space on the other lanes will also be filled up with cars. The result is more gridlock. — Sylvia Adcock

BY MICHAEL DORMAN

More than 4,000 monkeys a month were flown during the mid-1950s from India and the Philippines to a desolate laboratory along the bank of a small river near Bluffton, S.C. Those monkeys would play pivotal roles in helping provide the vaccine used in the largest polio-vaccination test program in the United States — conducted on Long Island in 1954.

The monkeys' kidneys were removed and the organs' cells were injected with polio virus. The cells then multiplied, and the virus was scientifically treated so that it would not transmit the disease. The process produced a vaccine that, when injected into humans, would develop antibodies designed to fight polio and its crippling effects.

On April 27, 1954, about 15,000 Suffolk children began rolling up their sleeves for the first of three shots in a nationwide test of the polio vaccine, developed by Dr. Jonas Salk of the University of Pittsburgh Medical School. Six days later, Nassau began inoculating 50,000 children. Half the children in each county received Salk vaccine. The other half got a harmless liquid, enabling medical researchers to gauge the vaccine's effectiveness.

It is almost impossible to exaggerate the terror posed by polio at the time. Parents lived in constant dread that their children would be stricken — perhaps killed, perhaps condemned by paralysis to pass their days in iron-lung machines. Many had grown up with constant reminders of polio's ravages in the person of the nation's most celebrated victim of the disease, President Franklin D. Roosevelt. Some parents who could afford it took their children to summer resorts each year to remove them from crowded urban and suburban neighborhoods reputed to provide breeding grounds for polio.

Although there was concern among parents about the safety of the injections, more than 90 percent of the eligible children turned out to receive their shots on Long Island. Initially, the injections were given to children in the first, second and third grades but eventually were provided to older children and adults. Some children involved in the initial tests smiled self-consciously as the needles slid into their arms. Others cried. Many held their arms afterward. All received lollipops as rewards for their fortitude.

Physicians and nurses from throughout both counties volunteered their services in visiting schools to administer the shots. At the Meadowlawn School in East Meadow, school nurse Ruth Foote supervised the vaccination of 540 children. As one small boy emerged from a booth after receiving his shot, he told a friend: "You know, that doctor was telling me jokes — trying to take my mind off the needle."

Another student, 9-year-old Danny Billings, wore an unworried expression — even a trace of a smile — as he received his shot at the Meadowlawn School. But Ellen Engel, 7, yowled as she received hers at Central School in Long Beach. Robert Lange, 7, his broken right arm in a cast, gamely offered his left so Dr. Michael Lorenzo could inject him with vaccine at the North Side School in East Williston.

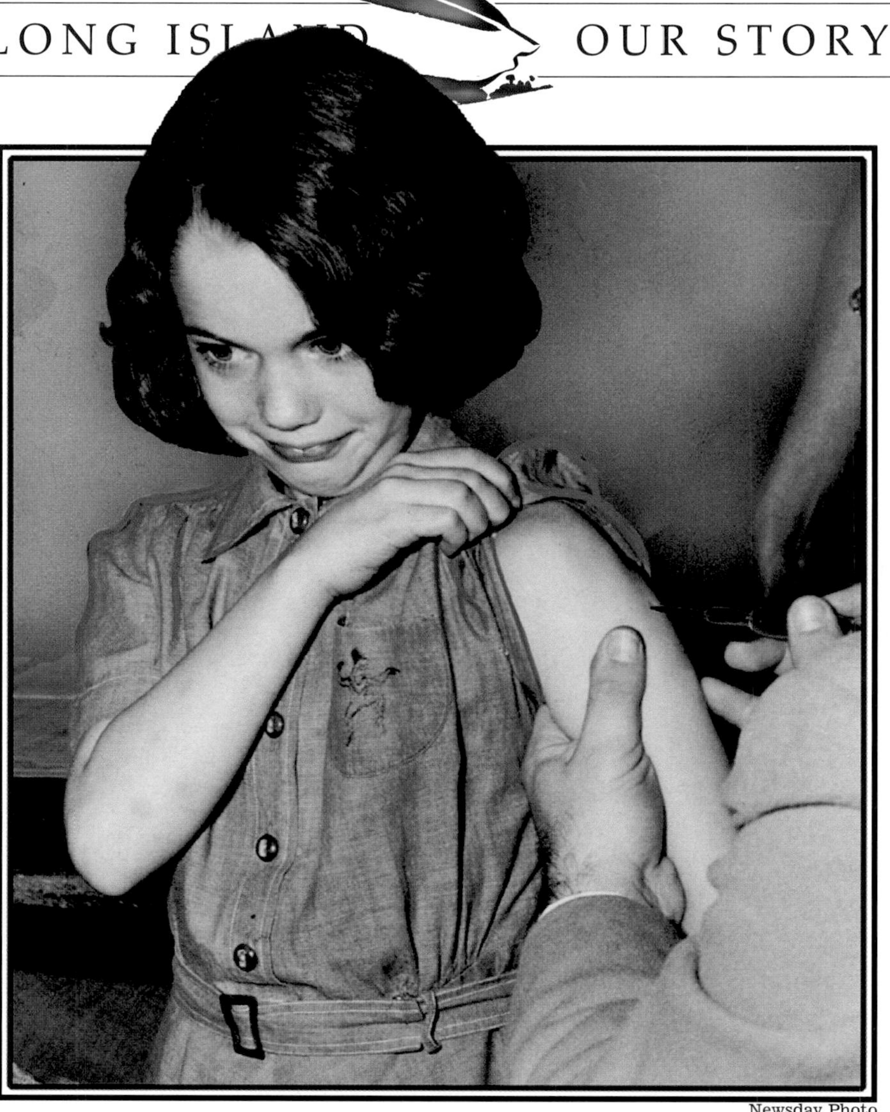

Newsday Photo

Nine-year-old Martha Prime of Huntington braces for a polio vaccination. The disease struck fear in adults, who worried that children would die or be condemned to paralysis.

In '54, thousands line up to fight polio — taking the shots felt around the world

LI's Vaccine Volunteers

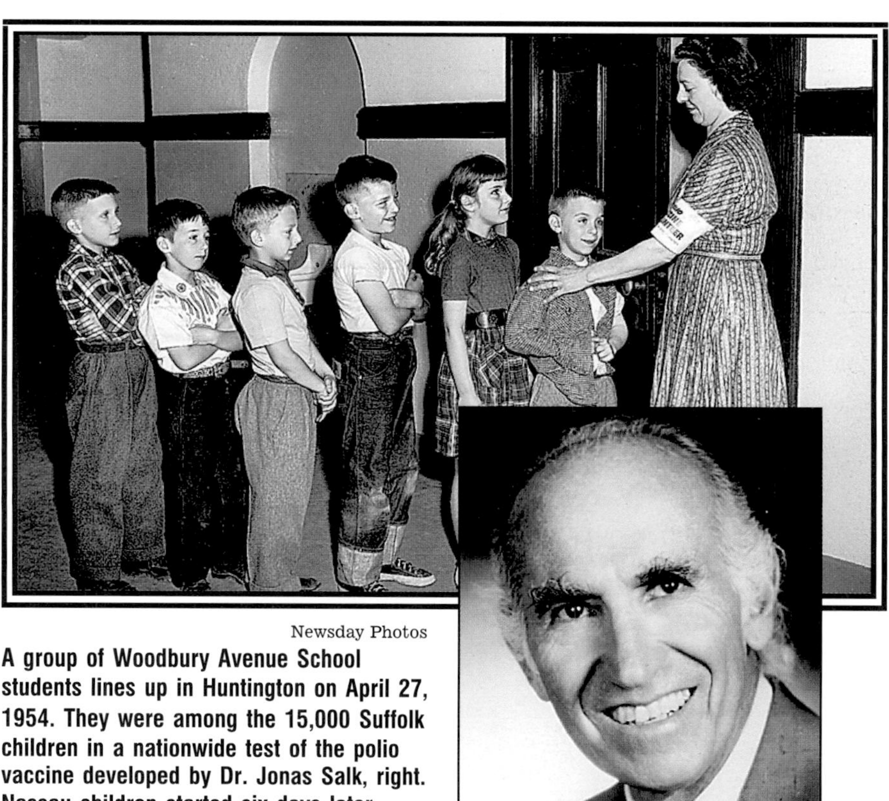

Newsday Photos

A group of Woodbury Avenue School students lines up in Huntington on April 27, 1954. They were among the 15,000 Suffolk children in a nationwide test of the polio vaccine developed by Dr. Jonas Salk, right. Nassau children started six days later.

Nassau and Suffolk medical officials said they were confident the vaccine was safe. The National Foundation for Infantile Paralysis, sponsoring the tests, pointed out that Jonas Salk's own children had taken the vaccine along with 8,000 Pittsburgh children and there had been no ill effects.

A second shot would be injected a week after the first and a third shot four weeks later. Before being used, each batch of vaccine was tested in three independent laboratories to ensure that it could not transmit the disease. It was also tested to be sure it contained no live virus causing any other disease.

As had been predicted, the injection program occasionally ran into problems. There were, for example, periodic shortages of vaccine. Nassau officials at one point proposed stretching the supply by giving only one injection to each child — using the rest to spread the coverage to additional children. But the plan was reversed when a national committee of 33 polio experts expressed unanimous disapproval.

Even when shots were taken, some recipients still contracted polio and small numbers even died. In 1955, a Bethpage child, Donita Lent, became the first in the state to contract polio after receiving one shot of vaccine. Bruce Spiegel, an 8-year-old second-grader at Oceanside Central School, came down with a mild case of polio a short time later. Bruce had received two injections. He initially ran a high fever, then complained that his left arm felt "awfully heavy." He was taken to a doctor, who immediately hospitalized him. Relatives said they were sure he would have suffered a more severe case of polio if he had not taken the two shots.

In August, 1959, a Sayville mother became the first person on Long Island to die of polio after taking three shots of Salk vaccine. Mary Fleming, 38, died in Southside Hospital in Bay Shore two days after coming down with bulbar polio — the most serious form of the disease. She, her husband and their five children had all taken the vaccine. That same week, Nassau Health Commissioner Earle Brown disclosed that eight children in his county who had taken Salk shots had contracted polio during that year. "No vaccine is 100 percent perfect," Brown said. "But this vaccine, I have faith in it."

There seemed good reason for such faith. The vaccine clearly worked.

During a typical pre-Salk year, 1950, there were 309 reported polio cases and 19 deaths in Nassau. By the time of Mary Fleming's death eight months into 1959, there were only 10 cases and no additional deaths on all of Long Island. Throughout New York State, there were 1,910 polio cases and 187 deaths in 1950. In 1960, there were only 138 cases and 26 deaths statewide.

Eventually, polio would be all but eradicated in the United States. Long Island health officials said recently that no polio cases have been reported to them in at least three years. Jonas Salk, who died of a heart ailment in 1995 at the age of 80, surely deserves most of the credit. But some say a word of gratitude is due those thousands of monkeys that helped bring Salk's vaccine to the world.

Michael Dorman is a freelance writer.

When the 7-year-old Manorville boy falls into a shaft, he gets the world's attention

Benny's Well-Wishers

BY MICHAEL DORMAN

The sand would not stop falling. He was trapped beneath a foot and a half of grit. There was sand caked around his mouth, sand in his eyes, sand in his nose, sand in his ears. And still it would not stop falling.

Seven-year-old Benjamin Hooper Jr. had no way of knowing it, but his terrifying predicament had become the biggest news story in the nation on May 16, 1957. Well-wishers worldwide were praying that his life would be saved.

Benny had fallen into the sandy shaft of a 21-foot well just dug by his father in the backyard of the family's bungalow on Ryerson Avenue in Manorville. The shaft was 3 feet wide at its mouth, but narrowed to 6 inches. Benny was stuck 18½ feet below ground, his feet wedged in that 6-inch trap.

The struggle for survival had begun — as such crises often do — with intimations of the utterly mundane. Benny and his best friend, 7-year-old Mike Molinaro, were playing a game of soldiers in the Hooper backyard about 7:30 p.m. "We saw a piece of pipe across the yard and were going to make it a gun," Mike said a short time later.

"Race you to it," Benny challenged. A lean, sandy-haired beanpole — all arms and legs — Benny easily pulled ahead. "He got there first," Mike said.

But, in his haste, Benny failed to spot the shaft for a new well. Suddenly, he plunged feet first down the hole.

"I only saw his arms go down it," Mike said. "He only made a sound like 'umm, umm.' "

Benny's father, Benjamin Hooper, was still working in the yard, scarcely 10 feet from the shaft and not far from a thick clump of woods. Mike ran to him. "Benny fell in a hole."

At first, Hooper did not believe him. "Benny must be in the woods," he said. When Benjamin Hooper looked into the hole, all he could see were his son's upstretched arms. "Wiggle your hand if you're all right," he shouted. A small hand wiggled obediently below.

Rescue workers soon descended on Ryerson Avenue. Benny's mother, Betty Hooper, was at work as a switchboard operator at the nearby Riverhead telephone exchange — manually plugging in calls. When one light flashed on, she was jolted to overhear in her headset the voice of a detective, Joseph Townsend, calling Brookhaven police headquarters from her home. "There's trouble at the Hooper home," Townsend said. "The kid's fallen in a well."

Screaming, Betty Hooper was led to a car and driven home.

Emergency workers tried to rescue Benny with grappling hooks, but could not budge him. Inadvertently, though, a rescuer's hook snared Benny's red poplin jacket and pulled it up his outstretched arms and over his head — providing both an air pocket and a partial shield against the falling sand.

The Hooper family physician, Dr. Joseph Kris, rushed to the home. An oxygen hose had been dropped deep into the well to help Benny breathe. But the steady force of the flowing oxygen was causing ever more sand to cascade over him. Some workers wanted to remove the hose, but Kris persuaded them to gamble on leaving it in place. Without the oxygen, the doctor said, there could be no hope at all. As it was, he said, it was improbable Benny was alive — it would take a miracle for him to survive.

Attempts to work that miracle began with a decision to dig a second shaft parallel to the well shaft and then excavate a tunnel connecting the two shafts as a rescue route. A Patchogue contractor, Michael Stiriz, offering his expertise and equipment, assumed supervision of hordes of volunteers. Stiriz began digging the rescue shaft with a power shovel late on the night of May 16. But the sand kept crumbling around the shovel, and Stiriz decided by 1 a.m. May 17 that the remainder of the shoveling would have to be done by hand. Teams of volunteers digging in shifts — their bodies smeared with sweat and grime — heaved sand from the hole for hour after hour. By daybreak, the Hooper yard was aswarm with more than 500 people. Arrayed around the property were two cranes, an ambulance, two fire trucks, a civil-defense wagon and a welding truck.

The volunteers shoveled their shaft 11 feet deep, shored up the sides, then dug some more until they reached the point where the tunnel would begin. At one point, a cave-in wiped out their work. Still, they persevered.

At 12:35 p.m. the Rev. Paul Mastalski of St. John the Baptist Catholic Church in Wading River stood above the well and gave Benny conditional rites.

At 2 o'clock, a Brookhaven National Laboratory engineer, Edward Hunter, arrived with a vacuum-pump machine. By 4:45, the machine had removed much of the sand atop Benny. Hunter also brought three smooth steel drums in descending sizes. With their tops and bottoms cut off, they fit together in telescope fashion — so they could form a solid passageway for the tunnel. By 6:45, the third drum was put in place. Three volunteers — Sam Woodson of Riverhead and John Rambo and John Remick of Wading River — stretched out on their stomachs in the tunnel, snatching sand with their bare hands. Woodson passed the sand behind him to Rambo, who passed it to Remick, who pushed it back to the rescue shaft, where it was carried away by conveyor belt.

"That sand was really abrasive," Rambo would recall recently. "There wasn't enough room in that small hole to work with a shovel. So I dug with my hands until my fingers were almost worn down to the quick."

At 7:30 p.m., 24 hours after the saga had begun, Sam Woodson clawed his way through still another 6 inches of sand. Suddenly, Benny Hopper was sprawled before him.

Woodson reached out tentatively and touched the boy. He felt Benny move. "Oh, Lordy, the boy's alive," he shouted.

When Woodson tried to pull Benny free, sand came caving into the narrow spot where well and tunnel met. Woodson dug frantically through the sand, flung a protective arm around Benny's head and shoulders and dragged him into the tunnel. Other hands lifted Benny to the surface.

Det. Joseph Townsend burst inside the family home, where Betty and Ben Hooper were awaiting word.

"He's alive!" Townsend yelled.

Betty Hooper grabbed his jacket lapels and shook him. "Before God, you wouldn't fool me," she said.

"I wouldn't fool you," Townsend assured her. "Benny's alive."

The Hoopers rode in the ambulance that rushed Benny to Bayview Hospital in Mastic Beach. On the way, he uttered his first words since the rescue: "Mommy. Daddy." After a week in the hospital — part of it in an oxygen tent — Benny Hooper went home. He was adamant on one point about his experience in the well: "I wasn't scared."

It all came to be known as the miracle of Manorville.

Michael Dorman is a freelance writer.

AP Photo, 1957

Newsday Photos

With floodlights shining on them, workers dig in sandy soil in 1957 to reach the boy who fell into a backyard well shaft 21 feet deep. Top right, the father, Benjamin Hooper, smiles after seeing Benny in a hospital. Sam Woodson, above right, reached out and pulled Benny to safety.

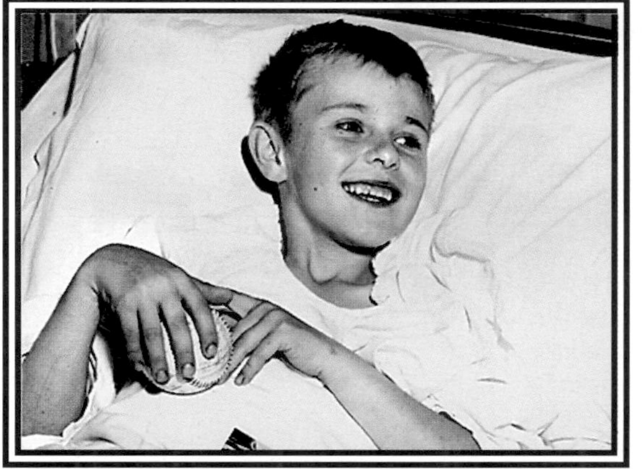

Newsday Photo

At left, Benny recovers from his fall at Bayview Hospital.

As an adult, Benjamin Hooper Jr. went to work for LILCO. He lives with his family in Ridge. He has declined in recent years to discuss his ordeal in the well.

The Vatican forms the Diocese of Rockville Centre from Nassau and Suffolk

LI Gets a Bishop of Its Own

BY STUART VINCENT
STAFF WRITER

Church bells pealed a welcome to the motorcade as it rolled through Valley Stream and Lynbrook, stopping at Catholic churches just long enough for pastors and parochial schoolchildren to deliver greetings. At Rockville Centre, the cars linked up with 11 marching bands and 4,000 marchers for a parade down North Village Avenue to Quealy Place.

There, on this Sunday afternoon of May 26, 1957, Bishop Walter P. Kellenberg stepped from an open car into a crowd of about 10,000 in front of St. Agnes Roman Catholic Cathedral and took possession of the church and the newly formed Roman Catholic Diocese of Rockville Centre.

During the next 15 years, in the midst of an unprecedented growth spurt, Kellenberg carved a diocese out of burgeoning subdivisions, farmland and pine barrens. Challenged from the start by the demand for more schools, churches and offices, Kellenberg jokingly dubbed himself "Kick-off Kellenberg," forever asking for donations or dedicating a new building.

Indeed, all the pomp and ceremony of that Sunday in 1957 celebrated more than the arrival of a new church leader. It marked a turning point for Long Island, a recognition by no less than Pope Pius XII that Nassau and Suffolk had arrived on the American scene. Pius was no stranger to Long Island. As Cardinal Eugenio Pacelli, the papal secretary of state, he had used Inisfada, the Manhasset estate of Nicholas and Genevieve Brady, in 1936 as his U.S. headquarters.

On April 6, 1957, Pius had issued a papal bull cleaving Nassau and Suffolk Counties from the Diocese of Brooklyn and creating *Dioecesis Petropolitana In Insula Longa* — Latin for Diocese of Rockville Centre on Long Island. At Kellenberg's installation May 27 at the newly designated cathedral of St. Agnes, New York's Cardinal Francis Spellman spoke of "this new, great and rapidly growing" diocese.

The creation of the new diocese was prompted by the rapid growth of the Brooklyn diocese's two eastern counties. In a sense, it was history repeating itself. Just over a century earlier, in 1853, the Brooklyn diocese was formed from the Archdiocese of New York, encompassing Long Island from Coney Island to Montauk Point. Creation of a second Long Island diocese didn't become a reality until after the death in November, 1956, of Brooklyn's Archbishop Thomas E. Molloy, who was said to have opposed it.

When Kellenberg arrived, he found new parishes using temporary quarters. St. Rose of Lima, Massapequa, was holding mass in a converted bar; in Wantagh, St. Francis de Chantal was using a firehouse; St. James in Plainedge was housed in a converted chicken coop.

Newsday Photo

Long Island's new Roman Catholic bishop, Walter P. Kellenberg, is welcomed in 1957 during a rally held on a field between St. Agnes Cathedral and the Rockville Centre railroad station.

Kellenberg, who arrived a week before his 57th birthday, was a logical choice to head the new diocese. A New York native, he had 20 years of administrative experience in the Archdiocese of New York. Kellenberg was Spellman's secretary when he was made an auxiliary bishop in 1953, and six months later he headed upstate to Ogdensberg to take over that diocese. After just three years there, he was named Rockville Centre's first bishop.

"I come to you in the name of God," he said at his installation in St. Agnes. "I am yours."

One church official, who was a young priest at the time at St. Anne's Parish in Brentwood, recalled that Long Island Catholics generally liked the idea of their own diocese.

"The way it had been run previously, everything of importance was in Brooklyn," said Bishop John R. McGann, now 73, who succeeded Kellenberg as bishop. "If you had outstanding priests out here, they kept getting moved west." Parishioners in Nassau and Suffolk helped support diocesan high schools, he said, even though there weren't any in either county.

Rockville Centre, the only village in the United States to serve as a diocesan seat, was chosen primarily because of the large church complex that existed there — a convent, schools, a rectory, an athletic field and a large Norman Gothic church capable of seating at least 1,300 people. In fact, the church was "intended by its builder to be a cathedral long before an episcopal See was envisioned by anyone except Rockville Centre's extraordinary pastor, the Right Reverend Monsignor Peter Quealy," wrote Sister Joan de Lourdes Leonard in "Richly Blessed," her 1991 history of the diocese.

Quealy, born in County Waterford, Ireland, served 50 years as pastor of St. Agnes' parish, which upon his arrival included Island Park, Long Beach, Oceanside, Malverne, Baldwin and Lynbrook. Besides the church complex on the street that would eventually bear his name, he bought land on which Mercy Hospital and Molloy College would be built. When Kellenberg arrived, he visited the 91-year-old Quealy in his rectory. Only after receiving Quealy's blessing and giving him his blessing in return did Kellenberg present his credentials as bishop to Diocese of Brooklyn officials, Leonard wrote.

The festivities were hardly over when Kellenberg got to work, forming an administrative staff to run a diocese of 1,2?2 square miles containing almost 483 000 Catholics out of a population of about 1.6 million. Setting up a temporary chancery in the St. Agnes High School basement, Kellenberg chose Msgr. Vincent Baldwin — later the diocese's first auxiliary bishop — as chancellor and vicar general, Msgr. Thomas Daley as co-chancellor and the Rev. Francis Williams as his secretary. McGann, who later succeeded Williams, was named an assistant chancellor.

The toughest job, McGann recalled, was keeping up with the baby boomers who threatened to overwhelm churches and schools. "Everything was inadequate," McGann said recently, "so you had to constantly enlarge the churches, add onto the schools, build convents, start new parishes."

Within five years, Kellenberg established seven new parishes and St. Pius X Preparatory Seminary for high school students considering the priesthood. In his first four years as bishop, 28 elementary schools were built along with 27 additions to existing schools. In 1963, Kellenberg raised $24 million in pledges for four diocesan high schools.

But the times already were changing for the church and Long Island. Within a decade, it became increasingly difficult to find priests, nuns and brothers to staff churches and schools. By the time McGann took over in 1976, the Baby Boom was over. McGann eventually had to close two diocesan high schools, consolidate elementary schools and close the preparatory seminary.

Still it fell to him to heed Kellenberg's exhortation to the crowd at St. Agnes that Sunday in 1957: "Follow me in my work to spread the kingdom of Christ in this wonderful Long Island."

Nassau County Museum Collection

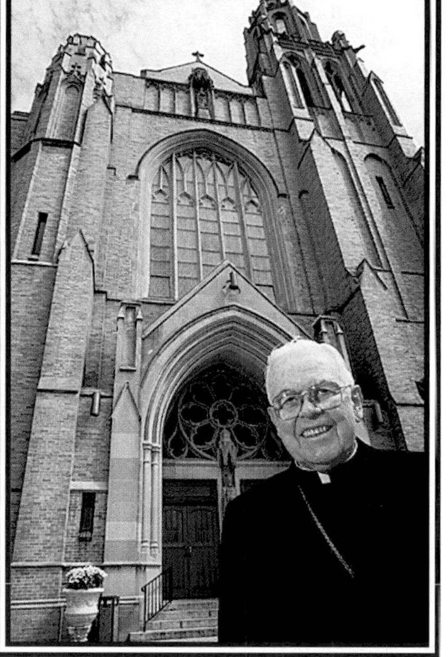

Newsday Photo / Bill Davis

Above right, the future Pope Pius XII, who later authorized the Diocese of Rockville Centre, stayed on Long Island during a 1936 visit. Right, Bishop John McGann, Kellenberg's successor, at St. Agnes Cathedral

BY JOYE BROWN
STAFF WRITER

Polite protests come to an end as Long Island activists accelerat

'The Movement'

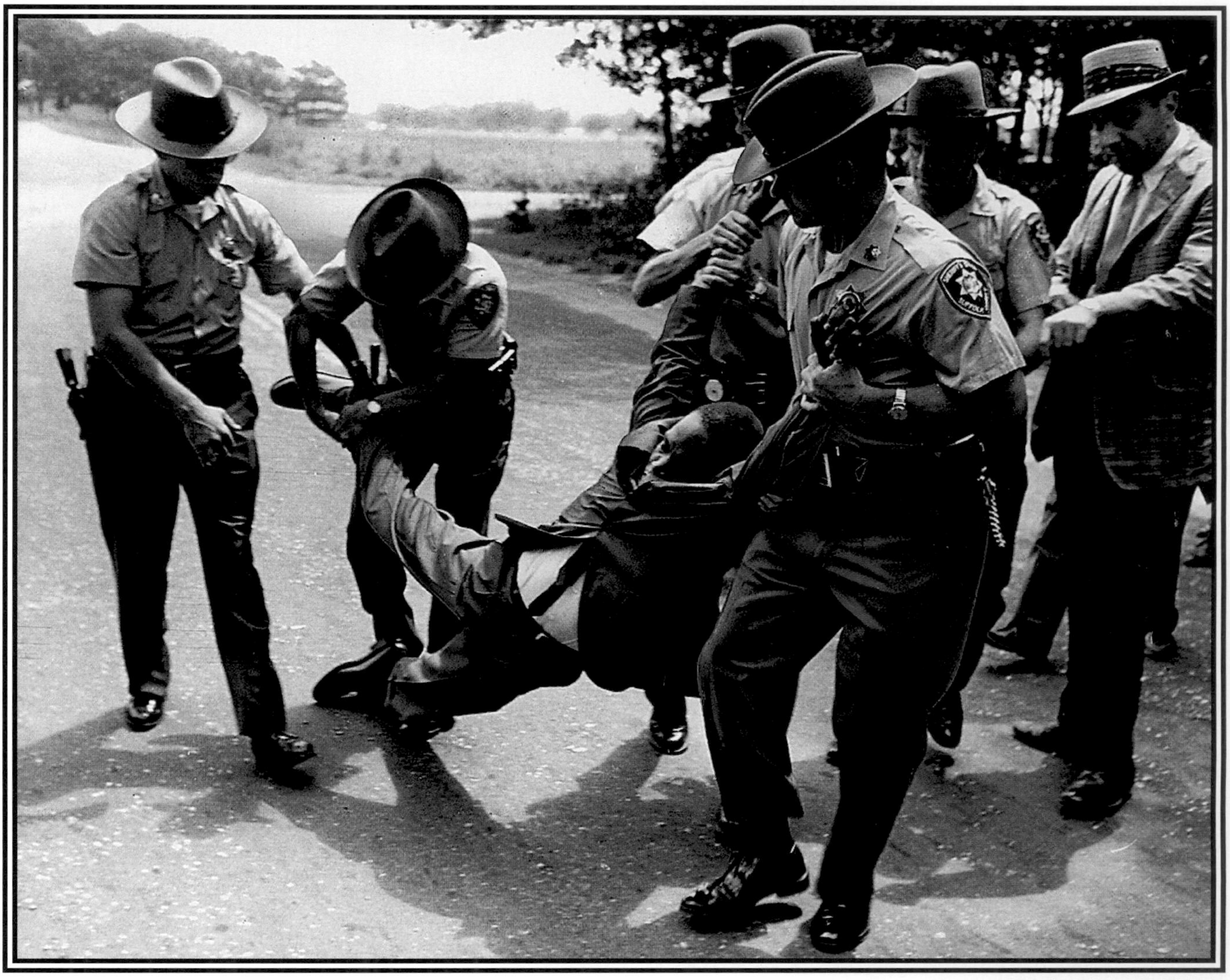

Newsday Photo / Ike Eichorn

Lincoln O. Lynch, CORE's L.I. director, is put under arrest on a charge of trespassing during a protest at a duck farm in Riverhead in 1964.

One hundred years after Abraham Lincoln freed the slaves, a black man, also named Lincoln, walked to a podium at the Garden City Hotel. He was there, on the first day of January, 1963, the centennial of the Emancipation Proclamation, to receive an award from the NAACP.

Lincoln O. Lynch, clean cut and conservatively dressed, carried several handwritten sheets of notebook paper and placed them gently on the stand. When the polite applause died down, the recently appointed chairman of the Long Island branch of the Congress of Racial Equality looked out over the audience of almost 1,000, most of them black Long Islanders, and began to speak.

It was not what his audience expected.

"Here in Nassau County," Lynch began, "and indeed in the very Village of Garden City in which we now meet, racial discrimination and segregation cry out loud for correction.

"All over Nassau, from Inwood to Oyster Bay, from Glen Cove and Manhasset and Port Washington, on our supposedly fabulous North Shore, to Freeport and Farmingdale and Roosevelt and across the border into Amityville, there exists shameless evidence of undisguised discrimination . . . "

His conclusion left many in the audience stunned: "The largest portion of the blame for this situation must be laid, squarely, at the door of the Negro himself, especially so of those who claim to have achieved middle-class status." Black suburbanites, he said, were engaging in a "mad scramble to attain middle-class status and to acquire the trappings of false values dictated by the same society which holds him in contempt." Worse, he said, they seemed to have forgotten that "no Negro can attain freedom until all Negroes attain freedom."

Until then, polite protest had typified the civil rights movement on Long Island. Now Lynch was advocating direct action and defiance. He issued a call to arms, urging black Long Islanders to "prepare and finance lawsuits, badger elected officials for legislation, to picket or sit in or boycott, if necessary, to win equal rights."

In the next several months, many would heed his call. Lynch would become a catalyst, spurring on a coalition of individuals and organizations that crossed racial, economic and geographic lines. Across Long Island, CORE, the NAACP and a host of local activists would work together and separately, picketing and protesting, suing and negotiating for equal access to housing, jobs and schools.

"Before Lincoln, things were pretty quiet," Thomas A. Johnson, who was hired as Newsday's first black reporter a few months after the speech, said recently. "Lincoln brought things to the foreground."

With Lynch's call to activism, civil rights groups battled publicly and aggressively for school desegregation, good housing for migrant workers, an end to urban renewal's destruction of black neighborhoods, more jobs for blacks in banking, malls, insurance and other businesses, and integrated fire departments.

The effort came at a particularly crucial time, as whites were fleeing racially changing neighborhoods in New York City while increasing numbers of upwardly mobile blacks were seeking their place in suburbia as well. "As the African-American population grew on Long Island, the civil rights movement had to respond to new demands and greater pressures," said Charles F. Howlett of West Islip, a historian and specialist on the local civil rights movement.

That response was extraordinarily well organized, with activists schooled in everything from making protest signs and "testing" housing for discrimination to lodging effective complaints and staying calm under pressure. Still, their fight got ugly at times, with scuffles, arrests and even cross-burnings marking school integration efforts in Malverne and Amityville.

For a time, at least, the activists were successful at opening up government, jobs and a few neighborhoods for black residents. Their greatest success, however, was in focusing attention on racial discrimination in Nassau and Suffolk.

"We had hope; we had vision," said Annette Triquere of Westbury, one of many now in their 60s and 70s who were active in what they still proudly call "The Movement." "We changed people's lives," said Hazel Dukes of Roslyn, who walked a picket line at Suffolk County duck farms, protesting the conditions under which black migrants worked, long before she would become state conference president of the NAACP.

Certainly the activism did not end the quest for equal rights. "Things have changed," acknowledged Alan Singer, a professor at Hofstra University's school of education who has studied the era. "But to say they've changed is not to say that everything is solved. In some ways, Long Island today represents the inability of the civil rights movement to successfully build an equal, integrated community. It failed to break down the barriers."

Added Lynda R. Day, an assistant professor of Africana studies at Brooklyn College and author of a history of blacks on Long Island, "The problem was that no one understood how entrenched racism was."

Still, the activist period, which peaked roughly from 1963 through 1969, is significant, historians and activists agree, because for a stretch of time in Nassau and Suffolk, as it was across the United States, the civil rights movement spoke with one voice.

And that voice was powerful.

"What you had was a network of people on many different levels and in many different places who were organized, who were struggling on many fronts," Singer said. "So when it came to them getting what they wanted, there were no accidents."

Long before Lynch walked to that podium, African-Americans on Long Island had been working toward equal rights. Some sued for their freedom and property in the years of slavery. And, as their descendents settled down in segregated communities in Nassau and Suffolk, it was not uncommon to press

the drive to secure a range of civil rights

for Equality

for equal access to education. Charles Brewster's fight to get his son in a new, all-white school in Amityville in 1895, for example, led to a change in state law that limited segregation in public schools.

With the founding of the National Association for the Advancement of Colored People in 1909, black Long Islanders continued to address grievances. The trend accelerated after World War II, as the Island's black population slowly began to grow — despite racial covenants in many housing developments.

"After the war, there was all this patriotic preaching about equality," said Eugene Reed, a retired Amityville dentist who served in the Army and went on to become an NAACP state conference president. "And, of course, it wasn't true for us. That knowledge stimulated more rebellion, more fighting of a system that did not include us."

That rebellion drew more attention during the 1950s, as the Montgomery, Ala., bus boycott and the U.S. Supreme Court's ruling on Brown vs. Board of Education focused national awareness on racial equality. During that period, which paralleled a boom in Long Island's population, the non-white population grew but at a rate far slower than that of the white population. The percentage of black residents crept from 3.2 percent in 1950 to only 3.6 percent in 1960.

As the black population grew, the NAACP seemed to be everywhere. In 1957, it publicly criticized hiring practices of Long Island school districts, charging an "almost conspiracy" between college placement bureaus and the growing local school systems in "cheating qualified Negro teachers out of jobs in Nassau and Suffolk." School districts denied the allegations, saying they couldn't find qualified candidates. "The fact that I don't know if we have any Negro teachers now should be important to show we don't think that way," the president of one Nassau school board said.

By the early 1960s, with demonstrations and sit-ins generating publicity in the South, other organizations dedicated to racial equality began to spring up on Long Island. In 1961, the newly formed Huntington Committee on Human Relations collected 1,000 pledges from residents to welcome new black residents. "The effort was inspired not only because Huntington's population of lower-income Negroes had grown greatly but because the town had wished to engage a high school music teacher of exceptional qualifications," read a news report. "But he was a Negro and Huntington discovered, to its chagrin, that no suitable housing accommodations were available to him." During the decade, about 30 other communities would establish similar committees.

By 1962, after a number of meetings with NAACP officials, Nassau County set up its own 27-member human rights commission. "We handled complaints about everything from police to employment," the agency's first director, Farrell Jones, said recently.

The quest for civil rights on Long Island was moving slowly until the Nassau NAACP gave Lynch, a resident of

Please see RIGHTS on Page 341

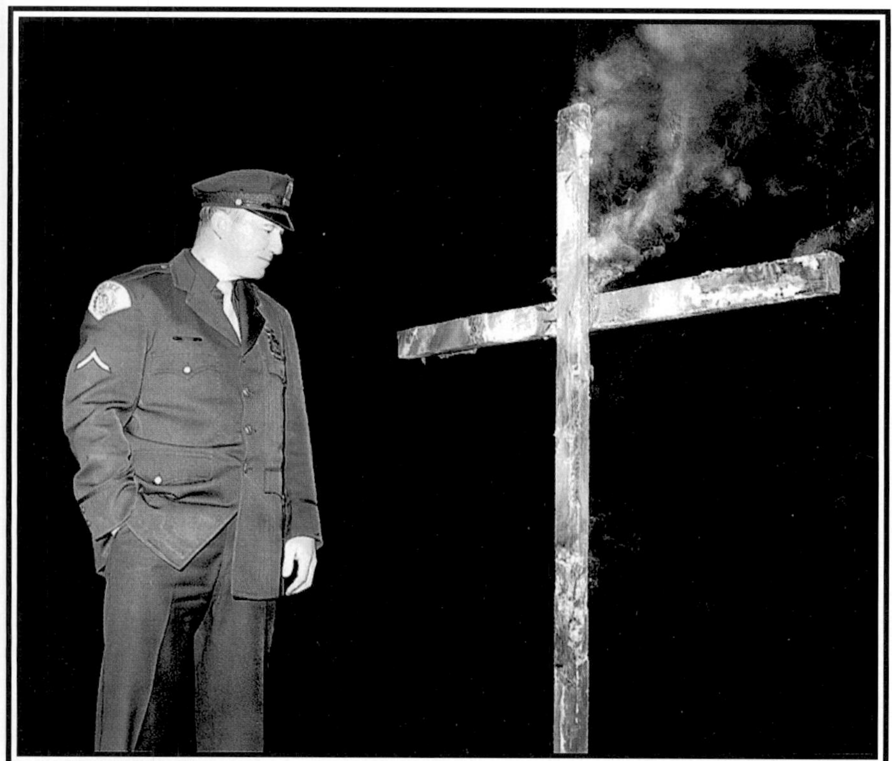

Newsday Photo, 1966

Patrolman Donald Hagen with a cross that was burned on the grounds of Malverne High School in 1966. In the next year, Malverne implemented a school integration plan.

FAST FORWARD

FIGURES FROM LONG ISLAND'S CIVIL RIGHTS MOVEMENT

Lincoln O. Lynch, 78, Manhattan

Then: Long Island chairman of the Congress of Racial Equality
Now: Retired
Most Successful Achievement: "We made people aware of the conditions that existed and what they could do about it . . . no one else had dared to meet the situation head on."
Least Successful: Bringing more black students into the movement. "We made the mistake of educating white people on Long Island too much rather than educating black students on how to be effective activists."
Looking Forward: "I would advise the young people to be smart and to be vigilant, to develop a set of principles, to achieve respect and dignity and to demand acceptance with no strings attached."

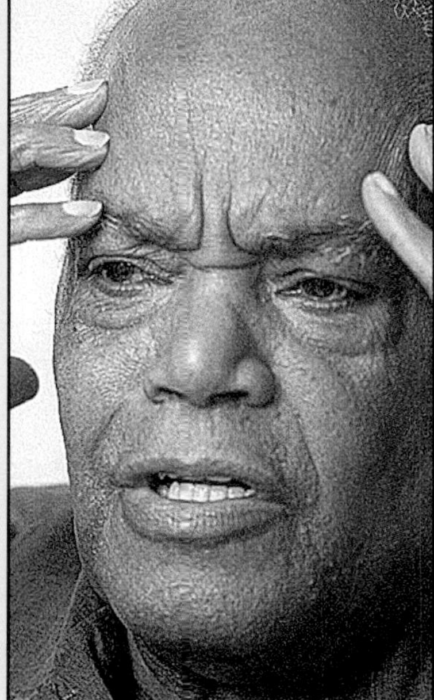

Newsday Photos / Bill Davis

Lynch today: "We made people aware."

Annette Triquere, Westbury

Then: director of the Freedom School, a summer program for youth that operated in conjunction with the Hempstead school system; member of CORE.
Now: Retired. Teaches voice.
Most Successful Achievement: "We found a way for everybody to contribute. We were able to do it and and prove by our example that it can be done."
Least Successful: Unable to maintain momentum, coalitions. "All of a sudden, when school integregation became an issue, all hell broke loose. People didn't want integration too close to home."
Looking Forward: "People have to unite for equality and have to be willing to work, and work together, for it."

Triquere with daughter Peggy Kern: "People have to unite for equality."

Eugene Reed, 75, Amityville

Then: State, local, national NAACP official; attended funeral of his friend, slain activist Medgar Evers in Jackson, Miss., with the Rev. Martin Luther King Jr.; active in the South during the most violent times of the national civil rights movement.
Now: Retired dentist.
Most Successful Achievement: Planning and organization, whether for demonstrations or lawsuits, that led to results. "We were good at letting the punishment fit the crime."
Least Successful: Cultivating new activists. "I'm 75 years old and I'm not going to be on the front lines anymore. Someone has to take my place. And they will have to organize, organize, organize."
Looking Forward: "There is always the need to root out subtle discrimination; it is not on the surface anymore."

Reed: "They will have to organize . . ."

Integration Dream Lost In Roosevelt

BY JOYE BROWN
STAFF WRITER

Once upon a time, there was a place in virtually all-white Long Island that civil rights activists pointed to as integrated. That place was Roosevelt, one square mile of homes and businesses.

At that time, the community of 14,000 was also about 30 percent black. Yet, "there has been little, if any, racial tension and bitterness," noted a 1965 newspaper story.

The community boasted a movie theater, bowling alley and skating rink. It was not uncommon for residents to leave their doors unlocked as they walked to plentiful shopping nearby. But cracks already were beginning to show. That same year, the newspaper reported, black civic activists "launched a fight to keep a stabilized neighborhood of single-family homes, a community that ranks in the middle-income group or higher, a place that would be free of blighted areas."

But in the next few years, as the community increasingly became a place where blacks wanted to live, it became a place whites rushed to leave. And they took with them many businesses, services and the guarantee of schools that graduated mostly college-bound students. Like many communities, such as Lakeview and Uniondale, Roosevelt's years of blacks and whites sharing equally in suburban life were fleeting. "Study after study shows that white people have little tolerance for racial minorities living nearby, especially African-Americans," said Marc Silver, a sociologist at Hofstra University. "Unfortunately, with white flight comes an association with declining property values, higher taxes, absentee landlords and decreasing community services." In the late '60s, when fights over integrating Roosevelt schools landed in court, white flight accelerated. Real estate speculators moved in. And properties owned by absentee landlords opened up a lucrative rental market. By 1970, the transformation was complete; Roosevelt became almost all black. Now, it has a sizable black middle-class population. But community life is not what it was. "One problem is that single-family homeowners were not replaced with single-family homeowners," said Robert Francis, commissioner of planning and economic development for the Town of Hempstead and a Roosevelt resident for 33 years. "Over time, there were more people per home, which caused overcrowding and strained services, especially in the schools. The problem became not so much race as economics."

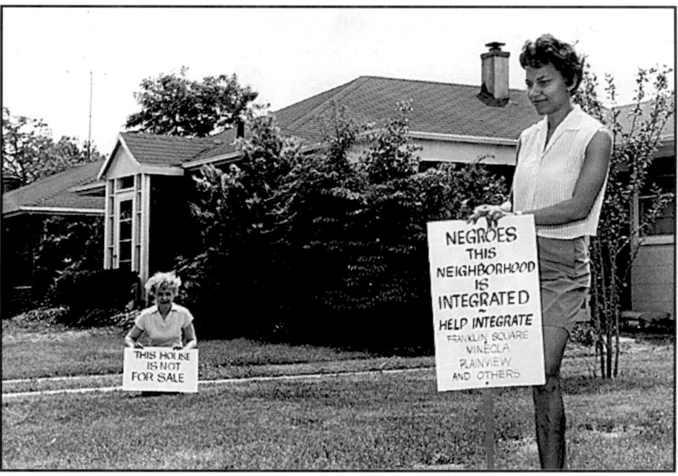

Newsday Photo / Dick Kraus

Seeking racial balance in 1961: Mrs. Michael Zaffe, left, said she would not leave as more blacks moved to Lakeview. Mrs. Lincoln Lynch, then wife of the local rights leader, urged blacks to buy in segregated areas.

In that, Roosevelt could be a lesson on what went wrong in the maturing of suburbia. In his study of the 22 counties surrounding New York City in 1957, Harvard sociologist Oscar Hadlin accurately predicted that more and more blacks would seek their place in the suburbs. He predicted that blacks probably would settle together — just as other immigrants had. But, he warned that without acceptance from whites, blacks would not share the amenities suburbia had to offer. "When color and ethnic identity cease to be unbearable burdens, when opportunity for jobs, education and housing becomes genuinely equal . . . the Negroes . . . will at least have a firm base upon which to construct a sound communal life . . . The alternative in a democratic society is almost unthinkable," Hadlin wrote.

In Roosevelt, civic leaders today contend with the unthinkable, continuing efforts to bring Roosevelt back to the community it was three decades ago. "I see single-family homes being built," said Francis, "and that's a good sign. But are we where we were back in the 1960s? I don't think so."

A Civil Rights History

Long Island

1947. Levittown barred African-American homeowners and renters.

1949. Levittown dropped racial exclusion clause from lease, but continued discrimination.

1957. State NAACP official charged "near conspiracy" between college placement agencies and local school authorities to keep blacks out of teaching jobs on Long Island.

1961. Census results showed more African-Americans moving to New York City suburbs. Huntington human-relations group said it would welcome black residents.

1962. Nassau County established Committee on Human Rights. Urged on by civil-rights groups, New York State investigated allegations of blockbusting in Nassau.

1963. L.I. Congress of Racial Equality chairman Lincoln Lynch called on blacks to sue, boycott, hold sit-ins to end racial discrimination. NAACP charged that urban renewal projects were being used to drive out black families, including in Rockville Centre and Long Beach. CORE campaigned for job opportunities for African-Americans in banking, insurance and other professions. State ordered Malverne school integration.

United States

1947. Jackie Robinson joined the Brooklyn Dodgers and became the 20th Century's first black player in the major leagues.

1954. In Brown vs. Board of Education, the Supreme Court found racial segregation in public schools unconstitutional.

1955. Rosa Parks refused to change seats on a Montgomery, Ala., bus. On Dec. 5, blacks began boycott of the bus system, which continued until shortly after Dec. 13, 1956, when the Supreme Court outlawed bus segregation in the city.

1957. Federal troops enforced school integration in Little Rock, Ark. The Southern Christian Leadership Conference was formed with the Rev. Martin Luther King Jr. as president. Congress passed the Voting Rights Bill of 1957, the first major civil rights legislation in more than 75 years.

1960. Sit-ins in Greensboro, N.C., initiated wave of similar protests throughout the South.

1962. James Meredith desegregated the University of Mississippi.

Aftermath of church bombing

1963. Four black girls died in the bombing of the 16th Street Baptist Church in Birmingham, Ala. Medgar Evers killed in Mississippi. The March on Washington was the largest civil rights demonstration to date as King delivered his "I Have a Dream" speech.

Activists Push For Civil Rights

RIGHTS from Page 339

Lakeview, an award for leadership. He planned long and hard what he would say that night. "Things were moving," he said in a recent interview, "but much, much too slowly. And not everybody was involved in the effort."

On that New Year's Day, Lynch brandished segregated housing, along with de facto school segregation in Malverne, Westbury and Hempstead, as "examples of the dwarf-like steps this fastest-growing county" has taken to address equal rights. From there, he moved to employment, citing businesses that long had been closed to all but a few black Long Islanders.

"Notwithstanding the valiant efforts of a few well-meaning individuals and organizations in the field of race relations," Lynch told his audience, which included Nassau County Executive Eugene Nickerson, a Democrat, and state Assembly Speaker Joseph Carlino, a Long Beach Republican, "a moral and psychological wilderness exists on Long Island, as barren as one would find anywhere south of the Mason-Dixon line." Newsday ran a story about the speech with the headline: "LI Negroes Let Race Down."

The next day, Newsday ran an editorial, "Right Way, Wrong Way," chiding Lynch for his remarks and recommending moderation rather than direct action. "The answer is not a call to arms," the editorial said. "The answer is the gradual absorption of the Negro into the American community on every level . . . Time, and not very much of it, is a far better catalyst, a far better solution to an acknowledged problem that is rapidly working out anyway."

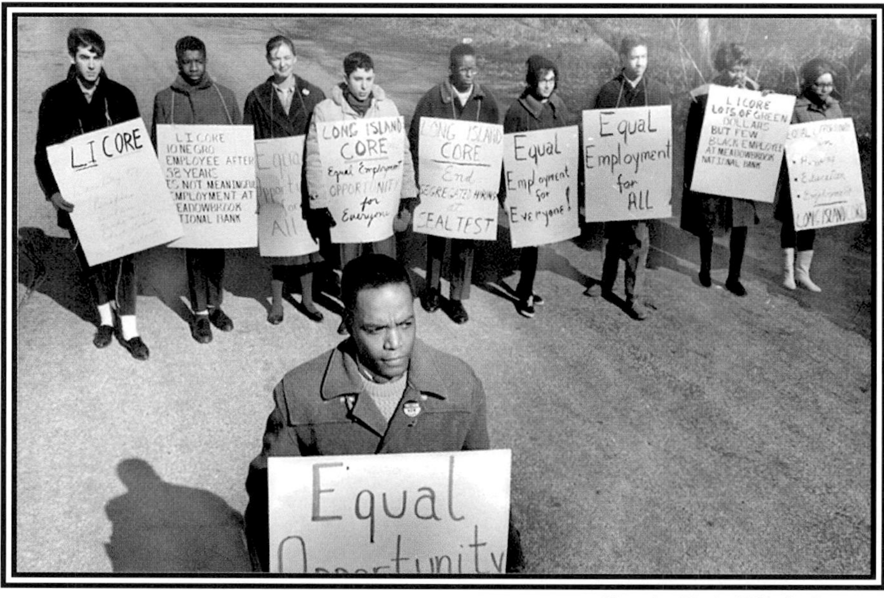

Newsday Photo / Marvin Sussman

Lynch, as head of Long Island's CORE, leads a march in West Hempstead in 1963 to call for more jobs for minorities at local employers such as Sealtest Dairy and Meadowbrook National Bank.

The editorial ignited still more controversy. And the state NAACP immediately jumped into the fray. "We . . . abhor and denounce the gradualism suggested by Newsday," the group said in a statement. "We stand shoulder to shoulder with Mr. Lynch, with CORE and with other organizations seeking the active participation of Negroes in the historic struggle of the Negro in the attainment of full citizenship."

With a flurry of publicity and the blessing of the venerable NAACP, Lynch moved quickly, charging that Sealtest Dairy and Franklin National Bank did not have enough black employees and urging a boycott in leaflets distributed in Nassau and New York City. Both firms agreed to hire more blacks at all employment levels. CORE, with the active participation of supporters, black and white, moved just as quickly to seek concessions from Meadowbrook National Bank, Hempstead Bank and other financial institutions, along with defense firms and employment agencies.

While Lynch and CORE dominated the headlines — at one demonstration for integrating fire departments, Lynch scaled a fence at a firefighters contest and lay down on a track, forcing a truck to stop inches from his head — other activists across the Island were spreading their efforts over an astounding range of issues. "It seemed we were out there making trouble every day," said Mel Jackson, an NAACP member who went on to succeed Lynch. "Sometimes we would bring people to meetings and lock the doors. We wanted them to have an emotional experience."

The activists took on some Nassau and Suffolk fire departments, complaining that membership requirements barred blacks from joining. They took on local governments, including Rockville Centre and Long Beach, contending that urban renewal was being used to displace black residents rather than provide them with better housing. And they took on real estate agencies and other businesses they believed engaged in blockbusting, racial steering and redlining — tactics designed to cause white flight or steer blacks into and away from certain communities.

They were aided by sympathetic

Please see RIGHTS on Next Page

Struggle for school integration in Amityville. Cross-burning in Amityville. State Sen. Norman Lent (R-East Rockaway) introduced bill in Albany to block school busing for integration.

1964-66. White parents in Malverne defied integration plan.

1965. Rev. Martin Luther King Jr. toured Hempstead, Long Beach and West Hempstead. He received honorary degree from Hofstra.

1966. Opponents of school integration won control of Malverne school board.

1967. Protests against white-only volunteer fire departments in Wyandanch and Amityville. School integration plan implemented in Malverne. Proposal made to bus New York City schoolchildren to Great Neck schools.

1968. Racial tension in Westbury schools. King visited Rockville Centre.

1969-70. Students demanded King birthday observance. NAACP challenged unfair zoning practices. Great Neck school integration plan defeated in advisory referendum. Racial incidents in Freeport, Roosevelt, Central Islip, Amityville, Bellport, Hempstead and Glen Cove.

1964. Three civil rights workers murdered in Mississippi. Beginning in Harlem, serious racial disturbances occurred in more than six major cities. The 24th Amendment forbade use of poll tax to prevent voting. King was awarded the Nobel Prize.

1965. Malcolm X was assassinated in New York City. The Southern Christian Leadership Conference launched a voter drive in Selma, Ala., which escalated into a nationwide protest movement. Watts riots erupted in Los Angeles.

1966. Congress of Racial Equality endorsed the concept of "black power" as militancy and black nationalism grew. The Black Panther Party was founded by Huey P. Newton and Bobby Seale in Oakland, Calif.

Bobby Seale, left, and Huey Newton

Destruction from rioting in Boston

1967. In the worst summer for racial disturbances in U.S. history, there were more than 40 riots.

1968. Kerner Commission report described racial division in the United States. King was assassinated in Memphis, Tenn. In the following week, riots occurred in at least 125 places throughout the country.

1969. The Supreme Court ruled that school districts must end racial segregation.

SOURCE: "Chronology of African American History," by Alton Hornsby Jr.; "The Civil Rights Movement on Long Island, A Local Curriculum Guide for Middle School and High School," Hofstra University

Newsday / Linda McKenney

FAST FORWARD

FIGURES FROM THE LI CIVIL RIGHTS MOVEMENT

Newsday Photo / Bill Davis

The Quintynes: Focus on children.

Delores Quintyne, 64; Irvin Quintyne, 71, Amityville

Then: Among the founders of Suffolk County CORE.
Now: She works part time with Hempstead Town; he is retired.
Most Successful Achievement: Opening up jobs in a variety of businesses for blacks. "We had a job bank," said Delores Quintyne. "So when employers said they couldn't find anyone who was qualified, we'd give them a list." Voter registration, education.
Least Successful: Education, employment and housing. Fielding a successful black candidate for local public office.
Looking Forward: Focus on improving education for children; consolidating the efforts of national civil rights organizations into one specialized push for equal rights.

Newsday Photo, 1993 / K. Wiles Stabile

Jones: ". . . still much to be done."

Farrell Jones, 72, Port Washington

Then: First director, Nassau County Human Rights Commission.
Now: Justice, Village of Manorhaven.
Most Successful Achievement: "Raising public consciousness that there was a problem. It was hard to ignore something that was out there, in public, day after day."
Least Successful: "We really did not change the housing situation."
Looking Forward: "There is still much to be done on the housing, economic and education fronts."

Newsday Photo / William J. Senft

As members of the Congress of Racial Equality picket in front of a real estate office in Hicksville in 1964, counter-demonstrators display a Confederate flag. One of the main goals of the civil rights activists was to end discrimination in housing.

Activists Push For Civil Rights

RIGHTS from **Preceding Page**

public officials, including Farrell Jones. "I was the inside guy," he said. "Some of us [in the movement] would come across as angry. Some of us would come across as reasonable. That was our front. We would go to whomever and say, 'Who would you rather talk to, Lincoln or me?' and we would negotiate what we needed from there."

There was also support from clergy, including Bishop Walter Kellenberg of the Diocese of Rockville Centre. "It is necessary that each individual examine his own conscience in matters of interracial and social justice," he said in a pastoral letter to Catholics in August, 1963. "It is further necessary that each of us by private and public prayer beg the Good God, unceasingly, to teach Americans that only equal opportunity for all can make the American dream of justice a reality for all of our citizens."

The activists were also aided by state and national legislation. In 1964, for example, Congress passed the Economic Opportunity Act. That, in turn, led to creation of the Economic Opportunity Commission in Nassau, which would grow to become the county's largest antipoverty agency. John Kearse, who would become the agency's first black director, headed the EOC's program in the Five Towns, where the group was successful in getting housing for the area's minority residents. "That was a short, compact period of time that was so beautiful," Kearse, who still runs the EOC, said recently, "and so fulfilling."

Local efforts were also helped by the national civil rights movement, which relied heavily on Long Island for funds, manpower and leadership.

Two influential activists were Doris and Donald Shaffer, founders of the Great Neck Committee for Human Rights. They were responsible for two of the most successful civil rights fund raisers in the United States. Both took place on Long Island and were attended by the Rev. Martin Luther King Jr.

On a fund-raising trip in 1965, King toured segregated neighborhoods in Lakeview, Hempstead, Long Beach and West Hempstead. A few months later, he spoke at Hofstra University's commencement, where he was awarded an honorary degree. "It is one thing for the white person of good will in the North to rise up with righteous indignation when a bus is burned with freedom riders in Alabama, or when a church is bombed . . . " he told students, as a group of protesters attempted to disrupt his address.

"But it is just as important for the white person in the North to rise up with righteous indignation when a Negro cannot live in your neighborhood or when a Negro cannot get a job at your particular firm . . . "

Activist efforts often included "consciousness raising" sessions with blacks and whites. The tactics of choice, however, continued to be demonstrations, leafleting, picketing and sit-ins. And although they worked, the methods over time were attacked by whites. "As far as the Negro goes much of his shortcomings are of his own making," a Floral Park woman wrote in a letter to the editor in Newsday. "CORE and other organizations would do well to lead their people to win respect and admiration of the white man by their way of living rather than a show of force." A Northport man agreed: "I think it is pitiful when a group of self-appointed troublemakers such as CORE can dictate the policies of an institution as large as the Franklin National Bank."

Still, the civil rights workers went on, attempting the colossal tasks of integrating housing and schools. "Those were the toughest," Dukes said. "But thank God, CORE was the NAACP and the NAACP was CORE. And we had

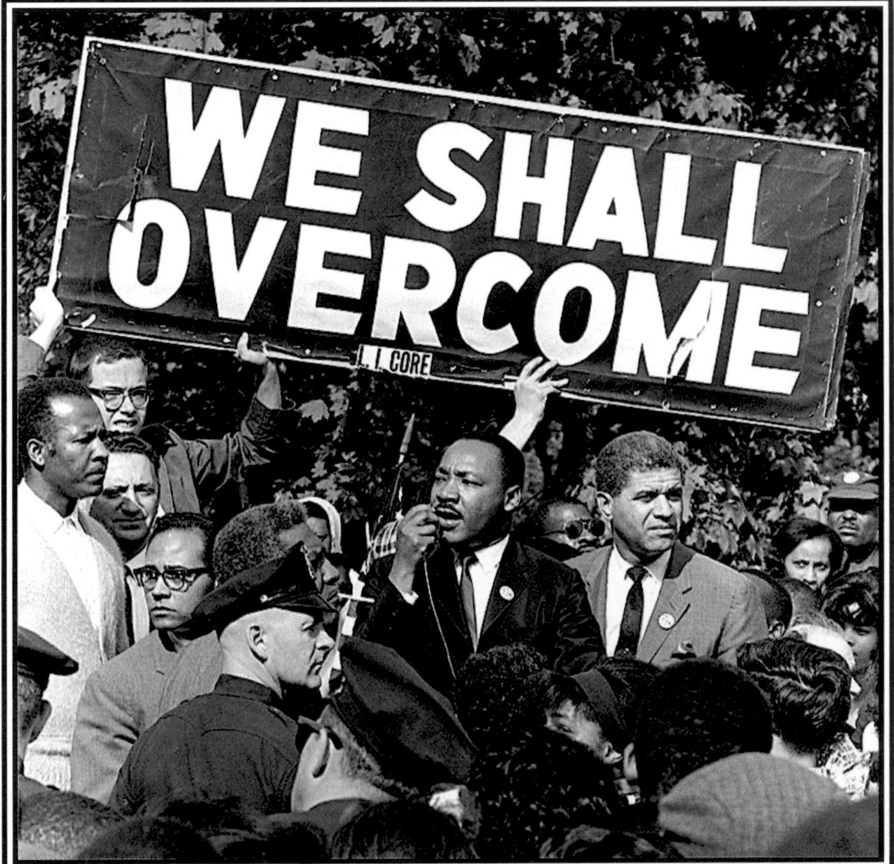

Newsday Photo / Alan Raia

The Rev. Martin Luther King Jr. addresses a rally in Lakeview in 1965. He toured several communities and few months later spoke at Hofstra University's commencement ceremony.

The Hard Life in Migrant Alley

BY BILL BLEYER
STAFF WRITER

They came every spring, making the trip on their own or transported by middlemen known as crew leaders. They toiled six or even seven long days a week under a searing sun, sorting potatoes, picking strawberries or planting at nurseries. At night, they slept on cots in crowded, tar paper-covered barracks usually lacking indoor plumbing and cooking facilities, and where the windows were chicken wire-covered openings and the greasy walls were covered with flies.

This was the scene in Migrant Alley, the nickname for farmland on the North Fork in the late 1950s and early 1960s.

In those years, thousands of temporary workers filled about 100 migrant farm labor camps between Huntington and Greenport. Others lived in more traditional neighborhoods that had grown into slums.

The migrants were as essential to Long Island farmers as seed and fertilizer. Agriculture in Suffolk was a $50 million-a-year industry, and even small family farms needed supplemental hands to bring in their vegetables and fruit. Four decades ago, most of the migrants were southern blacks who followed the picking season north and then returned to their permanent homes in the South in late fall to repeat the cycle.

Newsday Photo / Harvey Weber

Migrant workers bag potatoes in 1961. There was no minimum wage, no medical insurance or workmen's compensation coverage. Union organizing efforts usually failed.

Some of the farmhands traveled to Long Island alone or with their families. Others signed up in the South with crew leaders who recruited workers, brought them north, made deals with farmers and handled the wages. The trip north was free; but there was usually a price for a ride home. Each year, migrants who couldn't afford the return trip remained on Long Island, living in poverty or on welfare.

Their work and their income were dependent on the weather and the crop yield. Sometimes the migrants could be busy for months without a break but often work came sporadically. "I ain't had no steady work for three weeks," a black migrant from South Carolina told a reporter in 1961. "Just sometimes maybe a day and a half, and then nothing."

There was no minimum wage, no medical insurance or workmen's compensation coverage. Union organizing efforts were usually unproductive.

Some migrants made $70 to $90 for a six-day week on Long Island, but a survey conducted by Suffolk officials in 1959 showed the average weekly wage was $26.23. An elderly black woman told a congressional committee in 1960 that her crew leader in Suffolk never gave her more than $16 a week for six days work that ran from 6 a.m. to midnight. "They taken out Social Security on me with no number," she testified. "I paid $1 for union fees, and I don't know what kind of union I was in."

Whether they made $90 or $16, migrants who lived in the camps paid the going rate of $12 a week for a place to sleep and 50 cents a meal or sometimes $12.50 a week for room and board. Or they might share a shack or house nearby, usually filled far beyond what the zoning laws allowed.

Conditions at the farm labor camps — situated on private property and run by individual farmers or farm cooperative groups — varied widely. Most were on the tar paper-covered shack end of the spectrum.

State law specified that any farmer who housed more than five migrant workers would be considered the operator of a labor camp that had to be licensed. State building code regulations would then apply. Some farmers dodged these rules by hiding workers in shacks far from the nearest road.

The substandard living conditions sometimes proved fatal. In 1961 a leaky kerosene stove exploded in a barracks in Suffolk's largest migrant camp in Cutchogue, killing four workers.

Conditions at the camps began to improve in 1958 when Gov. W. Averell Harriman imposed more stringent requirements for heating, sanitation and living space. In 1961 and 1962, federal and state legislation provided for licensing and regulation of crew leaders In 1965 a law was passed to require employers with a migrant payroll of more than $1,200 to cover the workers with workmen's compensation insurance.

In 1960, of the more than 4,500 migrant workers in Suffolk, more than 3,500 were black and 500 were from Puerto Rico. By 1971, the number of migrant workers had dropped to 1,700, in part because of mechanization and dwindling farm acreage. But the number of migrants who decided to remain on Long Island year-round rose from 1,000 in 1964 to 1,600 in 1971.

This trend toward staying put has continued to the point where almost no temporary farm workers migrate from the South to follow the harvests anymore. The current farm work force in Suffolk is about 8,000, at least half of them "seasonal agricultural workers" who come to Long Island for the farm season, then return to their homes.

"Today's farm labor comes from Mexico, Guatemala, South America, Poland, from all over the world," said Joseph Gergela, executive director of the Long Island Farm Bureau, which represents local farmers. The crew leader system died out when most of the seasonal workers began coming from other countries.

For those doing farm work, the money is better these days. "People don't want to work on farms," Gergela said. So the seasonals are paid "minimum wage at least," sometimes more than $10 an hour.

But finding a decent and affordable place to live remains difficult. "We don't have a lot of labor camps left," said Sister Margaret Quigley, coordinator of the Eastern Suffolk BOCES Migrant Education Outreach Program. "Farmers stay away from providing housing because of all of the restrictions" and government regulation.

The 20 remaining farm labor camps in the Riverhead area are strictly regulated by county and federal agencies, Gergela said.

help from a lot of local human rights groups. We worked together and kept each other's spirits high."

They needed to. In housing, they ran up against years of entrenched patterns of segregation. In some communities, African-Americans lived in substandard housing although they could afford better. Their problem: They couldn't buy or rent houses in areas where whites did not want them. On the East End, the NAACP took the problem to local officials. One Southampton official appeared unconcerned about the situation. "There are a lot of white people in this and other towns that don't live in the kinds of homes they want to live in," he said.

In 1964, Suffolk CORE and Huntington Township Committee for Human Relations camped out in tents for three days protesting an Amityville housing development that refused to sell to blacks. "Suffolk's first sit-in and sleep-in for housing equality ended . . . with a victory for the civil rights movement," Newsday reported. "Mr. and Mrs. Colin Smith, of Amityville, signed a one-year lease for a $130-a-month, three and a half room apartment. Direct-action protest at last accomplished a quick response."

Later that year, in Syosset, a picket line sprang up when a homeowner backed off on a deal to sell to an African-American electrical engineer and his wife after receiving telephone threats, apparently from neighbors. "The 20 CORE members, who demonstrated quietly, got some unexpected support from a 12-year-old girl who left her playmates, walked to the middle of the tree-lined street and, with a piece of chalk, printed in neat, three-foot letters, 'Freedom for All,' " said a news report. The sale went through.

It was not so easy in Hicksville, where a protest against a real estate firm, Vigilant, sparked violence. Activists contended that the firm refused to show homes to blacks. A shoving match at a demonstration was broken up by scores of police

"That was the only time I was ever afraid on a picket line," said Delores Quintyne, one of the founders of CORE in Suffolk. After eight days, CORE stopped the picketing Vigilant's offices and the firm pledged to adhere to a state law barring discrimination.

In 1963, state Commissioner of Education James Allen Jr. recommended that local districts consider busing to integrate schools. Several school boards on Long Island resisted, including those

Please see RIGHTS on Next Page

FAST FORWARD

FIGURES FROM THE LI CIVIL RIGHTS MOVEMENT

Newsday Photo / Viorel Florescu

Dukes: "The fight is not over."

Hazel Dukes, 66, Roslyn

Then: Worked with NAACP and supported CORE in demonstrations and other activities.
Now: State Council president, NAACP.
Most Successful Achievement: "People called it like it was, took on government, private businesses and people who were denying people their God-given rights."
Least Successful: "The schools."
Looking Forward: "It's up to the young people. The fight is not over in housing, education or economics. And there are new fights. They have to find the zest and the zeal to go for true equality. Nobody is going to give it to anyone."

Newsday Photo / Bill Davis

Jackson: "We are always working..."

Mel Jackson, 65, Hempstead

Then: Active in NAACP, became head of L.I. CORE.
Now: Executive director, Leadership Training Institute.
Most Successful Achievement: Building a coalition of people inside and outside the system to get jobs, housing. "We did a good job getting their attention."
Least Successful: Maintaining the momentum.
Looking Forward: "We are always working and will continue to do so."

COMPILED BY JOYE BROWN

Activists Push For Civil Rights

RIGHTS from **Preceding Page**

in Malverne, Manhasset and Westbury. The civil rights supporters launched demonstrations in the districts. And in Amityville, residents fought a separate proposal to build schools in the black and white sections of the community. Most of the communities ultimately reached some compromise.

In the years that followed, schools continued to be a source of conflict, as the civil rights groups attempted to fight de facto segregation and foster integration wherever they could. In Roosevelt, one-third of its students stayed home for two days in 1965 during an NAACP protest. In Great Neck, activists — most of them white — pushed a proposal in 1967 to bus in New York City children to integrate the schools. It was voted down in an advisory referendum two years later.

The fight that generated the most controversy, however, was in Malverne. The NAACP complained to the state that black children were getting an inferior education in the district because they were largely segregated in one elementary school. The complaint led to Allen's directing Malverne to become the first district in the state to end de facto segregation. In response, more than 1,500 residents gathered in Lynbrook to protest his directive. And a community group, Taxpayers and Parents Association, urged the district to sue.

In turn, the NAACP and its supporters launched a series of sit-ins. The protests continued, culminating in a school boycott, more sit-ins and picketing. Five protestors, including Lynch, were arrested. And Eugene Reed was thrown to the floor during a struggle in one school.

Whites resisted, saying they feared the loss of their neighborhood schools, which they said were adequately integrated. At one point, a court invalidated Allen's directive. The NAACP and its supporters were incensed. "We will sit in, crawl in, lie in, stand in, chain in, pray in and the jails hold no terror for us," one protestor, Lloyd Delaney, shouted during a school board meeting.

In 1965, State Sen. Norman F. Lent Jr. (R-East Rockaway), in an attempt to preserve neighborhood schools, unsuccessfully proposed two amendments to state law that would ban students from being assigned to schools on the basis of race. Later that year, a state Court of Appeals reinstated Allen's desegregation order. In 1966, a cross was burned on the lawn of the Malverne High School. The plan was finally implemented in 1967.

"This was one of the early mobilizations in the fight for school integration in the nation, one of the early proving grounds," Alan Singer said.

Even before King was assassinated in April, 1968, the nature of the civil rights movement on Long Island began changing. Mirroring the national trend, the movement went from activist to militant. With the rise of black power, it also, by design, became less integrated. After King's death, black

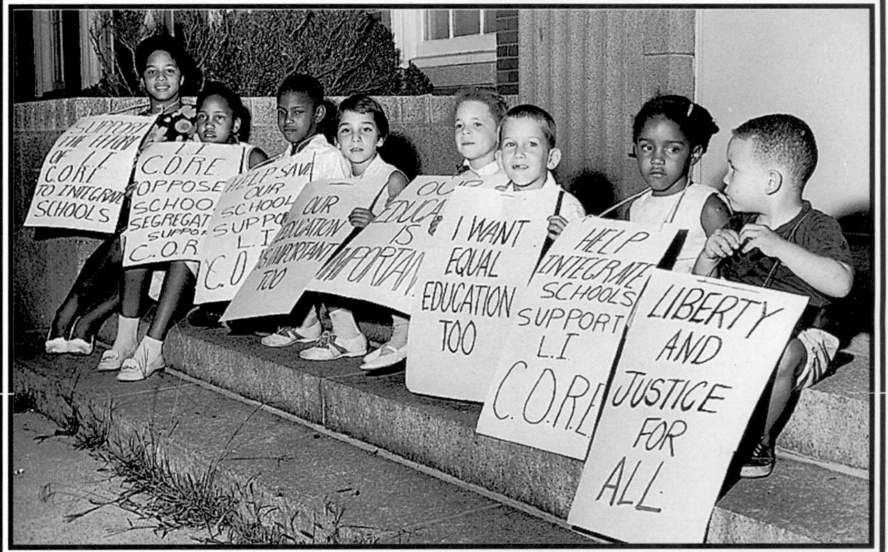

Newsday Photo / Marvin Sussman

Children rest from picket line duty in 1962 at Malverne High School. In 1963, several LI school boards, including Malverne, resisted a state plan to use busing to achieve integration.

students on Long Island demanded courses on African history, black history and recognition of King's efforts through special programs. Sometimes there was conflict, including boycotts and fights between black and white students. The NAACP and CORE also continued their efforts, concentrating more in black communities.

Lincoln O. Lynch became a national CORE official and left Lakeview. Eventually, he settled down in Harlem, where he now lives surrounded by African art and family photographs. Looking back, Lynch, now 78, is pleased with what occurred on Long Island almost four decades ago. He bristles at the suggestion that some at the time considered the tactics he and others used a form of blackmail.

"If that was blackmail," he said, voice rising and eyes glaring, "it was long overdue and served its purpose." If he had it to do all over again, he said, he would have involved African-American children more actively in the movement with the hope that they might have continued the fight to this day.

After all, he recalled, it was a poem he learned as a child on the island of Jamaica that moved him toward raising the stakes in the civil rights movement on Long Island. The poem, by British historian Thomas Babington Macaulay, speaks of haves and have nots, insiders and outsiders, patricians and plebians in ancient Rome.

Lynch can still recite that inspiration from memory, his voice becoming deeper and measured:

". . . When our latest hope is fled, ye taste of our despair,
And learn by proof, in some wild hour, how much the wretched dare."

The civil rights activists on Long Island certainly dared, historians agree. But what did they accomplish? Their spotlight on inequities on Long Island opened up housing in some neighborhoods and made urban renewal work in a few others. Their work opened up the possibility of jobs for blacks in a variety of places, from Newsday to the State University at Stony Brook to some of the regional malls.

"The struggle of the civil rights movement cracked open Long Island to blacks, gave blacks some access to communities, to schools, to jobs," Singer said. "But it has never been full access. And it won't be unless there is some change in attitudes."

Many of the issues activists identified and fought to correct remain unresolved to this day.

Long Island remains segregated, with 95 percent of black residents in Nassau and Suffolk concentrated in 5 percent of the Island's census tracts. For residents in black communities, the quality of life is substantially different from that of their white counterparts. Black communities generally are more crowded, pay higher taxes, and have fewer businesses and fewer services than white communities. And they generally have little political clout. It took a lawsuit in Nassau to clear the way for two blacks to be elected to the county Legislature; in Suffolk, no black has ever been elected. The same holds true in many town and local governments.

Fire departments remain segregated, with the racially mixed department in the black community of Roosevelt being the exception rather than the rule — even when the department serves a predominately black community such as Wyandanch. Schools remain segregated, largely as a function of the 126 communities they serve. Teachers of any color remain in woefully short supply, as 50 of Long Island's 126 school districts last year did not employ a single black teacher. And only half of the districts employed more than one.

All of these things trouble the civil rights activists. "My heart just aches," Dukes said. "We didn't go far enough," Lynch said.

Day believes Long Island could go further, with more consciousness-raising among the increasingly diverse races and ethnic groups who now live in Nassau and Suffolk. She believes that to be essential. "Without it, our kids will continue to grow up culturally limited and unprepared to be in a world that is much more culturally diverse."

Marc Silver, a sociologist at Hofstra, also points to the increasing diversity of Long Island. In six years, demographers say, one in four Long Islanders will be black, Asian or Hispanic. By 2010, it will be one in three. (Currently, it is almost one in five.)

"Either things change or you create points of crisis," he said. "At this point, it's impossible to predict how it will get resolved."

A Newsday reporter recalls spinning bottles, flying crockery, other unexplained events

A Home's Bad Vibrations

BY DAVID KAHN
STAFF WRITER

One of the strangest mysteries in Long Island history was the case of the popping bottles and flying globe. I know. I heard them pop and saw it fly.

When I came to work in the old Newsday building in Garden City on Feb. 10, 1958, I saw a story headlined "Balmy Bouncing Bottles Jar LIer's Home." It told how, in the Seaford house of Air France employee James Herrmann, bottles of hair tonic, perfume, bleach, even holy water, had spontaneously unscrewed their tops and fallen over. His wife, Lucille, actually saw one bottle spin off its top, turn on the shelf and fall on the floor. Herrmann watched a bottle of medicine hop at least 6 inches across a bathroom vanity into the sink. Their son, Jimmy, 12, was pictured looking at broken glassware.

Years earlier, I had written about psychic phenomena, including poltergeists. The German word, which means "rattling ghosts," refers to unseen spirits that cause strange noises, movements of furniture and breakages of crockery that have been recorded for hundreds of years from all parts of the world. A teenager often is present. I told my city editor that a poltergeist might be at large in Seaford. He assigned me the story.

The events began Feb. 3 in the Herrmann's six-room ranch house. They came in spurts, but averaged about two a day. On Feb. 20, they grew more numerous and malicious. A bottle of ink flew from the dinette table against the front door, spattering the door, the rug and the wallpaper. A porcelain figurine hurled itself twice against a wooden desk, 10 feet away, denting it and then shattering. The sugar bowl crashed onto the dining room floor. Lucille Herrmann, alone in the house, went to a neighbor's.

Nor were the Herrmanns the only ones to witness the events. A British reporter saw a flashbulb leap from an end table, carom into drapes and bounce twice on the floor. A Nassau County detective, Joseph Tozzi, twice heard noises, ran into adjoining rooms, and found that a sugar bowl in the dinette had flipped three feet and that a porcelain statuette had flown 10 feet across the living room and smashed into a wooden secretary. I myself several times heard and once observed an event.

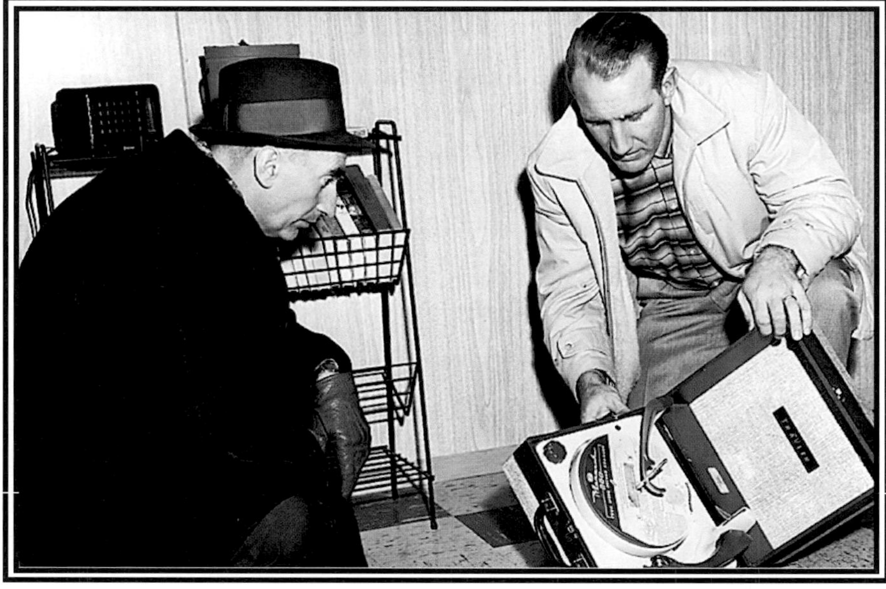

Newsday Photo, 1958 / Cliff DeBear

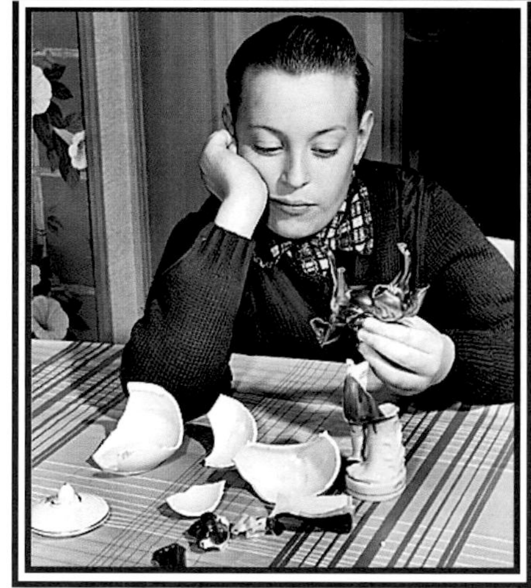

Newsday Photo, 1958 / Jim Nightingale

James Herrmann, above right, shows Det. Sgt. Bert McConnell a phonograph found on the floor. Jimmy, left, with broken crockery.

At about 8:10 p.m. on Feb. 24, the children in bed, Herrmann and I were talking about the disturbances. Suddenly, there was a crash from the living room behind me. We rushed in; Jimmy was there before us. A porcelain figurine of a Colonial man had smashed against the wooden desk, denting it. The figurine was in pieces. Fifty minutes later, hoping to see one of the events, I positioned myself on the living room couch facing Jimmy's darkened bedroom. Suddenly, a 10-inch cardboard globe of the world flipped silently out of Jimmy's room in my direction and bounced into the opposite corner of the living room. I jumped up, ran into Jimmy's room, and snapped on the light. He was sitting up in bed, the covers over his legs. Could he have thrown it? I thought it was possible, but improbable.

Jim Herrmann sought an explanation. Air officials at Mitchel Field said none of their equipment could produce those effects. A neighbor suggested that vibrations from an underground stream might be causing the movements, but a vibration detector set up by the Long Island Lighting Co. found nothing out of the ordinary. Technicians from RCA, covering most of the radio spectrum, found no abnormal signals. The head of the Hempstead Town Building Department found no defects in the 5-year-old house, in which only the Herrmanns had lived.

As the events escalated — from statuettes flying to bureaus falling over — and the story went national, more than 250 letters poured in. A Chicago man proposed, "Leave out a pad and pencil, and write on the pad, 'Who are you? Can we help?' "

Was it a hoax? Neither Tozzi nor I thought so. The family — there was also a daughter, Lucille, 13 — didn't seem the type.

But what about young Jimmy? Many thought he was the culprit, including my night city editor. "Catch the kid!" he ordered.

It is true that in many of these strange events, it was possible for the bright and lively seventh-grade honor student to have done them. But he would have had to have been extraordinarily strong and agile. When the statuettes struck objects, they did so with an almost explosive sound. It's unlikely that he could have thrown them with such force.

Tozzi agreed. Moreover, both of us felt that he had no desire to harass his parents and no need for attention. We both thought Jimmy was not doing this.

In the end, after 67 occurrences, the events stopped. The last took place on March 10. A 45-page study by a Duke University parapsychologist, likewise exonerating Jimmy, concluded that the events would remain forever a mystery.

When asked what the answer is, I say that all we can do is class the events as an instance of a poltergeist and await an explanation of that phenomenon. As Hamlet said, "There are more things in heaven and earth, Horatio, / Than are dreamt of in your philosophy."

LEGACY

THE ENDURING MYSTERY OF THE WEEPING ICONS

Pagona Catsounis was kneeling before an icon of the Virgin Mary on March 16, 1960, when she saw something almost unbelievable — a small tear quivering on the cheek of the Blessed Mother.

She waited for almost a week as the tears continued to appear and then told her story. The announcement drew droves of pilgrims, skeptics and sightseers to her Island Park home.

Catsounis' weeping icon was the first of three that would be discovered on Long Island that year. The second appeared one month later in the Oceanside home of Catsounis' aunt, Antonia Koulis. Four Newsday staff members, including reporter Jim Hadjin, witnessed the event.

"I had to be convinced. I was skeptical," said Hadjin, who retired from Newsday in 1986. But after a priest allowed him to examine the lithograph icon, he changed his mind."Miracle is a pretty strong word, but I don't see what else it could have been," he said.

Chemists, engineers, art experts and others were unable to explain the phenomenon. Skeptics dismissed the tears as the result of condensation. One team of chemists tested a sample and concluded the liquid did not contain enough salt or nitrogen to be human tears.

The first two icons are now enshrined at St. Paul's Greek Orthodox Cathedral in Hempstead, and draw more than 3,000 visitors a year, according to Rev. Nicholas J. Magoulias, who arrived at the church shortly after the icons were discovered. "Tearing icons are not unusual. They happened before the fall of Constantinople, before the fall of France in the Second World War. . . The '60s were turbulent times," Magoulias said, explaining why he believes the weeping icons appeared at the dawn of the decade.

The third icon, discovered by Koulis shortly after the second, is still in her family's home. Although all three icons continue to perform what Magoulias called "miracles" — helping to heal the sick — only the third shows physical signs of its paranormal past.

According to Catsounis, who now lives in Oceanside, "If you go and pray with all your heart, sometimes the eyes open and close."

— **Katie Thomas**

Greek Orthodox Archbishop Iakovos studies a weeping icon in the Oceanside home of Antonia Koulis in 1960.

Newsday Photo / Richard Morseman

In the 1960s, Democrats win both county executive positions, reshaping LI politics

Breaking the GOP's Grip

BY MICHAEL DORMAN

The unthinkable became not only thinkable but palpable in the 1960s: Two-party government swept across Long Island.

In 1960, Democrat H. Lee Dennison took office as Suffolk County executive. In 1962, Democrat Eugene H. Nickerson was sworn in as Nassau County executive.

Their election victories broke the choke hold long maintained by Republicans over Long Island politics and led the way for fellow Long Island Democrats to win other county and town offices, as well as seats in Congress and the State Legislature. The arrival of two-party government thus redesigned the face of Long Island politics.

Dennison and Nickerson, the chief players in this political revolution, had little in common except that each had forsaken his Republican upbringing to become a Democrat. Dennison, the son of a Republican mayor of Hornell, N.Y., was a blunt — some said gruff — engineer. He dreamed an engineer's dreams of vast public-works projects and gave an outward appearance of being apolitical.

Nickerson, a descendant of John Adams, was often called patrician in tones that seemed to question his toughness. But he proved he was tough as early as his college years at Harvard. A right-handed athlete, he was stricken at 17 by polio — restricting use of his right arm. He then taught himself to play squash left-handed, became the college team's top player and was named Harvard athlete of the year. As an adult, Nickerson was very much a political animal — dreaming of a career in public service that would elevate him to ever-higher elected offices.

Dennison and Nickerson were never close. "He simply goes his way and I go my way," Dennison once said.

Dennison went to work in 1927 as an engineer for Suffolk County. In 1951, after writing a scathing report on the Republican county administration's planning operations, he was fired and became a private engineer.

He played no active role in politics until Dominick Baranello, then as now Suffolk Democratic chairman, urged him in 1959 to run for Brookhaven supervisor. "To get rid of him, I indicated I would run for county executive and that was all," Dennison would recall. "The next time I heard from him I was in a campaign for county executive." In a stunning upset, Dennison defeated a former Huntington supervisor, Joseph Cermak, by 559 votes to win election to the newly established office.

Democrats took 6-4 control of the county board of supervisors. But the Democratic majority — the first on the Suffolk board since the early 1900s — was illusory. Seven votes were needed for approval of all financial measures. Dennison fought stiff battles with the Republicans in attempts to gain that critical seventh vote.

He was re-elected twice and served 12 years before retiring at the end of 1971. One description of Dennison's approach to politics and life was offered by John V. N. Klein, who succeeded him as county executive. Although Klein headed Dennison's Republican opposition on the board, the two men got along well.

One night, driving Klein home from a meeting, Dennison encountered a muddy, flooded road described by Klein as "literally soup." Klein suggested taking another road. "Nonsense!" Dennison snorted. "I can handle the situation. Just brace yourself." He backed up, gunned his motor and raced through the muck. "Head down and plow forward," Klein said, summarizing Dennison's approach to life. "He got an idea and ran with it. Sometimes he scored and sometimes he got his transmission removed."

Among Dennison's accomplishments were the creation of Suffolk Community College; open-space acquisitions of 15,000 acres for conservation; creation of a county planning department; an ambitious building program that included the county office building later named for him in Hauppauge, and creation of a human rights commission.

Dennison died in 1983, at the age of 79, in Florida.

Eugene Nickerson, after graduation from Columbia Law School, became law secretary to Chief Justice of the United States Harlan F. Stone. Later, while practicing law, he began working in Democratic politics as Roslyn campaign chairman and rose to vice chairman of the Nassau organization.

Nickerson, who was born in New Jersey but later moved to Roslyn, first sought elective office in 1959 with a race for Nassau surrogate. He tells of enduring interminable candidates' nights, sitting in meeting halls waiting to speak. Candidates for more glamorous offices were always called before him. And, after those candidates had spoken, spectators tended to drift away. One night, when Nickerson was finally introduced, only one man was seated before him.

"Gosh, you must really be interested in the surrogate's race," Nickerson said.

"Actually, no," the man replied. "I'm the next speaker."

Nickerson lost the surrogate's race, but two years later the Democrats nominated him for county executive. He had two major advantages in the race. One was the campaign direction of John F. English, a brilliant political strategist who was Nassau Democratic chairman and a close associate of President John F. Kennedy. The other advantage was the ineptitude of Nickerson's Republican opponent, Robert Dill, a former Customs official.

At one point, Dill called the Democrats "a bunch of greasy, slimy pigs." English responded with ridicule — sending Democrats in pig masks, and even a live pig, to Dill rallies. When Dill refused to debate Nickerson, English offered $10,000 to Dill's campaign fund if he would debate. When Dill still refused, English offered that same $10,000 if Dill would "debate the issues with any eighth-grader in a Nassau school to be chosen by lot." Dill again refused.

Although an underdog — there had never been a Democratic Nassau County executive — Nickerson won. He was re-elected twice, but defeated in races for the Democratic nomination for governor and U.S. senator.

When he left office in 1970, he was considered an effective county executive. He lost the fight to build an educational and cultural center on the old Mitchel Field property, but his plan did result in construction of the Nassau Coliseum. He expanded county parks, brought greater professionalism to the county police and eliminated hundreds of patronage jobs.

President Jimmy Carter later appointed Nickerson to a federal judgeship that he still holds in the Eastern District of New York, headquartered in Brooklyn. He has presided over many organized crime cases.

John Klein, who dealt with Nickerson as well as Dennison, assessed their careers this way: "They were unique individuals in the context of their particular executive branches. They were not just Democrats in Republican counties. Their contributions and perspectives for the future of both counties were very original and unusual."

Michael Dorman is a freelance writer.

Newsday Photo / John H. Cornell Jr.

Democratic County Executives H. Lee Dennison, left, of Suffolk and Eugene H. Nickerson of Nassau led their party's surge into office on Long Island.

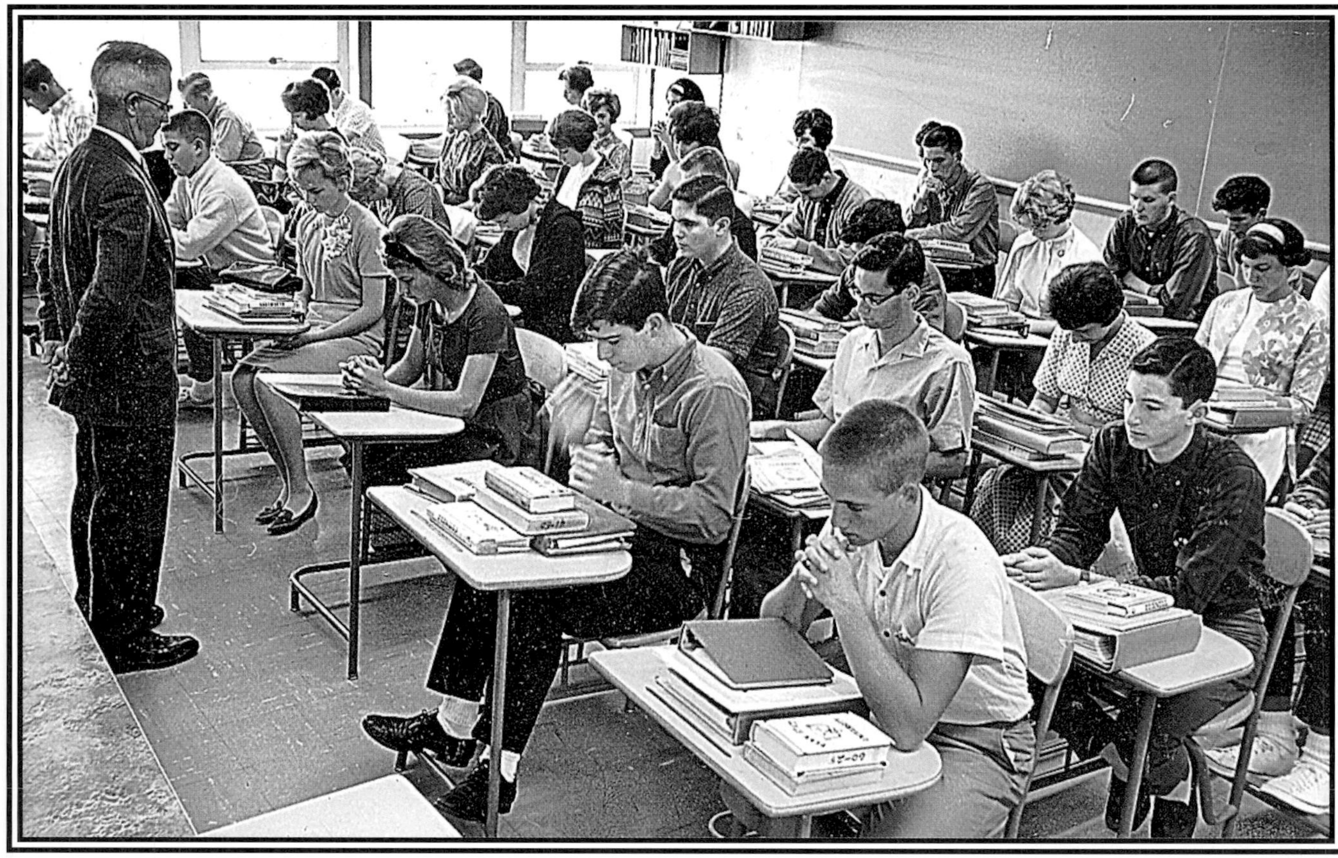

Newsday Photo / Thomas H. Maguire

Baldwin High School students bow their heads for a "minute of silence" on Sept. 6, 1962, instead of reciting a Regents-sponsored prayer outlawed by the Supreme Court the preceding June 25. Teacher Ezra Reed, left, called the prayer ban "a shame."

TWO OTHER CASES REACH TOP COURT

In addition to the Herricks suit, two other major U.S. Supreme Court cases were generated on Long Island.

In 1982, the court ruled that it was an unconstitutional suppression of ideas for the Island Trees school district in Levittown to remove books considered offensive from the high school library. In 1976, the school board had removed nine books on the grounds that they were "anti-American, anti-Christian, anti-Semitic and just plain filthy." The books included Bernard Malamud's "The Fixer" and Kurt Vonnegut's "Slaughterhouse Five."

In 1974, the court upheld an "antigrouper" law passed by the Village of Belle Terre near Port Jefferson that prohibited more than two persons unrelated by blood or marriage from living together in a one-family house. The law was challenged in 1972 by six students at the State University at Stony Brook who had jointly rented a 14-room Tudor house in the village.

— George DeWan

U.S. Supreme Court agrees with parents who oppose prayer in a Herricks school

School Prayer Divides LI

BY GEORGE DEWAN
STAFF WRITER

One day in the fall of 1958, Steven Engel visited his son's classroom in the Searington Elementary School in the Herricks school district. Engel, a Jew, was not prepared for what he saw his son doing.

"I saw one of my children with his hands clasped and his head bent," Engel, now 75, recalled recently from his home in Great Neck, where he has since moved. "After, I asked him, 'What were you doing?' He said, 'I was saying my prayers.' I said, 'That's not the way we say prayers.' "

The prayer in question was Regents-sponsored, school board-approved and nonsectarian, and students were not required to say it. But after being challenged by Engel and four other parents in the district early in 1959, the prayer was ruled unconstitutional in 1962 by the U.S. Supreme Court in a landmark First Amendment decision. Engel vs. Vitale (William Vitale was the school board president at the time) went into the history books.

The parents — who had a total of 10 children in the district's schools — had lost at trial in State Supreme Court in Nassau and lost every appeal until the case got to the U.S. Supreme Court. When the high court's decision was announced on June 25, 1962, it was met with a storm of protest. Newsday editorialized against the decision, and religious leaders and some polititicans opposed it.

"I am shocked and frightened that the Supreme Court has declared unconstitutional a simple and voluntary declaration of belief in God by public school children," said the Roman Catholic archbishop of New York, Cardinal Francis Spellman. "The decision strikes at the very heart of the Godly tradition in which America's children have for so long been raised."

"It means that asking divine guidance in the schools is wrong," said Rep. Steven B. Derounian (R-Roslyn). "I think to ask divine guidance is right anytime and anywhere."

The reaction locally was more vicious. Parents who brought the suit were bombarded with crank calls and obscene and threatening messages calling them Communists and atheists. The assault included the burning of gasoline-soaked rags in the form of a large cross in the driveway of one of the plaintiffs, Lawrence Roth, who lived near Engel.

"When we won the case, all hell broke loose," Engel, a businessman, said recently. "The dirty letters, the midnight phone calls. I once received a call at work: 'We've got your children.' I took a taxi home from work in New York. I went to the school, but everything was OK."

Another plaintiff was Monroe Lerner, also from Roslyn Heights. "There were neighbors who stopped talking to us," Lerner's wife, Julia, said recently. "But they've gotten over it. It took them time to understand that no one in this group was interested in preventing religion in their lives. We had to take our phone off the hook . . . terrible things were said to us. We got letters, with the words cut out of papers. This is how intense the feelings were."

A postcard was mailed to all five plaintiffs. It began: "You damn Jews with your liberal viewpoint are ruining a wonderful country." In fact, two of the plaintiffs were Jews, one a Unitarian, one a Protestant, the fifth an agnostic.

Some people approved of what Engel and the others had done. A schoolteacher wrote: "Congratulations for the victory you have won for the United States and mankind. Your courage and determination serve as a most welcome inspiration and example to those of us who, although seeing the right, may often hesitate to capture and preserve it."

The prayer, composed by the State Board of Regents and recommended for use by school districts, was brief: "Almighty God, we acknowledge our dependence upon Thee, and we beg Thy blessings upon us, our parents, our teachers and our country."

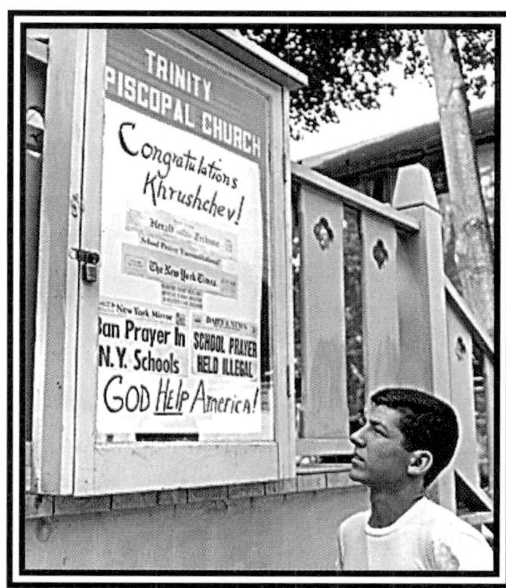

Newsday Photo / Walter Del Toro

Gary De Angelis reads a Northport church bulletin board in 1962 displaying headlines on the ruling, plus the rector's comments.

In its 6-1 decision, with the majority opinion written by Justice Hugo Black, the Supreme Court concluded that the prayer violated the First Amendment, which begins, "Congress shall make no law respecting an establishment of religion . . ." On the normally nine-member court, one justice was ill and another did not vote because he had not been on the court during the oral arguments.

"In this country," Black wrote, "it is no part of the business of government to compose official prayers for any group of the American people to recite as part of a religious program carried on by government . . . By the time of the adoption of the Constitution our history shows that there was a widespread awareness among many Americans of the dangers of a union of Church and State."

William J. Butler, the attorney who argued the plaintiffs' case before the court, was asked recently whether he thought the 1962 decision was vulnerable to attack.

"I think it's written in stone, Engel vs. Vitale," he said. 'Every year since then there's been an attempt to introduce a constitutional amendment to overrule the case. That has never happened. It can't . . . for that to happen, they'd have to monkey around with the First Amendment. They can't do that."

Engel said he had mixed feelings about the national publicity. "I know my name is in history," he said. "But I really wish it could have been resolved with the board of education. I'm proud of one thing: The Nassau Chapter of the American Civil Liberties Union evolved out of this case."

He was asked if, knowing what he knows now, he would do it again. "That's a strange question that I don't know the answer to. Knowing what happened . . . somebody had to do it. If religious freedom was going to have any meaning in America, somebody had to do it."

Her public slaying in Queens becomes a symbol of Americans' failure to get involved

The Killing of Kitty Genovese

BY MICHAEL DORMAN

It was just after 3 a.m.

A red Fiat rolled slowly through the darkness into a parking space adjacent to the Long Island Rail Road station in Kew Gardens. The young woman behind the wheel emerged from the car and locked it. She began the 100-foot walk toward her apartment house at 82-70 Austin St.

But then she spotted a man standing along her route. Apparently afraid, she changed direction and headed toward the intersection of Austin and Lefferts Boulevard — where there was a police call box.

Suddenly, the man overtook her and grabbed her. She screamed. Residents of nearby apartment houses turned on their lights and threw open their windows. The woman screamed again: "Oh, my God, he stabbed me! Please help me!"

A man in a window shouted: "Let that girl alone." The attacker walked away. Apartment lights went out and windows slammed shut. The victim staggered toward her apartment. But the attacker returned and stabbed her again.

"I'm dying!" she cried.

Windows opened again. The attacker entered a car and drove away. Windows closed, but the attacker soon came back again. His victim had crawled inside the front door of an apartment house at 82-62 Austin St. He found her sprawled on the floor and stabbed her still again. This time he killed her.

It was not until 3:50 that morning — March 13, 1964 — that a neighbor of the victim called police. Officers arrived two minutes later and found the body. They identified the victim as Catherine Genovese, 28, who had been returning from her job as manager of a bar in Hollis. Neighbors knew her not as Catherine but as Kitty.

Kitty Genovese: It was a name that would become symbolic in the public mind for a dark side of the national character. It would stand for Americans who were too indifferent or too frightened or too alienated or too self-absorbed to "get involved" in helping a fellow human being in dire trouble. A term "the Genovese syndrome" would be coined to describe the attitude.

Detectives investigating Genovese's murder discovered that no fewer than 38 of her neighbors had witnessed at least one of her killer's three attacks but had neither come to her aid nor called the police. The one call made to the police came after Genovese was already dead.

Assistant Chief Insp. Frederick Lussen, commander of Queens detectives, said that nothing in his 25 years of police work had shocked him so much as the apathy encountered on the Genovese murder. "As we have reconstructed the crime, the assailant had three chances to kill this woman during a 35-minute period," Lussen said. "If we had been called when he first attacked, this woman might not be dead now."

Expressions of outrage cascaded not only from public officials and private citizens in the New York area but from across the country. When detectives asked Genovese's neighbors why they had not taken action, many said they had been afraid or had not wanted to get involved. But Lt. Bernard Jacobs, in charge of the investigation, asked: "Where they are in their homes, near phones, why should they be afraid to call the police?"

Madeline Hartmann, a native of France, was 68 at the time of the murder and lived in the building where Genovese died. On the 20th anniversary of the murder, she said in an interview she did not feel bad about failing to call the police. "So many, many [other] times in the night, I heard screaming," she said. "I'm not the police and my English speaking is not perfect."

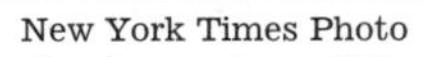

New York Times Photo

The scene above in Kew Gardens where Kitty Genovese, left, 1) parked in a station lot, 2) was attacked, 3) was assaulted again, and 4) was attacked for the third time.

AP Photo

There was no law, police officials conceded, that required someone witnessing a crime to report it to police. But they contended that morality should oblige a witness to do so.

Six days after the Genovese murder, police arrested a suspect — Winston Moseley, 29, a business-machine operator who lived with his wife and two children in Ozone Park. Moseley had no criminal record. But detectives said he swiftly confessed to killing not only Genovese but also two other women.

Moseley said he had "an uncontrollable urge to kill." He told detectives he prowled the streets at night while his wife, Elizabeth, was at work. "I chose women to kill because they were easier and didn't fight back," Moseley said.

Three months after Genovese's death, Moseley went on trial for her murder in State Supreme Court in Queens. He pleaded insanity and testified in painstaking detail about how he had stalked and stabbed Genovese to satisfy his supposedly uncontrollable urge. On June 11, 1964, a jury found him guilty. The following month, he was sentenced by Justice J. Irwin Shapiro to die in the electric chair at Sing Sing prison. "When I see this monster, I wouldn't hesitate to pull the switch myself," the judge said.

But in 1967 the State Court of Appeals reduced the punishment to life imprisonment on the ground that Shapiro had erred in refusing to admit evidence on Moseley's mental condition at a pre-sentence hearing.

A year later, taken from prison to a Buffalo hospital for minor surgery, Moseley struck a prison guard and escaped. He obtained a gun, held five persons hostage, raped one of them and squared off for a showdown with FBI agents in an apartment building. Neil Welch, agent in charge of the Buffalo FBI office, entered the second-floor apartment where Moseley made his stand. Welch and Moseley pointed guns at each other for half an hour as they negotiated. Finally, Moseley surrendered.

Moseley's periodic requests for parole have repeatedly been denied. During one parole hearing in 1984, Moseley volunteered that he had written Genovese's relatives a letter "to apologize for the inconvenience I caused."

A parole commissioner responded acidly: "That's a good way to say it. They were inconvenienced."

Moseley also told the board the murder was as difficult for him as his victim. "For a victim outside, it's a one-time or one-hour or one-minute affair," he said. "But, for the person who's caught, it's forever."

In 1995, seeking a new trial, Moseley obtained a hearing in Brooklyn federal court. Some of Genovese's relatives, unable to bring themselves to attend the original trial, appeared at the hearing. Genovese's sister, Susan Wakeman, said outside the courtroom: "We don't blame the people who were there that night and might have heard her crying. Only one person killed my sister, and he should die the way she did."

The court denied Moseley's petition. He is now convict No. 64A0102 at the Great Meadow state prison in Comstock, N.Y.

Over the years, there have been various scholarly studies of "the Genovese syndrome." At a three-day Catherine Genovese Memorial Conference on Bad Samaritanism at Fordham University in 1984, City University of New York psychology professor Stanley Milgram capsulized the questions raised by the Genovese murder.

"The case touched on a fundamental issue of the human condition, our primordial nightmare," Milgram said. "If we need help, will those around us stand around and let us be destroyed or will they come to our aid? Are those other creatures out there to help us sustain our life and values, or are we individual flecks of dust just floating around in a vacuum?"

Michael Dorman is a freelance writer.

Land deals are a gold mine for corrupt officials, until the reporters begin digging

LI Muckrakers Strike Pay Dirt

BY BOB KEELER
STAFF WRITER

As the wave of population growth swept eastward across Long Island after World War II, it created both immense wealth and boundless opportunities for some corrupt politicians to convert part of that wealth to their own uses.

Both the wealth and the corruption were rooted in the land, the vast, evergreen commodity that played the same role on Long Island that oil and cattle played in Texas.

For those with a sharp real estate eye, the population surge wrought a lucrative transformation: On land that formerly had nurtured only large trees and small wildlife, the owners could prosper by offering what the arriving multitudes needed — shopping centers, apartment complexes and gas stations.

In the late 1960s, the land and the corruption became the raw materials of an extensive Newsday investigation that broke new ground in investigative journalism and educated readers about pervasive abuses of power.

Using insider knowledge, for example, a politician could learn where the exits for the Long Island Expressway would be, buy that land cheap, and sell it profitably for the construction of gas stations.

At the time, doing that wasn't illegal, said Bob Greene, the top investigative journalist who led Newsday's investigation, but it was wrong. "There should be a level playing field for every citizen," Greene said.

Another key was town government's power of zoning. By changing the zoning of land, politicians increase its value, because an acre zoned for stores or garden apartments produces more income than one zoned for houses. Some officials voted to rezone land in which they or associates had an interest.

For years, nobody noticed.

The first scandals broke in 1955, when state auditors learned that the Suffolk County treasurer's office had used improper procedures in selling land that the county acquired from owners who had not paid property taxes.

That triggered investigations by special prosecutors, lent impetus to a countywide vote to adopt a more professional charter form of government, and helped elect a Democratic Board of Supervisors and county executive, H. Lee Dennison, in a Republican-dominated county. But the corruption didn't end.

In 1964, a Newsday reporter, Manny Topol, became curious about an announcement that the Town of Islip planned to buy land near town hall and build more office space. When Topol asked who owned the property, he got no immediate answer from Walter Conlon, the town attorney. Topol told another Newsday reporter, Alan Eysen (now a consultant to Republicans).

Digging through records, Eysen found that the brother of Conlon's law partner was president of the corporation that owned the property. Later, Eysen found this pattern: The town would reject rezoning applications from ordinary citizens, who grew weary and sold the land. The new owners, well-connected politicians and cronies, hiding behind dummy corporations, got rezonings easily.

Eysen and others, including Greene, tried to elicit interest in the story from Kirk Price, the Suffolk editor. But Price was quietly acquiring land near MacArthur Airport and pushing in Newsday for airport expansion, which would increase the value of this property.

Early in 1967, Price died. His successor, Art Perfall, was enthusiastic about investigating. So Greene, Eysen and another reporter, Ray Larsen, began the long investigation into what became known as "the Suffolk scandals."

Newsday Photo / Ike Eichorn

Babylon Town Republican leader Fred Fellman leaves court in Riverhead in 1971 on his way to jail after sentencing; he had pleaded guilty to grand larceny.

Quickly, Greene developed a source, dubbed Zip, who fed the "Greene Team" information on dummy corporations and the politicians behind them. Another member of the team, Ken Crowe, had a genius for examining real estate records and figuring out the complex deals at the heart of the corruption. Greene's skill lay in tying it all together.

"Greene had an incredible ability to see connections that the rest of us hadn't seen," said one team member, Brian Donovan.

The first stories on Islip began running on Sept. 28, 1967. The third day of the series showed how Councilman Donald Kuss had supervised airport development for Islip, while acquiring an undisclosed interest in land at the airport entrance. It also contained a separate story, "Editor Tied to Kuss Deal," about Kirk Price's $33,000 profit on land at the airport. Conlon and Kuss later went on trial and drew one-year jail terms.

In the aftermath of the series on Islip Republicans, Greene noticed what happened in towns not included in the series: Voters ousted incumbents. "The people themselves, reading that series, could see the same things happening in their own towns," Greene said.

Newsday Photo, 1966

Newsday Suffolk editor Kirk Price, who profited from a questionable land deal

From Islip, the team turned its attention to Brookhaven. There, they had no source like Zip. So they relied on documents. "We would put a zoning map on the wall and draw a circle around every gas station, garden apartment and major shopping center rezoning and just backtrack it," Crowe said.

Among other things, the 1968 Brookhaven stories showed how Councilmen George Fuchs and Clarence Hough voted for the rezoning that made Smith Haven Mall possible, and private firms in which the two were involved got $700,000 worth of business on constructing the mall. Fuchs was acquitted at trial, but later pleaded guilty to a misdmeanor income tax charge and drew a $2,500 fine. Hough died before his case could be tried.

The stories also showed how town Republican leader Richard Zeidler, as chairman of the Suffolk County Water Authority, profited by helping to place a county well near land in which he had a hidden interest.

In 1969, the team focused on Babylon, where a feud between town Republican leader Fred Fellman and his wife produced revealing documents about Fellman's questionable practices at a trailer park that he ran. He later pleaded guilty to grand larceny for stealing from a trailer firm and went to jail.

For the three-year investigation, Newsday won a Pulitzer Prize for public service in 1970. Before his sentencing, Fellman showed up at the paper's Pulitzer party and told the staff that Newsday couldn't have won it without him.

Perhaps more important than the few jail sentences, the long investigation pioneered document-based investigative reporting, led to some tightening of laws and showed Long Islanders the underlying corruption.

"None of the latter-day scandals had anywhere near the impact that the one in the '50s did because the one in the '50s led to a complete revolution in the form of the government," said Lee Koppelman, executive director of the Long Island Regional Planning Board. But during the '60s scandals, Koppelman quipped that Newsday should be district attorney.

Greene, who now teaches journalism at Hofstra University, summed it up this way: "We educated future reporters to the fact that this is one of the ways that politicians steal." But journalists must remain vigilant. "Reform just makes people figure out ways to do it a different way."

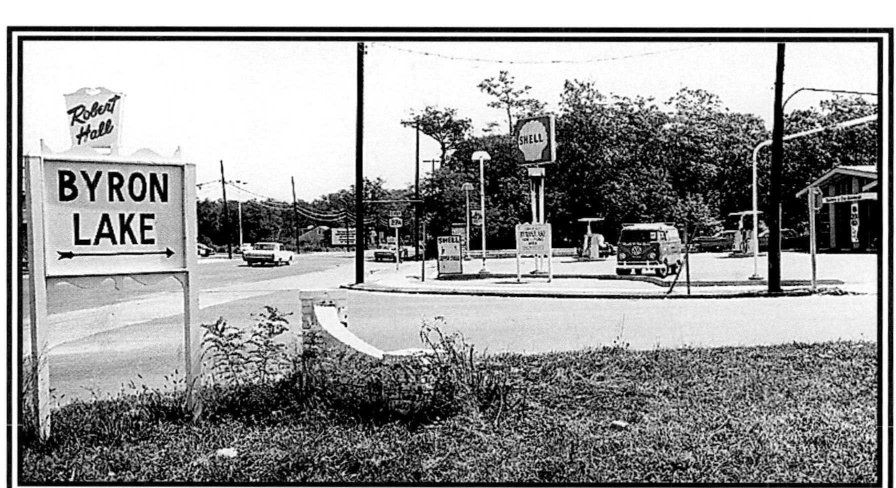

Newsday Photo, 1967 / Walter del Toro

Newsday's 1967 series revealed that a service station was built at Bay View Drive and Montauk Highway in Oakdale in the early '60s after rezoning was granted to a corporation co-owned by the wife of the Suffolk Republican Party treasurer. A previous owner had failed to win rezoning.

FAST FORWARD

Newsday Photo / Harvey Weber

A 1965 photo shows a buildup of detergent foam in Centerport.

DETERGENTS AND POLLUTION

The Suffolk County Legislature was on an environmental roll in 1971. Having dispensed with DDT, county officials turned to a menace bubbling in the county's water supply — washday detergents. Suffolk passed the nation's first ban on the sale of all detergents, forcing residents to use regular soap for laundry.

As early as 1955, the county health department had been receiving complaints, mostly from homeowners in Islip and Babylon, of bad-smelling, bad-tasting and foaming water. The Suffolk law banned alcohol sulfate, the dirt-loosening agent in detergents, which was not breaking down in the underground water supply.

But times and detergents changed. Most detergents became biodegradable. Most neighborhoods with cesspools were connected to public sewer systems. In 1981, the health department reported that lifting the ban would have "no significant harmful environmental impact."

Legis. Joseph Rizzo (R-Islip Terrace), sponsor of repeal, voiced a more commercial rationale: Suffolk shoppers were slipping across the border to Nassau County where the sale of detergents was not banned. They were also purchasing other household items in Nassau supermarkets. Suffolk was losing the sales tax, and Nassau was gaining.

The 10-year-old ordinance was repealed.

— Rhoda Amon

Suffolk activists lead the fight to save wildlife in the 1960s

The Anti-DDT Vanguard

BY RHODA AMON
STAFF WRITER

A massive fish kill in a Yaphank lake jump-started a whole national movement.

The spraying of DDT had been wreaking havoc with America's wildlife for several decades, but it was the dying fish in Yaphank that brought together 20 scientists and a lawyer in a pioneer court action that probably improved the lives of most Long Islanders. Possibly, most Americans. Certainly, all osprey and most fish.

In 1966, a Patchogue attorney, Victor J. Yannacone, brought suit against the Suffolk County Mosquito Control Commission to stop the spraying of the deadly pesticide in local marshes. He was prompted, he said, by the insistence of his wife, Carol, a biologist, that he "do something" about the fish massacre.

Sounding the alarm at the same time was the Brookhaven Town Natural Resources Committee, an informal group of scientists and baymen. Vanishing birds, crabs and butterflies were signaling that something was definitely wrong in the Long Island environment.

One of those scientists, Charles Wurster, wrote a letter to the editor — Yannacone saw the letter and the union of science and law resulted. It led to Suffolk becoming the first county in the nation to ban DDT. New York State followed in 1970, and in 1972, DDT was banned nationwide, resulting in a rebound of populations of osprey, bald eagles and other imperiled birdlife.

"We were a handful of people with one goal. The whole movement that would develop was beyond our wildest dreams," recalls Wurster, then an associate professor at the State University at Stony Brook and one of the founders of the Environmental Defense Fund, which operated out of a one-room attic of the Stony Brook post office.

In support of the class-action suit (which stated that Carol A. Yannacone and everyone else had the right to enjoy a clean environment), the scientists wrote: "Continuing to use DDT against mosquitoes in Suffolk County would be like using atomic weapons to control criminals in New York City."

A Brookhaven naturalist, Dennis Puleston, explained recently: "DDT was effective against malarial mosquitoes in New Guinea during World War II. After the war, it went into high production. Massive amounts were produced to spray all insects. No one knew what effect it would have on nontargeted organisms." Aerial sprays spread, he said. Traces of DDT were found in dead penguins in the Antarctic.

Appeals from the scientists had no effect on the Suffolk commission bent on "largely unsuccessful efforts to reduce mosquito populations," Puleston said.

But in 1966, a State Supreme Court judge ordered the commission to show why it should not stop spraying the chemical. Puleston painted seven watercolors to show a trial judge how DDT was destroying the health of Long Island's creatures.

One watercolor depicted how the blue-claw crab ingested DDT from the mussels it ate. "So that's why there are no more crabs in Great South Bay," Justice Jack Stanislaw exclaimed.

Though the court ultimately ruled against the suit, it didn't matter. The Suffolk County Legislature ordered the commission to stop using DDT to kill mosquitoes.

The scientists, incorporating as the Environmental Defense Fund in 1967, adopted Yannacone's motto: "Sue the ———."

Puleston, then technical information director at the Brookhaven National Laboratory, was the first chairman. Now 92, he recalls the early struggles with little funding. "And the big chemical industry fought tenaciously to stop the bans."

But a new age of environmental enthusiasm was dawning. The Suffolk scientists filed a suit to stop a Michigan plan to spray the toxic chemical dieldrin against Japanese beetles. "Appeals for our aid in fighting environmental threats were pouring in," Puleston said. The first Earth Day was celebrated in 1970.

Surprisingly, although the conservation movement started before Puleston was born, few thought of litigation to stop pollution. "There was no such subject as environmental law," Yannacone says. "We were the first to sue a chemical."

Another Long Islander, President Theodore Roosevelt, hosted the first White House Conference on the conservation ethic in 1908. With characteristic vigor, he jacked up the nation's stock of preserved forests to 194 million acres. Forest conservation continued during Franklin Roosevelt's New Deal, but was shelved by World War II.

Then in 1962 Rachel Carson's book, "Silent Spring," alerted the public to the wide destruction of wildlife being caused by toxic pesticides.

"But even Rachel Carson didn't know the full effects of DDT," Puleston says. He came to the realization after years of studying the osprey on Gardiners Island, starting in 1948 with permission from the Gardiner family. "There were 300 nesting ospreys, one of the world's highest concentrations," he says. "By the '60s we could find only two or three chicks."

Wurster had a similar experience studying songbirds at Dartmouth before coming to Stony Brook. Now 67 and retired, he continues the battle for the ecosystem as an Environmental Defense Fund trustee, along with Art Cooley, leader of the original Brookhaven group.

Much of the effort among scientists is now focused on reducing carbon dioxide emissions, which they say are accelerating dangerous global warming.

Newsday Photo / Thomas A. Ferrara

Naturalist Dennis Puleston, above, painted the osprey at right. In the 1960s, he argued against the use of DDT by reporting the harm done to the osprey and other species.

Grumman's lunar module ferries astronauts on a dangerous mission to the moon

A Giant Step for LI

By Michael Dorman

'Quantity light."

Astronaut Edwin (Buzz) Aldrin signaled an alert to Neil Armstrong — commander of the first manned spacecraft attempting to land on the moon. The signal light indicated they had only 114 seconds' worth of fuel remaining for the descent engine taking them to the lunar surface. If the fuel ran out, they would have to abort the Apollo 11 mission and attempt a risky return to Earth.

But they had not yet found a suitable landing spot. Their lunar excursion module, code-named Eagle and built on Long Island by Grumman Aircraft Engineering Corp., was operating on a computer inadvertently taking them down into a boulder-strewn crater. A landing there might be fatal. The LEM might crash into a boulder. They might topple over. They might land at an angle greater than 30 degrees from the vertical — making a return takeoff impossible.

NASA Photo

With Earth rising above the moon's horizon, the lunar module returns to the command module in 1969 after Neil Armstrong and Edwin (Buzz) Aldrin took their historic walks. So far, the Grumman-made lunar module had performed as planned.

Armstrong made a crucial decision. He took control of the spacecraft away from the computer and flew manually past the rocky crater.

Over the radio crackled the voice of Charlie Duke, the capsule communicator at Mission Control in Houston.

"Thirty seconds."

Thirty seconds of fuel — and maybe not even that, for estimates were not infallibly precise. Finding a spot smoother and more level than the rocky field, Armstrong descended toward it.

"Forty feet," Aldrin reported to Mission Control. "Things look good. Picking up some dust. Drifting to the right a little. Contact light! OK. Engine stop." When the engine stopped, by some estimates, the fuel tank was empty.

A short time later, Armstrong reported: "Houston. Tranquility Base here. The Eagle has landed."

It was 4:17 p.m., July 20, 1969. Wild applause, cheers and tears filled Mission Control and Grumman's Bethpage plant — scenes mirrored at a seemingly countless number of locations throughout the world. In one of the great adventures in the history of mankind, humans had made the 225,000-mile journey to the moon.

But back on Long Island the jubilation was mixed with deep concern. Grumman engineers were troubled by doubts largely unrecognized by the public. The astronauts' journey back from the moon would be far more difficult and infinitely more dangerous than the trip to the lunar surface. The question was: Would they actually be able to return safely to Earth?

* * *

Thomas J. Kelly, the propulsion expert who headed Grumman's space-exploration operations and became known as the father of the LEM, had been troubleshooting problems constantly throughout the flight. He was stationed in the Spacecraft Analysis Room adjacent to Mission Control at the National Aeronautics and Space Administration Center in Houston.

A short, dark-haired man with a soft voice and an unflappable air, Kelly had first come under Grumman's wing when he won a scholarship from the company upon graduation from Mepham High School in North Bellmore. He used the scholarship to study engineering at Cornell University, then took a master's from Columbia. Throughout college, he worked summers as an apprentice engineer at Grumman. After college, he served as a Grumman propulsion engineer on missile and military aircraft projects. Now, at 50, he found himself directing Grumman's mission to the moon.

The critical byword for Kelly and other Grumman engineers designing the LEM had been redundancy. The moon mission presented so many risks to the astronauts' lives that the engineers installed a seemingly endless array of redundant backup systems to guard against possible operations failures. In some cases, there were backups upon backups upon backups. But weight limitations made total redundancy impossible.

So there could be no backup for the critical rocket engine designed to lift the Eagle from the moon for the return trip toward Earth. If that engine failed, the astronauts would be stranded forever on the moon.

"There would be nothing we could do except watch them die a long, slow death," Kelly said recently.

* * *

Tom Kelly and Grumman had ridden a long, tortuous flight path merely to gain the opportunity to prevent such an unthinkable disaster. In the early 1960s, Grumman — known chiefly as a manufacturer of Navy warplanes — bid unsuccessfully on a series of government aerospace contracts. Then, with NASA's encouragement, the company volunteered to develop at its own expense a proposal for the space vehicle intended to land on the moon — a vehicle then called simply the Bug.

There was stiff competition among various companies for the contract to build the Bug. NASA was considering three methods of carrying out the mission — a direct ascent to the lunar surface using a gigantic rocket; an Earth-orbiting rendezvous technique; and a plan that would put a command vehicle in lunar orbit, where it would release a two-stage spacecraft for a round trip to the moon, then a return trip to Earth.

"We thought the rendezvous in lunar orbit was much more efficient than the other ideas," Kelly said. "It wouldn't take all the weight to the moon that the others would. You could leave a lot of the weight in lunar orbit."

While the engineers were drawing their plans, political forces were at work to bring the LEM contract to Grumman — with its contemplated millions of dollars and thousands of jobs for the Long Island economy. Nassau Democratic chairman John F. English, a close associate of President John F. Kennedy, made frequent visits to the White House with Nassau County Executive Eugene H. Nickerson to lobby on Grumman's behalf. As English would put it in an interview not long before his death in 1987: "I was up to my ——— in the LEM program."

On Nov. 7, 1962 — deliberately waiting until a day after Election Day so it would not be accused of playing politics with a huge government project — the space agency awarded Grumman the LEM contract. It approved the company's plan for a rendezvous in lunar orbit. Whoops and hollers resounded through the Grumman plant at news of the contract award. The initial contract called for $350 million worth of work. But, in the end, the job would be worth $2.3 billion. At its peak, 7,000 Grumman employees would be assigned to the LEM.

Many of those who worked on the LEM said a contagious enthusiasm and camaraderie swept through the work force during the project. Lifetime friendships were forged. "It was a very exciting time," Tom Kelly said. "We let our imaginations run wild — figuring out how to do every step we had to do."

Often, Grumman employees could be seen in the parking lots after work — drawing diagrams in the dust on their cars to demonstrate how certain problems on the LEM could be solved.

Although the acronym LEM stood for lunar excursion module, NASA dropped the word "excursion" from the name on the theory that it sounded frivolous — perhaps calling up visions of picnic journeys — and changed the acronym to LM. But the original LEM tag stuck. The space vehicle that emerged from Bethpage actually did resemble a bug, and not a particularly graceful one at that. Atop four spindly legs stood a lumpy body with what appeared to be spare parts sticking out at bizarre angles. The spacecraft basically consisted of two stages — a descent stage to carry the astronauts from the command vehicle to the moon and an ascent stage to separate from the other section on the moon and return the astronauts to the command vehicle for the trip back to Earth.

"Form followed function," Kelly explained. "It came out the way it came out." Grumman engineers realized, for instance, they could reduce the LEM's weight by cutting back the number of certain rocket-propellant tanks from four to two. But that would remove a semblance of symmetry. "It made it look as if the LEM had mumps," Kelly said. "But so what? So we did it with two tanks."

Roger Carpenter, who served on the LEM engineering materials review board, said recently that there was a general misconception about how the spacecraft was built. "The LEM was not mass-produced," he said. "It was entirely handmade." The LEM had more than a million parts, and human hands worked on every one of them. Grumman would eventually build more than a dozen LEMs, and all would be different.

"My job was to fix problems," Carpenter said. "Every day, we had some. We had some windows, for example, that were giving us problems. The LEM, of course, had to be able to withstand very high temperatures. But, when heated, these windows would crack into thousands of pieces. We worked and worked on it, and determined it was a bonding problem. We worked with the supplier and corrected it."

Steven Hornacek, a telemetry engineer, recalls taking part in sensitive tests on the critical engine designed to lift the spacecraft from the moon. There were numerous valves on the engine. "All of them had to open at exactly the same time and with the same force," Hornacek says. "The tests had to assure that they would do that." Hornacek also recalls tests where the LEM was taken into a hangar and, in conditions approximating the moon's gravity, was dropped from a height of about 20 feet to simulate a lunar landing.

There were also two preparatory LEM flights only months before the first manned moon landing. In the second, Apollo 10, the LEM flew within 50,000 feet of the moon and sent back vivid pictures of the surface.

For seven years, Kelly and his team labored toward the moment when the LEM would be carried aloft on the first manned moon trip. They progressed through simulated flights, actual test flights and the final preparatory flights — with hundreds of failures, bumps and course corrections along the way. They were still troubled by their main concern — whether the astronauts could be safely returned to Earth. But they were forced to move ahead. It was time, at last, for the main event.

* * *

The Saturn V rocket sat majestically on the launching pad at Cape Kennedy, Fla., bathed in the brilliant glow of floodlights during the early morning hours of July 16. Poised to send the Apollo 11 crew into the heavens, it would be the heaviest vehicle ever fired aloft — 6,484,289 pounds.

Joseph Gavin, Tom Kelly's boss and Grumman's senior vice president in charge of space operations, was at Cape Kennedy to supervise the LEM preparations for the launch. "There had been a meeting three days before the launch of all the senior people involved in getting ready for the flight," Gavin recalled in a recent interview.

"My job was to say the LEM was ready. I said it was. Then, the night before the launch, there were some questions about the loading of a critical helium tank on the LEM. I stayed at the Cape until about 9 o'clock to review and approve the procedures being used. Then I went back to my motel to catch a few hours' sleep, but was back at the Cape by 1 a.m."

Neil Armstrong and Buzz Aldrin, each 39, boarded the spacecraft on the launching pad along with Michael Collins, 38, the third astronaut chosen for the mission. Collins would not descend to the lunar surface. Instead,

FAST FORWARD

AN EMERGENCY CALL TO KELLY: TROUBLE ON APOLLO 13

On April 13, 1970, nine months after the first lunar landing, another spacecraft on a manned moon mission was speeding through the heavens 205,000 miles from Earth. Suddenly, there was a loud bang.

There had been an explosion in a liquid oxygen tank aboard the Apollo 13 spacecraft, endangering the flight and its three astronauts — James Lovell, Fred Haise and Jack Swigert.

Thomas J. Kelly, the Grumman engineer known as the father of the LEM spacecraft, was on temporary leave at the time to take a management course at the Massachusetts Institute of Technology. An urgent telephone call asked him to return immediately to Grumman's Bethpage headquarters and help direct attempts to rescue the astronauts.

Kelly quickly chartered an airplane and flew to Bethpage. There, he worked ceaselessly for three days to find a way to bring the astronauts safely back. Teaming with John Aaron, a NASA mission controller, Kelly refined various rescue suggestions — making adjustments to meet objections by various experts that this plan or that was too ambitious or impractical. In the end, all the work succeeded. The astronauts made a safe emergency return to Earth.

For the broad range of his work on the space program, Kelly was awarded NASA's Distinguished Public Service Medal in 1973.

Now 79 and retired, Kelly lives in Cutchogue. He peers often through a telescope perched in his living room — capturing glimpses of waterfowl taking flight over Peconic Bay. That seems only appropriate for a man who devoted much of his working life to devising means of flight — to the moon and back.

— Michael Dorman

Newsday Photo / Bill Davis

Tom Kelly holds a model of his proudest creation, the LEM.

Northrop Grumman Photo

Tom Kelly, center, and Grumman co-workers on the lunar lander project pose after the launch of Apollo X in May, 1969. From left are Arnold Whitaker, Robert Carbee, company president Llewellyn Evans, Kelly, Jim Leather, Frank Canning and John Coursen. During the Apollo X dress rehearsal, astronauts orbited the moon in the lunar module but did not land.

he would pilot a command vehicle called the Columbia, from which the LEM would be launched to the moon. Collins would orbit the moon until Armstrong and Aldrin returned to the command vehicle in the LEM for the trip back to Earth.

"It was tense waiting for the launch," Joe Gavin said. "The LEM had been tested again and again. I'd already made the commitment to launch. I was pretty confident, but there's always doubt."

After a smooth countdown, the Saturn V rocket lifted off launching pad 39A with wave after wave of thunderous roar and a sense of limitless power. It was 9:32 a.m., just 724 milliseconds behind schedule. As the rocket rose, it shook loose more than 1,000 pounds of ice that had formed on its sides.

The spacecraft was boosted by a rocket into Earth orbit 12 minutes after liftoff. Two and a half hours into the flight, an engine fired for five minutes and sent the vehicle racing through space at 24,245 mph — pulling it out of the Earth's gravitational force and speeding it toward the moon. Lunar gravity took hold 43,495 miles from the moon.

The astronauts said little during the moon-bound flight. "It's all dead air and static," a Mission Control official reported. But the conversation picked up after the LEM separated from the moon-orbiting command vehicle — sending Armstrong and Aldrin cruising toward the lunar surface.

"Eagle has wings," Armstrong reported. As the astronauts later circled the moon, searching for a landing spot and sending back to Earth television pictures of the surface, a Mission Control capsule communicator asked: "Would you care to comment on some of those craters as we go by?"

"Just going over Mount Marilyn," Armstrong replied, describing a peak NASA had named for the wife of another astronaut, James Lovell. "Now we're looking at what we call Boot Hill."

* * *

Only minutes after the LEM landed on the moon, there was a demonstration of just how many potential catastrophes confronted the mission. Tom Kelly abruptly found himself in the middle of tense deliberations aimed at averting disaster.

He and other experts in Houston noticed on their flight-monitoring screens alarming increases in the temperature and pressure readings on one of the Eagle's descent-stage fuel lines. After the descent engine shut down, a blockage had apparently developed in the fuel line. Kelly assumed that liquid helium had frozen a slug of fuel left in the line. Residual heat from the engine, which had been operating at 5,000 degrees Fahrenheit when the spacecraft landed, was moving up toward the frozen fuel.

"We got nervous because, if the fuel gets hot enough, it's liable to detonate," Kelly said in a recent interview. Such an explosion could injure the astronauts or wreck the spacecraft. The fuel temperature rose from 20 degrees to 200. One expert said: "Another 50 degrees and all bets are off."

Some engineers called for an immediate abort of the flight, but that was impossible for technical reasons. Kelly suggested "burping" the engine, restarting it at 10 percent power for an instant to relieve the pressure.

"But then, guess what?" Kelly said. "The problem went away." Without any corrective action, the temperature inexplicably dropped to normal.

Kelly knew, however, that the mission could not get that lucky often. And he could not forget the risks inherent in the liftoff from the moon.

* * *

Armstrong and Aldrin were supposed to take a rest period after the LEM landed on the moon. But they were keyed up and not sleepy, so they received permission to move directly to their next scheduled activity — actually walking on the moon. NASA officials hurriedly called on duty Mission Control's so-called Green Team, assigned to monitor the moon walk.

John Devaney, a Grumman engineer on duty in Houston, had one particular concern about the walk. "The landing gear on the LEM was designed to crush during the landing on the moon," Devaney said in a recent interview. "It was full of crunched tinfoil, so it would crush on touchdown. But Armstrong and Aldrin put the LEM down so gently that the landing gear didn't crush. That left the LEM higher off the moon's surface than we expected. I was worried that, when Armstrong dropped off the ladder to the surface, the bottom of the ladder would be so high that he couldn't climb back into the LEM."

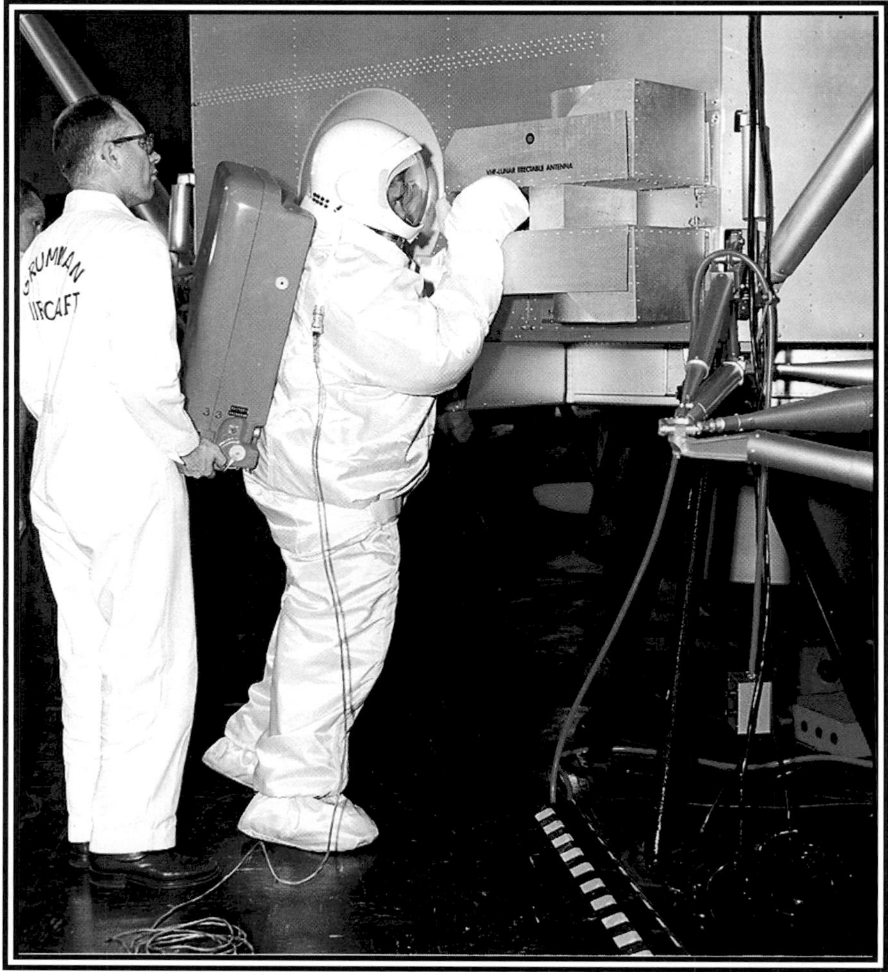

Northrop Grumman Photo

Astronaut Roger Chaffee, above right, practices removing an antenna from stowage on a lunar module mockup in 1964. Three years later, Chaffee and two other astronauts were killed in a fire at Cape Kennedy. Below, Edwin Aldrin walks on the moon near the lunar module during the Apollo 11 mission in July, 1969.

NASA Photo

At 10:56 p.m. July 20, Armstrong began descending the ladder in his bulky pressurized suit for the long-anticipated space walk. He seemed to drop gingerly from the bottom step.

"That's one small step for man, one giant leap for mankind," he said as he became the first human to set foot on the moon. Those were the words he spoke. Those were the words recorded for posterity. But actually he had misspoken, and the words — as delivered — did not quite make sense. It later developed that what he had actually meant to say was: "That's one small step for *a* man, one giant leap for mankind."

In what seemed a cautious gait, Armstrong shuffled about the lunar landscape. "The surface is fine and powdery," he reported. "It adheres in fine layers, like powdered charcoal, to the soles and sides of my foot. I can see the footprints of my boots and the treads in the fine, sandy particles."

Aldrin soon joined him. They walked and jumped across the lunar surface for two hours and 14 minutes as a television camera they had set up nearby transmitted live pictures back to millions of fascinated viewers. They deployed the equipment for a batch of continuing experiments and gathered 21 moon rocks. They also planted an American flag on the moon, not as a sign of conquest but as a symbol of national pride. When it was time to return to the LEM, they had no trouble negotiating their way back up the ladder — uncrushed landing gear or no uncrushed landing gear.

* * *

Armstrong and Aldrin were poised in the LEM for takeoff from the moon, knowing full well they were about to stake their lives on the 172-pound ascent engine designed to lift them off the lunar surface. Grumman had tested the engine successfully more than 3,000 times. But, if it somehow failed, the astronauts were well aware they would be stranded on the moon.

Since there was only one ascent engine, Grumman had built a simple — and, it was hoped, problem-free — device. "It was pressure-fed, with no pumps," Tom Kelly said. "The propellants ignited on contact, with no ignition system."

Now, as the engine awaited its critical test, Mission Control radioed: "You're clear for takeoff."

"Roger, understand," Aldrin replied. "We're No. 1 on the runway."

Seconds later, the engine fired with a burst of energy. The LEM's ascent stage separated from the descent stage and rose smoothly from the moon. The Grumman engine had performed flawlessly.

Tom Kelly, in the Spacecraft Analysis Room in Houston, knew immediately the liftoff was successful. "Once you get the signal for liftoff, it goes very quickly — bang, like that," he said. "We were very worried about it because the engine and a lot of other things have to work simultaneously. It either goes or it doesn't. Fortunately, it went."

After a four-hour flight, the LEM rendezvoused on the dark side of the moon with the Columbia command vehicle piloted by Michael Collins. The two vehicles docked. Armstrong and

Please see **MOON** on **Next Page**

Grumman LEM Visits the Moon

MOON from **Preceding Page**

Aldrin were so eager to rejoin Collins that they slid through the passage into the command vehicle even before Houston directed them to do so. A Mission Control official, with a touch of pique, told them: "You beat us to the punch."

Columbia's long journey back to Earth was so smooth that only one of three scheduled course-correcting rocket firings actually became necessary. The astronauts slept and relaxed for such long periods that Mission Control once radioed: "Apollo 11, this is Houston. Are you still up there?"

At dawn on July 24, Apollo 11 splashed into the South Pacific near the Navy aircraft carrier Hornet. The Columbia was almost instantly capsized by 6-foot ocean swells. But a recovery team from the Hornet quickly righted the spacecraft by using large flotation bags. On a rubber life raft, the astronauts were scrubbed down with disinfectants to ward off health hazards encountered on the mission. They were then lifted by helicopter to the Hornet to begin 18 days of quarantine.

At Mission Control, where swarms of people were breaking out the traditional splashdown cigars, a 20-by-10-foot television screen usually employed to display flight information was showing John F. Kennedy's challenge to Americans: "I believe that this nation should commit itself to achieving the goal, before this decade is out, of landing a man on the moon and returning him safely to Earth."

Now, a new message flashed across the screen:

"Mission accomplished — July, 1969."

* * *

Since the LEM mission effectively ended when the vehicle docked with Columbia, Tom Kelly returned to Long Island to await the end of Apollo 11's journey. He and about 100 other Grumman employees watched the splashdown on television in the Mission Support Room at Bethpage.

"It was a moment of triumph," Kelly said. "We were watching the people in Mission Control on television, lighting cigars. We didn't have any cigars, so we cheered and patted each others' backs."

Looking back on the Apollo 11 Mission with the perspective of almost three decades, Kelly says, "It was the greatest thing in my career. And, in hindsight, it was even more significant than we thought at the time. It got NASA finally moving on some broad-based programs that are producing some marvels today. We've now made unmanned landings on Mars. We're learning an enormous amount about the universe. And none of this would have happened without Apollo 11."

Michael Dorman is a freelance writer.

FAST FORWARD

NEIL ARMSTRONG'S LI CONNECTION

It would seem any company would boast if Neil A. Armstrong, the first human to step foot on the moon, had been named its chairman.

Not AIL Systems Inc., the Deer Park defense electroncs company.

Armstrong, who landed on the moon July 20, 1969, was named AIL's chairman in January, 1989, long after he left the U.S. space program for civilian life. But neither AIL nor its parent at the time, Eaton Corp. of Cleveland, made any public announcement of Armstrong's appointment. It came out during an interview an AIL executive had with a Newsday reporter on an unrelated matter.

AIL and Eaton said there was nothing secret about the appointment. It had, they said, more to do with Armstrong's long-held, deeply rooted desire for personal privacy. After his historic moon landing, watched by the entire world, Armstrong retreated to the anonymity of the business world, shunning most interviews.

Newsday Photo, 1993 / Dick Kraus

Armstrong, first man on the moon and, more recently, chairman of AIL Systems

Armstrong, an Ohio native, had been a board member of Eaton, a company that makes auto parts and other machinery, and which owned AIL. In the late 1980s, AIL was struggling to build defense electronics equipment for the Air Force's B-1B nuclear bomber. The company's work had been sharply criticized by the Air Force and some members of Congress. Eaton asked Armstrong to take rein of the company and help it wade through its B-1B work, as well as through the company's problems with the Air Force and Congress.

AIL's day-to-day business is run by James Smith, the company's president and chief executive officer, who reports to Armstrong. Armstrong, 67, does not spend much time on the Island, appearing about once a month at AIL for board meetings. He maintains a residence in Ohio.

— **James Bernstein**

KEEPERS OF THE FLAME AT NORTHROP GRUMMAN

Newsday Photos / Bill Davis

Members of a volunteer group of retirees at Northrop Grumman in Bethpage who restore old aircraft. Behind them is a F4F Wildcat bound for Long Island's Cradle of Aviation Museum. They also are rebuilding an F8F Bearcat fighter for the government of Thailand.

A lawyer in Alaska wants to rebuild an old Grumman Goose seaplane. A British military expert needs data on Norway's Penguin missile. A historian seeks specifics about the lunar module.

They turn to the History Center at Northrop Grumman in Bethpage. The center holds hundreds of items, from founder Leroy Grumman's pilot's license to early models of classic Grumman aircraft.

Because it is maintained only part time by a handful of retired engineers, it cannot be opened to the public. Still, those volunteers, men passionate about aircraft, work Mondays and Wednesdays to catalog and burnish Grumman's history.

"We answer mail from all over the world," says Lawrence Feliu, 73, of Uniondale. "We don't like to say to the person that we can't answer the question."

Another group in Bethpage also is keeping Grumman history alive. In a Plant 1 hangar, about 20 volunteers, also retirees, work each Tuesday on old Grumman aircraft. Headed by retired production worker Augie Ripp of Babylon, the group restores planes for the likes of the Smithsonian Institution and Long Island's Cradle of Aviation Museum.

Volunteers Roger Seybel, Lawrence Feliu, Lynn McDonald and Robert Tallman, from left, pose with a model of an F6F Hellcat at the Northrop Grumman History Center.

Home Was So Close, Yet So Far

An astronaut's view of the Island

By Georgina Martorella
STAFF WRITER

Every morning for a week in the summer of 1996, Kevin Kregel would wake up, have his breakfast and take a look out the window at Long Island.

It was some view. His window was on the flight deck of a spaceship.

On his second mission for NASA, the Amityville astronaut was the pilot on a 16-day Life and Microgravity Spacelab that served as a model for studies on the future International Space Station.

The weather was clear for a week as the ship orbited Earth, and those were the days Kregel could see home. About three hours after wake-up, Long Island could be spotted through the cloudless atmosphere. Kregel would set aside 10 minutes a day to take pictures of his hometown as he passed over.

Even though they were traveling at 5 miles per second, Kregel could pick out Kennedy and LaGuardia Airports, Lake Ronkonkoma, major roadways such as the Northern State and Southern State Parkways, bridges and parks.

"The city was gray, as was the western end of Long Island, because of all the buildings, but would get gradually greener and greener as you looked east," Kregel said. He could pick out his hometown, Amityville, by identifying landmarks — the barrier islands, Robert Moses State Park, the Long Beach Bridge. "At 5 miles per second, you can only pick out marks. I'd aim the camera in the general direction, adjust the speed and focus, and get Amityville right in the center."

When Kregel was growing up, he was inspired to set his sights on space by the activity going on at nearby Grumman, where inventors, scientists and engineers were building the lunar excursion module that would land men on the moon in 1969. His next ambition is to see Long Island from the moon.

"I was only 150 miles from home, but right outside of the spaceship, there is no way to survive. I could see my hometown, where my family lived, where I grew up, and I thought, that was my starting point, and even though I've come so far, I'm not finished yet."

Kregel, 41, has flown three space missions. But it was only on his second mission that he was able to see the place he has such fond memories of. "Long Island has a lot to offer a kid. It was a great place to grow up — we were close to the beach, close to the big city. I always enjoy coming back to the Island and sharing my experiences."

NASA Photos

Long Island seen from the Space Shuttle

LONG ISLANDERS REACHING FOR THE STARS

Space travel — been there, done that and some of these Long Islanders even have the T-shirts to prove it. Here are the nine NASA astronauts who have spent their formative years in Queens, Nassau or Suffolk stargazing from these very shores.

Ellen S. Baker. Born April 27, 1953, in Fayetteville, N.C., but raised in Queens. Daughter of Queens Borough President Claire Shulman. A graduate of Bayside High School, she received a bachelor of arts degree in geology from the State University at Buffalo, a doctorate of medicine from Cornell University and a master's in public health from the University of Texas. Joined NASA in 1981 as a medical officer at the Lyndon B. Johnson Space Center. Has been an astronaut since 1985 — logging more than 686 hours in space on three flights. Most recent mission was aboard the STS-71 Atlantis in 1995, the first shuttle to dock with the Russian space station Mir and exchange crew.

Fernando (Frank) Caldeiro. Born June 12, 1958, in Buenos Aires. Graduated from W.C. Bryant High School in Long Island City. Received an associate's degree in applied science in aerospace technology from the State College of Technology at Farmingdale, a bachelor of science degree in mechanical engineering from the University of Arizona and a master of science degree in engineering management from the University of Central Florida. Hired by NASA Kennedy Space Center in 1991 as a lead engineer in the Systems Assurance Office. Selected as an astronaut candidate in 1996 and is now qualified as a mission specialist. Assigned to the Operations Planning Branch.

Charles J. Camarda. Born May 8, 1952, in Queens. Graduated from Archbishop Molloy High School in Jamaica. Received a bachelor of science degree in aerospace engineering from Polytechnic Institute of Brooklyn, a master of science degree in engineering science from George Washington University, and a doctorate in aerospace engineering from Virginia Polytechnic Institute and State University. Selected as an astronaut candidate by NASA in 1996. Now qualified for flight assignment as a mission specialist. Assigned to the Astronaut Office Spacecraft Systems, Operations Branch.

Mary Louise Cleave. Born Feb. 5, 1947, in Southampton. Grew up in Great Neck, where she attended Great Neck North High School. Received a bachelor of science degree in biological sciences from Colorado State University. Earned a master of science degree in microbial ecology, and a doctorate in civil and environmental engineering from Utah State. Mission specialist on two space flights. First mission included two space walks and deployment of three communications satellites. Second mission aboard the orbiter Atlantis in 1989. Crew members successfully deployed the Magellan Venus-exploration spacecraft — the first U.S. planetary science mission launched since 1978. Magellan arrived at Venus in mid-1990 to map its entire surface. Assigned to NASA's Goddard Space Flight Center in Greenbelt, Md.

Robert L. (Hoot) Gibson. Born Oct. 30, 1946, in Cooperstown, N.Y. Lived for several years on Long Island, graduating from Huntington High School. Received an associate's degree in engineering science from Suffolk County Community College and a bachelor of science degree in aeronautical engineering from California Polytechnic State University. Made his first solo flight over Long Island at 16 and earned his pilot's license at 17. Became a Navy pilot and was selected by NASA in 1978. Has flown five missions. On his last mission, in 1995, Gibson commanded the crew of the first space shuttle mission to dock with the Russian space station Mir to exchange crews. Chief of the Astronaut Office from October, 1993, to September, 1994, he participated in the investigation of the space shuttle Challenger accident. Retired from NASA in November, 1996.

Kevin R. Kregel. Born Sept. 16, 1956, and grew up in Amityville. Graduate of Amityville Memorial High School, where he played varsity baseball and soccer. Received a bachelor of science degree in astronautical engineering from the Air Force Academy and a master's degree in public administration from Troy State University in 1988. A Navy pilot prior to joining NASA as an aerospace engineer and instructor pilot. Kregel has been on three space flights and has logged more than 600 hours as a shuttle mission pilot. Last mission was the fourth U.S. microgravity payload flight, which focused on experiments that dealt with the weightless environment of space and how it affects physical functioning.

Michael J. Massimino. Born Aug. 19, 1962, in Oceanside and grew up in Franklin Square. Graduate of H. Frank Carey High School in Franklin Square. Received a bachelor of science degree in industrial engineering from Columbia University in 1984 and master of science degrees in mechanical engineering and in technology and policy from the Massachusetts Institute of Technology, where he also earned a doctorate in mechanical engineering. Selected as an astronaut candidate by NASA in 1996 and is now qualified for flight assignment as a mission specialist. Currently assigned to the Astronaut Office Robotics Branch.

William M. Shepherd. Born July 26, 1949, and considers Babylon his hometown. A graduate of Arcadia High School in Scottsdale, Ariz., he received a bachelor of science degree in aerospace engineering from the U.S. Naval Academy, and the degrees of ocean engineer and master of science in mechanical engineering from the Massachusetts Institute of Technology in 1978. Served with the Navy Seals. Joined NASA in 1984 and has served as a mission specialist aboard three space flights, logging 440 hours. Received training in Russia and is scheduled to be the first U.S. astronaut to command the international space station in July, 1999.

James D. Wetherbee. Born Nov. 27, 1952, in Flushing and grew up in Huntington Station. Graduated from Holy Family Diocesan High School in South Huntington. Bachelor of science degree in aerospace engineering from the University of Notre Dame in 1974. A Navy pilot, he became an astronaut in 1985, logging more than 955 hours on four space flights. Was the mission commander of STS-63 Discovery (1995), the first joint flight of the Russian-American space program. Mission commander for STS-86 Atlantis (1997), the seventh mission to meet and dock with Mir. This mission successfully delivered a control computer, exchanged U.S. crew members and executed a spacewalk to retrieve experiments previously deployed on Mir. Now serves as deputy director of the Johnson Space Center in Houston.

— Georgina Martorella

1968's police sweep at Stony Brook, a national first of its kind, ignites controversy

A Drug Raid on Campus

BY MICHAEL DORMAN

There were 165 uniformed Suffolk police officers and plainclothes detectives out there in the darkness at 5 a.m.

They were holding warrants for 38 suspects named in a sealed indictment. Also in their hands were copies of an elaborate manual drawn up for the raid. Bearing the crest of the county police narcotics squad, the manual included pictures of a marijuana leaf and a poppy. It contained maps of all the places to be raided and descriptions of the suspects and their associates ("subject in the past has worn an American flag as a cape"). The manual emphasized the need for caution and strict radio silence.

On signal, the officers pounced — fanning out across the lawns of the State University at Stony Brook. They were hunting college students and their associates. The charges ranged from possession to use to sale of substances from marijuana to hallucinogens.

It was Jan. 17, 1968 — the day of the great Stony Brook drug bust. It was the first known case in the nation where police had penetrated the presumed academic sanctity of a major university for such a raid. Some said the bust was a bust.

In their first sweep, the raiders picked up 20 suspects — mostly students and a few campus hangers-on. But there would be more arrests later. Students complained that the officers had torn their dorm rooms apart in searches for evidence. Police retorted that those searches had uncovered a pistol and quantities of marijuana, hashish and hallucinogens.

A sharp debate erupted about the legitimacy of the raid — a debate that mirrored the larger disagreement raging nationally between the establishment and the counterculture on issues from drugs to the Vietnam War. Some argued that the police had no place on a college campus and that marijuana should be legalized. Police and public officials said they were just enforcing the law.

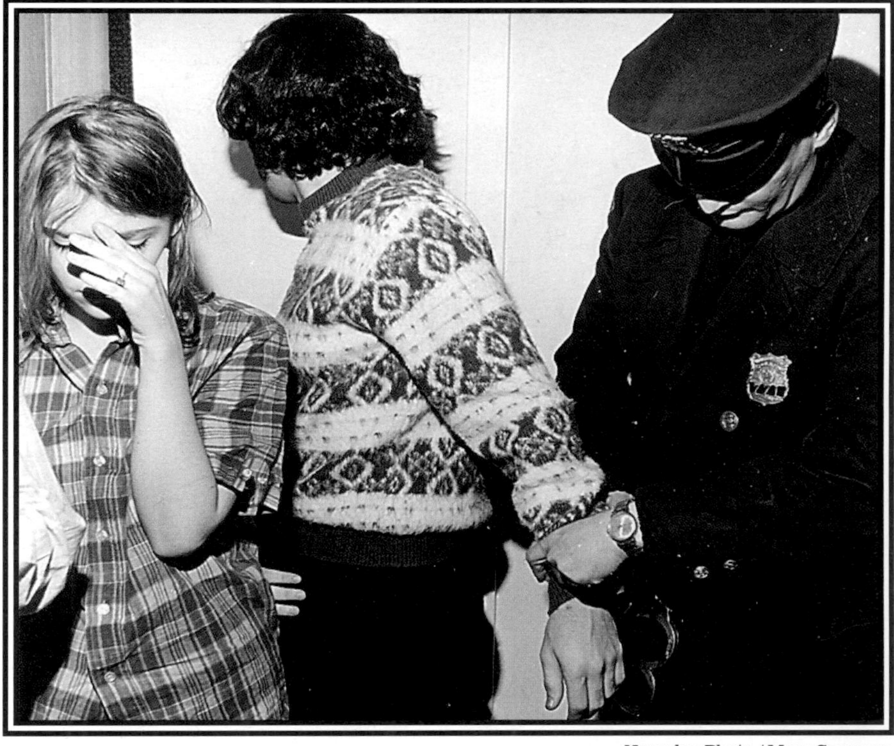

Newsday Photo / Marv Sussman

A woman masks her face as her boyfriend is handcuffed during a drug raid by 165 Suffolk officers on the Stony Brook campus in 1968. The legitimacy of the raid was debated.

The raids precipitated a wave of events stretching for several months. There was a long grand jury investigation, followed by two state legislative investigations. Two professors were jailed on contempt charges for refusing to cooperate. Two university officials were transferred. There was a second police raid that touched off a student riot. And, deserved or not, Stony Brook gained the reputation of being a "drug school."

Among the more volatile issues debated after the initial raid was the strategy police had used in conducting their initial investigation. Two young police officers, Frank Gennari and John Colby, went undercover on the Stony Brook campus — posing as nonstudents and making small-time drug connections.

Some students, suspecting Colby was a federal narcotics agent, took to calling him "John the Fed." But many would later say they could not conceive of police coming onto campus. The notion of a university being a sanctuary irritated Henry O'Brien, the assistant district attorney supervising the case. "I just felt that the university was to blame for a lot of this," O'Brien said later.

University officials did not dispute that there was a drug problem on the campus. One official said a survey disclosed that at least a third of Stony Brook students had smoked marijuana. But the officials bristled at police officers' contention that they could not notify campus administrators of the pending raid for fear of a leak.

The current Stony Brook president, Shirley Strum Kenny, said in a recent interview that — although she was not there at the time — what she had heard about 1968 raids made her believe "the response was maximal to what was not a very dangerous situation for our nation."

She said there is not the sort of drug-use problem at Stony Brook that there was on many campuses in the 1960s. As for police coming on campus, Kenny said, "We have our own security force — certainly able to handle most situations. If ever an emergency arises that our security force can't handle, we would go to the Suffolk police. But, if police came on campus uninvited, that would be a bad situation."

After all the commotion, the law-enforcement results of the raid were hardly stunning. Only about a third of those arrested served even a day of jail time. "Not one went to trial," Henry O'Brien said. "Every one was a plea. They didn't plead to felonies. Why ruin the kids?"

The police narcotics squad commander, Det. Sgt. Robert Cummins, complained that penalties should have been heavier — that "people were getting off on misdemeanors." Five years later, Cummins himself was indicted on charges of siphoning off $40,000 in money that was supposed to be used to make undercover drug buys.

Cummins pleaded guilty and was sentenced to a year in jail — bigger trouble than any of the Stony Brook Suffolk defendants confronted.

Michael Dorman is a freelance writer.

LEGACY

A LONG ISLAND STUDENT DIES AT KENT STATE

No one who lived through the turmoil of the Vietnam War will ever forget the image of Jeffrey Miller's death.

It occurred during a time of protests on college campuses. Some were spurred by crackdowns on drug use, but the most intense centered on the war in Vietnam.

Jeffrey Miller

Miller was a 20-year-old junior at Kent State University in Ohio protesting American involvement in Southeast Asia when National Guardsmen fired on the demonstrators. The Plainview High graduate, who hoped to become a psychologist, was killed. A student's photograph of a runaway teenage girl, shrieking with pain as she knelt at his lifeless and bleeding body, was printed and shown everywhere. It became an icon for the antiwar movement and a symbol of the nation's rift over Vietnam.

The 13-second fusillade by the 28-man detachment on May 4, 1970, killed four students and wounded nine others. The victims' parents filed criminal charges against the guardsmen, which were dismissed. A $40-million lawsuit against the State of Ohio was settled for $675,000.

AP Photo / Copyright 1970, Valley Daily News, John Filo

Jeffrey Miller lies lifeless on the Kent State campus as runaway Mary Ann Vecchio kneels at his body, screaming.

After Miller's death, his mother, a retired social worker, remarried and moved to Queens. Elaine Holstein traveled to Kent State for the 15th anniversary but refused to attend the 20th because of the school's decision not to include the victims' names on a memorial. When the college relented, she went back three years ago for the 25th anniversary.

"It made me a different person," she said of the shooting. Besides the loss of her son, she had to endure a flood of hate mail.

In a recent interview, Holstein said she is satisfied that Jeffrey's memory will not be forgotten on the campus. "The memorial is fairly substantial. There's a big field of flowers; it was more than just a little plaque." And her son's name is kept alive at his old high school by an annual scholarship.

Holstein said there is not one day when she doesn't think about her son and Kent State. "It's something that's always there. Jeff's still part of the family." — **Bill Bleyer**

The decade-long conflict kills hundreds of LIers and leaves many veterans embittered

Vietnam War's Deep Wounds

BY DAVID BEHRENS
STAFF WRITER

The war in Vietnam left deep wounds in nearly every Long Island community and, three decades later, the scars are still visible whenever veterans bare their souls.

More than 58,000 Americans were killed in the decade-long conflict. When the war ended in 1975, 574 servicemen from the villages and hamlets of Nassau and Suffolk counties were among the dead. In Queens, hundreds more were killed, with the Jamaica, Flushing, Woodside and Astoria sections bearing the greatest losses.

In Nassau, East Meadow, Hempstead, Levittown, Massapequa, Merrick and New Hyde Park each lost more than a dozen servicemen. So did Brentwood, Central Islip, Huntington and Lindenhurst in Suffolk.

In the mid-1960s, many young men enlisted without hesitation. Before the war became one of the great divisive issues in American history, they signed up for many reasons.

Ron Kovic, who grew up in Massapequa, dreamed of being a war hero like John Wayne, joining in the fight against communism. He was 18 when he enlisted in the summer of 1964.

Robert Fountain, now a Baldwin resident, signed up as an officer-candidate because the Navy promised to pay for two years of college and teach him to fly.

Bobby Muller, as a senior at Hofstra University, thought his 125-pound frame might look more dashing in the dress blues of the Marine Corps. He enlisted in 1967 and by September, 1968, he was a combat lieutenant leading a Marine platoon.

To many, enlisting in the military was a patriotic thing to do, said Muller, who grew up in Great Neck. It was also a smart move to go in before the seemingly inevitable arrival of a draft notice. By 1967, the war was heating up. During the year, American manpower in Vietnam almost doubled, to more than 490,000. The 1968 draft call was scheduled to bring in 300,000.

But when they came home, few of the veterans felt like heroes. There were no welcome-home parades, no street celebrations, none of the crazy joy that marked the end of two world wars.

Ron Kovic and Bobby Muller, both 52 now, came home to Long Island to testify passionately about the futility of the war. Both returned as paraplegics and saw themselves and their comrades as victims of an immoral, pointless war.

Other servicemen came back with a different sort of bitterness: the feeling they were betrayed by the American people who failed to honor them and by the American government, which failed to commit itself to ultimate victory.

The war continues to be a matter of divisive debate when the subject comes up. But by now, many Vietnam veterans would rather not talk about the war and very few have joined veterans organizations, said Mario Lombardi, vice commander of the American Legion post in Hicksville. "The way they were treated when they got home was an atrocity," Lombardi, a World War II veteran, said.

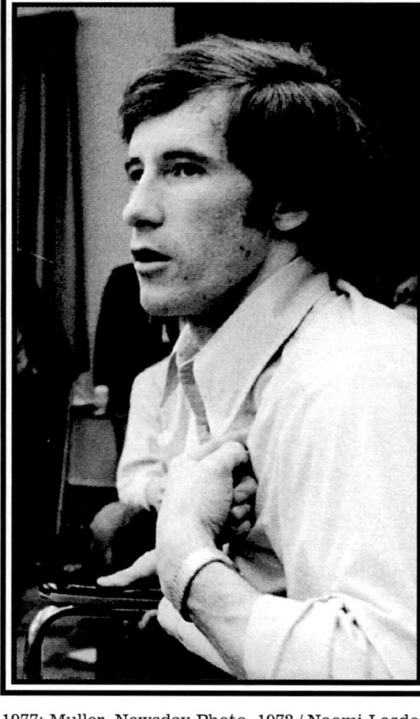

Kovic, UPI Photo, 1977; Muller, Newsday Photo, 1972 / Naomi Lasdon

Ron Kovic, left, of Massapequa, and Bobby Muller, who attended Hofstra, are both 52 now. They came home to testify about the futility of the war, speaking from their wheelchairs.

Kovic, who grew up in a blue-collar family, emerged as a national figure. At age 21, he returned home in a wheelchair — paralyzed from the chest down when a 30-cal. bullet shattered his spine. After three years of despair, Kovic signed on with the antiwar movement and began to speak at Long Island teach-ins. A year later, he and Muller, in wheelchairs, heckled President Richard Nixon from the floor of the 1972 Republican National Convention. "Stop the bombing, stop the war," they chanted until they were ejected from the hall.

Kovic was on the podium in 1976 addressing the Democratic National Convention and he recorded the scene in his wrenching 1976 bestseller, "Born on the Fourth of July." When the film version was released in 1989, he became, arguably, the nation's best-known Vietnam veteran. "I never thought I would say this but I believe my wound has become a blessing in disguise," he told Newsday when the film opened. "It's enabled me to reach millions of people with a message of peace and a message of hope."

For many veterans such as Robert Fountain, Kovic's message has brought little solace. Fountain, who was wounded twice during his 1965-66 tour of duty, came home believing in the rightness of the war.

"Like any military men, we were there to do a job. If the politicians had just kept out of it and let the military people run the war, we'd have done a hell of a lot better," he said. In his mid-50s, he belongs to an American Legion post in Baldwin where Vietnam veterans number only 10 or so of a roster of 190.

Fountain is still bitter about the Vietnamese in the south. "They didn't really care about us — just wanted to sell us dope and make money," he said. But he has no apologies for his role in Vietnam. As a Navy lieutenant with a medevac unit, Fountain said he saved many American lives. "And at the time, I didn't think our men were dying in vain . . . We didn't know the government was going to let us down."

Muller, who was wounded eight months into his Vietnam tour, also felt betrayed when he came home in a wheelchair. In college, he said, "I trusted the government to do the right thing." But he soon came to feel the war was a moral mistake from the start. In early 1971, Muller organized the Vietnam Veterans Against the War and appeared at rallies throughout Nassau and Suffolk. He later founded the International Campaign to Ban Landmines, which won the 1997 Nobel Peace Prize.

The first antiwar teach-in on Long Island had been conducted at Adelphi University, on May 10, 1965. At the time, most citizens here supported the U.S. military involvement, recalled Charles Howlett, a Long Island historian and writer. "But as Vietnam became a quagmire, Long Island mirrored the nation's disillusionment with the war." Sadly, he noted, for civilian opponents of the government's policy in Vietnam, their opposition to the war evolved into "contempt for those who fought it."

LEGACY

VIETNAM WAR'S MEDAL OF HONOR RECIPIENTS FROM LI

Vietnam War Medal of Honor recipients from Nassau, Suffolk and Queens:

STEPHEN E. KAROPCZYC, of Bethpage, Army first lieutenant, was fatally wounded when he leaped to cover a live grenade with his helmet to save two of his men. He continued to direct his men until he died two hours later.

JOHN J. KEDENBURG, of Baldwin, Army specialist fifth class, died after staying behind to hold off the enemy as his men were evacuated in an airlift.

GEORGE C. LANG, now of Seaford, specialist fourth class, used rifle fire and grenades to wipe out three enemy bunkers. He was seriously wounded.

GARFIELD M. LANGHORN, of Riverhead, Army private, was killed when he threw himself on a grenade to protect wounded colleagues.

THOMAS P. NOONAN JR., of Astoria, Marine Corps lance corporal, was mortally wounded as he dragged a wounded colleague to safety.

ROBERT E. O'MALLEY, Woodside, now living in Texas, Marine Corps sergeant, protected his men until all were evacuated from battle, although he was wounded.

Newsday Photo / Bill Davis

The Vietnam Veterans Memorial, in Farmingville

LI's Allard Lowenstein mobilizes a national effort to stop the Vietnam conflict

Fighting Against the War

BY DAVID BEHRENS
STAFF WRITER

In the spring of 1970, a few days after National Guardsmen killed four students at Kent State University in Ohio, Rep. Allard Lowenstein met with antiwar demonstrators on the Hofstra University campus.

The students were angry about the Kent State killings and bitter about the mounting death toll in Vietnam. Student strikes had spread to more than 400 American colleges and there was talk on many campuses of "shutting down the system."

Lowenstein, a Democrat elected in 1968 from the Long Beach congressional district, flashed a modest two-fingered peace sign and then quietly urged the Hofstra students to remain within the political system, working to defeat "every man who sits in elected office . . . and votes for war."

The soft-spoken man in his trademark rumpled suit never gave up on the possibility of orderly social change or the notion of winning hearts and minds with rational discourse. "As a kid," he once recalled, "I was always being beaten up and I was funny-looking and ended up feeling left out. I find I can always identify with the people who are left out."

Newsday Photos / Stan Wolfson

Allard Lowenstein, a Democratic congressman from the Long Beach district from 1968-70, speaks at a peace rally in Mineola in 1971.

It was Lowenstein who had won national attention as the architect of the campaign to dump President Lyndon B. Johnson as the Democratic party's candidate in the 1968 election. At first, Lowenstein had attempted to recruit Robert F. Kennedy to lead the charge, then persuaded Sen. Eugene McCarthy of Minnesota to serve as the antiwar challenger.

On March 12, 1968, with the help of hundreds of "Get Clean for Gene" college students, McCarthy won 42 percent of the vote in the New Hampshire primary, a tally widely regarded as a stunning setback for Johnson. Four days later, Robert Kennedy entered the race and by the end of the month, Johnson announced on national television that he would not seek re-election.

It was McCarthy's candidacy, in fact, that brought Lowenstein to Long Island in 1968.

After the Wisconsin primary, Don Shaffer, a long-time civil rights activist who headed Long Island's McCarthy for President Committee, wrote a letter inviting Lowenstein to run for office in the Fifth Congressional District, to represent the liberal Long Beach area. A Yale-trained lawyer, Lowenstein was teaching law at the City University of New York at the time. "He accepted the offer in a matter of days," recalled Shaffer, who had been searching for a strong antiwar candidate.

Lowenstein won a bitter primary battle with another antiwar candidate, but after winning election in the fall, he served just one term. By 1970, however, he had become the personification of peaceful protest across the country, a distinction he retained until his violent death in 1980. At the age of 51, he was shot to death in his mid-Manhattan office by a mentally unstable assassin, Dennis Sweeney, a former friend and colleague in the civil rights movement.

During Lowenstein's term in Congress, the antiwar movement engulfed Long Island. Demonstrations sponsored by the Long Island Peace Coalition became a matter of routine. There were rallies in village parks and on the main streets of Long Island. Many protesters were in their teens and early 20s, drawn into political action for the first time.

Freeport citizens, for instance, gathered every Sunday in 1967 and 1968 for a silent peace vigil at the local post office. Just before New Hampshire's primary in 1968, Huntington's Resistance Against the War held a large rally on the Village Green. An often-seen sign read: "We Condemn the Illegal War." Members of Women Strike for Peace often were in the forefront. At the Smith Haven Mall, mothers held a continuing peace vigil. High school students carried placards reading: "Stop the Bloody Massacre."

In 1969, students picketed the Manhasset draft board with signs that read "Stop the Nixon Death Lottery." In 1970, after the Kent State killings, Long Island colleges held "alternative" classes and high school students joined a candlelight procession to Oyster Bay Town Hall. The antiwar debate had spread to almost every corner of Long Island, dividing communities, families and generations.

In the late '60s, there were also rallies to counter the growing protest. In 1967, older veterans marched outside a Pete Seeger concert carrying signs that read: "Support Our Boys in Vietnam." At Hempstead Village Hall, demonstrators gathered to cheer young men reporting for army induction.

But the antiwar sentiment continued to grew until the war came to an end in 1975. By then, 547 Long Island residents were officially listed as killed in action. In Congress, Lowenstein did not survive his 1970 re-election bid, when he was branded the "Viet Cong-ressman" by supporters of Republican Norman Lent. Two years later, the state Legislature had redrawn district lines to break up the Long Beach coalition of Jewish and black voters. Lowenstein, then 43, did not give up the dream of returning to Congress and, unsuccessfully, entered six more contests, on Long Island and in Manhattan and Brooklyn.

A peace sign flies with the American flag at the same 1971 rally at State Supreme Court in Mineola.

Many voters considered Lowenstein too radical, his backers said; It was an ironic fate for a man committed to seeking change within the system. But for activists on Long Island, Lowenstein remains a vivid memory.

Nancy Mitzman still reveres the lessons Lowenstein taught. Just 30 when she joined Women Strike for Peace in 1968, she attended countless rallies, gathered signatures on endless petitions, entered into numerous neighborhood debates.

"Allard Lowenstein was such a good teacher, showing people how to have a direct influence on their government — and we saw it really could work," said Mitzman, now 60 and living in Blue Point. "My husband and I felt we were living through a time of enormous change, really taking part in democracy. It was such a hopeful period, because the war did end, perhaps sooner than it might have."

Later, the protest movement drew women like Mitzman into mainstream politics. "Some of us went on to found the Suffolk Women's Political Caucus, and many of us continue to try to improve our communities." It was another product of the protest era, she said.

For Michael D'Innocenzo, a Hofstra history professor who was teaching on campus when Lowenstein made his post-Kent State talk, the congressman left a powerful legacy. "He could make people understand complex issues," D'Innocenzo said. "His extraordinary achievement was putting together a mainstream movement as an alternative when so many people were ready to dump both political parties."

1970s planners seeking to prevent chaos tangle with reluctant local officials

Face-Off With A Grim Future

BY BILL BLEYER
STAFF WRITER

Hodgepodge development. Open space at a premium. Traffic at a standstill. High taxes strangling home sales. Housing for renters and senior citizens almost nonexistent.

That's what regional planners saw when they peered into their crystal ball in 1970 to predict what Long Island would look like in 15 years if nothing was done to hold off the dark forces of sprawl and gridlock.

The haphazard development that followed World War II had already created plenty of problems by 1970 — more than enough to give the comprehensive plan released that summer by the Nassau-Suffolk Regional Planning Board a sense of urgency.

"We can't afford to wait," Lee Koppelman, executive director of the board since its inception in 1965, said when the plan was released. He contended the Island had one last chance to detour around a disastrous future, and the plan was the road map.

The "Comprehensive Plan for 1985" called for sweeping changes in the way Long Island went about its business:

- Transportation: Expand the highway network, build two bridges over Long Island Sound, revamp the Long Island Rail Road and establish an integrated bi-county bus system.
- Housing: Build 400,000 new units by 1985, including 128,500 rental apartments for residents under 25 and over 65.
- Land use: Cluster construction to preserve open land, acquire parkland, limit development in North Shore estate areas and on the East End, and preserve at least 30,000 acres of farmland.
- Taxes: Create countywide taxing districts to pay for schools and impose county sales taxes to prevent an anticipated doubling of the average Long Island homeowner's tax bill in 15 years to pay for increased public services.

Suffolk officials adopted the plan but implemented only pieces. Nassau balked at adopting it but still implemented parts of it. Almost three decades later — as anyone who drives the Long Island Expressway can testify — many of the problems remain. "In certain areas we had very strong implementation and in certain areas there have been frustrating failures," Koppelman said recently.

At the time the plan was developed, Suffolk and Nassau were two of the fastest growing suburban counties in the country. "The regional plan was an attempt to tie the two counties together for the first time," Koppelman said.

"The traffic was already a mess," so much so that an additional 18 lanes of east-west highway would be needed by 1985 unless mass transit was improved, he added. The plan advocated a 40-mile limited-access highway along the North Shore, a north-south expressway in central Nassau and reconstruction of Route 110 into a limited access highway. It called for replacing LIRR trains with express buses east of Northport, Riverhead and Patchogue. None of these projects materialzed.

The recommended electrification of the LIRR main line to Calverton was only carried out to Ronkonkoma — and not until 1988.

What did fly was the recommended expansion of Long Island MacArthur Airport and Brookhaven Airport. Progress also was served when both counties set up intersecting bus systems to replace privately operated routes offering inadequate service.

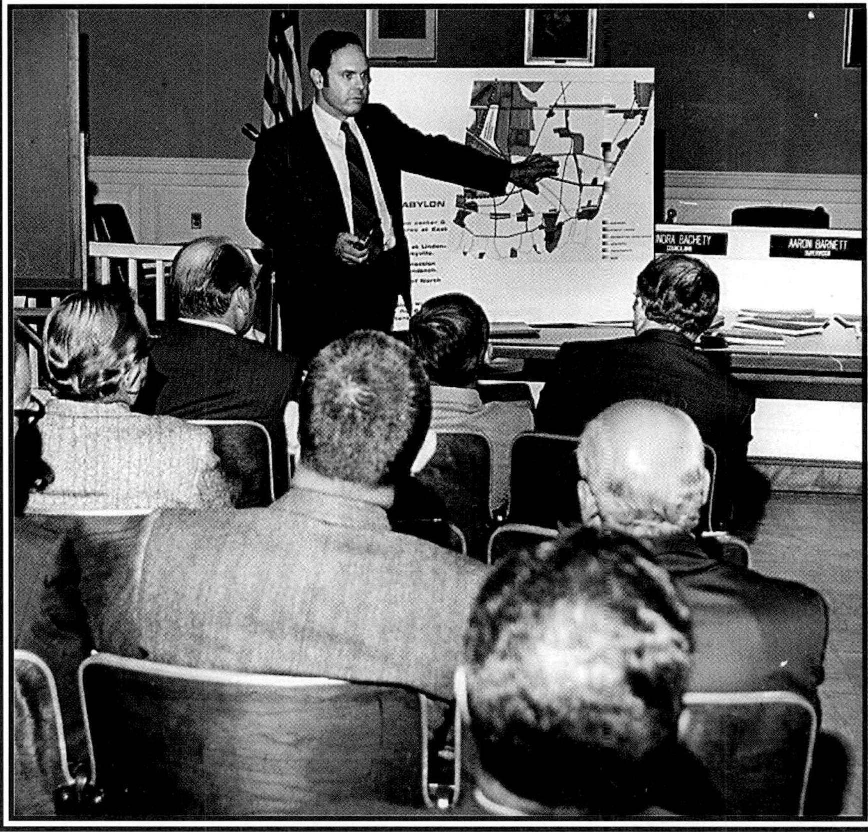

Newsday Photo / Mitch Turner

In 1970, Lee Koppelman, head of the Nassau-Suffolk Regional Planning Board, explains a proposed plan for Babylon. Below, a 1970 rendering of a proposed Long Island Sound bridge.

When it came to housing, civic associations slammed the door shut. "Whenever anyone would suggest any housing other than single-family detached, they vigorously opposed it," Koppelman said. A few innovative projects such as the Leisure Village senior citizens complex in Brookhaven Town were built in areas with few residents to oppose them. "At that time most of the local governments fought against clustering because they didn't understand it." Now, he said, it's a standard government planning tool.

The idea of countywide school taxing districts went nowhere because districts refused to yield control. But county sales taxes were created and helped hold down property tax increases.

"In the environmental field, the plan was a tremendous success," Koppelman said. The fledgling Suffolk County open-space program was expanded. Recommendations for preservation of wetlands led to the state's Tidal and Freshwater Wetlands Act of 1972. The Suffolk farm preservation program was adopted.

But the recommendation that virtually all of the undeveloped land remaining in Nassau be preserved for parks or open space was bulldozed.

The planning board knew that it would be impossible to get Long Island's 13 towns, two cities and 93 villages to agree to all the proposals. Another problem was that officials in Suffolk embraced the plan while those in Nassau distrusted the planning board as a Suffolk-dominated entity.

Owen Smith, a Nassau attorney who helped set up the regional planning board, said recently, "There was a lot of concern in Nassau with what was perceived to be the regional agency getting involved in local land use planning."

Koppelman stressed the fact that the plan was not a one-shot deal. The Long Island Regional Planning Board, as it now is called, periodically updates it. Despite the mixed results, Koppelman said, "If that plan had not been prepared, the Island today would be in an altogether different situation."

WETLANDS SINK THE BAYVILLE-RYE BRIDGE

Master planner Robert Moses called it a "gossamer thread over an arm of the sea." But opponents of his proposed Bayville-Rye Bridge viewed it as a rope that would strangle the North Shore.

Moses proposed the span to Westchester in 1965 when traffic jammed his Throgs Neck and Whitestone Bridges. He argued that the bridge would help end Long Island's dead-end status. Critics said it would generate more traffic than it would relieve, never pay for itself and citify Nassau. The opponents came up with the perfect roadblock in 1968 — about 5,000 acres of wetlands ringing Oyster Bay Harbor in the path of the bridge and its access roads. The land, mostly owned by the Town of Oyster Bay, was donated to the U.S. Department of the Interior to create the Oyster Bay National Wildlife Refuge. U.S. law prohibits any construction through the marshes.

But Gov. Nelson Rockefeller didn't give up until 1973 when the Legislature approved for the third time a bill repealing the state's authority to construct the bridge. After two previous vetos, Rockefeller stunned everybody by signing it.

The focus then shifted to a bridge from Suffolk to Connecticut. But a state study found that none of the proposed routes would pay for themselves. And Connecticut officials were as opposed to the idea as they had been to the Bayville Bridge. "You can't build it half way," said Lee Koppelman, executive director of the Long Island Regional Planning Board.

Planners now advocate high-speed ferries as the only practical way to improve traffic across the Sound. But this concept also has been blocked by concerns about noise, traffic and development. — **Bill Bleyer**

MTA Bridges and Tunnels Special Archive

For greed, corruption and cost overruns, the Suffolk scandal is at the top of the heap

The Sewer District Stench

BY AMANDA HARRIS
STAFF WRITER

In 1969, when Suffolk officials were desperately trying to convince citizens to approve installing sewers in the southwest corner of the county, one officer of the county's sewer agency stood up at a public meeting and declared: "I know you have a lack of faith in government, but this agency is apolitical. We are honorable."

It was the last time those terms were used to describe Suffolk's Southwest Sewer District.

Over the years, Long Island has had plenty of big political scandals, but the sewer district mess was the longest-running and the most expensive. It had all the standard ingredients: greedy contractors, corrupt politicians, massive cost overruns and even the predawn murder of a key official who was eager to tell prosecutors everything he knew. "It was a disaster," summed up Howard Scarrow, a political science professor at the State University at Stony Brook.

When the long-overdue Bergen Point treatment plant in West Babylon was finally finished, at first it stank, made loud noises and didn't work. The district's finances have never been on a steady footing and residents have been continually fearful of dramatic rate increases. The project began in the mid-1960s, when Suffolk's population was exploding and it became clear that the southern portions of Babylon and Islip Towns lay too low to depend on cesspools without polluting the Island's underground water supply. In the need to install hundreds of miles of underground sewer pipes and a massive waste treatment system, contractors and politicians saw their opportunity and they took it.

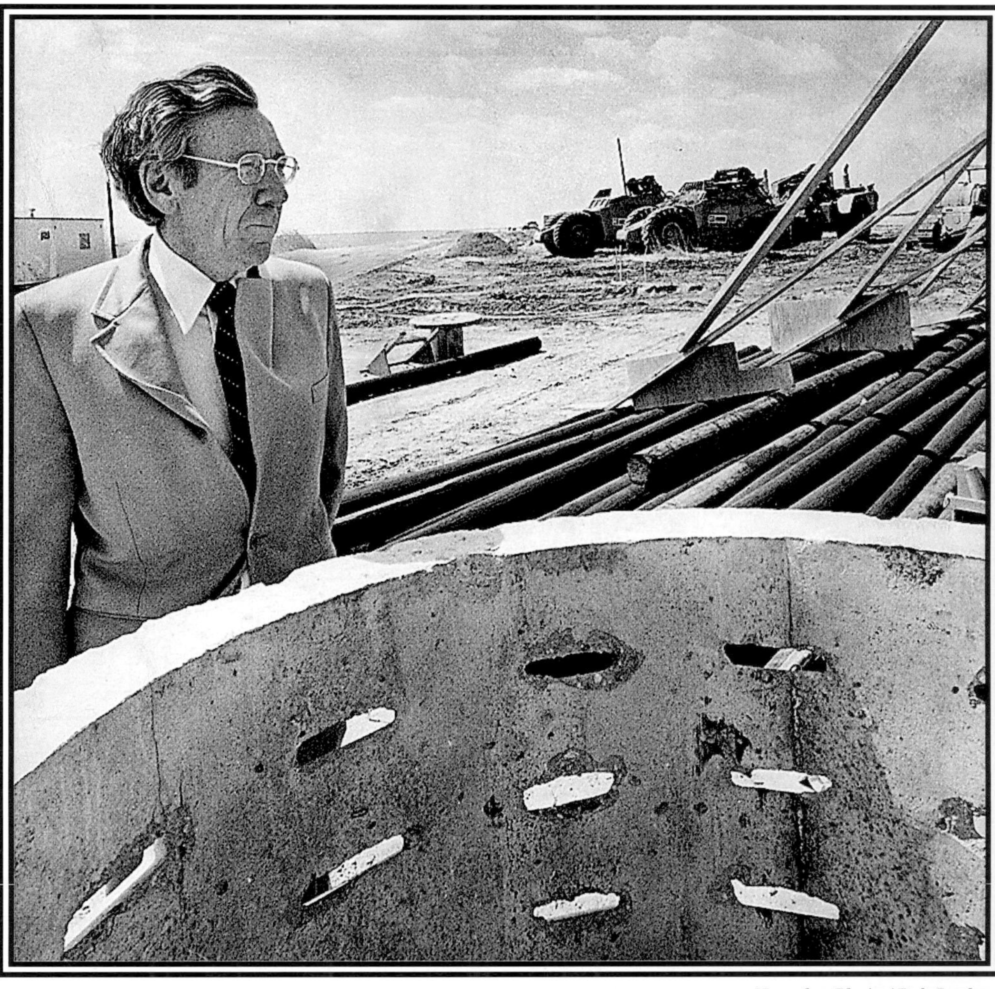

Newsday Photo / Bob Luckey

John Flynn, who was directly in charge of the Southwest Sewer District project, at the Bergen Point plant in 1975. After being indicted, he promised to tell all. But before he could, he was killed by his lover.

The first ambitious plan for sewers was turned down by voters in the proposed district in a referendum in 1967, but two years later, a second, trimmed-down version was narrowly approved, 53 percent to 47 percent, after alarmists warned voters that their children would get their drinking water out of toilets if they didn't OK sewers. County officials promised their constituents that the whole project would cost $291 million, including interest on borrowing.

Officials were supposed to be scouring the nation for the best engineering firm for the job, reviewing the qualifications of 70 companies. But the winner was a small, comparatively inexperienced firm in Melville run by Charles Walsh of Huntington. The company was picked by Arthur Cromarty, who doubled at the time as county Republican leader and chairman of the Suffolk Board of Supervisors.

Walsh's company, Bowe Walsh and Associates, secured an open-ended contract under which the firm's fee was based on the total cost of the project; it was paid $54 million for the job and an audit years later showed that $31 million of the fee was based on fraudulent claims. Walsh, who was later captured on videotape describing himself as "a natural-born master criminal," was eventually convicted of charges connected with channeling money from sewer contractors to key politicians. The final cost of the project was more than $1 billion.

At one time more than a dozen official investigations, in addition to one by the newly activist Suffolk Legislature, tried to detect the scams behind the project. A bipartisan "Gang of Three" — Legis. Anthony Noto (R-Babylon), Michael Grant (R-Brentwood) and Martin Feldman (D-Dix Hills) — regularly and dramatically revealed various sins of the project: watered-down concrete in sewer pipes, a rigged bid for lab equipment, an audit sanitized to remove any suggestion of kickbacks. It was then that the first suggestion was made to abolish the county legislature and return Suffolk to the tranquility of a county board of supervisors.

The legislature's inquiries helped establish Suffolk's tradition of two-party government and led to passage of several local reforms, including laws protecting government whistle-blowers, requiring legislative permission to employ relatives of top county officials and mandating that top officials disclose their sources of outside income.

The scandal also had a huge impact on many political careers. For years, the most significant division in Suffolk politics was not party affiliation, but whether lawmakers came from inside or outside the sewer district.

Newsday Photo / George Argeroplos

Sue Thurber Quinn, who admitted killing Flynn, leaves a police station in 1979.

"We're having a civil war here in Suffolk County," Assemb. John Flanagan (R-Huntington) said during a 1984 debate on state legislation to bail out the district. "This is brother against brother. Party lines have disappeared." The issue created such deep animosity that there is no bronze plaque on the treatment plant listing the officials responsible for the facility because no one wanted his name listed.

The bitterest fight was waged when Islip Supervisor Peter F. Cohalan challenged incumbent County Executive John V.N. Klein of Smithtown, a popular official whose promising career was tarnished by his steadfast championing of the project. At the county Republican convention in June, 1979, Cohalan's supporters tried to wrest from Klein the party's designation for county executive.

The convention atmosphere at GOP headquarters in Blue Point grew so tense that two committeemen almost slugged each other and the band belted out "God Bless America" until the two sat down. Cohalan went on to beat Klein in the Republican primary, an almost inconceivable development in local politics, and then beat Feldman in the general election.

But the most dramatic moment in the long saga came in June, 1979, when a Suffolk grand jury indicted John Flynn, the county official directly in charge of the project, for lying about the project to a Suffolk grand jury. Within hours of being charged, Flynn told an assistant district attorney he would tell all, adding, "I'm fed up with covering up for everyone else." But before he revealed the project's secrets, he was stabbed to death in the back with a fishing knife by Sue Thurber Quinn, his lover and former employee. Quinn eventually told authorities she killed Flynn because he had cheated on her, not because of the sewer district scandal. She pleaded guilty to manslaughter and was sentenced to five to 15 years in prison.

These days, the treatment process works smoothly and residents no longer have to worry that their cesspools will overflow. Many businesses outside the original boundaries in Babylon and Islip have eagerly petitioned their way into the district, a move supporters see as a tribute to the value of sewering. At present, the district has 63,000 connections.

"The plant has become a good neighbor . . . and we're proud of it," said Suffolk Public Works Commissioner Charles Bartha, who joined county government 26 years ago as a Southwest Sewer District worker.

But the financial problems continue. For almost 20 years, numerous refinancing schemes and bailouts have been used to keep the project solvent. And another crisis is brewing: County budget director Kenneth Weiss said the district faces a $12-million to $14-million deficit next year unless the county devises yet another financial solution.

Evolution of a Highway

Long Island's post-World War II growing pains and the steps needed to relieve them are written in stone — and asphalt.

At right is the Southern State Parkway in 1952, looking east toward the Park Avenue Bridge in Roosevelt. Below is the same section in 1998. Originally, the road was designed to accommodate traffic of the 1930s as a 42-foot-wide, four-lane undivided highway, with touches by master builder Robert Moses that included wooden light poles, stone bridges and brown-and-white signs.

THEN & NOW

But by the 1950s, heavier traffic created by the postwar housing boom was clogging the arteries. Before the war, traffic on the Southern State was estimated by the state Department of Transportation at about 15,000 vehicles per day. By 1951, that figure had risen to 71,000 per day and to 107,000 by the mid-1950s. Today, the department estimates, 190,000 vehicles a day move through this section in Roosevelt.

A partial response on the Southern State Parkway in 1950, according to Christopher Cotter, a senior landscape architect with the state agency, was to build a 15-inch-thick concrete median barrier with a 5-inch-diameter steel tube on top, as shown in the photo at right.

But a radical transformation was needed just a few years later. A completely new parkway was built next to the original, with a wide grass median strip. New bridges, such as the one completed in 1956 over the westbound lanes in the bottom photo, were constructed next to the originals, using stone from the same quarries.

In the mid-1980s, lighting was updated with aluminum poles that were colored brown to blend with the landscape. Signs have evolved, Cotter noted, with the last improvements being made in the 1980s. Early in the 1990s, he said, median barriers were installed to prevent crossover accidents.

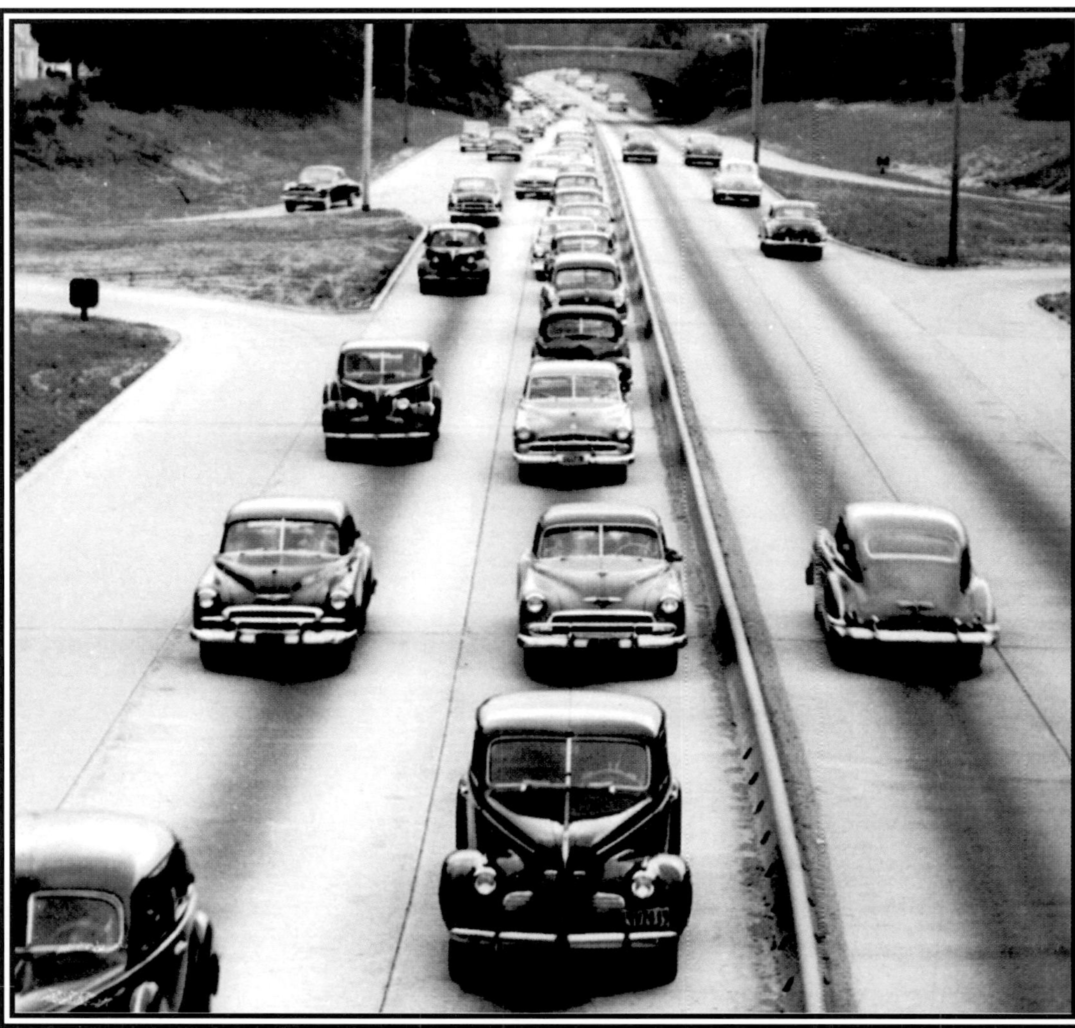

Newsday Photo, 1952

TIME MACHINE

PICTURING THE PAST AND PRESENT

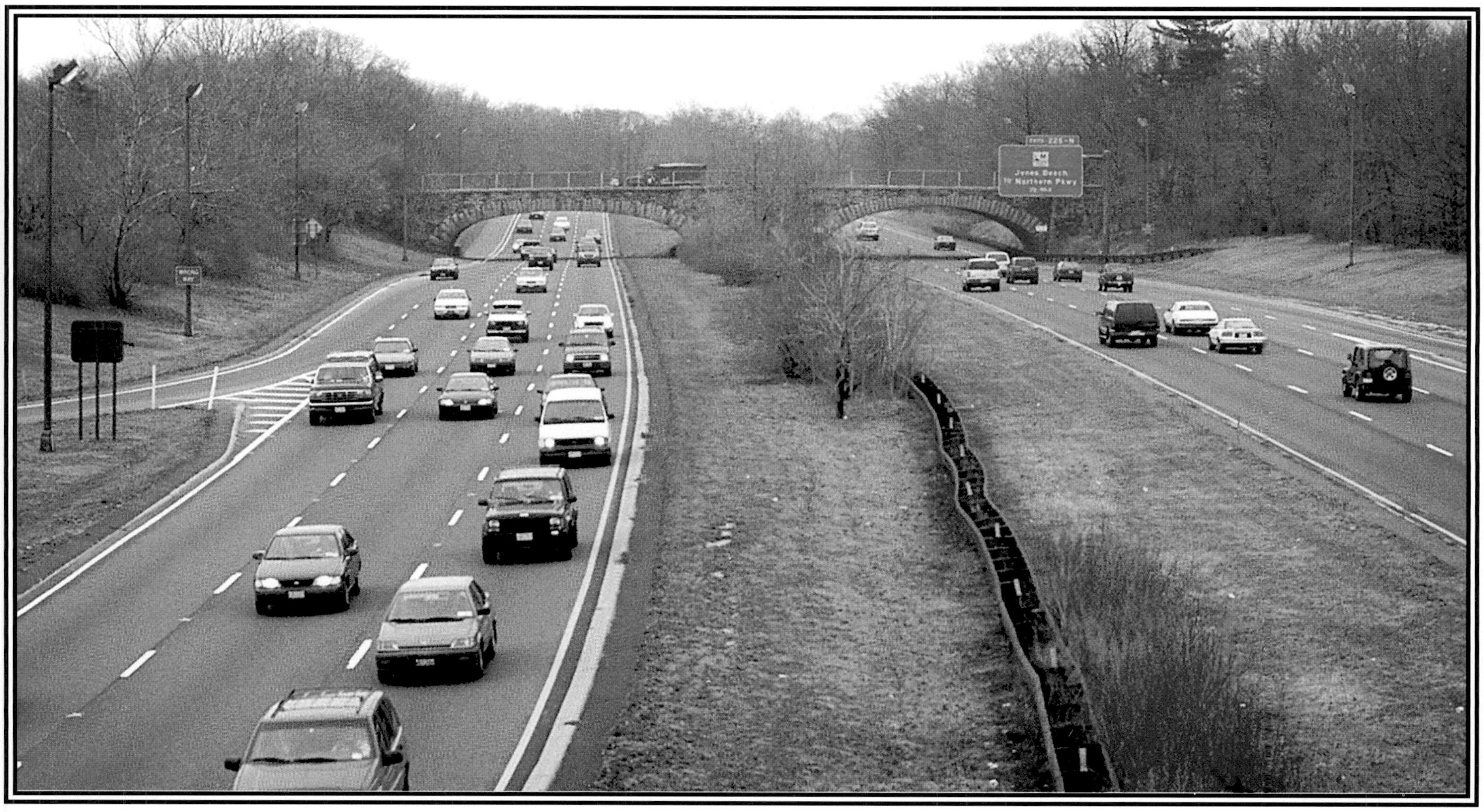

Newsday Photo / Bill Davis

Newsday File Photo / Dick Kraus

TIME MACHINE

PICTURING THE PAST AND PRESENT

Newsday Photo / Bill Davis

Air Tragedy On Cove Neck

For one night, a two-lane road on secluded Cove Neck was a scene of mayhem — a thunderous crash, cries for help, sirens, shouting and death.

It was 9:34 p.m. on Jan. 25, 1990, when Avianca Flight 52, bound for Kennedy International Airport from Bogota, Colombia, crashed on Tennis Court Road. The Boeing 707 had run out of fuel after enduring three holding patterns, miscommunication between crew and air-traffic controllers and an abortive landing attempt. Seventy-three people died — and 85 survived.

IT HAPPENED **HERE**

A police officer had seen the jet dive that foggy night, and so when controllers reported a plane lost, local police already knew about the crash. Vehicles quickly clogged the road, forcing many rescuers to walk miles on foot. Investigations followed and it would be weeks before the wreckage was removed.

CHAPTER 9

Transformation

From the closing of the frontier to the maturing of suburbia

In the past quarter century, LIers learn to cope with the end of unbridled growth

The Land of Limits

BY STEVE WICK
STAFF WRITER

CHAPTER 9 – 1973-98

For Long Island, the last quarter century has been marked by such defining episodes as the failure of Shoreham and the decline of Grumman — not to mention the odyssey of the Garbage Barge, the trial of Joe Margiotta, and the "Amityville Horror," the murder case that grew into a bizarre social phenomenon. But there were some uplifting moments, too: the triumph of the Islanders, even the poignant tale of Physty the Whale.

This final chapter of "Long Island: Our Story" brings history up to date with the stories that best reflect these last 25 years — and some that were simply too interesting to ignore.

One summer day at the end of June, 1972, a stream of cars got on the Long Island Expressway in Queens and got off in Riverhead, a 91-mile journey from the city to the country. It marked the culmination of an 18-year effort to extend the expressway from the Queens-Midtown Tunnel to the heart of the last concentration of farms on Long Island. The roadway was now in place to bring the west end to the East End.

But only a year later, the explosive growth that had driven Long Island for a generation sputtered to a halt. Coming just as the LIE finally made it all the way east, the timing couldn't have been more ironic — or symbolic.

That year, 1973, marked the end of the Island's long history as an inviting frontier — first for the Indians who lived here for 500 generations, then for the Dutch and English who arrived to build new lives, and finally for the Levittowners, who almost instantly created a vast suburb atop thousands of acres of old potato farms. As a national recession bloomed and housing construction plummeted, Long Island began a transformation that would come to shape the next quarter-century.

It was as if a curtain had been dropped. For 25 years, Long Island had been a region of seemingly boundless growth and unbridled optimism. Now, it was suddenly defined less by its promise than by its limitations.

The history of the last quarter-century will not be found in dusty archives or in the attics of historical societies. It is in the collective memory of the 2.5 million people who lived the flip side of the suburban dream as Long Island moved into middle age.

Like so many city dwellers before them, Judy and Barry Shivak left Queens for a suburban home in a good school district. They found a four-bedroom house in a new Stony Brook development, and bought it for $35,000 in 1972. "But within a year the economy went bad," recalls Judy Shivak, "and there were 'For Sale' signs all over the neighborhood. Then interest rates began to go up. It was a very scary time." By the early '80s, house prices began to soar, and new home buyers like the Shivaks could not find a house they could afford.

"We were certainly a more cynical place after that," said Roy Fedelem, a demographer with the Long Island Regional Planning Board. "You can see a measure of bitterness beginning at that time." It would take the better part of 25 years for the mood of the region to rise again.

For latter-day Long Islanders — an older and more racially and culturally diverse population than the generation before — the postmodern era has been a time of soaring costs and diminished expectations. The urban expatriates of the late '40s, '50s and '60s had little more than crabgrass and late trains to worry about. But life changed in the '70s, '80s and '90s.

Property taxes rose to keep up with the costs of education and municipal services — and it began to dawn on many people that perhaps they could no longer afford the schools that had been one of the foundations of suburban life. After years of work and an expenditure of approximately $5 billion, the Shoreham Nuclear Power Plant was shut down. And Long Islanders watched — helplessly, until the recent state takeover of LILCO — as their electrical rates rose to the highest in the continental United States.

Grumman Aerospace, for so many years the great engine of the Island's economy as well as a major component of its identity, laid off more than 22,000 workers and was sold. And in perhaps the ultimate indignity, Long Islanders came face-to-face with their inability to figure out what to do with their own garbage: landfills overflowed and a barge of Long Island trash sailed the Eastern Seaboard, rejected by four states and three countries — including the tiny republic of Belize — as Johnny Carson quipped on late-night TV, "Why not send it to Iran?"

And life got more crowded still. As more and more cars choked our roads, the most basic issue of transportation — how do we get to work and home again — grew considerably worse. Between 1973 and 1997, the number of passenger cars in Nassau and Suffolk grew by nearly 50 percent: from about 1.2 million to nearly 1.8 million. Add a smaller percentage increase in Queens, and that means an additional 674,000 cars in the three counties during these last 25 years — more than the total number of cars in Suffolk in 1973.

Almost overnight, Long Island was no longer a place where the environment was seen as purely an attraction. Now many people worried about the safety of their drinking water, the pollution of the Island's clam-rich bays and the question of whether something in the environment was causing what struck many as an alarming incidence

Farmland is tilled in Melville, but a development has already bloomed next door. Much East End farmland has been spared the bulldozer.

Newsday Photos / Bill Davis

Looking westward along Jericho Turnpike from a point just east of Route 110 in Huntington, Oheka Castle looms on the horizon as a symbol of a long-gone era when clogged roads were not a concern. A telephoto lens makes the castle seem closer than it would normally appear from Route 110.

of breast cancer.

The landscape changed, too, if in a more subtle way than in the years of the postwar boom. Shopping centers kept creeping across the land, virtually doubling their space in Suffolk, from 17 million square feet to 33 million square feet since 1973. There wasn't much room for new roads, but the Long Island Expressway expanded to include the modern symbol of traffic bursting at the seams — the high-occupancy lane.

But the transformation of Long Island from a land of opportunity to a land of limits transcended even these particular episodes and developments. It was the Island itself that changed — not so much the way it looked as the way it felt.

As Long Islanders became increasingly preoccupied with such fundamental issues of modern suburban life as taxes, traffic, garbage and electric bills, they also became gripped by a loss of communal confidence. The Islanders hockey team brought a measure of civic pride with their four straight Stanley Cups in the early '80s, but it was eclipsed by a series of image-tarnishing events — first the garbage barge and then Joey Buttafuoco: Somehow, a Baldwin auto mechanic and the teenage girl who shot his wife, had come to represent Long Island beyond the boom. It seemed that any number of our crimes had something to say about the underside of life in this particular late-century American suburb.

"I think the thing about Long Island is that we spoiled it more than it spoiled us," said Barbara Kelly, curator of the Long Island Studies Institute at Hofstra. "The landscape changed all around us . . . Life seemed to get away from us."

But while these years have been a period of constriction and struggle, they also arguably provided a new opportunity: a chance for Long Island to take a collective breath and begin to redefine the region as it prepares to move into the next century.

After 1973, Long Island was no longer a place where government agencies rubber-stamped development projects; now they slowed them down. Lot sizes grew to reduce density. The rapidly dwindling supply of farmland was saved from further uncontrolled development, and so was Long Island's last great forest — the Suffolk pine barrens, formed by the glaciers that created the Island 20,000 years ago. "As everything was slowing down and the recession kicked in, I took a helicopter ride to the East End," remembers John V.N. Klein, who was elected Suffolk County executive in 1971. "It was late November. I looked down over this incredibly beautiful scene of winter rye grass. I thought to myself, this stuff will disappear just like it did in Nassau and western Suffolk. I grew up in Smithtown. I had seen prime farmland disappear."

As the economic door shut, the environmental door opened even wider. Klein noticed that land speculators who'd bought up property on the East End were now stuck, and began a county program to buy development rights to farmland. As a result, thousands of acres of farmland on the East End were spared the bulldozer. Today, these same East End farms grow more products than any other part of New York State. "Had the boom continued unabated, we would have lost all that farmland," Klein said.

"The '60s were growth, growth, growth," said Lee Koppelman, executive director of the Long Island Regional Planning Board, recalling the decade when Suffolk was the fastest growing county in the United States. "Certainly, the recession, and a tremendous change in attitude by Long Island, allowed for open space to be set aside."

There were also the beginnings of changes in the Island's social makeup. With an increasing mix of cultures and races, and a population that was aging, it was less strikingly the prototypical suburb of young, white, middle-class families. Just as it did in the previous generation, Long Island reflected a version of the demographic patterns of the city. In 1970, Nassau County was 95 percent white. In 1996, it was 86 percent white. The largest increases were in blacks and Latin Americans. In Queens, the percentage of the borough's population that was white dropped from 85 percent to 58 percent between 1970 and 1990.

Meanwhile, just as all those years of frenetic development led ultimately to preservation, it was the sudden decline of the defense industry in the late 1980s and early '90s — triggered by major cutbacks in federal spending — that forced Long Island to move toward a more dynamic economy for the millennium.

"The defense build-up of the 1980s served to delay the maturation process of Long Island from a post-World War II economy," said James LaRocca, former head of the Long Island Association, a business group, and a candidate for the Democratic nomination for governor. "We were still on a government-financed, defense-based mindset past the point where we should have been. The economy that has evolved from this, which we see in computers, software and biotechnologies, is the path to the future. And very importantly, it is an economy built up by our own assets — a high-quality education system, a labor force that is highly educated and that demands a solid quality of life."

Long Island lost 100,000 jobs during the recession of the late '80s — half in the defense industry — but with a healthier national and local economy, it's gotten back approximately 73,000. Meanwhile, the real estate market has come back strong, and with the partial state takeover of LILCO, there is even some good news in electric bills. "There is still a high capacity for good living here," says LaRocca.

Has the curtain gone back up? If it has, the stage is looking different. Call it a revival.

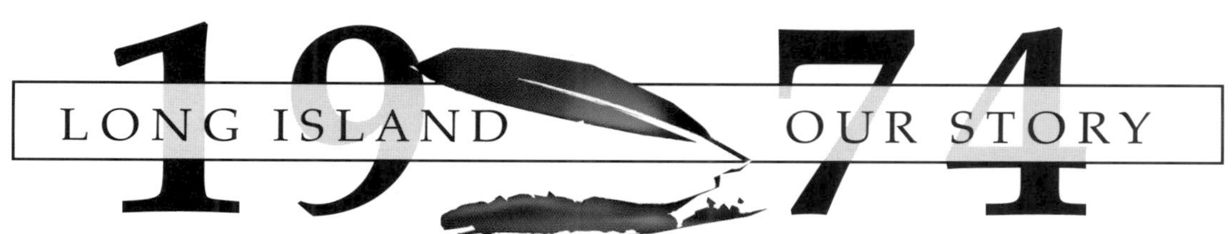

Six murders on Ocean Avenue become a media circus rippling around the world

The Horrors In Amityville

BY ED LOWE
NEWSDAY COLUMNIST

In the middle of the night of Nov. 13, 1974, a 23-year-old, disaffected, recovering teenager, Ronald (Butch) DeFeo Jr., who by using drugs, stealing outboard motors and posturing pathetically in a local saloon already had demonstrated that he was hell-bent on becoming a loser, sneaked around the rooms of his parents' handsome Dutch Colonial house at 112 Ocean Ave. in Amityville, brandishing a .35-cal. rifle, with which he shot to death every member of his immediate family: father, mother, two brothers and two sisters. His siblings were 18, 13, 12 and 7.

Later that evening, DeFeo presented himself to persons familiar with him two blocks north, at a bar then called Henry's, on the corner of Merrick Road and Ocean Avenue, where he announced with melodramatic anguish that he had happened upon a horrible murder scene in his house. A friend and several patrons visited the house and could not believe what they saw. They summoned the Amityville police, who summoned the homicide squad of the Suffolk County Police Department.

Because of the DeFeo family's size and the range of ages of the children — this in a 2½-square-mile, notoriously insular village — nearly everybody in Amityville felt connected in one or another way to the DeFeo family, through kids, teachers, shoe store proprietors, auto mechanics or St. Martin of Tours Catholic Church.

My late father, Lt. Ed Lowe, was second in command of the village police department at the time, and thus was charged with maintaining the crime scene. A classmate of mine from high school was the DeFeo family's favorite priest and confessor. And because I was something of a saloonist myself, I knew both the partners and the patrons of Henry's, whom I quietly introduced to the Newsday police reporter covering the story.

Assigned to Newsday's Nassau County office, and with the crime having occurred one-eighth of a mile into Suffolk, I was spared from officially having to work on the story as a reporter. Unprofessional as it may seem, I felt lucky to avoid the certain animosity of my neighbors.

Because of collectively felt hurt and humiliation, the media invariably becomes the enemy of an otherwise quiet and tight-knit place at the time of so spectacular a tragedy, though the neighbors understandably are even more curious than the rest of the world about what actually happened.

But no one could have predicted how the antipathy would escalate and how the story would become twisted, nor how protracted and ultimately global the media assault would be.

My luck finally ran out with this assignment, to review what would have been merely one of the most horrific true-crime stories in the history of Long Island, but which instead became buried under the hoopla and folderol of "The Amityville Horror — A True Story," among the nation's most commercially successful scams.

Despite self-serving protestations that DeFeo had heard mystical voices and only followed their phantasmagorical orders to kill, the State of New York convicted him in 1975 and he was sentenced to serve six consecutive 25-year prison terms, or 150 years, for the murders.

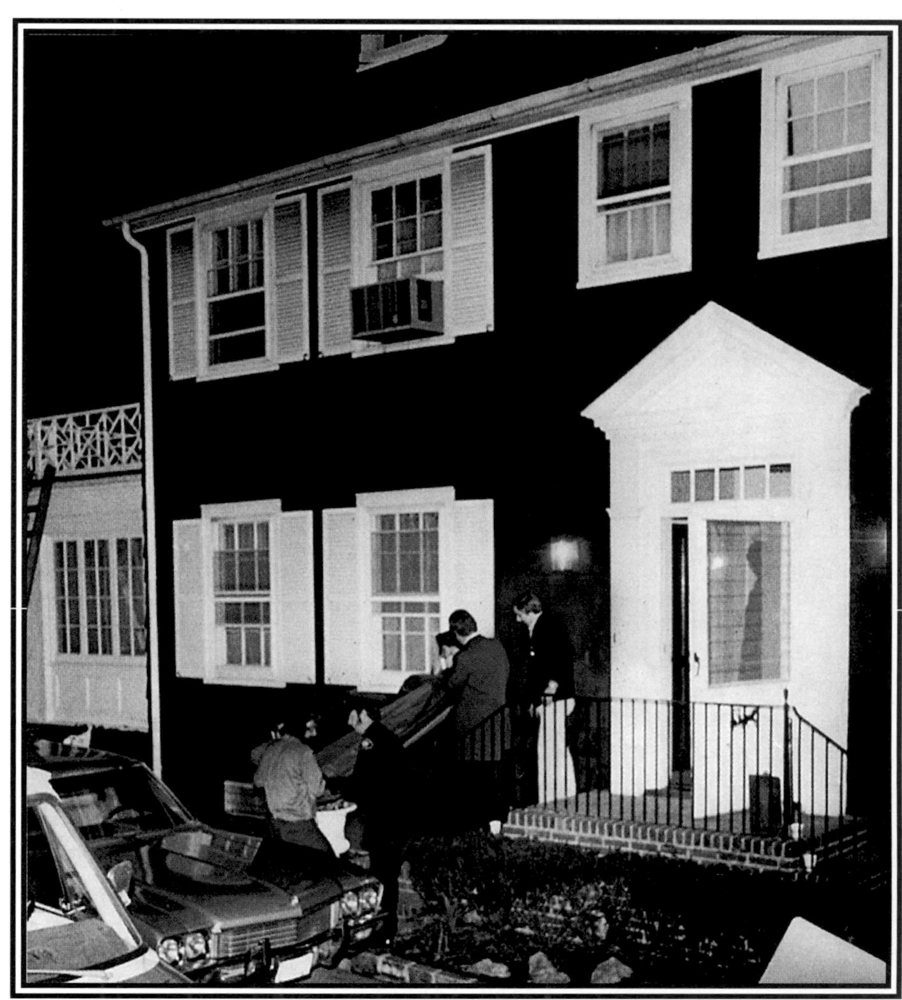

Newsday Photo / Mitch Turner

Newsday Photo / Don Jacobson

Six people died in Amityville on the night of Nov. 13, 1974, at 112 Ocean Ave., above, the smart Dutch Colonial house where Ronald DeFeo Jr., right, killed his family — both parents and four siblings. It became the site of the celebrated "Amityville Horror" book, which focused on alleged paranormal phenomena. The crime ultimately was obscured by attention to the book and, later, a Hollywood movie.

Under normally abnormal circumstances, that would have been the gruesome end of it. But in December, 1975, George and Kathy Lutz — he a land surveyor whose business had just declared bankruptcy — suddenly bought the DeFeo house for roughly the market value, $80,000, a figure mysteriously above their means. They lived in the house for 28 days, during which time they never once called the Amityville Police Department, and after which they held a press conference, of all things, at which they claimed to be abandoning the place in terror of its demons.

Previously, they had registered no complaints about so much as a creaky floorboard (let alone a free-floating, window-peeping piggy's head, a violently unhinged front door, swarms of carnivorous flies or an ominously whispering, disembodied voice).

For months, neighbors and residents of Amityville periodically witnessed visitations alternately as bizarre as they were comedic, as ghost-hunters from all over the country — some wearing tweed suits and carrying notepads, others wearing flowing black robes and wielding medieval scepters — paraded about the house and yard, occasionally chanting incantations and even prying off shingles, presumably for future psychic analysis.

And we in Amityville thought that was annoying.

The Lutzes moved to California. People wondered how they could afford to do that.

"The Amityville Horror — A True Story" was published in 1977, by Prentice-Hall. A pedestrian piece of imitative fiction penned by the late soap-opera writer Jay Anson, it included a series of episodic scenes reminiscent of recently successful horror films, notably "The Exorcist," with its projectile vomiting, ominous voices, visiting swarms of flies and scenes of doors being violently ripped off their hinges, presumably in full view of anybody living across the street.

Aside from the Lutzes, only one true name was included in the book, that of Amityville Police Sgt. Pat Cammarato, who threatened to sue after he saw it, so that future editions of the book referred to his fictional counterpart as Pat Zammarato.

Still, with its jacket emblazened with the words, "A True Story" — in blood red, of course — the book invaded the nonfiction sections of stores and libraries and sold out everywhere across the country. New hordes of people descended on Amityville: unofficial ghost-hunters, curiosity hounds, believing and disbelieving readers, and obnoxious drunks.

Meanwhile, the house had traded again, for $55,000 — the reduction in price due to the notoriety — but after a year or two, and especially after the release of the movie starring James Brolin and Margot Kidder, the new owners moved out. Amityville saw the entire country, and later emissaries from the world, through a prism of mass hysteria and unfathomable stupidity.

Friends of mine bought the house but sold out, too, because it seemed the harassment would never end. As recently as last Halloween, a local radio station offered prizes to any listener with the gall to knock on the door of the house while simultaneously talking to the radio DJ on a cell phone. When a protective next-door neighbor intervened, he involuntarily wound up on-air as "the angry neighbor," a character in a cruelly intrusive would-be comedy bit.

Always, hopelessly obscured in all the hype and media madness was this: Dawn DeFeo would be about 42, had she lived; her sister, Allison, 37; brothers Mark, 36, and John, 31. By now they might all have provided their parents, Ronald and Louise, with grandchildren. They might own other houses in Amityville. Instead, Ronald DeFeo murdered them, and their memory has been all but lost to our collective and evidently boundless fascination with events that never happened.

Levittown leads an 8-year court struggle but fails to overturn state's funding policy

The Fight for School Dollars

BY JERRY MARKON
STAFF WRITER

It was a basic premise of suburbia: the right to a good education in a neighborhood school. And few communities prized their schools more than Levittown.

In the boom years of the 1950s and '60s, enrollment soared in America's quintessential suburb. Programs expanded. "The school district was our identity," says Levittown resident and former PTA leader Clare Worthing.

But as the growth stopped and the economy slipped, Levittown found itself in a financial squeeze, lacking the wealth to pay for the education residents had come to expect. So the district went to court in 1974, leading 27 of New York's less wealthy communities in a lawsuit seeking to overturn the state's method of relying on local property taxes to finance education.

The case would last eight years and involve 23,000 pages of testimony. In the end, the schools would lose, and subsequent efforts to alter the wealth disparities among Long Island's 125 districts would fail. Today, the "Levittown case" is barely a footnote in the history of national school reform. Yet it endures in importance locally. It raised issues of taxation and fairness in education still fiercely debated — and galvanized Long Island school districts into a potent lobbying force for change.

Above all, the case served as a symbolic end to the era of plenty for Long Island schools, a painful transition from unparalleled growth to the modern age of aging buildings, budget battles and shrinking dollars to fund rising academic standards.

Those struggles were unthinkable in the halcyon days, when the masses migrated to Long Island, bringing along their high expectations for schools. "They wanted their children's lives to be better than theirs, and the key was education," said Lorraine Deller, a former president of the Nassau-Suffolk School Board Association who moved to Baldwin in 1964.

Levittown's school enrollment peaked about 1968, then started declining, which meant reduced state aid. Then, in 1973, a national recession hit Long Island hard — and in districts like Levittown, state mandates for everything from special education to energy-efficient boilers drained resources.

As they wrestled with tightening budgets, Levittown administrators found that the district's lack of industry and relatively low property wealth meant that they couldn't raise as much money as richer districts could. Levittown was forced to increase class sizes and cut back on electives and supplies.

"We just didn't have any money," recalled Robert Neidich, Levittown's superintendent at the time. "I thought our only hope was to change the system."

By the mid-1970s, the timing seemed right. Several lawsuits had been filed in other states seeking to change education financing, and a landmark 1971 ruling in California had declared that state's system of funding schools through property taxes unconstitutional.

The California case galvanized a national school equity reform movement, fueled by the social activism of the times.

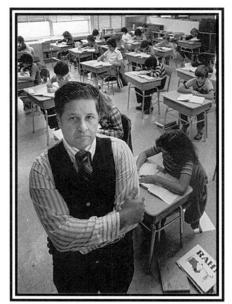

Robert Neidich, who as Levittown schools superintendent in 1974 led the lawsuit over funding of public education

"The whole equity spirit started with the civil rights movement, the Great Society," said Margaret Goertz, a school finance expert and education professor at the University of Pennsylvania.

Neidich picked up the telephone in 1974, and within days, he had rounded up support from 26 other property-poor suburban and rural districts, including 12 on Long Island ranging from Brentwood to Roosevelt.

"He was a dynamo, the principal actor," said Daniel Levitt, who represented the districts in the lawsuit they filed in 1974 in State Supreme Court in Mineola. The plaintiffs were later joined by the Cities of New York, Rochester, Buffalo and Syracuse, which argued that since their resources had to finance everything from police to firefighters, there was not enough left for education.

During the eight-month trial, the suburban and rural districts argued that the state formula enacted in 1925 was unconstitutional because it relied too heavily on property taxes and tied education to property wealth. They urged a fairer distribution of funds, though they didn't make any specific proposals.

Attorneys for the state countered that the current system met the requirements of New York's constitution — that children be given a free, basic education. Only the Legislature could make changes, they argued, and the state could not afford the money for reform.

In 1978, Justice L. Kingsley Smith backed the Levittown forces, ruling that the state's funding system was unconstitutional because it favored property-rich districts. The Appellate Division upheld the ruling.

But the State Court of Appeals in 1982 ruled against the school districts. Though it found "significant inequalities" in school financing, it agreed with the state's arguments and upheld the current system. The loss shocked those arguing for change.

"Most people were surprised at how the Court of Appeals chickened out," said Levitt, a Manhattan lawyer. "This system is crazy."

His opposing counsel, Amy Herz Juviler, sounded ready to re-argue a case that she said "lasted so long it was like being in prison." While the system may have inequalities, she said, they should be debated in the Legislature, not the courts. "The school districts were 100 percent wrong," said Juviler, who retired in 1993 as a New York City criminal court judge.

In the last decade the Legislature has adjusted the school-aid formula to provide some additional money to low-wealth districts, but it hasn't satisfied these districts A subsequent suit filed by low-wealth Long Island districts was thrown out in 1995, and the system is still riddled with disparities and heavily dependent on property taxes. New York State pays about 40 percent of school costs; the national average is 49 percent. Meanwhile, about 20 other states have been ordered by courts to replace systems similar to New York's in the past two decades. Those states have generally spent more on low-wealth districts, with a few restricting spending of wealthier districts.

Today, Levittown schools still face large classes and limits on supplies and extracurricular activities. Superintendent Herman Sirois says the old lawsuit gave the district an unfair "stigma" as poor; it did not participate in the second suit.

But Sirois said he understands what his predecessors felt compelled to do. "They were honor-bound to carry a banner for the needs of their citizens," he said. "At some point, even if you're crying into the night, you have to speak out."

Newsday Photos / Dick Kraus

Students at Abbey Lane School in Levittown ask Lt. Gov. Mary Anne Krupsak, left, about the district's financial problems during a visit in 1977. As the economy slipped, Levittown found itself in a financial squeeze, lacking the wealth to pay for the education residents had come to expect.

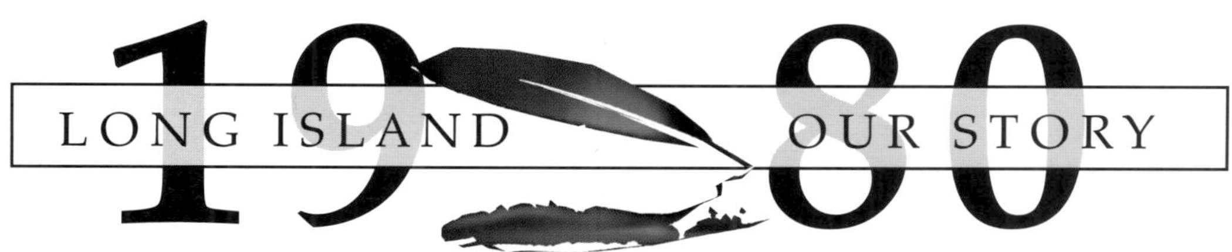

An NHL team puts 'Islanders' on its jerseys, and LI on the map of sports legends

They Shoot, They Score!

BY JOHN JEANSONNE
STAFF WRITER

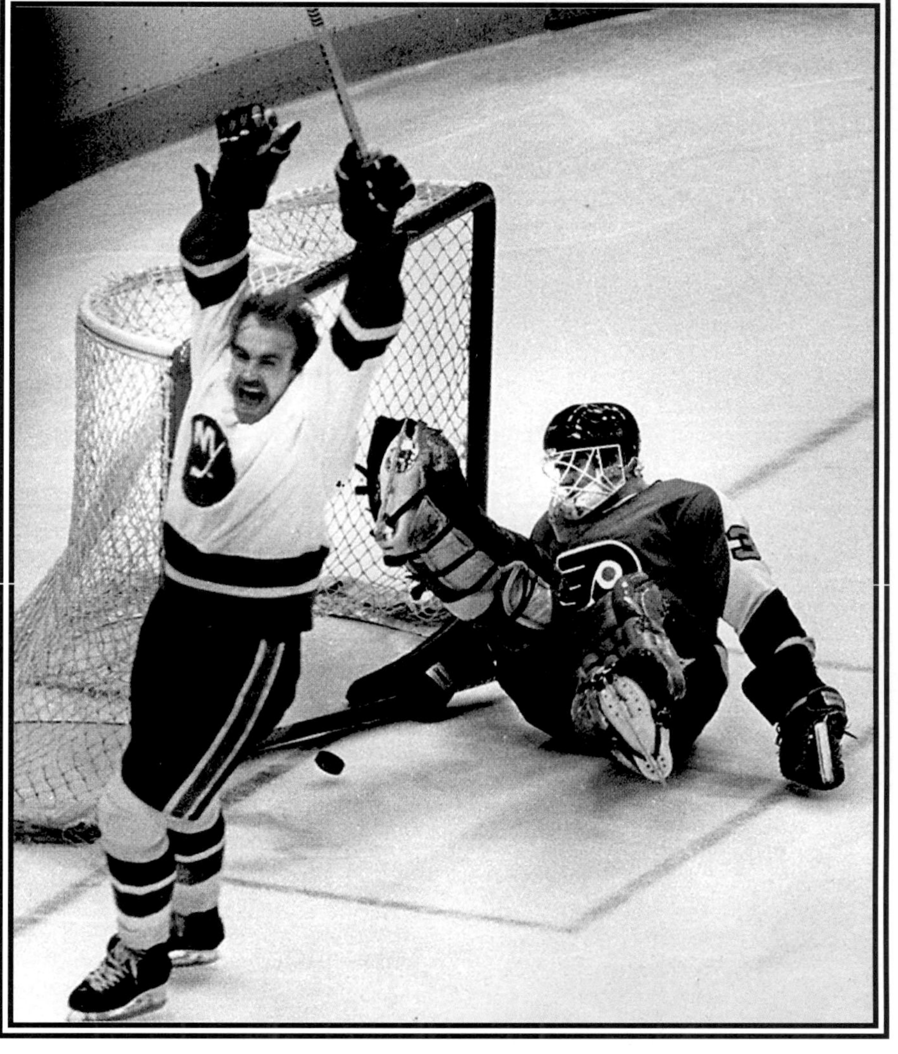

Newsday Photo / David L. Pokress

In 1980, Bobby Nystrom of the Islanders scores the goal that gave the team its first Stanley Cup. Below, Denis Potvin celebrates the Isles' second of four straight Stanley Cups.

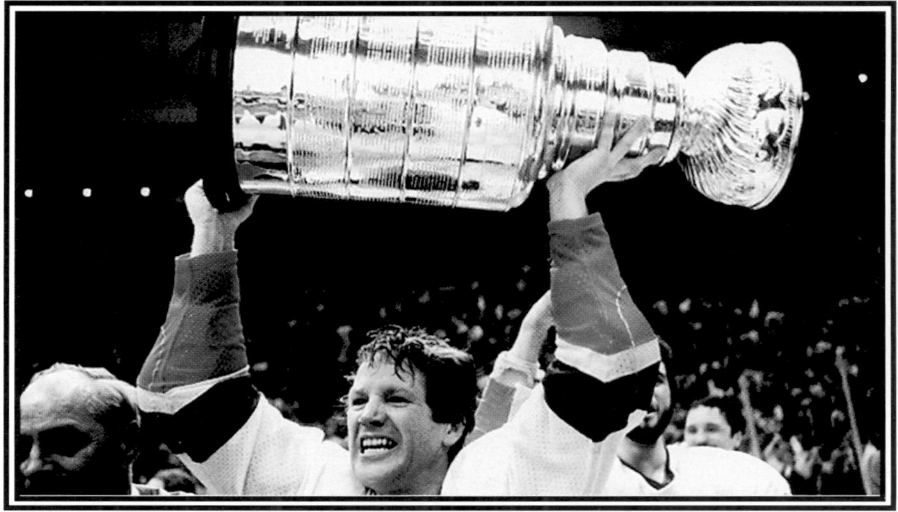

Newsday Photo / Ozier Muhammad

We can say with certainty that Long Island put the map on the New York Islanders. But besides the design of the hockey team's logo, the converse is also true: When Bobby Nystrom scored an overtime goal on May 24, 1980, to secure the first of the Islanders' four consecutive hockey championships, the only surviving big-time sports team east of the Queens-Nassau border left its mark on Long Island as well.

Though composed entirely of Canadians at the time, the Islanders became "Our Boys." They became part of the public memory, the flip side of such later identifiers as Hurricane Gloria or the Long Island Lolita. They made headlines; they worked their way into the *lingua franca* at the local deli or barbershop.

"Sometimes a place gets a bad identity; there's a lot of bad news," said Michael D'Innocenzo, a Hofstra University history professor who has taught courses on sports history. "But the very name, 'Islanders,' helped to give a thrust of territoriality — our area against other areas — and that is something that some people respond to, particularly young people."

At the time, Newsday columnist Steve Jacobson wrote that the Islanders were "worth a good substantial yell for their contribution to our sense of well-being. They made a lot of us feel better about ourselves." An estimated 30,000 hockey fans and Long Island chauvinists showed up for a parade along the Nassau Coliseum access roads to celebrate, and then-Nassau County Executive Francis Purcell proclaimed that the Islanders' championship "gives us an identity we've been striving for for a long time. People won't say, 'Where's Long Island?' "

Maybe people do ask, nearly two decades later. After all, the Islanders have spent the 1990s muddling in mediocrity; attendance is down and there have been threats to move the team, whose ownership recently changed hands. But the issue of Long Island's ongoing search for its identity, in the shadow of the Center of the Universe known as New York City, did resonate with the Islanders' birth here in 1972 and with their quick road to the top.

As a National Hockey League expansion team, the Islanders — like most of the younger generation on Long Island in the 1970s — had not come from somewhere else. They fit the description of all those residents "not choosing suburbia anymore, those born to it," D'Innocenzo said. They grew up in the equivalent of Levitt housing: the no-frills, affordable Nassau Coliseum.

"There was a sense of community with the Islanders," said Art Feeney of Seaford, an Islander season-ticket holder through all 26 years of their existence. "From the early '70s on, even those first couple of terrible years, there was a sense of difference from New York City, which we never had before."

What made the difference even better was that the team the Islanders dismissed in their first trip to the playoffs was the team of Long Islanders' parents, the New York Rangers. It was the Islanders' bar mitzvah.

They may not have thoroughly represented the Island's expanding cultural diversity — mostly Canadian, thoroughly Anglo-Saxon, the NHL still has no Latino players and few black players — but the Islanders were rare evidence that the Island could offer something the equal of what Manhattan had. "It was like trumping the city," D'Innocenzo said.

And, adding to the hominess of the team was the fact that its officials and players were suburbanites to the core, decidedly *not* New York City people. Coach Al Arbour, the architect of their four championships, had to be flown to the Island from his previous job in St. Louis and shown the trees and grass to convince him this was not the skylines and concrete of Manhattan. When the Islanders won their first Stanley Cup, and it was called New York's first such victory since the Rangers had won in 1940, Islander goalie Bill Smith responded pointedly, "The Stanley Cup is not in New York. It's on Long Island."

Longtime fan Feeney remembers driving away from the Coliseum the afternoon the Islanders won the Cup and being stopped "on Wantagh Avenue by a 70-year-old man who wanted to know what the fuss was. I asked him if he ever had heard of the Islanders and he said no. But when I explained that Long Island's team had just won the hockey championships, he turned the lights on his car and joined the celebration."

Before the Islanders, there were the Long Island Ducks, a minor-league team (1959-73) whose owner, Brooklyn-born Al Baron, called the proximity to New York City "the good news-bad news situation" for sports franchises on the Island. In 1972, the NHL hurriedly had placed an expansion team here, primarily to block competition from the fledgling World Hockey Association. Both leagues recognized that Long Island was the 11th largest metropolitan community in the nation. It had more people than Cleveland, Miami, Atlanta and Denver.

But marketing research done by the Arrows, an indoor soccer team that failed to survive a brief existence at the Coliseum, soon found that there was no clearly defined "Long Island sports market." Television, history and day-to-day business all tied much of the Island to the "New York market." Even the name used by the team — *New York* Islanders — purposely played on the perceived marquee value of Big Town.

The basketball Nets never were quite accepted on Long Island, in spite of featuring two superstars: Rick Barry and, later, Julius Erving. It was widely believed that the Nets were league-impaired — they were in the newer, less-accepted American Basketball Association until 1976, their final year on the Island before moving to New Jersey. Also, in the early 1970s, all of professional basketball wrestled for a time with a perception that largely white audiences wouldn't support a sport beginning to be dominated by black players.

Just as obviously, long before the Islanders materialized in 1972, Long Island was world famous for "The Great Gatsby" and Levittown, Grumman's lunar module and the Hamptons. But the Islanders' high-profile presence did have something to do with tying together this difficult-to-label place: We are not a state, not a county, not a city. Just home to a four-time hockey champion.

It helped that the Islanders deepened their local roots with years of community service and the fact that several of their players settled here after retirement, among them Bobby Nystrom and original captain Ed Westfall.

And when management changed the team's logo three years ago — to a design that seemed to be an ad for fish sticks — it was shouted down by fans. They got the Long Island map back on the Islanders. And perhaps subliminally, vice versa.

More Than A Troubadour

When he died on the LIE, Harry Chapin left a rich legacy of generosity and commitment

BY FRED BRUNING
STAFF WRITER

Once upon the 1970s, Harry Chapin did a concert at a high school in Patchogue. It was like many other Chapin appearances — equal parts hoedown, pep rally, political seminar, kaffeeklatsch and sensitivity session.

Alone on the stage, Chapin sang and sang and sang. "Cat's in the Cradle," "W*O*L*D," "Taxi," "Circle" and assorted others. When not crooning his "story" songs, Chapin was jawboning. Hunger, peace, brotherhood — Chapin's sermon was vintage stuff for a decade defined by images of emaciated African children, Vietnam casualties and racial discord. An onlooker could not help but marvel at the man's energy. Chapin might never deplete his supply of music, subject matter or stamina. In doubt only was the strength of his audience. As Allan Pepper, co-owner of the Bottom Line nightclub in Greenwich Village, observed recently: "Harry could be a steamroller."

From the time he moved to Huntington Bay in 1972 until he perished July 16, 1981, in a traffic accident on the Long Island Expressway at the age of 38, Chapin was a one-man civic improvement campaign — a fellow who used celebrity as a potent force for the common good. His stunning death — on Long Island's quintessential thoroughfare and only hours before a free performance at Eisenhower Park — robbed the community of an unyielding advocate and irreplacable friend.

"You looked to Harry for inspiration," said Barbara Hoffman, a folksinger from Brookhaven hamlet who sang with a local group that once appeared on the same bill with Chapin. "He wasn't afraid to do what needed to be done or sing the songs that needed to be sung."

Since Chapin's death, other stars have rallied to Long Island causes — Billy Joel works on behalf of East End baymen; Paul Simon staged summer concerts at Deep Hollow Ranch to save open space in Montauk; Alec Baldwin established a breast cancer research center at the State University at Stony Brook in the name of his mother, Carol, who was treated for the disease. But, in or out of show business, no one compares to the minstrel who evidently took seriously the lyrics to his own song, "Could you put your light on please?"

Born into a family of New Yorkers who extolled art, music, philosophy, academic achievement and the glories of city life, Harry Forster Chapin nevertheless was resolved to leave his imprint on Long Island — the balkanized megaburb he had come to embrace as home.

"He thought Long Island represented a remarkable opportunity," said Chapin's widow, Sandy, who still lives in the big house with the water view where the couple reared five children. "Harry was not an elitist, at all."

Chapin envisioned an Island where the arts flourished and universities expanded and humane discourse was the norm. Whether or not his idea had a prayer, Chapin proceeded as though divinely inspired. "Every time he got something under way, he started something else," his wife said.

Manic, maybe, but Chapin was unstoppable. He served on the boards of the Eglevsky Ballet, the Long Island Philharmonic, Hofstra University. He energized the now-defunct Performing Arts Foundation (PAF) of Huntington. Connecting as easily with high-powered corporate leaders as with teenagers in tie-dyes, Chapin persuaded Long Island executives to donate money and manpower to his cultural campaign. Blitzed by a whirlwind, who could say no?

Newsday Photo / David L. Pokress

Folksinger Harry Chapin plays host at a benefit barbecue at his Huntington Bay home in the summer of 1975 for the now-defunct Performing Arts Foundation of Huntington.

Larry Austin, chief executive officer of Austin Travel in Melville and president of the Long Island Philharmonic, recalled the night an outdoor PAF gala on the North Shore was threatened by a downpour.

"The parking lot turned to mud," Austin said. "There was a long line of cars coming through the rain and there was Harry, his hair all over his face. As each car came by, he would knock on the windshield and say, 'Hi, I'm Harry Chapin. It's gonna stop. You're gonna have a wonderful time.' "

Chapin found time for politics, too. A Democrat, he wrote campaign literature for Allard Lowenstein, the passionate opponent of the Vietnam War who represented south Nassau for one term in Congress. He backed — and befriended — the Island's political wunderkind, Rep. Tom Downey. Sandy Chapin says her husband even was considering a run himself — against Alfonse D'Amato for U.S. Senate.

Chapin learned how government worked from close range. He lobbied on behalf of food programs — if turned away from a congressman's office, Chapin often would await the official in the men's room — and served on Jimmy Carter's Presidential Commission on World Hunger. Once he was jabbering so enthusiastically at a White House meeting that the president implored Chapin to pipe down.

Back home, Chapin worked for the hungry, too. He helped start the food bank called Long Island Cares and co-founded World Hunger Year, an organization that continues to aid grassroots groups across the nation. He did numerous benefits for hunger and other causes — half of his more than 200 annual performances. Now the Harry Chapin Foundation in Huntington, chaired by his wife, supports arts, environmental and agricultural efforts intended to aid poor Americans. "Harry always said he wasn't afraid to fail," said Bill Ayres of Huntington, the other co-founder of World Hunger Year who still serves as executive director of the Manhattan-based organization. "He said the greatest successes were built on failure."

Chapin's ambitious agenda was undercut not by a shortage of spirit, commitment or talent but, if anything, common sense. The singer was a notoriously bad driver and may have made a fateful mistake near Exit 40 of the LIE when, heading west, he maneuvered his blue Volkswagen Rabbit into the path of a truck. Chapin — whose license had been revoked after several suspensions — was pulled from the flaming wreckage but died of massive internal bleeding. Distraught fans in Eisenhower Park that night passed candles, hugged one another and, soothed themselves with lyrics from Chapin's philosophical sign-off number. "All my life's a circle," the crowd sang. Said one admirer: "My God, how he touched me."

Though all his dreams did not come true, Chapin accomplished more than any mere troubadour might have dared expect. On Long Island and elsewhere, he put in place institutions that endure. His name is synonymous with generosity and commitment, and his music endures. Sandy Chapin says she often gets letters from people who tell her that when life gets rough, they put on a record by Harry.

Chapin's goal to transform Long Island was audacious and most likely impossible. Some may argue that while the Island has made much progress in the areas of art and education, it lacks the identity Chapin believed necessary. Peter Coan, author of the 1987 biography, "Taxi: the Harry Chapin Story," wonders if anyone will emerge to assume Chapin's role. "When he died, there was no one to carry that torch," Coan said.

But Chapin may have seen things differently. At a 1977 Nassau-Suffolk volunteer conference, he said, "We all have the potential to move the world — and the world is ready to move." As Chapin demonstrated, all it takes is a push.

On July 16, 1981, Harry Chapin was on his way to a free performance when his car and a truck collided on the LIE. He was 38.

Newsday Photo / Walter del Toro

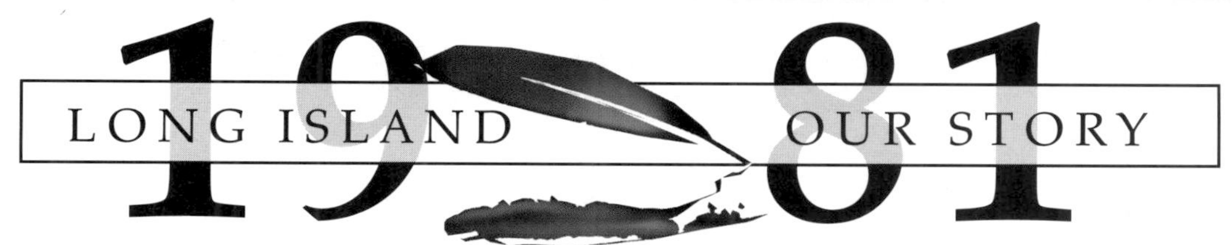

The Nassau GOP chairman's powerful machine sputters when he goes to jail

The Fall of Joseph Margiotta

BY RITA CIOLLI
STAFF WRITER

GOP-1. The license plates of the chairman of the local Republican Party told who was boss.

By the 1970s, Nassau County's suburban political machine had become the single most powerful GOP organization in the country, and Joseph Margiotta was being compared to the nation's legendary political leaders. From the newest town councilman to the president of the United States, Margiotta was Long Island's influential wheeler-dealer who linked them all.

Other Nassau Republican leaders had commanded wide influence. J. Russel Sprague, for instance, was instrumental in the nomination of Dwight D. Eisenhower, and the party had dominated county politics for most of the last century. But when Margiotta took over as chairman in 1967, he created what was to become an electoral juggernaut. He returned power to local leaders who owed their own power to the chairman. He also centralized fund-raising, introduced polling techniques and wrote a handbook, "How to Run an Election District."

In the end, Margiotta may have been too successful in dispensing patronage, the lifeblood of any political party. His increasing power over municipal hiring, promotions and contracts attracted the attention of federal and state prosecutors who spent much of the 1970s looking for evidence that he had crossed the line separating the political from the criminal. Finally, on Dec. 9, 1981, Margiotta's unchallenged power came to a crashing end when a federal jury convicted him on charges that he had presided over an illegal insurance fee-splitting scheme that enriched his political cronies. A judge later sentenced Margiotta to two years in prison, despite a parade of character witnesses that read like a Who's Who of the Island's community leaders.

The specific charge in the case was that under Margiotta, $678,000 in county insurance commissions was kicked back to politically connected brokers. But the premise of the case was perhaps more significant: Prosecutors contended that Margiotta was so powerful a political leader that he virtually ran the governments of Hempstead Town and Nassau County. Therefore, in a novel legal theory, the prosecutors argued that it was Margiotta, as much as any elected official, who owed a duty of honest government.

The shocking downfall of the state's pre-eminent party leader was the most important political story of its time on Long Island, and its repercussions are still influencing GOP politics. His throne was taken by Alfonse D'Amato, who in 1980 had begged Margiotta for permission to challenge Jacob Javits, the incumbent Republican U.S. senator. D'Amato has been the state's most important Republican kingmaker ever since.

Margiotta appealed his conviction all the way to the U.S. Supreme Court, but when the high court refused to hear the case in 1983, Margiotta resigned as party leader in Nassau and passed control to his hand-picked successor, Joseph Mondello. His choice of a little known party leader led some to believe that there was an agreement that Mondello would give control back to Margiotta after he served his sentence. But when the former party chairman returned from prison, he found no seat for him at the GOP table. Mondello remains in control 15 years later, and by all accounts, the personal and political rift between the two men has never healed.

It also took several years for the Nassau GOP to recover from the wounds of the Margiotta case. The party suffered so many financial setbacks in the late 1980s that it was even forced to give up its four season seats to the Islanders. The party lost control of the Towns of North Hempstead and Oyster Bay, though feuding Nassau Democrats were never able to parlay these gains into parity with the long-entrenched Republicans.

By 1991, Mondello also closed the books on another vestige of Margiotta's old party machine by making the final payment in a $1.3-million settlement of what had been known as the "1 percent case." The GOP had to repay Town of Hempstead workers who said that in the early 1970s they had to kick back 1 percent of their salaries to the party in return for jobs, promotions and overtime.

Margiotta's downfall, and the end of his political system, had grown out of a 1978 State Investigation Commission report charging that municipal governments throughout the state were giving their insurance business to politically connected brokers. The main broker in Nassau, Richard Williams, split those fees with other brokers — Republican leaders designated by Margiotta. Although it was a legal, statewide practice, and the Democrats also did it when they held the county executive seat in the 1960s, prosecutors later said that Margiotta was targeted because of the way he had institutionalized the practice.

"Everyone was doing 70 miles an hour in a 65-mile-an-hour zone. Margiotta was doing 100," was how the patronage system was described at the time by Edward Korman, then the U.S. attorney for the Eastern District of New York. The indictment charging Margiotta with extortion and mail fraud was handed down in November, 1979.

While the legal theories used in the prosecution raised cries of a witch hunt from the party faithful, the case revealed how patronage and party loyalty were intertwined. At Margiotta's trial, William Cahn, the former Nassau district attorney, told of how he went to the party leader for money after he lost his bid for re-election in 1974 to Denis Dillon. Cahn testified that for the next five years, even after he was convicted of charges of double billing while in office, his family received $2,000 a month from Williams for little or no work.

After eight days of deliberations, jurors said they were deadlocked, 8-4 in favor of acquittal, and a mistrial was declared. Korman got permission to retry the case from his supervisor at the Justice Department — Rudolph Giuliani. With a different jury and more tightly focused prosecution, Margiotta was convicted on all counts.

Throughout the ordeal, he refused to consider any plea bargain to a misdemeanor. "I thought I hadn't done anything wrong. I didn't do anything wrong," he said in a recent interview.

Margiotta, now 70, regained his license to practice law in 1991 and still works out of his old power base of Uniondale. He does most of his political consulting these days for the rising Republican leader in Suffolk, John Powell. And he is still a powerful fund raiser for charities, mostly for Hofstra University, where he once played football.

From his box in the new stadium, Margiotta can see the top of the federal courthouse where he was convicted. He acknowledges the irony but shares very little of his emotions about the experience he still calls "my problem." "People always ask me about revenge," he says. "The way I am going to get my revenge is to be happy and successful."

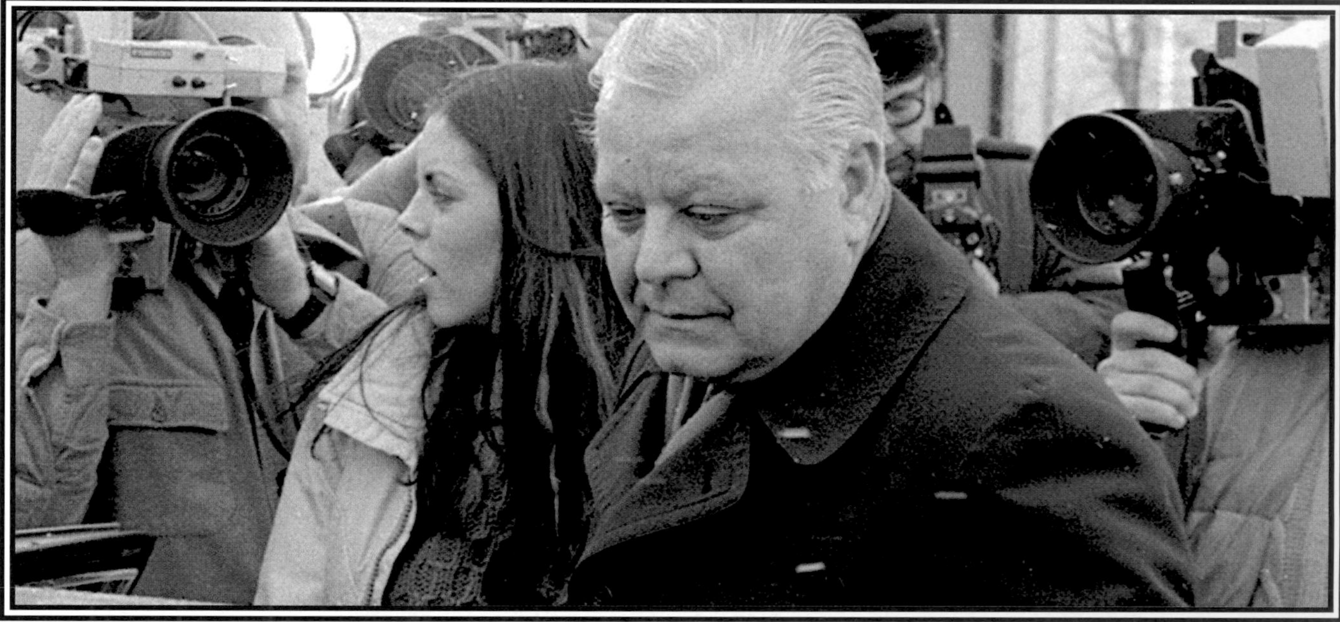

Newsday Photo / Alan Raia

GOP leader Joseph Margiotta gets into his car in 1982 after being sentenced to two years in prison for an insurance kickback scheme.

LEGACY

Newsday Photo / Bill Davis

A MAN, HIS COLLEGE, HIS MONUMENT

Joseph Margiotta, a Hofstra alumnus, football player, former trustee and president of the Hofstra Pride Club, stands in front of the new athletic department building, Joseph M. Margiotta Hall.

Marine biologist Sam Sadove examines the condition of Physty, the 6-year-old, 25-foot-long, 12-ton sperm whale that spent nine days in April, 1981, at Captree Boat Basin, where tens of thousands of humans came together for a close encounter. Physty was eventually nursed back to health and escorted back out to sea by a flotilla of ships.

Newsday Photo / Bob Luckey

Thanks to caring Long Islanders, he fights off pneumonia and returns to sea

Physty, the Big, Brave Whale

By Irene Virag
STAFF WRITER

He swam to us, sick and foundering, out of the deepest deeps and for one shining moment he called to what is good in all of us. We named him after the Latin for his species, *Physeter macrocephalus,* the largest of the toothed whales.

Physty for short.

The story of Physty is a whale of a tale suited for this place called Paumonok. Long Island is after all an island and it deserves a great fish story. And even if whales are red-blooded mammals, they rule the sea and so what better story than the saga of the 12-ton sperm whale that visited our shores for nine days in April of 1981. A saga that was part soap opera, part deathwatch, part rescue mission.

The story's ending is still at sea. But it began when a 6-year-old sperm whale fell behind his pod somewhere in the Atlantic. According to the best guesses of experts who know about such things, Physty swam through polluted waters and contracted bacteria that turned into a form of pneumonia. The currents pulled him into Fire Island Inlet. Soon after, on the morning of April 16, a motorist driving on Oak Beach Road spotted a slate-colored mound offshore and thought it was a sinking boat. Instead, he found a stranded 25-foot-long whale struggling in water 3 feet deep.

Marine biologist Sam Sadove, founder and then director of the Okeanos Ocean Research Foundation, was among the first to be called. "I was told it was a dead 10- to 12-foot whale," Sadove recalls. "I figured it was a pilot whale and I could pick it up in my truck. When I got there, I realized it wasn't a pilot whale and it wasn't dead."

But before Physty swam into legend, he had to be towed a mile and a half east to the deeper waters of Captree Boat Basin, where tens of thousands of humans came together for a close encounter. They watched from the dock and the beach as a 12-ton E.T. struggled to survive on the edge of suburbia. Faith healers came with holy water and state officials — with little faith — made funeral plans. Children offered chicken soup and Easter eggs and divers carried squid laced with antibiotics.

As marine scientists turned the 500-foot-wide basin into a giant marine E.R., a kinship grew between creatures great and small. And Physty got his name. "The name," says Sam Sadove, "was a play on words based on the Latin *Physeter* and on "feisty," which, at the risk of anthropomorphizing, this whale definitely was."

From the beginning the key was to get antibiotics into the cetacean. At first, scientists tried unsuccessfully to pry open his jaws with a two-by-four and pump antibiotic tablets down his throat with a hose. But like an obstinate child, or perhaps a suspicious stranger, Physty refused to open his mouth. Rescuers feared he wouldn't make it through the night.

The significance of what finally happened in the boat basin is perhaps best measured by the humans who touched the great whale — and in turn, were touched by him. One of them was Michael Sandlofer, a Vietnam veteran who learned to dive in the Navy and had just opened a marine museum on City Island in the Bronx. On a chilly spring night, Sandlofer, a member of the rescue team, dove into the choppy basin and called to the wild.

"I made a sound, a whale sound," he recalls. "I'd stop, move, stop, move. His eye followed my movements. I could see he wanted a human encounter. I took off my gloves as a sign of respect and rubbed my hands together for warmth.

"I moved toward him with my hands outstretched. My mind kept saying, 'Get out of here,' but my heart said, 'Come to me, Physty.' He swam toward me. I was petrified. I swam under him, he opened his mouth like a giant Castro convertible and I fed him a squid."

Now there was a way to make the medicine go down. The next night, the squid were laced with hundreds of 500-mg. tablets of an antibiotic. The diver hand-fed Physty nightly until more than five pounds of antibiotics were in the whale's system.

"I'm the person who put my hand in Physty's mouth," says Sandlofer, whose museum features an exhibit and video that tells the whale's story. "I know that whale trusted me and I trusted him. I was touched by a whale and I'll never forget it."

Physty left Long Island 17 years ago, at 1:45 p.m. on the 25th of April, 1981, as thousands of humans cheered from the dock. "Go Physty, go. Go," they yelled, lost in the group dynamic of the first successful effort in the United States to nurse a stranded whale back to health and send it out to sea.

Physty was herded out of the basin by a flotilla of ships that included three Coast Guard vessels and an inflatable skiff. He stopped three times and flicked his tail. When he was about 100 feet from the basin, Physty rolled over and gave three strong calls and blew spray from his blowhole.

"Whale gone bye-bye," a 3-year-old watching from his father's shoulders cried out. And Physty swam home.

It would be nice to think that Physty spread his own legend among his species — the story of a fish-shaped island of two-legged mammals who cared. It is a romantic thought, and it has not been lost on Sam Sadove, whose very calling — the saving of aquatic creatures — is a measure of how far we have come from the days when Long Islanders went into the sea to kill whales. Normally, the down-to-sea scientist does not like to attribute human characteristics to wildlife, but it seems different when it comes to Physty.

"It's hard to say if Physty has a memory of his time on Long Island," he says. "He was a young whale and maybe like with humans, memory from youth is thin. Is it possible that Physty has that ability to remember? There's no real way of knowing. But I can tell you this. When you look into the eye of a sperm whale, you get a sense that there's something going on in there. Does Physty remember? Even if it's just a fanciful thought, it's a nice thought."

Two years after Physty left our shores, Sam Sadove was on a sea-life survey flight over the Atlantic when he saw a group of sperm whales. One of them had the telltale marks left on Physty's tail by the nylon rope used to tow him into Captree Basin.

"Physty was seen alive," Sam Sadove says. "Exactly when and where I won't answer. It was a significant amount of time after the stranding for me to be sure he recovered. I saw the scar on the tail flukes — and I knew it was Physty. He'll have those scars for as long as he lives. And a sperm whale can live for more than 70 years.

"I'd like to think Physty's still out there," says Sadove.

As would we all. It is nice to think that Physty is surging through the ocean, sounding in the deepest deeps and remembering the kindness of strangers. And if we believe in Physty, we can trust that our own tomorrow is out there, too, waiting on the far horizon.

Newsday Photo / Bob Luckey

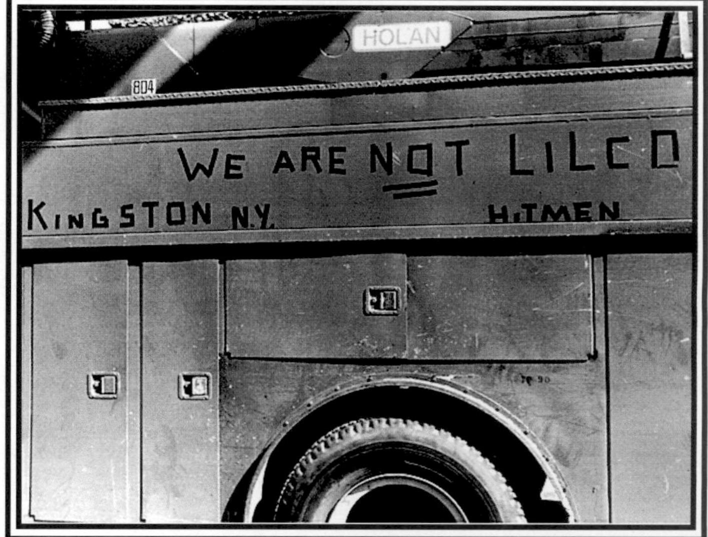

Newsday Photo / Dick Yarwood

At left, some of Hurricane Gloria's destruction on Ponquogue Avenue in Hampton Bays in 1985. Above, workers on a truck brought in by an upstate utility make clear their nonaffiliation with LILCO, whose response furthered its reputation as the utility Long Islanders loved to hate.

An epic hurricane transforms LI, its people and, eventually, its power company

Life in the Wake of Gloria

BY STEVE WICK
STAFF WRITER

Eleven days and eight hours after Hurricane Gloria knocked out their electrical service, the lights finally went on in Richard and Carol Mogil's Centereach home.

"We were among the very last to get our power back," Richard Mogil recalled. "It was very painful for us. We waited and we waited. We boiled water and did all our cooking on a gas grill in the backyard. We couldn't take hot showers, and you can't believe how you miss that after a while.

"It really got old quick," he added. "It was such a relief to see the truck coming down our street that last day."

On Oct. 8, 1985, a terse statement read by a Long Island Lighting Co. spokesman said the utility's power system, devastated when Hurricane Gloria roared ashore on Sept. 27, had been restored to normal. All over Long Island, homeowners who had not been able to flush their toilets, take a shower, cook dinner in an electric oven or flick on the lights, breathed deep sighs of relief. Their regional nightmare was over.

As hurricanes go, there had been far worse ones than Gloria — the storm of 1938, for instance. Photographs of Westhampton Beach after the hurricane of 1938 showing overturned cars and mountains of lumber from wrecked houses have an unreal quality to them, as if no storm could possibly have done such damage. Gloria, though, did far more to change Long Island than any previous storm. As soon as the lights blinked out on Sept. 27 — to stay out, in some neighborhoods, for a week or more — Gloria became as much a political storm as a weather event.

First, Gloria showed Long Island's weak underbelly: Without power from the region's principal supplier, LILCO, the nearly 750,000 customers who lost it could barely carry on their day-to-day lives. Routine events were turned into ordeals. Because Long Island Rail Road crossings did not work, train service was cut back dramatically, and trip times were extended. A commuter train from Southampton that normally took two hours to reach Manhattan took eight hours. Hundreds of schools were closed because buildings were too dark to conduct classes in, and consumers across the region complained of being gouged for such items as water, ice, generators, milk and bread.

Second, Gloria — and the long time it took to get electrical service back to normal — greatly magnified the antagonism toward LILCO many Long Islanders already felt. It embittered homeowners who had never given more than a thought to the utility, and drew thousands of converts to a burgeoning anti-LILCO movement, which eventually forced the closing of the utility's Shoreham nuclear power plant and, earlier this month, the sale of the company itself.

"There is no question that Hurricane Gloria changed Long Island in profound ways," said Lee Koppelman, executive director of the Long Island Regional Planning Board. "We were a different kind of place after Gloria."

Born in the south Atlantic Ocean, Gloria plodded its way up the East Coast before landing on Long Island with 100 mph winds one morning in early fall. Of the 11 deaths attributed to the storm across the Northeast, only one was on Long Island. However, a third of the $300 million damage caused by the storm occurred here. On South Shore barrier beaches, 48 summer homes were ripped off their foundations and smashed to pieces.

As the storm passed to the north, more than two-thirds of LILCO's customers were left without power. In many communities without municipal water systems, that meant — in addition to having no electricity — they were also without water for household use. Toilets could not be flushed and clothes could not be washed. "It was hard from the beginning," Mogil said, "but as the days added up and there was no remedy in sight, it got horrible. We kept calling and calling LILCO, but we could never get through."

To attack the widespread destruction of their supply system, LILCO brought in utilities from across the Northeast. But the pace of recovery was slow, and as power was restored unevenly in many communities, crews were jeered and booed by angry homeowners.

Four days after Gloria struck, Long Islanders were increasingly feeling the pinch — from the long waits for ice and commuter trains to the long days and nights without power. But the brunt of their criticism went to LILCO, and its chairman, William Catacosinos, who was on vacation in Italy when Gloria brought the worst disaster in the utility's history. That the chairman chose not to rush home was the final indignity to many Long Islanders. "If it was me, I would have gotten my ass on the first plane back," Nassau County Executive Francis Purcell declared at the time. "I would have swum back if I had to."

Catacosinos did come home a few days after the storm hit — and promptly announced that LILCO wanted to charge ratepayers for the estimated $40 million storm repair bill. In defending the proposal, LILCO said it had no hurricane insurance, and a storm reserve fund had a negative balance. Who else but the ratepayers could pick up the costs?

Gov. Mario Cuomo characterized the idea of billing customers for the damage as "chutzpah," adding that Long Islanders "aren't that stupid" to accept it. Purcell called it "outrageous," and Suffolk County Executive Peter Cohalan said it was "unconscionable." By the 11th day, as power came back on in Centereach and other neighborhoods hardest hit, the public backlash against LILCO reached a crescendo. That day, a group called Citizens to Replace LILCO announced plans to take over the company and operate it as a public utility. During the next 13 years, the Long Island Power Authority was created, Shoreham was abandoned, and the most reviled company on Long Island ceased to exist.

OTHER BOUTS WITH NATURE

Sorry, Gloria, wild as you were, you weren't the worst. You were just No. 2. The nor'easter that slammed into Long Island on Dec. 11, 1992 — and in 48 furious hours rearranged coastlines shaped at the close of the Ice Age 12,000 years ago — got the most respect from the National Weather Service meteorologists at Brookhaven National Lab in Upton. Ask any former homeowner on Dune Road in Westhampton Beach.

After Hurricane Gloria, here are nature's most serious troublemakers in the past 25 years, ranked by Brookhaven meteorologist-in-charge Mike Wyllie as follows: **3)** the blizzard of '78, more damaging than **4)** the blizzard of January, '96, which dumped 20 inches of snow on most of Long Island, and **5)** the superstorm of March, '93, which might be called the messiest after snow turned to sleet and freezing rain.

Then there was **6)** the October Halloween Surprise of '96, as it was unaffectionately called, and **7)** Hurricane Bob of '91, our last great coastal-flooding, tree-uprooting, power-outaging hurricane. Then we came through the record-breaking winter of '95-'96, which blanketed 70 to 90 inches of snow across Long Island. Call it **8)**, **9)** and **10)**. — Rhoda Amon

CHAPTER 9 TRANSFORMATION 1986

Donald Manes' attempted suicide points the way to corruption in the city's agencies

A Queens-Size Scandal

BY PAUL MOSES
STAFF WRITER

He was the king of Queens, alone on a highway in the middle of the night with a bleeding wrist and a 10½-inch fillet knife at his side. Driving erratically on the Grand Central Parkway, he was pulled over by two police officers who found none other than Donald Manes, the Queens borough president and Democratic leader.

"I'm cut," Manes told them, his explanation for the two-inch, Y-shaped gash on his left wrist.

So began the saga of one of the largest political corruption scandals in New York City's considerable history in such matters. From payoffs made in return for contracts to collect parking-ticket debts, it burgeoned to engulf dozens of lobbyists and officials of a wide range of agencies during the next two years. It spurred some modest changes in ethics laws, imperiled Edward I. Koch's mayoralty and helped lift Rudolph Giuliani's career.

The scandal was propelled by the sheer mystery of why the powerful, politically savvy "Donny" Manes had come to such desperate straits in the early morning darkness of Jan. 10, 1986.

Rather than admit an attempt to take his own life, Manes lied to police at first, claiming kidnapers had cut him. The four-term borough president's power was such that even after the city's detective chief announced he believed Manes had attempted suicide, prominent Queens Democrats attending a birthday party for the hospitalized Manes that same night said they believed him and not the police.

Giuliani, the U.S. attorney in Manhattan, had a pretty good idea of what was going on, though. A shady informer had led the FBI to a collection agent, Bernard Sandow, who had been paying off Geoffrey Lindenauer, deputy director of the city Parking Violations Bureau, to get contracts. And Lindenauer was a buddy of Manes.

Giuliani could have waited to follow all the leads and quietly built a case. But he seized the day and had Lindenauer arrested immediately.

Lindenauer later said he and Manes had both discussed suicide as a way out, and ended up tearfully embracing in Manes' living room as Lindenauer pledged he would never confess they had been taking bribes together.

But Lindenauer quickly turned informant after his arrest, and the scheme unraveled quicker than a videotape on rewind. He told investigators that he and Manes had shared a half-million dollars in bribes for collection agency contracts. But the big payoff, it was later charged, came from Bronx Democratic boss Stanley Friedman, who secretly cut Lindenauer and Manes in on stock in Citisource Inc., in return for giving the company a $22.7-million city contract for hand-held computers for issuing parking tickets.

By the time Manes actually did kill himself — with a kitchen knife in his Jamaica Estates home on March 13, 1986, two months after the first attempt — the shadow of scandal had begun to spread from the parking bureau to other agencies. Prosecutors and the news media, for the most part caught snoozing, rushed into their own investigations and for the next two years, political corruption dominated the city's agenda.

Giuliani led the derby, starting with a victory in Friedman's trial, which he prosecuted personally. But his biggest political corruption probe resulted in a series of convictions involving payoffs made by Wedtech, a Bronx-based defense contractor. Rep. Mario Biaggi (D-Bronx) and Bronx Borough President Stanley Simon were among those convicted.

Federal and local prosecutors around the city also made a variety of other public corruption cases, leading to convictions of such figures as Brooklyn Democratic boss Meade Esposito; Jay Turoff, head of the city taxi commission; Richard Rubin, executive secretary of the Queens Democratic Party, and Queens Administrative Judge Francis X. Smith.

Koch, who'd won re-election easily in 1985, was slowly dragged down by the scandal, which started just 10 days into his third term. The normally buoyant Koch had to admit he'd gotten too close to the political bosses and that his own investigations department bungled a good chance to uncover corruption in the parking bureau.

Giuliani, on the other hand, was the man of the hour. He'd already been successful in indicting mob bosses, but the municipal corruption scandal made him a player on the political scene, a crusader whose advice on changing the system was constantly sought. He took one major false step: a bribery-conspiracy case against Koch confidante Bess Myerson, who was acquitted in a resounding defeat for Giuliani.

Within months after resigning as U.S. attorney, Giuliani was running for mayor as a Republican, lambasting Koch for letting "crooks" control hiring in City Hall. The once-unassailable Koch sought an unprecedented fourth term but never made it to the general election; he lost the 1989 Democratic primary to Manhattan Borough President David Dinkins, who narrowly defeated Giuliani to become mayor. Giuliani won the return match four years later.

The scandal led to creation of two commissions aimed at passing reforms to end what many said was systemic corruption in city government. But the success of those efforts is debatable.

The city investigations department was expanded and given control over the inspectors general in each agency, but is still criticized as too close to the mayor. County political leaders were barred from being elected city officials, as Manes was. But Queens Democratic leader Tom Manton is still allowed to serve in Congress.

Limits have also been placed on campaign contributions, which once ran up to $50,000 in mayoral campaigns. But just last year, the city Campaign Finance Board found the rules were often dodged when related companies gave numerous donations at the legal limit, $7,700.

And there are stricter rules to keep former city officials from lobbying city government, as Friedman did. But the rules continue to have major loopholes, often rendering them meaningless.

As for Manes, he was never convicted or even indicted. But as the late Newsday columnist Murray Kempton wrote, "There cannot, after all, be much left to say about Donald Manes once you have said that no sin of his could have been half so awful as what he suffered for it."

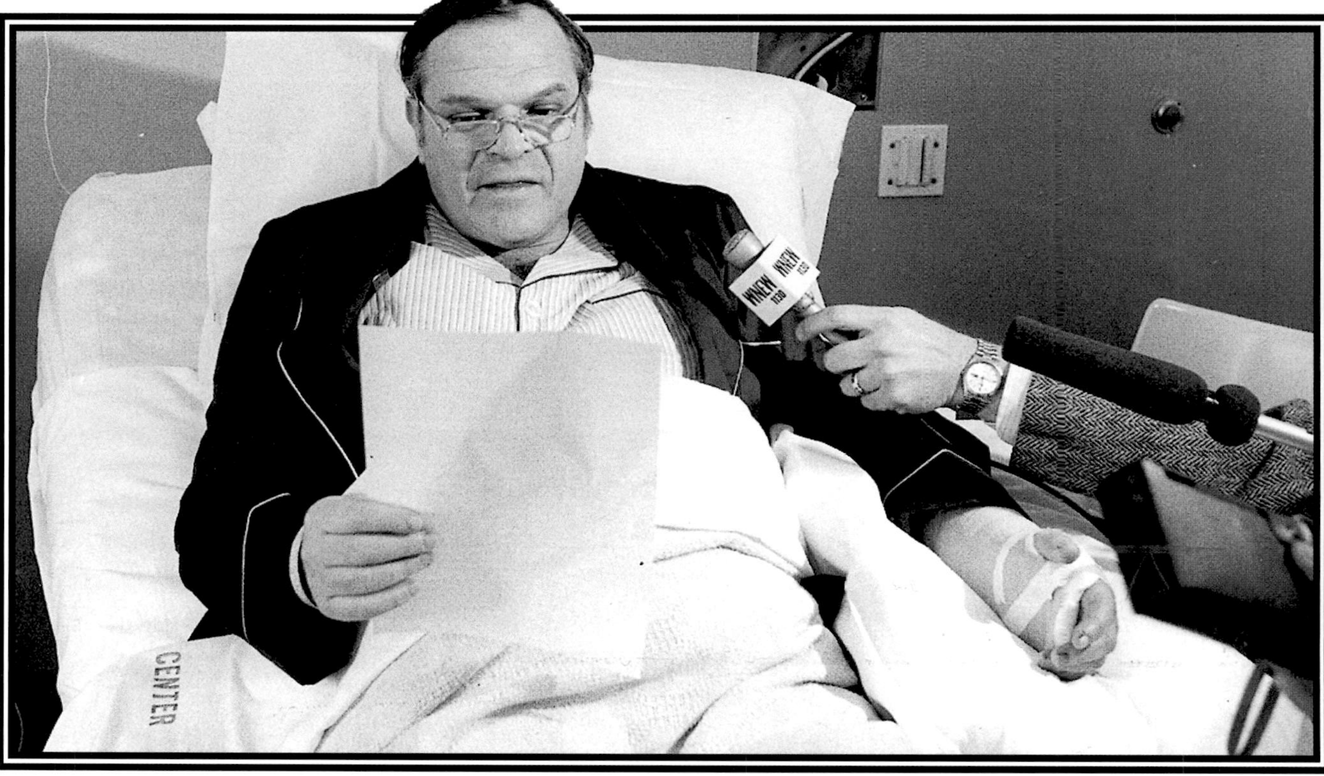

AP Photo

Newsday Photo

Queens Borough President Donald Manes, his left wrist bandaged in 1986, admits he made a suicide attempt. At left, in 1985, he greets Mayor Ed Koch, who had to admit that he was too close to bosses such as Manes.

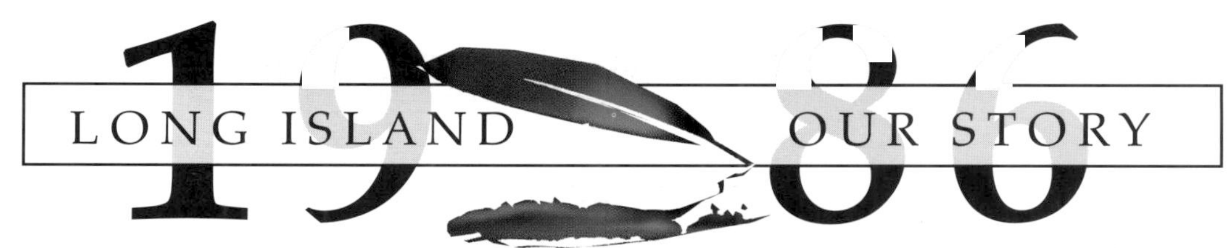

An assault on blacks by mob of whites in Howard Beach becomes a symbol of racism

An Ugly Racial Attack

BY PETE BOWLES
STAFF WRITER

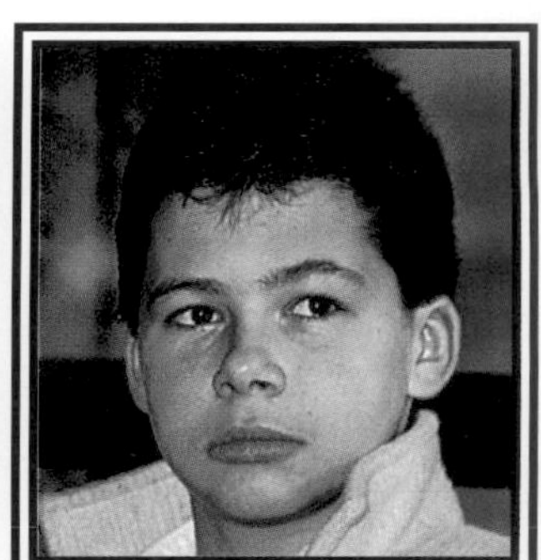

Ladone, Newsday Photo / Richard Lee; Riley, Photo by Paul Demaria; Lester, Newsday Photo / Alan Raia

THE PURSUERS: From left, Jason Ladone, Scott Kern, Robert Riley and Jon Lester were convicted in the attack that led to Michael Griffith's death.

Grimes, Newsday Photo / Jeffrey A. Salter; Sandiford, Newsday Photo / Donna Dietrich

THE PURSUED: From left, Michael Griffith, Timothy Grimes and Cedric Sandiford were victims of attack.

The tragedy of Howard Beach — a mob attack on three black men that turned a quiet Queens neighborhood into a national symbol of racism — began on the night of Dec. 19, 1986.

The three blacks from Brooklyn — Michael Griffith, Cedric Sandiford and Timothy Grimes — found themselves stranded in Howard Beach when their car broke down. They quickly discovered they were in the wrong neighborhood. Leaving their car to look for a tow truck, they walked along Cross Bay Boulevard and were harangued by a carload of white teenagers who were driving a friend home from a birthday party. Angry words and racial epithets were exchanged.

The car sped off and Griffith, Sandiford and Grimes continued to the New Park Pizza, where each had a slice.

Back at the party, according to trial evidence, Jon Lester, then 17, roused the crowd by shouting, "There's ——— at the New Park, let's go kill them."

Shortly after leaving the pizzeria — it was now early in the morning of Dec. 20 — the three black men were confronted on Cross Bay Boulevard by a dozen white youths wielding baseball bats and tree limbs. They bolted.

Grimes wielded a knife and managed to escape without injury. Sandiford was slammed across the back with a baseball bat. "Everybody jumped in," Sandiford later testified, 'beating me with tree limbs and sticks and kicking me. I said, 'Oh God, I'm dead.' "

Griffith turned and ran north on 90th Street. Shouting racial epithets, ordering the young construction worker to "get out of the neighborhood," Lester, Robert Riley, Scott Kern and Jason Ladone chased the lone black man into traffic on the Belt Parkway, according to testimony. There, he was struck by a car, his body thrown in the air and hurled about 100 feet forward before landing on the highway. The impact shattered the car's windshield. Witnesses who saw the body lying on the highway said it did not look like a human being — only a clump of rags. Michael Griffith was dead at 23.

Three Howard Beach youths were eventually convicted of manslaughter and assault in the case, and three others were convicted of riot charges. But the aftermath lingered for years. Demonstrators shouted "Howard Beach, have you heard? This is not Johannesburg!" and the resulting trials, along with a book and an NBC docudrama, focused national attention on a racially troubled city. The name "Howard Beach" became synonymous with racism — much to the dismay of residents of the small enclave adjacent to Kennedy Airport. Years later, recalling the reaction of white residents of Howard Beach following the last trial, special state prosecutor Charles J. Hynes — now the Brooklyn district attorney — said, "It is sad to me that an American jury, leaving an American courtroom, is booed. That's a tragedy. That's one of the many tragedies of this case."

The incident — one of the most controversial and potentially volatile cases in New York City in the 1980s — also made important public figures of a number of people who became associated with the case, including Hynes. The tragedy also brought one of the first sound stages for civil rights activists Alton Maddox, C. Vernon Mason and the Rev. Al Sharpton.

In his closing statement at the second trial, Assistant State Special Prosecutor James Kohler told the jury: "I have apologized for the obscene language used at this trial, but the greatest obscenity was this: That the actions of this group of 12 young men were based on racial hatred, and that what took place in Howard Beach on Dec. 20, 1986, was a race riot in every ugly sense of the word."

When he sentenced Lester to 10 to 30 years in prison a year after the attack, State Supreme Court Justice Thomas Demakos said the youth "exhibited such a hatred and such a callousness toward the life of another human being which must not go unpunished."

In 1989, when the Appellate Division upheld the manslaughter convictions of Lester, Ladone and Kern, Justice Milton Mollen said, "A message loud and clear must go forth that racial violence by any person or group, whatever their race, will not be tolerated by a just and civilized society, and that when it does occur it must be appropriately punished."

About three years after the attack, Sandiford, who was 36 when he was badly beaten, married Jean Griffith, the mother of Michael Griffith. He later died of complications from AIDS. Grimes, 18 at the time of the attack, was later sentenced to 16 years in a Virginia prison for shooting his brother in the face with a shotgun.

In a prison interview in 1994, Jon Lester said the college education he pursued behind bars has changed his life. He earned a degree in business administration. Like his co-defendants, he remains in prison.

"I can't stand racists," said Lester, now 28. "They're small and frightened and ignorant." He also admitted his role in the Howard Beach case. "No excuses for me," he said. "I take responsibility for my actions. I'm responsible for someone being dead. I can never undo that, and I will live with it every day forever."

Seven years after the vicious attack, the city agreed to pay the families of Griffith and Sandiford a total of $50,000 to settle a civil suit charging that the police treated the victims like crime suspects because they were black. With the settlement, the victims' families called for peace and an end to racial hatred in the city. Said Griffith's brother, Christopher Griffith, "We are challenging the people to work toward a day when every citizen can walk in any neighborhood without fearing for his life."

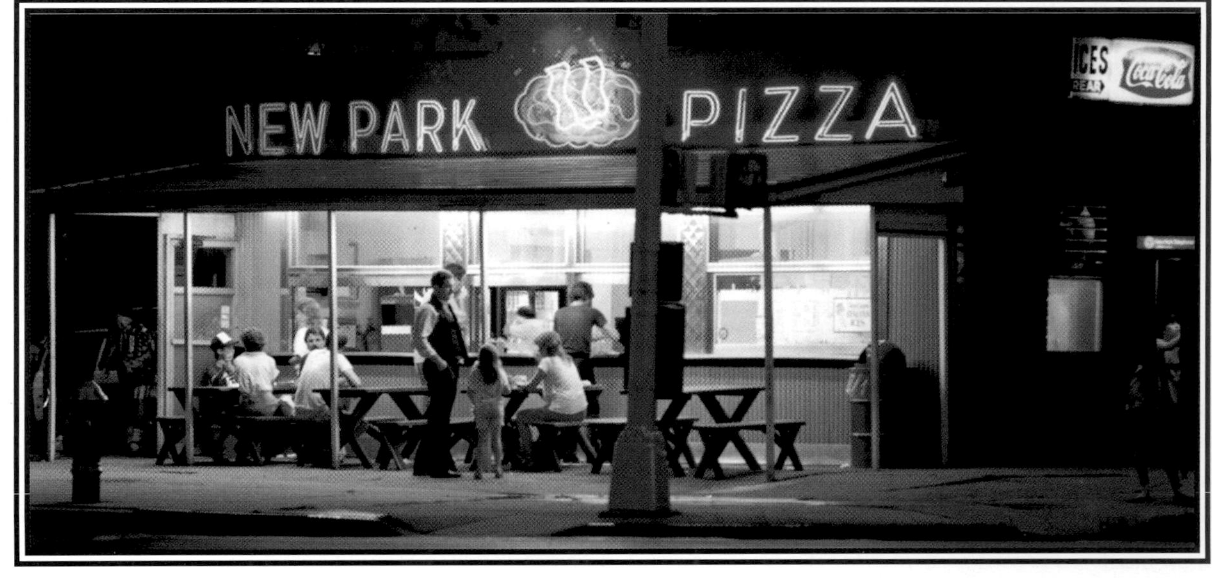

Newsday Photo, 1988 / Daniel Sheehan

Griffith, Grimes and Sandiford stopped at this pizza place on Cross Bay Boulevard before the attack began.

A plan to send Long Island garbage south becomes a national joke — but helps solve a problem

Barging Into A Trashy Saga

BY SHIRLEY PERLMAN
STAFF WRITER

It was 1987 and America was awash in trashy news, most notably the sex scandals involving former U.S. Sen. Gary Hart and television evangelist Jim Bakker.

But the trash story that eclipsed all others was the saga of Long Island's wandering garbage barge and its futile 6,000-mile search for a home.

Towed by the tugboat Break of Dawn, the ill-fated scow and its outcast cargo sailed into the national consciousness late that winter, the brainchild of Lowell Harrelson, a flamboyant Alabama businessman who thought he could turn trash into treasure by barging it off the Island to cheap dumping sites down south.

Instead of profit, he found a maelstrom of protest and ridicule that drew headlines across the country. As the barge sailed up and down the coast, its travails were chronicled not only on the nightly news, but on the nightly monologue: It provided Johnny Carson more material than Gary Hart's Monkey Business.

The odyssey of the garbage barge was an indignity that perfectly, and inevitably, symbolized the Long Island garbage crisis of the 1980s. What to do with trash had become an issue throughout the country, but on Long Island the problem was especially acute. After the Island's landfills were identified as a major source of groundwater contamination, the state Legislature passed a law in 1983 banning all landfilling by 1990. So what to do with the trash?

In 1987, 80 percent of the area's garbage was dumped in landfills. But with the 1990 deadline fast approaching, politicians scrambled for a solution. Incineration plants tended to be inefficient and also were considered a source of air pollution. Recycling had been unsuccessful. In desperation, some towns were now trucking their trash off the Island, mainly to upstate sites. The price, almost $100 a ton, was at least twice the cost at landfills. But by 1987, this method accounted for the disposal of 13 percent of Long Island's garbage — more than twice the percentage of trash that was burned in local incinerators.

Into this picture sailed Harrelson and his barge. His plan was to lease the vessels he saw rusting on the Mississippi River, abandoned by the offshore oil industry, and load them with New York trash that could be dumped in farm fields in the South. He traveled to New York and met with Thomas Hroncich, who ran Waste Alternatives Inc., a transfer station in Islip where garbage was loaded on trucks and hauled away. Hroncich contacted Thomas Gesuale, a Dix Hills man who owned a dockside business in Queens, and together they brought in four Long Island carting companies as partners. Each carter put up $50,000, and United Marine Transport Services — the garbage barge people — was born. The partners envisioned leasing four barges to haul 10,000 tons a day — at a profit of $200,000 a day. "He said when he first came here this was better than oil," Gesuale said of Harrelson.

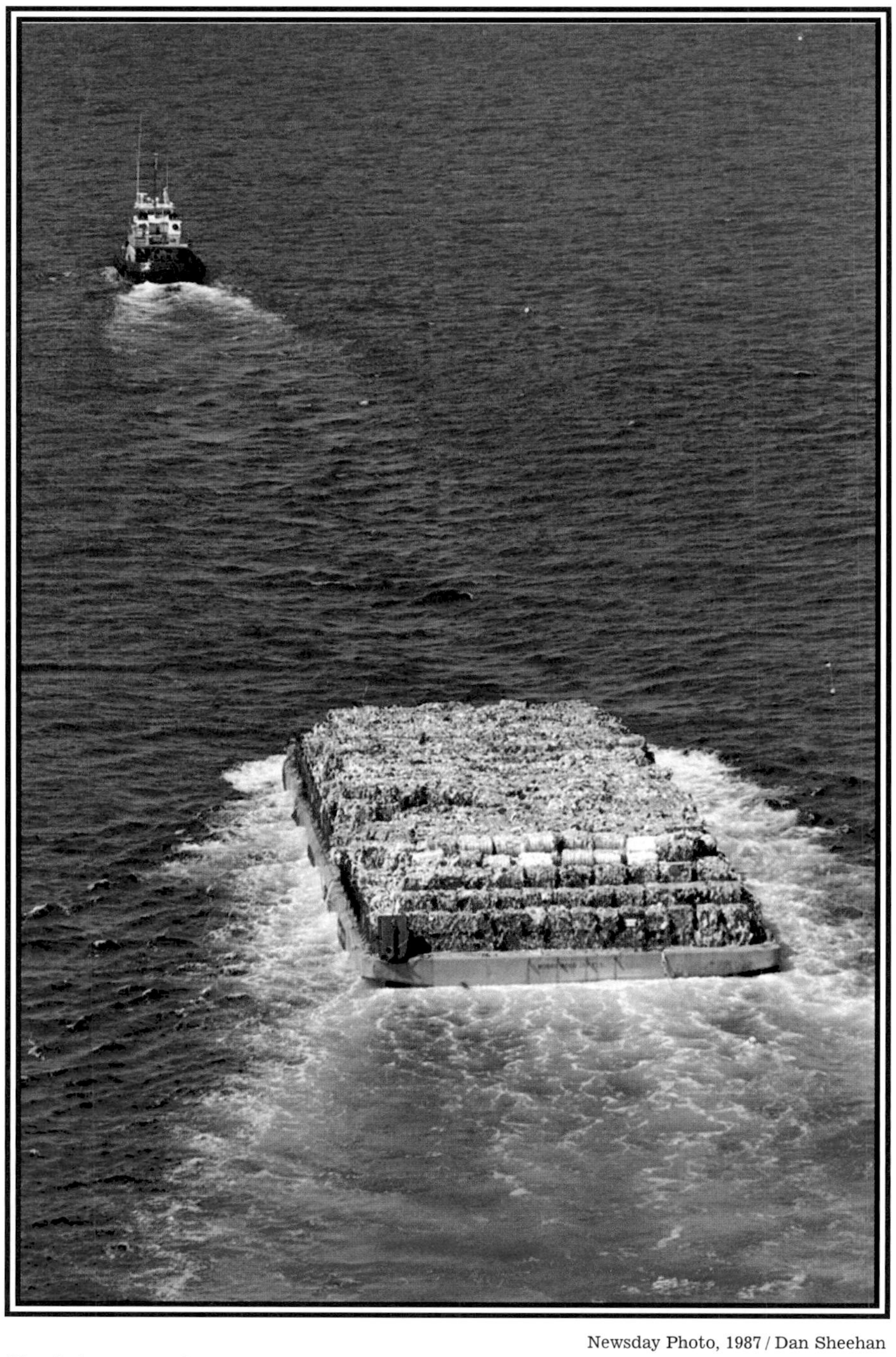

On March 22, the Break of Dawn pulled out of New York with 3,186 tons of baled Islip trash in tow. At the helm was Duffy St. Pierre, a soft-spoken Cajun sea captain from New Orleans, with a crew of three men. Three days later, the barge docked in North Carolina, where Harrelson had verbal agreements with a few farmers to use some of their land for dump sites. And then . . .

"There were these two little old ladies in Morehead City living in a house near the dock where the barge pulled up," Hroncich recalled recently. "They called the mayor's office, and one thing led to another. They really started it."

The mayor called the governor. The governor barred the barge from docking anywhere in the state. The same thing happened in Louisiana (where Harrelson had written agreements to dump the trash in landfills), Texas and Florida. By then, nobody wanted Long Island's garbage, but everyone was talking about it.

Hroncich, now a solid waste manager in Cape May County, N.J., says that things might have been different had the cargo been covered. The partners decided against a $6,000 tarpaulin because the Coast Guard told them it wasn't necessary. But if the little old ladies from Morehead City hadn't gotten a look at the cargo, Hroncich says wistfully, "It could have been a different story."

As the barge continued from port to port, the story was the same: Cuba said no, and so did the little country of Belize. Mexico said it would dispatch gunboats if the barge tried to approach the Yucatan Peninsula. On the "Tonight" show, Johnny Carson had an idea for Capt. St. Pierre: "Do a U-e at Yemen . . . a hard left at Oman, up into the Gulf of Persia and — there is Iran. Dump it right there."

On May 16, after two months at sea, the beleaguered garbage barge sailed back into New York Harbor under police escort and then dropped anchor in Brooklyn's Gravesend Bay. There it became a tourist attraction for almost four months while state and local officials battled in court about what to do with the trash, and others fretted over allegations by state investigators that three of the project's five silent partners had connections to organized crime.

Finally, in August, after four months of legal wrangling, an agreement was reached to burn the trash in Brooklyn and bury the ash at the Islip landfill. On Sept. 1, the first truckload of ash was deposited atop the landfill without protest or fanfare. Frank Jones, then the Islip town supervisor, breathed a sigh of relief. "I am without question sick of the story," he said at the time.

A decade later, garbage is no longer much in the news, thanks, in part, to the way the barge focused attention on the problem. Nassau and Suffolk still generate about seven pounds of garbage per person per day, one of the highest rates in the country. But now, about half of Long Island's waste is incinerated in local waste-to-energy plants, while about 20 percent is now burned or buried off Long Island. And about 35 percent is recycled, a huge increase from pre-barge days. There are now only four active landfills in Nassau and Suffolk, and they only accept ash or clean fill — no raw municipal garbage.

"The barge was one of those things that probably tweaked what we were already doing and made it more of a public issue than it would have otherwise," said R.L. Swanson, director of the Waste Reduction and Management Institute at the State University at Stony Brook. "The public got on the towns a little more."

For his part, Hroncich said, "We were just a little bit ahead of our time." He notes that the barge venture continues to be a topic of discussion at disposal seminars. "They always refer back to the Islip garbage barge as the turning point in waking up the politicians," he said. If nothing else, "It was an adventure."

Newsday Photo, 1987 / Dan Sheehan

After being spurned at every port, the barge sails back to New York after a two-month odyssey.

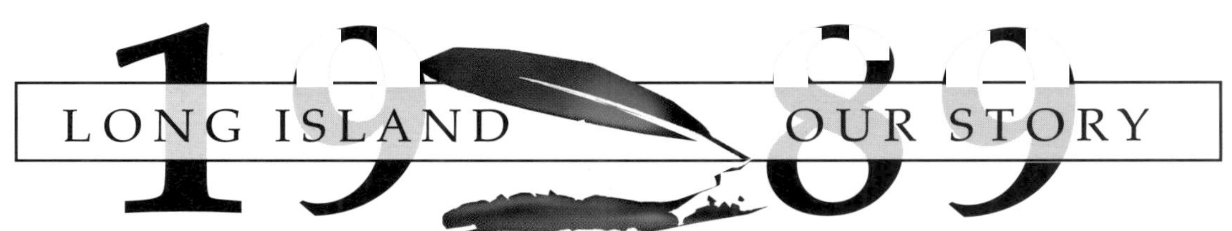

Lights Out At Shoreham

Anti-nuclear activism spurs the closing of a new $6 billion plant

BY DAN FAGIN
STAFF WRITER

It was only concrete and steel, after all. A tangled mass of pipes and circuitry wrapped around a cavernous core of superheated water. A machine to harness the breakneck energy released when atoms are split in chain reactions, and to channel that energy into the prosaic chore of lighting lights and heating homes.

But the Shoreham Nuclear Power Station was never just a machine. Not to the people of Long Island, who made the 25-year saga of the doomed plant on Brookhaven's north shore the defining political struggle of the Island's modern era. Shoreham launched an anti-authoritarian brand of citizen activism that transformed local politics, especially in Suffolk County, and against all odds vanquished the massed power of the federal government, Wall Street and the electric utility industry, preventing a completed and fully licensed nuclear power plant from operating for the only time in American history.

The chain reaction set off by the Shoreham fight rippled far beyond the confines of the plant itself, and even beyond the nuclear industry whose decline it came to symbolize. By the time Shoreham was fully decommissioned on Oct. 12, 1994, its $6 billion price tag — about *85 times* higher than the original estimate — had nearly wrecked the regional economy by saddling Long Island with some of the highest electric rates in the nation.

The Shoreham reactor never produced a kilowatt of commercial power, but it proved to be an accomplished breeder of cynicism and distrust. Like Frankenstein's monster, Shoreham ultimately destroyed its own progenitor, the Long Island Lighting Co., and forever changed the way Long Islanders view authority. Born in an era of boundless optimism, even naivete, about the future, Shoreham died a slow and tortuous death at a time when Long Islanders were finally facing the consequences of supercharged growth, and weren't liking much of what they saw.

"The pattern changed, and on Long Island a lot of that is because of Shoreham and the arrogance of LILCO," said veteran planner Lee Koppelman, the director of the Center for Regional Policy Studies at the State University at Stony Brook. "There's a much greater cynicism toward institutions, and the citizens have become far more sophisticated. They don't take things at face value anymore, with some justification."

In 1965, when LILCO first announced its intention to build a nuclear plant somewhere in Suffolk County, elected officials fervently embraced the project. Within a year, LILCO had bought a 455-acre site between the sparsely populated hamlets of Shoreham and Wading River, and was declaring its new plant would be on line by 1973, at a cost of $65 million-$75 million.

Then, LILCO made the first of many mistakes. Swept away by the enthusiastic response to Shoreham and the nuclear boosterism of the federal Atomic Energy Commission, and mindful that demand for power was rising by more than 10 percent per year on Long Island, LILCO bought land for a second nuclear plant, this time in affluent Lloyd Harbor. Appalled, the peninsula's residents organized a well-funded opposition effort that by 1969 had killed the proposal.

But LILCO remained as enamored as ever with the technology that proponents famously predicted would produce power "too cheap to meter." In 1968, LILCO decided to increase the size of Shoreham from 540 to 820 megawatts. That decision — and a plan to build two more reactors in Jamesport that never got off the drawing board — delayed the timetable and ballooned the costs of Shoreham. Most important, the delays provided crucial time for anti-nuclear activism to spread beyond Lloyd Harbor and take root across Long Island.

The company's demeanor didn't help its case. "Early in the game, the opposition was treated sort of disdainfully," remembers Ira Freilicher, a former LILCO vice president who served as the company's chief spokesman and Shoreham strategist. "We handled them in a more confrontational and patronizing way than we should have. It was an arrogance on our part."

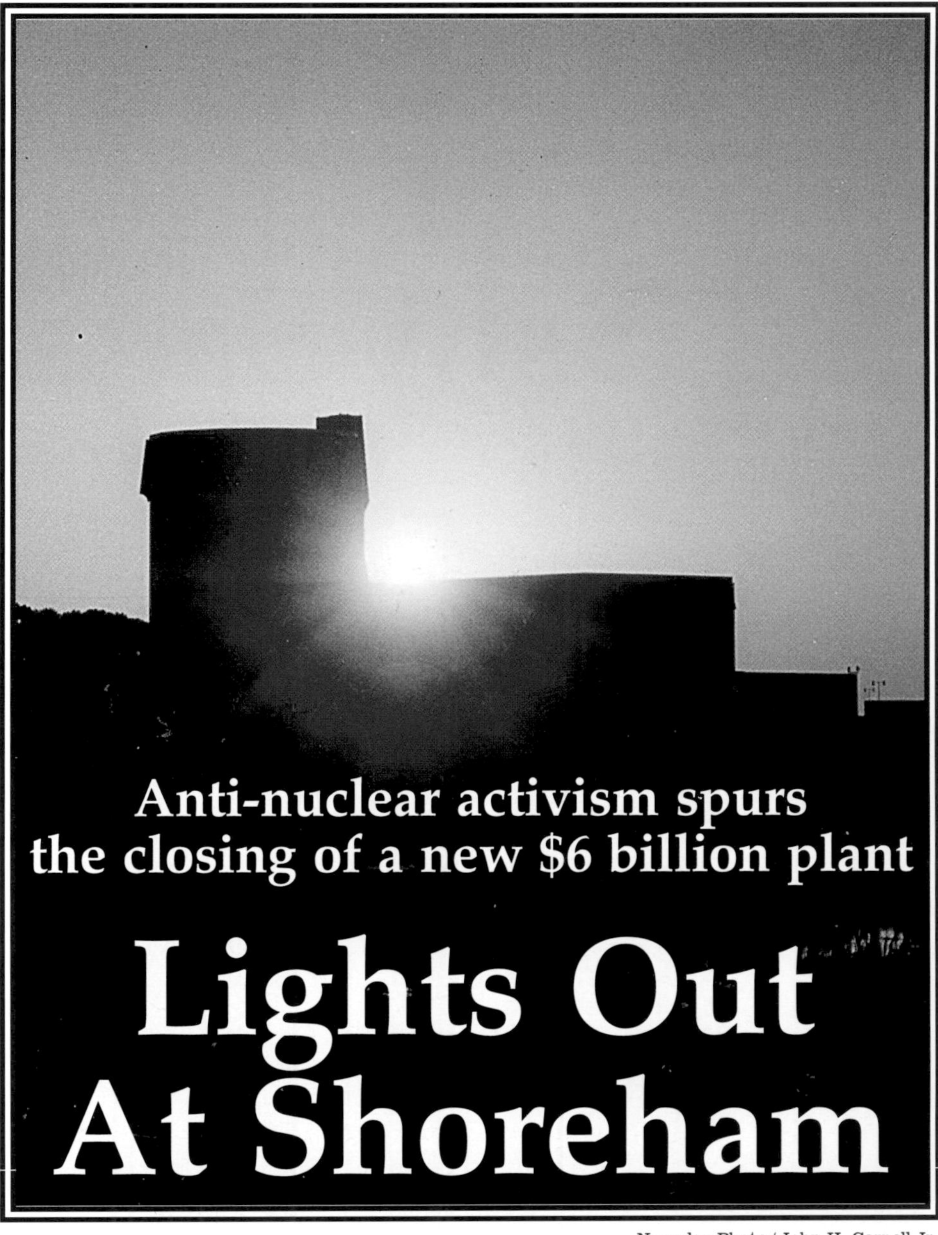
Newsday Photo / John H. Cornell Jr.
The Shoreham Nuclear Power Station in 1988, a year before LILCO agreed to close it.

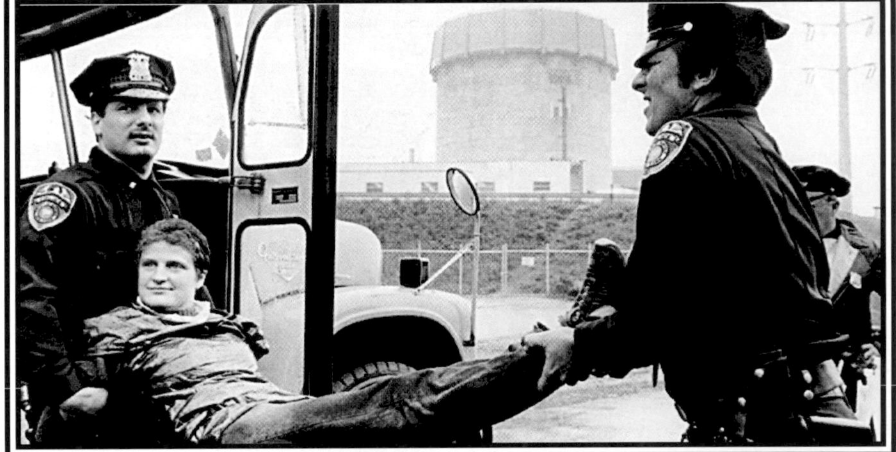
Newsday Photo / Jim Peppler
Shoreham launched citizens, such as this man being carried into a police truck in 1979, into anti-establishment protests that transformed local politics, especially in Suffolk County.

LILCO was similarly its own worst enemy in its inept management of Shoreham's construction. By the late 1970s, the plant's price tag was approaching $2 billion, mostly because of astonishingly low worker productivity as well as design changes ordered by federal regulators.

Then, fatefully for Shoreham, the 1978 Three Mile Island reactor accident in Pennsylvania galvanized the anti-nuclear movement nationwide, and Shoreham became a focal point. On a rainy Sunday in June, 1979, 15,000 protesters showed up at Shoreham for the largest demonstration in Long Island history. Police made 571 arrests. Meanwhile, Three Mile Island prompted federal regulators to declare that operators of nuclear plants would have to work out evacuation plans in cooperation with state and local governments.

As opposition spread and electric rates soared, big cracks developed in what was formerly a united pro-Shoreham front among Long Island's political and business leaders. A key turning point came on Feb. 17, 1983, when the Suffolk Legislature flatly declared in a 15-1 vote that the county could not be safely evacuated. A few minutes before that vote, New York's newly elected governor, Mario Cuomo, ordered state officials not to approve any LILCO-sponsored evacuation plan.

"That's the day that everything crystalized and came together," remembers Wayne Prospect, the first anti-Shoreham member of the county legislature. "You felt that we were at least in the game, and that the county, with the state, at least had a fighting chance."

Although its own projections were now questioning whether the region really needed Shoreham's electricity, LILCO plowed ahead and managed to complete Shoreham in 1984, winning federal permission for low-power tests the following year. But by the late 1980s, the evacuation fight was still delaying an operating license for the plant, and anti-LILCO fervor was spreading, fueled in part by anger over the utility's poor performance in restoring power after Hurricane Gloria struck in 1985. Finally, the state Legislature created the Long Island Power Authority as a vehicle to close Shoreham and take over the company.

On Feb. 28, 1989, after more than two years of negotiations and abortive deals, Cuomo and LILCO chairman William J. Catacosinos signed off on an agreement that shuttered the plant forever but made ratepayers responsible for most of Shoreham's cost.

Even after Shoreham was taken apart, it remained a towering presence on the political landscape of Long Island. In 1995, LILCO's sky-high rates, and residual public anger over Shoreham, prodded Cuomo's successor, George Pataki, to reverse himself and broker a partial public takeover of LILCO by LIPA that was finally completed last month. But electric rates are still among the nation's highest and Pataki's LILCO takeover remains a major controversy.

Evidently, Long Island isn't finished hating Shoreham yet.

The F-14's demise cripples a major employer and plunges LI defense work into a steep dive

Grumman in Decline

BY JAMES BERNSTEIN
STAFF WRITER

On a cloudy day in the nation's capital nine years ago, Defense Secretary Dick Cheney sat behind a dark wooden table in an ornate hearing room in the House of Representatives and made an announcement that would echo across Long Island for years.

Testifying before the House Armed Services Committee on April 25, 1989, Cheney revealed that as part of a massive effort to reduce government spending, the Pentagon no longer would buy a host of new weapons. Among those on the hit list was the F-14 Tomcat jet fighter, the sleek swing-wing airplane built by Grumman Corp.

For years, the F-14 line had been Grumman's largest and most important program, employing a quarter of the company's 20,000 workers through the '70s and '80s, and representing some 20 percent of the company's $4 billion in annual sales. It was so crucial, not only to Grumman but to the entire Long Island economy, that the Nassau-Suffolk congressional delegation and other Grumman supporters waged a fierce battle in the next few months to reverse the Pentagon's decision.

They were able to win a slight reprieve: The company would build 18 more F-14s during the next three years. But by 1992, 20 years after it began, the Tomcat program would end. And not too long after that, so would Grumman itself. Only five years after the Pentagon's decision, Grumman — the company that had been Long Island's largest private employer for 60 years, famous for the warplanes and space vehicles it had built for America — would itself go the way of the F-14.

In May, 1994, Grumman was acquired by rival Northrop Corp. of Los Angeles, and the merged company became known as Northrop Grumman Corp. And now, the final act is playing out: The Grumman name will disappear entirely if a proposed acquisition of the company by Lockheed Martin Corp. of

Newsday Photo / Don Jacobsen

Grumman Corp. headquarters in Bethpage — before the sale to Northrop Corp. of Los Angeles

Bethesda, Md., goes through. The Justice Department has filed suit to block the deal, and the case is to be heard in federal court in Washington, D.C., in September.

The decline and fall of the region's most prominent business was a landmark in the economic as well as social history of postwar Long Island. It came amid massive consolidation in the nation's aerospace and defense industry, which was responding to vastly reduced Pentagon spending after the Cold War ended. Only six months after that morning in Washington when Cheney said he was ending the F-14 program, the Berlin Wall fell. What was good for the advance of democracy was not necessarily good for jobs on Long Island.

"From that point on, it was downhill" for Grumman, said former Rep. George Hochbrueckner (D-Coram), a member of the House Armed Services Committee who became known for his tireless defense of the Tomcat and Grumman in Washington.

Perhaps Cheney's announcement should not have come as such a shock. The first F-14, after all, was delivered to the Navy in 1972. Hundreds were based aboard aircraft carriers at sea. And all military airplane programs eventually end. Nonetheless, there was shock throughout Grumman's Bethpage headquarters. "Grumman people never believed it would happen," said one former company executive.

Without the F-14, many company insiders thought, there would be no Grumman. True, the company had other businesses: electronics, truck building, space and even other airplane programs. But the F-14 was the company's heart and soul — "it's known as the F-14 company," a defense expert said at the time — and its other programs would not be enough to sustain the company's work force.

"I knew it was the beginning of the end," said Scott Schimmel, who worked in production and control in Bethpage. "We were all just asking, when are we going to get laid off?"

Schimmel was among thousands of Grumman workers who lost their jobs just as Long Island's defense industry was rapidly dwindling. Fairchild Republic Co., Grumman's neighbor in Farmingdale, had closed in 1987, after 56 years of building Air Force airplanes. The Island's other big defense contractor, Sperry Corp. in Great Neck, was laying people off. The year before Fairchild shut down, Sperry had merged with Detroit-based Burroughs Corp. to form Unisys Corp.

The defense industry on Long Island had been the engine of the region's economy for decades, and it became superhot in the 1980s, when President Ronald Reagan spent more than $1 trillion on a military buildup. The cancellation of the F-14, however, was a strong signal that aircraft manufacturing on Long Island — an industry that employed as many as 80,000 people in 1986 — was coming to an end.

In mid-1989 — within months of the Pentagon's F-14 decision — the Island officially went into a recession. It was the beginning of a three-year economic slump that would cost the region a staggering 100,000 jobs, a downturn brought about in large part by the decline of the defense industry. As F-14 production began to wind down at Grumman, the company reduced the size of its Long Island work force. Local suppliers also began to feel the pinch. Some laid off workers. Others sought nondefense work. Still others were forced to shut their doors.

Between 1986 and 1997, the defense industry on Long Island lost an astonishing 49,000 jobs, according to state Labor Department figures. Only about 31,000 people are still employed in the industry on the Island.

There were cries for retraining, new directions, ways to lure new companies to Long Island "None of it happened," said Lee Koppelman, the veteran bi-county planning chief. What brought the economy out of recession, economists and planners agree, was an improved national economy and a burgeoning Long Island software and electronics industry, which gave rise to companies such as Computer Associates International in Islandia and Symbol Technologies in Holtsville.

At Grumman, as F-14 production wound down, company executives tried to come up with ways to survive, but the choices were few. As one of the smaller companies in the aerospace industry, Grumman was out of the business of building new military airplanes. It had not won a contract to build new planes in 20 years. Pentagon spending for new planes was expected to be scarce. For the company founded in 1929 by Leroy Grumman, and which was embedded in the fabric of Long Island life, merger with another company seemed the best choice.

For a few weeks in the spring of '94, a war of nerves was waged for Grumman between Martin Marietta Corp. of Bethesda, Md., and Northrop. Martin offered $55 a share for Grumman, which the company had accepted, even announcing the deal to the public. But a few days later, Northrop offered shareholders $62, winning the bidding war when Martin refused to budge from its original offer.

Grumman as anyone on Long Island knew it was gone.

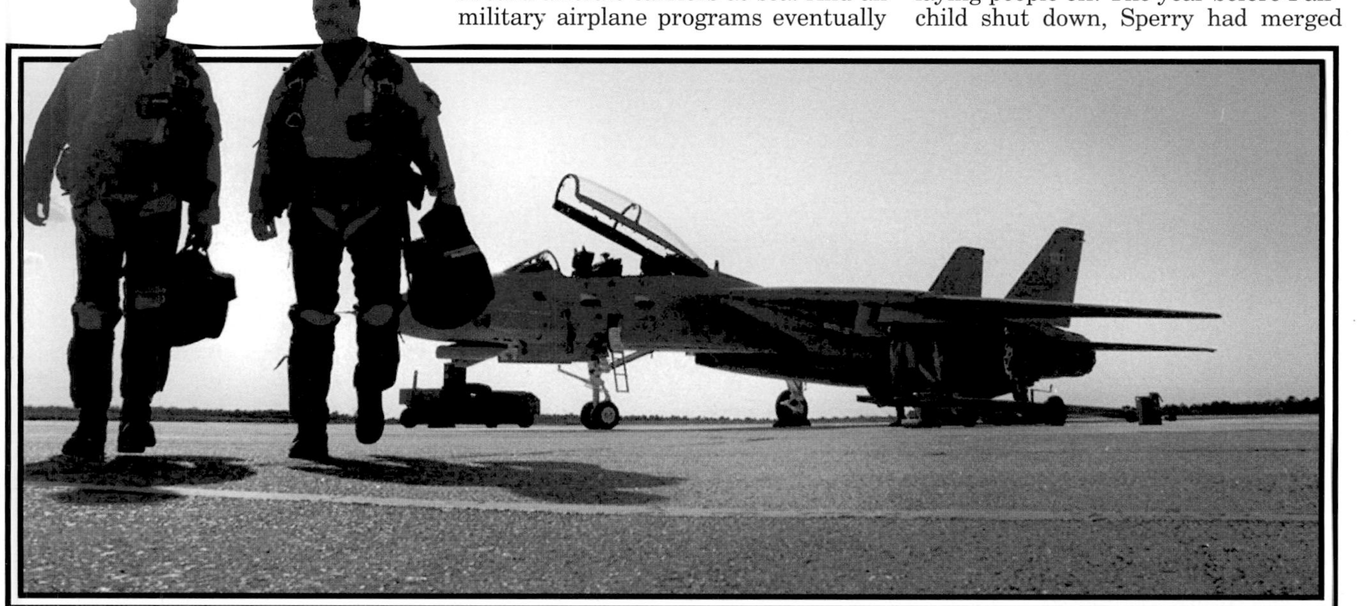

Newsday Photo / J. Michael Dombroski

Pilots leave the last F-14 after the test flight: The plane had long been the most important program for Grumman, Long Island's largest private employer for 60 years.

Colin Ferguson opens fire on a rush-hour LIRR train, killing six in a shocking spree

Gunfire On the 5:33

By Paul Vitello
NEWSDAY COLUMNIST

The commuter train pulled out of the station carrying people of all kinds home from work on a Wednesday evening — secretaries and stockbrokers and sellers and buyers and students, and in their laps were bags and bundles, and in their heads were all the thousands of threads of unfinished business that is human life in progress.

When it pulled into the Merillon Avenue station in Garden City, 30 minutes later, that life was over. It was the "before" on the stranded side of a before-and-after dividing line gouged out of the lives of everyone there.

There were only two kinds of people left on the train, the living and the dead.

It is almost impossible to make sense of the acts of a madman. Psychiatrists and historians try. But most often it is left to the survivors and their families to salvage some vestige of meaning from the carnage of a loner like Jeffrey Dahmer or a leader like Pol Pot, or a paranoid gunman like Colin Ferguson, who got on a packed homebound Long Island Rail Road train on Dec. 7, 1993, and shot 25 people at point blank range to settle his imaginary scores with the world.

Six people died and 19 were wounded on the 5:33 out of Penn Station that evening. More might have been shot if two passengers had not tackled Ferguson as he paused to reload his gun.

Here was our homicidal postal worker. Our McDonald's gunman.

Of all the connections that have defined us as Americans in the past quarter century — regardless of race, religion or time zone — this was the most terrifying: the realization that at any time, at any place, our lives might end at the hands of a madman with a gun.

It is part of the culture, like jazz or baseball or the opportunity to become incredibly rich. There is the opportunity of sudden death by the Second Amendment.

That Ferguson was a madman was not the universal judgment. A court said he was competent to stand trial, even competent to act as his own attorney. But anyone who saw him pacing before the jury in 1994, talking about the years-long racist government conspiracy against him — scoffing at the 93-count indictment against him as a fiction based on the fact that "it matches the year 1993" — could not help but see him that way.

He was probably crazy. Whether he was competent to stand trial, whether there is racism in America, whether and how mental illness coincides with social ills are all interesting questions. But the questions that people really had to answer were tougher than those: How can you be sitting on a train one moment with a shopping bag full of Christmas presents between your feet and the next moment find yourself in the equivalent of a foxhole with the enemy coming over the top, killing you?

How could a man as disturbed as this one obtain a legal license to carry a firearm?

How could this happen? And happen over and over and over again — in trains and fast food restaurants and post offices and tourist attractions and schools and on the streets every day — each time triggering the same tired debate about the right to bear arms. We may ponder these questions from the safety of our intact lives. But the survivors and their families have had to tackle them in the flesh, in the trenches.

How they have answered them is as much a part of the story of the Long Island Rail Road Massacre as the massacre itself.

Among the survivors, Kevin McCarthy and his mother, Carolyn McCarthy, are probably the best known — he for his miraculous recovery from a life-threatening head wound, she for her triple transformation from homemaker to widow, to gun-control advocate, to congresswoman. Her husband, Denis, was killed by the gunman.

Joyce Gorycki and her daughter moved away for a while from Long Island to try to recover from the loss of their husband and father, James, one of the six killed. Then they moved back because this was where they had connections to the world. Joyce is an officer now in a statewide gun-control advocacy group.

Arlene and Jack LoCicero kept a vigil for five days at the bedside of their daughter, Amy LoCicero, whose thoracic artery was severed by one of Ferguson's bullets. Amy was a religious young woman, which had helped sustain her in 1992 when, just married, she lost her 27-year-old husband to pancreatic cancer.

Now the parents struggled to maintain hope for Amy's life, then struggled to let go when they were told there was no hope, then decided on Dec. 12, after the doctors explained for them one more time the meaning of brain death, to donate her heart, kidneys and liver for transplants.

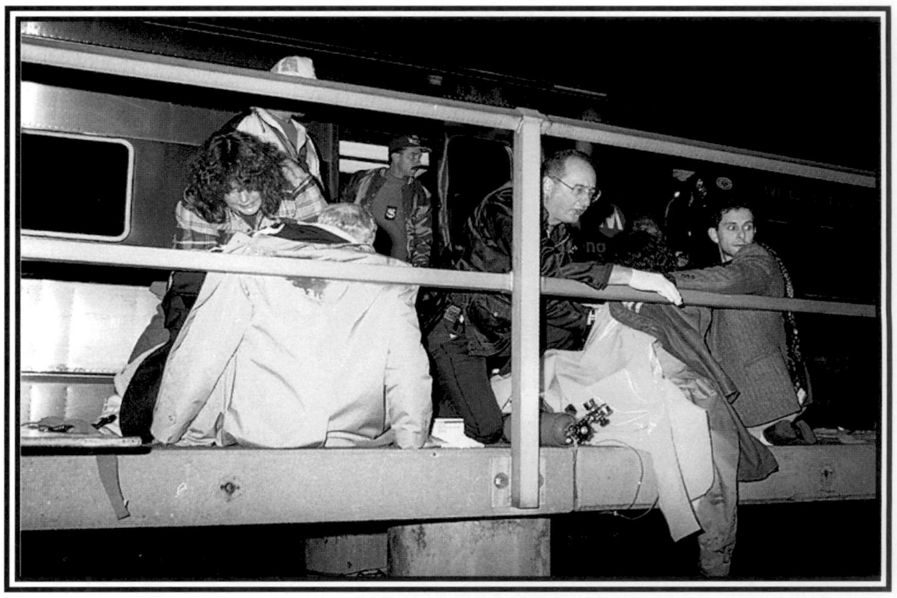

The heart went to an Islip mother of seven, Theresa Caravella, whom Arlene would meet months later. "I was having a difficult time," Arlene said. "And I asked her if I could just hold her because she was so real and all the things that were happening to us were just so surreal . . . And Theresa said, 'Remember, the heart that beats in me is the same heart that beat in your womb.' "

That touched her. She'll never forget it.

The struggle of all the survivors, in a way, has been to re-establish connections to the world. The psychiatrists all tell you that when violence happens it leaves not only wounds of the flesh but the pain of isolation. How can anyone understand what they have been through? No one can.

It is as if Ferguson, the madman, had been armed not only with bullets but with a contagion that threatened everyone he touched with becoming a stranger in a strange land like himself.

There are survivors who now, five years later, and probably forever, will wake up in the middle of the night in a cold sweat, reliving the moment when they looked up and saw his face.

"It was the most awful thing I ever saw," said Mary Anne Phillips, who was the first one wounded when Ferguson stood up, removed the semi-automatic pistol from his gym bag and began to shoot the people who by some accident of fate were sitting in the places where his mind saw enemies.

In her testimony before the jury, she described the look on Ferguson's face as "searing." Outside in the hall, talking to reporters, she had used another word.

"Evil," she said.

Like many of the survivors, though, Kevin McCarthy still takes the railroad to work and home again. He is married now. He walks stiffly because of his injuries, but was recently seen trotting and weaving through the rush hour crowd at the Merillon Avenue Long Island Rail Road station, trying to catch his train, a bundle under his arm. And from the look of him, there were a hundred things on his mind.

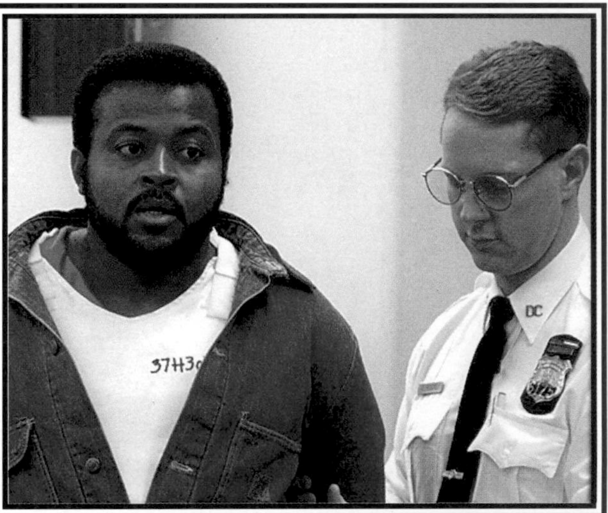

Above, two wounded passengers are cared for on the platform at the LIRR's Merillon Avenue station. Left, Colin Ferguson, who was convicted as the gunman, is brought before a judge at County Court in Mineola in 1994.

Top, Newsday Photo / Alan Raia; Newsday Photo / K. Wiles Stabile

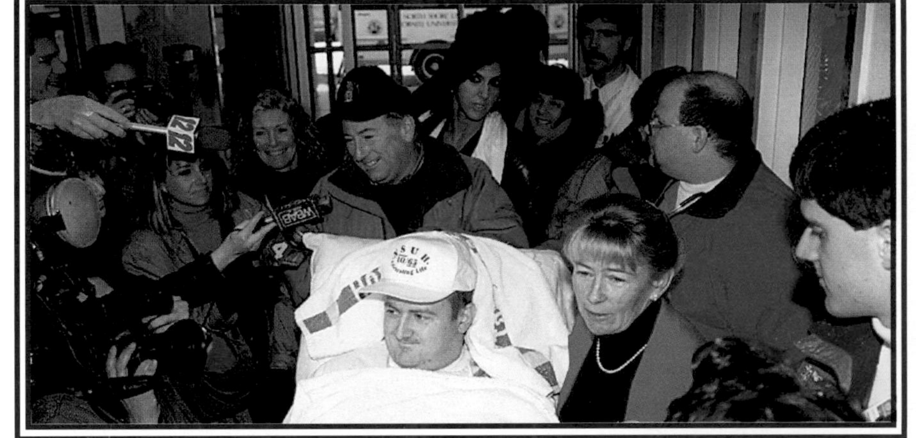

Newsday Photo / Dick Kraus

Carolyn McCarthy accompanies her wounded son, Kevin, into North Shore University Hospital, Glen Cove, in 1994. Later she was elected to Congress on a gun-control platform.

The pine barrens helps to protect LI's water supply — but it took a fight to save it

The War of the Woods

BY DAN FAGIN
STAFF WRITER

It is an Everglades with humility, a Yosemite without the grandeur. No sea of grass, but shallow ponds and reed-choked swamps. No redwood canopy over a rich forest floor, but spindly pines and bushy scrub oaks pushing up through parched sand.

Born thousands of years ago in the outwash of the last glacier, the pine barrens is a humble wilderness, and that has been its salvation in Long Island's modern era.

Luck, fear and altruism are what spared 100,000 acres of pine barrens in east-central Suffolk County, the remnant of vast pine and hardwood forests that once blanketed Long Island but were obliterated, first by farms and then by the eastward march of suburbia.

Farmers for centuries spurned the dry soil and poor lumber of the land they called "barren," and the economic slowdowns of the 1970s and 1980s stalled suburban sprawl at its western edge. That was the lucky part. Then came the fear, as many Long Islanders decided that their roads would get more congested and their drinking water more polluted if development continued unchecked.

But it took the foresight of planners, activists, business people, voters and politicians to capitalize on the luck and channel the fear into a series of remarkable actions, capped by a state law and a comprehensive plan that ensured that Long Island's last wilderness will remain forever wild.

"Long Island was headed toward becoming Everywhere, USA, and to some extent is still headed that way. The pine barrens agreement is a major step in preventing that from happening. That's the most important legacy," said John Turner, who co-founded the Long Island Pine Barrens Society as a college student in 1977.

The saving of the pine barrens actually began in the 1960s, when Suffolk County bought its first properties along the Peconic River. But in the mid-1970s, when Turner and two friends took their first hikes in the pine barrens, almost all of the land was still in the hands of people who one day planned to build on it.

"It was nothing short of mind-blowing to walk through landscapes that were the same as what the Indians saw," Turner remembered. "Slowly, that excitement transformed into fear, once we realized there was no guarantee that this landscape was something that would be permanent."

Pressure from environmentalists and the lobbying of local planners such as Lee Koppelman, executive director of the Long Island Regional Planning Board, steered more county and state money into pine barrens purchases in the early 1980s. Then in 1987 Suffolk voters overwhelmingly approved a sweeping land-acquisition program funded by a quarter-cent sales tax.

By then, Long Islanders had learned that there were self-interested reasons to preserve the pine barrens. Many of the Island's shallowest water wells had been tainted by fertilizers, solvents, pesticides and detergents, and hydrologists were discovering that deeper wells were at risk, too.

The key, the experts concluded, was to protect undeveloped land in areas along the central spine of Long Island where rain penetrates the sandy soil and slowly moves down into the deep aquifers that hold 70 trillion gallons of water and supply almost all of the Island's drinking water. These "deep recharge zones" were already mostly developed, with one exception: the pine barrens.

The burst of land-buying by Suffolk and the state eventually locked up more than 35,000 acres in the central pine barrens, but developer Wilbur Breslin and other major builders were still moving ahead with plans to put up a checkerboard of subdivisions and shopping malls amid the forest. Town governments in Brookhaven, Southampton and Riverhead were encouraging those plans and rejecting calls by Koppelman and others for low-density building in watershed areas.

The Long Island Pine Barrens Society, then still a shoestring organization, decided in 1989 that its case-by-case approach to battling development proposals wasn't working well enough. Its new executive director, a tenacious public-relations man named Richard Amper, was thinking bigger. Much bigger.

On Nov. 21, 1989, the society filed the biggest environmental lawsuit in state history and quickly won a court order blocking 238 pending projects valued at $11.2 billion. The group's key argument was that before the three towns approved any more proposals to build in the pine barrens, they should be forced to study the "cumulative impact" of all of those proposals.

The lawsuit snaked through the court system for almost three years. The towns won in state Supreme Court, but the pine barrens society triumphed on appeal. The final decision rested with New York's highest court, the Court of Appeals, which delivered its unanimous verdict on Nov. 24, 1992. It declared that the court couldn't force the towns to do a cumulative impact study, despite what it called "the risk of irreversible harm to the environment" without it.

But even though they had won, Breslin and the other developers didn't relish the prospect of continued guerrilla warfare about hundreds of individual projects in the pine barrens. What they wanted was certainty: a map that would tell them where they could build and where they couldn't and what the rules would be. Developers began meeting with Amper and other environmentalists to devise a sweeping plan to ban new development inside a 52,500-acre core and to tighten restrictions on building in a 47,500-acre buffer zone that would include some of the most controversial proposals, including Breslin's.

In mid-1993, after marathon negotiations, the state Legislature passed a bill formalizing the agreement. That July, in a sunlit ceremony in South Haven County Park near Mastic, Gov. Mario Cuomo signed the Long Island Pine Barrens Preservation Act, calling it "something you can wrap your soul around."

The war of the woods still isn't entirely over. Though the plan includes a method of compensating pine barrens property owners, some of those landowners remain convinced the plan is an illegal confiscation of their land. But their legal challenges have failed so far, and some prominent former skeptics now consider the pine barrens agreement a huge success.

When the comprehensive plan for the pine barrens was finally completed on June 29, 1995, an opponent appeared at the signing ceremony dressed as a hobo. He carried a sign that read: "This will be the future of the building industry if the plan is not changed."

He was E. M. Schwenk, the executive director of the Long Island Builders Institute, and he was disheartened with the outcome of a plan he had helped devise. But Schwenk, who resigned the following year, now sees the pine barrens agreement as a model to control development throughout eastern Suffolk.

"On balance, it's good that it all happened," Schwenk said. "For the present, and especially for the future."

And for the past as well. The pine barrens agreement preserves the hardscrabble forest that is the last unaltered legacy of the great glacier that sculpted Long Island a thousand generations ago.

Newsday Photo, 1997 / Jim Peppler

The setting sun silhouettes a pine cone in the Dwarf Pine Barrens in Westhampton.

Cuomo, Newsday Photo / Kathy Kmonicek; Newsday Photo / John H. Cornell Jr.

Gov. Mario Cuomo, left, speaks at a ceremony before signing the pine barrens legislation in 1993; above, Edwin (Buzz) Schwenk, left, and Richard Amper in 1997; both now support the measure, which protects an important water resource.

A deadly parade of violence brings pain to peaceful neighborhoods

Crime in the Suburbs

BY TOM DEMORETCKY
STAFF WRITER

A MURDERERS ROW

1975: Dr. Charles Friedgood poisoned his wife and tried to flee.

1979: Adam Berwid stabbed his ex-wife and called authorities.

1987: Newlywed Matthew Solomon killed his wife, Lisa, on Christmas Eve.

1993: Joel Rifkin said he killed 17 women.

1987: Nurse Richard Angelo killed seven patients with a paralyzing drug.

1988: Martin Tankleff killed his parents, apparently over his desire for a new car.

1989: Robert Golub was arrested for the death of neighbor Kelly Tinyes, 13.

Newsday Photos; Rifkin Photo by Bill Turnbull

For the postwar generation of baby boomers and their parents, Long Island was seen largely as a refuge, away from the big city and, of course, away from crime. "I never thought anything like that would happen here," reporters covering crimes would often hear. "That's why we left the city."

But in the past 25 years, the quiet suburbs have spawned enough murder and mayhem to keep both prosecutors and movie-of-the-week producers busy. From Colin Ferguson's horrific slaughter of commuters on the Long Island Rail Road to the antics of Joey Buttafuoco and Amy Fisher, local crime has often become national news — and network entertainment.

Long Island has the dubious honor of being the home of New York State's worst serial killer: Joel Rifkin, arrested in June, 1993, after state troopers spotted his pickup truck without license plates on the Southern State Parkway. A high-speed chase ended in Mineola, where the unemployed 34-year-old landscaper from East Meadow crashed into a utility pole. Troopers detected an odor from the back of the truck. It came from the dead body of Tiffany Bresciani, 22, one of 17 women, mostly prostitutes, Rifkin would confess to killing. He was sentenced to more than 200 years in seven murder convictions.

Besides Amy Fisher, other high-profile cases featuring young defendants included that of Selden High School cheerleader Cheryl Pierson, who in 1986 arranged to have a homeroom classmate, Sean Pica, murder her father; Pierson said she made the deal to protect herself and her sister from sexual assault by their father. She was sentenced to six months in jail. Pica got eight to 24 years. In 1988, Martin Tankleff murdered his parents, Seymour and Arlene in Belle Terre, apparently because they wouldn't buy him a new car. He was sentenced to 50 years to life. Huntington Station newlywed Matthew Solomon, meanwhile, was convicted of killing his wife, Lisa, on Christmas Eve, 1987, then stuffing her body into a plastic garbage bag and pretending to take part in a neighborhood search for her. He was sentenced to 18 years to life.

The "Amityville Horror" — in which 23-year-old Ronald DeFeo murdered his family — was undoubtedly Long Island's most sensational crime story of the 1970s, but it wasn't the only one. The body of Sophie Friedgood, 48, was found in her Great Neck bed by a maid early in the afternoon of June 18, 1975. Her husband, Dr. Charles Friedgood, then 57, hurried home from his Brooklyn medical office that day and signed a medical certificate saying she died of a stroke. Friedgood had his wife hurriedly buried, looted her estate of $650,000, took her jewelry and was rushing off to join his lover in Denmark when he was stopped on a plane at Kennedy Airport. Autopsies revealed that Demerol had been injected into Mrs. Friedgood's liver. Almost 80, Friedgood is still serving his sentence of 25 years to life.

Another ill-fated relationship, one deeply affected by severe mental disorder, ended on Dec. 6, 1979, with the violent death of Ewa Berwid. Despite a label on his file jacket at Pilgrim Psychiatric Center saying that authorities should be notified if Adam Berwid escaped, and despite letters from authorities urging that he not be released, Berwid was given a weekend pass and went to the home in Mineola where his ex-wife and children, ages 4 and 7, were living.

Berwid, then 43, killed his ex-wife with a knife he had bought for the purpose, washed the body, cleaned up the blood and then placed the corpse on a cot with candles on each side. Then he calmly called the Nassau district attorney's office to tell what he had done. Convicted of murder, he was sentenced to 35 years to life.

Good Samaritan Hospital in West Islip was the setting for the case of Richard Angelo, a 26-year-old nurse who came to be known as the Angel of Death. Angelo was tried in 1989 for the deaths of seven patients in the hospital in the fall of 1987. The deaths came from injections of the paralyzing drug Pavulon. He was convicted of murder in two of the deaths and lesser charges for others. The motive: a feeling of inadequacy. "I wanted to create a situation where I would cause the patient to have some respiratory distress or some problem and through my intervention or suggested intervention or whatever, come out looking like I knew what I was doing," he said during a videotaped confession shown at his trial. "I had no confidence in myself. I felt very inadequate." It was enough to send him to prison for at least 50 years.

Some cases shed light on the darker side of suburbia. On April 29, 1979, a 13-year-old boy in Smithtown threatened to report four other teenagers for stealing a beat-up old minibike. It would lead to a horrible death for the boy, John Pius, and a long court case with very mixed results for the four accused of killing him by stuffing pebbles down his throat, causing him to choke to death. The four were convicted of the killing in 1981 but were later granted retrials. Only two, Michael Quartararo and Thomas Ryan, are still in prison.

The March, 1989, killing in Valley Stream of 13-year-old Kelly Anne Tinyes was a crime among neighbors. Kelly's mutilated body was found by police in a basement closet of the nearby Golub home the morning after she had walked down the block after getting a phone call from someone at the Golub home. Robert Golub, 21 at the time, was convicted of the murder. The two families have remained on the same street ever since. Golub, now 30 and serving 25 years to life, denied any involvement.

A murder in the woods put an eerie spotlight on Northport in the summer of 1984 after police initially described Ricky Kasso, 17, and James Troiano, 18, as Satanists who took large quantities of powerful hallucinogens. But the tales turned out to be greatly exaggerated: The investigation would eventually show that Kasso stabbed 17-year-old Gary Lauwers to death largely because of a drug dispute. Kasso confessed to police, and two days after his arrest hanged himself in the Suffolk County Police lockup. Nine months later, Troiano was acquitted of being an accomplice to the killing.

The quarter century also brought two notorious kidnapings of children. On March 6, 1974, 8-year-old John Calzadilla was taken off a Dix Hills street three blocks from his home as he was returning from school. He was released a day later, after his family paid $50,000 ransom. According to testimony at their trials, the kidnapers, five New Jersey men, decided to return the boy when they heard the FBI was on the case. They never got the ransom, either. The drop point was a railroad bridge, and the money was taken by two railroad workers. They were caught and most of the money was returned.

More recently, Katie Beers, a Mastic Beach 10-year-old, was rescued by police on Jan. 13, 1993, after spending 16 days in a dungeon John Esposito had especially built for the purpose in his Bay Shore home. Esposito was sentenced to 15 years to life in prison.

But perhaps no crime shocked Long Island more than the spree that involved 100 people and occurred in two places — the Sea Crest Diner in Old Westbury and a house party in Plainview — in the early morning hours of Saturday, May 29, 1982.

Five men, all from Brooklyn, invaded the Plainview party, forced 20 persons to take off their clothes, robbed them and sexually abused and raped women. Then they went to the diner, where they held about 75 people at gunpoint and ordered several men and women to have sex. One woman was raped in front of several diner patrons, people were pistol-whipped, blackjacked, shot in the buttocks; they were all made to strip and throw their valuables on the floor. Witnesses got a description of the car the men were in, and all five ultimately were arrested. All — including two later convicted of a 1981 murder — remain in prison. It was called by one judge "the most violent and obscene crime spree in the history of Nassau County."

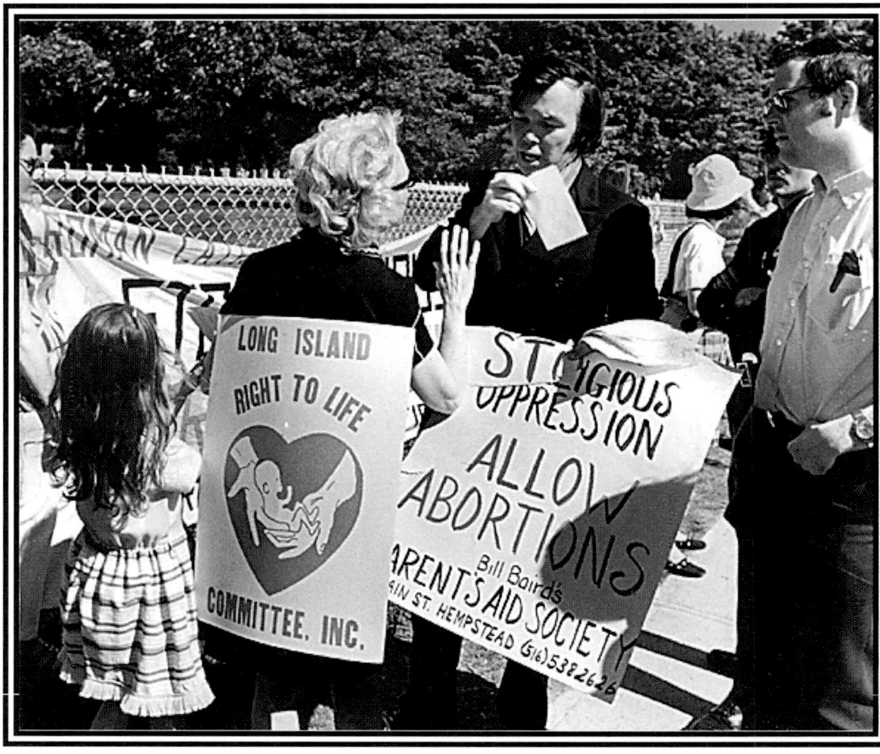

Newsday Photo / Stanley Wolfson

A woman gives a mass card to abortion-rights activist Bill Baird at competing abortion rallies in East Meadow in 1972. Baird opened one of the first U.S. clinics, in Hempstead in 1964.

From civil rights to abortion, LI serves as a stage for many heated controversies

A Long-Running Morality Play

BY RHODA AMON
STAFF WRITER

Long Island has been center stage for some of the most heated social controversies of the past quarter century: civil rights, abortion rights, freedom of speech, the right to live and the right to die.

With an older and more diverse population than it had in the Baby Boom years of the '50s and '60s, the Island saw a host of morality plays that drew national attention and spawned several landmark court decisions.

In the early '70s, much of the heat swirled around Bill Baird, an abortion-rights activist who opened one of the nation's first clinics in Hempstead in 1964 — six years before abortion became legal in New York State and a decade before the U.S. Supreme Court's 1973 Roe vs. Wade decision threw out most state laws prohibiting abortion. To many in the abortion-rights movement, Baird was a courageous crusader. But anti-abortion activists called him "a blasphemer and a no-holds-barred master of deceit." Some called him Dr. Death.

Actually, Baird, raised as a Lutheran in Hollis, had only a year in New York Medical College before dropping out in 1963 to support his family by taking a job with a pharmaceutical company that made contraceptive foam. His reproductive-rights activism was galvanized, he said, on seeing a woman die in a Manhattan hospital after attempting an abortion with a metal coat hanger.

At his peak in the '70s and '80s, Baird operated abortion clinics in Hempstead, Hauppauge and Boston and said he served 10,000 women a year. This fell away to 2,000 annually in Hempstead before he was forced to close his debt-ridden, often-sabotaged clinic in 1993 and was evicted from his Hauppauge site the following year. Known nationally for his feisty antics, including picketing Catholic churches carrying a 6-foot cross, Baird's name was attached in the '70s to three U.S. Supreme Court decisions — one that extended access to birth-control information to single women and two others in which the court ruled that states cannot require women under 18 to obtain parental consent and permitted minors to get permission from a judge instead of their parents.

After closing the clinics, Baird founded the Pro-Choice League. Now 66 and living in Huntington, he works out of a clinic-on-wheels, from which, he says, he "teaches poor people about AIDS, birth control and abortion." When interviewed recently, he was looking forward to picketing the National Right to Life Convention 1998 in Orlando, Fla., which was scheduled to close Saturday.

Another abortion issue that attracted national attention involved an Upper Brookville man who sought to terminate his comatose wife's pregnancy to improve her chances for recovery. Nancy Klein, who was 17 weeks pregnant, was in a deep coma after sustaining head injuries in a 1988 auto accident. Two Long Island anti-abortion groups sued for legal guardianship of the woman and her fetus in an effort to block the abortion. After a panel of judges ruled against the activists as "absolute strangers" to the Kleins and the U.S. Supreme Court declined to stop the procedure, the abortion was performed. Nancy Klein partially recovered. In a less-than-happy ending, her husband, Martin, sued for divorce in 1991.

Another poignant legal struggle in which outsiders thrust an unwilling young Long Island couple into the national spotlight was the case of Baby Jane Doe, as it became known. In 1983, Linda and Dan A. had decided against surgery for their infant daughter, born severely handicapped with spina bifida. Doctors had told them she would be severely retarded and suffer numerous other medical problems but could live as long as 20 years if the open-spine condition was corrected through surgery and excess fluid drained from her brain.

Although doctors at the University Hospital at Stony Brook accepted the parents' decision to simply provide nutrition, medication and coverings for the open-spine condition, attorney Lawrence Washburn, acting on a tip from Birthright, a Long Island group that monitors such cases, filed a petition in State Supreme Court seeking to mandate the surgery. It sparked a national debate and private soul-searching about the moral and ethical factors in court-ordered medical care.

After the Appellate Division of the State Supreme Court, reversing an earlier State Supreme Court decision, ruled that the parents were acting responsibly, the administration of President Ronald Reagan entered the case. The Department of Health and Human Services sued the hospital on the ground that the handicapped infant had been denied her civil rights under the Rehabilitation Act of 1973. The court ruled that the handicap-discrimination law did not apply to medical treatment in this case, according to the couple's attorney, Paul Gianelli.

"It was a very sad case and yet satisfying," Gianelli now says. Although doctors had told the courts that the infant would die within two years without surgery, Gianelli said that Jane Doe, now nearly 15, resides with her parents, who are still guarding their privacy and hers. He would not say anything more.

And there was a satisfying finale for Dr. Vincent Montemarano, whose "mercy killing" trial in 1974 was a Long Island forerunner to the current controversy of Michigan's Dr. Jack Kevorkian. Montemarano was charged with giving a fatal injection to a terminally ill cancer patient in Nassau County Medical Center. Nassau District Attorney William Cahn called it "a murder of convenience." The jury did not agree, and a free Montemarano left Long Island for a quieter life in rural Wisconsin.

Long Island's school boards were embroiled in controversies throughout the last 25 years, but none attained the prominence of Levittown's Island Trees school board, whose banning of 11 books from the school libraries in 1976 was catapulted into a national freedom-of-speech issue. The board contended that the books contained material that was anti-Christian, anti-Semitic, anti-black, anti-American and "just plain filthy." Among the banned books were "Slaughterhouse-Five" by Kurt Vonnegut, "The Fixer" by Bernard Malamud, which won the Pulitzer Prize for fiction in 1967, and "Soul on Ice," by Eldridge Cleaver.

Steven Pico, then a 17-year-old senior, and four other students sued, charging that the book-banning violated their First Amendment rights. Almost seven years later the case reached the U.S. Supreme Court. In a decision hailed as a victory by the students backed by the New York Civil Liberties Union, the court declared that public school boards could not ban books from school libraries merely because they dislike the ideas expressed in them.

"Students do not shed rights to freedom of speech or expression at the schoolhouse gate," wrote Justice William Brennan. The books were returned to the shelves.

Outside the U.S. Supreme Court in 1982 for the book-banning case: Steven Pico, center, with Island Trees board members, from left, Frank Martin, Richard Ahrens, Richard Michaels, Christina Fasulo, Patrick Hughes, Richard Melchers, Louis Nessim

Newsday Photo / Dick Kraus

LI by the Numbers

A look at how Nassau, Suffolk and Queens populations and lifestyle have changed in the last quarter century:

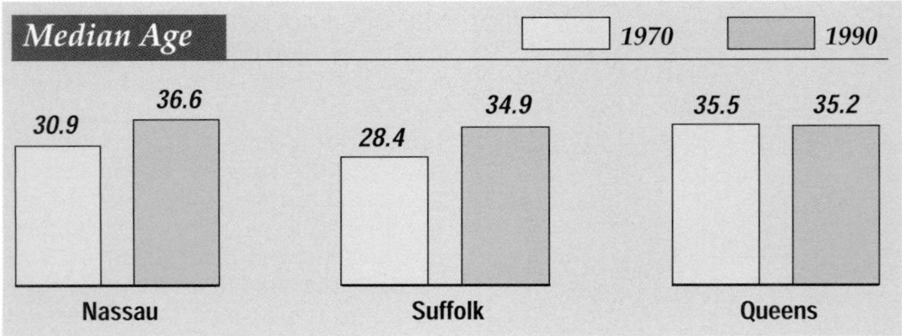

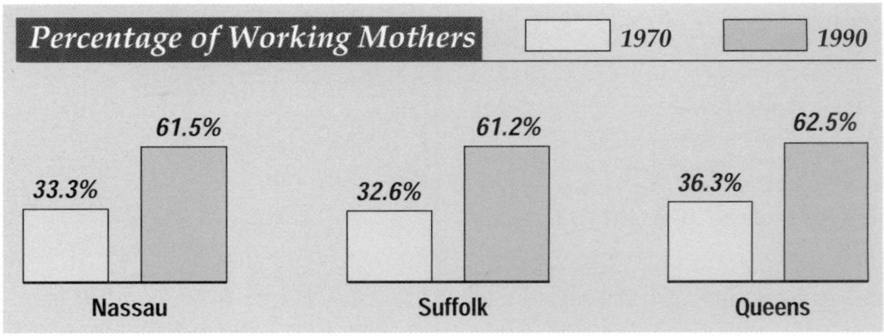

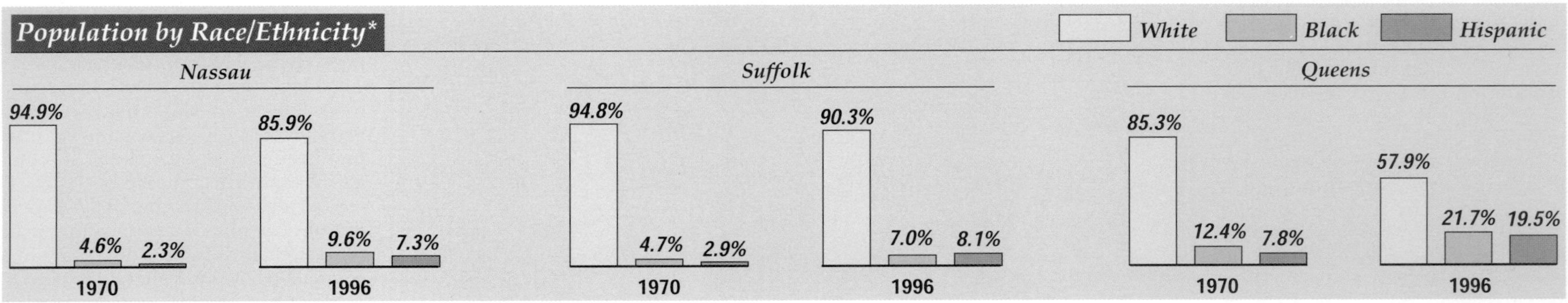

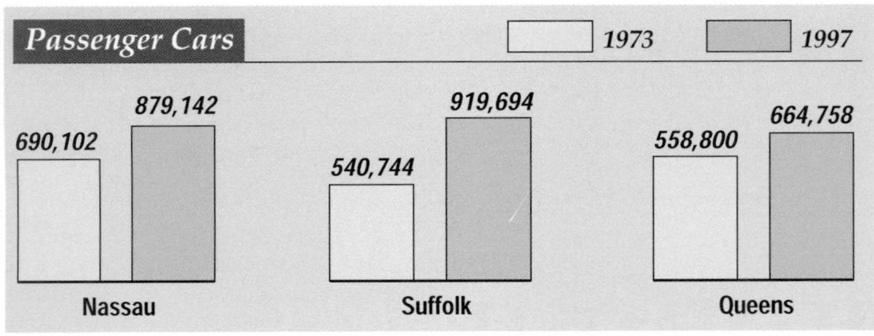

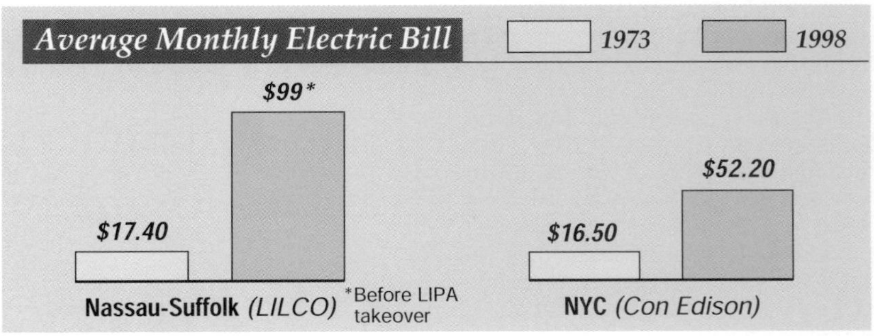

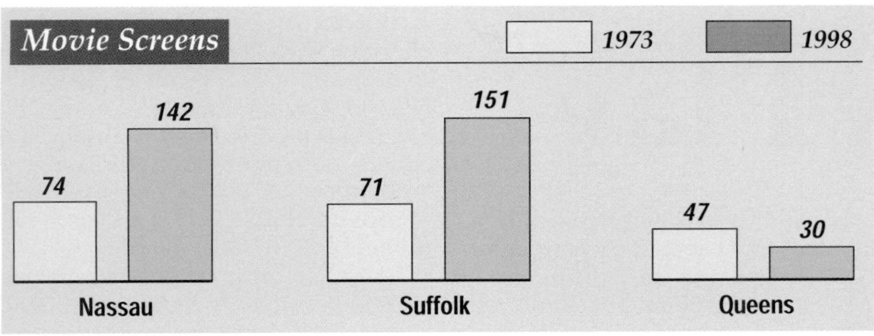

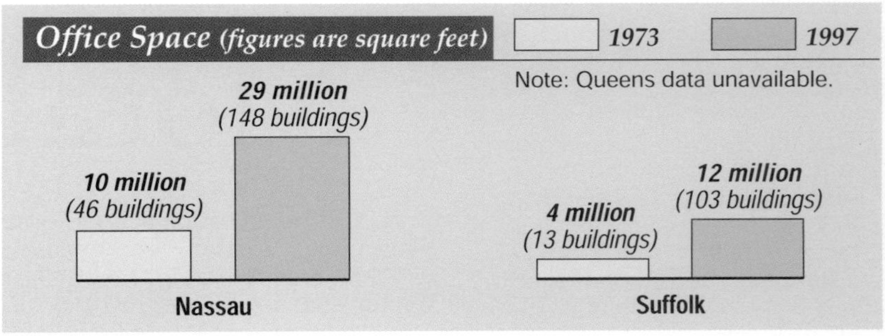

*- Figures total more than 100 percent because Hispanics are counted both as Hispanic and as black or white.

Major Events in the Last 25 Years

Jan. 15, 1973. Original Garden City Hotel razed.

Dec. 9, 1974. Franklin National Bank collapsed; largest U.S. bank failure.

June 24, 1975. Eastern Airlines flight crashed at Kennedy Airport, killing 114.

Dec. 29, 1975. Eleven killed as bomb exploded at LaGuardia.

Aug. 11, 1977. "Son of Sam" David Berkowitz arrested.

Oct. 19, 1977. Concorde SST arrived at JFK.

March 14, 1980. Former LI Rep. Allard Lowenstein murdered.

Nov. 4, 1980. Al D'Amato elected to U.S. Senate.

July 29, 1981. Robert Moses died.

May 17, 1983. Islanders won fourth straight Stanley Cup.

Sept. 27, 1985. Hurricane Gloria struck Long Island.

Dec. 20, 1986. Michael Griffith killed in Howard Beach racial incident.

March 13, 1987. Fairchild Republic closed.

Jan. 27, 1988. Big Duck moved to Flanders.

Feb. 28, 1989. Gov. Mario Cuomo and LILCO head William Catacosinos signed deal to shut down Shoreham plant.

Dec. 15, 1989. Citicorp building, tallest in Queens, opened.

Jan. 25, 1990. Avianca jet crashed in Cove Neck.

Dec. 7, 1993. Colin Ferguson shot 25 commuters.

Jan. 28, 1994. Levittown builder William Levitt died.

Aug. 21, 1995. Wildfires burned pine barrens.

July 17, 1996. TWA Flight 800 exploded off East Moriches, killing 230.

May 28, 1998. LILCO ceased to exist.

SOURCE: U.S. Census Bureau; Long Island Regional Planning Board; New York City Planning Department; New York State Department of Motor Vehicles; LILCO; Con Edison; Cushman & Wakefield of Long Island

Compiled by Rhoda Amon

Newsday / Linda McKenney

Newsday / Gary Viskupic

Moving Ahead, Looking Back

BY HARVEY ARONSON

When I was a child in Queens, my family used to go on Sunday drives through our own borough and Brooklyn. As our Packard or Studebaker — there was even a Buick with a rumble seat — purred along the city streets, my father would glance at a store or a factory or an apartment building and turn to my mother. "Look, Anna," he would say, "remember, it was just a lot. We could have bought it for a song."

I used to wonder. I couldn't believe there were ever that many empty lots. In Queens perhaps, but not in Brooklyn. Now I understand. I drive through my adopted Long Island along an expressway bordered by ugly sound barriers and on highways ever more spangled with gas stations and fast-food chains and strip malls and I echo my father's refrain.

The changes are subtle yet telling, and they have come like quicksilver. It is like aging — a wrinkle here, a gray hair there and suddenly you are older. A Price Club here and a Home Depot there and the frontier vanishes. Perhaps it has something to do with celebrating my 69th birthday. On the cusp of 70, the world accelerates — childhood lingers gracefully in the halls of memory but the recent past flashes by.

So it is with the last quarter-century. Corporate monoliths have squeezed out sod farms on Pinelawn Road in Melville. Houses stand where dairy cows once grazed along a stretch of Jericho Turnpike in Huntington. Golf courses are replacing potato fields in Riverhead, strip malls spot the road to the East End, Saturday morning at the town dump is a rite of the past, and a lonely drive-in movie in Westbury is the last of its kind.

I bought a house in East Northport in 1959 on what seemed to be the edge of the world and was for the moment the far frontier of suburbia. All of us — my neighbors and I — were settlers. We hacked up our half-acres with three-pronged rakes — we couldn't afford to rent rototillers — and the neighborhood show-off was a rich guy who drove his ride-on mower to the gas station. We were all young and the laughter of kids filled the backyards. Many of the men worked in New York City. In the evening, they got off the train in the haze of steam engines and the wives in the waiting cars slid over to the passenger seats so the men could drive home.

The frontier had moved east to Setauket by the 1970s and the boom was over. The kids were going to college and almost half the houses in the neighborhood had second owners. But I could still keep up with the changes. It was the next quarter-century — the last 25 years — that would leave me breathless like a body surfer in time, trying to stay on top of the waves. And all around me on the shore, the change is ever more visible.

The settlers are in their 60s and 70s now and retirement is a lifestyle that in the last few decades has bred condo communities and senior housing across the Island. Schools my children attended no longer exist. Equally telling, only one or two kids come to my house on Halloween in the neighborhood where I now live. The Long Island they know is graced with parks and beaches but it is much less sylvan than the one my own children grew up in. And I wonder — where have all the sod farms gone?

There are, of course, statistics to quantify the changes that have come so quickly during the past 25 years.

These days I live in a house that cost three times what I sold the split level for in the early 1980s — the closing costs alone were more than the price I paid for my first home.

But if such statistics are inviolate in themselves, they too often mean what we interpret them to mean. I can only point to my own statistics, my own profile. The landscape of my life mirrors many of the changes Long Island has lived through in these post-pioneer days. Some of the elements, like computers and cell phones and fax machines and television remotes, are universal. Some, like mauve rhododendrons and Montauk daisies, are essentially Long Island. Some others are just me. But let me hold up the mirror and reflect change.

I have been divorced and I have lived with someone and I have remarried. I have two daughters, one of whom is gay and one who is divorced but planning another marriage. Only my son still lives on Long Island but I do not think he will stay here forever. My wife, who is a year younger than my oldest daughter, is a breast cancer survivor. There are many statistics about breast cancer and how it may relate to Long Island. All I know is that a woman who has transformed my life lives with a shadow that will never go away.

Twenty-five years ago, I wore a shirt and jacket and usually a tie when I went out to eat on Saturday night. Today, I'm likely to wear jeans and a sweater and I don't wait for the weekend. I see movies in multiplexes instead of neighborhood theaters. I go to a gym and work out with a trainer.

These days I live in a house that cost three times what I sold the split level for in the early 1980s — the closing costs alone were more than the price I paid for my first home. I pay somebody what I once made in a week to mow my lawn. My wife and I both work and we have a cleaning person who comes every Monday. We live on a pond and we don't sail but we do have a rowboat and an electric motor with a battery I can't lift. I drive a sports utility vehicle and I find a small adventure in standing on the running board and waving my cowboy hat.

Such things are part of a dichotomy that governs our days. As the suburbs become more urban, as farms and fields vanish and mega-stores replace main streets, we search for adventures. We seek romance and that is part of what drew us to Levittown and beyond and why we are drawn to the water's edge and keep moving east.

I drive around my adopted Long Island and marvel at the changes of a quarter century I echo my father's refrain. It's important to go forward. And it's important to remember the past.

Harvey Aronson, a former Newsday columnist, is the editor of the daily series "Long Island: Our Story."

TIME MACHINE

PICTURING THE PAST AND PRESENT

Village's Volunteers

The Rockville Centre Fire Department has relied on the same basic component — volunteers — since 1875, when Hook and Ladder Co. No. 1 was formed. But the volunteers of 1913, pictured above, received a major boost when the department spent $700 for a "motorized chassis" to go under an existing wagon, according to Tony Walsh, a volunteer for Defender Hose Co. No. 1 and de facto historian for the department. Before that, volunteers either relied on horses or pulled the wagons themselves to fires.

Nowadays, a new truck with all the whistles and bells (and sirens) can cost well over $350,000, Walsh said.

Of course, the department has greater demands than it did at the beginning of the century. In 1908, volunteers responded to seven calls, Walsh said, compared with 2,200 last year.

There is another basic difference between 1913 and 1998: women volunteers. Eileen Lapkowski, on the third row's right side in the photo at right, is one of five women in the 330-volunteer department. Rockville Centre has had female firefighters for about 10 years, said Chief John V. Murray, second from right in the front row. His uncle, at the far left of the front row, is Mayor Eugene Murray.

— **Andrew Salomon**

Newsday Photo / Bill Davis

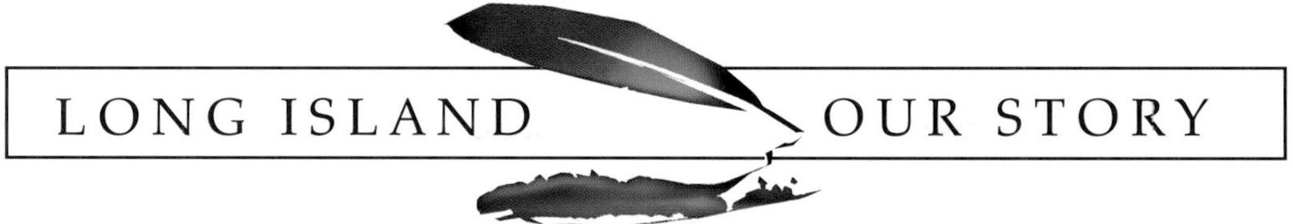

Extras

What follows are selected stories, graphics, maps and special features from "Long Island: Our Story"

It Happened Here First

LONG ISLAND OUR STORY

Moonwalk: Grumman Corp. of Bethpage built the lunar lander used when men walked on the moon in 1969.

America's First Black Poet: Jupiter Hammon, a slave born in 1711 and owned by the Lloyd family of Lloyd Neck

Medals of Honor: In 1782, America's first Purple Heart was awarded to Elijah Churchill of Connecticut for his role in successful raids against the British in Coram and Fort Salonga.

Under the Sea: The first American submarine base, the Holland Torpedo Boat Station, was located in New Suffolk in 1899-1905.

And All the Ships at Sea: In 1901, wireless inventor Guglielmo Marconi transmitted the first shore-to-ship commercial message from Babylon.

First in War: The first guided-missile tests were done in Amityville in 1917.

First in Peace: The United Nations was based in Lake Success from 1945 until the cornerstone of the present UN building in Manhattan was laid in 1951.

On the Air: The first commercial wireless station in America for ship-to-shore radio communication was erected in a Babylon shack in 1900 by Henry J. Kellum.

Across the Pond: In 1922, RCA built the first transatlantic radio-telephone transmitting station at Rocky Point.

On Ramp: Vanderbilt Motor Parkway became the nation's first toll highway when it opened in 1908.

Scout's Honor: Arthur R. Eldred of Rockville Centre became the first Eagle Scout in 1912.

Before Jackie: The country's first black professional baseball team was formed in Babylon in 1885. It was called the Cuban Giants and was composed of employees of the Argyle Hotel.

Links to the Past: Shinnecock Hills Country Club, established in Southampton in 1891, was the first private 18-hole golf club in America.

Macy's Who? In 1842, Hildreth's Department Store in Southampton became the first family-owned and -operated department store in America.

Budding Industry: The first nursery in the country was the Prince nursery in Flushing, established 1737.

Show Me the Plastic: Long Island's Franklin National Bank (now EAB) was the first bank in the country to issue a credit card, about 1952.

The Big Store: King Kullen opened the first self-service supermarket in Jamaica in 1930.

Gentlemen, Start Your Engines: On Oct. 8, 1904, William K. Vanderbilt II acted as referee for the Vanderbilt Cup Race, the first international auto race in America. The grandstand was on Jericho Turnpike in Westbury.

Brainstorms: Invented on Long Island

Ball bearings: Oliver Perry Robinson found in his woodshop in Bellport one day in 1866 that tiny steel balls of buckshot made a board move easily across a flat surface.

Sand digger: In 1883, Nicholas Godrey of Bayville invented a steam-driven machine that combined the tedious tasks of digging and separating sand.

Water skis: The brainchild of Fred Waller of Huntington, who invented and patented them in 1925.

Cinerama: Waller came up with this wide-screen movie format in 1948.

TV "rabbit ear" antenna: One of many patents for consumer electronics was awarded to Marvin Middlemark, a self-made millionaire from Old Westbury, between 1956 and 1968.

MRI: Magnetic resonance imaging was invented by Raymond Damadian of Fonar Corp. and patented in 1974.

Bar code: Jerome Swartz, founder and chairman of Symbol Technologies in Holtsville, was credited with inventing laser bar-code scanners. The first hand-held laser bar-code scanner was introduced in 1980.

Eye in the Sky: The first aerial traffic reports came from a Goodyear blimp operating from the Holmes Airport in Queens in 1936.

They're Off! The first measured racetrack in the colonies was the New Market track on the Hempstead Plains in 1665.

Lucky Lindy: Charles Lindbergh left from Roosevelt Field for Paris on May 20, 1927, on the first solo, nonstop, transatlantic flight.

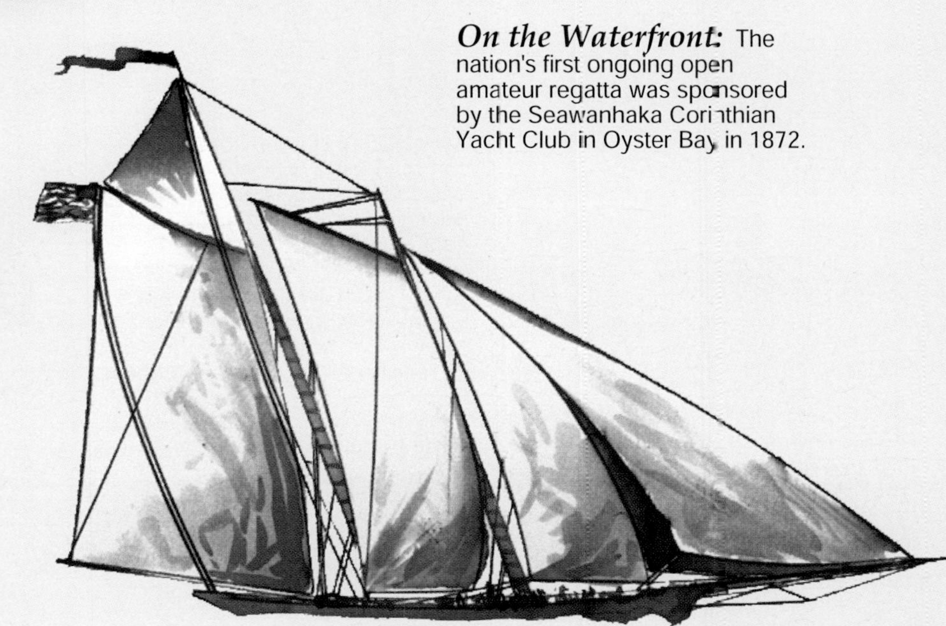

On the Waterfront: The nation's first ongoing open amateur regatta was sponsored by the Seawanhaka Corinthian Yacht Club in Oyster Bay in 1872.

Staying Power: Glenn Curtiss flew a plane over a distance of 25 kilometers in Mineola on July 7, 1909, winning the Scientific American Trophy and a prize of $10,000 for the first sustained flight.

Breaking the Gender Barrier: In 1911, Long Island's Harriet Quimby became the first woman in America to get her pilot's license.

Air Mail: America's first air-mail delivery occurred in 1911, when local flier Earl Ovington carried a bag of 640 letters and 1,280 postcards, from Garden City to Mineola.

Easy Withdrawal: The nation's first ATM was installed in 1969, when Chemical Bank put a machine in its Rockville Centre branch.

And the Rest Is History: The first paid-admission baseball championship games were held July 29, 1858, on the Fashion Race Course in present-day Corona, Queens.

LI Firsts

Twenty milestones for Queens, Nassau, and Suffolk Counties.

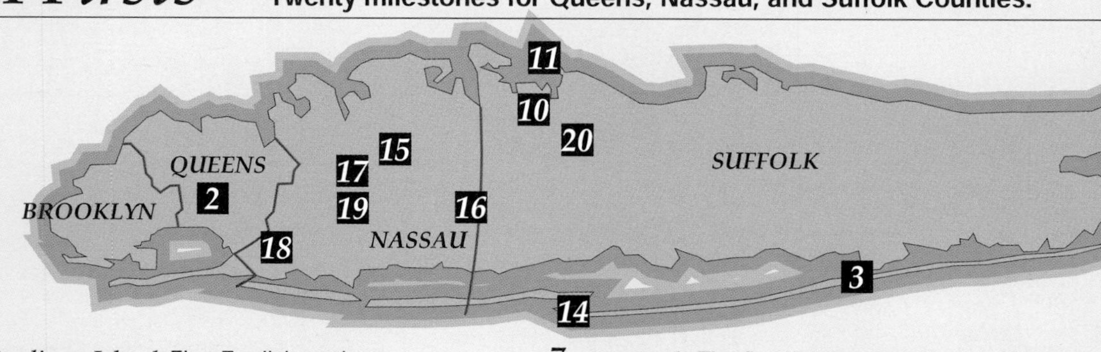

1. ***Gardiners Island:*** First English settlement in New York State was Gardiners Island, purchased by Lion Gardiner in 1639.

2. ***South Jamaica and Southold:*** The first cemeteries, begun in 1640, were Prospect Cemetery off Jamaica Avenue, and the Old Burying Ground off Route 25A.

3. ***Fire Island:*** The Dutch ship Prince Maurice, the first recorded shipwreck, sank in 1657.

4. ***East Hampton:*** Clinton Academy, the first chartered academic institution in the state, was founded in 1784.

5. ***Sag Harbor:*** The first newspaper, the Long Island Herald, was published in 1791.

6. ***Sag Harbor:*** The first book – "A Plain and Serious Address to the Master of a Family on the subject of Family Religion," by Philip Doddridge – was published in 1791.

7. ***Montauk:*** The first lighthouse in New York State, built in 1796, was the Montauk Lighthouse.

8. ***Southold:*** The first incorporated library was founded in 1797.

9. ***Sag Harbor:*** Sag Harbor Fire Department, the oldest volunteer company, was established 1803.

10. ***Huntington:*** Silas Wood published the first history of Long Island, "A Sketch of the First Settlement of the Several Towns on Long-Island," in 1824.

11. ***Eatons Neck:*** The first life-saving station opened in 1849.

12. ***Greenport:*** First National Bank of Greenport, the first commercial bank, opened in 1864.

13. ***Southampton:*** The Parrish Art Museum, the first art museum, opened in 1898.

14. ***Robert Moses State Park:*** The first state park was Fire Island State Park, authorized in 1908 and later renamed for Robert Moses.

15. ***Mineola:*** The first airport was Mineola Flying Field, established in 1909.

16. ***Farmingdale:*** The state School of Agriculture was the first public college in 1912.

17. ***Garden City:*** Adelphi moved here from Brooklyn in 1929 and became the first private four-year college.

18. ***Valley Stream:*** The first drive-in movie theater opened in 1938.

19. ***Garden City:*** The first major shopping mall was Roosevelt Field in 1956.

20. ***Commack:*** The Long Island Ducks hockey team, the first sports franchise, began playing in 1959.

Newsday graphic by Linda McKenney
Illustrations by Bob Newman

Research by Georgina Martorella

Milestones in Transportation

Maritime

1657. Long Island's first recorded shipwreck: Prins Maurits ran aground off Fire Island; all 180 crewmen and Dutch immigrants saved by Indians.

1789. Sag Harbor named one of America's first ports of entry by first Congress.

1796. Montauk Lighthouse, New York State's first, completed.

1797. John Willse, L.I.'s first known shipbuilder, launched maiden ship from what is now Poquott.

New Bedford Whaling Museum

1843. Southampton whaling Capt. Mercator Cooper sailed on the Manhattan, above, from Sag Harbor on voyage that took him to Japan, which was closed to foreigners.

1847. Schooner Edward L. Frost, first U.S. ship to bring cargo from Japan, built in Port Jefferson.

Sag Harbor Whaling Museum Photo

1848. Sag Harbor whale ship commanded by Capt. Thomas Roys became first ever to sail through Bering Strait and into Arctic Ocean to hunt bowhead whales.

1851. Port Jefferson sailmaker Reuben Wilson made sails for victorious schooner America in first race against England; race became known as America's Cup.

1871. The Myra became last whaler to sail from Sag Harbor.

1872. Nation's first ongoing open amateur regatta, sponsored by Seawanhaka Corinthian Yacht Club in Centre Island.

1883. Bridgeport and Port Jefferson Steamboat Co. formed first regular L.I.-Connecticut ferry service.

1895. Islip Capt. Hank Haff skippered Defender to victory in the America's Cup, using first all-American crew.

1899. First modern submarine for U.S. Navy tested in New Suffolk.

Photo Courtesy of James R. McNamara

1901. The 201-foot Martha Wallace, above left, last and largest sailing ship built on Long Island, was launched in Port Jefferson.

1943. U.S. Merchant Marine Academy in Kings Point dedicated.

Newsday File Photo / Kathy Kmonicek

1946. Grumman engineer John Achilich designed first widely marketed aluminum canoe.

1949. Webb Institute, founded in 1889 as America's first naval architecture college, moved to Glen Cove.

Aviation

1833. Charles F. Durant landed balloon at Union Race Course in Jamaica, becoming the first person to set foot on L.I. from the air.

1909. Glenn Curtiss, L.I.'s first flier, took off from Mineola field, remaining aloft half an hour. A month later, Curtiss took Scientific American Trophy for longest flight by an American – 28 miles in 58 minutes.

1910. Elmo Neale Pickerill achieved first air-to-ground telegraphic communication during flight from Mineola to Manhattan Beach. First international air meet in America was held at Belmont Park; record set at 61 mph.

1911. After 49 days and many forced landings, Calbraith P. Rodgers completed first transcontinental air trip, Mineola to Long Beach, Calif. Also Earle Ovington made first U.S. air-mail flight, from Garden City to Mineola.

1912. Long Islander Harriet Quimby, first licensed female pilot, died in airplane accident.

1918. "Aerial torpedos," considered country's first guided missiles, were successfully test-launched from Amityville to Fire Island.

1919. Navy aircraft built in Garden City and Rockaway Beach became first plane to fly across the Atlantic. It stopped in Newfoundland, the Azores, Lisbon and finally England.

1923. Two military fliers made first nonstop coast-to-coast flight, reaching San Diego from Mitchel Field in 27 hours.

UPI Photo

May 19, 1927. Charles Lindbergh began the first nonstop solo transatlantic flight, taking off from Roosevelt Field, landing 33 hours later at Le Bourget Airport, France.

Nassau County Museum, Long Island Studies Institute Photo

1929. Elinor Smith set women's solo endurance record by staying aloft for 26 hours, 23 minutes and 13 seconds over Roosevelt Field.

1930. Grumman Aircraft Engineering Co. opened in cinderblock garage in Baldwin.

1939. LaGuardia Field opened.

1942. U.S. Civil Aeronautics Authority opened MacArthur Airport in Islip.

1948. President Harry Truman dedicated Idlewild Airport.

1951. Roosevelt Field closed to air traffic to make way for construction of L.I.'s first major shopping mall.

1963. One month after president's assassination, Idlewild renamed John F. Kennedy International Airport.

1966. NASA awarded billion-dollar contract to Grumman to produce 15 modules to land men on moon.

NASA Photo

July 20, 1969. Bethpage-built Grumman module landed on moon.

1977. First Concorde supersonic transport arrived at Kennedy Airport.

1987. Fairchild Republic Co. closed, leaving 3,500 jobless.

Newsday File Photo

1990. Avianca jet from Colombia crashed in Cove Neck on way to Kennedy Airport, killing 73.

1994. Grumman acquired by Northrop Corp.

1996. Paris-bound TWA Flight 800 exploded and plunged into Atlantic off East Moriches, killing all 230 aboard.

Centuries of progress – and setbacks – at sea, in the air, on the road and on the rails for Long Islanders

Trains

1834. Long Island Rail Road chartered by state for a Brooklyn-to-Boston rail-sea route.

1836. LIRR became first U.S. railroad to mount steam whistles on locomotives.

1837. First section of LIRR main line completed, from Jamaica to Hicksville.

1842. Main line reached Suffolk with opening of Deer Park station.

1844. LIRR main line, 10 years in making, reached last stop, Greenport; first trip from Brooklyn took 3 hours, 45 minutes.

1848. New Haven Rail Road opened, making LIRR route to Boston via Greenport obsolete.

1864. South Side Railroad completed a line serving the South Shore from Brooklyn to Patchogue.

1876. LIRR merged with Flushing and North Side Railroad and began freight service. Biggest freight item: manure from city streets and stables for LI farmers.

Photo Courtesy of Vincent Seyfried

1881. Austin Corbin took charge of LIRR.

1895. LIRR reached Montauk.

Suffolk County Historical Society Photo

1899. Mile-A-Minute Murphy made bicycling history by riding one mile in 57.8 seconds behind LIRR train.

1900. Pennsylvania Railroad took control of the LIRR.

Nassau County Museum, Long Island Studies Institute Photo

1901. Mineola, Hempstead and Freeport Trolley Co. gained first franchise to operate street-surface railroad from Mineola to Freeport.

1905. LIRR purchased first all-steel passenger car and became first railroad to use extensive main-line electrification.

1910. Pennsylvania Station opened in New York; 43 trains headed for L.I.

1926. LIRR put nation's first diesel locomotive in service. Later that year, a train crashed into Golden's Pickle Works in Calverton, killing six people.

1949. Pennsylvania Railroad put LIRR into bankruptcy court.

AP File Photo

1950. Nation's worst rail wreck happened on Thanksgiving eve. Babylon-bound train crashed into stalled train west of Jamaica station, killing 79, injuring 334.

1951. LIRR emerged from bankruptcy as a railroad redevelopment corporation.

1966. LIRR purchased by Metropolitan Commuter Transportation Authority, later succeeded by the Metropolitan Transportation Authority.

1979. All-female conducting crew, first in country, worked the 4:35 p.m. from Port Washington.

1993. Six LIRR riders were killed, 19 injured, when Colin Ferguson fired a semi-automatic gun on a train in Garden City.

Roads and Cars

1600s. Indians blazed L.I.'s first through route, from what is now Brooklyn to what is now Jericho, 30 miles east; route later known as Jericho Turnpike.

1733. Three main roads running length of L.I. laid out: North Country (now parts of Route 25A), Middle Country (now parts of Jericho Turnpike), and South Country Roads (now parts of Montauk Highway).

1801. Flushing and Newtown Bridge and Turnpike Co. incorporated, a turning point in L.I. road improvement.

1807. Charter issued for Jamaica-Hempstead Plank Road, later to become Hempstead Turnpike.

1836. North Hempstead and Flushing Turnpike Road and Bridge Co. formed to build road from Flushing to Roslyn, now western portion of Route 25A.

1852. Merrick Road, one of L.I.'s longest pioneer highways, developed from Jamaica to Merrick as plank road.

1883. Brooklyn Bridge opened as longest suspension bridge in world.

1892. Queens County began public, tax-financed management of roads, ending private ownership and tolls.

1903. Williamsburg Bridge opened.

Newsday Photo / Bill Davis

1904. William Kissam Vanderbilt II acted as referee for Vanderbilt Cup Race, starting and ending in Westbury – first international auto race in America.

1906. Spectator died at third Vanderbilt race when crowds surged onto road to see cars, forcing Vanderbilt to build a private race course that would later become part of his Motor Parkway.

1908. Vanderbilt's L.I. Motor Parkway opened for nine miles, from Westbury to Bethpage. Toll: $2.

Newsday Archive

1910. Seventh and last Vanderbilt Cup race on L.I. Four fatalities convinced car makers and drivers course was unsafe.

1912. Unprofitable L.I. Motor Parkway reduced toll to $1.50.

1914. L.I. Motor Parkway reached 43 miles, from Flushing to Lake Ronkonkoma.

1922. L.I.'s first divided "super highway" opened: Long Beach Road.

NYS Parks, Recreation and Historic Preservation Photo

1929. Jones Beach State Park, above, Southern State and Wantagh Parkways and Sunrise Highway opened.

1933. Toll on L.I. Motor Parkway reduced to 40 cents.

1936. Grand Central Parkway and Triborough Bridge completed.

1938. L.I. Motor Parkway given to Queens, Nassau and Suffolk Counties in lieu of tax payments. Only Suffolk kept it as roadway.

Triborough Bridge and Tunnel Authority Photo

1949. Queens-Midtown Tunnel opened.

1952. Northern State and Sagtikos Parkways completed.

1958. Gov. Averill Harriman opened first section of Long Island Expressway – five miles from Queens line to Roslyn Heights.

1969. Seaford-Oyster Bay Expressway opened.

1972. Long Island Expressway completed to Riverhead.

1976. Right turns on red lights permitted in Nassau and Suffolk.

Compiled by Georgina Martorella

Graphic by Linda McKenney

Black History: 41

These are some of the prominent African-Americans with ties to Nassau, Suffolk and Queens:

Jupiter Hammon (1712-1800). America's first black published poet was born in Lloyd Neck and lived and died a slave.

Venture Smith (about 1729-1805). Was kidnaped from West Africa into slavery and taken to Fishers Island when he was 7. He bought his freedom and lived in Suffolk County before moving to Connecticut.

Paul Cuffee (1757-1812). The Wading River resident, a missionary of Indian and African descent, traveled throughout Long Island preaching to Indians, slaves and whites.

Southampton Historical Museum Photo

Pyrrhus Concer bought his freedom, became a whaler and sailed to Japan.

Sojourner Truth walked on Long Island, advocating rights.

Benjamin Whitecuff and his son, **Benjamin.** The Hempstead men fought in the Revolutionary War. The elder Whitecuff, a prosperous landowner, joined the Continental Army. The younger joined the British.

Pyrrhus Concer (1814-1897). Concer, of Southampton, bought his freedom and became a seaman on a whaling ship that was one of the first to sail into Japanese waters.

Sojourner Truth (1797-1883). Walked from New York City to Huntington in 1843, advocating abolition, women's rights and other causes.

Wilson Rantus (1807-1861). He was an abolitionist instrumental in establishing a weekly black newspaper and a school for black children in Jamaica.

Joseph Cinque. Led the slave rebellion on the slave ship Amistad in 1839.

Frederick Douglass, the most famous black abolitionist, spoke in Hempstead.

Henry Highland Garnet (1815-1882). Briefly an indentured servant to Epenetus Smith II of Smithtown before going on to become a famous Presbyterian minister and abolitionist.

Frederick Douglass (1817-1895). The most famous black abolitionist was in regular contact with the Quaker community in Westbury and spoke in Brooklyn and in Hempstead.

Harriet Tubman (1823-1913). "The Moses of Her People," she freed 300 slaves via the Underground Railroad, which may have included stops in Port Washington and Sag Harbor.

Gilbert Jackson (1846-1916). Hempstead resident, member of the 20th Regiment, U.S. Colored Infantry, one of many in the Civil War.

Samuel Ballton (1838-1917). The "Pickle King" of Greenlawn began a lucrative life as an entrepreneur by buying the local pickle works. He went on to real estate development.

Lewis Howard Latimer (1848-1928). Inventor from Flushing who worked with Alexander Graham Bell on patent drawings and received a patent for using carbon filaments in light bulbs.

Centerport-Greenlawn Historical Association

Samuel Ballton gained renown as the Pickle King of Greenlawn.

Booker T. Washington (1856-1915). "Up From Slavery" author and founder of Alabama's Tuskegee Institute, had a summer home in Fort Salonga.

William Edward Burghardt Du Bois (1868-1963). Famed author and historian lived in St. Albans.

Father Divine (1879-1965), preacher who founded the Peace Mission Church, lived in Sayville and Brooklyn.

Significant Events Through the Years

1626: Slavery was introduced in New York, then called the colony of New Netherlands, as 11 blacks were brought in for enforced work.

1706: New York colonial law prohibited slaves from testifying for or against a free man in civil or criminal cases.

1712: Slave revolt in New York City ended with nine whites killed and 21 blacks executed.

1741: Thirteen blacks were burned at the stake; 17 blacks and four whites were hanged after New York mistakenly charged slaves with plotting an insurrection.

1761: Black poet Jupiter Hammon of Lloyd Neck published his poem, "Salvation by Christ With Penetential Cries."

1799: New York passed the first in a series of gradual emancipation laws. Children born to slaves after July 4 were free but had to continue working for their parents' owners for a specified number of years.

1811: The congregation of the Macedonia African Methodist Episcopal Church in Flushing was formed. In the next few years, congregations were formed in Amityville, Port Washington, Roslyn and Setauket.

1827: Slavery ended in New York State.

1839: Slaves on the Spanish ship Amistad revolted. Ship was seized off of Montauk. The Africans aboard eventually won their freedom in a case taken to the U.S. Supreme Court.

1843: Sojourner Truth left Manhattan to begin a trek to Huntington, preaching about God and abolition along the way.

1861: Beginning of the Civil War. Blacks from Long Island served in the 20th, 22nd, 26th and 26th U.S. Colored Troops. Among them was George Lyons of Amityville, who served as a drummer boy, and Joachim Pease, a gunner on the USS Kearsarge who won a Medal of Honor.

1867: African and Indian community near what now is Lake Success built a school with $267 raised at the local church fair.

1885: First black professional baseball team in the country was founded in Babylon.

1895: Desegregation of Amityville schools. The community's black school was closed after Charles Brewster, a black parent, complained that his child had been barred from attending a new school built for white children. Five years later, state legislation limited racial segregation in public schools.

1898: Spanish American War. The 10th Calvary trained in Yaphank and, on returning from Cuba, landed in Montauk.

1906: First black fraternity, Alpha Phi Alpha, was established at Cornell University in upstate Ithaca.

1909: The NAACP was founded in New York City.

1917: Outbreak of World War I. Many black soldiers, assigned to segregated units, trained in Yaphank.

1920: Marcus Garvey's national convention of the Universal Negro Improvement Association met in New York City.

Names to Remember

Inventor Lewis Howard Latimer of Flushing patented carbon filaments for light bulbs.

Rev. Martin Luther King Jr. (1929-1968). He visited Hempstead, Long Beach and West Hempstead in 1965. In 1968 he spoke in Rockville Centre.

William H. Johnson (1901-1970). An artist, whose work has increasingly become more famous, spent his last years in a hospital in Kings Park.

Louis Armstrong (1900-1971). The legendary trumpeter who pushed jazz to a new level lived in Corona. The area also has been home to other entertainers, including **(Count) William Basie** (1904-1984), **James Brown** (1933-), **Mercer Ellington** (1919-1996), **Ella Fitzgerald** (1918-1996), **Lena Horne** (1917-), **Thomas (Fats) Waller** (1904-1943), all in St. Albans; **Billie Holiday** (1915-1959), Flushing; **John Coltrane** (1926-1967), Dix Hills; **Eddie Murphy** (1961-), Roosevelt; **LL Cool J** (1969-), St. Albans; **Mariah Carey** (1970-), Huntington.

Journalist Dennis P. Bell of Uniondale won a Pulitzer Prize.

Roy Wilkins (1901-1981). A civil rights activist and former director of the NAACP who lived the last 30 years of his life in Flushing.

Ralph J. Bunche (1904-1971). Won a Nobel Peace Prize in 1950 and lived in Kew Gardens.

Dennis P. Bell (1949-1995), of Uniondale, a journalist at Newsday who won a Pulitzer Prize in 1985, with reporter Josh Friedman and photographer Ozier Muhammad, for reporting on the famine in Ethiopia. Bell started at the paper as a floor sweeper and worked his way up to reporter and local editor.

Photo by Paul Hoeffler, 1957

Singer Billie Holiday was a Flushing resident, and jazz great Louis Armstrong made his home in Corona.

Joseph McNeil (1942-), now of Hempstead, at age 17 was one of four students who launched the era of "sit in" protests in 1960 at a whites-only lunch counter at Woolworths in Greensboro, N.C. The students refused to move to the store's blacks-only stand-up counter and were arrested. Their protest led to desegregation of local lunch counters.

Newsday Photo / Bruce Gilbert

Popular singer Mariah Carey grew up in Huntington.

Jackie Robinson (1919-1972). The great baseball player who broke the color line in baseball lived in St. Albans. Queens was also home for a time for **Joe Louis** (1914-1981), world heavyweight boxing champion. Football great **Jim Brown** (1936-) grew up in Manhasset, basketball legend **Julius Erving** (1950-) lived in Roosevelt and **Roy Campanella** (1921-1993), Brooklyn Dodger All-Star catcher, lived at different times in Queens and Glen Cove.

AP Photo, 1986

Roosevelt's Julius Erving

1922: The Harlem Renaissance, a golden age of black literature and art in the United States, began, lasting until 1929.

1941: Beginning of World War II. "Brown Bomber" Joe Louis, the heavyweight champion, took Army training in Yaphank. He reported for duty in a limousine, accompanied by a crowd of reporters and photographers.
- Spann Watson of Westbury trained as a pilot at Tuskegee Institute in Alabama. He was one of the first black pilots to fight an air battle in the war.

1947: Jackie Robinson joined the Brooklyn Dodgers, becoming the first black player in Major League Baseball's modern era.
- Levittown's restrictive covenants barred black homeowners and renters.

1950: Ralph J. Bunche, who lived in Kew Gardens, won the Nobel Peace Prize for his work as a mediator in Palestine.

1963: State ordered Malverne school district to desegregate. School boards in Manhasset, Westbury and Amityville were also pressured to integrate schools. Cross burning occurred in Amityville.

1964: Beginning in Harlem, serious racial disturbances occurred in more than six major cities. The 24th Amendment forbids use of poll tax to prevent voting.

1965: Malcolm X was assassinated in New York City.
- The Rev. Martin Luther King Jr. visited Hempstead, Long Beach and West Hempstead. He received an honorary degree from Hofstra University and addressed graduating students.

1967: In the worst summer for racial unrest in U.S. history, more than 40 riots and 100 other disturbances occurred.

1968: The Rev. Martin Luther King Jr. spoke in Rockville Centre. Eight days later, he was assassinated in Memphis. In the following week, riots occurred in at least 125 places throughout the country.
- Shirley Chisholm of Brooklyn became the first black woman elected to Congress.

1972: Shirley Chisholm made an unsuccessful bid for Democratic nomination for president.

1982: Barbara Patton of Freeport became the first black woman to represent a suburban district in the State Assembly.

1989: James Garner of Hempstead was elected Long Island's first black village mayor.

1994: H. Carl McCall was elected comptroller, becoming the first black elected official at the state level.

1996: Roger Corbin of Westbury and Darlene Harris of Uniondale were elected as first black members in the newly created Nassau County Legislature. The county's Board of Supervisors and its weighted voting system had been declared unconstitutional by a federal court as a result of a lawsuit that contended that the system deprived minorities of fair and effective representation.

COMPILED BY JOYE BROWN

SOURCES: "Chronology of African American History," by Alton Hornsby Jr.; "The Civil Rights Movement on Long Island, A Local Curriculum Guide for Middle School and High School," Hofstra University; Library of Congress black history timeline; "Making a Way to Freedom: A History of African Americans on Long Island," by Lynda R. Day, and Newsday files.

LI's Coming-of-Age Party

BY MICHELE INGRASSIA
STAFF WRITER

And a party of a lifetime it was, as the Gold Coast celebrated the presence of the prince of Wales

AS A chauffeur's son, Stewart Donaldson wasn't likely to be invited to many Gold Coast soirees, unless it was a servants' ball. But on Sept. 6, 1924, when the fabulously rich Clarence Mackay feted England's wildly popular prince of Wales, the 17-year-old Donaldson had a window on the most glorious party of all.

Perched atop the main house of Harbor Hill, Mackay's 600-acre Roslyn estate, he took in the sweep: the mile-long driveway shimmering with tiny blue candles, the two-story ballroom set with thousands of American Beauty roses, the tables of lobster piled 6 feet high. As he watched, Donaldson helped wield four giant spotlights, which were set up to bathe the Italian gardens in alternating hues of red, yellow, blue, green and white.

"And when the prince of Wales arrived, all the spots were put on and pointed at the gardens, fountain and rose trellis," Donaldson recalled in the meticulously typed diaries he compiled decades later. "It was some show. I'll never forget it. That night they said there were over 1,000 people on the floor of the ballroom. That's hard to believe, but it is supposed to be true." And, indeed, it was true. But that's not all.

It was the most gilded party of Long Island's most gilded age, the capstone of the prince's 23-day Gold Coast holiday and the personification of the era when America's mightiest families transformed the North Shore into a playground for the rich and richer. Surely, flashy parties were nothing new — the mansion set was as competitive in the ballroom as it was in the boardroom — but no one ever matched Mackay's audacious bash: 1,200 guests, an army of servants and four frantic weeks of preparation, down to the last white light bulb fastened to the last Mackay (pronounced Mack-EE) rosebush.

Everyone clamored for a piece of it. Assistant Secretary of the Navy Theodore Roosevelt Jr. was there. So was World War I Gen. John J. Pershing and much of *haute* New York, from (Mr. and Mrs. Frederick) Allen to (Mr. and Mrs. Payne) Whitney; there also were enough counts, countesses, lords, ladies, marquis and marchionesses to populate a small duchy. But the real prize was the prince, whose appearance cemented the Gold Coast's coming-of-age, branding it, at last, a rival worthy of the more established Newport. "I don't know whether the people of Newport would agree, but if this party didn't bring Long Island to the same level, it certainly put it on the same playing field," says Nassau County historian Edward Smits.

Bryant Library Local History Collection Photo

The prince of Wales, center, stands by his mustachioed party host, Clarence Mackay, in 1924.

Even the prince, who ostensibly had come to watch the international polo matches at the Meadow Brook Club, was awed. As he recalled in "A King's Story," his 1947 autobiography, "My American hosts spared no expense in demonstrating the splendor of a modern industrial republic." Certainly none more eagerly than Mackay, whose father, John W. Mackay, made his fortune in the Comstock Lode and who, with a $500 million inheritance, was every bit the profligate son. The dance music alone, the prince noted, "was provided by two bands directed by the great Paul Whiteman, who at a later stage was inspired to lead his musicians in a march around the hall, weaving in and out of the shadowy figures in armor."

To understand the seismic impact of the prince's visit, it's important to remember that, at the time, Edward Albert Christian George Andrew Patrick David was, quite simply, the most popular man in the universe, a blond, waiflike figure who combined the androgynous sexiness of Leonardo DiCaprio with the megawattage of Princess Diana. Of course, this was his age of innocence. It would be nearly a decade before he would fall in love with Wallis Warfield Simpson and a dozen years before he would become King Edward VIII, only to give up the throne 11 months later to marry the twice-divorced American — a decision that threatened the future of the monarchy and left Edward with the meaningless title of duke of Windsor.

IT WASN'T only power and riches that made him so attractive. With his melancholy blue eyes, his hunger for bathtub gin and his love of parties and polo, the elegant 30-year-old prince was the quintessential guy's guy, the ultimate ladies' man. HERE HE IS, GIRLS — THE MOST ELIGIBLE BACHELOR YET UNCAUGHT, screamed a headline inside the New York Daily News on Aug. 29, 1924, the day Edward arrived in New York aboard the liner Berengaria.

Actually, the frenzy began even before he set sail. Traveling under the name Lord Renfrew, the prince slipped aboard ship and into his five-room, $5,400 suite at 4 a.m. — 14½ hours early — hoping to avoid "that ubiquitous fraternity of photographers," as the New

York Times called the paparazzi following him. It was a fleeting victory. Daily came shipboard reports of all things royal, from the prince's clothes (the world's best-dressed man wore only two suits, one gray, one brown) to his exercise routine (the ship's boxing instructor declared him so limber "he can touch his knuckles to the ground without bending his knees").

Even more enticing to the tabloids were the ship's sweet young "debbies," the blushing society girls vying for a royal nod. Only Lenora Cahill, a dark-haired St. Louis girl, succeeded, spinning around the dance floor with the prince not once but twice in a row. The next day, she was front-page news.

And by the time Edward landed in New York with two tons of luggage, the press was panting.

"Have you become engaged to an American girl?" one of the 150 reporters who met up with him asked.

"Would you marry an American girl if you fell in love with one?" asked another, with eerie premonition.

IN FACT, the only thing the prince wanted was to be left alone. Not a chance. The more he demanded privacy — he even threatened to run off to his Canadian ranch — the more the press and public jockeyed for another glimpse. As Edward boarded the yacht Black Watch for the final leg of the journey to Long Island, more than 10,000 locals waved him on, filling bay and inlets with rafts and yachts and North Shore landings with buntings and bands.

Finally, he stepped onto a float at the Pratt estate in Glen Cove, then sped off to the 140-acre Syosset home of James A. Burden, who had, graciously enough, decamped to New York. Though Edward and Wallis would later develop reputations as world-class freeloaders, it was apparent even in 1924 that this wasn't a guy who paid his own way. Besides, who would ask him to? "These people were in cutthroat wars over dahlias and who grew the best," says Glen Cove historian Dan Russell. "This was even better — who could get to the prince of Wales to stay at their house or come to their party."

Yet, for all his press-dodging — there were so many reporters covering him that Western Union opened temporary press headquarters at the LIRR station in Syosset — the prince did as he pleased. And, for the most part, that meant he played polo, sometimes at the W.R. Grace estate, other times at the Howard Phipps estate or anywhere else he was invited. In between, the "indefatigable vacationist," as the papers dubbed him, swam, raced speedboats and rushed off to Belmont Park to watch as Epinard lost to Wise Counsellor.

To be sure, Edward was an eager sportsman but hardly a graceful one. The press relentlessly poked fun at his inability to stay on his horse — and those weren't his only disasters. One day, an opponent's polo pony kicked a clod of dirt into his right eye, conjuring one heck of a royal shiner. Another day, Clarence Mackay's 17-year-old son, John William, beaned him with a tennis ball. "The prince was so nice and so wonderful about it, but my husband was so embarrassed he almost died," John's 90-year-old widow, Gwendolyn, said recently.

But not even an eye patch could keep Edward from the parties — swim parties, polo parties, lunch parties, dinner parties, supper parties, middle-of-the-night parties — that were thrown in his name, usually two or three a day. One of the most raucous was the dinner at the Piping Rock Club in Locust Valley to honor the British contenders for the international polo title. While Edward and

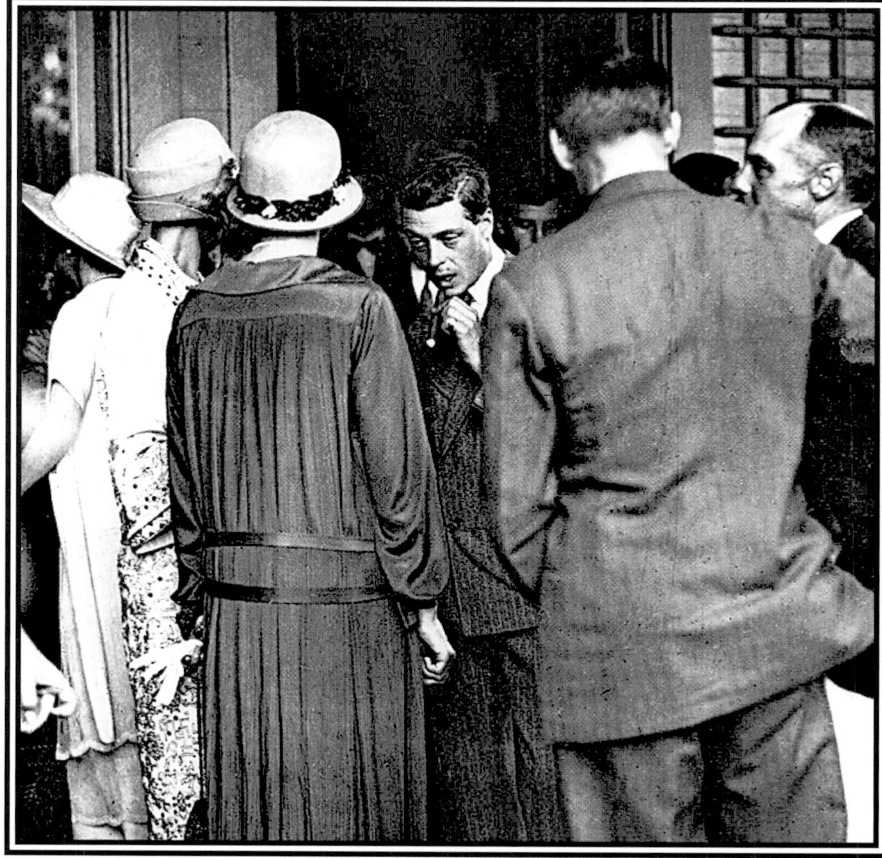

New York Daily News Photo

The prince meets guests at a lawn party at the Pratt estate in Glen Cove.

New York Daily News Photo

The prince liked horseback riding, but he fell off a lot, to the delight of the New York press.

the others supped on cantaloupe, lobster Newburg and vanilla ice cream, Ziegfeld Follies star Will Rogers roasted the prince's polo foibles and late-night escapades.

In a New York Times column the following week, Rogers admitted to a bit of stage fright. "I didn't get scared until just before it came time to go (on). Then I happened to think of the Tower of London and remembered its whole reputation was built on obituary notices of people who had displeased Princes and Kings." But Edward laughed loudest of all, and Rogers admitted it was easier to tease the prince than keep up with him. "Say, no foreigner comes to America to sleep. He can sleep when he gets to England," the humorist wrote. "A man leaving England for this country should have enough sleep stored up to do him a lifetime."

Indeed, the royal party boy seemed hell-bent on cramming in every last dance, to the endless delight of the princess wannabes lined up to be his partner. At a party at the Oyster Bay estate of Rodman Wanamaker, they literally wore out the floor, and so, at 1:30 a.m., a car was dispatched into town, where, the Times reported, "druggists were rousted out of bed to turn over all the floor wax and talcum they had on hand," all to smooth the way for "the shuffling of royal feet."

But, in the end, those were merely dress rehearsals for Mackay's ball. Planning began early that summer when Mackay — whose mother, Louise, had often entertained the prince's grandfather, Edward VII, in London — announced he would fete the young king-to-be. And, truth be told, there could have been no more regal setting. Situated on the second-highest spot on Long Island, Harbor Hill was twice the size of the principality of Monaco and offered breathtaking views of Hempstead Harbor and Long Island Sound.

The interiors were just as fabulous. The main house, a French chateau designed by the renowned McKim, Mead & White, spared no expense — indeed, Stanford White was accused of pillaging any number of European palaces to furnish it. The two-story main hall bulged with tapestries, ancient battle flags and the finest collection of armor this side of the Atlantic. Outside, an extravagant Italian garden unfolded, its fountain set off with Paul Manship statues, its terrace with the horses of Marly, copied from the Champs de Elysees.

And Mackay — Clarie, as everyone called him — was determined to show off Harbor Hill's grandeur at its glittering best. There were blue-lit Chinese lanterns set into the maple trees along the main drive, orange lights in the trees lining the walk to the mansion, spotlights trained on the gardens and, towering above the rooftop, the Stars and Stripes done in red, white and blue bulbs. In his diaries, now stored in the Bryant Library in Roslyn, Stewart Donaldson recalled how "the power company had to dig up the electric cable and spot transformers at certain locations and put a fence around each one." In all, he wrote, "it took many electricians, carpenters, laborers, plumbers, etc., and L.I.L.Co." four weeks just to finish the electric work.

For the floral arrangements, Mackay turned to head gardener Frank Demak and New York florist Wadley & Smythe. Indoors, they filled the galleries with American Beauty roses snipped from Mackay's private greenhouse. Outside, Donaldson wrote, they transformed the north terrace into "a pavilion of flowers. No one could believe that it wasn't an integral part of the house."

Mackay left no detail untended. The tables were set with pieces from the $125,000 service that Tiffany & Co. had created for the elder Mackay, using nearly 15,000 ounces of silver from his mines. Cars were fetched using a relay system involving telephones wired to the trees and chauffeurs positioned at holding stations, waiting for their cars to be called. And the music was provided by society's bandleader of the moment, Paul Whiteman.

"About 3 PM that day, two large moving vans pulled up to the front and out came two baby grands and all of the trunks of musical instruments," Donaldson wrote. ". . . The pianos and instruments were taken up to the balcony above the ballroom . . . and at 4 PM, Mrs. Louise Mackay seated herself in the great hall and had Whiteman and his 45-piece orchestra play Strauss waltzes just for her." Later that night, Whiteman split the orchestra in half, so one band could spell the other.

THE FINAL TAB: $1.5 million — serious bucks to impress a guest of honor who reportedly skipped the 3-foot-wide salmon in favor of a simple sandwich, then bowed out at 11 p.m.

Still, there was no doubt the party, like the prince's three weeks on Long Island, left an indelible impression on Edward. "By the time I had to return to Great Britain," he wrote in his autobiography, "I had picked up quite a full line of American slang, acquired a taste for bathtub gin and had decided that every Briton in a position to do so should make a practice of visiting that great country at least once every two or three years."

Unfortunately, his father didn't agree. With stunning swiftness, reports of the prince's frolicking had sped across the ocean, to the great displeasure of the Teutonic King George V. And although the prince tried to wave it away as nothing more than "uninhibited journalism," George was furious. It "would not be correct to say that he actually banned my returning to the United States," Edward wrote. "Yes, whenever my brothers and I tentatively advanced some project that would take us there, a series of vague but irremovable obstacles always appeared to block us." Others, though, needed nothing grander; it had been the party of a lifetime.

Pioneers In The Air

Flash In The Sky

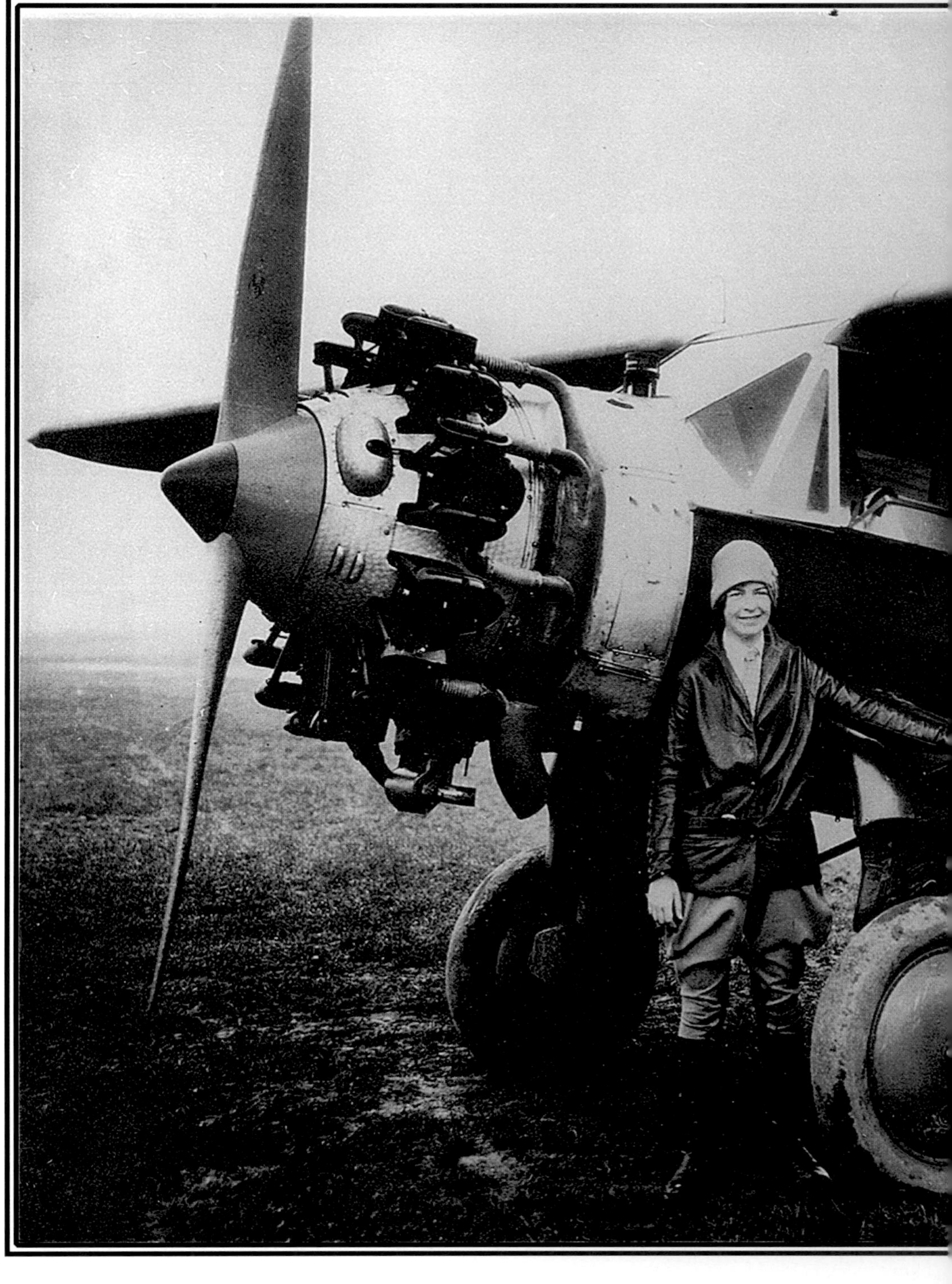

Elinor Smith was a world-class pilot before she was out of her teens – and probably a better one than the more famous Amelia Earhart

BY LAURA MUHA

Elinor Smith wrapped both hands around the control stick and held on tightly as her open-cockpit biplane pitched and jounced through the night sky.

WHAM! A violent jolt of turbulence sent the plane plummeting. Quickly, Smith jammed the throttle open, regaining control just as — *WHAM!* — more turbulence rocked the little craft.

Anxiously, she peered at her watch. It was just before midnight on Jan. 30, 1929 — 10 hours since the Freeport teenager had taken off from Mitchel Field in an attempt to break the women's solo endurance record.

The temperature had been dropping rapidly since sundown, and was now 8 degrees. The bitter cold seeped through Smith's leather flight suit; inside her fur-lined gloves, her fingers were numb. The chamois mask she wore to protect her face was unbearably itchy, despite the layer of cold cream her mother had rubbed into her skin before takeoff. And with every breath, moisture built up inside the mask, steaming up her goggles.

Clumsily, Smith loosened her seatbelt, hoping to ease the cramps that wracked her legs after hours of sitting. *WHAM!* A moment later, turbulence hurled her half out of the cockpit.

Her heart pounding, she managed to tighten the belt again — only to discover that the stabilizer, which enabled her to keep the plane level as the aircraft's center of gravity changed, was frozen in one position.

For the next few hours, the 17-year-old aviator battled exhaustion, cold, turbulence and equipment problems as she desperately tried to figure out what to do. She circled central Nassau County, then headed south and flew up and down Sunrise Highway, figuring it would make a good emergency landing strip. Although she had planned to stay aloft for 18 hours, breaking the old endurance record of 12 hours by a wide margin, it was rapidly becoming obvious to Smith she couldn't hold out that long.

But ending her flight before daybreak presented another problem. Despite her considerable experience as a pilot — Smith had been taking flying lessons since she was 8 — she had never landed a plane at night, and wasn't sure she'd be able to.

In the days before the invention of sophisticated instrumentation, a pilot's ability to land an aircraft depended largely on his or her depth perception, which Smith knew could be seriously impaired in the dark. Couple that with an icy, dimly lit field and an airplane half-full of high-test gasoline, and she was facing a potential disaster. "If I hit something," she recalls, "I knew what the outcome would be: KA-BOOM!"

Still, what choice did she have? She couldn't bail out and risk the possibility of her pilotless plane plunging into someone's house. So bracing her knees against the stick to keep the plane level, she reached for her flare gun and fired it once, to let the ground crew know she was coming in.

Almost simultaneously, Smith saw another aircraft circling slowly, deliberately below her. The pilot — whom she later learned was famed Army flier Jimmy Doolittle, returning from a test flight to Philadelphia — had realized she was in trouble and was showing her how to line up her ship for a night landing.

Afraid to so much as blink, she cut the throttle and followed him in, setting her plane easily on the frozen field. "I just sat there for a minute and thanked God I was down," recalls Smith, now 86 and living in Santa Cruz, Calif. "It was the worst flight of my life!"

Still, when she landed at Mitchel Field at 3:30 a.m. on Jan. 31, 1929, she had been in the air for 13 hours, 16 minutes and 45 seconds.

Elinor Patricia Smith, a petite, freckle-faced teenager, had just set the first of her many world's records.

Her name is not nearly as recognizable as that of her friend and fellow flier Amelia Earhart. But Smith was widely acclaimed as one of the great pilots of her era. Many considered her more accomplished than Earhart, whose longer career and eventual disappearance in the Pacific in 1937 burnished her mystique in the annals of early aviation.

Smith was among the flashiest and most colorful of

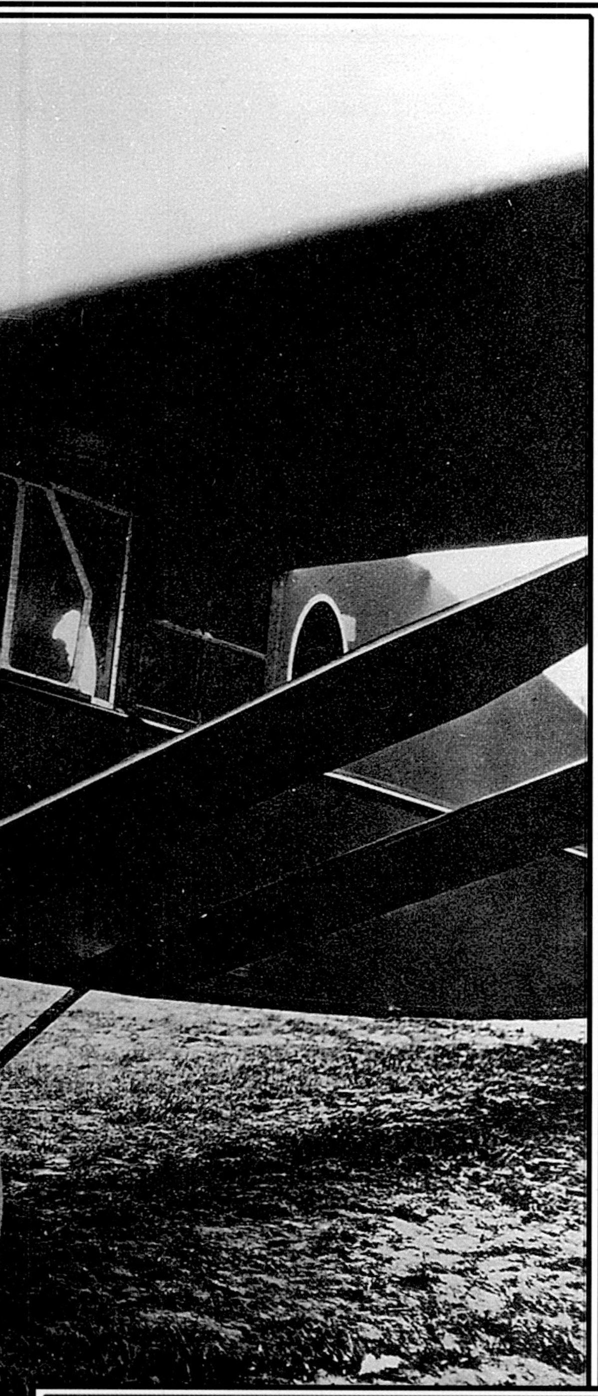

early aviators. Newsreels of her feats played in movie houses around the country, front-page headlines proclaimed her the "youthful air queen," and in 1930, when she was only 19, she was voted best female pilot in the country by her fellow fliers. At the Smithsonian Institution's National Air and Space Museum in Washington, D.C., where Smith's name hangs in the Golden Age of Flight gallery, curator Dorothy Cochrane says Smith deserves far more public recognition than she gets: "She's not a household word, but she probably should be, because she did some really significant flying."

"We were always waiting to see what Ellie would do next," recalls Glen Head resident George Dade, 85, who grew up on Curtiss Field and watched admiringly as Smith flew longer, higher, faster than any woman before her.

Smith knew she was destined to be a pilot almost from the minute she saw her first airplane, at age 6. She had gone on a Sunday drive with her parents and younger brother and saw a sign on a road near Hicksville: "Airplane Rides — $5 and $10." Parked nearby in a potato field was a contraption that looked as if it had been made from Tinkertoys, with a bullet-shaped object that turned out to be the cockpit jutting from the front. "To my brother Joe and I, it was Star Wars!" Smith recalls, laughing.

Smith's father, vaudevillian Tom Smith, pulled over and began talking to the pilot. Eighty years later, his daughter still remembers every detail of what happened next: how Tom Smith tied her blond braids together so they wouldn't blow around; how he lifted her and Joe into the cockpit and buckled the seatbelt over them, the thrill she felt as the plane lurched across the field and into the sky. Then there was the view, more breathtaking than she could have imagined.

"I could see out over the Atlantic Ocean, I could see the fields, I could even see the Sound," she recalls. "And the clouds on that particular day had just broken open so there were these shafts of light coming down and lighting up this whole landscape in various greens and yellows."

From that moment on, she wanted to be a pilot.

Of course, becoming a pilot in 1917 was a radical choice for anyone, especially a little girl. Only 14 years had passed since the Wright brothers' historic flight. Airplanes were primitive — they had no radios or brakes and few instruments — and crashes were an everyday occurrence. Pilots were viewed as a cross between daredevils and heroes, risking their lives for a moment of glory — hardly the sort of behavior a woman of that era was expected to engage in.

"Women were not thought to have the temperament to fly," explains Cochrane. "It wouldn't be feminine for them to go up in these machines, get oil smeared all over themselves. And they weren't supposed to be in pants!"

Still, a very few women were making their mark in aviation. In 1910, a Mineola housewife named Bessica Raiche had taken off from the Hempstead Plains in a homemade silk and bamboo airplane, landing in the record books as the first American woman to make an official solo flight. A year later, Harriet Quimby, a New York drama critic who had learned to fly in Mineola, became the first American woman to receive a pilot's license. And in Texas, aviator Katherine Stinson, Smith's idol, was making headlines with her aerial loops and rolls.

In her bid to learn to fly, Smith had two things going for her: a mother who didn't want to deny her daughter opportunities just because of her gender — "She felt very strongly that women shouldn't be considered second-class citizens," explains Smith — and a father who was passionate about airplanes.

When he wasn't on the vaudeville circuit, Tom Smith spent much of his time hanging out at Curtiss Field in Mineola, and he invariably took his daughter with him. The pilots gave her rides, and, when they saw how much she loved it, let her take the controls. "It was almost like a viral thing. It got into your bloodstream," Smith says of flying. "You wanted to do it every day."

By the time she was a teenager, that's exactly what she was doing. Rising before daybreak, she'd pull on argyle socks, her brother's knickers and an old leather jacket — "My mother wasn't crazy about that getup!" — and jump into the family car, which her father had taught her to drive when she was 11. Then she'd head for a small field in Wantagh, where her instructor kept his plane, and together they'd fly to Curtiss Field, which had a longer runway for her to practice on. She'd spend a half hour doing takeoffs and landings, then rush home, change clothes, grab her bicycle and hurry to school, trying to slip quietly into her seat so no one would realize she was late.

It didn't take long before Smith's hard work paid off. At 15, she became the youngest woman in the world to fly solo; a year later, she became the youngest person in the United States to earn a pilot's license. And barely a month after that, she pulled off a hair-raising stunt that made news around the world.

It had started in September, 1928, when another pilot, an obscure barnstormer who'd flown in from the Midwest, decided a good way to get publicity would be to fly under the Hell Gate Bridge between Astoria and Wards Island — a stunt anyone familiar with the area would have shunned because of air turbulence near the surface of the East River (not to mention that flying under bridges was forbidden in New York City). Sure enough, the barnstormer crashed into one of the piers and, although uninjured, wound up with a suspended license.

Undeterred, the man began hanging out at Curtiss Field, bragging about what a wonderful pilot he was, and claiming that only engine failure had prevented him from completing the feat.

Finally, one of the aerial photographers who worked at the field got irritated. "When are you going to knock it off? Why, even Ellie here could do it!" He turned to Smith. "Couldn't you?"

"Sure," said Smith with a shrug, although she had no intention of trying.

The next thing she knew, the barnstormer was spreading rumors that she'd agreed to duplicate his flight, then chickened out.

"I was furious!" recalls Smith, who saw only one recourse: to prove him wrong by flying under not one East River bridge, but four — starting with the Queensboro, then moving south to the Williamsburg, Manhattan and Brooklyn Bridges. (She avoided the treacherous Hell Gate, however.)

"She's a Daredevil!" headlined The Daily News, reporting on Smith's planned exploit.

"We said, 'She's crazy — she'll lose her plane!' " recalls Paul Rizzo, now 94, a former flight instructor at the field who still lives in East Meadow.

But Smith was undaunted. On Oct. 21, 1928, after

Top Photo, Nassau County Museum Collection, Long Island Studies Institute; Above, Newsday Photo / Bill Davis

Elinor Smith Sullivan, above, at the Cradle of Aviation Museum in Garden City with a plane similar to the one she flew at Mitchel Field to a women's endurance record in January, 1929, and, top, at age 17 a few months after setting the record.

Please see SMITH on Next Page

SMITH from Preceding Page

several weeks of checking tide tables for bridge clearances and practicing low-level flying around the masts of boats in Manhasset Bay, she took off from Curtiss Field and headed for New York City.

The next day's Daily News told the rest of story: "Elinor Smith, Freeport's 17-year-old aviatrix, nonchalantly ducked under four East River bridges yesterday afternoon in a Waco biplane and reported the stunt was easy . . . 'I had to dodge a couple of ships near the bridges, but there was plenty of room,' the high school aviatrix reported." The story was accompanied by a photograph of Smith back at the airfield, casually powdering her nose as if to say, "It was nothing."

To this day, Smith is the only person ever to have piloted a landplane under all the bridges — something she considers a mixed blessing. "The flight only lasted five minutes, yet when people referred to me in the later years, it was invariably [as] the girl who flew under the four East River bridges," she says in mock dismay.

The feat made her an instant celebrity — by evening, newsreels of her flight were playing in Broadway movie houses — but Smith couldn't rest on her laurels if she wanted to achieve her goal of becoming a professional pilot.

By the late 1920s, a handful of companies were starting to hire women to demonstrate their planes — "The message was that if a woman could fly it, anyone could," says the Smithsonian's Cochrane — but there were also about three dozen licensed female pilots in the United States, giving Smith plenty of competition.

In March, 1929, two months after Smith, at 17, set the women's solo endurance record at 13-plus hours, Californian Louise Thaden topped Smith by nearly nine hours. Later that same year, Phoebe Omlie became the first woman to fly to an altitude of 25,000 feet. Then there was Earhart, who had set a number of speed records and even had her own publicity manager.

Without such an advantage, Smith knew the only way to land the contracts she needed to fly professionally would be to drum up her own publicity.

So a month after Thaden broke her endurance record, Smith took it back by staying aloft over Nassau County for 26 hours, 23 minutes and 16 seconds. Later the same year, she and a California pilot named Bobbi Trout teamed up on a two-person endurance flight, setting a joint record of 42 hours and becoming the first women to refuel a plane in midair — a feat that involved having a second plane flying overhead drop a gas line to them.

There were other firsts, too: At 18, Smith became the youngest person, male or female, to receive a transport pilot's license, authorizing her to fly passengers commercially. The same year, she became the first woman — and possibly the only one of her era — to pilot a military aircraft, after Adm. William Moffett invited her to test one of his Navy training planes in Hampton Bays. (Moffett was so impressed by Smith's demonstration that he gave her his gold admiral's wings, which she made into a ring that she still wears.)

As she'd hoped, Smith's piloting skills were in demand. In 1929, she was hired as the first female executive pilot of the Irvin Chute Co., to demonstrate parachute drops on a nationwide tour; a year after that, she became the first woman test pilot for Long Island's Fairchild Aviation Corp. She endorsed goggles and motor oil. And NBC radio hired her as a commentator covering international flights and air races. But she wasn't finished breaking records.

In 1931, Smith became the first woman to fly to over 30,000 feet. Her first attempt almost ended in disaster when the engine of her plane died at 25,000 feet. Trying to restart it, Smith accidentally cut off her oxygen supply and passed out; the plane plunged 23,000 feet. "When I came to, I was in a power dive right into the Hempstead Reservoir," she recalls. She managed to steer to a landing on a rough patch of ground near Mitchel Field, only to realize there were two trees looming ahead of her. Rather than crash into them and damage the plane — "I wanted to go back up the next week!" — she slammed on the brakes and deliberately flipped the ship over, crouching in her seat to protect herself. (The only damage to the plane was a bent propeller.)

"Aviatrix, 18, Saves Self by Keeping Head," The New York World-Telegram headlined the next day (she was actually 19 at the time). The paper

'Bad Boy of the Air'

Of all the pilots who used Curtiss Field as a base in the early 1920s, few were more skilled — or more colorful — than Bert Acosta.

"He could have flown a barn door if it had wings," says Paul Rizzo, a former flight instructor who knew Acosta well.

But Acosta, a test pilot for the Curtiss Corp., also had a reckless streak that earned him the title "bad boy of the air." He delighted in flying under bridges and rolling a wheel over the roofs of Manhattan skyscrapers as he passed overhead; on more than one occasion, his license was suspended for "stunting."

On another occasion, a passenger asked him what time it was. "I don't know, but I'll find out," said Acosta, and promptly headed for Manhattan, where he buzzed the clock tower of the Metropolitan Life building. ("That story is completely true!" says Rizzo.)

On the ground, Acosta's love of women and alcohol repeatedly landed him in hot water, and occasionally in jail. (Acosta was twice divorced — the second time, newspapers reported, after his wife discovered love letters from a woman who said she was pregnant with his child.)

But Acosta's reputation as a pilot didn't suffer. In April, 1927, he and fellow flier Clarence Chamberlin set a joint endurance record of 51 hours, 11 minutes and 25 seconds aloft. And less than two weeks after Charles Lindbergh's historic crossing of the Atlantic, Acosta flew from Long Island to France with Commander Richard Byrd.

In 1936, Acosta signed on as anti-Franco mercenary during the Spanish Civil War. But after he returned to the United States, his drinking worsened, and in December of 1951, he collapsed in a New York City saloon. Acosta was taken to the hospital, where it was discovered that he had tuberculosis.

He died in a Colorado sanitorium in 1954 at age 59.

— Laura Muha

Long Island Studies Institute

Test pilot Bert Acosta in 1917

The Guggenheims, Allies of Aviators

Cradle of Aviation Museum Photo

Charles Lindbergh and Harry Guggenheim, right, around 1928

Daniel Guggenheim died in 1930 without ever having flown, even as a passenger. Yet it if weren't for the contributions of this wealthy Sands Point industrialist, "you couldn't hop on an airplane and fly where you can fly today," says Bob van der Linden, an aviation historian with the Smithsonian Institution.

In the last five years of his life, between 1925 and 1930, Guggenheim pumped more than $3.3 million into a series of aviation-related initiatives — money that led to the development of safer, more reliable engines; instruments enabling pilots to navigate without looking at the ground, and public acceptance of aviation as a viable means of transportation. But Guggenheim was in his 70s in these experimental years and was happy to leave the actual flying to younger people.

People like his son, Harry, whose experience as a Navy pilot during World War I had first sparked Guggenheim's interest in aviation. Harry Guggenheim was convinced that the nation's future was in air travel, and in 1925 he talked his father into donating $500,000 to create a school of aeronautical engineering at New York University — the first of eight such schools the father and son would eventually endow. "It is not too much to say that they really established the profession of aeronautical engineering in the U.S. as we know it," says Richard P. Hallion, U.S. Air Force historian and author of a 1977 book, "Legacy of Flight: The Guggenheim Contribution to American Aviation."

Daniel Guggenheim also set up a fund to promote aviation, including research. One of its most important projects was a "town marking" campaign that encouraged communities to paint their names on the roofs of large buildings so pilots who were lost would be able to reorient themselves. (In those days pilots navigated by looking at the ground.) "It was a simple idea, yet it had such a profound impact on aviation safety," says Hallion.

In 1926, the elder Guggenheim announced a "safe aircraft" competition with a $100,000 prize that led to the development of an engine that could fly at low speeds without stalling, the main cause of crashes. Two years after that, he established a flight laboratory at Mitchel Field to develop instruments that would enable pilots to fly even when it was too foggy for them to see the ground. Together the Guggenheims also established a model airline in California to demonstrate that air travel was safe and reliable.

After Daniel's death in 1930, Harry, who co-founded Newsday with his wife, Alicia Patterson, in 1940, continued the family's aviation-related philanthropies, going on to sponsor rocketry pioneer Robert Goddard. Harry Guggenheim died in 1971. He and his father's contributions to aviation are celebrated in a short documentary at the National Air and Space Museum in Washington, D.C.

— Muha

reported that the first people on the scene found Smith walking around her overturned plane, muttering, "It makes me mad. It makes me mad."

Uninjured and undeterred, Smith went up again a week later, this time setting a new women's altitude record of 34,500 feet.

But of all the honors Smith received, her proudest moment came in 1930, when the American Society for the Promotion of Aviation asked the nation's licensed fliers to name the best male and female pilots in the United States. When the ballots were counted, Smith — who'd assumed Earhart would take the title — was stunned to learn she had won. "It was such an honor to know that my peers considered me the best," she says.

Then, a year later, happenstance led indirectly to the end of Smith's flying career. Barely 20, she had gone to Albany to lobby for legislation to bar electric companies from stringing power lines around airports. While there, she met state Aviation Commissioner Patrick Sullivan, a political appointee who, she was disgusted to learn, "didn't know beans about aviation. Nothing. Zilch!"

However, Sullivan, an attorney and legislator from New York City, did know that he liked the feisty blond aviator. He asked her for a date. Two years later, they were married. Like other women aviators of the time, she continued to use her maiden name professionally.

For several years and two children after that, Smith kept flying. Then one afternoon, while pregnant with her third child, she was piloting a balky aircraft. "It just struck me: Maybe this is not so smart. I've got two [children], and they need a mother more than I need to fly."

Shortly after that, Smith quit cold turkey to stay home and raise her children; nearly 25 years would pass before she piloted a plane again (in 1956, when the Air Force invited her to help out with training exercises at Mitchel Field).

But even when Smith wasn't flying, aviation was never far from her mind. "At the dinner table, it was always like this," recalls Smith's daughter, Patricia Sullivan of Manhattan, banking her hand like an airplane to demonstrate her mother's favorite topic of conversation.

These days, Smith still flies occasionally with her son at an airport near her California home. But nothing, she says, will ever top the freedom of those early days in the skies above Long Island.

"It was a wonderful, wonderful time," she says wistfully. "I just loved every part of it!"

Laura Muha is a freelance writer.

More Than Just Hot Air

In June, 1833, a crowd of more than 100,000 people gathered to watch Jersey City native Charles Durant lift off from Manhattan's Castle Garden in a hot-air balloon.

A strong wind made liftoff difficult, but on the fourth attempt, Durant finally cleared the Castle walls and floated across the East River toward Jamaica. He landed at Union Race Course, about 40 yards from the course's starting post, earning the distinction of becoming the first person to set foot on Long Island from the air.

At the time of his historic flight, Durant, then in his late 20s, had already been making headlines for several years with his aerial exploits. In September, 1830, he had become the first person to fly from New York to New Jersey; as he drifted over Staten Island, he dropped a note to friends, saying he'd be by for tea that afternoon.

Cradle of Aviation Museum Photo

Announcing an ascension by Charles Durant in 1830

On another occasion, he had reportedly managed to land his balloon on the deck of a steamer on the Chesapeake Bay. And at the start of each flight, Durant would toss to the crowd printed copies of verses that he wrote himself, including this one:

Perhaps I may touch at the moon
To give your respects as I pass, sirs
And learn if the spheres are in tune
Or if they are lighted with gas, sirs.

In 1834, Durant retired from ballooning, having made a mere 12 flights. In later years, he pursued lithography, cultivated silkworms (he produced the first silk made in the United States) and studied marine biology. He died in 1875 — some 50 years before people began taking to the air over Long Island on a regular basis. — **Laura Muha**

'First Woman Aviator of America'

While studying in France in the early 1900s, Mineola resident Bessica Medlar Raiche became interested in aviation — so much so that when she and her husband returned to the United States, they built a silk-and-bamboo biplane. The couple transported the finished aircraft to the Hempstead Plains, and on Sept. 26, 1910, Raiche climbed aboard and took off, landing in the history books as the first American woman to make a solo flight — though the flight lasted only a few minutes and ended in a crash.

One local paper described the aftermath this way: "She scrambled to her feet and before any one of the mechanicians and others who had witnessed the fall of the biplane could reach her, she had shut off the engine and stopped the propeller. She calmly said she was not injured to those who ran to her aid, and then she directed the men to drag the wrecked plane back to the shed."

In the next few weeks, Raiche made several more flights; for her efforts, the Aeronautical Society later awarded her a gold-and-diamond medal inscribed "First Woman Aviator of America." (She might have been more accurately described as the first woman to fly *intentionally*. Rochester native Blanche Stuart Scott had soloed two weeks before Raiche, but the society refused to give her credit because her flight was accidental: She'd been practicing her taxiing along the ground when a gust of wind lifted her plane 40 feet into the air.) Raiche and her husband later built and sold two more planes, but eventually she gave up flying and became a physician.

— **Laura Muha**

Mineola's Bessica Raiche was recognized as the first woman to make a solo flight.

Smithsonian Institution Photo

A Woman's Will to Fly

Long Island's black communities turned out nearly 1,000 strong for the big air show at Curtiss Field in Mineola in September, 1922. The cause of all the excitement was Bessie Coleman, making her first flight in America since her return from France, where she had become the first licensed black pilot in the world.

Coleman, then 29, had gone to France to train after being rejected by American aviation schools because she was black and a woman. She soared three times that September day in a tiny Curtiss JN4D, the first American-made plane she had flown. Her performance, she said, was to "honor the 115th Infantry, the colored regiment" and to "create an interest in aviation" among her people. She went on to barnstorm the country, returning several times to perform in Mineola air shows.

Born in Texas in 1893, Coleman determined after World War I to learn to fly. The climate was inhospitable for women pilots as well as blacks. A year before Coleman's first appearance in Mineola, Laura Bromwell, a daring young aviator, had crashed while looping over the same field, causing The New York Times to suggest that women be excluded from an activity "in which their presence certainly is unnecessary."

Four years later Coleman met the same fate over Florida. But her causes survived. Bessie Coleman Aero Groups, organized after her death, staged the first all-black air show in 1931. Elinor Smith of Freeport established women's endurance and altitude records in the late '20s. And Amelia Earhart, with the aid of a good publicist, became America's darling. — **Rhoda Amon**

AP Photo

Bessie Coleman performed in Mineola.

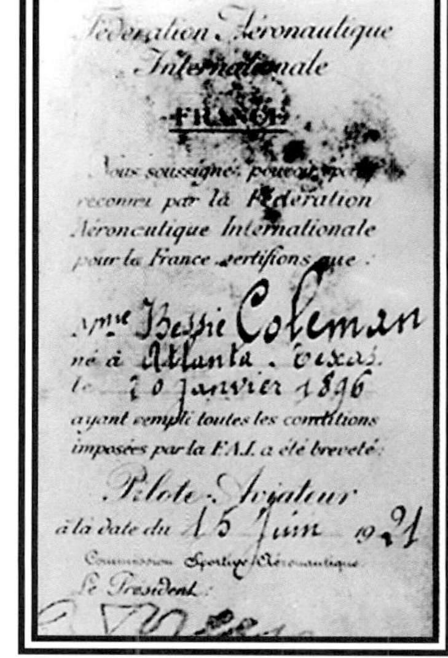
Fédération Aéronautique Internationale
FRANCE
Nous soussignés, pouvoir ... reconnu par la Fédération Aéronautique Internationale pour la France certifions que :
Mlle Bessie Coleman
né à Atlanta, Texas
le 20 Janvier 1896
ayant rempli toutes les conditions imposées par la F.A.I. a été breveté :
Pilote-Aviateur
à la date du 15 Juin 1921
Commission Sportive Aéronautique
Le Président :

Long Island Studies Institute

Her pilot's license, issued in France

Track Stars

Cassidy Family Photo

William Edward Cassidy, wearing gloves, stands at right on the front of a locomotive in about 1912 at the Jamaica station. He joined the Long Island Rail Road at age 16 in 1909 — the second of five generations of Cassidys to work for the LIRR.

BY AL BAKER
STAFF WRITER

LIRR workers since 1875, the Cassidys have forged family ties as strong as the iron rails that helped create Long Island

ANOTHER FAMILY holiday party was boiling away inside Willie and Lottie Cassidy's house in Richmond Hill that Christmas Eve night, 1939, when the ring of the stand-up phone jangled above the din of laughter, songs and poetry.

It was the past on the line, and the future, too. It was the Long Island Rail Road calling, offering work to young Joe Cassidy, then just six months shy of his 20th birthday.

His dad, Willie, always ready with a flash of wit, grabbed the receiver from a living room table. Nobody knows exactly what he said, but it could have been one of his staple jokes.

"Lottie's house of pain," or "Breyer's Ice Cream!"

Or he could have just said, "Cassidys," and offered a holiday hello.

Willie listened for a good second, gave the receiver to his son and said, "Joe, do you want to go firing on the railroad?"

The boy's soul is said to have suddenly appeared on his face.

"When?" he asked.

"Tonight!"

All young Joe Cassidy knew as he stood on a Chinese rug in the freshly painted living room at 130-02 95th Ave., Richmond Hill, Queens, a neighborhood where wind-blown soot from the nearby LIRR yard misted walls and windows, was that he yearned to work the trains like his dad and his granddad. Never mind that it was Christmas Eve. Forget the party, the home-cooked food, the warmth of relatives you could reach out and hug. Forget that a pretty young woman was waiting eagerly for him to pick her up for a late-night formal dance or that he was dressed — as dapper as ever — in a black tuxedo with dancing shoes and a dash of sweet-smelling cologne.

Forget it all.

Within hours, the muscular black-haired Irishman named Joseph Anthony Cassidy, the third of Willie and Lottie Cassidy's five children, was smack in the belly of a sooty old steam engine barreling along on its silver-slick iron rails somewhere through the Long Island night.

"And he had to shovel several tons of coal," his son, Joseph A. Cassidy Jr., 55, says today of his father's job keeping the train engine stoked. "One hundred and sixteen miles. From Long Island City to Montauk," Joe Jr. says, shaking his head. "On Christmas Eve."

But Joe Jr. probably would have done the same

thing as his father. The Cassidys were Irish immigrants and they worked the Long Island Rail Road. Joe's instant "Yes!" made him third in a line of five generations whose cumulative record stands today at 123 years of unbroken service on the LIRR. Joe's father and grandfather had worked for the line before him and his son and granddaughter would come after him.

Four generations of men with bodies cut like the trains they rode and repaired, their thighs and forearms chiseled like iron, their jaws jutting straight out like a locomotive. And a woman who, with the same steely intensity of her forebears, is now in training to run the smooth electric cars or diesels that have replaced steam engines.

They are the Cassidys — all of them drawn to the iron rails, the steady clank of metal on metal and the familiar whistle of the locomotive. They ran the trains that helped build Long Island. They rode through storms. They derailed. They crashed. That, too. Their trains hit people who wandered out onto the tracks, and the Cassidys agonized forever over each sad death. They worked hard, they stank of steam and soot and tried to scrub the filthy smell from the walls of their houses. They suffered so much time away from home, on holidays and weekends. They missed their children's ball games after school. They could only lay off for burials or weddings.

But they earned good livings, and when they got off duty, they surrounded themselves with family. They shined their shoes and ironed knife-sharp creases into their slacks. They prayed for the dead and for the living and went to church on Sundays and had grand suppers after mass. They smoked cigarettes, drank whiskey and homemade beer, wrote poetry and sang until morning. And they tried, one generation after another, to do better than the last.

"We are a microcosm of what millions of Irish-American families have experienced," Joe Jr. says today from the dining room of his two-story home in Garden City, where soot never falls.

They worked hard, sacrificed, suffered discrimination and succeeded.

They did it generation by generation, working on the railroad.

* * *

Chartered in 1834, the Long Island Rail Road was only 41 years old when Patrick Cassidy joined on to clean steam engines in 1875. The nation had not even celebrated the centennial when he landed the job at the Morris Park roundhouse and found a place to live with his wife, the former Delia Murphy, down the road in Richmond Hill, in a Queens neighborhood where the houses were close together but unattached.

Each of the couple's parents had set sail from Ireland, probably with hundreds of thousands of others on the heels of the potato famine in the late 1840s. The Murphys came from a place the family knows only as Sandy Hill. The Cassidys, by most accounts, came from County Fermanagh, tranquil with isle-dotted Lough Erne in Ulster Province.

Patrick's parents, William and Mary, and their ancestors are a bit of a mystery. Some members of the family like to playfully describe their forebears as a wild band of horse thieves driven from the homeland. Others say this is probably a romantic fiction, enriched with the passing of years, embellished by each generation. It's never been confirmed.

What seems clear is that Patrick, born about 1853 in St. Michael's parish, Flushing, thrived on the railroad, though some despised the Irish at that time.

"That there is a strong dislike among our native population to the Irish cannot well be denied," reads a Hempstead Inquirer article from Sept. 6, 1867. The article went on to describe the Irish as the most "clannish, presumptious and fond of exercising political power of any of our foreign born citizens."

Not many specifics are known about Patrick's career. He eventually became a train mechanic, working in the maintenance of equipment department in Long Island City before rising to the rank of foreman. What is known is that he worked 16-hour days, seven days a week. He and Delia raised seven girls and three boys, none of whom survive. Patrick

Cassidy Family Photo

Willie Cassidy and his grandson, Joe Jr., play in the back of the Richmond Hill house in 1944.

Cassidy Family Photo

Joe Cassidy, who got his job with the LIRR on Christmas Eve, 1939, takes a break in the cab of a train in the mid-1940s.

Newsday Photo / Bill Davis

Kelly Cassidy, an engineer trainee, and her dad, Joe Jr., the tyke shown in the photo at left, stand in the Richmond Hill yard.

Cassidy Family Photo

Willie Cassidy, right, with an unidentified man and two children on the back of a 1,000-hp locomotive in 1951

Track Stars

may have dreamed of operating a train, but that would have to wait until the next generation.

* * *

William Edward Cassidy was born Oct. 9, 1884, the second child and first son of Patrick and Delia Cassidy. He joined the LIRR as a hostler 16 years later, on July 4, 1900, lying about his age to pass the minimum 18-year-old age limit at the time.

"He got $2.50 a week as a track worker," says his oldest grandson, Donald Douglas, 68, of Piscataway, N.J. "He told me he bought a pair of yellow shoes with his first week's pay."

In 1902, that same 5-foot-7 Willie Cassidy became a fireman for the LIRR and joined a union, the Brotherhood of Locomotive Engineers. He became an engineer in 1910, two years after Henry Ford introduced the Model T car, the same year that William Howard Taft led the nation while a baseball manager named Connie Mack led the Philadelphia Athletics to a world championship.

Willie got up in the middle of the night to go to work, his daughter, Gertrude Douglas, 88, remembers. On hearing him leave the house on winter nights — carrying the lunch pail and the Thermos full of coffee his wife prepared — young Gertrude would lie in her bed upstairs in the six-room clapboard house in Richmond Hill and worry.

"It was always a bitter cold night," she remembered recently from her home in Ponte Vedra, Fla. "He always took night jobs because they paid more money than day jobs did. I was always so concerned that he would catch a cold. He worked so many days."

When people talk about Willie, they do it with smiles and with music in their voices. They describe his good humor, impeccable cleanliness, warmth and lust for life. Willie worked hard, that's for sure, but seemed to chuckle all the way.

He called his wife "The Kaiser." Charlotte (Lottie) Cassidy was the daughter of German immigrants. She was a stolid woman who surrounded herself with loved ones each Sunday — her mother, Caroline Kohler, and five strapping brothers. There was always homemade lemon meringue pie, white bread and sauerbraten-and-spaetzle dinners. And Willie Cassidy delighted the grandchildren — rhyming, talking out of the side of his mouth and kidding his wife.

"I remember my granddad in the living room," Michael Cassidy, 47, said recently from his home in Arlington, Va. "He would sit in one chair. Lottie would sit in another chair, with a table betwen them. He would sit on the chair with his hands on his rather rotund belly and he would say, 'Lottie, Lottie,' and she wouldn't turn to him. And he would talk and talk and she would just stare straight ahead, ignoring him.

"Then, he would say to us, 'Watch this,' and he would whisper, 'money,' and suddenly, she would turn to him and say, 'What'd you say?' And he would laugh."

Sundays were important for a railroad man. On freight runs to Montauk, Willie was often forced to stay overnight in towns such as Greenport or Port Jefferson. Because of his vast time away from home, he made what time he had with family worth remembering.

Despite the kidding, Willie had great pride in his German bride, adored her brothers, and instilled that pride in his children. And his wages kept his family financially secure even through the 1929 stock market crash, and the sustained gloom of the Great Depression.

"We never knew what depression was or never knew what being deprived of anything was," Gertrude Douglas, the only survivor among her parents' five children, said over the phone. "We never were. We had a wonderful childhood."

Railroad pay afforded Willie and Lottie the ability to buy the Richmond Hill house for $4,000 in 1912. Lottie's sister, Nora, lived next door with her husband, Frank, and their five kids. Lang's Country Store was down the block, where proprietor Haddie Lang always set aside sugar for the Cassidys. And the house was a short walk from the Dunton tower station where Willie met his engine every night.

Cassidy Family Photo

Patrick Cassidy, father of William, started the LIRR dynasty.

Living close to the yard had a down side. Lottie and the children had to clean the windows once a week and paint the house each year due to what Gertrude calls "that lovely soot from the Long Island Rail Road. It was terrible."

"When your mother dies, I am going to put a paintbrush in her hand," went another of Willie's jokes.

The kids would laugh. And then Willie might head down to the basement, take out his teeth and have a jar of homemade beer or go down the block to Gus' saloon, where he met with other railroad men to lift a pint, sing, tell stories, or talk work or politics.

Through the years, the kids and grandkids each took turns retrieving "Uncle Will" from Gus'. One Sunday, after church, one of Gertrude's sons, Bruce Douglas, who was 8 years old at the time, was dispatched to the saloon to get Willie for dinner. Now 63, Douglas remembers stepping into a warm dark room where men in overalls and red bandannas gathered in a circle by a big mirror on the back wall.

Willie welcomed Bruce, "introduced me to all the boys" and asked him sing "Too Raloo Raloora, Too Raloo Ralai," or "Going My Way," from the Bing Crosby movie.

There was lunchmeat on the bar and sawdust on the floor and the swirl of cigar smoke in the air.

As they walked home, Willie's good spirits suddenly disintegrated into gloom as if the drink and his own memories had conspired to sadden him.

"I took him home and he was all emotional and he was thinking of all the kids who were killed on the railroad tracks," Douglas said. "In those days they didn't have the crossing controls and switches and a couple of kids got killed when he was operating the engine, and that just stayed with him all the time. The kids were playing on the tracks or trestles, and, for one reason or another, they couldn't get out of the way."

Willie was involved in about 30 accidental deaths as a locomotive engineer, his grandson, Joe Jr., says today. He was handcuffed to his train for 10 hours after one of these deaths until the cops finally understood that a train can't steer around a child or stop on a dime.

Once, some kids threw a switch as a prank and a freight train Willie was taking to Greenport veered off onto an abandoned sidetrack that ended abruptly in front of a house.

"The train didn't stop, as much as he braked it. It kept going," said Bruce Douglas, who heard the story many times. The train slammed through the house. Luckily, nobody was home. Willie was shaken. He thought the wreck a terrible thing. But, as the years passed, he poked some fun at the incident.

"He said that some guy was upstairs in a bathtub when the train hit," Douglas said. "All those Cassidys had a great Irish wit. Sort of a black sense of humor, not unlike Yiddish humor: No matter how bad things get, there is always some humor."

Willie brushed himself off and went back to work after each mishap. Unlike today, there was no time off between tragedies. Willie had no counseling program to attend. No stress management expert to speak with. He dealt with his demons on his own, Joe Jr. says.

Willie retired in 1952.

A photo in the February-March issue of that year's Long Island Railroader noted the occasion. "Bill, bug on cleanliness, was once presented with a broom by buddies," the caption read.

William Edward Cassidy died at 81 on Oct. 14, 1965. His son, Joe, was already a legend on the railroad.

* * *

Besides Gertrude, who was born on Aug. 27, 1909, Willie and Lottie had four sons: William, born on Nov. 2, 1911; Joseph, born on June 15, 1920; John Edward, born on March 5, 1926, and Francis, who died when he was just 9 months old in September, 1918, of what now might be diagnosed as sudden infant death syndrome.

John Edward Cassidy forged a career on Broadway, TV and the silver screen, where he would be known as Jack; William went to work on the stock exchange, and Gertrude married Charles Douglas and spent her time raising a family. It was left to Joe to keep up the family tradition.

Joe was a strong kid and an even stronger adult, though he died early, at 59, of a heart attack in 1979, just months after he was named the LIRR's director of training.

"My mother always said that if he was 6-foot instead of 5-8, he would have looked like Hercules," said Joe's daughter, Kathleen Cassidy-Barthelme, 51, of Oakhurst, N.J. "We had covered posts in the basement and he would grab those posts and lift himself up." Kids watching this would marvel at the man stuck straight out from the pole, parallel to the floor, like a flag. Feats of strength were common at work, too, where Joe was known to shovel coal with one arm.

His relatives say that for Joe, the railroad wasn't just a job, but a passion. He became an engineer in 1941, at the age of 21, got married and learned the ins and outs of railroading so well that in 1949, he won a job testing others in their working knowledge of the LIRR's so-called book of rules and characteristics.

"He knew railroad theory backward and forward," said Joe Jr.

Many a morning the children would wake at 7 to find 10 men around the kitchen table at their house in Richmond Hill not far from their father's boyhood home, all eyes glued to Joe Cassidy as he taught "the art" of braking, engineering or firing. Firemen did not merely shovel the coals into the firebox — they had to keep the coals hot and the steam pressure at its highest for the train to run most efficiently, but they

Track Stars

had to be careful not to let the smoke escaping the stack turn black. It was a delicate balance for such a mighty machine. "There is an art to doing that," he told his son, who never shoveled coal because by the time he became a fireman, there were no steam engines.

"He loved teaching, and I am dead serious when I say he was responsible for thousands of people getting qualified on the railroad, both among trainmen and railroad service individuals," said Joe Jr. "Because he loved the intricacies of the railroad so much, he could inflect that verve into his teaching and it made the classes interesting, and I can tell you from first-hand knowledge because he taught me."

Joe eventually had a building named after him, the J.A. Cassidy Training Center, in Jamaica. Though he enjoyed the classroom, his true love always remained the running of the trains, and, like Willie before him, he kept his engine spic and span.

In their early years, Joe's children, Joseph Jr., Kathleen and Brian, often hung out the second-floor windows of their house to see the nearby tracks and catch a glimpse of dad zooming by in the seat of his shiny engine, heading west to Kew Gardens. With a nod of his head or a tip of his denim engineer's cap, he always waved or blew the whistle.

"There was a glamor about the railroad that still holds true for me today," Kathleen Cassidy-Barthelme says. "Having my dad come in on the front end of the engine, in the engineer's seat, and just the overwhelming pride that he was in charge — I wanted to be an engineer."

Some summer days, Joe's wife, Miriam, would pack the kids into her car and drive to Hewlett Beach for afternoons at the shore. Sometimes, as the car was stopped at the Hewlett rail crossing, a train would pass and up in the engineer's seat, leading the way, was proud Joe Cassidy.

Joe's nephew, the former teen idol and now writer-producer Shaun Cassidy, remembers how lucky he felt when he came to New York in 1964, and his Uncle Joe was the engineer who ran the railroad exhibit at the World's Fair. "It was a magical time," said Shaun, one of Jack Cassidy's sons. "He was the king because he was running the thing that every kid in the world wanted to get on."

Growing up in California, amid the glamor of Hollywood, Shaun listened to his father talk about the family's roots being back in the East, in New York, in the railroad.

"That sense of history was something he took great pride in and something he wanted us to take great pride in even if we never grew up to be engineers," Shaun Cassidy said.

Jack Cassidy even wrote a play, "A Waltz for Willie Ryan" — a drama he never finished — about a man modeled on his father. The man goes home and comes to terms with the good and bad in his family. It is a story filled with the difficulty of being working-class Irish at the turn of the century with characters who could have been Willie or Joe Cassidy's colleagues in real life.

Cassidy Family Photo

Willie Cassidy, left, and his son Joe watch as actress Shirley Jones boards a train in 1963. She was married to Joe's brother Jack, an actor on Broadway, in movies and on television.

Actor Jack idolized his big brother Joe, many in the family said, and often called him for counsel. Joe usually could find time for family, despite his long hours working nights, weekends and holidays.

An exception, of course, was that fateful Christmas Eve, 1939, when the phone rang and Joe Cassidy left his family party and broke a date with a woman waiting for him to take her to a formal dance.

Miriam Cassidy, who might not have met Joe had he gone on that date and who married him two years later, remembers the story her husband often told. "He was very nice and sweet to the girl and he called her and explained to her that, 'This could be the whole pattern of my life.' She said, 'Go ahead.' And so, consequently, he did. And from that moment on it was like that."

It took a special kind of woman to be a railroad man's wife — to withstand the long lonely hours and the missed appointments, but Miriam managed. Joe always brought home good wages and worshiped his days off. This set him apart a bit from his father — it wasn't until Lottie Cassidy saw her son's first pay envelope for handling freight that she realized Willie had been holding back.

The subsequent confrontation became a legend on the LIRR, where rumor traveled faster than trains, and a colleague drew a cartoon of Willie making his explanation to his wife. "I'll tell you why your son Joe makes more than I do," the caption reads. "He hauls the loads and I handle the empties."

Professionally, Joe battled prejudice against Irish Catholics but suffered less bias than his father or grandfather before him. At one time, Willie faced the slogan "Irish Need Not Apply." But Joe Jr. says his father, like others of his generation, "was able to rise above the prejudices and secure a management job. What the Irish did was to fight their way out of the streets and into the classrooms and into the professions that made the Irish an integral part of the backbone of this country. We had to overcome the same kind of prejudices that have been heaped upon Italian people, Jewish people, African-American people and Native American people as well as others."

In 1968, Joe became supervisor of operations training. A 51-day strike in 1972, however, soured 52-year-old Joe Cassidy on management. When he and some 30 other men thought management had broken an agreement on what work they would have to do during the strike, they went back to working on the train.

"As a result of that, the railroad swore that none of those people would ever be in management, ever, ever again," said Joe Jr. "And they treated my father and the rest of those people pretty shabbily."

Joe ran trains for the next seven years, which wasn't so bad, considering he loved it so much. On days off, he continued to teach the book of rules in his kitchen. Then, in March, 1979, because of Joe's legendary status as a teacher, the executive vice president of the railroad, A. Norman Gandia, gave Joe the job of director of training.

The family tells this story of the exchange between the two men.

"What if I don't live to fulfill your dream of what the training message should be?" Joe asked.

"By God, you'll come back from the grave to teach," Gandia answered.

Joe Cassidy died on Oct. 26 of that year.

His wake was held at R. Stutzmann & Son Inc. funeral home in Queens Village. Some 2,800 people came to pay their respects during the three-day period. "Second only to the owner of Nathan's, in Coney Island," Joe Jr. said of the hordes of mourners. "So the funeral director said at the time."

Joe Jr. had big shoes to fill.

* * *

At age 17, Joe Cassidy Jr. was awarded the Michael J. Cashman trophy as Brooklyn Prep's outstanding high-school athlete of 1961. He posed for a picture with star athletes Gil Hodges, Paul Hornung and Mike Ditka. He still has the program with their autographs. And the menu, with the beverage choices, "demi tasse" and "milk for boys."

Built like a truck — just like his dad — Joe Jr. joined the Marines after graduation, became a sergeant and taught drill, marksmanship and general military subjects at Parris Island, S.C.

But he wasn't all brawn. Blessed with the same Irish wit of his Uncle Jack, Joe Jr. polished public speaking skills in his high school oratorical society.

The mix of strength and smarts would come in handy down the road.

Joe Jr. joined the railroad on June 18, 1970, and, at the same time, took classes at St. John's University. Disappointed in management because of his father's experience with the strike, he graduated college in 1972, got married two months later and — with his wedding ring on one hand and his college ring on the other — went out and ran for office with the Brotherhood of Locomotive Engineers. He was elected a local committeeman in 1973, and never looked back.

"What soured my father lit the fire in my belly, and that's how I became involved in the union business," said Joe Jr., who today serves as an international vice president of the BLE, the oldest active union in the nation. "I had my family's good name, which always worked in my favor when it came to elections."

He was elected vice chairman of the union in 1976, and became general chairman in 1983. In August, 1991, he was elected to his current job and has been crisscrossing the country ever since, negotiating contracts, handling grievances, resolving issues and giving speeches.

But he still keeps his hand at the throttle. On a leave of absence as an

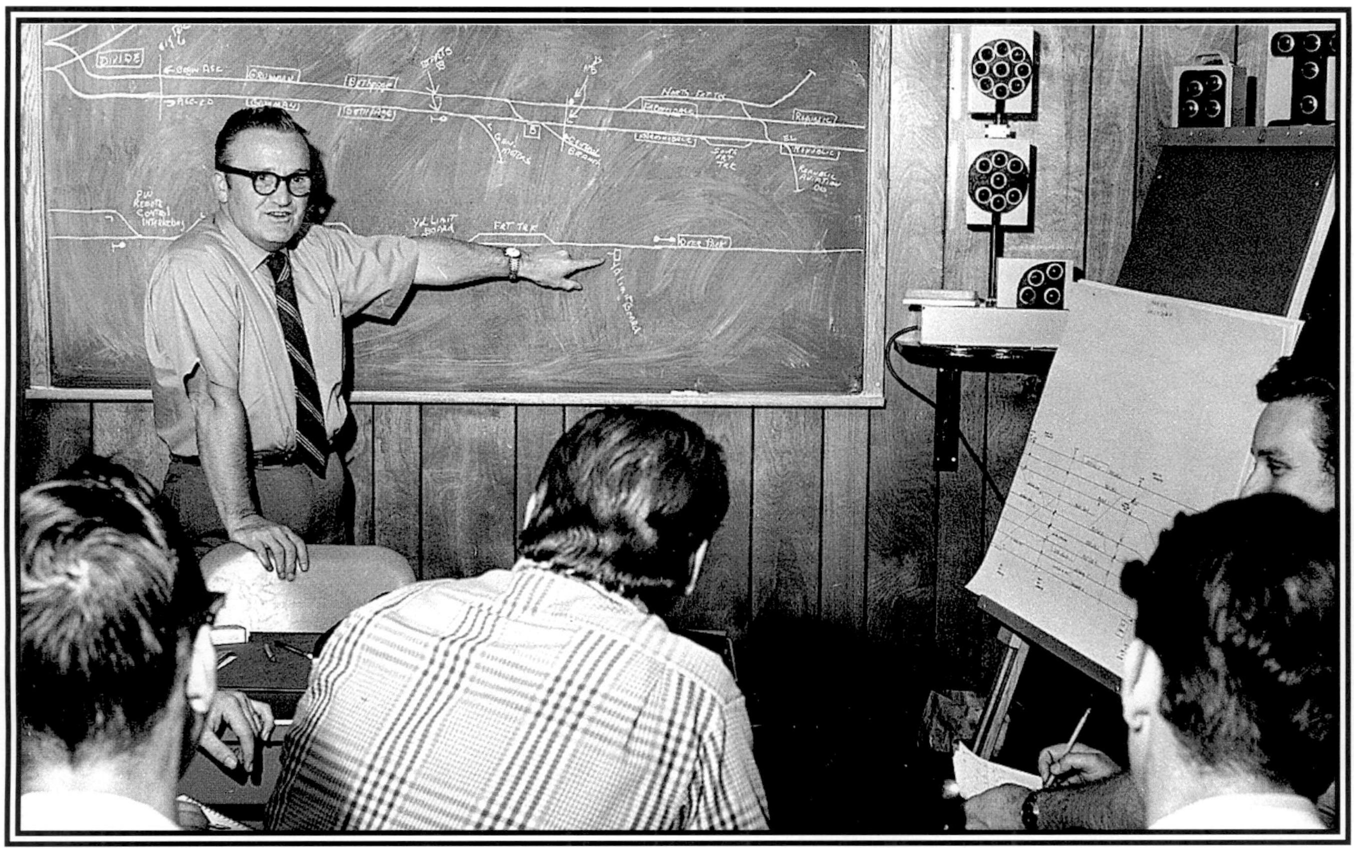

Cassidy Family Photo

Joe Cassidy, who loved teaching, instructs a class of trainmen in a converted passenger coach in Jamaica in 1970.

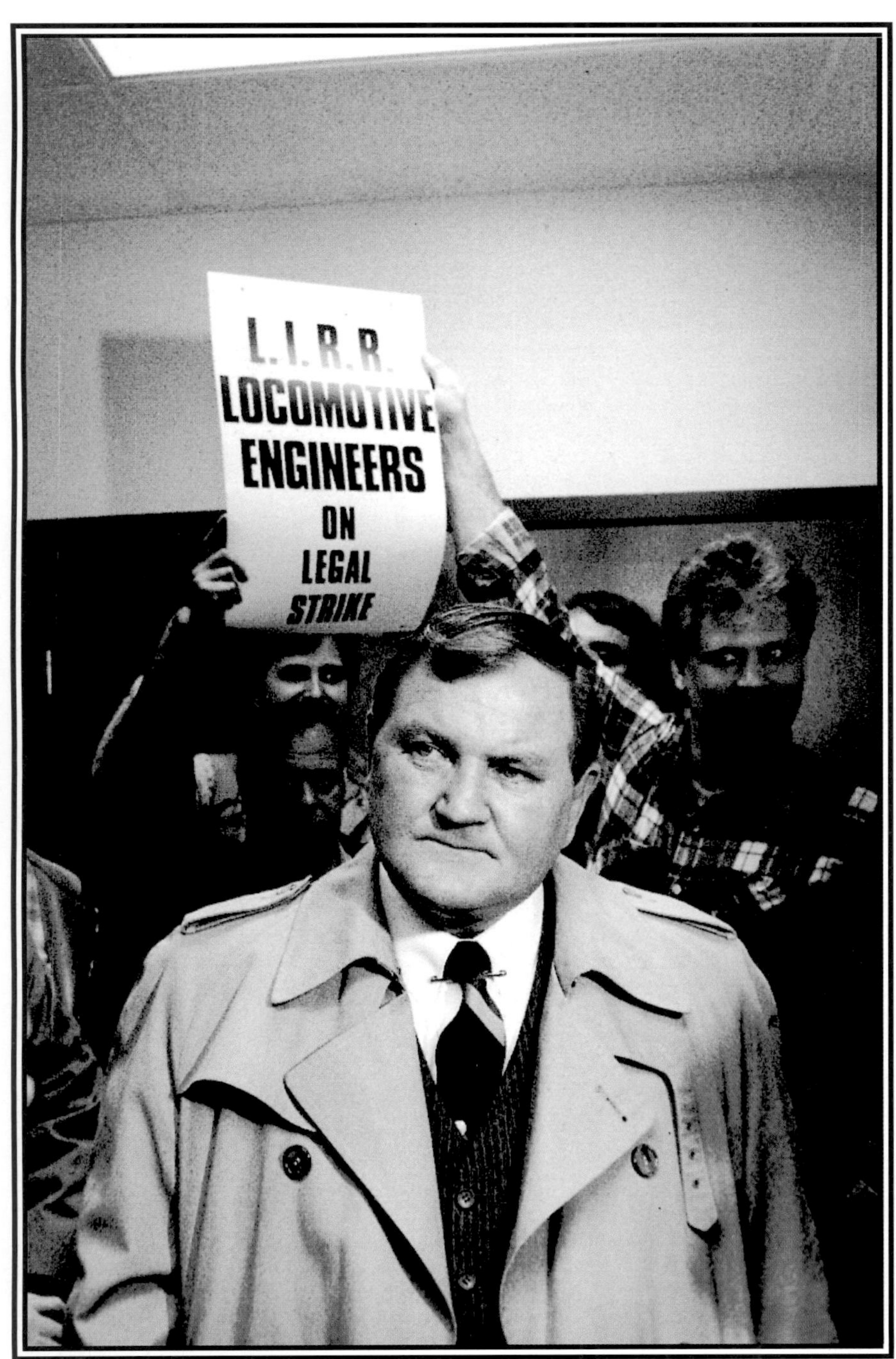

Newsday Photo

Joe Cassidy Jr. stands with fellow union members during a labor dispute in 1987.

LIRR engineer, Joe Jr. runs two trains a year to remain qualified.

He wonders what his grandfather Willie would make of his success.

When Willie joined, most union leaders and the people in the upper echelons of the railroad industry heirarchy were non-Catholics, Joe Jr. says. "In the early days, if you were Irish Catholic on the railroad, you were restricted to the more strenuous manual labor."

But Joe Jr. points out that Willie "knew that the railroads and the union would overcome their basic prejudices, so he stayed. And he was right in his assumption."

Irish immigrants had learned to "be more cooperative with the unions," says St. John's University professor William D. Griffin. "Organized labor, when it was at its peak of power, was very much dominated by the Irish-Americans."

Even as they struggled against stereotypes that painted them as silly, drunken "Micks" or "Paddys," the Irish worked to gain footholds of power, mostly finding them in the Democratic Party. They campaigned fiercely, built organizations and worked for common goals.

Willie Cassidy sowed those seeds. His son nurtured them and his grandson reaped the harvest.

"I think the first thing he would wonder," Joe Jr. says of Willie, "is how an Irish-Catholic like his grandson became the international vice president of the BLE, because at one time you simply couldn't be Irish-Catholic. But, ah, to know that we are not discriminated against because of our religious affiliation — he would be gratified."

Last year, on New Year's Eve, Joe Jr. made one of his mandatory train runs. Just east of the Garden City station, he passed a train going in the opposite direction. He looked at the person in the cab of the other train to give the customary wave. And then he saw who it was. "Hi, Kelly," he said over the transmitter.

"Hi, Dad," his daughter, the engineer trainee, answered.

* * *

In a classroom at the LIRR's Hillside training facility in February, Kelly Cassidy, 24, sits for tests to become a railroad engineer.

She quit her job as a teacher's aide with the city Board of Education to live out a dream to carry on her legacy: to become the fifth-generation Cassidy to work on the railroad, the first woman in a string of men.

"I think that is kind of extraordinary in itself," her uncle Brian, 49, says from his office in Chicago, where he is a corporate director of sales for Hyatt.

When Kelly walks through the training department, she passes a plaque with her grandfather Joe's picture on the wall. When she goes to the Morris Park rail yard or to the Long Island City engineer's room, she sees an image remembered from childhood of her grandfather Joe sitting on a bench talking to other engineers and firemen.

Now people tell her stories about Willie and Joe. She remembers the ones about Patrick that her father told her when he used to let her sit up on his lap in the engineer's cab. "He would let me blow the horn. He'd say, 'Okay, Kelly, I want you to blow two long, one short and one long.'"

During her training sessions, when she is sitting high in a cab, riding the same rails her father, grandfather, great-grandfather and great-great-grandfather knew so well, Kelly wonders.

"I look around. I wonder, 'Is this the way my grandfather ran a train? Are these the things he saw?' A lot has changed since he passed on, but a lot has stayed the same."

Her voice trails off. The ghosts of Cassidys past are everywhere for Kelly Cassidy because she is in the place where they spent so much time.

"When people find out who I am, one of the first statements out of their mouth is, 'I knew your grandfather very well,' or 'Your grandfather taught me the book of rules and without him I would never have understood it.'

"I come from such a long history," Kelly says. "It is something that started five generations ago with relatives I have never known. My grandfather was a legend, still is a legend, on the railroad. My father is a leader in our union and is still one of the strongest voices we have. And then comes me."

For every ounce of excitement there is an equal measure of nervousness. Sometimes, the pressure to succeed is almost crushing.

"I am not expected to fail," she says. "I have anxiety about not carrying forward. In a way, it's harder because I don't want to disappoint those who want me to be an engineer. They all have one saying, all the bosses, all the engineers, all the union leaders. Their one line is, 'Make me proud.' I've heard that since I started."

Kelly doesn't know how far she will go or if she will continue the trend of each generation of railroad Cassidys outdoing their predecessors. But she knows she has one bond with Willie and Patrick, with her dad and granddad. It's a trait that's in her blood.

"All I want to do is run trains," she says.

She's a Cassidy.

Field Of Dreams, 50 Years Later

THEN & NOW

They were one-tract finds, and they came from a man with a one-track mind: Bill Levitt, the brash developer who practically invented the suburb, lived the dream of building dreams.

In 1947, he planted the seeds of modern living in a Nassau potato field. Levittown was born.

More than 17,000 homes dotted the landscape in neat, treeless rows. Here — in 1947 at right, and today, below — is a section bordered in both photos by Wolcott Road on the bottom right and Newbridge Road at the extreme top left.

Today, the properties have trees, extensions, driveways — and families. And the dream lives on. — **Jerry Zezima**

Newsday Photo

TIME MACHINE

PICTURING THE PAST AND PRESENT

Newsday Photo / Jim Peppler

The pages that follow tell the story of Levittown, the most mythologized community in America. But no less compelling is the life of William J. Levitt, the man who planted the seeds of modern suburbia in a Long Island potato field.

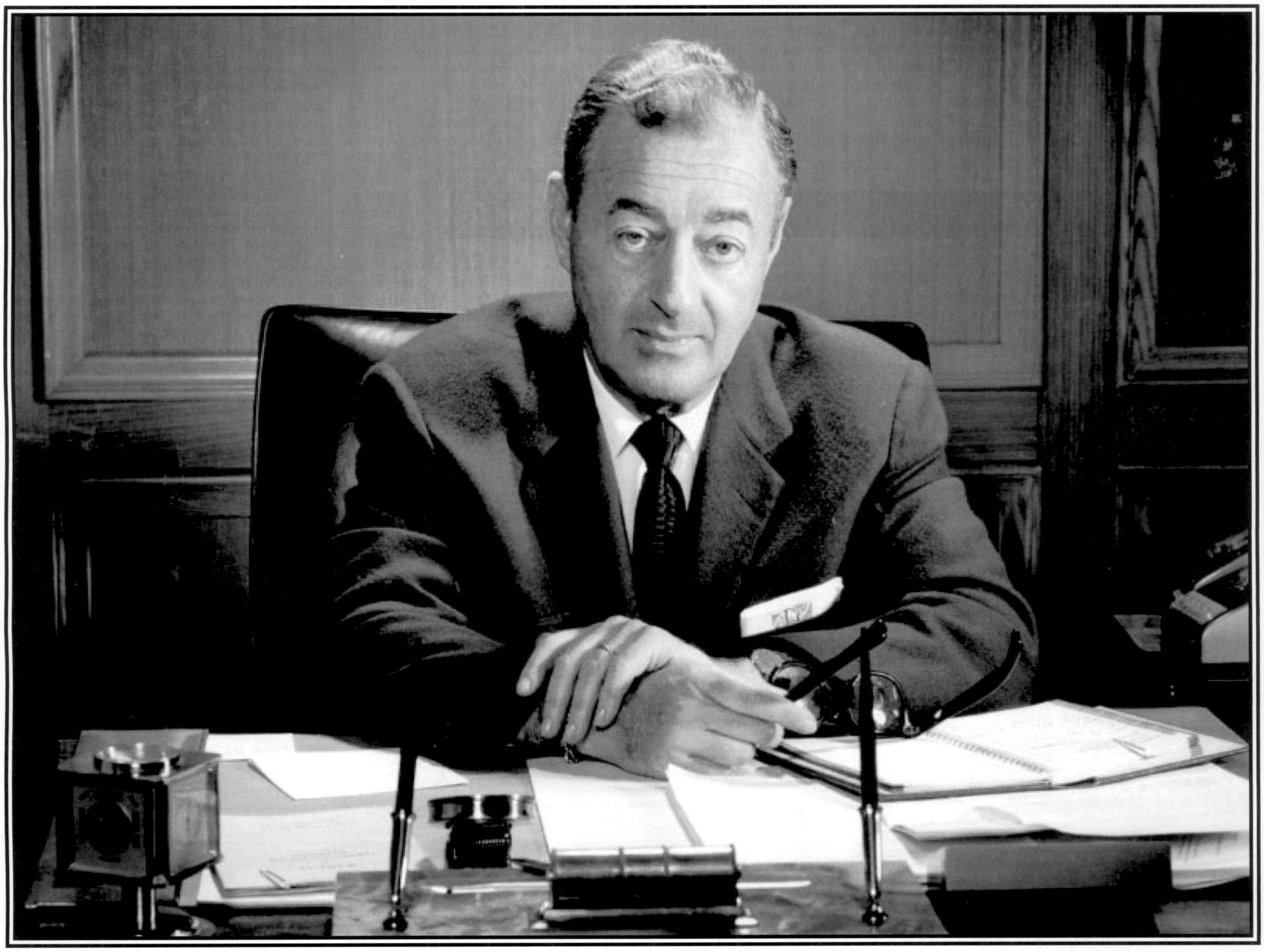

Newsday File Photo

The Dream Builder

BY CHARLIE ZEHREN
STAFF WRITER

Unable to pay for treatment at the hospital he gave millions of dollars to build, a dying Bill Levitt was still hoping for another roll of the dice.

Forty-two years after he completed his last house in Levittown and 26 years after he sold his company for $92 million, Levitt teetered on the verge of bankruptcy, amid allegations that he looted family charities and cheated homebuyers. Still, the man who once claimed to be America's biggest homebuilder was sure he could save his business and his family's good name.

"I have a regular organization ready to punch in full time," Levitt rasped during his last interview late in 1993. "I need another six months."

But at 86, he'd outlived success, a victim of changing economics, questionable business practices, worse luck and a lifestyle that far exceeded his means. Three months later, Levitt was dead.

"Bill was having dreams of this supposed comeback that simply wasn't there," said Charles Biederman, nephew and trusted business partner, who visited him at North Shore University Hospital. "But he believed so intensely, you found yourself believing, too, even though you knew it wasn't true."

Newsday Photo / Daniel Sheehan

William J. Levitt in 1986: In its cover story on him in 1950, Time magazine described Levitt as "a cocky, rambunctious hustler with brown hair, cow-sad eyes, a hoarse voice (from smoking three packs of cigarettes a day), and a liking for hyperbole . . ."

Dreams are what Bill Levitt sold. And his biggest came to pass starting in 1947 on 7.3 square miles of land near what was then called Island Trees in Nassau County. Today, Levittown's 17,447 mass-produced Cape Cod and ranch houses form the core of a still vibrant community that critics once dismissed as an incipient slum.

This original $50 million development — along with dozens of other mass projects he produced throughout the world over the course of a 64-year-career — offers testament to Levitt's prowess as a pitchman and financier who grasped the seductive appeal of homeownership for young families.

William J. Levitt did not invent the suburb. However, with his father, Abraham, and younger brother, Alfred, Bill Levitt combined the entrepreneurial spirit of Henry Ford with the self-promotional bluster of P.T. Barnum to change the American landscape. Levitt revolutionized the home construction industry by unsnarling arcane building codes and union rules and employing new technologies to get quality building jobs done fast and cheap. And he did it all with flair in the New York media spotlight.

Until the magic wore off late in life, Levitt displayed a genius for calculating the risk, seizing opportunity, exploiting the forces swirling around him, extemporizing, and amassing fortunes for himself and others. Going through three wives, a couple of yachts and a massive fortune, Levitt lived life with zest.

There was always time for a party. Tapped out after cavorting at the Havana Yacht Club shortly before the Cuban Revolution, Levitt quickly moved to raise capital for yet another gamble. Weaving down the aisle of his corporate plane as it arced northward across the Caribbean, Levitt scraped together about $80 from his lieutenants. Checking his coordinates, Levitt ordered the pilot to divert course and land in Nassau, the Bahamas.

Once on the ground, Levitt moved on to a local casino and boldy parlayed the meager stake into about $2,500 in 10 straight passes at the craps table. Wrangling a loan from the house, Levitt kept rolling until he bankrolled a weeklong vacation for the entire entourage. "That's Bill," said Nelson Kamuf, who was there. "A good gambler who knew how to play the odds."

And Levitt knew how to play both sides against the middle.

In public, Levitt derided "the people of Park Avenue" and reveled in the adulation heaped on him by middle-class homeowners. And when Hofstra University professor Stuart Bird asked him to state his legacy shortly before he died, Levitt looked into the camera and said he would like to be remembered as "a guy that, I suppose, gave value for low-cost housing. Not somebody that gave value for half-million-dollar houses. Anybody can do that." But in private, close relatives say, Levitt fancied himself part of the jet set and exhibited contempt for the "masses" he dismissed as "asses."

In business, Levitt could be just as disingenuous. Despite testifying before Congress that it was impossible for him to discriminate because he was Jewish, Levitt wouldn't sell to Jews in his upscale developments and excluded blacks right up through the mid-1960s, well after the adoption of landmark federal civil rights legislation. In politics, Levitt aligned his views with whoever could help him. When anti-Communist Sen. Joseph R. McCarthy (R-Wis.) took control of crucial housing legislation, Levitt railed against the Red Menace. Later, in order to build low-cost housing outside of Paris, Levitt allied himself with the socialist government.

"The end always justified the means — within the four corners of reason, of course," Levitt said in 1948.

Those who knew him say Levitt was generous and never claimed perfection. He was a complex man leading a complex life and like any great salesman, skillfully told people what they wanted to hear.

"I loved my father very much and idolized him," summed up his son, James, in a recent interview. "So did a lot of people. He was good at that."

Brooklyn Beginnings

Bill Levitt's father, Abraham, was born into poverty on July 1, 1880, in the Williamsburg section of Brooklyn, the youngest of five sons of Louis Levitt, a rabbi who emigrated from Russia, and Nellie Levitt, who was born in Austria. Leaving school at 10 to do odd jobs in the neighborhood, Abraham Levitt educated himself, reading avidly and attending meetings at literary clubs. A romantic in a classic sense, he found city life harsh and sought beauty in flowers and gardens. Passing a state Regents exam at 20, Abraham won entrance to New York University Law School, earning his degree in 1902 with a specialty in real estate law.

Admitted to the bar, Levitt started practicing in New York City. He married Pauline A. Biederman on Jan. 9, 1906. The couple had two sons, first William Jaird on Feb. 11, 1907, and then Alfred Stuart five years later. Life in the four-story brownstone on Macon Street was comfortable — and argumentative.

Abraham, physically compact and quietly philosophical, was a devotee of the German philosopher Ernst Haeckel, who believed there was no such thing as free will, only fate. Abraham grew close to the shy and intense Alfred, who, even at a young age, showed artistic talent. "Alfred is a genius, and I use that term advisedly," Abraham would later say. Bill, boisterous and brimming with self-confidence, held a special spot in his strong-willed mother's heart.

Relatives say that in adulthood Alfred reminisced that his mother would beckon, pull her young son to her breast, and whisper in his ear: "Where's your brother Bill?"

Even before he was a teenager, Bill would don a suit, bound into the parlor and announce plans to go into Manhattan, make money and live the high life.

Bill attended PS 44 and Boys High School in Bedford-Stuyvesant, playing lacrosse and joining the swim team. At NYU, he majored in mathematics and English. But Bill was later quoted saying that in his third year, at age 19, he quit because, "I got itchy, I wanted to make a lot of money. I wanted a big car and a lot of clothes." Levitt later contradicted himself, saying he graduated in 1927, a claim records can't back up.

During these years, Abraham represented real estate clients, and occasionally dabbled in buying and selling properties. Family lore has it that Abraham used money Pauline made taking in sewing to buy some of his first vacant lots in Brooklyn. Then, around 1925, Abraham accepted 100 plots in Rockville Centre from a bankrupt client. Abraham bankrolled builders who bought the land and began building houses.

But Abraham was forced to take control of some 40 partially finished homes in the late 1920s, when a real estate slump forced their builders out of business. Facing steep losses, Abraham took a chance and encouraged Bill and Alfred to team up and finish the job.

Bill never intended to be a builder, and as Abraham once recalled, "Alfred loved to draw, but he didn't know what a two-by-four was." Yet feeding off each other's enthusiasm, the brothers managed to work with existing crews to quickly complete and then sell the 40 homes. Emboldened by success, Abraham formed Levitt & Sons to develop the rest of the property, adopting the project's existing name, Strathmore.

LI HISTORY.COM

For more on Levittown pioneering, visit Newsday's special Internet site, http://www.lihistory.com, and see vintage movie clips, including amateur footage of Frank Lloyd Wright at the Great Neck construction project that inspired Alfred Levitt in 1936. Also, you can see more photos from the early days in Levittown and read excerpts from the transcript of Hofstra professor Stuart Bird's interview with William J. Levitt in 1993.

Abraham established the corporate hierarchy that would later yield Levittown. Bill, 22, served as president, handling advertising, sales and financing, while Alfred — who was still in his teens and would also drop out of NYU — became vice president of design. Without benefit of license or formal architectural training, Alfred then drafted plans for the first entirely Levitt house. The half-timbered, six-room, two-bathroom Tudor sold for $14,500 on Aug. 2, 1929, just two months before the onset of the Great Depression.

That November, as financial panic swept the nation, Bill married Rhoda Kirshner, his teenage sweetheart, who blossomed into a patron of the arts. Bill Levitt was 26 when his first son, William Jr., was born in 1933.

Abraham's risky bet selling upper-middle-class housing into the teeth of the Depression paid off. He sold another 18 upscale Strathmore houses before pressing ahead for a total of 600 in four years.

"Bill wouldn't be a success without Alfred, and Alfred wouldn't be a success without Bill," Abraham liked to say in his later years. "Together they are terrific."

Bill Levitt won a reputation as the young man to see for high-end housing along Long Island's North Shore — the Gold Coast. Indeed, by the fall of 1933, the Levitts were growing rich building the 200-house North Strathmore development in Manhasset — priced between $9,100 and $18,500. Through 1941, the Levitts built another 1,200 homes in Manhasset, Great Neck and Westchester County.

Network radio stars, big-time newspapermen, surgeons, Madison Avenue types, $10,000-a-year lawyers and a brace of Manhattan celebrities flocked to Levitt homes. But before laws and mores changed, Bill Levitt — grandson of a rabbi — also restricted Jews from his North Shore "pride of the company" developments, said Yale University historian John Thomas Liell.

In recent interviews, relatives said Levitt opposed what he called "institutionalized religion." But his relatives and contemporaries say it is ludicrous to brand Levitt an anti-Semite. They point out how Levitt made large contributions to Israel starting in 1947, when he handed a $1 million check to future Jerusalem Mayor Teddy Kollek, as a loan for weapons. Throughout his life, Levitt gave millions of dollars more to Jewish charities.

Nevertheless, Levitt rationalized the policy as an unfortunate cost of doing business, said Paul Townsend, Levitt's former public relations man, who now publishes the Long Island Business News.

"Sure, he went along with the local practice of real-estate agents not selling to Jews," Townsend said. "History should show that Levitt was part of the ugly gentlemen's agreement."

Levitt Family Photo

The high profile and voluble style of William J. Levitt, left, created tension in his relationship with his more reserved younger brother, Alfred S. Levitt, the designer of the Levittown homes.

The Navy Years

As the New Deal expanded and the nation lurched into World War II, the Levitts took their first tentative steps away from custom, upscale homes toward cheaper housing backed by federal credit. While far from successful, Bill and Alfred later said they learned valuable lessons mass producing Navy housing near Norfolk, Va., in 1942. In fact, Bill Levitt would say that experience proved far more valuable than his days as a lieutenant in the Navy Seabees in wartime Hawaii.

Levitt was 36 with a wife, a 10-year-old son and a baby boy, James, when he shipped out to Oahu in 1944 with the famed Navy construciton unit, serving as a personnel manager for 260 men. If anything, Levitt later recalled, the Seabees didn't give him experience, he helped the Seabees. "What experience?" Levitt once said. "It was the other way around."

The only thing Levitt built in Hawaii was a reputation as an officer who cared for his men and knew how to have a good time, said Kamuf, an engineer who roomed with Levitt in the officers' barracks and later became president of the Levitt organization.

In bearing, Lt. Levitt more resembled Ensign Pulver than John Wayne, Kamuf said, recalling that his future boss spent much of the war shooting craps, playing jazz piano and drinking. "Johnny Walker Red," Kamuf said. "And martinis — dry, straight up."

Even though he was in the Pacific, Levitt's thoughts were back on the Atlantic Coast, where Abraham and Alfred were drawing up a detailed building plan of grandiose proportions. Naval buddies recalled Levitt saying, "Beg, borrow or steal the money and then build and build," because whoever developed immense tracts of low-cost housing after the war was going to become extremely wealthy.

Levitt Family Photo

Even while in the Navy, Levitt's thoughts were on home construction.

"The dice were loaded," Levitt, the inveterate gambler, later recalled thinking. "The market was there, and the government was ready with backing. How could we lose?"

As World War II drew to a close, Abraham and Alfred Levitt were convinced they had the right idea for the right place at the perfect time — a Levitt town on the farm fields of the Hempstead Plains.

In Bill's absence, Abraham took over as company president and by 1944 exercised options to buy land and began lining up materials to build a community of 6,000 low-priced homes — dwarfing the nation's largest development.

The mass-production techniques, the niftily designed homes, the layout of the development grew from all the tricks of the trade that Alfred had saved up for years, according to relatives and business associates.

"Alfred was the creator," said Ralph Della Ratta, 75, who worked closely with Bill for four decades after the war. "It was his product that sold."

Everyone involved in the creation of Levittown agrees, though, that Alfred and Abraham would not have been able to build the project without Bill's strengths as a financier and enthusiastic promoter.

It was Bill who persuaded politicians from the Hempstead Town Board to the U.S. Senate to rewrite the laws that would make Levittown possible.

Abraham, by this time in his late 60s, had ceded control to his sons, dedicating himself to directing the planting of trees, shrubs and flowering plants at the new development. Alfred, a drawing-board idealist, and Bill, a bottom-line realist, clashed.

Biederman and others said Alfred's principles continued to frustrate Bill, who even lost an argument with Alfred over whether a garage should be included with the first Levittown model. (Alfred compromised and later versions included a carport.) "Until people are decently housed," Alfred said, "I believe we have no moral right to house autos."

For his part, Bill said he barely had to advertise Levittown because the response to the first offering in 1947 was overwhelming. "Any damn fool can build homes. What counts is how many can you sell for how little," Levitt said. But for years he wouldn't sell or rent to blacks, even after courts struck down racial covenants. Levitt — whose family, fearing a decline in property value, moved to Long Island from Brooklyn after a black attorney moved next door to them — said he wouldn't have been able to compete if he didn't follow the discriminatory practices of the time.

In all, Levitt & Sons built 15 other projects throughout the Island.

In 1952, they moved the mass production operation to Bucks County, Pa., near Philadelphia, for another 17,000-home Levittown. Completing that in 1958, Levitt crossed the Delaware and built a 12,000-home Willingboro, N.J., project.

Celebrity Status

Monogramed, pinstriped, bow-tied, and arrogant, Bill Levitt looked and acted every inch the mogul as he worked the two telephone lines and interoffice buzzers atop his massive desk within the oak-paneled offices of Levitt & Sons in Manhasset. By the late 1940s, Levitt was growing richer and gaining national attention as the cheeky guy stamping out houses at a rate of one every 16 minutes.

Newsreel interviewers and congressmen lauded Levitt, who was introduced to America on the July 3, 1950, cover of Time magazine — the most influential publication of its day — as the "cocky rambunctious hustler" prone to hyberbole and smoking three packs of cigarettes a day.

Rougish with wavy hair and heavy-lidded eyes, Levitt, then 43, lived in a big Manhattan apartment, and warmed to celebrity status as he lectured America on what it needed to stoke the postwar economy.

Yet behind the scenes, tension continued to mount between Bill and the reserved Abraham and Alfred, who were increasingly uncomfortable with Bill's high-profile and voluble style. Bill favored Cadillac convertibles and believed Alfred had grown too impractical. Alfred favored Fords and thought Bill believed too much in his own press.

Relations among the Levitts deteriorated in 1951 after Alfred divorced his wife, Silvia, to marry a 19-year-old fashion model he fell in love with on a shopping trip to Paris. "It was me," Monique, Alfred's widow, who remarried and now lives in Hawaii, said in a recent interview. "I clashed with Bill."

Later, she said, Bill offered her $25,000 to not submit a profile she wrote of Alfred to Reader's Digest. "I was insulted and told him to keep the money." She said she decided to withhold the article to avoid further family tension.

"It was Bill who craved all the publicity," Monique said.

Finally, the brothers, who had so much success as a team, split their business affairs in 1954 and grew estranged, bumping into each other occasionally at their parents' home in Kings Point. Alfred went on to develop Queens apartment complexes and Suffolk housing developments before he died at 54 in 1966.

"Alfred and Bill were brothers, but there was clearly a rivalry," said Les Dembitzer, Bill Levitt's longtime personal accountant and investment banker. "I think it's fair to say that Alfred resented Bill running the show. That Bill would make all the major decisions.

They simply came to a parting of the ways."

Without his brother, Bill Levitt continued thinking big. Levitt's company, which he had taken public in 1960, lost $1.4 million a year later as housing demand fell and huge tracts of land near metropolitan areas grew scarce. Yet Levitt adapted quickly and changed tactics, branching out geogrpahically — Chicago, Washington, D.C., France — reducing the scale of projects, dabbling in townhouse projects, delegating authority and decentralizing management.

Hooking up with young homebuilder Dick Bernhard in the bar of the Caribe Hilton in Puerto Rico, Levitt then launched a highly successful 12,000-home development west of San Juan. Completing the transition from heading a family business to running a thoroughly modern corporation, Levitt was back on track, posting a 20 percent average annual increase in sales into the late 1960s.

Bill Levitt was on a roll. Favoring royal-blue sport coats, light slacks and fawn-colored oxfords, he would fly to San Juan during the winter months, hit the hotels and casinos, not bothering to check in at the local office, before departing days later. Levitt bosses in Puerto Rico often found themselves dispatching employees to pick up foreign merchandise and personal gifts Bill routed from points throughout the world through the local airport to save on U.S. taxes.

Financially, Levitt grew even more successful. On the strength of Puerto Rico and his other projects, Levitt cut a deal to sell the company to the International Telephone & Telegraph Corp. for $92 million in July, 1967. At age 60, Levitt went from being very rich to incredibly wealthy, personally netting $62 million in the form of ITT stock.

"If it was for a penny less than $92 million, I'd walk out right now," the fanatically punctual Levitt roared when ITT chief executive Harold Geneen, a legendary dealmaker, kept him waiting at the closing.

As part of the deal, ITT changed the name of its new subsiary to Levitt Corp. Levitt agreed not to build in the United States for 10 years. In effect, the man who renamed Island Trees to honor his family sold his right to use his good name, and "that never stopped bothering him," said Dembitzer, Levitt's accountant.

Business associates now say Levitt went into the deal thinking he would play a greater role in ITT affairs. But Geneen — who later called the merger one of his biggest mistakes — froze Levitt out. ITT executives felt Levitt was already getting too old to take on more responsibility. In the office, Levitt stewed on the sidelines. But at home and on the road, Levitt lived it up, collecting expensive art and building a chateau.

Friends, family members and business associates said that while he was married, Levitt did little to hide his ongoing love affair with his secretary, Alice Kenny. He married her in 1959, divorcing Rhoda after 29 years of marriage, but not before taking his then-14-year-old son, Jim, to a Manhattan restaurant to break the news. "Until then," Jim recently recalled, "I had no idea that my parents were not going to be going on together."

In 1969, Levitt divorced his second wife, Alice, and married Simone Korchin, an art dealer from France more than 20 years his junior, two weeks after she divorced her husband in Rome.

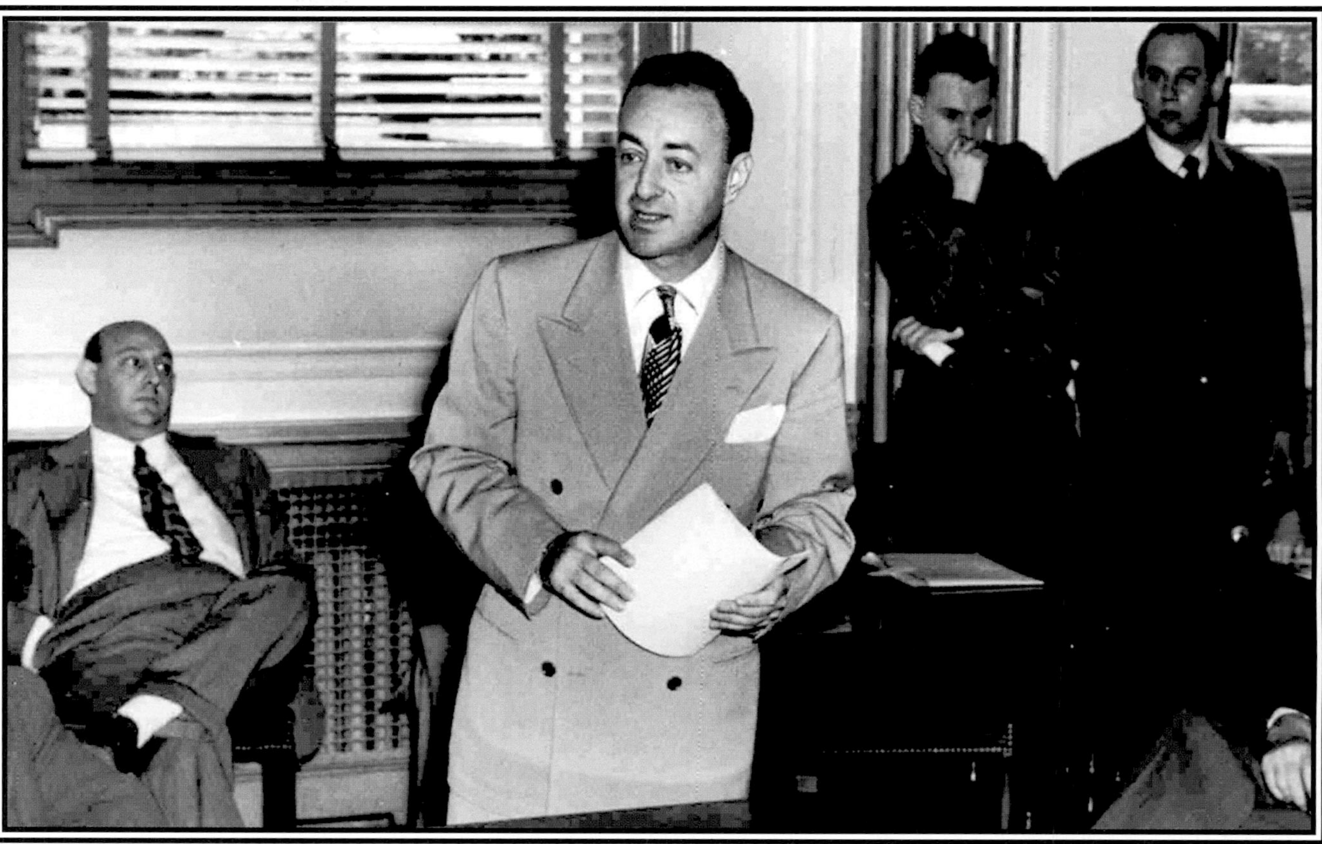

Newsday File Photo

In an undated photo, Levitt speaks to the Board of Supervisors at Hempstead Town Hall.

Lavish Living

Life was grand at La Colline, Levitt's $3 million, 26-room, French-provincial mansion on 68 acres in Mill Neck, said Nicole Bernstein, Levitt's eldest stepdaughter by Simone. A parade of Broadway stars, famous politicians and media luminaries made their way up the winding drive, through the ornate courtyard, past outsized birdcages, into Bill Levitt's salon. Despite an attentive household staff, Bill liked to personally tend bar and care for his seven dogs. The family vacationed in Europe and went on African safari.

Several of his two children, three stepchildren and others he helped raise said Levitt proved as distant as he was demanding. But they also expressed their respect, admiration and love for the man who lavished gifts along with admonitions.

"Bill was driven and determined to educate us. To help us become the people he believed we could be," Bernstein said. "I loved Bill. I appreciated him even more in later years."

During these heady days, Simone and Bill gave each other expensive gifts, celebrating their wedding anniversary each month for years. Financial records later showed the presents included some $3 million in jewelry. Levitt's art collection also grew to include paintings by Renoir, Monet, Degas and Chagall. Much later, Levitt actually flaunted his wealth, showing how far he had come from Williamsburg by assembling the New York media corps to view his sumptuous 237-foot yacht, La Belle Simone, moored in front of the Brooklyn Bridge. The license plate on his Rolls Royce parked on the pier read "WL-1"

It was troubling, Kamuf said, that Levitt never seemed to invest his money to maintain a stream of income. "Bill always looked for projects to generate money, but didn't really invest," Kamuf said.

For Levitt, that made the sting of Wall Street's early-1970s bear market even more painful. To avoid taxes, Levitt had not converted ITT to cash. Instead, he borrowed against it. When ITT shares crashed, Levitt's holdings were worth about 10 percent of their original value. Chase Manhattan Bank seized Levitt's stock as collateral. Bill Levitt's luck started to run out.

Levitt scrambled for a comeback by forming a new real-estate company when his non-compete clause with ITT expired in 1978. But Dembitzer said, "Bill was never really able to recover."

Levitt tried and failed to build mass developments in Florida, Iran, Venezuela and Nigeria. Trapped in a financial nightmare, Levitt began siphoning millions of dollars out of what he was able to build to support his lifestyle and prop up new ventures.

Regulators who later barred Levitt from doing business in New York said he diverted homeowners' deposits for the Florida homes and money that should have been used for repairs and maintenance. Investigators said Levitt also took at least $17 million from his family's charities to cover personal expenses. Levitt sold La Colline to make payments.

"Bill did more good for more people than any other businessman in the world," said Fred VanderKloot, Levitt's stepson-in-law and Florida business partner, during a recent interview. "But at the end he was running out of capital and not reinvesting the profits."

James Levitt said his father did not adjust to changing consumer tastes and increased government controls: "He just didn't realize how tough things were going to be."

Desperately hunting for partners, Levitt managed to wrangle a meeting with executives from a major New York investment group, Biederman said. They asked why they should risk the money given that Levitt had not completed a serious project in 15 years. "At that point, Bill reached into his pocket and pulled out 10 to 15 yellowed articles. 'Look what I've done,' he said. It was very awkward," Biederman recalled. "Bill stayed at the party too long."

In 1985, Levitt then 78, made a last-ditch attempt to save the Florida development by entering into negotiations with Long Island developer Ron Parr. Critical to the deal was Levitt's getting more financing from the troubled Old Court Savings and Loan of Maryland.

"Bill said he was perfectly willing to give up financial control. He just wanted to make sure that his name would be associated with the project. He was just looking for a way to recover his reputation, his family name," Parr said.

Finally, a critical meeting was scheduled. Old Court officials were to fly by private plane to a meeting with Levitt and Parr at Brookhaven Airport. When Parr arrived, Levitt was already there, alone. 'Someone gave Bill a ride and dropped him off," Parr recalled.

The appointed time came and passed and for 2½ hours Levitt — a compulsively punctual executive — poured his heart out to Parr, talking about Levittown, his family, how the business had changed, sketching his hopes for the Florida development. When it became clear that Old Court executives were not going to show, Levitt grew quiet, embarrassed. Parr gave Levitt a lift back to Mill Neck.

"It was the first time I ever saw Bill Levitt dejected," Parr said. "Bill Levitt was beat."

Still, Della Ratta said, his boss had a great ride.

"No one should ever feel sorry for Bill," he said. "What difference does it make if you die with $100 million in the bank or nothing in the bank if you had Bill Levitt's life? He had a huge estate, a huge yacht, three gorgeous wives and was generous to boot. What the hell more do you want? It was the American dream." ●

It was 1947 and thousands came to a former Long Island potato field to find a piece of the American Dream — a home of their own

Suburban Pioneers

BY GEOFFREY MOHAN
STAFF WRITER

At the time, no one could have known what the dust clouds rising from the Hempstead Plains would mean. Not the young veteran Herb Kalisman, who regarded them from a train in the Hicksville station as he headed from his rented Brooklyn attic to the relief of a Suffolk County beach.

"I asked the conductor, 'What is that?' " Kalisman recalled. "He said, 'This guy is out there building all these houses.' I said, 'Who the hell would live out there?'

"A few years later," Kalisman said, "I was one of the who-the-hells."

Ernie Knoell Jr., the burly son of a farmer, stood amid that dust and watched with mild bemusement as wood skeletons rose from the neighboring fields while he cut spinach on his father's farm in the summer of 1947.

"We worked hours sometimes out in the field at 4 or 5 o'clock in the morning, in the dark, and you'd hear these guys hammering across the street," the 73-year-old Farmingdale resident said. "You'd relax after supper, and these guys were still hammering at 10 o'clock at night."

The full import of that hammering wasn't even clear to the charismatic dreamer William Jaird Levitt, his subdued architect brother, Alfred, and the family patriarch, Abraham, who were building 2,000 Spartan, look-alike boxes on old farmland beside the Wantagh Parkway in a place called Island Trees.

What started in 1947 as affordable rental homes for house-hungry World War II veterans would mutate rapidly over the next four years. By 1951 a complex of 17,447 homes blanketed the farms of Island Trees, spilling over into Wantagh, Hicksville and Westbury.

Levittown, as it came to be known, would help usher in the era of home ownership on a massive scale for a class that previously held only the faintest dream of a house in the country.

It would help transform the building industry from a piecemeal, custom enterprise into an assembly-line industry and create a template for the way the American middle class would settle into the second half of the 20th Century.

Yet by most accounts, Levittown was an ad-hoc revolution that surprised even William Levitt, who found himself at the juncture where unprecedented social, political and financial currents crossed as America came out of World War II.

"There was an amazing, almost voodoo-like combination of circumstances that made the Levittown projects work," said Peter Hales, an art historian from the University of Illinois at Chicago who studies postwar suburbs. ". . . It was almost a can't-lose phenomenon."

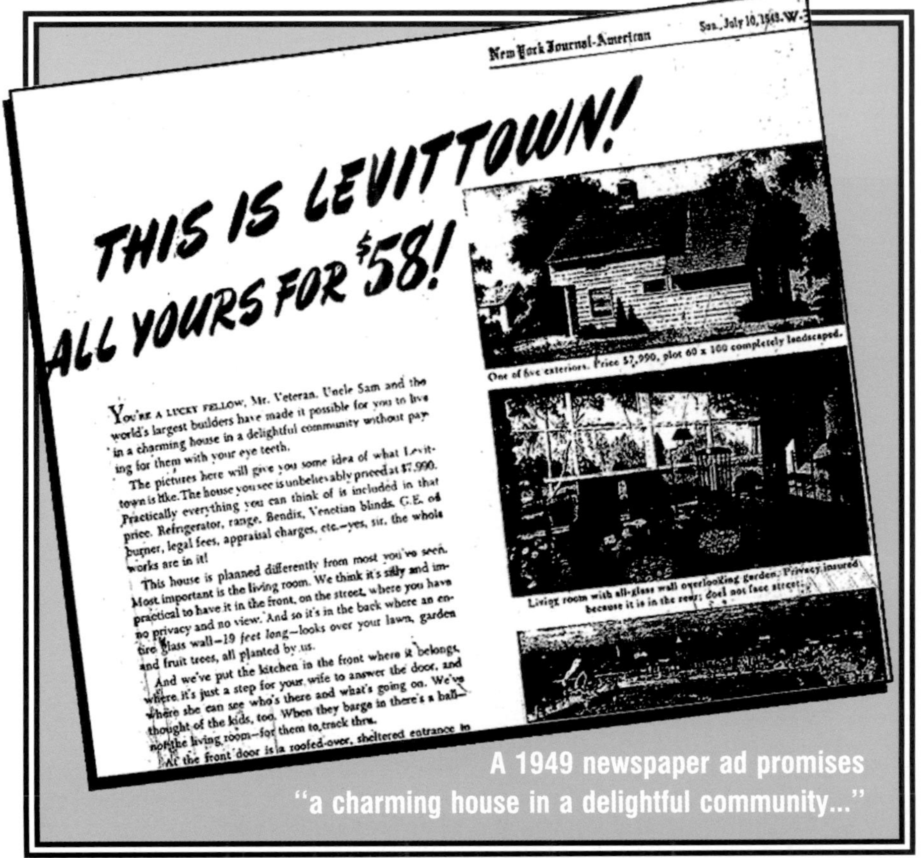
New York Journal-American Sun., July 10, 1949

THIS IS LEVITTOWN!
ALL YOURS FOR $58!

YOU'RE A LUCKY FELLOW, Mr. Veteran. Uncle Sam and the world's largest builders have made it possible for you to live in a charming house in a delightful community without paying for them with your eye teeth.

The pictures here will give you some idea of what Levittown is like. The house you see is unbelievably priced at $7,990. Practically everything you can think of is included in that price. Refrigerator, range, Bendix, Venetian blinds, G.E. oil burner, legal fees, appraisal charges, etc.—yes, sir, the whole works are in it!

This house is planned differently from most you've seen. Most important is the living room. We think it's silly and impractical to have it in the front, on the street, where you have no privacy and no view. And so it's in the back where an entire glass wall—19 *feet long*—looks over your lawn, garden and fruit trees, all planted by us.

And we've put the kitchen in the front where it belongs, where it's just a step for your wife to answer the door, and where she can see who's there and what's going on. We've thought of the kids, too. When they barge in there's a ball— not the living room—for them to track thru.

At the front door is a roofed-over, sheltered entrance to

One of five exteriors. Price $7,990, plot 60 x 100 completely landscaped.

Living room with all-glass wall overlooking garden. Privacy insured because it is in the rear; does not face street.

A 1949 newspaper ad promises "a charming house in a delightful community..."

Squeezed first by the hard times of the Great Depression and later the military needs of the war, developers had built precious little since the real-estate market crashed in the 1930s. Young men and women then went to fight fascism, but 12 million GIs came home to live in attics, basements and Quonset huts.

The houses were their reward. But as the Cold War replaced the World War, they took on added symbolism. Defeating communism in Europe meant making capitalism shine here. A single-family house in the suburbs, fully equipped with the best appliances, became a patriotic mission, and Levittown its best example.

"How can we expect to sell democracy in Europe until we prove that within the democratic system we can provide decent homes for our people?" President Harry Truman pleaded during his 1948 campaign.

Truman and Congress unleashed the largest amount of financing ever made available to the building industry — tens of billions of dollars that gave an entire generation a boost into the middle class.

Levitt played these forces like a conductor. He pitted postwar patriotism against unions and political machines, red-baited his enemies, banned all but white residents and courted power brokers to convert his colony of renters into a community of homeowners on an unprecedented scale.

Levittown happened through luck, fear, financial aid and force of will. It

Newsday File Photo

Owen (Bill) Drugan spreads fertilizer on the lawn outside his new ranch-style house in Levittown on April 18, 1950.

was on Oct. 1, 1947, that the first 300 families moved into the Cape Cods clustered in Island Trees.

Five decades later, Levittown has become the most studied, scorned and mythologized community in America — idealized by some as a planned utopia, pilloried by others as the grandfather of the sprawling conformity that came to mark modern suburbs.

History shows neither is entirely true.

The Levitts, especially financier-salesman William Levitt, draw credit for inventing suburbia, assembly-line homes and cellarless houses.

None of that is entirely true, either.

But time blanches the detail of Levittown's story, leaving only the boldest outlines. The liberation returning GIs felt to have their own homes. The struggle to confound critics who foresaw a blue-collar slum. The dreams veterans realized by increments, chronicled in the additions that so transformed these houses it is difficult to find a Levitt original.

Levittowners tell their story with the spare morality of a Western. They speak reverently of "Mr. Levitt" and his "plan." Sometimes they mean Bill. Sometimes they mean Abraham, a diminutive figure who would tour their town and lecture them on the proper care of the peach, elm, maple and oak trees that acquired such grace over time.

"When you saw a Cadillac driving through Levittown and you couldn't see anyone behind the wheel, you always knew it was Abraham Levitt," recalled Robert Abrams, a Levittown pioneer who founded the Levittown Tribune.

"It's hard for me to tell you how I felt about [Bill] Levitt except to say in my book, Levitt will go down as a great guy," Abrams said. "He responded to a need when my wife and I needed a house. He provided us with more than a decent life. He gave us a start in life."

Levittowners wax nostalgic about the "village greens" and their mom-and-pop stores within baby-stroller distance of their homes; they point to the empty lots for sandlot ball, and the nine swimming pools that became summertime shrines, where being tall enough to hold your head above the water became a rite of passage for Levittown youth.

They point with pride to the fact that with no outside help and little experience they filled in the pieces of the puzzle that Levitt left out — a school district, a chamber of commerce, Little League, a library and a volunteer fire district.

"You know, Levitt built the houses," said Beth Dalton, of Dalton Funeral Homes, a fixture in Levittown. "It's the vets that moved in, that created Levittown. He just built houses. They're the ones. It's their values and their energy that created this community."

But they bristle at the intrusion of

Nassau County Museum Collection, Long Island Studies Institute Photo

Before becoming the most studied, criticized and mythologized community in America, Levittown, then known as Island Trees, was farmland. Levittown, shown here in 1949, was the brainchild of William J. Levitt, who built 17,447 homes. All were sold at well below market value.

Corbis-Bettmann Photo

unflattering details, some of them not of their making: the racial covenants, the schools Levitt left out of his plans and that became a financial burden, the book-banning and mudslinging battles, the choking traffic, the spiraling taxes, the death of businesses in the village greens, the sprawl that scarred Hempstead Turnpike, and fences that cut off the camaraderie of the pioneer days.

The burden of history lies heavily on these pioneers. And all they wanted 50 years ago was a home.

$60-a-Month Rentals

Bob Abrams was a brash former combat correspondent, and his wife, Eleanor, was in the last trimester of pregnancy. They lived with Eleanor's parents in Brooklyn.

"It was a fairly large apartment for two people," Eleanor Abrams said. "It was not fairly large for four people."

As he rode the subway to his typesetting job in Manhattan, Abrams spied a story in the Herald-Tribune, his favorite newspaper, about a rental development on Long Island.

"By the time I got to work, I'd written out a postcard, and I put it in the mail," Abrams said.

Abrams never even saw the white Cape Cod he agreed to rent for $60 a month until he walked up to it on Oct. 1, 1947, the day the first 300 residents moved into Levittown's first phase, north of Hempstead Turnpike, east of the Wantagh Parkway.

Edgar and Pat Daniels waited until 1949 to come to Levittown. Edgar was a Marine Corps veteran from Chester, Pa., fresh from a three-year hitch in the South Pacific. Pat was from Omaha.

They can tick off the meager details of their pre-Levitt life in Queens: "Seventy dollars a month, hardly furnished, stall shower, ice box," Edgar Daniels said. "The door down to the basement got water rats. They were banging on the door."

Daniels stood on a frigid line outside a model of a Levitt ranch in Roslyn. Warmed by fires in barrels, he made new friends who would become neighbors when the Daniels family moved into a house at 37 Hook Lane on July 26, 1949.

Pat Daniels didn't get the exact model she wanted, but it didn't matter.

"I was so happy to get out of Flushing I would have taken anything that was clean and neat," Pat Daniels recalled. "And I mean it was; it was like a little doll house."

In 1949, Mildred Glaser and her husband, David, a graphic artist and poet, were just as happy to get out of a Brownsville walk-up and into a house with $80 to spare.

Downhill Lane was just a muddy track when they came out to check the progress on the house they had bought.

"They just paved it, but it was covered with mud," David Glaser said. "And I said, 'Oh, that's our house right there.' We walk up. 'Downhill [Lane], thirty-three, there it is.' We walk up and there's this slab in the ground, and believe it or not, we're

looking at it, and I said, 'Well, let's see: The bathroom's over here; there's where the bedroom is. And I laid down right on it. The wet slab. She said, 'Get up, you fool.' I said, 'Nah, look how wonderful it is.' "

They had a house but not much else. There were no personal telephones in the early days, and the pioneers went to Hicksville to pick up their mail. Many had no cars. They could not afford babysitters. They had no churches, no schools, no front lawns.

What they had was each other.

"There was a spirit that I've never seen since," said Frank Wolff, who moved to Gardiners Avenue in the summer of 1948 from a basement in Jamaica. "There was an automatic neighborliness which is completely lost today."

Levittown tested pioneers early and often. Over the community's first Christmas, a record-setting blizzard buried the stubby saplings Levitt & Sons had planted at each home. The following year, 1948, another storm hit.

Mary Heron Quinn, who moved into Levittown in November, 1947, left work in Manhattan at 2 p.m. and arrived the next day at 5 a.m., walking the last leg from Hicksville with fellow commuters, behind a plow truck.

"There was a lot of people sick here with the flu," Quinn recalled. Levittown's first druggist, Lester Smith, managed to get hold of a snowplow. "He hired it himself, and he got in the plow with the guys who drove it, and drove to all of these houses where the people were so sick, and got the prescription filled. Saved their lives, actually. He was out all night trying to get through that snow."

Levittown's settlers, fresh from the hard living in the city, started early trying to personalize the sturdy boxes they now called home.

I Remember Levittown . . .

Connie Nisito

She lives in the same Levitt ranch she moved into with her husband in 1951.

"The first thing that happened when we moved here was the milkmen. There were two milkmen waiting for us the day we took occupancy on Oct. 31, 1951. And my husband flipped a coin to pick out which of the two men would get the milk contract. And Merrick Dairy got it . . . I still have the milk box. It's right outside . . .

"And that was the great milk that was delivered in the bottles, with the cream that came up to the top in the freezing-cold weather, and it was like having your own natural ice cream. Then followed by the Dugan man. The Dugan man was indispensable. This man provided us with eggs, bacon, cakes, you know, and all kinds of great breads, butter, so that was our lifeline.

Newsday Photo / John Paraskevas

"Because you know here in those days there was no such thing as getting out to a supermarket in two or three minutes. First of all, very many of the women didn't have cars. The women that had cars were the women that drove their husbands to the Long Island Rail Road station at five o'clock in the morning for them to pick up their trains. And they were the fortunate ones, that ended up with a car for the day. They were very sought after, these women that had cars. The rest of us, that didn't have cars, were really in bad shape. I didn't have a car for eight years."

In the summer of 1948, Wolff watched residents "borrow" lumber and materials from homes being built along Gardiners Avenue to floor their attics or convert them to bedrooms. A man who traipsed through his yard one twilight, with several children in tow, explained he was "improving Mr. Levitt's property."

Finally, Levitt & Sons hired a retired New York City cop who patrolled the area in a black 1936 Chevrolet with dimmed lights. Wolff resisted temptation until the very end. Then he went across the street and stole the sign warning residents not to steal.

"I thought that was the ultimate theft," Wolff said. "They didn't need it anymore anyhow."

There were other petty larcenies that fall in the category of getting by. One involved the pay phone on the lane behind Wolff's house. The phone's coin box was inadvertently left unlocked.

"Everybody got wise and they just pulled the drawer open, took the nickel out, put it in the slot, got connected, then walked away," Wolff said.

"It sounds like larceny, but it wasn't," said Wolff, his voice still tinctured by his native Breslau, Germany. "You must remember one thing. Ninety-nine percent of the people were veterans, right? All about the same age. All with growing families, or trying to have growing families. And all struggling. And it was actually no different than it was in the service, you know. If you'd get away without doing KP, OK."

Getting by and making do quickly built new friendships.

Like many residents fresh from the city, Wolff had no car. Each day, he'd walk to Hempstead Turnpike and Loring Road and put out his thumb to catch a ride to Jamaica, where he worked at a trucking company. No more than two cars would pass before he got a ride. Pretty soon, the same guy started picking him up.

"He said, 'Instead of standing out here — you know it may rain or anything like that — why don't you just come to the house and we'll start from there?' " The two soon were playing chess together in a chess group.

Levittowners knew how to join. There were more than 200 groups, from Kiwanis to knitting, by the 1950s. Scouting was big. Little League was huge. There were soap-box derbies on the few roads that offered any elevation.

Children roamed the open yards — Levitt prohibited fences. While parents lamented an infestation of Japanese beetles — an unintended result of plowing up the fields for houses — kids collected them.

"I can remember the children, you know what the boys' favorite pastime was in the summertime? It was beetle time," Connie Nisito, who moved into a Levitt ranch in October, 1951, recalled. "How many beetles can they get in a mayonnaise jar with a little oil in it. And then they would fill these jars up and at the end of the night, they would count the beetles."

Levittown houses were housewife-centered. For that matter, so was America. Advertisements touted a mother's ability to mind her children from the window of the kitchen, which was well-appointed with a Bendix washer, a General Electric refrigerator and stainless-steel cabinets.

"And we've put the kitchen in the front where it belongs, where it's just a step for your wife to answer the door, and where she can see who's there and what's going on," read a Levitt & Sons advertisement from 1949.

Levitt laid down the law with his tenants. Laundry could be hung only on umbrella-stand dryers, and it could not be hung at all on weekends.

If lawns weren't cut, Levitt would send a crew and bill the tenant. On weekends, the men learned to share their lawn mowers, and they chipped in to do repairs.

"Nobody knew how to change a fuse; nobody knew how to repair an appliance," Abrams said. "If you had to do something, you'd have 15 guys over watching because they wanted to know how to do it when they had to do it themselves . . . Everybody was there to share whatever they knew with everyone else.'

The Conception

None of it could have happened without a massive federal program that steered developers toward affordable housing, providing them with up-front, government-guaranteed financing.

The Serviceman's Readjustment Act of 1944, better known as the GI Bill, was piggybacked with housing

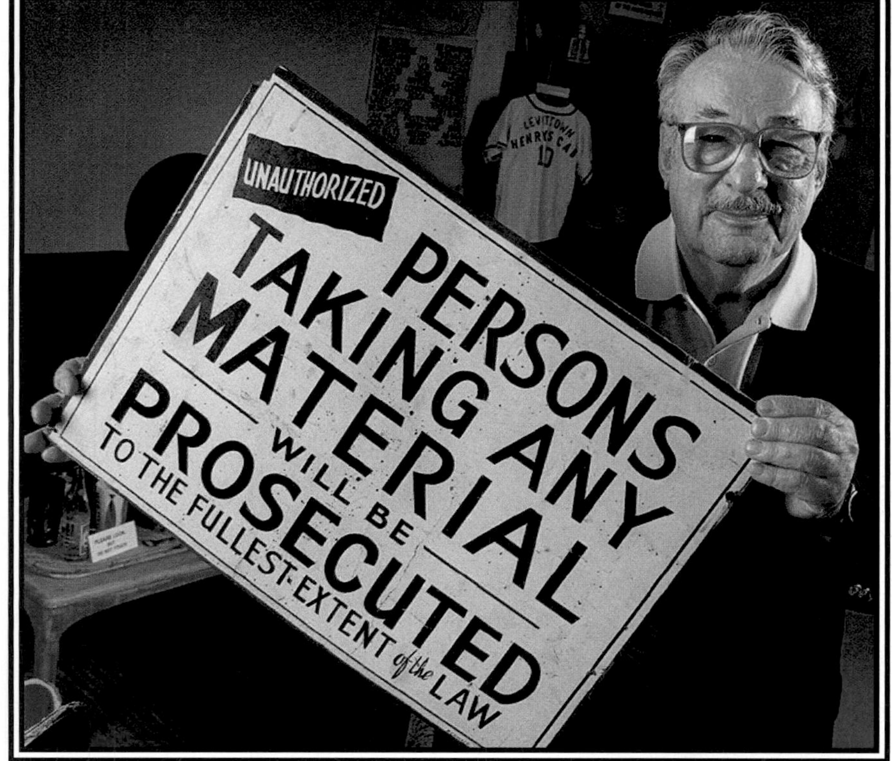

Newsday Photo / John Paraskevas

Levittown pioneer Frank Wolff with a souvenir he took from a Levitt construction site in 1948. "They didn't need it anymore," he says.

legislation that had created the Federal Housing Administration a decade earlier. The two operated in tandem to put the government in the business of guaranteeing financing for developers first, and then risk-free individual mortgages for GIs that required little money down.

It pumped $20 billion into the industry in its first four years and was the closest thing to free money the housing trades had ever seen.

The GI Bill also gave veterans the shot at a college education.

For the first time, two ingredients of the American dream were placed within the grasp of an entire generation — higher education and a house. They took them and ran, crossing over into a territory we now recognize as the modern middle class.

It brought the common person to a place called suburbia, and made suburbia commonplace.

With the provision that also sent soldiers to college, the GI bill erased the image of the leafy suburbs as a blue-blooded domain, and the definition of the middle class changed with it, according to Barbara Kelly, a Hofstra University assistant professor whose 1993 book, "Expanding the American Dream," chronicles Levittown's social and economic evolution.

"The markers of education and home ownership were so strong that, even if you worked at Grumman or Republic, nobody referred to you as a factory worker," Kelly said.

With Bill Levitt at the helm, Levitt & Sons was ready for the wave, and they rode it.

"He saw housing for workers was the place to be, and he went there fast," Kelly said. "There was a lot of it going on everywhere. But he managed to get the credit, cornering the market on the media. He was the Barnum of the postwar suburbs."

Out in California, David Bohannon had built large-scale suburbs from 1939 through 1944 in the exact way that Levitt planned to do it in Levittown — on slabs, by assembly line, at a rate of one every 45 minutes at its peak. But he never built more than 1,492 in one year. Levitt was aiming for 2,000 and would later surpass even that.

Levitt's original Cape Cods weren't new, either. They came almost whole cloth from FHA manuals on affordable housing, according to Kelly.

"The idea of large-scale suburban housing developments — everything that Levitt did, practically, was discussed in the Thirties," said Elizabeth Ewen, a State College at Old Westbury professor of history working on a book with colleague Rosalyn Baxandall about suburban development on Long Island.

But no one had put it together like the Levitts.

William Levitt built and stoked a brassy house-building machine that stretched from a California lumber mill to a Roslyn assembly shop. It was a process that would be studied and copied for decades to come.

Alfred Levitt, as introverted as he was intellectual, wrestled with the limits of a Cape Cod cottage and came out with more airy ranches. He centered them around neighborhood pools and small village greens that people could walk to and apportioned them lots that started at 60 by 100 feet and often ranged longer and wider. He left vest-pocket parks and ballfields like scraps from a textile cutter — and everywhere, Abraham Levitt adorned them with his beloved fruit trees and shrubs.

The Levitts would abide no fences, no curbside utility poles, and no clotheslines to break up the pastoral effect they desired.

They had both time and money to develop their plan, and paths that led them to Island Trees.

Before the war, the parkways of Robert Moses made the idea of living in the suburbs and commuting to the city seem possible for a growing number of people. Levitt & Sons had entered the housing business in the late 1920s with relatively upscale homes called Strathmore, in Rockville Centre and Manhasset.

Just before Bill Levitt left for a stint in the Navy Seabees during the war, the Levitts took out options on 1,200 acres of land in Island Trees held by the Merillon Corp. — part of the old estate of A.T. Stewart, the department-store magnate who built Garden City.

By the end of the war, the Levitts had capital ranging into the millions, had exercised their option in Island Trees, and were talking big.

Newsday File Photo

Oct. 1, 1947: The first day renters took occupancy of Levitt houses.

Upon Potato Fields

When Levitt got there, Island Trees was a flat and dusty prairie with a one-room schoolhouse amid a patchwork of farms and fallow land. Except for a small colony of a dozen homes built in 1933, houses were scattered. The old Vanderbilt Motor Parkway had fallen into disuse. There was an aviation club and a skeet-shooting range.

Dutch and German farm families, many of them linked by marriage or distant kin, had farmed in Island Trees for generations. But a wormlike pest called the golden nematode put their land in quarantine, and kept their potatoes off anything but local markets.

Levitt may have seen the golden nematode as his golden opportunity. But farmers saw suburbia coming, and it was only a matter of time before they sold, according to some who were there at the time.

"That was the talk, that nematodes forced them out, and in a sense maybe it is, but they were ready to go," said former farmer Ernie Knoell Jr.

There were still potato fields when Levitt got to Island Trees, Knoell said, but many farmers had switched to vegetable crops.

Knoell's wife, Muriel, comes from a farm family, and can remember the trips to Hunts Point, where prices set by middlemen often didn't cover the cost of the crates that held the squash or spinach.

"The truth was, the farmers weren't getting anything for their produce, so to them this was a godsend," Muriel Knoell said. "They sold. At least they put money in their pocket."

Ernie Knoell's father had seen it before. He had been a tenant farmer in Queens before suburban development pushed him out to his own 12.5-acre plot beside what then was called Jerusalem Avenue — now Gardiners Avenue.

Knoell waited until Levitt's back yards came up against his farm before he sold his acreage for about $30,000 in 1948 — to a Levitt competitor who built his own homes in the middle of Levittown. The same land today would be worth about $3.5 million.

Levitt didn't buy all the land at once for what would become Levittown. After the first purchase, he

In the summer of 1947, Ernie Knoell Jr. watched from his father's farm as houses sprouted in the Levittown subdivision. Today, Knoell tends to his garden in Farmingdale.

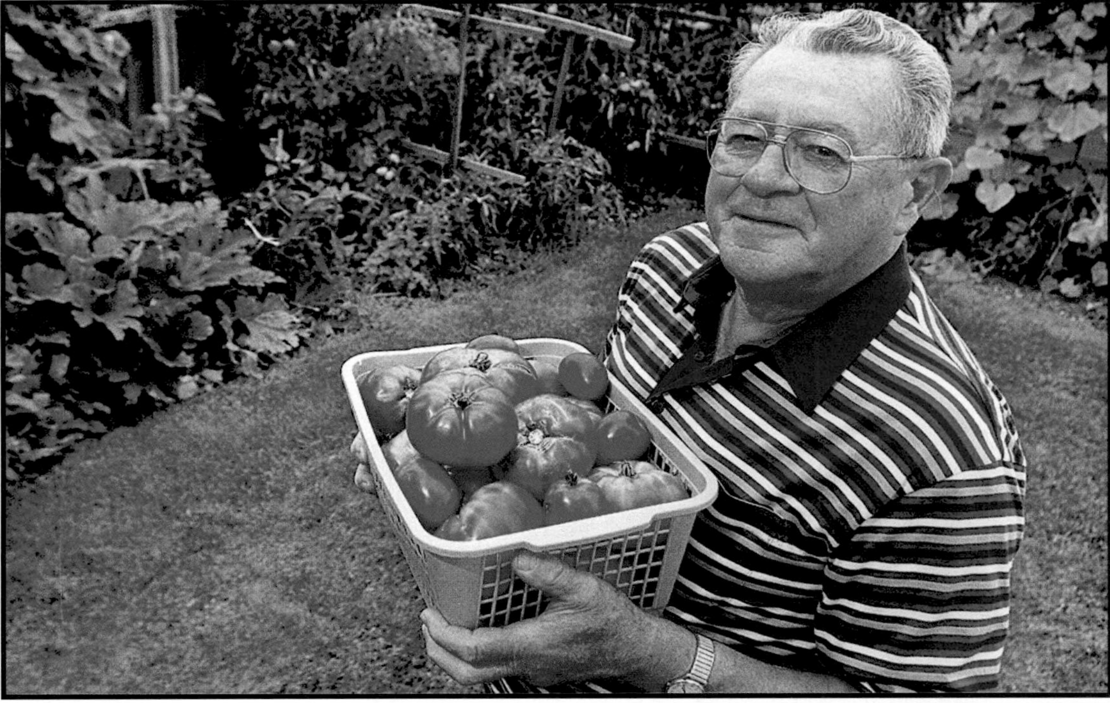

Newsday Photo / John Paraskevas

Levitt's Defenses Of Racist Policies

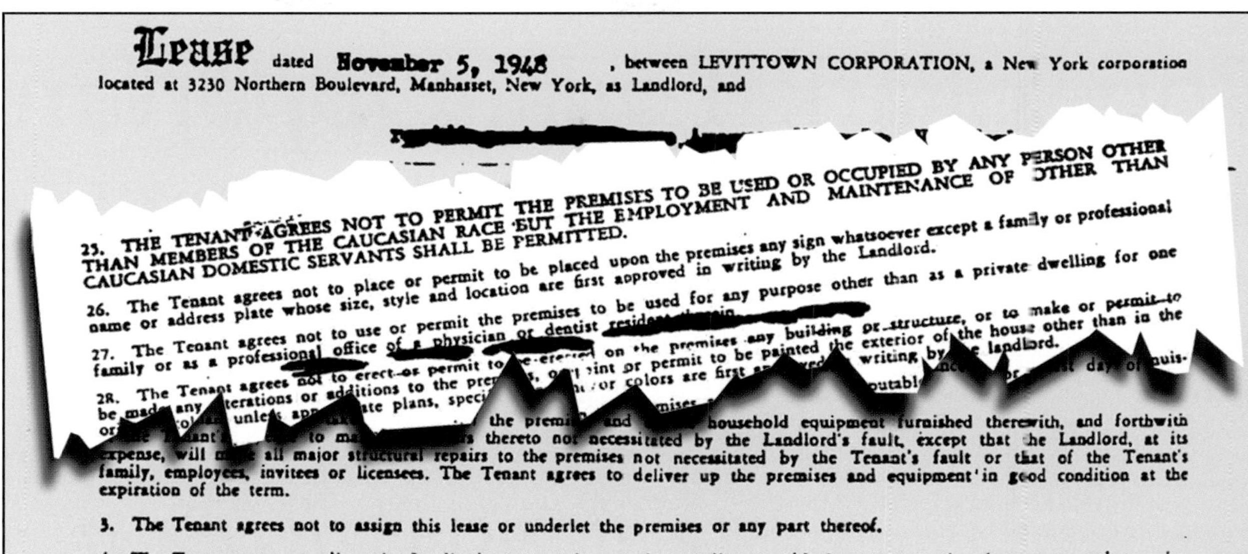

Lease dated November 5, 1948, between LEVITTOWN CORPORATION, a New York corporation located at 3230 Northern Boulevard, Manhasset, New York, as Landlord, and

25. THE TENANT AGREES NOT TO PERMIT THE PREMISES TO BE USED OR OCCUPIED BY ANY PERSON OTHER THAN MEMBERS OF THE CAUCASIAN RACE BUT THE EMPLOYMENT AND MAINTENANCE OF OTHER THAN CAUCASIAN DOMESTIC SERVANTS SHALL BE PERMITTED.

26. The Tenant agrees not to place or permit to be placed upon the premises any sign whatsoever except a family or professional name or address plate whose size, style and location are first approved in writing by the Landlord.

27. The Tenant agrees not to use or permit the premises to be used for any purpose other than as a private dwelling for one family or as a professional office of a physician or dentist

28. The Tenant agrees not to erect or permit to

household equipment furnished therewith, and forthwith thereto not necessitated by the Landlord's fault, except that the Landlord, at its expense, will make all major structural repairs to the premises not necessitated by the Tenant's fault or that of the Tenant's family, employees, invitees or licensees. The Tenant agrees to deliver up the premises and equipment in good condition at the expiration of the term.

3. The Tenant agrees not to assign this lease or underlet the premises or any part thereof.

The Caucasians-only covenant in a Levitt lease

BY GEOFFREY MOHAN
STAFF WRITER

William Levitt's explanations for openly barring blacks from Levittown and his other developments varied over time, but one theme persisted — segregation was the common coin and good for business.

"I knew that if I declared for open housing, my worst enemies would be my colleagues in the building industry," Levitt told Newsday in 1977, 30 years after Levittown's founding. "It was a business decision. We would have been driven out of business if we were alone."

Levitt at first passed the blame to the Federal Housing Administration, which backed his financing and recommended against "inharmonious racial or nationality groups."

The agency's underwriting manual at the time warned, "If a neighborhood is to retain stability, it is necessary that properties shall continue to be occupied by the same social and racial classes." It recommended use of "suitable restrictive covenants."

So Levitt used such a covenant: "THE TENANT AGREES NOT TO PERMIT THE PREMISES TO BE USED OR OCCUPIED BY ANY PERSON OTHER THAN MEMBERS OF THE CAUCASIAN RACE. BUT THE EMPLOYMENT AND MAINTENANCE OF OTHER THAN CAUCASIAN DOMESTIC SERVANTS SHALL BE PERMITTED."

However, in 1948, the U.S. Supreme Court declared such provisions "unenforceable as law and contrary to public policy."

A year later, the FHA announced that beginning the following year, it would not back mortgages linked to segregationist covenants.

Levitt eliminated the racial covenants, but pledged to practice discrimination nonetheless, according to a Levitt news release at the time.

Testimony, interviews and published accounts show that Levitt later changed his mind about whites-only practices, but only when faced with state laws or political and public pressure.

When Levitt & Sons moved to Pennsylvania and New Jersey, the public-relations team of Tex McCrary and Paul Townsend convinced him to relent on his policies supporting racial exclusion, Townsend said. But first, Levitt unsuccessfully sued New Jersey over its newly enacted antidiscrimination law, saying it interfered with his constitutional rights to engage in private enterprise.

"We insisted if we're going to handle public relations with him in Pennsylvania, that he didn't go through with that," Townsend said. "At that time there was a growing consensus that you couldn't discriminate against blacks."

Levitt reverted to restrictive covenants in a Maryland development called Belair in 1963 and was called to task for it by a House committee weighing antidiscrimination legislation in 1966.

"Any home builder who chooses to operate on an open-occupancy basis, where it is not customary or required by law, runs the grave risk of losing business to his competitor who chooses to discriminate," Levitt testified. "That, in a nutshell, is why we follow our present policy in Maryland."

Levitt ultimately became a convert at the congressional hearing — not on moral grounds, he argued, but on economic ones. A federal law was the only way, he said, to remove the competitive advantage that he felt segregationist developers had.

In the end, the original Levittown never had more than a handful of black families well into the 1980s, and today, it remains 97 percent white.

Samuel Miller, executive director of Long Island Housing Services, believes some blacks were steered away from Levittown, but many others choose to stay away because of its history. "Who wants to be a pioneer in this day and age?" Miller said.

Levitt frequently told interviewers that he could solve the nation's housing problem, but not its race problems. On the 30th anniversary of Levittown, he compared the plight of blacks to that of Jews.

"Blacks are trying to do in 300 years what Jews couldn't do in 6,000 years," Levitt, the grandson of a rabbi, told Newsday in 1977. "I don't want blacks to wait 6,000 years. But it cannot be done at once."

What Levitt did not mention at the time was that he also had agreed to use restrictive covenants to ban Jews from his early Manhasset developments. It was strictly business.

"He was a very market-oriented fella," Townsend said. "When the market said you don't sell to Jews or you don't sell to blacks, he went along with it. I never heard him say any nasty words about Jews or blacks. He just went along with the market." •

hitched his wagon to Milton Levin, a young real-estate broker working for his father-in-law, Max Gruber, in Roslyn Heights.

Levin and Levitt got along famously. Each year, Bill Levitt would ask Milton Levin what he had available. If it didn't border his project, he wasn't interested. Even if it turned out later that he'd need that land.

Levin got wise, and started buying whatever he could in and around Island Trees, at first for as little as $300 an acre but later for 10 times that much.

"We kept buying in advance of his progress and became an unofficial holding company," Levin said. "He didn't want to give up his cash to buy a lot of land."

And when it came to buying land, Max Gruber knew how to talk to farmers. They chewed the fat about potatoes, beans, weather. It drove Levin nuts to watch.

"I said, 'What are you doing talking about vegetables and farming? We're here to buy and sell land,' " Levin said.

"He said, 'That man knows why I'm there, and he knows that I know that he knows.' He says, 'The time will come. He's not ready to give me a number yet. The time will come.' "

Some held out, and some sold quickly. But the time came for all of them.

"They sold their farms there and went five miles further out and bought one of the farms at farm prices," Levin said.

The Levitts took the land and began laying out streets, dictated more by the boundaries of the old farms than by any sense of a master plan for traffic.

The winding lanes were an old touch, borrowed from earlier suburbs, that lent a country air and slowed traffic. Each section had thematic names. There were the tree streets, the bird section, the tradesmen streets, the celestial section. By the end, they resorted to alphabetical sections. Every so often, the Levitts penciled in a village green or a school.

Because they never got control of prime patches of land along Hempstead Turnpike, residents watched as other developers lined what once was a dusty one-lane road with strip malls and asphalt meadows that siphoned business from the village greens and created the need to expand Hempstead Turnpike into the six-lane highway that now bisects their community.

The Levitts donated land for churches and a temple. But they didn't donate land for the schools, as folklore has it.

Property records show the Levitts and other property owners sold the land well above its original cost to the school district, which had to float bonds and raise taxes to pay for it. All told, taxpayers in Levittown School District 5 paid $772,325 in the

Ronek Park, Equal-Opportunity Suburb

BY SIDNEY C. SCHAER
STAFF WRITER

There are no signs welcoming you to Ronek Park.

Perhaps that is to be expected, because Ronek Park was one of the thousands of subdivisions built in the post-World War II housing boom that transformed the Long Island landscape.

And like those other housing developments that sprang up across Nassau and Suffolk Counties to provide housing for World War II veterans, its once-distinctive parade of new homes gradually disappeared as time blurred the borders from one section of new homes to another, and the skinny saplings became trees, and what began as starter homes for some became lifetime investments.

But one thing made Ronek Park different from those other developments: It was colorblind.

"We had looked for five years and had all but given up, when a friend of ours told us about it," says Ann Gilmore, an African-American who remembers Valentine's Day, 1953, the day she and her husband, Gil, and their daughter moved from St. Albans to a three-bedroom house on Prospect Street.

Ronek Park had been built in stages beginning in 1950, with earlier homes having flat roofs and later ones peaked. But it wasn't its architecture that distinguished this community of homes tucked along and between Albany Avenue and Great Neck Road in what eventually became North Amityville, it was the simple fact that you didn't have to be Caucasian to buy in.

"We felt welcome here," Gilmore says, recalling an earlier experience when she and her husband had taken two different buses to get to the model homes in Levittown, only to receive the cold shoulder.

"It was a Sunday, and when we got there sometime in 1948, well, it was strange, because when we finally approached a salesman to ask for an application, well, he didn't say anything, but just walked away from us. It was as if we were invisible," she says.

If Ann Gilmore's American dream was destroyed at a Levittown model home, it was restored at a modest ranch house in Ronek Park. She was not alone.

In 1950, when the first model at Ronek Park went on display, its distinction was clear. Builder Thomas Romano declared that his homes would be available to all persons, "regardless of race, creed, or color."

The plans called for building 1,000 homes on a 147-acre tract. The first house went on display at the intersection of Somerset and Great Neck Roads, and listed for $6,990. By the end of the first day, nearly 3,000 people had come to see it, and Newsday reported that the majority coming were "Negroes."

"They may not have been the best places in the world, but I have to tip my hat to him [Romano]," said Lenny Canton, who came with his parents to Ronek Park in 1953, and still owns the home his parents bought on Great Neck Road. "Except for a place like St. Albans and South Jamaica, this was the only place a black veteran could come."

Canton, acting chairman of the North Amityville Community Economic Council, has no illusions about what Ronek Park was and is today. It began modestly and, for the most part, remains that way.

"It became a place where people speculated. It became a dumping ground for social services, and if you didn't own it, how much do you take care of it?" Canton says, describing the difficulties that occurred when nearby Republic Aviation shut down in the 1960s and people began losing their homes.

At the very center of Ronek Park, there evolved a piece of real estate that became known as "The Corner." And the corner became infamous for drug dealing, a haven for crime. As a result, Ronek Park's reputation suffered.

Now, things may be changing. A brand-new 10,000-square-foot child care center is about to open. A bank branch and a police substation also are coming, according to Canton, and across the road a new pharmacy is being built.

There is no question that some of Ronek Park homes are disheveled. But there also are homes that have been expanded, landscaped, built up and built out.

James Merrick came to Ronek Park when there was only the flat-roofed model, dubbed the Hollywood. Those early years were exciting, said Merrick, who had moved to New York from Washington and was living in Harlem when he saw an advertisement for the homes.

"We all had new homes . . . We had never owned a home, most of us," he said.

Merrick added a 16-by-23-foot extension. Others, such as Mildred Browne, added a second floor. Ann Gilmore and her husband, now in a Queens Veterans Administration nursing home, added a porch, moved the front door, relocated the kitchen and built a garage.

In a way, it sounds very much like what happened in Levittown.

But ask Ann Gilmore about Levittown and she still bristles.

"If they gave me a Levittown house today," she said, "I wouldn't take it." •

Unlike other postwar housing developments, Ronek Park did not discriminate. In 1950, when houses went on display, builder Thomas Romano said all could buy, "regardless of race, creed or color." Penndale Avenue, above, was part of Ronek Park, but is now part of North Amityville.

Newsday Photo / John Paraskevas

first decade of the community for land for schools within the boundaries of the Levitt development, according to school and property records.

The Levitts admitted later there was no grand design for Levittown. They planned it a section at a time and made corrections as they went along.

"On Long Island, we never knew from one year to the next how much more we could build, so we never had an overall master plan," Alfred Levitt wrote in Architectural Forum years after Levittown was finished.

"Levittown has no through-road system. That is its most glaring deficiency," Bill Levitt told Newsday for the 10th anniversary of his creation. "If we could have planned Levittown, L.I., at its present size, we would have provided different price classes to appeal to a greater market, and to make a better, more well-rounded community," Levitt added.

The original "plan" simply was repeated in pieces with modest changes until it had multiplied out to more than 17,000 homes.

Basements or Slabs?

When Levitt & Sons built its first 2,000 homes in 1947, the project had already set a national record for houses built in a year.

The houses were for rent only, though Levitt told newspapers in May, 1947, that the homes would be available for purchase at $6,990 at some future date. Most veterans could move into Levittown for a total monthly cost of $60.

The Levitts waited to see what would happen. By May 22, they had 4,495 applicants who forked over a $60 deposit, and Bill Levitt, before a single house had been built, announced plans for 2,000 more.

When the veterans handed Levitt their deposits, he gave them a letter enlisting their help in overcoming the last obstacle to actually building the houses — the local building code. There would be no houses in Island Trees, Levitt knew, if the Hempstead Town Board did not approve Alfred's proposal to use a shallow cement slab embedded with copper hot-water heating tubes instead of a basement and conventional heating system. Both were crucial to the Levitt formula for a house costing less than $7,000. It would cut out material that was hard to get and decrease labor costs.

"This is the most important part of all: Be at the public hearing at the town hall in Hempstead on Tuesday, May 27th at 10:30 a.m. for the public hearing to determine whether these houses can be built as we have designed them," he wrote to the veterans. "The town board has called this public hearing, and unless you and your friends are there, it may not be approved. If you want modern, comfortable, beautiful housing at a rental

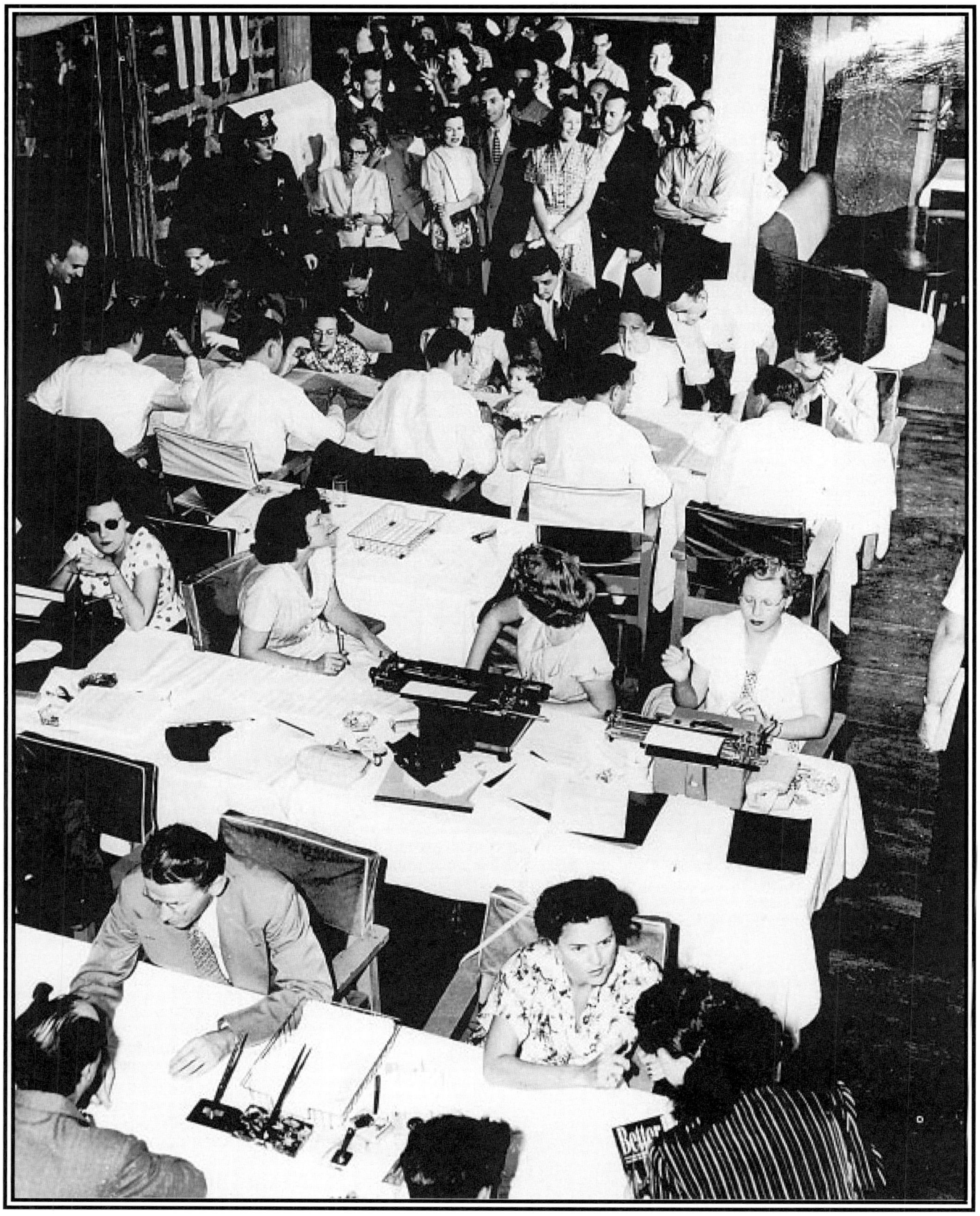

Nassau County Museum Collection, Long Island Studies Institute Photo

People hoping to buy Levitt homes crowd the Levitt & Sons sales office on Aug. 18, 1949. Buyers took title on the same day.

within your reach, you must be there! We're doing our part; you must do yours!"

With every new house meaning a potential new subscriber, local newspapers, including Newsday, got behind the Island Trees development from the beginning. The same day Newsday reported Levitt's plans, on May 8, it ran an editorial that portrayed cellars as outdated lairs for rotting apples, coal bins and floodwaters.

"Maybe it was good enough for grandpappy to live in a baroque chateau, propped up over a hole in the ground, but it is not good enough for us," Newsday wrote.

A young veteran named Paul Townsend was on separation pay from the service, working for local veterans groups. Newsday Managing Editor Alan Hathway enlisted his help.

"Alan Hathway was very much in Bill Levitt's corner," Townsend said. "Newsday asked us to get behind it. We met with Bill Levitt and Alan Hathway. They were working very close."

By the time the hearing came around, pressure was intense. Years later, political insiders told Newsday biographer Bob Keeler that Levitt softened the opposition in a backroom deal that shuttled business to politically connected insurance firms.

Eight hundred people attended the hearing, which lasted only 20 minutes. Levitt and two veterans made impassioned speeches before the vote was taken. The board, led by Presiding Supervisor A. Holly Patterson, capitulated.

William Levitt bragged to the Christian Science Monitor in April, 1948, that he had used the press to drum up support for his project at the hearing.

"It was a joke," Levitt said. "The place was stormed, jammed every inch. Veterans with their wives and babies overflowed into the streets demanding homes. Very quickly, breaking all precedent, the building code was changed. A small builder could not have brought that about."

Levitt had the endorsement of the board. Now he had to face the old-

I Remember Levittown . . .

Bernadette (Herbie) Fisher Wheeler

She was the reporter who chronicled the birth of Levittown for Newsday, including the crucial May 27, 1947, meeting of the Hempstead Town Board packed by veterans and their families.

"My eyes popped when I got to town hall because the lobby and the stairs leading up to the hearing room were loaded with people. The upstairs hallway was jammed and the room was packed. People were standing along the walls. I remember there were a lot of children, toddlers — some in strollers — and many babies held by men and women. We expected there would be quite a turnout. But the extent of the crowd was a big surprise to me . . . The meeting itself was rather brief. There were some speeches. No screaming and yelling the way people do at town meetings today. Everyone was quiet, anxious. I remember one guy in uniform, holding a baby, made a strong statement. These people were desperate. It was very moving. When the decision was announced, the crowd broke into applause."

Then, despite her skepticism about Levitt's plans and oft-stated dislike of the proposal for "thousands of little boxes," Wheeler and her husband wound up buying a Levittown ranch house in 1958.

"Levittown was the last place on the planet I thought I would be living. But, as it turned out, we moved there because the house was such a good buy, even though it was one of three lemons on the block. We loved living there. I came into work and told [managing editor Alan] Hathway I would be eating crow for the rest of my days."

Bernadette (Herbie) Fisher Wheeler in the 1960s.

time union system that had a lock on the construction trades.

William C. DeKoning Sr. was the most powerful labor boss on Long Island — before he was jailed on extortion and grand larceny charges in 1954. DeKoning headed Local 138 of the International Union of Operating Engineers.

As the project got under way, the unions picketed Levitt's construction site, but after a few days, inexplicably broke off the picket and allowed workers to cross the lines.

Some 40 years later, Local 138 reformers lamented the deal to Keeler for his history of the paper.

"It was the most drastic blow that he could deal to labor," said John DeKoning, the union boss' nephew. "We could have broke Levitt."

Contractors paid off the union for the ability to operate machinery with nonunion labor, explained William Wilkens, a Local 138 reformer. "There were union machines on the job in Levittown, and he was letting the contractor use them without [union] engineers and having people go there and collect from the contractor," Wilkens said.

Levitt now was free to set in motion a system that eliminated dependence on union labor.

He broke tasks down to their simplest components, providing pre-cut materials at each house site. Contractors worked directly for Levitt and got paid on a piecework basis. The more roofs they shingled, the more they earned.

"Even if they didn't have the skills, by the time they built the fifth house, they had the skills," explained Ralph DellaRatta, a vice president in the Levitt organization for 39 years. "He didn't set the system up to get around a union. He didn't need a trained person. And by the way, you couldn't get the production any other way."

The last thing veteran Tom Pepper wanted to do was shell out money he didn't have in order to get a union card. So building Levittown looked like a good deal to him in the summers of 1947 and 1948, between semesters at Syracuse University.

"That's why it was so popular — you didn't have to join the union," Pepper said. "We used to get $28 a roof in 1947. Then we went to the interior, where we'd put the shelves up, and the trim around the window. We got $45 for that. There were guys in there from Finland."

The Levitts had their construction method figured out.

Inside the Roslyn warehouses of the Levitts' North Shore Supply Co., workers gathered and assembled elements of the houses for Island Trees — trusses, planks, gypsum board, nails. Levitt's own trucks brought the material to the work sites to await the roaming construction gangs. To eliminate waste, all building elements were in multiples of 4 and 8, a notion that has since become standard practice in the industry.

Levitt inspectors prowled the sites, taking measurements, counting nails, watching the contractors like hawks.

"Sometimes we would make a mistake and make the wrong cut," Pepper said. "Everything was lined up in front of the houses. We would sneak across the street and steal it from the other houses."

Newsday File Photo

William Levitt, right, shows Sen. Joseph McCarthy a washing machine in a Levitt house in 1947.

Help From Washington

The Levitts began attracting attention.

Even as the rental phase of the Island Trees development was going up in 1947, Congress began fumbling for a better solution to the housing crisis, which still vexed the Truman Administration and became a successful reelection issue.

At the forefront of the movement were the American Legion, at the time the strongest lobby involved in the housing issue, and an obscure Republican senator from Wisconsin named Joseph McCarthy, who was looking for a spotlight issue.

Levitt courted them both at Island Trees.

Newly elected to the Senate and four years away from the days as a vetter of Americanism, McCarthy wanted to ensure America kept a promise it had implied to veterans before the war began: a home.

McCarthy bullied his way onto a select committee investigating the housing shortage and convened a series of hearings that would set the terms of the housing debate.

Island Trees was one of his first stops.

Levitt led McCarthy, the American Legion National Housing Committee and top FHA officials on a tour of his project in August, 1947. He was photographed with McCarthy peering into one of the Bendix automatic washers that were standard equipment in the Levitt Capes.

McCarthy, who hated unions and public housing, favored the Levitt model of single homes on suburban plots. He believed "that public housing projects were nests for communism. They produced it environmentally," said Richard Fried, a Cold War historian at the University of Illinois at Chicago.

Like most builders, Levitt wanted to keep government from competing with the private sector. He also had a distaste for the government's methods — he testified that those methods ensured defense housing Levitt built in Norfolk, Va., in the early part of the war turned out to be "junk."

Levitt wanted federal officials to extend and further liberalize the FHA program that so far had provided the up-front financing for developments such as Levittown. He wanted help easing building codes. He wanted rationing to be lifted on building materials. He wanted to cement his reputation as the foremost builder of economical housing.

Levitt served McCarthy's purposes, and McCarthy served Levitt's, eventually penning the 1948 legislation that helped spur the homeownership phase of Levittown.

Levitt also wanted to sell to nonveterans, who did not enjoy the same financial preferences at the time.

"I can build houses for eighteen and nineteen thousand dollars, if I want to, and I cannot give them to a nonveteran, who can afford it, and vacate a $50-a-month apartment," Levitt argued during a January, 1948, hearing before McCarthy.

"You let me clear a thousand or two thousand families within the city of New York who want to come out, the nonveteran, and the veteran now has accommodations available to him."

During frequent trips he made to Capitol Hill, Levitt adopted the rhetoric of anticommunism to further his cause, repeating slogans like, "No man who owns his own house can be a communist. He's has too much to do."

Levitt got much of what he wanted from McCarthy and the 80th Congress. The 1948 Housing Bill, written as a replacement amendment by McCarthy, liberalized lending, making it possible for anyone to buy a home with 5 percent down, and extending mortgage terms to 30 years. Veterans could get in with no money down.

But Truman also extended rent control.

These changes, and the fact that Levitt needed to get his capital out of houses and into the next phase of land purchases, pushed Levitt out of the rental market.

Together, they inspired the creation of the homeowner phase of Levittown — the ranch models of 1949, 1950 and 1951, all of which were for sale right from the start.

As Levitt tried to make the transition from Long Island's biggest landlord to its biggest home seller, his image as a savior became tarnished when he pressured residents to rename Island Trees in his honor, boosted their rents and pushed tenants to buy their homes.

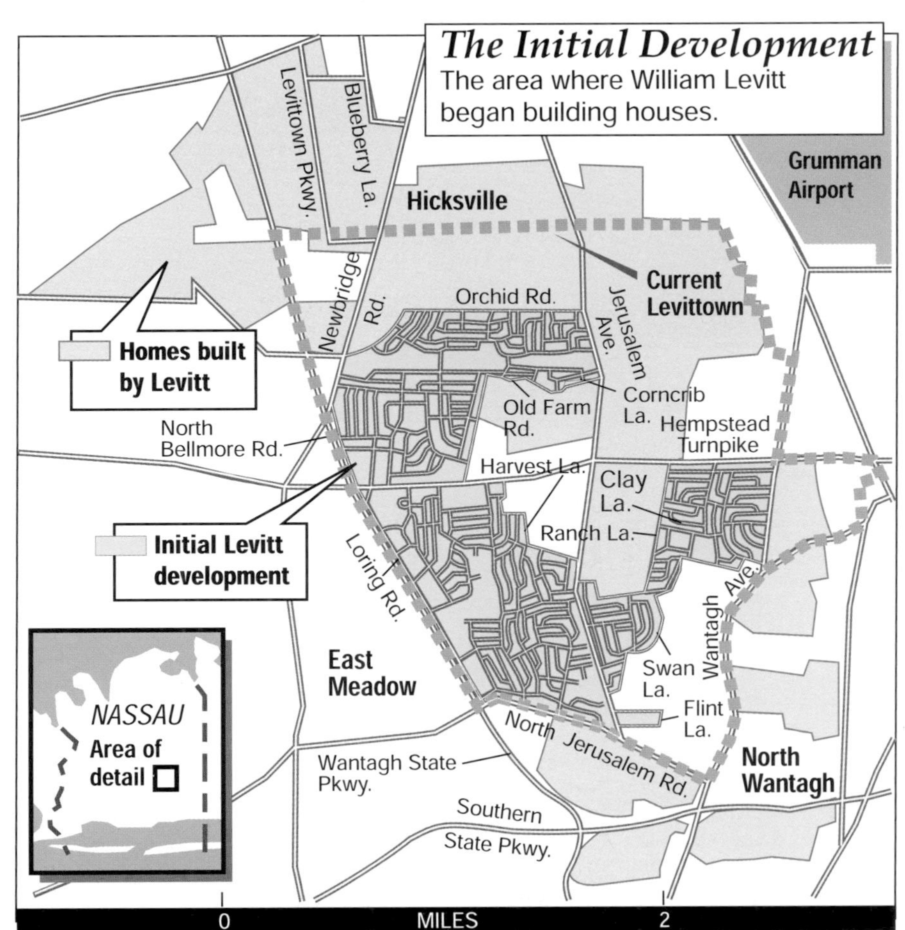

Newsday/Richard Cornett

A New Name: Levittown

Levittown pioneer Robert Abrams had begun publishing the Tribune in December, 1947, while a few blocks away, his neighbor, Ira Cahn, began publishing the Eagle.

To both men, Bill Levitt was a news mill — announcing new plans, stores, village green shopping centers and pools.

They covered every move. When Ira G. Goldman, a vice president of Levitt & Sons, celebrated the 1,000th family to move into the Island Trees development on Dec. 1, 1947, the Eagle quoted Goldman referring to "a Levitt town" that would house 20,000 residents.

A week later, a mysterious letter to the editor, signed "Mac," appeared in the Eagle, suggesting the community take on the name of its builder.

"Each month we honor the Levitts with our check for rent," wrote Mac, "but how about something to show how much we appreciate the good deal we've gotten?"

In its next edition, the Eagle said Levitt had an "informal poll among several companies and organizations" and some 300 letters in support of the name change.

On the last day of 1947, Levitt announced his Island Trees development would henceforth be known as Levittown. Abrams told him it was a lousy idea. Island Trees was a more romantic name.

"I wanted the new name as a kind of monument to my family," William Levitt told Coronet Magazine in September, 1948. "And, by gosh, I wasn't going to brook any interference."

In February, 1948, Levitt announced a rent increase, from $60 to $65, which would go into effect when leases expired by the end of the year. At the same time, he broached the idea of selling the homes to tenants — for $7,990, a full $1,000 higher than what he advertised when he announced the ground-breaking of Levittown on May 7, 1947.

Veterans groups accused Levitt of breaking his promise to war heroes. The Island Trees Civic Association also rebelled, and in March refused to adopt Levittown in its name, a symbolic slap at Levitt.

Levitt moved to buy one of the newspapers — making an offer for the Eagle that Cahn rebuffed, but finding Abrams more than willing to sell out of his struggling operation and stay on as editor. As he did with other tenants he found undesirable, Levitt later refused to renew Cahn's lease.

Left, Newsday Photo / John Paraskevas

Bob Abrams, above, in the office of the Levittown Tribune in 1949, and today. "[William] Levitt will go down as a great guy," Abrams says.

Abrams said Levitt never interfered in the editorial content. But thereafter, controversy over the name and rent increase on the pages of the Tribune died down.

Levitt then moved to pacify another hotbed of dissent. He took aim at the Island Trees Civic Association, going so far as to packing a meeting with Levitt employees to incorporate Levittown in the group's name.

Another mysterious missive appeared. This one promised an organized effort to oppose the rent hikes. It was signed, "Island Trees Communist Party."

No such party ever existed, and no one ever was able to find its author. It set the stage for a pamphlet Levitt delivered to tenants' doorsteps in July, 1948, in which he branded dissenters as communist dupes by referring to a Cold War essay by Supreme Court Justice William O. Douglas, called "The Way to Win Without War."

"Too often idealistic people are seduced because they find the Communists again and again on the reform side of current arguments," Douglas wrote.

"Sound familiar?" Levitt asked. "Despite the skeptics and the professional critics and the communists," he continued, "we believe in Levittown, in its honesty and goodness. What's more, we believe most of the tenants feel as we do."

Levitt also branded as communists anyone who challenged his decision not to rent to blacks, a choice he defended as one forced upon him by the free market.

"Our policy as to whom we sell or do not sell is the same as that of any other builder in the metropolitan area," Levitt said when a group of Levittowners complained about the policy to the FHA in Washington.

Racial Covenants

Eugene Burnett paid a visit to Levittown in December, 1949. He was an Army veteran of World War II, living in Manhattan. He also was black.

"We got there and looked at the house, the model house," Burnett said. "There were other persons looking at the model house. I didn't see any blacks We were the only ones . . . and we walked around the house and then I walked up to the salesman and I said to him, 'Pretty nice house. I'm interested. Would you give me an outline of the procedure, how do I apply? Do you have an application of some sort?

"And he became very solemn, he looked me in the eye, braced himself and said, 'It's not me.' He wasn't hostile at all. So, don't get that impression. But he said, 'It's not me, but the owners of this development have not as yet decided whether or not they're going to sell these homes to Negroes.'

"I left," Burnett said. "I will never forget that long ride back to Harlem . . . How I didn't start World War III is beyond me. Because that was the feeling I had."

Levitt had decided not to sell to blacks from the outset. At first, he wrote that restriction into the leases — a practice recommended at the time by the FHA, which was backing the financing and preferred "homogeneous" neighborhoods.

After the Supreme Court in 1948 declared racial covenants "unenforceable," Levitt dropped the restrictions against occupancy by "non-Caucasians."

But he kept the unwritten policy.

"Levittown has been and is now progressing as a private enterprise job, and it is entirely in the discretion and judgment of Levitt & Sons as to whom it will rent or sell," Levitt explained in a 1949 announcement in the Levittown Tribune. ". . . The elimination of the clause has changed

I Remember Levittown . . .

Newsday File Photo

Robert W. Greene

A journalism professor at Hofstra University, Greene is a retired Newsday reporter and editor. He was 22 with a wife, two kids, a new job, and nearly no money when he scraped together the $500 down payment to buy a Levittown cape. He lived there from 1951 to 1957.

'My next-door neighbor was Leo O'Connell, who had come down from Canada, originally from Liverpool. Like us, I would say he was poor. Every morning Leo would go out ahead of me to work. And he would call me and tell me if he saw any good sofas or bureaus put out in anyone else's garbage. I would hustle out with the car, pick it up quick, and put it in the back yard. Then on Saturdays, after the wives learned how to sew slipcovers and Leo and I learned how to tie things with twine and work with springs, we repaired everything, and literally furnished our houses — for the first couple of years until we got more money — with stuff we picked up from the trash . . .

"We had wonderful parties. Everyone would chip in for a keg of beer on the Fourth of July or whatever. We would choose a back yard; no one had fences then so it didn't really matter. . . . All of the women and all of the men made stuff. The party starts about ten in the morning and winds up about five o'clock the next morning! Everyone would be wandering, lurching through each others' backyards to get home . . . Everyone took care of each other. It was just a wonderful community . . . We still exchange Christmas cards, what is it, more than 40 years ago now? Good God, that's a long time."

absolutely nothing."

Picketers were beginning to appear at Levitt & Sons offices, angry over the restrictive covenants. They were quickly labeled communists by Levitt, residents and Newsday.

"Organizations which appear to be either Communist-dominated or Communist-inspired have been attempting to raise a racial issue at Levittown," Newsday wrote in an editorial on March 12, 1949. "The issue did not exist until it was fostered by people not immediately affected by it. Their only real motive seems to be to set race against race, and if possible, to bog down the Levitt building program, which means homes for thousands of people."

In September, 1950, Levitt told two renters who had begun an interracial play group that their leases would not be renewed. Gertrude Novick and Lillian Ross did not need to be told why they faced eviction.

"We decided to have a little play group, an integrated play group, so we had families from Hempstead bring children in," Novick explained. "It was just two houses on the same street. Our neighbors loved it. Their kids came and played, too. It was just a fun thing. The neighbors enjoyed it and had a fun time. Obviously someone told Levitt about it."

Novick was active in Levittown's Committee to End Discrimination, a small group that met in living rooms and occasionally protested the racial covenants.

"Nobody went out to look for it; you just happened to meet some people who had the same ideologies," she said of the group. "A few people asked us why we moved there if we knew about those covenants."

Novick said she moved in knowing all about the covenants, which she found repulsive, for a simple reason: "We really had no place to live . . . Sometimes your hands are tied, and you hope you can get in and change the world a little bit."

From 1950 to 1953, a handful of black families managed to quietly buy or sublet Levitt homes without his knowledge.

Newsday Photo / John Paraskevas

Because of Levitt & Sons' restrictive policy against blacks, Eugene Burnett, a World War II veteran, could not buy a Levitt house. Instead, he bought one in Ronek Park. Today, Burnett lives in Wyandanch.

Levitt was losing control of his community because he no longer owned much of it. Enticed by the $7.50 monthly difference between his newly hiked rents and a mortgage, tenants leaped into ownership.

The Herons were first, in the fall of 1948, and like everything about Levittown, they were celebrated. When Phil Heron and his sister Adele went to Levitt's Manhasset office to sign the papers, Levitt greeted them at the door.

"They said who they were, and he said, 'Oh, I'm so glad to see you, I didn't think anybody was going to buy these things,' " Mary Heron Quinn recalled of her siblings' trip. "He knew how many he had, and he knew that it would be better to sell them."

By the end of 1949, Levitt moved to divest what remained of his stake in the rental Levittown in a deal that let him avert a steep tax. The mystery transaction was revealed three months later, in March, 1950. By selling a subsidiary that controlled the remaining 4,020 rental houses to a Phildelphia-based educational group, Levitt paid a long-term capital gain of about 25 percent rather than income taxes of up to 77 percent.

'Rabbittown'

By 1951, there were 6,000 Cape Cods, and almost 12,000 ranches sprawling over the boundaries of two towns and three school districts. Island Trees was reduced to a school-district designation, and Rand McNally gave Levittown a dot.

Traffic was outgrowing Abe Levitt's prized trees, and the yards and streets were filling so quickly with children that Levittown acquired the nickname of "Rabbittown."

It had no central governing body, no group of elders to look to for guidance, and no industry to share its tax burden.

Social and architectural critics looked at the endless expanse of cookie-cutter homes and similar families and shuddered.

There were subtle variations in style — the Lookout Cape, the Snug Harbor Cape, the Green Hills, the Mariner. There were differences in color. From 1949 to 1951, Levitt also offered ranch houses in five varieties.

But the similarity and scale couldn't help but inspire the cartoon of a drunken commuter stumbling into the wrong house to commit an accidental infidelity.

A subdivision in California would inspire the 1962 Malvina Reynolds song, "Little Boxes," which described tract houses "all made of ticky tacky and [that] all look the same." But the line stuck to Levittown.

Social critic Lewis Mumford accused the Levitts of using "new-fashioned methods to compound old-fashioned mistakes."

"It's a suburb, and suburbs are just an expansion of a mistaken policy to build without industry," Mumford said. "We have to build complete, well-integrated 'new towns,' not monotonous suburbs with great picture windows that look out onto clotheslines."

I Remember Levittown . . .

Billy Joel

The singer and composer grew up on Meeting Lane in the Hicksville part of Levittown.

'When we got older, my friends and I would take the train into the city. We'd go to movies, museums, we'd just walk around. We were getting away, and we thought the city was where things were great. It was a place to go . . .

"As kids, we'd hang out at the Carvel. Then there was the Levittown pool, where a lot of kids went. There were different places we'd go and hang out and not do much. We'd hang out at the Parkway Village Green. We'd listen to rock and roll. In '64, we started a band, the Echoes. We played at Holy Family Church, teen nights in different places.

"The first gig I remember getting paid for was at Holy Family. I had a crush on a girl named Virginia. I was on stage, and she was looking at me. It was great — it was the coolest thing I could have done."

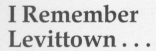

Washington Post Photo / Tom Allen

Billy Joel in 1978, a hometown booster

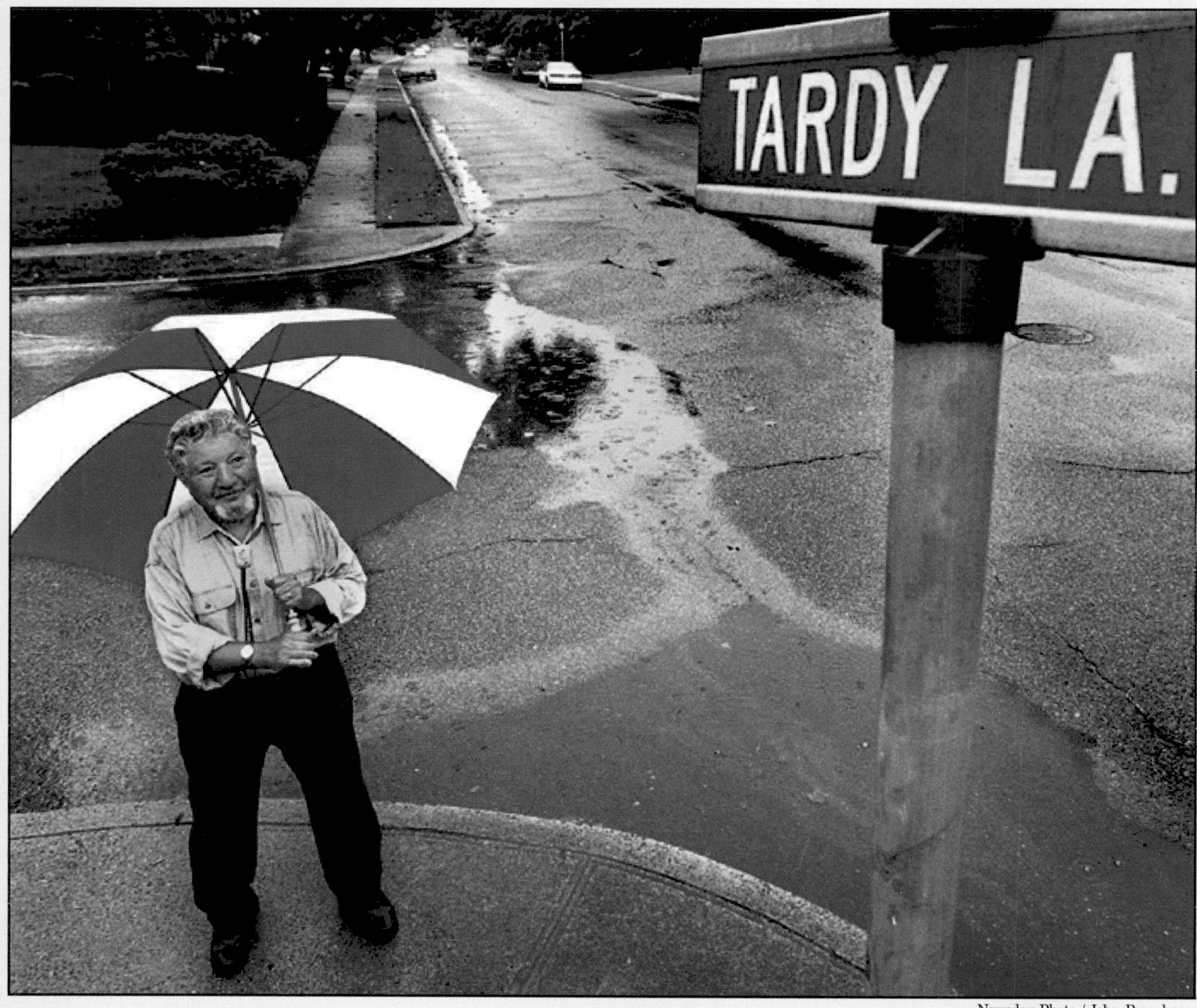

I Remember Levittown . . .

Herb Kalisman
Moved into Levittown in 1951.

"People were interested to see how it would work out. There were dire predictions that it would turn into a slum. In fact, it turned out to be one of the best communities in the state . . . They said it would be all made of ticky tacky and they were all just the same. If you look at it now, all the houses are different now . . . I think the word 'Levittown' became like the postwar substitution for the word 'Brooklyn' or 'Texas.' You just said Brooklyn or Texas and everyone would laugh."

Herb Kalisman on his street, where the last Levittown houses were built before Levitt & Sons moved on to other states.

Newsday Photo / John Paraskevas

Other critics thought that Levittown lowered both the standards of the housing and the standards of the culture.

Levittowners were stung by the criticism, and the persistent prediction that their new town would become a slum.

Eight months after Pat Daniels moved in, she went to Manhattan to Trader Vic's with a friend. "We were talking to the bartender, and he says, 'Hey, where you young ladies from?' "

Daniels tried to think of something other than Levittown.

"I said I was from Hicksville," she said, laughing. "I should have said Wantagh. Hicksville was worse than Levittown."

When William Levitt gamely defended his creation in Good Housekeeping 10 years after he broke ground for Levittown, he summed up his critics:

"The new postwar suburbs are stereotyped, drab and dull. The people who live in them, adapting like chameleons to the color of their surroundings, tend to become stereotyped, drab and dull. There is no privacy. To get along with neighbors, conformity is a must."

Levitt admitted the uniformity of his houses. It was what people could afford, he argued. America should "glory in" its ability to mass-produce everything from houses to the furniture and appliances in them, he said.

"Too much has been made of the goldfish-bowl-picture-window notion," Levitt complained. "All they have to do is hang draperies and maintain a decent reserve in personal manners."

Residents confounded the critics. They loved their homes. They believed all you needed to live in the new suburbia was faith in the future and an imagination.

Connie Nisito put up sheets until she could afford draperies. She furnished her Levitt ranch with the same bed, two chairs, two dressers, coffee table, desk and hooked rug that graced her apartment in her mother's house in Jackson Heights, Queens.

"I had no sofa, but that was all right, we didn't need a sofa," said Nisito, who still lives in the ranch she purchased with her husband in 1951. "I had a rocker, and two velvet chairs . . . a bed with no headboard, and two nice mahogany dressers.

"It was adorable," Nisito said. "Really cute. It really was like a little doll house, and I wish it was that way again."

As families grew, doll houses sprang dormers, garages, breezeways and wings. Thousand Lanes, a publication put out mainly by contractors and designers, filled its pages with tips, from "Beauty at Bedtime" to "Attic Conversions."

Sunrise Lumber Corp. sold "attic room material" for $109, or 95 cents a week. Botto Brothers, then on Broadway in Hicksville, was an authorized dealer for the stainless-steel Tracy cabinets and sinks.

An interior decorator for J.C. Penney wrote "Live Better, Eat Better in a Well-Decorated Home."

Ben Zino, who lived just east of Levittown, started in the home-renovation business in 1952, and Levittown became his specialty. By the time he retired in 1992, Zino Construction had done about 4,000 projects in Levittown.

"One of the first things they needed was a little more space in the kitchen," said Zino, now retired and living in Fort Myers, Fla. "There was this little outside foyer that we took out and enlarged the kitchen, that was done for $230.

"The next thing we did was put in a bedroom in the attic and put in a stairwell. There was nothing but a trapdoor."

With some innovation and help from people like Zino, Levittowners remade their houses and remade themselves. Thousand Lanes was full of self-effacing references to the new suburbanites' humble beginnings and sendups of the patrician suburbia it was replacing. There would be no antique furniture, paisley shawls or lustrous silver culled from their grandparents' attics, Helen Gregutt wrote in one edition.

"Our grandmothers counted themselves lucky if they could make house room for their numerous offspring, the goat and the cow," Gregutt wrote. "One day we would have the capital and space for power tools and a sewing machine. One day we might even learn to use them to our mutual advantage. Meanwhile, we yearned for pleasant surroundings."

By 1951, when Levitt sold his last house on the aptly named Tardy Lane, the Census Bureau decided it had found the "average" American, and he lived in Levittown. He was male, 30, married with two children, earned $3,000 year and owned a refrigerator, a radio and a telephone as well as a stake in a mortgaged home.

But another feature was creeping into the picture of middle America — high taxes. Levittowners faced the task of raising funds for 15 schools in a decade. They also faced the upkeep of the swimming pools and parks Levitt deeded over to local jurisdictions — all of which required special tax districts.

The cost of building those amenities had already been figured into the Levitt profit margins, a Levitt & Sons secret. "You can't tell people you're charging them for things they consider free,' Alfred Levitt told a Regional Planning Association meeting in December, 1950.

The Levitts, who had touted their creation as the "complete community concept " only sketched in schools before packing up and moving their formula for suburbia to Pennsylvania, New Jersey and beyond.

When it came time for pioneers to form a school board, float bonds for buildings and make decisions on curriculum, there was trouble in paradise. ●

EPILOGUE

Pine barrens fire, TWA crash show that residents can unite for a common purpose

Long Islanders Pull Together

From where he stood on the Sunrise Highway overpass, it seemed to Fred Daniels that the world was ablaze.

"It was one of the largest fires I'd ever seen," said Daniels, the Suffolk County deputy commissioner of Fire, Rescue and Emergency Services. "It was horizon to horizon."

Hundreds of homes and thousands of people were in the path of the raging fire as it burned more than 5,000 acres of pine forest on both sides of Sunrise Highway near Westhampton. The blaze began on the morning of Aug. 24, 1995.

"I was at home babysitting an infant grandson," recalled Rocky Oliveto, who lives in Westhampton. "My wife said, 'Look out the door; there's a fire out there.' I looked out the door and there was smoke toward Riverhead. It wasn't 10 minutes before the police evacuated us."

Just 11 months later, on July 17, 1996, boaters across the South Shore looked up into the sky and thought they saw ribbons of fire, like rockets ablaze. Tired from a long day of fishing, Frank Jackson of Hampton Bays was standing on his 55-foot trawler in Shinnecock Inlet when, "I looked out over the back deck to make sure everyone was on the boat when I saw a big fireball in the sky," he said at the time.

Newsday Photo / Bill Davis

Firefighters are silhouetted by the raging fire that consumed acres of pine forest on both sides of Sunrise Highway in August, 1995.

A few minutes later, Jackson untied his boat and headed out into the ocean, where the pieces of TWA Flight 800 had crashed. All 230 passengers had been killed.

The Sunrise fire and the explosion of Flight 800 are linked by a common theme — that in times of tragedy, hundreds of everyday Long Islanders will come together to offer help.

As the pine barrens burned, fire departments from all across Long Island responded, leaving homes and families to save other people's homes and families. In the dark ocean south of Long Island, hundreds of boaters worked through the night and into the next day to help the Coast Guard retrieve debris and bodies and bring them ashore.

Both tragedies show Long Islanders working together for a common purpose. At the fire scene, Long Islanders helped relocate families, protect homes and feed firefighters. At the crash scene, they helped retrieve debris from the water and bring the bodies of someone's mother or father, son or daughter back to a makeshift morgue onshore.

At that morgue that night was Msgr. James McDonald, of St. John the Evangelist Roman Catholic Church in Center Moriches. He was there to give last rites to the dead. He had officiated at the marriage of two of the victims, Eric and Virginia Holst. "It seemed so unreal, and yet it was happening," he said. "It was terribly sad." Seeing all the people working together in such a sad place was a kind of epiphany for McDonald.

"I would say it only intensified the goodness that is in people," he said. "And it will be permanently associated with Long Island."

But there is no guarantee that spirit will endure into the future because in some ways it is not part of our past. Historians caution that from the moment Europeans arrived on Long Island to build farms and villages, a strong independent streak manifested itself. The new villages were populated by people who needed only themselves and their immediate neighbors. What happened 25 miles to the west was of little concern. The Revolution and the Civil War brought hundreds of men together for a common purpose, but when the wars were over, and the mission accomplished, these men went home to their farms and villages to tend their futures.

Newsday Photo / John Keating

Relatives of victims of Flight 800 at a 1997 memorial service at Smith Point County Park

In modern times, efforts to work on a regional basis have often struck a wall of home-rule sentiment. One example occurred in 1970 when a proposed comprehensive Nassau-Suffolk master plan was only partially adopted.

But in both the brush fire and the plane crash, there was no hesitancy. Our regional history — if only for a few days — was rewritten. "The fires were a major event in that every part of our community responded, including every single fire department," said Suffolk County Executive Robert Gaffney. "I truly believe a strong sense of community emerged as everyone pitched in to help. It was like the moon landing — people felt so proud, even if you didn't have a Grumman relative. Long Islanders looked at themselves and said, 'We did it.' "

The people who worked side by side say they felt that they lived in a shared community, a regional village. Herb Davis, Brookhaven's former chief fire marshal, said, "The community response was overwhelming . . . I don't know if it takes a tragedy before people are good and kind. But it certainly showed everyone working together."

Barbara Kelly, director of special collections at the Long Island Studies Institute at Hofstra University, agrees that both events reminded Long Islanders that "we are all one community." But, she added, "we're all caught up in the hustle and bustle of everyday life. It is only when we are called to attention that we realize that we depend on one another. But it is important that we do come together periodically. We hear so much in the news that is negative that we sometimes forget how good people can be."

Looking back at the Sunrise fire, Fred Daniels said, "While the fires were an unfortunate incident, it strengthened our ability to cooperate and work together." He said that ability to work together on a large scale that week in August helped in the response to TWA 800 11 months later.

After hearing that a jet had exploded over the ocean, Jeffrey Irwin, a Red Cross volunteer, rushed to the Ramada Inn at Kennedy Airport to help relatives of the passengers. Looking back at his work, he thinks the response to the crash helped create a greater sense of community on Long Island.

"One day I had a Red Cross ID badge on and I stopped at a 7-Eleven to get my morning coffee," Irwin said. "And they said, 'No, no, no, you're not paying for anything.' People really rallied around. People and businesses were calling and saying, 'We can send somebody down to help. I have a spare truck. I can pick up ice. I can do whatever you need.' It was something small, but it showed a lot."

Bishop John McGann of the Diocese of Rockville Centre said the fire and the TWA explosion showed Long Island is, indeed, one community.

"I think the response to these events was typical of how Long Islanders have reacted in similar situations in the past and how they will continue to react in the future," McGann said. "I am convinced of the goodness of our people."

This story was reported by Bill Bleyer, Katie Thomas, George DeWan and Steve Wick, and was written by Wick.

LONG ISLAND OUR STORY

For more than two years, a team of Newsday reporters and editors worked on "Long Island: Our Story." The lead reporters were George DeWan and Steve Wick. The chief researcher was Georgina Martorella. The chief photographer was Bill Davis. In addition to those whose bylines appear in this book, the following were instrumental in its creation: Lawrence Striegel, layout and news editor; Richard L. Wiltamuth, copy chief; Robert Eisner, design director; Bob Newman and Linda McKenney, logo and design; Ned Levine, additional logos; Tim Drachlis and Bonnie Hede, graphics editors; Kathryn Sweeney and Susan King, photo research; Joye Brown, Richard C. Firstman and Alex Martin, editing; Mary Ann Skinner, Bob Henn, Barry Hooghkirk, Diane Ortiz and Julian Stein, book production; MeiPu Yang and Marilyn Sacrestano, marketing.

Jeffrey Schamberry was photo editor. Jack Millrod supervised editorial production. Harvey Aronson was the editor of the project, which was supervised by Peter Bengelsdorf and Howard Schneider.

The editors would like to thank Mary Wyman, Paul Fleishman and Newsday editor Tony Marro for their support and encouragement.

ACKNOWLEDGMENTS

The Newsday reporters, editors, photographers, artists and others who worked on "Long Island: Our Story" are grateful to many people and organizations for their enthusiastic cooperation. We regret that they are far too numerous to list in full, but we acknowledge some of those whose efforts and insights have been exceptionally valuable.

David Y. Allen, head, maps section, State University at Stony Brook library
William Asadorian, assistant manager, L.I. Division, Queens Borough Public Library
Fred Baker, art collector and dealer
Barbara Bart, director, Walt Whitman Birthplace State Historic Site and Interpretive Center
Rosalyn Baxandall, professor, American Studies Program, State University College at Old Westbury
Cliff Benfield, curator, Horton Point Lighthouse Museum
Antonia Booth, Southold Town Historian
Wallace Broege, director, Suffolk County Historical Society
Mitzi Caputo, curator, Huntington Historical Society
Louise and Mauro Cassano and members of the Levittown 50th Anniversary Committee
Joseph Coen, archivist, Diocese of Brooklyn
Stanley Cogan, president, Queens Historical Society
Robert Cooper, a Montaukett leader
Emma Cuesta, assistant dean of library services, Axinn Library, Hofstra University
Lynda R. Day, assistant professor of Africana studies, Brooklyn College
Mildred Murphy DeRiggi, historian, Museum Services Division, Nassau County Department of Recreation and Parks
James Driscoll, director of research, Queens Historical Society
Dick Dunne, director of public affairs, Northrop Grumman Corp.
John Eilertsen, director, Hallockville Museum Farm
Elizabeth Ewen, professor, American Studies Program, State University College at Old Westbury
Dean Failey, senior vice president and senior director of American furniture and decorative arts, Christie's auction house
Van Field, maritime historian
Roberta Fiore, Long Beach Historian
Guy Ladd Frost, Roslyn architect and preservationist
John A. Gable, executive director of the Theodore Roosevelt Association
Jeff Gottlieb, president, Central Queens Historical Society
Louise Hall, director, Smithtown Historical Society
Richard Hawkins, librarian, the Long Island History Room, the Smithtown Library
Charles F. Howlett, historian
Kathleen Kane, director of education, Society for the Preservation of Long Island Antiquities
Henry Keatts, Suffolk Community College professor and maritime historian
Barbara Kelly, curator, Long Island Studies Institute
Joan G. Kent, North Hempstead Town Historian
Dorothy King, librarian, Pennypacker Long Island Collection, East Hampton Library
Hugh King, East Hampton town crier
Lee Koppelman, executive director of Long Island Regional Planning Board
John Kordes, Garden City Village Historian
Tom Kuehhas, director, Oyster Bay Historical Society
Levittown Historical Society
Charles Lindner, director of library services, Immaculate Conception Center, Douglaston
Myron Luke, professor of history emeritus, Hofstra University
Robert MacKay, director, Society for the Preservation of Long Island Antiquities
J. Lance Mallamo, Suffolk County Historian
Arthur Mattson, Lynbrook Village Historian
Bishop John R. McGann, Diocese of Rockville Centre
James McKenna, site director, Old Bethpage Village Restoration
Herbert Mills, curator of geology, Nassau County Division of Museums
Natalie Naylor, director, Long Island Studies Institute at Hofstra University
New-York Historical Society
New York Public Library, rare books and manuscripts division
Winifred Latimer Norman, vice president, Latimer House Preservation Society
Florence Ogg, director of collections and exhibits, Vanderbilt Museum
Ronald Pisano, art historian
Public libraries: Brooklyn, Bryant, East Hampton, East Meadow, Emma Clark, Half Hollow Hills, Huntington, Levittown, Lindenhurst, Northport-East Northport, Smithtown, South Huntington
Gloria Rocchio, president, Ward Melville Heritage Organization
Kathleen D. Roe, principal archivist, New York State Archives and Records Administration
Marjorie Roe, president, Greater Patchogue Historical Society
Alice Ross, food historian
Dan Russell, Glen Cove Historian
Vincent F. Seyfried, Long Island Rail Road historian
Edward Smits, Nassau County Historian
Janet Spar, librarian, Levittown Public Library
Gaynell Stone, museum director of the Suffolk County Archaeological Association
John Strong, American studies professor at Southampton College, Long Island University
Anne Swezey, Patchogue Village Historian
Susana Tejada, regional archivist, State Documentary Heritage Program
Irene Tichenor, acting director, Brooklyn Historical Society
Carl Vail III, member of a venerable Long Island family
Deborah Van Cura, president, Greater Astoria Historical Society
Barbara Van Liew, editor, Society for the Preservation of Long Island Antiquities
Jean Wassong, archivist, Diocese of Rockville Centre
David Weiner, head, circulation-reserve services, Melville Library, State University at Stony Brook
Richard Welch, maritime historian
George Williams, North Hempstead Historic Commission
Roger Wunderlich, editor, the Long Island Historical Journal, associate professor of history, State University at Stony Brook
James York, Village of Hempstead Historian
Charles Young, L.I. Division director, retired, Queens Borough Public Library.

And special thanks to our Heritage and Legacy Partners for their support.

Index

Numbers in *italics* refer to illustrations.